P. Hamilton.

KU-165-070

Collins
Italian
Dictionary

HarperCollins Publishers
Westerhill Road
Bishopbriggs
Glasgow
G64 2QT
Great Britain

First Edition 2006

© HarperCollins Publishers 2006

ISBN-13   978-0-00-723144-7
ISBN-10   0-00-723144-x

www.collins.co.uk

A catalogue record for this book is
available from the British Library

Typeset by Thomas Callan

Printed and bound in Italy by
Legoprint S.P.A.

Acknowledgements
We would like to thank those
authors and publishers who kindly
gave permission for copyright
material to be used in the Collins
Word Web. We would also like to
thank Times Newspapers Ltd for
providing valuable data.

EDITORIAL DIRECTOR
Michela Clari

CONTRIBUTORS
G Bacchelli

EDITORIAL COORDINATION
Joyce Littlejohn

SERIES EDITOR
Lorna Knight

BASED ON THE COLLINS ITALIAN GEM
Catherine E Love
P L Rossi
D M Chaplin
F Villa
E Bilucaglia

INDICE

CONTENTS

I marchi registrati
I termini che a nostro parere costituiscono un marchio registrato sono stati designati come tali. In ogni caso, né la presenza né l'assenza di tale designazione implicano alcuna valutazione del loro reale stato giuridico.

Note on trademarks
Entered words that we have reason to believe constitute trademarks have been designated as such. However, neither the presence nor the absence of such designation should be regarded as affecting the legal status of any trademark.

INTRODUZIONE

Vi ringraziamo di aver scelto il Dizionario inglese Collins e ci auguriamo che esso si riveli uno strumento utile e piacevole da usare nello studio, in vacanza e sul lavoro.

INTRODUCTION

We are delighted that you have decided to buy the Collins Italian Dictionary and hope you will enjoy and benefit from using it at school, at home, on holiday or at work.

William Collins' dream of knowledge
for all began with the publication of his
first book in 1819. A self-educated mill
worker, he not only enriched millions
of lives, but also founded a flourishing
publishing house. Today, staying true to
this spirit, Collins books are packed with
inspiration, innovation, and practical
expertise. They place you at the centre
of a world of possibility and give you
exactly what you need to explore it.

Language is the key to this exploration,
and at the heart of Collins Dictionaries is
language as it is really used. New words,
phrases, and meanings spring up every
day, and all of them are captured and
analysed by the Collins Word Web.
Constantly updated, and with over 2.5
billion entries, this living language
resource is unique to our dictionaries.

Words are tools for life. And a Collins
Dictionary makes them work for you.

Collins. Do more.

ABBREVIAZIONI

ABBREVIATIONS

abbreviazione	*abbr*	abbreviation
aggettivo	*adj*	adjective
amministrazione	*Admin*	administration
avverbio	*adv*	adverb
aeronautica, viaggi aerei	*Aer*	flying, air travel
aggettivo	*ag*	adjective
agricoltura	*Agr*	agriculture
amministrazione	*Amm*	administration
anatomia	*Anat*	anatomy
architettura	*Archit*	architecture
articolo determinativo	*art def*	definite article
articolo indeterminativo	*art indef*	indefinite article
attributivo	*attrib*	attributive
ausiliare	*aus, aux*	auxiliary
automobile	*Aut*	motor car and motoring
avverbio	*av*	adverb
aeronautica, viaggi aerei	*Aviat*	flying, air travel
biologia	*Biol*	biology
botanica	*Bot*	botany
inglese britannico	*BRIT*	British English
consonante	*C*	consonant
chimica	*Chim, Chem*	chemistry
commercio, finanza	*Comm*	commerce, finance
comparativo	*compar*	comparative
informatica	*Comput*	computing
congiunzione	*cong, conj*	conjunction
edilizia	*Constr*	building
sostantivo usato come aggettivo, ma mai con funzione predicativa	*cpd*	compound element: noun used as adjective and which cannot follow the noun it qualifies
cucina	*Cuc, Culin*	cookery
davanti a	*dav*	before

ABBREVIAZIONI		ABBREVIATIONS
articolo determinativo	*def art*	definite article
determinativo; articolo, aggettivo dimostrativo o indefinito ecc	*det*	determiner: article, demonstrative etc
diminutivo	*dimin*	diminutive
diritto	*Dir*	law
economia	*Econ*	economics
edilizia	*Edil*	building
elettricità, elettronica	*Elettr, Elec*	electricity, electronics
esclamazione	*escl, excl*	exclamation
femminile	*f*	feminine
familiare (! da evitare)	*fam(!)*	colloquial usage (! particularly offensive)
ferrovia	*Ferr*	railways
senso figurato	*fig*	figurative use
fisiologia	*Fisiol*	physiology
fotografia	*Fot*	photography
verbo inglese la cui particella è inseparabile dal verbo	*fus*	(phrasal verb) where the particle cannot be separated from the main verb
nella maggior parte dei sensi; generalmente	*gen*	in most or all senses; generally
geografia, geologia	*Geo*	geography, geology
geometria	*Geom*	geometry
storia, storico	*Hist*	history, historical
impersonale	*impers*	impersonal
articolo indeterminativo	*indef art*	indefinite article
familiare (! da evitare)	*inf(!)*	colloquial usage (! particularly offensive)
infinito	*infin*	infinitive
informatica	*Inform*	computing

ABBREVIAZIONI		ABBREVIATIONS
insegnamento, sistema scolastico e universitario	*Ins*	schooling, schools and universities
invariabile	*inv*	invariable
irregolare	*irreg*	irregular
grammatica, linguistica	*Ling*	grammar, linguistics
maschile	*m*	masculine
matematica	*Mat(h)*	mathematics
termine medico, medicina	*Med*	medical term, medicine
il tempo, meteorologia	*Meteor*	the weather, meteorology
maschile o femminile	*m/f*	masculine or feminine
esercito, linguaggio militare	*Mil*	military matters
musica	*Mus*	music
sostantivo	*n*	noun
nautica	*Naut*	sailing, navigation
numerale (aggettivo, sostantivo)	*num*	numeral adjective or noun
	o.s.	oneself
peggiorativo	*peg, pej*	derogatory, pejorative
fotografia	*Phot*	photography
fisiologia	*Physiol*	physiology
plurale	*pl*	plural
politica	*Pol*	politics
participio passato	*pp*	past participle
preposizione	*prep*	preposition
pronome	*pron*	pronoun
psicologia, psichiatria	*Psic, Psych*	psychology, psychiatry
tempo passato	*pt*	past tense
qualcosa	*qc*	
qualcuno	*qn*	
religione, liturgia	*Rel*	religions, church service
sostantivo	*s*	noun
	sb	somebody

ABBREVIAZIONI		ABBREVIATIONS
insegnamento, sistema scolastico e universitario	*Scol*	schooling, schools and universities
singolare	*sg*	singular
soggetto (grammaticale)	*sog*	(grammatical) subject
	sth	something
congiuntivo	*sub*	subjunctive
soggetto (grammaticale)	*subj*	(grammatical) subject
superlativo	*superl*	superlative
termine tecnico, tecnologia	*Tecn, Tech*	technical term, technology
telecomunicazioni	*Tel*	telecommunications
tipografia	*Tip*	typography, printing
televisione	*TV*	television
tipografia	*Typ*	typography, printing
università	*Univ*	university
inglese americano	*US*	American English
vocale	*V*	vowel
verbo	*vb*	verb
verbo o gruppo verbale con funzione intransitiva	*vi*	verb or phrasal verb used intransitively
verbo pronominale o riflessivo	*vpr*	pronominal or reflexive verb
verbo o gruppo verbale con funzione transitiva	*vt*	verb or phrasal verb used transitively
zoologia	*Zool*	zoology
marchio registrato	®	registered trademark
introduce un'equivalenza culturale	≈	introduces a cultural equivalent

TRASCRIZIONE FONETICA

Consonanti		Consonants
NB **p, b, t, d, k, g** sono seguite da un'aspirazione in inglese.		NB **p, b, t, d, k, g** are not aspirated in Italian.

padre	p	**p**uppy
bambino	b	**b**a**b**y
tu**t**to	t	**t**en**t**
da**d**o	d	**d**a**dd**y
cane **ch**e	k	**c**ork **k**iss **ch**ord
gola **gh**iro	g	**g**a**g g**uess
sano	s	**s**o ri**c**e ki**ss**
svago e**s**ame	z	cou**s**in bu**zz**
scena	ʃ	**sh**eep **s**ugar
	ʒ	plea**s**ure bei**g**e
pe**c**e lan**ci**are	tʃ	**ch**ur**ch**
giro **g**ioco	dʒ	**j**ud**g**e **g**eneral
a**f**a **f**aro	f	**f**arm ra**ff**le
vero bra**v**o	v	**v**ery re**v**
	θ	**th**in ma**th**s
	ð	**th**at o**th**er
le**tt**o a**l**a	l	**l**itt**l**e ba**ll**
g**li**	ʎ	mi**lli**on
rete a**r**co	r	**r**at **r**a**r**e
ramo ma**dr**e	m	**m**u**mm**y co**mb**
no fu**m**ante	n	**n**o ra**n**
gnomo	ɲ	ca**ny**on
	ŋ	si**ng**ing ba**n**k
	h	**h**at re**h**eat
bu**i**o p**i**acere	j	**y**et
uomo g**u**aio	w	**w**all bewa**i**l
	x	lo**ch**

Varie		Miscellaneous
per l'inglese: la "r" finale viene pronunciata se seguita da una vocale	r	
precede la sillaba accentata	'	precedes the stressed syllable

PHONETIC TRANSCRIPTION

Vocali		Vowels
NB La messa in equivalenza di certi suoni indica solo una rassomiglianza approssimativa.		NB The pairing of some vowel sounds only indicates approximate equivalence.
vino idea	i i:	heel bead
	ɪ	hit pity
stella edera	e	
epoca eccetto	ɛ	set tent
mamma amore	a æ	bat apple
	ɑː	after car calm
	ã	fiancé
	ʌ	fun cousin
müsli	y	
	ə	over above
	əː	urn fern work
rosa occhio	ɔ	wash pot
	ɔː	born cork
ponte ognuno	o	
föhn	ø	
utile zucca	u	full soot
	uː	boon lewd

Dittonghi		Diphthongs
	ɪə	beer tier
	ɛə	tear fair there
	eɪ	date plaice day
	aɪ	life buy cry
	au	owl foul now
	əu	low no
	ɔɪ	boil boy oily
	uə	poor tour

ITALIAN PRONUNCIATION

Vowels

Where the vowel **e** or the vowel **o** appears in a stressed syllable it can be either open [ɛ], [ɔ] or closed [e], [o]. As the open or closed pronunciation of these vowels is subject to regional variation, the distinction is of little importance to the user of this dictionary. Phonetic transcription for headwords containing these vowels will therefore only appear where other pronunciation difficulties are present.

Consonants

c before "e" or "i" is pronounced like the *"tch"* in match.
ch is pronounced like the *"k"* in "kit".
g before "e" or "i" is pronounced like the *"j"* in "jet".
gh is pronounced like the *"g"* in "get".
gl before "e" or "i" is normally pronounced like the *"lli"* in "million", and in a few cases only like the *"gl"* in "glove".
gn is pronounced like the *"ny"* in "canyon"
sc before "e" or "i" is pronounced *"sh"*.
z is pronounced like the *"ts"* in "stetson", or like the *"d's"* in "bird's-eye".

Headwords containing the above consonants and consonantal groups have been given full phonetic transcription in this dictionary.

NB All double written consonants in Italian are fully sounded: e.g. the *tt* in "tutto" is pronounced as in "hat trick".

ITALIAN VERB FORMS

1 Gerundio 2 Participio passato 3 Presente 4 Imperfetto 5 Passato remoto
6 Futuro 7 Condizionale 8 Congiuntivo presente 9 Congiuntivo passato
10 Imperativo

andare 3 vado, vai, va, andiamo, andate, vanno 6 andrò *ecc.* 8 vada 10 va'!, vada!, andate!, vadano!

apparire 2 apparso 3 appaio, appari *o* apparisci, appare *o* apparisce, appaiono *o* appariscono 5 apparvi *o* apparsi, apparisti, apparve *o* apparì *o* apparse, apparvero *o* apparirono *o* apparsero 8 appaia *o* apparisca

aprire 2 aperto 3 apro 5 aprii, apristi 8 apra

AVERE 3 ho, hai, ha, abbiamo, avete, hanno 5 ebbi, avesti, ebbe, avemmo, aveste, ebbero 6 avrò *ecc.* 8 abbia *ecc.* 10 abbi!, abbia!, abbiate!, abbiano!

bere 1 bevendo 2 bevuto 3 bevo *ecc.* 4 bevevo *ecc.* 5 bevvi *o* bevetti, bevesti 6 berrò *ecc.* 8 beva *ecc.* 9 bevessi *ecc.*

cadere 5 caddi, cadesti 6 cadrò *ecc.*

cogliere 2 colto 3 colgo, colgono 5 colsi, cogliesti 8 colga

correre 2 corso 5 corsi, corresti

cuocere 2 cotto 3 cuocio, cociamo, cuociono 5 cossi, cocesti

dare 3 do, dai, dà, diamo, date, danno 5 diedi *o* detti, desti 6 darò *ecc.* 8 dia *ecc.* 9 dessi *ecc.* 10 da'!, dai!, date!, diano!

dire 1 dicendo 2 detto 3 dico, dici, dice, diciamo, dite, dicono 4 dicevo *ecc.* 5 dissi, dicesti 6 dirò *ecc.* 8 dica, diciamo, diciate, dicano 9 dicessi *ecc.* 10 di'!, dica!, dite!, dicano!

dolere 3 dolgo, duoli, duole, dolgono 5 dolsi, dolesti 6 dorrò *ecc.* 8 dolga

dovere 3 devo *o* debbo, devi, deve, dobbiamo, dovete, devono *o* debbono 6 dovrò *ecc.* 8 debba, dobbiamo, dobbiate, devano *o* debbano

ESSERE 2 stato 3 sono, sei, è, siamo, siete, sono 4 ero, eri, era, eravamo, eravate, erano 5 fui, fosti, fu, fummo, foste, furono 6 sarò *ecc.* 8 sia *ecc.* 9 fossi, fossi, fosse, fossimo, foste, fossero 10 sii!, sia!, siate!, siano!

fare 1 facendo 2 fatto 3 faccio, fai, fa, facciamo, fate, fanno 4 facevo *ecc.* 5 feci, facesti 6 farò *ecc.* 8 faccia *ecc.* 9 facessi *ecc.* 10 fa'!, faccia!, fate!, facciano!

FINIRE 1 finendo 2 finito 3 finisco, finisci, finisce, finiamo, finite, finiscono 4 finivo, finivi, finiva, finivamo, finivate, finivano 5 finii, finisti, finì, finimmo, finiste, finirono 6 finirò, finirai, finirà, finiremo, finirete, finiranno 7 finirei, finiresti, finirebbe, finiremmo, finireste, finirebbero 8 finisca, finisca, finisca, finiamo, finiate, finiscano 9 finissi, finissi, finisse, finissimo, finiste, finissero 10 finisci!, finisca!, finite!, finiscano!

giungere 2 giunto 5 giunsi, giungesti

leggere 2 letto 5 lessi, leggesti

mettere 2 messo 5 misi, mettesti

morire 2 morto 3 muoio, muori, muore, moriamo, morite, muoiono 6 morirò *o* morrò *ecc.* 8 muoia

muovere 2 mosso 5 mossi, movesti

nascere 2 nato 5 nacqui, nascesti

nuocere 2 nuociuto 3 nuoccio, nuoci, nuoce, nociamo *o* nuociamo, nuocete, nuocciono 4 nuocevo *ecc.* 5 nocqui, nuocesti 6 nuocerò *ecc.* 7 nuoccia

offrire 2 offerto 3 offro 5 offersi *o* offrii, offristi 8 offra

parere 2 parso 3 paio, paiamo, paiono 5 parvi *o* parsi, paresti 6 parrò *ecc.* 8 paia, paiamo, paiate, paiano

PARLARE 1 parlando **2** parlato **3** parlo, parli, parla, parliamo, parlate, parlano **4** parlavo, parlavi, parlava, parlavamo, parlavate, parlavano **5** parlai, parlasti, parlò, parlammo, parlaste, parlarono **6** parlerò, parlerai, parlerà, parleremo, parlerete, parleranno **7** parlerei, parleresti, parlerebbe, parleremmo, parlereste, parlerebbero **8** parli, parli, parli, parliamo, parliate, parlino **9** parlassi, parlassi, parlasse, parlassimo, parlaste, parlassero **10** parla!, parli!, parlate!, parlino!

piacere 2 piaciuto **3** piaccio, piacciamo, piacciono **5** piacqui, piacesti **8** piacci *ecc.*

porre 1 ponendo **2** posto **3** pongo, poni, pone, poniamo, ponete, pongono **4** ponevo *ecc.* **5** posi, ponesti **6** porrò *ecc.* **8** ponga, poniamo, poniate, pongano **9** ponessi *ecc.*

potere 3 posso, puoi, può, possiamo, potete, possono **6** potrò *ecc.* **8** possa, possiamo, possiate, possano

prendere 2 preso **5** presi, prendesti

ridurre 1 riducendo **2** ridotto **3** riduco *ecc.* **4** riducevo *ecc.* **5** ridussi, riducesti **6** ridurrò *ecc.* **8** riduca *ecc.* **9** riducessi *ecc.*

riempire 1 riempiendo **3** riempio, riempi, riempie, riempiono

rimanere 2 rimasto **3** rimango, rimangono **5** rimasi, rimanesti **6** rimarrò *ecc.* **8** rimanga

rispondere 2 risposto **5** risposi, rispondesti

salire 3 salgo, sali, salgono **8** salga

sapere 3 so, sai, sa, sappiamo, sapete, sanno **5** seppi, sapesti **6** saprò *ecc.* **8** sappia *ecc.* **10** sappi!, sappia!, sappiate!, sappiano!

scrivere 2 scritto **5** scrissi, scrivesti

sedere 3 siedo, siedi, siede, siedono **8** sieda

spegnere 2 spento **3** spengo, spengono **5** spensi, spegnesti **8** spenga

stare 2 stato **3** sto, stai, sta, stiamo, state, stanno **5** stetti, stesti **6** starò *ecc.* **8** stia *ecc.* **9** stessi *ecc.* **10** sta'!, stia!, state!, stiano!

tacere 2 taciuto **3** taccio, tacciono **5** tacqui, tacesti **8** taccia

tenere 3 tengo, tieni, tiene, tengono **5** tenni, tenesti **6** terrò *ecc.* **8** tenga

trarre 1 traendo **2** tratto **3** traggo, trai, trae, traiamo, traete, traggono **4** traevo *ecc.* **5** trassi, traesti **6** trarrò *ecc.* **8** tragga **9** traessi *ecc.*

udire 3 odo, odi, ode, odono **8** oda

uscire 3 esco, esci, esce, escono **8** esca

valere 2 valso **3** valgo, valgono **5** valsi, valesti **6** varrò *ecc.* **8** valga

vedere 2 visto *o* veduto **5** vidi, vedesti **6** vedrò *ecc.*

VENDERE 1 vendendo **2** venduto **3** vendo, vendi, vende, vendiamo, vendete, vendono **4** vendevo, vendevi, vendeva, vendevamo, vendevate, vendevano **5** vendei *o* vendetti, vendesti, vendé *o* vendette, vendemmo, vendeste, venderono *o* vendettero **6** venderò, venderai, venderà, venderemo, venderete, venderanno **7** venderei, venderesti, venderebbe, venderemmo, vendereste, venderebbero **8** venda, venda, venda, vendiamo, vendiate, vendano **9** vendessi, vendessi, vendesse, vendessimo, vendeste, vendessero **10** vendi!, venda!, vendete!, vendano!

venire 2 venuto **3** vengo, vieni, viene, vengono **5** venni, venisti **6** verrò *ecc.* **8** venga

vivere 2 vissuto **5** vissi, vivesti

volere 3 voglio, vuoi, vuole, vogliamo, volete, vogliono **5** volli, volesti **6** vorrò *ecc.* **8** voglia *ecc.* **10** vogli!, voglia!, vogliate!, vogliano!

ENGLISH VERB FORMS

present	pt	pp	present	pt	pp
arise	arose	arisen	feed	fed	fed
awake	awoke	awoken	feel	felt	felt
be (am, is, are; being)	was, were	been	fight	fought	fought
			find	found	found
bear	bore	born(e)	flee	fled	fled
beat	beat	beaten	fling	flung	flung
become	became	become	fly	flew	flown
begin	began	begun	forbid	forbade	forbidden
bend	bent	bent	forecast	forecast	forecast
bet	bet, betted	bet, betted	forget	forgot	forgotten
			forgive	forgave	forgiven
bid (at auction, cards)	bid	bid	forsake	forsook	forsaken
			freeze	froze	frozen
bid (say)	bade	bidden	get	got	got, (US) gotten
bind	bound	bound			
bite	bit	bitten	give	gave	given
bleed	bled	bled	go (goes)	went	gone
blow	blew	blown	grind	ground	ground
break	broke	broken	grow	grew	grown
breed	bred	bred	hang	hung	hung
bring	brought	brought	hang (execute)	hanged	hanged
build	built	built	have (has; having)	had	had
burn	burnt, burned	burnt, burned	hear	heard	heard
burst	burst	burst	hide	hid	hidden
buy	bought	bought	hit	hit	hit
can	could	(been able)	hold	held	held
cast	cast	cast	hurt	hurt	hurt
catch	caught	caught	keep	kept	kept
choose	chose	chosen	kneel	knelt, kneeled	knelt, kneeled
cling	clung	clung			
come	came	come	know	knew	known
cost	cost	cost	lay	laid	laid
cost (work out price of)	costed	costed	lead	led	led
			lean	leant, leaned	leant, leaned
creep	crept	crept			
cut	cut	cut	leap	leapt, leaped	leapt, leaped
deal	dealt	dealt			
dig	dug	dug	learn	learnt, learned	learnt, learned
do (does)	did	done			
draw	drew	drawn	leave	left	left
dream	dreamed, dreamt	dreamed, dreamt	lend	lent	lent
			let	let	let
drink	drank	drunk	lie (lying)	lay	lain
drive	drove	driven	light	lit, lighted	lit, lighted
dwell	dwelt	dwelt			
eat	ate	eaten	lose	lost	lost
fall	fell	fallen	make	made	made

present	pt	pp	present	pt	pp
may	might	—	spell	spelt, spelled	spelt, spelled
mean	meant	meant			
meet	met	met	spend	spent	spent
mistake	mistook	mistaken	spill	spilt, spilled	spilt, spilled
mow	mowed	mown, mowed			
			spin	spun	spun
must	(had to)	(had to)	spit	spat	spat
pay	paid	paid	split	split	split
put	put	put	spoil	spoiled, spoilt	spoiled, spoilt
quit	quit, quitted	quit, quitted			
			spread	spread	spread
read	read	read	spring	sprang	sprung
rid	rid	rid	stand	stood	stood
ride	rode	ridden	steal	stole	stolen
ring	rang	rung	stick	stuck	stuck
rise	rose	risen	sting	stung	stung
run	ran	run	stink	stank	stunk
saw	sawed	sawed, sawn	stride	strode	stridden
			strike	struck	struck, stricken
say	said	said			
see	saw	seen	strive	strove	striven
seek	sought	sought	swear	swore	sworn
sell	sold	sold	sweep	swept	swept
send	sent	sent	swell	swelled	swollen, swelled
set	set	set			
sew	sewed	sewn	swim	swam	swum
shake	shook	shaken	swing	swung	swung
shear	sheared	shorn, sheared	take	took	taken
			teach	taught	taught
shed	shed	shed	tear	tore	torn
shine	shone	shone	tell	told	told
shoot	shot	shot	think	thought	thought
show	showed	shown	throw	threw	thrown
shrink	shrank	shrunk	thrust	thrust	thrust
shut	shut	shut	tread	trod	trodden
sing	sang	sung	wake	woke, waked	woken, waked
sink	sank	sunk			
sit	sat	sat			
slay	slew	slain	wear	wore	worn
sleep	slept	slept	weave	wove, weaved	woven, weaved
slide	slid	slid			
sling	slung	slung	wed	wedded, wed	wedded, wed
slit	slit	slit			
smell	smelt, smelled	smelt, smelled			
			weep	wept	wept
sow	sowed	sown, sowed	win	won	won
			wind	wound	wound
speak	spoke	spoken	wring	wrung	wrung
speed	sped, speeded	sped, speeded	write	wrote	written

month; **pagato a ore** paid by the hour; **vendere qc a 2 euro il chilo** to sell sth at 2 euros a o per kilo

abbagli'ante [abbaʎ'ʎante] *ag* dazzling; **abbaglianti** *smpl* (*Aut*): **accendere gli abbaglianti** to put one's headlights on full (BRIT) o high (US) beam

abbagli'are [abbaʎ'ʎare] *vt* to dazzle; (*illudere*) to delude

abbai'are *vi* to bark

abbando'nare *vt* to leave, abandon, desert; (*trascurare*) to neglect; (*rinunciare a*) to abandon, give up; **abbandonarsi** *vpr* to let o.s. go; **abbandonarsi a** (*ricordi, vizio*) to give o.s. up to

abbas'sare *vt* to lower; (*radio*) to turn down; **abbassarsi** *vpr* (*chinarsi*) to stoop; (*livello, sole*) to go down; (*fig: umiliarsi*) to demean o.s.; **~ i fari** (*Aut*) to dip o dim (US) one's lights

ab'basso *escl* **~ il re!** down with the king!

abbas'tanza [abbas'tantsa] *av* (*a sufficienza*) enough; (*alquanto*) quite, rather, fairly; **non è ~ furbo** he's not shrewd enough; **un vino ~ dolce** quite a sweet wine; **averne ~ di qn/qc** to have had enough of sb/sth

ab'battere *vt* (*muro, casa*) to pull down; (*ostacolo*) to knock down; (*albero*) to fell; (: *vento*) to bring down; (*bestie da macello*) to slaughter; (*cane, cavallo*) to destroy, put down; (*selvaggina, aereo*) to shoot down; (*fig: malattia, disgrazia*) to lay low; **abbattersi** *vpr* (*avvilirsi*) to lose heart; **abbat'tuto, -a** *ag* (*fig*) depressed

abba'zia [abbat'tsia] *sf* abbey

'abbia *vb vedi* **avere**

abbi'ente *ag* well-to-do, well-off; **abbienti** *smpl* **gli abbienti** the well-to-do

abbiglia'mento [abbiʎʎa'mento] *sm* dress *no pl*; (*indumenti*) clothes *pl*; (*industria*) clothing industry

abbi'nare *vt* **~ (a)** to combine (with)

abboc'care *vi* (*pesce*) to bite; (*tubi*) to join; **~ (all'amo)** (*fig*) to swallow the bait

abbona'mento *sm* subscription; (*alle ferrovie ecc*) season ticket; **fare l'~** to take out a subscription (o season ticket)

abbo'narsi *vpr* **~ a un giornale** to take out a subscription to a newspaper; **~ al teatro/alle ferrovie** to take out a season ticket for the theatre/the train

abbon'dante *ag* abundant, plentiful; (*giacca*) roomy

abbon'danza [abbon'dantsa] *sf* abundance; plenty

abbor'dabile *ag* (*persona*) approachable; (*prezzo*) reasonable

a

A *abbr* (= autostrada) ≈ M (*motorway*)

PAROLA CHIAVE

a (*a + il* = **al**, *a + lo* = **allo**, *a + l'* = **all'**, *a + la* = **alla**, *a + i* = **ai**, *a + gli* = **agli**, *a + le* = **alle**) *prep*

1 (*stato in luogo*) at; (: *in*) in; **essere alla stazione** to be at the station; **essere a casa/a scuola/a Roma** to be at home/at school/in Rome; **è a 10 km da qui** it's 10 km from here, it's 10 km away

2 (*moto a luogo*) to; **andare a casa/a scuola** to go home/to school

3 (*tempo*) at; (*epoca, stagione*) in; **alle cinque** at five (o'clock); **a mezzanotte/ Natale** at midnight/Christmas; **al mattino** in the morning; **a maggio/primavera** in May/spring; **a cinquant'anni** at fifty (years of age); **a domani!** see you tomorrow!

4 (*complemento di termine*) to; **dare qc a qn** to give sth to sb

5 (*mezzo, modo*) with, by; **a piedi/cavallo** on foot/horseback; **fatto a mano** made by hand, handmade; **una barca a motore** a motorboat; **a uno a uno** one by one; **all'italiana** the Italian way, in the Italian fashion

6 (*rapporto*) a, per; (: *con prezzi*) at; **prendo 850 euro al mese** I get 850 euros a o per

abbotto'nare vt to button up, do up

abbracci'are [abbrat'tʃare] vt to embrace; (*persona*) to hug, embrace; (*professione*) to take up; (*contenere*) to include; **abbracciarsi** vpr to hug o embrace (one another); **ab'braccio** sm hug, embrace

abbrevi'are vt to shorten; (*parola*) to abbreviate

abbreviazi'one [abbrevjat'tsjone] sf abbreviation

abbron'zante [abbron'dzante] ag tanning, sun cpd

abbronzarsi vpr to tan, get a tan

abbron'zato, -a [abbron'dzato] ag (sun)tanned

abbrusto'lire vt (*pane*) to toast; (*caffè*) to roast; **abbrustolirsi** vpr to toast; (*fig: al sole*) to soak up the sun

abbuf'farsi vpr (*fam*): **~ (di qc)** to stuff o.s. (with sth)

abdi'care vi to abdicate; **~ a** to give up, renounce

a'bete sm fir (tree); **abete rosso** spruce

'abile ag (*idoneo*): **~ (a qc/a fare qc)** fit (for sth/to do sth); (*capace*) able; (*astuto*) clever; (*accorto*) skilful; **~ al servizio militare** fit for military service; **abilità** sf inv ability; cleverness; skill

a'bisso sm abyss, gulf

abi'tante sm/f inhabitant

abi'tare vt to live in, dwell in ▷ vi **~ in campagna/a Roma** to live in the country/in Rome; **dove abita?** where do you live?; **abitazi'one** sf residence; house

'abito sm dress no pl; (*da uomo*) suit; (*da donna*) dress; (*abitudine, disposizione, Rel*) habit; **abiti** smpl (*vestiti*) clothes; **in ~ da sera** in evening dress

abitu'ale ag usual, habitual; (*cliente*) regular

abitual'mente av usually, normally

abitu'are vt **~ qn a** to get sb used o accustomed to; **abituarsi a** to get used to, accustom o.s. to

abitudi'nario, -a ag of fixed habits ▷ sm/f regular customer

abi'tudine sf habit; **aver l'~ di fare qc** to be in the habit of doing sth; **d'~** usually; **per ~** from o out of habit

abo'lire vt to abolish; (*Dir*) to repeal

abor'tire vi (*Med*) to miscarry, have a miscarriage; (: *deliberatamente*) to have an abortion; (*fig*) to miscarry, fail; **a'borto** sm miscarriage; abortion

ABS [abɪɛse] sigla m (= *Anti-Blockier System*) ABS

'abside sf apse

abu'sare vi **~ di** to abuse, misuse; (*alcool*) to take to excess; (*approfittare, violare*) to take advantage of

abu'sivo, -a ag unauthorized, unlawful; **(occupante) ~** (*di una casa*) squatter

  ⬛ Attenzione! In inglese esiste la parola *abusive* che però vuol dire *ingiurioso*.

a.C. av abbr (= *avanti Cristo*) B.C.

a'cacia, -cie [a'katʃa] sf (*Bot*) acacia

ac'cadde vb vedi **accadere**

acca'demia sf (*società*) learned society; (*scuola: d'arte, militare*) academy

acca'dere vb impers to happen, occur

accal'dato ag hot

accalo'rarsi vpr (*fig*) to get excited

accampa'mento sm camp

accamparsi vpr to camp

acca'nirsi vpr (*infierire*) to rage; (*ostinarsi*) to persist; **acca'nito, -a** ag (*odio, gelosia*) fierce, bitter; (*lavoratore*) assiduous, dogged; (*fumatore*) inveterate

ac'canto av near, nearby; **~ a** prep near, beside, close to

accanto'nare vt (*problema*) to shelve; (*somma*) to set aside

accappa'toio sm bathrobe

accarez'zare [akkaret'tsare] vt to caress, stroke, fondle; (*fig*) to toy with

acca'sarsi vpr to set up house; to get married

accasci'arsi [akkaʃ'ʃarsi] vpr to collapse; (*fig*) to lose heart

accat'tone, -a sm/f beggar

accaval'lare vt (*gambe*) to cross

acce'care [attʃe'kare] vt to blind ▷ vi to go blind

ac'cedere [at'tʃedere] vi **~ a** to enter; (*richiesta*) to grant, accede to

accele'rare [attʃele'rare] vt to speed up ▷ vi (*Aut*) to accelerate; **~ il passo** to quicken one's pace; **accelera'tore** sm (*Aut*) accelerator

ac'cendere [at'tʃendere] vt (*fuoco, sigaretta*) to light; (*luce, televisione*) to put on, switch on, turn on; (*Aut: motore*) to switch on; (*Comm: conto*) to open; (*fig: suscitare*) to inflame, stir up; **ha da ~?** have you got a light?; **non riesco ad ~ il riscaldamento** I can't turn the heating on; **accen'dino, accendi'sigaro** sm (cigarette) lighter

accen'nare [attʃen'nare] vt (*Mus*) to pick out the notes of; to hum ▷ vi **~ a** (*fig: alludere a*) to hint at; (: *far atto di*) to make as if; **~ un saluto** (*con la mano*) to make as if to wave; (*col capo*) to half nod; **accenna a piovere** it looks as if it's going to rain

ac'cenno [at'tʃenno] sm (*cenno*) sign; nod; (*allusione*) hint

accensi'one [attʃen'sjone] sf (*vedi verbo*) lighting; switching on; opening; (*Aut*) ignition

ac'cento [at'tʃɛnto] *sm* accent; (*Fonetica, fig*) stress; (*inflessione*) tone (of voice)

accentu'are [attʃentu'are] *vt* to stress, emphasize; **accentuarsi** *vpr* to become more noticeable

accerchi'are [attʃer'kjare] *vt* to surround, encircle

accerta'mento [attʃerta'mento] *sm* check; assessment

accer'tare [attʃer'tare] *vt* to ascertain; (*verificare*) to check; (*reddito*) to assess; **accertarsi** *vpr* **accertarsi (di)** to make sure (of)

ac'ceso, -a [at'tʃeso] *pp di* **accendere** ▷ *ag* lit; on; open; (*colore*) bright

acces'sibile [attʃes'sibile] *ag* (*luogo*) accessible; (*persona*) approachable; (*prezzo*) reasonable

ac'cesso [at'tʃɛsso] *sm* (*anche Inform*) access; (*Med*) attack, fit; (*impulso violento*) fit, outburst

accessori *smpl* accessories

ac'cetta [at'tʃetta] *sf* hatchet

accet'tabile [attʃet'tabile] *ag* acceptable

accet'tare [attʃet'tare] *vt* to accept; **accettate carte di credito?** do you accept credit cards?; **~ di fare qc** to agree to do sth; **accettazi'one** *sf* acceptance; (*locale di servizio pubblico*) reception; **accettazione bagagli** (*Aer*) check-in (desk)

acchiap'pare [akkjap'pare] *vt* to catch

acciaie'ria [attʃaje'ria] *sf* steelworks *sg*

acci'aio [at'tʃajo] *sm* steel

acciden'tato, -a [attʃiden'tato] *ag* (*terreno ecc*) uneven

accigli'ato, -a [attʃiʎ'ʎato] *ag* frowning

ac'cingersi [at'tʃindʒersi] *vpr* **~ a fare qc** to be about to do sth

acciuf'fare [attʃuf'fare] *vt* to seize, catch

acci'uga, -ghe [at'tʃuga] *sf* anchovy

ac'cludere *vt* to enclose

accocco'larsi *vpr* to crouch

accogli'ente [akkoʎ'ʎɛnte] *ag* welcoming, friendly

ac'cogliere [ak'kɔʎʎere] *vt* (*ricevere*) to receive; (*dare il benvenuto*) to welcome; (*approvare*) to agree to, accept; (*contenere*) to hold, accommodate

ac'colgo *ecc vb vedi* **accogliere**

ac'colsi *ecc vb vedi* **accogliere**

accoltel'lare *vt* to knife, stab

accomoda'mento *sm* agreement, settlement

accomo'dante *ag* accommodating

accomo'darsi *vpr* (*sedersi*) to sit down; (*entrare*) to come in; **s'accomodi!** (*venga avanti*) come in!; (*si sieda*) take a seat!

accompagna'mento [akkompaɲɲa'mento] *sm* (*Mus*) accompaniment

accompa'gnare [akkompaɲ'ɲare] *vt* to accompany, come o go with; (*Mus*) to accompany; (*unire*) to couple; **~ la porta** to close the door gently

accompagna'tore, -trice *sm/f* companion; **~ turistico** courier

acconcia'tura [akkontʃa'tura] *sf* hairstyle

accondiscen'dente [akkondiʃʃen'dɛnte] *ag* affable

acconsen'tire *vi* **~ (a)** to agree o consent (to)

acconten'tare *vt* to satisfy; **accontentarsi** *vpr* **accontentarsi di** to be satisfied with, content o.s. with

ac'conto *sm* part payment; **pagare una somma in ~** to pay a sum of money as a deposit

acco'rato, -a *ag* heartfelt

accorci'are [akkor'tʃare] *vt* to shorten; **accorciarsi** *vpr* to become shorter

accor'dare *vt* to reconcile; (*colori*) to match; (*Mus*) to tune; (*Ling*): **~ qc con qc** to make sth agree with sth; (*Dir*) to grant; **accordarsi** *vpr* to agree, come to an agreement; (*colori*) to match

ac'cordo *sm* agreement; (*armonia*) harmony; (*Mus*) chord; **essere d'~** to agree; **andare d'~** to get on well together; **d'~!** all right!, agreed!; **accordo commerciale** trade agreement

ac'corgersi [ak'kɔrdʒersi] *vpr* **~ di** to notice; (*fig*) to realize

ac'correre *vi* to run up

ac'corto, -a *pp di* **accorgersi** ▷ *ag* shrewd; **stare ~** to be on one's guard

accos'tare *vt* (*avvicinare*): **~ qc a** to bring sth near to, put sth near to; (*avvicinarsi a*) to approach; (*socchiudere: imposte*) to half-close; (*: porta*) to leave ajar ▷ *vi* (*Naut*) to come alongside; **accostarsi** *vpr* **accostarsi a** to draw near, approach; (*fig*) to support

accredi'tare *vt* (*notizia*) to confirm the truth of; (*Comm*) to credit; (*diplomatico*) to accredit

ac'credito *sm* (*Comm: atto*) crediting; (*: effetto*) credit

accucci'arsi [akkut'tʃarsi] *vpr* (*cane*) to lie down

accu'dire *vt* (*anche: vi* **~ a**) to attend to

accumu'lare *vt* to accumulate; **accumularsi** *vpr* to accumulate; (*Finanza*) to accrue

accu'rato, -a *ag* (*diligente*) careful; (*preciso*) accurate

ac'cusa *sf* accusation; (*Dir*) charge; **la pubblica ~** the prosecution

accu'sare *vt* **~ qn di qc** to accuse sb of sth; (*Dir*) to charge sb with sth; **~ ricevuta di** (*Comm*) to acknowledge receipt of

accusa'tore, -'trice *sm/f* accuser ▷ *sm* (*Dir*) prosecutor

a'cerbo, -a [a'tʃɛrbo] *ag* bitter; (*frutta*) sour, unripe; (*persona*) immature

'acero ['atʃero] *sm* maple

a'cerrimo, -a [a'tʃɛrrimo] *ag* very fierce

a'ceto [a'tʃeto] *sm* vinegar

ace'tone [atʃe'tone] *sm* nail varnish remover

A.C.I. ['atʃi] *sigla m* = **Automobile Club d'Italia**

'acido, -a ['atʃido] *ag* (*sapore*) acid, sour; (*Chim*) acid ▷ *sm* (*Chim*) acid

'acino ['atʃino] *sm* berry; **acino d'uva** grape

'acne *sf* acne

'acqua *sf* water; (*pioggia*) rain; **acque** *sfpl* (*di mare, fiume ecc*) waters; **fare ~** (*Naut*) to leak, take in water; **~ in bocca!** mum's the word!; **acqua corrente** running water; **acqua dolce/salata** fresh/salt water; **acqua minerale/potabile/tonica** mineral/drinking/tonic water; **acque termali** thermal waters

a'cquaio *sm* sink

acqua'ragia [akkwa'radʒa] *sf* turpentine

a'cquario *sm* aquarium; (*dello zodiaco*): **A~** Aquarius

acquascooter [akkwas'kuter] *sm inv* Jet Ski®

ac'quatico, -a, -ci, -che *ag* aquatic; (*Sport, Scienza*) water *cpd*

acqua'vite *sf* brandy

acquaz'zone [akkwat'tsone] *sm* cloudburst, heavy shower

acque'dotto *sm* aqueduct; waterworks *pl*, water system

acque'rello *sm* watercolour

acqui'rente *sm/f* purchaser, buyer

acquis'tare *vt* to purchase, buy; (*fig*) to gain; **a'cquisto** *sm* purchase; **fare acquisti** to go shopping

acquo'lina *sf* **far venire l'~ in bocca a qn** to make sb's mouth water

a'crobata, -i, -e *sm/f* acrobat

a'culeo *sm* (*Zool*) sting; (*Bot*) prickle

a'cume *sm* acumen, perspicacity

a'custico, -a, ci, che *ag* acoustic ▷ *sf* (*scienza*) acoustics *sg*; (*di una sala*) acoustics *pl*; **cornetto ~** ear trumpet; **apparecchio ~** hearing aid

a'cuto, -a *ag* (*appuntito*) sharp, pointed; (*suono, voce*) shrill, piercing; (*Mat, Ling, Med*) acute; (*Mus*) high-pitched; (*fig: dolore,*

desiderio) intense; (*: perspicace*) acute, keen

a'dagio [a'dadʒo] *av* slowly ▷ *sm* (*Mus*) adagio; (*proverbio*) adage, saying

adatta'mento *sm* adaptation

adat'tare *vt* to adapt; (*sistemare*) to fit; **adattarsi** *vpr* **adattarsi (a)** (*ambiente, tempi*) to adapt (to); (*essere adatto*) to be suitable (for)

a'datto, -a *ag* **~ (a)** suitable (for), right (for)

addebi'tare *vt* **~ qc a qn** to debit sb with sth

ad'debito *sm* (*Comm*) debit

adden'tare *vt* to bite into

adden'trarsi *vpr* **~ in** to penetrate, go into

addestra'mento *sm* training

addes'trare *vt* to train

ad'detto, -a *ag* **~ a** (*persona*) assigned to; (*oggetto*) intended for ▷ *sm* employee; (*funzionario*) attaché; **gli addetti ai lavori** authorized personnel; (*fig*) those in the know; **addetto commerciale** commercial attaché; **addetto stampa** press attaché

ad'dio *sm, escl* goodbye, farewell

addirit'tura *av* (*veramente*) really, absolutely; (*perfino*) even; (*direttamente*) directly, right away

addi'tare *vt* to point out; (*fig*) to expose

addi'tivo *sm* additive

addizi'one *sf* addition

addob'bare *vt* to decorate; **ad'dobbo** *sm* decoration

addolo'rare *vt* to pain, grieve; **addolorarsi (per)** to be distressed (by)

addolo'rato, -a *ag* distressed, upset; **l'Addolorata** (*Rel*) Our Lady of Sorrows

ad'dome *sm* abdomen

addomesti'care *vt* to tame

addomi'nale *ag* abdominal; (**muscoli** *mpl*) **addominali** stomach muscles

addormen'tare *vt* to put to sleep; **addormentarsi** *vpr* to fall asleep, go to sleep

ad'dosso *av* on; **mettersi ~ il cappotto** to put one's coat on; **~ a** (*sopra*) on; (*molto vicino*) right next to; **stare ~ a qn** (*fig*) to breathe down sb's neck; **dare ~ a qn** (*fig*) to attack sb

adeguarsi *vpr* to adapt

adegu'ato, -a *ag* adequate; (*conveniente*) suitable; (*equo*) fair

a'dempiere *vt* to fulfil, carry out

ade'rente *ag* adhesive; (*vestito*) close-fitting ▷ *sm/f* follower

ade'rire *vi* (*stare attaccato*) to adhere, stick; **~ a** to adhere to, stick to; (*fig: società, partito*) to join; (*: opinione*) to support; (*richiesta*) to agree to

adesi'one *sf* adhesion; (*fig*) agreement,

acceptance; **ade'sivo, -a** *ag, sm* adhesive

a'desso *av (ora)* now; *(or ora, poco fa)* just now; *(tra poco)* any moment now

adia'cente [adja'tʃɛnte] *ag* adjacent

adi'bire *vt (usare):* **~ qc a** to turn sth into

adole'scente [adoleʃʃɛnte] *ag, sm/f* adolescent

adope'rare *vt* to use

ado'rare *vt* to adore; *(Rel)* to adore, worship

adot'tare *vt* to adopt; *(decisione, provvedimenti)* to pass; **adot'tivo, -a** *ag (genitori)* adoptive; *(figlio, patria)* adopted; **adozi'one** *sf* adoption; **adozione a distanza** child sponsorship

adri'atico, -a, -ci, -che *ag* Adriatic ▷ *sm* **l'A~, il mare A~** the Adriatic, the Adriatic Sea

adu'lare *vt* to adulate, flatter

a'dultero, -a *ag* adulterous ▷ *sm/f* adulterer (adulteress)

a'dulto, -a *ag* adult; *(fig)* mature ▷ *sm* adult, grown-up

a'ereo, -a *ag* air *cpd;* *(radice)* aerial ▷ *sm* aerial; *(aeroplano)* plane; **aereo da caccia** fighter (plane); **aereo di linea** airliner; **aereo a reazione** jet (plane); **ae'robica** *sf* aerobics *sg;* **aero'nautica** *sf (scienza)* aeronautics *sg;* **aeronautica militare** air force

aero'porto *sm* airport; **all'~ per favore** to the airport, please

aero'sol *sm inv* aerosol

'afa *sf* sultriness

af'fabile *ag* affable

affaccen'dato, -a [affattʃen'dato] *ag (persona)* busy

affacci'arsi [affat'tʃarsi] *vpr* **~ (a)** to appear (at)

affa'mato, -a *ag* starving; *(fig):* **~ (di)** eager (for)

affan'noso, -a *ag (respiro)* difficult; *(fig)* troubled, anxious

af'fare *sm (faccenda)* matter, affair; *(Comm)* piece of business, (business) deal; *(occasione)* bargain; *(Dir)* case; *(fam: cosa)* thing; **affari** *smpl (Comm)* business *sg;* **Ministro degli Affari esteri** Foreign Secretary (BRIT), Secretary of State (US)

affasci'nante [affaʃʃi'nante] *ag* fascinating

affasci'nare [affaʃʃi'nare] *vt* to bewitch; *(fig)* to charm, fascinate

affati'care *vt* to tire; **affaticarsi** *vpr (durar fatica)* to tire o.s. out; **affati'cato, -a** *ag* tired

af'fatto *av* completely; **non ... ~** not ... at all; **niente ~** not at all

affer'mare *vt (dichiarare)* to maintain,

affirm; **affermarsi** *vpr* to assert o.s., make one's name known; **affer'mato, -a** *ag* established, well-known; **affermazi'one** *sf* affirmation, assertion; *(successo)* achievement

affer'rare *vt* to seize, grasp; *(fig: idea)* to grasp; **afferrarsi** *vpr* **afferrarsi a** to cling to

affet'tare *vt (tagliare a fette)* to slice; *(ostentare)* to affect

affetta'trice [affetta'tritʃe] *sf* meat slicer

affet'tivo, -a *ag* emotional, affective

af'fetto *sm* affection; **affettu'oso, -a** *ag* affectionate

affezio'narsi [affettsjo'narsi] *vpr* **~ a** to grow fond of

affezio'nato, -a [affettsjo'nato] *ag* **~ a qn/qc** fond of sb/sth; *(attaccato)* attached to sb/sth

affia'tato, -a *ag* **essere molto affiatati** to get on very well

affibbi'are *vt (fig: dare)* to give

affi'dabile *ag* reliable

affida'mento *sm (Dir: di bambino)* custody; *(fiducia):* **fare ~ su qn** to rely on sb; **non dà nessun ~** he's not to be trusted

affi'dare *vt* **~ qc o qn a qn** to entrust sth o sb to sb; **affidarsi** *vpr* **affidarsi a** to place one's trust in

affi'lare *vt* to sharpen

affi'lato, -a *ag (gen)* sharp; *(volto, naso)* thin

affinché [affin'ke] *cong* in order that, so that

affit'tare *vt (dare in affitto)* to let, rent (out); *(prendere in affitto)* to rent; **af'fitto** *sm* rent; *(contratto)* lease

af'fliggere [af'fliddʒere] *vt* to torment; **affliggersi** *vpr* to grieve

af'flissi *ecc vb vedi* **affliggere**

afflosci'arsi [affloʃʃarsi] *vpr* to go limp

afflu'ente *sm* tributary

affo'gare *vt, vi* to drown

affol'lare *vt* to crowd; **affollarsi** *vpr* to crowd; **affol'lato, -a** *ag* crowded

affon'dare *vt* to sink

affran'care *vt* to free, liberate; *(Amm)* to redeem; *(lettera)* to stamp; *(: meccanicamente)* to frank (BRIT), meter (US)

af'fresco, -schi *sm* fresco

affret'tarsi *vpr* to hurry; **~ a fare qc** to hurry o hasten to do sth

affret'tato, -a *ag (veloce: passo, ritmo)* quick, fast; *(frettoloso: decisione)* hurried, hasty; *(: lavoro)* rushed

affron'tare *vt (pericolo ecc)* to face; *(nemico)* to confront; **affrontarsi** *vpr (reciproco)* to come to blows

affumi'cato, -a ag (prosciutto, aringa ecc) smoked

affuso'lato, -a ag tapering

Af'ganistan sm l'~ Afghanistan

a'foso, -a ag sultry, close

'Africa sf l'~ Africa; **afri'cano, -a** ag, sm/f African

a'genda [a'dʒɛnda] sf diary

> Attenzione! In inglese esiste la parola *agenda* che però vuol dire *ordine del giorno*.

a'gente [a'dʒɛnte] sm agent; **agente di cambio** stockbroker; **agente di polizia** police officer; **agente segreto** secret agent; **agen'zia** sf agency; (succursale) branch; **agenzia immobiliare** estate agent's (office) (BRIT), real estate office (US); **agenzia di collocamento/stampa** employment/press agency; **agenzia viaggi** travel agency

agevo'lare [adʒevo'lare] vt to facilitate, make easy

agevolazi'one [adʒevolat'tsjone] sf (facilitazione economica) facility; **agevolazione di pagamento** payment on easy terms; **agevolazioni creditizie** credit facilities; **agevolazioni fiscali** tax concessions

a'gevole [a'dʒevole] ag easy; (strada) smooth

aggianci'are [aggan'tʃare] vt to hook up; (Ferr) to couple

ag'geggio [ad'dʒeddʒo] sm gadget, contraption

agget'tivo [addʒet'tivo] sm adjective

agghiacci'ante [aggjat'tʃante] ag chilling

aggior'nare [addʒor'nare] vt (opera, manuale) to bring up-to-date; (seduta ecc) to postpone; **aggiornarsi** vpr to bring (o keep) o.s. up-to-date; **aggior'nato, -a** ag up-to-date

aggi'rare [addʒi'rare] vt to go round; (fig: ingannare) to trick; **aggirarsi** vpr to wander about; **il prezzo s'aggira sul milione** the price is around the million mark

aggi'ungere [ad'dʒundʒere] vt to add

aggi'unsi ecc [ad'dʒunsi] vb vedi **aggiungere**

aggius'tare [addʒus'tare] vt (accomodare) to mend, repair; (riassettare) to adjust; (fig: lite) to settle

aggrap'parsi vpr ~ **a** to cling to

aggra'vare vt (aumentare) to increase; (appesantire: anche fig) to weigh down, make heavy; (pena) to make worse; **aggravarsi** vpr to worsen, become worse

aggre'dire vt to attack, assault

aggressi'one sf aggression; (atto) attack, assault

aggres'sivo, -a ag aggressive

aggres'sore sm aggressor, attacker

aggrot'tare vt ~ **le sopracciglia** to frown

aggrovigliarsi vpr (fig) to become complicated

aggu'ato sm trap; (imboscata) ambush; **tendere un ~ a qn** to set a trap for sb

agguer'rito, -a ag fierce

agi'ato, -a [a'dʒato] ag (vita) easy; (persona) well-off, well-to-do

'agile ['adʒile] ag agile, nimble

'agio ['adʒo] sm ease, comfort; **mettersi a proprio ~** to make o.s. at home o comfortable; **agi** smpl comforts; **mettersi a proprio ~** to make o.s. at home o comfortable; **dare ~ a qn di fare qc** to give sb the chance of doing sth

a'gire [a'dʒire] vi to act; (esercitare un'azione) to take effect; (Tecn) to work, function; ~ **contro qn** (Dir) to take action against sb

agi'tare [adʒi'tare] vt (bottiglia) to shake; (mano, fazzoletto) to wave; (fig: turbare) to disturb; (: incitare) to stir (up); (: dibattere) to discuss; **agitarsi** vpr (mare) to be rough; (malato, dormitore) to toss and turn; (bambino) to fidget; (emozionarsi) to get upset; (Pol) to agitate; **agi'tato, -a** ag rough; restless; fidgety; upset, perturbed

'aglio ['aʎʎo] sm garlic

a'gnello [aɲ'ɲɛllo] sm lamb

'ago (pl **'aghi**) sm needle

ago'nistico, -a, -ci, -che ag athletic; (fig) competitive

agopun'tura sf acupuncture

a'gosto sm August

a'grario, -a ag agrarian, agricultural; (riforma) land cpd

a'gricolo, -a ag agricultural, farm cpd; **agricol'tore** sm farmer; **agricol'tura** sf agriculture, farming

agri'foglio [agri'foʎʎo] sm holly

agritu'rismo sm farm holidays pl

agrodolce ag bittersweet; (salsa) sweet and sour

a'grume sm (spesso al pl: pianta) citrus; (: frutto) citrus fruit

a'guzzo, -a [a'guttso] ag sharp

'ahi escl (dolore) ouch!

'Aia sf l'~ the Hague

'aids abbr m of Aids

airbag sm inv air bag

ai'rone sm heron

aiu'ola sf flower bed

aiu'tante sm/f assistant ▷ sm (Mil) adjutant; (Naut) master-at-arms; **aiutante di campo** aide-de-camp

aiu'tare vt to help; ~ **qn (a fare)** to help sb

(to do); **aiutarsi** *vpr* to help each other; **~ qn in qc/a fare qc** to help sb with sth/to do sth; **può aiutarmi?** can you help me?

ai'uto *sm* help, assistance, aid; *(aiutante)* assistant; **venire in ~ di qn** to come to sb's aid; **aiuto chirurgo** assistant surgeon

'ala *(pl* **'ali)** *sf* wing; **fare ~** to fall back, make way; **ala destra/sinistra** *(Sport)* right/left wing

ala'bastro *sm* alabaster

a'lano *sm* Great Dane

'alba *sf* dawn

alba'nese *ag, sm/f, sm* Albanian

Alba'nia *sf* **l'~** Albania

albe'rato, -a *ag (viale, piazza)* lined with trees, tree-lined

al'bergo, -ghi *sm* hotel; **albergo della gioventù** youth hostel

'albero *sm* tree; *(Naut)* mast; *(Tecn)* shaft; **albero genealogico** family tree; **albero a gomiti** crankshaft; **albero maestro** mainmast; **albero di Natale** Christmas tree; **albero di trasmissione** transmission shaft

albi'cocca, -che *sf* apricot

'album *sm* album; **album da disegno** sketch book

al'bume *sm* albumen

'alce ['altʃe] *sm* elk

'alcol *sm inv* = **alcool**

al'colico, -a, -ci, -che *ag* alcoholic ▷ *sm* alcoholic drink

alcoliz'zato, -a [alcolid'dzato] *sm/f* alcoholic

'alcool *sm inv* alcohol

al'cuno, -a *(det: dav sm:* **alcun** + *C, V,* **alcuno** + *s impura, gn, pn, ps, x, z; dav sf:* **alcuna** + *C,* **alcun'** +*V) det (nessuno):* **non ... ~** no, not any; **alcuni, e** *det pl* some, a few; **non c'è alcuna fretta** there's no hurry, there isn't any hurry; **senza alcun riguardo** without any consideration ▷ *pron pl* **alcuni, e** some, a few

alfa'betico, -a, ci, che *ag* alphabetical

alfa'beto *sm* alphabet

'alga, -ghe *sf* seaweed *no pl*, alga

'algebra ['aldʒebra] *sf* algebra

Alge'ria [aldʒe'ria] *sf* **l'~** Algeria

alge'rino, -a [aldʒe'rino] *ag, sm/f* Algerian

ali'ante *sm (Aer)* glider

'alibi *sm inv* alibi

a'lice [a'litʃe] *sf* anchovy

ali'eno, -a *ag (avverso):* **~ (da)** opposed (to), averse (to) ▷ *sm* alien

alimen'tare *vt* to feed; *(Tecn)* to feed; to supply; *(fig)* to sustain ▷ *ag* food *cpd*; **alimentari** *smpl* foodstuffs; *(anche:*

negozio di alimentari) grocer's shop; **alimentazi'one** *sf* feeding; supplying; sustaining; *(gli alimenti)* diet

a'liquota *sf* share; *(d'imposta)* rate; **aliquota d'imposta** tax rate

alis'cafo *sm* hydrofoil

'alito *sm* breath

all. *abbr* (= *allegato*) encl.

allaccia'mento [allattʃa'mento] *sm (Tecn)* connection

allacci'are [allat'tʃare] *vt (scarpe)* to tie, lace (up); *(cintura)* to do up, fasten; *(luce, gas)* to connect; *(amicizia)* to form

allaccia'tura [allattʃa'tura] *sf* fastening

alla'gare *vt* to flood; **allagarsi** *vpr* to flood

allar'gare *vt* to widen; *(vestito)* to let out; *(aprire)* to open; *(fig: dilatare)* to extend; **allargarsi** *vpr (gen)* to widen; *(scarpe, pantaloni)* to stretch; *(fig: problema, fenomeno)* to spread

allar'mare *vt* to alarm

al'larme *sm* alarm; **allarme aereo** air-raid warning

allat'tare *vt* to feed

alle'anza [alle'antsa] *sf* alliance

alle'arsi *vpr* to form an alliance; **alle'ato, -a** *ag* allied ▷ *sm/f* ally

alle'gare *vt (accludere)* to enclose; *(Dir: citare)* to cite, adduce; *(denti)* to set on edge; **alle'gato, -a** *ag* enclosed ▷ *sm* enclosure; *(di e-mail)* attachment; **in allegato** enclosed

allegge'rire [alleddʒe'rire] *vt* to lighten, make lighter; *(fig: lavoro, tasse)* to reduce

alle'gria *sf* gaiety, cheerfulness

al'legro, -a *ag* cheerful, merry; *(un po' brillo)* merry, tipsy; *(vivace: colore)* bright ▷ *sm (Mus)* allegro

allena'mento *sm* training

alle'nare *vt* to train; **allenarsi** *vpr* to train; **allena'tore** *sm (Sport)* trainer, coach

allen'tare *vt* to slacken; *(disciplina)* to relax; **allentarsi** *vpr* to become slack; *(ingranaggio)* to work loose

aller'gia, -'gie [aller'dʒia] *sf* allergy; **al'lergico, -a, -ci, -che** *ag* allergic; **sono allergico alla penicillina** I'm allergic to penicillin

alles'tire *vt (cena)* to prepare; *(esercito, nave)* to equip, fit out; *(spettacolo)* to stage

allet'tante *ag* attractive, alluring

alle'vare *vt (animale)* to breed, rear; *(bambino)* to bring up

allevi'are *vt* to alleviate

alli'bito, -a *ag* astounded

alli'evo *sm* pupil; *(apprendista)* apprentice; *(Mil)* cadet

alliga'tore *sm* alligator

alline'are vt (persone, cose) to line up; (Tip) to align; (fig: economia, salari) to adjust, align; **allinearsi** vpr to line up; (fig: a idee): **allinearsi a** to come into line with

al'lodola sf (sky)lark

alloggi'are [allod'dʒare] vt to accommodate ▷ vi to live; **al'loggio** sm lodging, accommodation (BRIT), accommodations (US)

allonta'nare vt to send away, send off; (impiegato) to dismiss; (pericolo) to avert, remove; (estraniare) to alienate; **allontanarsi** vpr **allontanarsi (da)** to go away (from); (estraniarsi) to become estranged (from)

al'lora av (in quel momento) then ▷ cong (in questo caso) well then; (dunque) well then, so; **la gente d'~** people then o in those days; **da ~ in poi** from then on

al'loro sm laurel

'alluce ['allutʃe] sm big toe

alluci'nante [allutʃi'nante] ag awful; (fam) amazing

allucinazi'one [allutʃinat'tsjone] sf hallucination

al'ludere vi **~ a** to allude to, hint at

allu'minio sm aluminium (BRIT), aluminum (US)

allun'gare vt to lengthen; (distendere) to prolong, extend; (diluire) to water down; **allungarsi** vpr to lengthen; (ragazzo) to stretch, grow taller; (sdraiarsi) to lie down, stretch out

al'lusi ecc vb vedi **alludere**

allusi'one sf hint, allusion

alluvi'one sf flood

al'meno av at least ▷ cong **(se) ~** if only; **(se) ~ piovesse!** if only it would rain!

a'logeno, -a [a'lɔdʒeno] ag **lampada alogena** halogen lamp

a'lone sm halo

'Alpi sfpl **le ~** the Alps

alpi'nismo sm mountaineering, climbing; **alpi'nista, -i, -e** sm/f mountaineer, climber

al'pino, -a ag Alpine; mountain cpd; **alpini** smpl (Mil) Italian Alpine troops

alt escl halt!, stop!

alta'lena sf (a funi) swing; (in bilico) seesaw

al'tare sm altar

alter'nare vt to alternate; **alternarsi** vpr to alternate; **alterna'tiva** sf alternative; **alterna'tivo, -a** ag alternative

al'terno, -a ag alternate; **a giorni alterni** on alternate days, every other day

al'tero, -a ag proud

al'tezza [al'tettsa] sf height; width, breadth; depth; pitch; (Geo) latitude;

(titolo) highness; (fig: nobiltà) greatness; **essere all'~ di** to be on a level with; (fig) to be up to o equal to

al'ticcio, -a, -ci, -ce [al'tittʃo] ag tipsy

alti'tudine sf altitude

'alto, -a ag high; (persona) tall; (tessuto) wide, broad; (sonno, acque) deep; (suono) high(-pitched); (Geo) upper; (settentrionale) northern ▷ sm top (part) ▷ av high; (parlare) aloud, loudly; **il palazzo è ~ 20 metri** the building is 20 metres high; **ad alta voce** aloud; **a notte alta** in the dead of night; **in ~** up, upwards; at the top; **dall'~ in** o **al basso** up and down; **degli alti e bassi** (fig) ups and downs; **alta fedeltà** high fidelity, hi-fi; **alta finanza/società** high finance/society; **alta moda** haute couture

altopar'lante sm loudspeaker

altopi'ano (pl altipi'ani) sm plateau, upland plain

altret'tanto, -a ag, pron as much; (pl) as many ▷ av equally; **tanti auguri! — grazie, ~** all the best! — thank you, the same to you

altri'menti av otherwise

 PAROLA CHIAVE

'altro, -a det 1 (diverso) other, different; **questa è un'altra cosa** that's another o a different thing

2 (supplementare) other; **prendi un altro cioccolatino** have another chocolate; **hai avuto altre notizie?** have you had any more o any other news?

3 (nel tempo): **l'altro giorno** the other day; **l'altr'anno** last year; **l'altro ieri** the day before yesterday; **domani l'altro** the day after tomorrow; **quest'altro mese** next month

4: **d'altra parte** on the other hand ▷ pron 1 (persona, cosa diversa o supplementare): **un altro, un'altra** another (one); **lo farà un altro** someone else will do it; **altri, e** others; **gli altri** (la gente) others, other people; **l'uno e l'altro** both (of them); **aiutarsi l'un l'altro** to help one another; **da un giorno all'altro** from day to day; (nel giro di 24 ore) from one day to the next; (da un momento all'altro) any day now

2 (sostantivato: solo maschile) something else; (: in espressioni interrogative) anything else; **non ho altro da dire** I have nothing else o I don't have anything else to say; **più che altro** above all; **se non altro** at least; **tra l'altro** among other things; **ci mancherebbe altro!** that's all we

need!; **non faccio altro che lavorare** I do nothing but work; **contento? — altro che!** are you pleased? — and how!; *vedi* **senza**; **noialtri**; **voialtri**; **tutto**

al'trove *av* elsewhere, somewhere else
altru'ista, -i, -e *ag* altruistic
a'lunno, -a *sm/f* pupil
alve'are *sm* hive
al'zare [al'tsare] *vt* to raise, lift; (*issare*) to hoist; (*costruire*) to build, erect; **alzarsi** *vpr* to rise; (*dal letto*) to get up; (*crescere*) to grow tall (*o taller*); **~ le spalle** to shrug one's shoulders; **alzarsi in piedi** to stand up, get to one's feet
a'maca, -che *sf* hammock
amalga'mare *vt* to amalgamate; **amalgamarsi** *vpr* to amalgamate
a'mante *ag* **~ di** (*musica ecc*) fond of ▷ *sm/f* lover/mistress
a'mare *vt* to love; (*amico, musica, sport*) to like; **amarsi** to love each other
amareggi'ato, -a [amared'dʒato] *ag* upset, saddened
ama'rena *sf* sour black cherry
ama'rezza [ama'rettsa] *sf* bitterness
a'maro, -a *ag* bitter ▷ *sm* bitterness; (*liquore*) bitters *pl*
amaz'zonico, -a, ci, che [amad'dzɔniko] *ag* Amazonian; Amazon *cpd*
ambasci'ata [ambaʃ'ʃata] *sf* embassy; (*messaggio*) message; **ambascia'tore, -'trice** *sm/f* ambassador/ambassadress
ambe'due *ag inv* **~ i ragazzi** both boys ▷ *pron inv* both
ambienta'lista, -i, e *ag* environmental ▷ *sm/f* environmentalist
ambien'tare *vt* to acclimatize; (*romanzo, film*) to set; **ambientarsi** *vpr* to get used to one's surroundings
ambi'ente *sm* environment; (*fig: insieme di persone*) milieu; (*stanza*) room
am'biguo, -a *ag* ambiguous
ambizi'one [ambit'tsjone] *sf* ambition; **ambizi'oso, -a** *ag* ambitious
'ambo *ag inv* both ▷ *sm* (*al gioco*) double
'ambra *sf* amber; **ambra grigia** ambergris
ambu'lante *ag* itinerant ▷ *sm* peddler
ambu'lanza [ambu'lantsa] *sf* ambulance; **chiamate un ~** call an ambulance
ambula'torio *sm* (*studio medico*) surgery
A'merica *sf* l'**~** America; l'**~ latina** Latin America; **ameri'cano, -a** *ag*, *sm/f* American
ami'anto *sm* asbestos
ami'chevole [ami'kevole] *ag* friendly
ami'cizia [ami'tʃittsja] *sf* friendship; **amicizie** *sfpl* (*amici*) friends
a'mico, -a, -ci, -che *sm/f* friend;

(*fidanzato*) boyfriend/girlfriend; **amico del cuore** bosom friend
'amido *sm* starch
ammac'care *vt* (*pentola*) to dent; (*persona*) to bruise
ammacca'tura *sf* dent; bruise
ammaes'trare *vt* (*animale*) to train
ammai'nare *vt* to lower, haul down
amma'larsi *vpr* to fall ill; **amma'lato, -a** *ag* ill, sick ▷ *sm/f* sick person; (*paziente*) patient
ammanet'tare *vt* to handcuff
ammas'sare *vt* (*ammucchiare*) to amass; (*raccogliere*) to gather together; **ammassarsi** *vpr* to pile up; to gather
ammat'tire *vi* to go mad
ammaz'zare [ammat'tsare] *vt* to kill; **ammazzarsi** *vpr* (*uccidersi*) to kill o.s.; (*rimanere ucciso*) to be killed; **ammazzarsi di lavoro** to work o.s. to death
am'mettere *vt* to admit; (*riconoscere: fatto*) to acknowledge, admit; (*permettere*) to allow, accept; (*supporre*) to suppose
amminis'trare *vt* to run, manage; (*Rel, Dir*) to administer; **amministra'tore** *sm* administrator; (*di condominio*) flats manager; **amministratore delegato** managing director; **amministrazi'one** *sf* management; administration
ammi'raglio [ammi'raʎʎo] *sm* admiral
ammi'rare *vt* to admire; **ammirazi'one** *sf* admiration
am'misi *ecc vb vedi* **ammettere**
ammobili'ato, -a *ag* furnished
am'mollo *sm* **lasciare in ~** to leave to soak
ammo'niaca *sf* ammonia
ammo'nire *vt* (*avvertire*) to warn; (*rimproverare*) to admonish; (*Dir*) to caution
ammonizi'one [ammonit'tsjone] *sf* (*monito: anche Sport*) warning; (*rimprovero*) reprimand; (*Dir*) caution
ammon'tare *vi* **~ a** to amount to ▷ *sm* (*total*) amount
ammorbi'dente *sm* fabric conditioner
ammorbi'dire *vt* to soften
ammortizza'tore *sm* (*Aut, Tecn*) shock-absorber
ammucchi'are [ammuk'kjare] *vt* to pile up, accumulate
ammuf'fire *vi* to go mouldy (BRIT) o moldy (US)
ammuto'lire *vi* to be struck dumb
amne'sia *sf* amnesia
amnis'tia *sf* amnesty
'amo *sm* (*Pesca*) hook; (*fig*) bait
a'more *sm* love; **amori** *smpl* love affairs; **il tuo bambino è un ~** your baby's a darling; **fare l'~ o all'~** to make love; **per ~ o per forza** by hook or by crook; **amor proprio**

self-esteem, pride

amo'roso, -a *ag (affettuoso)* loving, affectionate; *(d'amore: sguardo)* amorous; *(: poesia, relazione)* love cpd

'ampio, -a *ag* wide, broad; *(spazioso)* spacious; *(abbondante: vestito)* loose; *(: gonna)* full; *(: spiegazione)* ample, full

am'plesso *sm* intercourse

ampli'are *vt (ingrandire)* to enlarge; *(allargare)* to widen; **ampliarsi** *vpr* to grow, increase

amplifica'tore *sm (Tecn, Mus)* amplifier

ampu'tare *vt (Med)* to amputate

A.N. *sigla f (= Alleanza Nazionale)* Italian right-wing party

anabbaglianti *smpl* dipped (BRIT) *o* dimmed (US) headlights

anaboliz'zante *ag* anabolic ▷ *sm* anabolic steroid

anal'colico, -a, -ci, -che *ag* non-alcoholic ▷ *sm* soft drink

analfa'beta, -i, -e *ag, sm/f* illiterate

anal'gesico, -a, -ci, -che [anal'dʒɛziko] *ag, sm* analgesic

a'nalisi *sf inv* analysis; *(Med: esame)* test; **analisi del sangue** blood test *sg*

analiz'zare [analid'dzare] *vt* to analyse; *(Med)* to test

a'nalogo, -a, -ghi, -ghe *ag* analogous

'ananas *sm inv* pineapple

anar'chia [anar'kia] *sf* anarchy; **a'narchico, -a, -ci, -che** *ag* anarchic(al) ▷ *sm/f* anarchist

anarco-insurreziona'lista *ag* anarcho-revolutionary

'A.N.A.S. *sigla f (= Azienda Nazionale Autonoma delle Strade)* national roads department

anato'mia *sf* anatomy

'anatra *sf* duck

'anca, -che *sf (Anat)* hip

'anche ['anke] *cong (inoltre, pure)* also, too; *(perfino)* even; **vengo anch'io** I'm coming too; **~ se** even if

an'cora *av* still; *(di nuovo)* again; *(di più)* some more; *(persino)*: **~ più forte** even stronger; **non ~** not yet; **~ una volta** once more, once again; **~ un po'** a little more; *(di tempo)* a little longer

an'dare *sm* **a lungo ~** in the long run ▷ *vi* to go; *(essere adatto)*: **~ a** to suit; *(piacere)*: **il suo comportamento non mi va** I don't like the way he behaves; **ti va di ~ al cinema?** do you feel like going to the cinema?; **andarsene** to go away; **questa camicia va lavata** this shirt needs a wash *o* should be washed; **~ a cavallo** to ride; **~ in macchina/aereo** to go by car/plane; **~ a fare qc** to go and do sth; **~ a pescare/**

sciare to go fishing/skiing; **~ a male** to go bad; **come va?** *(lavoro, progetto)* how are things?; **come va? — bene, grazie!** how are you? — fine, thanks!; **va fatto entro oggi** it's got to be done today; **ne va della nostra vita** our lives are at stake; **an'data** *sf* going; *(viaggio)* outward journey; **biglietto di sola andata** single (BRIT) *o* one-way ticket; **biglietto di andata e ritorno** return (BRIT) *o* round-trip (US) ticket

andrò *ecc vb vedi* **andare**

a'neddoto *sm* anecdote

a'nello *sm* ring; *(di catena)* link; **anelli** *smpl (Ginnastica)* rings

a'nemico, -a, -ci, -che *ag* anaemic

aneste'sia *sf* anaesthesia

'angelo ['andʒelo] *sm* angel; **angelo custode** guardian angel

anghe'ria [ange'ria] *sf* vexation

angli'cano, -a *ag* Anglican

anglo'sassone *ag* Anglo-Saxon

'angolo *sm* corner; *(Mat)* angle; **angolo cottura** *(di appartamento ecc)* cooking area

an'goscia, -sce [an'gɔʃʃa] *sf* deep anxiety, anguish *no pl*

angu'illa *sf* eel

an'guria *sf* watermelon

'anice ['anitʃe] *sm (Cuc)* aniseed; *(Bot)* anise

'anima *sf* soul; *(abitante)* inhabitant; **non c'era ~ viva** there wasn't a living soul; **anima gemella** soul mate

ani'male *sm, ag* animal; **animale domestico** pet

anna'cquare *vt* to water down, dilute

annaffi'are *vt* to water; **annaffia'toio** *sm* watering can

an'nata *sf* year; *(importo annuo)* annual amount; **vino d'~** vintage wine

anne'gare *vt, vi* to drown

anne'rire *vt* to blacken ▷ *vi* to become black

annien'tare *vt* to annihilate, destroy

anniver'sario *sm* anniversary; **anniversario di matrimonio** wedding anniversary

'anno *sm* year; **ha 8 anni** he's 8 (years old)

anno'dare *vt* to knot, tie; *(fig: rapporto)* to form

annoi'are *vt* to bore; **annoiarsi** *vpr* to be bored

> Attenzione! In inglese esiste il verbo *to annoy* che però vuol dire *dare fastidio a*.

anno'tare *vt (registrare)* to note, note down; *(commentare)* to annotate

annu'ale *ag* annual

annu'ire *vi* to nod; *(acconsentire)* to agree

annul'lare *vt* to annihilate, destroy;

(*contratto, francobollo*) to cancel; (*matrimonio*) to annul; (*sentenza*) to quash; (*risultati*) to declare void

annunci'are [annun'tʃare] *vt* to announce; (*dar segni rivelatori*) to herald

an'nuncio [an'nuntʃo] *sm* announcement; (*fig*) sign; **annunci economici** classified advertisements, small ads; **annunci mortuari** (*colonna*) obituary column; **annuncio pubblicitario** advertisement

'annuo, -a *ag* annual, yearly

annu'sare *vt* to sniff, smell; **~ tabacco** to take snuff

a'nomalo, -a *ag* anomalous

a'nonimo, -a *ag* anonymous ▷ *sm* (*autore*) anonymous writer (*o* painter *ecc*); **società anonima** (*Comm*) joint stock company

anores'sia *sf* anorexia

ano'ressico, -a, -ci, che *ag* anorexic

anor'male *ag* abnormal ▷ *sm/f* subnormal person

ANSA *sigla f* (= *Agenzia Nazionale Stampa Associata*) press agency

'ansia *sf* anxiety

ansi'mare *vi* to pant

ansi'oso, -a *ag* anxious

'anta *sf* (*di finestra*) shutter; (*di armadio*) door

An'tartide *sf* **l'~** Antarctica

an'tenna *sf* (*Radio, TV*) aerial; (*Zool*) antenna, feeler; (*Naut*) yard; **antenna parabolica** satellite dish

ante'prima *sf* preview; **anteprima di stampa** (*Inform*) print preview

anteri'ore *ag* (*ruota, zampa*) front; (*fatti*) previous, preceding

antiade'rente *ag* non-stick

antibi'otico, -a, -ci, -che *ag, sm* antibiotic

anti'camera *sf* anteroom; **fare ~** to wait (for an audience)

antici'pare [antitʃi'pare] *vt* (*consegna, visita*) to bring forward, anticipate; (*somma di denaro*) to pay in advance; (*notizia*) to disclose ▷ *vi* to be ahead of time; **an'ticipo** *sm* anticipation; (*di denaro*) advance; **in anticipo** early, in advance; **occorre che prenoti in anticipo?** do I need to book in advance?

an'tico, -a, -chi, -che *ag* (*quadro, mobili*) antique; (*dell'antichità*) ancient; **all'antica** old-fashioned

anticoncezio'nale [antikontʃettsjo'nale] *sm* contraceptive

anticonfor'mista, -i, -e *ag, sm/f* nonconformist

anti'corpo *sm* antibody

antidolo'rifico, -ci *sm* painkiller

anti'doping *sm* drug testing ▷ *ag inv* **test ~ drugs** (*BRIT*) *o* **drug** (*US*) **test**

an'tifona *sf* (*Mus, Rel*) antiphon; **capire l'~** (*fig*) to take the hint

anti'forfora *ag inv* anti-dandruff

anti'furto *sm* anti-theft device

anti'gelo [anti'dʒelo] *ag inv* **(liquido) ~** (*per motore*) antifreeze; (*per cristalli*) de-icer

antiglobalizzazione [antiglobalidd zat'tsjone] *ag inv* **movimento ~** anti-globalization movement

An'tille *sfpl* **le ~** the West Indies

antin'cendio [antin'tʃendjo] *ag inv* fire *cpd*

anti'nebbia *sm inv* (*anche:* **faro ~**: *Aut*) fog lamp

antinfiamma'torio, -a *ag, sm* anti-inflammatory

antio'rario [antio'rarjo] *ag* **in senso ~** anticlockwise

anti'pasto *sm* hors d'œuvre

antipa'tia *sf* antipathy, dislike; **anti'patico, -a, -ci, -che** *ag* unpleasant, disagreeable

antiproi'ettile *ag inv* bulletproof

antiquari'ato *sm* antique trade; **un oggetto d'~** an antique

anti'quario *sm* antique dealer

anti'quato, -a *ag* antiquated, old-fashioned

anti'rughe *ag inv* (*crema, prodotto*) anti-wrinkle

antitraspi'rante *ag* antiperspirant

anti'vipera *ag inv* **siero ~** remedy for snake bites

antivirus [anti'virus] *sm inv* antivirus software *no pl* ▷ *ag inv* antivirus

antolo'gia, -'gie [antolo'dʒia] *sf* anthology

anu'lare *ag* ring *cpd* ▷ *sm* third finger

'anzi ['antsi] *av* (*invece*) on the contrary; (*o meglio*) or rather, or better still

anzi'ano, -a [an'tsjano] *ag* old; (*Amm*) senior ▷ *sm/f* old person; senior member

anziché [antsi'ke] *cong* rather than

a'patico, -a, -ci, -che *ag* apathetic

'ape *sf* bee

aperi'tivo *sm* apéritif

aperta'mente *av* openly

a'perto, -a *pp di* **aprire** ▷ *ag* open; **all'~** in the open (air); **è ~ al pubblico?** is it open to the public?; **quando è ~ il museo?** when is the museum open?

aper'tura *sf* opening; (*ampiezza*) width; (*Fot*) aperture; **apertura alare** wing span; **apertura mentale** open-mindedness

ap'nea *sf* **immergersi in ~** to dive without breathing apparatus

a'postrofo *sm* apostrophe

ap'paio ecc vb vedi **apparire**

ap'palto sm (Comm) contract; **dare/ prendere in ~ un lavoro** to let out/ undertake a job on contract

appannarsi vpr to mist over; to grow dim

apparecchi'are [apparek'kjare] vt to prepare; (tavola) to set ▷ vi to set the table

appa'recchio [appa'rekkjo] sm piece of apparatus, device; (aeroplano) aircraft inv; **apparecchio acustico** hearing aid; **apparecchio telefonico** telephone; **apparecchio televisivo** television set

appa'rente ag apparent

appa'rire vi to appear; (sembrare) to seem, appear

apparta'mento sm flat (BRIT), apartment (US)

appar'tarsi vpr to withdraw

apparte'nere vi **~ a** to belong to

ap'parvi ecc vb vedi **apparire**

appassio'nare vt to thrill; (commuovere) to move; **appassionarsi** vpr **appassionarsi a qc** to take a great interest in sth; **appassio'nato, -a** ag passionate; (entusiasta): **appassionato (di)** keen (on)

appas'sire vi to wither

appas'sito, -a ag dead

ap'pello sm roll-call; (implorazione, Dir) appeal; **fare ~ a** to appeal to

ap'pena av (a stento) hardly, scarcely; (solamente, da poco) just ▷ cong as soon as; **(non) ~ furono arrivati ...** as soon as they had arrived ...; **~ ... che** o **quando** no sooner ... than

ap'pendere vt to hang (up)

appen'dice [appen'ditfe] sf appendix; **romanzo d'~** popular serial

appendi'cite [appendi'tfite] sf appendicitis

Appen'nini smpl **gli ~** the Apennines

appesan'tire vt to make heavy; **appesantirsi** vpr to grow stout

appe'tito sm appetite

appic'care vt **~ il fuoco a** to set fire to, set on fire

appicci'care [appittfi'kare] vt to stick; **appiccicarsi** vpr to stick; (fig: persona) to cling

appiso'larsi vpr to doze off

applau'dire vt, vi to applaud; **ap'plauso** sm applause

appli'care vt to apply; (regolamento) to enforce; **applicarsi** vpr to apply o.s.

appoggi'are [appod'dʒare] vt (mettere contro): **~ qc a qc** to lean o rest sth against sth; (fig: sostenere) to support; **appoggiarsi** vpr **appoggiarsi a** to lean against; (fig) to rely upon; **ap'poggio** sm support

apposita'mente av specially; (apposta) on purpose

ap'posito, -a ag appropriate

ap'posta av on purpose, deliberately

appos'tarsi vpr to lie in wait

ap'prendere vt (imparare) to learn

appren'dista, -i, -e sm/f apprentice

apprensi'one sf apprehension

apprez'zare [appret'tsare] vt to appreciate

appro'dare vi (Naut) to land; (fig): **non ~ a nulla** to come to nothing

approfit'tare vi **~ di** to make the most of; (peg) to take advantage of

approfon'dire vt to deepen; (fig) to study in depth

appropri'ato, -a ag appropriate

approssima'tivo, -a ag approximate, rough; (impreciso) inexact, imprecise

appro'vare vt (condotta, azione) to approve of; (candidato) to pass; (progetto di legge) to approve

appunta'mento sm appointment; (amoroso) date; **darsi ~** to arrange to meet (one another); **ho un ~ con...** I have an appointment with ...; **vorrei prendere un ~** I'd like to make an appointment

ap'punto sm note; (rimprovero) reproach ▷ av (proprio) exactly, just; **per l'~!, ~!** exactly!

apribot'tiglie [apribot'tiʎʎe] sm inv bottle opener

a'prile sm April

a'prire vt to open; (via, cadavere) to open up; (gas, luce, acqua) to turn on ▷ vi to open; **aprirsi** vpr to open; **aprirsi a qn** to confide in sb, open one's heart to sb; **a che ora aprite?** what time do you open?

apris'catole sm inv tin (BRIT) o can opener

APT sigla f (= Azienda di Promozione) ≈ tourist board

aquagym [akkwa'dʒim] sf aquaerobics

'aquila sf (Zool) eagle; (fig) genius

aqui'lone sm (giocattolo) kite; (vento) North wind

A/R abbr = **andata e ritorno** (biglietto) return ticket (BRIT), round-trip ticket (US)

A'rabia Sau'dita sf **l'~** Saudi Arabia

'arabo, -a ag, sm/f Arab ▷ sm (Ling) Arabic

a'rachide [a'rakide] sf peanut

ara'gosta sf crayfish; lobster

a'rancia, -ce [a'rantfa] sf orange; **aranci'ata** sf orangeade; **aranci'one** ag inv **(color) arancione** bright orange

a'rare vt to plough (BRIT), plow (US)

a'ratro sm plough (BRIT), plow (US)

a'razzo [a'rattso] sm tapestry

arbi'trare vt (Sport) to referee; to umpire; (Dir) to arbitrate

arbi'trario, -a *ag* arbitrary

'arbitro *sm* arbiter, judge; (*Dir*) arbitrator; (*Sport*) referee; (: *Tennis, Cricket*) umpire

ar'busto *sm* shrub

archeolo'gia [arkeolo'dʒia] *sf* arch(a)eology; **arche'ologo, -a, -gi, -ghe** *sm/f* arch(a)eologist

architet'tare [arkitet'tare] *vt* (*fig: ideare*) to devise; (: *macchinare*) to plan, concoct

archi'tetto [arki'tetto] *sm* architect; **architet'tura** *sf* architecture

ar'chivio [ar'kivjo] *sm* archives *pl*; (*Inform*) file

'arco *sm* (*arma, Mus*) bow; (*Archit*) arch; (*Mat*) arc

arcoba'leno *sm* rainbow

arcu'ato, -a *ag* curved, bent

'ardere *vt, vi* to burn

ar'desia *sf* slate

'area *sf* area; (*Edil*) land, ground; **area di rigore** (*Sport*) penalty area; **area di servizio** (*Aut*) service area

a'rena *sf* arena; (*per corride*) bullring; (*sabbia*) sand

are'narsi *vpr* to run aground

argente'ria [ardʒente'ria] *sf* silverware, silver

Argen'tina [ardʒen'tina] *sf* **l'~** Argentina; **argen'tino, -a** *ag, sm/f* Argentinian

ar'gento [ar'dʒento] *sm* silver; **argento vivo** quicksilver

ar'gilla [ar'dʒilla] *sf* clay

'argine ['ardʒine] *sm* embankment, bank; (*diga*) dyke, dike

argo'mento *sm* argument; (*motivo*) motive; (*materia, tema*) subject

'aria *sf* air; (*espressione, aspetto*) air, look; (*Mus: melodia*) tune; (*di opera*) aria; **mandare all'~ qc** to ruin o upset sth; **all'~ aperta** in the open (air)

'arido, -a *ag* arid

arieggi'are [arjed'dʒare] *vt* (*cambiare aria*) to air; (*imitare*) to imitate

ari'ete *sm* ram; (*Mil*) battering ram; (*dello zodiaco*): **A~** Aries

a'ringa, -ghe *sf* herring *inv*

arit'metica *sf* arithmetic

'arma, -i *sf* weapon, arm; (*parte dell'esercito*) arm; **chiamare alle armi** to call up (*BRIT*), draft (*US*); **sotto le armi** in the army (o forces); **alle armi!** to arms!; **arma atomica/nucleare** atomic/nuclear weapon; **arma da fuoco** firearm; **armi di distruzione di massa** weapons of mass destruction

arma'dietto *sm* (*di medicinali*) medicine cabinet; (*in palestra ecc*) locker; (*in cucina*) (kitchen) cupboard

ar'madio *sm* cupboard; (*per abiti*) wardrobe; **armadio a muro** built-in cupboard

ar'mato, -a *ag* **~ (di)** (*anche fig*) armed (with) ▷ *sf* (*Mil*) army; (*Naut*) fleet; **rapina a mano armata** armed robbery

arma'tura *sf* (*struttura di sostegno*) framework; (*impalcatura*) scaffolding; (*Storia*) armour *no pl*, suit of armour

armis'tizio [armis'tittsjo] *sm* armistice

armo'nia *sf* harmony

ar'nese *sm* tool, implement; (*oggetto indeterminato*) thing, contraption; **male in ~** (*malvestito*) badly dressed; (*di salute malferma*) in poor health; (*povero*) down-at-heel

'arnia *sf* hive

a'roma, -i *sm* aroma; fragrance; **aromi** *smpl* (*Cuc*) herbs and spices; **aromatera'pia** *sf* aromatherapy

'arpa *sf* (*Mus*) harp

arrabbi'are *vi* (*cane*) to be affected with rabies; **arrabbiarsi** *vpr* (*essere preso dall'ira*) to get angry, fly into a rage; **arrabbi'ato, -a** *ag* rabid, with rabies; furious, angry

arrampi'carsi *vpr* to climb (up)

arrangiarsi *vpr* to manage, do the best one can

arreda'mento *sm* (*studio*) interior design; (*mobili ecc*) furnishings *pl*

arre'dare *vt* to furnish

arre'ndersi *vpr* to surrender

arres'tare *vt* (*fermare*) to stop, halt; (*catturare*) to arrest; **arrestarsi** *vpr* (*fermarsi*) to stop; **ar'resto** *sm* (*cessazione*) stopping; (*fermata*) stop; (*cattura, Med*) arrest; **subire un arresto** to come to a stop o standstill; **mettere agli arresti** to place under arrest; **arresti domiciliari** house arrest *sg*

arre'trare *vt, vi* to withdraw; **arre'trato, -a** *ag* (*lavoro*) behind schedule; (*paese, bambino*) backward; (*numero di giornale*) back *cpd*; **arretrati** *smpl* arrears

arric'chire [arrik'kire] *vt* to enrich; **arricchirsi** *vpr* to become rich

arri'vare *vi* to arrive; (*accadere*) to happen, occur; **~ a** (*livello, grado ecc*) to reach; **a che ora arriva il treno da Londra?** what time does the train from London arrive?; **non ci arrivo** I can't reach it; (*fig: non capisco*) I can't understand it

arrive'derci [arrive'dertʃi] *escl* goodbye!

arri'vista, -i, -e *sm/f* go-getter

ar'rivo *sm* arrival; (*Sport*) finish, finishing line

arro'gante *ag* arrogant

arros'sire *vi* (*per vergogna, timidezza*) to blush, flush; (*per gioia, rabbia*) to flush

arros'tire *vt* to roast; (*pane*) to toast; (*ai*

ferri) to grill

ar'rosto *sm, ag inv* roast

arroto'lare *vt* to roll up

arroton'dare *vt* (*forma, oggetto*) to round; (*stipendio*) to add to; (*somma*) to round off

arruggi'nito, -a [arruddʒin'nito] *ag* rusty

'arsi *vb vedi* **ardere**

'arte *sf* art; (*abilità*) skill

ar'teria *sf* artery; **arteria stradale** main road

'artico, -a, -ci, -che *ag* Arctic

articolazi'one *sf* articulation; (*Anat, Tecn*) joint

ar'ticolo *sm* article; **articolo di fondo** (*Stampa*) leader, leading article

artifici'ale [artifi't∫ale] *ag* artificial

artigia'nato [artidʒa'nato] *sm* craftsmanship; craftsmen *pl*

artigi'ano, -a [arti'dʒano] *sm/f* craftsman/woman

ar'tista, -i, -e *sm/f* artist; **ar'tistico, -a, -ci, -che** *ag* artistic

ar'trite *sf* (*Med*) arthritis

a'scella [aʃ'ʃella] *sf* (*Anat*) armpit

ascen'dente [aʃʃen'dente] *sm* ancestor; (*fig*) ascendancy; (*Astr*) ascendant

ascen'sore [aʃʃen'sore] *sm* lift

a'scesso [aʃ'ʃesso] *sm* (*Med*) abscess

asciugaca'pelli [aʃʃugaka'pelli] *sm* hair-drier

asciuga'mano [aʃʃuga'mano] *sm* towel

asciu'gare [aʃʃu'gare] *vt* to dry; **asciugarsi** *vpr* to dry o.s.; (*diventare asciutto*) to dry

asci'utto, -a [aʃ'ʃutto] *ag* dry; (*fig: magro*) lean; (: *burbero*) curt; **restare a bocca asciutta** (*fig*) to be disappointed

ascol'tare *vt* to listen to

as'falto *sm* asphalt

'Asia *sf* l'~ Asia; **asi'atico, -a, -ci, -che** *ag*, *sm/f* Asiatic, Asian

a'silo *sm* refuge, sanctuary; **~ (d'infanzia)** nursery(-school); **asilo nido** crèche; **asilo politico** political asylum

'asino *sm* donkey, ass

ASL *sigla f* (= *Azienda Sanitaria Locale*) local health centre

'asma *sf* asthma

as'parago, -gi *sm* asparagus *no pl*

aspet'tare *vt* to wait for; (*anche Comm*) to await; (*aspettarsi*) to expect ▷ *vi* to wait; **aspettami, per favore** wait for me, please

as'petto *sm* (*apparenza*) aspect, appearance, look; (*punto di vista*) point of view; **di bell'~** good-looking

aspira'polvere *sm inv* vacuum cleaner

aspi'rare *vt* (*respirare*) to breathe in, inhale; (*apparecchi*) to suck (up) ▷ *vi* **~ a** to

aspire to

aspi'rina *sf* aspirin

'aspro, -a *ag* (*sapore*) sour, tart; (*odore*) acrid, pungent; (*voce, clima, fig*) harsh; (*superficie*) rough; (*paesaggio*) rugged

assaggi'are [assad'dʒare] *vt* to taste; **posso assaggiarlo?** can I have a taste?; **assaggino** [assad'dʒino] *sm* **assaggini** (*Cuc*) selection of first courses; **solo un assaggino** just a little

as'sai *av* (*molto*) a lot, much; (: *con ag*) very; (*a sufficienza*) enough ▷ *ag inv* (*quantità*) a lot of, much; (*numero*) a lot of, many; **~ contento** very pleased

as'salgo *ecc vb vedi* **assalire**

assa'lire *vt* to attack, assail

assal'tare *vt* (*Mil*) to storm; (*banca*) to raid; (*treno, diligenza*) to hold up

as'salto *sm* attack, assault

assassi'nare *vt* to murder; to assassinate; (*fig*) to ruin; **assas'sino, -a** *ag* murderous ▷ *sm/f* murderer; assassin

'asse *sm* (*Tecn*) axle; (*Mat*) axis ▷ *sf* board; **asse da stiro** ironing board

assedi'are *vt* to besiege

asse'gnare [assen'nare] *vt* to assign, allot; (*premio*) to award

as'segno [as'senno] *sm* allowance; (*anche:* **~ bancario**) cheque (BRIT), check (US); **contro ~** cash on delivery; **posso pagare con un ~?** can I pay by cheque?; **assegno circolare** bank draft; **assegni familiari** ≈ child benefit *no pl*; **assegno sbarrato** crossed cheque; **assegno di viaggio** traveller's cheque; **assegno a vuoto** dud cheque; **assegno di malattia/di invalidità** sick pay/disability benefit

assem'blea *sf* assembly

assen'tarsi *vpr* to go out

as'sente *ag* absent; (*fig*) faraway, vacant; **as'senza** *sf* absence

asse'tato, -a *ag* thirsty, parched

assicu'rare *vt* (*accertare*) to ensure; (*infondere certezza*) to assure; (*fermare, legare*) to make fast, secure; (*fare un contratto di assicurazione*) to insure; **assicurarsi** *vpr* (*accertarsi*): **assicurarsi (di)** to make sure (of); (*contro il furto ecc*): **assicurarsi (contro)** to insure o.s. (against); **assicurazi'one** *sf* assurance; insurance

assi'eme *av* (*insieme*) together; **~ a** (together) with

assil'lare *vt* to pester, torment

assis'tente *sm/f* assistant; **assistente sociale** social worker; **assistente di volo** (*Aer*) steward/stewardess

assis'tenza [assis'tɛntsa] *sf* assistance; **~ ospedaliera** free hospital treatment;

~ sociale welfare services pl; **assistenza sanitaria** health service

as'sistere vt (aiutare) to assist, help; (curare) to treat ▷ vi **- (a qc)** (essere presente) to be present (at sth), to attend (sth)

'**asso** sm ace; **piantare qn in ~** to leave sb in the lurch

associ'are [asso'tʃare] vt to associate; **associarsi** vpr to enter into partnership; **associarsi a** to become a member of, join; (dolori, gioie) to share in; **~ qn alle carceri** to take sb to prison

associazi'one [assotʃat'tsjone] sf association; (Comm) association, society; **~ a delinquere** (Dir) criminal association

as'solsi ecc vb vedi **assolvere**

assoluta'mente av absolutely

asso'luto, -a ag absolute

assoluzi'one [assolut'tsjone] sf (Dir) acquittal; (Rel) absolution

as'solvere vt (Dir) to acquit; (Rel) to absolve; (adempiere) to carry out, perform

assomigli'are [assomiʎ'ʎare] vi **~ a** to resemble, look like; **assomigliarsi** vpr to look alike; (nel carattere) to be alike

asson'nato, -a ag sleepy

asso'pirsi vpr to doze off

assor'bente ag absorbent ▷ sm: **assorbente interno** tampon; **assorbente esterno/igienico** sanitary towel

assor'bire vt to absorb

assor'dare vt to deafen

assorti'mento sm assortment

assor'tito, -a ag assorted; matched, matching

assuefazi'one [assuefat'tsjone] sf (Med) addiction

as'sumere vt (impiegato) to take on, engage; (responsabilità) to assume, take upon o.s.; (contegno, espressione) to assume, put on; (droga) to consume

as'sunsi ecc vb vedi **assumere**

assurdità sf inv absurdity; **dire delle ~** to talk nonsense

as'surdo, -a ag absurd

'**asta** sf pole; (vendita) auction

as'temio, -a ag teetotal ▷ sm/f teetotaller

Attenzione! In inglese esiste la parola abstemious che però vuol dire moderato.

aste'nersi vpr **~ (da)** to abstain (from), refrain (from); (Pol) to abstain (from)

aste'risco, -schi sm asterisk

'**astice** ['astitʃe] sm lobster

astig'matico, -a, -ci, che ag astigmatic

asti'nenza [asti'nɛntsa] sf abstinence; **essere in crisi di ~** to suffer from withdrawal symptoms

as'tratto, -a ag abstract

'**astro...** prefisso; **astrolo'gia** [astrolo'dʒia] sf astrology; **astro'nauta, -i, -e** sm/f astronaut; **astro'nave** sf space ship; **astrono'mia** sf astronomy; **astro'nomico, -a, -ci, -che** ag astronomic(al)

as'tuccio [as'tuttʃo] sm case, box, holder

as'tuto, -a ag astute, cunning, shrewd

A'tene sf Athens

'**ateo, -a** ag, sm/f atheist

at'lante sm atlas

at'lantico, -a, -ci, -che ag Atlantic ▷ sm l'**A~, l'Oceano A~** the Atlantic, the Atlantic Ocean

at'leta, -i, -e sm/f athlete; **at'letica** sf athletics sg; **atletica leggera** track and field events pl; **atletica pesante** weightlifting and wrestling

atmos'fera sf atmosphere

a'tomico, -a, -ci, -che ag atomic; (nucleare) atomic, atom cpd, nuclear

'**atomo** sm atom

'**atrio** sm entrance hall, lobby

a'troce [a'trotʃe] ag (che provoca orrore) dreadful; (terribile) atrocious

attac'cante sm/f (Sport) forward

attacca'panni sm hook, peg; (mobile) hall stand

attac'care vt (unire) to attach; (cucendo) to sew on; (far aderire) to stick (on); (appendere) to hang (up); (assalire: anche fig) to attack; (iniziare) to begin, start; (fig: contagiare) to pass on ▷ vi to stick, adhere; **attaccarsi** vpr to stick, adhere; (trasmettersi per contagio) to be contagious; (afferrarsi): **attaccarsi (a)** to cling (to); (fig: affezionarsi): **attaccarsi (a)** to become attached (to); **~ discorso** to start a conversation; **at'tacco, -chi** sm (azione offensiva: anche fig) attack; (Med) attack, fit; (Sci) binding; (Elettr) socket

atteggia'mento [atteddʒa'mento] sm attitude

at'tendere vt to wait for, await ▷ vi **~ a** to attend to

atten'dibile ag (storia) credible; (testimone) reliable

atten'tato sm attack; **~ alla vita di qn** attempt on sb's life

at'tento, -a ag attentive; (accurato) careful, thorough; **stare ~ a qc** to pay attention to sth; **~!** be careful!

attenzi'one [atten'tsjone] sf attention; **~!** watch out!, be careful!; **attenzioni** sfpl (premure) attentions; **fare ~ a** to watch out for; **coprire qn di attenzioni** to lavish attentions on sb

atter'raggio [atter'raddʒo] sm landing

atter'rare vt to bring down ▷ vi to land

at'tesa sf waiting; (tempo trascorso aspettando) wait; **essere in ~ di qc** to be waiting for sth

at'tesi ecc vb vedi **attendere**

at'teso, -a pp di **attendere**

'attico, -ci sm attic

attil'lato, -a ag (vestito) close-fitting

'attimo sm moment; **in un ~** in a moment

atti'rare vt to attract

atti'tudine sf (disposizione) aptitude; (atteggiamento) attitude

attività sf inv activity; (Comm) assets pl

at'tivo, -a ag active; (Comm) profit-making, credit cpd ▷ sm (Comm) assets pl; **in ~** in credit

'atto sm act; (azione, gesto) action, act, deed; (Dir: documento) deed, document; **atti** smpl (di congressi ecc) proceedings; **mettere in ~** to put into action; **fare ~ di fare qc** to make as if to do sth; **atto di morte/di nascita** death/birth certificate

at'tore, -'trice sm/f actor/actress

at'torno av round, around, about; **~ a** round, around, about

attrac'care vt, vi (Naut) to dock, berth

at'tracco, -chi sm (Naut) docking no pl; berth

at'trae ecc vb vedi **attrarre**

attra'ente ag attractive

at'traggo ecc vb vedi **attrarre**

at'trarre vt to attract

at'trassi ecc vb vedi **attrarre**

attraver'sare vt to cross; (città, bosco, fig: periodo) to go through; (fiume) to run through

attra'verso prep through; (da una parte all'altra) across

attrazi'one [attrat'tsjone] sf attraction

at'trezzo sm tool, instrument; (Sport) piece of equipment

at'trice [at'tritʃe] sf vedi **attore**

attu'ale ag (presente) present; (di attualità) topical

⬛ Attenzione! In inglese esiste la parola actual che però vuol dire effettivo.

attualità sf inv topicality; (avvenimento) current event

attual'mente av at the moment, at present

⬛ Attenzione! In inglese esiste la parola actually che però vuol dire effettivamente oppure veramente.

attu'are vt to carry out

attu'tire vt to deaden, reduce

'audio sm (TV, Radio, Cine) sound

audiovi'sivo, -a ag audiovisual

audizi'one [audit'tsjone] sf hearing; (Mus) audition

augu'rare vt to wish; **augurarsi qc** to hope for sth

au'guri smpl best wishes; **fare gli ~ a qn** to give sb one's best wishes; **tanti ~!** best wishes!; (per compleanno) happy birthday!

'aula sf (scolastica) classroom; (universitaria) lecture theatre; (di edificio pubblico) hall

aumen'tare vt, vi to increase; **au'mento** sm increase

au'rora sf dawn

ausili'are ag, sm, sm/f auxiliary

Aus'tralia sf **l'~** Australia; **australi'ano, -a** ag, sm/f Australian

'Austria sf **l'~** Austria; **aus'triaco, -a, -ci, -che** ag, sm/f Austrian

au'tentico, -a, -ci, -che ag authentic, genuine

au'tista, -i sm driver

'auto sf inv car

autoabbron'zante sm, ag self-tan

autoade'sivo, -a ag self-adhesive ▷ sm sticker

autobio'grafico, -a, ci, che ag autobiographic(al)

'autobus sm inv bus

auto'carro sm lorry (BRIT), truck

autocertificazi'one [autotʃertifikat'tsjone] sf self-declaration

autodistrut'tivo, -a ag self-destructive

auto'gol sm inv own goal

au'tografo, -a ag, sm autograph

auto'grill® sm inv motorway restaurant

auto'matico, -a, -ci, -che ag automatic ▷ sm (bottone) snap fastener; (fucile) automatic

auto'mobile sf (motor) car

automobi'lista, -i, -e sm/f motorist

autono'leggio sm car hire

autono'mia sf autonomy; (di volo) range

au'tonomo, -a ag autonomous, independent

autop'sia sf post-mortem, autopsy

auto'radio sf inv (apparecchio) car radio; (autoveicolo) radio car

au'tore, -'trice sm/f author

autoreggente [autored'dʒɛnte] ag **calze autoreggenti** hold ups

auto'revole ag authoritative; (persona) influential

autorica'ricabile ag **scheda ~** top-up card

autori'messa sf garage

autorità sf inv authority

autoriz'zare [autorid'dzare] vt (permettere) to authorize; (giustificare) to allow, sanction

autos'contro sm dodgem car (BRIT), bumper car (US)

autoscu'ola sf driving school
autos'tima sf self-esteem
autos'top sm hitchhiking; **autostop'pista, -i, -e** sm/f hitchhiker
autos'trada sf motorway (BRIT), highway (US); **autostrada informatica** information superhighway

● **AUTOSTRADE**
●
● You have to pay to use Italian
● motorways. They are indicated by an "A"
● followed by a number on a green sign.
● The speed limit on Italian motorways
● is 130 kph.

auto'velox® sm inv (police) speed camera
autovet'tura sf (motor) car
au'tunno sm autumn
avam'braccio [avam'brattʃo] (pl (f) **-cia**) sm forearm
avangu'ardia sf vanguard
a'vanti av (stato in luogo) in front; (moto: andare, venire) forward; (tempo: prima) before ▷ prep (luogo): **~ a** before, in front of; (tempo): **~ Cristo** before Christ ▷ escl (entrate) come (o go) in!; (Mil) forward!; (coraggio) come on! ▷ sm inv (Sport) forward; **~ e indietro** backwards and forwards; **andare ~** to go forward; (continuare) to go on; (precedere) to go (on) ahead; (orologio) to be fast; **essere ~ negli studi** to be well advanced with one's studies
avan'zare [avan'tsare] vt (spostare in avanti) to move forward, advance; (domanda) to put forward; (promuovere) to promote; (essere creditore): **~ qc da qn** to be owed sth by sb ▷ vi (andare avanti) to move forward, advance; (progredire) to make progress; (essere d'avanzo) to be left, remain
ava'ria sf (guasto) damage; (: meccanico) breakdown
a'varo, -a ag avaricious, miserly ▷ sm miser

O **PAROLA CHIAVE**

a'vere sm (Comm) credit; **gli averi** (ricchezze) wealth sg
▷ vt 1 (possedere) to have; **ha due bambini/una bella casa** she has (got) two children/a lovely house; **ha i capelli lunghi** he has (got) long hair; **non ho da mangiare/bere** I've (got) nothing to eat/drink, I don't have anything to eat/drink
2 (indossare) to wear, have on; **aveva una maglietta rossa** he was wearing o he had on a red tee-shirt; **ha gli occhiali** he wears

o has glasses
3 (ricevere) to get; **hai avuto l'assegno?** did you get o have you had the cheque?
4 (età, dimensione) to be; **ha 9 anni** he is 9 (years old); **la stanza ha 3 metri di lunghezza** the room is 3 metres in length; vedi **fame**; **paura** ecc
5 (tempo): **quanti ne abbiamo oggi?** what's the date today?; **ne hai per molto?** will you be long?
6 (fraseologia): **avercela con qn** to be angry with sb; **cos'hai?** what's wrong o what's the matter (with you)?; **non ha niente a che vedere** o **fare con me** it's got nothing to do with me
▷ vb aus 1 to have; **aver bevuto/ mangiato** to have drunk/eaten
2 (+ da + infinito) to have to do sth; **non hai che da chiederlo** you only have to ask him

aviazi'one [avjat'tsjone] sf aviation; (Mil) air force
'avido, -a ag eager; (peg) greedy
avo'cado sm avocado
a'vorio sm ivory
Avv. abbr = **avvocato**
avvantaggi'are [avvantad'dʒare] vt to favour; **avvantaggiarsi** vpr **avvantaggiarsi negli affari/sui concorrenti** to get ahead in business/of one's competitors
avvele'nare vt to poison
av'vengo ecc vb vedi **avvenire**
avveni'mento sm event
avve'nire vi, vb impers to happen, occur ▷ sm future
av'venni ecc vb vedi **avvenire**
avven'tato, -a ag rash, reckless
avven'tura sf adventure; (amorosa) affair
avventu'rarsi vpr to venture
avventu'roso, -a ag adventurous
avve'rarsi vpr to come true
av'verbio sm adverb
avverrò ecc vb vedi **avvenire**
avver'sario, -a ag opposing ▷ sm opponent, adversary
avver'tenza [avver'tentsa] sf (ammonimento) warning; (cautela) care; (premessa) foreword; **avvertenze** sfpl (istruzioni per l'uso) instructions
avverti'mento sm warning
avver'tire vt (avvisare) to warn; (rendere consapevole) to inform, notify; (percepire) to feel
avvi'are vt (mettere sul cammino) to direct; (impresa, trattative) to begin, start; (motore) to start; **avviarsi** vpr to set off, set out
avvici'nare [avvitʃi'nare] vt to bring

near; (*trattare con: persona*) to approach;
avvicinarsi *vpr* **avvicinarsi (a qn/qc)** to
approach (sb/sth), draw near (to sb/sth)
avvi'lito, -a *ag* discouraged
avvin'cente *ag* captivating
avvi'sare *vt* (*far sapere*) to inform;
(*mettere in guardia*) to warn; **av'viso** *sm*
warning; (*annuncio*) announcement;
(: *affisso*) notice; (*inserzione pubblicitaria*)
advertisement; **a mio avviso** in my
opinion; **avviso di chiamata** (*servizio*)
call waiting; (*segnale*) call waiting signal;
avviso di garanzia (*Dir*) notification (*of
impending investigation and of the right to
name a defence lawyer*)

> Attenzione! In inglese esiste la parola
> *advice* che però vuol dire *consiglio*.

avvis'tare *vt* to sight
avvi'tare *vt* to screw down (*o* in)
avvo'cato, -'essa *sm/f* (*Dir*) barrister
(*BRIT*), lawyer; (*fig*) defender, advocate
av'volgere [av'voldʒere] *vt* to roll up;
(*avviluppare*) to wrap up; **avvolgersi** *vpr*
(*avvilupparsi*) to wrap o.s. up; **avvol'gibile**
sm roller blind (*BRIT*), blind
av'volsi *ecc* *vb vedi* **avvolgere**
avvol'toio *sm* vulture
aza'lea [addza'lea] *sf* azalea
azi'enda [ad'dzjɛnda] *sf* business, firm,
concern; **azienda agricola** farm
azi'one [at'tsjone] *sf* action; (*Comm*) share
a'zoto [ad'dzɔto] *sm* nitrogen
azzar'dare [addzar'dare] *vt* (*soldi, vita*) to
risk, hazard; (*domanda, ipotesi*) to hazard,
venture; **azzardarsi** *vpr* **azzardarsi a fare**
to dare (to) do
az'zardo [ad'dzardo] *sm* risk
azzec'care [attsek'kare] *vt* (*risposta ecc*)
to get right
azzuf'farsi [attsuf'farsi] *vpr* to come to
blows
az'zurro, -a [ad'dzurro] *ag* blue ▷ *sm*
(*colore*) blue; **gli azzurri** (*Sport*) the Italian
national team

b

'babbo *sm* (*fam*) dad, daddy; **Babbo
Natale** Father Christmas
baby'sitter ['beɪbɪsitəʳ] *sm/f* *inv* baby-
sitter
'bacca, -che *sf* berry
baccalà *sm* dried salted cod; (*fig: peg*)
dummy
bac'chetta [bak'ketta] *sf* (*verga*) stick, rod;
(*di direttore d'orchestra*) baton; (*di tamburo*)
drumstick; **~ magica** magic wand
ba'checa, -che [ba'kɛka] *sf* (*mobile*)
showcase, display case; (*Univ, in ufficio*)
notice board (*BRIT*), bulletin board (*US*)
baci'are [ba'tʃare] *vt* to kiss; **baciarsi** *vpr*
to kiss (one another)
baci'nella [batʃi'nɛlla] *sf* basin
ba'cino [ba'tʃino] *sm* basin; (*Mineralogia*)
field, bed; (*Anat*) pelvis; (*Naut*) dock
'bacio ['batʃo] *sm* kiss
'baco, -chi *sm* worm; **baco da seta**
silkworm
ba'dare *vi* (*fare attenzione*) to take care, be
careful; (*occuparsi di*): **~ a** to look after, take
care of; (*dar ascolto*): **~ a** to pay attention
to; **bada ai fatti tuoi!** mind your own
business!
'baffi *smpl* moustache *sg*; (*di animale*)
whiskers; **ridere sotto i ~** to laugh up
one's sleeve; **leccarsi i ~** to lick one's lips
bagagli'aio [bagaʎ'ʎajo] *sm* luggage van

(BRIT) o car (US); (Aut) boot (BRIT), trunk (US)

ba'gaglio [ba'ɡaʎʎo] sm luggage no pl, baggage no pl; **fare/disfare i bagagli** to pack/unpack; **i nostri bagagli non sono arrivati** our luggage has not arrived; **può mandare qualcuno a prendere i nostri bagagli?** could you send someone to collect our luggage?; **bagaglio a mano** hand luggage

bagli'ore [baʎ'ʎore] sm flash, dazzling light; **un ~ di speranza** a ray of hope

ba'gnante [baɲ'ɲante] sm/f bather

ba'gnare [baɲ'ɲare] vt to wet; (inzuppare) to soak; (innaffiare) to water; (fiume) to flow through; (: mare) to wash, bathe; **bagnarsi** vpr to get wet; (al mare) to go swimming o bathing; (in vasca) to have a bath

ba'gnato, -a [baɲ'ɲato] ag wet

ba'gnino [baɲ'ɲino] sm lifeguard

'bagno [ˈbaɲɲo] sm bath; (stanza) bathroom; (toilette) toilet; **bagni** smpl (stabilimento) baths; **fare il ~** to have a bath; (nel mare) to go swimming o bathing; **dov'è il ~?** where's the toilet?; **fare il ~ a qn** to give sb a bath; **mettere a ~** to soak; **~ schiuma** bubble bath

bagnoma'ria [baɲɲoma'ria] sm **cuocere a ~** to cook in a double saucepan

bagnoschi'uma [baɲɲoskj'uma] sm inv bubble bath

'baia sf bay

balbet'tare vi to stutter, stammer; (bimbo) to babble ▷ vt to stammer out

bal'canico, -a, ci, che ag Balkan

bal'cone sm balcony; **avete una camera con ~?** do you have a room with a balcony?

bal'doria sf **fare ~** to have a riotous time

ba'lena sf whale

ba'leno sm flash of lightning; **in un ~** in a flash

bal'lare vt, vi to dance

balle'rina sf dancer; ballet dancer; (scarpa) ballet shoe

balle'rino sm dancer; ballet dancer

bal'letto sm ballet

'ballo sm dance; (azione) dancing no pl; **essere in ~** (fig: persona) to be involved; (: cosa) to be at stake

balne'are ag seaside cpd; (stagione) bathing

'balsamo sm (aroma) balsam; (lenimento, fig) balm

bal'zare [bal'tsare] vi to bounce; (lanciarsi) to jump, leap; **'balzo** sm bounce; jump, leap; (del terreno) crag

bam'bina ag, sf vedi **bambino**

bam'bino, -a sm/f child

'bambola sf doll

bambù sm bamboo

ba'nale ag banal, commonplace

ba'nana sf banana

'banca, -che sf bank; **banca dati** data bank

banca'rella sf stall

banca'rotta sf bankruptcy; **fare ~** to go bankrupt

ban'chetto [ban'ketto] sm banquet

banchi'ere [ban'kjere] sm banker

ban'china [ban'kina] sf (di porto) quay; (per pedoni, ciclisti) path; (di stazione) platform; **~ cedevole** (Aut) soft verge (BRIT) o shoulder (US)

'banco, -chi sm bench; (di negozio) counter; (di mercato) stall; (di officina) (work-)bench; (Geo, banca) bank; **banco di corallo** coral reef; **banco degli imputati** dock; **banco di prova** (fig) testing ground; **banco dei testimoni** witness box; **banco dei pegni** pawnshop; **banco di nebbia** bank of fog

Bancomat® sm inv automated banking; (tessera) cash card

banco'nota sf banknote

'banda sf band; (di stoffa) band, stripe; (lato, parte) side; **~ perforata** punch tape

bandi'era sf flag, banner

ban'dito sm outlaw, bandit

'bando sm proclamation; (esilio) exile, banishment; **~ alle chiacchiere!** that's enough talk!; **bando di concorso** announcement of a competition

bar sm inv bar

'bara sf coffin

ba'racca, -che sf shed, hut; (peg) hovel; **mandare avanti la ~** to keep things going

ba'rare vi to cheat

'baratro sm abyss

ba'ratto sm barter

ba'rattolo sm (di latta) tin; (di vetro) jar; (di coccio) pot

'barba sf beard; **farsi la ~** to shave; **farla in ~ a qn** (fig) to do sth to sb's face; **che ~!** what a bore!

barbabi'etola sf beetroot (BRIT), beet (US); **barbabietola da zucchero** sugar beet

barbi'ere sm barber

bar'bone sm (cane) poodle; (vagabondo) tramp

'barca, -che sf boat; **barca a motore** motorboat; **barca a remi** rowing boat; **barca a vela** sail(ing) boat

barcol'lare vi to stagger

ba'rella sf (lettiga) stretcher

ba'rile sm barrel, cask

ba'rista, -i, -e sm/f barman/maid; (proprietario) bar owner

ba'rocco, -a, -chi, -che *ag, sm* baroque
ba'rometro *sm* barometer
ba'rone *sm* baron; **baro'nessa** *sf* baroness
'barra *sf* bar; (*Naut*) helm; (*linea grafica*) line, stroke
bar'rare *vt* to bar
barri'carsi *vpr* to barricade o.s.
barri'era *sf* barrier; (*Geo*) reef
ba'ruffa *sf* scuffle
barzel'letta [bardzel'letta] *sf* joke, funny story
ba'sare *vt* to base, found; **basarsi** *vpr* **basarsi su** (*fatti, prove*) to be based o founded on; (: *persona*) to base one's arguments on
'basco, -a, -schi, -sche *ag* Basque ▷ *sm* (*copricapo*) beret
'base *sf* base; (*fig: fondamento*) basis; (*Pol*) rank and file; **di ~** basic; **in ~ a** on the basis of, according to; **a ~ di caffè** coffee-based
'baseball ['beɪsbɔːl] *sm* baseball
ba'sette *sfpl* sideburns
ba'silica, -che *sf* basilica
ba'silico *sm* basil
basket ['basket] *sm* basketball
bas'sista, -i, -e *sm/f* bass player
'basso, -a *ag* low; (*di statura*) short; (*meridionale*) southern ▷ *sm* bottom, lower part; (*Mus*) bass; **la bassa Italia** southern Italy
bassorili'evo *sm* bas-relief
bas'sotto, -a *ag* squat ▷ *sm* (*cane*) dachshund
'basta *escl* (that's) enough!, that will do!
bas'tardo, -a *ag* (*animale, pianta*) hybrid, crossbreed; (*persona*) illegitimate, bastard; (*peg*) ▷ *sm/f* illegitimate child, bastard (*peg*)
bas'tare *vi, vb impers* to be enough, be sufficient; **~ a qn** to be enough for sb; **basta chiedere o che chieda a un vigile** you have only to o need only ask a policeman; **basta così, grazie** that's enough, thanks
basto'nare *vt* to beat, thrash
baston'cino [baston'tʃino] *sm* (*Sci*) ski pole; **bastoncini di pesce** fish fingers
bas'tone *sm* stick; **~ da passeggio** walking stick
bat'taglia [bat'taʎʎa] *sf* battle; fight
bat'tello *sm* boat
bat'tente *sm* (*imposta: di porta*) wing, flap; (: *di finestra*) shutter; (*batacchio: di porta*) knocker; (: *di orologio*) hammer; **chiudere i battenti** (*fig*) to shut up shop
'battere *vt* to beat; (*grano*) to thresh; (*percorrere*) to scour ▷ *vi* (*bussare*) to knock; (*urtare*): **~ contro** to hit o strike against;

(*pioggia, sole*) to beat down; (*cuore*) to beat; (*Tennis*) to serve; **battersi** *vpr* to fight; **~ le mani** to clap; **~ i piedi** to stamp one's feet; **~ a macchina** to type; **~ bandiera italiana** to fly the Italian flag; **~ in testa** (*Aut*) to knock; **in un batter d'occhio** in the twinkling of an eye
batte'ria *sf* battery; (*Mus*) drums *pl*
bat'terio *sm* bacterium
batte'rista, -i, -e *sm/f* drummer
bat'tesimo *sm* (*rito*) baptism; christening
battez'zare [batted'dzare] *vt* to baptize; to christen
batti'panni *sm inv* carpet-beater
battis'trada *sm inv* (*di pneumatico*) tread; (*di gara*) pacemaker
'battito *sm* beat, throb; **battito cardiaco** heartbeat
bat'tuta *sf* blow; (*di macchina da scrivere*) stroke; (*Mus*) bar; beat; (*Teatro*) cue; (*frase spiritosa*) witty remark; (*di caccia*) beating; (*Polizia*) combing, scouring; (*Tennis*) service
ba'tuffolo *sm* wad
ba'ule *sm* trunk; (*Aut*) boot (BRIT), trunk (US)
'bava *sf* (*di animale*) slaver, slobber; (*di lumaca*) slime; (*di vento*) breath
bava'glino [bavaʎ'ʎino] *sm* bib
ba'vaglio [ba'vaʎʎo] *sm* gag
'bavero *sm* collar
ba'zar [bad'dzar] *sm inv* bazaar
BCE *sigla f* (= *Banca centrale europea*) ECB
be'ato, -a *ag* blessed; (*fig*) happy; **~ te!** lucky you!
bec'care *vt* to peck; (*fig: raffreddore*) to catch; **beccarsi** *vpr* (*fig*) to squabble; **beccarsi qc** to catch sth
beccherò *ecc* [bekke'rɔ] *vb vedi* **beccare**
'becco, -chi *sm* beak, bill; (*di caffettiera ecc*) spout; lip
be'fana *sf* hag, witch; **la B~** old woman who, according to legend, brings children their presents at the Epiphany; (*Epifania*) Epiphany

bef'fardo, -a *ag* scornful, mocking
'begli ['beʎʎi] *ag vedi* **bello**
'bei *ag vedi* **bello**

beige [bɛʒ] *ag inv* beige
bel *ag vedi* **bello**
be'lare *vi* to bleat
'belga, -gi, -ghe *ag, sm/f* Belgian
'Belgio ['bɛldʒo] *sm* **il ~** Belgium
'bella *sf* (*Sport*) decider; *vedi anche* **bello**
bel'lezza [bel'lettsa] *sf* beauty

 PAROLA CHIAVE

'bello, -a (*ag: dav sm* **bel** + C, **bell'** + V, **bello** + *s impura*, gn, pn, ps, x, z, *pl* **bei** + C, **begli** + *s impura ecc o* V) *ag* **1** (*oggetto, donna, paesaggio*) beautiful, lovely; (*uomo*) handsome; (*tempo*) beautiful, fine, lovely; **le belle arti** fine arts

2 (*quantità*): **una bella cifra** a considerable sum of money; **un bel niente** absolutely nothing

3 (*rafforzativo*): **è una truffa bella e buona!** it's a real fraud!; **è bell'e finito** it's already finished
▷ *sm* **1** (*bellezza*) beauty; (*tempo*) fine weather

2: **adesso viene il bello** now comes the best bit; **sul più bello** at the crucial point; **cosa fai di bello?** are you doing anything interesting?
▷ *av* **fa bello** the weather is fine, it's fine

'belva *sf* wild animal
belve'dere *sm inv* panoramic viewpoint
benché [ben'ke] *cong* although
'benda *sf* bandage; (*per gli occhi*) blindfold; **ben'dare** *vt* to bandage; to blindfold
'bene *av* well; (*completamente, affatto*): **è ben difficile** it's very difficult ▷ *ag inv* **gente ~** well-to-do people ▷ *sm* good; **beni** *smpl* (*averi*) property *sg*, estate *sg*; **io sto ~/poco ~** I'm well/not very well; **va ~** all right; **volere un ~ dell'anima a qn** to love sb very much; **un uomo per ~** a respectable man; **fare ~** to do the right thing; **fare ~ a** (*salute*) to be good for; **fare del ~ a qn** to do sb a good turn; **beni di consumo** consumer goods
bene'detto, -a *pp di* **benedire** ▷ *ag* blessed, holy
bene'dire *vt* to bless; to consecrate
benedu'cato, -a *ag* well-mannered
benefi'cenza [benefi'tʃɛntsa] *sf* charity
bene'ficio [bene'fitʃo] *sm* benefit; **con ~ d'inventario** (*fig*) with reservations
be'nessere *sm* well-being
benes'tante *ag* well-to-do
be'nigno, -a [be'niɲɲo] *ag* kind, kindly; (*critica ecc*) favourable; (*Med*) benign
benve'nuto, -a *ag, sm* welcome; **dare il ~ a qn** to welcome sb

ben'zina [ben'dzina] *sf* petrol (BRIT), gas (US); **fare ~** to get petrol (BRIT) o gas (US); **sono rimasto senza ~** I have run out of petrol (BRIT) o gas (US); **benzina verde** unleaded (petrol); **benzi'naio** *sm* petrol (BRIT) o gas (US) pump attendant
'bere *vt* to drink; **darla a ~ a qn** (*fig*) to fool sb; **vuoi qualcosa da ~?** would you like a drink?
ber'lina *sf* (*Aut*) saloon (car) (BRIT), sedan (US)
Ber'lino *sf* Berlin
ber'muda *smpl* (*calzoncini*) Bermuda shorts
ber'noccolo *sm* bump; (*inclinazione*) flair
ber'retto *sm* cap
berrò *ecc vb vedi* **bere**
ber'saglio [ber'saʎʎo] *sm* target
besciamella [beʃʃa'mɛlla] *sf* béchamel sauce
bes'temmia *sf* curse; (*Rel*) blasphemy
bestemmi'are *vi* to curse, swear; to blaspheme ▷ *vt* to curse, swear at; to blaspheme
'bestia *sf* animal; **andare in ~** (*fig*) to fly into a rage; **besti'ale** *ag* beastly; animal *cpd*; (*fam*): **fa un freddo bestiale** it's bitterly cold; **besti'ame** *sm* livestock; (*bovino*) cattle *pl*
be'tulla *sf* birch
be'vanda *sf* drink, beverage
'bevo *ecc vb vedi* **bere**
be'vuto, -a *pp di* **bere**
'bevvi *ecc vb vedi* **bere**
bianche'ria [bjanke'ria] *sf* linen; **~ da donna** ladies' underwear, lingerie; **biancheria femminile** lingerie; **biancheria intima** underwear
bi'anco, -a, -chi, -che *ag* white; (*non scritto*) blank ▷ *sm* white; (*intonaco*) whitewash ▷ *sm/f* white, white man/woman; **in ~** (*foglio, assegno*) blank; (*notte*) sleepless; **in ~ e nero** (*TV, Fot*) black and white; **mangiare in ~** to follow a bland diet; **pesce in ~** boiled fish; **andare in ~** (*non riuscire*) to fail; **bianco dell'uovo** egg-white
biasi'mare *vt* to disapprove of, censure
'Bibbia *sf* (*anche fig*) bible
bibe'ron *sm inv* feeding bottle
'bibita *sf* (soft) drink
biblio'teca, -che *sf* library; (*mobile*) bookcase
bicarbo'nato *sm* **~ (di sodio)** bicarbonate (of soda)
bicchi'ere [bik'kjɛre] *sm* glass
bici'cletta [bitʃi'kletta] *sf* bicycle; **andare in ~** to cycle
bidè *sm inv* bidet

bi'dello, -a *sm/f* (*Ins*) janitor
bi'done *sm* drum, can; (*anche:* **~ dell'immondizia**) (dust)bin; (*fam: truffa*) swindle; **fare un ~ a qn** (*fam*) to let sb down; to cheat sb
bien'nale *ag* biennial

● BIENNALE DI VENEZIA
●
● The **Biennale di Venezia** is an
● international contemporary art festival,
● which takes place every two years at
● Giardini in Venice. In its current form,
● it includes exhibits by artists from the
● many countries taking part, a thematic
● exhibition and a section for young
● artists.

bifamili'are *sf* ≈ semi-detached house
bifor'carsi *vpr* to fork
bigiotte'ria [bidʒotte'ria] *sf* costume jewellery; (*negozio*) jeweller's (*selling only costume jewellery*)
bigliet'taio, -a *sm/f* (*in treno*) ticket inspector; (*in autobus*) conductor
bigliette'ria [biλλette'ria] *sf* (*di stazione*) ticket office; booking office; (*di teatro*) box office
bigli'etto [biλ'λetto] *sm* (*per viaggi, spettacoli ecc*) ticket; (*cartoncino*) card; (*anche:* **~ di banca**) (bank)note; **biglietto d'auguri** greetings card; **biglietto da visita** visiting card; **biglietto d'andata e ritorno** return (ticket), round-trip ticket (*us*); **biglietto di sola andata** single (ticket)
bignè [bin'ɲe] *sm inv* cream puff
bigo'dino *sm* roller, curler
bi'gotto, -a *ag* over-pious ▷ *sm/f* church fiend
bi'kini *sm inv* bikini
bi'lancia, -ce [bi'lantʃa] *sf* (*pesa*) scales *pl*; (*: di precisione*) balance; (*dello zodiaco*): **B~** Libra; **bilancia commerciale** balance of trade; **bilancia dei pagamenti** balance of payments
bi'lancio [bi'lantʃo] *sm* (*Comm*) balance(-sheet); (*statale*) budget; **fare il ~ di** (*fig*) to assess; **bilancio consuntivo** (final) balance; **bilancio preventivo** budget
bili'ardo *sm* billiards *sg*; billiard table
bi'lingue *ag* bilingual
bilo'cale *sm* two-room flat (*Brit*) o apartment (*us*)
bi'nario, -a *ag* (*sistema*) binary ▷ *sm* (*railway*) track o line; (*piattaforma*) platform; **da che ~ parte il treno per Londra?** which platform does the train for

London go from?; **binario morto** dead-end track
bi'nocolo *sm* binoculars *pl*
bio... *prefisso*; **biodegra'dabile** *ag* biodegradable; **biodi'namico, -a, -ci, -che** *ag* biodynamic; **biogra'fia** *sf* biography; **biolo'gia** *sf* biology
bio'logico, -a, -ci, -che *ag* (*scienze, fenomeni ecc*)) biological; (*agricoltura, prodotti*) organic; **guerra biologica** biological warfare
bi'ondo, -a *ag* blond, fair
biotecnologia [bioteknolo'dʒia] *sf* biotechnology
biri'chino, -a [biri'kino] *ag* mischievous ▷ *sm/f* scamp, little rascal
bi'rillo *sm* skittle (*BRIT*), pin (*us*)
'biro® *sf inv* biro®
'birra *sf* beer; **a tutta ~** (*fig*) at top speed; **birra chiara/scura** ≈ lager/stout; **birre'ria** *sf* ≈ bierkeller
bis *escl, sm inv* encore
bis'betico, -a, -ci, -che *ag* ill-tempered, crabby
bisbigli'are [bisbiλ'λare] *vt, vi* to whisper
'bisca, -sche *sf* gambling-house
'biscia, -sce ['biʃʃa] *sf* snake; **biscia d'acqua** grass snake
biscot'tato, -a *ag* crisp; **fette biscottate** rusks
bis'cotto *sm* biscuit
bisessu'ale *ag, sm/f* bisexual
bises'tile *ag* **anno ~** leap year
bis'nonno, -a *sm/f* great grandfather/grandmother
biso'gnare [bizon'ɲare] *vb impers* **bisogna che tu parta/lo faccia** you'll have to go/do it; **bisogna parlargli** we'll (o I'll) have to talk to him
bi'sogno [bi'zoɲɲo] *sm* need; **ha ~ di qualcosa?** do you need anything?
bis'tecca, -che *sf* steak, beefsteak
bisticci'are [bistit'tʃare] *vi* to quarrel, bicker; **bisticciarsi** *vpr* to quarrel, bicker
'bisturi *sm* scalpel
'bivio *sm* fork; (*fig*) dilemma
biz'zarro, -a [bid'dzarro] *ag* bizarre, strange
blate'rare *vi* to chatter
blin'dato, -a *ag* armoured
bloc'care *vt* to block; (*isolare*) to isolate, cut off; (*porto*) to blockade; (*prezzi, beni*) to freeze; (*meccanismo*) to jam; **bloccarsi** *vpr* (*motore*) to stall; (*freni, porta*) to jam, stick; (*ascensore*) to stop, get stuck
blocche'rò *ecc* [blokke'rɔ] *vb vedi* **bloccare**
bloc'chetto [blok'ketto] *sm* notebook; (*di biglietti*) book

'**blocco, -chi** sm block; (Mil) blockade; (dei fitti) restriction; (quadernetto) pad; (fig: unione) coalition; (il bloccare) blocking; isolating, cutting-off; blockading; freezing; jamming; **in ~** (nell'insieme) as a whole; (Comm) in bulk; **blocco cardiaco** cardiac arrest; **blocco stradale** road block

blu ag inv, sm dark blue

'**blusa** sf (camiciotto) smock; (camicetta) blouse

'**boa** sm inv (Zool) boa constrictor; (sciarpa) feather boa ▷ sf buoy

bo'ato sm rumble, roar

bob [bɔb] sm inv bobsleigh

'**bocca, -che** sf mouth; **in ~ al lupo!** good luck!

boc'caccia, -ce [bok'kattʃa] sf (malalingua) gossip; **fare le boccacce** to pull faces

boc'cale sm jug; **boccale da birra** tankard

boc'cetta [bot'tʃetta] sf small bottle

'**boccia, -ce** [ˈbɔttʃa] sf bottle; (da vino) decanter, carafe; (palla) bowl; **gioco delle bocce** bowls sg

bocci'are [bot'tʃare] vt (proposta, progetto) to reject; (Ins) to fail; (Bocce) to hit

bocci'olo [bot'tʃɔlo] sm bud

boc'cone sm mouthful, morsel

boicot'tare vt to boycott

'**bolla** sf bubble; (Med) blister; **bolla di consegna** (Comm) delivery note; **bolla papale** papal bull

bol'lente ag boiling; boiling hot

bol'letta sf bill; (ricevuta) receipt; **essere in ~** to be hard up

bollet'tino sm bulletin; (Comm) note; **bollettino meteorologico** weather report; **bollettino di spedizione** consignment note

bollicina [bolli'tʃina] sf bubble

bol'lire vt, vi to boil

bolli'tore sm (Cuc) kettle; (per riscaldamento) boiler

'**bollo** sm stamp; **bollo per patente** driving licence tax; **bollo postale** postmark

'**bomba** sf bomb; **bomba atomica** atom bomb; **bomba a mano** hand grenade; **bomba ad orologeria** time bomb

bombarda'mento sm bombardment; bombing

bombar'dare vt to bombard; (da aereo) to bomb

'**bombola** sf cylinder

bombo'letta sf aerosol

bomboni'era sf box of sweets (as souvenir at weddings, first communions etc)

bo'nifico, -ci sm (riduzione, abbuono) discount; (versamento a terzi) credit transfer

bontà sf goodness; (cortesia) kindness; **aver la ~ di fare qc** to be good o kind enough to do sth

borbot'tare vi to mumble

'**borchia** [ˈbɔrkja] sf stud

bor'deaux [bor'do] ag inv, sm inv maroon

'**bordo** sm (Naut) ship's side; (orlo) edge; (striscia di guarnizione) border, trim; **a ~ di** (nave, aereo) aboard, on board; (macchina) in

bor'ghese [bor'geze] ag (spesso peg) middle-class; bourgeois; **abito ~** civilian dress

'**borgo, -ghi** sm (paesino) village; (quartiere) district; (sobborgo) suburb

boro'talco sm talcum powder

bor'raccia, -ce [bor'rattʃa] sf canteen, water-bottle

'**borsa** sf bag; (anche: **~ da signora**) handbag; (Econ): **la B~ (valori)** the Stock Exchange; **borsa dell'acqua calda** hot-water bottle; **borsa nera** black market; **borsa della spesa** shopping bag; **borsa di studio** grant; **borsel'lino** sm purse; **bor'setta** sf handbag

'**bosco, -schi** sm wood

bos'niaco, -a, ci, che ag, sm/f Bosnian

'**Bosnia Erze'govina** [ˈbɔsnja erdze'govina] sf **la ~** Bosnia Herzegovina

Bot, bot sigla m inv (= buono ordinario del Tesoro) short-term Treasury bond

bo'tanica sf botany

bo'tanico, -a, -ci, -che ag botanical ▷ sm botanist

'**botola** sf trap door

'**botta** sf blow; (rumore) bang

'**botte** sf barrel, cask

bot'tega, -ghe sf shop; (officina) workshop

bot'tiglia [bot'tiʎʎa] sf bottle; **bottiglie'ria** sf wine shop

bot'tino sm (di guerra) booty; (di rapina, furto) loot

'**botto** sm bang; crash; **di ~** suddenly

bot'tone sm button; **attaccare ~ a qn** (fig) to buttonhole sb

bo'vino, -a ag bovine; **bovini** smpl cattle

box [bɔks] sm inv (per cavalli) horsebox; (per macchina) lock-up; (per macchina da corsa) pit; (per bambini) playpen

boxe [bɔks] sf boxing

'**boxer** [ˈbɔkser] sm inv (cane) boxer ▷ smpl (mutande): **un paio di ~** a pair of boxer shorts

BR sigla fpl = **Brigate Rosse**

brac'cetto [brat'tʃetto] sm **a ~** arm in arm

braccia'letto sm bracelet, bangle

bracci'ata [brat'tʃata] sf (nel nuoto) stroke

'braccio ['brattʃo] (pl(f) braccia) sm (Anat) arm; (pl(m) bracci: di gru, fiume) arm; (: di edificio) wing; braccio di mare sound; bracci'olo sm (appoggio) arm

'bracco, -chi sm hound

'brace ['bratʃe] sf embers pl

braci'ola [bra'tʃola] sf (Cuc) chop

'branca, -che sf branch

'branchia ['brankja] sf (Zool) gill

'branco, -chi sm (di cani, lupi) pack; (di pecore) flock; (peg: di persone) gang, pack

bran'dina sf camp bed (BRIT), cot (US)

'brano sm piece; (di libro) passage

Bra'sile sm il ~ Brazil; brasili'ano, -a ag, sm/f Brazilian

'bravo, -a ag (abile) clever, capable, skilful; (buono) good, honest; (: bambino) good; (coraggioso) brave; ~! well done!; (a teatro) bravo!

bra'vura sf cleverness, skill

Bre'tagna [bre'taɲɲa] sf la ~ Brittany

bre'tella sf (Aut) link; bretelle sfpl (di calzoni) braces

'bretone ag, sm/f Breton

'breve ag brief, short; in ~ in short

brevet'tare vt to patent

bre'vetto sm patent; brevetto di pilotaggio pilot's licence (BRIT) o license (US)

'bricco, -chi sm jug; bricco del caffè coffeepot

briciola ['britʃola] sf crumb

'briciolo ['britʃolo] sm (specie fig) bit

'briga, -ghe sf (fastidio) trouble, bother; pigliarsi la ~ di fare qc to take the trouble to do sth

bri'gata sf (Mil) brigade; (gruppo) group, party; Brigate Rosse (Pol) Red Brigades

'briglia ['briʎʎa] sf rein; a ~ sciolta at full gallop; (fig) at full speed

bril'lante ag bright; (anche fig) brilliant; (che luccica) shining ▷ sm diamond

bril'lare vi to shine; (mina) to blow up ▷ vt (mina) to set off

'brillo, -a ag merry, tipsy

'brina sf hoarfrost

brin'dare vi ~ a qn/qc to drink o toast sb/sth

'brindisi sm inv toast

bri'oche [bri'ɔʃ] sf inv brioche

bri'tannico, -a, -ci, -che ag British

'brivido sm shiver; (di ribrezzo) shudder; (fig) thrill

brizzo'lato, -a [brittso'lato] ag (persona) going grey; (barba, capelli) greying

'brocca, -che sf jug

'broccoli smpl broccoli sg

'brodo sm broth; (per cucinare) stock; brodo ristretto consommé

bron'chite [bron'kite] sf (Med) bronchitis

bronto'lare vi to grumble; (tuono, stomaco) to rumble

'bronzo ['brondzo] sm bronze

'browser ['brauzer] sm inv (Inform) browser

brucia'pelo [brutʃa'pelo]: a ~ av point-blank

bruci'are [bru'tʃare] vt to burn; (scottare) to scald ▷ vi to burn; bruciarsi vpr to burn o.s.; (fallire) to ruin one's chances; ~ le tappe (fig) to shoot ahead; bruciarsi la carriera to ruin one's career

'bruco, -chi sm caterpillar; grub

'brufolo sm pimple, spot

'brullo, -a ag bare, bleak

'bruno, -a ag brown, dark; (persona) dark(-haired)

'brusco, -a, -schi, -sche ag (sapore) sharp; (modi, persona) brusque, abrupt; (movimento) abrupt, sudden

bru'sio sm buzz, buzzing

bru'tale ag brutal

'brutto, -a ag ugly; (cattivo) bad; (malattia, strada, affare) nasty, bad; ~ tempo bad weather

Bru'xelles [bry'sɛl] sf Brussels

BSE [biɛssɛ'e] sigla f (= encefalopatia spongiforme bovina) BSE

'buca, -che sf hole; (avvallamento) hollow; buca delle lettere letterbox

buca'neve sm inv snowdrop

bu'care vt (forare) to make a hole (o holes) in; (pungere) to pierce; (biglietto) to punch; bucarsi vpr (di eroina) to mainline; ~ una gomma to have a puncture

bu'cato sm (operazione) washing; (panni) wash, washing

'buccia, -ce ['buttʃa] sf skin, peel

bucherò ecc [buke'rɔ] vb vedi bucare

'buco, -chi sm hole

bud'dismo sm Buddhism

bu'dino sm pudding

'bue sm ox; carne di ~ beef

bu'fera sf storm

'buffo, -a ag funny; (Teatro) comic

bu'gia, -'gie [bu'dʒia] sf lie; dire una ~ to tell a lie; bugi'ardo, -a ag lying, deceitful ▷ sm/f liar

'buio, -a ag dark ▷ sm dark, darkness

'bulbo sm (Bot) bulb; bulbo oculare eyeball

Bulga'ria sf la ~ Bulgaria

'bulgaro, -a ag, sm/f, sm Bulgarian

buli'mia sf bulimia; bu'limico, -a, -ci, -che ag bulimic

bul'lone sm bolt

buona'notte escl good night! ▷ sf dare la

~ **a** to say good night to
buona'sera *escl* good evening!
buongi'orno [bwon'dʒorno] *escl* good morning (o afternoon)!
buongus'taio, -a *sm/f* gourmet

 PAROLA CHIAVE

bu'ono, -a (*ag: dav sm* **buon** + C o V, **buono** + s impura, gn, pn, ps, x, z; *dav sf* **buon'** +V) *ag*
1 (*gen*) good; **un buon pranzo/ristorante** a good lunch/restaurant; **(stai) buono!** behave!
2 (*benevolo*): **buono (con)** good (to), kind (to)
3 (*giusto, valido*) right; **al momento buono** at the right moment
4 (*adatto*): **buono a/da** fit for/to; **essere buono a nulla** to be no good o use at anything
5 (*auguri*): **buon anno!** happy New Year!; **buon appetito!** enjoy your meal!; **buon compleanno!** happy birthday!; **buon divertimento!** have a nice time!; **buona fortuna!** good luck!; **buon riposo!** sleep well!; **buon viaggio!** bon voyage!, have a good trip!
6: **a buon mercato** cheap; **di buon'ora** early; **buon senso** common sense; **alla buona** *ag* simple
▷ *av* in a simple way, without any fuss ▷ *sm*
1 (*bontà*) goodness, good
2 (*Comm*) voucher, coupon; **buono di cassa** cash voucher; **buono di consegna** delivery note; **buono del Tesoro** Treasury bill

buon'senso *sm* = **buon senso**
burat'tino *sm* puppet
'burbero, -a *ag* surly, gruff
buro'cratico, -a, ci, che *ag* bureaucratic
burocra'zia [burokrat'tsia] *sf* bureaucracy
bur'rasca, -sche *sf* storm
'burro *sm* butter
bur'rone *sm* ravine
bus'sare *vi* to knock
'bussola *sf* compass
'busta *sf* (*da lettera*) envelope; (*astuccio*) case; **in ~ aperta/chiusa** in an unsealed/sealed envelope; **busta paga** pay packet
busta'rella *sf* bribe, backhander
bus'tina *sf* (*piccola busta*) envelope; (*di cibi, farmaci*) sachet; (*Mil*) forage cap; **bustina di tè** tea bag
'busto *sm* bust; (*indumento*) corset, girdle; **a mezzo ~** (*foto*) half-length
but'tare *vt* to throw; (*anche: ~ via*) to throw away; **~ giù** (*scritto*) to scribble down; (*cibo*) to gulp down; (*edificio*) to pull down, demolish; (*pasta, verdura*) to put into boiling water; **buttarsi** *vpr* (*saltare*) to jump; **buttarsi dalla finestra** to jump out of the window
byte ['bait] *sm inv* byte

C

ca'bina sf (di nave) cabin; (da spiaggia) beach hut; (di autocarro, treno) cab; (di aereo) cockpit; (di ascensore) cage; **cabi'nato** sm cabin cruiser; **cabina di pilotaggio** cockpit; **cabina telefonica** call o (tele)phone box

ca'cao sm cocoa

'caccia ['kattʃa] sf hunting; (con fucile) shooting; (inseguimento) chase; (cacciagione) game ▷ sm inv (aereo) fighter; (nave) destroyer; **caccia grossa** big-game hunting; **caccia all'uomo** manhunt

cacci'are [kat'tʃare] vt to hunt; (mandar via) to chase away; (ficcare) to shove, stick ▷ vi to hunt; **cacciarsi** vpr **dove s'è cacciata la mia borsa?** where has my bag got to?; **cacciarsi nei guai** to get into trouble; **~ fuori qc** to whip o pull sth out; **~ un urlo** to let out a yell; **caccia'tore** sm hunter; **cacciatore di frodo** poacher

caccia'vite [kattʃa'vite] sm inv screwdriver

'cactus sm inv cactus

ca'davere sm (dead) body, corpse

'caddi ecc vb vedi **cadere**

ca'denza [ka'dɛntsa] sf cadence; (ritmo) rhythm; (Mus) cadenza

ca'dere vi to fall; (denti, capelli) to fall out; (tetto) to fall in; **questa gonna cade bene** this skirt hangs well; **lasciar ~** (anche fig) to drop; (anche: **~ dal sonno**) to be falling asleep on one's feet; **~ dalle nuvole** (fig) to be taken aback

cadrò ecc vb vedi **cadere**

ca'duta sf fall; **la ~ dei capelli** hair loss

caffè sm inv coffee; (locale) café; **caffè corretto** espresso coffee with a shot of spirits; **caffè macchiato** coffee with a dash of milk; **caffè macinato** ground coffee

caffel'latte sm inv white coffee

caffetti'era sf coffeepot

'cagna ['kaɲɲa] sf (Zool, peg) bitch

CAI sigla m = **Club Alpino Italiano**

cala'brone sm hornet

cala'maro sm squid

cala'mita sf magnet

calamità sf inv calamity, disaster

ca'lare vt (far discendere) to lower; (Maglia) to decrease ▷ vi (discendere) to go (o come) down; (tramontare) to set, go down; **~ di peso** to lose weight

cal'cagno [kal'kaɲɲo] sm heel

cal'care sm (incrostazione) (lime)scale

'calce ['kaltʃe] sm **in ~** at the foot of the page ▷ sf lime; **calce viva** quicklime

calci'are [kal'tʃare] vt, vi to kick; **calcia'tore** sm footballer

'calcio ['kaltʃo] sm (pedata) kick; (sport) football, soccer; (di pistola, fucile) butt; (Chim) calcium; **calcio d'angolo** (Sport) corner (kick); **calcio di punizione** (Sport) free kick; **calcio di rigore** penalty

calco'lare vt to calculate, work out, reckon; (ponderare) to weigh (up); **calcola'tore, -'trice** ag calculating ▷ sm calculator; (fig) calculating person; **calcolatore elettronico** computer; **calcola'trice** sf calculator

'calcolo sm (anche Mat) calculation; (infinitesimale ecc) calculus; (Med) stone; **fare i propri calcoli** (fig) to weigh the pros and cons; **per ~** out of self-interest

cal'daia sf boiler

'caldo, -a ag warm; (molto caldo) hot; (fig: appassionato) keen; hearty ▷ sm heat; **ho ~** I'm warm; I'm hot; **fa ~** it's warm; it's hot

caleidos'copio sm kaleidoscope

calen'dario sm calendar

'calibro sm (di arma) calibre, bore; (Tecn) callipers pl; (fig) calibre; **di grosso ~** (fig) prominent

'calice ['kalitʃe] sm goblet; (Rel) chalice

Cali'fornia sf California

californi'ano, -a ag Californian

calligra'fia sf (scrittura) handwriting; (arte) calligraphy

'callo sm callus; (ai piedi) corn

'calma sf calm

cal'mante sm tranquillizer

cal'mare vt to calm; (lenire) to soothe; **calmarsi** vpr to grow calm, calm down; (vento) to abate; (dolori) to ease

'calmo, -a ag calm, quiet

'calo sm (Comm: di prezzi) fall; (: di volume) shrinkage; (: di peso) loss

ca'lore sm warmth; heat; **in ~** (Zool) on heat

calo'ria sf calorie

calo'rifero sm radiator

calo'roso, -a ag warm

calpes'tare vt to tread on, trample on; **"è vietato ~ l'erba"** "keep off the grass"

ca'lunnia sf slander; (scritta) libel

cal'vizie [kal'vittsje] sf baldness

'calvo, -a ag bald

'calza ['kaltsa] sf (da donna) stocking; (da uomo) sock; **fare la ~** to knit; **calze di nailon** nylons, (nylon) stockings

calza'maglia [kaltsa'maʎʎa] sf tights pl; (per danza, ginnastica) leotard

calzet'tone [kaltset'tone] sm heavy knee-length sock

cal'zino [kal'tsino] sm sock

calzo'laio [kaltso'lajo] sm shoemaker; (che ripara scarpe) cobbler

calzon'cini [kaltson'tʃini] smpl shorts; **calzoncini da bagno** (swimming) trunks

cal'zone [kal'tsone] sm trouser leg; (Cuc) savoury turnover made with pizza dough; **calzoni** smpl (pantaloni) trousers (BRIT), pants (US)

camale'onte sm chameleon

cambia'mento sm change

cambi'are vt to change; (modificare) to alter, change; (barattare) **~ (qc con qn/qc)** to exchange (sth with sb/for sth) ▷ vi to change, alter; **cambiarsi** vpr (d'abito) to change; **~ casa** to move (house); **~ idea** to change one's mind; **~ treno** to change trains; **dove posso ~ dei soldi?** where can I change some money?; **ha da ~?** have you got any change?; **posso cambiarlo, per favore?** could I exchange this, please?

cambiava'lute sm inv exchange office

'cambio sm change; (modifica) alteration, change; (scambio, Comm) exchange; (corso dei cambi) rate (of exchange); (Tecn, Aut) gears pl; **in ~ di** in exchange for; **dare il ~ a qn** to take over from sb

'camera sf room; (anche: **~ da letto**) bedroom; (Pol) chamber, house; **camera ardente** mortuary chapel; **camera d'aria** inner tube; (di pallone) bladder; **camera di commercio** Chamber of Commerce; **Camera dei Deputati** Chamber of Deputies, ≈ House of Commons (BRIT), ≈ House of Representatives (US); **camera a gas** gas chamber; **camera a un letto/due letti** single/twin-bedded room; **camera matrimoniale** double room; **camera oscura** (Fot) dark room

Attenzione! In inglese esiste la parola camera, che però significa macchina fotografica.

came'rata, -i, -e sm/f companion, mate ▷ sf dormitory

cameri'era sf (domestica) maid; (che serve a tavola) waitress; (che fa le camere) chambermaid

cameri'ere sm (man)servant; (di ristorante) waiter

came'rino sm (Teatro) dressing room

'camice ['kamitʃe] sm (Rel) alb; (per medici ecc) white coat

cami'cetta [kami'tʃetta] sf blouse

ca'micia, -cie [ka'mitʃa] sf (da uomo) shirt; (da donna) blouse; **camicia di forza** straitjacket; **camicia da notte** (da donna) nightdress; (da uomo) nightshirt

cami'netto sm hearth, fireplace

ca'mino sm chimney; (focolare) fireplace, hearth

'camion sm inv lorry (BRIT), truck (US)

camio'nista, -i sm lorry driver (BRIT), truck driver (US)

cam'mello sm (Zool) camel; (tessuto) camel hair

cammi'nare vi to walk; (funzionare) to work, go

cam'mino sm walk; (sentiero) path; (itinerario, direzione, tragitto) way; **mettersi in ~** to set o start off

camo'milla sf camomile; (infuso) camomile tea

ca'moscio [ka'moʃʃo] sm chamois; **di ~** (scarpe, borsa) suede cpd

cam'pagna [kam'paɲɲa] sf country, countryside; (Pol, Comm, Mil) campaign; **in ~** in the country; **andare in ~** to go to the country; **fare una ~** to campaign; **campagna pubblicitaria** advertising campaign

cam'pana sf bell; (anche: **~ di vetro**) bell jar; **campa'nello** sm (all'uscio, da tavola) bell

campa'nile sm bell tower, belfry

cam'peggio sm camping; (terreno) camp site; **fare (del) ~** to go camping

camper ['kamper] sm inv motor caravan (BRIT), motor home (US)

campio'nario, -a ag **fiera campionaria** trade fair ▷ sm collection of samples

campio'nato sm championship

campi'one, -'essa sm/f (Sport) champion ▷ sm (Comm) sample

'campo sm field; (Mil) field; (accampamento) camp; (spazio delimitato: sportivo ecc) ground; field; (di quadro) background; **i campi** (campagna) the countryside; **campo da aviazione** airfield; **campo di battaglia** (Mil, fig) battlefield; **campo di concentramento** concentration camp; **campo da golf** golf course; **campo profughi** refugee camp; **campo sportivo** sports ground; **campo da tennis** tennis court; **campo visivo** field of vision

'Canada sm **il ~** Canada; **cana'dese** ag, sm/f Canadian ▷ sf (anche: **tenda canadese**) ridge tent

ca'naglia [ka'naʎʎa] sf rabble, mob; (persona) scoundrel, rogue

ca'nale sm (anche fig) channel; (artificiale) canal

'canapa sf hemp; **canapa indiana** (droga) cannabis

cana'rino sm canary

cancel'lare [kantʃel'lare] vt (con la gomma) to rub out, erase; (con la penna) to strike out; (annullare) to annul, cancel; (disdire) to cancel

cancelle'ria [kantʃelle'ria] sf chancery; (materiale per scrivere) stationery

can'cello [kan'tʃello] sm gate

'cancro sm (Med) cancer; (dello zodiaco): **C~** Cancer

candeg'gina [kanded'dʒina] sf bleach

can'dela sf candle; **candela (di accensione)** (Aut) spark(ing) plug

cande'labro sm candelabra

candeli'ere sm candlestick

candi'dare vt to present as candidate; **candidarsi** vpr to present o.s. as candidate

candi'dato, -a sm/f candidate; (aspirante a una carica) applicant

'candido, -a ag white as snow; (puro) pure; (sincero) sincere, candid

can'dito, -a ag candied

'cane sm dog; (di pistola, fucile) cock; **fa un freddo ~** it's bitterly cold; **non c'era un ~** there wasn't a soul; **cane da caccia/da guardia** hunting/guard dog; **cane lupo** Alsatian; **cane pastore** sheepdog

ca'nestro sm basket

can'guro sm kangaroo

ca'nile sm kennel; (di allevamento) kennels pl; **canile municipale** dog pound

'canna sf (pianta) reed; (: indica, da zucchero) cane; (bastone) stick, cane; (di fucile) barrel; (di organo) pipe; (fam: droga) joint; **canna fumaria** chimney flue; **canna da pesca** (fishing) rod; **canna da zucchero** sugar cane

cannel'loni smpl pasta tubes stuffed with sauce and baked

cannocchi'ale [kannok'kjale] sm telescope

can'none sm (Mil) gun; (Storia) cannon; (tubo) pipe, tube; (piega) box pleat; (fig) ace

can'nuccia, -ce [kan'nuttʃa] sf (drinking) straw

ca'noa sf canoe

'canone sm canon, criterion; (mensile, annuo) rent; fee

canot'taggio [kanot'taddʒo] sm rowing

canotti'era sf vest

ca'notto sm small boat, dinghy; canoe

can'tante sm/f singer

can'tare vt, vi to sing; **cantau'tore, -'trice** sm/f singer-composer

canti'ere sm (Edil) (building) site; (cantiere navale) shipyard

can'tina sf cellar; (bottega) wine shop; **cantina sociale** cooperative winegrowers' association

> Attenzione! In inglese esiste la parola **canteen**, che però significa **mensa**.

'canto sm song; (arte) singing; (Rel) chant, chanting; (poesia) poem, lyric; (parte di una poesia) canto; (parte, lato): **da un ~** on the one hand; **d'altro ~** on the other hand

canzo'nare [kantso'nare] vt to tease

can'zone [kan'tsone] sf song; (Poesia) canzone

'caos sm inv chaos; **ca'otico, -a, -ci, -che** ag chaotic

CAP sigla m = **codice di avviamento postale**

ca'pace [ka'patʃe] ag able, capable; (ampio, vasto) large, capacious; **sei ~ di farlo?** can you o are you able to do it?; **capacità** sf inv ability; (Dir, di recipiente) capacity

ca'panna sf hut

capan'none sm (Agr) barn; (fabbricato industriale) (factory) shed

ca'parbio, -a ag stubborn

ca'parra sf deposit, down payment

ca'pello sm hair; **capelli** smpl (capigliatura) hair sg

ca'pezzolo [ka'pettsolo] sm nipple

ca'pire vt to understand; **non capisco** I don't understand

capi'tale ag (mortale) capital; (fondamentale) main, chief ▷ sf (città) capital ▷ sm (Econ) capital

capi'tano sm captain

capi'tare vi (giungere casualmente) to happen to go, find o.s.; (accadere) to happen; (presentarsi: cosa) to turn up, present itself ▷ vb impers to happen; **mi è capitato un guaio** I've had a spot of trouble

capi'tello sm (Archit) capital

ca'pitolo sm chapter

capi'tombolo sm headlong fall, tumble

'capo sm head; (persona) head, leader; (: in ufficio) head, boss; (: in tribù) chief; (di oggetti) head; top; end; (Geo) cape; **andare a ~** to start a new paragraph; **da ~** over again; **capo di bestiame** head inv of cattle; **capo di vestiario** item of clothing; **Capo'danno** sm New Year; **capo'giro** sm dizziness no pl; **capola'voro, -i** sm masterpiece; **capo'linea** (pl **capi'linea**) sm terminus; (pena) imprisonment; **capostazi'one** (pl **capistazi'one**) sm station master

capo'tavola (pl(m) **capi'tavola**) pl(f) inv sm/f (persona) head of the table; **sedere a ~** to sit at the head of the table

capo'volgere [kapo'voldʒere] vt to overturn; (fig) to reverse; **capovolgersi** vpr to overturn; (barca) to capsize; (fig) to be reversed

'cappa sf (mantello) cape, cloak; (del camino) hood

cap'pella sf (Rel) chapel

cap'pello sm hat

'cappero sm caper

cap'pone sm capon

cap'potto sm (over)coat

cappuc'cino [kapput'tʃino] sm (frate) Capuchin monk; (bevanda) cappuccino, frothy white coffee

cap'puccio [kap'puttʃo] sm (copricapo) hood; (della biro) cap

'capra sf (she-)goat

ca'priccio [ka'prittʃo] sm caprice, whim; (bizza) tantrum; **fare i capricci** to be very naughty; **capricci'oso, -a** ag capricious, whimsical; naughty

Capri'corno sm Capricorn

capri'ola sf somersault

capri'olo sm roe deer

'capro sm **~ espiatorio** scapegoat

ca'prone sm billy-goat

'capsula sf capsule; (di arma, per bottiglie) cap

cap'tare vt (Radio, TV) to pick up; (cattivarsi) to gain, win

carabini'ere sm member of Italian military police force

● CARABINIERI
●
● Originally part of the armed forces, the
● **carabinieri** are police who perform
● both military and civil duties. They
● include paratroopers and mounted
● divisions.

ca'raffa sf carafe

Ca'raibi smpl **il mar dei ~** the Caribbean (Sea)

cara'mella sf sweet

ca'rattere sm character; (caratteristica) characteristic, trait; **avere un buon ~** to be good-natured; **carattere jolly** wild card; **caratte'ristica, -che** sf characteristic, trait, peculiarity; **caratte'ristico, -a, -ci, -che** ag characteristic

car'bone sm coal

carbu'rante sm (motor) fuel

carbura'tore sm carburettor

carce'rato, -a [kartʃe'rato] sm/f prisoner

'carcere ['kartʃere] sm prison; (pena) imprisonment

carci'ofo [kar'tʃɔfo] sm artichoke

cardel'lino sm goldfinch

car'diaco, -a, -ci, -che ag cardiac, heart cpd

cardi'nale ag, sm cardinal

'cardine sm hinge

'cardo sm thistle

ca'rente ag **~ di** lacking in

cares'tia sf famine; (penuria) scarcity, dearth

ca'rezza [ka'rettsa] sf caress

'carica, -che sf (mansione ufficiale) office, position; (Mil, Tecn, Elettr) charge; **ha una forte ~ di simpatia** he's very likeable; vedi anche **carico**

caricabatte'ria sm inv battery charger

cari'care vt (merce, Inform) to load; (orologio) to wind up; (batteria, Mil) to charge

'carico, -a, -chi, -che ag (che porta un peso): **~ di** loaded o laden with; (fucile) loaded; (orologio) wound up; (batteria) charged; (colore) deep; (caffè, tè) strong ▷ sm (il caricare) loading; (ciò che si carica) load; (fig: peso) burden, weight; **persona a ~** dependent; **essere a ~ di qn** (spese ecc) to be charged to sb

'carie sf (dentaria) decay

ca'rino, -a ag (grazioso) lovely, pretty, nice; (riferito a uomo, anche simpatico) nice

carità sf charity; **per ~!** (escl di rifiuto) good heavens, no!

carnagi'one [karna'dʒone] sf complexion

'carne sf flesh; (bovina, ovina ecc) meat; **non mangio ~** I don't eat meat; **carne di maiale/manzo/pecora** pork/beef/mutton; **carne in scatola** tinned o canned meat; **carne tritata** o **macinata** mince (BRIT), hamburger meat (US), minced (BRIT) o ground (US) meat

carne'vale sm carnival

● CARNEVALE

● **Carnevale** is the period between
Epiphany (Jan. 6th) and the beginning
of Lent. People wear fancy dress, and
there are parties, processions of floats
and bonfires. It culminates immediately
before Lent in the festivities of **martedì
grasso** (Shrove Tuesday).

'caro, -a ag (amato) dear; (costoso) dear,
expensive; **è troppo ~** it's too expensive
ca'rogna [ka'roɲɲa] sf carrion; (anche: **fig**:
fam) swine
ca'rota sf carrot
caro'vana sf caravan
car'poni av on all fours
car'rabile ag suitable for vehicles; **"passo
~"** "keep clear"
carreggi'ata [karred'dʒata] sf
carriageway (BRIT), (road)way
car'rello sm trolley; (Aer) undercarriage;
(Cinema) dolly; (di macchina da scrivere)
carriage
carri'era sf career; **fare ~** to get on; **a gran
~** at full speed
carri'ola sf wheelbarrow
'carro sm cart, wagon; **carro armato**
tank; **carro attrezzi** breakdown van
car'rozza [kar'rottsa] sf carriage, coach
carrozze'ria [karrottse'ria] sf body,
coachwork (BRIT); (officina) coachbuilder's
workshop (BRIT), body shop
carroz'zina [karrot'tsina] sf pram (BRIT),
baby carriage (US)
'carta sf paper; (al ristorante) menu; (Geo)
map; plan; (documento) card; (costituzione)
charter; **carte** sfpl (documenti) papers,
documents; **alla ~** (al ristorante) à la
carte; **carta assegni** bank card; **carta
assorbente** blotting paper; **carta bollata**
o **da bollo** official stamped paper; **carta
(da gioco)** playing card; **carta di credito**
credit card; **carta (geografica)** map;
carta d'identità identity card; **carta
igienica** toilet paper; **carta d'imbarco**
(Aer, Naut) boarding card; **carta da lettere**
writing paper; **carta da pacchi** wrapping
paper; **carta da parati** wallpaper; **carta
libera** (Amm) unstamped paper; **carta
stradale** road map; **carta verde** (Aut)
green card; **carta vetrata** sandpaper;
carta da visita visiting card
car'taccia, -ce [kar'tattʃa] sf waste paper
carta'pesta sf papier-mâché
car'tella sf (scheda) card; (Inform, custodia:
di cartone) folder; (: di uomo d'affari ecc)

briefcase; (: di scolaro) schoolbag, satchel;
cartella clinica (Med) case sheet
cartel'lino sm (etichetta) label; (su porta)
notice; (scheda) card; **timbrare il ~**
(all'entrata) to clock in; (all'uscita) to clock
out; **cartellino di presenza** clock card,
timecard
car'tello sm sign; (pubblicitario) poster;
(stradale) sign, signpost; (Econ) cartel; (in
dimostrazioni) placard; **cartello stradale**
sign; **cartel'lone** sm (della tombola)
scoring frame; (Teatro) playbill; **tenere il
cartellone** (spettacolo) to have a long run;
cartellone pubblicitario advertising
poster
car'tina sf (Aut, Geo) map; **può
indicarmelo sulla ~?** can you show it to
me on the map?
car'toccio [kar'tɔttʃo] sm paper bag
cartole'ria sf stationer's (shop)
carto'lina sf postcard; **cartolina postale**
ready-stamped postcard
car'tone sm cardboard; (Arte) cartoon;
cartoni animati (Cinema) cartoons
car'tuccia, -ce [kar'tuttʃa] sf cartridge
'casa sf house; (in senso astratto) home;
(Comm) firm, house; **essere a ~** to be at
home; **vado a ~ mia/tua** I'm going home/
to your house; **vino della ~** house wine;
casa di cura nursing home; **casa editrice**
publishing house; **Casa delle Libertà**
centre-right coalition; **casa di riposo** (old
people's) home, care home; **case popolari**
≈ council houses (o flats) (BRIT), ≈ public
housing units (US); **casa dello studente**
student hostel
ca'sacca, -che sf military coat; (di fantino)
blouse
casa'linga, -ghe sf housewife
casa'lingo, -a, -ghi, -ghe ag household,
domestic; (fatto a casa) home-made;
(semplice) homely; (amante della casa)
home-loving
cas'care vi to fall; **cas'cata** sf fall;
(d'acqua) cascade, waterfall
cascherò ecc [kaske'rɔ] vb vedi **cascare**
'casco, -schi sm helmet; (del parrucchiere)
hair-drier; (di banane) bunch; **casco blu**
(Mil) blue helmet (UN soldier)
casei'ficio [kazei'fitʃo] sm creamery
ca'sella sf pigeon-hole; **casella postale**
post office box
ca'sello sm (di autostrada) toll-house
ca'serma sf barracks pl
ca'sino (fam) sm brothel; (confusione) row,
racket
casinò sm inv casino
'caso sm chance; (fatto, vicenda) event,
incident; (possibilità) possibility; (Med,

Ling) case; **a ~** at random; **per ~** by chance, by accident; **in ogni ~, in tutti i casi** in any case, at any rate; **al ~** should the opportunity arise; **nel ~ che** in case; **~ mai** if by chance; **caso limite** borderline case

caso'lare *sm* cottage

'caspita *escl* (*di sorpresa*) good heavens!; (*di impazienza*) for goodness' sake!

'cassa *sf* case, crate, box; (*bara*) coffin; (*mobile*) chest; (*involucro: di orologio ecc*) case; (*macchina*) cash register, till; (*luogo di pagamento*) checkout (counter); (*fondo*) fund; (*istituto bancario*) bank; **cassa automatica prelievi** cash dispenser; **cassa continua** night safe; **cassa mutua** *o* **malattia** health insurance scheme; **cassa integrazione: mettere in cassa integrazione** ≈ to lay off; **cassa di risparmio** savings bank; **cassa toracica** (*Anat*) chest

cassa'forte (*pl* **casse'forti**) *sf* safe; **lo potrebbe mettere nella ~?** could you put this in the safe, please?

cassa'panca (*pl* **cassa'panche** *o* **casse'panche**) *sf* settle

casseru'ola *sf* saucepan

cas'setta *sf* box; (*per registratore*) cassette; (*Cinema, Teatro*) box-office takings *pl*; **film di ~** box-office draw; **cassetta di sicurezza** strongbox; **cassetta delle lettere** letterbox

cas'setto *sm* drawer

cassi'ere, -a *sm/f* cashier; (*di banca*) teller

casso'netto *sm* wheelie-bin

cas'tagna [kas'taɲɲa] *sf* chestnut

cas'tagno [kas'taɲɲo] *sm* chestnut (tree)

cas'tano, -a *ag* chestnut (brown)

cas'tello *sm* castle; (*Tecn*) scaffolding

casti'gare *vt* to punish; **cas'tigo, -ghi** *sm* punishment

cas'toro *sm* beaver

casu'ale *ag* chance *cpd*; (*Inform*) random *cpd*

catalizza'tore [kataliddza'tore] *sm* (*anche fig*) catalyst; (*Aut*) catalytic converter

ca'talogo, -ghi *sm* catalogue

catarifran'gente [katarifran'dʒɛnte] *sm* (*Aut*) reflector

ca'tarro *sm* catarrh

ca'tastrofe *sf* catastrophe, disaster

catego'ria *sf* category

ca'tena *sf* chain; **catena di montaggio** assembly line; **catene da neve** (*Aut*) snow chains; **cate'nina** *sf* (*gioiello*) (thin) chain

cate'ratta *sf* cataract; (*chiusa*) sluice-gate

ca'tino *sm* basin

ca'trame *sm* tar

'cattedra *sf* teacher's desk; (*di docente*)

chair

catte'drale *sf* cathedral

catti'veria *sf* malice, spite; naughtiness; (*atto*) spiteful act; (*parole*) malicious *o* spiteful remark

cat'tivo, -a *ag* bad; (*malvagio*) bad, wicked; (*turbolento: bambino*) bad, naughty; (: *mare*) rough; (*odore, sapore*) nasty, bad

cat'tolico, -a, -ci, -che *ag, sm/f* (Roman) Catholic

cattu'rare *vt* to capture

'causa *sf* cause; (*Dir*) lawsuit, case, action; **a ~ di, per ~ di** because of; **fare** *o* **muovere ~ a qn** to take legal action against sb

cau'sare *vt* to cause

cau'tela *sf* caution, prudence

'cauto, -a *ag* cautious, prudent

cauzi'one [kaut'tsjone] *sf* security; (*Dir*) bail

'cava *sf* quarry

caval'care *vt* (*cavallo*) to ride; (*muro*) to sit astride; (*ponte*) to span; **caval'cata** *sf* ride; (*gruppo di persone*) riding party

cavalca'via *sm inv* flyover

cavalci'oni [kaval'tʃoni]: **a ~ di** *prep* astride

cavali'ere *sm* rider; (*feudale, titolo*) knight; (*soldato*) cavalryman; (*al ballo*) partner

caval'letta *sf* grasshopper

caval'letto *sm* (*Fot*) tripod; (*da pittore*) easel

ca'vallo *sm* horse; (*Scacchi*) knight; (*Aut: anche: ~ **vapore**) horsepower; (*dei pantaloni*) crotch; **a ~** on horseback; **a ~ di** astride, straddling; **cavallo di battaglia** (*fig*) hobby-horse; **cavallo da corsa** racehorse; **cavallo a dondolo** rocking horse

ca'vare *vt* (*togliere*) to draw out, extract, take out; (: *giacca, scarpe*) to take off; (: *fame, sete, voglia*) to satisfy; **cavarsela** to manage, get on all right; (*scamparla*) to get away with it

cava'tappi *sm inv* corkscrew

ca'verna *sf* cave

'cavia *sf* guinea pig

cavi'ale *sm* caviar

ca'viglia [ka'viʎʎa] *sf* ankle

'cavo, -a *ag* hollow ▷ *sm* (*Anat*) cavity; (*corda, Elettr, Tel*) cable

cavo'letto *sm* **~ di Bruxelles** Brussels sprout

cavolfi'ore *sm* cauliflower

'cavolo *sm* cabbage; (*fam*): **non m'importa un ~** I don't give a damn

'cazzo ['kattso] *sm* (*fam!: pene*) prick (!); **non gliene importa un ~** (*fig fam!*) he doesn't give a damn about it; **fatti i**

cazzi tuoi (*fig fam!*) mind your own damn business

C.C.D. *sigla m* (= *Centro Cristiano Democratico*) *Italian political party of the centre*

CD *sm inv* CD; (*lettore*) CD player

CD-Rom [tʃidi'rɔm] *sm inv* CD-ROM

C.D.U. *sigla m* (= *Cristiano Democratici Uniti*) *Italian centre-right political party*

ce [tʃe] *pron, av vedi* **ci**

Ce'cenia [tʃe'tʃɛnja] *sf* **la ~** Chechnya

ce'ceno, -a [tʃe'tʃɛno] *sm/f, ag* Chechen

'ceco, -a, -chi, -che ['tʃɛko] *ag, sm/f* Czech; **la Repubblica Ceca** the Czech Republic

'cedere ['tʃɛdere] *vt* (*concedere posto*) to give up; (*Dir*) to transfer, make over ▷ *vi* (*cadere*) to give way, subside; **~ (a)** to surrender (to), yield (to), give in (to)

'cedola ['tʃɛdola] *sf* (*Comm*) coupon; voucher

'ceffo ['tʃeffo] (*peg*) *sm* ugly mug

cef'fone [tʃef'fone] *sm* slap, smack

cele'brare [tʃele'brare] *vt* to celebrate

'celebre ['tʃɛlebre] *ag* famous, celebrated

ce'leste [tʃe'lɛste] *ag* celestial; heavenly; (*colore*) sky-blue

'celibe ['tʃɛlibe] *ag* single, unmarried

'cella ['tʃɛlla] *sf* cell; **cella frigorifera** cold store

'cellula ['tʃɛllula] *sf* (*Biol, Elettr, Pol*) cell; **cellulare** *sm* cellphone

cellu'lite [tʃellu'lite] *sf* cellulite

cemen'tare [tʃemen'tare] *vt* (*anche fig*) to cement

ce'mento [tʃe'mento] *sm* cement; **cemento armato** reinforced concrete

'cena ['tʃena] *sf* dinner; (*leggera*) supper

ce'nare [tʃe'nare] *vi* to dine, have dinner

'cenere ['tʃenere] *sf* ash

'cenno ['tʃenno] *sm* (*segno*) sign, signal; (*gesto*) gesture; (*col capo*) nod; (*con la mano*) wave; (*allusione*) hint, mention; (*breve esposizione*) short account; **far ~ di sì/no** to nod (one's head)/shake one's head

censi'mento [tʃensi'mento] *sm* census

cen'sura [tʃen'sura] *sf* censorship; censor's office; (*fig*) censure

cente'nario, -a [tʃente'narjo] *ag* (*che ha cento anni*) hundred-year-old; (*che ricorre ogni cento anni*) centennial, centenary *cpd* ▷ *sm/f* centenarian ▷ *sm* centenary

cen'tesimo, -a [tʃen'tezimo] *ag, sm* hundredth; (*di euro, dollaro*) cent

cen'tigrado, -a [tʃen'tigrado] *ag* centigrade; **20 gradi centigradi** 20 degrees centigrade

cen'timetro [tʃen'timetro] *sm* centimetre

centi'naio [tʃenti'najo] (*pl(f)* **-aia**) *sm* **un ~ (di)** a hundred; about a hundred

'cento ['tʃento] *num* a hundred, one hundred

cento'mila [tʃento'mila] *num* a o one hundred thousand; **te l'ho detto ~ volte** (*fig*) I've told you a thousand times

cen'trale [tʃen'trale] *ag* central ▷ *sf*: **centrale telefonica** (telephone) exchange; **centrale elettrica** electric power station; **centrali'nista** *sm/f* operator; **centra'lino** *sm* (telephone) exchange; (*di albergo ecc*) switchboard; **centralizzato, -a** [tʃentralid'dzato] *ag* central

cen'trare [tʃen'trare] *vt* to hit the centre of; (*Tecn*) to centre

cen'trifuga [tʃen'trifuga] *sf* spin-drier

'centro ['tʃentro] *sm* centre; **centro civico** civic centre; **centro commerciale** shopping centre; (*città*) commercial centre

'ceppo ['tʃeppo] *sm* (*di albero*) stump; (*pezzo di legno*) log

'cera ['tʃera] *sf* wax; (*aspetto*) appearance

ce'ramica, -che [tʃe'ramika] *sf* ceramic; (*Arte*) ceramics *sg*

cerbi'atto [tʃer'bjatto] *sm* (*Zool*) fawn

cer'care [tʃer'kare] *vt* to look for, search for ▷ *vi* **~ di fare qc** to try to do sth; **stiamo cercando un albergo/ristorante** we're looking for a hotel/restaurant

cercherò *ecc* [tʃerke'rɔ] *vb vedi* **cercare**

'cerchia ['tʃerkja] *sf* circle

cerchietto [tʃer'kjetto] *sm* (*per capelli*) hairband

'cerchio ['tʃerkjo] *sm* circle; (*giocattolo, di botte*) hoop

cereali [tʃere'ali] *smpl* cereal *sg*

ceri'monia [tʃeri'mɔnja] *sf* ceremony

ce'rino [tʃe'rino] *sm* wax match

'cernia ['tʃɛrnja] *sf* (*Zool*) stone bass

cerni'era [tʃer'njera] *sf* hinge; **cerniera lampo** zip (fastener) (BRIT), zipper (US)

'cero ['tʃero] *sm* (church) candle

ce'rotto [tʃe'rɔtto] *sm* sticking plaster

certa'mente [tʃerta'mente] *av* certainly

certifi'cato *sm* certificate; **certificato medico** medical certificate; **certificato di nascita/di morte** birth/death certificate

PAROLA CHIAVE

'certo, -a ['tʃɛrto] *ag* (*sicuro*): **certo (di/ che)** certain o sure (of/that)
▷ *det* **1** (*tale*) certain; **un certo signor Smith** a (certain) Mr Smith
2 (*qualche: con valore intensivo*) some; **dopo un certo tempo** after some time; **un fatto di una certa importanza** a matter of some importance; **di una certa età**

past one's prime, not so young
▷ *pron* **certi, e** *pl* some ▷ *av* (*certamente*) certainly; (*senz'altro*) of course; **di certo** certainly; **no (di) certo!, certo che no!** certainly not!; **sì certo** yes indeed, certainly

cer'vello, -i [tʃer'vɛllo] (*Anat*) (*pl*(*f*) **-a**) *sm* brain; **cervello elettronico** computer
'cervo, -a [tʃɛrvo] *sm/f* stag/doe ▷ *sm* deer; **cervo volante** stag beetle
ces'puglio [tʃes'puʎʎo] *sm* bush
ces'sare [tʃes'sare] *vi, vt* to stop, cease; **~ di fare qc** to stop doing sth
ces'tino [tʃes'tino] *sm* basket; (*per la carta straccia*) wastepaper basket; **cestino da viaggio** (*Ferr*) packed lunch (*o* dinner)
'cesto [tʃesto] *sm* basket
'ceto [tʃɛto] *sm* (*social*) class
cetrio'lino [tʃetrio'lino] *sm* gherkin
cetri'olo [tʃetri'ɔlo] *sm* cucumber
Cfr. *abbr* (= *confronta*) cf.
CGIL *sigla f* (= *Confederazione Generale Italiana del Lavoro*) trades union organization
chat line [tʃæt'laen] *sf inv* chat room
chattare [tʃat'tare] *vi* (*Inform*) to chat online

PAROLA CHIAVE

che [ke] *pron* **1** (*relativo: persona: soggetto*) who; (: *oggetto*) whom, that; (: *cosa, animale*) which, that; **il ragazzo che è venuto** the boy who came; **l'uomo che io vedo** the man (whom) I see; **il libro che è sul tavolo** the book which *o* that is on the table; **il libro che vedi** the book (which *o* that) you see; **la sera che ti ho visto** the evening I saw you
2 (*interrogativo, esclamativo*) what; **che (cosa) fai?** what are you doing?; **a che (cosa) pensi?** what are you thinking about?; **non sa che (cosa) fare** he doesn't know what to do; **ma che dici!** what are you saying!
3 (*indefinito*): **quell'uomo ha un che di losco** there's something suspicious about that man; **un certo non so che** an indefinable something
▷ *det* **1** (*interrogativo: tra tanti*) what; (: *tra pochi*) which; **che tipo di film preferisci?** what sort of film do you prefer?; **che vestito ti vuoi mettere?** what (*o* which) dress do you want to put on?
2 (*esclamativo: seguito da aggettivo*) how; (: *seguito da sostantivo*) what; **che buono!** how delicious!; **che bel vestito!** what a lovely dress!
▷ *cong* **1** (*con proposizioni subordinate*) that;

credo che verrà I think he'll come; **voglio che tu studi** I want you to study; **so che tu c'eri** I know (that) you were there; **non che, non che sia sbagliato, ma ...** not that it's wrong, but ...
2 (*finale*) so that; **vieni qua, che ti veda** come here, so (that) I can see you
3 (*temporale*): **arrivai che eri già partito** you had already left when I arrived; **sono anni che non lo vedo** I haven't seen him for years
4 (*in frasi imperative, concessive*): **che venga pure!** let him come by all means!; **che tu sia benedetto!** may God bless you!
5 (*comparativo: con più, meno*) than; *vedi anche* **più**; **meno**; **così** *ecc*

chemiotera'pia [kemjotera'pia] *sf* chemotherapy
chero'sene [kero'zɛne] *sm* kerosene

PAROLA CHIAVE

chi [ki] *pron* **1** (*interrogativo: soggetto*) who; (: *oggetto*) who, whom; **chi è?** who is it?; **di chi è questo libro?** whose book is this?, whose is this book?; **con chi parli?** who are you talking to?; **a chi pensi?** who are you thinking about?; **chi di voi?** which of you?; **non so a chi rivolgermi** I don't know who to ask
2 (*relativo*) whoever, anyone who; **dillo a chi vuoi** tell whoever you like
3 (*indefinito*): **chi ... chi ...** some ... others ...; **chi dice una cosa, chi dice un'altra** some say one thing, others say another

chiacchie'rare [kjakkje'rare] *vi* to chat; (*discorrere futilmente*) to chatter; (*far pettegolezzi*) to gossip; **chi'acchiere** *sfpl* **fare due** *o* **quattro chiacchiere** to have a chat
chia'mare [kja'mare] *vt* to call; (*rivolgersi a qn*) to call (in), send for; **chiamarsi** *vpr* (*aver nome*) to be called; **come ti chiami?** what's your name?; **mi chiamo Paolo** my name is Paolo, I'm called Paolo; **~ alle armi** to call up; **~ in giudizio** to summon; **chia'mata** *sf* (*Tel*) call; (*Mil*) call-up
chia'rezza [kja'rettsa] *sf* clearness; clarity
chia'rire [kja'rire] *vt* to make clear; (*fig: spiegare*) to clear up, explain
chi'aro, -a ['kjaro] *ag* clear; (*luminoso*) clear, bright; (*colore*) pale, light
chi'asso ['kjasso] *sm* uproar, row
chi'ave ['kjave] *sf* key ▷ *ag inv* key *cpd*; **posso avere la mia ~?** can I have my key?; **chiave d'accensione** (*Aut*) ignition key;

chiave di volta keystone; **chiave inglese** monkey wrench

chi'azza ['kjattsa] *sf* stain; splash

'chicco, -chi ['kikko] *sm* grain; *(di caffè)* bean; **chicco d'uva** grape

chi'edere ['kjɛdere] *vt (per sapere)* to ask; *(per avere)* to ask for ▷ *vi* ~ **di qn** to ask after sb; *(al telefono)* to ask for o want sb; ~ **qc a qn** to ask sb sth; to ask sb for sth; **chiedersi** *vpr* **chiedersi (se)** to wonder (whether)

chi'esa ['kjɛza] *sf* church

chi'esi *ecc* ['kjɛzi] *vb vedi* **chiedere**

'chiglia ['kiʎʎa] *sf* keel

'chilo ['kilo] *sm* kilo; **chi'lometro** *sm* kilometre

'chimica ['kimika] *sf* chemistry

'chimico, -a, -ci, -che ['kimiko] *ag* chemical ▷ *sm/f* chemist

chi'nare [ki'nare] *vt* to lower, bend; **chinarsi** *vpr* to stoop, bend

chi'occiola ['kjɔttʃola] *sf* snail; *(di indirizzo e-mail)* at sign, @; **scala a ~** spiral staircase

chi'odo ['kjɔdo] *sm* nail; *(fig)* obsession; **chiodo di garofano** *(Cuc)* clove

chi'osco, -schi ['kjɔsko] *sm* kiosk, stall

chi'ostro ['kjɔstro] *sm* cloister

chiro'mante [kiro'mante] *sm/f* palmist

chirur'gia [kirur'dʒia] *sf* surgery; **chirurgia estetica** cosmetic surgery; **chi'rurgo, -ghi** *o* **gi** *sm* surgeon

chissà [kis'sa] *av* who knows, I wonder

chi'tarra [ki'tarra] *sf* guitar

chitar'rista, -i, e [kitar'rista] *sm/f* guitarist, guitar player

chi'udere ['kjudere] *vt* to close, shut; *(luce, acqua)* to put off, turn off; *(definitivamente: fabbrica)* to close down, shut down; *(strada)* to close; *(recingere)* to enclose; *(porre termine a)* to end ▷ *vi* to close, shut; to close down, shut down; to end; **chiudersi** *vpr* to shut, close; *(ritirarsi: anche fig)* to shut o.s. away; *(ferita)* to close up; **a che ora chiudete?** what time do you close?

chi'unque [ki'unkwe] *pron (relativo)* whoever; *(indefinito)* anyone, anybody; ~ **sia** whoever it is

'chiusi *ecc* ['kjusi] *vb vedi* **chiudere**

chi'uso, -a ['kjuso] *pp di* **chiudere** ▷ *sf (di corso d'acqua)* sluice, lock; *(recinto)* enclosure; *(di discorso ecc)* conclusion, ending; **chiu'sura** *sf (vedi* **chiudere)** closing; shutting; closing o shutting down; enclosing; putting o turning off; ending; *(dispositivo)* catch; fastening; fastener; **chiusura lampo®** zip (fastener) *(BRIT)*, zipper *(US)*

C.I. *abbr* = **carta d'identità**

⭕ **PAROLA CHIAVE**

ci [tʃi] *(dav* **lo, la, li, le, ne** *diventa* **ce)** *pron* **1** *(personale: complemento oggetto)* us; *(: a noi: complemento di termine)* (to) us; *(: riflessivo)* ourselves; *(: reciproco)* each other, one another; *(impersonale):* **ci si veste** we get dressed; **ci ha visti** he's seen us; **non ci ha dato niente** he gave us nothing; **ci vestiamo** we get dressed; **ci amiamo** we love one another o each other

2 *(dimostrativo: di ciò, su ciò, in ciò ecc)* about (o on o of) it; **non so cosa farci** I don't know what to do about it; **che c'entro io?** what have I got to do with it?

▷ *av (qui)* here; *(lì)* there; *(moto attraverso luogo):* **ci passa sopra un ponte** a bridge passes over it; **non ci passa più nessuno** nobody comes this way any more; **esserci** *vedi* **essere**

cia'batta [tʃa'batta] *sf* slipper; *(pane)* ciabatta

ciam'bella [tʃam'bɛlla] *sf (Cuc)* ring-shaped cake; *(salvagente)* rubber ring

ci'ao ['tʃao] *escl (all'arrivo)* hello!; *(alla partenza)* cheerio! bye!

cias'cuno, -a [tʃas'kuno] *(det: dav sm:* **ciascun** +C, V, **ciascuno** +s impura, gn, pn, ps, x, z; *dav sf:* **ciascuna** +C, **ciascun'** +V) *det* every, each; *(ogni)* every ▷ *pron* each (one); *(tutti)* everyone, everybody

ci'barie [tʃi'barje] *sfpl* foodstuffs

cibernauta, -i, -e [tʃiber'nauta] *sm/f* Internet surfer

ciberspazio [tʃiber'spattsjo] *sm* cyberspace

'cibo ['tʃibo] *sm* food

ci'cala [tʃi'kala] *sf* cicada

cica'trice [tʃika'tritʃe] *sf* scar

'cicca ['tʃikka] *sf* cigarette end

'ciccia ['tʃittʃa] *(fam) sf* fat

cicci'one, -a [tʃit'tʃone] *sm/f (fam)* fatty

cicla'mino [tʃikla'mino] *sm* cyclamen

ci'clismo [tʃi'klizmo] *sm* cycling; **ci'clista, -i, -e** *sm/f* cyclist

'ciclo ['tʃiklo] *sm* cycle; *(di malattia)* course

ciclomo'tore [tʃiklomo'tore] *sm* moped

ci'clone [tʃi'klone] *sm* cyclone

ci'cogna [tʃi'koɲɲa] *sf* stork

ci'eco, -a, -chi, -che ['tʃɛko] *ag* blind ▷ *sm/f* blind man/woman

ci'elo ['tʃɛlo] *sm* sky; *(Rel)* heaven

'cifra ['tʃifra] *sf (numero)* figure; numeral; *(somma di denaro)* sum, figure; *(monogramma)* monogram, initials *pl*; *(codice)* code, cipher 'ciglio, -i ['tʃiʎʎo] (delle palpebre) (pl(f) ciglia) sm (margine) edge, verge; (eye)lash; (eye)lid; (sopracciglio) eyebrow

'cigno ['tʃiɲɲo] sm swan

cigo'lare [tʃigo'lare] vi to squeak, creak

'Cile ['tʃile] sm il ~ Chile

ci'leno, -a [tʃi'lɛno] ag, sm/f Chilean

cili'egia, -gie o ge [tʃi'ljedʒa] sf cherry

ciliegina [tʃilje'dʒina] sf glacé cherry

cilin'drata [tʃilin'drata] sf (Aut) (cubic) capacity; una macchina di grossa ~ a big-engined car

ci'lindro [tʃi'lindro] sm cylinder; (cappello) top hat

'cima ['tʃima] sf (sommità) top; (di monte) top, summit; (estremità) end; in ~ a at the top of; da ~ a fondo from top to bottom; (fig) from beginning to end

'cimice ['tʃimitʃe] sf (Zool) bug; (puntina) drawing pin (BRIT), thumbtack (US)

cimini'era [tʃimi'njɛra] sf chimney; (di nave) funnel

cimi'tero [tʃimi'tɛro] sm cemetery

'Cina ['tʃina] sf la ~ China

cin'cin [tʃin'tʃin] escl cheers!

'cinema ['tʃinema] sm inv cinema

ci'nese [tʃi'nese] ag, sm/f, sm Chinese inv

'cinghia ['tʃingja] sf strap; (cintura, Tecn) belt

cinghi'ale [tʃin'gjale] sm wild boar

cinguet'tare [tʃingwet'tare] vi to twitter

'cinico, -a, -ci, -che ['tʃiniko] ag cynical ▷ sm/f cynic

cin'quanta [tʃin'kwanta] num fifty; cinquan'tesimo, -a num fiftieth

cinquan'tina [tʃinkwan'tina] sf (serie): una ~ (di) about fifty; (età): essere sulla ~ to be about fifty

'cinque ['tʃinkwe] num five; avere ~ anni to be five (years old); il ~ dicembre 1998 the fifth of December 1998; alle ~ (ora) at five (o'clock)

cinque'cento [tʃinkwe'tʃɛnto] num five hundred ▷ sm il C~ the sixteenth century

cin'tura [tʃin'tura] sf belt; cintura di salvataggio lifebelt (BRIT), life preserver (US); cintura di sicurezza (Aut, Aer) safety o seat belt

cintu'rino [tʃintu'rino] sm strap; ~ dell'orologio watch strap

ciò [tʃɔ] pron this; that; ~ che what; ~ nonostante o nondimeno nevertheless, in spite of that

ci'occa, -che ['tʃɔkka] sf (di capelli) lock

ciocco'lata [tʃokko'lata] sf chocolate; (bevanda) (hot) chocolate; cioccola'tino sm chocolate

cioè [tʃo'ɛ] av that is (to say)

ci'otola ['tʃɔtola] sf bowl

ci'ottolo [tʃi'ɔttolo] sm pebble; (di strada) cobble(stone)

ci'polla [tʃi'polla] sf onion; (di tulipano ecc) bulb

cipol'lina [tʃipol'lina] sf cipolline sottaceto pickled onions

ci'presso [tʃi'prɛsso] sm cypress (tree)

'cipria ['tʃiprja] sf (face) powder

'Cipro ['tʃipro] sm Cyprus

'circa ['tʃirka] av about, roughly ▷ prep about, concerning; a mezzogiorno ~ about midday

'circo, -chi ['tʃirko] sm circus

circo'lare [tʃirko'lare] vi to circulate; (Aut) to drive (along), move (along) ▷ ag circular ▷ sf (Amm) circular; (di autobus) circle (line)

'circolo ['tʃirkolo] sm circle

circon'dare [tʃirkon'dare] vt to surround; circondarsi vpr circondarsi di to surround o.s. with

circonvallazi'one [tʃirkonvallat'tsjone] sf ring road (BRIT), beltway (US); (per evitare una città) by-pass

circos'petto, -a [tʃirkos'petto] ag circumspect, cautious

circos'tante [tʃirkos'tante] ag surrounding, neighbouring

circos'tanza [tʃirkos'tantsa] sf circumstance; (occasione) occasion

cir'cuito [tʃir'kuito] sm circuit

CISL sigla f (= Confederazione Italiana Sindacati Lavoratori) trades union organization

cis'terna [tʃis'tɛrna] sf tank, cistern

'cisti ['tʃisti] sf cyst

cis'tite [tʃis'tite] sf cystitis

ci'tare [tʃi'tare] vt (Dir) to summon; (autore) to quote; (a esempio, modello) to cite

ci'tofono [tʃi'tɔfono] sm entry phone; (in uffici) intercom

città [tʃit'ta] sf inv town; (importante) city; città universitaria university campus

cittadi'nanza [tʃittadi'nantsa] sf citizens pl; (Dir) citizenship

citta'dino, -a [tʃitta'dino] ag town cpd; city cpd ▷ sm/f (di uno Stato) citizen; (abitante di città) townsman, city dweller

ci'uccio ['tʃuttʃo] sm (fam) comforter, dummy (BRIT), pacifier (US)

ci'uffo ['tʃuffo] sm tuft

ci'vetta [tʃi'vetta] sf (Zool) owl; (fig: donna) coquette, flirt ▷ ag inv auto/nave ~ decoy car/ship

'civico, -a, -ci, -che ['tʃiviko] ag civic; (museo) municipal, town cpd; city cpd

ci'vile [tʃi'vile] ag civil; (non militare) civilian; (nazione) civilized ▷ sm civilian

civiltà [tʃivilˈta] *sf* civilization; (*cortesia*) civility

'clacson *sm inv* (*Aut*) horn

clandes'tino, -a *ag* clandestine; (*Pol*) underground, clandestine; (*immigrato*) illegal ▷ *sm/f* stowaway; (*anche:* **immigrato ~**) illegal immigrant

'classe *sf* class; **di ~** (*fig*) with class, of excellent quality; **classe operaia** working class; **classe turistica** (*Aer*) economy class

'classico, -a, -ci, -che *ag* classical; (*tradizionale: moda*) classic(al) ▷ *sm* classic; classical author

clas'sifica *sf* classification; (*Sport*) placings *pl*

classifi'care *vt* to classify; (*candidato, compito*) to grade; **classificarsi** *vpr* to be placed

'clausola *sf* (*Dir*) clause

clavi'cembalo [klaviˈtʃembalo] *sm* harpsichord

cla'vicola *sf* (*Anat*) collar bone

clic'care *vi* (*Inform*): **~ su** to click on

cli'ente *sm/f* customer, client

'clima, -i *sm* climate; **climatizzatore** *sm* air conditioning system

'clinica, -che *sf* (*scienza*) clinical medicine; (*casa di cura*) clinic, nursing home; (*settore d'ospedale*) clinic

clo'nare *vt* to clone; **clonazione** [klonaˈtsjone] *sf* cloning

'cloro *sm* chlorine

club *sm inv* club

c.m. *abbr* = **corrente mese**

cm *abbr* (= *centimetro*) cm

coalizi'one [koalitˈtsjone] *sf* coalition

'COBAS *sigla mpl* (= *Comitati di base*) *independent trades unions*

'coca *sf* (*bibita*) Coke®; (*droga*) cocaine

coca'ina *sf* cocaine

cocci'nella [kottʃiˈnɛlla] *sf* ladybird (*BRIT*), ladybug (*US*)

cocci'uto, -a [kotˈtʃuto] *ag* stubborn, pigheaded

'cocco, -chi *sm* (*pianta*) coconut palm; (*frutto*): **noce di ~** coconut ▷ *sm/f* (*fam*) darling

cocco'drillo *sm* crocodile

cocco'lare *vt* to cuddle, fondle

cocerò *ecc* [kotʃeˈrɔ] *vb vedi* **cuocere**

co'comero *sm* watermelon

'coda *sf* tail; (*fila di persone, auto*) queue (*BRIT*), line (*US*); (*di abiti*) train; **con la ~ dell'occhio** out of the corner of one's eye; **mettersi in ~** to queue (up) (*BRIT*), line up (*US*); to join the queue (*BRIT*) *o* line (*US*); **coda di cavallo** (*acconciatura*) ponytail

co'dardo, -a *ag* cowardly ▷ *sm/f* coward

'codice [ˈkoditʃe] *sm* code; **codice di avviamento postale** postcode (*BRIT*), zip code (*US*); **codice a barre** bar code; **codice civile** civil code; **codice fiscale** tax code; **codice penale** penal code; **codice segreto** (*di tessera magnetica*) PIN (number); **codice della strada** highway code

coe'rente *ag* coherent

coe'taneo, -a *ag, sm/f* contemporary

'cofano *sm* (*Aut*) bonnet (*BRIT*), hood (*US*); (*forziere*) chest

'cogliere [ˈkɔʎʎere] *vt* (*fiore: frutto*) to pick, gather; (*sorprendere*) to catch, surprise; (*bersaglio*) to hit; (*fig: momento opportuno ecc*) to grasp, seize, take; (*: capire*) to grasp; **~ qn in flagrante** *o* **in fallo** to catch sb red-handed

co'gnato, -a [koɲˈɲato] *sm/f* brother-/sister-in-law

co'gnome [koɲˈɲome] *sm* surname

coinci'denza [kointʃiˈdɛntsa] *sf* coincidence; (*Ferr, Aer, di autobus*) connection

coin'cidere [koinˈtʃidere] *vi* to coincide

coin'volgere [koinˈvɔldʒere] *vt* **~ in** to involve in

cola'pasta *sm inv* colander

co'lare *vt* (*liquido*) to strain; (*pasta*) to drain; (*oro fuso*) to pour ▷ *vi* (*sudore*) to drip; (*botte*) to leak; (*cera*) to melt; **~ a picco** *vt, vi* (*nave*) to sink

colazi'one [kolatˈtsjone] *sf* breakfast; **fare ~** to have breakfast; **a che ora è servita la ~?** what time is breakfast?

co'lera *sm* (*Med*) cholera

'colgo *ecc vb vedi* **cogliere**

'colica *sf* (*Med*) colic

co'lino *sm* strainer

'colla *sf* glue; (*di farina*) paste

collabo'rare *vi* to collaborate; **~ a** to collaborate on; (*giornale*) to contribute to; **collabora'tore, -'trice** *sm/f* collaborator; contributor; **collaboratore esterno** freelance; **collaboratrice familiare** home help

col'lana *sf* necklace; (*collezione*) collection, series

col'lant [kɔˈlã] *sm inv* tights *pl*

col'lare *sm* collar

col'lasso *sm* (*Med*) collapse

collau'dare *vt* to test, try out

col'lega, -ghi, -ghe *sm/f* colleague

collega'mento *sm* connection; (*Mil*) liaison

colle'gare *vt* to connect, join, link; **collegarsi** *vpr* (*Radio, TV*) to link up; **collegarsi con** (*Tel*) to get through to

col'legio [kolˈlɛdʒo] *sm* college; (*convitto*)

boarding school; **collegio elettorale** (*Pol*) constituency

'**collera** *sf* anger

col'**lerico, -a, -ci, -che** *ag* quick-tempered, irascible

col'**letta** *sf* collection

col'**letto** *sm* collar

collezio'**nare** [kollettsjo'nare] *vt* to collect

collezi'**one** [kollet'tsjone] *sf* collection

col'**lina** *sf* hill

col'**lirio** *sm* eyewash

'**collo** *sm* neck; (*di abito*) neck, collar; (*pacco*) parcel; **collo del piede** instep

colloca'**mento** *sm* (*impiego*) employment; (*disposizione*) placing, arrangement

collo'**care** *vt* (*libri, mobili*) to place; (*Comm: merce*) to find a market for

collocazi'**one** [kollokat'tsjone] *sf* placing; (*di libro*) classification

col'**loquio** *sm* conversation, talk; (*ufficiale, per un lavoro*) interview; (*Ins*) preliminary oral exam

col'**mare** *vt* ~ **di** (*anche fig*) to fill with; (*dare in abbondanza*) to load o overwhelm with

co'**lombo, -a** *sm/f* dove; pigeon

co'**lonia** *sf* colony; (*per bambini*) holiday camp; **(acqua di) ~** (eau de) cologne

co'**lonna** *sf* column; **colonna sonora** (*Cinema*) sound track; **colonna vertebrale** spine, spinal column

colon'**nello** *sm* colonel

colo'**rante** *sm* colouring

colo'**rare** *vt* to colour; (*disegno*) to colour in

co'**lore** *sm* colour; **a colori** in colour, colour *cpd*; **farne di tutti i colori** to get up to all sorts of mischief; **vorrei un ~ diverso** I'd like a different colour

colo'**rito, -a** *ag* coloured; (*viso*) rosy, pink; (*linguaggio*) colourful ▷ *sm* (*tinta*) colour; (*carnagione*) complexion

'**colpa** *sf* fault; (*biasimo*) blame; (*colpevolezza*) guilt; (*azione colpevole*) offence; (*peccato*) sin; **di chi è la ~?** whose fault is it?; **è ~ sua** it's his fault; **per ~ di** through, owing to; **col'pevole** *ag* guilty

col'**pire** *vt* to hit, strike; (*fig*) to strike; **rimanere colpito da qc** to be amazed o struck by sth

'**colpo** *sm* (*urto*) knock; (*: affettivo*) blow, shock; (*: aggressivo*) blow; (*di pistola*) shot; (*Med*) stroke; (*rapina*) raid; **di ~** suddenly; **fare ~** to make a strong impression; **colpo d'aria** chill; **colpo in banca** bank job o raid; **colpo basso** (*Pugilato, fig*) punch below the belt; **colpo di fulmine** love at first sight; **colpo di grazia** coup de grâce; **colpo di scena** (*Teatro*) coup de théâtre; (*fig*) dramatic turn of events; **colpo di sole** sunstroke; **colpo di Stato** coup d'état; **colpo di telefono** phone call; **colpo di testa** (sudden) impulse o whim; **colpo di vento** gust (of wind); **colpi di sole** (*nei capelli*) highlights

'**colsi** *ecc vb vedi* **cogliere**

col'**tellata** *sf* stab

col'**tello** *sm* knife; **coltello a serramanico** clasp knife

colti'**vare** *vt* to cultivate; (*verdura*) to grow, cultivate

'**colto, -a** *pp di* **cogliere** ▷ *ag* (*istruito*) cultured, educated

'**coma** *sm inv* coma

comanda'**mento** *sm* (*Rel*) commandment

coman'**dante** *sm* (*Mil*) commander, commandant; (*di reggimento*) commanding officer; (*Naut, Aer*) captain

coman'**dare** *vi* to be in command ▷ *vt* to command; (*imporre*) to order, command; ~ **a qn di fare** to order sb to do

combaci'**are** [komba'tʃare] *vi* to meet; (*fig: coincidere*) to coincide

com'**battere** *vt, vi* to fight

combi'**nare** *vt* to combine; (*organizzare*) to arrange; (*fam: fare*) to make, cause; **combinazi'one** *sf* combination; (*caso fortuito*) coincidence; **per combinazione** by chance

combus'**tibile** *ag* combustible ▷ *sm* fuel

 PAROLA CHIAVE

'**come** *av* **1** (*alla maniera di*) like; **ti comporti come lui** you behave like him o like he does; **bianco come la neve** (as) white as snow; **come se** as if, as though

2 (*in qualità di*) as a; **lavora come autista** he works as a driver

3 (*interrogativo*) how; **come ti chiami?** what's your name?; **come sta?** how are you?; **com'è il tuo amico?** what is your friend like?; **come? (prego?)** pardon?, sorry?; **come mai?** how come?; **come mai non ci hai avvertiti?** why on earth didn't you warn us?

4 (*esclamativo*): **come sei bravo!** how clever you are!; **come mi dispiace!** I'm terribly sorry!

▷ *cong* **1** (*in che modo*) how; **mi ha spiegato come l'ha conosciuto** he told me how he met him

2 (*correlativo*) as; (*con comparativi di maggioranza*) than; **non è bravo come pensavo** he isn't as clever as I thought; **è**

meglio di come pensassi it's better than I thought

3 (*appena che, quando*) as soon as; **come arrivò, iniziò a lavorare** as soon as he arrived, he set to work; *vedi* **così**; **tanto**

'comico, -a, -ci, -che *ag* (*Teatro*) comic; (*buffo*) comical ▷ *sm* (*attore*) comedian, comic actor

cominci'are [komin'tʃare] *vt, vi* to begin, start; **~ a fare/col fare** to begin to do/by doing; **a che ora comincia il film?** when does the film start?

comi'tato *sm* committee

comi'tiva *sf* party, group

co'mizio [ko'mittsjo] *sm* (*Pol*) meeting, assembly

com'media *sf* comedy; (*opera teatrale*) play; (: *che fa ridere*) comedy; (*fig*) playacting *no pl*

commemo'rare *vt* to commemorate

commen'tare *vt* to comment on; (*testo*) to annotate; (*Radio, TV*) to give a commentary on

commerci'ale [kommer'tʃale] *ag* commercial, trading; (*peg*) commercial

commercia'lista, -i, e [kommertʃa'lista] *sm/f* (*laureato*) graduate in economics and commerce; (*consulente*) business consultant

commerci'ante [kommer'tʃante] *sm/f* trader, dealer; (*negoziante*) shopkeeper

commerci'are [kommer'tʃare] *vt, vi* **~ in** to deal *o* trade in

com'mercio [kom'mertʃo] *sm* trade, commerce; **essere in ~** (*prodotto*) to be on the market *o* on sale; **essere nel ~** (*persona*) to be in business; **commercio al dettaglio/all'ingrosso** retail/wholesale trade; **commercio elettronico** e-commerce

com'messo, -a *pp di* **commettere** ▷ *sm/f* shop assistant (BRIT), sales clerk (US) ▷ *sm* (*impiegato*) clerk; **commesso viaggiatore** commercial traveller

commes'tibile *ag* edible

com'mettere *vt* to commit

com'misi *ecc vb vedi* **commettere**

commissari'ato *sm* (*Amm*) commissionership; (: *sede*) commissioner's office; **commissariato di polizia** police station

commis'sario *sm* commissioner; (*di pubblica sicurezza*) ≈ (police) superintendent (BRIT), ≈ (police) captain (US); (*Sport*) steward; (*membro di commissione*) member of a committee *o* board

commissi'one *sf* (*incarico*) errand;

(*comitato, percentuale*) commission; (*Comm: ordinazione*) order; **commissioni** *sfpl* (*acquisti*) shopping *sg*; **commissioni bancarie** bank charges; **commissione d'esame** examining board

com'mosso, -a *pp di* **commuovere**

commo'vente *ag* moving

commozi'one [kommot'tsjone] *sf* emotion, deep feeling; **commozione cerebrale** (*Med*) concussion

commu'overe *vt* to move, affect; **commuoversi** *vpr* to be moved

como'dino *sm* bedside table

comodità *sf inv* comfort; convenience

'comodo, -a *ag* comfortable; (*facile*) easy; (*conveniente*) convenient; (*utile*) useful, handy ▷ *sm* comfort; convenience; **con ~** at one's convenience *o* leisure; **fare il proprio ~** to do as one pleases; **far ~** to be useful *o* handy

compa'gnia [kompaɲ'ɲia] *sf* company; (*gruppo*) gathering

com'pagno, -a [kom'paɲɲo] *sm/f* (*di classe, gioco*) companion; (*Pol*) comrade

com'paio *ecc vb vedi* **comparire**

compa'rare *vt* to compare

compara'tivo, -a *ag, sm* comparative

compa'rire *vi* to appear

com'parvi *ecc vb vedi* **comparire**

compassi'one *sf* compassion, pity; **avere ~ di qn** to feel sorry for sb, to pity sb

com'passo *sm* (pair of) compasses *pl*; callipers *pl*

compa'tibile *ag* (*scusabile*) excusable; (*conciliabile, Inform*) compatible

compa'tire *vt* (*aver compassione di*) to sympathize with, feel sorry for; (*scusare*) to make allowances for

com'patto, -a *ag* compact; (*roccia*) solid; (*folla*) dense; (*fig: gruppo, partito*) united

compen'sare *vt* (*equilibrare*) to compensate for, make up for; **~ qn di** (*rimunerare*) to pay *o* remunerate sb for; (*risarcire*) to pay compensation to sb for; (*fig: fatiche, dolori*) to reward sb for; **com'penso** *sm* compensation payment, remuneration; reward; **in compenso** (*d'altra parte*) on the other hand

compe'rare *vt* = **comprare**

'compere *sfpl* **fare ~** to do the shopping

compe'tente *ag* competent; (*mancia*) apt, suitable

com'petere *vi* to compete, vie; (*Dir: spettare*): **~ a** to lie within the competence of; **competizi'one** *sf* competition

compi'angere [kom'pjandʒere] *vt* to sympathize with, feel sorry for

'compiere *vt* (*concludere*) to finish, complete; (*adempiere*) to carry out, fulfil;

compiersi *vpr* (*avverarsi*) to be fulfilled, come true; **~ gli anni** to have one's birthday

compi'lare *vt* (*modulo*) to fill in; (*dizionario, elenco*) to compile

'compito *sm* (*incarico*) task, duty; (*dovere*) duty; (*Ins*) exercise; (: *a casa*) piece of homework; **fare i compiti** to do one's homework

comple'anno *sm* birthday

complessità *sf* complexity

comples'sivo, -a *ag* (*globale*) comprehensive, overall; (*totale: cifra*) total

com'plesso, -a *ag* complex ▷ *sm* (*Psic, Edil*) complex; (*Mus: corale*) ensemble; (: *orchestrina*) band; (: *di musica pop*) group; **in** o **nel ~** on the whole; **complesso alberghiero** hotel complex; **complesso edilizio** building complex; **complesso vitaminico** vitamin complex

completa'mente *av* completely

comple'tare *vt* to complete

com'pleto, -a *ag* complete; (*teatro, autobus*) full ▷ *sm* suit; **al ~** full; (*tutti presenti*) all present; **completo da sci** ski suit

compli'care *vt* to complicate; **complicarsi** *vpr* to become complicated

'complice [ˈkɔmplitʃe] *sm/f* accomplice

complicità [komplitʃiˈta] *sf inv* complicity; **un sorriso/uno sguardo di ~** a knowing smile/look

complimen'tarsi *vpr* **~ con** to congratulate

compli'mento *sm* compliment; **complimenti** *smpl* (*cortesia eccessiva*) ceremony *sg*; (*ossequi*) regards, compliments; **complimenti!** congratulations!; **senza complimenti!** don't stand on ceremony!; make yourself at home!; help yourself!

complot'tare *vi* to plot, conspire

com'plotto *sm* plot, conspiracy

com'pone *ecc vb vedi* **comporre**

compo'nente *sm/f* member ▷ *sm* component

com'pongo *ecc vb vedi* **comporre**

componi'mento *sm* (*Dir*) settlement; (*Ins*) composition; (*poetico, teatrale*) work

com'porre *vt* (*musica, testo*) to compose; (*mettere in ordine*) to arrange; (*Dir: lite*) to settle; (*Tip*) to set; (*Tel*) to dial; **comporsi** *vpr* **comporsi di** to consist of, be composed of

comporta'mento *sm* behaviour

compor'tare *vt* (*implicare*) to involve; **comportarsi** *vpr* to behave

com'posi *ecc vb vedi* **comporre**

composi'tore, -'trice *sm/f* composer;

(*Tip*) compositor, typesetter

com'posto, -a *pp di* **comporre** ▷ *ag* (*persona*) composed, self-possessed; (: *decoroso*) dignified; (*formato da più elementi*) compound *cpd* ▷ *sm* compound

com'prare *vt* to buy; **dove posso ~ delle cartoline?** where can I buy some postcards?

com'prendere *vt* (*contenere*) to comprise, consist of; (*capire*) to understand

compren'sibile *ag* understandable

comprensi'one *sf* understanding

compren'sivo, -a *ag* (*prezzo*): **~ di** inclusive of; (*indulgente*) understanding

> Attenzione! In inglese esiste la parola *comprehensive*, che però in genere significa *completo*.

com'preso, -a *pp di* **comprendere** ▷ *ag* (*incluso*) included; **il servizio è ~?** is service included?

com'pressa *sf* (*Med: garza*) compress; (: *pastiglia*) tablet; *vedi anche* **compresso**

com'primere *vt* (*premere*) to press; (*Fisica*) to compress; (*fig*) to repress

compro'messo, -a *pp di* **compromettere** ▷ *sm* compromise

compro'mettere *vt* to compromise; **compromettersi** *vpr* to compromise o.s.

com'puter *sm inv* computer

comu'nale *ag* municipal, town *cpd*, ≈ borough *cpd*

co'mune *ag* common; (*consueto*) common, everyday; (*di livello medio*) average; (*ordinario*) ordinary ▷ *sm* (*Amm*) town council; (: *sede*) town hall ▷ *sf* (*di persone*) commune; **fuori del ~** out of the ordinary; **avere in ~** to have in common, share; **mettere in ~** to share

comuni'care *vt* (*notizia*) to pass on, convey; (*malattia*) to pass on; (*ansia ecc*) to communicate; (*trasmettere: calore ecc*) to transmit, communicate; (*Rel*) to administer communion to ▷ *vi* to communicate

comuni'cato *sm* communiqué; **comunicato stampa** press release

comunicazi'one [komunikatˈtsjone] *sf* communication; (*annuncio*) announcement; (*Tel*): **dare la ~ a qn** to put sb through; **ottenere la ~** to get through; **comunicazione (telefonica)** (telephone) call

comuni'one *sf* communion; **comunione di beni** (*Dir*) joint ownership of property

comu'nismo *sm* communism

comunità *sf inv* community; **Comunità Europea** European Community

co'munque *cong* however, no matter how ▷ *av* (*in ogni modo*) in any case; (*tuttavia*) however, nevertheless

con prep with; **partire col treno** to leave by train; **~ mio grande stupore** to my great astonishment; **~ tutto ciò** for all that

con'cedere [kon'tʃedere] vt (accordare) to grant; (ammettere) to admit, concede; **concedersi qc** to treat o.s. to sth, to allow o.s. sth

concentrarsi vpr to concentrate

concentrazi'one sf concentration

conce'pire [kontʃe'pire] vt (bambino) to conceive; (progetto, idea) to conceive (of); (metodo, piano) to devise

con'certo [kon'tʃerto] sm (Mus) concert; (: componimento) concerto

con'cessi ecc [kon'tʃessi] vb vedi **concedere**

con'cetto [kon'tʃetto] sm (pensiero, idea) concept; (opinione) opinion

concezi'one [kontʃet'tsjone] sf conception

con'chiglia [kon'kiʎʎa] sf shell

conci'are [kon'tʃare] vt (pelli) to tan; (tabacco) to cure; (fig: ridurre in cattivo stato) to beat up; **conciarsi** vpr (sporcarsi) to get in a mess; (vestirsi male) to dress badly

concili'are [kontʃi'ljare] vt to reconcile; (contravvenzione) to pay on the spot; (sonno) to be conducive to, induce; **conciliarsi qc** to gain o win o sth (for o.s.); **conciliarsi qn** to win sb over; **conciliarsi con** to be reconciled with

con'cime [kon'tʃime] sm manure; (chimico) fertilizer

con'ciso, -a [kon'tʃizo] ag concise, succinct

concitta'dino, -a [kontʃitta'dino] sm/f fellow citizen

con'cludere vt to conclude; (portare a compimento) to conclude, finish, bring to an end; (operare positivamente) to achieve ▷ vi (essere convincente) to be conclusive; **concludersi** vpr to come to an end, close

concor'dare vt (tregua, prezzo) to agree on; (Ling) to make agree ▷ vi to agree

con'corde ag (d'accordo) in agreement; (simultaneo) simultaneous

concor'rente sm/f competitor; (Ins) candidate; **concor'renza** sf competition

concorrenzi'ale [konkorren'tsjale] ag competitive

con'correre vi **~ (in)** (Mat) to converge o meet (in); **~ (a)** (competere) to compete (for); (: Ins: a una cattedra) to apply (for); (partecipare: a un'impresa) to take part (in), contribute (to); **con'corso, -a** pp di **concorrere** ▷ sm competition; (Ins) competitive examination; **concorso di colpa** (Dir) contributory negligence

con'creto, -a ag concrete

con'danna sf sentence; conviction; condemnation

condan'nare vt (Dir): **~ a** to sentence to; **~ per** to convict of; (disapprovare) to condemn

conden'sare vt to condense

condi'mento sm seasoning; dressing

con'dire vt to season; (insalata) to dress

condi'videre vt to share

condizio'nale [kondittsjo'nale] ag conditional ▷ sm (Ling) conditional ▷ sf (Dir) suspended sentence

condizio'nare [kondittsjo'nare] vt to condition; **ad aria condizionata** air-conditioned; **condiziona'tore** sm air conditioner

condizi'one [kondit'tsjone] sf condition

condogli'anze [kondoʎ'ʎantse] sfpl condolences

condo'minio sm joint ownership; (edificio) jointly-owned building

con'dotta sf (modo di comportarsi) conduct, behaviour; (di un affare ecc) handling; (di acqua) piping; (incarico sanitario) country medical practice controlled by a local authority

condu'cente [kondu'tʃente] sm driver

con'duco ecc vb vedi **condurre**

con'durre vt to conduct; (azienda) to manage; (accompagnare: bambino) to take; (automobile) to drive; (trasportare: acqua, gas) to convey, conduct; (fig) to lead ▷ vi to lead

con'dussi ecc vb vedi **condurre**

confe'renza [konfe'rentsa] sf (discorso) lecture; (riunione) conference; **conferenza stampa** press conference

con'ferma sf confirmation

confer'mare vt to confirm

confes'sare vt to confess; **confessarsi** vpr to confess; **andare a confessarsi** (Rel) to go to confession

con'fetto sm sugared almond; (Med) pill
Attenzione! In inglese esiste la parola confetti, che però significa coriandoli.

confet'tura sf (gen) jam; (di arance) marmalade

confezio'nare [konfettsjo'nare] vt (vestito) to make (up); (merci, pacchi) to package

confezi'one [konfet'tsjone] sf (di abiti: da uomo) tailoring; (: da donna) dressmaking; (imballaggio) packaging; **confezioni per signora** ladies' wear; **confezioni da uomo** menswear; **confezione regalo** gift pack

confi'care vt **~ qc in** to hammer o drive sth into; **conficcarsi** vpr to stick

confi'dare vi **~ in** to confide in, rely on ▷ vt to confide; **confidarsi con qn** to confide

in sb
configu'rare vt (Inform) to set
configurazi'one [konfigurat'tsjone] sf
configuration; (Inform) setting
confi'nare vi ~ **con** to border on ▷ vt (Pol)
to intern; (fig) to confine
Confin'dustria sigla f (= Confederazione
Generale dell'Industria Italiana) employers'
association; ≈ CBI (BRIT)
con'fine sm boundary; (di paese) border,
frontier
confis'care vt to confiscate
con'flitto sm conflict
conflu'enza [konflu'entsa] sf (di fiumi)
confluence; (di strade) junction
con'fondere vt to mix up, confuse;
(imbarazzare) to embarrass; **confondersi**
vpr (mescolarsi) to mingle; (turbarsi) to be
confused; (sbagliare) to get mixed up
confor'tare vt to comfort, console
confron'tare vt to compare
con'fronto sm comparison; **in** o **a ~ di** in
comparison with, compared to; **nei miei**
(o **tuoi** ecc) **confronti** towards me (o you
ecc)
con'fusi ecc vb vedi **confondere**
confusi'one sf confusion; (chiasso) racket,
noise; (imbarazzo) embarrassment
con'fuso, -a pp di **confondere** ▷ ag (vedi
confondere) confused; embarrassed
conge'dare [kondʒe'dare] vt to dismiss;
(Mil) to demobilize; **congedarsi** vpr to
take one's leave
con'gegno [kon'dʒeɲɲo] sm device, mechanism
conge'lare [kondʒe'lare] vt to freeze;
congelarsi vpr to freeze; **congela'tore**
sm freezer
congesti'one [kondʒes'tjone] sf
congestion
conget'tura [kondʒet'tura] sf conjecture
con'giungere [kon'dʒundʒere] vt to
join (together); **congiungersi** vpr to join
(together)
congiunti'vite [kondʒunti'vite] sf
conjunctivitis
congiun'tivo [kondʒun'tivo] sm (Ling)
subjunctive
congi'unto, -a [kon'dʒunto] pp di
congiungere ▷ ag (unito) joined ▷ sm/f
relative
congiunzi'one [kondʒun'tsjone] sf (Ling)
conjunction
congi'ura [kon'dʒura] sf conspiracy
congratu'larsi vpr ~ **con qn per qc** to
congratulate sb on sth
congratulazi'oni [kongratulat'tsjoni]
sfpl congratulations
con'gresso sm congress
C.O.N.I. sigla m (= Comitato Olimpico

Nazionale Italiano) Italian Olympic Games
Committee
coni'are vt to mint, coin; (fig) to coin
co'niglio [ko'niʎʎo] sm rabbit
coniu'gare vt (Ling) to conjugate;
coniugarsi vpr to get married
'coniuge ['kɔnjudʒe] sm/f spouse
connazio'nale [konnattsjo'nale] sm/f
fellow-countryman/woman
connessi'one sf connection
con'nettere vt to connect, join ▷ vi (fig) to
think straight
'cono sm cone; **cono gelato** ice-cream
cone
co'nobbi ecc vb vedi **conoscere**
cono'scente [konoʃʃente] sm/f
acquaintance
cono'scenza [konoʃʃɛntsa] sf (il sapere)
knowledge no pl; (persona) acquaintance;
(facoltà sensoriale) consciousness no pl;
perdere ~ to lose consciousness
co'noscere [ko'noʃʃere] vt to know; **ci
siamo conosciuti a Firenze** we (first) met
in Florence; **conoscersi** vpr to know o.s.;
(reciproco) to know each other; (incontrarsi)
to meet; **~ qn di vista** to know sb by
sight; **farsi ~** (fig) to make a name for o.s.;
conosci'uto, -a pp di **conoscere** ▷ ag
well-known
con'quista sf conquest
conquis'tare vt to conquer; (fig) to gain,
win
consa'pevole ag ~ **di** aware o conscious of
'conscio, -a, -sci, -sce ['kɔnʃo] ag ~ **di**
aware o conscious of
consecu'tivo, -a ag consecutive;
(successivo: giorno) following, next
con'segna [kon'seɲɲa] sf delivery; (merce
consegnata) consignment; (custodia) care,
custody; (Mil: ordine) orders pl; (: punizione)
confinement to barracks; **pagamento
alla ~** cash on delivery; **dare qc in ~ a qn**
to entrust sth to sb
conse'gnare [konseɲ'ɲare] vt to deliver;
(affidare) to entrust, hand over; (Mil) to
confine to barracks
consegu'enza [konse'gwɛntsa] sf
consequence; **per** o **di ~** consequently
con'senso sm approval, consent;
consenso informato informed consent
consen'tire vi ~ **a** to consent o agree to
▷ vt to allow, permit
con'serva sf (Cuc) preserve; **conserva
di frutta** jam; **conserva di pomodoro**
tomato purée
conser'vante sm (per alimenti)
preservative
conser'vare vt (Cuc) to preserve;
(custodire) to keep; (: dalla distruzione ecc) to

preserve, conserve

conserva'tore, -'trice sm/f (Pol) conservative

conserva'torio sm (di musica) conservatory

conservazi'one [konservat'tsjone] sf preservation; conservation

conside'rare vt to consider; (reputare) to consider, regard; **considerarsi** vpr to consider o.s.

consigli'are [konsiʎ'ʎare] vt (persona) to advise; (metodo, azione) to recommend, advise, suggest; **mi può ~ un buon ristorante?** can you recommend a good restaurant?; **con'siglio** sm (suggerimento) advice no pl, piece of advice; (assemblea) council; **consiglio d'amministrazione** board; **Consiglio d'Europa** Council of Europe; **Consiglio dei Ministri** (Pol): **il Consiglio dei Ministri** ≈ the Cabinet

consis'tente ag thick; solid; (fig) sound, valid

con'sistere vi ~ **in** to consist of

conso'lare ag consular ▷ vt (confortare) to console, comfort; (rallegrare) to cheer up; **consolarsi** vpr to be comforted; to cheer up

conso'lato sm consulate

consolazi'one [konsolat'tsjone] sf consolation, comfort

'console sm consul

conso'nante sf consonant

'consono, -a ag ~ **a** consistent with, consonant with

con'sorte sm/f consort

consta'tare vt to establish, verify

consu'eto, -a ag habitual, usual

consu'lente sm/f consultant

consul'tare vt to consult; **consultarsi** vpr **consultarsi con qn** to seek the advice of sb

consul'torio sm ~ **familiare** family planning clinic

consu'mare vt (logorare: abiti, scarpe) to wear out; (usare) to consume, use up; (mangiare, bere) to consume; (Dir) to consummate; **consumarsi** vpr to wear out; to be used up; (anche fig) to be consumed; (combustibile) to burn out

con'tabile ag accounts cpd, accounting ▷ sm/f accountant

contachi'lometri [kontaki'lɔmetri] sm inv ≈ mileometer

conta'dino, -a sm/f countryman/ woman, farm worker; (peg) peasant

contagi'are [konta'dʒare] vt to infect

contagi'oso, -a ag infectious; contagious

conta'gocce [konta'gottʃe] sm inv (Med) dropper

contami'nare vt to contaminate

con'tante sm cash; **pagare in contanti** to pay cash; **non ho contanti** I haven't got any cash

con'tare vt to count; (considerare) to consider ▷ vi to count, be of importance; ~ **su qn** to count o rely on sb; ~ **di fare qc** to intend to do sth; **conta'tore** sm meter

contat'tare vt to contact

con'tatto sm contact

'conte sm count

conteggi'are [konted'dʒare] vt to charge, put on the bill

con'tegno [kon'teɲɲo] sm (comportamento) behaviour; (atteggiamento) attitude; **darsi un ~** to act nonchalant; to pull o.s. together

contemporanea'mente av simultaneously; at the same time

contempo'raneo, -a ag, sm/f contemporary

conten'dente sm/f opponent, adversary

conte'nere vt to contain; **conteni'tore** sm container

conten'tezza [konten'tettsa] sf contentment

con'tento, -a ag pleased, glad; ~ **di** pleased with

conte'nuto sm contents pl; (argomento) content

con'tessa sf countess

contes'tare vt (Dir) to notify; (fig) to dispute

con'testo sm context

continen'tale ag, sm/f continental

conti'nente ag continent ▷ sm (Geo) continent; (: terra ferma) mainland

contin'gente [kontin'dʒɛnte] ag contingent ▷ sm (Comm) quota; (Mil) contingent

continua'mente av (senza interruzione) continuously, nonstop; (ripetutamente) continually

continu'are vt to continue (with), go on with ▷ vi to continue, go on; ~ **a fare qc** to go on o continue doing sth

continuità sf continuity

con'tinuo, -a ag (numerazione) continuous; (pioggia) continual, constant; (Elettr): **corrente continua** direct current; **di ~** continually

'conto sm (calcolo) calculation; (Comm, Econ) account; (di ristorante, albergo) bill; (fig: stima) consideration, esteem; **il ~, per favore** can I have the bill, please?; **lo metta sul mio ~** put it on my bill; **fare i conti con qn** to settle one's account with sb; **fare ~ su qn/qc** to count o rely on sb; **rendere ~ a qn di qc** to be accountable to sb for sth; **tener ~ di qn/qc** to take sb/sth into account; **per ~ di** on behalf of; **per ~ mio** as far as I'm concerned; **a conti fatti, in fin dei conti** all things considered; **conto corrente** current account; **conto alla rovescia** countdown

con'torno sm (linea) outline, contour; (ornamento) border; (Cuc) vegetables pl

con'torto, -a pp di **contorcere**

contrabbandi'ere, -a sm/f smuggler

contrab'bando sm smuggling, contraband; **merce di ~** contraband, smuggled goods pl

contrab'basso sm (Mus) (double) bass

contraccambi'are vt (favore ecc) to return

contraccet'tivo, -a [kontrattʃet'tivo] ag, sm contraceptive

contrac'colpo sm rebound; (di arma da fuoco) recoil; (fig) repercussion

contrad'dire vt to contradict; **contraddirsi** vpr to contradict o.s.; (uso reciproco: persone) to contradict each other o one another; (: testimonianze ecc) to be contradictory

contraf'fare vt (persona) to mimic; (alterare: voce) to disguise; (firma) to forge, counterfeit

contraria'mente av **~ a** contrary to

contrari'are vt (contrastare) to thwart, oppose; (irritare) to annoy, bother

con'trario, -a ag opposite; (sfavorevole) unfavourable ▷ sm opposite; **essere ~ a qc** (persona) to be against sth; **in caso ~** otherwise; **avere qc in ~** to have some objection; **al ~** on the contrary

contrasse'gnare [kontrassen'ɲare] vt to mark

contras'tare vt (avversare) to oppose; (impedire) to bar; (negare: diritto) to contest, dispute ▷ vi **~ (con)** (essere in disaccordo) to contrast (with); (lottare) to struggle (with)

contrat'tacco sm counterattack

contrat'tare vt, vi to negotiate

contrat'tempo sm hitch

con'tratto, -a pp di **contrarre** ▷ sm contract

contravvenzi'one [contravven'tsjone] sf contravention; (ammenda) fine

contrazi'one [kontrat'tsjone] sf contraction; (di prezzi ecc) reduction

contribu'ente sm/f taxpayer; ratepayer (BRIT), property tax payer (US)

contribu'ire vi to contribute

'contro prep against; **~ di me/lui** against me/him; **pastiglie ~ la tosse** throat lozenges; **~ pagamento** (Comm) on payment ▷ prefisso: **controfi'gura** sf (Cinema) double

control'lare vt (accertare) to check; (sorvegliare) to watch, control; (tenere nel proprio potere, fig: dominare) to control; **controllarsi** vpr to control o.s.; **con'trollo** sm check; watch; control; **controllo delle nascite** birth control; **control'lore** sm (Ferr, Autobus) (ticket) inspector

contro'luce [kontro'lutʃe] sf inv (Fot) backlit shot ▷ av **(in) ~** against the light; (fotografare) into the light

contro'mano av **guidare ~** to drive on the wrong side of the road; (in un senso unico) to drive the wrong way up a one-way street

controprodu'cente [kontroprodu'tʃente] ag counterproductive

contro'senso sm (contraddizione) contradiction in terms; (assurdità) nonsense

controspio'naggio [kontrospio'naddʒo] sm counterespionage

contro'versia sf controversy; (Dir) dispute

contro'verso, -a ag controversial

contro'voglia [kontro'vɔʎʎa] av unwillingly

contusi'one sf (Med) bruise

convale'scente [konvaleʃʃente] ag, sm/f convalescent

convali'dare vt (Amm) to validate; (fig: sospetto, dubbio) to confirm

con'vegno [kon'veɲɲo] sm (incontro) meeting; (congresso) convention, congress; (luogo) meeting place

conve'nevoli smpl civilities

conveni'ente ag suitable; (vantaggioso) profitable; (: prezzo) cheap

> Attenzione! In inglese esiste la parola convenient, che però significa comodo.

conve'nire vi (riunirsi) to gather, assemble; (concordare) to agree; (tornare utile) to be worthwhile ▷ vb impers **conviene fare questo** it is advisable to do this; **conviene andarsene** we should go; **ne convengo** I agree

con'vento sm (di frati) monastery; (di suore) convent

convenzio'nale [konventsjo'nale] ag conventional

convenzi'one [konven'tsjone] sf (Dir) agreement; (nella società) convention

conver'sare vi to have a conversation, converse

conversazi'one [konversat'tsjone] sf conversation; **fare ~** to chat, have a chat

conversi'one sf conversion; **conversione ad U** (Aut) U-turn

conver'tire vt (trasformare) to change; (Pol, Rel) to convert; **convertirsi** vpr **convertirsi (a)** to be converted (to)

con'vesso, -a ag convex

convin'cente [konvin'tʃɛnte] *ag* convincing

con'vincere [kon'vintʃere] *vt* to convince; **~ qn di qc** to convince sb of sth; **~ qn a fare qc** to persuade sb to do sth; **convincersi** *vpr* **convincersi (di qc)** to convince o.s. (of sth); **~ qn di qc** to convince sb of sth; **~ qn a fare qc** to convince sb to do sth

convi'vente *sm/f* common-law husband/wife

con'vivere *vi* to live together

convo'care *vt* to call, convene; (*Dir*) to summon

convulsi'one *sf* convulsion

coope'rare *vi* **~ (a)** to cooperate (in); **coopera'tiva** *sf* cooperative

coordi'nare *vt* to coordinate

co'perchio [ko'pɛrkjo] *sm* cover; (*di pentola*) lid

co'perta *sf* cover; (*di lana*) blanket; (*da viaggio*) rug; (*Naut*) deck

coper'tina *sf* (*Stampa*) cover, jacket

co'perto, -a *pp di* **coprire** ▷ *ag* covered; (*cielo*) overcast ▷ *sm* place setting; (*posto a tavola*) place; (*al ristorante*) cover charge; **~ di** covered in o with

coper'tone *sm* (*Aut*) rubber tyre

coper'tura *sf* (*anche Econ, Mil*) cover; (*di edificio*) roofing

'copia *sf* copy; **brutta/bella ~** rough/final copy

copi'are *vt* to copy

copi'one *sm* (*Cinema, Teatro*) script

'coppa *sf* (*bicchiere*) goblet; (*per frutta, gelato*) dish; (*trofeo*) cup, trophy; **coppa dell'olio** oil sump (BRIT) o pan (US)

'coppia *sf* (*di persone*) couple; (*di animali, Sport*) pair

coprifu'oco, -chi *sm* curfew

copri'letto *sm* bedspread

copripiu'mino *sm* duvet cover

co'prire *vt* to cover; (*occupare: carica, posto*) to hold; **coprirsi** *vpr* (*cielo*) to cloud over; (*vestirsi*) to wrap up, cover up; (*Econ*) to cover o.s.; **coprirsi di** (*macchie, muffa*) to become covered in

coque [kɔk] *sf* **uovo alla ~** boiled egg

co'raggio [ko'raddʒo] *sm* courage, bravery; **~!** (*forza!*) come on!; (*animo!*) cheer up!

co'rallo *sm* coral

Co'rano *sm* (*Rel*) Koran

co'razza [ko'rattsa] *sf* armour; (*di animali*) carapace, shell; (*Mil*) armour(-plating)

'corda *sf* cord; (*fune*) rope; (*spago, Mus*) string; **dare ~ a qn** to let sb have his (*o* her) way; **tenere sulla ~ qn** to keep sb on tenterhooks; **tagliare la ~** to slip away, sneak off; **corda vocale** vocal cords

cordi'ale *ag* cordial, warm ▷ *sm* (*bevanda*) cordial

'cordless ['kɔːdlɪs] *sm inv* cordless phone

cor'done *sm* cord, string; (*linea: di polizia*) cordon; **cordone ombelicale** umbilical cord

Co'rea *sf* **la ~** Korea

coreogra'fia *sf* choreography

cori'andolo *sm* (*Bot*) coriander; **coriandoli** *smpl* confetti *sg*

cor'nacchia [kor'nakkja] *sf* crow

corna'musa *sf* bagpipes *pl*

cor'netta *sf* (*Mus*) cornet; (*Tel*) receiver

cor'netto *sm* (*Cuc*) croissant; (*gelato*) cone

cor'nice [kor'nitʃe] *sf* frame; (*fig*) setting, background

cornici'one [korni'tʃone] *sm* (*di edificio*) ledge; (*Archit*) cornice

'corno (*pl(f)* **-a**) *sm* (*Zool*) horn; (*pl(m)* **-i**: *Mus*) horn; **fare le corna a qn** to be unfaithful to sb

Corno'vaglia [korno'vaʎʎa] *sf* **la ~** Cornwall

cor'nuto, -a *ag* (*con corna*) horned; (*fam!: marito*) cuckolded ▷ *sm* (*fam!*) cuckold; (: *insulto*) bastard (!)

'coro *sm* chorus; (*Rel*) choir

co'rona *sf* crown; (*di fiori*) wreath

'corpo *sm* body; (*militare, diplomatico*) corps *inv*; **prendere ~** to take shape; **a ~ ~** hand-to-hand; **corpo di ballo** corps de ballet; **corpo insegnante** teaching staff

corpora'tura *sf* build, physique

cor'reggere [kor'rɛddʒere] *vt* to correct; (*compiti*) to correct, mark

cor'rente *ag* (*acqua: di fiume*) flowing; (: *di rubinetto*) running; (*moneta, prezzo*) current; (*comune*) everyday ▷ *sm* **essere al ~ (di)** to be well-informed (about); **mettere al ~ (di)** to inform (of) ▷ *sf* (*d'acqua*) current, stream; (*spiffero*) draught; (*Elettr, Meteor*) current; (*fig*) trend, tendency; **la vostra lettera del 5 ~ mese** (*Comm*) your letter of the 5th of this month; **corrente alternata/continua** alternate/direct current; **corrente'mente** *av* commonly; **parlare una lingua correntemente** to speak a language fluently

'correre *vi* to run; (*precipitarsi*) to rush; (*partecipare a una gara*) to race; (*fig: diffondersi*) to go round ▷ *vt* (*Sport: gara*) to compete in; (*rischio*) to run; (*pericolo*) to face; **~ dietro a qn** to run after sb; **corre voce che ...** it is rumoured that ...

cor'ressi *ecc vb vedi* **correggere**

correzi'one [korret'tsjone] *sf* correction; marking; **correzione di bozze** proofreading

corri'doio *sm* corridor; (*in aereo, al cinema*)

aisle; **vorrei un posto sul ~** I'd like an aisle seat

corri'dore *sm* (*Sport*) runner; (: *su veicolo*) racer

corri'era *sf* coach (BRIT), bus

corri'ere *sm* (*diplomatico, di guerra, postale*) courier; (*Comm*) carrier

corri'mano *sm* handrail

corrispon'dente *ag* corresponding ▷ *sm/f* correspondent

corrispon'denza [korrispon'dɛntsa] *sf* correspondence

corris'pondere *vi* (*equivalere*): **~ (a)** to correspond (to) ▷ *vt* (*stipendio*) to pay; (*fig: amore*) to return

cor'rodere *vt* to corrode

cor'rompere *vt* to corrupt; (*comprare*) to bribe

cor'roso, -a *pp di* **corrodere**

cor'rotto, -a *pp di* **corrompere** ▷ *ag* corrupt

corru'gare *vt* to wrinkle; **~ la fronte** to knit one's brows

cor'ruppi *ecc vb vedi* **corrompere**

corruzi'one [korrut'tsjone] *sf* corruption; bribery

'corsa *sf* running *no pl*; (*gara*) race; (*di autobus, taxi*) journey, trip; **fare una ~** to run, dash; (*Sport*) to run a race; **corsa campestre** cross-country race

'corsi *ecc vb vedi* **correre**

cor'sia *sf* (*Aut, Sport*) lane; (*di ospedale*) ward

'Corsica *sf* **la ~** Corsica

cor'sivo *sm* cursive (writing); (*Tip*) italics *pl*

'corso, -a *pp di* **correre** ▷ *sm* course; (*strada cittadina*) main street; (*di unità monetaria*) circulation; (*di titoli, valori*) rate, price; **in ~** in progress, under way; (*annata*) current; **corso d'acqua** river, stream; (*artificiale*) waterway; **corso d'aggiornamento** refresher course; **corso serale** evening class

'corte *sf* (court)yard; (*Dir, regale*) court; **fare la ~ a qn** to court sb; **corte marziale** court-martial

cor'teccia, -ce [kor'tettʃa] *sf* bark

corteggi'are [korted'dʒare] *vt* to court

cor'teo *sm* procession

cor'tese *ag* courteous; **corte'sia** *sf* courtesy; **per cortesia ...** excuse me, please ...

cor'tile *sm* (court)yard

cor'tina *sf* curtain; (*anche fig*) screen

'corto, -a *ag* short; **essere a ~ di qc** to be short of sth; **corto circuito** short-circuit

'corvo *sm* raven

'cosa *sf* thing; (*faccenda*) affair, matter, business *no pl*; (*che*) **~?** what?; (*che*)

cos'è? what is it?; **a ~ pensi?** what are you thinking about?

'coscia, -sce ['kɔʃa] *sf* thigh; **coscia di pollo** (*Cuc*) chicken leg

cosci'ente [koʃ'ʃente] *ag* conscious; **~ di** conscious o aware of

 PAROLA CHIAVE

così *av* **1** (*in questo modo*) like this, (in) this way; (*in tal modo*) so; **le cose stanno così** this is the way things stand; **non ho detto così!** I didn't say that!; **come stai? — (e) così** how are you? — so-so; **e così via** and so on; **per così dire** so to speak

2 (*tanto*) so; **così lontano** so far away; **un ragazzo così intelligente** such an intelligent boy

▷ *ag inv* (*tale*): **non ho mai visto un film così** I've never seen such a film ▷ *cong* **1** (*perciò*) so, therefore

2: **così ... come** as ... as; **non è così bravo come te** he's not as good as you; **così ... che** so ... that

cosid'detto, -a *ag* so-called

cos'metico, -a, -ci, -che *ag, sm* cosmetic

cos'pargere [kos'pardʒere] *vt* **~ di** to sprinkle with

cos'picuo, -a *ag* considerable, large

cospi'rare *vi* to conspire

'cossi *ecc vb vedi* **cuocere**

'costa *sf* (*tra terra e mare*) coast(line); (*litorale*) shore; (*Anat*) rib; **la C~ Azzurra** the French Riviera

cos'tante *ag* constant; (*persona*) steadfast ▷ *sf* constant

cos'tare *vi, vt* to cost; **quanto costa?** how much does it cost?; **~ caro** to be expensive, cost a lot

cos'tata *sf* (*Cuc*) large chop

costeggi'are [kosted'dʒare] *vt* to be close to; to run alongside

costi'ero, -a *ag* coastal, coast *cpd*

costitu'ire *vt* (*comitato, gruppo*) to set up, form; (*elementi, parti: comporre*) to make up, constitute; (*rappresentare*) to constitute; (*Dir*) to appoint; **costituirsi** *vpr* **costituirsi alla polizia** to give o.s. up to the police

costituzi'one [kostitut'tsjone] *sf* setting up; building up; constitution

'costo *sm* cost; **a ogni** o **qualunque ~, a tutti i costi** at all costs

'costola *sf* (*Anat*) rib

cos'toso, -a *ag* expensive, costly

cos'tringere [kos'trindʒere] *vt* **~ qn a fare qc** to force sb to do sth

costru'ire *vt* to construct, build;

45 | costruire

costruzi'one *sf* construction, building
cos'tume *sm* (*uso*) custom; (*foggia di vestire, indumento*) costume; **costume da bagno** bathing *o* swimming costume (BRIT), swimsuit; (*da uomo*) bathing *o* swimming trunks *pl*
co'tenna *sf* bacon rind
coto'letta *sf* (*di maiale, montone*) chop; (*di vitello, agnello*) cutlet
co'tone *sm* cotton; **cotone idrofilo** cotton wool (BRIT), absorbent cotton (US)
'cotta *sf* (*fam: innamoramento*) crush
'cottimo *sm* **lavorare a ~** to do piecework
'cotto, -a *pp di* **cuocere** ▷ *ag* cooked; (*fam: innamorato*) head-over-heels in love; **ben ~** (*carne*) well done
cot'tura *sf* cooking; (*in forno*) baking; (*in umido*) stewing
co'vare *vt* to hatch; (*fig: malattia*) to be sickening for; (: *odio, rancore*) to nurse ▷ *vi* (*fuoco, fig*) to smoulder
'covo *sm* den
co'vone *sm* sheaf
'cozza ['kɔttsa] *sf* mussel
coz'zare [kot'tsare] *vi* **~ contro** to bang into, collide with
'crampo *sm* cramp; **ho un ~ alla gamba** I've got cramp in my leg
'cranio *sm* skull
cra'tere *sm* crater
cra'vatta *sf* tie
cre'are *vt* to create
'crebbi *ecc vb vedi* **crescere**
cre'dente *sm/f* (*Rel*) believer
cre'denza [kre'dɛntsa] *sf* belief; (*armadio*) sideboard
'credere *vt* to believe ▷ *vi* **~ in, ~ a** to believe in; **~ qn onesto** to believe sb (to be) honest; **~ che** to believe *o* think that; **credersi furbo** to think one is clever
'credito *sm* (*anche Comm*) credit; (*reputazione*) esteem, repute; **comprare a ~** to buy on credit
'crema *sf* cream; (*con uova, zucchero ecc*) custard; **crema pasticcera** confectioner's custard; **crema solare** sun cream
cre'mare *vt* to cremate
'crepa *sf* crack
cre'paccio [kre'pattʃo] *sm* large crack, fissure; (*di ghiacciaio*) crevasse
crepacu'ore *sm* broken heart
cre'pare *vi* (*fam: morire*) to snuff it, kick the bucket; **~ dalle risa** to split one's sides laughing
crêpe [krɛp] *sf inv* pancake
cre'puscolo *sm* twilight, dusk
'crescere ['kreʃʃere] *vi* to grow ▷ *vt* (*figli*) to raise
'cresima *sf* (*Rel*) confirmation

'crespo, -a *ag* (*capelli*) frizzy; (*tessuto*) puckered ▷ *sm* crêpe
'cresta *sf* crest; (*di polli, uccelli*) crest, comb
'creta *sf* chalk; clay
creti'nata *sf* (*fam*): **dire/fare una ~** to say/do a stupid thing
cre'tino, -a *ag* stupid ▷ *sm/f* idiot, fool
CRI *sigla f* = **Croce Rossa Italiana**
cric *sm inv* (*Tecn*) jack
cri'ceto [kri'tʃɛto] *sm* hamster
crimi'nale *ag, sm/f* criminal
criminalità *sf* crime; **criminalità organizzata** organized crime
'crimine *sm* (*Dir*) crime
crip'tare *vt* (*TV: programma*) to encrypt
crisan'temo *sm* chrysanthemum
'crisi *sf inv* crisis; (*Med*) attack, fit; **crisi di nervi** attack *o* fit of nerves
cris'tallo *sm* crystal; **cristalli liquidi** liquid crystals
cristia'nesimo *sm* Christianity
cristi'ano, -a *ag, sm/f* Christian
'Cristo *sm* Christ
cri'terio *sm* criterion; (*buon senso*) (common) sense
'critica, -che *sf* criticism; **la ~** (*attività*) criticism; (*persone*) the critics *pl*; *vedi anche* **critico**
criti'care *vt* to criticize
'critico, -a, -ci, -che *ag* critical ▷ *sm* critic
cro'ato, -a *ag, sm/f* Croatian, Croat
Croa'zia [kroa'tsja] *sf* Croatia
croc'cante *ag* crisp, crunchy
'croce ['krotʃe] *sf* cross; **in ~** (*di traverso*) crosswise; (*fig*) on tenterhooks; **Croce Rossa** Red Cross
croci'ata [kro'tʃata] *sf* crusade
croci'era [kro'tʃera] *sf* (*viaggio*) cruise; (*Archit*) transept
croci'fisso, -a *pp di* **crocifiggere**
crol'lare *vi* to collapse; **'crollo** *sm* collapse; (*di prezzi*) slump, sudden fall; **crollo in Borsa** slump in prices on the Stock Exchange
cro'mato, -a *ag* chromium-plated
'cromo *sm* chrome, chromium
'cronaca, -che *sf* (*Stampa*) news *sg*; (: *rubrica*) column; (*TV, Radio*) commentary; **fatto *o* episodio di ~** news item; **cronaca nera** crime news *sg*; crime column
'cronico, -a, -ci, -che *ag* chronic
cro'nista, -i *sm* (*Stampa*) reporter
cro'nometro *sm* chronometer; (*a scatto*) stopwatch
'crosta *sf* crust
cros'tacei [kros'tatʃei] *smpl* shellfish
cros'tata *sf* (*Cuc*) tart
cros'tino *sm* (*Cuc*) crouton; (: *da antipasto*) canapé

cruci'ale [kru'tʃale] *ag* crucial
cruci'verba *sm inv* crossword (puzzle)
cru'dele *ag* cruel
'crudo, -a *ag* (*non cotto*) raw; (*aspro*) harsh, severe
cru'miro (*peg*) *sm* blackleg (BRIT), scab
'crusca *sf* bran
crus'cotto *sm* (*Aut*) dashboard
CSI *sigla f inv* (= *Comunità Stati Indipendenti*) CIS
CSM [tʃiesse'emme] *sigla m* (= *consiglio superiore della magistratura*) Magistrates' Board of Supervisors
'Cuba *sf* Cuba
cu'bano, -a *ag, sm/f* Cuban
cu'betto *sm*; **cubetto di ghiaccio** ice cube
'cubico, -a, -ci, -che *ag* cubic
cu'bista, -i, -e *ag* (*Arte*) Cubist ▷ *sf* (*in discoteca*) podium dancer
'cubo, -a *ag* cubic ▷ *sm* cube; **elevare al ~** (*Mat*) to cube
cuc'cagna [kuk'kaɲɲa] *sf* **paese della ~** land of plenty; **albero della ~** greasy pole (*fig*)
cuc'cetta [kut'tʃetta] *sf* (*Ferr*) couchette; (*Naut*) berth
cucchiai'ata [kukja'jata] *sf* spoonful
cucchia'ino [kukkja'ino] *sm* teaspoon; coffee spoon
cucchi'aio [kuk'kjajo] *sm* spoon
'cuccia, -ce ['kuttʃa] *sf* dog's bed; **a ~!** down!
'cucciolo ['kuttʃolo] *sm* cub; (*di cane*) puppy
cu'cina [ku'tʃina] *sf* (*locale*) kitchen; (*arte culinaria*) cooking, cookery; (*le vivande*) food, cooking; (*apparecchio*) cooker; **cucina componibile** fitted kitchen; **cuci'nare** *vt* to cook
cu'cire [ku'tʃire] *vt* to sew, stitch; **cuci'trice** *sf* stapler
cucù *sm inv* cuckoo
'cuffia *sf* bonnet, cap; (*da infermiera*) cap; (*da bagno*) (bathing) cap; (*per ascoltare*) headphones *pl*, headset
cu'gino, -a [ku'dʒino] *sm/f* cousin

 PAROLA CHIAVE

'cui *pron* **1** (*nei complementi indiretti: persona*) whom; (*: oggetto, animale*) which; **la persona/le persone a cui accennavi** the person/people you were referring to o to whom you were referring; **i libri di cui parlavo** the books I was talking about o about which I was talking; **il quartiere in cui abito** the district where I live; **la ragione per cui** the reason why
2 (*inserito tra articolo e sostantivo*) whose;

la donna i cui figli sono scomparsi the woman whose children have disappeared; **il signore, dal cui figlio ho avuto il libro** the man from whose son I got the book

culi'naria *sf* cookery
'culla *sf* cradle
cul'lare *vt* to rock
'culmine *sm* top, summit
'culo (*fam!*) *sm* arse (BRIT!), ass (US!); (*fig: fortuna*): **aver ~** to have the luck of the devil
'culto *sm* (*religione*) religion; (*adorazione*) worship, adoration; (*venerazione: anche fig*) cult
cul'tura *sf* culture; education, learning; **cultu'rale** *ag* cultural
cultu'rismo *sm* body-building
cumula'tivo, -a *ag* cumulative; (*prezzo*) inclusive; (*biglietto*) group *cpd*
'cumulo *sm* (*mucchio*) pile, heap; (*Meteor*) cumulus
cu'netta *sf* (*avvallamento*) dip; (*di scolo*) gutter
cu'ocere ['kwɔtʃere] *vt* (*alimenti*) to cook; (*mattoni ecc*) to fire ▷ *vi* to cook; **~ al forno** (*pane*) to bake; (*arrosto*) to roast; **cu'oco, -a, -chi, -che** *sm/f* cook; (*di ristorante*) chef
cu'oio *sm* leather; **cuoio capelluto** scalp
cu'ore *sm* heart; **cuori** *smpl* (*Carte*) hearts; **avere buon ~** to be kind-hearted; **stare a ~ a qn** to be important to sb
'cupo, -a *ag* dark; (*suono*) dull; (*fig*) gloomy, dismal
'cupola *sf* dome; cupola
'cura *sf* care; (*Med: trattamento*) (course of) treatment; **aver ~ di** to look after; **a ~ di** (*libro*) edited by; **cura dimagrante** diet
cu'rare *vt* (*malato, malattia*) to treat; (*: guarire*) to cure; (*aver cura di*) to take care of; (*testo*) to edit; **curarsi** *vpr* to take care of o.s.; (*Med*) to follow a course of treatment; **curarsi di** to pay attention to
curio'sare *vi* to look round, wander round; (*tra libri*) to browse; **~ nei negozi** to look o wander round the shops
curiosità *sf inv* curiosity; (*cosa rara*) curio, curiosity
curi'oso, -a *ag* curious; **essere ~ di** to be curious about
cur'sore *sm* (*Inform*) cursor
'curva *sf* curve; (*stradale*) bend, curve
cur'vare *vt* to bend ▷ *vi* (*veicolo*) to take a bend; (*strada*) to bend, curve; **curvarsi** *vpr* to bend; (*legno*) to warp
'curvo, -a *ag* curved; (*piegato*) bent
cusci'netto [kuʃʃi'netto] *sm* pad; (*Tecn*) bearing ▷ *ag inv* **stato ~** buffer state; **cuscinetto a sfere** ball bearing

cu'scino [kuʃˈʃino] *sm* cushion; (*guanciale*) pillow

cus'tode *sm/f* keeper, custodian

cus'todia *sf* care; (*Dir*) custody; (*astuccio*) case, holder

custo'dire *vt* (*conservare*) to keep; (*assistere*) to look after, take care of; (*fare la guardia*) to guard

CV *abbr* (= *cavallo vapore*) h.p.

cybercaffè [tʃiberkaˈfɛ] *sm inv* cybercafé

cybernauta, -i, -e *sm/f* Internet surfer

cyberspazio *sm* cyberspace

 PAROLA CHIAVE

da (*da+il* = **dal**, *da+lo* = **dallo**, *da+l'* = **dall'**, *da+la* = **dalla**, *da+i* = **dai**, *da+gli* = **dagli**, **da+le** = **dalle**) *prep* **1** (*agente*) by; **dipinto da un grande artista** painted by a great artist

2 (*causa*) with; **tremare dalla paura** to tremble with fear

3 (*stato in luogo*) at; **abito da lui** I'm living at his house *o* with him; **sono dal giornalaio/da Francesco** I'm at the newsagent's/Francesco's (house)

4 (*moto a luogo*) to; (*moto per luogo*) through; **vado da Pietro/dal giornalaio** I'm going to Pietro's (house)/to the newsagent's; **sono passati dalla finestra** they came in through the window

5 (*provenienza, allontanamento*) from; **arrivare/partire da Milano** to arrive/ depart from Milan; **scendere dal treno/ dalla macchina** to get off the train/out of the car; **si trova a 5 km da qui** it's 5 km from here

6 (*tempo: durata*) for; (: *a partire da:* nel passato) since; (: *nel futuro*) from; **vivo qui da un anno** I've been living here for a year; **è dalle 3 che ti aspetto** I've been waiting for you since 3 (o'clock); **da oggi in poi** from today onwards; **da bambino** as a

child, when I (*o he ecc*) was a child
7 (*modo, maniera*) like; **comportarsi da uomo** to behave like a man; **l'ho fatto da me** I did it (by) myself
8 (*descrittivo*): **una macchina da corsa** a racing car; **una ragazza dai capelli biondi** a girl with blonde hair; **un vestito da 60 euro** a 60 euros dress

dà *vb vedi* **dare**
dac'capo *av* (*di nuovo*) (once) again; (*dal principio*) all over again, from the beginning
'dado *sm* (*da gioco*) dice *o* die; (*Cuc*) stock (BRIT) *o* bouillon (US) cube; (*Tecn*) (screw)nut; **dadi** *smpl* (game of) dice; **giocare a dadi** to play dice
'daino *sm* (fallow) deer *inv*; (*pelle*) buckskin
dal'tonico, -a, -ci, -che *ag* colour-blind
'dama *sf* lady; (*nei balli*) partner; (*gioco*) draughts *sg* (BRIT), checkers *sg* (US)
damigi'ana [dami'dʒana] *sf* demijohn
da'nese *ag* Danish ▷ *sm/f* Dane ▷ *sm* (*Ling*) Danish
Dani'marca *sf* **la ~** Denmark
dannazi'one *sf* damnation
danneggi'are [danned'dʒare] *vt* to damage; (*rovinare*) to spoil; (*nuocere*) to harm
'danno *sm* damage; (*a persona*) harm, injury; **danni** *smpl* (*Dir*) damages; **dan'noso, -a** *ag* **dannoso (a, per)** harmful (to), bad (for)
Da'nubio *sm* **il ~** the Danube
'danza ['dantsa] *sf* **la ~** dancing; **una ~** a dance
dan'zare [dan'tsare] *vt, vi* to dance
dapper'tutto *av* everywhere
dap'prima *av* at first
'dare *sm* (*Comm*) debit ▷ *vt* to give; (*produrre: frutti, suono*) to produce ▷ *vi* (*guardare*): **~ su** to look (out) onto; **darsi** *vpr* **darsi a** to dedicate o.s. to; **darsi al commercio** to go into business; **darsi al bere** to take to drink; **~ da mangiare a qn** to give sb sth to eat; **~ per certo qc** to consider sth certain; **~ per morto qn** to give sb up for dead; **darsi per vinto** to give in
'data *sf* date; **~ limite d'utilizzo** *or* **di consumo** best-before date; **~ di nascita** date of birth; **data di scadenza** expiry date
'dato, -a *ag* (*stabilito*) given ▷ *sm* datum; **dati** *smpl* data *pl*; **~ che** given that; **un ~ di fatto** a fact; **dati sensibili** personal information
da'tore, -'trice *sm/f*; **datore di lavoro** employer
'dattero *sm* date

dattilogra'fia *sf* typing
datti'lografo, -a *sm/f* typist
da'vanti *av* in front; (*dirimpetto*) opposite ▷ *ag inv* front ▷ *sm* front; **~ a** in front of; facing, opposite; (*in presenza di*) before, in front of
davan'zale [davan'tsale] *sm* windowsill
dav'vero *av* really, indeed
d.C. *adv abbr* (= *dopo Cristo*) A.D.
'dea *sf* goddess
'debbo *ecc vb vedi* **dovere**
'debito, -a *ag* due, proper ▷ *sm* debt; (*Comm: dare*) debit; **a tempo ~** at the right time
'debole *ag* weak, feeble; (*suono*) faint; (*luce*) dim ▷ *sm* weakness; **debo'lezza** *sf* weakness
debut'tare *vi* to make one's debut
deca'denza [deka'dɛntsa] *sf* decline; (*Dir*) loss, forfeiture
decaffei'nato, -a *ag* decaffeinated
decapi'tare *vt* to decapitate, behead
decappot'tabile *ag, sf* convertible
de'cennio [de'tʃɛnnjo] *sm* decade
de'cente [de'tʃɛnte] *ag* decent, respectable, proper; (*accettabile*) satisfactory, decent
de'cesso [de'tʃɛsso] *sm* death
de'cidere [de'tʃidere] *vt* **~ qc** to decide on sth; (*questione, lite*) to settle sth; **~ di fare/ che** to decide to do/that; **~ di qc** (*cosa*) to determine sth; **decidersi (a fare)** to decide (to do), make up one's mind (to do)
deci'frare [detʃi'frare] *vt* to decode; (*fig*) to decipher, make out
deci'male [detʃi'male] *ag* decimal
'decimo, -a ['dɛtʃimo] *num* tenth
de'cina [de'tʃina] *sf* ten; (*circa dieci*): **una ~ (di)** about ten
de'cisi *ecc* [de'tʃizi] *vb vedi* **decidere**
decisi'one [detʃi'zjone] *sf* decision; **prendere una ~** to make a decision
deci'sivo, -a [detʃi'zivo] *ag* (*gen*) decisive; (*fattore*) deciding
de'ciso, -a [de'tʃizo] *pp di* **decidere**
decli'nare *vi* (*pendio*) to slope down; (*fig: diminuire*) to decline ▷ *vt* to decline
declinazi'one *sf* (*Ling*) declension
de'clino *sm* decline
decodifica'tore *sm* (*Tel*) decoder
decol'lare *vi* (*Aer*) to take off; **de'collo** *sm* take-off
deco'rare *vt* to decorate; **decorazi'one** *sf* decoration
de'creto *sm* decree; **decreto legge** *decree with the force of law*
'dedica, -che *sf* dedication
dedi'care *vt* to dedicate; **dedicarsi** *vpr* **dedicarsi a** to devote o.s. to

dedicherò ecc [dedike'rɔ] vb vedi **dedicare**

'dedito, -a ag **~ a** (studio ecc) dedicated o devoted to; (vizio) addicted to

de'duco ecc vb vedi **dedurre**

de'durre vt (concludere) to deduce; (defalcare) to deduct

de'dussi ecc vb vedi **dedurre**

defici'ente [defi'tʃɛnte] ag (mancante): **~ di** deficient in; (insufficiente) insufficient ▷ sm/f mental defective; (peg: cretino) idiot

'deficit ['dɛfitʃit] sm inv (Econ) deficit

defi'nire vt to define; (risolvere) to settle; **defini'tiva** sf **in ~** (dopotutto) in the end; (dunque) hence; **defini'tivo, -a** ag definitive, final; **definizi'one** sf definition; settlement

defor'mare vt (alterare) to put out of shape; (corpo) to deform; (pensiero, fatto) to distort; **deformarsi** vpr to lose its shape

de'forme ag deformed; disfigured

de'funto, -a ag late cpd ▷ sm/f deceased

degene'rare [dedʒene'rare] vi to degenerate

de'gente [de'dʒɛnte] sm/f (in ospedale) in-patient

deglu'tire vt to swallow

de'gnare [deɲ'ɲare] vt **~ qn della propria presenza** to honour sb with one's presence; **degnarsi** vpr **degnarsi di fare qc** to deign o condescend to do sth

'degno, -a ag dignified; **~ di** worthy of; **~ di lode** praiseworthy

de'grado sm; **degrado urbano** urban decline

'delega, -ghe sf (procura) proxy

dele'terio, -a ag damaging; (per salute ecc) harmful

del'fino sm (Zool) dolphin; (Storia) dauphin; (fig) probable successor

deli'cato, -a ag delicate; (salute) delicate, frail; (fig: gentile) thoughtful, considerate; (: che dimostra tatto) tactful

delin'quente sm/f criminal, delinquent; **delinquente abituale** regular offender, habitual offender; **delin'quenza** sf criminality, delinquency; **delinquenza minorile** juvenile delinquency

deli'rare vi to be delirious, rave; (fig) to rave

de'lirio sm delirium; (ragionamento insensato) raving; (fig): **andare/mandare in ~** to go/send into a frenzy

de'litto sm crime

delizi'oso, -a ag delightful; (cibi) delicious

delta'plano sm hang-glider; **volo col ~** hang-gliding

delu'dente ag disappointing

de'ludere vt to disappoint; **delusi'one** sf disappointment; **de'luso, -a** pp di **deludere**

'demmo vb vedi **dare**

demo'cratico, -a, -ci, -che ag democratic

democra'zia [demokrat'tsia] sf democracy

demo'lire vt to demolish

de'monio sm demon, devil; **il D~** the Devil

de'naro sm money

densità sf inv density

'denso, -a ag thick, dense

den'tale ag dental

'dente sm tooth; (di forchetta) prong; **al ~** (Cuc: pasta) al dente; **denti del giudizio** wisdom teeth; **denti da latte** milk teeth; **denti'era** sf (set of) false teeth pl

denti'fricio [denti'fritʃo] sm toothpaste

den'tista, -i, -e sm/f dentist

'dentro av inside; (in casa) indoors; (fig: nell'intimo) inwardly ▷ prep **~ (a)** in; **piegato in ~** folded over; **qui/là ~** in here/ there; **~ di sé** (pensare, brontolare) to oneself

de'nuncia, -ce o **cie** [de'nuntʃa] sf denunciation; declaration; **denuncia dei redditi** (income) tax return

denunci'are [denun'tʃare] vt to denounce; (dichiarare) to declare; (persona, smarrimento ecc) report; **vorrei ~ un furto** I'd like to report a theft

denu'trito, -a ag undernourished

denutrizi'one [denutrit'tsjone] sf malnutrition

deodo'rante sm deodorant

depe'rire vi to waste away

depi'larsi vpr **~ (le gambe)** (con rasoio) to shave (one's legs); (con ceretta) to wax (one's legs)

depila'torio, -a ag hair-removing cpd, depilatory

dépli'ant [depli'ɑ̃] sm inv leaflet; (opuscolo) brochure

deplo'revole ag deplorable

de'pone, de'pongo ecc vb vedi **deporre**

de'porre vt (depositare) to put down; (rimuovere: da una carica) to remove; (: re) to depose; (Dir) to testify

depor'tare vt to deport

de'posi ecc vb vedi **deporre**

deposi'tare vt (gen, Geo, Econ) to deposit; (lasciare) to leave; (merci) to store; **depositarsi** vpr (sabbia, polvere) to settle

de'posito sm deposit; (luogo) warehouse; depot; (: Mil) depot; **deposito bagagli** left-luggage office

deposizi'one [depozit'tsjone] sf deposition; (da una carica) removal

depra'vato, -a ag depraved ▷ sm/f degenerate

depre'dare vt to rob, plunder

depressi'one sf depression
de'presso, -a pp di **deprimere** ▷ ag depressed
deprez'zare [depret'tsare] vt (Econ) to depreciate
depri'mente ag depressing
de'primere vt to depress
depu'rare vt to purify
depu'tato sm (Pol) deputy, ≈ Member of Parliament (BRIT), ≈ Member of Congress (US)
deragli'are [deraʎ'ʎare] vi to be derailed; **far ~** to derail
de'ridere vt to mock, deride
de'risi ecc vb vedi **deridere**
de'riva sf (Naut, Aer) drift; **andare alla ~** (anche fig) to drift
deri'vare vi **~ da** to derive from ▷ vt to derive; (corso d'acqua) to divert
derma'tologo, -a, -gi, -ghe sm/f dermatologist
deru'bare vt to rob
des'crivere vt to describe; **descrizi'one** sf description
de'serto, -a ag deserted ▷ sm (Geo) desert; **isola deserta** desert island
deside'rare vt to want, wish for; (sessualmente) to desire; **~ fare/che qn faccia** to want o wish to do/sb to do; **desidera fare una passeggiata?** would you like to go for a walk?
desi'derio sm wish; (più intenso, carnale) desire
deside'roso, -a ag **~ di** longing o eager for
desi'nenza [dezi'nɛntsa] sf (Ling) ending, inflexion
de'sistere vi **~ da** to give up, desist from
deso'lato, -a ag (paesaggio) desolate; (persona: spiacente) sorry
'dessi ecc vb vedi **dare**
'deste ecc vb vedi **dare**
desti'nare vt to destine; (assegnare) to appoint, assign; (indirizzare) to address; **~ qc a qn** to intend to give sth to sb, intend sb to have sth; **destina'tario, -a** sm/f (di lettera) addressee
destinazi'one [destinat'tsjone] sf destination; (uso) purpose
des'tino sm destiny, fate
destitu'ire vt to dismiss, remove
'destra sf (mano) right hand; (parte) right (side); (Pol): **la ~** the Right; **a ~** (essere) on the right; (andare) to the right
destreggi'arsi [destred'dʒarsi] vpr to manoeuvre (BRIT), maneuver (US)
des'trezza [des'trettsa] sf skill, dexterity
'destro, -a ag right, right-hand
dete'nuto, -a sm/f prisoner
deter'gente [deter'dʒɛnte] ag (crema, latte) cleansing ▷ sm cleanser

 Attenzione! In inglese esiste la parola detergent che però significa detersivo.

determi'nare vt to determine
determina'tivo, -a ag determining; **articolo ~** (Ling) definite article
determi'nato, -a ag (gen) certain; (particolare) specific; (risoluto) determined, resolute
deter'sivo sm detergent
detes'tare vt to detest, hate
de'trae, de'traggo ecc vb vedi **detrarre**
de'trarre vt **~ (da)** to deduct (from), take away (from)
de'trassi ecc vb vedi **detrarre**
'detta sf **a ~ di** according to
det'taglio [det'taʎʎo] sm detail; (Comm): **il ~** retail; **al ~** (Comm) retail; separately
det'tare vt to dictate; **~ legge** (fig) to lay down the law; **det'tato** sm dictation
'detto, -a pp di **dire** ▷ ag (soprannominato) called, known as; (già nominato) above-mentioned ▷ sm saying; **~ fatto** no sooner said than done
devas'tare vt to devastate; (fig) to ravage
devi'are vi **~ (da)** to turn off (from) ▷ vt to divert; **deviazi'one** sf (anche Aut) diversion
'devo ecc vb vedi **dovere**
de'volvere vt (Dir) to transfer, devolve
de'voto, -a ag (Rel) devout, pious; (affezionato) devoted
devozi'one [devot'tsjone] sf devoutness; (anche Rel) devotion

⦿ PAROLA CHIAVE

di (di+il = **del**, di+lo = **dello**, di+l' = **dell'**, di+la = **della**, di+i = **dei**, di+gli = **degli**, di+le = **delle**) prep **1** (possesso, specificazione) of; (composto da, scritto da) by; **la macchina di Paolo/mio fratello** Paolo's/my brother's car; **un amico di mio fratello** a friend of my brother's, one of my brother's friends; **un quadro di Botticelli** a painting by Botticelli
2 (caratterizzazione, misura) of; **una casa di mattoni** a brick house, a house made of bricks; **un orologio d'oro** a gold watch; **un bimbo di 3 anni** a child of 3, a 3-year-old child
3 (causa, mezzo, modo) with; **tremare di paura** to tremble with fear; **morire di cancro** to die of cancer; **spalmare di burro** to spread with butter
4 (argomento) about, of; **discutere di sport** to talk about sport
5 (luogo: provenienza) from; out of; **essere**

di Roma to be from Rome; **uscire di casa** to come out of o leave the house
6 (*tempo*) in; **d'estate/d'inverno** in (the) summer/winter; **di notte** by night, at night; **di mattina/sera** in the morning/evening; **di lunedì** on Mondays
▷ *det* (*una certa quantità di*) some; (: *negativo*) any; (*interrogativo*) any; some; **del pane** (some) bread; **delle caramelle** (some) sweets; **degli amici miei** some friends of mine; **vuoi del vino?** do you want some o any wine?

dia'bete *sm* diabetes *sg*
dia'betico, -a, ci, che *ag, sm/f* diabetic
dia'framma, -i *sm* (*divisione*) screen; (*Anat, Fot, contraccettivo*) diaphragm
di'agnosi [di'aɲɲozi] *sf* diagnosis *sg*
diago'nale *ag, sf* diagonal
dia'gramma, -i *sm* diagram
dia'letto *sm* dialect
di'alisi *sf* dialysis *sg*
di'alogo, -ghi *sm* dialogue
dia'mante *sm* diamond
di'ametro *sm* diameter
diaposi'tiva *sf* transparency, slide
di'ario *sm* diary
diar'rea *sf* diarrhoea
di'avolo *sm* devil
di'battito *sm* debate, discussion
'dice ['ditʃe] *vb vedi* **dire**
di'cembre [di'tʃembre] *sm* December
dice'ria [ditʃe'ria] *sf* rumour, piece of gossip
dichia'rare [dikja'rare] *vt* to declare; **dichiararsi** *vpr* to declare o.s.; (*innamorato*) to declare one's love; **dichiararsi vinto** to acknowledge defeat; **dichiarazi'one** *sf* declaration; **dichiarazione dei redditi** statement of income; (*modulo*) tax return
dician'nove [ditʃan'nɔve] *num* nineteen
dicias'sette [ditʃas'sɛtte] *num* seventeen
dici'otto [di'tʃɔtto] *num* eighteen
dici'tura [ditʃi'tura] *sf* words *pl*, wording
'dico *ecc vb vedi* **dire**
didasca'lia *sf* (*di illustrazione*) caption; (*Cine*) subtitle; (*Teatro*) stage directions *pl*
di'eci ['djɛtʃi] *num* ten
di'edi *ecc vb vedi* **dare**
'diesel ['dizəl] *sm inv* diesel engine
dies'sino, -a *sm/f* member of the DS political party
di'eta *sf* diet; **essere a ~** to be on a diet
di'etro *av* behind; (*in fondo*) at the back ▷ *prep* behind; (*tempo: dopo*) after ▷ *sm* back, rear ▷ *ag inv* back *cpd*; **le zampe di ~** the hind legs; **~ richiesta** on demand; (*scritta*) on application

di'fendere *vt* to defend; **difendersi** *vpr* (*cavarsela*) to get by; **difendersi da/contro** to defend o.s. from/against; **difendersi dal freddo** to protect o.s. from the cold; **difen'sore, -a** *sm/f* defender; **avvocato difensore** counsel for the defence; **di'fesa** *sf* defence
di'fesi *ecc vb vedi* **difendere**
di'fetto *sm* (*mancanza*): **~ di** lack of; shortage of; (*di fabbricazione*) fault, flaw, defect; (*morale*) fault, failing, defect; (*fisico*) defect; **far ~** to be lacking; **in ~** at fault; in the wrong; **difet'toso, -a** *ag* defective, faulty
diffe'rente *ag* different
diffe'renza [diffe'rɛntsa] *sf* difference; **a ~ di** unlike
diffe'rire *vt* to postpone, defer ▷ *vi* to be different
diffe'rita *sf* **in ~** (*trasmettere*) prerecorded
dif'ficile [dif'fitʃile] *ag* difficult; (*persona*) hard to please, difficult (to please); (*poco probabile*): **è ~ che sia libero** it is unlikely that he'll be free ▷ *sm* difficult part; difficulty; **difficoltà** *sf inv* difficulty
diffi'dente *ag* suspicious, distrustful
diffi'denza *sf* suspicion, distrust
dif'fondere *vt* (*luce, calore*) to diffuse; (*notizie*) to spread, circulate; **diffondersi** *vpr* to spread
dif'fusi *ecc vb vedi* **diffondere**
dif'fuso, -a *pp di* **diffondere** ▷ *ag* (*malattia, fenomeno*) widespread
'diga, -ghe *sf* dam; (*portuale*) breakwater
dige'rente [didʒe'rɛnte] *ag* (*apparato*) digestive
dige'rire [didʒe'rire] *vt* to digest; **digesti'one** *sf* digestion; **diges'tivo, -a** *ag* digestive ▷ *sm* (after-dinner) liqueur
digi'tale [didʒi'tale] *ag* digital; (*delle dita*) finger *cpd*, digital ▷ *sf* (*Bot*) foxglove
digi'tare [didʒi'tare] *vt, vi* (*Inform*) to key (in)
digiu'nare [didʒu'nare] *vi* to starve o.s.; (*Rel*) to fast; **digi'uno, -a** *ag* **essere digiuno** not to have eaten ▷ *sm* fast; **a digiuno** on an empty stomach
dignità [diɲɲi'ta] *sf inv* dignity
'DIGOS ['digɔs] *sigla f* (= *Divisione Investigazioni Generali e Operazioni Speciali*) police department dealing with political security
digri'gnare [digriɲ'ɲare] *vt* **~ i denti** to grind one's teeth
dilapi'dare *vt* to squander, waste
dila'tare *vt* to dilate; (*gas*) to cause to expand; (*passaggio, cavità*) to open (up); **dilatarsi** *vpr* to dilate; (*Fisica*) to expand
dilazio'nare [dilattsjo'nare] *vt* to delay,

defer

di'lemma, -i sm dilemma

dilet'tante sm/f dilettante; (anche Sport) amateur

dili'gente [dili'dʒɛnte] ag (scrupoloso) diligent; (accurato) careful, accurate

dilu'ire vt to dilute

dilun'garsi vpr (fig): ~ **su** to talk at length on o about

diluvi'are vb impers to pour (down)

di'luvio sm downpour; (inondazione, fig) flood

dima'grante ag slimming cpd

dima'grire vi to get thinner, lose weight

dime'nare vt to wave, shake; **dimenarsi** vpr to toss and turn; (fig) to struggle; ~ **la coda** (cane) to wag its tail

dimensi'one sf dimension; (grandezza) size

dimenti'canza [dimenti'kantsa] sf forgetfulness; (errore) oversight, slip; **per ~** inadvertently

dimenti'care vt to forget; **ho dimenticato la chiave/il passaporto** I forgot the key/my passport; **dimenticarsi** vpr **dimenticarsi di qc** to forget sth

dimesti'chezza [dimesti'kettsa] sf familiarity

di'mettere vt ~ **qn da** to dismiss sb from; (dall'ospedale) to discharge sb from; **dimettersi** vpr **dimettersi (da)** to resign (from)

dimez'zare [dimed'dzare] vt to halve

diminu'ire vt to reduce, diminish; (prezzi) to bring down, reduce ▷ vi to decrease, diminish; (rumore) to die down, die away; (prezzi) to fall, go down

diminu'tivo, -a ag, sm diminutive

diminuzi'one sf decreasing, diminishing

di'misi ecc vb vedi **dimettere**

dimissi'oni sfpl resignation sg; **dare** o **presentare le ~** to resign, hand in one's resignation

dimos'trare vt to demonstrate, show; (provare) to prove, demonstrate; **dimostrarsi** vpr **dimostrarsi molto abile** to show o.s. o prove to be very clever; **dimostra 30 anni** he looks about 30 (years old); **dimostrazi'one** sf demonstration; proof

di'namica sf dynamics sg

di'namico, -a, -ci, -che ag dynamic

dina'mite sf dynamite

'dinamo sf inv dynamo

dino'sauro sm dinosaur

din'torni smpl outskirts; **nei ~ di** in the vicinity o neighbourhood of

'dio (pl **'dei**) sm god; **D~** God; **gli dei** the gods; **D~ mio!** my goodness!, my God!

diparti'mento sm department

dipen'dente ag dependent ▷ sm/f employee; **dipendente statale** state employee

di'pendere vi ~ **da** to depend on; (finanziariamente) to be dependent on; (derivare) to come from, be due to

di'pesi ecc vb vedi **dipendere**

di'pingere [di'pindʒere] vt to paint

di'pinsi ecc vb vedi **dipingere**

di'pinto, -a pp di **dipingere** ▷ sm painting

di'ploma, -i sm diploma

diplo'matico, -a, -ci, -che ag diplomatic ▷ sm diplomat

diploma'zia [diplomat'tsia] sf diplomacy

di'porto: **imbarcazione da ~** sf pleasure craft

dira'dare vt to thin (out); (visite) to reduce, make less frequent; **diradarsi** vpr to disperse; (nebbia) to clear (up)

'dire vt to say; (segreto, fatto) to tell; ~ **qc a qn** to tell sb sth; ~ **a qn di fare qc** to tell sb to do sth; ~ **di sì/no** to say yes/no; **si dice che ...** they say that ...; **si ~bbe che ...** it looks (o sounds) as though ...; **dica, signora?** (in un negozio) yes, Madam, can I help you?; **come si dice in inglese...?** what's the English (word) for ...?

di'ressi ecc vb vedi **dirigere**

di'retta sf vedi **diretto**

di'retto, -a pp di **dirigere** ▷ ag direct ▷ sm (Ferr) through train

diret'tore, -'trice sm/f (di azienda) director: manager/ess; (di scuola elementare) head (teacher) (BRIT), principal (US); **direttore d'orchestra** conductor; **direttore vendite** sales director o manager

direzi'one [diret'tsjone] sf board of directors; management; (senso di movimento) direction; **in ~ di** in the direction of, towards

diri'gente [diri'dʒɛnte] sm/f executive; (Pol) leader ▷ ag **classe ~** ruling class

di'rigere [di'ridʒere] vt to direct; (impresa) to run, manage; (Mus) to conduct; **dirigersi** vpr **dirigersi verso** o **a** to make o head for

dirim'petto av opposite; ~ **a** opposite, facing

di'ritto, -a ag straight; (onesto) straight, upright ▷ av straight, directly; **andare ~** to go straight on ▷ sm right side; (Tennis) forehand; (Maglia) plain stitch; (prerogativa) right; (leggi, scienza): **il ~** law; **diritti** smpl (tasse) duty sg; **stare ~** to stand up straight; **aver ~ a qc** to be entitled to sth; **diritti d'autore** royalties

dirotta'mento sm; **dirottamento**

(aereo) hijack

dirot'tare vt (nave, aereo) to change the course of; (aereo sotto minaccia) to hijack; (traffico) to divert ▷ vi (nave, aereo) to change course; **dirotta'tore, -'trice** sm/f hijacker

di'rotto, -a ag (pioggia) torrential; (pianto) unrestrained; **piovere a ~** to pour; **piangere a ~** to cry one's heart out

di'rupo sm crag, precipice

di'sabile sm/f disabled person ▷ ag disabled; **i disabili** the disabled

disabi'tato, -a ag uninhabited

disabitu'arsi vpr **~ a** to get out of the habit of

disac'cordo sm disagreement

disadat'tato, -a ag (Psic) maladjusted

disa'dorno, -a ag plain, unadorned

disagi'ato, -a [diza'dʒato] ag poor, needy; (vita) hard

di'sagio [di'zadʒo] sm discomfort; (disturbo) inconvenience; (fig: imbarazzo) embarrassment; **essere a ~** to be ill at ease

disappro'vare vt to disapprove of; **disapprovazi'one** sf disapproval

disap'punto sm disappointment

disar'mare vt, vi to disarm; **di'sarmo** sm (Mil) disarmament

di'sastro sm disaster

disas'troso, -a ag disastrous

disat'tento, -a ag inattentive; **disattenzi'one** sf carelessness, lack of attention

disavven'tura sf misadventure, mishap

dis'capito sm **a ~ di** to the detriment of

dis'carica, -che sf (di rifiuti) rubbish tip o dump

di'scendere [diʃ'ʃɛndere] vt to go (o come) down ▷ vi to go (o come) down; (strada) to go down; (smontare) to get off; **~ da** (famiglia) to be descended from; **~ dalla macchina/dal treno** to get out of the car/out of o off the train; **~ da cavallo** to dismount, get off one's horse

di'scesa [diʃ'ʃesa] sf descent; (pendio) slope; **in ~** (strada) downhill cpd, sloping; **discesa libera** (Sci) downhill (race)

disci'plina [diʃʃi'plina] sf discipline

'disco, -schi sm disc; (Sport) discus; (fonografico) record; (Inform) disk; **disco orario** (Aut) parking disc; **disco rigido** (Inform) hard disk; **disco volante** flying saucer

disco'grafico, -a, ci, che ag record cpd, recording cpd ▷ sm record producer; **casa discografica** record(ing) company

dis'correre vi **~ (di)** to talk (about)

dis'corso, -a pp di **discorrere** ▷ sm speech; (conversazione) conversation, talk

disco'teca, -che sf (raccolta) record library; (locale) disco

discre'panza [diskre'pantsa] sf disagreement

dis'creto, -a ag discreet; (abbastanza buono) reasonable, fair

discriminazi'one [diskriminat'tsjone] sf discrimination

dis'cussi ecc vb vedi **discutere**

discussi'one sf discussion; (litigio) argument; **fuori ~** out of the question

dis'cutere vt to discuss, debate; (contestare) to question ▷ vi (conversare): **~ (di)** to discuss; (litigare) to argue

dis'detta sf (di prenotazione ecc) cancellation; (sfortuna) bad luck

dis'dire vt (prenotazione) to cancel; (Dir): **~ un contratto d'affitto** to give notice (to quit); **vorrei ~ la mia prenotazione** I want to cancel my booking

dise'gnare [disen'nare] vt to draw; (progettare) to design; (fig) to outline

disegna'tore, -'trice sm/f designer

di'segno [di'senno] sm drawing; design; outline; **disegno di legge** (Dir) bill

diser'bante sm weed-killer

diser'tare vt, vi to desert

dis'fare vt to undo; (valigie) to unpack; (meccanismo) to take to pieces; (neve) to melt; **disfarsi** vpr to come undone; (neve) to melt; **~ il letto** to strip the bed; **disfarsi di qn** (liberarsi) to get rid of sb; **dis'fatto, -a** pp di **disfare**

dis'gelo [diz'dʒɛlo] sm thaw

dis'grazia [diz'grattsja] sf (sventura) misfortune; (incidente) accident, mishap

disgu'ido sm hitch; **disguido postale** error in postal delivery

disgus'tare vt to disgust

dis'gusto sm disgust; **disgus'toso, -a** ag disgusting

disidra'tare vt to dehydrate

disimpa'rare vt to forget

disinfet'tante ag, sm disinfectant

disinfet'tare vt to disinfect

disini'bito, -a ag uninhibited

disinstal'lare vt (software) to uninstall

disinte'grare vt, vi to disintegrate; **disintegrarsi** vpr to disintegrate

disinteres'sarsi vpr **~ di** to take no interest in

disinte'resse sm indifference; (generosità) unselfishness

disintossicarsi vpr to clear out one's system; (alcolizzato, drogato) to be treated for alcoholism (o drug addiction)

disin'volto, -a ag casual, free and easy

dismi'sura sf excess; **a ~** to excess, excessively

disoccu'pato, -a ag unemployed ▷ sm/f unemployed person; **disoccupazi'one** sf unemployment

diso'nesto, -a ag dishonest

disordi'nato, -a ag untidy; (privo di misura) irregular, wild

di'sordine sm (confusione) disorder, confusion; (sregolatezza) debauchery; **disordini** smpl (Pol ecc) disorder sg; (tumulti) riots

disorien'tare vt to disorientate

disorien'tato, -a ag disorientated

'dispari ag inv odd, uneven

dis'parte: in ~ av (da lato) aside, apart; **tenersi o starsene in ~** to keep to o.s., hold o.s. aloof

dispendi'oso, -a ag expensive

dis'pensa sf pantry, larder; (mobile) sideboard; (Dir) exemption; (Rel) dispensation; (fascicolo) number, issue

dispe'rato, -a ag (persona) in despair; (caso, tentativo) desperate

disperazi'one sf despair

dis'perdere vt (disseminare) to disperse; (Mil) to scatter, rout; (fig: consumare) to waste, squander; **disperdersi** vpr to disperse; to scatter; **dis'perso, -a** pp di **disperdere** ▷ sm/f missing person

dis'petto sm spite no pl, spitefulness no pl; **fare un ~ a qn** to play a (nasty) trick on sb; **a ~ di** in spite of; **dispet'toso, -a** ag spiteful

dispia'cere [dispja'tʃere] sm (rammarico) regret, sorrow; (dolore) grief; **dispiaceri** smpl (preoccupazioni) troubles, worries vi ~ **a** to displease vb impers **mi dispiace (che)** I am sorry (that); **le dispiace se…?** do you mind if…?

dis'pone, dis'pongo ecc vb vedi **disporre**

dispo'nibile ag available

dis'porre vt (sistemare) to arrange; (preparare) to prepare; (Dir) to order; (persuadere) ~ **qn a** to incline o dispose sb towards ▷ vi (decidere) to decide; (usufruire): ~ **di** to use, have at one's disposal; (essere dotato): ~ **di** to have

dis'posi ecc vb vedi **disporre**

disposi'tivo sm (meccanismo) device

disposizi'one [dispozit'tsjone] sf arrangement, layout; (stato d'animo) mood; (tendenza) bent, inclination; (comando) order; (Dir) provision, regulation; **a ~ di qn** at sb's disposal

dis'posto, -a pp di **disporre**

disprez'zare [dispret'tsare] vt to despise

dis'prezzo [dis'prettso] sm contempt

'disputa sf dispute, quarrel

dispu'tare vt (contendere) to dispute, contest; (gara) to take part in ▷ vi to

quarrel; ~ **di** to discuss; **disputarsi qc** to fight for sth

'disse vb vedi **dire**

dissente'ria sf dysentery

dissen'tire vi ~ **(da)** to disagree (with)

disse'tante ag refreshing

'dissi vb vedi **dire**

dissimu'lare vt (fingere) to dissemble; (nascondere) to conceal

dissi'pare vt to dissipate; (scialacquare) to squander, waste

dissu'adere vt ~ **qn da** to dissuade sb from

distac'care vt to detach, separate; (Sport) to leave behind; **distaccarsi** vpr to be detached; (fig) to stand out; **distaccarsi da** (fig: allontanarsi) to grow away from

dis'tacco, -chi sm (separazione) separation; (fig: indifferenza) detachment; (Sport): **vincere con un ~ di …** to win by a distance of …

dis'tante av far away ▷ ag ~ **(da)** distant (from), far away (from)

dis'tanza [dis'tantsa] sf distance

distanzi'are [distan'tsjare] vt to space out, place at intervals; (Sport) to outdistance; (fig: superare) to outstrip, surpass

dis'tare vi **distiamo pochi chilometri da Roma** we are only a few kilometres (away) from Rome; **quanto dista il centro da qui?** how far is the town centre?

dis'tendere vt (coperta) to spread out; (gambe) to stretch (out); (mettere a giacere) to lay; (rilassare: muscoli, nervi) to relax; **distendersi** vpr (rilassarsi) to relax; (sdraiarsi) to lie down

dis'tesa sf expanse, stretch

dis'teso, -a pp di **distendere**

distil'lare vt to distil

distille'ria sf distillery

dis'tinguere vt to distinguish; **distinguersi** vpr (essere riconoscibile) to be distinguished; (emergere) to stand out, be conspicuous, distinguish o.s.

dis'tinta sf (nota) note; (elenco) list; **distinta di versamento** pay-in slip

distin'tivo, -a ag distinctive; distinguishing ▷ sm badge

dis'tinto, -a pp di **distinguere** ▷ ag (dignitoso ed elegante) distinguished; **"distinti saluti"** (in lettera) yours faithfully

distinzi'one [distin'tsjone] sf distinction

dis'togliere [dis'tɔʎʎere] vt ~ **da** to take away from; (fig) to dissuade from

distorsi'one sf (Med) sprain; (Fisica, Ottica) distortion

dis'trarre vt to distract; (divertire) to entertain, amuse; **distrarsi** vpr (non

fare attenzione) to be distracted, let one's
mind wander; (*svagarsi*) to amuse o enjoy
o.s.; **dis'tratto, -a** *pp di* **distrarre** ▷ *ag*
absent-minded; (*disattento*) inattentive;
distrazi'one *sf* absent-mindedness;
inattention; (*svago*) distraction,
entertainment
dis'tretto *sm* district
distribu'ire *vt* to distribute; (*Carte*) to
deal (out); (*posta*) to deliver; (*lavoro*) to
allocate, assign; (*ripartire*) to share out;
distribu'tore *sm* (*di benzina*) petrol (BRIT)
o gas (US) pump; (*Aut, Elettr*) distributor;
distributore automatico vending
machine
distri'care *vt* to disentangle, unravel;
districarsi *vpr* (*tirarsi fuori*): **districarsi da**
to get out of, disentangle o.s. from
dis'truggere [dis'truddʒere] *vt* to
destroy; **distruzi'one** *sf* destruction
distur'bare *vt* to disturb, trouble; (*sonno,
lezioni*) to disturb, interrupt; **disturbarsi**
vpr to put o.s. out
dis'turbo *sm* trouble, bother,
inconvenience; (*indisposizione*) (slight)
disorder, ailment; **scusi il ~** I'm sorry to
trouble you
disubbidi'ente *ag* disobedient
disubbi'dire *vi* **~ (a qn)** to disobey (sb)
disu'mano, -a *ag* inhuman
di'tale *sm* thimble
'dito (*pl(f)* **'dita**) *sm* finger; (*misura*) finger,
finger's breadth; **dito (del piede)** toe
'ditta *sf* firm, business
ditta'tore *sm* dictator
ditta'tura *sf* dictatorship
dit'tongo, -ghi *sm* diphthong
di'urno, -a *ag* day *cpd*, daytime *cpd*
'diva *sf vedi* **divo**
di'vano *sm* sofa; divan; **divano letto** bed
settee, sofa bed
divari'care *vt* to open wide
di'vario *sm* difference
diven'tare *vi* to become; **~ famoso/
professore** to become famous/a teacher
diversifi'care *vt* to diversify, vary;
to differentiate; **diversificarsi** *vpr*
diversificarsi (per) to differ (in)
diversità *sf inv* difference, diversity;
(*varietà*) variety
diver'sivo *sm* diversion, distraction
di'verso, -a *ag* (*differente*): **~ (da)** different
(from); **diversi, -e** *det pl* several, various;
(*Comm*) sundry *pron pl* several (people),
many (people)
diver'tente *ag* amusing
diverti'mento *sm* amusement, pleasure;
(*passatempo*) pastime, recreation
diver'tire *vt* to amuse, entertain;

divertirsi *vpr* to amuse o enjoy o.s.
di'videre *vt* (*anche Mat*) to divide;
(*distribuire, ripartire*) to divide (up), split
(up); **dividersi** *vpr* (*separarsi*) to separate;
(*strade*) to fork
divi'eto *sm* prohibition; **"~ di sosta"** (*Aut*)
"no parking"
divinco'larsi *vpr* to wriggle, writhe
di'vino, -a *ag* divine
di'visa *sf* (*Mil ecc*) uniform; (*Comm*) foreign
currency
di'visi *ecc vb vedi* **dividere**
divisi'one *sf* division
'divo, -a *sm/f* star
divo'rare *vt* to devour
divorzi'are [divor'tsjare] *vi* **~ (da qn)** to
divorce (sb)
di'vorzio [di'vɔrtsjo] *sm* divorce
divul'gare *vt* to divulge, disclose; (*rendere
comprensibile*) to popularize
dizio'nario [ditsjo'narjo] *sm* dictionary
DJ [di'dʒei] *sigla m/f* (= *Disk Jockey*) DJ
do *sm* (*Mus*) C; (: *solfeggiando*) do(h)
dobbi'amo *vb vedi* **dovere**
D.O.C. [dɔk] *abbr* (= *denominazione di origine
controllata*) label guaranteeing the quality
of wine
'doccia, -ce ['dɔttʃa] *sf* (*bagno*) shower;
fare la ~ to have a shower
do'cente [do'tʃente] *ag* teaching ▷ *sm/f*
teacher; (*di università*) lecturer
'docile ['dɔtʃile] *ag* docile
documen'tario *sm* documentary
documentarsi *vpr* **~ (su)** to gather
information o material (about)
docu'mento *sm* document; **documenti**
smpl (*d'identità ecc*) papers
dodi'cesimo, -a [dodi'tʃɛzimo] *num*
twelfth
'dodici ['dɔditʃi] *num* twelve
do'gana *sf* (*ufficio*) customs *pl*; (*tassa*)
(customs) duty; **passare la ~** to go
through customs; **dogani'ere** *sm*
customs officer
'doglie ['dɔʎʎe] *sfpl* (*Med*) labour *sg*, labour
pains
'dolce ['dɔltʃe] *ag* sweet; (*carattere, persona*)
gentle, mild; (*fig: mite: clima*) mild; (*non
ripido: pendio*) gentle ▷ *sm* (*sapore dolce*)
sweetness, sweet taste; (*Cuc: portata*)
sweet, dessert; (: *torta*) cake; **dolcifi'cante**
sm sweetener
'dollaro *sm* dollar
Dolo'miti *sfpl* **le ~** the Dolomites
do'lore *sm* (*fisico*) pain; (*morale*) sorrow,
grief; **dolo'roso, -a** *ag* painful; sorrowful,
sad
do'manda *sf* (*interrogazione*) question;
(*richiesta*) demand; (: *cortese*) request;

(Dir: richiesta scritta) application; (Econ): **la ~** demand; **fare una ~ a qn** to ask sb a question; **fare ~ (per un lavoro)** to apply (for a job)

doman'dare vt (per avere) to ask for; (per sapere) to ask; (esigere) to demand; **domandarsi** vpr to wonder; to ask o.s.; **~ qc a qn** to ask sb for sth; to ask sb sth

do'mani av tomorrow ▷ sm **il ~** (il futuro) the future; (il giorno successivo) the next day; **~ l'altro** the day after tomorrow

do'mare vt to tame

doma'tore, -'trice sm/f (gen) tamer; **domatore di cavalli** horsebreaker; **domatore di leoni** lion tamer

domat'tina av tomorrow morning

do'menica, -che sf Sunday; **di** o **la ~** on Sundays

do'mestico, -a, -ci, -che ag domestic ▷ sm/f servant, domestic

domi'cilio [domi'tʃiljo] sm (Dir) domicile, place of residence

domi'nare vt to dominate; (fig: sentimenti) to control, master ▷ vi to be in the dominant position

do'nare vt to give, present; (per beneficenza ecc) to donate ▷ vi (fig): **~ a** to suit, become; **~ sangue** to give blood; **dona'tore, -'trice** sm/f donor; **donatore di sangue/di organi** blood/organ donor

dondo'lare vt (cullare) to rock; **dondolarsi** vpr to swing, sway; **'dondolo** sm **sedia/cavallo a dondolo** rocking chair/horse

'donna sf woman; **donna di casa** housewife; home-loving woman; **donna di servizio** maid

donnai'olo sm ladykiller

'donnola sf weasel

'dono sm gift

doping ['dɔpiŋ] sm doping

'dopo av (tempo) afterwards; (più tardi) later; (luogo) after, next ▷ prep after ▷ cong (temporale): **~ aver studiato** after having studied; **~ mangiato va a dormire** after having eaten o after a meal he goes for a sleep ▷ ag inv **il giorno ~** the following day; **un anno ~** a year later; **~ di me/lui** after me/him; **~, a ~!** see you later!

dopo'barba sm inv after-shave

dopodo'mani av the day after tomorrow

doposci [dopoʃ'ʃi] sm inv après-ski outfit

dopo'sole sm inv aftersun (lotion)

dopo'tutto av (tutto considerato) after all

doppi'aggio [dop'pjaddʒo] sm (Cinema) dubbing

doppi'are vt (Naut) to round; (Sport) to lap; (Cinema) to dub

'doppio, -a ag double; (fig: falso) double-dealing, deceitful ▷ sm (quantità): **il ~**

(di) twice as much (o many), double the amount (o number) of; (Sport) doubles pl ▷ av double

doppi'one sm duplicate (copy)

doppio'petto sm double-breasted jacket

dormicchi'are [dormik'kjare] vi to doze

dormigli'one, -a [dormiʎ'ʎone] sm/f sleepyhead

dor'mire vt, vi to sleep; **andare a ~** to go to bed; **dor'mita** sf **farsi una dormita** to have a good sleep

dormi'torio sm dormitory

dormi'veglia [dormi'veʎʎa] sm drowsiness

'dorso sm back; (di montagna) ridge, crest; (di libro) spine; **a ~ di cavallo** on horseback

do'sare vt to measure out; (Med) to dose

'dose sf quantity, amount; (Med) dose

do'tato, -a ag **~ di** (attrezzature) equipped with; (bellezza, intelligenza) endowed with; **un uomo ~** a gifted man

'dote sf (di sposa) dowry; (assegnata a un ente) endowment; (fig) gift, talent

Dott. abbr (= dottore) Dr.

dotto'rato sm degree; **dottorato di ricerca** doctorate, doctor's degree

dot'tore, -essa sm/f doctor; **chiamate un ~** call a doctor

○ **DOTTORE**
○
○ In Italy, anyone who has a degree in any
○ subject can use the title **dottore**. Thus
○ a person who is addressed as **dottore** is
○ not necessarily a doctor of medicine.

dot'trina sf doctrine

Dott.ssa abbr (= dottoressa) Dr.

'dove av (gen) where; (in cui) where, in which; (dovunque) wherever ▷ cong (mentre, laddove) whereas; **~ sei?/vai?** where are you?/are you going?; **dimmi dov'è** tell me where it is; **di ~ sei?** where are you from?; **per ~ si passa?** which way should we go?; **la città ~ abito** the town where o in which I live; **siediti ~ vuoi** sit wherever you like

do'vere sm (obbligo) duty ▷ vt (essere debitore): **~ qc (a qn)** to owe (sb) sth ▷ vi (seguito dall'infinito: obbligo) to have to; **rivolgersi a chi di ~** to apply to the appropriate authority o person; **lui deve farlo** he has to do it, he must do it; **quanto le devo?** how much do I owe you?; **è dovuto partire** he had to leave; **ha dovuto pagare** he had to pay; (: intenzione): **devo partire domani** I'm (due) to leave tomorrow; (: probabilità): **dev'essere tardi** it must be late; **come**

si deve (*lavorare, comportarsi*) properly; **una persona come si deve** a respectable person

dove'roso, -a *ag* (*right and*) proper

dovrò *ecc vb vedi* **dovere**

do'vunque *av* (*in qualunque luogo*) wherever; (*dappertutto*) everywhere; **~ io vada** wherever I go

do'vuto, -a *ag* (*causato*): **~ a** due to

doz'zina [dod'dzina] *sf* dozen; **una ~ di uova** a dozen eggs

dozzi'nale [doddzi'nale] *ag* cheap, second-rate

'drago, -ghi *sm* dragon

'dramma, -i *sm* drama; **dram'matico, -a, -ci, -che** *ag* dramatic

'drastico, -a, -ci, -che *ag* drastic

'dritto, -a *ag, av* = **diritto**

'droga, -ghe *sf* (*sostanza aromatica*) spice; (*stupefacente*) drug; **droghe leggere/pesanti** soft/hard drugs

drogarsi *vpr* to take drugs

dro'gato, -a *sm/f* drug addict

droghe'ria [droge'ria] *sf* grocer's shop (BRIT), grocery (store) (US)

drome'dario *sm* dromedary

DS [di'esse] *sigla mpl* (= *Democratici di Sinistra*) *Italian left-wing party*

'dubbio, -a *ag* (*incerto*) doubtful, dubious; (*ambiguo*) dubious ▷ *sm* (*incertezza*) doubt; **avere il ~ che** to be afraid that, suspect that; **mettere in ~ qc** to question sth

dubi'tare *vi* **~ di** to doubt; (*risultato*) to be doubtful of

Dub'lino *sf* Dublin

'duca, -chi *sm* duke

du'chessa [du'kessa] *sf* duchess

'due *num* two

due'cento [due'tʃento] *num* two hundred ▷ *sm* **il D~** the thirteenth century

due'pezzi [due'pettsi] *sm* (*costume da bagno*) two-piece swimsuit; (*abito femminile*) two-piece suit

'dunque *cong* (*perciò*) so, therefore; (*riprendendo il discorso*) well (then) ▷ *sm inv* **venire al ~** to come to the point

du'omo *sm* cathedral

> Attenzione! In inglese esiste la parola *dome*, che però significa *cupola*.

dupli'cato *sm* duplicate

'duplice ['duplitʃe] *ag* double, twofold; **in ~ copia** in duplicate

du'rante *prep* during

du'rare *vi* to last; **~ fatica a** to have difficulty in

du'rezza [du'rettsa] *sf* hardness; stubbornness; harshness; toughness

'duro, -a *ag* (*pietra, lavoro, materasso, problema*) hard; (*persona: ostinato*) stubborn, obstinate; (*severo*) harsh, hard; (*voce*) harsh; (*carne*) tough ▷ *sm* hardness; (*difficoltà*) hard part; (*persona*) tough guy; **tener ~** to stand firm, hold out; **~ d'orecchi** hard of hearing

DVD [divu'di] *sigla m* (= *digital versatile (or) video disc*) DVD; (*lettore*) DVD player

e (dav V spesso **ed**) cong and; **e lui?** what about him?; **e compralo!** well buy it then!

E abbr (= est) E

è vb vedi **essere**

eb'bene cong well (then)

'ebbi ecc vb vedi **avere**

e'braico, -a, -ci, -che ag Hebrew, Hebraic ▷ sm (Ling) Hebrew

e'breo, -a ag Jewish ▷ sm/f Jew/ess

EC abbr (= Eurocity) fast train connecting Western European cities

ecc. av abbr (= eccetera) etc

eccel'lente [ettʃel'lɛnte] ag excellent

ec'centrico, -a, -ci, -che [et'tʃɛntriko] ag eccentric

ecces'sivo, -a [ettʃes'sivo] ag excessive

ec'cesso [et'tʃɛsso] sm excess; **all'~** (gentile, generoso) to excess, excessively; **eccesso di velocità** (Aut) speeding

ec'cetera [et'tʃɛtera] av et cetera, and so on

ec'cetto [et'tʃɛtto] prep except, with the exception of; **~ che** except, other than; **~ che (non)** unless

eccezio'nale [ettʃettsjo'nale] ag exceptional

eccezi'one [ettʃet'tsjone] sf exception; (Dir) objection; **a ~ di** with the exception of, except for; **d'~** exceptional

ecci'tare [ettʃi'tare] vt (curiosità, interesse) to excite, arouse; (folla) to incite; **eccitarsi** vpr to get excited; (sessualmente) to become aroused

'ecco av (per dimostrare): **~ il treno!** here's o here comes the train!; (dav pron): **~mi!** here I am!; **~ne uno!** here's one (of them)!; (dav pp): **~ fatto!** there, that's it done!

ec'come av rather; **ti piace? — ~!** do you like it? — I'll say! o and how! o rather! (BRIT)

e'clisse sf eclipse

'eco (pl(m) **'echi**) sm o f echo

ecogra'fia sf (Med) scan

ecolo'gia [ekolo'dʒia] sf ecology

eco'logico, -a, ci, che [eko'lɔdʒiko] ag ecological

econo'mia sf economy; (scienza) economics sg; (risparmio: azione) saving; **fare ~** to economize, make economies; **eco'nomico, -a, -ci, -che** ag economic; (poco costoso) economical

ecstasy ['ekstazi] sf Ecstasy

'edera sf ivy

e'dicola sf newspaper kiosk o stand (US)

edi'ficio [edi'fitʃo] sm building

e'dile ag building cpd

Edim'burgo sf Edinburgh

edi'tore, -'trice ag publishing cpd ▷ sm/f publisher

> Attenzione! In inglese esiste la parola *editor*, che però significa *redattore*.

edizi'one [edit'tsjone] sf edition; (tiratura) printing; **edizione straordinaria** special edition

edu'care vt to educate; (gusto, mente) to train; **~ qn a fare** to train sb to do; **edu'cato, -a** ag polite, well-mannered; **educazi'one** sf education; (familiare) upbringing; (comportamento) (good) manners pl; **educazione fisica** (Ins) physical training o education

> Attenzione! In inglese esiste la parola *educated*, che però significa *istruito*.

educherò ecc [eduke'rɔ] vb vedi **educare**

effemi'nato, -a ag effeminate

efferve'scente [efferveʃ'ʃɛnte] ag effervescent

effet'tivo, -a ag (reale) real, actual; (impiegato, professore) permanent; (Mil) regular ▷ sm (Mil) strength; (di patrimonio ecc) sum total

ef'fetto sm effect; (Comm: cambiale) bill; (fig: impressione) impression; **in effetti** in fact, actually; **effetto serra** greenhouse effect; **effetti personali** personal effects, personal belongings

effi'cace [effi'katʃe] ag effective

effici'ente [effi'tʃɛnte] ag efficient

E'geo [e'dʒɛo] sm **l'~, il mare ~** the Aegean (Sea)

E'gitto [e'dʒitto] sm **l'~** Egypt

egizi'ano, -a [edʒit'tsjano] ag, sm/f Egyptian

'egli ['eʎʎi] pron he; **~ stesso** he himself

ego'ismo sm selfishness, egoism; **ego'ista, -i, -e** ag selfish, egoistic ▷ sm/f egoist

Egr. abbr = **egregio**

e'gregio, -a, -gi, -gie [e'grɛdʒo] ag (nelle lettere): **E~ Signore** Dear Sir

E.I. abbr = **Esercito Italiano**

elabo'rare vt (progetto) to work out, elaborate; (dati) to process

elasticiz'zato, -a [elastit'ʃid'dzato] ag stretch cpd

e'lastico, -a, -ci, -che ag elastic; (fig: andatura) springy; (: decisione, vedute) flexible ▷ sm (di gomma) rubber band; (per il cucito) elastic no pl

ele'fante sm elephant

ele'gante ag elegant

e'leggere [e'lɛddʒere] vt to elect

elemen'tare ag elementary; **le (scuole) elementari** sfpl primary (BRIT) o grade (US) school

ele'mento sm element; (parte componente) element, component, part; **elementi** smpl (della scienza ecc) elements, rudiments

ele'mosina sf charity, alms pl; **chiedere l'~** to beg

elen'care vt to list

elencherò ecc [elenke'rɔ] vb vedi **elencare**

e'lenco, -chi sm list; **elenco telefonico** telephone directory

e'lessi ecc vb vedi **eleggere**

eletto'rale ag electoral, election cpd

elet'tore, -'trice sm/f voter, elector

elet'trauto sm inv workshop for car electrical repairs; (tecnico) car electrician

elettri'cista, -i [elettri'tʃista] sm electrician

elettricità [elettritʃi'ta] sf electricity

e'lettrico, -a, -ci, -che ag electric(al)

elettriz'zante [elettrid'dzante] ag (fig) electrifying, thrilling

elettriz'zare [elettrid'dzare] vt to electrify; **elettrizzarsi** vpr to become charged with electricity

e'lettro... prefisso; **elettrodo'mestico, -a, -ci, -che** ag **apparecchi elettrodomestici** domestic (electrical) appliances; **elet'tronico, -a, -ci, -che** ag electronic

elezi'one [elet'tsjone] sf election; **elezioni** sfpl (Pol) election(s)

'elica, -che sf propeller

eli'cottero sm helicopter

elimi'nare vt to eliminate

elisoc'corso sm helicopter ambulance

el'metto sm helmet

elogi'are [elo'dʒare] vt to praise

elo'quente ag eloquent

e'ludere vt to evade

e'lusi ecc vb vedi **eludere**

e-mail [i'mɛil] sf inv (messaggio, sistema) e-mail ▷ ag inv (indirizzo) e-mail

emargi'nato, -a [emardʒi'nato] sm/f outcast; **emarginazione** [emardʒinat'tsjone] sf marginalization

embri'one sm embryo

emenda'mento sm amendment

emer'genza [emer'dʒɛntsa] sf emergency; **in caso di ~** in an emergency

e'mergere [e'mɛrdʒere] vi to emerge; (sommergibile) to surface; (fig: distinguersi) to stand out

e'mersi ecc vb vedi **emergere**

e'mettere vt (suono, luce) to give out, emit; (onde radio) to send out; (assegno, francobollo, ordine) to issue

emi'crania sf migraine

emi'grare vi to emigrate

emis'fero sm hemisphere; **emisfero australe** southern hemisphere; **emisfero boreale** northern hemisphere

e'misi ecc vb vedi **emettere**

emit'tente ag (banca) issuing; (Radio) broadcasting, transmitting ▷ sf (Radio) transmitter

emorra'gia, -'gie [emorra'dʒia] sf haemorrhage

emor'roidi sfpl haemorrhoids pl (BRIT), hemorrhoids pl (US)

emo'tivo, -a ag emotional

emozio'nante [emottsjo'nante] ag exciting, thrilling

emozionare [emottsjo'nare] vt (commuovere) to move; (agitare) to make nervous; (elettrizzare) to excite; **emozionarsi** vpr to be moved; to be nervous; to be excited; **emozionato, -a** [emottsjo'nato] ag (commosso) moved; (agitato) nervous; (elettrizzato) excited

emozi'one [emot'tsjone] sf emotion; (agitazione) excitement

enciclope'dia [entʃiklope'dia] sf encyclopaedia

endove'noso, -a ag (Med) intravenous

'E.N.E.L. ['enel] sigla m (= Ente Nazionale per l'Energia Elettrica) national electricity company

ener'getico, -a, ci, che [ener'dʒɛtiko] ag (risorse, crisi) energy cpd; (sostanza, alimento) energy-giving

ener'gia, -'gie [ener'dʒia] sf (Fisica) energy; (fig) energy, strength, vigour; **energia eolica** wind power; **energia solare** solar energy, solar power;

e'**nergico, -a, -ci, -che** ag energetic, vigorous

'**enfasi** sf emphasis; (peg) bombast, pomposity

en'**nesimo, -a** ag (Mat, fig) nth; **per l'ennesima volta** for the umpteenth time

e'**norme** ag enormous, huge

'**ente** sm (istituzione) body, board, corporation; (Filosofia) being; **enti pubblici** public bodies; **ente di ricerca** research organization

en'**trambi, -e** pron pl both (of them) ▷ ag pl **~ i ragazzi** both boys, both of the boys

en'**trare** vi to go (o come) in; **~ in** (luogo) to enter, go (o come) into; (trovar posto, poter stare) to fit into; (essere ammesso a: club ecc) to join, become a member of; **~ in automobile** to get into the car; **far ~ qn** (visitatore ecc) to show sb in; **questo non c'entra** (fig) that's got nothing to do with it; **en'trata** sf entrance, entry; **dov'è l'entrata?** where's the entrance?; **entrate** sfpl (Comm) receipts, takings; (Econ) income sg

'**entro** prep (temporale) within

entusias'**mare** vt to excite, fill with enthusiasm; **entusiasmarsi** vpr **entusiasmarsi (per qc/qn)** to become enthusiastic (about sth/sb); **entusi'asmo** sm enthusiasm; **entusi'asta, -i, -e** ag enthusiastic ▷ sm/f enthusiast

epa'**tite** sf hepatitis

epide'**mia** sf epidemic

epiles'**sia** sf epilepsy

epi'**lettico, -a, ci, che** ag, sm/f epileptic

epi'**sodio** sm episode

'**epoca, -che** sf (periodo storico) age, era; (tempo) time; (Geo) age

ep'**pure** cong and yet, nevertheless

EPT sigla m (= Ente Provinciale per il Turismo) district tourist bureau

equa'**tore** sm equator

equazi'**one** [ekwat'tsjone] sf (Mat) equation

e'**questre** ag equestrian

equi'**librio** sm balance, equilibrium; **perdere l'equilibrare** to lose one's balance

e'**quino, -a** ag horse cpd, equine

equipaggia'**mento** [ekwipaddʒa'mento] sm (operazione: di nave) equipping, fitting out; (: di spedizione, esercito) equipping, kitting out; (attrezzatura) equipment

equipaggi'**are** [ekwipad'dʒare] vt (di persone) to man; (di mezzi) to equip; **equipaggiarsi** vpr to equip o.s.; **equi'paggio** sm crew

equitazi'**one** [ekwitat'tsjone] sf (horse-)riding

equiva'**lente** ag, sm equivalent

e'**quivoco, -a, -ci, -che** ag equivocal, ambiguous; (sospetto) dubious ▷ sm misunderstanding; **a scanso di equivoci** to avoid any misunderstanding; **giocare sull'~** to equivocate

'**equo, -a** ag fair, just

'**era** sf era

'**era** ecc vb vedi **essere**

'**erba** sf grass; **in ~** (fig) budding; **erbe aromatiche** herbs; **erba medica** lucerne; **er'baccia, -ce** sf weed

erboriste'**ria** sf (scienza) study of medicinal herbs; (negozio) herbalist's (shop)

e'**rede** sm/f heir; **eredità** sf (Dir) inheritance; (Biol) heredity; **lasciare qc in eredità a qn** to leave o bequeath sth to sb; **eredi'tare** vt to inherit; **eredi'tario, -a** ag hereditary

ere'**mita, -i** sm hermit

er'**gastolo** sm (Dir: pena) life imprisonment

'**erica** sf heather

er'**metico, -a, -ci, -che** ag hermetic

'**ernia** sf (Med) hernia

'**ero** vb vedi **essere**

e'**roe** sm hero

ero'**gare** vt (somme) to distribute; (gas, servizi) to supply

e'**roico, -a, -ci, -che** ag heroic

ero'**ina** sf heroine; (droga) heroin

erosi'**one** sf erosion

e'**rotico, -a, -ci, -che** ag erotic

er'**rato, -a** ag wrong

er'**rore** sm error, mistake; (morale) error; **per ~** by mistake; **ci dev'essere un ~** there must be some mistake; **errore giudiziario** miscarriage of justice

eruzi'**one** [erut'tsjone] sf eruption

esacer'**bare** [ezatʃer'bare] vt to exacerbate

esage'**rare** [ezadʒe'rare] vt to exaggerate ▷ vi to exaggerate; (eccedere) to go too far

esal'**tare** vt to exalt; (entusiasmare) to excite, stir

e'**same** sm examination; (Ins) exam, examination; **fare o dare un ~** to sit o take an exam; **esame di guida** driving test; **esame del sangue** blood test

esami'**nare** vt to examine

esaspe'**rare** vt to exasperate; to exacerbate

esatta'**mente** av exactly; accurately, precisely

esat'**tezza** [ezat'tettsa] sf exactitude, accuracy, precision

e'**satto, -a** pp di **esigere** ▷ ag (calcolo, ora) correct, right, exact; (preciso) accurate,

precise; (*puntuale*) punctual
esau'dire *vt* to grant, fulfil
esauri'ente *ag* exhaustive
esauri'mento *sm* exhaustion;
esaurimento nervoso nervous
breakdown
esau'rire *vt* (*stancare*) to exhaust, wear
out; (*provviste, miniera*) to exhaust;
esaurirsi *vpr* to exhaust o.s., wear o.s.
out; (*provviste*) to run out; **esau'rito, -a**
ag exhausted; (*merci*) sold out; **registrare
il tutto esaurito** (*Teatro*) to have a full
house; **e'sausto, -a** *ag* exhausted
'esca (*pl* **'esche**) *sf* bait
'esce ['eʃʃe] *vb vedi* **uscire**
eschi'mese [eski'mese] *ag, sm/f* Eskimo
'esci ['eʃʃi] *vb vedi* **uscire**
escla'mare *vi* to exclaim, cry out
esclama'tivo, -a *ag* **punto ~** exclamation
mark
esclamazi'one *sf* exclamation
es'cludere *vt* to exclude
es'clusi *ecc vb vedi* **escludere**
esclusi'one *sf* exclusion; **a ~ di, fatta
~ per** except (for), apart from; **senza ~
(alcuna)** without exception; **procedere
per ~** to follow a process of elimination;
senza ~ di colpi (*fig*) with no holds barred;
esclusione sociale social exclusion
esclu'siva *sf* (*Dir, Comm*) exclusive *o* sole
rights *pl*
esclusiva'mente *av* exclusively, solely
esclu'sivo, -a *ag* exclusive
es'cluso, -a *pp di* **escludere**
'esco *vb vedi* **uscire**
escogi'tare [eskodʒi'tare] *vt* to devise,
think up
'escono *vb vedi* **uscire**
escursi'one *sf* (*gita*) excursion, trip;
(: *a piedi*) hike, walk; (*Meteor*) range;
escursione termica temperature range
esecuzi'one [ezekut'tsjone] *sf* execution,
carrying out; (*Mus*) performance;
esecuzione capitale execution
esegu'ire *vt* to carry out, execute; (*Mus*) to
perform, execute
e'sempio *sm* example; **per ~** for example,
for instance; **fare un ~** to give an example;
esem'plare *ag* exemplary ▷ *sm* example;
(*copia*) copy
eserci'tare [ezertʃi'tare] *vt* (*professione*)
to practise (BRIT), practice (US); (*allenare:
corpo, mente*) to exercise, train; (*diritto*)
to exercise; (*influenza, pressione*) to exert;
esercitarsi *vpr* to practise; **esercitarsi
alla lotta** to practise fighting
e'sercito [e'zɛrtʃito] *sm* army
eser'cizio [ezer'tʃittsjo] *sm* practice;
exercising; (*fisico: di matematica*) exercise;

(*Econ*) financial year; (*azienda*) business,
concern; **in ~** (*medico ecc*) practising;
esercizio pubblico (*Comm*) commercial
concern
esi'bire *vt* to exhibit, display; (*documenti*)
to produce, present; **esibirsi** *vpr* (*attore*)
to perform; (*fig*) to show off; **esibizi'one**
sf exhibition; (*di documento*) presentation;
(*spettacolo*) show, performance
esi'gente [ezi'dʒɛnte] *ag* demanding
e'sigere [e'zidʒere] *vt* (*pretendere*) to
demand; (*richiedere*) to demand, require;
(*imposte*) to collect
'esile *ag* (*persona*) slender, slim; (*stelo*) thin;
(*voce*) faint
esili'are *vt* to exile; **e'silio** *sm* exile
esis'tenza [ezis'tɛntsa] *sf* existence
e'sistere *vi* to exist
esi'tare *vi* to hesitate
'esito *sm* result, outcome
'esodo *sm* exodus
esone'rare *vt* to exempt
e'sordio *sm* debut
esor'tare *vt* **~ qn a fare** to urge sb to do
e'sotico, -a, -ci, -che *ag* exotic
es'pandere *vt* to expand; (*confini*) to
extend; (*influenza*) to extend, spread;
espandersi *vpr* to expand; **espansi'one**
sf expansion; **espansione di memoria**
(*Inform*) memory upgrade; **espan'sivo, -a**
ag expansive, communicative
espatri'are *vi* to leave one's country
espedi'ente *sm* expedient
es'pellere *vt* to expel
esperi'enza [espe'rjɛntsa] *sf* experience
esperi'mento *sm* experiment
es'perto, -a *ag, sm* expert
espi'rare *vt, vi* to breathe out
es'plicito, -a [es'plitʃito] *ag* explicit
es'plodere *vi* (*anche fig*) to explode ▷ *vt*
to fire
esplo'rare *vt* to explore
esplosi'one *sf* explosion
es'pone *ecc vb vedi* **esporre**
es'pongo, es'poni *ecc vb vedi* **esporre**
es'porre *vt* (*merci*) to display; (*quadro*)
to exhibit, show; (*fatti, idee*) to explain,
set out; (*porre in pericolo, Fot*) to expose:
esporsi *vpr* **esporsi a** (*sole, pericolo*) to
expose o.s. to; (*critiche*) to lay o.s. open to
espor'tare *vt* to export
es'pose *ecc vb vedi* **esporre**
esposizi'one [espozit'tsjone] *sf*
displaying; exhibiting; setting out;
(*anche Fot*) exposure; (*mostra*) exhibition;
(*narrazione*) explanation, exposition
es'posto, -a *pp di* **esporre** ▷ *ag* **~ a nord**
facing north ▷ *sm* (*Amm*) statement,
account; (: *petizione*) petition

espressi'one sf expression

espres'sivo, -a ag expressive

es'presso, -a pp di esprimere ▷ ag express ▷ sm (lettera) express letter; (anche: treno ~) express train; (anche: caffè ~) espresso

es'primere vt to express; esprimersi vpr to express o.s.

es'pulsi ecc vb vedi espellere

espulsi'one sf expulsion

es'senza [es'sɛntsa] sf essence; essenzi'ale ag essential; l'essenziale the main o most important thing

○ PAROLA CHIAVE

'essere sm being; essere umano human being
▷ vb copulativo 1 (con attributo, sostantivo) to be; sei giovane/simpatico you are o you're young/nice; è medico he is o he's a doctor
2 (+ di: appartenere) to be; di chi è la penna? whose pen is it?; è di Carla it is o it's Carla's, it belongs to Carla
3 (+ di: provenire) to be; è di Venezia he is o he's from Venice
4 (data, ora): è il 15 agosto/lunedì it is o it's the 15th of August/Monday; che ora è?, che ore sono? what time is it?; è l'una it is o it's one o'clock; sono le due it is o it's two o'clock
5 (costare): quant'è? how much is it?; sono 10 euro it's 10 euros
▷ vb aus 1 (attivo): essere arrivato/venuto to have arrived/come; è già partita she has already left
2 (passivo) to be; essere fatto da to be made by; è stata uccisa she has been killed
3 (riflessivo): si sono lavati they washed, they got washed
4 (+ da + infinito): è da farsi subito it must be o is to be done immediately
▷ vi 1 (esistere, trovarsi) to be; sono a casa I'm at home; essere in piedi/seduto to be standing/sitting
2: esserci: c'è there is; ci sono there are; che c'è? what's the matter?, what is it?; ci sono! (fig: ho capito) I get it!; vedi anche ci
▷ vb impers è tardi/Pasqua it's late/Easter; è possibile che venga he may come; è così that's the way it is

'essi pron mpl vedi esso

'esso, -a pron it; (riferito a persona: soggetto) he/she; (: complemento) him/her

est sm east

es'tate sf summer

esteri'ore ag outward, external

es'terno, -a ag (porta, muro) outer, outside; (scala) outside; (alunno, impressione) external ▷ sm outside, exterior ▷ sm/f (allievo) day pupil; all'~ outside; per uso ~ for external use only; esterni smpl (Cinema) location shots

'estero, -a ag foreign ▷ sm all'~ abroad

es'teso, -a pp di estendere ▷ ag extensive, large; scrivere per ~ to write in full

es'tetico, -a, -ci, -che ag aesthetic ▷ sf (disciplina) aesthetics sg; (bellezza) attractiveness; este'tista, -i, -e sm/f beautician

es'tinguere vt to extinguish, put out; (debito) to pay off; estinguersi vpr to go out; (specie) to become extinct

es'tinsi ecc vb vedi estinguere

estin'tore sm (fire) extinguisher

estinzi'one sf putting out; (di specie) extinction

estir'pare vt (pianta) to uproot, pull up; (fig: vizio) to eradicate

es'tivo, -a ag summer cpd

es'torcere [es'tortʃere] vt ~ qc (a qn) to extort sth (from sb)

estradizi'one [estradit'tsjone] sf extradition

es'trae, es'traggo ecc vb vedi estrarre

es'traneo, -a ag foreign ▷ sm/f stranger; rimanere ~ a qc to take no part in sth

es'trarre vt to extract; (minerali) to mine; (sorteggiare) to draw

es'trassi ecc vb vedi estrarre

estrema'mente av extremely

estre'mista, -i, e sm/f extremist

estremità sf inv extremity, end ▷ sf pl (Anat) extremities

es'tremo, -a ag extreme; (ultimo: ora, tentativo) final, last ▷ sm extreme; (di pazienza, forze) limit, end; estremi smpl (Amm: dati essenziali) details, particulars; l'~ Oriente the Far East

estro'verso, -a ag, sm extrovert

età sf inv age; all'~ di 8 anni at the age of 8, at 8 years of age; ha la mia ~ he (o she) is the same age as me o as I am; raggiungere la maggiore ~ to come of age; essere in ~ minore to be under age

'etere sm ether

eternità sf eternity

e'terno, -a ag eternal

etero'geneo, -a [etero'dʒɛneo] ag heterogeneous

eterosessu'ale ag, sm/f heterosexual

'etica sf ethics sg; vedi anche etico

eti'chetta [eti'ketta] sf label; (cerimoniale): l'~ etiquette

'etico, -a, -ci, -che *ag* ethical
eti'lometro *sm* Breathalyzer®
etimolo'gia, -'gie [etimolo'dʒia] *sf*
  etymology
Eti'opia *sf* l'~ Ethiopia
'etnico, -a, -ci, -che *ag* ethnic
e'trusco, -a, -schi, -sche *ag, sm/f*
  Etruscan
'ettaro *sm* hectare (= 10,000 m²)
'etto *sm abbr* (= ettogrammo) 100 grams
'euro *sm inv* (*divisa*) euro
Eu'ropa *sf* l'~ Europe
europarlamen'tare *sm/f* Member of the
  European Parliament, MEP
euro'peo, -a *ag, sm/f* European
eutana'sia *sf* euthanasia
evacu'are *vt* to evacuate
e'vadere *vi* (*fuggire*): ~ **da** to escape from
  ▷ *vt* (*sbrigare*) to deal with, dispatch; (*tasse*)
  to evade
evapo'rare *vi* to evaporate
e'vasi *ecc vb vedi* **evadere**
evasi'one *sf* (*vedi* evadere) escape;
  dispatch; **evasione fiscale** tax evasion
eva'sivo, -a *ag* evasive
e'vaso, -a *pp di* **evadere** ▷ *sm* escapee
e'vento *sm* event
eventu'ale *ag* possible
> ■ Attenzione! In inglese esiste la parola
> *eventual*, che però significa *finale*.

eventual'mente *av* if necessary
> ■ Attenzione! In inglese esiste la
> parola *eventually*, che però significa
> *alla fine*.

evi'dente *ag* evident, obvious
evidente'mente *av* evidently;
  (*palesemente*) obviously, evidently
evi'tare *vt* to avoid; ~ **di fare** to avoid
  doing; ~ **qc a qn** to spare sb sth
evoluzi'one [evolut'tsjone] *sf* evolution
e'volversi *vpr* to evolve
ev'viva *escl* hurrah!; ~ **il re!** long live the
  king!, hurrah for the king!
ex *prefisso* ex, former
'extra *ag inv* first-rate; top-quality ▷ *sm*
  inv extra; **extracomuni'tario, -a** *ag* from
  outside the EC ▷ *sm/f* non-EC citizen
extrater'restre *ag, sm/f* extraterrestrial

fa *vb vedi* **fare** ▷ *sm inv* (Mus) F;
  (: *solfeggiando la scala*) fa ▷ *av* **10 anni fa** 10
  years ago
'fabbrica *sf* factory; **fabbri'care** *vt* to
  build; (*produrre*) to manufacture, make;
  (*fig*) to fabricate, invent
> ■ Attenzione! In inglese esiste la parola
> *fabric*, che però significa *stoffa*.

fac'cenda [fat'tʃɛnda] *sf* matter, affair;
  (*cosa da fare*) task, chore
fac'chino [fak'kino] *sm* porter
'faccia, -ce ['fattʃa] *sf* face; (*di moneta,*
  medaglia) side; **faccia a faccia** face to face
facci'ata [fat'tʃata] *sf* façade; (*di pagina*)
  side
'faccio ['fattʃo] *vb vedi* **fare**
fa'cessi *ecc* [fa'tʃessi] *vb vedi* **fare**
fa'cevo *ecc* [fa'tʃevo] *vb vedi* **fare**
'facile ['fatʃile] *ag* easy; (*disposto*): ~ **a**
  inclined to, prone to; (*probabile*): **è ~ che**
  piova it's likely to rain
facoltà *sf inv* faculty; (*autorità*) power
facolta'tivo, -a *ag* optional; (*fermata*
  d'autobus) request cpd
'faggio ['faddʒo] *sm* beech
fagi'ano [fa'dʒano] *sm* pheasant
fagio'lino [fadʒo'lino] *sm* French (BRIT) o
  string bean
fagi'olo [fa'dʒɔlo] *sm* bean
'fai *vb vedi* **fare**

'fai-da-'te sm inv DIY, do-it-yourself
'falce ['faltʃe] sf scythe; **falci'are** vt to cut; (fig) to mow down
falcia'trice [faltʃa'tritʃe] sf (per fieno) reaping machine; (per erba) mowing machine
'falco, -chi sm hawk
'falda sf layer, stratum; (di cappello) brim; (di cappotto) tails pl; (di monte) lower slope; (di tetto) pitch
fale'gname [faleɲ'ɲame] sm joiner
falli'mento sm failure; bankruptcy
fal'lire vi (non riuscire): ~ **(in)** to fail (in); (Dir) to go bankrupt ▷ vt (colpo, bersaglio) to miss
'fallo sm error, mistake; (imperfezione) defect, flaw; (Sport) foul; fault; **senza ~** without fail
falò sm inv bonfire
falsifi'care vt to forge; (monete) to forge, counterfeit
'falso, -a ag false; (errato) wrong; (falsificato) forged; fake; (: oro, gioielli) imitation cpd ▷ sm forgery; **giurare il ~** to commit perjury
'fama sf fame; (reputazione) reputation, name
'fame sf hunger; **aver ~** to be hungry
fa'miglia [fa'miʎʎa] sf family
famili'are ag (della famiglia) family cpd; (ben noto) familiar; (rapporti, atmosfera) friendly; (Ling) informal, colloquial ▷ sm/f relative, relation
fa'moso, -a ag famous, well-known
fa'nale sm (Aut) light, lamp (BRIT); (luce stradale, Naut) light; (di faro) beacon
fa'natico, -a, -ci, -che ag fanatical; (del teatro, calcio ecc): ~ **di** o **per** mad o crazy about ▷ sm/f fanatic; (tifoso) fan
'fango, -ghi sm mud
'fanno vb vedi **fare**
fannul'lone, -a sm/f idler, loafer
fantasci'enza [fantaʃʃɛntsa] sf science fiction
fanta'sia sf fantasy, imagination; (capriccio) whim, caprice ▷ ag inv **vestito ~** patterned dress
fan'tasma, -i sm ghost, phantom
fan'tastico, -a, -ci, -che ag fantastic; (potenza, ingegno) imaginary
fan'tino sm jockey
fara'butto sm crook
fard sm inv blusher

PAROLA CHIAVE

'fare sm 1 (modo di fare): **con fare distratto** absent-mindedly; **ha un fare simpatico** he has a pleasant manner

2: **sul far del giorno/della notte** at daybreak/nightfall

▷ vt 1 (fabbricare, creare) to make; (: casa) to build; (: assegno) to make out; **fare un pasto/una promessa/un film** to make a meal/a promise/a film; **fare rumore** to make a noise

2 (effettuare: lavoro, attività, studi) to do; (: sport) to play; **cosa fa?** (adesso) what are you doing?; (di professione) what do you do?; **fare psicologia/italiano** (Ins) to do psychology/Italian; **fare un viaggio** to go on a trip o journey; **fare una passeggiata** to go for a walk; **fare la spesa** to do the shopping

3 (funzione) to be; (Teatro) to play, be; **fare il medico** to be a doctor; **fare il malato** (fingere) to act the invalid

4 (suscitare: sentimenti): **fare paura a qn** to frighten sb; **(non) fa niente** (non importa) it doesn't matter

5 (ammontare): **3 più 3 fa 6** 3 and 3 are o make 6; **fanno 3 euro** that's 3 euros; **Roma fa 2.000.000 di abitanti** Rome has 2,000,000 inhabitants; **che ora fai?** what time do you make it?

6 (+ infinito): **far fare qc a qn** (obbligare) to make sb do sth; (permettere) to let sb do sth; **fammi vedere** let me see; **far partire il motore** to start (up) the engine; **far riparare la macchina/costruire una casa** to get o have the car repaired/a house built

7: **farsi: farsi una gonna** to make o.s. a skirt; **farsi un nome** to make a name for o.s.; **farsi la permanente** to get a perm; **farsi tagliare i capelli** to get one's hair cut; **farsi operare** to have an operation

8 (fraseologia): **farcela** to succeed, manage; **non ce la faccio più** I can't go on; **ce la faremo** we'll make it; **me l'hanno fatta!** (imbrogliare) I've been done!; **lo facevo più giovane** I thought he was younger; **fare sì/no con la testa** to nod/shake one's head

▷ vi 1 (agire) to act, do; **fate come volete** do as you like; **fare presto** to be quick; **fare da** to act as; **non c'è niente da fare** it's no use; **saperci fare con qn/qc** to know how to deal with sb/sth; **faccia pure!** go ahead!

2 (dire) to say; **"davvero?" fece** "really?" he said

3: **fare per** (essere adatto) to be suitable for; **fare per fare qc** to be about to do sth; **fece per andarsene** he made as if to leave

4: **farsi: si fa così** this is the way it's done; **non si fa così!** (rimprovero) that's no way to behave!; **la festa non si fa** the party is off

5: **fare a gara con qn** to compete o vie with sb; **fare a pugni** to come to blows; **fare in tempo a fare** to be in time to do ▷ vb impers **fa bel tempo** the weather is fine; **fa caldo/freddo** it's hot/cold; **fa notte** it's getting dark ▷ vpr **farsi 1** (diventare) to become; **farsi prete** to become a priest; **farsi grande/vecchio** to grow tall/old

2 (spostarsi): **farsi avanti/indietro** to move forward/back

3 (fam: drogarsi) to be a junkie

far'falla sf butterfly

fa'rina sf flour

farma'cia, -'cie [farma'tʃia] sf pharmacy; (negozio) chemist's (shop) (BRIT), pharmacy; **farma'cista, -i, -e** sm/f chemist (BRIT), pharmacist

farmaco, -ci o **chi** sm drug, medicine

'faro sm (Naut) lighthouse; (Aer) beacon; (Aut) headlight

'fascia, -sce ['faʃʃa] sf band, strip; (Med) bandage; (di sindaco, ufficiale) sash; (parte di territorio) strip, belt; (di contribuenti ecc) group, band; **essere in fasce** (anche fig) to be in one's infancy; **fascia oraria** time band

fasci'are [faʃ'ʃare] vt to bind; (Med) to bandage

fa'scicolo [faʃ'ʃikolo] sm (di documenti) file, dossier; (di rivista) issue, number; (opuscolo) booklet, pamphlet

'fascino ['faʃʃino] sm charm, fascination

fa'scismo [faʃ'ʃizmo] sm fascism

'fase sf phase; (Tecn) stroke; **fuori ~** (motore) rough

fas'tidio sm bother, trouble; **dare ~ a qn** to bother o annoy sb; **sento ~ allo stomaco** my stomach's upset; **avere fastidi con la polizia** to have trouble o bother with the police; **fastidi'oso, -a** ag annoying, tiresome

Attenzione! In inglese esiste la parola _fastidious_, che però significa _pignolo_.

'fata sf fairy

fa'tale ag fatal; (inevitabile) inevitable; (fig) irresistible

fa'tica, -che sf hard work, toil; (sforzo) effort; (di metalli) fatigue; **a ~** with difficulty; **fare ~ a fare qc** to have a job doing sth; **fati'coso, -a** ag tiring, exhausting; (lavoro) laborious

'fatto, -a pp di **fare** ▷ ag **un uomo ~** a grown man; **~ a mano/in casa** hand-/home-made ▷ sm fact; (azione) deed; (avvenimento) event, occurrence; (di romanzo, film) action, story; **cogliere qn sul ~** to catch sb red-handed; **il ~ sta** o **è**

che the fact remains o is that; **in ~ di** as for, as far as … is concerned

fat'tore sm (Agr) farm manager; (Mat, elemento costitutivo) factor; **fattore di protezione** (di lozione solare) factor; **vorrei una crema solare con ~ di protezione 15** I'd like a factor 15 suntan cream

fatto'ria sf farm; farmhouse

Attenzione! In inglese esiste la parola _factory_, che però significa _fabbrica_.

fatto'rino sm errand-boy; (di ufficio) office-boy; (d'albergo) porter

fat'tura sf (Comm) invoice; (di abito) tailoring; (malia) spell

fattu'rato sm (Comm) turnover

'fauna sf fauna

'fava sf broad bean

'favola sf (fiaba) fairy tale; (d'intento morale) fable; (fandonia) yarn; **favo'loso, -a** ag fabulous; (incredibile) incredible

fa'vore sm favour; **per ~** please; **fare un ~ a qn** to do sb a favour

favo'rire vt to favour; (il commercio, l'industria, le arti) to promote, encourage; **vuole ~?** won't you help yourself?; **favorisca in salotto** please come into the sitting room

fax sm inv fax; **mandare qc via ~** to fax sth

fazzo'letto [fattso'letto] sm handkerchief; (per la testa) (head)scarf; **fazzoletto di carta** tissue

feb'braio sm February

'febbre sf fever; **aver la ~** to have a high temperature; **febbre da fieno** hay fever

'feci ecc ['fɛtʃi] vb vedi **fare**

fecondazi'one [fekondat'tsjone] sf fertilization; **fecondazione artificiale** artificial insemination

fe'condo, -a ag fertile

'fede sf (credenza) belief, faith; (Rel) faith; (fiducia) faith, trust; (fedeltà) loyalty; (anello) wedding ring; (attestato) certificate; **aver ~ in qn** to have faith in sb; **in buona/cattiva ~** in good/bad faith; **"in ~"** (Dir) "in witness whereof"; **fe'dele** ag **fedele (a)** faithful (to) ▷ sm/f follower; **i fedeli** (Rel) the faithful

'federa sf pillowslip, pillowcase

fede'rale ag federal

'fegato sm liver; (fig) guts pl, nerve

'felce ['feltʃe] sf fern

fe'lice [fe'litʃe] ag happy; (fortunato) lucky; **felicità** sf happiness

felici'tarsi [felitʃi'tarsi] vpr (congratularsi): **~ con qn per qc** to congratulate sb on sth

fe'lino, -a ag, sm feline

'felpa sf sweatshirt

'femmina sf (Zool, Tecn) female; (figlia) girl, daughter; (spesso peg) woman;

femmi'nile *ag* feminine; (*sesso*) female; (*lavoro, giornale, moda*) woman's ▷ *sm* (*Ling*) feminine

'femore *sm* thighbone, femur

fe'nomeno *sm* phenomenon

feri'ale *ag* **giorno ~** weekday

'ferie *sfpl* holidays (BRIT), vacation *sg* (US); **andare in ~** to go on holiday *o* vacation

fe'rire *vt* to injure; (*deliberatamente: Mil ecc*) to wound; (*colpire*) to hurt; **ferirsi** *vpr* to hurt o.s., injure o.s; **fe'rita** *sf* injury, wound; **fe'rito, -a** *sm/f* wounded *o* injured man/woman

fer'maglio [fer'maʎʎo] *sm* clasp; (*per documenti*) clip

fer'mare *vt* to stop, halt; (*Polizia*) to detain, hold ▷ *vi* to stop; **fermarsi** *vpr* to stop, halt; **fermarsi a fare qc** to stop to do sth; **può fermarsi qui/all'angolo?** could you stop here/at the corner?

fer'mata *sf* stop; **fermata dell'autobus** bus stop

fer'menti *smpl* **~ lattici** probiotic bacteria

fer'mezza [fer'mettsa] *sf* (*fig*) firmness, steadfastness

'fermo, -a *ag* still, motionless; (*veicolo*) stationary; (*orologio*) not working; (*saldo: anche fig*) firm; (*voce, mano*) steady ▷ *escl* stop!; keep still! ▷ *sm* (*chiusura*) catch, lock; (*Dir*): **fermo di polizia** police detention

fe'roce [fe'rɔtʃe] *ag* (*animale*) fierce, ferocious; (*persona*) cruel, fierce; (*fame, dolore*) raging; **le bestie feroci** wild animals

ferra'gosto *sm* (*festa*) feast of the Assumption; (*periodo*) August holidays *pl*

● **FERRAGOSTO**

● **Ferragosto**, August 15th, is a national
● holiday. Marking the Feast of the
● Assumption, its origins are religious
● but in recent years it has simply become
● the most important public holiday of
● the summer season. Most people take
● some extra time off work and head out
● of town to the holiday resorts.

ferra'menta *sfpl* **negozio di ~** ironmonger's (BRIT), hardware shop *o* store (US)

'ferro *sm* iron; **una bistecca ai ferri** a grilled steak; **ferro battuto** wrought iron; **ferro da calza** knitting needle; **ferro di cavallo** horseshoe; **ferro da stiro** iron

ferro'via *sf* railway (BRIT), railroad (US); **ferrovi'ario, -a** *ag* railway *cpd* (BRIT), railroad *cpd* (US); **ferrovi'ere** *sm*

railwayman (BRIT), railroad man (US)

'fertile *ag* fertile

'fesso, -a *pp di* **fendere** ▷ *ag* (*fam: sciocco*) crazy, cracked

fes'sura *sf* crack, split; (*per gettone, moneta*) slot

'festa *sf* (*religiosa*) feast; (*pubblica*) holiday; (*compleanno*) birthday; (*onomastico*) name day; (*ricevimento*) celebration, party; **far ~** to have a holiday; to live it up; **far ~ a qn** to give sb a warm welcome

festeggi'are [fested'dʒare] *vt* to celebrate; (*persona*) to have a celebration for

fes'tivo, -a *ag* (*atmosfera*) festive; **giorno ~** holiday

'feto *sm* foetus (BRIT), fetus (US)

'fetta *sf* slice

fettuc'cine [fettut'tʃine] *sfpl* (*Cuc*) ribbon-shaped pasta

FF.SS. *abbr* = **Ferrovie dello Stato**

FI *sigla* = **Firenze** ▷ *abbr* (= **Forza Italia**) *Italian centre-right political party*

fi'aba *sf* fairy tale

fi'acca *sf* weariness; (*svogliatezza*) listlessness

fi'acco, -a, -chi, -che *ag* (*stanco*) tired, weary; (*svogliato*) listless; (*debole*) weak; (*mercato*) slack

fi'accola *sf* torch

fi'ala *sf* phial

fi'amma *sf* flame

fiam'mante *ag* (*colore*) flaming; **nuovo ~** brand new

fiam'mifero *sm* match

fiam'mingo, -a, -ghi, -ghe *ag* Flemish ▷ *sm/f* Fleming ▷ *sm* (*Ling*) Flemish; **i Fiamminghi** the Flemish

fi'anco, -chi *sm* side; (*Mil*) flank; **di ~** sideways, from the side; **a ~ a ~** side by side

fi'asco, -schi *sm* flask; (*fig*) fiasco; **fare ~** to fail

fia'tare *vi* (*fig: parlare*): **senza ~** without saying a word

fi'ato *sm* breath; (*resistenza*) stamina; **avere il ~ grosso** to be out of breath; **prendere ~** to catch one's breath

'fibbia *sf* buckle

'fibra *sf* fibre; (*fig*) constitution

fic'care *vt* to push, thrust, drive; **ficcarsi** *vpr* (*andare a finire*) to get to

ficcherò *ecc* [fikke'rɔ] *vb vedi* **ficcare**

'fico, -chi *sm* (*pianta*) fig tree; (*frutto*) fig; **fico d'India** prickly pear; **fico secco** dried fig

fidanza'mento [fidantsa'mento] *sm* engagement

fidan'zarsi [fidan'tsarsi] *vpr* to get engaged; **fidan'zato, -a** *sm/f* fiancé/

fiancée
fi'darsi vpr **~ di** to trust; **fi'dato, -a** ag
reliable, trustworthy
fi'ducia [fi'dutʃa] sf confidence,
trust; **incarico di ~** position of trust,
responsible position; **persona di ~**
reliable person
fie'nile sm barn; hayloft
fi'eno sm hay
fi'era sf fair
fi'ero, -a ag proud; (audace) bold
'fifa (fam) sf **aver ~** to have the jitters
fig. abbr (= figura) fig.
'figlia ['fiʎʎa] sf daughter
figli'astro, -a [fiʎ'ʎastro] sm/f stepson/
daughter
'figlio ['fiʎʎo] sm son; (senza distinzione di
sesso) child; **figlio di papà** spoilt, wealthy
young man; **figlio unico** only child
fi'gura sf figure; (forma, aspetto esterno)
form, shape; (illustrazione) picture,
illustration; **far ~** to look smart; **fare una
brutta ~** to make a bad impression
figu'rina sf figurine; (cartoncino) picture
card
'fila sf row, line; (coda) queue; (serie) series,
string; **di ~** in succession; **fare la ~** to
queue; **in ~ indiana** in single file
fi'lare vt to spin ▷ vi (baco, ragno) to spin;
(formaggio fuso) to go stringy; (discorso) to
hang together; (fam: amoreggiare) to go
steady; (muoversi a forte velocità) to go at
full speed; **~ diritto** (fig) to toe the line; **~
via** to dash off
filas'trocca, -che sf nursery rhyme
filate'lia sf philately, stamp collecting
fi'letto sm (di vite) thread; (di carne) fillet
fili'ale ag filial ▷ sf (di impresa) branch
film sm inv film
'filo sm (anche fig) thread; (filato) yarn;
(metallico) wire; (di lama, rasoio) edge; **per ~
e per segno** in detail; **con un ~ di voce** in
a whisper; **filo d'erba** blade of grass; **filo
interdentale** dental floss; **filo di perle**
string of pearls; **filo spinato** barbed wire
fi'lone sm (di minerali) seam, vein; (pane)
≈ Vienna loaf; (fig) trend
filoso'fia sf philosophy; **fi'losofo, -a** sm/f
philosopher
fil'trare vt, vi to filter
'filtro sm filter; **filtro dell'olio** (Aut) oil filter
fi'nale ag final ▷ sm (di opera) end, ending;
(: Mus) finale ▷ sf (Sport) final; **final'mente**
av finally, at last
fi'nanza [fi'nantsa] sf finance; **finanze**
sfpl (di individuo, Stato) finances
finché [fin'ke] cong (per tutto il tempo che)
as long as; (fino al momento in cui) until;
aspetta ~ io (non) sia ritornato wait

until I get back
'fine ag (lamina, carta) thin; (capelli,
polvere) fine; (vista, udito) keen, sharp;
(persona: raffinata) refined, distinguished;
(osservazione) subtle ▷ sf end ▷ sm aim,
purpose; (esito) result, outcome; **secondo
~** ulterior motive; **in o alla ~** in the end,
finally
fi'nestra sf window; **fines'trino** sm
window; **vorrei un posto vicino al
finestrino** I'd like a window seat
'fingere ['findʒere] vt to feign; (supporre)
to imagine, suppose; **fingersi** vpr **fingersi
ubriaco/pazzo** to pretend to be drunk/
mad; **~ di fare** to pretend to do
fi'nire vt to finish ▷ vi to finish, end;
quando finisce lo spettacolo? when
does the show finish?; **~ di fare** (compiere)
to finish doing; (smettere) to stop doing; **~
in galera** to end up o finish up in prison
finlan'dese ag, sm (Ling) Finnish ▷ sm/f
Finn
Fin'landia sf **la ~** Finland
'fino, -a ag (capelli, seta) fine; (oro) pure;
(fig: acuto) shrewd ▷ av (spesso troncato in
fin: pure, anche) even ▷ prep (spesso troncato
in **fin**: tempo): **fin quando?** till when?;
(: luogo): **fin qui** as far as here; **~ a** (tempo)
until, till; (luogo) as far as, (up) to; **fin da
domani** from tomorrow onwards; **fin
da ieri** since yesterday; **fin dalla nascita**
from o since birth
fi'nocchio [fi'nɔkkjo] sm fennel; (fam: peg:
omosessuale) queer
fi'nora av up till now
'finsi ecc vb vedi **fingere**
'finta sf pretence, sham; (Sport) feint; **far ~
(di fare)** to pretend (to do)
'finto, -a pp di **fingere** ▷ ag false;
artificial
finzi'one [fin'tsjone] sf pretence, sham
fi'occo, -chi sm (di nastro) bow; (di stoffa,
lana) flock; (di neve) flake; (Naut) jib; **coi
fiocchi** (fig) first-rate; **fiocchi di avena**
oatflakes; **fiocchi di granturco** cornflakes
fi'ocina ['fjɔtʃina] sf harpoon
fi'oco, -a, -chi, -che ag faint, dim
fi'onda sf catapult
fio'raio, -a sm/f florist
fi'ore sm flower; **fiori** smpl (Carte) clubs; **a
fior d'acqua** on the surface of the water;
avere i nervi a fior di pelle to be on edge;
fior di latte cream; **fiori di campo** wild
flowers
fioren'tino, -a ag Florentine
fio'retto sm (Scherma) foil
fio'rire vi (rosa) to flower; (albero) to
blossom; (fig) to flourish
Fi'renze [fi'rɛntse] sf Florence

'firma sf signature
Attenzione! In inglese esiste la parola firm, che però significa ditta.

fir'mare vt to sign; **un abito firmato** a designer suit; **dove devo ~?** where do I sign?

fisar'monica, -che sf accordion

fis'cale ag fiscal, tax cpd; **medico ~** doctor employed by Social Security to verify cases of sick leave

fischi'are [fis'kjare] vi to whistle ▷ vt to whistle; (attore) to boo, hiss

fischi'etto [fis'kjetto] sm (strumento) whistle

'fischio ['fiskjo] sm whistle

'fisco sm tax authorities pl, ≈ Inland Revenue (BRIT), ≈ Internal Revenue Service (US)

'fisica sf physics sg

'fisico, -a, -ci, -che ag physical ▷ sm/f physicist ▷ sm physique

fisiotera'pia sf physiotherapy

fisiotera'pista sm/f physiotherapist

fis'sare vt to fix, fasten; (guardare intensamente) to stare at; (data, condizioni) to fix, establish, set; (prenotare) to book; **fissarsi** vpr **fissarsi su** (sguardo, attenzione) to focus on; (fig: idea) to become obsessed with

'fisso, -a ag fixed; (stipendio, impiego) regular ▷ av **guardare ~ qc/qn** to stare at sth/sb

'fitta sf sharp pain; vedi anche **fitto**

fit'tizio, -a ag fictitious, imaginary

'fitto, -a ag thick, dense; (pioggia) heavy ▷ sm depths pl, middle; (affitto, pigione) rent

fi'ume sm river

fiu'tare vt to smell, sniff; (animale) to scent; (fig: inganno) to get wind of, smell; **~ tabacco/cocaina** to take snuff/cocaine

fla'grante ag **cogliere qn in ~** to catch sb red-handed

fla'nella sf flannel

flash [flaʃ] sm inv (Fot) flash; (giornalistico) newsflash

'flauto sm flute

fles'sibile ag pliable; (fig: che si adatta) flexible

flessibili'tà sf (anche fig) flexibility

flessi'one sf (gen) bending; (Ginnastica: a terra) sit-up; (: in piedi) forward bend; (: sulle gambe) knee-bend; (diminuzione) slight drop, slight fall; (Ling) inflection; **fare una ~** to bend; **una ~ economica** a downward trend in the economy

'flettere vt to bend

'flipper sm inv pinball machine

F.lli abbr (= fratelli) Bros.

'flora sf flora

'florido, -a ag flourishing; (fig) glowing with health

'floscio, -a, -sci, -sce ['floʃʃo] ag (cappello) floppy, soft; (muscoli) flabby

'flotta sf fleet

'fluido, -a ag, sm fluid

flu'oro sm fluorine

'flusso sm flow; (Fisica, Med) flux; **~ e ri~** ebb and flow

fluvi'ale ag river cpd, fluvial

FMI sigla m (= Fondo Monetario Internazionale) IMF

'foca, -che sf (Zool) seal

fo'caccia, -ce [fo'kattʃa] sf kind of pizza; (dolce) bun

'foce ['fotʃe] sf (Geo) mouth

foco'laio sm (Med) centre of infection; (fig) hotbed

foco'lare sm hearth, fireside; (Tecn) furnace

'fodera sf (di vestito) lining; (di libro, poltrona) cover

'fodero sm (di spada) scabbard; (di pugnale) sheath; (di pistola) holster

'foga sf enthusiasm, ardour

'foglia ['fɔʎʎa] sf leaf; **foglia d'argento/ d'oro** silver/gold leaf

'foglio ['fɔʎʎo] sm (di carta) sheet (of paper); (di metallo) sheet; **foglio di calcolo** (Inform) spreadsheet; **foglio rosa** (Aut) provisional licence; **foglio di via** (Dir) expulsion order; **foglio volante** pamphlet

'fogna ['foɲɲa] sf drain, sewer

föhn [føːn] sm inv hair dryer

'folla sf crowd, throng

'folle ag mad, insane; (Tecn) idle; **in ~** (Aut) in neutral

fol'lia sf folly, foolishness; foolish act; (pazzia) madness, lunacy

'folto, -a ag thick

fon sm inv hair dryer

fondamen'tale ag fundamental, basic

fonda'mento sm foundation; **fondamenta** sfpl (Edil) foundations

fon'dare vt to found; (fig: dar base): **~ qc su** to base sth on

fon'dente ag **cioccolato ~** plain o dark chocolate

'fondere vt (neve) to melt; (metallo) to fuse, melt; (fig: colori) to merge, blend; (: imprese, gruppi) to merge ▷ vi to melt; **fondersi** vpr to melt; (fig: partiti, correnti) to unite, merge

'fondo, -a ag deep ▷ sm (di recipiente, pozzo) bottom; (di stanza) back; (quantità di liquido che resta, deposito) dregs pl; (sfondo) background; (unità immobiliare) property, estate; (somma di denaro) fund; (Sport)

long-distance race; **fondi** *smpl* (*denaro*)
funds; **a notte fonda** at dead of night; **in ~
a** at the bottom of; at the back of; (*strada*)
at the end of; **andare a ~** (*nave*) to sink;
conoscere a ~ to know inside out; **dar ~
a** (*fig: provviste, soldi*) to use up; **in ~** (*fig*)
after all, all things considered; **andare
fino in ~ a** (*fig*) to examine thoroughly; **a ~
perduto** (*Comm*) without security; **fondi
di magazzino** old *o* unsold stock *sg*; **fondi
di caffè** coffee grounds; **fondo comune di
investimento** investment trust
fondo'tinta *sm inv* (*cosmetico*) foundation
fo'netica *sf* phonetics *sg*
fon'tana *sf* fountain
'fonte *sf* spring, source; (*fig*) source ▷ *sm*:
fonte battesimale (*Rel*) font; **fonte
energetica** source of energy
fo'raggio [fo'raddʒo] *sm* fodder, forage
fo'rare *vt* to pierce, make a hole in;
(*pallone*) to burst; (*biglietto*) to punch; **~
una gomma** to burst a tyre (*BRIT*) *o* tire
(*US*)
'forbici ['fɔrbitʃi] *sfpl* scissors
'forca, -che *sf* (*Agr*) fork, pitchfork;
(*patibolo*) gallows *sg*
for'chetta [for'ketta] *sf* fork
for'cina [for'tʃina] *sf* hairpin
fo'resta *sf* forest
foresti'ero, -a *ag* foreign ▷ *sm/f* foreigner
'forfora *sf* dandruff
'forma *sf* form; (*aspetto esteriore*) form,
shape; (*Dir: procedura*) procedure; (*per
calzature*) last; (*stampo da cucina*) mould
formag'gino [formad'dʒino] *sm*
processed cheese
for'maggio [for'maddʒo] *sm* cheese
for'male *ag* formal
for'mare *vt* to form, shape, make; (*numero
di telefono*) to dial; (*fig: carattere*) to form,
mould; **formarsi** *vpr* to form, take shape;
for'mato *sm* format, size; **formazi'one**
sf formation; (*fig: educazione*) training;
formazione professionale vocational
training
for'mica¹, -che *sf* ant
formica®² ['fɔrmika] *sf* (*materiale*)
Formica®
formi'dabile *ag* powerful, formidable;
(*straordinario*) remarkable
'formula *sf* formula; **formula di cortesia**
courtesy form
formu'lare *vt* to formulate; to express
for'naio *sm* baker
for'nello *sm* (*elettrico, a gas*) ring; (*di pipa*)
bowl
for'nire *vt* **~ qn di qc, ~ qc a qn** to provide
o supply sb with sth, supply sth to sb
'forno *sm* (*di cucina*) oven; (*panetteria*)

bakery; (*Tecn: per calce ecc*) kiln; (: *per
metalli*) furnace; **forno a microonde**
microwave oven
'foro *sm* (*buco*) hole; (*Storia*) forum;
(*tribunale*) (law) court
'forse *av* perhaps, maybe; (*circa*) about;
essere in ~ to be in doubt
'forte *ag* strong; (*suono*) loud; (*spesa*)
considerable, great; (*passione, dolore*)
great, deep ▷ *av* strongly; (*velocemente*)
fast; (*a voce alta*) loud(ly); (*violentemente*)
hard ▷ *sm* (*edificio*) fort; (*specialità*) forte,
strong point; **essere ~ in qc** to be good
at sth
for'tezza *sf* (*morale*) strength;
(*luogo fortificato*) fortress
for'tuito, -a *ag* fortuitous, chance
for'tuna *sf* (*destino*) fortune, luck; (*buona
sorte*) success, fortune; (*eredità, averi*)
fortune; **per ~** luckily, fortunately; **di ~**
makeshift, improvised; **atterraggio di
~** emergency landing; **fortu'nato, -a** *ag*
lucky, fortunate; (*coronato da successo*)
successful
'forza ['fɔrtsa] *sf* strength; (*potere*) power;
(*Fisica*) force; **forze** *sfpl* (*fisiche*) strength
sg; (*Mil*) forces *escl* come on!; **per ~** against
one's will; (*naturalmente*) of course; **a viva
~** by force; **a ~ di** by dint of; **~ maggiore**
circumstances beyond one's control; **la
~ pubblica** the police *pl*; **forze armate**
armed forces; **forze dell'ordine** the forces
of law and order; **Forza Italia** *Italian
centre-right political party*; **forza di pace**
peacekeeping force
for'zare [for'tsare] *vt* to force; **~ qn a fare**
to force sb to do
for'zista, -i, e [for'tsista] *ag* of Forza Italia
▷ *sm/f* member (*o* supporter) of Forza
Italia
fos'chia [fos'kia] *sf* mist, haze
'fosco, -a, -schi, -sche *ag* dark, gloomy
'fosforo *sm* phosphorous
'fossa *sf* pit; (*di cimitero*) grave; **fossa
biologica** septic tank
fos'sato *sm* ditch; (*di fortezza*) moat
fos'setta *sf* dimple
'fossi *ecc vb vedi* **essere**
'fossile *ag, sm* fossil
'fosso *sm* ditch; (*Mil*) trench
'foste *ecc vb vedi* **essere**
'foto *sf* photo; **può farci una ~, per
favore?** would you take a picture of us,
please? ▷ *prefisso*: **foto ricordo** souvenir
photo; **foto tessera** passport(-type)
photo; **foto'camera** *sf* **fotocamera
digitale** digital camera; **foto'copia** *sf*
photocopy; **fotocopi'are** *vt* to photocopy;
fotocopia'trice [fotokopja'tritʃe]

sf photocopier; **fotogra'fare** *vt* to photograph; **fotogra'fia** *sf* (*procedimento*) photography; (*immagine*) photograph; **fare una fotografia** to take a photograph; **una fotografia a colori/in bianco e nero** a colour/black and white photograph; **foto'grafico, -a, ci, che** *ag* photographic; **macchina fotografica** camera; **fo'tografo, -a** *sm/f* photographer; **fotoro'manzo** *sm* romantic picture story

fou'lard[fu'lar] *sm inv* scarf

fra *prep* = **tra**

'fradicio, -a, -ci, -ce['fraditʃo] *ag* (*molto bagnato*) soaking (wet); **ubriaco ~** blind drunk

'fragile['fradʒile] *ag* fragile; (*fig: salute*) delicate

'fragola *sf* strawberry

fra'grante *ag* fragrant

frain'tendere *vt* to misunderstand

fram'mento *sm* fragment

'frana *sf* landslide; (*fig: persona*): **essere una ~** to be useless

fran'cese[fran'tʃeze] *ag* French ▷ *sm/f* Frenchman/woman ▷ *sm* (*Ling*) French; **i Francesi** the French

'Francia['frantʃa] *sf* **la ~** France

'franco, -a, -chi, -che *ag* (*sincero*) frank, open, sincere ▷ *sm* (*moneta*) franc; **farla franca** (*fig*) to get off scot-free; **prezzo ~ fabbrica** ex-works price; **franco di dogana** duty-free

franco'bollo *sm* (postage) stamp

'frangia, -ge['frandʒa] *sf* fringe

frap'pé *sm* milk shake

'frase *sf* (*Ling*) sentence; (*locuzione, espressione, Mus*) phrase; **frase fatta** set phrase

'frassino *sm* ash (tree)

frastagli'ato, -a[frasta'ʎʎato] *ag* (*costa*) indented, jagged

frastor'nare *vt* to daze; to befuddle

frastu'ono *sm* hubbub, din

'frate *sm* friar, monk

fratel'lastro *sm* stepbrother; (*con genitore in comune*) half-brother

fra'tello *sm* brother; **fratelli** *smpl* brothers; (*nel senso di fratelli e sorelle*) brothers and sisters

fra'terno, -a *ag* fraternal, brotherly

frat'tempo *sm* **nel ~** in the meantime, meanwhile

frat'tura *sf* fracture; (*fig*) split, break

frazi'one[frat'tsjone] *sf* fraction; (*di comune*) small town

'freccia, -ce['frettʃa] *sf* arrow; **freccia di direzione** (*Aut*) indicator

fred'dezza[fred'dettsa] *sf* coldness

'freddo, -a *ag, sm* cold; **fa ~** it's cold;

aver ~ to be cold; **a ~** (*fig*) deliberately; **freddo'loso, -a** *ag* sensitive to the cold

fre'gare *vt* to rub; (*fam: truffare*) to take in, cheat; (: *rubare*) to swipe, pinch; **fregarsene** (*fam!*): **chi se ne frega?** who gives a damn (about it)?

fregherò *ecc* [frege'rɔ] *vb vedi* **fregare**

fre'nare *vt* (*veicolo*) to slow down; (*cavallo*) to rein in; (*lacrime*) to restrain, hold back ▷ *vi* to brake; **frenarsi** *vpr* (*fig*) to restrain o.s., control o.s.

'freno *sm* brake; (*morso*) bit; **tenere a ~** to restrain; **freno a disco** disc brake; **freno a mano** handbrake

frequen'tare *vt* (*scuola, corso*) to attend; (*locale, bar*) to go to, frequent; (*persone*) to see (often)

frequen'tato, -a *ag* (*locale*) busy

fre'quente *ag* frequent; **di ~** frequently

fres'chezza[fres'kettsa] *sf* freshness

'fresco, -a, -schi, -sche *ag* fresh; (*temperatura*) cool; (*notizia*) recent, fresh ▷ *sm* **godere il ~** to enjoy the cool air; **stare ~** (*fig*) to be in for it; **mettere al ~** to put in a cool place

'fretta *sf* hurry, haste; **in ~** in a hurry; **in ~ e furia** in a mad rush; **aver ~** to be in a hurry

friggere['friddʒere] *vt* to fry ▷ *vi* (*olio ecc*) to sizzle

'frigido, -a['fridʒido] *ag* (*Med*) frigid

'frigo *sm* fridge

frigo'bar *sm inv* minibar

frigo'rifero, -a *ag* refrigerating ▷ *sm* refrigerator

fringu'ello *sm* chaffinch

'frissi *ecc vb vedi* **friggere**

frit'tata *sf* omelette; **fare una ~** (*fig*) to make a mess of things

frit'tella *sf* (*Cuc*) fritter

'fritto, -a *pp di* **friggere** ▷ *ag* fried ▷ *sm* fried food; **fritto misto** mixed fry

frit'tura *sf* (*Cuc*): **frittura di pesce** mixed fried fish

'frivolo, -a *ag* frivolous

frizi'one[frit'tsjone] *sf* friction; (*sulla pelle*) rub, rub-down; (*Aut*) clutch

friz'zante[frid'dzante] *ag* (*anche fig*) sparkling

fro'dare *vt* to defraud, cheat

'frode *sf* fraud; **frode fiscale** tax evasion

'fronda *sf* (leafy) branch; (*di partito politico*) internal opposition; **fronde** *sfpl* (*di albero*) foliage *sg*

fron'tale *ag* frontal; (*scontro*) head-on

'fronte *sf* (*Anat*) forehead; (*di edificio*) front, façade ▷ *sm* (*Mil, Pol, Meteor*) front; **a ~, di ~** facing, opposite; **di ~ a** (*posizione*) opposite, facing, in front of; (*a paragone di*) compared with

fronti'era sf border, frontier

'frottola sf fib

fru'gare vi to rummage ▷ vt to search

frugherò ecc [fruge'rɔ] vb vedi **frugare**

frul'lare vt (Cuc) to whisk ▷ vi (uccelli) to flutter; **frul'lato** sm milk shake; fruit drink; **frulla'tore** sm electric mixer

fru'mento sm wheat

fru'scio [fruʃʃio] sm rustle; rustling; (di acque) murmur

'frusta sf whip; (Cuc) whisk

frus'tare vt to whip

frus'trato, -a ag frustrated

'frutta sf fruit; (portata) dessert; **frutta candita** candied fruit; **frutta secca** dried fruit

frut'tare vi to bear dividends, give a return

frut'teto sm orchard

frutti'vendolo, -a sm/f greengrocer (BRIT), produce dealer (US)

'frutto sm fruit; (fig: risultato) result(s); (Econ: interesse) interest; (: reddito) income; **frutti di bosco** berries; **frutti di mare** seafood sg

FS abbr = **Ferrovie dello Stato**

fu vb vedi **essere** ▷ ag inv **il fu Paolo Bianchi** the late Paolo Bianchi

fuci'lare [futʃi'lare] vt to shoot

fu'cile [fu'tʃile] sm rifle, gun; (da caccia) shotgun, gun

'fucsia sf fuchsia

'fuga sf escape, flight; (di gas, liquidi) leak; (Mus) fugue; **fuga di cervelli** brain drain

fug'gire [fud'dʒire] vi to flee, run away; (fig: passar veloce) to fly ▷ vt to avoid

'fui vb vedi **essere**

fu'liggine [fu'liddʒine] sf soot

'fulmine sm thunderbolt; lightning no pl

fu'mare vi to smoke; (emettere vapore) to steam ▷ vt to smoke; **le dà fastidio se fumo?** do you mind if I smoke?; **fuma'tore, -'trice** sm/f smoker

fu'metto sm comic strip; **giornale** sm, **a fumetti** comic

'fummo vb vedi **essere**

'fumo sm smoke; (vapore) steam; (il fumare tabacco) smoking; **fumi** smpl (industriali ecc) fumes; **i fumi dell'alcool** the after-effects of drink; **vendere ~** to deceive, cheat; **fumo passivo** passive smoking

'fune sf rope, cord; (più grossa) cable

'funebre ag (rito) funeral; (aspetto) gloomy, funereal

fune'rale sm funeral

'fungere ['fundʒere] vi **~ da** to act as

'fungo, -ghi sm fungus; (commestibile) mushroom; **fungo velenoso** toadstool

funico'lare sf funicular railway

funi'via sf cable railway

'funsi ecc vb vedi **fungere**

funzio'nare [funtsjo'nare] vi to work, function; (fungere): **~ da** to act as; **come funziona?** how does this work?; **la TV non funziona** the TV isn't working

funzio'nario [funtsjo'narjo] sm official; **funzionario statale** civil servant

funzi'one [fun'tsjone] sf function; (carica) post, position; (Rel) service; **in ~** (meccanismo) in operation; **in ~ di** (come) as; **fare la ~ di qn** (farne le veci) to take sb's place

fu'oco, -chi sm fire; (fornello) ring; (Fot, Fisica) focus; **dare ~ a qc** to set fire to sth; **far ~** (sparare) to fire; **al ~!** fire!; **fuoco d'artificio** firework

fuorché [fwor'ke] cong, prep except

fu'ori av outside; (all'aperto) outdoors, outside; (fuori di casa, Sport) out; (esclamativo) get out! ▷ prep **~ (di)** out of, outside ▷ sm outside; **lasciar ~ qc/qn** to leave sth/sb out; **far ~ qn** (fam) to kill sb, do sb in; **essere ~ di sé** to be beside o.s.; **~ luogo** (inopportuno) out of place, uncalled for; **~ mano** out of the way, remote; **~ pericolo** out of danger; **~ uso** old-fashioned; obsolete; **fuorigi'oco** sm offside; **fuori'strada** sm (Aut) cross-country vehicle

'furbo, -a ag clever, smart; (peg) cunning

fu'rente ag **~ (contro)** furious (with)

fur'fante sm rascal, scoundrel

fur'gone sm van

'furia sf (ira) fury, rage; (fig: impeto) fury, violence; (fretta) rush; **a ~ di** by dint of; **andare su tutte le furie** to get into a towering rage; **furi'bondo, -a** ag furious

furi'oso, -a ag furious

'furono vb vedi **essere**

fur'tivo, -a ag furtive

'furto sm theft; **vorrei denunciare un ~** I'd like to report a theft; **furto con scasso** burglary

'fusa sfpl **fare le ~** to purr

fu'seaux smpl inv leggings

'fusi ecc vb vedi **fondere**

fu'sibile sm (Elettr) fuse

fusi'one sf (di metalli) fusion, melting; (colata) casting; (Comm) merger; (fig) merging

'fuso, -a pp di **fondere** ▷ sm (Filatura) spindle; **fuso orario** time zone

fus'tino sm (di detersivo) tub

'fusto sm stem; (Anat, di albero) trunk; (recipiente) drum, can

fu'turo, -a ag, sm future

g

'**gabbia** sf cage; (da imballaggio) crate; **gabbia dell'ascensore** lift (BRIT) o elevator (US) shaft; **gabbia toracica** (Anat) rib cage

gabbi'ano sm (sea)gull

gabi'netto sm (Med ecc) consulting room; (Pol) ministry; (WC) toilet, lavatory; (Ins: di fisica ecc) laboratory

'**gaffe** [gaf] sf inv blunder

ga'lante ag gallant, courteous; (avventura) amorous

ga'lassia sf galaxy

ga'lera sf (Naut) galley; (prigione) prison

'**galla** sf **a ~** afloat; **venire a ~** to surface, come to the surface; (fig: verità) to come out

galleggi'are [galled'dʒare] vi to float

galle'ria sf (traforo) tunnel; (Archit, d'arte) gallery; (Teatro) circle; (strada coperta con negozi) arcade

'**Galles** sm **il ~** Wales

gal'lina sf hen

'**gallo** sm cock

galop'pare vi to gallop

ga'loppo sm gallop; **al o di ~** at a gallop

'**gamba** sf leg; (asta: di lettera) stem; **in ~** (in buona salute) well; (bravo, sveglio) bright, smart; **prendere qc sotto ~** (fig) to treat sth too lightly

gambe'retto sm shrimp

'**gambero** sm (di acqua dolce) crayfish; (di mare) prawn

'**gambo** sm stem; (di frutta) stalk

'**gamma** sf (Mus) scale; (di colori, fig) range

'**gancio** ['gantʃo] sm hook

'**gara** sf competition; (Sport) competition; contest; match; (: corsa) race; **fare a ~** to compete, vie

ga'rage [ga'raʒ] sm inv garage

garan'tire vt to guarantee; (debito) to stand surety for; (dare per certo) to assure

garan'zia [garan'tsia] sf guarantee; (pegno) security

gar'bato, -a ag courteous, polite

gareggi'are [gared'dʒare] vi to compete

garga'rismo sm gargle; **fare i gargarismi** to gargle

ga'rofano sm carnation; **chiodo di ~** clove

'**garza** ['gardza] sf (per bende) gauze

gar'zone [gar'dzone] sm (di negozio) boy

gas sm inv gas; **sento odore di ~** I can smell gas; **a tutto ~** at full speed; **dare ~** (Aut) to accelerate

ga'solio sm diesel (oil)

gas'sato, -a ag fizzy

gast'rite sf gastritis

gastrono'mia sf gastronomy

gat'tino sm kitten

'**gatto, -a** sm/f cat, tomcat/she-cat; **gatto delle nevi** (Aut, Sci) snowcat; **gatto selvatico** wildcat

'**gazza** ['gaddza] sf magpie

gel [dʒɛl] sm inv gel

ge'lare [dʒe'lare] vt, vi, vb impers to freeze

gelate'ria [dʒelate'ria] sf ice-cream shop

gela'tina [dʒela'tina] sf gelatine; **gelatina esplosiva** dynamite; **gelatina di frutta** fruit jelly

ge'lato, -a [dʒe'lato] ag frozen ▷ sm ice cream

'**gelido, -a** ['dʒɛlido] ag icy, ice-cold

'**gelo** ['dʒɛlo] sm (temperatura) intense cold; (brina) frost; (fig) chill

gelo'sia [dʒelo'sia] sf jealousy

ge'loso, -a [dʒe'loso] ag jealous

'**gelso** ['dʒɛlso] sm mulberry (tree)

gelso'mino [dʒelso'mino] sm jasmine

ge'mello, -a [dʒe'mɛllo] ag, sm/f twin; **gemelli** smpl (di camicia) cufflinks; (dello zodiaco): **Gemelli** Gemini sg

'**gemere** ['dʒɛmere] vi to moan, groan; (cigolare) to creak

'**gemma** ['dʒɛmma] sf (Bot) bud; (pietra preziosa) gem

gene'rale [dʒene'rale] ag, sm general; **in ~** (per sommi capi) in general terms; (di solito) usually, in general

gene'rare [dʒene'rare] vt (dar vita) to give birth to; (produrre) to produce; (causare)

to arouse; (*Tecn*) to produce, generate;
generazi'one *sf* generation

'genere ['dʒɛnere] *sm* kind, type, sort;
(*Biol*) genus; (*merce*) article, product;
(*Ling*) gender; (*Arte, Letteratura*) genre;
in ~ generally, as a rule; **genere umano**
mankind; **generi alimentari** foodstuffs

ge'nerico, -a, -ci, -che [dʒe'nɛriko] *ag*
generic; (*vago*) vague, imprecise

'genero ['dʒɛnero] *sm* son-in-law

gene'roso, -a [dʒene'roso] *ag* generous

ge'netica [dʒe'nɛtika] *sf* genetics *sg*

ge'netico, -a, -ci, -che [dʒe'nɛtiko] *ag*
genetic

gen'giva [dʒen'dʒiva] *sf* (*Anat*) gum

geni'ale [dʒen'jale] *ag* (*persona*) of genius;
(*idea*) ingenious, brilliant

'genio ['dʒɛnjo] *sm* genius; **andare a ~ a
qn** to be to sb's liking, appeal to sb

geni'tore [dʒeni'tore] *sm* parent, father
o mother; **i miei genitori** my parents, my
father and mother

gen'naio [dʒen'najo] *sm* January

'Genova ['dʒɛnova] *sf* Genoa

'gente ['dʒɛnte] *sf* people *pl*

gen'tile [dʒen'tile] *ag* (*persona, atto*) kind;
(*: garbato*) courteous, polite; (*nelle lettere*):
G~ Signore Dear Sir; (*: sulla busta*): **G~
Signor Fernando Villa** Mr Fernando Villa

genu'ino, -a [dʒenu'ino] *ag* (*prodotto*)
natural; (*persona, sentimento*) genuine,
sincere

geogra'fia [dʒeogra'fia] *sf* geography

geolo'gia [dʒeolo'dʒia] *sf* geology

ge'ometra, -i, -e [dʒe'ɔmetra] *sm/f*
(*professionista*) surveyor

geome'tria [dʒeome'tria] *sf* geometry

ge'ranio [dʒe'ranjo] *sm* geranium

gerar'chia [dʒerar'kia] *sf* hierarchy

'gergo, -ghi ['dʒɛrgo] *sm* jargon; slang

geria'tria [dʒerja'tria] *sf* geriatrics *sg*

Ger'mania [dʒer'manja] *sf* **la ~** Germany;
la ~ occidentale/orientale West/East
Germany

'germe ['dʒɛrme] *sm* germ; (*fig*) seed

germogli'are [dʒermoʎ'ʎare] *vi* to sprout;
to germinate

gero'glifico, -ci [dʒero'glifiko] *sm*
hieroglyphic

ge'rundio [dʒe'rundjo] *sm* gerund

'gesso ['dʒesso] *sm* chalk; (*Scultura, Med,
Edil*) plaster; (*statua*) plaster figure;
(*minerale*) gypsum

gesti'one [dʒes'tjone] *sf* management

ges'tire [dʒes'tire] *vt* to run, manage

'gesto ['dʒesto] *sm* gesture

Gesù [dʒe'zu] *sm* Jesus

gesu'ita, -i [dʒezu'ita] *sm* Jesuit

get'tare [dʒet'tare] *vt* to throw; (*anche:*

~ via) to throw away *o* out; (*Scultura*) to
cast; (*Edil*) to lay; (*acqua*) to spout; (*grido*)
to utter; **gettarsi** *vpr* **gettarsi in** (*fiume*)
to flow into; **~ uno sguardo su** to take a
quick look at

'getto ['dʒetto] *sm* (*di gas, liquido, Aer*) jet;
a ~ continuo uninterruptedly; **di ~** (*fig*)
straight off, in one go

get'tone [dʒet'tone] *sm* token; (*per giochi*)
counter; (*: roulette ecc*) chip; **gettone
telefonico** telephone token

ghiacci'aio [gjat'tʃajo] *sm* glacier

ghiacci'ato, -a *ag* frozen; (*bevanda*)
ice-cold

ghi'accio ['gjattʃo] *sm* ice

ghiacci'olo [gjat'tʃɔlo] *sm* icicle; (*tipo di
gelato*) ice lolly (BRIT), Popsicle® (US)

ghi'aia ['gjaja] *sf* gravel

ghi'anda ['gjanda] *sf* (*Bot*) acorn

ghi'andola ['gjandola] *sf* gland

ghi'otto, -a ['gjotto] *ag* greedy; (*cibo*)
delicious, appetizing

ghir'landa [gir'landa] *sf* garland, wreath

'ghiro ['giro] *sm* dormouse

'ghisa ['giza] *sf* cast iron

già [dʒa] *av* already; (*ex, in precedenza*)
formerly ▷ *escl* of course!, yes indeed!

gi'acca, -che ['dʒakka] *sf* jacket; **giacca
a vento** windcheater (BRIT), windbreaker
(US)

giacché [dʒak'ke] *cong* since, as

giac'cone [dʒak'kone] *sm* heavy jacket

gi'ada ['dʒada] *sf* jade

giagu'aro [dʒa'gwaro] *sm* jaguar

gi'allo ['dʒallo] *ag* yellow; (*carnagione*)
sallow ▷ *sm* yellow; (*anche:* **romanzo ~**)
detective novel; (*anche:* **film ~**) detective
film; **giallo dell'uovo** yolk

Giamaica [dʒa'maika] *sf* **la ~** Jamaica

Giap'pone [dʒap'pone] *sm* Japan;
giappo'nese *ag, sm/f, sm* Japanese *inv*

giardi'naggio [dʒardi'naddʒo] *sm*
gardening

giardini'ere, -a [dʒardi'njere] *sm/f*
gardener

giar'dino [dʒar'dino] *sm* garden; **giardino
d'infanzia** nursery school; **giardino
pubblico** public gardens *pl*, (public) park;
giardino zoologico zoo

giavel'lotto [dʒavel'lɔtto] *sm* javelin

gigabyte [dʒiga'bait] *sm inv* gigabyte

gi'gante, -'essa [dʒi'gante] *sm/f* giant
▷ *ag* giant, gigantic; (*Comm*) giant-size

'giglio ['dʒiʎʎo] *sm* lily

gilè [dʒi'le] *sm inv* waistcoat

gin [dʒin] *sm inv* gin

gine'cologo, -a, -gi, -ghe [dʒine'kɔlogo]
sm/f gynaecologist

gi'nepro [dʒi'nepro] *sm* juniper

gi'nestra [dʒi'nɛstra] *sf* (*Bot*) broom

Gi'nevra [dʒi'nevra] *sf* Geneva

gin'nastica *sf* gymnastics *sg*; (*esercizio fisico*) keep-fit exercises; (*Ins*) physical education

gi'nocchio [dʒi'nɔkkjo] (*pl(m)* **gi'nocchi**, *o pl(f)* **gi'nocchia**) *sm* knee; **stare in ~** to kneel, be on one's knees; **mettersi in ~** to kneel (down)

gio'care [dʒo'kare] *vt* to play; (*scommettere*) to stake, wager, bet; (*ingannare*) to take in ▷ *vi* to play; (*a roulette ecc*) to gamble; (*fig*) to play a part, be important; **~ a** (*gioco, sport*) to play; (*cavalli*) to bet on; **giocarsi la carriera** to put one's career at risk; **gioca'tore, -'trice** *sm/f* player; gambler

gio'cattolo [dʒo'kattolo] *sm* toy

giocherò *ecc* [dʒoke'rɔ] *vb vedi* **giocare**

gi'oco, -chi ['dʒɔko] *sm* game; (*divertimento, Tecn*) play; (*al casinò*) gambling; (*Carte*) hand; (*insieme di pezzi ecc necessari per un gioco*) set; **per ~** for fun; **fare il doppio ~ con qn** to double-cross sb; **i Giochi Olimpici** the Olympic Games; **gioco d'azzardo** game of chance; **gioco degli scacchi** chess set

giocoli'ere [dʒoko'ljɛre] *sm* juggler

gi'oia ['dʒɔja] *sf* joy, delight; (*pietra preziosa*) jewel, precious stone

gioielle'ria [dʒojelle'ria] *sf* jeweller's craft; jeweller's (shop)

gioielli'ere, -a [dʒojel'ljɛre] *sm/f* jeweller

gioi'ello [dʒo'jello] *sm* jewel, piece of jewellery; **i miei gioielli** my jewels *o* jewellery; **gioielli** *smpl* (*anelli, collane ecc*) jewellery; **i gioielli della Corona** the crown jewels

Gior'dania [dʒor'danja] *sf* **la ~** Jordan

giorna'laio, -a [dʒorna'lajo] *sm/f* newsagent (BRIT), newsdealer (US)

gior'nale [dʒor'nale] *sm* (news) paper; (*diario*) journal, diary; (*Comm*) journal; **giornale di bordo** log; **giornale radio** radio news *sg*

giornali'ero, -a [dʒorna'ljɛro] *ag* daily; (*che varia: umore*) changeable ▷ *sm* day labourer

giorna'lismo [dʒorna'lizmo] *sm* journalism

giorna'lista, -i, -e [dʒorna'lista] *sm/f* journalist

gior'nata [dʒor'nata] *sf* day; **giornata lavorativa** working day

gi'orno ['dʒorno] *sm* day; (*opposto alla notte*) day, daytime; (*anche*: **luce del ~**) daylight; **al ~** per day; **di ~** by day; **al ~ d'oggi** nowadays

gi'ostra ['dʒɔstra] *sf* (*per bimbi*) merry-go-round; (*torneo storico*) joust

gi'ovane ['dʒovane] *ag* young; (*aspetto*) youthful ▷ *sm/f* youth/girl, young man/woman; **i giovani** young people

gio'vare [dʒo'vare] *vi* **~ a** (*essere utile*) to be useful to; (*far bene*) to be good for ▷ *vb impers* (*essere bene, utile*) to be useful; **giovarsi di qc** to make use of sth

giovedì [dʒove'di] *sm inv* Thursday; **di** *o* **il ~** on Thursdays

gioven'tù [dʒoven'tu] *sf* (*periodo*) youth; (*i giovani*) young people *pl*, youth

G.I.P. [dʒip] *sigla m inv* (= *Giudice per le Indagini Preliminari*) judge for preliminary enquiries

gira'dischi [dʒira'diski] *sm inv* record player

gi'raffa [dʒi'raffa] *sf* giraffe

gi'rare [dʒi'rare] *vt* (*far ruotare*) to turn; (*percorrere, visitare*) to go round; (*Cinema*) to shoot; to make; (*Comm*) to endorse ▷ *vi* to turn; (*più veloce*) to spin; (*andare in giro*) to wander, go around; **girarsi** *vpr* to turn; **~ attorno a** to go round; to revolve round; **al prossimo incrocio giri a destra/sinistra** turn right/left at the next junction; **far ~ la testa a qn** to make sb dizzy; (*fig*) to turn sb's head

girar'rosto [dʒirar'rɔsto] *sm* (*Cuc*) spit

gira'sole [dʒira'sole] *sm* sunflower

gi'revole [dʒi'revole] *ag* revolving, turning

gi'rino [dʒi'rino] *sm* tadpole

'giro ['dʒiro] *sm* (*circuito, cerchio*) circle; (*di chiave, manovella*) turn; (*viaggio*) tour, excursion; (*passeggiata*) stroll, walk; (*in macchina*) drive; (*in bicicletta*) ride; (*Sport: della pista*) lap; (*di denaro*) circulation; (*Carte*) hand; (*Tecn*) revolution; **prendere in ~ qn** (*fig*) to pull sb's leg; **fare un ~** to go for a walk (o a drive o a ride); **andare in ~** to go about, walk around; **a stretto ~ di posta** by return of post; **nel ~ di un mese** in a month's time; **essere nel ~** (*fig*) to belong to a circle (of friends); **giro d'affari** (*Comm*) turnover; **giro di parole** circumlocution; **giro di prova** (*Aut*) test drive; **giro turistico** sightseeing tour; **giro'collo** *sm* **a girocollo** crew-neck *cpd*

gironzo'lare [dʒirondzo'lare] *vi* to stroll about

'gita ['dʒita] *sf* excursion, trip; **fare una ~** to go for a trip, go on an outing

gi'tano, -a [dʒi'tano] *sm/f* gipsy

giù [dʒu] *av* down; (*dabbasso*) downstairs; **in ~** downwards, down; **~ di lì** (*pressappoco*) thereabouts; **bambini dai 6 anni in ~** children aged 6 and under; **~ per, cadere ~ per le scale** to fall down the stairs; **essere ~** (*fig: di salute*) to be run down; (: *di spirito*) to be depressed

giub'botto [dʒub'bɔtto] *sm* jerkin; **giubbotto antiproiettile** bulletproof vest; **giubbotto salvagente** life jacket

giudi'care [dʒudi'kare] *vt* to judge; (*accusato*) to try; (*lite*) to arbitrate in; **~ qn/qc bello** to consider sb/sth (to be) beautiful

gi'udice ['dʒuditʃe] *sm* judge; **giudice conciliatore** justice of the peace; **giudice istruttore** examining (BRIT) o committing (US) magistrate; **giudice popolare** member of a jury

giu'dizio [dʒu'dittsjo] *sm* judgment; (*opinione*) opinion; (*Dir*) judgment, sentence; (: *processo*) trial; (: *verdetto*) verdict; **aver ~** to be wise o prudent; **citare in ~** to summons

gi'ugno ['dʒuɲɲo] *sm* June

gi'ungere ['dʒundʒere] *vi* to arrive ▷ *vt* (*mani ecc*) to join; **~ a** to arrive at, reach

gi'ungla ['dʒungla] *sf* jungle

gi'unsi *ecc* ['dʒunsi] *vb vedi* **giungere**

giura'mento [dʒura'mento] *sm* oath; **giuramento falso** perjury

giu'rare [dʒu'rare] *vt* to swear ▷ *vi* to swear, take an oath

giu'ria [dʒu'ria] *sf* jury

giu'ridico, -a, -ci, -che [dʒu'ridiko] *ag* legal

giustifi'care [dʒustifi'kare] *vt* to justify; **giustificazi'one** *sf* justification; (*Ins*) (note of) excuse

gius'tizia [dʒus'tittsja] *sf* justice; **giustizi'are** *vt* to execute, put to death

gi'usto, -a ['dʒusto] *ag* (*equo*) fair, just; (*vero*) true, correct; (*adatto*) right, suitable; (*preciso*) exact, correct ▷ *av* (*esattamente*) exactly, precisely; (*per l'appunto, appena*) just; **arrivare ~** to arrive just in time; **ho ~ bisogno di te** you're just the person I need

glaci'ale [gla'tʃale] *ag* glacial

gli [ʎi] (*davV, s impura, gn, pn, ps, x, z*) *det mpl* the ▷ *pron* (*a lui*) to him; (*a esso*) to it; (*in coppia con lo, la, li, le, ne: a lui, a lei, a loro ecc*): **~ele do** I'm giving them to him (o her o them); *vedi anche* **il**

glo'bale *ag* overall

'globo *sm* globe

'globulo *sm* (*Anat*): **globulo rosso/bianco** red/white corpuscle

'gloria *sf* glory

'gnocchi ['ɲɔkki] *smpl* (*Cuc*) small dumplings made of semolina pasta or potato

'gobba *sf* (*Anat*) hump; (*protuberanza*) bump

'gobbo, -a *ag* hunchbacked; (*ricurvo*) round-shouldered ▷ *sm/f* hunchback

'goccia, -ce ['gottʃa] *sf* drop; **goccio'lare**

vi, vt to drip

go'dere *vi* (*compiacersi*): **~ (di)** to be delighted (at), rejoice (at); (*trarre vantaggio*): **~ di** benefit from ▷ *vt* to enjoy; **godersi la vita** to enjoy life; **godersela** to have a good time, enjoy o.s.

godrò *ecc vb vedi* **godere**

'goffo, -a *ag* clumsy, awkward

'gola *sf* (*Anat*) throat; (*golosità*) gluttony, greed; (*di camino*) flue; (*di monte*) gorge; **fare ~** (*anche fig*) to tempt

golf *sm inv* (*Sport*) golf; (*maglia*) cardigan

'golfo *sm* gulf

go'loso, -a *ag* greedy

gomi'tata *sf* **dare una ~ a qn** to elbow sb; **farsi avanti a (forza o furia di) gomitate** to elbow one's way through; **fare a gomitate per qc** to fight to get sth

'gomito *sm* elbow; (*di strada ecc*) sharp bend

go'mitolo *sm* ball

'gomma *sf* rubber; (*per cancellare*) rubber, eraser; (*di veicolo*) tyre (BRIT), tire (US); **gomma americana** o **da masticare** chewing gum; **gomma a terra** flat tyre (BRIT) o tire (US); **ho una ~ a terra** I've got a flat tyre; **gom'mone** *sm* rubber dinghy

gonfi'are *vt* (*pallone*) to blow up, inflate; (*dilatare, ingrossare*) to swell; (*fig: notizia*) to exaggerate; **gonfiarsi** *vpr* to swell; (*fiume*) to rise; **'gonfio, -a** *ag* swollen; (*stomaco*) bloated; (*vela*) full; **gonfi'ore** *sm* swelling

'gonna *sf* skirt; **gonna pantalone** culottes *pl*

'gorgo, -ghi *sm* whirlpool

gorgogli'are [gorgoʎ'ʎare] *vi* to gurgle

go'rilla *sm inv* gorilla; (*guardia del corpo*) bodyguard

'gotico, -a, ci, che *ag, sm* Gothic

'gotta *sf* gout

gover'nare *vt* (*stato*) to govern, rule; (*pilotare, guidare*) to steer; (*bestiame*) to tend, look after

go'verno *sm* government

GPL *sigla m* (= *Gas di Petrolio Liquefatto*) LPG

GPS *sigla m* (= *Global Positioning System*) GPS

graci'dare [gratʃi'dare] *vi* to croak

'gracile ['gratʃile] *ag* frail, delicate

gradazi'one [gradat'tsjone] *sf* (*sfumatura*) gradation; **gradazione alcolica** alcoholic content, strength

gra'devole *ag* pleasant, agreeable

gradi'nata *sf* flight of steps; (*in teatro, stadio*) tiers *pl*

gra'dino *sm* step; (*Alpinismo*) foothold

gra'dire *vt* (*accettare con piacere*) to accept; (*desiderare*) to wish, like; **gradisce una tazza di tè?** would you like a cup of tea?

'grado *sm* (*Mat, Fisica ecc*) degree; (*stadio*)

degree, level; (Mil, sociale) rank; **essere in ~ di fare** to be in a position to do

gradu'ale ag gradual

graf'fetta sf paper clip

graffi'are vt to scratch; **graffiarsi** vpr to get scratched; (con unghie) to scratch o.s.

'graffio sm scratch

gra'fia sf spelling; (scrittura) handwriting

'grafico, -a, -ci, -che ag graphic ▷ sm graph; (persona) graphic designer

gram'matica, -che sf grammar

'grammo sm gram(me)

'grana sf (granello, di minerali, corpi spezzati) grain; (fam: seccatura) trouble; (: soldi) cash ▷ sm inv Parmesan (cheese)

gra'naio sm granary, barn

gra'nata sf (proiettile) grenade

Gran Bre'tagna [-bre'taɲɲa] sf la ~ Great Britain

'granchio ['grankjo] sm crab; (fig) blunder; **prendere un ~** (fig) to blunder

'grande (qualche volta **gran** + C, **grand'** + V) ag (grosso, largo, vasto) big, large; (alto) tall; (lungo) long; (in sensi astratti) great ▷ sm/f (persona adulta) adult, grown-up; (chi ha ingegno e potenza) great man/woman; **fare le cose in ~** to do things in style; **una gran bella donna** a very beautiful woman; **non è una gran cosa** o **un gran che** it's nothing special; **non ne so gran che** I don't know very much about it

gran'dezza [gran'dettsa] sf (dimensione) size; magnitude; (fig) greatness; **in ~ naturale** life-size(d)

grandi'nare vb impers to hail

'grandine sf hail

gra'nello sm (di cereali, uva) seed; (di frutta) pip; (di sabbia, sale ecc) grain

gra'nito sm granite

'grano sm (in quasi tutti i sensi) grain; (frumento) wheat; (di rosario, collana) bead; **grano di pepe** peppercorn

gran'turco sm maize

'grappa sf rough, strong brandy

'grappolo sm bunch, cluster

gras'setto sm (Tip) bold (type)

'grasso, -a ag fat; (cibo) fatty; (pelle) greasy; (terreno) rich; (fig: guadagno, annata) plentiful ▷ sm (di persona, animale) fat; (sostanza che unge) grease

'grata sf grating

gra'ticola sf grill

'gratis av free, for nothing

grati'tudine sf gratitude

'grato, -a ag grateful; (gradito) pleasant, agreeable

gratta'capo sm worry, headache

grattaci'elo [gratta'tʃɛlo] sm skyscraper

gratta e vinci ['gratta e 'vintʃi] sm inv (biglietto) scratchcard; (lotteria) scratchcard lottery

grat'tare vt (pelle) to scratch; (raschiare) to scrape; (pane, formaggio, carote) to grate; (fam: rubare) to pinch ▷ vi (stridere) to grate; (Aut) to grind; **grattarsi** vpr to scratch o.s.; **grattarsi la pancia** (fig) to twiddle one's thumbs

grat'tugia, -gie [grat'tudʒa] sf grater; **grattugi'are** vt to grate; **pane grattugiato** breadcrumbs pl

gra'tuito, -a ag free; (fig) gratuitous

'grave ag (danno, pericolo, peccato ecc) grave, serious; (responsabilità) heavy, grave; (contegno) grave, solemn; (voce, suono) deep, low-pitched; (Ling): **accento ~** grave accent; **un malato ~** a person who is seriously ill

grave'mente av (ammalato, ferito) seriously

gravi'danza [gravi'dantsa] sf pregnancy

gravità sf seriousness; (anche Fisica) gravity

gra'voso, -a ag heavy, onerous

'grazia ['grattsja] sf grace; (favore) favour; (Dir) pardon

'grazie ['grattsje] escl thank you!; **~ mille!** o **tante!** o **infinite!** thank you very much!; **~ a** thanks to

grazi'oso, -a [grat'tsjoso] ag charming, delightful; (gentile) gracious

'Grecia ['grɛtʃa] sf la ~ Greece; **'greco, -a, -ci, -che** ag, sm/f, sm Greek

'gregge ['greddʒe] (pl(f) **-i**) sm flock

grembi'ule sm apron; (sopravveste) overall

'grembo sm lap; (ventre della madre) womb

'grezzo, -a ['greddzo] ag raw, unrefined; (diamante) rough, uncut; (tessuto) unbleached

gri'dare vi (per chiamare) to shout, cry (out); (strillare) to scream, yell ▷ vt to shout (out), yell (out); **~ aiuto** to cry o shout for help

'grido (pl(m) **-i**, o pl(f) **-a**) sm shout, cry; scream, yell; (di animale) cry; **di ~** famous

'grigio, -a, -gi, -gie ['gridʒo] ag, sm grey

'griglia ['griʎʎa] sf (per arrostire) grill; (Elettr) grid; (inferriata) grating; **alla ~** (Cuc) grilled

gril'letto sm trigger

'grillo sm (Zool) cricket; (fig) whim

'grinta sf grim expression; (Sport) fighting spirit

gris'sino sm bread-stick

Groen'landia sf la ~ Greenland

gron'daia sf gutter

gron'dare vi to pour; (essere bagnato): **~ di** to be dripping with ▷ vt to drip with

'groppa sf (di animale) back, rump; (fam:

dell'uomo) back, shoulders pl

gros'sezza [gros'settsa] *sf* size; thickness

gros'sista, -i, -e *sm/f* (*Comm*) wholesaler

'grosso, -a *ag* big, large; (*di spessore*) thick; (*grossolano: anche fig*) coarse; (*grave, insopportabile*) serious, great; (*tempo, mare*) rough ▷ *sm* **il ~ di** the bulk of; **un pezzo ~** (*fig*) a VIP, a bigwig; **farla grossa** to do something very stupid; **dirle grosse** to tell tall stories; **sbagliarsi di ~** to be completely wrong

'grotta *sf* cave; grotto

grot'tesco, -a, -schi, -sche *ag* grotesque

gro'viglio [gro'viʎʎo] *sm* tangle; (*fig*) muddle

gru *sf inv* crane

'gruccia, -ce ['gruttʃa] *sf* (*per camminare*) crutch; (*per abiti*) coat-hanger

'grumo *sm* (*di sangue*) clot; (*di farina ecc*) lump

'gruppo *sm* group; **gruppo sanguigno** blood group

GSM *sigla m* (= *Global System for Mobile Communication*) GSM

guada'gnare [gwada'ɲɲare] *vt* (*ottenere*) to gain; (*soldi, stipendio*) to earn; (*vincere*) to win; (*raggiungere*) to reach

gua'dagno [gwa'daɲɲo] *sm* earnings pl; (*Comm*) profit; (*vantaggio, utile*) advantage, gain; **guadagno lordo/netto** gross/net earnings pl

gu'ado *sm* ford; **passare a ~** to ford

gu'ai *escl* **~ a te (***o* **lui** *ecc***)!** woe betide you (*o* him *ecc*)!

gu'aio *sm* trouble, mishap; (*inconveniente*) trouble, snag

gua'ire *vi* to whine, yelp

gu'ancia, -ce ['gwantʃa] *sf* cheek

guanci'ale [gwan'tʃale] *sm* pillow

gu'anto *sm* glove

guarda'linee *sm inv* (*Sport*) linesman

guar'dare *vt* (*con lo sguardo: osservare*) to look at; (*film, televisione*) to watch; (*custodire*) to look after, take care of ▷ *vi* to look; (*badare*): **~ a** to pay attention to; (*luoghi: esser orientato*): **~ a** to face; **guardarsi** *vpr* to look at o.s.; **guardarsi da** (*astenersi*) to refrain from; (*stare in guardia*) to beware of; **guardarsi dal fare** to take care not to do; **guarda di non sbagliare** try not to make a mistake; **~ a vista qn** to keep a close watch on sb

guarda'roba *sm inv* wardrobe; (*locale*) cloakroom

gu'ardia *sf* (*individuo, corpo*) guard; (*sorveglianza*) watch; **fare la ~ a qc/qn** to guard sth/sb; **stare in ~** (*fig*) to be on one's guard; **di ~** (*medico*) on call; **guardia carceraria** (*prison*) warder; **guardia del**

corpo bodyguard; **Guardia di finanza** (*corpo*) customs pl; (*persona*) customs officer; **guardia medica** emergency doctor service

○ **GUARDIA DI FINANZA**
○
○ The **Guardia di Finanza** is a military
○ body which deals with infringements
○ of the laws governing income tax and
○ monopolies. It reports to the Ministers
○ of Finance, Justice or Agriculture,
○ depending on the function it is
○ performing.

guardi'ano, -a *sm/f* (*di carcere*) warder; (*di villa ecc*) caretaker; (*di museo*) custodian; (*di zoo*) keeper; **guardiano notturno** night watchman

guarigi'one [gwari'dʒone] *sf* recovery

gua'rire *vt* (*persona, malattia*) to cure; (*ferita*) to heal ▷ *vi* to recover, be cured; to heal (up)

guar'nire *vt* (*ornare: abiti*) to trim; (*Cuc*) to garnish

guasta'feste *sm/f inv* spoilsport

guastarsi *vpr* (*cibo*) to go bad; (*meccanismo*) to break down; (*tempo*) to change for the worse

gu'asto, -a *ag* (*non funzionante*) broken; (: *telefono ecc*) out of order; (*andato a male*) bad, rotten; (: *dente*) decayed, bad; (*fig: corrotto*) depraved ▷ *sm* breakdown; (*avaria*) failure; **guasto al motore** engine failure

gu'erra *sf* war; (*tecnica: atomica, chimica ecc*) warfare; **fare la ~ (a)** to wage war (against); **guerra mondiale** world war; **guerra preventiva** preventive war

'gufo *sm* owl

gu'ida *sf* (*libro*) guidebook; (*persona*) guide; (*comando, direzione*) guidance, direction; (*Aut*) driving; (*tappeto: di tenda, cassetto*) runner; **avete una ~ in italiano?** do you have a guidebook in Italian?; **c'è una ~ che parla italiano?** is there an Italian-speaking guide?; **guida a destra/a sinistra** (*Aut*) right-/left-hand drive; **guida telefonica** telephone directory; **guida turistica** tourist guide

gui'dare *vt* to guide; (*squadra, rivolta*) to lead; (*auto*) to drive; (*aereo, nave*) to pilot; **sai ~?** can you drive?; **guida'tore, -trice** *sm/f* (*conducente*) driver

guin'zaglio [gwin'tsaʎʎo] *sm* leash, lead

'guscio ['guʃʃo] *sm* shell

gus'tare *vt* (*cibi*) to taste; (: *assaporare con piacere*) to enjoy, savour; (*fig*) to enjoy, appreciate ▷ *vi*: **~ a** to please; **non mi**

gusta affatto I don't like it at all
'gusto *sm* taste; (*sapore*) flavour; (*godimento*) enjoyment; **che gusti avete?** which flavours do you have?; **al ~ di fragola** strawberry-flavoured; **mangiare di ~** to eat heartily; **prenderci ~: ci ha preso ~** he's acquired a taste for it, he's got to like it; **gus'toso, -a** *ag* tasty; (*fig*) agreeable

H, h ['akka] *sf o m inv* (*lettera*) H, h ▷ *abbr* (= *ora*) hr; (= *etto, altezza*) h; **H come hotel** ≈ H for Harry (*BRIT*), H for How (*US*)
ha, 'hai [a, ai] *vb vedi* **avere**
ha'cker [hæ'kəʳ] *sm inv* hacker
hall [hɔl] *sf inv* hall, foyer
hamburger [am'burger] *sm inv* (*carne*) hamburger; (*panino*) burger
'handicap ['handikap] *sm inv* handicap; **handicap'pato, -a** *ag* handicapped ▷ *sm/f* handicapped person, disabled person
'hanno ['anno] *vb vedi* **avere**
hard discount [ardi'kaunt] *sm inv* discount supermarket
hard disk [ar'disk] *sm inv* hard disk
hardware ['ardwer] *sm inv* hardware
hascisch [aʃʃiʃ] *sm* hashish
Hawaii [a'vai] *sfpl* **le ~** Hawaii *sg*
help [ɛlp] *sm inv* (*Inform*) help
'herpes ['ɛrpes] *sm* (*Med*) herpes *sg*; **herpes zoster** shingles *sg*
'hi-fi ['haifai] *sm inv, ag inv* hi-fi
ho [ɔ] *vb vedi* **avere**
'hobby ['hɔbi] *sm inv* hobby
'hockey ['hɔki] *sm* hockey; **hockey su ghiaccio** ice hockey
home page ['hoʊm'pɛidʒ] *sf inv* home page
Hong Kong ['ɔ̃kɔ̃g] *sf* Hong Kong
'hostess ['houstis] *sf inv* air hostess (*BRIT*)

o stewardess
hot dog ['hɔtdɔg] *sm inv* hot dog
ho'tel *sm inv* hotel
humour ['hju:mə] *sm inv* (sense of) humour
'humus *sm* humus
husky ['aski] *sm inv* (cane) husky *m inv*

i *det mpl* the
IC *abbr* (= *Intercity*) Intercity
ICI ['itʃi] *sigla f* (= *Imposta Comunale sugli Immobili*) ≈ Council Tax
i'cona *sf* (*Rel, Inform, fig*) icon
i'dea *sf* idea; (*opinione*) opinion, view; (*ideale*) ideal; **dare l'~ di** to seem, look like; **neanche** *o* **neppure per ~!** certainly not!; **idea fissa** obsession
ide'ale *ag, sm* ideal
ide'are *vt* (*immaginare*) to think up, conceive; (*progettare*) to plan
i'dentico, -a, -ci, -che *ag* identical
identifi'care *vt* to identify; **identificarsi** *vpr* **identificarsi (con)** to identify o.s. (with)
identità *sf inv* identity
ideolo'gia, -'gie [ideolo'dʒia] *sf* ideology
idio'matico, -a, -ci, -che *ag* idiomatic; **frase idiomatica** idiom
idi'ota, -i, -e *ag* idiotic ▷ *sm/f* idiot
'idolo *sm* idol
idoneità *sf* suitability
i'doneo, -a *ag* ~ **a** suitable for, fit for; (*Mil*) fit for; (*qualificato*) qualified for
i'drante *sm* hydrant
idra'tante *ag* moisturizing ▷ *sm* moisturizer
i'draulico, -a, -ci, -che *ag* hydraulic ▷ *sm* plumber

idroe'lettrico, -a, -ci, -che *ag* hydroelectric

i'drofilo, -a *ag vedi* cotone

i'drogeno [i'drɔdʒeno] *sm* hydrogen

idrovo'lante *sm* seaplane

i'ena *sf* hyena

i'eri *av, sm* yesterday; **il giornale di ~** yesterday's paper; **~ l'altro** the day before yesterday; **~ sera** yesterday evening

igi'ene [i'dʒɛne] *sf* hygiene; **igiene pubblica** public health; **igi'enico, -a, -ci, -he** *ag* hygienic; *(salubre)* healthy

i'gnaro, -a [iɲ'ɲaro] *ag* **~ di** unaware of, ignorant of

i'gnobile [iɲ'ɲɔbile] *ag* despicable, vile

igno'rante [iɲɲo'rante] *ag* ignorant

igno'rare [iɲɲo'rare] *vt (non sapere, conoscere)* to be ignorant o unaware of, not to know; *(fingere di non vedere, sentire)* to ignore

i'gnoto, -a [iɲ'ɲɔto] *ag* unknown

 PAROLA CHIAVE

il *(pl(m)* i; *diventa* lo *(pl* gli) *davanti a s impura, gn, pn, ps, x, z;* f la *(pl* le)) *det m* 1 the; **il libro/lo studente/l'acqua** the book/the student/the water; **gli scolari** the pupils
2 *(astrazione)*: **il coraggio/l'amore/la giovinezza** courage/love/youth
3 *(tempo)*: **il mattino/la sera** in the morning/evening; **il venerdì** *ecc (abitualmente)* on Fridays *ecc; (quel giorno)* on (the) Friday *ecc;* **la settimana prossima** next week
4 *(distributivo)* a, an; **2 euro il chilo/paio** 2 euros a o per kilo/pair
5 *(partitivo)* some, any; **hai messo lo zucchero?** have you added sugar?; **hai comprato il latte?** did you buy (some o any) milk?
6 *(possesso)*: **aprire gli occhi** to open one's eyes; **rompersi la gamba** to break one's leg; **avere i capelli neri/il naso rosso** to have dark hair/a red nose
7 *(con nomi propri)*: **il Petrarca** Petrarch; **il Presidente Bush** President Bush; **dov'è la Francesca?** where's Francesca?
8 *(con nomi geografici)*: **il Tevere** the Tiber; **l'Italia** Italy; **il Regno Unito** the United Kingdom; **l'Everest** Everest

ille'gale *ag* illegal

illeg'gibile [illed'dʒibile] *ag* illegible

ille'gittimo, -a [ille'dʒittimo] *ag* illegitimate

il'leso, -a *ag* unhurt, unharmed

illimi'tato, -a *ag* boundless; unlimited

ill.mo *abbr* = illustrissimo

il'ludere *vt* to deceive, delude; **illudersi** *vpr* to deceive o.s., delude o.s.

illumi'nare *vt* to light up, illuminate; *(fig)* to enlighten; **illuminarsi** *vpr* to light up; **~ a giorno** to floodlight; **illuminazi'one** *sf* lighting; illumination; floodlighting; *(fig)* flash of inspiration

il'lusi *ecc vb vedi* illudere

illusi'one *sf* illusion; **farsi delle illusioni** to delude o.s.; **illusione ottica** optical illusion

il'luso, -a *pp di* illudere

illus'trare *vt* to illustrate; **illustrazi'one** *sf* illustration

il'lustre *ag* eminent, renowned; **illus'trissimo, -a** *ag (negli indirizzi)* very revered

imbal'laggio [imbal'laddʒo] *sm* packing *no pl*

imbal'lare *vt* to pack; *(Aut)* to race

imbalsa'mare *vt* to embalm

imbambo'lato, -a *ag (sguardo)* vacant, blank

imbaraz'zante [imbarat'tsante] *ag* embarrassing, awkward

imbaraz'zare [imbarat'tsare] *vt (mettere a disagio)* to embarrass; *(ostacolare movimenti)* to hamper

imbaraz'zato, -a [imbarat'tsato] *ag* embarrassed; **avere lo stomaco ~** to have an upset stomach

imba'razzo [imba'rattso] *sm (disagio)* embarrassment; *(perplessità)* puzzlement, bewilderment; **imbarazzo di stomaco** indigestion

imbar'care *vt (passeggeri)* to embark; *(merci)* to load; **imbarcarsi** *vpr* **imbarcarsi su** to board; **imbarcarsi per l'America** to sail for America; **imbarcarsi in** *(fig: affare ecc)* to embark on

imbarcazi'one [imbarkat'tsjone] *sf (small)* boat, *(small)* craft *inv;* **imbarcazione di salvataggio** lifeboat

im'barco, -chi *sm* embarkation; loading; boarding; *(banchina)* landing stage

imbas'tire *vt (cucire)* to tack; *(fig: abbozzare)* to sketch, outline

im'battersi *vpr* **~ in** *(incontrare)* to bump o run into

imbat'tibile *ag* unbeatable, invincible

imbavagli'are [imbavaʎ'ʎare] *vt* to gag

imbe'cille [imbe'tʃille] *ag* idiotic ▷ *sm/f* idiot; *(Med)* imbecile

imbian'care *vt* to whiten; *(muro)* to whitewash ▷ *vi* to become o turn white

imbian'chino [imbjan'kino] *sm (house)* painter, painter and decorator

imboc'care *vt (bambino)* to feed; *(entrare: strada)* to enter, turn into

imbocca'tura *sf* mouth; (*di strada, porto*) entrance; (*Mus, del morso*) mouthpiece

imbos'cata *sf* ambush

imbottigli'are [imbotti(λ)'ʎare] *vt* to bottle; (*Naut*) to blockade; (*Mil*) to hem in; **imbottigliarsi** *vpr* to be stuck in a traffic jam

imbot'tire *vt* to stuff; (*giacca*) to pad; **imbottirsi** *vpr* **imbottirsi di** (*rimpinzarsi*) to stuff o.s. with; **imbot'tito, -a** *ag* stuffed; (*giacca*) padded; **panino imbottito** filled roll

imbra'nato, -a *ag* clumsy, awkward ▷ *sm/f* clumsy person

imbrogli'are [imbroʎ'ʎare] *vt* to mix up; (*fig: raggirare*) to deceive, cheat; (: *confondere*) to confuse, mix up; **imbrogli'one, -a** *sm/f* cheat, swindler

imbronci'ato, -a *ag* sulky

imbu'care *vt* to post; **dove posso ~ queste cartoline?** where can I post these cards?

imbur'rare *vt* to butter

im'buto *sm* funnel

imi'tare *vt* to imitate; (*riprodurre*) to copy; (*assomigliare*) to look like

immagazzi'nare [immagaddzi'nare] *vt* to store

immagi'nare [immadʒi'nare] *vt* to imagine; (*supporre*) to suppose; (*inventare*) to invent; **s'immagini!** don't mention it!, not at all!; **immaginazi'one** *sf* imagination; (*cosa immaginata*) fancy

im'magine [im'madʒine] *sf* image; (*rappresentazione grafica, mentale*) picture

imman'cabile *ag* certain; unfailing

im'mane *ag* (*smisurato*) enormous; (*spaventoso*) terrible

immangi'abile [imman'dʒabile] *ag* inedible

immatrico'lare *vt* to register; **immatricolarsi** *vpr* (*Ins*) to matriculate, enrol

imma'turo, -a *ag* (*frutto*) unripe; (*persona*) immature; (*prematuro*) premature

immedesi'marsi *vpr* ~ **in** to identify with

immediata'mente *av* immediately, at once

immedi'ato, -a *ag* immediate

im'menso, -a *ag* immense

im'mergere [im'merdʒere] *vt* to immerse, plunge; **immergersi** *vpr* to plunge; (*sommergibile*) to dive, submerge; (*dedicarsi a*): **immergersi in** to immerse o.s. in

immeri'tato, -a *ag* undeserved

immersi'one *sf* immersion; (*di sommergibile*) submersion, dive; (*di palombaro*) dive

im'mettere *vt* ~ **(in)** to introduce (into); ~ **dati in un computer** to enter data on a computer

immi'grato, -a *sm/f* immigrant

immi'nente *ag* imminent

immischiarsi *vpr* ~ **in** to interfere o meddle in

im'mobile *ag* motionless, still; **immobili'are** *ag* (*Dir*) property *cpd*

immon'dizia [immon'dittsja] *sf* dirt, filth; (*spesso al pl: spazzatura, rifiuti*) rubbish *no pl*, refuse *no pl*

immo'rale *ag* immoral

immor'tale *ag* immortal

im'mune *ag* (*esente*) exempt; (*Med, Dir*) immune

immu'tabile *ag* immutable; unchanging

impacchet'tare [impakket'tare] *vt* to pack up

impacci'ato, -a *ag* awkward, clumsy; (*imbarazzato*) embarrassed

im'pacco, -chi *sm* (*Med*) compress

impadro'nirsi *vpr* ~ **di** to seize, take possession of; (*fig: apprendere a fondo*) to master

impa'gabile *ag* priceless

impa'lato, -a *ag* (*fig*) stiff as a board

impalca'tura *sf* scaffolding

impalli'dire *vi* to turn pale; (*fig*) to fade

impa'nato, -a *ag* (*Cuc*) coated in breadcrumbs

impanta'narsi *vpr* to sink (in the mud); (*fig*) to get bogged down

impappi'narsi *vpr* to stammer, falter

impa'rare *vt* to learn

impar'tire *vt* to bestow, give

imparzi'ale [impar'tsjale] *ag* impartial, unbiased

impas'sibile *ag* impassive

impas'tare *vt* (*pasta*) to knead

impastic'carsi *vpr* to pop pills

im'pasto *sm* (*l'impastare: di pane*) kneading; (: *di cemento*) mixing; (*pasta*) dough; (*anche fig*) mixture

im'patto *sm* impact

impau'rire *vt* to scare, frighten ▷ *vi* (*anche*: **impaurirsi**) to become scared o frightened

impazi'ente [impat'tsjɛnte] *ag* impatient

impaz'zata [impat'tsata] *sf* **all'~** (*precipitosamente*) at breakneck speed

impaz'zire [impat'tsire] *vi* to go mad; ~ **per qn/qc** to be crazy about sb/sth

impec'cabile *ag* impeccable

impedi'mento *sm* obstacle, hindrance

impe'dire *vt* (*vietare*): ~ **a qn di fare** to prevent sb from doing; (*ostruire*) to obstruct; (*impacciare*) to hamper, hinder

impegnarsi *vpr* (*vincolarsi*): **~ a fare** to undertake to do; (*mettersi risolutamente*): **~ in qc** to devote o.s. to sth; **~ con qn** (*accordarsi*) to come to an agreement with sb

impegna'tivo, -a *ag* binding; (*lavoro*) demanding, exacting

impe'gnato, -a *ag* (*occupato*) busy; (*fig: romanzo, autore*) committed, engagé

im'pegno [im'peɲɲo] *sm* (*obbligo*) obligation; (*promessa*) promise, pledge; (*zelo*) diligence, zeal; (*compito, d'autore*) commitment

impel'lente *ag* pressing, urgent

impen'narsi *vpr* (*cavallo*) to rear up; (*Aer*) to nose up; (*fig*) to bridle

impensie'rire *vt* to worry; **impensierirsi** *vpr* to worry

impera'tivo, -a *ag, sm* imperative

impera'tore, -'trice *sm/f* emperor/ empress

imperdo'nabile *ag* unforgivable, unpardonable

imper'fetto, -a *ag* imperfect ▷ *sm* (*Ling*) imperfect (tense)

imperi'ale *ag* imperial

imperi'oso, -a *ag* (*persona*) imperious; (*motivo, esigenza*) urgent, pressing

imperme'abile *ag* waterproof ▷ *sm* raincoat

im'pero *sm* empire; (*forza, autorità*) rule, control

imperso'nale *ag* impersonal

imperso'nare *vt* to personify; (*Teatro*) to play, act (the part of)

imperter'rito, -a *ag* fearless, undaunted; impassive

imperti'nente *ag* impertinent

'impeto *sm* (*moto, forza*) force, impetus; (*assalto*) onslaught; (*fig: impulso*) impulse; (*: slancio*) transport; **con ~** energetically; vehemently

impet'tito, -a *ag* stiff, erect

impetu'oso, -a *ag* (*vento*) strong, raging; (*persona*) impetuous

impi'anto *sm* (*installazione*) installation; (*apparecchiature*) plant; (*sistema*) system; **impianto elettrico** wiring; **impianto di risalita** (*Sci*) ski lift; **impianto di riscaldamento** heating system; **impianto sportivo** sports complex

impic'care *vt* to hang; **impiccarsi** *vpr* to hang o.s.

impicciarsi [impit'tʃarsi] *vpr* (*immischiarsi*): **~ (in)** to meddle (in); **impicciati degli affari tuoi!** mind your own business!

impicci'one, -a [impit'tʃone] *sm/f* busybody

impie'gare *vt* (*usare*) to use, employ; (*spendere: denaro, tempo*) to spend; (*investire*) to invest; **impie'gato, -a** *sm/f* employee

impi'ego, -ghi *sm* (*uso*) use; (*occupazione*) employment; (*posto di lavoro*) (regular) job, post; (*Econ*) investment

impieto'sire *vt* to move to pity; **impietosirsi** *vpr* to be moved to pity

impigli'arsi *vpr* to get caught up o entangled

impi'grirsi *vpr* to grow lazy

impli'care *vt* to imply; (*coinvolgere*) to involve

im'plicito, -a [im'plitʃito] *ag* implicit

implo'rare *vt* to implore; (*pietà ecc*) to beg for

impolve'rarsi *vpr* to get dusty

im'pone *ecc vb vedi* **imporre**

impo'nente *ag* imposing, impressive

im'pongo *ecc vb vedi* **imporre**

impo'nibile *ag* taxable ▷ *sm* taxable income

impopo'lare *ag* unpopular

im'porre *vt* to impose; (*costringere*) to force, make; (*far valere*) to impose, enforce; **imporsi** *vpr* (*persona*) to assert o.s.; (*cosa: rendersi necessario*) to become necessary; (*aver successo: moda, attore*) to become popular; **~ a qn di fare** to force sb to do, make sb do

impor'tante *ag* important; **impor'tanza** *sf* importance; **dare importanza a qc** to attach importance to sth; **darsi importanza** to give o.s. airs

impor'tare *vt* (*introdurre dall'estero*) to import ▷ *vi* to matter, be important ▷ *vb impers* (*essere necessario*) to be necessary; (*interessare*) to matter; **non importa!** it doesn't matter!; **non me ne importa!** I don't care!

im'porto *sm* (*total*) amount

importu'nare *vt* to bother

im'posi *ecc vb vedi* **imporre**

imposizi'one [impozit'tsjone] *sf* imposition; order, command; (*onere, imposta*) tax

imposses'sarsi *vpr* **~ di** to seize, take possession of

impos'sibile *ag* impossible; **fare l'~** to do one's utmost, do all one can

im'posta *sf* (*di finestra*) shutter; (*tassa*) tax; **imposta sul reddito** income tax; **imposta sul valore aggiunto** value added tax (*BRIT*), sales tax (*US*)

impos'tare *vt* (*imbucare*) to post; (*preparare*) to plan, set out; (*avviare*) to begin, start off; (*voce*) to pitch

impostazi'one [impostat'tsjone] *sf*
(*di lettera*) posting (BRIT), mailing (US);
(*di problema, questione*) formulation,
statement; (*di lavoro*) organization,
planning; (*di attività*) setting up; (*Mus:
di voce*) pitch; **impostazioni** *sfpl* (*di
computer*) settings

impo'tente *ag* weak, powerless; (*anche
Med*) impotent

impratí'cabile *ag* (*strada*) impassable;
(*campo da gioco*) unplayable

impre'care *vi* to curse, swear; **~ contro** to
hurl abuse at

imprecazi'one [imprekat'tsjone] *sf*
abuse, curse

impre'gnare [impreɲ'ɲare] *vt* **~ (di)**
(*imbevere*) to soak o impregnate (with);
(*riempire*) to fill (with)

imprendi'tore *sm* (*industriale*)
entrepreneur; (*appaltatore*) contractor;
piccolo ~ small businessman

im'presa *sf* (*iniziativa*) enterprise; (*azione*)
exploit; (*azienda*) firm, concern

impressio'nante *ag* impressive;
upsetting

impressio'nare *vt* to impress; (*turbare*) to
upset; (*Fot*) to expose; **impressionarsi** *vpr*
to be easily upset

impressi'one *sf* impression; (*fig:
sensazione*) sensation, feeling; (*stampa*)
printing; **fare ~** (*colpire*) to impress;
(*turbare*) to frighten, upset; **fare
buona/cattiva ~ a** to make a good/bad
impression on

impreve'dibile *ag* unforeseeable;
(*persona*) unpredictable

impre'visto, -a *ag* unexpected,
unforeseen ▷ *sm* unforeseen event; **salvo
imprevisti** unless anything unexpected
happens

imprigio'nare [impridʒo'nare] *vt* to
imprison

impro'babile *ag* improbable, unlikely

im'pronta *sf* imprint, impression, sign;
(*di piede, mano*) print; (*fig*) mark, stamp;
impronta digitale fingerprint

improvvisa'mente *av* suddenly;
unexpectedly

improvvi'sare *vt* to improvise

improv'viso, -a *ag* (*imprevisto*)
unexpected; (*subitaneo*) sudden; **all'~**
unexpectedly; suddenly

impru'dente *ag* unwise, rash

impu'gnare [impuɲ'ɲare] *vt* to grasp,
grip; (*Dir*) to contest

impul'sivo, -a *ag* impulsive

im'pulso *sm* impulse

impun'tarsi *vpr* to stop dead, refuse to
budge; (*fig*) to be obstinate

impu'tato, -a *sm/f* (*Dir*) accused,
defendant

 PAROLA CHIAVE

in (*in + il* = **nel**, *in + lo* = **nello**, *in + l'* = **nell'**, *in
+ la* = **nella**, *in + i* = **nei**, *in + gli* = **negli**, *in + le*
= **nelle**) *prep* **1** (*stato in luogo*) in; **vivere in
Italia/città** to live in Italy/town; **essere in
casa/ufficio** to be at home/the office; **se
fossi in te** if I were you

2 (*moto a luogo*) to; (: *dentro*) into; **andare
in Germania/città** to go to Germany/
town; **andare in ufficio** to go to the office;
entrare in macchina/casa to get into the
car/go into the house

3 (*tempo*) in; **nel 1989** in 1989; **in giugno/
estate** in June/summer

4 (*modo, maniera*) in; **in silenzio** in silence;
in abito da sera in evening dress; **in
guerra** at war; **in vacanza** on holiday;
Maria Bianchi in Rossi Maria Rossi née
Bianchi

5 (*mezzo*) by; **viaggiare in autobus/treno**
to travel by bus/train

6 (*materia*) made of; **in marmo** made of
marble, marble *cpd*; **una collana in oro** a
gold necklace

7 (*misura*) in; **siamo in quattro** there are
four of us; **in tutto** in all

8 (*fine*) **dare in dono** to give as a gift;
spende tutto in alcool he spends all his
money on drink; **in onore di** in honour of

inabi'tabile *ag* uninhabitable

inacces'sibile [inattʃes'sibile] *ag* (*luogo*)
inaccessible; (*persona*) unapproachable

inaccet'tabile [inattʃet'tabile] *ag*
unacceptable

ina'datto, -a *ag* **~ (a)** unsuitable o unfit
(for)

inadegu'ato, -a *ag* inadequate

inaffi'dabile *ag* unreliable

inami'dato, -a *ag* starched

inar'care *vt* (*schiena*) to arch; (*sopracciglia*)
to raise

inaspet'tato, -a *ag* unexpected

inas'prire *vt* (*disciplina*) to tighten up,
make harsher; (*carattere*) to embitter;
inasprirsi *vpr* to become harsher; to
become bitter; to become worse

inattac'cabile *ag* (*anche fig*) unassailable;
(*alibi*) cast-iron

inatten'dibile *ag* unreliable

inat'teso, -a *ag* unexpected

inattu'abile *ag* impracticable

inau'dito, -a *ag* unheard of

inaugu'rare *vt* to inaugurate, open;
(*monumento*) to unveil

inaugurazi'one [inaugurat'tsjone] *sf* inauguration; unveiling

incal'lito, -a *ag* calloused; (*fig*) hardened, inveterate; (: *insensibile*) hard

incande'scente [inkandeʃʃɛnte] *ag* incandescent, white-hot

incan'tare *vt* to enchant, bewitch; **incantarsi** *vpr* (*rimanere intontito*) to be spellbound; to be in a daze; (*meccanismo: bloccarsi*) to jam; **incan'tevole** *ag* charming, enchanting

in'canto *sm* spell, charm, enchantment; (*asta*) auction; **come per ~** as if by magic; **mettere all'~** to put up for auction

inca'pace [inka'patʃe] *ag* incapable

incarce'rare [inkartʃe'rare] *vt* to imprison

incari'care *vt* **~ qn di fare** to give sb the responsibility of doing; **incaricarsi di** to take care o charge of

in'carico, -chi *sm* task, job

incarta'mento *sm* dossier, file

incar'tare *vt* to wrap (in paper)

incas'sare *vt* (*merce*) to pack (in cases); (*gemma: incastonare*) to set; (*Econ: riscuotere*) to collect; (*Pugilato: colpi*) to take, stand up to; **in'casso** *sm* cashing, encashment; (*introito*) takings *pl*

incas'trare *vt* to fit in, insert; (*fig: intrappolare*) to catch; **incastrarsi** *vpr* (*combaciare*) to fit together; (*restare bloccato*) to become stuck

incate'nare *vt* to chain up

in'cauto, -a *ag* imprudent, rash

inca'vato, -a *ag* hollow; (*occhi*) sunken

incendi'are [intʃen'djare] *vt* to set fire to; **incendiarsi** *vpr* to catch fire, burst into flames

in'cendio [in'tʃendjo] *sm* fire

inceneri'tore [intʃeneri'tore] *sm* incinerator

in'censo [in'tʃɛnso] *sm* incense

incensu'rato, -a [intʃensu'rato] *ag* (*Dir*): **essere ~** to have a clean record

incenti'vare [intʃenti'vare] *vt* (*produzione, vendite*) to boost; (*persona*) to motivate

incen'tivo [intʃen'tivo] *sm* incentive

incep'parsi *vpr* to jam

incer'tezza [intʃer'tettsa] *sf* uncertainty

in'certo, -a [in'tʃɛrto] *ag* uncertain; (*irresoluto*) undecided, hesitating ▷ *sm* uncertainty

in'cetta [in'tʃetta] *sf* buying up; **fare ~ di qc** to buy up sth

inchi'esta [in'kjɛsta] *sf* investigation, inquiry

inchi'narsi *vpr* to bend down; (*per riverenza*) to bow; (: *donna*) to curtsy

inchio'dare [inkjo'dare] *vt* to nail (down); **~ la macchina** (*Aut*) to jam on the brakes

inchi'ostro [in'kjɔstro] *sm* ink; **inchiostro simpatico** invisible ink

inciam'pare [intʃam'pare] *vi* to trip, stumble

inci'dente [intʃi'dɛnte] *sm* accident; **ho avuto un ~** I've had an accident; **incidente automobilistico** o **d'auto** car accident; **incidente diplomatico** diplomatic incident

in'cidere [in'tʃidere] *vi* **~ su** to bear upon, affect ▷ *vt* (*tagliare incavando*) to cut into; (*Arte*) to engrave; to etch; (*canzone*) to record

in'cinta [in'tʃinta] *ag f* pregnant

incipri'are [intʃi'prjare] *vt* to powder **incipriarsi** ▷ *vpr* to powder one's face

in'circa [in'tʃirka] *av* **all'~** more or less, very nearly

in'cisi *ecc* [in'tʃizi] *vb vedi* **incidere**

incisi'one [intʃi'zjone] *sf* cut; (*disegno*) engraving; etching; (*registrazione*) recording; (*Med*) incision

in'ciso, -a [in'tʃizo] *pp di* **incidere** ▷ *sm* **per ~** incidentally, by the way

inci'tare [intʃi'tare] *vt* to incite

inci'vile [intʃi'vile] *ag* uncivilized; (*villano*) impolite

incl. *abbr* (= *incluso*) encl.

incli'nare *vt* to tilt; **inclinarsi** *vpr* (*barca*) to list; (*aereo*) to bank

in'cludere *vt* to include; (*accludere*) to enclose; **in'cluso, -a** *pp di* **includere** ▷ *ag* included; enclosed

incoe'rente *ag* incoherent; (*contraddittorio*) inconsistent

in'cognita [in'koɲɲita] *sf* (*Mat, fig*) unknown quantity

in'cognito, -a [in'koɲɲito] *ag* unknown ▷ *sm* **in ~** incognito

incol'lare *vt* to glue, gum; (*unire con colla*) to stick together

inco'lore *ag* colourless

incol'pare *vt* **~ qn di** to charge sb with

in'colto, -a *ag* (*terreno*) uncultivated; (*trascurato: capelli*) neglected; (*persona*) uneducated

in'colume *ag* safe and sound, unhurt

incom'benza [inkom'bɛntsa] *sf* duty, task

in'combere *vi* (*sovrastare minacciando*): **~ su** to threaten, hang over

incominci'are [inkomin'tʃare] *vi, vt* to begin, start

incompe'tente *ag* incompetent

incompi'uto, -a *ag* unfinished, incomplete

incom'pleto, -a *ag* incomplete

incompren'sibile *ag* incomprehensible

inconce'pibile [inkontʃe'pibile] *ag*

inconceivable

inconcili'abile[inkontʃi'ljabile] *ag* irreconcilable

inconclu'dente *ag* inconclusive; (*persona*) ineffectual

incondizio'nato, -a[inkondittsjo'nato] *ag* unconditional

inconfon'dibile *ag* unmistakable

inconsa'pevole *ag* ~ **di** unaware of, ignorant of

in'conscio, -a, -sci, -sce[in'kɔnʃo] *ag* unconscious ▷ *sm* (*Psic*): **l'~** the unconscious

inconsis'tente *ag* insubstantial; unfounded

inconsu'eto, -a *ag* unusual

incon'trare *vt* to meet; (*difficoltà*) to meet with; **incontrarsi** *vpr* to meet

in'contro *av* ~ **a** (*verso*) towards ▷ *sm* meeting; (*Sport*) match; meeting; **incontro di calcio**football match

inconveni'ente *sm* drawback, snag

incoraggia'mento[inkoraddʒa'mento] *sm* encouragement

incoraggi'are[inkorad'dʒare] *vt* to encourage

incornici'are[inkorni'tʃare] *vt* to frame

incoro'nare *vt* to crown

in'correre *vi* ~ **in** to meet with, run into

incosci'ente[inkoʃʃente] *ag* (*inconscio*) unconscious; (*irresponsabile*) reckless, thoughtless

incre'dibile *ag* incredible, unbelievable

in'credulo, -a *ag* incredulous, disbelieving

incremen'tare *vt* to increase; (*dar sviluppo a*) to promote

incre'mento *sm* (*sviluppo*) development; (*aumento numerico*) increase, growth

incresci'oso, -a[inkreʃ'ʃoso] *ag* (*incidente ecc*) regrettable

incrimi'nare *vt* (*Dir*) to charge

incri'nare *vt* to crack; (*fig: rapporti, amicizia*) to cause to deteriorate; **incrinarsi** *vpr* to crack; to deteriorate

incroci'are[inkro'tʃare] *vt* to cross; (*incontrare*) to meet ▷ *vi* (*Naut, Aer*) to cruise; **incrociarsi** *vpr* (*strade*) to cross, intersect; (*persone, veicoli*) to pass each other; **~ le braccia/le gambe** to fold one's arms/cross one's legs

in'crocio[in'krotʃo] *sm* (*anche Ferr*) crossing; (*di strade*) crossroads

incuba'trice[inkuba'tritʃe] *sf* incubator

'incubo *sm* nightmare

incu'rabile *ag* incurable

incu'rante *ag* ~ **(di)** heedless (of), careless (of)

incurio'sire *vt* to make curious; **incuriosirsi** *vpr* to become curious

incursi'one *sf* raid

incur'vare *vt* to bend, curve; **incurvarsi** *vpr* to bend, curve

incusto'dito, -a *ag* unguarded, unattended

in'cutere *vt* ~ **timore/rispetto a qn** to strike fear into sb/command sb's respect

'indaco *sm* indigo

indaffa'rato, -a *ag* busy

inda'gare *vt* to investigate

in'dagine[in'dadʒine] *sf* investigation, inquiry; (*ricerca*) research, study; **indagine di mercato**market survey

indebi'tarsi *vpr* to run o get into debt

indebo'lire*vt, vi* (*anche*: **indebolirsi**) to weaken

inde'cente[inde'tʃɛnte] *ag* indecent

inde'ciso, -a[inde'tʃizo] *ag* indecisive; (*irresoluto*) undecided

indefi'nito, -a *ag* (*anche Ling*) indefinite; (*impreciso, non determinato*) undefined

in'degno, -a[in'deɲɲo] *ag* (*atto*) shameful; (*persona*) unworthy

indemoni'ato, -a *ag* possessed (by the devil)

in'denne *ag* unhurt, uninjured

indenniz'zare[indennid'dzare] *vt* to compensate

indetermina'tivo, -a *ag* (*Ling*) indefinite

'India *sf* **l'~** India; **indi'ano, -a** *ag* Indian ▷ *sm/f* (*d'India*) Indian; (*d'America*) Native American, (American) Indian

indi'care *vt* (*mostrare*) to show, indicate; (: *col dito*) to point to, point out; (*consigliare*) to suggest, recommend; **indica'tivo, -a** *ag* indicative ▷ *sm* (*Ling*) indicative (mood); **indicazi'one** *sf* indication; (*informazione*) piece of information

'indice['inditʃe] *sm* index; (*fig*) sign; (*dito*) index finger, forefinger; **indice di gradimento**(*Radio, TV*) popularity rating

indicherò *ecc* [indike'rɔ] *vb vedi* **indicare**

indi'cibile[indi'tʃibile] *ag* inexpressible

indietreggi'are[indietred'dʒare] *vi* to draw back, retreat

indi'etro *av* back; (*guardare*) behind, back; (*andare, cadere: anche*: **all'~**) backwards; **rimanere ~** to be left behind; **essere ~** (*col lavoro*) to be behind; (*orologio*) to be slow; **rimandare qc ~** to send sth back

indi'feso, -a *ag* (*città ecc*) undefended; (*persona*) defenceless

indiffe'rente *ag* indifferent

in'digeno, -a[in'didʒeno] *ag* indigenous, native ▷ *sm/f* native

indigesti'one[indidʒes'tjone] *sf* indigestion

indi'gesto, -a[indi'dʒɛsto] *ag* indigestible

indi'gnare [indiɲ'nare] *vt* to fill with indignation; **indignarsi** *vpr* to get indignant

indimenti'cabile *ag* unforgettable

indipen'dente *ag* independent

in'dire *vt* (*concorso*) to announce; (*elezioni*) to call

indi'retto, -a *ag* indirect

indiriz'zare [indirit'tsare] *vt* (*dirigere*) to direct; (*mandare*) to send; (*lettera*) to address

indi'rizzo [indi'rittso] *sm* address; (*direzione*) direction; (*avvio*) trend, course; **il mio ~ è...** my address is ...

indis'creto, -a *ag* indiscreet

indis'cusso, -a *ag* unquestioned

indispen'sabile *ag* indispensable, essential

indispet'tire *vt* to irritate, annoy ▷ *vi* (*anche:* **indispettirsi**) to get irritated o annoyed

individu'ale *ag* individual

individu'are *vt* (*dar forma distinta a*) to characterize; (*determinare*) to locate; (*riconoscere*) to single out

indi'viduo *sm* individual

indizi'ato, -a *ag* suspected ▷ *sm/f* suspect

in'dizio [in'dittsjo] *sm* (*segno*) sign, indication; (*Polizia*) clue; (*Dir*) piece of evidence

'indole *sf* nature, character

indolen'zito, -a [indolen'tsito] *ag* stiff, aching; (*intorpidito*) numb

indo'lore *ag* painless

indo'mani *sm* **l'~** the next day, the following day

Indo'nesia *sf* **l'~** Indonesia

indos'sare *vt* (*mettere indosso*) to put on; (*avere indosso*) to have on; **indossa'tore, -'trice** *sm/f* model

indottri'nare *vt* to indoctrinate

indovi'nare *vt* (*scoprire*) to guess; (*immaginare*) to imagine, guess; (*il futuro*) to foretell; **indovi'nello** *sm* riddle

indubbia'mente *av* undoubtedly

in'dubbio, -a *ag* certain, undoubted

in'duco *ecc vb vedi* **indurre**

indugi'are [indu'dʒare] *vi* to take one's time, delay

in'dugio [in'dudʒo] *sm* (*ritardo*) delay; **senza ~** without delay

indul'gente [indul'dʒɛnte] *ag* indulgent; (*giudice*) lenient

indu'mento *sm* article of clothing, garment

indu'rire *vt* to harden ▷ *vi* (*anche:* **indurirsi**) to harden, become hard

in'durre *vt* **~ qn a fare qc** to induce o persuade sb to do sth; **~ qn in errore** to mislead sb

in'dussi *ecc vb vedi* **indurre**

in'dustria *sf* industry; **industri'ale** *ag* industrial ▷ *sm* industrialist

inecce'pibile [inettʃe'pibile] *ag* unexceptionable

i'nedito, -a *ag* unpublished

ine'rente *ag* **~ a** concerning, regarding

i'nerme *ag* unarmed; defenceless

inerpi'carsi *vpr* **~ (su)** to clamber (up)

i'nerte *ag* inert; (*inattivo*) indolent, sluggish

ine'satto, -a *ag* (*impreciso*) inexact; (*erroneo*) incorrect; (*Amm: non riscosso*) uncollected

inesis'tente *ag* non-existent

inesperi'enza [inespe'rjɛntsa] *sf* inexperience

ines'perto, -a *ag* inexperienced

inevi'tabile *ag* inevitable

i'nezia [i'nɛttsja] *sf* trifle, thing of no importance

infagot'tare *vt* to bundle up, wrap up; **infagottarsi** *vpr* to wrap up

infal'libile *ag* infallible

infa'mante *ag* defamatory

in'fame *ag* infamous; (*fig: cosa, compito*) awful, dreadful

infan'gare *vt* to cover with mud; (*fig: reputazione*) to sully; **infangarsi** *vpr* to get covered in mud; to be sullied

infan'tile *ag* child *cpd*; childlike; (*adulto, azione*) childish; **letteratura ~** children's books *pl*

in'fanzia [in'fantsja] *sf* childhood; (*bambini*) children *pl*; **prima ~** babyhood, infancy

infari'nare *vt* to cover with (*o* sprinkle with *o* dip in) flour; **infarina'tura** *sf* (*fig*) smattering

in'farto *sm* (*Med*) heart attack

infasti'dire *vt* to annoy, irritate; **infastidirsi** *vpr* to get annoyed *o* irritated

infati'cabile *ag* tireless, untiring

in'fatti *cong* actually, as a matter of fact

> Attenzione! In inglese esiste l'espressione *in fact* che però vuol dire *in effetti*.

infatu'arsi *vpr* **~ di** to become infatuated with, fall for

infe'dele *ag* unfaithful

infe'lice [infe'litʃe] *ag* unhappy; (*sfortunato*) unlucky, unfortunate; (*inopportuno*) inopportune, ill-timed; (*mal riuscito: lavoro*) bad, poor

inferi'ore *ag* lower; (*per intelligenza, qualità*) inferior ▷ *sm/f* inferior; **~ a** (*numero, quantità*) less *o* smaller than;

(*meno buono*) inferior to; **~ alla media** below average; **inferiorità** *sf* inferiority

inferme'ria *sf* infirmary; (*di scuola, nave*) sick bay

infermi'ere, -a *sm/f* nurse

infermità *sf inv* illness; infirmity; **infermità mentale** mental illness; (*Dir*) insanity

in'fermo, -a *ag* (*ammalato*) ill; (*debole*) infirm

infer'nale *ag* infernal; (*proposito, complotto*) diabolical

in'ferno *sm* hell

inferri'ata *sf* grating

infes'tare *vt* to infest

infet'tare *vt* to infect; **infettarsi** *vpr* to become infected; **infezi'one** *sf* infection

infiam'mabile *ag* inflammable

infiam'mare *vt* to set alight; (*fig, Med*) to inflame; **infiammarsi** *vpr* to catch fire; (*Med*) to become inflamed; **infiammazi'one** *sf* (*Med*) inflammation

infie'rire *vi* **~ su** (*fisicamente*) to attack furiously; (*verbalmente*) to rage at

infi'lare *vt* (*ago*) to thread; (*mettere: chiave*) to insert; (: *anello, vestito*) to slip o put on; (*strada*) to turn into, take; **infilarsi** *vpr* to slip into; (*indossare*) to slip on; **~ l'uscio** to slip in; to slip out

infil'trarsi *vpr* to penetrate, seep through; (*Mil*) to infiltrate

infil'zare [infil'tsare] *vt* (*infilare*) to string together; (*trafiggere*) to pierce

'infimo, -a *ag* lowest

in'fine *av* finally; (*insomma*) in short

infinità *sf* infinity; (*in quantità*): **un'~ di** an infinite number of

infi'nito, -a *ag* infinite; (*Ling*) infinitive ▷ *sm* infinity; (*Ling*) infinitive; **all'~** (*senza fine*) endlessly

infinocchi'are [infinok'kjare] (*fam*) *vt* to hoodwink

infischi'arsi [infis'kjarsi] *vpr* **~ di** not to care about

in'fisso, -a (*pp*) *di* **infiggere** *sm* fixture; (*di porta, finestra*) frame

inflazi'one [inflat'tsjone] *sf* inflation

in'fliggere [in'fliddʒere] *vt* to inflict

in'flissi *ecc vb vedi* **infliggere**

influ'ente *ag* influential; **influ'enza** *sf* influence; (*Med*) influenza, flu

influen'zare [influen'tsare] *vt* to influence, have an influence on

influ'ire *vi* **~ su** to influence

in'flusso *sm* influence

infon'dato, -a *ag* unfounded, groundless

in'fondere *vt* **~ qc in qn** to instill sth in sb

infor'mare *vt* to inform, tell; **informarsi**

vpr **informarsi (di** o **su)** to inquire (about)

infor'matica *sf* computer science

informa'tivo, -a *ag* informative

infor'mato, -a *ag* informed; **tenersi ~** to keep o.s. (well-)informed

informa'tore *sm* informer

informazi'one [informat'tsjone] *sf* piece of information; **prendere informazioni sul conto di qn** to get information about sb; **chiedere un'~** to ask for (some) information

in'forme *ag* shapeless

informico'larsi *vpr* to have pins and needles

infortu'nato, -a *ag* injured, hurt ▷ *sm/f* injured person

infor'tunio *sm* accident; **infortunio sul lavoro** industrial accident, accident at work

infra'dito *sm inv* (*calzatura*) flip flop (BRIT), thong (US)

infrazi'one [infrat'tsjone] *sf* **~ a** breaking of, violation of

infredda'tura *sf* slight cold

infreddo'lito, -a *ag* cold, chilled

infu'ori *av* out; **all'~** outwards; **all'~ di** (*eccetto*) except, with the exception of

infuri'arsi *vpr* to fly into a rage

infusi'one *sf* infusion

in'fuso, -a *pp di* **infondere** ▷ *sm* infusion

Ing. *abbr* = **ingegnere**

ingaggi'are [ingad'dʒare] *vt* (*assumere con compenso*) to take on, hire; (*Sport*) to sign on; (*Mil*) to engage

ingan'nare *vt* to deceive; (*fisco*) to cheat; (*eludere*) to dodge, elude; (*fig: tempo*) to while away ▷ *vi* (*apparenza*) to be deceptive; **ingannarsi** *vpr* to be mistaken, be wrong

in'ganno *sm* deceit, deception; (*azione*) trick; (*menzogna, frode*) cheat, swindle; (*illusione*) illusion

inge'gnarsi [indʒeɲ'ɲarsi] *vpr* to do one's best, try hard; **~ per vivere** to live by one's wits

inge'gnere [indʒeɲ'ɲɛre] *sm* engineer; **~ civile/navale** civil/naval engineer; **ingegne'ria** *sf* engineering; **ingegnere genetica** genetic engineering

in'gegno [in'dʒeɲɲo] *sm* (*intelligenza*) intelligence, brains *pl*; (*capacità creativa*) ingenuity; (*disposizione*) talent; **inge'gnoso, -a** *ag* ingenious, clever

ingelo'sire [indʒelo'zire] *vt* to make jealous ▷ *vi* (*anche*: **ingelosirsi**) to become jealous

in'gente [in'dʒɛnte] *ag* huge, enormous

ingenuità [indʒenui'ta] *sf* ingenuousness

in'genuo, -a [in'dʒɛnuo] *ag* naïve
Attenzione! In inglese esiste la parola *ingenious*, che però significa *ingegnoso*.

inge'rire [indʒe'rire] *vt* to ingest

inges'sare [indʒes'sare] *vt* (*Med*) to put in plaster; **ingessa'tura** *sf* plaster

Inghil'terra [ingil'tɛrra] *sf* l'~ England

inghiot'tire [ingjot'tire] *vt* to swallow

ingial'lire [indʒal'lire] *vi* to go yellow

inginocchi'arsi [indʒinok'kjarsi] *vpr* to kneel (down)

ingiù [in'dʒu] *av* down, downwards

ingi'uria [in'dʒurja] *sf* insult; (*fig: danno*) damage

ingius'tizia [indʒus'tittsja] *sf* injustice

ingi'usto, -a [in'dʒusto] *ag* unjust, unfair

in'glese *ag* English ▷ *sm/f* Englishman/woman ▷ *sm* (*Ling*) English; **gli Inglesi** the English; **andarsene** *o* **filare all'~** to take French leave

ingoi'are *vt* to gulp (down); (*fig*) to swallow (up)

ingol'farsi *vpr* to flood

ingom'brante *ag* cumbersome

ingom'brare *vt* (*strada*) to block; (*stanza*) to clutter up

in'gordo, -a *ag* ~ **di** greedy for; (*fig*) greedy *o* avid for

in'gorgo, -ghi *sm* blockage, obstruction; (*anche:* ~ **stradale**) traffic jam

ingoz'zarsi *vpr* ~ (**di**) to stuff o.s. (with)

ingra'naggio [ingra'naddʒo] *sm* (*Tecn*) gear; (*di orologio*) mechanism; **gli ingranaggi della burocrazia** the bureaucratic machinery

ingra'nare *vi* to mesh, engage ▷ *vt* to engage; ~ **la marcia** to get into gear

ingrandi'mento *sm* enlargement; extension

ingran'dire *vt* (*anche Fot*) to enlarge; (*estendere*) to extend; (*Ottica, fig*) to magnify ▷ *vi* (*anche:* **ingrandirsi**) to become larger *o* bigger; (*aumentare*) to grow, increase; (*espandersi*) to expand

ingras'sare *vt* to make fat; (*animali*) to fatten; (*lubrificare*) to oil, lubricate ▷ *vi* (*anche:* **ingrassarsi**) to get fat, put on weight

in'grato, -a *ag* ungrateful; (*lavoro*) thankless, unrewarding

ingredi'ente *sm* ingredient

in'gresso *sm* (*porta*) entrance; (*atrio*) hall; (*l'entrare*) entrance, entry; (*facoltà di entrare*) admission; **ingresso libero** admission free

ingros'sare *vt* to increase; (*folla, livello*) to swell ▷ *vi* (*anche:* **ingrossarsi**) to increase; to swell

in'grosso *av* **all'~** (*Comm*) wholesale;

(*all'incirca*) roughly, about

ingua'ribile *ag* incurable

'inguine *sm* (*Anat*) groin

ini'bire *vt* to forbid, prohibit; (*Psic*) to inhibit; **inibirsi** *vpr* to restrain o.s.

ini'bito, -a *ag* inhibited ▷ *sm/f* inhibited person

iniet'tare *vt* to inject; **iniezi'one** *sf* injection

ininterrotta'mente *av* non-stop, continuously

ininter'rotto, -a *ag* unbroken; uninterrupted

inizi'ale [init'tsjale] *ag, sf* initial

inizi'are [init'tsjare] *vi, vt* to begin, start; **a che ora inizia il film?** when does the film start?; ~ **qn a** to initiate sb into; (*pittura ecc*) to introduce sb to; ~ **a fare qc** to start doing sth

inizia'tiva [inittsja'tiva] *sf* initiative; **iniziativa privata** private enterprise

i'nizio [i'nittsjo] *sm* beginning; **all'~** at the beginning, at the start; **dare** ~ **a qc** to start sth, get sth going

innaffi'are *ecc* = **annaffiare** *ecc*

innamo'rarsi *vpr* ~ (**di qn**) to fall in love (with sb); **innamo'rato, -a** *ag* (*che nutre amore*): **innamorato (di)** in love (with); (*appassionato*): **innamorato di** very fond of ▷ *sm/f* lover; sweetheart

innanzi'tutto *av* first of all

in'nato, -a *ag* innate

innatu'rale *ag* unnatural

inne'gabile *ag* undeniable

innervo'sire *vt* ~ **qn** to get on sb's nerves; **innervosirsi** *vpr* to get irritated *o* upset

innes'care *vt* to prime

'inno *sm* hymn; **inno nazionale** national anthem

inno'cente [inno'tʃɛnte] *ag* innocent

in'nocuo, -a *ag* innocuous, harmless

inno'vativo, -a *ag* innovative

innume'revole *ag* innumerable

inol'trare *vt* (*Amm*) to pass on, forward

i'noltre *av* besides, moreover

inon'dare *vt* to flood

inoppor'tuno, -a *ag* untimely, ill-timed; inappropriate; (*momento*) inopportune

inorri'dire *vt* to horrify ▷ *vi* to be horrified

inosser'vato, -a *ag* (*non notato*) unobserved; (*non rispettato*) not observed, not kept

inossi'dabile *ag* stainless

INPS *sigla m* (= *Istituto Nazionale Previdenza Sociale*) social security service

inqua'drare *vt* (*foto, immagine*) to frame; (*fig*) to situate, set

inqui'eto, -a *ag* restless; (*preoccupato*) worried, anxious

inqui'lino, -a sm/f tenant

inquina'mento sm pollution

inqui'nare vt to pollute

insabbi'are vt (fig: pratica) to shelve;
insabbiarsi vpr (arenarsi: barca) to run
aground; (fig: pratica) to be shelved

insac'cati smpl (Cuc) sausages

insa'lata sf salad; **insalata mista** mixed
salad; **insalata russa** (Cuc) Russian salad
(comprised of cold diced cooked vegetables in
mayonnaise); **insalati'era** sf salad bowl

insa'nabile ag (piaga) which cannot be
healed; (situazione) irremediable; (odio)
implacable

insa'puta sf **all'~ di qn** without sb
knowing

inse'diarsi vpr to take up office; (popolo,
colonia) to settle

in'segna [in'seɲɲa] sf sign; (emblema)
sign, emblem; (bandiera) flag, banner

insegna'mento [inseɲɲa'mento] sm
teaching

inse'gnante [inseɲ'ɲante] ag teaching
▷ sm/f teacher

inse'gnare [inseɲ'ɲare] vt, vi to teach; **~ a
qn qc** to teach sb sth; **~ a qn a fare qc** to
teach sb (how) to do sth

insegui'mento sm pursuit, chase

insegu'ire vt to pursue, chase

insena'tura sf inlet, creek

insen'sato, -a ag senseless, stupid

insen'sibile ag (nervo) insensible; (persona)
indifferent

inse'rire vt to insert; (Elettr) to connect;
(allegare) to enclose; (annuncio) to put in,
place; **inserirsi** vpr (fig): **inserirsi in** to
become part of

inservi'ente sm/f attendant

inserzi'one [inser'tsjone] sf insertion;
(avviso) advertisement; **fare un'~ sul
giornale** to put an advertisement in the
paper

insetti'cida, -i [insetti'tʃida] sm
insecticide

in'setto sm insect

insi'curo, -a ag insecure

insi'eme av together ▷ prep **~ a** o **con**
together with ▷ sm whole; (Mat, servizio,
assortimento) set; (Moda) ensemble, outfit;
tutti ~ all together; **tutto ~** all together;
(in una volta) at one go; **nell'~** on the
whole; **d'~** (veduta ecc) overall

in'signe [in'siɲɲe] ag (persona) famous,
distinguished; (città, monumento) notable

insignifi'cante [insiɲɲifi'kante] ag
insignificant

insinu'are vt (introdurre): **~ qc in** to slip
o slide sth into; (fig) to insinuate, imply;
insinuarsi vpr **insinuarsi in** to seep into;

(fig) to creep into; to worm one's way into

in'sipido, -a ag insipid

insis'tente ag insistent; persistent

in'sistere vi **~ su qc** to insist on sth; **~ in
qc/a fare** (perseverare) to persist in sth/in
doing

insoddis'fatto, -a ag dissatisfied

insoffe'rente ag intolerant

insolazi'one [insolat'tsjone] sf (Med)
sunstroke

inso'lente ag insolent

in'solito, -a ag unusual, out of the
ordinary

inso'luto, -a ag (non risolto) unsolved

in'somma av (in conclusione) in short;
(dunque) well ▷ escl for heaven's sake!

in'sonne ag sleepless; **in'sonnia** sf
insomnia, sleeplessness

insonno'lito, -a ag sleepy, drowsy

insoppor'tabile ag unbearable

in'sorgere [in'sordʒere] vi (ribellarsi) to
rise up, rebel; (apparire) to come up, arise

in'sorsi ecc vb vedi **insorgere**

insospet'tire vt to make suspicious
▷ vi (anche: **insospettirsi**) to become
suspicious

inspi'rare vt to breathe in, inhale

in'stabile ag (carico, indole) unstable;
(tempo) unsettled; (equilibrio) unsteady

instal'lare vt to install

instan'cabile ag untiring, indefatigable

instau'rare vt to introduce, institute

insuc'cesso [insut'tʃesso] sm failure, flop

insuffici'ente [insuffi'tʃente] ag
insufficient; (compito, allievo) inadequate;
insuffici'enza sf insufficiency;
inadequacy; (Ins) fail; **insufficienza di
prove** (Dir) lack of evidence; **insufficienza
renale** renal insufficiency

insu'lina sf insulin

in'sulso, -a ag (sciocco) inane, silly;
(persona) dull, insipid

insul'tare vt to insult, affront

in'sulto sm insult, affront

intac'care vt (fare tacche) to cut into;
(corrodere) to corrode; (fig: cominciare ad
usare: risparmi) to break into; (: ledere) to
damage

intagli'are [intaʎ'ʎare] vt to carve

in'tanto av (nel frattempo) meanwhile,
in the meantime; (per cominciare) just to
begin with; **~ che** while

inta'sare vt to choke (up), block (up);
(Aut) to obstruct, block; **intasarsi** vpr to
become choked o blocked

intas'care vt to pocket

in'tatto, -a ag intact; (puro) unsullied

intavo'lare vt to start, enter into

inte'grale ag complete; (pane, farina)

wholemeal (BRIT), whole-wheat (US); (Mat): **calcolo ~** integral calculus

inte'grante ag ~ integral part

inte'grare vt to complete; (Mat) to integrate; **integrarsi** vpr (persona) to become integrated

integra'tore sm **integratori alimentari** nutritional supplements

integrità sf integrity

'integro, -a ag (intatto, intero) complete, whole; (retto) upright

intelaia'tura sf frame; (fig) structure, framework

intel'letto sm intellect; **intellettu'ale** ag, sm/f intellectual

intelli'gente [intelli'dʒente] ag intelligent

intem'perie sfpl bad weather sg

in'tendere vt (avere intenzione): **~ fare qc** to intend o mean to do sth; (comprendere) to understand; (udire) to hear; (significare) to mean; **intendersi** vpr (conoscere): **intendersi di** to know a lot about, be a connoisseur of; (accordarsi) to get on (well); **intendersela con qn** (avere una relazione amorosa) to have an affair with sb; **intendi'tore, -'trice** sm/f connoisseur, expert

inten'sivo, -a ag intensive

in'tenso, -a ag intense

in'tento, -a ag (teso, assorto): **~ (a)** intent (on), absorbed (in) ▷ sm aim, purpose

intenzio'nale [intentsjo'nale] ag intentional

intenzi'one [inten'tsjone] sf intention; (Dir) intent; **avere ~ di fare qc** to intend to do sth, have the intention of doing sth

interat'tivo, -a ag interactive

intercet'tare [intertʃet'tare] vt to intercept

intercity [ɪntəsɪ'tɪ] sm inv (Ferr) ≈ intercity (train)

inter'detto, -a pp di **interdire** ▷ ag forbidden, prohibited; (sconcertato) dumbfounded ▷ sm (Rel) interdict

interes'sante ag interesting; **essere in stato ~** to be expecting (a baby)

interes'sare vt to interest; (concernere) to concern, be of interest to; (far intervenire): **~ qn a** to draw sb's attention to ▷ vi **~ a** to interest, matter to; **interessarsi** vpr (mostrare interesse): **interessarsi a** to take an interest in, be interested in; (occuparsi): **interessarsi di** to take care of

inte'resse sm (anche Comm) interest

inter'faccia, -ce [inter'fattʃa] sf (Inform) interface

interfe'renza [interfe'rentsa] sf interference

interfe'rire vi to interfere

interiezi'one [interjet'tsjone] sf exclamation, interjection

interi'ora sfpl entrails

interi'ore ag interior, inner, inside, internal; (fig) inner

inter'medio, -a ag intermediate

inter'nare vt (arrestare) to intern; (Med) to commit (to a mental institution)

inter'nauta sm/f Internet user

internazio'nale [internattsjo'nale] ag international

'Internet ['internet] sf Internet; **in ~** on the Internet

in'terno, -a ag (di dentro) internal, interior, inner; (: mare) inland; (nazionale) domestic; (allievo) boarding ▷ sm inside, interior; (di paese) interior; (fodera) lining; (di appartamento) flat (number); (Tel) extension ▷ sm/f (Ins) boarder; **interni** smpl (Cinema) interior shots; **all'~** inside; **Ministero degli Interni** Ministry of the Interior, ≈ Home Office (BRIT), Department of the Interior (US)

in'tero, -a ag (integro, intatto) whole, entire; (completo, totale) complete; (numero) whole; (non ridotto: biglietto) full; (latte) full-cream

interpel'lare vt to consult

interpre'tare vt to interpret; **in'terprete** sm/f interpreter; (Teatro) actor/actress, performer; (Mus) performer; **ci potrebbe fare da interprete?** could you act as an interpreter for us?

interregio'nale [interredʒo'nale] sm train that travels between two or more regions of Italy, stopping frequently

interro'gare vt to question; (Ins) to test; **interrogazi'one** sf questioning no pl; (Ins) oral test

inter'rompere vt to interrupt; (studi, trattative) to break off, interrupt; **interrompersi** vpr to break off, stop

interrut'tore sm switch

interruzi'one [interrut'tsjone] sf interruption; break

interur'bana sf trunk o long-distance call

inter'vallo sm interval; (spazio) space, gap

interve'nire vi (partecipare): **~ a** to take part in; (intromettersi: anche Pol) to intervene; (Med: operare) to operate; **inter'vento** sm participation; (intromissione) intervention; (Med) operation; **fare un intervento nel corso di** (dibattito, programma) to take part in

inter'vista sf interview; **intervis'tare** vt to interview

intes'tare vt (lettera) to address; (proprietà): **~ a** to register in the name of;

~ **un assegno a qn** to make out a cheque to sb

intestato, -a *ag (proprietà, casa, conto)* in the name of; *(assegno)* made out to; **carta intestata** headed paper

intes'tino *sm (Anat)* intestine

intimidazi'one [intimidat'tsjone] *sf* intimidation

intimi'dire *vt* to intimidate ▷ *vi (intimidirsi)* to grow shy

intimità *sf* intimacy; privacy; *(familiarità)* familiarity

'intimo, -a *ag* intimate; *(affetti, vita)* private; *(fig: profondo)* inmost ▷ *sm (persona)* intimate *o* close friend; *(dell'animo)* bottom, depths *pl*; **parti intime** *(Anat)* private parts

in'tingolo *sm* sauce; *(pietanza)* stew

intito'lare *vt* to give a title to; *(dedicare)* to dedicate; **intitolarsi** *vpr (libro, film)* to be called

intolle'rabile *ag* intolerable

intolle'rante *ag* intolerant

in'tonaco, -ci *o* **chi** *sm* plaster

into'nare *vt (canto)* to start to sing; *(armonizzare)* to match; **intonarsi** *vpr (colori)* to go together; **intonarsi a** *(carnagione)* to suit; *(abito)* to go with, match

inton'tito, -a *ag* stunned, dazed; ~ **dal sonno** stupid with sleep

in'toppo *sm* stumbling block, obstacle

in'torno *av* around; ~ **a** *(attorno a)* around; *(riguardo, circa)* about

intossi'care *vt* to poison; **intossicazi'one** *sf* poisoning

intralci'are [intral'tʃare] *vt* to hamper, hold up

intransi'tivo, -a *ag, sm* intransitive

intrapren'dente *ag* enterprising, go-ahead

intra'prendere *vt* to undertake

intrat'tabile *ag* intractable

intratte'nere *vt* to entertain; to engage in conversation; **intrattenersi** *vpr* to linger; **intrattenersi su qc** to dwell on sth

intrave'dere *vt* to catch a glimpse of; *(fig)* to foresee

intrecci'are [intret'tʃare] *vt (capelli)* to plait, braid; *(intessere: anche fig)* to weave, interweave, intertwine

intri'gante *ag* scheming ▷ *sm/f* schemer, intriguer

in'trinseco, -a, -ci, -che *ag* intrinsic

in'triso, -a *ag* ~ **(di)** soaked (in)

intro'durre *vt* to introduce; *(chiave ecc)*: ~ **qc in** to insert sth into; *(persone: far entrare)* to show in; **introdursi** *vpr (moda, tecniche)* to be introduced; **introdursi in** *(persona:* penetrare) to enter; *(: entrare furtivamente)* to steal *o* slip into; **introduzi'one** *sf* introduction

in'troito *sm* income, revenue

intro'mettersi *vpr* to interfere, meddle; *(interporsi)* to intervene

in'truglio [in'truʎʎo] *sm* concoction

intrusi'one *sf* intrusion; interference

in'truso, -a *sm/f* intruder

intu'ire *vt* to perceive by intuition; *(rendersi conto)* to realize; **in'tuito** *sm* intuition; *(perspicacia)* perspicacity

inu'mano, -a *ag* inhuman

inumi'dire *vt* to dampen, moisten; **inumidirsi** *vpr* to become damp *o* wet

i'nutile *ag* useless; *(superfluo)* pointless, unnecessary

inutil'mente *av* unnecessarily; *(senza risultato)* in vain

inva'dente *ag (fig)* interfering, nosey

in'vadere *vt* to invade; *(affollare)* to swarm into, overrun; *(acque)* to flood

inva'ghirsi [inva'girsi] *vpr* ~ **di** to take a fancy to

invalidità *sf* infirmity; disability; *(Dir)* invalidity

in'valido, -a *ag (infermo)* infirm, invalid; *(al lavoro)* disabled; *(Dir: nullo)* invalid ▷ *sm/f* invalid; disabled person

in'vano *av* in vain

invasi'one *sf* invasion

inva'sore, invadi'trice [invadi'tritʃe] *ag* invading ▷ *sm* invader

invecchi'are [invek'kjare] *vi (persona)* to grow old; *(vino, popolazione)* to age; *(moda)* to become dated ▷ *vt* to age; *(far apparire più vecchio)* to make look older

in'vece [in'vetʃe] *av* instead; *(al contrario)* on the contrary; ~ **di** instead of

inve'ire *vi* ~ **contro** to rail against

inven'tare *vt* to invent; *(pericoli, pettegolezzi)* to make up, invent

inven'tario *sm* inventory; *(Comm)* stocktaking *no pl*

inven'tore *sm* inventor

invenzi'one [inven'tsjone] *sf* invention; *(bugia)* lie, story

inver'nale *ag* winter *cpd*; *(simile all'inverno)* wintry

in'verno *sm* winter

invero'simile *ag* unlikely

inversi'one *sf* inversion; reversal; **"divieto d'~"** *(Aut)* "no U-turns"

in'verso, -a *ag* opposite; *(Mat)* inverse ▷ *sm* contrary, opposite; **in senso ~** in the opposite direction; **in ordine ~** in reverse order

inver'tire *vt* to invert, reverse; ~ **la marcia** *(Aut)* to do a U-turn

investi'gare vt, vi to investigate; **investiga'tore, -'trice** sm/f investigator, detective; **investigatore privato** private investigator

investi'mento sm (Econ) investment

inves'tire vt (denaro) to invest; (veicolo: pedone) to knock down; (: altro veicolo) to crash into; (apostrofare) to assail; (incaricare): **~ qn di** to invest sb with

invi'are vt to send; **invi'ato, -a** sm/f envoy; (Stampa) correspondent; **inviato speciale** (Pol) special envoy; (di giornale) special correspondent

in'vidia sf envy; **invidi'are** vt **invidiare qn (per qc)** to envy sb for sth; **invidiare qc a qn** to envy sb sth; **invidi'oso, -a** ag envious

in'vio, -'vii sm sending; (insieme di merci) consignment; (tasto) Return (key), Enter (key)

invipe'rito, -a ag furious

invi'sibile ag invisible

invi'tare vt to invite; **~ qn a fare** to invite sb to do; **invi'tato, -a** sm/f guest; **in'vito** sm invitation

invo'care vt (chiedere: aiuto, pace) to cry out for; (appellarsi: la legge, Dio) to appeal to, invoke

invogli'are [invoʎ'ʎare] vt **~ qn a fare** to tempt sb to do, induce sb to do

involon'tario, -a ag (errore) unintentional; (gesto) involuntary

invol'tino sm (Cuc) roulade

in'volto sm (pacco) parcel; (fagotto) bundle

in'volucro sm cover, wrapping

inzup'pare [intsup'pare] vt to soak; **inzupparsi** vpr to get soaked

'io pron I ▷ sm inv **l'~** the ego, the self; **~ stesso(a)** I myself

i'odio sm iodine

l'onio sm **lo ~, il mar ~** the Ionian (Sea)

ipermer'cato sm hypermarket

ipertensi'one sf high blood pressure, hypertension

iper'testo sm hypertext

ip'nosi sf hypnosis; **ipnotiz'zare** vt to hypnotize

ipocri'sia sf hypocrisy

i'pocrita, -i, -e ag hypocritical ▷ sm/f hypocrite

ipo'teca, -che sf mortgage

i'potesi sf inv hypothesis

'ippica sf horseracing

'ippico, -a, -ci, -che ag horse cpd

ippocas'tano sm horse chestnut

ip'podromo sm racecourse

ippo'potamo sm hippopotamus

'ipsilon sf o m inv (lettera) Y, y; (: dell'alfabeto greco) epsilon

IR abbr (= Interregionale) long distance train which stops frequently

ira'cheno, -a [ira'kɛno] ag, sm/f Iraqi

l'ran sm **l'~** Iran

irani'ano, -a ag, sm/f Iranian

l'raq sm **l'~** Iraq

'iride sf (arcobaleno) rainbow; (Anat, Bot) iris

'iris sm inv iris

Ir'landa sf **l'~** Ireland; **l'~ del Nord** Northern Ireland, Ulster; **la Repubblica d'~** Eire, the Republic of Ireland; **irlan'dese** ag Irish ▷ sm/f Irishman/woman; **gli Irlandesi** the Irish

iro'nia sf irony; **i'ronico, -a, -ci, -che** ag ironic(al)

irragio'nevole [irradʒo'nevole] ag irrational; unreasonable

irrazio'nale [irrattsjo'nale] ag irrational

irre'ale ag unreal

irrego'lare ag irregular; (terreno) uneven

irremo'vibile ag (fig) unshakeable, unyielding

irrequi'eto, -a ag restless

irresis'tibile ag irresistible

irrespon'sabile ag irresponsible

irri'gare vt (annaffiare) to irrigate; (fiume ecc) to flow through

irrigi'dire [irridʒi'dire] vt to stiffen; **irrigidirsi** vpr to stiffen

irri'sorio, -a ag derisory

irri'tare vt (mettere di malumore) to irritate, annoy; (Med) to irritate; **irritarsi** vpr (stizzirsi) to become irritated o annoyed; (Med) to become irritated

ir'rompere vi **~ in** to burst into

irru'ente ag (fig) impetuous, violent

ir'ruppi ecc vb vedi **irrompere**

irruzi'one [irrut'tsjone] sf **fare ~ in** to burst into; (polizia) to raid

is'crissi ecc vb vedi **iscrivere**

is'critto, -a pp di **iscrivere** ▷ sm/f member; **per o in ~** in writing

is'crivere vt to register, enter; (persona): **~ (a)** to register (in), enrol (in); **iscriversi** vpr **iscriversi (a)** (club, partito) to join; (università) to register o enrol (at); (esame, concorso) to register o enter (for); **iscrizi'one** sf (epigrafe ecc) inscription; (a scuola, società) enrolment, registration; (registrazione) registration

Is'lam sm **l'~** Islam

Is'landa sf **l'~** Iceland

islan'dese ag Icelandic ▷ sm/f Icelander ▷ sm (Ling) Icelandic

'isola sf island; **isola pedonale** (Aut) pedestrian precinct

isola'mento sm isolation; (Tecn) insulation

iso'lante ag insulating ▷ sm insulator

iso'lare vt to isolate; (Tecn) to insulate; (: acusticamente) to soundproof; **isolarsi** vpr to isolate o.s.; **iso'lato, -a** ag isolated; insulated ▷ sm (gruppo di edifici) block

ispet'tore sm inspector

ispezio'nare [ispettsjo'nare] vt to inspect

'ispido, -a ag bristly, shaggy

ispi'rare vt to inspire

Isra'ele sm l'~ Israel; **israeli'ano, -a** ag, sm/f Israeli

is'sare vt to hoist

istan'taneo, -a ag instantaneous ▷ sf (Fot) snapshot

is'tante sm instant, moment; **all'~, sull'~** instantly, immediately

is'terico, -a, -ci, -che ag hysterical

isti'gare vt to incite

is'tinto sm instinct

institu'ire vt (fondare) to institute, found; (porre: confronto) to establish; (intraprendere: inchiesta) to set up

isti'tuto sm institute; (di università) department; (ente, Dir) institution; **istituto di bellezza** beauty salon; **istituto di credito** bank, banking institution; **istituto di ricerca** research institute

istituzi'one [istitut'tsjone] sf institution

'istmo sm (Geo) isthmus

'istrice ['istritfe] sm porcupine

istru'ito, -a ag educated

istrut'tore, -'trice sm/f instructor ▷ ag **giudice ~** vedi **giudice**

istruzi'one sf education; training; (direttiva) instruction; **istruzioni** sfpl (norme) instructions; **istruzioni per l'uso** instructions for use; **~ obbligatoria** (Scol) compulsory education

l'talia sf l'~ Italy

itali'ano, -a ag Italian ▷ sm/f Italian ▷ sm (Ling) Italian; **gli Italiani** the Italians

itine'rario sm itinerary

'ittico, -a, -ci, -che ag fish cpd; fishing cpd

lugos'lavia = **Jugoslavia**

IVA ['iva] sigla f (= imposta sul valore aggiunto) VAT

jazz [dʒaz] sm jazz

jeans [dʒinz] smpl jeans

jeep® [dʒip] sm inv jeep

'jogging ['dʒɔgiŋ] sm jogging; **fare ~** to go jogging

'jolly ['dʒɔli] sm inv joker

joystick [dʒɔis'tik] sm inv joystick

ju'do [dʒu'dɔ] sm judo

Jugos'lavia [jugoz'lavja] sf (Storia): **la ~** Yugoslavia; **la ex-~** former Yugoslavia; **jugos'lavo, -a** ag, sm/f (Storia) Yugoslav(ian)

K l

K, k ['kappa] *sf o m inv (lettera)* K, k ▷ *abbr*
(= *kilo-, chilo-*) k; (*Inform*) K; **K come**
Kursaal ≈ K for King
kamikaze [kami'kaddze] *sm inv* kamikaze
karaoke [ka'raokɛ] *sm inv* karaoke
karatè *sm* karate
ka'yak [ka'jak] *sm inv* kayak
Kenia ['kenja] *sm* **il ~** Kenya
kg *abbr* (= *chilogrammo*) kg
'killer *sm inv* gunman, hired gun
kitsch [kitʃ] *sm* kitsch
'kiwi ['kiwi] *sm inv* kiwi fruit
km *abbr* (= *chilometro*) km
K.O. [kappa'o] *sm inv* knockout
ko'ala [ko'ala] *sm inv* koala (bear)
koso'varo, -a [koso'varo] *ag, sm/f*
Kosovan
Ko'sovo *sm* Kosovo
'krapfen *sm inv* (*Cuc*) doughnut
Kuwait [ku'vait] *sm* **il ~** Kuwait

l' *det vedi* **la; lo; il**
la (*dav V* **l'**) *det f* the ▷ *pron* (*oggetto: persona*)
her; (: *cosa*) it; (: *forma di cortesia*) you; *vedi*
anche **il**
là *av* there; **di là** (*da quel luogo*) from there;
(*in quel luogo*) in there; (*dall'altra parte*)
over there; **di là di** beyond; **per di là** that
way; **più in là** further on; (*tempo*) later
on; **fatti in là** move up; **là dentro/**
sopra/sotto in/up (*o on*)/under there;
vedi anche **quello**
'labbro (*pl(f)* **labbra**) (*solo nel senso Anat*)
sm lip
labi'rinto *sm* labyrinth, maze
labora'torio *sm* (*di ricerca*) laboratory;
(*di arti, mestieri*) workshop; **laboratorio**
linguistico language laboratory
labori'oso, -a *ag* (*faticoso*) laborious;
(*attivo*) hard-working
'lacca, -che *sf* lacquer
'laccio ['lattʃo] *sm* noose; (*legaccio, tirante*)
lasso; (*di scarpa*) lace; **laccio emostatico**
tourniquet
lace'rare [latʃe'rare] *vt* to tear to shreds,
lacerate; **lacerarsi** *vpr* to tear
'lacrima *sf* tear; **in lacrime** in tears;
lacri'mogeno, -a *ag* **gas lacrimogeno**
tear gas
la'cuna *sf* (*fig*) gap
'ladro *sm* thief

laggiù [lad'dʒu] *av* down there; (*di là*) over there

la'gnarsi [laɲ'ɲarsi] *vpr* **~ (di)** to complain (about)

'lago, -ghi *sm* lake

la'guna *sf* lagoon

'laico, -a, -ci, -che *ag* (*apostolato*) lay; (*vita*) secular; (*scuola*) non-denominational ▷ *sm/f* layman/woman

'lama *sm inv* (*Zool*) llama; (*Rel*) lama ▷ *sf* blade

lamentarsi *vpr* (*emettere lamenti*) to moan, groan; (*rammaricarsi*): **~ (di)** to complain (about)

lamen'tela *sf* complaining *no pl*

la'metta *sf* razor blade

'lamina *sf* (*lastra sottile*) thin sheet (*o* layer *o* plate); **lamina d'oro** gold leaf; gold foil

'lampada *sf* lamp; **lampada a gas** gas lamp; **lampada da tavolo** table lamp

lampa'dario *sm* chandelier

lampa'dina *sf* light bulb; **lampadina tascabile** pocket torch (BRIT) *o* flashlight (US)

lam'pante *ag* (*fig: evidente*) crystal clear, evident

lampeggi'are [lamped'dʒare] *vi* (*luce, fari*) to flash ▷ *vb impers* **lampeggia** there's lightning; **lampeggia'tore** *sm* (*Aut*) indicator

lampi'one *sm* street light *o* lamp (BRIT)

'lampo *sm* (*Meteor*) flash of lightning; (*di luce: fig*) flash

lam'pone *sm* raspberry

'lana *sf* wool; **pura ~ vergine** pure new wool; **lana d'acciaio** steel wool; **lana di vetro** glass wool

lan'cetta [lan'tʃetta] *sf* (*indice*) pointer, needle; (*di orologio*) hand

'lancia ['lantʃa] *sf* (*arma*) lance; (: *picca*) spear; (*di pompa antincendio*) nozzle; (*imbarcazione*) launch; **lancia di salvataggio** lifeboat

lanciafi'amme [lantʃa'fjamme] *sm inv* flamethrower

lanci'are [lan'tʃare] *vt* to throw, hurl, fling; (*Sport*) to throw; (*far partire: automobile*) to get up to full speed; (*bombe*) to drop; (*razzo, prodotto, moda*) to launch; **lanciarsi** *vpr* **lanciarsi contro/su** to throw *o* hurl *o* fling o.s. against/on; **lanciarsi in** (*fig*) to embark on

lanci'nante [lantʃi'nante] *ag* (*dolore*) shooting, throbbing; (*grido*) piercing

'lancio ['lantʃo] *sm* throwing *no pl*; throw; dropping *no pl*; drop; launching *no pl*; launch; **lancio del disco** (*Sport*) throwing the discus; **lancio del peso** putting the shot

'languido, -a *ag* (*fiacco*) languid, weak; (*tenero, malinconico*) languishing

lan'terna *sf* lantern; (*faro*) lighthouse

'lapide *sf* (*di sepolcro*) tombstone; (*commemorativa*) plaque

'lapsus *sm inv* slip

'lardo *sm* bacon fat, lard

lar'ghezza [lar'gettsa] *sf* width; breadth; looseness; generosity; **larghezza di vedute** broad-mindedness

'largo, -a, -ghi, -ghe *ag* wide; broad; (*maniche*) wide; (*abito: troppo ampio*) loose; (*fig*) generous ▷ *sm* width; breadth; (*mare aperto*): **il ~** the open sea ▷ *sf* **stare** *o* **tenersi alla larga (da qn/qc)** to keep one's distance (from sb/sth), keep away (from sb/sth); **~ due metri** two metres wide; **~ di spalle** broad-shouldered; **di larghe vedute** broad-minded; **su larga scala** on a large scale; **di manica larga** generous, open-handed; **al ~ di Genova** off (the coast of) Genoa; **farsi ~ tra la folla** to push one's way through the crowd

'larice ['laritʃe] *sm* (*Bot*) larch

larin'gite [larin'dʒite] *sf* laryngitis

'larva *sf* larva; (*fig*) shadow

la'sagne [la'zaɲɲe] *sfpl* lasagna *sg*

lasci'are [laʃʃare] *vt* to leave; (*abbandonare*) to leave, abandon, give up; (*cessare di tenere*) to let go of ▷ *vb* **~ fare qn** to let sb do; **~ andare** *o* **correre** *o* **perdere** to let things go their own way; **~ stare qc/qn** to leave sth/sb alone; **lasciarsi** *vpr* (*persone*) to part; (*coppia*) to split up; **lasciarsi andare** to let o.s. go

'laser ['lazer] *ag, sm inv* **(raggio) ~** laser (beam)

lassa'tivo, -a *ag, sm* laxative

'lasso *sm*; **lasso di tempo** interval, lapse of time

lassù *av* up there

'lastra *sf* (*di pietra*) slab; (*di metallo, Fot*) plate; (*di ghiaccio, vetro*) sheet; (*radiografica*) X-ray (plate)

lastri'cato *sm* paving

late'rale *ag* lateral, side *cpd*; (*uscita, ingresso ecc*) side *cpd* ▷ *sm* (*Calcio*) half-back

la'tino, -a *ag, sm* Latin

lati'tante *sm/f* fugitive (from justice)

lati'tudine *sf* latitude

'lato, -a *ag* (*fig*) wide, broad ▷ *sm* side; (*fig*) aspect, point of view; **in senso ~** broadly speaking

'latta *sf* tin (plate); (*recipiente*) tin, can

lat'tante *ag* unweaned

'latte *sm* milk; **latte detergente** cleansing milk *o* lotion; **latte intero** full-cream milk;

latte a lunga conservazione UHT milk, long-life milk; **latte magro** o **scremato** skimmed milk; **latte in polvere** dried o powdered milk; **latte solare** suntan lotion; **latti'cini** smpl dairy products

lat'tina sf (di birra ecc) can

lat'tuga, -ghe sf lettuce

'laurea sf degree; **laurea in ingegneria** engineering degree; **laurea in lettere** ≈ arts degree

○ **LAUREA**
○
○ The **laurea** is awarded to students
○ who successfully complete their
○ degree courses. Traditionally,
○ this takes between four and six
○ years; a major element of the final
○ examinations is the presentation
○ and discussion of a dissertation. A
○ shorter, more vocational course of
○ study, taking from two to three years,
○ is also available; at the end of this time
○ students receive a diploma called the
○ **laurea breve**.

laure'arsi vpr to graduate

laure'ato, -a ag, sm/f graduate

'lauro sm laurel

'lauto, -a ag (pranzo, mancia) lavish

'lava sf lava

la'vabo sm washbasin

la'vaggio [la'vaddʒo] sm washing no pl; **lavaggio del cervello** brainwashing no pl; **lavaggio a secco** dry-cleaning

la'vagna [la'vaɲɲa] sf (Geo) slate; (di scuola) blackboard

la'vanda sf (anche Med) wash; (Bot) lavender; **lavande'ria** sf laundry; **lavanderia automatica** launderette; **lavanderia a secco** dry-cleaner's; **lavan'dino** sm sink

lavapi'atti sm/f dishwasher

la'vare vt to wash; **lavarsi** vpr to wash, have a wash; **~ a secco** to dry-clean; **lavarsi le mani/i denti** to wash one's hands/clean one's teeth

lava'secco sm o f inv dry cleaner's

lavasto'viglie [lavasto'viʎʎe] sm o f inv (macchina) dishwasher

lava'trice [lava'tritʃe] sf washing machine

lavo'rare vi to work; (fig: bar, studio ecc) to do good business ▷ vt to work; **lavorarsi qn** (persuaderlo) to work on sb; **~ a** to work on; **~ a maglia** to knit; **lavora'tivo, -a** ag working; **lavora'tore, -'trice** sm/f worker ▷ ag working

la'voro sm work; (occupazione) job, work no pl; (opera) piece of work, job; (Econ) labour; **che ~ fa?** what do you do?; **lavori forzati** hard labour; **lavoro interinale** o **in affitto** temporary work

le det fpl the ▷ pron (oggetto) them; (: a lei, a essa) (to) her; (: forma di cortesia) (to) you; vedi anche **il**

le'ale ag loyal; (sincero) sincere; (onesto) fair

'lecca 'lecca sm inv lollipop

leccapi'edi (peg) sm/f inv toady, bootlicker

lec'care vt to lick; (gatto: latte ecc) to lick o lap up; (fig) to flatter; **leccarsi i baffi** to lick one's lips

leccherò ecc [lekke'rɔ] vb vedi **leccare**

'leccio ['lettʃo] sm holm oak, ilex

leccor'nia sf titbit, delicacy

'lecito, -a ['lɛtʃito] ag permitted, allowed

'lega, -ghe sf league; (di metalli) alloy

le'gaccio [le'gattʃo] sm string, lace

le'gale ag legal ▷ sm lawyer; **legaliz'zare** vt to authenticate; (regolarizzare) to legalize

le'game sm (corda, fig: affettivo) tie, bond; (nesso logico) link, connection

le'gare vt (prigioniero, capelli, cane) to tie (up); (libro) to bind; (Chim) to alloy; (fig: collegare) to bind, join ▷ vi (far lega) to unite; (fig) to get on well

le'genda [le'dʒɛnda] sf (di carta geografica ecc) = **leggenda**

'legge ['leddʒe] sf law

leg'genda [led'dʒɛnda] sf (narrazione) legend; (di carta geografica ecc) key, legend

'leggere ['lɛddʒere] vt, vi to read

legge'rezza [ledddʒe'rettsa] sf lightness; thoughtlessness; fickleness

leg'gero, -a [led'dʒɛro] ag light; (agile, snello) nimble, agile, light; (tè, caffè) weak; (fig: non grave, piccolo) slight; (: spensierato) thoughtless; (: incostante) fickle; free and easy; **alla leggera** thoughtlessly

leg'gio, -'gii [led'dʒio] sm lectern; (Mus) music stand

legherò ecc [lege'rɔ] vb vedi **legare**

legisla'tivo, -a [ledʒizla'tivo] ag legislative

legisla'tura [ledʒizla'tura] sf legislature

le'gittimo, -a [le'dʒittimo] ag legitimate; (fig: giustificato, lecito) justified, legitimate; **legittima difesa** (Dir) self-defence

'legna ['leɲɲa] sf firewood

'legno ['leɲɲo] sm wood; (pezzo di legno) piece of wood; **di ~** wooden; **legno compensato** plywood

'lei pron (soggetto) she; (oggetto: per dare rilievo, con preposizione) her; (forma di cortesia: anche: **L~**) you ▷ sm **dare del ~**

a qn to address sb as "lei"; **~ stessa** she herself; you yourself

lenta'mente *av* slowly

'lente *sf* (*Ottica*) lens *sg*; **lenti a contatto o corneali** contact lenses; **lenti (a contatto) morbide/rigide** soft/hard contact lenses; **lente d'ingrandimento** magnifying glass; **lenti** *sfpl* (*occhiali*) lenses

len'tezza [len'tettsa] *sf* slowness

len'ticchia [len'tikkja] *sf* (*Bot*) lentil

len'tiggine [len'tiddʒine] *sf* freckle

'lento, -a *ag* slow; (*molle: fune*) slack; (*non stretto: vite, abito*) loose ▷ *sm* (*ballo*) slow dance

'lenza ['lɛntsa] *sf* fishing-line

lenzu'olo [len'tswɔlo] *sm* sheet

le'one *sm* lion; (*dello zodiaco*): **L~** Leo

lepo'rino, -a *ag* **labbro ~** harelip

'lepre *sf* hare

'lercio, -ci, -cie ['lɛrtʃo] *ag* filthy

lesi'one *sf* (*Med*) lesion; (*Dir*) injury, damage; (*Edil*) crack

les'sare *vt* (*Cuc*) to boil

'lessi *ecc vb vedi* **leggere**

'lessico, -ci *sm* vocabulary; lexicon

'lesso, -a *ag* boiled ▷ *sm* boiled meat

le'tale *ag* lethal; fatal

leta'maio *sm* dunghill

le'tame *sm* manure, dung

le'targo, -ghi *sm* lethargy; (*Zool*) hibernation

'lettera *sf* letter; **lettere** *sfpl* (*letteratura*) literature *sg*; (*studi umanistici*) arts (subjects); **alla ~** literally; **in lettere** in words, in full

letteral'mente *av* literally

lette'rario, -a *ag* literary

lette'rato, -a *ag* well-read, scholarly

lettera'tura *sf* literature

let'tiga, -ghe *sf* (*barella*) stretcher

let'tino *sm* cot (BRIT), crib (US); **lettino solare** sunbed

'letto, -a *pp di* **leggere** ▷ *sm* bed; **andare a ~** to go to bed; **letto a castello** bunk beds *pl*; **letto a una piazza** single; **letto a due piazze o matrimoniale** double bed

let'tore, -'trice *sm/f* reader; (*Ins*) (foreign language) assistant (BRIT), (foreign) teaching assistant (US) ▷ *sm* (*Tecn*): **~ ottico** optical character reader; **lettore**

CD CD player; **lettore DVD** DVD player

let'tura *sf* reading

leuce'mia [leutʃe'mia] *sf* leukaemia

'leva *sf* lever; (*Mil*) conscription; **far ~ su qn** to work on sb; **leva del cambio** (*Aut*) gear lever

le'vante *sm* east; (*vento*) East wind; **il L~** the Levant

le'vare *vt* (*occhi, braccio*) to raise; (*sollevare, togliere: tassa, divieto*) to lift; (*indumenti*) to take off, remove; (*rimuovere*) to take away; (: *dal di sopra*) to take off; (: *dal di dentro*) to take out

leva'toio, -a *ag* **ponte ~** drawbridge

lezi'one [let'tsjone] *sf* lesson; (*Univ*) lecture; **fare ~** to teach; to lecture; **dare una ~ a qn** to teach sb a lesson; **lezioni private** private lessons

li *pron pl* (*oggetto*) them

lì *av* there; **di o da lì** from there; **per di lì** that way; **di lì a pochi giorni** a few days later; **lì per lì** there and then; at first; **essere lì (lì) per fare** to be on the point of doing, be about to do; **lì dentro** in there; **lì sotto** under there; **lì sopra** on there; up there; *vedi anche* **quello**

liba'nese *ag, sm/f* Lebanese *inv*

Li'bano *sm* **il ~** the Lebanon

'libbra *sf* (*peso*) pound

li'beccio [li'bettʃo] *sm* south-west wind

li'bellula *sf* dragonfly

libe'rale *ag, sm/f* liberal

liberaliz'zare [liberalid'dzare] *vt* to liberalize

libe'rare *vt* (*rendere libero: prigioniero*) to release; (: *popolo*) to free, liberate; (*sgombrare: passaggio*) to clear; (: *stanza*) to vacate; (*produrre: energia*) to release; **liberarsi** *vpr* **liberarsi di qc/qn** to get rid of sth/sb; **liberazi'one** *sf* liberation, freeing; release; rescuing

'libero, -a *ag* free; (*strada*) clear; (*non occupato: posto ecc*) vacant; free; not taken; empty; not engaged; **~ di fare qc** free to do sth; **~ da** free from; **è ~ questo posto?** is this seat free?; **~ arbitrio** free will; **~ professionista** self-employed professional person; **~ scambio** free trade;

liber'tà *sf inv* freedom; (*tempo disponibile*) free time ▷ *sfpl* (*licenza*) liberties; **in libertà provvisoria/vigilata** released without bail/on probation

'Libia *sf* **la ~** Libya; **'libico, -a, -ci, -che** *ag, sm/f* Libyan

li'bidine *sf* lust

li'braio *sm* bookseller

li'brarsi *vpr* to hover

libre'ria *sf* (*bottega*) bookshop; (*mobile*) bookcase

Attenzione! In inglese esiste la parola *library*, che però significa *biblioteca*.

li'bretto *sm* (*permesso*) booklet; (*taccuino*) notebook; (*Mus*) libretto; **libretto degli assegni** cheque book; **libretto di circolazione** (*Aut*) logbook; **libretto di risparmio** (*savings*) bank-book, passbook; **libretto universitario** student's report book

'libro *sm* book; **libro di cassa** cash book; **libro mastro** ledger; **libro paga** payroll; **libro di testo** textbook

li'cenza [li'tʃɛntsa] *sf* (*permesso*) permission, leave; (*di pesca, caccia, circolazione*) permit, licence; (*Mil*) leave; (*Ins*) school leaving certificate; (*libertà*) liberty; licence; licentiousness; **andare in ~** (*Mil*) to go on leave

licenzia'mento [litʃentsja'mento] *sm* dismissal

licenzi'are [litʃen'tsjare] *vt* (*impiegato*) to dismiss; (*Comm: per eccesso di personale*) to make redundant; (*Ins*) to award a certificate to; **licenziarsi** *vpr* (*impiegato*) to resign, hand in one's notice; (*Ins*) to obtain one's school-leaving certificate

li'ceo [li'tʃɛo] *sm* (*Ins*) secondary (*BRIT*) o high (*US*) school (*for 14- to 19-year-olds*)

'lido *sm* beach, shore

Liechtenstein ['liktənstain] *sm* **il ~** Liechtenstein

li'eto, -a *ag* happy, glad; **"molto ~"** (*nelle presentazioni*) "pleased to meet you"

li'eve *ag* light; (*di poco conto*) slight; (*sommesso: voce*) faint, soft

lievi'tare *vi* (*anche fig*) to rise ▷ *vt* to leaven

li'evito *sm* yeast; **lievito di birra** brewer's yeast

'ligio, -a, -gi, -gie ['lidʒo] *ag* faithful, loyal

'lilla *sm inv* lilac

'lillà *sm inv* lilac

'lima *sf* file; **lima da unghie** nail file

limacci'oso, -a [limat'tʃoso] *ag* slimy; muddy

li'mare *vt* to file (down); (*fig*) to polish

limi'tare *vt* to limit, restrict; (*circoscrivere*) to bound, surround; **limitarsi** *vpr* **limitarsi nel mangiare** to limit one's

eating; **limitarsi a qc/a fare qc** to limit o.s. to sth/to doing sth

'limite *sm* limit; (*confine*) border, boundary; **limite di velocità** speed limit

limo'nata *sf* lemonade (*BRIT*), (*lemon*) soda (*US*); lemon squash (*BRIT*), lemonade (*US*)

li'mone *sm* (*pianta*) lemon tree; (*frutto*) lemon

'limpido, -a *ag* clear; (*acqua*) limpid, clear

'lince ['lintʃe] *sf* lynx

linci'are *vt* to lynch

'linea *sf* line; (*di mezzi pubblici di trasporto: itinerario*) route; (: *servizio*) service; **a grandi linee** in outline; **mantenere la ~** to look after one's figure; **aereo di ~** airliner; **nave di ~** liner; **volo di ~** scheduled flight; **linea aerea** airline; **linea di partenza/ d'arrivo** (*Sport*) starting/finishing line; **linea di tiro** line of fire

linea'menti *smpl* features; (*fig*) outlines

line'are *ag* linear; (*fig*) coherent, logical

line'etta *sf* (*trattino*) dash; (*d'unione*) hyphen

lin'gotto *sm* ingot, bar

'lingua *sf* (*Anat, Cuc*) tongue; (*idioma*) language; **mostrare la ~** to stick out one's tongue; **di ~ italiana** Italian-speaking; **che lingue parla?** what languages do you speak?; **una ~ di terra** a spit of land; **lingua madre** mother tongue

lingu'aggio [lin'gwaddʒo] *sm* language

lingu'etta *sf* (*di strumento*) reed; (*di scarpa, Tecn*) tongue; (*di busta*) flap

'lino *sm* (*pianta*) flax; (*tessuto*) linen

li'noleum *sm inv* linoleum, lino

liposuzi'one [liposut'tsjone] *sf* liposuction

lique'fatto, -a *pp di* **liquefare**

liqui'dare *vt* (*società, beni: persona: uccidere*) to liquidate; (*persona: sbarazzarsene*) to get rid of; (*conto, problema*) to settle; (*Comm: merce*) to sell off, clear; **liquidazi'one** *sf* liquidation; settlement; clearance sale

liquidità *sf* liquidity

'liquido, -a *ag, sm* liquid; **liquido per freni** brake fluid

liqui'rizia [likwi'rittsja] *sf* liquorice

li'quore *sm* liqueur

'lira *sf* (*Storia: unità monetaria*) lira; (*Mus*) lyre; **lira sterlina** pound sterling

'lirico, -a, -ci, -che *ag* lyric(al); (*Mus*) lyric; **cantante/teatro ~** opera singer/house

Lis'bona *sf* Lisbon

'lisca *sf* (*di pesce*) fishbone

lisci'are [liʃʃare] *vt* to smooth; (*fig*) to flatter

'liscio, -a, -sci, -sce ['liʃʃo] *ag* smooth;

(capelli) straight; (mobile) plain; (bevanda alcolica) neat; (fig) straightforward, simple ▷ av **andare ~** to go smoothly; **passarla liscia** to get away with it

'liso, -a ag worn out, threadbare

'lista sf (elenco) list; **lista elettorale** electoral roll; **lista delle spese** shopping list; **lista dei vini** wine list; **lista delle vivande** menu

lis'tino sm list; **listino dei cambi** (foreign) exchange rate; **listino dei prezzi** price list

'lite sf quarrel, argument; (Dir) lawsuit

liti'gare vi to quarrel; (Dir) to litigate

li'tigio [li'tidʒo] sm quarrel

lito'rale ag coastal, coast cpd ▷ sm coast

'litro sm litre

livel'lare vt to level, make level

li'vello sm level; (fig) level, standard; **ad alto ~** (fig) high-level; **livello del mare** sea level

'livido, -a ag livid; (per percosse) bruised, black and blue; (cielo) leaden ▷ sm bruise

Li'vorno sf Livorno, Leghorn

'lizza ['littsa] sf lists pl; **scendere in ~** to enter the lists

lo (dav s impura, gn, pn, ps, x, z; dav V **l'**) det m the ▷ pron (oggetto: persona) him; (: cosa) it; **lo sapevo** I knew it; **lo so** I know; **sii buono, anche se lui non lo è** be good, even if he isn't; vedi anche **il**

lo'cale ag local ▷ sm room; (luogo pubblico) premises pl; **locale notturno** nightclub; **località** sf inv locality

lo'canda sf inn

locomo'tiva sf locomotive

locuzi'one [lokut'tsjone] sf phrase, expression

lo'dare vt to praise

'lode sf praise; (Ins) **laurearsi con 110 e ~ ≈** to graduate with a first-class honours degree (BRIT), graduate summa cum laude (US)

'loden sm inv (stoffa) loden; (cappotto) loden overcoat

lo'devole ag praiseworthy

loga'ritmo sm logarithm

'loggia, -ge ['lɔddʒa] sf (Archit) loggia; (circolo massonico) lodge; **loggi'one** sm (di teatro): **il loggione** the Gods sg

'logico, -a, -ci, -che ['lɔdʒiko] ag logical

logo'rare vt to wear out; (sciupare) to waste; **logorarsi** vpr to wear out; (fig) to wear o.s. out

'logoro, -a ag (stoffa) worn out, threadbare; (persona) worn out

Lombar'dia sf **la ~** Lombardy

lom'bata sf (taglio di carne) loin

lom'brico, -chi sm earthworm

londi'nese ag London cpd ▷ sm/f Londoner

'Londra sf London

lon'gevo, -a [lon'dʒevo] ag long-lived

longi'tudine [londʒi'tudine] sf longitude

lonta'nanza [lonta'nantsa] sf distance; absence

lon'tano, -a ag (distante) distant, faraway; (assente) absent; (vago: sospetto) slight, remote; (tempo: remoto) far-off, distant; (parente) distant, remote ▷ av far; **è lontana la casa?** is it far to the house?, is the house far from here?; **è ~ un chilometro** it's a kilometre away o a kilometre from here; **più ~** farther; **da o di ~** from a distance; **~ da** a long way from; **è molto ~ da qui?** is it far from here?; **alla lontana** slightly, vaguely

lo'quace [lo'kwatʃe] ag talkative, loquacious; (fig: gesto ecc) eloquent

'lordo, -a ag dirty, filthy; (peso, stipendio) gross

'loro pron pl (oggetto, con preposizione) them; (complemento di termine) to them; (soggetto) they; (forma di cortesia: anche: **L~**) you; to you; **il(la) ~, i(le) ~** det their; (forma di cortesia: anche: **L~**) your ▷ pron theirs; (forma di cortesia: anche: **L~**) yours; **~ stessi(e)** they themselves; you yourselves

'losco, -a, -schi, -sche ag (fig) shady, suspicious

'lotta sf struggle, fight; (Sport) wrestling; **lotta libera** all-in wrestling; **lot'tare** vi to fight, struggle; to wrestle

lotte'ria sf lottery; (di gara ippica) sweepstake

'lotto sm (gioco) (state) lottery; (parte) lot; (Edil) site

● **Lotto**
●
● The **Lotto** is an official lottery run by the
● Italian Finance Ministry. It consists of
● a weekly draw of numbers and is very
● popular.

lozi'one [lot'tsjone] sf lotion

lubrifi'cante sm lubricant

lubrifi'care vt to lubricate

luc'chetto [luk'ketto] sm padlock

lucci'care [luttʃi'kare] vi to sparkle, glitter, twinkle

'luccio ['luttʃo] sm (Zool) pike

'lucciola ['luttʃola] sf (Zool) firefly; glowworm

'luce ['lutʃe] sf light; (finestra) window; **alla ~ di** by the light of; **fare ~ su qc** (fig) to shed o throw light on sth; **~ del sole/della luna**

sun/moonlight

lucer'nario [lutʃer'narjo] *sm* skylight

lu'certola [lu'tʃertola] *sf* lizard

luci'dare [lutʃi'dare] *vt* to polish

lucida'trice [lutʃida'tritʃe] *sf* floor polisher

'lucido, -a ['lutʃido] *ag* shining, bright; (*lucidato*) polished; (*fig*) lucid ▷ *sm* shine, lustre; (*disegno*) tracing; **lucido per scarpe** shoe polish

'lucro *sm* profit, gain

'luglio ['luʎʎo] *sm* July

'lugubre *ag* gloomy

'lui *pron* (*soggetto*) he; (*oggetto: per dare rilievo, con preposizione*) him; **~ stesso** he himself

lu'maca, -che *sf* slug; (*chiocciola*) snail

lumi'noso, -a *ag* (*che emette luce*) luminous; (*cielo, colore, stanza*) bright; (*sorgente*) of light, light *cpd*; (*fig: sorriso*) bright, radiant

'luna *sf* moon; **luna nuova/piena** new/full moon; **luna di miele** honeymoon; **siamo in ~ di miele** we're on honeymoon

'luna park *sm inv* amusement park, funfair

lu'nare *ag* lunar, moon *cpd*

lu'nario *sm* almanac; **sbarcare il ~ to** make ends meet

lu'natico, -a, -ci, -che *ag* whimsical, temperamental

lunedì *sm inv* Monday; **di** *o* **il ~** on Mondays

lun'ghezza [lun'gettsa] *sf* length; **lunghezza d'onda** (*Fisica*) wavelength

'lungo, -a, -ghi, -ghe *ag* long; (*lento: persona*) slow; (*diluito: caffè, brodo*) weak, watery, thin ▷ *sm* length ▷ *prep* along; **~ 3 metri** 3 metres long; **a ~** for a long time; **a ~ andare** in the long run; **di gran lunga** (*molto*) by far; **andare in ~** *o* **per le lunghe** to drag on; **saperla lunga** to know what's what; **in ~ e in largo** far and wide, all over; **~ il corso dei secoli** throughout the centuries

lungo'mare *sm* promenade

lu'notto *sm* (*Aut*) rear *o* back window; **lunotto termico** heated rear window

lu'ogo, -ghi *sm* place; (*posto: di incidente ecc*) scene, site; (*punto, passo di libro*) passage; **in ~ di** instead of; **in primo ~** in the first place; **aver ~** to take place; **dar ~ a** to give rise to; **luogo di nascita** birthplace; (*Amm*) place of birth; **luogo di provenienza** place of origin; **luogo comune** commonplace

'lupo, -a *sm/f* wolf

'luppolo *sm* (*Bot*) hop

'lurido, -a *ag* filthy

lusin'gare *vt* to flatter

Lussem'burgo *sm* (*stato*): **il ~** Luxembourg ▷ *sf* (*città*) Luxembourg

'lusso *sm* luxury; **di ~** luxury *cpd*; **lussu'oso, -a** *ag* luxurious

lus'suria *sf* lust

lus'trino *sm* sequin

'lutto *sm* mourning; **essere in/portare il ~** to be in/wear mourning

m. *abbr* = **mese**; **metro**; **miglia**; **monte**

ma *cong* but; **ma insomma!** for goodness sake!; **ma no!** of course not!

'macabro, -a *ag* gruesome, macabre

macché [mak'ke] *escl* not at all!, certainly not!

macche'roni [makke'rɔni] *smpl* macaroni *sg*

'macchia ['makkja] *sf* stain, spot; (*chiazza di diverso colore*) spot, splash, patch; (*tipo di boscaglia*) scrub; **alla ~** (*fig*) in hiding; **macchi'are** *vt* (*sporcare*) to stain, mark; **macchiarsi** *vpr* (*persona*) to get o.s. dirty; (*stoffa*) to stain; to get stained o marked

macchi'ato, -a [mak'kjato] *ag* (*pelle, pelo*) spotted; **~ di** stained with; **caffè ~** coffee with a dash of milk

'macchina ['makkina] *sf* machine; (*motore, locomotiva*) engine; (*automobile*) car; (*fig: meccanismo*) machinery; **andare in ~** (*Aut*) to go by car; (*Stampa*) to go to press; **macchina da cucire** sewing machine; **macchina fotografica** camera; **macchina da presa** cine o movie camera; **macchina da scrivere** typewriter; **macchina a vapore** steam engine

macchi'nario [makki'narjo] *sm* machinery

macchi'nista, -i [makki'nista] *sm* (*di treno*) engine-driver; (*di nave*) engineer

---

Macedonia [matʃe'dɔnja] *sf* **la ~** Macedonia

mace'donia [matʃe'dɔnja] *sf* fruit salad

macel'laio [matʃel'lajo] *sm* butcher

macelle'ria *sf* butcher's (shop)

ma'cerie [ma'tʃɛrje] *sfpl* rubble *sg*, debris *sg*

ma'cigno [ma'tʃiɲɲo] *sm* (*masso*) rock, boulder

maci'nare [matʃi'nare] *vt* to grind; (*carne*) to mince (BRIT), grind (US)

macrobi'otico, -a *ag* macrobiotic ▷ *sf* macrobiotics *sg*

Ma'donna *sf* (*Rel*) Our Lady

mador'nale *ag* enormous, huge

'madre *sf* mother; (*matrice di bolletta*) counterfoil ▷ *ag inv* mother *cpd*; **ragazza ~** unmarried mother; **scena ~** (*Teatro*) principal scene; (*fig*) terrible scene

madre'lingua *sf* mother tongue, native language

madre'perla *sf* mother-of-pearl

ma'drina *sf* godmother

maestà *sf inv* majesty

ma'estra *sf vedi* **maestro**

maes'trale *sm* north-west wind, mistral

ma'estro, -a *sm/f* (*Ins: anche:* **~ di scuola o elementare**) primary (BRIT) o grade school (US) teacher; (*esperto*) expert ▷ *sm* (*artigiano, fig: guida*) master; (*Mus*) maestro ▷ *ag* (*principale*) main; (*di grande abilità*) masterly, skilful; **maestra d'asilo** nursery teacher; **~ di cerimonie** master of ceremonies

'mafia *sf* Mafia

'maga *sf* sorceress

ma'gari *escl* (*esprime desiderio*): **~ fosse vero!** if only it were true!; **ti piacerebbe andare in Scozia? — ~!** would you like to go to Scotland? — and how! ▷ *av* (*anche*) even; (*forse*) perhaps

magaz'zino [magad'dzino] *sm* warehouse; **grande ~** department store

Attenzione! In inglese esiste la parola *magazine* che però significa *rivista*.

'maggio ['maddʒo] *sm* May

maggio'rana [maddʒo'rana] *sf* (*Bot*) (sweet) marjoram

maggio'ranza [maddʒo'rantsa] *sf* majority

maggior'domo [maddʒor'dɔmo] *sm* butler

maggi'ore [mad'dʒore] *ag* (*comparativo: più grande*) bigger, larger; taller; greater; (*: più vecchio: sorella, fratello*) older, elder; (*: di grado superiore*) senior; (*: più importante: Mil, Mus*) major; (*superlativo*) biggest, largest; tallest; greatest; oldest, eldest ▷ *sm/f* (*di grado*) superior; (*di età*) elder;

(*Mil*) major; (: *Aer*) squadron leader; **la maggior parte** the majority; **andare per la ~** (*cantante ecc*) to be very popular; **maggio'renne** *ag* of age ▷ *sm/f* person who has come of age

ma'gia [ma'dʒia] *sf* magic; '**magico, -a, -ci, -che** *ag* magic; (*fig*) fascinating, charming, magical

magis'trato [madʒis'trato] *sm* magistrate

'maglia ['maʎʎa] *sf* stitch; (*lavoro ai ferri*) knitting *no pl*; (*tessuto, Sport*) jersey; (*maglione*) jersey, sweater; (*di catena*) link; (*di rete*) mesh; **maglia diritta/rovescia** plain/purl; **magli'etta** *sf* (*canottiera*) vest; (*tipo camicia*) T-shirt

magli'one *sm* sweater, jumper

ma'gnetico, -a, -ci, -che *ag* magnetic

ma'gnifico, -a, -ci, -che [maɲ'ɲifiko] *ag* magnificent, splendid; (*ospite*) generous

ma'gnolia [maɲ'ɲɔlja] *sf* magnolia

'mago, -ghi *sm* (*stregone*) magician, wizard; (*illusionista*) magician

ma'grezza [ma'grettsa] *sf* thinness

'magro, -a *ag* (*very*) thin, skinny; (*carne*) lean; (*formaggio*) low-fat; (*fig: scarso, misero*) meagre, poor; (: *meschino: scusa*) poor, lame; **mangiare di ~** not to eat meat

'mai *av* (*nessuna volta*) never; (*talvolta*) ever; **non ... ~** never; **~ più** never again; **non sono ~ stato in Spagna** I've never been to Spain; **come ~?** why (*o* how) on earth?; **chi/dove/quando ~?** whoever/wherever/ whenever?

mai'ale *sm* (*Zool*) pig; (*carne*) pork

maio'nese *sf* mayonnaise

'mais *sm inv* maize

maiu'scolo, -a *ag* (*lettera*) capital; (*fig*) enormous, huge

mala'fede *sf* bad faith

malan'dato, -a *ag* (*persona: di salute*) in poor health; (: *di condizioni finanziarie*) badly off; (*trascurato*) shabby

ma'lanno *sm* (*disgrazia*) misfortune; (*malattia*) ailment

mala'pena *sf* **a ~** hardly, scarcely

ma'laria *sf* (*Med*) malaria

ma'lato, -a *ag* ill, sick; (*gamba*) bad; (*pianta*) diseased ▷ *sm/f* sick person; (*in ospedale*) patient; **malat'tia** *sf* (*infettiva ecc*) illness, disease; (*cattiva salute*) illness, sickness; (*di pianta*) disease

mala'vita *sf* underworld

mala'voglia [mala'vɔʎʎa] *sf* **di ~** unwillingly, reluctantly

Mala'ysia *sf* Malaysia

mal'concio, -a, -ci, -ce [mal'kontʃo] *ag* in a sorry state

malcon'tento *sm* discontent

malcos'tume *sm* immorality

mal'destro, -a *ag* (*inabile*) inexpert, inexperienced; (*goffo*) awkward

'male *av* badly ▷ *sm* (*ciò che è ingiusto, disonesto*) evil; (*danno, svantaggio*) harm; (*sventura*) misfortune; (*dolore fisico, morale*) pain, ache; **di ~ in peggio** from bad to worse; **sentirsi ~** to feel ill; **far ~** (*dolere*) to hurt; **far ~ alla salute** to be bad for one's health; **far del ~ a qn** to hurt *o* harm sb; **restare** *o* **rimanere ~** to be sorry; to be disappointed; to be hurt; **andare a ~** to go bad; **come va? — non c'è ~** how are you? — not bad; **avere mal di gola/testa** to have a sore throat/a headache; **aver ~ ai piedi** to have sore feet; **mal d'auto** carsickness; **mal di cuore** heart trouble; **male di dente** toothache; **mal di mare** seasickness

male'detto, -a *pp di* **maledire** ▷ *ag* cursed, damned; (*fig: fam*) damned, blasted

male'dire *vt* to curse; **maledizi'one** *sf* curse; **maledizione!** damn it!

maledu'cato, -a *ag* rude, ill-mannered

maleducazi'one [maledukat'tsjone] *sf* rudeness

ma'lefico, -a, -ci, -che *ag* (*influsso, azione*) evil

ma'lessere *sm* indisposition, slight illness; (*fig*) uneasiness

malfa'mato, -a *ag* notorious

malfat'tore, -'trice *sm/f* wrongdoer

mal'fermo, -a *ag* unsteady, shaky; (*salute*) poor, delicate

mal'grado *prep* in spite of, despite ▷ *cong* although; **mio** (*o* **tuo** *ecc*) **~** against my (*o* your *ecc*) will

ma'ligno, -a [ma'liɲɲo] *ag* (*malvagio*) malicious, malignant; (*Med*) malignant

malinco'nia *sf* melancholy, gloom; **malin'conico, -a, -ci, -che** *ag* melancholy

malincu'ore: **a ~** *av* reluctantly, unwillingly

malin'teso, -a *ag* misunderstood; (*riguardo, senso del dovere*) mistaken, wrong ▷ *sm* misunderstanding; **c'è stato un ~** there's been a misunderstanding

ma'lizia [ma'littsja] *sf* (*malignità*) malice; (*furbizia*) cunning; (*espediente*) trick; **mali'zioso, -a** *ag* malicious; cunning; (*vivace, birichino*) mischievous

malme'nare *vt* to beat up

ma'locchio [ma'lɔkkjo] *sm* evil eye

ma'lora *sf* **andare in ~** to go to the dogs

ma'lore *sm* (*sudden*) illness

mal'sano, -a *ag* unhealthy

'malta *sf* (*Edil*) mortar

mal'tempo *sm* bad weather

'malto sm malt

maltrat'tare vt to ill-treat

malu'more sm bad mood; (*irritabilità*) bad temper; (*discordia*) ill feeling; **di ~** in a bad mood

'malva sf (Bot) mallow ▷ ag, sm inv mauve

mal'vagio, -a, -gi, -gie [mal'vadʒo] ag wicked, evil

malvi'vente sm criminal

malvolenti'eri av unwillingly, reluctantly

'mamma sf mummy, mum; **~ mia!** my goodness!

mam'mella sf (Anat) breast; (*di vacca, capra ecc*) udder

mam'mifero sm mammal

ma'nata sf (*colpo*) slap; (*quantità*) handful

man'canza [man'kantsa] sf lack; (*carenza*) shortage, scarcity; (*fallo*) fault; (*imperfezione*) failing, shortcoming; **per ~ di tempo** through lack of time; **in ~ di meglio** for lack of anything better

man'care vi (*essere insufficiente*) to be lacking; (*venir meno*) to fail; (*sbagliare*) to be wrong, make a mistake; (*non esserci*) to be missing, not to be there; (*essere lontano*): **~ (da)** to be away (from) ▷ vt to miss; **~ di** to lack; **~ a** (*promessa*) to fail to keep; **tu mi manchi** I miss you; **mancò poco che morisse** he very nearly died; **mancano ancora 10 sterline** we're still £10 short; **manca un quarto alle 6** it's a quarter to 6

mancherò ecc [manke'rɔ] vb vedi **mancare**

'mancia, -ce ['mantʃa] sf tip; **quanto devo lasciare di ~?** how much should I tip?; **~ competente** reward

manci'ata [man'tʃata] sf handful

man'cino, -a [man'tʃino] ag (*braccio*) left; (*persona*) left-handed; (*fig*) underhand

manda'rancio [manda'rantʃo] sm clementine

man'dare vt to send; (*far funzionare: macchina*) to drive; (*emettere*) to send out; (: *grido*) to give, utter, let out; **~ a chiamare qn** to send for sb; **~ avanti** (*fig: famiglia*) to provide for; (: *fabbrica*) to run, look after; **~ giù** to send down; (*anche fig*) to swallow; **~ via** to send away; (*licenziare*) to fire

manda'rino sm mandarin (orange); (*cinese*) mandarin

man'data sf (*quantità*) lot, batch; (*di chiave*) turn; **chiudere a doppia ~** to double-lock

man'dato sm (*incarico*) commission; (*Dir: provvedimento*) warrant; (*di deputato ecc*) mandate; (*ordine di pagamento*) postal o money order; **mandato d'arresto** warrant for arrest

man'dibola sf mandible, jaw

'mandorla sf almond; **'mandorlo** sm almond tree

'mandria sf herd

maneggi'are [maned'dʒare] vt (*creta, cera*) to mould, work, fashion; (*arnesi, utensili*) to handle; (: *adoperare*) to use; (*fig: persone, denaro*) to handle, deal with; **ma'neggio** sm moulding; handling; use; (*intrigo*) plot, scheme; (*per cavalli*) riding school

ma'nesco, -a, -schi, -sche ag free with one's fists

ma'nette sfpl handcuffs

manga'nello sm club

mangi'are [man'dʒare] vt to eat; (*intaccare*) to eat into o away; (*Carte, Scacchi ecc*) to take ▷ vi to eat ▷ sm eating; (*cibo*) food; (*cucina*) cooking; **possiamo ~ qualcosa?** can we have something to eat?; **mangiarsi le parole** to mumble; **mangiarsi le unghie** to bite one's nails

man'gime [man'dʒime] sm fodder

'mango, -ghi sm mango

ma'nia sf (Psic) mania; (*fig*) obsession, craze; **ma'niaco, -a, -ci, -che** ag suffering from a mania; **maniaco (di)** obsessed (by), crazy (about)

'manica sf sleeve; (*fig: gruppo*) gang, bunch; (Geo): **la M~, il Canale della M~** the (English) Channel; **essere di ~ larga/ stretta** to be easy-going/strict; **manica a vento** (Aer) wind sock

mani'chino [mani'kino] sm (*di sarto, vetrina*) dummy

'manico, -ci sm handle; (Mus) neck

mani'comio sm mental hospital; (*fig*) madhouse

mani'cure sm o f inv manicure ▷ sf inv manicurist

mani'era sf way, manner; (*stile*) style, manner; **maniere** sfpl (*comportamento*) manners; **in ~ che** so that; **in ~ da** so as to; **in tutte le maniere** at all costs

manifes'tare vt to show, display; (*esprimere*) to express; (*rivelare*) to reveal, disclose ▷ vi to demonstrate; **manifestazi'one** sf show, display; expression; (*sintomo*) sign, symptom; (*dimostrazione pubblica*) demonstration; (*cerimonia*) event

mani'festo, -a ag obvious, evident ▷ sm poster, bill; (*scritto ideologico*) manifesto

ma'niglia [ma'niʎʎa] sf handle; (*sostegno: negli autobus ecc*) strap

manipo'lare vt to manipulate; (*alterare: vino*) to adulterate

man'naro: lupo ~ sm werewolf

'mano, -i sf hand; (*strato: di vernice ecc*) coat; **di prima ~** (*notizia*) first-hand; **di**

seconda ~ second-hand; **man ~** little by little, gradually; **man ~ che** as; **darsi o stringersi la** ~ to shake hands; **mettere le mani avanti** (fig) to safeguard o.s.; **restare a mani vuote** to be left empty-handed; **venire alle mani** to come to blows; **a ~** by hand; **mani in alto!** hands up!

mano'dopera sf labour

ma'nometro sm gauge, manometer

mano'mettere vt (alterare) to tamper with; (aprire indebitamente) to break open illegally

ma'nopola sf (dell'armatura) gauntlet; (guanto) mitt; (di impugnatura) hand-grip; (pomello) knob

manos'critto, -a ag handwritten ▷ sm manuscript

mano'vale sm labourer

mano'vella sf handle; (Tecn) crank

ma'novra sf manoeuvre (BRIT), maneuver (US); (Ferr) shunting

man'sarda sf attic

mansi'one sf task, duty, job

mansu'eto, -a ag gentle, docile

man'tello sm cloak; (fig: di neve ecc) blanket, mantle; (Zool) coat

mante'nere vt to maintain; (adempiere: promesse) to keep, abide by; (provvedere a) to support, maintain; **mantenersi** vpr **mantenersi calmo/giovane** to stay calm/young

'Mantova sf Mantua

manu'ale ag manual ▷ sm (testo) manual, handbook

ma'nubrio sm handle; (di bicicletta ecc) handlebars pl; (Sport) dumbbell

manutenzi'one [manuten'tsjone] sf maintenance, upkeep; (d'impianti) maintenance, servicing

'manzo ['mandzo] sm (Zool) steer; (carne) beef

'mappa sf (Geo) map; **mappa'mondo** sm map of the world; (globo girevole) globe

mara'tona sf marathon

'marca, -che sf (Comm: di prodotti) brand; (contrassegno, scontrino) ticket, check; **prodotto di ~** (di buona qualità) high-class product; **marca da bollo** official stamp

mar'care vt (munire di contrassegno) to mark; (a fuoco) to brand; (Sport: gol) to score; (: avversario) to mark; (accentuare) to stress; **~ visita** (Mil) to report sick

marcherò ecc [marke'tɔ] vb vedi **marcare**

mar'chese, -a [mar'keze] sm/f marquis o marquess/marchioness

marchi'are [mar'kjare] vt to brand

'marcia, -ce ['martʃa] sf (anche Mus, Mil) march; (funzionamento) running; (il camminare) walking; (Aut) gear; **mettere in ~** to start; **mettersi in ~** to get moving; **far ~ indietro** (Aut) to reverse; (fig) to back-pedal

marciapi'ede [martʃa'pjɛde] sm (di strada) pavement (BRIT), sidewalk (US); (Ferr) platform

marci'are [mar'tʃare] vi to march; (andare: treno, macchina) to go; (funzionare) to run, work

'marcio, -a, -ci, -ce ['martʃo] ag (frutta, legno) rotten, bad; (Med) festering; (fig) corrupt, rotten

mar'cire [mar'tʃire] vi (andare a male) to go bad, rot; (suppurare) to fester; (fig) to rot, waste away

'marco, -chi sm (unità monetaria) mark

'mare sm sea; **in ~** at sea; **andare al ~** (in vacanza ecc) to go to the seaside; **il M~ del Nord** the North Sea

ma'rea sf tide; **alta/bassa ~** high/low tide

mareggi'ata [mared'dʒata] sf heavy sea

mare'moto sm seaquake

maresci'allo [mareʃʃallo] sm (Mil) marshal; (: sottufficiale) warrant officer

marga'rina sf margarine

marghe'rita [marge'rita] sf (ox-eye) daisy, marguerite; (di stampante) daisy wheel

'margine ['mardʒine] sm margin; (di bosco, via) edge, border

mariju'ana [mæri'wa:nə] sf marijuana

ma'rina sf navy; (costa) coast; (quadro) seascape; **marina mercantile/militare** navy/merchant navy (BRIT) o marine (US)

mari'naio sm sailor

mari'nare vt (Cuc) to marinate; **~ la scuola** to play truant

ma'rino, -a ag sea cpd, marine

mario'netta sf puppet

ma'rito sm husband

ma'rittimo, -a ag maritime, sea cpd

marmel'lata sf jam; (di agrumi) marmalade

mar'mitta sf (recipiente) pot; (Aut) silencer; **marmitta catalitica** catalytic converter

'marmo sm marble

mar'motta sf (Zool) marmot

maroc'chino, -a [marok'kino] ag, sm/f Moroccan

Ma'rocco sm **il ~** Morocco

mar'rone ag inv brown ▷ sm (Bot) chestnut

> Attenzione! In inglese esiste la parola *maroon*, che però indica un altro colore, il rosso bordeaux.

mar'supio sm pouch; (per denaro) bum bag; (per neonato) sling

martedì sm inv Tuesday; **di** o **il ~** on

Tuesdays; **martedì grasso** Shrove Tuesday

martel'lare vt to hammer ▷ vi (pulsare) to throb; (: cuore) to thump

mar'tello sm hammer; (: di uscio) knocker; **martello pneumatico** pneumatic drill

'martire sm/f martyr

mar'xista, -i, -e ag, sm/f Marxist

marza'pane [martsa'pane] sm marzipan

'marzo ['martso] sm March

mascal'zone [maskal'tsone] sm rascal, scoundrel

mas'cara sm inv mascara

ma'scella [maʃʃella] sf (Anat) jaw

'maschera ['maskera] sf mask; (travestimento) disguise; (: per un ballo ecc) fancy dress; (Teatro, Cinema) usher/usherette; (personaggio del teatro) stock character; **masche'rare** vt to mask; (travestire) to disguise; to dress up; (fig: celare) to hide, conceal; (Mil) to camouflage; **mascherarsi da** to disguise o.s. as; to dress up as; (fig) to masquerade as

mas'chile [mas'kile] ag masculine; (sesso, popolazione) male; (abiti) men's; (per ragazzi: scuola) boys'

mas'chilista, -i, -e ag, sm/f (uomo) (male) chauvinist, sexist; (donna) sexist

'maschio, -a ['maskjo] ag (Biol) male; (virile) manly ▷ sm (anche Zool, Tecn) male; (uomo) man; (ragazzo) boy; (figlio) son

masco'lino, -a ag masculine

'massa sf mass; (di errori ecc): **una ~ di** heaps of, masses of; (di gente) mass, multitude; (Elettr) earth; **in ~** (Comm) in bulk; (tutti insieme) en masse; **adunata in ~** mass meeting; **di ~** (cultura, manifestazione) mass cpd

mas'sacro sm massacre, slaughter; (fig) mess, disaster

massaggi'are [massad'dʒare] vt to massage

mas'saggio [mas'saddʒo] sm massage; **massaggio cardiaco** cardiac massage

mas'saia sf housewife

masse'rizie [masse'rittsje] sfpl (household) furnishings

mas'siccio, -a, -ci, -ce [mas'sittʃo] ag (oro, legno) solid; (palazzo) massive; (corporatura) stout ▷ sm (Geo) massif

'massima sf (sentenza, regola) maxim; (Meteor) maximum temperature; **in linea di ~** generally speaking; vedi **massimo**

massi'male sm maximum

'massimo, -a ag, sm maximum; **al ~** at (the) most

'masso sm rock, boulder

masteriz'zare [masterid'dzare] vt (CD, DVD) to burn

masterizza'tore [masteriddza'tore] sm CD burner o writer

masti'care vt to chew

'mastice ['mastitʃe] sm mastic; (per vetri) putty

mas'tino sm mastiff

ma'tassa sf skein

mate'matica sf mathematics sg

mate'matico, -a, -ci, -che ag mathematical ▷ sm/f mathematician

materas'sino sm mat; **materassino gonfiabile** air bed

mate'rasso sm mattress; **materasso a molle** spring o interior-sprung mattress

ma'teria sf (Fisica) matter; (Tecn, Comm) material, matter no pl; (disciplina) subject; (argomento) subject matter, material; **in ~ di** (per quanto concerne) on the subject of; **materie prime** raw materials

materi'ale ag material; (fig: grossolano) rough, rude ▷ sm material; (insieme di strumenti ecc) equipment no pl, materials pl

maternità sf motherhood, maternity; (reparto) maternity ward

ma'terno, -a ag (amore, cura ecc) maternal, motherly; (nonno) maternal; (lingua, terra) mother cpd

ma'tita sf pencil; **matite colorate** coloured pencils; **matita per gli occhi** eyeliner (pencil)

ma'tricola sf (registro) register; (numero) registration number; (nell'università) freshman, fresher

ma'trigna [ma'triɲɲa] sf stepmother

matrimoni'ale ag matrimonial, marriage cpd

matri'monio sm marriage, matrimony; (durata) marriage, married life; (cerimonia) wedding

mat'tina sf morning

'matto, -a ag mad, crazy; (fig: falso) false, imitation ▷ sm/f madman/woman; **avere una voglia matta di qc** to be dying for sth

mat'tone sm brick; (fig): **questo libro/ film è un ~** this book/film is heavy going

matto'nella sf tile

matu'rare vi (anche: maturarsi: frutta, grano) to ripen; (ascesso) to come to a head; (fig: persona, idea, Econ) to mature ▷ vt to ripen, to (make) mature

maturità sf maturity; (di frutta) ripeness, maturity; (Ins) school-leaving examination, ≈ GCE A-levels (BRIT)

ma'turo, -a ag mature; (frutto) ripe, mature

max. abbr (= massimo) max

maxischermo [maxis'kermo] sm giant screen

'mazza ['mattsa] sf (bastone) club;

(*martello*) sledge-hammer; (*Sport: da golf*) club; (: *da baseball, cricket*) bat

maz'zata [mat'tsata] *sf* (*anche fig*) heavy blow

'mazzo ['mattso] *sm* (*di fiori, chiavi ecc*) bunch; (*di carte da gioco*) pack

me *pron* me; **me stesso(a)** myself; **sei bravo quanto me** you are as clever as I (am) *o* as me

mec'canico, -a, -ci, -che *ag* mechanical ▷ *sm* mechanic; **può mandare un ~?** can you send a mechanic?

mecca'nismo *sm* mechanism

me'daglia [me'daʎʎa] *sf* medal

me'desimo, -a *ag* same; (*in persona*): **io ~** I myself

'media *sf* average; (*Mat*) mean; (*Ins: voto*) end-of-term average; **le medie** *sfpl* = **scuola media**; **in ~** on average; *vedi anche* **medio**

medi'ante *prep* by means of

media'tore, -'trice *sm/f* mediator; (*Comm*) middle man, agent

medi'care *vt* to treat; (*ferita*) to dress

medi'cina [medi'tʃina] *sf* medicine; **medicina legale** forensic medicine

'medico, -a, -ci, -che *ag* medical ▷ *sm* doctor; **chiamate un ~** call a doctor; **medico generico** general practitioner, GP

medie'vale *ag* medieval

'medio, -a *ag* average; (*punto, ceto*) middle; (*altezza, statura*) medium ▷ *sm* (*dito*) middle finger; **licenza media** *leaving certificate awarded at the end of 3 years of secondary education*; **scuola media** *first 3 years of secondary school*

medi'ocre *ag* mediocre, poor

medi'tare *vt* to ponder over, meditate on; (*progettare*) to plan, think out ▷ *vi* to meditate

mediter'raneo, -a *ag* Mediterranean; **il (mare) M~** the Mediterranean (Sea)

me'dusa *sf* (*Zool*) jellyfish

mega'byte *sm inv* (*Comput*) megabyte

me'gafono *sm* megaphone

'meglio ['mɛʎʎo] *av, ag inv* better; (*con senso superlativo*) best ▷ *sm* (*la cosa migliore*): **il ~** the best (thing); **faresti ~ ad andartene** you had better leave; **alla ~** as best one can; **andar di bene in ~** to get better and better; **fare del proprio ~** to do one's best; **per il ~** for the best; **aver la ~ su qn** to get the better of sb

'mela *sf* apple; **mela cotogna** quince

mela'grana *sf* pomegranate

melan'zana [melan'dzana] *sf* aubergine (*BRIT*), eggplant (*US*)

melato'nina *sf* melatonin

'melma *sf* mud, mire

'melo *sm* apple tree

melo'dia *sf* melody

me'lone *sm* (musk)melon

'membro *sm* member (*pl(f)* **membra**) (*arto*) limb

memo'randum *sm inv* memorandum

me'moria *sf* memory; **memorie** *sfpl* (*opera autobiografica*) memoirs; **a ~** (*imparare, sapere*) by heart; **a ~ d'uomo** within living memory

mendi'cante *sm/f* beggar

 PAROLA CHIAVE

'meno *av* **1** (*in minore misura*) less; **dovresti mangiare meno** you should eat less, you shouldn't eat so much

2 (*comparativo*): **meno ... di** not as ... as, less ... than; **sono meno alto di te** I'm not as tall as you (are), I'm less tall than you (are); **meno ... che** not as ... as, less ... than; **meno che mai** less than ever; **è meno intelligente che ricco** he's more rich than intelligent; **meno fumo più mangio** the less I smoke the more I eat

3 (*superlativo*) least; **il meno dotato degli studenti** the least gifted of the students; **è quello che compro meno spesso** it's the one I buy least often

4 (*Mat*) minus; **8 meno 5** 8 minus 5, 8 take away 5; **sono le 8 meno un quarto** it's a quarter to 8; **meno 5 gradi** 5 degrees below zero, minus 5 degrees; **1 euro in meno** 1 euro less

5 (*fraseologia*): **quanto meno poteva telefonare** he could at least have phoned; **non so se accettare o meno** I don't know whether to accept or not; **fare a meno di qc/qn** to do without sth/sb; **non potevo fare a meno di ridere** I couldn't help laughing; **meno male!** thank goodness!; **meno male che sei arrivato** it's a good job that you've come

▷ *ag inv* (*tempo, denaro*) less; (*errori, persone*) fewer; **ha fatto meno errori di tutti** he made fewer mistakes than anyone, he made the fewest mistakes of all ▷ *sm inv* **1**: **il meno** (*il minimo*) the least; **parlare del più e del meno** to talk about this and that **2** (*Mat*) minus

▷ *prep* (*eccetto*) except (for), apart from; **a meno che, a meno di** unless; **a meno che non piova** unless it rains; **non posso, a meno di prendere ferie** I can't, unless I take some leave

---

meno'pausa *sf* menopause

'mensa *sf* (*locale*) canteen; (: *Mil*) mess; (: *nelle università*) refectory

men'sile *ag* monthly ▷ *sm* (*periodico*) monthly (magazine); (*stipendio*) monthly salary

'mensola *sf* bracket; (*ripiano*) shelf; (*Archit*) corbel

'menta *sf* mint; (*anche*: **~ piperita**) peppermint; (*bibita*) peppermint cordial; (*caramella*) mint, peppermint

men'tale *ag* mental; **mentalità** *sf inv* mentality

'mente *sf* mind; **imparare/sapere qc a ~** to learn/know sth by heart; **avere in ~ qc** to have sth in mind; **passare di ~ a qn** to slip sb's mind

men'tire *vi* to lie

'mento *sm* chin

'mentre *cong* (*temporale*) while; (*avversativo*) whereas

menù *sm inv* menu; **ci può portare il ~?** could we see the menu?; **menù turistico** set menu

menzio'nare [mentsjo'nare] *vt* to mention

men'zogna [men'tsɔɲɲa] *sf* lie

mera'viglia [mera'viʎʎa] *sf* amazement, wonder; (*persona, cosa*) marvel, wonder; **a ~** perfectly, wonderfully; **meravigli'are** *vt* to amaze, astonish; **meravigliarsi (di)** to marvel (at); (*stupirsi*) to be amazed (at), be astonished (at); **meravigli'oso, -a** *ag* wonderful, marvellous

mer'cante *sm* merchant; **mercante d'arte** art dealer

merca'tino *sm* (*rionale*) local street market; (*Econ*) unofficial stock market

mer'cato *sm* market; **mercato dei cambi** exchange market; **mercato nero** black market

'merce ['mɛrtʃe] *sf* goods *pl*, merchandise

mercé [mer'tʃe] *sf* mercy

merce'ria [mertʃe'ria] *sf* (*articoli*) haberdashery (BRIT), notions *pl* (US); (*bottega*) haberdasher's shop (BRIT), notions store (US)

mercoledì *sm inv* Wednesday; **di** *o* **il ~ on** Wednesdays; **mercoledì delle Ceneri** Ash Wednesday

mer'curio *sm* mercury

'merda (*fam!*) *sf* shit (!)

me'renda *sf* afternoon snack

meren'dina *sf* snack

meridi'ana *sf* (*orologio*) sundial

meridi'ano, -a *ag* meridian; midday *cpd*, noonday ▷ *sm* meridian

meridio'nale *ag* southern ▷ *sm/f* southerner

meridi'one *sm* south

me'ringa, -ghe *sf* (*Cuc*) meringue

meri'tare *vt* to deserve, merit ▷ *vb impers*

merita andare it's worth going

meri'tevole *ag* worthy

'merito *sm* merit; (*valore*) worth; **in ~ a** as regards, with regard to; **dare ~ a qn di** to give sb credit for; **finire a pari ~** to finish joint first (*o* second *ecc*); to tie

mer'letto *sm* lace

'merlo *sm* (*Zool*) blackbird; (*Archit*) battlement

mer'luzzo [mer'luttso] *sm* (*Zool*) cod

mes'chino, -a [mes'kino] *ag* wretched; (*scarso*) scanty, poor; (*persona*: *gretta*) mean; (: *limitata*) narrow-minded, petty

mesco'lare *vt* to mix; (*vini, colori*) to blend; (*mettere in disordine*) to mix up, muddle up; (*carte*) to shuffle

'mese *sm* month

'messa *sf* (*Rel*) mass; (*il mettere*): **messa in moto** starting; **messa in piega** set; **messa a punto** (*Tecn*) adjustment; (*Aut*) tuning; (*fig*) clarification; **messa in scena** = **messinscena**

messag'gero [messad'dʒεro] *sm* messenger

messaggino [messad'dʒino] *sm* (*di telefonino*) text (message)

mes'saggio [mes'saddʒo] *sm* message; **posso lasciare un ~?** can I leave a message?; **ci sono messaggi per me?** are there any messages for me?; **messaggio di posta elettronica** e-mail message

messag'gistica [messad'dʒistica] *sf* **~ immediata** (*Inform*) instant messaging; **programma di ~ immediata** instant messenger

mes'sale *sm* (*Rel*) missal

messi'cano, -a *ag, sm/f* Mexican

'Messico *sm* **il ~** Mexico

messin'scena [messin'ʃena] *sf* (*Teatro*) production

'messo, -a *pp di* **mettere** ▷ *sm* messenger

mesti'ere *sm* (*professione*) job; (: *manuale*) trade; (: *artigianale*) craft; (*fig*: *abilità nel lavoro*) skill, technique; **essere del ~** to know the tricks of the trade

'mestolo *sm* (*Cuc*) ladle

mestruazi'one [mestruat'tsjone] *sf* menstruation

'meta *sf* destination; (*fig*) aim, goal

metà *sf inv* half; (*punto di mezzo*) middle; **dividere qc a** *o* **per ~** to divide sth in half, halve sth; **fare a ~ (di qc con qn)** to go halves (with sb in sth); **a ~ prezzo** at half price; **a ~ strada** halfway

meta'done *sm* methadone

me'tafora *sf* metaphor

me'tallico, -a, -ci, -che *ag* (*di metallo*) metal *cpd*; (*splendore, rumore ecc*) metallic

me'tallo *sm* metal

metalmec'canico, -a, -ci, -che *ag* engineering *cpd* ▷ *sm* engineering worker

me'tano *sm* methane

me'ticcio, -a, -ci, -ce [me'tittʃo] *sm/f* half-caste, half-breed

me'todico, -a, -ci, -che *ag* methodical

'metodo *sm* method

'metro *sm* metre; (*nastro*) tape measure; (*asta*) (metre) rule

metropoli'tana *sf* underground, subway

'mettere *vt* to put; (*abito*) to put on; (: *portare*) to wear; (*installare: telefono*) to put in; (*fig: provocare*): **~ fame/allegria a qn** to make sb hungry/happy; (*supporre*): **mettiamo che ...** let's suppose o say that ...; **mettersi** *vpr* (*persona*) to put o.s.; (*oggetto*) to go; (*disporsi: faccenda*) to turn out; **mettersi a sedere** to sit down; **mettersi a letto** to get into bed; (*per malattia*) to take to one's bed; **mettersi il cappello** to put on one's hat; **mettersi a** (*cominciare*) to begin to, start to; **mettersi al lavoro** to set to work; **mettersi con qn** (*in società*) to team up with sb; (*in coppia*) to start going out with sb; **metterci: metterci molta cura/molto tempo** to take a lot of care/a lot of time; **ci ho messo 3 ore per venire** it's taken me 3 hours to get here; **mettercela tutta** to do one's best; **~ a tacere qn/qc** to keep sb/sth quiet; **~ su casa** to set up house; **~ su un negozio** to start a shop; **~ via** to put away

mezza'notte [meddza'nɔtte] *sf* midnight

'mezzo, -a ['mɛddzo] *ag* half; **un ~ litro/panino** half a litre/roll ▷ *ag* half-; **~ morto** half-dead ▷ *sm* (*metà*) half; (*parte centrale: di strada ecc*) middle; (*per raggiungere un fine*) means *sg*; (*veicolo*) vehicle; (*nell'indicare l'ora*): **le nove e ~** half past nine; **~giorno e ~** half past twelve; **mezzi** *smpl* (*possibilità economiche*) means; **di mezza età** middle-aged; **un soprabito di mezza stagione** a spring (*o* autumn) coat; **di ~** middle, in the middle; **andarci di ~** (*patir danno*) to suffer; **levarsi** *o* **togliersi di ~** to get out of the way; **in ~ a** in the middle of; **per** *o* **a ~ di** by means of; **mezzi di comunicazione di massa** mass media *pl*; **mezzi pubblici** public transport *sg*; **mezzi di trasporto** means of transport

mezzogi'orno [meddzo'dʒorno] *sm* midday, noon; **a ~** at 12 (o'clock) *o* midday *o* noon; **il ~ d'Italia** southern Italy

mi (*dav lo, la, li, le, ne diventa* **me**) *pron* (*oggetto*) me; (*complemento di termine*) to me; (*riflessivo*) myself ▷ *sm* (*Mus*) E; (: *solfeggiando la scala*) mi

miago'lare *vi* to miaow, mew

'mica *av* (*fam*): **non ... ~** not ... at all; **non**

sono ~ stanco I'm not a bit tired; **non sarà ~ partito?** he wouldn't have left, would he?; **~ male** not bad

'miccia, -ce ['mittʃa] *sf* fuse

micidi'ale [mitʃi'djale] *ag* fatal; (*dannosissimo*) deadly

micro'fibra *sf* microfibre

mi'crofono *sm* microphone

micros'copio *sm* microscope

mi'dollo (*pl(f)* **midolla**) *sm* (*Anat*) marrow; **midollo osseo** bone marrow

mi'ele *sm* honey

'miglia ['miʎʎa] *sfpl di* **miglio**

migli'aio [miʎ'ʎajo] (*(pl)f* **migliaia**) *sm* thousand; **un ~ (di)** about a thousand; **a migliaia** by the thousand, in thousands

'miglio ['miʎʎo] *sm* (*Bot*) millet (*pl(f)* **miglia**) (*unità di misura*) mile; **~ marino** *o* **nautico** nautical mile

migliora'mento [miʎʎora'mento] *sm* improvement

miglio'rare [miʎʎo'rare] *vt, vi* to improve

migli'ore [miʎ'ʎore] *ag* (*comparativo*) better; (*superlativo*) best ▷ *sm* **il ~** the best (thing) ▷ *sm/f* **il(la) ~** the best (person); **il miglior vino di questa regione** the best wine in this area

'mignolo ['miɲɲolo] *sm* (*Anat*) little finger, pinkie; (: *dito del piede*) little toe

Mi'lano *sf* Milan

miliar'dario, -a *sm/f* millionaire

mili'ardo *sm* thousand million, billion (*us*)

mili'one *sm* million; **mille euro** one thousand euros

mili'tante *ag, sm/f* militant

mili'tare *vi* (*Mil*) to be a soldier, serve; (*fig: in un partito*) to be a militant ▷ *ag* military ▷ *sm* serviceman; **fare il ~** to do one's military service

'mille (*pl* **mila**) *num* a *o* one thousand; **dieci mila** ten thousand

mil'lennio *sm* millennium

millepi'edi *sm inv* centipede

mil'lesimo, -a *ag, sm* thousandth

milli'grammo *sm* milligram(me)

mil'limetro *sm* millimetre

'milza ['miltsa] *sf* (*Anat*) spleen

mimetiz'zare [mimetid'dzare] *vt* to camouflage; **mimetizzarsi** *vpr* to camouflage o.s.

'mimo *sm* (*attore, componimento*) mime

mi'mosa *sf* mimosa

min. *abbr* (= *minuto, minimo*) min.

'mina *sf* (*esplosiva*) mine; (*di matita*) lead

mi'naccia, -ce [mi'nattʃa] *sf* threat; **minacci'are** *vt* to threaten; **minacciare qn di morte** to threaten to kill sb; **minacciare di fare qc** to threaten to do sth

mi'nare vt (Mil) to mine; (fig) to undermine
mina'tore sm miner
mine'rale ag, sm mineral
mine'rario, -a ag (delle miniere) mining; (dei minerali) ore cpd
mi'nestra sf soup; **minestra in brodo** noodle soup; **minestra di verdure** vegetable soup
minia'tura sf miniature
mini'bar sm inv minibar
mini'era sf mine
mini'gonna sf miniskirt
'minimo, -a ag minimum, least, slightest; (piccolissimo) very small, slight; (il più basso) lowest, minimum ▷ sm minimum; **al ~** at least; **girare al ~** (Aut) to idle
minis'tero sm (Pol, Rel) ministry; (governo) government; **M~ delle Finanze** Ministry of Finance, ≈ Treasury
mi'nistro sm (Pol, Rel) minister
mino'ranza [mino'rantsa] sf minority
mi'nore ag (comparativo) less; (più piccolo) smaller; (numero) lower; (inferiore) lower, inferior; (meno importante) minor; (più giovane) younger; (superlativo) least; smallest; lowest; youngest ▷ sm/f = **minorenne**
mino'renne ag under age ▷ sm/f minor, person under age
mi'nuscolo, -a ag (scrittura, carattere) small; (piccolissimo) tiny ▷ sf small letter
mi'nuto, -a ag tiny, minute; (pioggia) fine; (corporatura) delicate, fine ▷ sm (unità di misura) minute; **al ~** (Comm) retail
'mio (f **'mia**, pl **mi'ei** or **'mie**) det **il ~, la mia** ecc my ▷ pron **il ~, la mia** ecc mine; **i miei** my family; **un ~ amico** a friend of mine
'miope ag short-sighted
'mira sf (anche fig) aim; **prendere la ~** to take aim; **prendere di ~ qn** (fig) to pick on sb
mi'racolo sm miracle
mi'raggio [mi'raddʒo] sm mirage
mi'rare vi **~ a** to aim at
mi'rino sm (Tecn) sight; (Fot) viewer, viewfinder
mir'tillo sm bilberry (BRIT), blueberry (US), whortleberry
mis'cela [miʃ'ʃela] sf mixture; (di caffè) blend
'mischia ['miskja] sf scuffle; (Rugby) scrum, scrummage
mis'cuglio [mis'kuʎʎo] sm mixture, hotchpotch, jumble
'mise vb vedi **mettere**
mise'rabile ag (infelice) miserable, wretched; (povero) poverty-stricken; (di scarso valore) miserable
mi'seria sf extreme poverty; (infelicità) misery

miseri'cordia sf mercy, pity
'misero, -a ag miserable, wretched; (povero) poverty-stricken; (insufficiente) miserable
'misi vb vedi **mettere**
mi'sogino [mi'zodʒino] sm misogynist
'missile sm missile
missio'nario, -a ag, sm/f missionary
missi'one sf mission
misteri'oso, -a ag mysterious
mis'tero sm mystery
'misto, -a ag mixed; (scuola) mixed, coeducational ▷ sm mixture
mis'tura sf mixture
mi'sura sf measure; (misurazione, dimensione) measurement; (taglia) size; (provvedimento) measure, step; (moderazione) moderation; (Mus) time; (: divisione) bar; (fig: limite) bounds pl, limit; **nella ~ in cui** inasmuch as, insofar as; **(fatto) su ~** made to measure
misu'rare vt (ambiente, stoffa) to measure; (terreno) to survey; (abito) to try on; (pesare) to weigh; (fig: parole ecc) to weigh up; (: spese, cibo) to limit ▷ vi to measure; **misurarsi** vpr **misurarsi con qn** to have a confrontation with sb; to compete with sb
'mite ag mild
'mitico, -a, ci, che ag mythical
'mito sm myth; **mitolo'gia, -'gie** sf mythology
'mitra sf (Rel) mitre ▷ sm inv (arma) sub-machine gun
mit'tente sm/f sender
mm abbr (= millimetro) mm
'mobile ag mobile; (parte di macchina) moving; (Dir: bene) movable, personal ▷ sm (arredamento) piece of furniture; **mobili** smpl (mobilia) furniture sg
mocas'sino sm moccasin
'moda sf fashion; **alla ~, di ~** fashionable, in fashion
modalità sf inv formality
mo'della sf model
mo'dello sm model; (stampo) mould ▷ ag inv model cpd
'modem sm inv modem
modera'tore, -'trice sm/f moderator
mo'derno, -a ag modern
mo'desto, -a ag modest
'modico, -a, -ci, -che ag reasonable, moderate
mo'difica, -che sf modification
modifi'care vt to modify, alter
'modo sm way, manner; (mezzo) means, way; (occasione) opportunity; (Ling) mood; (Mus) mode; **modi** smpl (comportamento) manners; **a suo ~, ~ suo** in his own way;

ad *o* **in ogni ~** anyway; **di** *o* **in ~ che** so that; **in ~ da** so as to; **in tutti i modi** at all costs; (*comunque sia*) anyway; (*in ogni caso*) in any case; **in qualche ~** somehow or other; **per ~ di dire** so to speak; **modo di dire** turn of phrase

'**modulo** *sm* (*modello*) form; (*Archit, lunare, di comando*) module

'**mogano** *sm* mahogany

'**mogio, -a, -gi, -gie** ['mɔdʒo] *ag* down in the dumps, dejected

'**moglie** ['moʎʎe] *sf* wife

mo'ine *sfpl* cajolery *sg*; (*leziosità*) affectation *sg*

mo'lare *sm* (*dente*) molar

'**mole** *sf* mass; (*dimensioni*) size; (*edificio grandioso*) massive structure

moles'tare *vt* to bother, annoy; **mo'lestia** *sf* annoyance, bother; **recar molestia a qn** to bother sb; **molestie sessuali** sexual harassment *sg*

'**molla** *sf* spring; **molle** *sfpl* (*per camino*) tongs

mol'lare *vt* to release, let go; (*Naut*) to ease; (*fig: ceffone*) to give ▷ *vi* (*cedere*) to give in

'**molle** *ag* soft; (*muscoli*) flabby

mol'letta *sf* (*per capelli*) hairgrip; (*per panni stesi*) clothes peg

'**mollica, -che** *sf* crumb, soft part

mol'lusco, -schi *sm* mollusc

'**molo** *sm* mole, breakwater; jetty

moltipli'care *vt* to multiply; **moltiplicarsi** *vpr* to multiply; to increase in number; **moltiplicazi'one** *sf* multiplication

 PAROLA CHIAVE

'**molto, -a** *det* (*quantità*) a lot of, much; (*numero*) a lot of, many; **molto pane/carbone** a lot of bread/coal; **molta gente** a lot of people, many people; **molti libri** a lot of books, many books; **non ho molto tempo** I haven't got much time; **per molto (tempo)** for a long time
▷ *av* **1** a lot, (very) much; **viaggia molto** he travels a lot; **non viaggia molto** he doesn't travel much *o* a lot
2 (*intensivo: con aggettivi, avverbi*) very; (: *con participio passato*) (very) much; **molto buono** very good; **molto migliore, molto meglio** much *o* a lot better
▷ *pron* much, a lot

momentanea'mente *av* at the moment, at present

momen'taneo, -a *ag* momentary, fleeting

mo'mento *sm* moment; **da un ~ all'altro** at any moment; (*all'improvviso*) suddenly; **al ~ di fare** just as I was (*o* you were *o* he was *ecc*) doing; **per il ~** for the time being; **dal ~ che** ever since; (*dato che*) since; **a momenti** (*da un momento all'altro*) any time *o* moment now; (*quasi*) nearly

'**monaca, -che** *sf* nun

'**Monaco** *sf* Monaco; **Monaco (di Baviera)** Munich

'**monaco, -ci** *sm* monk

monar'chia *sf* monarchy

monas'tero *sm* (*di monaci*) monastery; (*di monache*) convent

mon'dano, -a *ag* (*anche fig*) worldly; (*anche*: **dell'alta società**) society *cpd*; fashionable

mondi'ale *ag* (*campionato, popolazione*) world *cpd*; (*influenza*) world-wide

'**mondo** *sm* world; (*grande quantità*): **un ~ di** lots of, a host of; **il bel ~** high society

mo'nello, -a *sm/f* street urchin; (*ragazzo vivace*) scamp, imp

mo'neta *sf* coin; (*Econ: valuta*) currency; (*denaro spicciolo*) (small) change; **moneta estera** foreign currency; **moneta legale** legal tender

mongol'fiera *sf* hot-air balloon

'**monitor** *sm inv* (*Tecn, TV*) monitor

monolo'cale *sm* studio flat

mono'polio *sm* monopoly

mo'notono, -a *ag* monotonous

monovo'lume *ag inv, sf inv* (**automobile**) **~** people carrier, MPV

mon'sone *sm* monsoon

monta'carichi [monta'kariki] *sm inv* hoist, goods lift

mon'taggio [mon'taddʒo] *sm* (*Tecn*) assembly; (*Cinema*) editing

mon'tagna [mon'taɲɲa] *sf* mountain; (*zona montuosa*): **la ~** the mountains *pl*; **andare in ~** to go to the mountains; **montagne russe** roller coaster *sg*, big dipper *sg* (BRIT)

monta'naro, -a *ag* mountain *cpd* ▷ *sm/f* mountain dweller

mon'tano, -a *ag* mountain *cpd*; alpine

mon'tare *vt* to go (*o* come) up; (*cavallo*) to ride; (*apparecchiatura*) to set up, assemble; (*Cuc*) to whip; (*Zool*) to cover; (*incastonare*) to mount, set; (*Cinema*) to edit; (*Fot*) to mount ▷ *vi* to go (*o* come) up; (*a cavallo*): **~ bene/male** to ride well/badly; (*aumentare di livello, volume*) to rise

monta'tura *sf* assembling *no pl*; (*di occhiali*) frames *pl*; (*di gioiello*) mounting, setting; (*fig*): **montatura pubblicitaria** publicity stunt

'**monte** *sm* mountain; **a ~** upstream; **mandare a ~ qc** to upset sth, cause sth to fail; **il M~ Bianco** Mont Blanc; **monte di pietà** pawnshop; **monte premi** prize

mon'tone *sm* (*Zool*) ram; **carne di ~** mutton

montu'oso, -a *ag* mountainous

monu'mento *sm* monument

mo'quette [mɔ'kɛt] *sf inv* fitted carpet

'mora *sf* (*del rovo*) blackberry; (*del gelso*) mulberry; (*Dir*) delay; (: *somma*) arrears *pl*

mo'rale *ag* moral ▷ *sf* (*scienza*) ethics *sg*, moral philosophy; (*complesso di norme*) moral standards *pl*, morality; (*condotta*) morals *pl*; (*insegnamento morale*) moral ▷ *sm* morale; **essere giù di ~** to be feeling down

'morbido, -a *ag* soft; (*pelle*) soft, smooth
■ Attenzione! In inglese esiste la parola *morbid*, che però significa *morboso*.

mor'billo *sm* (*Med*) measles *sg*

'morbo *sm* disease

mor'boso, -a *ag* (*fig*) morbid

'mordere *vt* to bite; (*addentare*) to bite into

mori'bondo, -a *ag* dying, moribund

mo'rire *vi* to die; (*abitudine, civiltà*) to die out; **~ di fame** to die of hunger; (*fig*) to be starving; **~ di noia/paura** to be bored/scared to death; **fa un caldo da ~** it's terribly hot

mormo'rare *vi* to murmur; (*brontolare*) to grumble

'moro, -a *ag* dark(-haired), dark(-complexioned)

'morsa *sf* (*Tecn*) vice; (*fig: stretta*) grip

morsi'care *vt* to nibble (at), gnaw (at); (*insetto*) to bite

'morso, -a *pp di* **mordere** ▷ *sm* bite; (*di insetto*) sting; (*parte della briglia*) bit; **morsi della fame** pangs of hunger

morta'della *sf* (*Cuc*) mortadella (*type of salted pork meat*)

mor'taio *sm* mortar

mor'tale *ag, sm* mortal

'morte *sf* death

'morto, -a *pp di* **morire** ▷ *ag* dead ▷ *sm/f* dead man/woman; **i morti** the dead; **fare il ~** (*nell'acqua*) to float on one's back; **il Mar M~** the Dead Sea

mo'saico, -ci *sm* mosaic

'Mosca *sf* Moscow

'mosca, -sche *sf* fly; **mosca cieca** blind-man's-buff

mosce'rino [moʃʃe'rino] *sm* midge, gnat

mos'chea [mos'kɛa] *sf* mosque

'moscio, -a, -sci, -sce ['mɔʃʃo] *ag* (*fig*) lifeless

mos'cone *sm* (*Zool*) bluebottle; (*barca*) pedalo; (: *a remi*) kind of pedalo with oars

'mossa *sf* movement; (*nel gioco*) move

'mossi ecc *vb vedi* **muovere**

'mosso, -a *pp di* **muovere** ▷ *ag* (*mare*) rough; (*capelli*) wavy; (*Fot*) blurred

mos'tarda *sf* mustard; **mostarda di Cremona** pickled fruit with mustard

'mostra *sf* exhibition, show; (*ostentazione*) show; **in ~** on show; **far ~ di** (*fingere*) to pretend; **far ~ di sé** to show off

mos'trare *vt* to show; **può mostrarmi dov'è, per favore?** can you show me where it is, please?

'mostro *sm* monster; **mostru'oso, -a** *ag* monstrous

mo'tel *sm inv* motel

moti'vare *vt* (*causare*) to cause; (*giustificare*) to justify, account for

mo'tivo *sm* (*causa*) reason, cause; (*movente*) motive; (*letterario*) (central) theme; (*disegno*) motif, design, pattern; (*Mus*) motif; **per quale ~?** why?, for what reason?

'moto *sm* (*anche Fisica*) motion; (*movimento, gesto*) movement; (*esercizio fisico*) exercise; (*sommossa*) rising, revolt; (*commozione*) feeling, impulse ▷ *sf inv* (*motocicletta*) motorbike; **mettere in ~** to set in motion; (*Aut*) to start up

motoci'clista, -i, -e *sm/f* motorcyclist

mo'tore, -'trice *ag* motor; (*Tecn*) driving ▷ *sm* engine, motor; **a ~** motor *cpd*, power-driven; **~ a combustione interna/a reazione** internal combustion/jet engine; **motore di ricerca** (*Inform*) search engine; **moto'rino** *sm* moped; **motorino di avviamento** (*Aut*) starter

motos'cafo *sm* motorboat

'motto *sm* (*battuta scherzosa*) witty remark; (*frase emblematica*) motto, maxim

'mouse ['maus] *sm inv* (*Inform*) mouse

mo'vente *sm* motive

movi'mento *sm* movement; (*fig*) activity, hustle and bustle; (*Mus*) tempo, movement

mozi'one [mot'tsjone] *sf* (*Pol*) motion

mozza'rella [mottsa'rella] *sf* mozzarella, *a moist Neapolitan curd cheese*

mozzi'cone [mottsi'kone] *sm* stub, butt, end; (*anche:* **~ di sigaretta**) cigarette end

'mucca, -che *sf* cow; **mucca pazza** mad cow disease

'mucchio ['mukkjo] *sm* pile, heap; (*fig*): **un ~ di** lots of, heaps of

'muco, -chi *sm* mucus

'muffa *sf* mould, mildew

mug'gire [mud'dʒire] *vi* (*vacca*) to low, moo; (*toro*) to bellow; (*fig*) to roar

mu'ghetto [mu'getto] *sm* lily of the valley

mu'lino *sm* mill; **mulino a vento** windmill

'mulo *sm* mule

'multa *sf* fine

multi'etnico, -a, -ci, -che *ag* multiethnic
multirazziale [multirat'tsjale] *ag* multiracial
multi'sala *ag inv* multiscreen
multivitami'nico, -a, -ci, -che *ag*
  complesso ~ multivitamin
'mummia *sf* mummy
'mungere ['mundʒere] *vt* (*anche fig*) to milk
munici'pale [munitʃi'pale] *ag* municipal; town *cpd*
muni'cipio [muni'tʃipjo] *sm* town council, corporation; (*edificio*) town hall
munizi'oni [munit'tsjoni] *sfpl* (*Mil*) ammunition *sg*
'munsi *ecc vb vedi* **mungere**
mu'oio *ecc vb vedi* **morire**
mu'overe *vt* to move; (*ruota, macchina*) to drive; (*sollevare: questione, obiezione*) to raise, bring up; (: *accusa*) to make, bring forward; **muoversi** *vpr* to move; **muoviti!** hurry up!, get a move on!
'mura *sfpl vedi* **muro**
mu'rale *ag* wall *cpd*; mural
mura'tore *sm* mason; bricklayer
'muro *sm* wall
'muschio ['muskjo] *sm* (*Zool*) musk; (*Bot*) moss
musco'lare *ag* muscular, muscle *cpd*
'muscolo *sm* (*Anat*) muscle
mu'seo *sm* museum
museru'ola *sf* muzzle
'musica *sf* music; **musica da ballo/camera** dance/chamber music; **musi'cale** *ag* musical; **musi'cista, -i, -e** *sm/f* musician
'müsli ['mysli] *sm* muesli
'muso *sm* muzzle; (*di auto, aereo*) nose; **tenere il ~** to sulk
mussul'mano, -a *ag, sm/f* Muslim, Moslem
'muta *sf* (*di animali*) moulting; (*di serpenti*) sloughing; (*per immersioni subacquee*) diving suit; (*gruppo di cani*) pack
mu'tande *sfpl* (*da uomo*) (under)pants
'muto, -a *ag* (*Med*) dumb; (*emozione, dolore, Cinema*) silent; (*Ling*) silent, mute; (*carta geografica*) blank; **~ per lo stupore** *ecc* speechless with amazement *ecc*
'mutuo, -a *ag* (*reciproco*) mutual ▷ *sm* (*Econ*) (long-term) loan

n

N *abbr* (= nord) N
n. *abbr* (= numero) no.
'nafta *sf* naphtha; (*per motori diesel*) diesel oil
nafta'lina *sf* (*Chim*) naphthalene; (*tarmicida*) mothballs *pl*
'naia *sf* (*Mil*) slang term for national service
na'if [na'if] *ag inv* naïve
'nanna *sf* (*linguaggio infantile*): **andare a ~** to go to beddy-byes
'nano, -a *ag, sm/f* dwarf
napole'tano, -a *ag, sm/f* Neapolitan
'Napoli *sf* Naples
nar'ciso [nar'tʃizo] *sm* narcissus
nar'cotico, -ci *sm* narcotic
na'rice [na'ritʃe] *sf* nostril
nar'rare *vt* to tell the story of, recount; **narra'tiva** *sf* (*branca letteraria*) fiction
na'sale *ag* nasal
'nascere ['naʃʃere] *vi* (*bambino*) to be born; (*pianta*) to come o spring up; (*fiume*) to rise, have its source; (*sole*) to rise; (*dente*) to come through; (*fig: derivare, conseguire*): **~ da** to arise from, be born out of; **è nata nel 1952** she was born in 1952; **'nascita** *sf* birth
nas'condere *vt* to hide, conceal; **nascondersi** *vpr* to hide; **nascon'diglio** *sm* hiding place; **nascon'dino** *sm* (*gioco*) hide-and-seek; **nas'cosi** *ecc vb*

vedi **nascondere**; **nas'costo, -a** *pp di*
nascondere ▷ *ag* hidden; **di nascosto**
secretly
na'sello *sm* (*Zool*) hake
'naso *sm* nose
'nastro *sm* ribbon; (*magnetico, isolante,*
Sport) tape; **nastro adesivo** adhesive
tape; **nastro trasportatore** conveyor belt
nas'turzio [nas'turtsjo] *sm* nasturtium
na'tale *ag* of one's birth ▷ *sm* (*Rel*): **N~**
Christmas; (*giorno della nascita*) birthday;
nata'lizio, -a *ag* (*del Natale*) Christmas *cpd*
'natica, -che *sf* (*Anat*) buttock
'nato, -a *pp di* **nascere** ▷ *ag* **un attore ~** a
born actor; **nata Pieri** née Pieri
na'tura *sf* nature; **pagare in ~** to pay in
kind; **natura morta** still life
natu'rale *ag* natural
natural'mente *av* naturally; (*certamente,*
sì) of course
natu'rista, -i, e *ag, sm/f* naturist, nudist
naufra'gare *vi* (*nave*) to be wrecked;
(*persona*) to be shipwrecked; (*fig*) to fall
through; **'naufrago, -ghi** *sm* castaway,
shipwreck victim
'nausea *sf* nausea; **nause'ante** *ag* (*odore*)
nauseating; (*sapore*) disgusting; (*fig*)
sickening
'nautico, -a, -ci, -che *ag* nautical
na'vale *ag* naval
na'vata *sf* (*anche:* **~ centrale**) nave; (*anche:*
~ laterale) aisle
'nave *sf* ship, vessel; **nave cisterna**
tanker; **nave da guerra** warship; **nave**
passeggeri passenger ship
na'vetta *sf* shuttle; (*servizio di*
collegamento) shuttle (service)
navi'cella [navi't∫ella] *sf* (*di aerostato*)
gondola; **navicella spaziale** spaceship
navi'gare *vi* to sail; **~ in Internet** to surf
the Net; **navigazi'one** *sf* navigation
nazio'nale [nattsjo'nale] *ag* national ▷ *sf*
(*Sport*) national team; **nazionalità** *sf inv*
nationality
nazi'one [nat'tsjone] *sf* nation
naziskin ['nɑːtsiskin] *sm inv* Nazi
skinhead
NB *abbr* (= *nota bene*) NB

 PAROLA CHIAVE

ne *pron* **1** (*di lui, lei, loro*) of him/her/them;
about him/her/them; **ne riconosco la**
voce I recognize his (*o* her) voice
2 (*di questa, quella cosa*) of it; about it; **ne**
voglio ancora I want some more (of it *o*
them); **non parliamone più!** let's not talk
about it any more!
3 (*con valore partitivo*): **hai dei libri? — sì,**

ne ho have you any books? — yes, I have
(some); **hai del pane? — no, non ne ho**
have you any bread? — no, I haven't any;
quanti anni hai? — ne ho 17 how old are
you? — I'm 17
▷ *av* (*moto da luogo: da lì*) from there; **ne**
vengo ora I've just come from there

né *cong* **né ... né** neither ... nor; **né l'uno**
né l'altro lo vuole neither of them wants
it; **non parla né l'italiano né il tedesco**
he speaks neither Italian nor German, he
doesn't speak either Italian or German;
non piove né nevica it isn't raining or
snowing
ne'anche [ne'anke] *av, cong* not even;
non ... ~ not even; **~ se volesse**
potrebbe venire he couldn't even come
if he wanted to; **non l'ho visto — ~ io**
I didn't see him — neither did I *o* I didn't
either; **~ per idea** *o* **sogno!** not on your
life!
'nebbia *sf* fog; (*foschia*) mist
necessaria'mente [net∫essarjamɛnte]
av necessarily
neces'sario, -a [net∫es'sarjo] *ag*
necessary
necessità [net∫essi'ta] *sf inv* necessity;
(*povertà*) need, poverty
necro'logio [nekro'lɔdʒo] *sm* obituary
notice
ne'gare *vt* to deny; (*rifiutare*) to deny,
refuse; **~ di aver fatto/che** to deny
having done/that; **nega'tivo, -a** *ag, sf, sm*
negative
negherò *ecc* [nege'rɔ] *vb vedi* **negare**
negli'gente [negli'dʒɛnte] *ag* negligent,
careless
negozi'ante [negot'tsjante] *sm/f* trader,
dealer; (*bottegaio*) shopkeeper (BRIT),
storekeeper (US)
negozi'are [negot'tsjare] *vt* to negotiate
▷ *vi* **~ in** to trade *o* deal in; **negozi'ato** *sm*
negotiation
ne'gozio [ne'gɔttsjo] *sm* (*locale*) shop
(BRIT), store (US)
'negro, -a *ag, sm/f* Negro
ne'mico, -a, -ci, -che *ag* hostile; (*Mil*)
enemy *cpd* ▷ *sm/f* enemy; **essere ~ di** to be
strongly averse *o* opposed to
nem'meno *av, cong* = **neanche**
'neo *sm* mole; (*fig*) (slight) flaw
'neon *sm* (*Chim*) neon
neo'nato, -a *ag* newborn ▷ *sm/f* newborn
baby
neozelan'dese [neoddzelan'dese] *ag*
New Zealand *cpd* ▷ *sm/f* New Zealander
'Nepal *sm* **il ~** Nepal
nep'pure *av, cong* = **neanche**

'**nero, -a** *ag* black; (*scuro*) dark ▷ *sm* black;
il Mar N~ the Black Sea

'**nervo** *sm* (*Anat*) nerve; (*Bot*) vein; **avere
i nervi** to be on edge; **dare sui nervi a
qn** to get on sb's nerves; **ner'voso, -a** *ag*
nervous; (*irritabile*) irritable ▷ *sm* (*fam*):
far venire il nervoso a qn to get on sb's
nerves

'**nespola** *sf* (*Bot*) medlar; (*fig*) blow, punch

'**nesso** *sm* connection, link

PAROLA CHIAVE

nes'suno, -a (*det: dav sm* **nessun** +C,V,
nessuno +*s impura, gn, pn, ps, x, z; dav sf*
nessuna +C, **nessun'** +V) *det* **1** (*non uno*)
no; (, *espressione negativa* +) any; **non c'è
nessun libro** there isn't any book, there
is no book; **nessun altro** no one else,
nobody else; **nessun'altra cosa** nothing
else; **in nessun luogo** nowhere
2 (*qualche*) any; **hai nessuna obiezione?**
do you have any objections?
▷ *pron* **1** (*non uno*) no one, nobody; (,
espressione negativa +) any(one); (: *cosa*)
none; (, *espressione negativa* +) any;
**nessuno è venuto, non è venuto
nessuno** nobody came
2 (*qualcuno*) anyone, anybody; **ha
telefonato nessuno?** did anyone phone?

net'tare *vt* to clean

net'tezza [net'tettsa] *sf* cleanness,
cleanliness; **nettezza urbana** cleansing
department

'**netto, -a** *ag* (*pulito*) clean; (*chiaro*) clear,
clear-cut; (*deciso*) definite; (*Econ*) net

nettur'bino *sm* dustman (BRIT), garbage
collector (US)

neu'trale *ag* neutral

'**neutro, -a** *ag* neutral; (*Ling*) neuter ▷ *sm*
(*Ling*) neuter

'**neve** *sf* snow; **nevi'care** *vb impers* to
snow; **nevi'cata** *sf* snowfall

ne'vischio [ne'viskjo] *sm* sleet

ne'voso, -a *ag* snowy; snow-covered

nevral'gia [nevral'dʒia] *sf* neuralgia

nevras'tenico, -a, -ci, -che *ag* (*Med*)
neurasthenic; (*fig*) hot-tempered

ne'vrosi *sf* neurosis

ne'vrotico, -a, ci, che *ag, sm/f* (*anche fig*)
neurotic

'**nicchia** ['nikkja] *sf* niche; (*naturale*) cavity,
hollow; **nicchia di mercato** (*Comm*) niche
market

nicchi'are [nik'kjare] *vi* to shilly-shally,
hesitate

'**nichel** ['nikel] *sm* nickel

nico'tina *sf* nicotine

'**nido** *sm* nest; **a ~ d'ape** (*tessuto ecc*)
honeycomb *cpd*

PAROLA CHIAVE

ni'ente *pron* **1** (*nessuna cosa*) nothing;
niente può fermarlo nothing can stop
him; **niente di niente** absolutely nothing;
nient'altro nothing else; **nient'altro che**
nothing but, just, only; **niente affatto**
not at all, not in the least; **come se niente
fosse** as if nothing had happened; **cose da
niente** trivial matters; **per niente** (*gratis,
invano*) for nothing
2 (*qualcosa*): **hai bisogno di niente?** do
you need anything?
3: **non ... niente** nothing; (*espressione
negativa* +) anything; **non ho visto niente**
I saw nothing, I didn't see anything; **non
ho niente da dire** I have nothing o haven't
anything to say
▷ *sm* nothing; **un bel niente** absolutely
nothing; **basta un niente per farla
piangere** the slightest thing is enough to
make her cry ▷ *av* (*in nessuna misura*): **non
... niente** not ... at all; **non è (per) niente
buono** it isn't good at all

Ni'geria [ni'dʒɛrja] *sf* **la ~** Nigeria

'**ninfa** *sf* nymph

nin'fea *sf* water lily

ninna-'nanna *sf* lullaby

'**ninnolo** *sm* (*gingillo*) knick-knack

ni'pote *sm/f* (*di zii*) nephew/niece; (*di
nonni*) grandson/daughter, grandchild

'**nitido, -a** *ag* clear; (*specchio*) bright

ni'trire *vi* to neigh

ni'trito *sm* (*di cavallo*) neighing *no pl*; neigh;
(*Chim*) nitrite

nitroglice'rina [nitroglitʃe'rina] *sf*
nitroglycerine

no *av* (*risposta*) no; **vieni o no?** are you
coming or not?; **perché no?** why not?;
lo conosciamo? — tu no ma io sì do we
know him? — you don't but I do; **verrai,
no?** you'll come, won't you?

'**nobile** *ag* noble ▷ *sm/f* noble, nobleman/
woman

'**nocca, -che** *sf* (*Anat*) knuckle

'**noccio** *ecc* ['nɔttʃo] *vb vedi* **nuocere**

nocci'ola [not'tʃɔla] *ag inv* (*colore*) hazel,
light brown ▷ *sf* hazelnut

noccio'lina [nottʃo'lina] *sf*: **nocciolina
americana** peanut

'**nocciolo** ['nɔttʃolo] *sm* (*di frutto*) stone;
(*fig*) heart, core

'**noce** ['nɔtʃe] *sm* (*albero*) walnut tree ▷ *sf*
(*frutto*) walnut; **noce di cocco** coconut;
noce moscata nutmeg

no'cevo *ecc* [no't∫evo] *vb vedi* **nuocere**
no'civo, -a [no't∫ivo] *ag* harmful, noxious
'nocqui *ecc vb vedi* **nuocere**
'nodo *sm* (*di cravatta, legname, Naut*) knot; (*Aut, Ferr*) junction; (*Med, Astr, Bot*) node; (*fig: legame*) bond, tie; (: *punto centrale*) heart, crux; **avere un ~ alla gola** to have a lump in one's throat
no-'global *sm/f* anti-globalization protester ▷ *ag* (*movimento, manifestante*) anti-globalization
'noi *pron* (*soggetto*) we; (*oggetto: per dare rilievo, con preposizione*) us; **~ stessi(e)** we ourselves; (*oggetto*) ourselves
'noia *sf* boredom; (*disturbo, impaccio*) bother *no pl*, trouble *no pl*; **avere qn/qc a ~** not to like sb/sth; **mi è venuto a ~** I'm tired of it; **dare ~ a** to annoy; **avere delle noie con qn** to have trouble with sb
noi'oso, -a *ag* boring; (*fastidioso*) annoying, troublesome

> Attenzione! In inglese esiste la parola *noisy*, che però significa *rumoroso*.

noleggi'are [noled'dʒare] *vt* (*prendere a noleggio*) to hire (BRIT); (*dare a noleggio*) to hire out (BRIT), rent (out); (*aereo, nave*) to charter; **vorrei ~ una macchina** I'd like to hire a car; **no'leggio** *sm* hire (BRIT), rental; charter
'nomade *ag* nomadic ▷ *sm/f* nomad
'nome *sm* name; (*Ling*) noun; **in/a ~ di** in the name of; **di o per ~** (*chiamato*) called, named; **conoscere qn di ~** to know sb by name; **nome d'arte** stage name; **nome di battesimo** Christian name; **nome di famiglia** surname
no'mignolo [no'miɲɲolo] *sm* nickname
'nomina *sf* appointment
nomi'nale *ag* nominal; (*Ling*) noun *cpd*
nomi'nare *vt* to name; (*eleggere*) to appoint; (*citare*) to mention
nomina'tivo, -a *ag* (*Ling*) nominative; (*Econ*) registered ▷ *sm* (*Ling: anche:* **caso ~**) nominative (case); (*Amm*) name
non *av* not ▷ *prefisso* non-; *vedi* **affatto; appena** *ecc*
nonché [non'ke] *cong* (*tanto più, tanto meno*) let alone; (*e inoltre*) as well as
noncu'rante *ag* **~ (di)** careless (of), indifferent (to)
'nonno, -a *sm/f* grandfather/mother; (*in senso più familiare*) grandma/grandpa; **i nonni** *smpl* the grandparents
non'nulla *sm inv* **un ~** nothing, a trifle
'nono, -a *ag, sm* ninth
nonos'tante *prep* in spite of, notwithstanding ▷ *cong* although, even though
nontiscordardimé *sm inv* (*Bot*) forget-

me-not
nord *sm* North ▷ *ag inv* north; northern; **il Mare del N~** the North Sea; **nor'dest** *sm* north-east; **nor'dovest** *sm* north-west
'norma *sf* (*principio*) norm; (*regola*) regulation, rule; (*consuetudine*) custom, rule; **a ~ di legge** according to law, as laid down by law; **norme per l'uso** instructions for use; **norme di sicurezza** safety regulations
nor'male *ag* normal; standard *cpd*
normal'mente *av* normally
norve'gese [norve'dʒese] *ag, sm/f, sm* Norwegian
Nor'vegia [nor'vedʒa] *sf* **la ~** Norway
nostal'gia [nostal'dʒia] *sf* (*di casa, paese*) homesickness; (*del passato*) nostalgia
nos'trano, -a *ag* local; national; home-produced
'nostro, -a *det* **il (la) ~(-a)** *ecc* our ▷ *pron* **il (la) ~(-a)** *ecc* ours ▷ *sm* **il ~** our money; our belongings; **i nostri** our family; our own people; **è dei nostri** he's one of us
'nota *sf* (*segno*) mark; (*comunicazione scritta, Mus*) note; (*fattura*) bill; (*elenco*) list; **degno di ~** noteworthy, worthy of note
no'taio *sm* notary
no'tare *vt* (*segnare: errori*) to mark; (*registrare*) to note (down), write down; (*rilevare, osservare*) to note, notice; **farsi ~** to get o.s. noticed
no'tevole *ag* (*talento*) notable, remarkable; (*peso*) considerable
no'tifica, -che *sf* notification
no'tizia [no'tittsja] *sf* (*piece of*) news *sg*; (*informazione*) piece of information; **notizi'ario** *sm* (*Radio, TV, Stampa*) news *sg*
'noto, -a *ag* (well-)known
notori'età *sf* fame; notoriety
no'torio, -a *ag* well-known; (*peg*) notorious
not'tambulo, -a *sm/f* night-bird; (*fig*)
not'tata *sf* night
'notte *sf* night; **di ~** at night; (*durante la notte*) in the night, during the night; **notte bianca** sleepless night
not'turno, -a *ag* nocturnal; (*servizio, guardiano*) night *cpd*
no'vanta *num* ninety; **novan'tesimo, -a** *num* ninetieth
'nove *num* nine
nove'cento [nove't∫ento] *num* nine hundred ▷ *sm* **il N~** the twentieth century
no'vella *sf* (*Letteratura*) short story
no'vello, -a *ag* (*piante, patate*) new; (*insalata, verdura*) early; (*sposo*) newly-married
no'vembre *sm* November
novità *sf inv* novelty; (*innovazione*)

innovation; (*cosa originale, insolita*)
something new; (*notizia*) (piece of) news
sg; **le ~ della moda** the latest fashions
nozi'one [not'tsjone] *sf* notion, idea
'**nozze** ['nɔttse] *sfpl* wedding *sg*, marriage
sg; **nozze d'argento/d'oro** silver/golden
wedding *sg*
'**nubile** *ag* (*donna*) unmarried, single
'**nuca** *sf* nape of the neck
nucle'are *ag* nuclear
'**nucleo** *sm* nucleus; (*gruppo*) team,
unit, group; (*Mil, Polizia*) squad; **nucleo
familiare** family unit
nu'dista, -i, -e *sm/f* nudist
'**nudo, -a** *ag* (*persona*) bare, naked, nude;
(*membra*) bare, naked; (*montagna*) bare
▷ *sm* (*Arte*) nude
'**nulla** *pron, av* = **niente** ▷ *sm* = **il nulla**
nothing
nullità *sf inv* nullity; (*persona*) nonentity
'**nullo, -a** *ag* useless, worthless; (*Dir*) null
(and void); (*Sport*): **incontro ~** draw
nume'rale *ag, sm* numeral
nume'rare *vt* to number
nu'merico, -a, -ci, -che *ag* numerical
'**numero** *sm* number; (*romano, arabo*)
numeral; (*di spettacolo*) act, turn; **numero
civico** house number; **numero di scarpe**
shoe size; **numero di telefono** telephone
number; **nume'roso, -a** *ag* numerous,
many; (*con sostantivo sg*) large
nu'occio *ecc* ['nwɔttʃo] *vb vedi* **nuocere**
nu'ocere ['nwɔtʃere] *vi* **~ a** to harm,
damage
nu'ora *sf* daughter-in-law
nuo'tare *vi* to swim; (*galleggiare: oggetti*) to
float; **nuota'tore, -'trice** *sm/f* swimmer;
nu'oto *sm* swimming
nu'ova *sf* (*notizia*) (piece of) news *sg*; *vedi
anche* **nuovo**
nuova'mente *av* again
Nu'ova Ze'landa [-dze'landa] *sf* **la ~** New
Zealand
nu'ovo, -a *ag* new; **di ~** again; **~
fiammante** *o* **di zecca** brand-new
nutri'ente *ag* nutritious, nourishing
nutri'mento *sm* food, nourishment
nu'trire *vt* to feed; (*fig: sentimenti*) to
harbour, nurse; **nutrirsi** *vpr* **nutrirsi di** to
feed on, to eat
'**nuvola** *sf* cloud; **nuvo'loso, -a** *ag* cloudy
nuzi'ale [nut'tsjale] *ag* nuptial; wedding
cpd
'**nylon** ['nailən] *sm* nylon

O

o (*davV spesso* **od**) *cong* or; **o ... o** either ...
or; **o l'uno o l'altro** either (of them)
O *abbr* (= *ovest*) W
'**oasi** *sf inv* oasis
obbedi'ente *ecc* = **ubbidiente** *ecc*
obbli'gare *vt* (*costringere*): **~ qn a fare**
to force *o* oblige sb to do; (*Dir*) to bind;
obbliga'torio, -a *ag* compulsory,
obligatory; '**obbligo, -ghi** *sm* obligation;
(*dovere*) duty; **avere l'obbligo di fare** to be
obliged to do; **essere d'obbligo** (*discorso,
applauso*) to be called for
o'beso, -a *ag* obese
obiet'tare *vt* **~ che** to object that; **~
su qc** to object to sth, raise objections
concerning sth
obiet'tivo, -a *ag* objective ▷ *sm* (*Ottica,
Fot*) lens *sg*, objective; (*Mil, fig*) objective
obiet'tore *sm* objector; **obiettore di
coscienza** conscientious objector
obiezi'one [objet'tsjone] *sf* objection
obi'torio *sm* morgue, mortuary
o'bliquo, -a *ag* oblique; (*inclinato*)
slanting; (*fig*) devious, underhand
oblite'rare *vt* (*biglietto*) to stamp;
(*francobollo*) to cancel
oblò *sm inv* porthole
'**oboe** *sm* (*Mus*) oboe
'**oca** (*pl* '**oche**) *sf* goose
occasi'one *sf* (*caso favorevole*) opportunity;

(*causa, motivo, circostanza*) occasion; (*Comm*) bargain; **d'~** (*a buon prezzo*) bargain *cpd*; (*usato*) secondhand

occhi'aia [ok'kjaja] *sf* **avere le occhiaie** to have shadows under one's eyes

occhi'ali [ok'kjali] *smpl* glasses, spectacles; **occhiali da sole/da vista** sunglasses/(prescription) glasses

occhi'ata [ok'kjata] *sf* look, glance; **dare un'~ a** to have a look at

occhi'ello [ok'kjɛllo] *sm* buttonhole; (*asola*) eyelet

'occhio ['ɔkkjo] *sm* eye; **~!** careful!, watch out!; **a ~ nudo** with the naked eye; **a quatt'rocchi** privately, tête-à-tête; **dare all'~** o **nell'~ a qn** to catch sb's eye; **fare l'~ a qc** to get used to sth; **tenere d'~ qn** to keep an eye on sb; **vedere di buon/mal ~ qc** to look favourably/unfavourably on sth

occhio'lino [okkjo'lino] *sm* **fare l'~ a qn** to wink at sb

occiden'tale [ottʃiden'tale] *ag* western ▷ *sm/f* Westerner

occi'dente [ottʃi'dɛnte] *sm* west; (*Pol*): **l'O~** the West; **a ~** in the west

occor'rente *ag* necessary ▷ *sm* all that is necessary

occor'renza [okkor'rɛntsa] *sf* necessity, need; **all'~** in case of need

oc'correre *vi* to be needed, be required ▷ *vb impers* **occorre farlo** it must be done; **occorre che tu parta** you must leave, you'll have to leave; **mi occorrono i soldi** I need the money

> Attenzione! In inglese esiste il verbo *to occur*, che però significa *succedere*.

oc'culto, -a *ag* hidden, concealed; (*scienze, forze*) occult

occu'pare *vt* to occupy; (*manodopera*) to employ; (*ingombrare*) to occupy, take up; **occuparsi** *vpr* to occupy o.s., keep o.s. busy; (*impiegarsi*) to get a job; **occuparsi di** (*interessarsi*) to take an interest in; (*prendersi cura di*) to look after, take care of; **occu'pato, -a** *ag* (*Mil, Pol*) occupied; (*persona: affaccendato*) busy; (*posto, sedia*) taken; (*toilette, Tel*) engaged; **la linea è occupata** the line's engaged; **è occupato questo posto?** is this seat taken?; **occupazi'one** *sf* occupation; (*impiego, lavoro*) job; (*Econ*) employment

o'ceano [o'tʃeano] *sm* ocean

'ocra *sf* ochre

'OCSE *sigla f* (= *Organizzazione per la Cooperazione e lo Sviluppo Economico*) OECD (*Organization for Economic Cooperation and Development*)

ocu'lare *ag* ocular, eye *cpd*; **testimone ~** eye witness

ocu'lato, -a *ag* (*attento*) cautious, prudent; (*accorto*) shrewd

ocu'lista, -i, -e *sm/f* eye specialist, oculist

odi'are *vt* to hate, detest

odi'erno, -a *ag* today's, of today; (*attuale*) present

'odio *sm* hatred; **avere in ~ qc/qn** to hate o detest sth/sb; **odi'oso, -a** *ag* hateful, odious

odo'rare *vt* (*annusare*) to smell; (*profumare*) to perfume, scent ▷ *vi* **~ (di)** to smell (of)

o'dore *sm* smell; **odori** *smpl* (*Cuc*) (aromatic) herbs

of'fendere *vt* to offend; (*violare*) to break, violate; (*insultare*) to insult; (*ferire*) to hurt; **offendersi** *vpr* (*con senso reciproco*) to insult one another; (*risentirsi*): **offendersi (di)** to take offence (at), be offended (by)

offe'rente *sm* (*in aste*): **al maggior ~** to the highest bidder

of'ferta *sf* offer; (*donazione, anche Rel*) offering; (*in gara d'appalto*) tender; (*in aste*) bid; (*Econ*) supply; **fare un'~** to make an offer; to tender; to bid; **"offerte d'impiego"** "situations vacant"; **offerta speciale** special offer

of'fesa *sf* insult, affront; (*Mil*) attack; (*Dir*) offence; *vedi anche* **offeso**

of'feso, -a *pp di* **offendere** ▷ *ag* offended; (*fisicamente*) hurt, injured ▷ *sm/f* offended party; **essere ~ con qn** to be annoyed with sb; **parte offesa** (*Dir*) plaintiff

offi'cina [offi'tʃina] *sf* workshop

of'frire *vt* to offer; **offrirsi** *vpr* (*proporsi*) to offer (o.s.), volunteer; (*occasione*) to present itself; (*esporsi*): **offrirsi a** to expose o.s. to; **ti offro da bere** I'll buy you a drink

offus'care *vt* to obscure, darken; (*fig: intelletto*) to dim, cloud; (: *fama*) to obscure, overshadow; **offuscarsi** *vpr* to grow dark; to cloud, grow dim; to be obscured

ogget'tivo, -a [odd3et'tivo] *ag* objective

og'getto [od'd3etto] *sm* object; (*materia, argomento*) subject (matter); **oggetti smarriti** lost property *sg*

'oggi ['ɔdd3i] *av, sm* today; **~ a otto** a week today; **oggigi'orno** *av* nowadays

OGM *sigla m* (= *organismo geneticamente modificato*) GMO

'ogni ['ɔɲɲi] *det* every, each; (*tutti*) all; (*con valore distributivo*) every; **~ uomo è mortale** all men are mortal; **viene ~ due giorni** he comes every two days; **~ cosa** everything; **ad ~ costo** at all costs, at any price; **in ~ luogo** everywhere; **~ tanto** every so often; **~ volta che** every time that

Ognis'santi [oɲɲis'santi] *sm* All Saints' Day

o'gnuno [oɲ'ɲuno] *pron* everyone,

everybody

O'landa sf l'~ Holland; **olan'dese** ag Dutch ▷ sm (Ling) Dutch ▷ sm/f Dutchman/woman; **gli Olandesi** the Dutch

ole'andro sm oleander

oleo'dotto sm oil pipeline

ole'oso, -a ag oily; (che contiene olio) oil-yielding

ol'fatto sm sense of smell

oli'are vt to oil

oli'era sf oil cruet

Olim'piadi sfpl Olympic games; **o'limpico, -a, -ci, -che** ag Olympic

'olio sm oil; **sott'~** (Cuc) in oil; **~ di fegato di merluzzo** cod liver oil; **olio d'oliva** olive oil; **olio di semi** vegetable oil

o'liva sf olive; **o'livo** sm olive tree

'olmo sm elm

OLP sigla f (= Organizzazione per la Liberazione della Palestina) PLO

ol'traggio [ol'traddʒo] sm outrage; offence, insult; **~ a pubblico ufficiale** (Dir) insulting a public official; **oltraggio al pudore** (Dir) indecent behaviour

ol'tranza [ol'trantsa] sf **a ~** to the last, to the bitter end

'oltre av (più in là) further; (di più: aspettare) longer, more ▷ prep (di là da) beyond, over, on the other side of; (più di) more than, over; (in aggiunta a) besides; (eccetto): **~ a** except, apart from; **oltrepas'sare** vt to go beyond, exceed

o'maggio [o'maddʒo] sm (dono) gift; (segno di rispetto) homage, tribute; **omaggi** smpl (complimenti) respects; **rendere ~ a** to pay homage o tribute to; **in ~** (copia, biglietto) complimentary

ombe'lico, -chi sm navel

'ombra sf (zona non assolata, fantasma) shade; (sagoma scura) shadow; **sedere all'~** to sit in the shade; **restare nell'~** (fig) to remain in obscurity

om'brello sm umbrella; **ombrel'lone** sm beach umbrella

om'bretto sm eye shadow

O.M.C. sigla f (= Organizzazione Mondiale del Commercio) WTO

ome'lette [ɔma'lɛt] sf inv omelet(te)

ome'lia sf (Rel) homily, sermon

omeopa'tia sf homoeopathy

omertà sf conspiracy of silence

o'mettere vt to omit, leave out; **~ di fare** to omit o fail to do

omi'cida, -i, -e [omi'tʃida] ag homicidal, murderous ▷ sm/f murderer/eress

omi'cidio [omi'tʃidjo] sm murder; **omicidio colposo** culpable homicide

o'misi ecc vb vedi **omettere**

omissi'one sf omission; **omissione di soccorso** (Dir) failure to stop and give assistance

omogeneiz'zato [omodʒeneid'dzato] sm baby food

omo'geneo, -a [omo'dʒɛneo] ag homogeneous

o'monimo, -a sm/f namesake ▷ sm (Ling) homonym

omosessu'ale ag, sm/f homosexual

O.M.S. sigla f (= Organizzazione Mondiale della Sanità) WHO

On. abbr (Pol) = **onorevole**

'onda sf wave; **mettere** o **mandare in ~** (Radio, TV) to broadcast; **andare in ~** (Radio, TV) to go on the air; **onde corte/lunghe/medie** short/long/medium wave

'onere sm burden; **oneri fiscali** taxes

onestà sf honesty

o'nesto, -a ag (probo, retto) honest; (giusto) fair; (casto) chaste, virtuous

ONG sigla f inv **Organizzazione Non Governativa** NGO

onnipo'tente ag omnipotent

ono'mastico, -ci sm name-day

ono'rare vt to honour; (far onore a) to do credit to

ono'rario, -a ag honorary ▷ sm fee

o'nore sm honour; **in ~ di** in honour of; **fare gli onori di casa** to play host (o hostess); **fare ~ a** to honour; (pranzo) to do justice to; (famiglia) to be a credit to; **farsi ~** to distinguish o.s.; **ono'revole** ag honourable ▷ sm/f (Pol) ≈ Member of Parliament (BRIT), ≈ Congressman/woman (US)

on'tano sm (Bot) alder

'O.N.U. ['ɔnu] sigla f (= Organizzazione delle Nazioni Unite) UN, UNO

o'paco, -a, -chi, -che ag (vetro) opaque; (metallo) dull, matt

o'pale sm o f opal

'opera sf work; (azione rilevante) action, deed, work; (Mus) work; opus; (: melodramma) opera; (: teatro) opera house; (ente) institution, organization; **opere pubbliche** public works; **opera d'arte** work of art; **opera lirica** (grand) opera

ope'raio, -a ag working-class; workers' ▷ sm/f worker; **classe operaia** working class

ope'rare vt to carry out, make; (Med) to operate on ▷ vi to operate, work; (rimedio) to act, work; (Med) to operate; **operarsi** vpr (Med) to have an operation; **operarsi d'appendicite** to have one's appendix out; **operazi'one** sf operation

ope'retta sf (Mus) operetta, light opera

opini'one *sf* opinion; **opinione pubblica** public opinion

'oppio *sm* opium

op'pongo *ecc vb vedi* **opporre**

op'porre *vt* to oppose; **opporsi** *vpr* **opporsi (a qc)** to oppose (sth); to object (to sth); ~ **resistenza/un rifiuto** to offer resistance/refuse

opportu'nista, -i, -e *sm/f* opportunist

opportunità *sf inv* opportunity; *(convenienza)* opportuneness, timeliness

oppor'tuno, -a *ag* timely, opportune

op'posi *ecc vb vedi* **opporre**

opposizi'one [oppozit'tsjone] *sf* opposition; *(Dir)* objection

op'posto, -a *pp di* **opporre** ▷ *ag* opposite; *(opinioni)* conflicting ▷ *sm* opposite, contrary; **all'~** on the contrary

oppressi'one *sf* oppression

oppri'mente *ag* *(caldo, noia)* oppressive; *(persona)* tiresome; *(deprimente)* depressing

op'primere *vt* *(premere, gravare)* to weigh down; *(estenuare: caldo)* to suffocate, oppress; *(tiranneggiare: popolo)* to oppress

op'pure *cong* or (else)

op'tare *vi* ~ **per** to opt for

o'puscolo *sm* booklet, pamphlet

opzi'one [op'tsjone] *sf* option

'ora *sf* (60 *minuti*) hour; *(momento)* time; **che ~ è?, che ore sono?** what time is it?; **a che ~ apre il museo/negozio?** what time does the museum/shop open?; **non veder l'~ di fare** to long to do, look forward to doing; **di buon'~** early; **alla buon'~!** at last!; ~ **legale** *o* **estiva** summer time (BRIT), daylight saving time (US); **ora di cena** dinner time; **ora locale** local time; **ora di pranzo** lunchtime; **ora di punta** (Aut) rush hour

o'racolo *sm* oracle

o'rale *ag, sm* oral

o'rario, -a *ag* hourly; *(fuso, segnale)* time *cpd*; *(velocità)* per hour ▷ *sm* timetable, schedule; *(di ufficio, visite ecc)* hours *pl*, time(s *pl*); **in ~** on time

o'rata *sf* (Zool) sea bream

ora'tore, -'trice *sm/f* speaker; orator

'orbita *sf* (Astr, Fisica) orbit; (Anat) (eye-)socket

or'chestra [or'kɛstra] *sf* orchestra

orchi'dea [orki'dɛa] *sf* orchid

or'digno [or'diɲɲo] *sm* *(esplosivo)* explosive device

ordi'nale *ag, sm* ordinal

ordi'nare *vt* *(mettere in ordine)* to arrange, organize; *(Comm)* to order; *(prescrivere: medicina)* to prescribe; *(comandare)*: **posso ~ per favore?** can I order now please?; ~ **a qn di fare qc** to order *o* command sb to do

sth; (Rel) to ordain

ordi'nario, -a *ag (comune)* ordinary; everyday; standard; *(grossolano)* coarse, common ▷ *sm* ordinary; *(Ins: di università)* full professor

ordi'nato, -a *ag* tidy, orderly

ordinazi'one [ordinat'tsjone] *sf* (Comm) order; (Rel) ordination; **eseguire qc su ~** to make sth to order

'ordine *sm* order; *(carattere)*: **d'~ pratico** of a practical nature; **all'~** (Comm: *assegno*) to order; **di prim'~** first-class; **fino a nuovo ~** until further notice; **essere in ~** *(documenti)* to be in order; *(stanza, persona)* to be tidy; **mettere in ~** to put in order, tidy (up); **l'~ pubblico** law and order; **ordini (sacri)** (Rel) holy orders; **ordine del giorno** *(di seduta)* agenda; (Mil) order of the day; **ordine di pagamento** (Comm) order for payment

orec'chino [orek'kino] *sm* earring

o'recchio [o'rekkjo] *(pl(f)* **o'recchie**) *sm* (Anat) ear

orecchi'oni [orek'kjoni] *smpl* (Med) mumps *sg*

o'refice [o'rɛfitʃe] *sm* goldsmith; jeweller; **orefice'ria** *sf (arte)* goldsmith's art; *(negozio)* jeweller's (shop)

'orfano, -a *ag* orphan(ed) ▷ *sm/f* orphan; ~ **di padre/madre** fatherless/motherless

orga'netto *sm* barrel organ; *(fam: armonica a bocca)* mouth organ; *(: fisarmonica)* accordion

or'ganico, -a, -ci, -che *ag* organic ▷ *sm* personnel, staff

organi'gramma, -i *sm* organization chart

orga'nismo *sm* (Biol) organism; *(corpo umano)* body; (Amm) body, organism

organiz'zare [organid'dzare] *vt* to organize; **organizzarsi** *vpr* to get organized; **organizzazi'one** *sf* organization

'organo *sm* organ; *(di congegno)* part; *(portavoce)* spokesman, mouthpiece

'orgia, -ge ['ɔrdʒa] *sf* orgy

or'goglio [or'gɔʎʎo] *sm* pride; **orgogli'oso, -a** *ag* proud

orien'tale *ag* oriental; eastern; east

orienta'mento *sm* positioning; orientation; direction; **senso di ~** sense of direction; **perdere l'~** to lose one's bearings; **orientamento professionale** careers guidance

orien'tarsi *vpr* to find one's bearings; *(fig: tendere)* to orient, lean; *(: indirizzarsi)*: ~ **verso** to take up, go in for

ori'ente *sm* east; **l'O~** the East, the Orient; **a ~** in the east o'rigano sm oregano

origi'nale [oridʒi'nale] ag original; (bizzarro) eccentric ▷ sm original

origi'nario, -a [oridʒi'narjo] ag original; **essere ~ di** to be a native of; (provenire da) to originate from; to be native to

o'rigine [o'ridʒine] sf origin; **all'~** originally; **d'~ inglese** of English origin; **dare ~ a** to give rise to

origli'are [oriʎ'ʎare] vi **~ (a)** to eavesdrop (on)

o'rina sf urine

ori'nare vi to urinate ▷ vt to pass

orizzon'tale [oriddzon'tale] ag horizontal

oriz'zonte [orid'dzonte] sm horizon

'orlo sm edge, border; (di recipiente) rim, brim; (di vestito ecc) hem

'orma sf (di persona) footprint; (di animale) track; (impronta, traccia) mark, trace

or'mai av by now, by this time; (adesso) now; (quasi) almost, nearly

ormeggi'are [ormed'dʒare] vt (Naut) to moor

or'mone sm hormone

ornamen'tale ag ornamental, decorative

or'nare vt to adorn, decorate; **ornarsi** vpr **ornarsi (di)** to deck o.s. (out) (with)

ornitolo'gia [ornitolo'dʒia] sf ornithology

'oro sm gold; **d'~, in ~** gold cpd; **d'~** (colore, occasione) golden; (persona) marvellous

oro'logio [oro'lɔdʒo] sm clock; (da tasca, da polso) watch; **orologio al quarzo** quartz watch; **orologio da polso** wristwatch

o'roscopo sm horoscope

or'rendo, -a ag (spaventoso) horrible, awful; (bruttissimo) hideous

or'ribile ag horrible

or'rore sm horror; **avere in ~ qn/qc** to loathe o detest sb/sth; **mi fanno ~** I loathe o detest them

orsacchi'otto [orsak'kjotto] sm teddy bear

'orso sm bear; **orso bruno/bianco** brown/polar bear

or'taggio [or'taddʒo] sm vegetable

or'tensia sf hydrangea

or'tica, -che sf (stinging) nettle

orti'caria sf nettle rash

'orto sm vegetable garden, kitchen garden; (Agr) market garden (BRIT), truck farm (US); **orto botanico** botanical garden(s) (pl)

orto'dosso, -a ag orthodox

ortogra'fia sf spelling

orto'pedico, -a, -ci, -che ag orthopaedic ▷ sm orthopaedic specialist

orzai'olo [ordza'jɔlo] sm (Med) stye

'orzo ['ordzo] sm barley

o'sare vt, vi to dare; **~ fare** to dare (to) do

oscenità [oʃʃeni'ta] sf inv obscenity

o'sceno, -a [oʃ'ʃeno] ag obscene; (ripugnante) ghastly

oscil'lare [oʃʃil'lare] vi (pendolo) to swing; (dondolare: al vento ecc) to rock; (variare) to fluctuate; (Tecn) to oscillate; (fig): **~ fra** to waver o hesitate between

oscu'rare vt to darken, obscure; (fig) to obscure; **oscurarsi** vpr (cielo) to darken, cloud over; (persona): **si oscurò in volto** his face clouded over

oscurità sf (vedi ag) darkness; obscurity

os'curo, -a ag dark; (fig) obscure; humble, lowly ▷ sm **all'~** in the dark; **tenere qn all'~ di qc** to keep sb in the dark about sth

ospe'dale sm hospital; **dov'è l'~ più vicino?** where's the nearest hospital?

ospi'tale ag hospitable

ospi'tare vt to give hospitality to; (albergo) to accommodate

'ospite sm/f (persona che ospita) host/hostess; (persona ospitata) guest

os'pizio [os'pittsjo] sm (per vecchi ecc) home

osser'vare vt to observe, watch; (esaminare) to examine; (notare, rilevare) to notice, observe; (Dir: la legge) to observe, respect; (mantenere: silenzio) to keep, observe; **far ~ qc a qn** to point sth out to sb; **osservazi'one** sf observation; (di legge ecc) observance; (considerazione critica) observation, remark; (rimprovero) reproof; **in osservazione** under observation

ossessio'nare vt to obsess, haunt; (tormentare) to torment, harass

ossessi'one sf obsession

os'sia cong that is, to be precise

'ossido sm oxide; **ossido di carbonio** carbon monoxide

ossige'nare [ossidʒe'nare] vt to oxygenate; (decolorare) to bleach; **acqua ossigenata** hydrogen peroxide

os'sigeno sm oxygen

'osso (pl(f) ossa) (nel senso Anat) sm bone; **d'~** (bottone ecc) of bone, bone cpd; **osso di seppia** cuttlebone

osta'colare vt to block, obstruct

os'tacolo sm obstacle; (Equitazione) hurdle, jump

os'taggio [os'taddʒo] sm hostage

os'tello sm; **ostello della gioventù** youth hostel

osten'tare vt to make a show of, flaunt

oste'ria sf inn

os'tetrico, -a, -ci, -che ag obstetric ▷ sm obstetrician

'ostia sf (Rel) host; (per medicinali) wafer

'ostico, -a, -ci, -che ag (fig) harsh; hard, difficult; unpleasant

os'tile ag hostile

osti'narsi *vpr* to insist, dig one's heels in; **~ a fare** to persist (obstinately) in doing; **osti'nato, -a** *ag* (*caparbio*) obstinate; (*tenace*) persistent, determined

'ostrica, -che *sf* oyster

Attenzione! In inglese esiste la parola *ostrich*, che però significa *struzzo*.

ostru'ire *vt* to obstruct, block

o'tite *sf* ear infection

ot'tanta *num* eighty

ot'tavo, -a *num* eighth

otte'nere *vt* to obtain, get; (*risultato*) to achieve, obtain

'ottica *sf* (*scienza*) optics *sg*; (*Fot: lenti, prismi ecc*) optics *pl*

'ottico, -a, -ci, -che *ag* (*della vista: nervo*) optic; (*dell'ottica*) optical ▷ *sm* optician

ottima'mente *av* excellently, very well

otti'mismo *sm* optimism; **otti'mista, -i, -e** *sm/f* optimist

'ottimo, -a *ag* excellent, very good

'otto *num* eight

ot'tobre *sm* October

otto'cento [otto'tʃento] *num* eight hundred ▷ *sm* **l'O~** the nineteenth century

ot'tone *sm* brass; **gli ottoni** (*Mus*) the brass

ottu'rare *vt* to close (up); (*dente*) to fill; **il lavandino è otturato** the sink is blocked; **otturarsi** *vpr* to become o get blocked up; **otturazi'one** *sf* closing (up); (*dentaria*) filling

ot'tuso, -a *ag* (*Mat, fig*) obtuse; (*suono*) dull

o'vaia *sf* (*Anat*) ovary

o'vale *ag, sm* oval

o'vatta *sf* cotton wool; (*per imbottire*) padding, wadding

'ovest *sm* west

o'vile *sm* pen, enclosure

ovulazi'one [ovulat'tsjone] *sf* ovulation

'ovulo *sm* (*Fisiol*) ovum

o'vunque *av* = **dovunque**

ovvi'are *vi* **~ a** to obviate

'ovvio, -a *ag* obvious

ozi'are [ot'tsjare] *vi* to laze, idle

'ozio ['ɔttsjo] *sm* idleness; (*tempo libero*) leisure; **ore d'~** leisure time; **stare in ~** to be idle

o'zono [o'dzɔno] *sm* ozone

P *abbr* (= *parcheggio*) P; (*Aut:* = *principiante*) L

p. *abbr* (= *pagina*) p.

pac'chetto [pak'ketto] *sm* packet; **pacchetto azionario** (*Comm*) shareholding

'pacco, -chi *sm* parcel; (*involto*) bundle; **pacco postale** parcel

'pace ['patʃe] *sf* peace; **darsi ~** to resign o.s.; **fare la ~ con** to make it up with

pa'cifico, -a, -ci, -che [pa'tʃiːfiko] *ag* (*persona*) peaceable; (*vita*) peaceful; (*fig: indiscusso*) indisputable; (: *ovvio*) obvious, clear ▷ *sm* **il P~, l'Oceano P~** the Pacific (Ocean)

paci'fista, -i, -e [patʃi'fista] *sm/f* pacifist

pa'della *sf* frying pan; (*per infermi*) bedpan

padigli'one [padiʎ'ʎone] *sm* pavilion

'Padova *sf* Padua

'padre *sm* father

pa'drino *sm* godfather

padro'nanza [padro'nantsa] *sf* command, mastery

pa'drone, -a *sm/f* master/mistress; (*proprietario*) owner; (*datore di lavoro*) employer; **essere ~ di sé** to be in control of o.s.; **padrone(a) di casa** master/mistress of the house; (*per gli inquilini*) landlord/lady

pae'saggio [pae'zaddʒo] sm landscape
pa'ese sm (nazione) country, nation; (terra) country, land; (villaggio) village, (small) town; **i Paesi Bassi** the Netherlands; **paese di provenienza** country of origin
'paga, -ghe sf pay, wages pl
paga'mento sm payment
pa'gare vt to pay; (acquisto, fig: colpa) to pay for; (contraccambiare) to repay, pay back ▷ vi to pay; **quanto l'hai pagato?** how much did you pay for it?; **posso ~ con la carta di credito?** can I pay by credit card?; **~ in contanti** to pay cash
pa'gella [pa'dʒella] sf (Ins) report card
pagherò [page'rɔ] sm inv acknowledgement of a debt, IOU
'pagina ['padʒina] sf page; **pagine bianche** phone book, telephone directory; **pagine gialle** Yellow Pages
'paglia ['paʎʎa] sf straw
pagli'accio [paʎ'ʎattʃo] sm clown
pagli'etta [paʎ'ʎetta] sf (cappello per uomo) (straw) boater; (per tegami ecc) steel wool
pa'gnotta [paɲ'ɲɔtta] sf round loaf
'paio (pl(f) **'paia**) sm pair; **un ~ di** (alcuni) a couple of
'Pakistan sm **il ~** Pakistan
'pala sf shovel; (di remo, ventilatore, elica) blade; (di ruota) paddle
pa'lato sm palate
pa'lazzo [pa'lattso] sm (reggia) palace; (edificio) building; **palazzo di giustizia** courthouse; **palazzo dello sport** sports stadium
'palco, -chi sm (Teatro) box; (tavolato) platform, stand; (ripiano) layer
palco'scenico, -ci [palkoʃʃeniko] sm (Teatro) stage
pa'lese ag clear, evident
Pales'tina sf **la ~** Palestine
palesti'nese ag, sm/f Palestinian
pa'lestra sf gymnasium; (esercizio atletico) exercise, training; (fig) training ground, school
pa'letta sf spade; (per il focolare) shovel; (del capostazione) signalling disc
pa'letto sm stake, peg; (spranga) bolt
'palio sm (gara): **il P~** horse race run at Siena; **mettere qc in ~** to offer sth as a prize

● **PALIO**

● The **palio** is a horse race which takes
● place in a number of Italian towns, the
● most famous being the one in Siena.
● This is usually held twice a year on July
● 2nd and August 16th in the Piazza del
● Campo in Siena. 10 of the 17 **contrade** or

● districts take part, each represented by
● a horse and rider. The winner is the first
● horse to complete the course, whether
● it has a rider or not.

'palla sf ball; (pallottola) bullet; **palla di neve** snowball; **palla ovale** rugby ball; **pallaca'nestro** sf basketball; **palla'mano** sf handball; **pallanu'oto** sf water polo; **palla'volo** sf volleyball
palleggi'are [palled'dʒare] vi (Calcio) to practise with the ball; (Tennis) to knock up
pallia'tivo sm palliative; (fig) stopgap measure
'pallido, -a ag pale
pal'lina sf (bilia) marble
pallon'cino [pallon'tʃino] sm balloon; (lampioncino) Chinese lantern
pal'lone sm (palla) ball; (Calcio) football; (aerostato) balloon; **gioco del ~** football
pal'lottola sf pellet; (proiettile) bullet
'palma sf (Anat) = **palmo**; (Bot, simbolo) palm; **palma da datteri** date palm
'palmo sm (Anat) palm; **restare con un ~ di naso** to be badly disappointed
'palo sm (legno appuntito) stake; (sostegno) pole; **fare da** o **il ~** (fig) to act as look-out
palom'baro sm diver
pal'pare vt to feel, finger
'palpebra sf eyelid
pa'lude sf marsh, swamp
pan'cetta [pan'tʃetta] sf (Cuc) bacon
pan'china [pan'kina] sf garden seat; (di giardino pubblico) (park) bench
'pancia, -ce [pantʃa] sf belly, stomach; **mettere** o **fare ~** to be getting a paunch; **avere mal di ~** to have stomachache o a sore stomach
panci'otto [pan'tʃɔtto] sm waistcoat
'pancreas sm inv pancreas
'panda sm inv panda
'pane sm bread; (pagnotta) loaf (of bread); (forma): **un ~ di burro** a pat of butter; **guadagnarsi il ~** to earn one's living; **pane a cassetta** sliced bread; **pane di Spagna** sponge cake; **pane integrale** wholemeal bread; **pane tostato** toast
panette'ria sf (forno) bakery; (negozio) baker's (shop), bakery
panetti'ere, -a sm/f baker
panet'tone sm a kind of spiced brioche with sultanas, eaten at Christmas
pangrat'tato sm breadcrumbs pl
'panico, -a, -ci, -che ag, sm panic
pani'ere sm basket
pani'ficio [pani'fitʃo] sm (forno) bakery; (negozio) baker's (shop), bakery
pa'nino sm roll; **panino caldo** toasted sandwich; **panino imbottito** filled roll;

sandwich

'panna *sf* (*Cuc*) cream; (*Tecn*) = **panne**; **panna da cucina** cooking cream; **panna montata** whipped cream

'panne *sf inv* **essere in ~** (*Aut*) to have broken down

pan'nello *sm* panel; **pannello solare** solar panel

'panno *sm* cloth; **panni** *smpl* (*abiti*) clothes; **mettiti nei miei panni** (*fig*) put yourself in my shoes

pan'nocchia [pan'nɔkkja] *sf* (*di mais ecc*) ear

panno'lino *sm* (*per bambini*) nappy (BRIT), diaper (US)

pano'rama, -i *sm* panorama

panta'loni *smpl* trousers (BRIT), pants (US), pair *sg*, of trousers o pants

pan'tano *sm* bog

pan'tera *sf* panther

pan'tofola *sf* slipper

'Papa, -i *sm* pope

papà *sm inv* dad(dy)

pa'pavero *sm* poppy

'pappa *sf* baby cereal; **pappa reale** royal jelly

pappa'gallo *sm* parrot; (*fig: uomo*) Romeo, wolf

pa'rabola *sf* (*Mat*) parabola; (*Rel*) parable

para'bolico, -a, ci, che *ag* (*Mat*) parabolic; *vedi anche* **antenna**

para'brezza [para'breddza] *sm inv* (*Aut*) windscreen (BRIT), windshield (US)

paraca'dute *sm inv* parachute

para'diso *sm* paradise

parados'sale *ag* paradoxical

para'fulmine *sm* lightning conductor

pa'raggi [pa'raddʒi] *smpl* **nei ~** in the vicinity, in the neighbourhood

parago'nare *vt* **~ con/a** to compare with/to

para'gone *sm* comparison; (*esempio analogo*) analogy, parallel; **reggere al ~** to stand comparison

'paragrafo *sm* paragraph

pa'ralisi *sf* paralysis

paral'lelo, -a *ag* parallel ▷ *sm* (*Geo*) parallel; (*comparazione*): **fare un ~ tra** to draw a parallel between

para'lume *sm* lampshade

pa'rametro *sm* parameter

para'noia *sf* paranoia; **para'noico, -a, -ci, -che** *ag, sm/f* paranoid

para'occhi [para'ɔkki] *smpl* blinkers

para'petto *sm* balustrade

pa'rare *vt* (*addobbare*) to adorn, deck; (*proteggere*) to shield, protect; (*scansare: colpo*) to parry; (*Calcio*) to save ▷ *vi* **dove**

vuole andare a ~? what are you driving at?

pa'rata *sf* (*Sport*) save; (*Mil*) review, parade

para'urti *sm inv* (*Aut*) bumper

para'vento *sm* folding screen; **fare da ~ a qn** (*fig*) to shield sb

par'cella [par'tʃɛlla] *sf* account, fee (*of lawyer etc*)

parcheggi'are [parked'dʒare] *vt* to park; **posso ~ qui?** can I park here?; **parcheggiatore, -trice** [parkeddʒa'tore] *sm/f* (*Aut*) parking attendant

par'cheggio *sm* parking *no pl*; (*luogo*) car park; (*singolo posto*) parking space

par'chimetro [par'kimetro] *sm* parking meter

'parco, -chi *sm* park; (*spazio per deposito*) depot; (*complesso di veicoli*) fleet

par'cometro *sm* (pay-and-display) ticket machine

pa'recchio, -a [pa'rekkjo] *det* quite a lot of; (*tempo*) quite a lot of, a long

pareggi'are [pared'dʒare] *vt* to make equal; (*terreno*) to level, make level; (*bilancio, conti*) to balance ▷ *vi* (*Sport*) to draw; **pa'reggio** *sm* (*Econ*) balance; (*Sport*) draw

pa'rente *sm/f* relative, relation

> Attenzione! In inglese esiste la parola **parent**, che però significa *genitore*.

paren'tela *sf* (*vincolo di sangue, fig*) relationship

pa'rentesi *sf* (*segno grafico*) bracket, parenthesis; (*frase incisa*) parenthesis; (*digressione*) parenthesis, digression

pa'rere *sm* (*opinione*) opinion; (*consiglio*) advice, opinion; **a mio ~** in my opinion ▷ *vi* to seem, appear ▷ *vb impers* **pare che** it seems o appears that; they say that; **mi pare che** it seems to me that; **mi pare di sì** I think so; **fai come ti pare** do as you like; **che ti pare del mio libro?** what do you think of my book?

pa'rete *sf* wall

'pari *ag inv* (*uguale*) equal, same; (*in giochi*) equal; drawn, tied; (*Mat*) even ▷ *sm inv* (*Pol: di Gran Bretagna*) peer ▷ *sm/f inv* peer, equal; **copiato ~ ~** copied word for word; **alla ~** on the same level; **ragazza alla ~** au pair girl; **mettersi alla ~ con** to place o.s. on the same level as; **mettersi in ~ con** to catch up with; **andare di ~ passo con qn** to keep pace with sb

Pa'rigi [pa'ridʒi] *sf* Paris

pari'gino, -a [pari'dʒino] *ag, sm/f* Parisian

parità *sf* parity, equality; (*Sport*) draw, tie

parlamen'tare *ag* parliamentary ▷ *sm/f* ≈ Member of Parliament (BRIT), ≈ Congressman/woman (US) ▷ *vi* to

negotiate, parley
parla'mento sm parliament

● **PARLAMENTO**
●
● The Italian **Parlamento** is made
● up of two chambers, the **Camera**
● **dei deputati** and the **Senato**.
● Parliamentary elections are held every
● 5 years.

parlan'tina (fam) sf talkativeness; **avere ~**
to have the gift of the gab
par'lare vi to speak, talk; (confidare cose
segrete) to talk ▷ vt to speak; **~ (a qn) di** to
speak o talk (to sb) about; **posso ~ con…?**
can I speak to …?; **parla italiano?** do you
speak Italian?; **non parlo inglese** I don't
speak English
parmigi'ano [parmi'dʒano] sm (grana)
Parmesan (cheese)
pa'rola sf word; (facoltà) speech; **parole**
sfpl (chiacchiere) talk sg; **chiedere la ~** to
ask permission to speak; **prendere la ~**
to take the floor; **parola d'onore** word of
honour; **parola d'ordine** (Mil) password;
parole incrociate crossword (puzzle) sg;
paro'laccia, -ce sf bad word, swearword
parrò ecc vb vedi **parere**
par'rocchia [par'rɔkkja] sf parish; parish
church
par'rucca, -che sf wig
parrucchi'ere, -a [parruk'kjɛre] sm/f
hairdresser ▷ sm barber
'parte sf part; (lato) side; (quota spettante a
ciascuno) share; (direzione) direction; (Pol)
party; faction; (Dir) party; **a ~** ag separate
▷ av separately; **scherzi a ~** joking aside;
a ~ ciò apart from that; **da ~** (in disparte)
to one side, aside; **d'altra ~** on the other
hand; **da ~ di** (per conto di) on behalf of; **da
~ mia** as far as I'm concerned, as for me;
da ~ a ~ right through; **da ogni ~** on all
sides, everywhere; (moto da luogo) from all
sides; **da nessuna ~** nowhere; **da questa
~** (in questa direzione) this way; **prendere
~ a qc** to take part in sth; **mettere da ~**
to put aside; **mettere qn a ~ di** to inform
sb of
parteci'pare [partetʃi'pare] vi **~ a** to take
part in, participate in; (utili ecc) to share in;
(spese ecc) to contribute to; (dolore, successo
di qn) to share (in)
parteggi'are [parted'dʒare] vi **~ per** to
side with, be on the side of
par'tenza [par'tɛntsa] sf departure;
(Sport) start; **essere in ~** to be about to
leave, be leaving
parti'cipio [parti'tʃipjo] sm participle

partico'lare ag (specifico) particular;
(proprio) personal, private; (speciale)
special, particular; (caratteristico)
distinctive, characteristic; (fuori dal
comune) peculiar ▷ sm detail, particular; **in
~** in particular, particularly
par'tire vi to go, leave; (allontanarsi) to go
(o drive ecc) away o off; (petardo, colpo) to
go off; (fig: avere inizio, Sport) to start; **sono
partita da Roma alle 7** I left Rome at 7; **a
che ora parte il treno/l'autobus?** what
time does the train/bus leave?; **il volo
parte da Ciampino** the flight leaves from
Ciampino; **a ~ da** from
par'tita sf (Comm) lot, consignment; (Econ:
registrazione) entry, item; (Carte, Sport:
gioco) game; (: competizione) match, game;
partita di caccia hunting party; **partita
IVA** VAT registration number
par'tito sm (Pol) party; (decisione) decision,
resolution; (persona da maritare) match
'parto sm (Med) delivery, (child)birth;
labour
'parvi ecc vb vedi **parere**
parzi'ale [par'tsjale] ag (limitato) partial;
(non obiettivo) biased, partial
pasco'lare vt, vi to graze
'pascolo sm pasture
'Pasqua sf Easter; **Pas'quetta** sf Easter
Monday
pas'sabile ag fairly good, passable
pas'saggio [pas'saddʒo] sm passing no
pl, passage; (traversata) crossing no pl,
passage; (luogo, prezzo della traversata,
brano di libro ecc) passage; (su veicolo altrui)
lift (BRIT), ride; (Sport) pass; **di ~** (persona)
passing through; **può darmi un ~ fino
alla stazione?** can you give me a lift to the
station?; **passaggio a livello** level (BRIT) o
grade (US) crossing; **passaggio pedonale**
pedestrian crossing
passamon'tagna [passamon'taɲɲa] sm
inv balaclava
pas'sante sm/f passer-by ▷ sm loop
passa'porto sm passport
pas'sare vi (andare) to go; (veicolo, pedone)
to pass (by), go by; (fare una breve sosta:
postino ecc) to come, call; (: amico: per fare
una visita) to call o drop in; (sole, aria, luce)
to get through; (trascorrere: giorni, tempo)
to pass, go by; (fig: proposta di legge) to
be passed; (: dolore) to pass, go away;
(Carte) to pass ▷ vt (attraversare) to cross;
(trasmettere: messaggio): **~ qc a qn** to pass
sth on to sb; (dare): **~ qc a qn** to pass sth to
sb, give sb sth; (trascorrere: tempo) to spend;
(superare: esame) to pass; (triturare: verdura)
to strain; (approvare) to pass, approve;
(oltrepassare, sorpassare: anche fig) to go

beyond, pass; (*fig: subire*) to go through; **mi passa il sale/l'olio per favore?** could you pass the salt/oil please?; **~ da ... a** to pass from ... to; **~ di padre in figlio** to be handed down *o* to pass from father to son; **~ per** (*anche fig*) to go through; **~ per stupido/un genio** to be taken for a fool/a genius; **~ sopra** (*anche fig*) to pass over; **~ attraverso** (*anche fig*) to go through; **~ alla storia** to pass into history; **~ a un esame** to go up (to the next class) after an exam; **~ inosservato** to go unnoticed; **~ di moda** to go out of fashion; **le passo il Signor X** (*al telefono*) here is Mr X; I'm putting you through to Mr X; **lasciar ~ qn/qc** to let sb/sth through; **come te la passi?** how are you getting on *o* along?

passa'tempo *sm* pastime, hobby

pas'sato, -a *ag* past; (*sfiorito*) faded ▷ *sm* past; (*Ling*) past (tense); **passato prossimo/remoto** (*Ling*) present perfect/past historic; **passato di verdura** (*Cuc*) vegetable purée

passeg'gero, -a [passed'dʒero] *ag* passing ▷ *sm/f* passenger

passeggi'are [passed'dʒare] *vi* to go for a walk; (*in veicolo*) to go for a drive; **passeggi'ata** *sf* walk; drive; (*luogo*) promenade; **fare una passeggiata** to go for a walk (*o* drive); **passeg'gino** *sm* pushchair (*BRIT*), stroller (*US*)

passe'rella *sf* footbridge; (*di nave, aereo*) gangway; (*pedana*) catwalk

'passero *sm* sparrow

passi'one *sf* passion

pas'sivo, -a *ag* passive ▷ *sm* (*Ling*) passive; (*Econ*) debit; (: *complesso dei debiti*) liabilities *pl*

'passo *sm* step; (*andatura*) pace; (*rumore*) (foot)step; (*orma*) footprint; (*passaggio, fig: brano*) passage; (*valico*) pass; **a ~ d'uomo** at walking pace; **~ (a) ~** step by step; **fare due** *o* **quattro passi** to go for a walk *o* a stroll; **di questo ~** at this rate; **"passo carraio"** "vehicle entrance – keep clear"

'pasta *sf* (*Cuc*) dough; (: *impasto per dolce*) pastry; (: *anche*: **~ alimentare**) pasta; (*massa molle di materia*) paste; (*fig: indole*) nature; **paste** *sfpl* (*pasticcini*) pastries; **pasta in brodo** noodle soup; **pasta sfoglia** puff pastry *o* paste (*US*)

pastasci'utta [pastaʃ'ʃutta] *sf* pasta

pas'tella *sf* batter

pas'tello *sm* pastel

pasticce'ria [pastittʃe'ria] *sf* (*pasticcini*) pastries *pl*, cakes *pl*; (*negozio*) cake shop; (*arte*) confectionery

pasticci'ere, -a [pastit'tʃere] *sm/f* pastrycook; confectioner

pastic'cino [pastit'tʃino] *sm* petit four

pas'ticcio [pas'tittʃo] *sm* (*Cuc*) pie; (*lavoro disordinato, imbroglio*) mess; **trovarsi nei pasticci** to get into trouble

pas'tiglia [pas'tiʎʎa] *sf* pastille, lozenge

pas'tina *sf* *small pasta shapes used in soup*

'pasto *sm* meal

pas'tore *sm* shepherd; (*Rel*) pastor, minister; (*anche*: **cane ~**) sheepdog; **pastore tedesco** (*Zool*) Alsatian, German shepherd

pa'tata *sf* potato; **patate fritte** chips (*BRIT*), French fries; **pata'tine** *sfpl* (*potato*) crisps; **patatine fritte** chips

pa'tente *sf* licence; **patente di guida** driving licence (*BRIT*), driver's license (*US*); **patente a punti** *driving licence with penalty points*

> Attenzione! In inglese esiste la parola *patent*, che però significa *brevetto*.

paternità *sf* paternity, fatherhood

pa'tetico, -a, -ci, -che *ag* pathetic; (*commovente*) moving, touching

pa'tibolo *sm* gallows *sg*, scaffold

'patina *sf* (*su rame ecc*) patina; (*sulla lingua*) fur, coating

pa'tire *vt*, *vi* to suffer

pa'tito, -a *sm/f* enthusiast, fan, lover

patolo'gia [patolo'dʒia] *sf* pathology

'patria *sf* homeland

pa'trigno [pa'triɲɲo] *sm* stepfather

patri'monio *sm* estate, property; (*fig*) heritage

pa'trono *sm* (*Rel*) patron saint; (*socio di patronato*) patron; (*Dir*) counsel

patteggi'are [patted'dʒare] *vt*, *vi* to negotiate; (*Dir*) to plea-bargain

patti'naggio [patti'naddʒo] *sm* skating; **pattinaggio a rotelle/sul ghiaccio** roller-/ice-skating

patti'nare *vi* to skate; **~ sul ghiaccio** to ice-skate; **pattina'tore, -'trice** *sm/f* skater; **'pattino** *sm* skate; (*di slitta*) runner; (*Aer*) skid; (*Tecn*) sliding block; **pattini in linea** Rollerblades®; **pattini da ghiaccio/a rotelle** ice/roller skates

'patto *sm* (*accordo*) pact, agreement; (*condizione*) term, condition; **a ~ che** on condition that

pat'tuglia [pat'tuʎʎa] *sf* (*Mil*) patrol

pattu'ire *vt* to reach an agreement on

pattumi'era *sf* (*dust*)bin (*BRIT*), ashcan (*US*)

pa'ura *sf* fear; **aver ~ di/di fare/che** to be frightened *o* afraid of/of doing/that; **far ~ a** to frighten; **per ~ di/che** for fear of/that; **pau'roso, -a** *ag* (*che fa paura*) frightening; (*che ha paura*) fearful, timorous

'pausa sf (sosta) break; (nel parlare, Mus) pause

pavi'mento sm floor

> Attenzione! In inglese esiste la parola pavement, che però significa marciapiede.

pa'vone sm peacock

pazien'tare [pattsjen'tare] vi to be patient

pazi'ente [pat'tsjɛnte] ag, sm/f patient; **pazi'enza** sf patience

paz'zesco, -a, -schi, -sche [pat'tsesko] ag mad, crazy

paz'zia [pat'tsia] sf (Med) madness, insanity; (azione) folly; (di azione, decisione) madness, folly

'pazzo, -a ['pattso] ag (Med) mad, insane; (strano) wild, mad ▷ sm/f madman/woman; **~ di** (gioia, amore ecc) mad o crazy with; **~ per qc/qn** mad o crazy about sth/sb

PC [pit'tʃi] sigla sm inv (= personal computer) PC; **PC portatile** laptop

pec'care vi to sin; (fig) to err

pec'cato sm sin; **è un ~ che** it's a pity that; **che ~!** what a shame o pity!

peccherò ecc [pekke'rɔ] vb vedi **peccare**

pece ['petʃe] sf pitch

Pe'chino [pe'kino] sf Beijing

'pecora sf sheep; **peco'rino** sm sheep's milk cheese

pe'daggio [pe'daddʒo] sm toll

pedago'gia [pedago'dʒia] sf pedagogy, educational methods pl

peda'lare vi to pedal; (andare in bicicletta) to cycle

pe'dale sm pedal

pe'dana sf footboard; (Sport: nel salto) springboard; (: nella scherma) piste

pe'dante ag pedantic ▷ sm/f pedant

pe'data sf (impronta) footprint; (colpo) kick; **prendere a pedate qn/qc** to kick sb/sth

pedi'atra, -i, -e sm/f paediatrician

pedi'cure sm/f inv chiropodist

pe'dina sf (della dama) draughtsman (BRIT), draftsman (US); (fig) pawn

pedi'nare vt to shadow, tail

pe'dofilo, -a ag, sm/f paedophile

pedo'nale ag pedestrian

pe'done, -a sm/f pedestrian ▷ sm (Scacchi) pawn

'peggio ['pɛddʒo] av, ag inv worse ▷ sm o f **il o la ~** the worst; **alla ~** at worst, if the worst comes to the worst; **peggio'rare** vt to make worse, worsen ▷ vi to grow worse, worsen; **peggi'ore** ag (comparativo) worse; (superlativo) worst ▷ sm/f **il(la) peggiore** the worst (person)

'pegno ['peɲɲo] sm (Dir) security, pledge; (nei giochi di società) forfeit; (fig) pledge, token; **dare in ~ qc** to pawn sth

pe'lare vt (spennare) to pluck; (spellare) to skin; (sbucciare) to peel; (fig) to make pay through the nose

pe'lato, -a ag **pomodori pelati** tinned tomatoes

'pelle sf skin; (di animale) skin, hide; (cuoio) leather; **avere la ~ d'oca** to have goose pimples o goose flesh

pellegri'naggio [pellegri'naddʒo] sm pilgrimage

pelle'rossa (pl **pelli'rosse**) sm/f Red Indian

pelli'cano sm pelican

pel'liccia, -ce [pel'littʃa] sf (mantello di animale) coat, fur; (indumento) fur coat; **pelliccia ecologica** fake fur

pel'licola sf (membrana sottile) film, layer; (Fot, Cinema) film

'pelo sm hair; (pelame) coat, hair; (pelliccia) fur; (di tappeto) pile; (di liquido) surface; **per un ~: per un ~ non ho perduto il treno** I very nearly missed the train; **c'è mancato un ~ che affogasse** he escaped drowning by the skin of his teeth; **pe'loso, -a** ag hairy

peltro sm pewter

pe'luche [pə'lyʃ] sm plush; **giocattoli di ~** soft toys

pe'luria sf down

'pena sf (Dir) sentence; (punizione) punishment; (sofferenza) sadness no pl, sorrow; (fatica) trouble no pl, effort; (difficoltà) difficulty; **far ~** to be pitiful; **mi fai ~** I feel sorry for you; **prendersi o darsi la ~ di fare** to go to the trouble of doing; **pena di morte** death sentence; **pena pecuniaria** fine; **pe'nale** ag penal

pen'dente ag hanging; leaning ▷ sm (ciondolo) pendant; (orecchino) drop earring

'pendere vi (essere appeso): **~ da** to hang from; (essere inclinato) to lean; (fig: incombere): **~ su** to hang over

pen'dio, -'dii sm slope, slant; (luogo in pendenza) slope

'pendola sf pendulum clock

pendo'lare sm/f commuter

pendo'lino sm high-speed train

pene'trante ag piercing, penetrating

pene'trare vi to come o get in ▷ vt to penetrate; **~ in** to enter; (proiettile) to penetrate; (: acqua, aria) to go o come into

penicil'lina [penitʃil'lina] sf penicillin

pe'nisola sf peninsula

penitenzi'ario [peniten'tsjarjo] sm prison

'penna sf (di uccello) feather; (per scrivere) pen; **penne** sfpl (Cuc) quills (type of pasta); **penna a sfera** ballpoint pen; **penna stilografica** fountain pen

penna'rello sm felt-(tip) pen

pen'nello sm brush; (per dipingere) (paint)brush; **a ~** (perfettamente) to perfection, perfectly; **pennello per la barba** shaving brush

pe'nombra sf half-light, dim light

pen'sare vi to think ▷ vt to think; (inventare, escogitare) to think out; **~ a** to think of; (amico, vacanze) to think of o about; (problema) to think about; **~ di fare qc** to think of doing sth; **ci penso io** I'll see to o take care of it

pensi'ero sm thought; (modo di pensare, dottrina) thinking no pl; (preoccupazione) worry, care, trouble; **stare in ~ per qn** to be worried about sb; **pensie'roso, -a** ag thoughtful

'pensile ag hanging

pensio'nato, -a sm/f pensioner

pensi'one sf (al prestatore di lavoro) pension; (vitto e alloggio) board and lodging; (albergo) boarding house; **andare in ~** to retire; **mezza ~** half board; **pensione completa** full board

pen'tirsi vpr **~ di** to repent of; (rammaricarsi) to regret, be sorry for

'pentola sf pot; **pentola a pressione** pressure cooker

pe'nultimo, -a ag last but one (BRIT), next to last, penultimate

penzo'lare [pendzo'lare] vi to dangle, hang loosely

'pepe sm pepper; **pepe in grani/macinato** whole/ground pepper

peperon'cino [peperon'tʃino] sm chilli pepper

pepe'rone sm pepper, capsicum; (piccante) chili

pe'pita sf nugget

PAROLA CHIAVE

per prep **1** (moto attraverso luogo) through; **i ladri sono passati per la finestra** the thieves got in (o out) through the window; **l'ho cercato per tutta la casa** I've searched the whole house o all over the house for it

2 (moto a luogo) for, to; **partire per la Germania/il mare** to leave for Germany/the sea; **il treno per Roma** the Rome train, the train for o to Rome

3 (stato in luogo): **seduto/sdraiato per terra** sitting/lying on the ground

4 (tempo) for; **per anni/lungo tempo** for years/a long time; **per tutta l'estate** throughout the summer, all summer long; **lo rividi per Natale** I saw him again at Christmas; **lo faccio per lunedì** I'll do it for Monday

5 (mezzo, maniera) by; **per lettera/via aerea/ferrovia** by letter/airmail/rail; **prendere qn per un braccio** to take sb by the arm

6 (causa, scopo) for; **assente per malattia** absent because of o through o owing to illness; **ottimo per il mal di gola** excellent for sore throats

7 (limitazione) for; **è troppo difficile per lui** it's too difficult for him; **per quel che mi riguarda** as far as I'm concerned; **per poco che sia** however little it may be; **per questa volta ti perdono** I'll forgive you this time

8 (prezzo, misura) for; (distributivo) a, per; **venduto per 3 milioni** sold for 3 million; **1 euro per persona** 1 euro a o per person; **uno per volta** one at a time; **uno per uno** one by one; **5 per cento** 5 per cent; **3 per 4 fa 12** 3 times 4 equals 12; **dividere/moltiplicare 12 per 4** to divide/multiply 12 by 4

9 (in qualità di) as; (al posto di) for; **avere qn per professore** to have sb as a teacher; **ti ho preso per Mario** I mistook you for Mario, I thought you were Mario; **dare per morto qn** to give sb up for dead

10 (seguito da vb: finale): **per fare qc** so as to do sth, in order to do sth; (: causale): **per aver fatto qc** for having done sth; (: consecutivo): **è abbastanza grande per andarci da solo** he's big enough to go on his own

'pera sf pear

per'bene ag inv respectable, decent ▷ av (con cura) properly, well

percentu'ale [pertʃentu'ale] sf percentage

perce'pire [pertʃe'pire] vt (sentire) to perceive; (ricevere) to receive

PAROLA CHIAVE

perché [per'ke] av why; **perché no?** why not?; **perché non vuoi andarci?** why don't you want to go?; **spiegami perché l'hai fatto** tell me why you did it
▷ cong **1** (causale) because; **non posso uscire perché ho da fare** I can't go out because o as I've a lot to do
2 (finale) in order that, so that; **te lo do perché tu lo legga** I'm giving it to you so (that) you can read it

3 (*consecutivo*): **è troppo forte perché si possa batterlo** he's too strong to be beaten
▷ *sm inv* reason; **il perché di** the reason for

perciò [per'tʃɔ] *cong* so, for this (*o* that) reason

per'correre *vt* (*luogo*) to go all over; (: *paese*) to travel up and down, go all over; (*distanza*) to cover

per'corso, -a *pp di* **percorrere** ▷ *sm* (*tragitto*) journey; (*tratto*) route

percu'otere *vt* to hit, strike

percussi'one *sf* percussion; **strumenti a ~** (*Mus*) percussion instruments

'perdere *vt* to lose; (*lasciarsi sfuggire*) to miss; (*sprecare: tempo, denaro*) to waste ▷ *vi* to lose; (*serbatoio ecc*) to leak; **perdersi** *vpr* (*smarrirsi*) to get lost; (*svanire*) to disappear, vanish; **mi sono perso** I'm lost; **ho perso il portafoglio/passaporto** I've lost my wallet/passport; **abbiamo perso il treno** we missed our train; **saper ~** to be a good loser; **lascia ~!** forget it!, never mind!

perdigi'orno [perdi'dʒorno] *sm/f inv* idler, waster

'perdita *sf* loss; (*spreco*) waste; (*fuoriuscita*) leak; (*Comm*) we are running at a loss; **a ~ d'occhio** as far as the eye can see

perdo'nare *vt* to pardon, forgive; (*scusare*) to excuse, pardon

per'dono *sm* forgiveness; (*Dir*) pardon

perduta'mente *av* desperately, passionately

pe'renne *ag* eternal, perpetual, perennial; (*Bot*) perennial

perfetta'mente *av* perfectly; **sai ~ che ...** you know perfectly well that ...

per'fetto, -a *ag* perfect ▷ *sm* (*Ling*) perfect (tense)

perfeziona'mento [perfettsjona'mento] *sm* **~ (di)** improvement (in), perfection (of); **corso di ~** proficiency course

perfezio'nare [perfettsjo'nare] *vt* to improve, perfect; **perfezionarsi** *vpr* to improve

perfezi'one [perfet'tsjone] *sf* perfection

per'fino *av* even

perfo'rare *vt* to perforate, to punch a hole (*o* holes) in; (*banda, schede*) to punch; (*trivellare*) to drill

perga'mena *sf* parchment

perico'lante *ag* precarious

pe'ricolo *sm* danger; **mettere in ~** to endanger, put in danger; **perico'loso, -a** *ag* dangerous

perife'ria *sf* (*di città*) outskirts *pl*

pe'rifrasi *sf* circumlocution

pe'rimetro *sm* perimeter

peri'odico, -a, -ci, -che *ag* periodic(al); (*Mat*) recurring ▷ *sm* periodical

pe'riodo *sm* period

peripe'zie [peripet'tsie] *sfpl* ups and downs, vicissitudes

pe'rito, -a *ag* expert, skilled ▷ *sm/f* expert; (*agronomo, navale*) surveyor; **perito chimico** qualified chemist

peri'zoma, -i [peri'dzoma] *sm* G-string

'perla *sf* pearl; **per'lina** *sf* bead

perlus'trare *vt* to patrol

perma'loso, -a *ag* touchy

perma'nente *ag* permanent ▷ *sf* permanent wave, perm; **perma'nenza** *sf* permanence; (*soggiorno*) stay

perme'are *vt* to permeate

per'messo, -a *pp di* **permettere** ▷ *sm* (*autorizzazione*) permission, leave; (*dato a militare, impiegato*) leave; (*licenza*) licence, permit; (*Mil: foglio*) pass; **~?, è ~?** (*posso entrare?*) may I come in?; (*posso passare?*) excuse me; **permesso di lavoro/pesca** work/fishing permit; **permesso di soggiorno** residence permit

per'mettere *vt* to allow, permit; **~ a qn qc/di fare qc** to allow sb sth/to do sth; **permettersi qc/di fare qc** to allow o.s. sth/to do sth; (*avere la possibilità*) to afford sth/to do sth

per'misi *ecc vb vedi* **permettere**

per'nacchia [per'nakkja] (*fam*) *sf* **fare una ~** to blow a raspberry

per'nice [per'nitʃe] *sf* partridge

'perno *sm* pivot

pernot'tare *vi* to spend the night, stay overnight

'pero *sm* pear tree

però *cong* (*ma*) but; (*tuttavia*) however, nevertheless

perpendico'lare *ag, sf* perpendicular

per'plesso, -a *ag* perplexed; uncertain, undecided

perqui'sire *vt* to search; **perquisizi'one** *sf* (*police*) search

'perse *ecc vb vedi* **perdere**

persecuzi'one [persekut'tsjone] *sf* persecution

persegui'tare *vt* to persecute

perseve'rante *ag* persevering

'persi *ecc vb vedi* **perdere**

persi'ana *sf* shutter; **persiana avvolgibile** roller shutter

per'sino *av* = **perfino**

persis'tente *ag* persistent

'perso, -a *pp di* **perdere**

per'sona *sf* person; (*qualcuno*): **una ~** someone, somebody; (*espressione interrogativa +*) anyone *o* anybody

perso'naggio [perso'naddʒo] *sm* (*persona*

ragguardevole) personality, figure; (*tipo*) character, individual; (*Letteratura*) character

perso'nale *ag* personal ▷ *sm* staff; personnel; (*figura fisica*) build

personalità *sf inv* personality

perspi'cace [perspi'katʃe] *ag* shrewd, discerning

persu'adere *vt* ~ **qn (di qc/a fare)** to persuade sb (of sth/to do)

per'tanto *cong* (*quindi*) so, therefore

'pertica, -che *sf* pole

perti'nente *ag* ~ **(a)** relevant (to), pertinent (to)

per'tosse *sf* whooping cough

perturbazi'one [perturbat'tsjone] *sf* disruption; perturbation; **perturbazione atmosferica** *sf* atmospheric disturbance

per'vadere *vt* to pervade

per'verso, -a *ag* depraved; perverse

perver'tito, -a *sm/f* pervert

p.es. *abbr* (= *per esempio*) e.g.

pe'sante *ag* heavy; **è troppo ~** it's too heavy

pe'sare *vt* to weigh ▷ *vi* (*avere un peso*) to weigh; (*essere pesante*) to be heavy; (*fig*) to carry weight; ~ **su** (*fig*) to lie heavy on; to influence; to hang over; **pesarsi** *vpr* to weigh o.s.; ~ **le parole** to weigh one's words; ~ **sulla coscienza** to weigh on sb's conscience; **mi pesa ammetterlo** I don't like admitting it; **tutta la responsabilità pesa su di lui** all the responsibility rests on him; **è una situazione che mi pesa** I find the situation difficult; **il suo parere pesa molto** his opinion counts for a lot

'pesca (*pl* **pesche**) (: *frutto*) *sf* peach; (*il pescare*) fishing; **andare a ~** to go fishing; ~ **con la lenza** angling; **pesca di beneficenza** (*lotteria*) lucky dip

pes'care *vt* (*pesce*) to fish for; to catch; (*qc nell'acqua*) to fish out; (*fig: trovare*) to get hold of, find; **andare a ~** to go fishing

pesca'tore *sm* fisherman; angler

'pesce ['peʃʃe] *sm* fish *gen inv*; **Pesci** (*dello zodiaco*) Pisces; **pesce d'aprile!** April Fool!; **pesce rosso** goldfish; **pesce spada** swordfish; **pesce'cane** *sm* shark

pesche'reccio [peske'rettʃo] *sm* fishing boat

pesche'ria [peske'ria] *sf* fishmonger's (shop) (BRIT), fish store (US)

pescherò *ecc* [peske'rɔ] *vb vedi* **pescare**

'peso *sm* weight; (*Sport*) shot; **rubare sul ~** to give short weight; **essere di ~ a qn** (*fig*) to be a burden to sb; **peso lordo/netto** gross/net weight; **peso massimo/medio** (*Pugilato*) heavy/middleweight

pessi'mismo *sm* pessimism; **pessi'mista,**

-i, -e *ag* pessimistic ▷ *sm/f* pessimist

'pessimo, -a *ag* very bad, awful

pes'tare *vt* to tread on, trample on; (*sale, pepe*) to grind; (*uva, aglio*) to crush; (*fig: picchiare*): ~ **qn** to beat sb up

'peste *sf* plague; (*persona*) nuisance, pest

pes'tello *sm* pestle

'petalo *sm* (Bot) petal

pe'tardo *sm* firecracker, banger (BRIT)

petizi'one [petit'tsjone] *sf* petition

petroli'era *sf* (*nave*) oil tanker

pe'trolio *sm* oil, petroleum; (*per lampada, fornello*) paraffin

> Attenzione! In inglese esiste la parola *petrol* che però significa *benzina*.

pettego'lare *vi* to gossip

pettego'lezzo [pettego'leddzo] *sm* gossip *no pl*; **fare pettegolezzi** to gossip

pet'tegolo, -a *ag* gossipy ▷ *sm/f* gossip

petti'nare *vt* to comb (the hair of); **pettinarsi** *vpr* to comb one's hair; **pettina'tura** *sf* (*acconciatura*) hairstyle

'pettine *sm* comb; (*Zool*) scallop

petti'rosso *sm* robin

'petto *sm* chest; (*seno*) breast, bust; (*Cuc: di carne bovina*) brisket; (: *di pollo ecc*) breast; **a doppio ~** (*abito*) double-breasted

petu'lante *ag* insolent

'pezza ['pettsa] *sf* piece of cloth; (*toppa*) patch; (*cencio*) rag, cloth

pez'zente [pet'tsɛnte] *sm/f* beggar

'pezzo ['pettso] *sm* (*gen*) piece; (*brandello, frammento*) piece, bit; (*di macchina, arnese ecc*) part; (*Stampa*) article; (*di tempo*): **aspettare un ~** to wait quite a while o some time; **in** o **a pezzi** in pieces; **andare in pezzi** to break into pieces; **un bel ~ d'uomo** a fine figure of a man; **abito a due pezzi** two-piece suit; **pezzo di cronaca** (*Stampa*) report; **pezzo grosso** (*fig*) bigwig; **pezzo di ricambio** spare part

pi'accio *ecc* ['pjattʃo] *vb vedi* **piacere**

pia'cente [pja'tʃɛnte] *ag* attractive

pia'cere [pja'tʃere] *vi* to please; **una ragazza che piace** a likeable girl; an attractive girl; ~ **a: mi piace** I like it; **quei ragazzi non mi piacciono** I don't like those boys; **gli ~bbe andare al cinema** he would like to go to the cinema ▷ *sm* pleasure; (*favore*) favour; **"~!"** (*nelle presentazioni*) "pleased to meet you!"; ~ **(di conoscerla)** nice to meet you; **con ~** certainly, with pleasure; **per ~!** please; **fare un ~ a qn** to do sb a favour; **pia'cevole** *ag* pleasant, agreeable

pi'acqui *ecc* *vb vedi* **piacere**

pi'aga, -ghe *sf* (*lesione*) sore; (*ferita: anche fig*) wound; (*fig: flagello*) scourge, curse; (: *persona*) pest, nuisance

piagnuco'lare [pjaɲɲuko'lare] vi to whimper

pianeggi'ante [pjaned'dʒante] ag flat, level

piane'rottolo sm landing

pia'neta sm (Astr) planet

pi'angere ['pjandʒere] vi to cry, weep; (occhi) to water ▷ vt to cry, weep; (lamentare) to bewail, lament; **~ la morte di qn** to mourn sb's death

pianifi'care vt to plan

pia'nista, -i, -e sm/f pianist

pi'ano, -a ag (piatto) flat, level; (Mat) plane; (chiaro) clear, plain ▷ av (adagio) slowly; (a bassa voce) softly; (con cautela) slowly, carefully ▷ sm (Mat) plane; (Geo) plain; (livello) level, plane; (di edificio) floor; (programma) plan; (Mus) piano; **a che ~ si trova?** what floor is it on?; **pian ~** very slowly; (poco a poco) little by little; **in primo/secondo ~** in the foreground/background; **di primo ~** (fig) prominent, high-ranking

piano'forte sm piano, pianoforte

piano'terra sm inv ground floor

pi'ansi ecc vb vedi **piangere**

pi'anta sf (Bot) plant; (Anat: anche: **~ del piede**) sole (of the foot); (grafico) plan; (topografica) map; **in ~ stabile** on the permanent staff; **pian'tare** vt to plant; (conficcare) to drive o hammer in; (tenda) to put up, pitch; (fig: lasciare) to leave, desert; **piantarsi** vpr **piantarsi davanti a qn** to plant o.s. in front of sb; **piantala!** (fam) cut it out!

pianter'reno sm = **pianoterra**

pia'nura sf plain

pi'astra sf plate; (di pietra) slab; (di fornello) hotplate; **panino alla ~** ≈ toasted sandwich; **piastra di registrazione** tape deck

pias'trella sf tile

pias'trina sf (Mil) identity disc

piatta'forma sf (anche fig) platform

piat'tino sm saucer

pi'atto, -a ag flat; (fig: scialbo) dull ▷ sm (recipiente, vivanda) dish; (portata) course; (parte piana) flat (part); **piatti** smpl (Mus) cymbals; **piatto fondo** soup dish; **piatto forte** main course; **piatto del giorno** dish of the day, plat du jour; **piatto del giradischi** turntable; **piatto piano** dinner plate

pi'azza ['pjattsa] sf square; (Comm) market; **far ~ pulita** to make a clean sweep; **piazza d'armi** (Mil) parade ground; **piaz'zale** sm (large) square; **piaz'zola** [pjat'tsɔla] sf (Aut) lay-by; (di tenda) pitch

pic'cante ag hot, pungent; (fig) racy; biting

pic'chetto [pik'ketto] sm (Mil, di scioperanti) picket; (di tenda) peg

picchi'are [pik'kjare] vt (persona: colpire) to hit, strike; (: prendere a botte) to beat (up); (battere) to beat; (sbattere) to bang ▷ vi (bussare) to knock; (: con forza) to bang; (colpire) to hit, strike; (sole) to beat down; **picchi'ata** sf (Aer) dive

'picchio ['pikkjo] sm woodpecker

pic'cino, -a [pit'tʃino] ag tiny, very small

picci'one [pit'tʃone] sm pigeon

'picco, -chi sm peak; **a ~** vertically

'piccolo, -a ag small; (oggetto, mano, di età: bambino) small, little; (dav sostantivo: di breve durata: viaggio) short; (fig) mean, petty ▷ sm/f child, little one

pic'cone sm pick(-axe)

pic'cozza [pik'kɔttsa] sf ice-axe

'picnic sm inv picnic

pi'docchio [pi'dɔkkjo] sm louse

pi'ede sm foot; (di mobile) leg; **in piedi** standing; **a piedi** on foot; **a piedi nudi** barefoot; **su due piedi** (fig) at once; **prendere ~** (fig) to gain ground, catch on; **sul ~ di guerra** (Mil) ready for action; **piede di porco** crowbar

pi'ega, -ghe sf (piegatura, Geo) fold; (di gonna) pleat; (di pantaloni) crease; (grinza) wrinkle, crease; **prendere una brutta ~** (fig) to take a turn for the worse

pie'gare vt to fold; (braccia, gambe, testa) to bend ▷ vi to bend; **piegarsi** vpr to bend; (fig): **piegarsi (a)** to yield (to), submit (to)

piegherò ecc [pjege'rɔ] vb vedi **piegare**

pie'ghevole ag pliable, flexible; (porta) folding

Pie'monte sm **il ~** Piedmont

pi'ena sf (di fiume) flood, spate

pi'eno, -a ag full; (muro, mattone) solid ▷ sm (colmo) height, peak; (carico) full load; **~ di** full of; **in ~ giorno** in broad daylight; **il ~, per favore** (Aut) fill it up, please

piercing ['pirsing] sm piercing; **farsi il ~ all'ombelico** to have one's navel pierced

pietà sf pity; (Rel) piety; **senza ~** pitiless, merciless; **avere ~ di** (compassione) to pity, feel sorry for; (misericordia) to have pity o mercy on

pie'tanza [pje'tantsa] sf dish, course

pie'toso, -a ag (compassionevole) pitying, compassionate; (che desta pietà) pitiful

pi'etra sf stone; **pietra preziosa** precious stone, gem

'piffero sm (Mus) pipe

pigi'ama, -i [pi'dʒama] sm pyjamas pl

pigli'are [piʎ'ʎare] vt to take, grab; (afferrare) to catch

'pigna ['pinna] *sf* pine cone
pi'gnolo, -a [pin'nolo] *ag* pernickety
pi'grizia [pi'grittsja] *sf* laziness
'pigro, -a *ag* lazy
PIL *sigla m* (= *prodotto interno lordo*) GDP
'pila *sf* (*catasta, di ponte*) pile; (*Elettr*) battery; (*torcia*) torch (BRIT), flashlight
pi'lastro *sm* pillar
'pile ['pail] *sm inv* fleece
'pillola *sf* pill; **prendere la ~** to be on the pill
pi'lone *sm* (*di ponte*) pier; (*di linea elettrica*) pylon
pi'lota, -i, -e *sm/f* pilot; (*Aut*) driver
▷ *ag inv* pilot *cpd*; **pilota automatico** automatic pilot
pinaco'teca, -che *sf* art gallery
pi'neta *sf* pinewood
ping-'pong [piŋ'pɔŋ] *sm* table tennis
pingu'ino *sm* (*Zool*) penguin
'pinna *sf* (*di pesce*) fin; (*di cetaceo, per nuotare*) flipper
'pino *sm* pine (tree); **pi'nolo** *sm* pine kernel
'pinza ['pintsa] *sf* pliers *pl*; (*Med*) forceps *pl*; (*Zool*) pincer
pinzette [pin'tsette] *sfpl* tweezers
pi'oggia, -ge ['pjɔddʒa] *sf* rain; **pioggia acida** acid rain
pi'olo *sm* peg; (*di scala*) rung
piom'bare *vi* to fall heavily; (*gettarsi con impeto*): **~ su** to fall upon, assail ▷ *vt* (*dente*) to fill; **piomba'tura** *sf* (*di dente*) filling
piom'bino *sm* (*sigillo*) (lead) seal; (*del filo a piombo*) plummet; (*Pesca*) sinker
pi'ombo *sm* (*Chim*) lead; **a ~** (*cadere*) straight down; **senza ~** (*benzina*) unleaded
pioni'ere, -a *sm/f* pioneer
pi'oppo *sm* poplar
pi'overe *vb impers* to rain ▷ *vi* (*fig: scendere dall'alto*) to rain down; (*lettere, regali*) to pour in; **pioviggi'nare** *vb impers* to drizzle; **pio'voso, -a** *ag* rainy
pi'ovra *sf* octopus
pi'ovve *ecc vb vedi* **piovere**
'pipa *sf* pipe
pipì (*fam*) *sf* **fare ~** to have a wee (wee)
pipis'trello *sm* (*Zool*) bat
pi'ramide *sf* pyramid
pi'rata, -i *sm* pirate; **pirata della strada** hit-and-run driver; **pirata informatica** hacker
Pire'nei *smpl* **i ~** the Pyrenees
pi'romane *sm/f* pyromaniac; arsonist
pi'roscafo *sm* steamer, steamship
pisci'are [piʃʃare] (*fam!*) *vi* to piss (!), pee (!)
pi'scina [piʃʃina] *sf* (*swimming*) pool; (*stabilimento*) (*swimming*) baths *pl*
pi'sello *sm* pea

piso'lino *sm* nap
'pista *sf* (*traccia*) track, trail; (*di stadio*) track; (*di pattinaggio*) rink; (*da sci*) run; (*Aer*) runway; (*di circo*) ring; **pista da ballo** dance floor
pis'tacchio [pis'takkjo] *sm* pistachio (tree); pistachio (nut)
pis'tola *sf* pistol, gun
pis'tone *sm* piston
pi'tone *sm* python
pit'tore, -'trice *sm/f* painter; **pitto'resco, -a, -schi, -sche** *ag* picturesque
pit'tura *sf* painting; **pittu'rare** *vt* to paint

 PAROLA CHIAVE

più *av* **1** (*in maggiore quantità*) more; **più del solito** more than usual; **in più, di più** more; **ne voglio di più** I want some more; **ci sono 3 persone in o di più** there are 3 more o extra people; **più o meno** more or less; **per di più** (*inoltre*) what's more, moreover
2 (*comparativo*) more; (*aggettivo corto +*) ...er; **più ... di/che** more ... than; **lavoro più di te/Paola** I work harder than you/Paola; **è più intelligente che ricco** he's more intelligent than rich
3 (*superlativo*) most; (*aggettivo corto +*) ...est; **il più grande/intelligente** the biggest/most intelligent; **è quello che compro più spesso** that's the one I buy most often; **al più presto** as soon as possible; **al più tardi** at the latest
4 (*negazione*): **non ... più** no more, no longer; **non ho più soldi** I've got no more money, I don't have any more money; **non lavoro più** I'm no longer working, I don't work any more; **a più non posso** (*gridare*) at the top of one's voice; (*correre*) as fast as one can
5 (*Mat*) plus; **4 più 9 fa 9** 4 plus 5 equals 9; **più 5 gradi** 5 degrees above freezing, plus 5
▷ *prep* plus ▷ *ag inv*: **più ... (di)** more ... (than); **più denaro/tempo** more money/time; **più persone di quante ci aspettassimo** more people than we expected
2 (*numerosi, diversi*) several; **l'aspettai per più giorni** I waited for it for several days
▷ *sm* **1** (*la maggior parte*): **il più è fatto** most of it is done
2 (*Mat*) plus (sign)
3: **i più** the majority

pi'uma *sf* feather; **piu'mino** *sm* (eider)down; (*per letto*) eiderdown; (: *tipo* *danese*) duvet, continental quilt; (*giacca*) quilted jacket (*with goose-feather padding*); (*per cipria*) powder puff; (*per spolverare*) feather duster

piut'tosto *av* rather; **~ che** (*anziché*) rather than

'**pizza** ['pittsa] *sf* pizza; **pizze'ria** *sf* place where pizzas are made, sold or eaten

pizzi'care [pittsi'kare] *vt* (*stringere*) to nip, pinch; (*pungere*) to sting; to bite; (*Mus*) to pluck ▷ *vi* (*prudere*) to itch, be itchy; (*cibo*) to be hot o spicy

'**pizzico, -chi** ['pittsiko] *sm* (*pizzicotto*) pinch, nip; (*piccola quantità*) pinch, dash; (*d'insetto*) sting; bite

pizzi'cotto [pittsi'kɔtto] *sm* pinch, nip

'**pizzo** ['pittso] *sm* (*merletto*) lace; (*barbetta*) goatee beard

plagi'are [pla'dʒare] *vt* (*copiare*) to plagiarize

plaid [plɛd] *sm inv* (travelling) rug (BRIT), lap robe (US)

pla'nare *vi* (*Aer*) to glide

'**plasma** *sm* plasma

plas'mare *vt* to mould, shape

'**plastica, -che** *sf* (*arte*) plastic arts *pl*; (*Med*) plastic surgery; (*sostanza*) plastic; **plastica facciale** face lift

'**platano** *sm* plane tree

pla'tea *sf* (*Teatro*) stalls *pl*

'**platino** *sm* platinum

plau'sibile *ag* plausible

pleni'lunio *sm* full moon

'**plettro** *sm* plectrum

pleu'rite *sf* pleurisy

'**plico, -chi** *sm* (*pacco*) parcel; **in ~ a parte** (*Comm*) under separate cover

plo'tone *sm* (*Mil*) platoon; **plotone d'esecuzione** firing squad

plu'rale *ag, sm* plural

PM *abbr* (*Pol*) = **Pubblico Ministero**; (= *Polizia Militare*) MP (*Military Police*)

pneu'matico, -a, -ci, -che *ag* inflatable; pneumatic ▷ *sm* (*Aut*) tyre (BRIT), tire (US)

po' *av, sm vedi* **poco**

⭕ PAROLA CHIAVE

'**poco, -a, -chi, -che** *ag* (*quantità*) little, not much; (*numero*) few, not many; **poco pane/denaro/spazio** little o not much bread/money/space; **poche persone/ idee** few o not many people/ideas; **ci vediamo tra poco** (*sottinteso: tempo*) see you soon

▷ *av* 1 (*in piccola quantità*) little, not much; (*numero limitato*) few, not many; **guadagna poco** he doesn't earn much, he earns little

2 (*con ag, av*) (a) little, not very; **sta poco bene** he isn't very well; **è poco più vecchia di lui** she's a little o slightly older than him

3 (*tempo*): **poco dopo/prima** shortly afterwards/before; **il film dura poco** the film doesn't last very long; **ci vediamo molto poco** we don't see each other very often, we hardly ever see each other

4: **un po'** a little, a bit; **è un po' corto** it's a little o a bit short; **arriverà fra un po'** he'll arrive shortly o in a little while

5: **a dir poco** to say the least; **a poco a poco** little by little; **per poco non cadevo** I nearly fell; **è una cosa da poco** it's nothing, it's of no importance; **una persona da poco** a worthless person

▷ *pron* (a) little

po'dere *sm* (*Agr*) farm

'**podio** *sm* dais, platform; (*Mus*) podium

po'dismo *sm* (*Sport*) track events *pl*

poe'sia *sf* (*arte*) poetry; (*componimento*) poem

po'eta, -'essa *sm/f* poet/poetess

poggi'are [pod'dʒare] *vt* to lean, rest; (*posare*) to lay, place; **poggia'testa** *sm inv* (*Aut*) headrest

'**poggio** ['pɔddʒo] *sm* hillock, knoll

'**poi** *av* then; (*alla fine*) finally, at last; **e ~** (*inoltre*) and besides; **questa ~ (è bella)!** (*ironico*) that's a good one!

poiché [poi'ke] *cong* since, as

'**poker** *sm* poker

po'lacco, -a, -chi, -che *ag* Polish ▷ *sm/f* Pole

po'lare *ag* polar

po'lemica, -che *sf* controversy

po'lemico, -a, -ci, -che *ag* polemic(al), controversial

po'lenta *sf* (*Cuc*) sort of thick porridge made with maize flour

polio(mie'lite) *sf* polio(myelitis)

'**polipo** *sm* polyp

polisti'rolo *sm* polystyrene

po'litica, -che *sf* politics *sg*; (*linea di condotta*) policy; (*anche*: **politico**); **politica'mente** *av* politically; **politicamente corretto** politically correct

po'litico, -a, -ci, -che *ag* political ▷ *sm/f* politician

poli'zia [polit'tsia] *sf* police; **polizia giudiziaria** ≈ Criminal Investigation Department (BRIT), ≈ Federal Bureau of Investigation (US); **polizia stradale** traffic police; **polizi'esco, -a, -schi, -sche** *ag* police *cpd*; (*film, romanzo*) detective *cpd*; **polizi'otto** *sm* policeman; **cane poliziotto** police dog; **donna poliziotto**

policewoman; **poliziotto di quartiere** local police officer

'polizza ['pɔlittsa] sf (Comm) bill; **~ di assicurazione** insurance policy; **polizza di carico** bill of lading
pol'laio sm henhouse
'pollice ['pɔllitʃe] sm thumb
'polline sm pollen
'pollo sm chicken
pol'mone sm lung; **polmone d'acciaio** (Med) iron lung; **polmo'nite** sf pneumonia; **polmonite atipica** SARS
'polo sm (Geo, Fisica) pole; (gioco) polo; **polo nord/sud** North/South Pole
Po'lonia sf **la ~** Poland
'polpa sf flesh, pulp; (carne) lean meat
pol'paccio [pol'pattʃo] sm (Anat) calf
polpas'trello sm fingertip
pol'petta sf (Cuc) meatball
'polpo sm octopus
pol'sino sm cuff
'polso sm (Anat) wrist; (pulsazione) pulse; (fig: forza) drive, vigour
pol'trire vi to laze about
pol'trona sf armchair; (Teatro: posto) seat in the front stalls (BRIT) o orchestra (US)
'polvere sf dust; (sostanza ridotta minutissima) powder, dust; **latte in ~** dried o powdered milk; **caffè in ~** instant coffee; **sapone in ~** soap powder; **polvere da sparo/pirica** gunpowder
po'mata sf ointment, cream
po'mello sm knob
pome'riggio [pome'riddʒo] sm afternoon
'pomice ['pɔmitʃe] sf pumice
'pomo sm (mela) apple; (ornamentale) knob; (di sella) pommel; **pomo d'Adamo** (Anat) Adam's apple
pomo'doro sm tomato; **pomodori pelati** skinned tomatoes
'pompa sf pump; (sfarzo) pomp (and ceremony); **pompe funebri** funeral parlour sg (BRIT), undertaker's sg; **pompa di benzina** petrol (BRIT) o gas (US) pump; (distributore) filling o gas (US) station; **pom'pare** vt to pump; (trarre) to pump out; (gonfiare d'aria) to pump up
pom'pelmo sm grapefruit
pompi'ere sm fireman

po'nente sm west
pongo, poni ecc vb vedi **porre**
'ponte sm bridge; (di nave) deck; (: anche: **~ di comando**) bridge; (impalcatura) scaffold; **fare il ~** (fig) to take the extra day off (between 2 public holidays); **governo ~** interim government; **ponte aereo** airlift; **ponte levatoio** drawbridge; **ponte sospeso** suspension bridge
pon'tefice [pon'tefitʃe] sm (Rel) pontiff
'popcorn ['pɔpkɔːn] sm inv popcorn
popo'lare ag popular; (quartiere, clientela) working-class ▷ vt (rendere abitato) to populate; **popolarsi** vpr to fill with people, get crowded; **popolazi'one** sf population
'popolo sm people
'poppa sf (di nave) stern; (seno) breast
porcel'lana [portʃel'lana] sf porcelain, china; piece of china
porcel'lino, -a [portʃel'lino] sm/f piglet; **porcellino d'India** guinea pig
porche'ria [porke'ria] sf filth, muck; (fig: oscenità) obscenity; (: azione disonesta) dirty trick; (: cosa mal fatta) rubbish
por'cile [por'tʃile] sm pigsty
por'cino, -a [por'tʃino] ag of pigs, pork cpd ▷ sm (fungo) type of edible mushroom
'porco, -ci sm pig; (carne) pork
porcos'pino sm porcupine
'porgere ['pɔrdʒere] vt to hand, give; (tendere) to hold out
pornogra'fia sf pornography; **porno'grafico, -a, -ci, -che** ag pornographic
'poro sm pore
'porpora sf purple
'porre vt (mettere) to put; (collocare) to place; (posare) to lay (down), put (down); (fig: supporre): **poniamo (il caso) che ...** let's suppose that ...
'porro sm (Bot) leek; (Med) wart
'porsi ecc vb vedi **porgere**
'porta sf door; (Sport) goal; **portaba'gagli** sm inv (facchino) porter; (Aut, Ferr) luggage rack; **porta-CD** [portatʃi'di] sm inv (mobile) CD rack; (astuccio) CD holder; **porta'cenere** sm inv ashtray; **portachi'avi** sm inv keyring; **porta'erei** sf inv (nave) aircraft carrier; **portafi'nestra** (pl **portefi'nestre**) sf French window; **porta'foglio** sm wallet; (Pol, Borsa) portfolio; **non trovo il portafoglio** I can't find my wallet; **portafor'tuna** sm inv lucky charm; mascot
por'tale sm (di chiesa, Inform) portal
porta'mento sm carriage, bearing
portamo'nete sm inv purse

por'tante ag (muro ecc) supporting, load-bearing

portan'tina sf sedan chair; (per ammalati) stretcher

portaom'brelli sm inv umbrella stand

porta'pacchi [porta'pakki] sm inv (di moto, bicicletta) luggage rack

por'tare vt (sostenere, sorreggere: peso, bambino, pacco) to carry; (indossare: abito, occhiali) to wear; (: capelli lunghi) to have; (avere: nome, titolo) to have, bear; (recare): ~ qc a qn to take (o bring) sth to sb; (fig: sentimenti) to bear

portasiga'rette sm inv cigarette case

por'tata sf (vivanda) course; (Aut) carrying (o loading) capacity; (di arma) range; (volume d'acqua) (rate of) flow; (fig: limite) scope, capability; (: importanza) impact, import; **alla ~ di tutti** (conoscenza) within everybody's capabilities; (prezzo) within everybody's means; **a/fuori ~ (di)** within/ out of reach (of); **a ~ di mano** within (arm's) reach

por'tatile ag portable

por'tato, -a ag (incline): ~ **a** inclined o apt to

portau'ovo sm inv eggcup

porta'voce [porta'votʃe] sm/f inv spokesman/woman

por'tento sm wonder, marvel

porti'era sf (Aut) door

porti'ere sm (portinaio) concierge, caretaker; (di hotel) porter; (nel calcio) goalkeeper

porti'naio, -a sm/f concierge, caretaker

portine'ria sf caretaker's lodge

'porto, -a pp di **porgere** ▷ sm (Naut) harbour, port ▷ sm inv port (wine); **porto d'armi** (documento) gun licence

Porto'gallo sm **il ~** Portugal; **porto'ghese** ag, sm/f, sm Portuguese inv

por'tone sm main entrance, main door

portu'ale ag harbour cpd, port cpd ▷ sm dock worker

porzi'one [por'tsjone] sf portion, share; (di cibo) portion, helping

'posa sf (Fot) exposure; (atteggiamento, di modello) pose

po'sare vt to put (down), lay (down) ▷ vi (ponte, edificio, teoria): ~ **su** to rest on; (Fot: atteggiarsi) to pose; **posarsi** vpr (aereo) to land; (uccello) to alight; (sguardo) to settle

po'sata sf piece of cutlery

pos'critto sm postscript

'posi ecc vb vedi **porre**

posi'tivo, -a ag positive

posizi'one [pozit'tsjone] sf position; **prendere ~** (fig) to take a stand; **luci di ~** (Aut) sidelights

pos'porre vt to place after; (differire) to postpone, defer

posse'dere vt to own, possess; (qualità, virtù) to have, possess

posses'sivo, -a ag possessive

pos'sesso sm ownership no pl; possession

posses'sore sm owner

pos'sibile ag possible ▷ sm **fare tutto il ~** to do everything possible; **nei limiti del ~** as far as possible; **al più tardi ~** as late as possible; **possibilità** sf inv possibility ▷ sfpl (mezzi) means; **aver la possibilità di fare** to be in a position to do; to have the opportunity to do

possi'dente sm/f landowner

possi'edo ecc vb vedi **possedere**

'posso ecc vb vedi **potere**

'posta sf (servizio) post, postal service; (corrispondenza) post, mail; (ufficio postale) post office; (nei giochi d'azzardo) stake; **Poste** sfpl (amministrazione) post office; **c'è ~ per me?** are there any letters for me?; **ministro delle Poste e Telecomunicazioni** Postmaster General; **posta aerea** airmail; **posta elettronica** E-mail, e-mail, electronic mail; **posta ordinaria** ≈ second-class mail; **posta prioritaria** ≈ first-class post; **pos'tale** ag postal, post office cpd

posteggi'are [posted'dʒare] vt, vi to park; **pos'teggio** sm car park (BRIT), parking lot (US); (di taxi) rank (BRIT), stand (US)

'poster sm inv poster

posteri'ore ag (dietro) back; (dopo) later ▷ sm (fam: sedere) behind

postici'pare [postitʃi'pare] vt to defer, postpone

pos'tino sm postman (BRIT), mailman (US)

'posto, -a pp di **porre** ▷ sm (sito, posizione) place; (impiego) job; (spazio libero) room, space; (di parcheggio) space; (sedile: al teatro, in treno ecc) seat; (Mil) post; **a ~** (in ordine) in place, tidy; (fig) settled; (: persona) reliable; **vorrei prenotare due posti** I'd like to book two seats; **al ~ di** in place of; **sul ~** on the spot; **mettere a ~** to tidy (up), put in order; (faccende) to straighten out; **posto di blocco** roadblock; **posto di lavoro** job; **posti in piedi** (in teatro, in autobus) standing room; **posto di polizia** police station

po'tabile ag drinkable; **acqua ~** drinking water

po'tare vt to prune

po'tassio sm potassium

po'tente ag (nazione) strong, powerful; (veleno, farmaco) potent, strong; **po'tenza** sf power; (forza) strength

potenzi'ale [poten'tsjale] *ag, sm*
potential

PAROLA CHIAVE

po'tere *sm* power; **al potere** (*partito ecc*)
in power; **potere d'acquisto** purchasing
power
▷ *vb aus* **1** (*essere in grado di*) can, be able
to; **non ha potuto ripararlo** he couldn't
o he wasn't able to repair it; **non è potuto
venire** he couldn't o he wasn't able to
come; **spiacente di non poter aiutare**
sorry not to be able to help
2 (*avere il permesso*) can, may, be allowed
to; **posso entrare?** can o may I come in?;
si può sapere dove sei stato? where on
earth have you been?
3 (*eventualità*) may, might, could;
potrebbe essere vero it might o could be
true; **può aver avuto un incidente** he
may o might o could have had an accident;
può darsi perhaps; **può darsi** o **essere
che non venga** he may o might not come
4 (*augurio*): **potessi almeno parlargli!** if
only I could speak to him!
5 (*suggerimento*): **potresti almeno
scusarti!** you could at least apologize!
▷ *vt* can, be able to; **può molto per noi** he
can do a lot for us; **non ne posso più** (*per
stanchezza*) I'm exhausted; (*per rabbia*) I
can't take any more

potrò *ecc vb vedi* **potere**
'povero, -a *ag* poor; (*disadorno*) plain, bare
▷ *sm/f* poor man/woman; **i poveri** the
poor; **~ di** lacking in, having little; **povertà**
sf poverty
poz'zanghera [pot'tsangera] *sf* puddle
'pozzo ['pottso] *sm* well; (*cava: di carbone*)
pit; (*di miniera*) shaft; **pozzo petrolifero**
oil well
P.R.A. [pra] *sigla m* (= *Pubblico Registro
Automobilistico*) ≈ DVLA
pran'zare [pran'dzare] *vi* to dine, have
dinner; (*a mezzogiorno*) to lunch, have lunch
'pranzo ['prandzo] *sm* dinner; (*a
mezzogiorno*) lunch
'prassi *sf* usual procedure
'pratica, -che *sf* practice; (*esperienza*)
experience; (*conoscenza*) knowledge,
familiarity; (*tirocinio*) training, practice;
(*Amm: affare*) matter, case; (: *incartamento*)
file, dossier; **in ~** (*praticamente*) in practice;
mettere in ~ to put into practice
prati'cabile *ag* (*progetto*) practicable,
feasible; (*luogo*) passable, practicable
pratica'mente *av* (*in modo pratico*)
in a practical way, practically; (*quasi*)

practically, almost
prati'care *vt* to practise; (*Sport: tennis ecc*)
to play; (: *nuoto, scherma ecc*) to go in for;
(*eseguire: apertura, buco*) to make; **~ uno
sconto** to give a discount
'pratico, -a, -ci, -che *ag* practical; **~ di**
(*esperto*) experienced o skilled in; (*familiare*)
familiar with
'prato *sm* meadow; (*di giardino*) lawn
preav'viso *sm* notice; **telefonata con ~**
personal o person to person call
pre'cario, -a *ag* precarious; (*Ins*)
temporary
precauzi'one [prekaut'tsjone] *sf* caution,
care; (*misura*) precaution
prece'dente [pretʃe'dɛnte] *ag* previous
▷ *sm* precedent; **il discorso/film ~** the
previous o preceding speech/film; **senza
precedenti** unprecedented; **precedenti
penali** criminal record *sg*; **prece'denza** *sf*
priority, precedence; (*Aut*) right of way
pre'cedere [pre'tʃɛdere] *vt* to precede, go
(o come) before
precipi'tare [pretʃipi'tare] *vi* (*cadere*) to
fall headlong; (*fig: situazione*) to get out
of control ▷ *vt* (*gettare dall'alto in basso*)
to hurl, fling; (*fig: affrettare*) to rush;
precipitarsi *vpr* (*gettarsi*) to hurl o fling
o.s.; (*affrettarsi*) to rush; **precipi'toso, -a**
ag (*caduta, fuga*) headlong; (*fig: avventato*)
rash, reckless; (: *affrettato*) hasty, rushed
preci'pizio [pretʃi'pittsjo] *sm* precipice; **a
~** (*fig: correre*) headlong
precisa'mente [pretʃiza'mente] *av* (*gen*)
precisely; (*con esattezza*) exactly
preci'sare [pretʃi'zare] *vt* to state, specify;
(*spiegare*) to explain (in detail)
precisi'one [pretʃi'zjone] *sf* precision;
accuracy
pre'ciso, -a [pre'tʃizo] *ag* (*esatto*) precise;
(*accurato*) accurate, precise; (*deciso: idee*)
precise, definite; (*uguale*): **2 vestiti precisi**
2 dresses exactly the same; **sono le 9
precise** it's exactly 9 o'clock
pre'cludere *vt* to block, obstruct
pre'coce [pre'kɔtʃe] *ag* early; (*bambino*)
precocious; (*vecchiaia*) premature
precon'cetto [prekon'tʃetto] *sm*
preconceived idea, prejudice
precur'sore *sm* forerunner, precursor
'preda *sf* (*bottino*) booty; (*animale, fig*) prey;
essere ~ di to fall prey to; **essere in ~ a** to
be prey to
'predica, -che *sf* sermon; (*fig*) lecture,
talking-to
predi'care *vt, vi* to preach
predi'cato *sm* (*Ling*) predicate
predi'letto, -a *pp di* **prediligere** ▷ *ag, sm/f*
favourite

predi'ligere [predi'lidʒere] *vt* to prefer, have a preference for

pre'dire *vt* to foretell, predict

predis'porre *vt* to get ready, prepare; **~ qn a qc** to predispose sb to sth

predizi'one [predit'tsjone] *sf* prediction

prefazi'one [prefat'tsjone] *sf* preface, foreword

prefe'renza [prefe'rentsa] *sf* preference

prefe'rire *vt* to prefer, like better; **~ il caffè al tè** to prefer coffee to tea, like coffee better than tea

pre'figgersi [pre'fiddʒersi] *vpr* **~ uno scopo** to set o.s. a goal

pre'fisso, -a *pp di* **prefiggere** ▷ *sm* (*Ling*) prefix; (*Tel*) dialling (BRIT) o dial (US) code; **qual è il ~ telefonico di Londra?** what is the dialling code for London?

pre'gare *vi* to pray ▷ *vt* (*Rel*) to pray to; (*implorare*) to beg; (*chiedere*): **~ qn di fare** to ask sb to do; **farsi ~** to need coaxing o persuading

pre'gevole [pre'dʒevole] *ag* valuable

pregherò *ecc* [prege'rɔ] *vb vedi* **pregare**

preghi'era [pre'gjera] *sf* (*Rel*) prayer; (*domanda*) request

pregi'ato, -a [pre'dʒato] *ag* (*di valore*) valuable; **vino ~** vintage wine

'pregio ['predʒo] *sm* (*stima*) esteem, regard; (*qualità*) (good) quality, merit; (*valore*) value, worth

pregiudi'care [predʒudi'kare] *vt* to prejudice, harm, be detrimental to

pregiu'dizio [predʒu'dittsjo] *sm* (*idea errata*) prejudice; (*danno*) harm *no pl*

'prego *escl* (*a chi ringrazia*) don't mention it!; (*invitando qn ad accomodarsi*) please sit down!; (*invitando qn ad andare prima*) after you!

pregus'tare *vt* to look forward to

prele'vare *vt* (*denaro*) to withdraw; (*campione*) to take; (*polizia*) to take, capture

preli'evo *sm* (*di denaro*) withdrawal; (*Med*): **fare un ~ (di)** to take a sample (of); **prelievo di sangue; fare un ~ di sangue** to take a blood sample

prelimi'nare *ag* preliminary

'premere *vt* to press ▷ *vi* **~ su** to press down on; (*fig*) to put pressure on; **~ a** (*fig: importare*) to matter to

pre'mettere *vt* to put before; (*dire prima*) to start by saying, state first

premi'are *vt* to give a prize to; (*fig: merito, onestà*) to reward

premiazi'one [premjat'tsjone] *sf* prize giving

'premio *sm* prize; (*ricompensa*) reward; (*Comm*) premium; (*Amm: indennità*) bonus

pre'misi *ecc vb vedi* **premettere**

premu'nirsi *vpr* **~ di** to provide o.s. with; **~ contro** to protect o.s. from, guard o.s. against

pre'mura *sf* (*fretta*) haste, hurry; (*riguardo*) attention, care; **premure** *sfpl* (*attenzioni, cure*) care *sg*; **aver ~** to be in a hurry; **far ~ a qn** to hurry sb; **usare ogni ~ nei riguardi di qn** to be very attentive to sb; **premu'roso, -a** *ag* thoughtful, considerate

'prendere *vt* to take; (*andare a prendere*) to get, fetch; (*ottenere*) to get; (*guadagnare*) to get, earn; (*catturare: ladro, pesce*) to catch; (*collaboratore, dipendente*) to take on; (*passeggero*) to pick up; (*chiedere: somma, prezzo*) to charge, ask; (*trattare: persona*) to handle ▷ *vi* (*colla, cemento*) to set; (*pianta*) to take; (*fuoco: nel camino*) to catch; (*voltare*): **~ a destra** to turn (to the) right; **prendersi** *vpr* (*azzuffarsi*): **prendersi a pugni** to come to blows; **dove si prende il traghetto per...?** where do we get the ferry to ...; **prendi qualcosa?** (*da bere, da mangiare*) would you like something to eat (o drink)?; **prendo un caffè** I'll have a coffee; **~ qn/qc per** (*scambiare*) to take sb/sth for; **~ fuoco** to catch fire; **~ parte a** to take part in; **prendersi cura di qn/qc** to look after sb/sth; **prendersela** (*adirarsi*) to get annoyed; (*preoccuparsi*) to get upset, worry

preno'tare *vt* to book, reserve; **vorrei ~ una camera doppia** I'd like to book a double room; **ho prenotato un tavolo al nome di ...** I booked a table in the name of ...; **prenotazi'one** *sf* booking, reservation; **ho confermato la prenotazione per fax/e-mail** I confirmed my booking by fax/e-mail

preoccu'pare *vt* to worry; to preoccupy; **preoccuparsi** *vpr* **preoccuparsi di qn/qc** to worry about sb/sth; **preoccuparsi per qn** to be anxious for sb; **preoccupazi'one** *sf* worry, anxiety

prepa'rare *vt* to prepare; (*esame, concorso*) to prepare for; **prepararsi** *vpr* (*vestirsi*) to get ready; **prepararsi a qc/a fare** to get ready o prepare (o.s.) for sth/to do; **~ da mangiare** to prepare a meal; **prepara'tivi** *smpl* preparations

preposizi'one [prepozit'tsjone] *sf* (*Ling*) preposition

prepo'tente *ag* (*persona*) domineering, arrogant; (*bisogno, desiderio*) overwhelming, pressing ▷ *sm/f* bully

'presa *sf* taking *no pl*; catching *no pl*; (*di città*) capture; (*indurimento: di cemento*) setting; (*appiglio, Sport*) hold; (*di acqua, gas*) (supply) point; (*piccola quantità: di sale* ecc) pinch; (Carte) trick; **far ~ (colla)** to set; **far ~ sul pubblico** to catch the public's imagination; **essere alle prese con** (fig) to be struggling with; **presa d'aria** air inlet; **presa (di corrente)** (Elettr) socket; (: al muro) point

pre'sagio [pre'zadʒo] sm omen

'presbite ag long-sighted

pres'crivere vt to prescribe

'prese ecc vb vedi **prendere**

presen'tare vt to present; (far conoscere): **~ qn (a)** to introduce sb (to); (Amm: inoltrare) to submit; **presentarsi** vpr (recarsi, farsi vedere) to present o.s., appear; (farsi conoscere) to introduce o.s.; (occasione) to arise; **presentarsi come candidato** (Pol) to stand as a candidate; **presentarsi bene/male** to have a good/poor appearance

pre'sente ag present; (questo) this ▷ sm present; **i presenti** those present; **aver ~ qc/qn** to remember sth/sb; **presenti** (persone) people present; **aver ~ qc/qn** to remember sth/sb; **tenere ~ qn/qc** to keep sth/sb in mind

presenti'mento sm premonition

pre'senza [pre'zentsa] sf presence; (aspetto esteriore) appearance; **presenza di spirito** presence of mind

pre'sepio, pre'sepe sm crib

preser'vare vt to protect; to save; **preservativo** sm sheath, condom

'presi ecc vb vedi **prendere**

'preside sm/f (Ins) head (teacher) (BRIT), principal (US); (di facoltà universitaria) dean; **preside di facoltà** (Univ) dean of faculty

presi'dente sm (Pol) president; (di assemblea, Comm) chairman; **presidente del consiglio** prime minister

presi'edere vt to preside over ▷ vi **~ a** to direct, be in charge of

pressap'poco av about, roughly

pres'sare vt to press

pressi'one sf pressure; **far ~ su qn** to put pressure on sb; **pressione sanguigna** blood pressure; **pressione atmosferica** atmospheric pressure

'presso av (vicino) nearby, close at hand ▷ prep (vicino a) near; (accanto a) beside, next to; (in casa di): **~ qn** at sb's home; (nelle lettere) care of, c/o; (alle dipendenze di): **lavora ~ di noi** he works for o with us ▷ smpl **nei pressi di** near, in the vicinity of

pres'tante ag good-looking

pres'tare vt **~ (qc a qn)** to lend (sb sth o sth to sb); **prestarsi** vpr (offrirsi): **prestarsi a fare** to offer to do; (essere adatto): **prestarsi a** to lend itself to, be suitable for; **mi può ~ dei soldi?** can you

lend me some money?; **~ aiuto** to lend a hand; **~ attenzione** to pay attention; **~ fede a qc/qn** to give credence to sth/sb; **~ orecchio** to listen; **prestazi'one** sf (Tecn, Sport) performance

prestigia'tore, -'trice [prestidʒa'tore] sm/f conjurer

pres'tigio [pres'tidʒo] sm (fama) prestige; (illusione): **gioco di ~** conjuring trick

'prestito sm lending no pl; loan; **dar in ~** to lend; **prendere in ~** to borrow

'presto av (tra poco) soon; (in fretta) quickly; (di buon'ora) early; **a ~** see you soon; **fare ~ a fare qc** to hurry up and do sth; (non costare fatica) to have no trouble doing sth; **si fa ~ a criticare** it's easy to criticize

pre'sumere vt to presume, assume

pre'sunsi ecc vb vedi **presumere**

presuntu'oso, -a ag presumptuous

presunzi'one [prezun'tsjone] sf presumption

'prete sm priest

preten'dente sm/f pretender ▷ sm (corteggiatore) suitor

pre'tendere vt (esigere) to demand, require; (sostenere): **~ che** to claim that; **pretende di aver sempre ragione** he thinks he's always right

> Attenzione! In inglese esiste il verbo to pretend, che però significa far finta.

pre'tesa sf (esigenza) claim, demand; (presunzione, sfarzo) pretentiousness; **senza pretese** unpretentious

pre'testo sm pretext, excuse

preva'lere vi to prevail

preve'dere vt (indovinare) to foresee; (presagire) to foretell; (considerare) to make provision for

preve'nire vt (anticipare) to forestall; to anticipate; (evitare) to avoid, prevent

preven'tivo, -a ag preventive ▷ sm (Comm) estimate

prevenzi'one [preven'tsjone] sf prevention; (preconcetto) prejudice

previ'dente ag showing foresight; prudent; **previ'denza** sf foresight; **istituto di previdenza** provident institution; **previdenza sociale** social security (BRIT), welfare (US)

pre'vidi ecc vb vedi **prevedere**

previsi'one sf forecast, prediction; **previsioni meteorologiche** weather forecast sg; **previsioni del tempo** weather forecast sg

pre'visto, -a pp di **prevedere** ▷ sm **più/meno del ~** more/less than expected

prezi'oso, -a ag precious; invaluable ▷ sm jewel; valuable

prez'zemolo [pret'tsemolo] sm parsley

'prezzo ['prɛttso] sm price; **prezzo d'acquisto/di vendita** buying/selling price

prigi'one [pri'dʒone] sf prison; **prigioni'ero, -a** ag captive ▷ sm/f prisoner

'prima sf (Teatro) first night; (Cinema) première; (Aut) first gear; vedi anche **primo** ▷ av before; (in anticipo) in advance, beforehand; (per l'addietro) at one time, formerly; (più presto) sooner, earlier; (in primo luogo) first ▷ cong **~ di fare/che parta** before doing/he leaves; **~ di** before; **~ o poi** sooner or later

pri'mario, -a ag primary; (principale) chief, leading, primary ▷ sm (Med) chief physician

prima'tista, -i, e sm/f (Sport) record holder

pri'mato sm supremacy; (Sport) record

prima'vera sf spring

primi'tivo, -a ag primitive; original

pri'mizie [pri'mittsje] sfpl early produce sg

'primo, -a ag first; (fig) initial; basic; prime ▷ sm/f first (one) ▷ sm (Cuc) first course; (in date): **il ~ luglio** the first of July; **le prime ore del mattino** the early hours of the morning; **ai primi di maggio** at the beginning of May; **viaggiare in prima** to travel first-class; **in ~ luogo** first of all, in the first place; **di prim'ordine** o **prima qualità** first-class, first-rate; **in un ~ tempo** at first; **prima donna** leading lady; (di opera lirica) prima donna

primordi'ale ag primordial

'primula sf primrose

princi'pale [printʃi'pale] ag main, principal ▷ sm manager, boss

principal'mente [printʃipal'mente] av mainly, principally

'principe ['printʃipe] sm prince; **principe ereditario** crown prince; **princi'pessa** sf princess

principi'ante [printʃi'pjante] sm/f beginner

prin'cipio [prin'tʃipjo] sm (inizio) beginning, start; (origine) origin, cause; (concetto, norma) principle; **al** o **in ~** at first; **per ~** on principle; **principi** smpl (concetti fondamentali) principles; **una questione di ~** a matter of principle

priorità sf priority

priori'tario, -a ag having priority, of utmost importance

pri'vare vt **~ qn di** to deprive sb of; **privarsi di** to go o do without

pri'vato, -a ag private ▷ sm/f private citizen; **in ~** in private

privilegi'are [privile'dʒare] vt to grant a privilege to

privilegi'ato, -a [privile'dʒato] ag (individuo, classe) privileged; (trattamento, Comm: credito) preferential; **azioni ~e** preference shares (BRIT), preferred stock (US)

privi'legio [privi'lɛdʒo] sm privilege

'privo, -a ag **~ di** without, lacking

pro prep for, on behalf of ▷ sm inv (utilità) advantage, benefit; **a che ~?** what's the use?; **il ~ e il contro** the pros and cons

pro'babile ag probable, likely; **probabilità** sf inv probability

probabil'mente av probably

pro'blema, -i sm problem

pro'boscide [pro'bɔʃʃide] sf (di elefante) trunk

pro'cedere [pro'tʃɛdere] vi to proceed; (comportarsi) to behave; (iniziare): **~ a** to start; **~ contro** (Dir) to start legal proceedings against; **proce'dura** sf (Dir) procedure

proces'sare [protʃes'sare] vt (Dir) to try

processi'one [protʃes'sjone] sf procession

pro'cesso [pro'tʃɛsso] sm trial; proceedings pl; (metodo) process

pro'cinto [pro'tʃinto] sm **in ~ di fare** about to do, on the point of doing

procla'mare vt to proclaim

procre'are vt to procreate

procu'rare vt **~ qc a qn** (fornire) to get o obtain sth for sb; (causare: noie ecc) to bring o give sb sth

pro'digio [pro'didʒo] sm marvel, wonder; (persona) prodigy

pro'dotto, -a pp di **produrre** ▷ sm product; **prodotti agricoli** farm produce sg

pro'duco ecc vb vedi **produrre**

pro'durre vt to produce

pro'dussi ecc vb vedi **produrre**

produzi'one sf production; (rendimento) output

Prof. abbr (= professore) Prof.

profa'nare vt to desecrate

profes'sare vt to profess; (medicina ecc) to practise

professio'nale ag professional

professi'one sf profession; **professio'nista, -i, -e** sm/f professional

profes'sore, -'essa sm/f (Ins) teacher; (: di università) lecturer; (: titolare di cattedra) professor

pro'filo sm profile; (breve descrizione) sketch, outline; **di ~** in profile

pro'fitto sm advantage, profit, benefit; (fig: progresso) progress; (Comm) profit

profondità sf inv depth

pro'fondo, -a ag deep; (rancore,

meditazione) profound ▷ *sm* depth(s *pl*), bottom; **quanto è profonda l'acqua?** how deep is the water?; **~ 8 metri** 8 metres deep

'**profugo, -a, -ghi, -ghe** *sm/f* refugee

profu'mare *vt* to perfume ▷ *vi* to be fragrant; **profumarsi** *vpr* to put on perfume o scent

profu'mato, -a *ag* (*fiore, aria*) fragrant; (*fazzoletto, saponetta*) (*Ins*) scented; (*pelle*) sweet-smelling; (*persona*) with perfume on

profume'ria *sf* perfumery; (*negozio*) perfume shop

pro'fumo *sm* (*prodotto*) perfume, scent; (*fragranza*) scent, fragrance

proget'tare [prodʒet'tare] *vt* to plan; (*edificio*) to plan, design; **pro'getto** *sm* plan; (*idea*) plan, project; **progetto di legge** bill

pro'gramma, -i *sm* programme; (*TV, Radio*) programmes *pl*; (*Ins*) syllabus, curriculum; (*Inform*) program; **program'mare** *vt* (*TV, Radio*) to put on; (*Inform*) to program; (*Econ*) to plan; **programma'tore, -'trice** *sm/f* (*Inform*) computer programmer

progre'dire *vi* to progress, make progress

pro'gresso *sm* progress *no pl*; **fare progressi** to make progress

proi'bire *vt* to forbid, prohibit

proiet'tare *vt* (*gen, Geom, Cinema*) to project; (: *presentare*) to show, screen; (*luce, ombra*) to throw, cast, project; **proi'ettile** *sm* projectile, bullet (*o* shell *ecc*); **proiet'tore** *sm* (*Cinema*) projector; (*Aut*) headlamp; (*Mil*) searchlight; **proiezi'one** *sf* (*Cinema*) projection; showing

prolife'rare *vi* (*fig*) to proliferate

pro'lunga, -ghe *sf* (*di cavo ecc*) extension

prolun'gare *vt* (*discorso, attesa*) to prolong; (*linea, termine*) to extend

prome'moria *sm inv* memorandum

pro'messa *sf* promise

pro'mettere *vt* to promise ▷ *vi* to be o look promising; **~ a qn di fare** to promise sb that one will do

promi'nente *ag* prominent

pro'misi *ecc vb vedi* **promettere**

promon'torio *sm* promontory, headland

promozi'one [promot'tsjone] *sf* promotion

promu'overe *vt* to promote

proni'pote *sm/f* (*di nonni*) great-grandchild, great-grandson/granddaughter; (*di zii*) great-nephew/niece

pro'nome *sm* (*Ling*) pronoun

pron'tezza [pron'tettsa] *sf* readiness; quickness, promptness

'**pronto, -a** *ag* ready; (*rapido*) fast, quick, prompt; **quando saranno pronte le mie foto?** when will my photos be ready?; **~!** (*Tel*) hello!; **~ all'ira** quick-tempered; **pronto soccorso** (*cure*) first aid; (*reparto*) A&E (*BRIT*), ER (*US*)

prontu'ario *sm* manual, handbook

pro'nuncia [pro'nuntʃa] *sf* pronunciation

pronunci'are [pronun'tʃare] *vt* (*parola, sentenza*) to pronounce; (*dire*) to utter; (*discorso*) to deliver; **come si pronuncia?** how do you pronounce it?

propa'ganda *sf* propaganda

pro'pendere *vi* **~ per** to favour, lean towards

propi'nare *vt* to administer

pro'porre *vt* (*suggerire*): **~ qc (a qn)** to suggest sth (to sb); (*candidato*) to put forward; (*legge, brindisi*) to propose; **~ di fare** to suggest o propose doing; **proporsi di fare** to propose o intend to do; **proporsi una meta** to set o.s. a goal

proporzio'nale [proportsjo'nale] *ag* proportional

proporzi'one [propor'tsjone] *sf* proportion; **in ~ a** in proportion to; **proporzioni** *sfpl* (*dimensioni*) proportions; **di vaste proporzioni** huge

pro'posito *sm* (*intenzione*) intention, aim; (*argomento*) subject, matter; **a ~ di** regarding, with regard to; **di ~** (*apposta*) deliberately, on purpose; **a ~** by the way; **capitare a ~** (*cosa, persona*) to turn up at the right time

proposizi'one [propozit'tsjone] *sf* (*Ling*) clause; (: *periodo*) sentence

pro'posta *sf* proposal; (*suggerimento*) suggestion; **proposta di legge** bill

proprietà *sf inv* (*ciò che si possiede*) property *gen no pl*, estate; (*caratteristica*) property; (*correttezza*) correctness; **proprietà privata** private property; **proprie'tario, -a** *sm/f* owner; (*di albergo ecc*) proprietor, owner; (*per l'inquilino*) landlord/lady

'**proprio, -a** *ag* (*possessivo*) own; (: *impersonale*) one's; (*esatto*) exact, correct, proper; (*senso, significato*) literal; (*Ling: nome*) proper; (*particolare*): **~ di** characteristic of, peculiar to ▷ *av* (*precisamente*) just, exactly; (*davvero*) really; (*affatto*): **non ... ~** not ... at all; **l'ha visto con i (suoi) propri occhi** he saw it with his own eyes

proro'gare *vt* to extend; (*differire*) to postpone, defer

'**prosa** *sf* prose

pro'sciogliere [proʃ'ʃɔʎʎere] *vt* to release; (*Dir*) to acquit

prosciu'gare [proʃʃu'gare] *vt* (*terreni*) to

drain, reclaim; **prosciugarsi** *vpr* to dry up
prosci'utto [proʃʃutto] *sm* ham;
prosciutto cotto/crudo cooked/cured
ham

prosegui'mento *sm* continuation; **buon
~!** all the best!; *(a chi viaggia)* enjoy the rest
of your journey!

prosegu'ire *vt* to carry on with, continue
▷ *vi* to carry on, go on

prospe'rare *vi* to thrive

prospet'tare *vt* *(esporre)* to point out,
show; **prospettarsi** *vpr* to look, appear

prospet'tiva *sf* *(Arte)* perspective; *(veduta)*
view; *(fig: previsione, possibilità)* prospect

pros'petto *sm* *(Disegno)* elevation; *(veduta)*
view, prospect; *(facciata)* façade, front;
(tabella) table; *(sommario)* summary;
prospetto informativo prospectus

prossimità *sf* nearness, proximity; **in ~ di**
near (to), close to

'**prossimo, -a** *ag* *(vicino)*: **~ a** near (to),
close to; *(che viene subito dopo)* next;
(parente) close ▷ *sm* neighbour, fellow man

prostitu'irsi *vpr* to prostitute o.s.

prosti'tuta *sf* prostitute

protago'nista, -i, -e *sm/f* protagonist

pro'teggere [pro'tɛddʒere] *vt* to protect

prote'ina *sf* protein

pro'tendere *vt* to stretch out

pro'testa *sf* protest

protes'tante *ag, sm/f* Protestant

protes'tare *vt, vi* to protest

pro'tetto, -a *pp di* **proteggere**

protezi'one [protet'tsjone] *sf* protection;
(patrocinio) patronage

pro'totipo *sm* prototype

pro'trarre *vt* *(prolungare)* to prolong;
protrarsi *vpr* to go on, continue

protube'ranza [protube'rantsa] *sf*
protuberance, bulge

'**prova** *sf* *(esperimento, cimento)* test,
trial; *(tentativo)* attempt, try; *(Mat,
testimonianza, documento ecc)* proof; *(Dir)*
evidence *no pl*, proof; *(Ins)* exam, test;
(Teatro) rehearsal; *(di abito)* fitting; **a ~ di**
(testimonianza di) as proof of; **a ~ di fuoco**
fireproof; **fino a ~ contraria** until it is
proved otherwise; **mettere alla ~** to put
to the test; **giro di ~** test o trial run; **prova
generale** *(Teatro)* dress rehearsal

pro'vare *vt* *(sperimentare)* to test; *(tentare)*
to try, attempt; *(assaggiare)* to try, taste;
(sperimentare in sé) to experience; *(sentire)*
to feel; *(cimentare)* to put to the test;
(dimostrare) to prove; *(abito)* to try on; **~ a
fare** to try o attempt to do

proveni'enza [prove'njɛntsa] *sf* origin,
source

prove'nire *vi* **~ da** to come from

pro'venti *smpl* revenue *sg*

pro'verbio *sm* proverb

pro'vetta *sf* test tube; **bambino in ~**
test-tube baby

pro'vider [pro'vaider] *sm inv* *(Inform)*
service provider

pro'vincia, -ce *o* **cie** [pro'vintʃa] *sf*
province

pro'vino *sm* *(Cinema)* screen test;
(campione) specimen

provo'cante *ag* *(attraente)* provocative

provo'care *vt* *(causare)* to cause, bring
about; *(eccitare: riso, pietà)* to arouse;
(irritare, sfidare) to provoke; **provocazi'one**
sf provocation

provve'dere *vi* *(disporre)*: **~ (a)** to provide
(for); *(prendere un provvedimento)* to take
steps, act; **provvedi'mento** *sm* measure;
(di previdenza) precaution

provvi'denza [provvi'dɛntsa] *sf* **la ~**
providence

provvigi'one [provvi'dʒone] *sf* *(Comm)*
commission

provvi'sorio, -a *ag* temporary

prov'viste *sfpl* supplies

'**prua** *sf* *(Naut)* bow(s) *(pl)*, prow

pru'dente *ag* cautious, prudent;
(assennato) sensible, wise; **pru'denza** *sf*
prudence, caution; wisdom

prudere *vi* to itch, be itchy

'**prugna** ['pruɲɲa] *sf* plum; **prugna secca**
prune

pru'rito *sm* itchiness *no pl*; itch

P.S. *abbr* (= *postscriptum*) P.S.; *(Polizia)*
= **Pubblica Sicurezza**

pseu'donimo *sm* pseudonym

psica'nalisi *sf* psychoanalysis

psicana'lista, -i, -e *sm/f* psychoanalyst

'**psiche** ['psike] *sf* *(Psic)* psyche

psichi'atra, -i, -e [psi'kjatra] *sm/f*
psychiatrist; **psichi'atrico, -a, -ci, -che** *ag*
psychiatric

psicolo'gia [psikolo'dʒia] *sf* psychology;
psico'logico, -a, -ci, -che *ag*
psychological; **psi'cologo, -a, -gi, -ghe**
sm/f psychologist

psico'patico, -a, -ci, -che *ag*
psychopathic ▷ *sm/f* psychopath

pubbli'care *vt* to publish

pubblicazi'one [pubblikat'tsjone] *sf*
publication

pubblicità [pubblitʃi'ta] *sf* *(diffusione)*
publicity; *(attività)* advertising; *(annunci nei
giornali)* advertisements *pl*

'**pubblico, -a, -ci, -che** *ag* public;
(statale: scuola ecc) state *cpd* ▷ *sm* public;
(spettatori) audience; **in ~** in public; **P~
Ministero** Public Prosecutor's Office; **la
Pubblica Sicurezza** the police; **pubblico**

funzionario civil servant

'**pube** sm (Anat) pubis

pubertà sf puberty

'**pudico, -a, -ci, -che** ag modest

pu'dore sm modesty

pue'rile ag childish

pugi'lato [pudʒi'lato] sm boxing

pugile ['pudʒile] sm boxer

pugna'lare [puɲɲa'lare] vt to stab

pu'gnale [puɲ'ɲale] sm dagger

'**pugno** ['puɲɲo] sm fist; (colpo) punch; (quantità) fistful

'**pulce** ['pultʃe] sf flea

pul'cino [pul'tʃino] sm chick

pu'lire vt to clean; (lucidare) to polish; **pu'lito, -a** ag (anche fig) clean; (ordinato) neat, tidy; **puli'tura** sf cleaning; **pulitura a secco** dry cleaning; **puli'zia** sf cleaning; cleanness; **fare le pulizie** to do the cleaning o the housework; **pulizia etnica** ethnic cleansing

'**pullman** sm inv coach

pull'over sm inv pullover, jumper

pullu'lare vi to swarm, teem

pul'mino sm minibus

'**pulpito** sm pulpit

pul'sante sm (push-)button

pul'sare vi to pulsate, beat

pul'viscolo sm fine dust; **pulviscolo atmosferico** specks pl of dust

'**puma** sm inv puma

pun'gente [pun'dʒɛnte] ag prickly; stinging; (anche fig) biting

'**pungere** ['pundʒere] vt to prick; (insetto, ortica) to sting; (: freddo) to bite

pungigli'one [pundʒiʎ'ʎone] sm sting

pu'nire vt to punish; **punizi'one** sf punishment; (Sport) penalty

'**punsi** ecc vb vedi **pungere**

'**punta** sf point; (parte terminale) tip, end; (di monte) peak; (di costa) promontory; (minima parte) touch, trace; **in ~ di piedi** on tip-toe; **ore di ~** peak hours; **uomo di ~** front-rank o leading man

pun'tare vt (piedi a terra, gomiti sul tavolo) to plant; (dirigere: pistola) to point; (scommettere) to bet ▷ vi (mirare): **~ a** to aim at; **~ su** (dirigersi) to head o make for; (fig: contare) to count o rely on

pun'tata sf (gita) short trip; (scommessa) bet; (parte di opera) instalment; **romanzo a puntate** serial

punteggia'tura [punteddʒa'tura] sf (Ling) punctuation

pun'teggio [pun'teddʒo] sm score

puntel'lare vt to support

pun'tello sm prop, support

pun'tina sf; **puntina da disegno** drawing pin

pun'tino sm dot; **fare qc a ~** to do sth properly

'**punto, -a** pp di **pungere** ▷ sm (segno, macchiolina) dot; (Ling) full stop; (di indirizzo e-mail) dot; (Mat, momento, di punteggio: fig: argomento) point; (posto) spot; (a scuola) mark; (nel cucire, nella maglia, Med) stitch ▷ av **non ... ~** not at all; **punto cardinale** point of the compass, cardinal point; **punto debole** weak point; **punto esclamativo** exclamation mark; **punto interrogativo** question mark; **punto nero** (comedone) blackhead; **punto di partenza** (anche fig) starting point; **punto di riferimento** landmark; (fig) point of reference; **punto (di) vendita** retail outlet; **punto e virgola** semicolon; **punto di vista** (fig) point of view

puntu'ale ag punctual

pun'tura sf (di ago) prick; (Med) puncture; (: iniezione) injection; (dolore) sharp pain; **puntura d'insetto** sting, bite

> Attenzione! In inglese esiste la parola *puncture*, che si usa per indicare la foratura di una gomma.

punzecchi'are [puntsek'kjare] vt to prick; (fig) to tease

può ecc, **-puo'i** vb vedi **potere**

pu'pazzo [pu'pattso] sm puppet

pu'pilla sf (Anat) pupil

purché [pur'ke] cong provided that, on condition that

'**pure** cong (tuttavia) and yet, nevertheless; (anche se) even if ▷ av (anche) too, also; **pur di** (al fine di) just to; **faccia ~!** go ahead!, please do!

purè sm (Cuc) purée; (: di patate) mashed potatoes

pu'rezza [pu'rettsa] sf purity

pur'gante sm (Med) purgative, purge

purga'torio sm purgatory

purifi'care vt to purify; (metallo) to refine

'**puro, -a** ag pure; (acqua) clear, limpid; (vino) undiluted; **puro'sangue** sm/f inv thoroughbred

pur'troppo av unfortunately

pus sm pus

'**pustola** sf pimple

puti'ferio sm rumpus, row

putre'fatto, -a pp di **putrefare**

put'tana (fam!) sf whore (!)

puz'zare [put'tsare] vi to stink

'**puzzo** ['puttso] sm stink, foul smell

'**puzzola** [puttsola] sf polecat

puzzo'lente [puttso'lɛnte] ag stinking

pvc [pivi'tʃi] sigla m (= polyvinyl chloride) PVC

q

q *abbr* (= *quintale*) q.

qua *av* here; **in ~** (*verso questa parte*) this way; **da un anno in ~** for a year now; **da ~ndo in ~?** since when?; **per di ~** (*passare*) this way; **al di ~ di** (*fiume, strada*) on this side of; **~ dentro/fuori** *ecc* in/out here *ecc*; *vedi anche* **questo**

qua'derno *sm* notebook; (*per scuola*) exercise book

qua'drante *sm* quadrant; (*di orologio*) face

qua'drare *vi* (*bilancio*) to balance, tally; (*descrizione*) to correspond ▷ *vt* (*Mat*) to square; **non mi quadra** I don't like it; **qua'drato, -a** *ag* square; (*fig: equilibrato*) level-headed, sensible; (*: peg*) square ▷ *sm* (*Mat*) square; (*Pugilato*) ring; **5 al quadrato** 5 squared

quadri'foglio [kwadri'fɔʎʎo] *sm* four-leaf clover

quadri'mestre *sm* (*periodo*) four-month period; (*Ins*) term

'quadro *sm* (*pittura*) painting, picture; (*quadrato*) square; (*tabella*) table, chart; (*Tecn*) board, panel; (*Teatro*) scene; (*fig: scena, spettacolo*) sight; (*: descrizione*) outline, description; **quadri** *smpl* (*Pol*) party organizers; (*Mil*) cadres; (*Comm*) managerial staff; (*Carte*) diamonds

'quadruplo, -a *ag, sm* quadruple

quaggiù [kwad'dʒu] *av* down here
'quaglia ['kwaʎʎa] *sf* quail

 PAROLA CHIAVE

'qualche ['kwalke] *det* **1** some, a few; (*in interrogative*) any; **ho comprato qualche libro** I've bought some *o* a few books; **qualche volta** sometimes; **hai qualche sigaretta?** have you any cigarettes?
2 (*uno*): **c'è qualche medico?** is there a doctor?; **in qualche modo** somehow
3 (*un certo, parecchio*) some; **un personaggio di qualche rilievo** a figure of some importance
4: **qualche cosa** = **qualcosa**

qual'cosa *pron* something; (*in espressioni interrogative*) anything; **qualcos'altro** something else; anything else; **~ di nuovo** something new; anything new; **~ da mangiare** something to eat; anything to eat; **c'è ~ che non va?** is there something *o* anything wrong?

qual'cuno *pron* (*persona*) someone, somebody; (*: in espressioni interrogative*) anyone, anybody; (*alcuni*) some; **~ è favorevole a noi** some are on our side; **qualcun altro** someone *o* somebody else; anyone *o* anybody else

 PAROLA CHIAVE

'quale (*spesso troncato in* **qual**) *det* **1** (*interrogativo*) what; (*: scegliendo tra due o più cose o persone*) which; **quale uomo/ denaro?** what man/money?, which man/ money?; **quali sono i tuoi programmi?** what are your plans?; **quale stanza preferisci?** which room do you prefer?
2 (*relativo: come*): **il risultato fu quale ci si aspettava** the result was as expected
3 (*esclamativo*) what; **quale disgrazia!** what bad luck!
▷ *pron* **1** (*interrogativo*) which; **quale dei due scegli?** which of the two do you want?
2 (*relativo*): **il (la) quale** (*persona: soggetto*) who; (*: oggetto, con preposizione*) whom; (*cosa*) which; (*possessivo*) whose; **suo padre, il quale è avvocato, ...** his father, who is a lawyer, ...; **il signore con il quale parlavo** the gentleman to whom I was speaking; **l'albergo al quale ci siamo fermati** the hotel where we stayed *o* which we stayed at; **la signora della quale ammiriamo la bellezza** the lady whose beauty we admire
3 (*relativo: in elenchi*) such as, like; **piante**

quali l'edera plants like o such as ivy; **quale sindaco di questa città** as mayor of this town

qua'lifica, -che *sf* qualification; (*titolo*) title

qualifi'cato, -a *ag* (*dotato di qualifica*) qualified; (*esperto, abile*) skilled; **non mi ritengo ~ per questo lavoro** I don't think I'm qualified for this job; **è un medico molto ~** he is a very distinguished doctor

qualificazi'one *sf* **gara di ~** (*Sport*) qualifying event

qualità *sf inv* quality; **in ~ di** in one's capacity as

qua'lora *cong* in case, if

qual'siasi *det inv* = **qualunque**

qua'lunque *det inv* any; (*quale che sia*) whatever; (*discriminativo*) whichever; (*posposto: mediocre*) poor, indifferent; ordinary; **mettiti un vestito ~** put on any old dress; **~ cosa** anything; **~ cosa accada** whatever happens; **a ~ costo** at any cost, whatever the cost; **l'uomo ~** the man in the street; **~ persona** anyone, anybody

'quando *cong, av* when; **~ sarò ricco** when I'm rich; **da ~** (*dacché*) since; (*interrogativo*): **da ~ sei qui?** how long have you been here?; **quand'anche** even if

quantità *sf inv* quantity; (*gran numero*): **una ~ di** a great deal of; a lot of; **in grande ~** in large quantities

 PAROLA CHIAVE

'quanto, -a *det* **1** (*interrogativo: quantità*) how much; (: *numero*) how many; **quanto pane/denaro?** how much bread/money?; **quanti libri/ragazzi?** how many books/boys?; **quanto tempo?** how long?; **quanti anni hai?** how old are you?

2 (*esclamativo*): **quante storie!** what a lot of nonsense!; **quanto tempo sprecato!** what a waste of time!

3 (*relativo: quantità*) as much … as; (: *numero*) as many … as; **ho quanto denaro mi occorre** I have as much money as I need; **prendi quanti libri vuoi** take as many books as you like

▷ *pron* **1** (*interrogativo: quantità*) how much; (: *numero*) how many; (: *tempo*) how long; **quanto mi dai?** how much will you give me?; **quanti me ne hai portati?** how many did you bring me?; **da quanto sei qui?** how long have you been here?; **quanti ne abbiamo oggi?** what's the date today?

2 (*relativo: quantità*) as much as; (: *numero*) as many as; **farò quanto posso** I'll do as much as I can; **possono venire quanti**

sono stati invitati all those who have been invited can come

▷ *av* **1** (*interrogativo: con ag, av*) how; (: *con vb*) how much; **quanto stanco ti sembrava?** how tired did he seem to you?; **quanto corre la tua moto?** how fast can your motorbike go?; **quanto costa?** how much does it cost?; **quant'è?** how much is it?

2 (*esclamativo: con ag, av*) how; (: *con vb*) how much; **quanto sono felice!** how happy I am!; **sapessi quanto abbiamo camminato!** if you knew how far we've walked!; **studierò quanto posso** I'll study as much as o all I can; **quanto prima** as soon as possible

3: **in quanto** (*in qualità di*) as; (*perché, per il fatto che*) as, since; **(in) quanto a** (*per ciò che riguarda*) as for, as regards

4: **per quanto** (*nonostante, anche se*) however; **per quanto si sforzi, non ce la farà** try as he may, he won't manage it; **per quanto sia brava, fa degli errori** however good she may be, she makes mistakes; **per quanto io sappia** as far as I know

qua'ranta *num* forty

quaran'tena *sf* quarantine

quaran'tesimo, -a *num* fortieth

quaran'tina *sf* **una ~ (di)** about forty

'quarta *sf* (*Aut*) fourth (gear); *vedi anche* **quarto**

quar'tetto *sm* quartet(te)

quarti'ere *sm* district, area; (*Mil*) quarters *pl*; **quartier generale** headquarters *pl*

'quarto, -a *ag* fourth ▷ *sm* fourth; (*quarta parte*) quarter; **le 6 e un ~** a quarter past six; **quarti di finale** quarter final; **quarto d'ora** quarter of an hour

'quarzo ['kwartso] *sm* quartz

'quasi *av* almost, nearly ▷ *cong* (*anche: ~ che*) as if; **(non) … ~ mai** hardly ever; **~ ~ me ne andrei** I've half a mind to leave

quas'sù *av* up here

quat'tordici [kwat'torditʃi] *num* fourteen

quat'trini *smpl* money *sg*, cash *sg*

'quattro *num* four; **in ~ e quattr'otto** in less than no time; **quattro'cento** *num* four hundred ▷ *sm* **il Quattrocento** the fifteenth century

 PAROLA CHIAVE

'quello, -a (*dav sm* **quel** + C, **quell'** + V, **quello** + *s impura, gn, pn, ps, x, z; pl* **quei** + C, **quegli** + V o *s impura, gn, pn, ps, x, z; dav sf* **quella** + C, **quell'** + V; *pl* **quelle**) *det* that; those *pl*; **quella casa** that house; **quegli**

uomini those men; **voglio quella camicia (lì o là)** I want that shirt
▷ *pron* **1** (*dimostrativo*) that (one), those (ones) *pl*; (*ciò*) that; **conosci quella?** do you know that woman?; **prendo quello bianco** I'll take the white one; **chi è quello?** who's that?; **prendi quello (lì o là)** take that one (there)
2 (*relativo*): **quello(a) che** (*persona*) the one (who); (*cosa*) the one (which), the one (that); **quelli(e) che** (*persone*) those who; (*cose*) those which; **è lui quello che non voleva venire** he's the one who didn't want to come; **ho fatto quello che potevo** I did what I could

'**quercia, -ce** ['kwɛrtʃa] *sf* oak (tree); (*legno*) oak
que'rela *sf* (*Dir*) (legal) action
que'sito *sm* question, query; problem
questio'nario *sm* questionnaire
questi'one *sf* problem, question; (*controversia*) issue; (*litigio*) quarrel; **in ~** in question; **è ~ di tempo** it's a matter o question of time

PAROLA CHIAVE

'**questo, -a** *det* **1** (*dimostrativo*) this; these *pl*; **questo libro (qui o qua)** this book; **io prendo questo cappotto, tu quello** I'll take this coat, you take that one; **quest'oggi** today; **questa sera** this evening
2 (*enfatico*): **non fatemi più prendere di queste paure** don't frighten me like that again
▷ *pron* (*dimostrativo*) this (one); these (ones) *pl*; (*ciò*) this; **prendo questo (qui o qua)** I'll take this one; **preferisci questi o quelli?** do you prefer these (ones) or those (ones)?; **questo intendevo io** this is what I meant; **vengono Paolo e Luca: questo da Roma, quello da Palermo** Paolo and Luca are coming: the former from Palermo, the latter from Rome

ques'tura *sf* police headquarters *pl*
qui *av* here; **da o di ~** from here; **di ~ in avanti** from now on; **di ~ a poco/una settimana** in a little while/a week's time; **~ dentro/sopra/vicino** in/up/near here; *vedi anche* **questo**
quie'tanza [kwje'tantsa] *sf* receipt
qui'ete *sf* quiet, quietness; calmness; stillness; peace
qui'eto, -a *ag* quiet; (*notte*) calm, still; (*mare*) calm
'**quindi** *av* then ▷ *cong* therefore, so

---

145 | quoziente

'**quindici** ['kwinditʃi] *num* fifteen; **~ giorni** a fortnight (BRIT), two weeks
quindi'cina [kwindi'tʃina] *sf* (*serie*): **una ~ (di)** about fifteen; **fra una ~ di giorni** in a fortnight
quinta *sf vedi* **quinto**
quin'tale *sm* quintal (100 kg)
'**quinto, -a** *num* fifth
quiz [kwidz] *sm inv* (*domanda*) question; (*anche*): **gioco a ~** quiz game
'**quota** *sf* (*parte*) quota, share; (*Aer*) height, altitude; (*Ippica*) odds *pl*; **prendere/ perdere ~** (*Aer*) to gain/lose height o altitude; **quota d'iscrizione** enrolment fee; (*a club*) membership fee
quotidi'ano, -a *ag* daily; (*banale*) everyday ▷ *sm* (*giornale*) daily (paper)
quozi'ente [kwot'tsjɛnte] *sm* (*Mat*) quotient; **quoziente d'intelligenza** intelligence quotient, IQ

R, r ['ɛrre] *sf o m (lettera)* R, r; **R come Roma**
≈ R for Robert (BRIT), R for Roger (US)

'rabbia *sf (ira)* anger, rage; *(accanimento, furia)* fury; *(Med: idrofobia)* rabies *sg*

rab'bino *sm* rabbi

rabbi'oso, -a *ag* angry, furious; *(facile all'ira)* quick-tempered; *(forze, acqua ecc)* furious, raging; *(Med)* rabid, mad

rabbo'nire *vt* to calm down

rabbrivi'dire *vi* to shudder, shiver

raccapez'zarsi [rakkapet'tsarsi] *vpr* **non ~** to be at a loss

raccapricci'ante [rakkaprit'ʃante] *ag* horrifying

raccatta'palle *sm inv (Sport)* ballboy

raccat'tare *vt* to pick up

rac'chetta [rak'ketta] *sf (per tennis)* racket; *(per ping-pong)* bat; **racchetta da neve** snowshoe; **racchetta da sci** ski stick

racchi'udere [rak'kjudere] *vt* to contain

rac'cogliere [rak'koʎʎere] *vt* to collect; *(raccattare)* to pick up; *(frutti, fiori)* to pick, pluck; *(Agr)* to harvest; *(approvazione, voti)* to win

rac'colta *sf* collecting *no pl*; collection; *(Agr)* harvesting *no pl*, gathering *no pl*; harvest, crop; *(adunata)* gathering; **raccolta differenziata** *(dei rifiuti)* separate collection of different kinds of household waste

rac'colto, -a *pp di* **raccogliere** ▷ *ag*
(persona: pensoso) thoughtful; *(luogo: appartato)* secluded, quiet ▷ *sm (Agr)* crop, harvest

raccoman'dabile *ag* (highly) commendable; **è un tipo poco ~** he is not to be trusted

raccoman'dare *vt* to recommend; *(affidare)* to entrust; *(esortare)*: **~ a qn di non fare** to tell o warn sb not to do; **raccoman'data** *sf (anche:* **lettera raccomandata)** recorded-delivery letter

raccon'tare *vt* **~ (a qn)** *(dire)* to tell (sb); *(narrare)* to relate (to sb), tell (sb) about; **rac'conto** *sm* telling *no pl*, relating *no pl*; *(fatto raccontato)* story, tale; **racconti per bambini** children's stories

rac'cordo *sm (Tecn: giunto)* connection, joint; *(Aut)*: **raccordo anulare** *(Aut)* ring road (BRIT), beltway (US); **raccordo autostradale** slip road (BRIT), entrance *(o exit)* ramp (US); **raccordo ferroviario** siding; **raccordo stradale** link road

racimo'lare [ratʃimo'lare] *vt (fig)* to scrape together, glean

'rada *sf (natural)* harbour

'radar *sm* radar

raddoppi'are *vt, vi* to double

raddriz'zare [raddrit'tsare] *vt* to straighten; *(fig: correggere)* to put straight, correct

'radere *vt (barba)* to shave off; *(mento)* to shave; *(fig: rasentare)* to graze; to skim; **radersi** *vpr* to shave (o.s.); **~ al suolo** to raze to the ground

radi'are *vt* to strike off

radia'tore *sm* radiator

radiazi'one [radjat'tsjone] *sf (Fisica)* radiation; *(cancellazione)* striking off

radi'cale *ag* radical ▷ *sm (Ling)* root

ra'dicchio [ra'dikkjo] *sm* chicory

ra'dice [ra'ditʃe] *sf* root

'radio *sf inv* radio ▷ *sm (Chim)* radium; **radioat'tivo, -a** *ag* radioactive; **radio'cronaca, -che** *sf* radio commentary; **radiogra'fia** *sf* radiography; *(foto)* X-ray photograph

radi'oso, -a *ag* radiant

radios'veglia [radjoz'veʎʎa] *sf* radio alarm

'rado, -a *ag (capelli)* sparse, thin; *(visite)* infrequent; **di ~** rarely

radu'nare *vt* to gather, assemble; **radunarsi** *vpr* to gather, assemble

ra'dura *sf* clearing

raf'fermo, -a *ag* stale

'raffica, -che *sf (Meteor)* gust (of wind); *(di colpi: scarica)* burst of gunfire

raffigu'rare *vt* to represent

raffi'nato, -a *ag* refined

raffor'zare [raffor'tsare] *vt* to reinforce
raffredda'mento *sm* cooling
raffred'dare *vt* to cool; (*fig*) to dampen, have a cooling effect on; **raffreddarsi** *vpr* to grow cool *o* cold; (*prendere un raffreddore*) to catch a cold; (*fig*) to cool (off)
raffred'dato, -a *ag* (*Med*): **essere ~** to have a cold
raffred'dore *sm* (*Med*) cold
raf'fronto *sm* comparison
'rafia *sf* (*fibra*) raffia
rafting ['rafting] *sm* white-water rafting
ra'gazza [ra'gattsa] *sf* girl; (*fam: fidanzato*) girlfriend; **nome da ~** maiden name; **ragazza madre** unmarried mother
ra'gazzo [ra'gattso] *sm* boy; (*fam: fidanzato*) boyfriend; **ragazzi** *smpl* (*figli*) kids; **ciao ragazzi!** (*gruppo*) hi guys!
raggi'ante [rad'dʒante] *ag* radiant, shining
'raggio ['raddʒo] *sm* (*di sole ecc*) ray; (*Mat, distanza*) radius; (*di ruota ecc*) spoke; **raggio d'azione** range; **raggi X** X-rays
raggi'rare [raddʒi'rare] *vt* to take in, trick
raggi'ungere [rad'dʒundʒere] *vt* to reach; (*persona: riprendere*) to catch up (with); (*bersaglio*) to hit; (*fig: meta*) to achieve
raggomito'larsi *vpr* to curl up
raggrane'llare *vt* to scrape together
raggrup'pare *vt* to group (together)
ragiona'mento [radʒona'mento] *sm* reasoning *no pl*; arguing *no pl*; argument
ragio'nare [radʒo'nare] *vi* to reason; **~ di** (*discorrere*) to talk about
ragi'one [ra'dʒone] *sf* reason; (*dimostrazione, prova*) argument, reason; (*diritto*) right; **aver ~** to be right; **aver ~ di qn** to get the better of sb; **dare ~ a qn** to agree with sb; to prove sb right; **perdere la ~** to become insane; (*fig*) to take leave of one's senses; **in ~ di** at the rate of; to the amount of; according to; **a o con ~** rightly, justly; **a ragion veduta** after due consideration; **ragione sociale** (*Comm*) corporate name
ragione'ria [radʒone'ria] *sf* accountancy; accounts department
ragio'nevole [radʒo'nevole] *ag* reasonable
ragioni'ere, -a [radʒo'njɛre] *sm/f* accountant
ragli'are [raʎ'ʎare] *vi* to bray
ragna'tela [raɲɲa'tela] *sf* cobweb, spider's web
'ragno ['raɲɲo] *sm* spider
ragù *sm inv* (*Cuc*) meat sauce; stew
RAI-TV [raiti'vu] *sigla f* = **Radio televisione italiana**
ralle'grare *vt* to cheer up; **rallegrarsi** *vpr*

to cheer up; (*provare allegrezza*) to rejoice; **rallegrarsi con qn** to congratulate sb
rallen'tare *vt* to slow down; (*fig*) to lessen, slacken ▷ *vi* to slow down
rallenta'tore *sm* (*Cinema*) slow-motion camera; **al ~** (*anche fig*) in slow motion
raman'zina [raman'dzina] *sf* lecture, telling-off
'rame *sm* (*Chim*) copper
rammari'carsi *vpr* **~ (di)** (*rincrescersi*) to be sorry (about), regret; (*lamentarsi*) to complain (about)
rammen'dare *vt* to mend; (*calza*) to darn
'ramo *sm* branch
ramo'scello [ramoʃ'ʃello] *sm* twig
'rampa *sf* flight (of stairs); **rampa di lancio** launching pad
rampi'cante *ag* (*Bot*) climbing
'rana *sf* frog
'rancido, -a ['rantʃido] *ag* rancid
ran'core *sm* rancour, resentment
ran'dagio, -a, -gi, -gie *o* **ge** [ran'dadʒo] *ag* (*gatto, cane*) stray
ran'dello *sm* club, cudgel
'rango, -ghi *sm* (*condizione sociale, Mil, riga*) rank
rannicchi'arsi [rannik'kjarsi] *vpr* to crouch, huddle
rannuvo'larsi *vpr* to cloud over, become overcast
'rapa *sf* (*Bot*) turnip
ra'pace [ra'patʃe] *ag* (*animale*) predatory; (*fig*) rapacious, grasping ▷ *sm* bird of prey
ra'pare *vt* (*capelli*) to crop, cut very short
rapida'mente *av* quickly, rapidly
rapidità *sf* speed
'rapido, -a *ag* fast; (*esame, occhiata*) quick, rapid ▷ *sm* (*Ferr*) express (train)
rapi'mento *sm* kidnapping; (*fig*) rapture
ra'pina *sf* robbery; **rapina in banca** bank robbery; **rapina a mano armata** armed robbery; **rapi'nare** *vt* to rob; **rapina'tore, -'trice** *sm/f* robber
ra'pire *vt* (*cose*) to steal; (*persone*) to kidnap; (*fig*) to enrapture, delight; **rapi'tore, -'trice** *sm/f* kidnapper
rap'porto *sm* (*resoconto*) report; (*legame*) relationship; (*Mat, Tecn*) ratio; **rapporti sessuali** sexual intercourse *sg*
rappre'saglia [rappre'saʎʎa] *sf* reprisal, retaliation
rappresen'tante *sm/f* representative
rappresen'tare *vt* to represent; (*Teatro*) to perform; **rappresentazi'one** *sf* representation; performing *no pl*; (*spettacolo*) performance
rara'mente *av* seldom, rarely
rare'fatto, -a *ag* rarefied
'raro, -a *ag* rare

ra'sare vt (barba ecc) to shave off; (siepi, erba) to trim, cut; **rasarsi** vpr to shave (o.s.)

raschi'are [ras'kjare] vt to scrape; (macchia, fango) to scrape off ▷ vi to clear one's throat

ra'sente prep ~ **(a)** close to, very near

'raso, -a pp di **radere** ▷ ag (barba) shaved; (capelli) cropped; (con misure di capacità) level; (pieno: bicchiere) full to the brim ▷ sm (tessuto) satin; **un cucchiaio** ~ a level spoonful; **raso terra** close to the ground

ra'soio sm razor; **rasoio elettrico** electric shaver o razor

ras'segna [ras'seɲɲa] sf (Mil) inspection, review; (esame) inspection, review; (resoconto) review, survey; (pubblicazione letteraria ecc) review; (mostra) exhibition, show; **passare in ~** (Mil, fig) to review

rassegnarsi vpr (accettare): ~ **(a qc/a fare)** to resign o.s. (to sth/to doing)

rassicu'rare vt to reassure

rasso'dare vt to harden, stiffen; **rassodarsi** vpr to harden, to strengthen

rassomigli'anza [rassomiʎ'ʎantsa] sf resemblance

rassomigli'are [rassomiʎ'ʎare] vi ~ **a** to resemble, look like

rastrel'lare vt to rake; (fig: perlustrare) to comb

ras'trello sm rake

'rata sf (quota) instalment; **pagare a rate** to pay by instalments o on hire purchase (BRIT)

ratifi'care vt (Dir) to ratify

'ratto sm (Dir) abduction; (Zool) rat

rattop'pare vt to patch

rattris'tare vt to sadden; **rattristarsi** vpr to become sad

'rauco, -a, -chi, -che ag hoarse

rava'nello sm radish

ravi'oli smpl ravioli sg

ravvi'vare vt to revive; (fig) to brighten up, enliven

razio'nale [rattsjo'nale] ag rational

razio'nare [rattsjo'nare] vt to ration

razi'one [rat'tsjone] sf ration; (porzione) portion, share

'razza ['rattsa] sf race; (Zool) breed; (discendenza, stirpe) stock, race; (sorta) sort, kind

razzi'ale [rat'tsjale] ag racial

raz'zismo [rat'tsizmo] sm racism, racialism

raz'zista, -i, -e [rat'tsista] ag, sm/f racist, racialist

'razzo ['raddzo] sm rocket

R.C. sigla m (= partito della Rifondazione Comunista) left-wing Italian political party

re sm inv king; (Mus) D; (: solfeggiando) re

rea'gire [rea'dʒire] vi to react

re'ale ag real; (di, da re) royal ▷ sm **il ~** reality

realiz'zare [realid'dzare] vt (progetto ecc) to realize, carry out; (sogno, desiderio) to realize, fulfil; (scopo) to achieve; (Comm: titoli ecc) to realize; (Calcio ecc) to score; **realizzarsi** vpr to be realized

real'mente av really, actually

realtà sf inv reality

re'ato sm offence

reat'tore sm (Fisica) reactor; (Aer: aereo) jet; (: motore) jet engine

reazio'nario, -a [reattsjo'narjo] ag (Pol) reactionary

reazi'one [reat'tsjone] sf reaction

'rebus sm inv rebus; (fig) puzzle; enigma

recapi'tare vt to deliver

re'capito sm (indirizzo) address; (consegna) delivery; **recapito a domicilio** home delivery (service); **recapito telefonico** phone number

re'cedere [re'tʃedere] vi to withdraw

recensi'one [retʃen'sjone] sf review

re'cente [re'tʃente] ag recent; **di ~** recently; **recente'mente** av recently

re'cidere [re'tʃidere] vt to cut off, chop off

recin'tare [retʃin'tare] vt to enclose, fence off

re'cinto [re'tʃinto] sm enclosure; (ciò che recinge) fence; surrounding wall

recipi'ente [retʃi'pjɛnte] sm container

re'ciproco, -a, -ci, -che [re'tʃiproko] ag reciprocal

'recita ['rɛtʃita] sf performance

reci'tare [retʃi'tare] vt (poesia, lezione) to recite; (dramma) to perform; (ruolo) to play o act (the part of)

recla'mare vi to complain ▷ vt (richiedere) to demand

re'clamo sm complaint

recli'nabile ag (sedile) reclining

reclusi'one sf (Dir) imprisonment

'recluta sf recruit

re'condito, -a ag secluded; (fig) secret, hidden

'record ag inv record cpd ▷ sm inv record; **in tempo ~, a tempo di ~** in record time; **detenere il ~ di** to hold the record for; **record mondiale** world record

recriminazi'one [rekriminat'tsjone] sf recrimination

recupe'rare vt (rientrare in possesso di) to recover, get back; (tempo perduto) to make up for; (Naut) to salvage; (: naufraghi) to rescue; (delinquente) to rehabilitate; ~ **lo svantaggio** (Sport) to close the gap

redargu'ire vt to rebuke

re'dassi *ecc vb vedi* **redigere**

reddi'tizio, -a [reddi'tittsjo] *ag* profitable

'reddito *sm* income; (*dello Stato*) revenue; (*di un capitale*) yield

re'digere [re'didʒere] *vt* to write; (*contratto*) to draw up

'redini *sfpl* reins

'reduce ['rɛdutʃe] *ag* ~ **da** returning from, back from ▷ *sm/f* survivor

refe'rendum *sm inv* referendum

refe'renze [refe'rɛntse] *sfpl* references

re'ferto *sm* medical report

rega'lare *vt* to give (as a present), make a present of

re'galo *sm* gift, present

re'gata *sf* regatta

'reggere ['rɛddʒere] *vt* (*tenere*) to hold; (*sostenere*) to support, bear, hold up; (*portare*) to carry, bear; (*resistere*) to withstand; (*dirigere: impresa*) to manage, run; (*governare*) to rule, govern; (*Ling*) to take, be followed by ▷ *vi* (*resistere*): ~ **a** to stand up to, hold out against; (*sopportare*): ~ **a** to stand; (*durare*) to last; (*fig: teoria ecc*) to hold water; **reggersi** *vpr* (*stare ritto*) to stand

'reggia, -ge ['rɛddʒa] *sf* royal palace

reggi'calze [reddʒi'kaltse] *sm inv* suspender belt

reggi'mento [reddʒi'mento] *sm* (*Mil*) regiment

reggi'seno [reddʒi'seno] *sm* bra

re'gia, -'gie [re'dʒia] *sf* (*TV, Cinema ecc*) direction

re'gime [re'dʒime] *sm* (*Pol*) regime; (*Dir: aureo, patrimoniale ecc*) system; (*Med*) diet; (*Tecn*) (engine) speed

re'gina [re'dʒina] *sf* queen

regio'nale [redʒo'nale] *ag* regional ▷ *sm* local train (*stopping frequently*)

regi'one [re'dʒone] *sf* region; (*territorio*) region, district, area

re'gista, -i, -e [re'dʒista] *sm/f* (*TV, Cinema ecc*) director

regis'trare [redʒis'trare] *vt* (*Amm*) to register; (*Comm*) to enter; (*notare*) to note, take note of; (*canzone, conversazione: strumento di misura*) to record; (*mettere a punto*) to adjust, regulate; (*bagagli*) to check in; **registra'tore** *sm* (*strumento*) recorder, register; (*magnetofono*) tape recorder; **registratore di cassa** cash register; **registratore a cassette** cassette recorder

re'gistro [re'dʒistro] *sm* (*libro, Mus, Tech*) register; ledger; logbook; (*Dir*) registry

re'gnare [reŋ'ɲare] *vi* to reign, rule

'regno ['reɲɲo] *sm* kingdom; (*periodo*) reign; (*fig*) realm; **il R~ Unito** the United Kingdom; **regno animale/vegetale** animal/vegetable kingdom

'regola *sf* rule; **a ~ d'arte** duly; perfectly; **in ~** in order

rego'labile *ag* adjustable

regola'mento *sm* (*complesso di norme*) regulations *pl*; (*di debito*) settlement; **regolamento di conti** (*fig*) settling of scores

rego'lare *ag* regular; (*in regola: domanda*) in order, lawful ▷ *vt* to regulate, control; (*apparecchio*) to adjust, regulate; (*questione, conto, debito*) to settle; **regolarsi** *vpr* (*moderarsi*): **regolarsi nel bere/nello spendere** to control one's drinking/ spending; (*comportarsi*) to behave, act

rela'tivo, -a *ag* relative

relazi'one [relat'tsjone] *sf* (*fra cose, persone*) relation(ship); (*resoconto*) report, account

rele'gare *vt* to banish; (*fig*) to relegate

religi'one [reli'dʒone] *sf* religion

re'liquia *sf* relic

re'litto *sm* wreck; (*fig*) down-and-out

re'mare *vi* to row

remini'scenze [reminiʃ'ʃɛntse] *sfpl* reminiscences

remis'sivo, -a *ag* submissive, compliant

'remo *sm* oar

re'moto, -a *ag* remote

'rendere *vt* (*ridare*) to return, give back; (*: saluto ecc*) to return; (*produrre*) to yield, bring in; (*esprimere, tradurre*) to render; ~ **qc possibile** to make sth possible; **rendersi** *vpr* **rendersi utile** to make o.s. useful; **rendersi conto di qc** to realize sth; ~ **qc possibile** to make sth possible; ~ **grazie a qn** give thanks to sb; ~ **omaggio a qn** to pay homage to sb; ~ **un servizio a qn** to do sb a service; ~ **una testimonianza** to give evidence; **non so se rendo l'idea** I don't know if I'm making myself clear

rendi'mento *sm* (*reddito*) yield; (*di manodopera, Tecn*) efficiency; (*capacità di produrre*) output; (*di studenti*) performance

'rendita *sf* (*di individuo*) private *o* unearned income; (*Comm*) revenue; **rendita annua** annuity

'rene *sm* kidney

'renna *sf* reindeer *inv*

re'parto *sm* department, section; (*Mil*) detachment

repel'lente *ag* repulsive

repen'taglio [repen'taʎʎo] *sm* **mettere a ~** to jeopardize, risk

repen'tino, -a *ag* sudden, unexpected

reper'torio *sm* (*Teatro*) repertory; (*elenco*) index, (alphabetical) list

'replica, -che *sf* repetition; reply, answer;

replicare | 150

(*obiezione*) objection; (*Teatro, Cinema*) repeat performance; (*copia*) replica

repli'care vt (*ripetere*) to repeat; (*rispondere*) to answer, reply

repressi'one sf repression

re'presso, -a pp di **reprimere**

re'primere vt to suppress, repress

re'pubblica, -che sf republic

reputazi'one [reputat'tsjone] sf reputation

requi'sire vt to requisition

requi'sito sm requirement

'resa sf (*l'arrendersi*) surrender; (*restituzione, rendimento*) return; **resa dei conti** rendering of accounts; (*fig*) day of reckoning

'resi ecc vb vedi **rendere**

resi'dente ag resident; **residenzi'ale** ag residential

re'siduo, -a ag residual, remaining ▷ sm remainder; (*Chim*) residue

'resina sf resin

resis'tente ag (*che resiste*): **~ a** resistant to; (*forte*) strong; (*duraturo*) long-lasting, durable; **~ al caldo** heat-resistant; **resis'tenza** sf resistance; (*di persona: fisica*) stamina, endurance; (*: mentale*) endurance, resistance

● **RESISTENZA**

● The **Resistenza** in Italy fought against
● the Nazis and the Fascists during the
● Second World War. Members of the
● **Resistenza** spanned a wide political
● spectrum and played a vital role in the
● Liberation and in the formation of the
● new democratic government at the end
● of the war.

re'sistere vi to resist; **~ a** (*assalto, tentazioni*) to resist; (*dolore: pianta*) to withstand; (*non patir danno*) to be resistant to

reso'conto sm report, account

res'pingere [res'pindʒere] vt to drive back, repel; (*rifiutare*) to reject; (*Ins: bocciare*) to fail

respi'rare vi to breathe; (*fig*) to get one's breath; to breathe again ▷ vt to breathe (in), inhale; **respirazi'one** sf breathing; **respirazione artificiale** artificial respiration; **res'piro** sm breathing no pl; (*singolo atto*) breath; (*fig*) respite, rest; **mandare un respiro di sollievo** to give a sigh of relief

respon'sabile ag responsible ▷ sm/f person responsible; (*capo*) person in charge; **~ di** responsible for; (*Dir*) liable for; **responsabilità** sf inv responsibility; (*legale*) liability

res'ponso sm answer

'ressa sf crowd, throng

'ressi ecc vb vedi **reggere**

res'tare vi (*rimanere*) to remain, stay; (*avanzare*) to be left, remain; **~ orfano/cieco** to become o be left an orphan/ become blind; **~ d'accordo** to agree; **non resta più niente** there's nothing left; **restano pochi giorni** there are only a few days left

restau'rare vt to restore

res'tio, -a, -'tii, -'tie ag **~ a** reluctant to

restitu'ire vt to return, give back; (*energie, forze*) to restore

'resto sm remainder, rest; (*denaro*) change; (*Mat*) remainder; **resti** smpl (*di cibo*) leftovers; (*di città*) remains; **del ~** moreover, besides; **tenga pure il ~** keep the change; **resti mortali** (mortal) remains

res'tringere [res'trindʒere] vt to reduce; (*vestito*) to take in; (*stoffa*) to shrink; (*fig*) to restrict, limit; **restringersi** vpr (*strada*) to narrow; (*stoffa*) to shrink

'rete sf net; (*fig*) trap, snare; (*di recinzione*) wire netting; (*Aut, Ferr, di spionaggio ecc*) network; **segnare una ~** (*Calcio*) to score a goal; **la R~** the Web; **rete ferroviaria** railway network; **rete del letto** (sprung) bed base; **rete stradale** road network; **rete (televisiva)** (*sistema*) network; (*canale*) channel

reti'cente [reti'tʃente] ag reticent

retico'lato sm grid; (*rete*) wire netting; (*di filo spinato*) barbed wire (fence)

'retina sf (*Anat*) retina

re'torico, -a, -ci, -che ag rhetorical

retribu'ire vt to pay

'retro sm inv back ▷ av (*dietro*): **vedi ~** see over(leaf)

retro'cedere [retro'tʃɛdere] vi to withdraw ▷ vt (*Calcio*) to relegate; (*Mil*) to degrade

re'trogrado, -a ag (*fig*) reactionary, backward-looking

retro'marcia [retro'martʃa] sf (*Aut*) reverse; (*: dispositivo*) reverse gear

retro'scena [retroʃ'ʃɛna] sm inv (*Teatro*) backstage; **i ~** (*fig*) the behind-the-scenes activities

retrovi'sore sm (*Aut*) (rear-view) mirror

'retta sf (*Mat*) straight line; (*di convitto*) charge for bed and board; (*fig: ascolto*): **dar ~ a** to listen to, pay attention to

rettango'lare ag rectangular

ret'tangolo, -a ag right-angled ▷ sm rectangle

ret'tifica, -che sf rectification, correction

'rettile sm reptile

retti'lineo, -a ag rectilinear

'retto, -a pp di **reggere** ▷ ag straight; (Mat): **angolo ~** right angle; (onesto) honest, upright; (giusto, esatto) correct, proper, right

ret'tore sm (Rel) rector; (di università) ≈ chancellor

reuma'tismo sm rheumatism

revisi'one sf auditing no pl; audit; servicing no pl; overhaul; review; revision; **revisione di bozze** proofreading

revi'sore sm; **revisore di bozze** proofreader; **revisore di conti** auditor

revival [ri'vaivəl] sm inv revival

'revoca sf revocation

revo'care vt to revoke

re'volver sm inv revolver

ri'abbia ecc vb vedi **riavere**

riabili'tare vt to rehabilitate

rianimazi'one [rianimat'tsjone] sf (Med) resuscitation; **centro di ~** intensive care unit

ria'prire vt to reopen, open again; **riaprirsi** vpr to reopen, open again

ri'armo sm (Mil) rearmament

rias'sumere vt (riprendere) to resume; (impiegare di nuovo) to re-employ; (sintetizzare) to summarize; **rias'sunto, -a** pp di **riassumere** ▷ sm summary

riattac'care vt (attaccare di nuovo): **~ (a)** (manifesto, francobollo) to stick back (on); (bottone) to sew back (on); (quadro, chiavi) to hang back up (on); **~ (il telefono o il ricevitore)** to hang up (the receiver)

ria'vere vt to have again; (avere indietro) to get back; (riacquistare) to recover; **riaversi** vpr to recover

riba'dire vt (fig) to confirm

ri'balta sf flap; (Teatro: proscenio) front of the stage; (fig) limelight; **luci della ~** footlights pl

ribal'tabile ag (sedile) tip-up

ribal'tare vt, vi (anche: **ribaltarsi**) to turn over, tip over

ribas'sare vt to lower, bring down ▷ vi to come down, fall

ri'battere vt to return, hit back; (confutare) to refute; **~ che** to retort that

ribel'larsi vpr **~ (a)** to rebel (against); **ri'belle** ag (soldati) rebel; (ragazzo) rebellious ▷ sm/f rebel

'ribes sm inv currant; **ribes nero** blackcurrant; **ribes rosso** redcurrant

ri'brezzo [ri'breddzo] sm disgust, loathing; **far ~ a** to disgust

ribut'tante ag disgusting, revolting

rica'dere vi to fall again; (scendere a terra: fig: nel peccato ecc) to fall back; (vestiti, capelli ecc) to hang (down); (riversarsi: fatiche, colpe): **~ su** to fall on; **rica'duta** sf (Med) relapse

rica'mare vt to embroider

ricambi'are vt to change again; (contraccambiare) to repay, return; **ri'cambio** sm exchange, return; (Fisiol) metabolism

ri'camo sm embroidery

ricapito'lare vt to recapitulate, sum up

ricari'care vt (arma, macchina fotografica) to reload; (pipa) to refill; (orologio) to rewind; (batteria) to recharge

ricat'tare vt to blackmail; **ri'catto** sm blackmail

rica'vare vt (estrarre) to draw out, extract; (ottenere) to obtain, gain

ric'chezza [rik'kettsa] sf wealth; (fig) richness

'riccio, -a ['rittʃo] ag curly ▷ sm (Zool) hedgehog; **riccio di mare** sea urchin; **'ricciolo** sm curl

'ricco, -a, -chi, -che ag rich; (persona, paese) rich, wealthy ▷ sm/f rich man/woman; **i ricchi** the rich; **~ di** full of; rich in

ri'cerca, -che [ri'tʃerka] sf search; (indagine) investigation, inquiry; (studio): **la ~** research; **una ~** piece of research; **ricerca di mercato** market research

ricer'care [ritʃer'kare] vt (motivi, cause) to look for, try to determine; (successo, piacere) to pursue; (onore, gloria) to seek; **ricer'cato, -a** ag (apprezzato) much sought-after; (affettato) studied, affected ▷ sm/f (Polizia) wanted man/woman

ricerca'tore, -'trice [ritʃerka'tore] sm/f (Ins) researcher

ri'cetta [ri'tʃetta] sf (Med) prescription; (Cuc) recipe; **mi può fare una ~ medica?** could you write me a prescription?

ricettazi'one [ritʃettat'tsjone] sf (Dir) receiving (stolen goods)

ri'cevere [ri'tʃevere] vt to receive; (stipendio, lettera) to get, receive; (accogliere: ospite) to welcome; (vedere: cliente, rappresentante) to see; **ricevi'mento** sm receiving no pl; (festa) reception; **ricevi'tore** sm (Tecn) receiver; **rice'vuta** sf receipt; **posso avere una ricevuta, per favore?** can I have a receipt, please?; **ricevuta fiscale** receipt for tax purposes; **ricevuta di ritorno** (Posta) advice of receipt

richia'mare [rikja'mare] vt (chiamare indietro, ritelefonare) to call back; (ambasciatore, truppe) to recall; (rimproverare) to reprimand; (attirare) to attract, draw; **può ~ più tardi?** can you call back later?; **richiamarsi a** (*riferirsi a*) to refer to

richi'edere [ri'kjɛdere] *vt* to ask again for; (*chiedere indietro*): **~ qc** to ask for sth back; (*chiedere: per sapere*) to ask; (: *per avere*) to ask for; (*Amm: documenti*) to apply for; (*esigere*) to need, require; **richi'esta** *sf* (*domanda*) request; (*Amm*) application, request; (*esigenza*) demand, request; **a richiesta** on request

rici'clare *vt* to recycle

'ricino ['ritʃino] *sm* **olio di ~** castor oil

ricognizi'one [rikoɲɲit'tsjone] *sf* (*Mil*) reconnaissance; (*Dir*) recognition, acknowledgement

ricominci'are [rikomin'tʃare] *vt, vi* to start again, begin again

ricom'pensa *sf* reward

ricompen'sare *vt* to reward

riconciliarsi *vpr* to be reconciled

ricono'scente [rikonoʃ'ʃente] *ag* grateful

rico'noscere [riko'noʃʃere] *vt* to recognize; (*Dir: figlio, debito*) to acknowledge; (*ammettere: errore*) to admit, acknowledge

rico'perto, -a *pp di* **ricoprire**

ricopi'are *vt* to copy

rico'prire *vt* (*coprire*) to cover; (*occupare: carica*) to hold

ricor'dare *vt* to remember, recall; (*richiamare alla memoria*): **~ qc a qn** to remind sb of sth; **ricordarsi** *vpr* **ricordarsi (di)** to remember; **ricordarsi di qc/di aver fatto** to remember sth/having done

ri'cordo *sm* memory; (*regalo*) keepsake, souvenir; (*di viaggio*) souvenir

ricor'rente *ag* recurrent, recurring; **ricor'renza** *sf* recurrence; (*festività*) anniversary

ri'correre *vi* (*ripetersi*) to recur; **~ a** (*rivolgersi*) to turn to; (: *Dir*) to appeal to; (*servirsi di*) to have recourse to

ricostitu'ente *ag* (*Med*): **cura ~** tonic

ricostru'ire *vt* (*casa*) to rebuild; (*fatti*) to reconstruct

ri'cotta *sf* soft white unsalted cheese made from sheep's milk

ricove'rare *vt* to give shelter to; **~ qn in ospedale** to admit sb to hospital

ri'covero *sm* shelter, refuge; (*Mil*) shelter; (*Med*) admission (to hospital)

ricreazi'one [rikreat'tsjone] *sf* recreation, entertainment; (*Ins*) break

ri'credersi *vpr* to change one's mind

ridacchi'are [ridak'kjare] *vi* to snigger

ri'dare *vt* to return, give back

'ridere *vi* to laugh; (*deridere, beffare*): **~ di** to laugh at, make fun of

ri'dicolo, -a *ag* ridiculous, absurd

ridimensio'nare *vt* to reorganize; (*fig*) to see in the right perspective

ri'dire *vt* to repeat; (*criticare*) to find fault with; to object to; **trova sempre qualcosa da ~** he always manages to find fault

ridon'dante *ag* redundant

ri'dotto, -a *pp di* **ridurre** ▷ *ag* (*biglietto*) reduced; (*formato*) small

ri'duco *ecc vb vedi* **ridurre**

ri'durre *vt* (*anche Chim, Mat*) to reduce; (*prezzo, spese*) to cut, reduce; (*accorciare: opera letteraria*) to abridge; (: *Radio, TV*) to adapt; **ridursi** *vpr* (*diminuirsi*) to be reduced, shrink; **ridursi a** to be reduced to; **ridursi pelle e ossa** to be reduced to skin and bone; **ri'dussi** *ecc vb vedi* **ridurre**; **ridut'tore** *sm* (*Elec*) adaptor; **riduzi'one** *sf* reduction; abridgement; adaptation; **ci sono riduzioni per i bambini/gli studenti?** is there a reduction for children/students?

ri'ebbi *ecc vb vedi* **riavere**

riem'pire *vt* to fill (up); (*modulo*) to fill in *o* out; **riempirsi** *vpr* to fill (up); **~ qc di** to fill sth (up) with

rien'tranza [rien'trantsa] *sf* recess; indentation

rien'trare *vi* (*entrare di nuovo*) to go (*o* come) back in; (*tornare*) to return; (*fare una rientranza*) to go in, curve inwards; to be indented; (*riguardare*): **~ in** to be included among, form part of

riepilo'gare *vt* to summarize ▷ *vi* to recapitulate

ri'esco *ecc vb vedi* **riuscire**

ri'fare *vt* to do again; (*ricostruire*) to make again; (*nodo*) to tie again, do up again; (*imitare*) to imitate, copy; **rifarsi** *vpr* (*risarcirsi*): **rifarsi di** to make up for; (*vendicarsi*): **rifarsi di qc su qn** to get one's own back on sb for sth; (*riferirsi*): **rifarsi a** to go back to; to follow; **~ il letto** to make the bed; **rifarsi una vita** to make a new life for o.s.

riferi'mento *sm* reference; **in o con ~ a** with reference to

rife'rire *vt* (*riportare*) to report ▷ *vi* to do a report; **riferirsi** *vpr* **riferirsi a** to refer to

rifi'nire *vt* to finish off, put the finishing touches to

rifiu'tare *vt* to refuse; **~ di fare** to refuse to do; **rifi'uto** *sm* refusal; **rifiuti** *smpl* (*spazzatura*) rubbish *sg*, refuse *sg*

riflessi'one *sf* (*Fisica, meditazione*) reflection; (*il pensare*) thought, reflection; (*osservazione*) remark

rifles'sivo, -a *ag* (*persona*) thoughtful, reflective; (*Ling*) reflexive

ri'flesso, -a pp di **riflettere** ▷ sm (di luce, allo specchio) reflection; (Fisiol) reflex; **di** o **per ~** indirectly

riflessologia [riflessolo'dʒia] sf reflexology

ri'flettere vt to reflect ▷ vi to think; **riflettersi** vpr to be reflected; **~ su** to think over

riflet'tore sm reflector; (proiettore) floodlight; searchlight

ri'flusso sm flowing back; (della marea) ebb; **un'epoca di ~** an era of nostalgia

ri'forma sf reform; **la R~** (Rel) the Reformation

riforma'torio sm (Dir) community home (BRIT), reformatory (US)

riforni'mento sm supplying, providing; restocking; **rifornimenti** smpl (provviste) supplies, provisions

rifor'nire vt (provvedere): **~ di** to supply o provide with; (fornire di nuovo: casa ecc) to restock; **rifornirsi** vpr **rifornirsi di qc** to stock up on sth

rifugi'arsi [rifu'dʒarsi] vpr to take refuge; **rifugi'ato, -a** sm/f refugee

ri'fugio [ri'fudʒo] sm refuge, shelter; (in montagna) shelter; **rifugio antiaereo** air-raid shelter

'riga, -ghe sf line; (striscia) stripe; (di persone, cose) line, row; (regolo) ruler; (scriminatura) parting; **mettersi in ~** to line up; **a righe** (foglio) lined; (vestito) striped

ri'gare vt (foglio) to rule ▷ vi **~ diritto** (fig) to toe the line

rigatti'ere sm junk dealer

righerò ecc [rige'rɔ] vb vedi **rigare**

'rigido, -a ['ridʒido] ag rigid, stiff; (membra ecc: indurite) stiff; (Meteor) harsh, severe; (fig) strict

rigogli'oso, -a [rigoʎ'ʎoso] ag (pianta) luxuriant; (fig: commercio, sviluppo) thriving

ri'gore sm (Meteor) harshness, rigours pl; (fig) severity, strictness; (anche: **calcio di ~**) penalty; **di ~** compulsory; **a rigor di termini** strictly speaking

riguar'dare vt to look at again; (considerare) to regard, consider; (concernere) to regard, concern; **riguardarsi** vpr (aver cura di sé) to look after o.s.

rigu'ardo sm (attenzione) care; (considerazione) regard, respect; **~ a** concerning, with regard to; **non aver riguardi nell'agire/nel parlare** to act/speak freely

rilasci'are [rilaʃ'ʃare] vt (rimettere in libertà) to release; (Amm: documenti) to issue

rilassarsi vpr to relax; (fig: disciplina) to become slack

rile'gare vt (libro) to bind

ri'leggere [ri'lɛddʒere] vt to reread, read again; (rivedere) to read over

ri'lento: a ~ av slowly

rile'vante ag considerable; important

rile'vare vt (ricavare) to find; (notare) to notice; (mettere in evidenza) to point out; (venire a conoscere: notizia) to learn; (raccogliere: dati) to gather, collect; (Topografia) to survey; (Mil) to relieve; (Comm) to take over

rili'evo sm (Arte, Geo) relief; (fig: rilevanza) importance; (Topografia) survey; **dar ~ a** o **mettere in ~ qc** (fig) to bring sth out, highlight sth

rilut'tante ag reluctant

'rima sf rhyme; (verso) verse

riman'dare vt to send again; (restituire, rinviare) to send back, return; (differire): **~ qc (a)** to postpone sth o put sth off (till); (fare riferimento): **~ qn a** to refer sb to; **essere rimandato** (Ins) to have to repeat one's exams

ri'mando sm (rinvio) return; (dilazione) postponement; (riferimento) cross-reference

rima'nente ag remaining ▷ sm rest, remainder; **i rimanenti** (persone) the rest of them, the others

rima'nere vi (restare) to remain, stay; (avanzare) to be left, remain; (restare stupito) to be amazed; (restare, mancare): **rimangono poche settimane a Pasqua** there are only a few weeks left till Easter; **rimane da vedere se** it remains to be seen whether; (diventare): **~ vedovo** to be left a widower; (trovarsi): **~ sorpreso** to be surprised

rimangi'are [riman'dʒare] vt to eat again; **~rsi la parola/una promessa** (fig) to go back on one's word/one's promise

ri'mango ecc vb vedi **rimanere**

rimargi'narsi vpr to heal

rimbal'zare [rimbal'tsare] vi to bounce back, rebound; (proiettile) to ricochet

rimbam'bito, -a ag senile, in one's dotage

rimboc'care vt (coperta) to tuck in; (maniche, pantaloni) to turn o roll up

rimbom'bare vi to resound

rimbor'sare vt to pay back, repay

rimedi'are vi **~ a** to remedy ▷ vt (fam: procurarsi) to get o scrape together

ri'medio sm (medicina) medicine; (cura, fig) remedy, cure

ri'mettere vt (mettere di nuovo) to put back; (indossare di nuovo): **~ qc** to put sth back on again; (affidare) to entrust; (: decisione) to refer; (condonare) to remit; (Comm: merci) to deliver; (: denaro) to remit; (*vomitare*) to bring up; (*perdere: anche:* **rimetterci**) to lose; **rimettersi al bello** (*tempo*) to clear up; **rimettersi in salute** to get better, recover one's health

ri'misi *ecc vb vedi* **rimettere**

'rimmel® *sm inv* mascara

rimoder'nare *vt* to modernize

rimorchi'are [rimor'kjare] *vt* to tow; (*fig: ragazza*) to pick up

ri'morchio [ri'morkjo] *sm* tow; (*veicolo*) trailer

ri'morso *sm* remorse

rimozi'one [rimot'tsjone] *sf* removal; (*da un impiego*) dismissal; (*Psic*) repression

rimpatri'are *vi* to return home ▷ *vt* to repatriate

rimpi'angere [rim'pjandʒere] *vt* to regret; (*persona*) to miss; **rimpi'anto, -a** *pp di* **rimpiangere** ▷ *sm* regret

rimpiaz'zare [rimpjat'tsare] *vt* to replace

rimpiccio'lire [rimpittʃo'lire] *vt* to make smaller ▷ *vi* (*anche:* **rimpicciolirsi**) to become smaller

rimpinzarsi [rimpin'tsarsi] *vpr* **~ (di qc)** to stuff o.s. (with sth)

rimprove'rare *vt* to rebuke, reprimand

rimu'overe *vt* to remove; (*destituire*) to dismiss

Rinasci'mento [rinaʃʃi'mento] *sm* **il ~** the Renaissance

ri'nascita [ri'naʃʃita] *sf* rebirth, revival

rinca'rare *vt* to increase the price of ▷ *vi* to go up, become more expensive

rinca'sare *vi* to go home

rinchi'udere [rin'kjudere] *vt* to shut (*o lock*) up; **rinchiudersi** *vpr* **rinchiudersi in** to shut o.s. up in; **rinchiudersi in se stesso** to withdraw into o.s.

rin'correre *vt* to chase, run after; **rin'corsa** *sf* short run

rin'crescere [rin'kreʃʃere] *vb impers* **mi rincresce che/di non poter fare** I'm sorry that/I can't do, I regret that/being unable to do

rinfacci'are [rinfat'tʃare] *vt* (*fig*): **~ qc a qn** to throw sth in sb's face

rinfor'zare [rinfor'tsare] *vt* to reinforce, strengthen ▷ *vi* (*anche:* **rinforzarsi**) to grow stronger

rinfres'care *vt* (*atmosfera, temperatura*) to cool (down); (*abito, pareti*) to freshen up ▷ *vi* (*tempo*) to grow cooler; **rinfrescarsi** *vpr* (*ristorarsi*) to refresh o.s.; (*lavarsi*) to freshen up; **rin'fresco, -schi** *sm* (*festa*) party; **rinfreschi** *smpl* refreshments

rin'fusa *sf* **alla ~** in confusion, higgledy-piggledy

ringhi'are [rin'gjare] *vi* to growl, snarl

ringhi'era [rin'gjɛra] *sf* railing; (*delle scale*)

banister(s) (*pl*)

ringiova'nire [rindʒova'nire] *vt* (*vestito, acconciatura ecc*): **~ qn** to make sb look younger; (: *vacanze ecc*) to rejuvenate ▷ *vi* (*anche:* **ringiovanirsi**) to become (*o look*) younger

ringrazia'mento [ringrattsja'mento] *sm* thanks *pl*

ringrazi'are [ringrat'tsjare] *vt* to thank; **~ qn di qc** to thank sb for sth

rinne'gare *vt* (*fede*) to renounce; (*figlio*) to disown, repudiate

rinnova'mento *sm* renewal; (*economico*) revival

rinno'vare *vt* to renew; (*ripetere*) to repeat, renew

rinoce'ronte [rinotʃe'ronte] *sm* rhinoceros

rino'mato, -a *ag* renowned, celebrated

rintracci'are [rintrat'tʃare] *vt* to track down

rintro'nare *vi* to boom, roar ▷ *vt* (*assordare*) to deafen; (*stordire*) to stun

rinunci'are [rinun'tʃare] *vi* **~ a** to give up, renounce; **~ a fare qc** to give up doing sth

rinvi'are *vt* (*rimandare indietro*) to send back, return; (*differire*): **~ qc (a)** to postpone sth o put sth off (till); to adjourn sth (till); (*fare un rimando*): **~ qn a** to refer sb to

rin'vio, -'vii *sm* (*rimando*) return; (*differimento*) postponement; (: *di seduta*) adjournment; (*in un testo*) cross-reference; **rinvio a giudizio** (*Dir*) indictment

riò *ecc vb vedi* **riavere**

ri'one *sm* district, quarter

riordi'nare *vt* (*rimettere in ordine*) to tidy; (*riorganizzare*) to reorganize

riorganiz'zare [riorganid'dzare] *vt* to reorganize

ripa'gare *vt* to repay

ripa'rare *vt* (*proteggere*) to protect, defend; (*correggere: male, torto*) to make up for; (: *errore*) to put right; (*aggiustare*) to repair ▷ *vi* (*mettere rimedio*): **~ a** to make up for; **ripararsi** *vpr* (*rifugiarsi*) to take refuge o shelter; **dove lo posso far ~?** where can I get this repaired?; **riparazi'one** *sf* (*di un torto*) reparation; (*di guasto, scarpe*) repairing *no pl*; repair; (*risarcimento*) compensation

ri'paro *sm* (*protezione*) shelter, protection; (*rimedio*) remedy

ripar'tire *vt* (*dividere*) to divide up; (*distribuire*) to share out ▷ *vi* to set off again; to leave again

ripas'sare *vi* to come (*o go*) back ▷ *vt* (*scritto, lezione*) to go over (again)

ripen'sare *vi* to think; (*cambiare pensiero*)

to change one's mind; (*tornare col pensiero*): **~ a** to recall

ripercu'otersi *vpr* **~ su** (*fig*) to have repercussions on

ripercussi'one *sf* (*fig*): **avere una ~ o delle ripercussioni su** to have repercussions on

ripes'care *vt* (*pesce*) to catch again; (*persona, cosa*) to fish out; (*fig: ritrovare*) to dig out

ri'petere *vt* to repeat; (*ripassare*) to go over; **può ~ per favore?** can you repeat that please?; **ripetizi'one** *sf* repetition; (*di lezione*) revision; **ripetizioni** *sfpl* (*Ins*) private tutoring *o* coaching *sg*

ripi'ano *sm* (*di mobile*) shelf

ri'picca *sf* **per ~** out of spite

'ripido, -a *ag* steep

ripie'gare *vt* to refold; (*piegare più volte*) to fold (up) ▷ *vi* (*Mil*) to retreat, fall back; (*fig: accontentarsi*): **~ su** to make do with

ripi'eno, -a *ag* full; (*Cuc*) stuffed; (*: panino*) filled ▷ *sm* (*Cuc*) stuffing

ri'pone, ri'pongo *ecc vb vedi* **riporre**

ri'porre *vt* (*porre al suo posto*) to put back, replace; (*mettere via*) to put away; (*fiducia, speranza*): **~ qc in qn** to place *o* put sth in sb

ripor'tare *vt* (*portare indietro*) to bring (*o* take) back; (*riferire*) to report; (*citare*) to quote; (*vittoria*) to gain; (*successo*) to have; (*Mat*) to carry; **riportarsi a** (*anche fig*) to go back to; (*riferirsi a*) to refer to; **~ danni** to suffer damage

ripo'sare *vt, vi* to rest; **riposarsi** *vpr* to rest

ri'posi *ecc vb vedi* **riporre**

ri'poso *sm* rest; (*Mil*): **~!** at ease!; **a ~** (*in pensione*) retired; **giorno di ~** day off

ripos'tiglio [ripos'tiʎʎo] *sm* lumber-room

ri'prendere *vt* (*prigioniero, fortezza*) to recapture; (*prendere indietro*) to take back; (*ricominciare: lavoro*) to resume; (*andare a prendere*) to fetch, come back for; (*riassumere: impiegati*) to take on again, re-employ; (*rimproverare*) to tell off; (*restringere: abito*) to take in; (*Cinema*) to shoot; **riprendersi** *vpr* to recover; (*correggersi*) to correct o.s.; **ri'presa** *sf* recapture; resumption; (*economica, da malattia, emozione*) recovery; (*Aut*) acceleration *no pl*; (*Teatro, Cinema*) rerun; (*Cinema: presa*) shooting *no pl*; shot; (*Sport*) second half; (*: Pugilato*) round; **a più riprese** on several occasions, several times; **ripresa cinematografica** shot

ripristi'nare *vt* to restore

ripro'durre *vt* to reproduce; **riprodursi** *vpr* (*Biol*) to reproduce; (*riformarsi*) to form again

ripro'vare *vt* (*provare di nuovo: gen*) to try

again; (*vestito*) to try on again; (*: sensazione*) to experience again ▷ *vi* (*tentare*): **~ (a fare qc)** to try (to do sth) again; **riproverò più tardi** I'll try again later

ripudi'are *vt* to repudiate, disown

ripu'gnante [ripuɲ'ɲante] *ag* disgusting, repulsive

ri'quadro *sm* square; (*Archit*) panel

ri'saia *sf* paddy field

risa'lire *vi* (*ritornare in su*) to go back up; **~ a** (*ritornare con la mente*) to go back to; (*datare da*) to date back to, go back to

risal'tare *vi* (*fig: distinguersi*) to stand out; (*Archit*) to project, jut out

risa'puto, -a *ag* **è ~ che ...** everyone knows that ..., it is common knowledge that ...

risarci'mento [risartʃi'mento] *sm* **~ (di)** compensation (for); **risarcimento danni** damages

risar'cire [risar'tʃire] *vt* (*cose*) to pay compensation for; (*persona*): **~ qn di qc** to compensate sb for sth

ri'sata *sf* laugh

riscalda'mento *sm* heating; **riscaldamento centrale** central heating

riscal'dare *vt* (*scaldare*) to heat; (*: mani, persona*) to warm; (*minestra*) to reheat; **riscaldarsi** *vpr* to warm up

ris'catto *sm* ransom; redemption

rischia'rare [riskja'rare] *vt* (*illuminare*) to light up; (*colore*) to make lighter; **rischiararsi** *vpr* (*tempo*) to clear up; (*cielo*) to clear; (*fig: volto*) to brighten up; **rischiararsi la voce** to clear one's throat

rischi'are [ris'kjare] *vt* to risk ▷ *vi* **~ di fare qc** to risk *o* run the risk of doing sth

'rischio ['riskjo] *sm* risk; **rischi'oso, -a** *ag* risky, dangerous

riscia'cquare [riʃʃa'kware] *vt* to rinse

riscon'trare *vt* (*rilevare*) to find

ris'cuotere *vt* (*ritirare: somma*) to collect; (*: stipendio*) to draw, collect; (*assegno*) to cash; (*fig: successo ecc*) to win, earn

'rise *ecc vb vedi* **ridere**

risenti'mento *sm* resentment

risen'tire *vt* to hear again; (*provare*) to feel ▷ *vi* **~ di** to feel (*o* show) the effects of; **risentirsi** *vpr* **risentirsi di** *o* **per** to take offence at, resent; **risen'tito, -a** *ag* resentful

ri'serbo *sm* reserve

ri'serva *sf* reserve; (*di caccia, pesca*) preserve; (*restrizione, di indigeni*) reservation; **di ~** (*provviste ecc*) in reserve

riser'vare *vt* (*tenere in serbo*) to keep, put aside; (*prenotare*) to book, reserve; **ho riservato un tavolo a nome...** I booked a table in the name of ...; **riser'vato,**

-a *ag* (*prenotato; fig: persona*) reserved; (*confidenziale*) confidential

'risi *ecc vb vedi* **ridere**

risi'edere *vi* ~ **a o in** to reside in

'risma *sf* (*di carta*) ream; (*fig*) kind, sort

'riso (*pl(f)* **risa**) (: *il ridere*) *sm* **il** ~ laughter; (*pianta*) rice ▷ *pp di* **ridere**

riso'lino *sm* snigger

ri'solsi *ecc vb vedi* **risolvere**

ri'solto, -a *pp di* **risolvere**

riso'luto, -a *ag* determined, resolute

risoluzi'one [risolut'tsjone] *sf* solving *no pl*; (*Mat*) solution; (*decisione, di schermo, immagine*) resolution

ri'solvere *vt* (*difficoltà, controversia*) to resolve; (*problema*) to solve; (*decidere*): ~ **di fare** to resolve to do; **risolversi** *vpr* (*decidersi*): **risolversi a fare** to make up one's mind to do; (*andare a finire*): **risolversi in** to end up, turn out; **risolversi in nulla** to come to nothing

riso'nanza [riso'nantsa] *sf* resonance; **aver vasta** ~ (*fig: fatto ecc*) to be known far and wide

ri'sorgere [ri'sordʒere] *vi* to rise again; **risorgi'mento** *sm* revival; **il Risorgimento** (*Storia*) the Risorgimento

● **RISORGIMENTO**
●
● The **Risorgimento** was the political
● movement which led to the
● proclamation of the Kingdom of Italy
● in 1861, and eventually to unification
● in 1871.

ri'sorsa *sf* expedient, resort; **risorse umane** human resources

ri'sorsi *ecc vb vedi* **risorgere**

ri'sotto *sm* (*Cuc*) risotto

risparmi'are *vt* to save; (*non uccidere*) to spare ▷ *vi* to save; ~ **qc a qn** to spare sb sth

ris'parmio *sm* saving *no pl*; (*denaro*) savings *pl*; **risparmi** *smpl* (*denaro*) savings

rispec'chiare [rispek'kjare] *vt* to reflect

rispet'tabile *ag* respectable

rispet'tare *vt* to respect; **farsi** ~ to command respect

rispet'tivo, -a *ag* respective

ris'petto *sm* respect; **rispetti** *smpl* (*saluti*) respects, regards; ~ **a** (*in paragone a*) compared to; (*in relazione a*) as regards, as for

ris'pondere *vi* to answer, reply; (*freni*) to respond; ~ **a** (*domanda*) to answer, reply to; (*persona*) to answer; (*invito*) to reply to; (*provocazione: veicolo, apparecchio*) to respond to; (*corrispondere a*) to correspond to; (: *speranze, bisogno*) to answer; ~ **di** to

answer for; **ris'posta** *sf* answer, reply; **in risposta a** in reply to

'rissa *sf* brawl

ris'tampa *sf* reprinting *no pl*; reprint

risto'rante *sm* restaurant; **mi può consigliare un buon** ~? can you recommend a good restaurant?

ris'tretto, -a *pp di* **restringere** ▷ *ag* (*racchiuso*) enclosed, hemmed in; (*angusto*) narrow; (*limitato*): ~ **(a)** restricted o limited (to); (*Cuc: brodo*) thick; (: *caffè*) extra strong

ristruttu'rare *vt* (*azienda*) to reorganize; (*edificio*) to restore; (*appartamento*) to alter; (*crema, balsamo*) to repair

risucchi'are [risuk'kjare] *vt* to suck in

risul'tare *vi* (*dimostrarsi*) to prove (to be), turn out (to be); (*riuscire*): ~ **vincitore** to emerge as the winner; ~ **da** (*provenire*) to result from, be the result of; **mi risulta che ...** I understand that ...; **non mi risulta** not as far as I know; **risul'tato** *sm* result

risuo'nare *vi* (*rimbombare*) to resound

risurrezi'one [risurret'tsjone] *sf* (*Rel*) resurrection

risusci'tare [risuʃʃi'tare] *vt* to resuscitate, restore to life; (*fig*) to revive, bring back ▷ *vi* to rise (from the dead)

ris'veglio [riz'veʎʎo] *sm* waking up; (*fig*) revival

ris'volto *sm* (*di giacca*) lapel; (*di pantaloni*) turn-up; (*di manica*) cuff; (*di tasca*) flap; (*di libro*) inside flap; (*fig*) implication

ritagli'are [ritaʎ'ʎare] *vt* (*tagliar via*) to cut out

ritar'dare *vi* (*persona, treno*) to be late; (*orologio*) to be slow ▷ *vt* (*rallentare*) to slow down; (*impedire*) to delay, hold up; (*differire*) to postpone, delay

ri'tardo *sm* delay; (*di persona aspettata*) lateness *no pl*; (*fig: mentale*) backwardness; **in** ~ late; **il volo ha due ore di** ~ the flight is two hours late; **scusi il** ~ sorry I'm late

ri'tegno [ri'teɲɲo] *sm* restraint

rite'nere *vt* (*trattenere*) to hold back; (: *somma*) to deduct; (*giudicare*) to consider, believe

ri'tengo, ri'tenni *ecc vb vedi* **ritenere**

riterrò, ritiene *ecc vb vedi* **ritenere**

riti'rare *vt* to withdraw; (*Pol: richiamare*) to recall; (*andare a prendere: pacco ecc*) to collect, pick up; **ritirarsi** *vpr* to withdraw; (*da un'attività*) to retire; (*stoffa*) to shrink; (*marea*) to recede

'ritmo *sm* rhythm; (*fig*) rate; (: *della vita*) pace, tempo

'rito *sm* rite; **di** ~ usual, customary

ritoc'care *vt* (*disegno, fotografia*) to touch up; (*testo*) to alter

ritor'nare *vi* to return, go (o come)

back, to get back; (ripresentarsi) to recur; (ridiventare): ~ ricco to become rich again ▷ vt (restituire) to return, give back; **quando ritorniamo?** when do we get back?

ritor'nello sm refrain

ri'torno sm return; **essere di ~** to be back; **avere un ~ di fiamma** (Aut) to backfire; (fig: persona) to be back in love again

ri'trarre vt (trarre indietro, via) to withdraw; (distogliere: sguardo) to turn away; (rappresentare) to portray, depict; (ricavare) to get, obtain

ritrat'tare vt (disdire) to retract, take back; (trattare nuovamente) to deal with again

ri'tratto, -a pp di ritrarre ▷ sm portrait

ritro'vare vt to find; (salute) to regain; (persona) to find; to meet again; **ritrovarsi** vpr (essere, capitare) to find o.s.; (raccapezzarsi) to find one's way; (con senso reciproco) to meet (again)

'ritto, -a ag (in piedi) standing, on one's feet; (levato in alto) erect, raised; (: capelli) standing on end; (posto verticalmente) upright

ritu'ale ag, sm ritual

riuni'one sf (adunanza) meeting; (riconciliazione) reunion

riu'nire vt (ricongiungere) to join (together); (riconciliare) to reunite, bring together (again); **riunirsi** vpr (adunarsi) to meet; (tornare insieme) to be reunited

riu'scire [riuʃˈʃire] vi (uscire di nuovo) to go out again, go back out; (aver esito: fatti, azioni) to go, turn out; (aver successo) to succeed, be successful; (essere, apparire) to be, prove; (raggiungere il fine) to manage, succeed; **~ a fare qc** to manage to do o succeed in doing o be able to do sth

'riva sf (di fiume) bank; (di lago, mare) shore

ri'vale sm/f rival; **rivalità** sf rivalry

rivalu'tare vt (Econ) to revalue

rive'dere vt to see again; (ripassare) to revise; (verificare) to check

rivedrò ecc vb vedi rivedere

rive'lare vt (divulgare) to reveal, disclose; (dare indizio) to reveal, show; **rivelarsi** vpr (manifestarsi) to be revealed; **rivelarsi onesto** ecc to prove to be honest ecc; **rivelazi'one** sf revelation

rivendi'care vt to claim, demand

rivendi'tore, -'trice sm/f retailer; **rivenditore autorizzato** (Comm) authorized dealer

ri'verbero sm (di luce, calore) reflection; (di suono) reverberation

rivesti'mento sm covering; coating

rives'tire vt to dress again; (ricoprire) to cover; to coat; (fig: carica) to hold

ri'vidi ecc vb vedi rivedere

ri'vincita [riˈvintʃita] sf (Sport) return match; (fig) revenge

ri'vista sf review; (periodico) magazine, review; (Teatro) revue; variety show

ri'volgere [riˈvoldʒere] vt (attenzione, sguardo) to turn, direct; (parole) to address; **rivolgersi** vpr to turn round; (fig: dirigersi per informazioni): **rivolgersi a** to go and see, go and speak to; (: ufficio) to enquire at

ri'volsi ecc vb vedi rivolgere

ri'volta sf revolt, rebellion

rivol'tella sf revolver

rivoluzio'nare [rivoluttsjoˈnare] vt to revolutionize

rivoluzio'nario, -a [rivoluttsjoˈnarjo] ag, sm/f revolutionary

rivoluzi'one [rivolutˈtsjone] sf revolution

riz'zare [ritˈtsare] vt to raise, erect; **rizzarsi** vpr to stand up; (capelli) to stand on end

'roba sf stuff, things pl; (possessi, beni) belongings pl, things pl, possessions pl; **~ da mangiare** things pl to eat, food; **~ da matti** sheer madness o lunacy

'robot sm inv robot

ro'busto, -a ag robust, sturdy; (solido: catena) strong

roc'chetto [rokˈketto] sm reel, spool

'roccia, -ce [ˈrɔttʃa] sf rock; **fare ~** (Sport) to go rock climbing

'roco, -a, chi, che ag hoarse

ro'daggio [roˈdaddʒo] sm running (BRIT) o breaking (US) in; **in ~** running (BRIT) o breaking (US) in

rodi'tore sm (Zool) rodent

rodo'dendro sm rhododendron

ro'gnone [ronˈɲone] sm (Cuc) kidney

'rogo, -ghi sm (per cadaveri) (funeral) pyre; (supplizio): **il ~** the stake

rol'lio sm roll(ing)

'Roma sf Rome

Roma'nia sf **la ~** Romania

ro'manico, -a, -ci, -che ag Romanesque

ro'mano, -a ag, sm/f Roman

ro'mantico, -a, -ci, -che ag romantic

romanzi'ere [romanˈdzjɛre] sm novelist

ro'manzo, -a [roˈmandzo] ag (Ling) romance cpd ▷ sm novel; **romanzo d'appendice** serial (story); **romanzo giallo/poliziesco** detective story; **romanzo rosa** romantic novel

'rombo sm rumble, thunder, roar; (Mat) rhombus; (Zool) turbot; brill

'rompere vt to break; (fidanzamento) to break off ▷ vi to break; **rompersi** vpr to break; **mi rompe le scatole** (fam) he (o she) is a pain in the neck; **rompersi un braccio** to break an arm; **mi si è rotta**

---

la macchina my car has broken down; **rompis'catole** (fam) sm/f inv pest, pain in the neck

'**rondine** sf (Zool) swallow

ron'zare [ron'dzare] vi to buzz, hum

ron'zio [ron'dzio] sm buzzing

'**rosa** sf rose ▷ ag inv, sm pink; **ro'sato, -a** ag pink, rosy ▷ sm (vino) rosé (wine)

rosicchi'are [rosik'kjare] vt to gnaw (at); (mangiucchiare) to nibble (at)

rosma'rino sm rosemary

roso'lare vt (Cuc) to brown

roso'lia sf (Med) German measles sg, rubella

ro'sone sm rosette; (vetrata) rose window

'**rospo** sm (Zool) toad

ros'setto sm (per labbra) lipstick

'**rosso, -a** ag, sm, sm/f red; **il mar R~** the Red Sea; **rosso d'uovo** egg yolk

rosticce'ria [rostittʃe'ria] sf shop selling roast meat and other cooked food

ro'taia sf rut, track; (Ferr) rail

ro'tella sf small wheel; (di mobile) castor

roto'lare vt, vi to roll; **rotolarsi** vpr to roll (about)

'**rotolo** sm roll; **andare a rotoli** (fig) to go to rack and ruin

ro'tondo, -a ag round

'**rotta** sf (Aer, Naut) course, route; (Mil) rout; **a ~ di collo** at breakneck speed; **essere in ~ con qn** to be on bad terms with sb

rotta'mare vt to scrap

rottamazione [rottama'tsjone] sf (come incentivo) the scrapping of old vehicles in return for incentives

rot'tame sm fragment, scrap, broken bit; **rottami** smpl (di nave, aereo ecc) wreckage sg

'**rotto, -a** pp di **rompere** ▷ ag broken; (calzoni) torn, split; **per il ~ della cuffia** by the skin of one's teeth

rot'tura sf breaking no pl; break; breaking off; (Med) fracture, break

rou'lotte [ru'lɔt] sf caravan

ro'vente ag red-hot

'**rovere** sm oak

ro'vescia [ro'veʃʃa] sf **alla ~** upside-down, inside-out; **oggi mi va tutto alla ~** everything is going wrong (for me) today

rovesci'are [roveʃʃare] vt (versare in giù) to pour; (: accidentalmente) to spill; (capovolgere) to turn upside down; (gettare a terra) to knock down; (: fig: governo) to overthrow; (piegare all'indietro: testa) to throw back; **rovesciarsi** vpr (sedia, macchina) to overturn; (barca) to capsize; (liquido) to spill; (fig: situazione) to be reversed

ro'vescio, -sci [ro'veʃʃo] sm other side, wrong side; (della mano) back; (di moneta) reverse; (pioggia) sudden downpour; (fig) setback; (Maglia: anche: **punto ~**) purl (stitch); (Tennis) backhand (stroke); **a ~** upside-down; inside-out; **capire qc a ~** to misunderstand sth

ro'vina sf ruin; **andare in ~** (andare a pezzi) to collapse; (fig) to go to rack and ruin; **rovine** sfpl (ruderi) ruins; **mandare in ~** to ruin

rovi'nare vi to collapse, fall down ▷ vt (danneggiare: fig) to ruin; **rovinarsi** vpr (persona) to ruin o.s.; (oggetto, vestito) to be ruined

rovis'tare vt (casa) to ransack; (tasche) to rummage in (o through)

'**rovo** sm (Bot) blackberry bush, bramble bush

'**rozzo, -a** ['roddzo] ag rough, coarse

ru'bare vt to steal; **~ qc a qn** to steal sth from sb; **mi hanno rubato il portafoglio** my wallet has been stolen

rubi'netto sm tap, faucet (us)

ru'bino sm ruby

ru'brica, -che sf (Stampa) column; (quadernetto) index book; address book; **rubrica d'indirizzi** address book; **rubrica telefonica** list of telephone numbers

'**rudere** sm (rovina) ruins pl

rudimen'tale ag rudimentary, basic

rudi'menti smpl rudiments; basic principles; basic knowledge sg

ruffi'ano sm pimp

'**ruga, -ghe** sf wrinkle

'**ruggine** ['ruddʒine] sf rust

rug'gire [rud'dʒire] vi to roar

rugi'ada [ru'dʒada] sf dew

ru'goso, -a ag wrinkled

rul'lino sm (Fot) spool; (: pellicola) film; **vorrei un ~ da 36 pose** I'd like a 36-exposure film

'**rullo** sm (di tamburi) roll; (arnese cilindrico, Tip) roller; **rullo compressore** steam roller; **rullo di pellicola** roll of film

rum sm rum

ru'meno, -a ag, sm/f, sm Romanian

rumi'nare vt (Zool) to ruminate

ru'more sm **un ~** a noise, a sound; **il ~** noise; **non riesco a dormire a causa del ~** I can't sleep for the noise; **rumo'roso, -a** ag noisy

Attenzione! In inglese esiste la parola *rumour*, che però significa *voce* nel senso *diceria*.

ru'olo sm (Teatro: fig) role, part; (elenco) roll, register, list; **di ~** permanent, on the permanent staff

ru'ota sf wheel; **ruota anteriore/**

posteriore front/back wheel; **ruota di scorta** spare wheel
ruo'tare vt, vi to rotate
'rupe sf cliff
'ruppi ecc vb vedi **rompere**
ru'rale ag rural, country cpd
ru'scello [ruʃʃello] sm stream
rus'sare vi to snore
'Russia sf **la ~** Russia; **'russo, -a** ag, sm/f, sm Russian
'rustico, -a, -ci, -che ag rustic; (fig) rough, unrefined
rut'tare vi to belch; **'rutto** sm belch
'ruvido, -a ag rough, coarse

S

S. abbr (= sud) S; (= santo) St
sa vb vedi **sapere**
'sabato sm Saturday; **di o il ~** on Saturdays
'sabbia sf sand; **sabbie mobili** quicksand(s); **sabbi'oso, -a** ag sandy
'sacca, -che sf bag; (bisaccia) haversack; **sacca da viaggio** travelling bag
sacca'rina sf saccharin(e)
saccheggi'are [sakked'dʒare] vt to sack, plunder
sac'chetto [sak'ketto] sm (small) bag, (small) sack; **sacchetto di carta/di plastica** paper/plastic bag
'sacco, -chi sm bag; (per carbone ecc) sack; (Anat, Biol) sac; (tela) sacking; (saccheggio) sack(ing); (fig: grande quantità): **un ~ di** lots of, heaps of; **sacco a pelo** sleeping bag; **sacco per i rifiuti** bin bag
sacer'dote [satʃer'dɔte] sm priest
sacrifi'care vt to sacrifice; **sacrificarsi** vpr to sacrifice o.s.; (privarsi di qc) to make sacrifices
sacri'ficio [sakri'fitʃo] sm sacrifice
'sacro, -a ag sacred
'sadico, -a, -ci, -che ag sadistic ▷ sm/f sadist
sa'etta sf arrow; (fulmine) thunderbolt; flash of lightning
sa'fari sm inv safari
sag'gezza [sad'dʒettsa] sf wisdom

'saggio, -a, -gi, -ge ['saddʒo] *ag* wise ▷ *sm* (*persona*) sage; (*esperimento*) test; (*fig: prova*) proof; (*campione*) sample; (*scritto*) essay

Sagit'tario [sadʒit'tarjo] *sm* Sagittarius

'sagoma *sf* (*profilo*) outline, profile; (*forma*) form, shape; (*Tecn*) template; (*bersaglio*) target; (*fig: persona*) character

'sagra *sf* festival

sagres'tano *sm* sacristan; sexton

sagres'tia *sf* sacristy

Sa'hara [sa'ara] *sm* **il (deserto del) ~** the Sahara (Desert)

'sai *vb vedi* **sapere**

'sala *sf* hall; (*stanza*) room; (*Cinema: Yyy: di proiezione*) cinema; **sala d'aspetto** waiting room; **sala da ballo** ballroom; **sala giochi** amusement arcade; **sala operatoria** operating theatre; **sala da pranzo** dining room; **sala per concerti** concert hall

sa'lame *sm* salami *no pl*, salami sausage

sala'moia *sf* (*Cuc*) brine

sa'lato, -a *ag* (*sapore*) salty; (*Cuc*) salted, salt *cpd*; (*fig: prezzo*) steep, stiff

sal'dare *vt* (*congiungere*) to join, bind; (*parti metalliche*) to solder; (*: con saldatura autogena*) to weld; (*conto*) to settle, pay

'saldo, -a *ag* (*resistente, forte*) strong, firm; (*fermo*) firm, steady, stable; (*fig*) firm, steadfast ▷ *sm* (*svendita*) sale; (*di conto*) settlement; (*Econ*) balance; **saldi** *smpl* (*Comm*) sales; **essere ~ nella propria fede** (*fig*) to stick to one's guns

'sale *sm* salt; (*fig*): **ha poco ~ in zucca** he doesn't have much sense; **sale fino** table salt; **sale grosso** cooking salt

'salgo *ecc vb vedi* **salire**

'salice ['salitʃe] *sm* willow; **salice piangente** weeping willow

sali'ente *ag* (*fig*) salient, main

sali'era *sf* salt cellar

sa'lire *vi* to go (*o* come) up; (*aereo ecc*) to climb, go up; (*passeggero*) to get on; (*sentiero, prezzi, livello*) to go up, rise ▷ *vt* (*scale, gradini*) to go (*o* come) up; **~ su** to climb (up); **~ sul treno/sull'autobus** to board the train/the bus; **~ in macchina** to get into the car; **sa'lita** *sf* climb, ascent; (*erta*) hill, slope; **in salita** *ag, av* uphill

sa'liva *sf* saliva

'salma *sf* corpse

'salmo *sm* psalm

sal'mone *sm* salmon

sa'lone *sm* (*stanza*) sitting room, lounge; (*in albergo*) lounge; (*su nave*) lounge, saloon; (*mostra*) show, exhibition; **salone di bellezza** beauty salon

sa'lotto *sm* lounge, sitting room; (*mobilio*) lounge suite

sal'pare *vi* (*Naut*) to set sail; (*anche:* **~ l'ancora**) to weigh anchor

'salsa *sf* (*Cuc*) sauce; **salsa di pomodoro** tomato sauce

sal'siccia, -ce [sal'sittʃa] *sf* pork sausage

sal'tare *vi* to jump, leap; (*esplodere*) to blow up, explode; (*: valvola*) to blow; (*venir via*) to pop off; (*non aver luogo: corso ecc*) to be cancelled ▷ *vt* to jump (over), leap (over); (*fig: pranzo, capitolo*) to skip, miss (out); (*Cuc*) to sauté; **far ~** to blow up; to burst open; **~ fuori** (*fig: apparire all'improvviso*) to turn up

saltel'lare *vi* to skip; to hop

'salto *sm* jump; (*Sport*) jumping; **fare un ~** to jump, leap; **fare un ~ da qn** to pop over to sb's (place); **salto in alto/lungo** high/long jump; **salto con l'asta** pole vaulting; **salto mortale** somersault

saltu'ario, -a *ag* occasional, irregular

sa'lubre *ag* healthy, salubrious

salume'ria *sf* delicatessen

sa'lumi *smpl* salted pork meats

salu'tare *ag* healthy; (*fig*) salutary, beneficial ▷ *vt* (*incontrandosi*) to greet; (*congedandosi*) to say goodbye to; (*Mil*) to salute

sa'lute *sf* health; **~!** (*a chi starnutisce*) bless you!; (*nei brindisi*) cheers!; **bere alla ~ di qn** to drink (to) sb's health

sa'luto *sm* (*gesto*) wave; (*parola*) greeting; (*Mil*) salute

salvada'naio *sm* money box, piggy bank

salva'gente [salva'dʒɛnte] *sm* (*Naut*) lifebuoy; (*ciambella*) life belt; (*giubbotto*) life jacket; (*stradale*) traffic island

salvaguar'dare *vt* to safeguard

sal'vare *vt* to save; (*trarre da un pericolo*) to rescue; (*proteggere*) to protect; **salvarsi** *vpr* to save o.s.; to escape; **salvaschermo** [salvas'kermo] *sm* (*Inform*) screen saver; **salvaslip** [salva'zlip] *sm inv* panty liner; **salva'taggio** *sm* rescue

'salve (*fam*) *escl* hi!

'salvia *sf* (*Bot*) sage

salvi'etta *sf* napkin; **salvietta umidificata** baby wipe

'salvo, -a *ag* safe, unhurt, unharmed; (*fuori pericolo*) safe, out of danger ▷ *sm* **in ~** safe ▷ *prep* (*eccetto*) except; **mettere qc in ~** to put sth in a safe place; **~ che** (*a meno che*) unless; (*eccetto che*) except (that); **~ imprevisti** barring accidents

sam'buco *sm* elder (tree)

'sandalo *sm* (*Bot*) sandalwood; (*calzatura*) sandal

'sangue *sm* blood; **farsi cattivo ~** to fret, get in a state; **sangue freddo** (*fig*) sang-froid, calm; **a ~ freddo** in cold blood;

sangui'nare *vi* to bleed

sanità *sf* health; (*salubrità*) healthiness; **Ministero della S~** Department of Health; **sanità mentale** sanity

sani'tario, -a *ag* health *cpd*; (*condizioni*) sanitary ▷ *sm* (*Amm*) doctor; **sanitari** *smpl* (*impianti*) bathroom o sanitary fittings

'sanno *vb vedi* **sapere**

'sano, -a *ag* healthy; (*denti, costituzione*) healthy, sound; (*integro*) whole, unbroken; (*fig: politica, consigli*) sound; **~ di mente** sane; **di sana pianta** completely, entirely; **~ e salvo** safe and sound

'santo, -a *ag* holy; (*fig*) saintly; (*seguito da nome proprio*) saint ▷ *sm/f* saint; **la Santa Sede** the Holy See

santu'ario *sm* sanctuary

sanzi'one [san'tsjone] *sf* sanction; (*penale, civile*) sanction, penalty

sa'pere *vt* to know; (*essere capace di*): **so nuotare** I know how to swim, I can swim ▷ *vi* **~ di** (*aver sapore*) to taste of; (*aver odore*) to smell of ▷ *sm* knowledge; **far ~ qc a qn** to inform sb about sth, let sb know sth; **mi sa che non sia vero** I don't think that's true; **non lo so** I don't know; **non so l'inglese** I don't speak English; **sa dove posso...?** do you know where I can ...?

sa'pone *sm* soap; **sapone da bucato** washing soap

sa'pore *sm* taste, flavour; **sapo'rito, -a** *ag* tasty

sappi'amo *vb vedi* **sapere**

saprò *ecc vb vedi* **sapere**

sarà *ecc vb vedi* **essere**

saraci'nesca [saratʃi'neska] *sf* (*serranda*) rolling shutter

sar'castico, -a, ci, che *ag* sarcastic

Sar'degna [sar'deɲɲa] *sf* **la ~** Sardinia

sar'dina *sf* sardine

sa'rei *ecc vb vedi* **essere**

SARS *sigla f* (*Med: = severe acute respiratory syndrome*) SARS

'sarta *sf vedi* **sarto**

'sarto, -a *sm/f* tailor/dressmaker

'sasso *sm* stone; (*ciottolo*) pebble; (*masso*) rock

sas'sofono *sm* saxophone

sas'soso, -a *ag* stony; pebbly

'Satana *sm* Satan

sa'tellite *sm, ag* satellite

'satira *sf* satire

'sauna *sf* sauna

sazi'are [sat'tsjare] *vt* to satisfy, satiate; **saziarsi** *vpr* **saziarsi (di)** to eat one's fill (of); (*fig*): **saziarsi di** to grow tired o weary of

'sazio, -a ['sattsjo] *ag* **~ (di)** sated (with), full (of); (*fig: stufo*) fed up (with), sick (of);

sono ~ I'm full (up)

sba'dato, -a *ag* careless, inattentive

sbadigli'are [zbadiʎ'ʎare] *vi* to yawn; **sba'diglio** *sm* yawn

sbagli'are [zbaʎ'ʎare] *vt* to make a mistake in, get wrong ▷ *vi* to make a mistake, be mistaken, be wrong; (*operare in modo non giusto*) to err; **sbagliarsi** *vpr* to make a mistake, be mistaken, be wrong; **~ strada/la mira** to take the wrong road/ miss one's aim

sbagli'ato, -a [zbaʎ'ʎato] *ag* (*gen*) wrong; (*compito*) full of mistakes; (*conclusione*) erroneous

'sbaglio *sm* mistake, error; (*morale*) error; **fare uno ~** to make a mistake

sbalor'dire *vt* to stun, amaze ▷ *vi* to be stunned, be amazed

sbal'zare [zbal'tsare] *vt* to throw, hurl ▷ *vi* (*balzare*) to bounce; (*saltare*) to leap, bound

sban'dare *vi* (*Naut*) to list; (*Aer*) to bank; (*Aut*) to skid

sba'raglio [zba'raʎʎo] *sm* rout; defeat; **gettarsi allo ~** to risk everything

sbaraz'zarsi [zbarat'tsarsi] *vpr* **~ di** to get rid of, rid o.s. of

sbar'care *vt* (*passeggeri*) to disembark; (*merci*) to unload ▷ *vi* to disembark

'sbarra *sf* bar; (*di passaggio a livello*) barrier; (*Dir*): **presentarsi alla ~** to appear before the court

sbar'rare *vt* (*strada ecc*) to block, bar; (*assegno*) to cross; **~ il passo** to bar the way; **~ gli occhi** to open one's eyes wide

'sbattere *vt* (*porta*) to slam, bang; (*tappeti, ali, Cuc*) to beat; (*urtare*) to knock, hit ▷ *vi* (*porta, finestra*) to bang; (*agitarsi: ali, vele ecc*) to flap; **me ne sbatto!** (*fam*) I don't give a damn!

sba'vare *vi* to dribble; (*colore*) to smear, smudge

'sberla *sf* slap

sbia'dire *vi, vt* to fade; **sbia'dito, -a** *ag* faded; (*fig*) colourless, dull

sbian'care *vt* to whiten; (*tessuto*) to bleach ▷ *vi* (*impallidire*) to grow pale o white

sbirci'ata [zbir'tʃata] *sf* **dare una ~ a qc** to glance at sth, have a look at sth

sbloc'care *vt* to unblock, free; (*freno*) to release; (*prezzi, affitti*) to decontrol; **sbloccarsi** *vpr* (*gen*) to become unblocked; (*passaggio, strada*) to clear, become unblocked

sboc'care *vi* **~ in** (*fiume*) to flow into; (*strada*) to lead into; (*persona*) to come (out) into; (*fig: concludersi*) to end (up) in

sboc'cato, -a *ag* (*persona*) foul-mouthed; (*linguaggio*) foul

sbocci'are [zbot'tʃare] *vi* (*fiore*) to bloom,

open (out)

sbol'lire vi (fig) to cool down, calm down

'sbornia (fam) sf **prendersi una ~** to get plastered

sbor'sare vt (denaro) to pay out

sbot'tare vi **~ in una risata/per la collera** to burst out laughing/explode with anger

sbotto'nare vt to unbutton, undo

sbrai'tare vi to yell, bawl

sbra'nare vt to tear to pieces

sbricio'lare [zbritʃo'lare] vt to crumble; **sbriciolarsi** vpr to crumble

sbri'gare vt to deal with; **sbrigarsi** vpr to hurry (up)

'sbronza ['zbrontsa] (fam) sf (ubriaco): **prendersi una ~** to get plastered

sbron'zarsi [zbron'tsarsi] vpr (fam) to get sozzled

'sbronzo, -a ['zbrontso] (fam) ag plastered

sbruf'fone, -a sm/f boaster

sbu'care vi to come out, emerge; (improvvisamente) to pop out (o up)

sbucci'are [zbut'tʃare] vt (arancia, patata) to peel; (piselli) to shell; **sbucciarsi un ginocchio** to graze one's knee

sbucherò ecc [zbuke'rɔ] vb vedi **sbucare**

sbuf'fare vi (persona, cavallo) to snort; (ansimare) to puff, pant; (treno) to puff

sca'broso, -a ag (fig: difficile) difficult, thorny; (: imbarazzante) embarrassing; (: sconcio) indecent

scacchi smpl (gioco) chess sg; **a ~** (tessuto) check(ed)

scacchi'era [skak'kjɛra] sf chessboard

scacci'are [skat'tʃare] vt to chase away o out, drive away o out

'scaddi ecc vb vedi **scadere**

sca'dente ag shoddy, of poor quality

sca'denza [ska'dɛntsa] sf (di cambiale, contratto) maturity; (di passaporto) expiry date; (di prodotto) maturity; **a breve/lunga ~** short-/long-term; **data di ~** expiry date

sca'dere vi (contratto ecc) to expire; (debito) to fall due; (valore, forze, peso) to decline, go down

sca'fandro sm (di palombaro) diving suit; (di astronauta) space-suit

scaf'fale sm shelf; (mobile) set of shelves

'scafo sm (Naut, Aer) hull

scagio'nare [skadʒo'nare] vt to exonerate, free from blame

'scaglia ['skaʎʎa] sf (Zool) scale; (scheggia) chip, flake

scagli'are [skaʎ'ʎare] vt (lanciare: anche fig) to hurl, fling; **scagliarsi** (anche: **vr**): **scagliarsi su** o **contro** to hurl o fling o.s. at; (fig) to rail at

'scala sf (a gradini ecc) staircase, stairs pl;

(a pioli, di corda) ladder; (Mus, Geo, di colori, valori, fig) scale; **scale** sfpl (scalinata) stairs; **su vasta ~/~ ridotta** on a large/small scale; **~ mobile (dei salari)** index-linked pay scale; **scala a libretto** stepladder; **scala mobile** escalator; (Econ) sliding scale

● **SCALA**
●
● Milan's world-famous **la Scala** theatre
● first opened its doors in 1778 with a
● performance of Salieri's opera, "L'Europa
● riconosciuta". It suffered serious
● damage in the bombing of Milan in 1943
● and reopened in 1946 with a concert
● conducted by Toscanini. It also has a
● famous classical dance school.

sca'lare vt (Alpinismo, muro) to climb, scale; (debito) to scale down, reduce

scalda'bagno [skalda'baɲɲo] sm water-heater

scal'dare vt to heat; **scaldarsi** vpr to warm up, heat up; (al fuoco, al sole) to warm o.s.; (fig) to get excited

scal'fire vt to scratch

scali'nata sf staircase

sca'lino sm (anche fig) step; (di scala a pioli) rung

'scalo sm (Naut) slipway; (: porto d'approdo) port of call; (Aer) stopover; **fare ~ (a)** (Naut) to call (at), put in (at); (Aer) to land (at), make a stop (at); **scalo merci** (Ferr) goods (BRIT) o freight yard

scalop'pina sf (Cuc) escalope

scal'pello sm chisel

scal'pore sm noise, row; **far ~** (notizia) to cause a sensation o a stir

'scaltro, -a ag cunning, shrewd

'scalzo, -a ['skaltso] ag barefoot

scambi'are vt to exchange; (confondere): **~ qn/qc per** to take o mistake sb/sth for; **mi hanno scambiato il cappello** they've given me the wrong hat; **scambiarsi** vpr (auguri, confidenze, visite) to exchange; **~ qn/qc per** (confondere) to mistake sth/sb for

'scambio sm exchange; (Ferr) points pl; **fare (uno) ~** to make a swap

scampa'gnata [skampaɲ'ɲata] sf trip to the country

scam'pare vt (salvare) to rescue, save; (evitare: morte, prigione) to escape ▷ vi **~ (a qc)** to survive (sth), escape (sth); **scamparla bella** to have a narrow escape

'scampo sm (salvezza) escape; (Zool) prawn; **cercare ~ nella fuga** to seek safety in flight

'scampolo sm remnant

scanala'tura *sf* (*incavo*) channel, groove
scandagli'are [skandaʎˈʎare] *vt* (*Naut*) to sound; (*fig*) to sound out; to probe
scandaliz'zare [skandalidˈdzare] *vt* to shock, scandalize; **scandalizzarsi** *vpr* to be shocked
'scandalo *sm* scandal
Scandi'navia *sf* **la ~** Scandinavia; **scandi'navo, -a** *ag*, *sm/f* Scandinavian
scanner ['skanner] *sm inv* (*Inform*) scanner
scansafa'tiche [skansafaˈtike] *sm/f inv* idler, loafer
scan'sare *vt* (*rimuovere*) to move (aside), shift; (*schivare*: *schiaffo*) to dodge; (*sfuggire*) to avoid; **scansarsi** *vpr* to move aside
scan'sia *sf* shelves *pl*; (*per libri*) bookcase
'scanso *sm* **a ~ di** in order to avoid, as a precaution against
scanti'nato *sm* basement
scapacci'one [skapatˈtʃone] *sm* clout
scapes'trato, -a *ag* dissolute
'scapola *sf* shoulder blade
'scapolo *sm* bachelor
scappa'mento *sm* (*Aut*) exhaust
scap'pare *vi* (*fuggire*) to escape; (*andare via in fretta*) to rush off; **lasciarsi ~ un'occasione** to let an opportunity go by; **~ di prigione** to escape from prison; **~ di mano** (*oggetto*) to slip out of one's hands; **~ di mente a qn** to slip sb's mind; **mi scappò detto** I let it slip; **scappa'toia** *sf* way out
scara'beo *sm* beetle
scarabocchi'are [skarabokˈkjare] *vt* to scribble, scrawl; **scara'bocchio** *sm* scribble, scrawl
scara'faggio [skaraˈfaddʒo] *sm* cockroach
scaraman'zia [skaramanˈtsia] *sf* **per ~** for luck
scaraven'tare *vt* to fling, hurl; **scaraventarsi** *vpr* to fling o.s.
scarce'rare [skartʃeˈrare] *vt* to release (from prison)
scardi'nare *vt* **~ una porta** to take a door off its hinges
scari'care *vt* (*merci, camion ecc*) to unload; (*passeggeri*) to set down, put off; (*arma*) to unload; (: *sparare, Elettr*) to discharge; (*corso d'acqua*) to empty, pour; (*fig: liberare da un peso*) to unburden, relieve; (*da Internet*) to download; **scaricarsi** *vpr* (*orologio*) to run o wind down; (*batteria, accumulatore*) to go flat o dead; (*fig: rilassarsi*) to unwind; (: *sfogarsi*) to let off steam
'scarico, -a, -chi, -che *ag* unloaded; (*orologio*) run down; (*accumulatore*) dead, flat ▷ *sm* (*di merci, materiali*) unloading; (*di immondizie*) dumping, tipping (BRIT); (*Tecn*:

deflusso) draining; (: *dispositivo*) drain; (*Aut*) exhaust
scarlat'tina *sf* scarlet fever
scar'latto, -a *ag* scarlet
'scarpa *sf* shoe; **scarpe da ginnastica/ tennis** gym/tennis shoes
scar'pata *sf* escarpment
scarpi'era *sf* shoe rack
scar'pone *sm* boot; **scarponi da montagna** climbing boots; **scarponi da sci** ski-boots
scarseggi'are [skarsedˈdʒare] *vi* to be scarce; **~ di** to be short of, lack
'scarso, -a *ag* (*insufficiente*) insufficient, meagre; (*povero: annata*) poor, lean; (*Ins: voto*) poor; **~ di** lacking in; **3 chili scarsi** just under 3 kilos, barely 3 kilos
scar'tare *vt* (*pacco*) to unwrap; (*idea*) to reject; (*Mil*) to declare unfit for military service; (*carte da gioco*) to discard; (*Calcio*) to dodge (past) ▷ *vi* to swerve
'scarto *sm* (*cosa scartata: anche Comm*) reject; (*di veicolo*) swerve; (*differenza*) gap, difference
scassi'nare *vt* to break, force
scate'nare *vt* (*fig*) to incite, stir up; **scatenarsi** *vpr* (*temporale*) to break; (*rivolta*) to break out; (*persona: infuriarsi*) to rage
'scatola *sf* box; (*di latta*) tin (BRIT), can; **cibi in ~** tinned (BRIT) o canned foods; **scatola cranica** cranium; **scato'lone** *sm* (big) box
scat'tare *vt* (*fotografia*) to take ▷ *vi* (*congegno, molla ecc*) to be released; (*balzare*) to spring up; (*Sport*) to put on a spurt; (*fig: per l'ira*) to fly into a rage; **~ in piedi** to spring to one's feet
'scatto *sm* (*dispositivo*) release; (: *di arma da fuoco*) trigger mechanism; (*rumore*) click; (*balzo*) jump, start; (*Sport*) spurt; (*fig: di ira ecc*) fit; (: *di stipendio*) increment; **di ~** suddenly
scaval'care *vt* (*ostacolo*) to pass (o climb) over; (*fig*) to get ahead of, overtake
sca'vare *vt* (*terreno*) to dig; (*legno*) to hollow out; (*pozzo, galleria*) to bore; (*città sepolta ecc*) to excavate
'scavo *sm* excavating *no pl*; excavation
'scegliere ['ʃeʎʎere] *vt* to choose, select
sce'icco, -chi [ʃeˈikko] *sm* sheik
'scelgo *ecc* ['ʃelgo] *vb vedi* **scegliere**
scel'lino [ʃelˈlino] *sm* shilling
'scelta ['ʃelta] *sf* choice; selection; **di prima ~** top grade o quality; **frutta o formaggi a ~** choice of fruit or cheese
'scelto, -a ['ʃelto] *pp di* **scegliere** ▷ *ag* (*gruppo*) carefully selected; (*frutta, verdura*) choice, top quality; (*Mil: specializzato*) crack *cpd*, highly skilled

'scemo, -a ['ʃemo] *ag* stupid, silly

'scena ['ʃɛna] *sf* (*gen*) scene; (*palcoscenico*) stage; **le scene** (*fig: teatro*) stage; **fare una ~** to make a scene; **andare in ~** to be staged *o* put on *o* performed; **mettere in ~** to stage

sce'nario [ʃe'narjo] *sm* scenery; (*di film*) scenario

sce'nata [ʃe'nata] *sf* row, scene

'scendere ['ʃɛndere] *vi* to go down (*o* come down); (*strada, sole*) to go down; (*notte*) to fall; (*passeggero: fermarsi*) to get out, alight; (*fig: temperatura, prezzi*) to go *o* come down, fall, drop ▷ *vt* (*scale, pendio*) to go (*o* come) down; **~ dalle scale** to come (*o* go) down the stairs; **~ dal treno** to get off *o* out of the train; **dove devo ~?** where do I get off?; **~ dalla macchina** to get out of the car; **~ da cavallo** to dismount, get off one's horse

sceneggi'ato [ʃeneddʒato] *sm* television drama

'scettico, -a, -ci, -che ['ʃɛttiko] *ag* sceptical

'scettro ['ʃɛttro] *sm* sceptre

'scheda ['skɛda] *sf* (index) card; **scheda elettorale** ballot paper; **scheda ricaricabile** (*Tel*) top-up card; **scheda telefonica** phone card; **sche'dario** *sm* file; (*mobile*) filing cabinet

sche'dina [ske'dina] *sf* ≈ pools coupon (BRIT)

'scheggia, -ge ['skeddʒa] *sf* splinter, sliver

'scheletro ['skɛletro] *sm* skeleton

'schema, -i ['skɛma] *sm* (*diagramma*) diagram, sketch; (*progetto, abbozzo*) outline, plan

'scherma ['skɛrma] *sf* fencing

scher'maglia [sker'maʎʎa] *sf* (*fig*) skirmish

'schermo ['skɛrmo] *sm* shield, screen; (*Cinema, TV*) screen

scher'nire [sker'nire] *vt* to mock, sneer at

scher'zare [sker'tsare] *vi* to joke

'scherzo ['skɛrtso] *sm* joke; (*tiro*) trick; (*Mus*) scherzo; **è uno ~!** (*una cosa facile*) it's child's play!, it's easy!; **per ~** in jest; for a joke *o* a laugh; **fare un brutto ~ a qn** to play a nasty trick on sb

schiaccia'noci [skjattʃa'notʃi] *sm inv* nutcracker

schiacci'are [skjat'tʃare] *vt* (*dito*) to crush; (*noci*) to crack; **~ un pisolino** to have a nap; **schiacciarsi** *vpr* (*appiattirsi*) to get squashed; (*frantumarsi*) to get crushed

schiaffeggi'are [skjaffed'dʒare] *vt* to slap

schi'affo ['skjaffo] *sm* slap

schiantarsi *vpr* to break (up), shatter

schia'rire [skja'rire] *vt* to lighten, make lighter; **schiarirsi** *vpr* to grow lighter; (*tornar sereno*) to clear, brighten up; **schiarirsi la voce** to clear one's throat

schiavitù [skjavi'tu] *sf* slavery

schi'avo, -a ['skjavo] *sm/f* slave

schi'ena ['skjɛna] *sf* (*Anat*) back; **schie'nale** *sm* (*di sedia*) back

schi'era ['skjɛra] *sf* (*Mil*) rank; (*gruppo*) group, band

schiera'mento [skjera'mento] *sm* (*Mil, Sport*) formation; (*fig*) alliance

schie'rare [skje'rare] *vt* (*esercito*) to line up, draw up, marshal; **schierarsi** *vpr* to line up; (*fig*): **schierarsi con** *o* **dalla parte di/contro qn** to side with/oppose sb

'schifo ['skifo] *sm* disgust; **fare ~** (*essere fatto male, dare pessimi risultati*) to be awful; **mi fa ~** it makes me sick, it's disgusting; **quel libro è uno ~** that book's rotten; **schi'foso, -a** *ag* disgusting, revolting; (*molto scadente*) rotten, lousy

schiocc'are [skjɔk'kare] *vt* (*frusta*) to crack; (*dita*) to snap; (*lingua*) to click; **~ le labbra** to smack one's lips

schiudersi *vpr* to open

schi'uma ['skjuma] *sf* foam; (*di sapone*) lather; (*di latte*) froth; (*fig: feccia*) scum

schi'vare [ski'vare] *vt* to dodge, avoid

'schivo, -a ['skivo] *ag* (*ritroso*) stand-offish, reserved; (*timido*) shy

schiz'zare [skit'tsare] *vt* (*spruzzare*) to spurt, squirt; (*sporcare*) to splash, spatter; (*fig: abbozzare*) to sketch ▷ *vi* to spurt, squirt; (*saltar fuori*) to dart up (*o* off *ecc*)

schizzi'noso, -a [skittsi'noso] *ag* fussy, finicky

'schizzo ['skittso] *sm* (*di liquido*) spurt; splash, spatter; (*abbozzo*) sketch

sci [ʃi] *sm* (*attrezzo*) ski; (*attività*) skiing; **sci d'acqua** water-skiing; **sci di fondo** cross-country skiing, ski touring (*us*); **sci nautico** water-skiing

'scia ['ʃia] (*pl* **scie**) *sf* (*di imbarcazione*) wake; (*di profumo*) trail

scià [ʃa] *sm inv* shah

sci'abola ['ʃabola] *sf* sabre

scia'callo [ʃa'kallo] *sm* jackal

sciac'quare [ʃak'kware] *vt* to rinse

scia'gura [ʃa'gura] *sf* disaster, calamity; misfortune

scialac'quare [ʃalak'kware] *vt* to squander

sci'albo, -a ['ʃalbo] *ag* pale, dull; (*fig*) dull, colourless

sci'alle ['ʃalle] *sm* shawl

scia'luppa [ʃa'luppa] *sf*; **scialuppa di salvataggio** lifeboat

sci'ame ['ʃame] *sm* swarm

sci'are [ʃi'are] *vi* to ski

sci'arpa ['ʃarpa] sf scarf; (fascia) sash

scia'tore, -'trice [ʃia'tore] sm/f skier

sci'atto, -a ['ʃatto] ag (persona) slovenly, unkempt

scien'tifico, -a, -ci, -che [ʃen'tifiko] ag scientific

sci'enza ['ʃɛntsa] sf science; (sapere) knowledge; **scienze** sfpl (Ins) science sg; **scienze naturali** natural sciences; **scienzi'ato, -a** sm/f scientist

'scimmia ['ʃimmja] sf monkey

scimpanzé [ʃimpan'tse] sm inv chimpanzee

scin'tilla [ʃin'tilla] sf spark; **scintil'lare** vi to spark; (acqua, occhi) to sparkle

scioc'chezza [ʃok'kettsa] sf stupidity no pl; stupid o foolish thing; **dire sciocchezze** to talk nonsense

sci'occo, -a, -chi, -che ['ʃɔkko] ag stupid, foolish

sci'ogliere ['ʃɔʎʎere] vt (nodo) to untie; (capelli) to loosen; (persona, animale) to untie, release; (fig: persona): **~ da** to release from; (neve) to melt; (nell'acqua: zucchero ecc) to dissolve; (fig: mistero) to solve; (porre fine a: contratto) to cancel; (: società, matrimonio) to dissolve; (: riunione) to bring to an end; **sciogliersi** vpr to loosen, come untied; to melt; to dissolve; (assemblea ecc) to break up; **~ i muscoli** to limber up; **scioglilingua** [ʃoʎʎi'lingwa] sm inv tongue-twister

sci'olgo ecc ['ʃɔlgo] vb vedi **sciogliere**

sci'olto, -a ['ʃɔlto] pp di **sciogliere** ▷ ag loose; (agile) agile, nimble; supple; (disinvolto) free and easy; **versi sciolti** (Poesia) blank verse

sciope'rare [ʃope'rare] vi to strike, go on strike

sci'opero ['ʃopero] sm strike; **fare ~** to strike; **sciopero bianco** work-to-rule (BRIT), slowdown (US); **sciopero selvaggio** wildcat strike; **sciopero a singhiozzo** on-off strike

scio'via [ʃio'via] sf ski lift

scip'pare [ʃip'pare] vt **~ qn** to snatch sb's bag; **mi hanno scippato** they snatched my bag

sci'rocco [ʃi'rɔkko] sm sirocco

sci'roppo [ʃi'rɔppo] sm syrup

'scisma, -i ['ʃizma] sm (Rel) schism

scissi'one [ʃis'sjone] sf (anche fig) split, division; (Fisica) fission

sciu'pare [ʃu'pare] vt (abito, libro, appetito) to spoil, ruin; (tempo, denaro) to waste

scivo'lare [ʃivo'lare] vi to slide o glide along; (involontariamente) to slip, slide; **'scivolo** sm slide; (Tecn) chute; **scivo'loso, -a** ag slippery

scle'rosi sf sclerosis

scoc'care vt (freccia) to shoot ▷ vi (guizzare) to shoot up; (battere: ora) to strike

scoccherò ecc [skokke'rɔ] vb vedi **scoccare**

scocci'are [skot'tʃare] (fam) vt to bother, annoy; **scocciarsi** vpr to be bothered o annoyed

sco'della sf bowl

scodinzo'lare [skodintso'lare] vi to wag its tail

scogli'era [skoʎ'ʎɛra] sf reef; cliff

'scoglio ['skɔʎʎo] sm (al mare) rock

scoi'attolo sm squirrel

scola'pasta sm inv colander

scolapi'atti sm inv drainer (for plates)

sco'lare ag **età scolare** school age ▷ vt to drain ▷ vi to drip

scola'resca sf schoolchildren pl, pupils pl

sco'laro, -a sm/f pupil, schoolboy/girl

▌ Attenzione! In inglese esiste la parola scholar, che però significa studioso.

sco'lastico, -a, -ci, -che ag school cpd; scholastic

scol'lato, -a ag (vestito) low-cut, low-necked; (donna) wearing a low-cut dress (o blouse ecc)

scolla'tura sf neckline

scolle'gare vt (fili, apparecchi) to disconnect

'scolo sm drainage

scolo'rire vt to fade; to discolour; **scolorirsi** vpr to fade; to become discoloured; (impallidire) to turn pale

scol'pire vt to carve, sculpt

scombusso'lare vt to upset

scom'messa sf bet, wager

scom'mettere vt, vi to bet

scomo'dare vt to trouble, bother; to disturb; **scomodarsi** vpr to put o.s. out; **scomodarsi a fare** to go to the bother o trouble of doing

'scomodo, -a ag uncomfortable; (sistemazione, posto) awkward, inconvenient

scompa'rire vi (sparire) to disappear, vanish; (fig) to be insignificant

scomparti'mento sm compartment; **uno ~ per non-fumatori** a non-smoking compartment

scompigli'are [skompiʎ'ʎare] vt (cassetto, capelli) to mess up, disarrange; (fig: piani) to upset

scomuni'care vt to excommunicate

'sconcio, -a, -ci, -ce ['skontʃo] ag (osceno) indecent, obscene ▷ sm disgrace

scon'figgere [skon'fiddʒere] vt to defeat, overcome

sconfi'nare vi to cross the border; (in proprietà privata) to trespass; (fig): **~ da** to stray o digress from

scon'fitta sf defeat

scon'forto sm despondency

sconge'lare [skondʒe'lare] vt to defrost

scongiu'rare [skondʒu'rare] vt (implorare) to entreat, beseech, implore; (eludere: pericolo) to ward off, avert; **scongi'uro** sm entreaty; (esorcismo) exorcism; **fare gli scongiuri** to touch wood (BRIT), knock on wood (US)

scon'nesso, -a ag incoherent

sconosci'uto, -a [skonoʃ'ʃuto] ag unknown; new, strange ▷ sm/f stranger; unknown person

sconsigli'are [skonsiʎ'ʎare] vt ~ **qc a qn** to advise sb against sth; ~ **qn dal fare qc** to advise sb not to do o against doing sth

sconso'lato, -a ag inconsolable; desolate

scon'tare vt (Comm: detrarre) to deduct; (: debito) to pay off; (: cambiale) to discount; (pena) to serve; (colpa, errori) to pay for, suffer for

scon'tato, -a ag (previsto) foreseen, taken for granted; **dare per ~ che** to take it for granted that

scon'tento, -a ag ~ **(di)** dissatisfied (with) ▷ sm dissatisfaction

'sconto sm discount; **fare uno ~** to give a discount; **ci sono sconti per studenti?** are there discounts for students?

scon'trarsi vpr (treni ecc) to crash, collide; (venire ad uno scontro, fig) to clash; ~ **con** to crash into, collide with

scon'trino sm ticket; (di cassa) receipt; **potrei avere lo ~ per favore?** can I have a receipt, please?

'scontro sm clash, encounter; crash, collision

scon'troso, -a ag sullen, surly; (permaloso) touchy

sconveni'ente ag unseemly, improper

scon'volgere [skon'vɔldʒere] vt to throw into confusion, upset; (turbare) to shake, disturb, upset; **scon'volto, -a** pp di **sconvolgere**

scooter ['skuter] sm inv scooter

'scopa sf broom; (Carte) Italian card game; **sco'pare** vt to sweep

sco'perta sf discovery

sco'perto, -a pp di **scoprire** ▷ ag uncovered; (capo) uncovered, bare; (macchina) open; (Mil) exposed, without cover; (conto) overdrawn

'scopo sm aim, purpose; **a che ~?** what for?

scoppi'are vi (spaccarsi) to burst; (esplodere) to explode; (fig) to break out; ~ **in pianto** o **a piangere** to burst out crying;

~ **dalle risa** o **dal ridere** to split one's sides laughing

scoppiet'tare vi to crackle

'scoppio sm explosion; (di tuono, arma ecc) crash, bang; (fig: di risa, ira) fit, outburst; (: di guerra) outbreak; **a ~ ritardato** delayed-action

sco'prire vt to discover; (liberare da ciò che copre) to uncover; (: monumento) to unveil; **scoprirsi** vpr to put on lighter clothes; (fig) to give o.s. away

scoraggi'are [skorad'dʒare] vt to discourage; **scoraggiarsi** vpr to become discouraged, lose heart

scorcia'toia [skortʃa'toja] sf short cut

'scorcio ['skortʃo] sm (Arte) foreshortening; (di secolo, periodo) end, close; **scorcio panoramico** vista

scor'dare vt to forget; **scordarsi** vpr **scordarsi di qc/di fare** to forget sth/to do

'scorgere ['skɔrdʒere] vt to make out, distinguish, see

scorpacci'ata [skorpat'tʃata] sf **fare una ~ (di)** to stuff o.s. (with), eat one's fill (of)

scorpi'one sm scorpion; (dello zodiaco): **S~** Scorpio

'scorrere vt (giornale, lettera) to run o skim through ▷ vi (liquido, fiume) to run, flow; (fune) to run; (cassetto, porta) to slide easily; (tempo) to pass (by)

scor'retto, -a ag incorrect; (sgarbato) impolite; (sconveniente) improper

scor'revole ag (porta) sliding; (fig: stile) fluent, flowing

'scorsi ecc vb vedi **scorgere**

'scorso, -a pp di **scorrere** ▷ ag last

scor'soio, -a ag **nodo ~** noose

'scorta sf (di personalità, convoglio) escort; (provvista) supply, stock

scor'tese ag discourteous, rude

'scorza ['skɔrdza] sf (di albero) bark; (di agrumi) peel, skin

sco'sceso, -a [skoʃ'ʃeso] ag steep

'scossa sf jerk, jolt, shake; (Elettr, fig) shock; **scossa di terremoto** earth tremor

'scosso, -a pp di **scuotere** ▷ ag (turbato) shaken, upset

scos'tante ag (fig) off-putting (BRIT), unpleasant

scotch [skɔtʃ] sm inv (whisky) Scotch; (nastro adesivo) Scotch tape®, Sellotape®

scot'tare vt (ustionare) to burn; (: con liquido bollente) to scald ▷ vi to burn; (caffè) to be too hot; **scottarsi** vpr to burn/scald o.s.; (fig) to have one's fingers burnt; **scotta'tura** sf burn; scald

'scotto, -a ag overcooked ▷ sm (fig):

pagare lo ~ (di) to pay the penalty (for)
sco'vare vt to drive out, flush out; (fig) to discover
'Scozia['skɔttsja] sf **la ~** Scotland; **scoz'zese** ag Scottish ▷ sm/f Scot
scredi'tare vt to discredit
screen saver['skriin'seɪvər] sm inv (Inform) screen saver
scre'mato, -a ag skimmed; **parzialmente ~** semi-skimmed
screpo'lato, -a ag (labbra) chapped; (muro) cracked
'screzio['skrettsjo] sm disagreement
scricchio'lare[skrikkjo'lare] vi to creak, squeak
'scrigno['skriɲɲo] sm casket
scrimina'tura sf parting
'scrissiecc vb vedi **scrivere**
'scritta sf inscription
'scritto, -a pp di **scrivere** ▷ ag written ▷ sm writing; (lettera) letter, note
scrit'toio sm writing desk
scrit'tore, -'trice sm/f writer
scrit'tura sf writing; (Comm) entry; (contratto) contract; (Rel): **la Sacra S~** the Scriptures pl
scrittu'rare vt (Teatro, Cinema) to sign up, engage; (Comm) to enter
scriva'nia sf desk
'scrivere vt to write; **come si scrive?** how is it spelt?, how do you write it?
scroc'cone, -a sm/f scrounger
'scrofa sf (Zool) sow
scrol'lare vt to shake; **scrollarsi** vpr (anche fig) to give o.s. a shake; (anche: **~ le spalle/il capo**) to shrug one's shoulders/ shake one's head
'scrupolo sm scruple; (meticolosità) care, conscientiousness
scrupo'loso, -a ag scrupulous; conscientious
scru'tare vt to scrutinize; (intenzioni, causa) to examine, scrutinize
scu'cire[sku'tʃire] vt (orlo ecc) to unpick, undo; **scucirsi** vpr to come unstitched
scude'ria sf stable
scu'detto sm (Sport) (championship) shield; (distintivo) badge
'scudo sm shield
sculacci'are[skulat'tʃare] vt to spank
scul'tore, -'trice sm/f sculptor
scul'tura sf sculpture
scu'ola sf school; **scuola elementare/ materna** primary (BRIT) o grade (US) /nursery school; **scuola guida** driving school; **scuola media** secondary (BRIT) o high (US) school; **scuola dell'obbligo** compulsory education; **scuola tecnica** technical college; **scuole serali** evening

classes, night school sg
scu'otere vt to shake
'scure sf axe
'scuro, -a ag dark; (fig: espressione) grim ▷ sm darkness; dark colour; (imposta) (window) shutter; **verde/rosso** ecc **~** dark green/red ecc
'scusa sf apology; (pretesto) excuse; **chiedere ~ a qn (per)** to apologize to sb (for); **chiedo ~** I'm sorry; (disturbando ecc) excuse me
scu'sare vt to excuse; **scusarsi** vpr **scusarsi (di)** to apologize (for); **(mi) scusi** I'm sorry; (per richiamare l'attenzione) excuse me
sde'gnato, -a[zdeɲ'nato] ag indignant, angry
'sdegno['zdeɲɲo] sm scorn, disdain
sdolci'nato, -a[zdoltʃi'nato] ag mawkish, oversentimental
sdrai'arsi vpr to stretch out, lie down
'sdraio sm **sedia a ~** deck chair
sdruccio'levole[zdruttʃo'levole] ag slippery

 PAROLA CHIAVE

se pron vedi **si**
▷ cong **1** (condizionale, ipotetica) if; **se nevica non vengo** I won't come if it snows; **sarei rimasto se me l'avessero chiesto** I would have stayed if they'd asked me; **non puoi fare altro se non telefonare** all you can do is phone; **se mai** if, if ever; **siamo noi se mai che le siamo grati** it is we who should be grateful to you; **se no** (altrimenti) or (else), otherwise **2** (in frasi dubitative, interrogative indirette) if, whether; **non so se scrivere o telefonare** I don't know whether o if I should write or phone

sé pron (gen) oneself; (esso, essa, lui, lei, loro) itself; himself; herself; themselves; **sé stesso(a)** pron oneself; itself; himself; herself
seb'bene cong although, though
sec. abbr (= secolo) c.
'secca sf (del mare) shallows pl; vedi anche **secco**
sec'care vt to dry; (prosciugare) to dry up; (fig: importunare) to annoy, bother ▷ vi to dry; to dry up; **seccarsi** vpr to dry; to dry up; (fig) to grow annoyed
sec'cato, -a ag (fig: infastidito) bothered, annoyed; (: stufo) fed up
secca'tura sf (fig) bother no pl, trouble no pl
seccheròecc [sekke'rɔ] vb vedi **seccare**

secchiello | 168

secchi'ello *sm* bucket; **secchiello del ghiaccio** ice bucket

'secchio ['sekkjo] *sm* bucket, pail

'secco, -a, -chi, -che *ag* dry; (*fichi, pesce*) dried; (*foglie, ramo*) withered; (*magro: persona*) thin, skinny; (*fig: risposta, modo di fare*) curt, abrupt; (: *colpo*) clean, sharp ▷ *sm* (*siccità*) drought; **restarci ~** (*fig: morire sul colpo*) to drop dead; **mettere in ~** (*barca*) to beach; **rimanere a ~** (*fig*) to be left in the lurch

seco'lare *ag* age-old, centuries-old; (*laico, mondano*) secular

'secolo *sm* century; (*epoca*) age

se'conda *sf* (*Aut*) second (gear); **viaggiare in ~** to travel second-class; *vedi anche* **secondo; seconda colazione** lunch

secon'dario, -a *ag* secondary

se'condo, -a *ag* second ▷ *sm* second; (*di pranzo*) main course ▷ *prep* according to; (*nel modo prescritto*) in accordance with; **~ me** in my opinion, to my mind; **di seconda mano** second-hand; **a seconda di** according to; in accordance with; **seconda classe** second-class

'sedano *sm* celery

seda'tivo, -a *ag, sm* sedative

'sede *sf* seat; (*di ditta*) head office; (*di organizzazione*) headquarters *pl*; **sede centrale** head office; **sede sociale** registered office

seden'tario, -a *ag* sedentary

se'dere *vi* to sit, be seated

'sedia *sf* chair; **sedia elettrica** electric chair; **sedia a rotelle** wheelchair

'sedici ['seditʃi] *num* sixteen

se'dile *sm* seat; (*panchina*) bench

sedu'cente [sedu'tʃɛnte] *ag* seductive; (*proposta*) very attractive

se'durre *vt* to seduce

se'duta *sf* session, sitting; (*riunione*) meeting; **seduta spiritica** séance; **seduta stante** (*fig*) immediately

seduzi'one [sedut'tsjone] *sf* seduction; (*fascino*) charm, appeal

SEeO *abbr* (= *salvo errori e omissioni*) E and OE

'sega, -ghe *sf* saw

'segale *sf* rye

se'gare *vt* to saw; (*recidere*) to saw off

'seggio ['sɛddʒo] *sm* seat; **seggio elettorale** polling station

'seggiola ['sɛddʒola] *sf* chair; **seggio'lone** *sm* (*per bambini*) highchair

seggio'via [sɛddʒo'via] *sf* chairlift

segherò *ecc* [sege'rɔ] *vb vedi* **segare**

segna'lare [seɲɲa'lare] *vt* (*manovra ecc*) to signal; to indicate; (*annunciare*) to announce; to report; (*fig: far conoscere*) to point out; (: *persona*) to single out

se'gnale [seɲ'ɲale] *sm* signal; (*cartello*): **segnale acustico** acoustic *o* sound signal; **segnale d'allarme** alarm; (*Ferr*) communication cord; **segnale orario** (*Radio*) time signal; **segnale stradale** road sign

segna'libro [seɲɲa'libro] *sm* (*anche Inform*) bookmark

se'gnare [seɲ'ɲare] *vt* to mark; (*prendere nota*) to note; (*indicare*) to indicate, mark; (*Sport: goal*) to score

'segno ['seɲɲo] *sm* sign; (*impronta, contrassegno*) mark; (*limite*) limit, bounds *pl*; (*bersaglio*) target; **fare ~ di sì/no** to nod (one's head)/shake one's head; **fare ~ a qn di fermarsi** to motion (to) sb to stop; **cogliere** *o* **colpire nel ~** (*fig*) to hit the mark; **segno zodiacale** star sign

segre'tario, -a *sm/f* secretary; **segretario comunale** town clerk; **Segretario di Stato** Secretary of State

segrete'ria *sf* (*di ditta, scuola*) (secretary's) office; (*d'organizzazione internazionale*) secretariat; (*Pol ecc: carica*) office of Secretary; **segreteria telefonica** answering service

se'greto, -a *ag* secret ▷ *sm* secret; secrecy *no pl*; **in ~** in secret, secretly

segu'ace [se'gwatʃe] *sm/f* follower, disciple

segu'ente *ag* following, next

segu'ire *vt* to follow; (*frequentare: corso*) to attend ▷ *vi* to follow; (*continuare: testo*) to continue

segui'tare *vt* to continue, carry on with ▷ *vi* to continue, carry on

'seguito *sm* (*scorta*) suite, retinue; (*discepoli*) followers *pl*; (*favore*) following; (*continuazione*) continuation; (*conseguenza*) result; **di ~** at a stretch, on end; **in ~** later on; **in ~ a, a ~ di** following; (*a causa di*) as a result of, owing to

'sei *vb vedi* **essere** ▷ *num* six

sei'cento [sei'tʃɛnto] *num* six hundred ▷ *sm* **il S~** the seventeenth century

selci'ato [sel'tʃato] *sm* cobbled surface

selezio'nare [selettsjo'nare] *vt* to select

selezi'one [selet'tsjone] *sf* selection

'sella *sf* saddle

sel'lino *sm* saddle

selvag'gina [selvad'dʒina] *sf* (*animali*) game

sel'vaggio, -a, -gi, -ge [sel'vaddʒo] *ag* wild; (*tribù*) savage, uncivilized; (*fig*) savage, brutal ▷ *sm/f* savage

sel'vatico, -a, -ci, -che *ag* wild

se'maforo *sm* (*Aut*) traffic lights *pl*

sem'brare vi to seem ▷ vb impers **sembra che** it seems that; **mi sembra che** it seems to me that, I think (that); **~ di essere** to seem to be

'**seme** sm seed; (*sperma*) semen; (*Carte*) suit

se'mestre sm half-year, six-month period

semifi'nale sf semifinal

semi'freddo sm ice-cream cake

semi'nare vt to sow

semi'nario sm seminar; (*Rel*) seminary

seminter'rato sm basement; (*appartamento*) basement flat

'**semola** sf; **semola di grano duro** durum wheat

semo'lino sm semolina

'**semplice** ['semplitʃe] ag simple; (*di un solo elemento*) single

'**sempre** av always; (*ancora*) still; **posso ~ tentare** I can always o still try; **da ~** always; **per ~** forever; **una volta per ~** once and for all; **~ che** provided (that); **~ più** more and more; **~ meno** less and less

sempre'verde ag, sm of (*Bot*) evergreen

'**senape** sf (*Cuc*) mustard

se'nato sm senate; **sena'tore, -'trice** sm/f senator

'**senno** sm judgment, (common) sense; **col ~ di poi** with hindsight

'**seno** sm (*Anat: petto, mammella*) breast; (*: grembo, fig*) womb; (*: cavità*) sinus

sen'sato, -a ag sensible

sensazio'nale [sensattsjo'nale] ag sensational

sensazi'one [sensat'tsjone] sf feeling, sensation; **avere ~ che** to have a feeling that; **fare ~** to cause a sensation, create a stir

sen'sibile ag sensitive; (*ai sensi*) perceptible; (*rilevante, notevole*) appreciable, noticeable; **~ a** sensitive to

⚠ Attenzione! In inglese esiste la parola *sensible*, che però significa *ragionevole*.

'**senso** sm (*Fisiol, istinto*) sense; (*impressione, sensazione*) feeling, sensation; (*significato*) meaning, sense; (*direzione*) direction; **sensi** smpl (*coscienza*) consciousness sg; (*sensualità*) senses; **ciò non ha ~** that doesn't make sense; **fare ~ a** (*ripugnare*) to disgust, repel; **in ~ orario/antiorario** clockwise/anticlockwise; **senso di colpa** sense of guilt; **senso comune** common sense; **senso unico** (*strada*) one-way; **senso vietato** (*Aut*) no entry

sensu'ale ag sensual; sensuous

sen'tenza [sen'tentsa] sf (*Dir*) sentence; (*massima*) maxim

senti'ero sm path

sentimen'tale ag sentimental; (*vita, avventura*) love cpd

senti'mento sm feeling

senti'nella sf sentry

sen'tire vt (*percepire al tatto, fig*) to feel; (*udire*) to hear; (*ascoltare*) to listen to; (*odore*) to smell; (*avvertire con il gusto, assaggiare*) to taste ▷ vi **~ di** (*avere sapore*) to taste of; (*avere odore*) to smell of; **sentirsi** vpr (*uso reciproco*) to be in touch; **sentirsi bene/male** to feel well/unwell o ill; **non mi sento bene** I don't feel well; **sentirsi di fare qc** (*essere disposto*) to feel like doing sth

sen'tito, -a ag (*sincero*) sincere, warm; **per ~ dire** by hearsay

'**senza** ['sɛntsa] prep, cong without; **~ dir nulla** without saying a word; **fare ~ qc** to do without sth; **~ di me** without me; **~ che io lo sapessi** without me o my knowing; **senz'altro** of course, certainly; **~ dubbio** no doubt; **~ scrupoli** unscrupulous; **~ amici** friendless

sepa'rare vt to separate; (*dividere*) to divide; (*tenere distinto*) to distinguish; **separarsi** vpr (*coniugi*) to separate, part; (*amici*) to part, leave each other; **separarsi da** (*coniuge*) to separate o part from; (*amico, socio*) to part company with; (*oggetto*) to part with; **sepa'rato, -a** ag (*letti, conto ecc*) separate; (*coniugi*) separated

seppel'lire vt to bury

'**seppi** ecc vb vedi **sapere**

'**seppia** sf cuttlefish ▷ ag inv sepia

se'quenza [se'kwentsa] sf sequence

seques'trare vt (*Dir*) to impound; (*rapire*) to kidnap; **se'questro** sm (*Dir*) impoundment; **sequestro di persona** kidnapping

'**sera** sf evening; **di ~** in the evening; **domani ~** tomorrow evening, tomorrow night; **se'rale** ag evening cpd; **se'rata** sf evening; (*ricevimento*) party

ser'bare vt to keep; (*mettere da parte*) to put aside; **~ rancore/odio verso qn** to bear sb a grudge/hate sb

serba'toio sm tank; (*cisterna*) cistern

'**Serbia** sf la ~ Serbia

'**serbo** ag Serbian ▷ sm/f Serbian, Serb ▷ sm (*Ling*) Serbian; (*il serbare*): **mettere/tenere** o **avere in ~ qc** to put/keep sth aside

se'reno, -a ag (*tempo, cielo*) clear; (*fig*) serene, calm

ser'gente [ser'dʒɛnte] sm (*Mil*) sergeant

'**serie** sf inv (*successione*) series inv; (*gruppo, collezione*) set; (*Sport*) division; league; (*Comm*): **modello di ~/fuori ~** standard/

custom-built model; **in ~** in quick succession; (*Comm*) mass *cpd*
serietà *sf* seriousness; reliability
'serio, -a *ag* serious; (*impiegato*) responsible, reliable; (*ditta, cliente*) reliable, dependable; **sul ~** (*davvero*) really, truly; (*seriamente*) seriously, in earnest
ser'pente *sm* snake; **serpente a sonagli** rattlesnake
'serra *sf* greenhouse; hothouse
ser'randa *sf* roller shutter
serra'tura *sf* lock
server ['sɛrver] *sm inv* (*Inform*) server
ser'vire *vt* to serve; (*clienti: al ristorante*) to wait on; (: *al negozio*) to serve, attend to; (*fig: giovare*) to aid, help; (*Carte*) to deal ▷ *vi* (*Tennis*) to serve; (*essere utile*): **~ a qn** to be of use to sb; **~ a qc/a fare** (*utensile ecc*) to be used for sth/for doing; **~ (a qn) da** to serve as (for sb); **servirsi** *vpr* (*usare*): **servirsi di** to use; (*prendere: cibo*): **servirsi (di)** to help o.s. (to); **serviti pure!** help yourself!; (*essere cliente abituale*): **servirsi da** to be a regular customer at, go to
servizi'evole [servit'tʃevole] *ag* obliging, willing to help
ser'vizio [ser'vittsjo] *sm* service; (*al ristorante: sul conto*) service (charge); (*Stampa, TV, Radio*) report; (*da tè, caffè ecc*) set, service; **servizi** *smpl* (*di casa*) kitchen and bathroom; (*Econ*) services; **essere di ~** to be on duty; **fuori ~** (*telefono ecc*) out of order; **~ compreso** service included; **servizio militare** military service; **servizio di posate** set of cutlery; **servizi segreti** secret service *sg*; **servizio da tè** tea set
ses'santa *num* sixty; **sessan'tesimo, -a** *num* sixtieth
sessi'one *sf* session
'sesso *sm* sex; **sessu'ale** *ag* sexual; sex *cpd*
ses'tante *sm* sextant
'sesto, -a *ag, sm* sixth
'seta *sf* silk
'sete *sf* thirst; **avere ~** to be thirsty
'setola *sf* bristle
'setta *sf* sect
set'tanta *num* seventy; **settan'tesimo, -a** *num* seventieth
set'tare *vt* (*Inform*) to set up
'sette *num* seven
sette'cento [sette'tʃento] *num* seven hundred ▷ *sm* **il S~** the eighteenth century
set'tembre *sm* September
settentrio'nale *ag* northern
settentri'one *sm* north

setti'mana *sf* week; **settima'nale** *ag, sm* weekly

● **SETTIMANA BIANCA**

● **Settimana bianca** is the name given
● to a week-long winter-sports holiday
● taken by many Italians some time in the
● skiing season.

'settimo, -a *ag, sm* seventh
set'tore *sm* sector
severità *sf* severity
se'vero, -a *ag* severe
sevizi'are [sevit'tsjare] *vt* to torture
sezio'nare [settsjo'nare] *vt* to divide into sections; (*Med*) to dissect
sezi'one [set'tsjone] *sf* section
sfacchi'nata [sfakki'nata] *sf* (*fam*) chore, drudgery *no pl*
sfacci'ato, -a [sfat'tʃato] *ag* (*maleducato*) cheeky, impudent; (*vistoso*) gaudy
sfa'mare *vt* to feed; (*cibo*) to fill; **sfamarsi** *vpr* to satisfy one's hunger, fill o.s. up
sfasci'are [sfaʃ'ʃare] *vt* (*ferita*) to unbandage; (*distruggere*) to smash, shatter; **sfasciarsi** *vpr* (*rompersi*) to smash, shatter
sfavo'revole *ag* unfavourable
'sfera *sf* sphere
sfer'rare *vt* (*fig: colpo*) to land, deal; (: *attacco*) to launch
'sfida *sf* challenge
sfi'dare *vt* to challenge; (*fig*) to defy, brave
sfi'ducia [sfi'dutʃa] *sf* distrust, mistrust
sfi'gato, -a (*fam*) *ag* (*sfortunato*) unlucky
sfigu'rare *vt* (*persona*) to disfigure; (*quadro, statua*) to deface ▷ *vi* (*far cattiva figura*) to make a bad impression
sfi'lare *vt* (*ago*) to unthread; (*abito, scarpe*) to slip off ▷ *vi* (*truppe*) to march past; (*atleti*) to parade; **sfilarsi** *vpr* (*perle ecc*) to come unstrung; (*orlo, tessuto*) to fray; (*calza*) to run, ladder; **sfi'lata** *sf* march past; parade; **sfilata di moda** fashion show
'sfinge ['sfindʒe] *sf* sphinx
sfi'nito, -a *ag* exhausted
sfio'rare *vt* to brush (against); (*argomento*) to touch upon
sfio'rire *vi* to wither, fade
sfo'cato, -a *ag* (*Fot*) out of focus
sfoci'are [sfo'tʃare] *vi* **~ in** to flow into; (*fig: malcontento*) to develop into
sfode'rato, -a *ag* (*vestito*) unlined
sfogarsi *vpr* (*sfogare la propria rabbia*) to give vent to one's anger; (*confidarsi*): **~ (con)** to pour out one's feelings (to); **non**

sfogarti su di me! don't take your bad temper out on me!

sfoggi'are [sfod'dʒare] *vt, vi* to show off

'sfoglia ['sfoʎʎa] *sf* sheet of pasta dough; **pasta ~** (*Cuc*) puff pastry

sfogli'are [sfoʎ'ʎare] *vt* (*libro*) to leaf through

'sfogo, -ghi *sm* (*eruzione cutanea*) rash; (*fig*) outburst; **dare ~ a** (*fig*) to give vent to

sfon'dare *vt* (*porta*) to break down; (*scarpe*) to wear a hole in; (*cesto, scatola*) to burst, knock the bottom out of; (*Mil*) to break through ▷ *vi* (*riuscire*) to make a name for o.s.

'sfondo *sm* background

sfor'mato *sm* (*Cuc*) type of soufflé

sfor'tuna *sf* misfortune, ill luck *no pl*; **avere ~** to be unlucky; **sfortu'nato, -a** *ag* unlucky; (*impresa, film*) unsuccessful

sforzarsi *vpr* **~ di** o **a** o **per fare** to try hard to do

'sforzo ['sfortso] *sm* effort; (*tensione eccessiva, Tecn*) strain; **fare uno ~** to make an effort

sfrat'tare *vt* to evict; **'sfratto** *sm* eviction

sfrecci'are [sfret'tʃare] *vi* to shoot o flash past

sfre'gare *vt* (*strofinare*) to rub; (*graffiare*) to scratch; **sfregarsi le mani** to rub one's hands; **~ un fiammifero** to strike a match

sfregi'are [sfre'dʒare] *vt* to slash, gash; (*persona*) to disfigure; (*quadro*) to deface

sfre'nato, -a *ag* (*fig*) unrestrained, unbridled

sfron'tato, -a *ag* shameless

sfrutta'mento *sm* exploitation

sfrut'tare *vt* (*terreno*) to overwork, exhaust; (*miniera*) to exploit, work; (*fig: operai, occasione, potere*) to exploit

sfug'gire [sfud'dʒire] *vi* to escape; **~ a** (*custode*) to escape (from); (*morte*) to escape; **~ a qn** (*dettaglio, nome*) to escape sb; **~ di mano a qn** to slip out of sb's hand (o hands)

sfu'mare *vt* (*colori, contorni*) to soften, shade off ▷ *vi* to shade (off), fade; (*fig: svanire*) to vanish, disappear; (*: speranze*) to come to nothing

sfuma'tura *sf* shading off *no pl*; (*tonalità*) shade, tone; (*fig*) touch, hint

sfuri'ata *sf* (*scatto di collera*) fit of anger; (*rimprovero*) sharp rebuke

sga'bello *sm* stool

sgabuz'zino [zgabud'dzino] *sm* lumber room

sgambet'tare *vi* to kick one's legs about

sgam'betto *sm* **far lo ~ a qn** to trip sb up; (*fig*) to oust sb

sganci'are [zgan'tʃare] *vt* to unhook; (*Ferr*) to uncouple; (*bombe: da aereo*) to release, drop; (*fig: fam: soldi*) to fork out; **sganciarsi** *vpr* (*fig*): **sganciarsi (da)** to get away (from)

sganghe'rato, -a [zgange'rato] *ag* (*porta*) off its hinges; (*auto*) ramshackle; (*risata*) wild, boisterous

sgar'bato, -a *ag* rude, impolite

'sgarbo *sm* **fare uno ~ a qn** to be rude to sb

sgargi'ante [zgar'dʒante] *ag* gaudy, showy

sgattaio'lare *vi* to sneak away o off

sge'lare [zdʒe'lare] *vi, vt* to thaw

sghignaz'zare [zgiɲɲat'tsare] *vi* to laugh scornfully

sgob'bare (*fam*) *vi* (*scolaro*) to swot; (*operaio*) to slog

sgombe'rare *vt* (*tavolo, stanza*) to clear; (*piazza, città*) to evacuate ▷ *vi* to move

'sgombro, -a *ag* **~ (di)** clear (of), free (from) ▷ *sm* (*Zool*) mackerel; (*anche:* **sgombero**) clearing; vacating; evacuation; (*: trasloco*) removal

sgonfi'are *vt* to let down, deflate; **sgonfiarsi** *vpr* to go down

'sgonfio, -a *ag* (*pneumatico, pallone*) flat

'sgorbio *sm* blot; scribble

sgra'devole *ag* unpleasant, disagreeable

sgra'dito, -a *ag* unpleasant, unwelcome

sgra'nare *vt* (*piselli*) to shell; **~ gli occhi** to open one's eyes wide

sgranchire [zgran'kire] *vt* (*anche:* **sgranchirsi**) to stretch; **~ le gambe** to stretch one's legs

sgranocchi'are [zgranok'kjare] *vt* to munch

'sgravio *sm* **~ fiscale** tax relief

sgrazi'ato, -a [zgrat'tsjato] *ag* clumsy, ungainly

sgri'dare *vt* to scold

sgual'cire [zgwal'tʃire] *vt* to crumple (up), crease

sgual'drina (*peg*) *sf* slut

sgu'ardo *sm* (*occhiata*) look, glance; (*espressione*) look (in one's eye)

sguaz'zare [zgwat'tsare] *vi* (*nell'acqua*) to splash about; (*nella melma*) to wallow; **~ nell'oro** to be rolling in money

sguinzagli'are [zgwintsaʎ'ʎare] *vt* to let off the leash; (*fig: persona*): **~ qn dietro a qn** to set sb on sb

sgusci'are [zguʃ'ʃare] *vt* to shell ▷ *vi* (*sfuggire di mano*) to slip; **~ via** to slip o slink away

'shampoo ['ʃampo] *sm inv* shampoo

shiatzu [ʃi'atstsu] *sm inv* shiatsu

shock [ʃɔk] *sm inv* shock

PAROLA CHIAVE

si (*dav lo, la, li, le, ne diventa* **se**) *pron* **1**
(*riflessivo: maschile*) himself; (: *femminile*)
herself; (: *neutro*) itself; (: *impersonale*)
oneself; (: *pl*) themselves; **lavarsi** to wash
(oneself); **si è tagliato** he has cut himself;
si credono importanti they think a lot of
themselves
2 (*riflessivo: con complemento oggetto*):
lavarsi le mani to wash one's hands; **si
sta lavando i capelli** he (*o* she) is washing
his (*o* her) hair
3 (*reciproco*) one another, each other; **si
amano** they love one another *o* each other
4 (*passivo*): **si ripara facilmente** it is easily
repaired
5 (*impersonale*): **si dice che ...** they *o*
people say that ...; **si vede che è vecchio**
one *o* you can see that it's old
6 (*noi*) we; **tra poco si parte** we're leaving
soon

sì *av* yes; **un giorno sì e uno no** every
other day

'sia *cong* **~ ... ~** (*o ... o*): **~ che lavori, ~ che
non lavori** whether he works or not;
(*tanto ... quanto*): **verranno ~ Luigi ~ suo
fratello** both Luigi and his brother will be
coming

si'amo *vb vedi* **essere**
si'cario *sm* hired killer
sicché [sik'ke] *cong* (*perciò*) so (that),
therefore; (*e quindi*) (and) so
siccità [sittʃi'ta] *sf* drought
sic'come *cong* since, as
Si'cilia [si'tʃilja] *sf* **la ~** Sicily
si'cura *sf* safety catch; (*Aut*) safety lock
sicu'rezza [siku'rettsa] *sf* safety; security;
(*fiducia*) confidence; (*certezza*) certainty; **di
~ safety** *cpd*; **la ~ stradale** road safety
si'curo, -a *ag* safe; (*ben difeso*) secure;
(*fiducioso*) confident; (*certo*) sure, certain;
(*notizia, amico*) reliable; (*esperto*) skilled
▷ *av* (*anche:* **di ~**) certainly; **essere/
mettere al ~** to be safe/put in a safe place;
~ di sé self-confident, sure of o.s.; **sentirsi
~** to feel safe *o* secure
si'edo *ecc vb vedi* **sedere**
si'epe *sf* hedge
si'ero *sm* (*Med*) serum; **sieronega'tivo,
-a** *ag* HIV-negative; **sieroposi'tivo, -a** *ag*
HIV-positive
si'ete *vb vedi* **essere**
si'filide *sf* syphilis
Sig. *abbr* (= *signore*) Mr
siga'retta *sf* cigarette

'sigaro *sm* cigar
Sigg. *abbr* (= *signori*) Messrs
sigil'lare [sidʒil'lare] *vt* to seal
si'gillo [si'dʒillo] *sm* seal
'sigla *sf* initials *pl*; acronym, abbreviation;
sigla automobilistica abbreviation of
province on vehicle number plate; **sigla
musicale** signature tune
Sig.na *abbr* (= *signorina*) Miss
signifi'care [siɲɲifi'kare] *vt* to mean;
signifi'cato *sm* meaning
si'gnora [si'ɲɲora] *sf* lady; **la ~ X** Mrs X;
buon giorno S~/Signore/Signorina
good morning; (*deferente*) good morning
Madam/Sir/Madam; (*quando si conosce
il nome*) good morning Mrs/Mr/Miss X;
Gentile S~/Signore/Signorina (*in una
lettera*) Dear Madam/Sir/Madam; **il signor
Rossi e ~** Mr Rossi and his wife; **signore e
signori** ladies and gentlemen
si'gnore [si'ɲɲore] *sm* gentleman;
(*padrone*) lord, master; (*Rel*): **il S~** the Lord;
il signor X Mr X; **i signori Bianchi** (*coniugi*)
Mr and Mrs Bianchi; *vedi anche* **signora**
signo'rile [siɲɲo'rile] *ag* refined
signo'rina [siɲɲo'rina] *sf* young lady; **la ~
X** Miss X; *vedi anche* **signora**
Sig.ra *abbr* (= *signora*) Mrs
silenzia'tore [silentsja'tore] *sm* silencer
si'lenzio [si'lentsjo] *sm* silence; **fare ~** to
be quiet, stop talking; **silenzi'oso, -a** *ag*
silent, quiet
si'licio [si'litʃo] *sm* silicon
sili'cone *sm* silicone
'sillaba *sf* syllable
si'luro *sm* torpedo
simboleggi'are [simboled'dʒare] *vt* to
symbolize
'simbolo *sm* symbol
'simile *ag* (*analogo*) similar; (*di questo tipo*):
un uomo ~ such a man, a man like this;
libri simili such books; **~ a** similar to; **i suoi
simili** one's fellow men; one's peers
simme'tria *sf* symmetry
simpa'tia *sf* (*qualità*) pleasantness;
(*inclinazione*) liking; **avere ~ per qn** to like
sb, have a liking for sb; **sim'patico, -a, -ci,
-che** *ag* (*persona*) nice, pleasant, likeable;
(*casa, albergo ecc*) nice, pleasant

> Attenzione! In inglese esiste la
> parola *sympathetic*, che però significa
> comprensivo.

simpatiz'zare [simpatid'dzare] *vi* **~ con**
to take a liking to
simu'lare *vt* to sham, simulate; (*Tecn*) to
simulate
simul'taneo, -a *ag* simultaneous
sina'goga, -ghe *sf* synagogue
sincerità [sintʃeri'ta] *sf* sincerity

sin'cero, -a [sin'tʃero] *ag* sincere; genuine; heartfelt

sinda'cale *ag* (trade-)union *cpd*

sinda'cato *sm* (*di lavoratori*) (trade) union; (*Amm, Econ, Dir*) syndicate, trust, pool

'sindaco, -ci *sm* mayor

sinfo'nia *sf* (*Mus*) symphony

singhioz'zare [singjot'tsare] *vi* to sob; to hiccup

singhi'ozzo [sin'gjottso] *sm* sob; (*Med*) hiccup; **avere il ~** to have the hiccups; **a ~** (*fig*) by fits and starts

single ['singol] *ag inv, sm/f inv* single

singo'lare *ag* (*insolito*) remarkable, singular; (*Ling*) singular ▷ *sm* (*Ling*) singular; (*Tennis*): **~ maschile/femminile** men's/women's singles

'singolo, -a *ag* single, individual ▷ *sm* (*persona*) individual; (*Tennis*) = **singolare**

si'nistra *sf* (*Pol*) left (wing); **a ~** on the left; (*direzione*) to the left

si'nistro, -a *ag* left, left-hand; (*fig*) sinister ▷ *sm* (*incidente*) accident

si'nonimo *sm* synonym; **~ di** synonymous with

sin'tassi *sf* syntax

'sintesi *sf* synthesis; (*riassunto*) summary, résumé

sin'tetico, -a, -ci, -che *ag* synthetic

sintetiz'zare [sintetid'dzare] *vt* to synthesize; (*riassumere*) to summarize

sinto'matico, -a, -ci, -che *ag* symptomatic

'sintomo *sm* symptom

sintonizzarsi *vpr* **~ su** to tune in to

si'pario *sm* (*Teatro*) curtain

si'rena *sf* (*apparecchio*) siren; (*nella mitologia, fig*) siren, mermaid

'Siria *sf* **la ~** Syria

si'ringa, -ghe *sf* syringe

'sismico, -a, -ci, -che *ag* seismic

sis'tema, -i *sm* system; method, way; **sistema nervoso** nervous system; **sistema operativo** (*Inform*) operating system; **sistema solare** solar system

siste'mare *vt* (*mettere a posto*) to tidy, put in order; (*risolvere: questione*) to sort out, settle; (*procurare un lavoro a*) to find a job for; (*dare un alloggio a*) to settle, find accommodation for; **sistemarsi** *vpr* (*problema*) to be settled; (*persona: trovare alloggio*) to find accommodation (*BRIT*) *o* accommodations (*US*); (: *trovarsi un lavoro*) to get fixed up with a job; **ti sistemo io!** I'll soon sort you out!

siste'matico, -a, -ci, -che *ag* systematic

sistemazi'one [sistemat'tsjone] *sf* arrangement, order; settlement; employment; accommodation (*BRIT*), accommodations (*US*)

'sito *sm* **~ Internet** website

situazi'one [situat'tsjone] *sf* situation

ski-lift ['ski:lift] *sm inv* ski tow

slacci'are [zlat'tʃare] *vt* to undo, unfasten

slanci'ato, -a [zlan'tʃato] *ag* slender

'slancio *sm* dash, leap; (*fig*) surge; **di ~** impetuously

'slavo, -a *ag* Slav(onic), Slavic

sle'ale *ag* disloyal; (*concorrenza ecc*) unfair

sle'gare *vt* to untie

slip [zlip] *sm inv* briefs *pl*

'slitta *sf* sledge; (*trainata*) sleigh

slit'tare *vi* to slip, slide; (*Aut*) to skid

s.l.m. *abbr* (= *sul livello del mare*) a.s.l.

slo'gare *vt* (*Med*) to dislocate

sloggi'are [zlod'dʒare] *vt* (*inquilino*) to turn out ▷ *vi* to move out

Slo'vacchia [zlo'vakkja] *sf* Slovakia

slo'vacco, -a, -chi, -che *ag, sm/f* Slovak

Slovenia [zlo'vɛnja] *sf* Slovenia

slo'veno, -a *ag, sm/f* Slovene, Slovenian ▷ *sm* (*Ling*) Slovene

smacchi'are [zmak'kjare] *vt* to remove stains from; **smacchia'tore** *sm* stain remover

'smacco, -chi *sm* humiliating defeat

smagli'ante [zmaʎ'ʎante] *ag* brilliant, dazzling

smaglia'tura [zmaʎʎa'tura] *sf* (*su maglia, calza*) ladder; (*della pelle*) stretch mark

smalizi'ato, -a [zmalit'tsjato] *ag* shrewd, cunning

smalti'mento *sm* (*di rifiuti*) disposal

smal'tire *vt* (*merce*) to sell off; (*rifiuti*) to dispose of; (*cibo*) to digest; (*peso*) to lose; (*rabbia*) to get over; **~ la sbornia** to sober up

'smalto *sm* (*anche: di denti*) enamel; (*per ceramica*) glaze; **smalto per unghie** nail varnish

smantel'lare *vt* to dismantle

smarri'mento *sm* loss; (*fig*) bewilderment; dismay

smar'rire *vt* to lose; (*non riuscire a trovare*) to mislay; **smarrirsi** *vpr* (*perdersi*) to lose one's way, get lost; (: *oggetto*) to go astray

smasche'rare [zmaske'rare] *vt* to unmask

SME *sigla m* (= *Sistema Monetario Europeo*) EMS (*European Monetary System*)

smen'tire *vt* (*negare*) to deny; (*testimonianza*) to refute; **smentirsi** *vpr* to be inconsistent

sme'raldo *sm* emerald

'smesso, -a *pp di* **smettere**

'smettere *vt* to stop; (*vestiti*) to stop wearing ▷ *vi* to stop, cease; **~ di fare** to stop doing

'smilzo, -a ['zmiltso] *ag* thin, lean
sminu'ire *vt* to diminish, lessen; (*fig*) to belittle
sminuz'zare [zminut'tsare] *vt* to break into small pieces; to crumble
'smisi *ecc vb vedi* **smettere**
smis'tare *vt* (*pacchi ecc*) to sort; (*Ferr*) to shunt
smisu'rato, -a *ag* boundless, immeasurable; (*grandissimo*) immense, enormous
smoking ['sməʊkɪŋ] *sm inv* dinner jacket
smon'tare *vt* (*mobile, macchina ecc*) to take to pieces, dismantle; (*fig: scoraggiare*) to dishearten ▷ *vi* (*scendere: da cavallo*) to dismount; (: *da treno*) to get off; (*terminare il lavoro*) to stop (work); **smontarsi** *vpr* to lose heart; to lose one's enthusiasm
'smorfia *sf* grimace; (*atteggiamento lezioso*) simpering; **fare smorfie** to make faces; to simper
'smorto, -a *ag* (*viso*) pale, wan; (*colore*) dull
smor'zare [zmor'tsare] *vt* (*suoni*) to deaden; (*colori*) to tone down; (*luce*) to dim; (*sete*) to quench; (*entusiasmo*) to dampen; **smorzarsi** *vpr* (*suono, luce*) to fade; (*entusiasmo*) to dampen
SMS *sigla m inv* (= *short message service*) text (message)
smu'overe *vt* to move, shift; (*fig: commuovere*) to move; (: *dall'inerzia*) to rouse, stir
snatu'rato, -a *ag* inhuman, heartless
'snello, -a *ag* (*agile*) agile; (*svelto*) slender, slim
sner'vante *ag* (*attesa, lavoro*) exasperating
snob'bare *vt* to snub
sno'dare *vt* (*rendere agile, mobile*) to loosen; **snodarsi** *vpr* to come loose; (*articolarsi*) to bend; (*strada, fiume*) to wind
sno'dato, -a *ag* (*articolazione, persona*) flexible; (*fune ecc*) undone
so *vb vedi* **sapere**
sobbar'carsi *vpr* ~ **a** to take on, undertake
'sobrio, -a *ag* sober
socchi'udere [sok'kjudere] *vt* (*porta*) to leave ajar; (*occhi*) to half-close; **socchi'uso, -a** *pp di* **socchiudere**
soc'correre *vt* to help, assist
soccorri'tore, -'trice *sm/f* rescuer
soc'corso, -a *pp di* **soccorrere** ▷ *sm* help, aid, assistance; **soccorso stradale** breakdown service
soci'ale [so'tʃale] *ag* social; (*di associazione*) club *cpd*, association *cpd*
socia'lismo [sotʃa'lizmo] *sm* socialism; **socia'lista, -i, -e** *ag, sm/f* socialist
società [sotʃe'ta] *sf inv* society; (*sportiva*) club; (*Comm*) company; ~ **a responsabilità limitata** *type of limited liability company*; **società per azioni** limited (BRIT) o incorporated (US) company
soci'evole [so'tʃevole] *ag* sociable
'socio ['sɔtʃo] *sm* (*Dir, Comm*) partner; (*membro di associazione*) member
'soda *sf* (*Chim*) soda; (*bibita*) soda (water)
soddisfa'cente [soddisfa'tʃente] *ag* satisfactory
soddis'fare *vt, vi* ~ **a** to satisfy; (*impegno*) to fulfil; (*debito*) to pay off; (*richiesta*) to meet, comply with; **soddis'fatto, -a** *pp di* **soddisfare** ▷ *ag* satisfied; **soddisfatto di** happy o satisfied with; pleased with; **soddisfazi'one** *sf* satisfaction
'sodo, -a *ag* firm, hard; (*uovo*) hard-boiled ▷ *av* (*picchiare, lavorare*) hard; (*dormire*) soundly
sofà *sm inv* sofa
soffe'renza [soffe'rɛntsa] *sf* suffering
sof'ferto, -a *pp di* **soffrire**
soffi'are *vt* to blow; (*notizia, segreto*) to whisper ▷ *vi* to blow; (*sbuffare*) to puff (and blow); **soffiarsi il naso** to blow one's nose; ~ **qc/qn a qn** (*fig*) to pinch o steal sth/sb from sb; ~ **via qc** to blow sth away
soffi'ata *sf* (*fam*) tip-off; **fare una ~ alla polizia** to tip off the police
'soffice ['sɔffitʃe] *ag* soft
'soffio *sm* (*di vento*) breath; **soffio al cuore** heart murmur
sof'fitta *sf* attic
sof'fitto *sm* ceiling
soffo'cante *ag* suffocating, stifling
soffo'care *vi* (*anche:* **soffocarsi**) to suffocate, choke ▷ *vt* to suffocate, choke; (*fig*) to stifle, suppress
sof'frire *vt* to suffer, endure; (*sopportare*) to bear, stand ▷ *vi* to suffer; to be in pain; ~ **(di) qc** (*Med*) to suffer from sth
sof'fritto, -a *pp di* **soffriggere** ▷ *sm* (*Cuc*) fried mixture of herbs, bacon and onions
sofisti'cato, -a *ag* sophisticated; (*vino*) adulterated
'software ['sɔftwɛə] *sm* ~ **applicativo** applications package
sogget'tivo, -a [sodd3et'tivo] *ag* subjective
sog'getto, -a [sod'd3etto] *ag* ~ **a** (*sottomesso*) subject to; (*esposto: a variazioni, danni ecc*) subject o liable to ▷ *sm* subject
soggezi'one [sodd3et'tsjone] *sf* subjection; (*timidezza*) awe; **avere ~ di qn** to stand in awe of sb; to be ill at ease in sb's presence
soggi'orno *sm* (*invernale, marino*) stay; (*stanza*) living room
'soglia ['sɔʎʎa] *sf* doorstep; (*anche fig*)

threshold

'**sogliola** ['sɔʎʎola] *sf* (*Zool*) sole
so'gnare [son'nare] *vt, vi* to dream; **~ a occhi aperti** to daydream
'**sogno** ['sonno] *sm* dream
'**soia** *sf* (*Bot*) soya
sol *sm* (*Mus*) G; (: *solfeggiando*) so(h)
so'laio *sm* (*soffitta*) attic
sola'mente *av* only, just
so'lare *ag* solar, sun *cpd*
'**solco, -chi** *sm* (*scavo, fig: ruga*) furrow; (*incavo*) rut, track; (*di disco*) groove
sol'dato *sm* soldier; **soldato semplice** private
soldi *smpl* (*denaro*) money *sg*; **non ho ~** I haven't got any money
'**sole** *sm* sun; (*luce*) sun(light); (*tempo assolato*) sun(shine); **prendere il ~** to sunbathe
soleggi'ato, -a [soled'dʒato] *ag* sunny
so'lenne *ag* solemn
soli'dale *ag* **essere ~ (con)** to be in agreement (with)
solidarietà *sf* solidarity
'**solido, -a** *ag* solid; (*forte, robusto*) sturdy, solid; (*fig: ditta*) sound, solid ▷ *sm* (*Mat*) solid
so'lista, -i, -e *ag* solo ▷ *sm/f* soloist
solita'mente *av* usually, as a rule
soli'tario, -a *ag* (*senza compagnia*) solitary, lonely; (*solo, isolato*) solitary, lone; (*deserto*) lonely ▷ *sm* (*gioiello, gioco*) solitaire
'**solito, -a** *ag* usual; **essere ~ fare** to be in the habit of doing; **di ~** usually; **più tardi del ~** later than usual; **come al ~** as usual
soli'tudine *sf* solitude
sol'letico *sm* tickling; **soffrire il ~** to be ticklish
solleva'mento *sm* raising; lifting; revolt; **sollevamento pesi** (*Sport*) weight-lifting
solle'vare *vt* to lift, raise; (*fig: persona: alleggerire*): **~ (da)** to relieve (of); (: *dar conforto*) to comfort, relieve; (: *questione*) to raise; (: *far insorgere*) to stir (to revolt); **sollevarsi** *vpr* to rise; (*fig: riprendersi*) to recover; (: *ribellarsi*) to rise up
solli'evo *sm* relief; (*conforto*) comfort
'**solo, -a** *ag* alone; (*in senso spirituale: isolato*) lonely; (*unico*): **un ~ libro** only one book, a single book; (*con ag numerale*): **veniamo noi tre soli** just o only the three of us are coming ▷ *av* (*soltanto*) only, just; **non ~ ... ma anche** not only ... but also; **fare qc da ~** to do sth (all) by oneself
sol'tanto *av* only
so'lubile *ag* (*sostanza*) soluble
soluzi'one [solut'tsjone] *sf* solution
sol'vente *ag, sm* solvent
so'maro *sm* ass, donkey

somigli'anza [somiʎ'ʎantsa] *sf* resemblance
somigli'are [somiʎ'ʎare] *vi* **~ a** to be like, resemble; (*nell'aspetto fisico*) to look like; **somigliarsi** *vpr* to be (o look) alike
'**somma** *sf* (*Mat*) sum; (*di denaro*) sum (of money)
som'mare *vt* to add up; (*aggiungere*) to add; **tutto sommato** all things considered
som'mario, -a *ag* (*racconto, indagine*) brief; (*giustizia*) summary ▷ *sm* summary
sommer'gibile [sommer'dʒibile] *sm* submarine
som'merso, -a *pp di* **sommergere**
sommità *sf inv* summit, top; (*fig*) height
som'mossa *sf* uprising
'**sonda** *sf* (*Med, Meteor, Aer*) probe; (*Mineralogia*) drill ▷ *ag inv* **pallone** *m* **~** weather balloon
son'daggio [son'daddʒo] *sm* sounding; probe; boring, drilling; (*indagine*) survey; **sondaggio d'opinioni** opinion poll
son'dare *vt* (*Naut*) to sound; (*atmosfera, piaga*) to probe; (*Mineralogia*) to bore, drill; (*fig: opinione ecc*) to survey, poll
so'netto *sm* sonnet
son'nambulo, -a *sm/f* sleepwalker
sonnel'lino *sm* nap
son'nifero *sm* sleeping drug (o pill)
'**sonno** *sm* sleep; **prendere ~** to fall asleep; **aver ~** to be sleepy
'**sono** *vb vedi* **essere**
so'noro, -a *ag* (*ambiente*) resonant; (*voce*) sonorous, ringing; (*onde, film*) sound *cpd*
sontu'oso, -a *ag* sumptuous; lavish
sop'palco, -chi *sm* mezzanine
soppor'tare *vt* (*subire: perdita, spese*) to bear, sustain; (*soffrire: dolore*) to bear, endure; (*cosa: freddo*) to withstand; (*persona: freddo, vino*) to take; (*tollerare*) to put up with, tolerate

> Attenzione! In inglese esiste il verbo *to support*, che però non significa *sopportare*.

sop'primere *vt* (*carica, privilegi, testimone*) to do away with; (*pubblicazione*) to suppress; (*parola, frase*) to delete
'**sopra** *prep* (*gen*) on; (*al di sopra di, più in alto di*) above; over; (*riguardo a*) on, about ▷ *av* on top; (*attaccato, scritto*) on it; (*al di sopra*) above; (*al piano superiore*) upstairs; **donne ~ i 30 anni** women over 30 (years of age); **abito di ~** I live upstairs; **dormirci ~** (*fig*) to sleep on it
so'prabito *sm* overcoat
soprac'ciglio [soprat'tʃiʎʎo] (*pl(f)* **soprac'ciglia**) *sm* eyebrow
sopraf'fare *vt* to overcome, overwhelm
sopral'luogo, -ghi *sm* (*di esperti*)

inspection; (*di polizia*) on-the-spot investigation

sopram'mobile *sm* ornament

soprannatu'rale *ag* supernatural

sopran'nome *sm* nickname

so'prano, -a *sm/f* (*persona*) soprano ▷ *sm* (*voce*) soprano

soprappensi'ero *av* lost in thought

sopras'salto *sm* **di ~** with a start; suddenly

soprasse'dere *vi* **~ a** to delay, put off

soprat'tutto *av* (*anzitutto*) above all; (*specialmente*) especially

sopravvalu'tare *vt* to overestimate

soprav'vento *sm* **avere/prendere il ~ su** to have/get the upper hand over

sopravvis'suto, -a *pp di* **sopravvivere**

soprav'vivere *vi* to survive; (*continuare a vivere*): **~ (in)** to live on (in); **~ a** (*incidente ecc*) to survive; (*persona*) to outlive

so'pruso *sm* abuse of power; **subire un ~** to be abused

soq'quadro *sm* **mettere a ~** to turn upside-down

sor'betto *sm* sorbet, water ice

sor'dina *sf* **in ~** softly; (*fig*) on the sly

'sordo, -a *ag* deaf; (*rumore*) muffled; (*dolore*) dull; (*odio, rancore*) veiled ▷ *sm/f* deaf person; **sordo'muto, -a** *ag* deaf-and-dumb ▷ *sm/f* deaf-mute

so'rella *sf* sister; **sorel'lastra** *sf* stepsister; (*con genitore in comune*) half-sister

sor'gente [sor'dʒɛnte] *sf* (*d'acqua*) spring; (*di fiume, Fisica, fig*) source

'sorgere ['sordʒere] *vi* to rise; (*scaturire*) to spring, rise; (*fig: difficoltà*) to arise

sorni'one, -a *ag* sly

sorpas'sare *vt* (*Aut*) to overtake; (*fig*) to surpass; (: *eccedere*) to exceed, go beyond; **~ in altezza** to be higher than; (*persona*) to be taller than

sorpren'dente *ag* surprising

sor'prendere *vt* (*cogliere: in flagrante ecc*) to catch; (*stupire*) to surprise; **sorprendersi** *vpr* **sorprendersi (di)** to be surprised (at); **sor'presa** *sf* surprise; **fare una sorpresa a qn** to give sb a surprise; **sor'preso, -a** *pp di* **sorprendere**

sor'reggere [sor'rɛddʒere] *vt* to support, hold up; (*fig*) to sustain; **sorreggersi** *vpr* (*tenersi ritto*) to stay upright

sor'ridere *vi* to smile; **sor'riso, -a** *pp di* **sorridere** ▷ *sm* smile

'sorsi *ecc vb vedi* **sorgere**

'sorso *sm* sip

'sorta *sf* sort, kind; **di ~** whatever, of any kind, at all

'sorte *sf* (*fato*) fate, destiny; (*evento fortuito*)

chance; **tirare a ~** to draw lots

sor'teggio [sor'teddʒo] *sm* draw

sorvegli'ante [sorveʎ'ʎante] *sm/f* (*di carcere*) guard, warder (BRIT); (*di fabbrica ecc*) supervisor

sorvegli'anza [sorveʎ'ʎantsa] *sf* watch; supervision; (*Polizia, Mil*) surveillance

sorvegli'are [sorveʎ'ʎare] *vt* (*bambino, bagagli, prigioniero*) to watch, keep an eye on; (*malato*) to watch over; (*territorio, casa*) to watch o keep watch over; (*lavori*) to supervise

sorvo'lare *vt* (*territorio*) to fly over ▷ *vi* **~ su** (*fig*) to skim over

S.O.S. *sigla m* mayday, SOS

'sosia *sm inv* double

sos'pendere *vt* (*appendere*) to hang (up); (*interrompere, privare di una carica*) to suspend; (*rimandare*) to defer; (*appendere*) to hang

sospet'tare *vt* to suspect ▷ *vi* **~ di** to suspect; (*diffidare*) to be suspicious of

sos'petto, -a *ag* suspicious ▷ *sm* suspicion; **sospet'toso, -a** *ag* suspicious

sospi'rare *vi* to sigh ▷ *vt* to long for, yearn for; **sos'piro** *sm* sigh

'sosta *sf* (*fermata*) stop, halt; (*pausa*) pause, break; **senza ~** non-stop, without a break

sostan'tivo *sm* noun, substantive

sos'tanza [sos'tantsa] *sf* substance; **sostanze** *sfpl* (*ricchezze*) wealth *sg*, possessions; **in ~** in short, to sum up

sos'tare *vi* (*fermarsi*) to stop (for a while), stay; (*fare una pausa*) to take a break

sos'tegno [sos'teɲɲo] *sm* support

soste'nere *vt* to support; (*prendere su di sé*) to take on, bear; (*resistere*) to withstand, stand up to; (*affermare*): **~ che** to maintain that; **sostenersi** *vpr* to hold o.s. up, support o.s.; (*fig*) to keep up one's strength; **~ gli esami** to sit exams

sostenta'mento *sm* maintenance, support

sostitu'ire *vt* (*mettere al posto di*): **~ qn/qc a** to substitute sb/sth for; (*prendere il posto di: persona*) to substitute for; (: *cosa*) to take the place of

sosti'tuto, -a *sm/f* substitute

sostituzi'one [sostitut'tsjone] *sf* substitution; **in ~ di** as a substitute for, in place of

sotta'ceti [sotta'tʃeti] *smpl* pickles

sot'tana *sf* (*sottoveste*) underskirt; (*gonna*) skirt; (*Rel*) soutane, cassock

sotter'fugio [sotter'fudʒo] *sm* subterfuge

sotter'raneo, -a *ag* underground ▷ *sm* cellar

sotter'rare *vt* to bury

sot'tile *ag* thin; (*figura, caviglia*) thin, slim,

slender; (*fine: polvere, capelli*) fine; (*fig: leggero*) light; (*: vista*) sharp, keen; (*: olfatto*) fine, discriminating; (*: mente*) subtle; shrewd ▷ *sm* **non andare per il ~** not to mince matters

sottin'teso, -a *pp di* **sottintendere** ▷ *sm* allusion; **parlare senza sottintesi** to speak plainly

'**sotto** *prep* (*gen*) under; (*più in basso di*) below ▷ *av* underneath, beneath; below; **(al piano) di ~** downstairs; **~ forma di** in the form of; **~ il monte** at the foot of the mountain; **siamo ~ Natale** it's nearly Christmas; **~ la pioggia/il sole** in the rain/sun(shine); **~ terra** underground; **chiuso ~ vuoto** vacuum-packed

sotto'fondo *sm* background; **sottofondo musicale** background music

sottoline'are *vt* to underline; (*fig*) to emphasize, stress

sottoma'rino, -a *ag* (*flora*) submarine; (*cavo, navigazione*) underwater ▷ *sm* (*Naut*) submarine

sottopas'saggio [sottopas'saddʒo] *sm* (*Aut*) underpass; (*pedonale*) subway, underpass

sotto'porre *vt* (*costringere*) to subject; (*fig: presentare*) to submit; **sottoporsi** *vpr* to submit; **sottoporsi a** (*subire*) to undergo

sottos'critto, -a *pp di* **sottoscrivere**

sotto'sopra *av* upside-down

sotto'terra *av* underground

sotto'titolo *sm* subtitle

sottovalu'tare *vt* to underestimate

sotto'veste *sf* underskirt

sotto'voce [sotto'votʃe] *av* in a low voice

sottovu'oto *av* **confezionare ~** to vacuum-pack ▷ *ag* **confezione** *f* **~** vacuum packed

sot'trarre *vt* (*Mat*) to subtract, take away; **~ qn/qc a** (*togliere*) to remove sb/sth from; (*salvare*) to save o rescue sb/sth from; **~ qc a qn** (*rubare*) to steal sth from sb; **sottrarsi** *vpr* **sottrarsi a** (*sfuggire*) to escape; (*evitare*) to avoid; **sottrazi'one** *sf* subtraction; removal

souve'nir [suv(ə)'niːr] *sm inv* souvenir

sovi'etico, -a, -ci, -che *ag* Soviet ▷ *sm/f* Soviet citizen

sovrac'carico, -a, chi, che *ag* **~ (di)** overloaded (with) ▷ *sm* excess load; **~ di lavoro** extra work

sovraffol'lato, -a *ag* overcrowded

sovrannatu'rale *ag* = **soprannatu'rale**

so'vrano, -a *ag* sovereign; (*fig: sommo*) supreme ▷ *sm/f* sovereign, monarch

sovrap'porre *vt* to place on top of, put on top of

sovvenzi'one [sovven'tsjone] *sf* subsidy, grant

'**sozzo, -a** ['sottso] *ag* filthy, dirty

S.P.A. *abbr* = **società per azioni**

spac'care *vt* to split, break; (*legna*) to chop; **spaccarsi** *vpr* to split, break; **spacca'tura** *sf* split

spaccherò *ecc* [spakke'rɔ] *vb vedi* **spaccare**

spacci'are [spat'tʃare] *vt* (*vendere*) to sell (off); (*mettere in circolazione*) to circulate; (*droga*) to peddle, push; **spacciarsi** *vpr* **spacciarsi per** (*farsi credere*) to pass o.s. off as, pretend to be; **spaccia'tore, -'trice** *sm/f* (*di droga*) pusher; (*di denaro falso*) dealer; '**spaccio** *sm* (*di merce rubata, droga*): **spaccio (di)** trafficking (in); **spaccio (di)** passing (of); (*vendita*) sale; (*bottega*) shop

'**spacco, -chi** *sm* (*fenditura*) split, crack; (*strappo*) tear; (*di gonna*) slit

spac'cone *sm/f* boaster, braggart

'**spada** *sf* sword

spae'sato, -a *ag* disorientated, lost

spa'ghetti [spa'getti] *smpl* (*Cuc*) spaghetti *sg*

'**Spagna** ['spaɲɲa] *sf* **la ~** Spain; **spa'gnolo, -a** *ag* Spanish ▷ *sm/f* Spaniard ▷ *sm* (*Ling*) Spanish; **gli Spagnoli** the Spanish

'**spago, -ghi** *sm* string, twine

spai'ato, -a *ag* (*calza, guanto*) odd

spalan'care *vt* to open wide; **spalancarsi** *vpr* to open wide

spa'lare *vt* to shovel

'**spalla** *sf* shoulder; (*fig: Teatro*) stooge; **spalle** *sfpl* (*dorso*) back

spalli'era *sf* (*di sedia ecc*) back; (*di letto: da capo*) head(board); (*: da piedi*) foot(board); (*Ginnastica*) wall bars *pl*

spal'lina *sf* (*bretella*) strap; (*imbottitura*) shoulder pad

spal'mare *vt* to spread

'**spalti** *smpl* (*di stadio*) terracing

'**spandere** *vt* to spread; (*versare*) to pour (out)

spa'rare *vt* to fire ▷ *vi* (*far fuoco*) to fire; (*tirare*) to shoot; **spara'toria** *sf* exchange of shots

sparecchi'are [sparek'kjare] *vt* **~ (la tavola)** to clear the table

spa'reggio [spa'reddʒo] *sm* (*Sport*) play-off

'**spargere** ['spardʒere] *vt* (*spargliare*) to scatter; (*versare: vino*) to spill; (*: lacrime, sangue*) to shed; (*diffondere*) to spread; (*emanare*) to give off (*o out*); **spargersi** *vpr* to spread

spa'rire *vi* to disappear, vanish

spar'lare *vi* **~ di** to run down, speak ill of

'**sparo** *sm* shot

spar'tire vt (eredità, bottino) to share out; (avversari) to separate

spar'tito sm (Mus) score

sparti'traffico sm inv (Aut) central reservation (BRIT), median (strip) (US)

sparvi'ero sm (Zool) sparrowhawk

spasi'mante sm suitor

spassio'nato, -a ag dispassionate, impartial

'spasso sm (divertimento) amusement, enjoyment; **andare a ~** to go out for a walk; **essere a ~** (fig) to be out of work; **mandare qn a ~** (fig) to give sb the sack

'spatola sf spatula; (di muratore) trowel

spa'valdo, -a ag arrogant, bold

spaventa'passeri sm inv scarecrow

spaven'tare vt to frighten, scare; **spaventarsi** vpr to be frightened, be scared; to get a fright; **spa'vento** sm fear, fright; **far spavento a qn** to give sb a fright; **spaven'toso, -a** ag frightening, terrible; (fig: fam) tremendous, fantastic

spazientirsi [spattsjen'tirsi] vpr to lose one's patience

'spazio ['spattsjo] sm space; **spazio aereo** airspace; **spazi'oso, -a** ag spacious

spazzaca'mino [spattsaka'mino] sm chimney sweep

spazza'neve [spattsa'neve] sm inv snowplough

spaz'zare [spat'tsare] vt to sweep; (foglie ecc) to sweep up; (cacciare) to sweep away; **spazza'tura** sf sweepings pl; (immondizia) rubbish; **spaz'zino** sm street sweeper

'spazzola ['spattsola] sf brush; **spazzola da capelli** hairbrush; **spazzola per abiti** clothesbrush; **spazzo'lare** vt to brush; **spazzo'lino** sm (small) brush; **spazzolino da denti** toothbrush

specchi'arsi [spek'kjarsi] vpr to look at o.s. in a mirror; (riflettersi) to be mirrored, be reflected

specchi'etto [spek'kjetto] sm (tabella) table, chart; **specchietto da borsetta** pocket mirror; **specchietto retrovisore** (Aut) rear-view mirror

'specchio ['spekkjo] sm mirror

speci'ale [spe'tʃale] ag special; **specia'lista, -i, -e** sm/f specialist; **specialità** sf inv speciality; (branca di studio) special field, speciality; **vorrei assaggiare una specialità del posto** I'd like to try a local speciality; **special'mente** av especially, particularly

'specie ['spetʃe] sf inv (Biol, Bot, Zool) species inv; (tipo) kind, sort ▷ av especially, particularly; **una ~ di** a kind of; **fare ~ a qn** to surprise sb; **la ~ umana** mankind

specifi'care [spetʃifi'kare] vt to specify, state

spe'cifico, -a, -ci, -che [spe'tʃifiko] ag specific

specu'lare vi **~ su** (Comm) to speculate in; (sfruttare) to exploit; (meditare) to speculate on; **speculazi'one** sf speculation

spe'dire vt to send

'spegnere ['speɲɲere] vt (fuoco, sigaretta) to put out, extinguish; (apparecchio elettrico) to turn o switch off; (gas) to turn off; (fig: suoni, passioni) to stifle; (debito) to extinguish; **spegnersi** vpr to go out; to go off; (morire) to pass away; **puoi ~ la luce?** could you switch off the light?; **non riesco a ~ il riscaldamento** I can't turn the heating off

spellarsi vpr to peel

'spendere vt to spend

'spengo ecc vb vedi **spegnere**

'spensi ecc vb vedi **spegnere**

spensie'rato, -a ag carefree

'spento, -a pp di **spegnere** ▷ ag (suono) muffled; (colore) dull; (sigaretta) out; (civiltà, vulcano) extinct

spe'ranza [spe'rantsa] sf hope

spe'rare vt to hope for ▷ vi **~ in** to trust in; **~ che/di fare** to hope that/to do; **lo spero, spero di sì** I hope so

sper'duto, -a ag (isolato) out-of-the-way; (persona: smarrita, a disagio) lost

sperimen'tale ag experimental

sperimen'tare vt to experiment with, test; (fig) to test, put to the test

'sperma, -i sm sperm

spe'rone sm spur

sperpe'rare vt to squander

'spesa sf (somma di denaro) expense; (costo) cost; (acquisto) purchase; (fam: acquisto del cibo quotidiano) shopping; **spese postali** postage sg; **spese di viaggio** travelling expenses

'spesso, -a ag (fitto) thick; (frequente) frequent ▷ av often; **spesse volte** frequently, often

spes'sore sm thickness

Spett. abbr vedi **spettabile**

spet'tabile (abbr: **Spett.**: in lettere) ag **~ Ditta X** Messrs X and Co.

spet'tacolo sm (rappresentazione) performance, show; (vista, scena) sight; **dare ~ di sé** to make an exhibition o a spectacle of o.s.

spet'tare vi **~ a** (decisione) to be up to; (stipendio) to be due to; **spetta a te decidere** it's up to you to decide

spetta'tore, -'trice sm/f (Cinema, Teatro) member of the audience; (di avvenimento) onlooker, witness

spettego'lare vi to gossip

spetti'nato, -a *ag* dishevelled

'**spettro** *sm* (*fantasma*) spectre; (*Fisica*) spectrum

'**spezie** [ˈspɛttsje] *sfpl* (*Cuc*) spices

spez'zare [spetˈtsare] *vt* (*rompere*) to break; (*fig: interrompere*) to break up; **spezzarsi** *vpr* to break

spezza'tino [spettsaˈtino] *sm* (*Cuc*) stew

spezzet'tare [spettsetˈtare] *vt* to break up (*o chop*) into small pieces

'**spia** *sf* spy; (*confidente della polizia*) informer; (*Elettr*) indicating light; warning light; (*fessura*) peep-hole; (*fig: sintomo*) sign, indication

spia'cente [spjaˈtʃɛnte] *ag* sorry; **essere ~ di qc/di fare qc** to be sorry about sth/for doing sth

spia'cevole [spjaˈtʃevole] *ag* unpleasant

spi'aggia, -ge [ˈspjaddʒa] *sf* beach; **spiaggia libera** public beach

spia'nare *vt* (*terreno*) to level, make level; (*edificio*) to raze to the ground; (*pasta*) to roll out; (*rendere liscio*) to smooth (out)

spi'are *vt* to spy on

spi'azzo [ˈspjattso] *sm* open space; (*radura*) clearing

'**spicchio** [ˈspikkjo] *sm* (*di agrumi*) segment; (*di aglio*) clove; (*parte*) piece, slice

spicciarsi *vpr* to hurry up

spiccioli *smpl* (small) change; **mi dispiace, non ho ~** sorry, I don't have any change

'**spicco, -chi** *sm* **di ~** outstanding; (*tema*) main, principal; **fare ~** to stand out

spie'dino *sm* (*utensile*) skewer; (*pietanza*) kebab

spi'edo *sm* (*Cuc*) spit

spie'gare *vt* (*far capire*) to explain; (*tovaglia*) to unfold; (*vele*) to unfurl; **spiegarsi** *vpr* to explain o.s., make o.s. clear; **~ qc a qn** to explain sth to sb; **spiegazi'one** *sf* explanation

spieghe'rò *ecc* [spjeˈɡero] *vb vedi* **spiegare**

spie'tato, -a *ag* ruthless, pitiless

spiffe'rare (*fam*) *vt* to blurt out, blab

'**spiffero** *sm* draught (BRIT), draft (US)

'**spiga, -ghe** *sf* (*Bot*) ear

spigli'ato, -a [spiʎˈʎato] *ag* self-possessed, self-confident

'**spigolo** *sm* corner; (*Mat*) edge

'**spilla** *sf* brooch; (*da cravatta, cappello*) pin; **~ di sicurezza** *o* **da balia** safety pin

'**spillo** *sm* pin; **spillo da balia** *o* **di sicurezza** safety pin

spi'lorcio, -a, -ci, -ce [spiˈlortʃo] *ag* mean, stingy

'**spina** *sf* (*Bot*) thorn, prickle; (*Zool*) spine, prickle; (*di pesce*) bone; (*Elettr*) plug; (*di botte*) bunghole; **birra alla ~** draught beer; **spina dorsale** (*Anat*) backbone

spinaci [spiˈnatʃi] *smpl* spinach *sg*

spi'nello *sm* (*Droga: gergo*) joint

'**spingere** [ˈspindʒere] *vt* to push; (*condurre: anche fig*) to drive; (*stimolare*): **~ qn a fare** to urge *o* press sb to do

spi'noso, -a *ag* thorny, prickly

'**spinsi** *ecc vb vedi* **spingere**

'**spinta** *sf* (*urto*) push; (*Fisica*) thrust; (*fig: stimolo*) incentive, spur; (: *appoggio*) string-pulling *no pl*; **dare una ~ a qn** (*fig*) to pull strings for sb

'**spinto, -a** *pp di* **spingere**

spio'naggio [spioˈnaddʒo] *sm* espionage, spying

spion'cino [spionˈtʃino] *sm* peephole

spi'raglio [spiˈraʎʎo] *sm* (*fessura*) chink, narrow opening; (*raggio di luce, fig*) glimmer, gleam

spi'rale *sf* spiral; (*contraccettivo*) coil; **a ~** spiral(-shaped)

spiri'tato, -a *ag* possessed; (*fig: persona, espressione*) wild

spiri'tismo *sm* spiritualism

'**spirito** *sm* (*Rel, Chim, disposizione d'animo, di legge ecc, fantasma*) spirit; (*pensieri, intelletto*) mind; (*arguzia*) wit; (*umorismo*) humour, wit; **lo S~ Santo** the Holy Spirit *o* Ghost

spirito'saggine [spiritoˈsaddʒine] *sf* witticism; (*peg*) wisecrack

spiri'toso, -a *ag* witty

spiritu'ale *ag* spiritual

'**splendere** *vi* to shine

'**splendido, -a** *ag* splendid; (*splendente*) shining; (*sfarzoso*) magnificent, splendid

splen'dore *sm* splendour; (*luce intensa*) brilliance, brightness

spogli'are [spoʎˈʎare] *vt* (*svestire*) to undress; (*privare, fig: depredare*): **~ qn di qc** to deprive sb of sth; (*togliere ornamenti: anche fig*): **~ qn/qc di** to strip sb/sth of; **spogliarsi** *vpr* to undress, strip; **spogliarsi di** (*ricchezze ecc*) to deprive o.s. of, give up; (*pregiudizi*) to rid o.s. of; **spoglia'rello** [spoʎʎaˈrello] *sm* striptease; **spoglia'toio** *sm* dressing room; (*di scuola ecc*) cloakroom; (*Sport*) changing room

'**spola** *sf* (*bobina di filo*) cop; **fare la ~ (fra)** to go to and fro *o* shuttle (between)

spolve'rare *vt* (*anche Cuc*) to dust; (*con spazzola*) to brush; (*con battipanni*) to beat; (*fig*) to polish off ▷ *vi* to dust

spon'taneo, -a *ag* spontaneous; (*persona*) unaffected, natural

spor'care *vt* to dirty, make dirty; (*fig*) to sully, mar; **sporcarsi** *vpr* to get dirty

spor'cizia [sporˈtʃittsja] *sf* (*stato*) dirtiness; (*sudiciume*) dirt, filth; (*cosa* *sporca*) dirt *no pl*, something dirty

'sporco, -a, -chi, -che *ag* dirty, filthy

spor'genza [spor'dʒentsa] *sf* projection

'sporgere ['spordʒere] *vt* to put out, stretch out ▷ *vi* (*venire in fuori*) to stick out; **sporgersi** *vpr* to lean out; **~ querela contro qn** (*Dir*) to take legal action against sb

'sporsi *ecc vb vedi* **sporgere**

sport *sm inv* sport

spor'tello *sm* (*di treno, auto ecc*) door; (*di banca, ufficio*) window, counter; **sportello automatico** (*Banca*) cash dispenser, automated telling machine

spor'tivo, -a *ag* (*gara, giornale, centro*) sports *cpd*; (*persona*) sporty; (*abito*) casual; (*spirito, atteggiamento*) sporting

'sposa *sf* bride; (*moglie*) wife

sposa'lizio [spoza'littsjo] *sm* wedding

spo'sare *vt* to marry; (*fig: idea, fede*) to espouse; **sposarsi** *vpr* to get married, marry; **sposarsi con qn** to marry sb, get married to sb; **spo'sato, -a** *ag* married

'sposo *sm* (*bride*)groom; (*marito*) husband

spos'sato, -a *ag* exhausted, weary

spos'tare *vt* to move, shift; (*cambiare: orario*) to change; **spostarsi** *vpr* to move; **può ~ la macchina, per favore?** can you move your car please?

'spranga, -ghe *sf* (*sbarra*) bar

spre'care *vt* to waste

spre'gevole [spre'dʒevole] *ag* contemptible, despicable

'spremere *vt* to squeeze

spremia'grumi *sm inv* lemon squeezer

spre'muta *sf* fresh juice; **spremuta d'arancia** fresh orange juice

sprez'zante [spret'tsante] *ag* scornful, contemptuous

sprofon'dare *vi* to sink; (*casa*) to collapse; (*suolo*) to give way, subside

spro'nare *vt* to spur (on)

sproporzio'nato, -a [sproportsjo'nato] *ag* disproportionate, out of all proportion

sproporzi'one [spropor'tsjone] *sf* disproportion

spro'posito *sm* blunder; **a ~** at the wrong time; (*rispondere, parlare*) irrelevantly

sprovve'duto, -a *ag* inexperienced, naïve

sprov'visto, -a *ag* (*mancante*): **~ di** lacking in, without; **alla sprovvista** unawares

spruz'zare [sprut'tsare] *vt* (*a nebulizzazione*) to spray; (*aspergere*) to sprinkle; (*inzaccherare*) to splash

'spugna ['spuɲɲa] *sf* (*Zool*) sponge; (*tessuto*) towelling

'spuma *sf* (*schiuma*) foam; (*bibita*) fizzy drink

spu'mante *sm* sparkling wine

spun'tare *vt* (*coltello*) to break the point of; (*capelli*) to trim ▷ *vi* (*uscire: germogli*) to sprout; (*: capelli*) to begin to grow; (*: denti*) to come through; (*apparire*) to appear (suddenly)

spun'tino *sm* snack

'spunto *sm* (*Teatro, Mus*) cuè; (*fig*) starting point; **dare lo ~ a** (*fig*) to give rise to

spu'tare *vt* to spit out; (*fig*) to belch (out) ▷ *vi* to spit

'squadra *sf* (*strumento*) (set) square; (*gruppo*) team, squad; (*di operai*) gang, squad; (*Mil*) squad; (*: Aer, Naut*) squadron; (*Sport*) team; **lavoro a squadre** teamwork

squagli'arsi [skwaʎ'ʎarsi] *vpr* to melt; (*fig*) to sneak off

squa'lifica *sf* disqualification

squalifi'care *vt* to disqualify

'squallido, -a *ag* wretched, bleak

'squalo *sm* shark

'squama *sf* scale

squarcia'gola [skwartʃa'gola]: **a ~** *av* at the top of one's voice

squattri'nato, -a *ag* penniless

squili'brato, -a *ag* (*Psic*) unbalanced

squil'lante *ag* shrill, sharp

squil'lare *vi* (*campanello, telefono*) to ring (out); (*tromba*) to blare; **'squillo** *sm* ring, ringing *no pl*; blare; **ragazza *f* squillo** *inv* call girl

squi'sito, -a *ag* exquisite; (*cibo*) delicious; (*persona*) delightful

squit'tire *vi* (*uccello*) to squawk; (*topo*) to squeak

sradi'care *vt* to uproot; (*fig*) to eradicate

srego'lato, -a *ag* (*senza ordine: vita*) disorderly; (*smodato*) immoderate; (*dissoluto*) dissolute

S.r.l. *abbr* = **società a responsabilità limitata**

sroto'lare *vt*, **sroto'larsi** ▷ *vpr* to unroll

SS *sigla* = **strada statale**

S.S.N. *abbr* (= *Servizio Sanitario Nazionale*) ≈ NHS

sta *ecc vb vedi* **stare**

'stabile *ag* stable, steady; (*tempo: non variabile*) settled; (*Teatro: compagnia*) resident ▷ *sm* (*edificio*) building

stabili'mento *sm* (*edificio*) establishment; (*fabbrica*) plant, factory

stabi'lire *vt* to establish; (*fissare: prezzi, data*) to fix; (*decidere*) to decide; **stabilirsi** *vpr* (*prendere dimora*) to settle

stac'care *vt* (*levare*) to detach, remove; (*separare: anche fig*) to separate, divide; (*strappare*) to tear off (*o* out); (*scandire: parole*) to pronounce clearly; (*Sport*) to leave behind; **staccarsi** *vpr* (*bottone ecc*) to come off; (*scostarsi*): **staccarsi (da)**

to move away (from); (fig: separarsi): **staccarsi da** to leave; **non ~ gli occhi da qn** not to take one's eyes off sb

'**stadio** sm (Sport) stadium; (periodo, fase) phase, stage

'**staffa** sf (di sella, Tecn) stirrup; **perdere le staffe** (fig) to fly off the handle

staf'**fetta** sf (messo) dispatch rider; (Sport) relay race

stagio'**nale** [stadʒo'nale] ag seasonal

stagio'**nato, -a** [stadʒo'nato] ag (vedi vb) seasoned; matured; (scherzoso: attempato) getting on in years

stagi'**one** [sta'dʒone] sf season; **alta/ bassa ~** high/low season

sta'**gista, -i, -e** [sta'd[gh]ista] sm/f trainee, intern (Us)

'**stagno, -a** ['stanɲo] ag watertight; (a tenuta d'aria) airtight ▷ sm (acquitrino) pond; (Chim) tin

sta'**gnola** [staɲ'ɲola] sf tinfoil

'**stalla** sf (per bovini) cowshed; (per cavalli) stable

stal'**lone** sm stallion

stamat'**tina** av this morning

stam'**becco, -chi** sm ibex

'**stampa** sf (Tip, Fot: tecnica) printing; (impressione, copia fotografica) print; (insieme di quotidiani, giornalisti ecc) press

stam'**pante** sf (Inform) printer

stam'**pare** vt to print; (pubblicare) to publish; (coniare) to strike, coin; (imprimere: anche fig) to impress

stampa'**tello** sm block letters pl

stam'**pella** sf crutch

'**stampo** sm mould; (fig: indole) type, kind, sort

sta'**nare** vt to drive out

stan'**care** vt to tire, make tired; (annoiare) to bore; (infastidire) to annoy; **stancarsi** vpr to get tired, tire o.s. out; **stancarsi (di)** to grow weary (of), grow tired (of)

stan'**chezza** [stan'kettsa] sf tiredness, fatigue

'**stanco, -a, -chi, -che** ag tired; **~ di** tired of, fed up with

stan'**ghetta** [stan'getta] sf (di occhiali) leg; (Mus, di scrittura) bar

'**stanno** vb vedi **stare**

sta'**notte** av tonight; (notte passata) last night

'**stante** prep a sé **~** (appartamento, casa) independent, separate

stan'**tio, -a, -'tii, -'tie** ag stale; (burro) rancid; (fig) old

stan'**tuffo** sm piston

'**stanza** ['stantsa] sf room; (Poesia) stanza; **stanza da bagno** bathroom; **stanza da letto** bedroom

stap'**pare** vt to uncork; to uncap

'**stare** vi (restare in un luogo) to stay, remain; (abitare) to stay, live; (essere situato) to be, be situated; (anche: **~ in piedi**) to be, stand; (essere, trovarsi) to be; (dipendere): **se stesse in me** if it were up to me, if it depended on me; (seguito da gerundio): **sta studiando** he's studying; **starci** (esserci spazio): **nel baule non ci sta più niente** there's no more room in the boot; (accettare) to accept; **ci stai?** is that okay with you?; **~ a** (attenersi a) to follow, stick to; (seguito dall'infinito): **stiamo a discutere** we're talking; (toccare a): **sta a te giocare** it's your turn to play; **~ per fare qc** to be about to do sth; **come sta?** how are you?; **io sto bene/male** I'm very well/not very well; **~ a qn** (abiti ecc) to fit sb; **queste scarpe mi stanno strette** these shoes are tight for me; **il rosso ti sta bene** red suits you

starnu'**tire** vi to sneeze; **star'nuto** sm sneeze

sta'**sera** av this evening, tonight

sta'**tale** ag state cpd; government cpd ▷ sm/f state employee, local authority employee; (nell'amministrazione) ≈ civil servant; **strada statale** ≈ trunk (Brit) o main road

sta'**tista, -i** sm statesman

sta'**tistica** sf statistics sg

'**stato, -a** pp di **essere; stare** ▷ sm (condizione) state, condition; (Pol) state; (Dir) status; **essere in ~ d'accusa** (Dir) to be committed for trial; **~ d'assedio/ d'emergenza** state of siege/emergency; **~ civile** (Amm) marital status; **gli Stati Uniti (d'America)** the United States (of America); **stato d'animo** mood; **stato maggiore** (Mil) staff

'**statua** sf statue

statuni'**tense** ag United States cpd, of the United States

sta'**tura** sf (Anat) height, stature; (fig) stature

sta'**tuto** sm (Dir) statute; constitution

sta'**volta** av this time

stazio'**nario, -a** [stattsjo'narjo] ag stationary; (fig) unchanged

stazi'**one** [stat'tsjone] sf station; (balneare, termale) resort; **stazione degli autobus** bus station; **stazione balneare** seaside resort; **stazione ferroviaria** railway (Brit) o railroad (Us) station; **stazione invernale** winter sports resort; **stazione di polizia** police station (in small town); **stazione di servizio** service o petrol (Brit) o filling station

'**stecca, -che** sf stick; (di ombrello) rib; (di sigarette) carton; (Med) splint; (stonatura):

fare una ~ to sing (o play) a wrong note
stec'cato sm fence
'**stella** sf star; **stella alpina**(Bot) edelweiss; **stella cadente**shooting star; **stella di mare**(Zool) starfish
'**stelo** sm stem; (asta) rod; **lampada a ~** standard lamp
'**stemma, -i** sm coat of arms
'**stemmo** vb vedi **stare**
stempi'ato, -a ag with a receding hairline
sten'dere vt (braccia, gambe) to stretch (out); (tovaglia) to spread (out); (bucato) to hang out; (mettere a giacere) to lay (down); (spalmare: colore) to spread; (mettere per iscritto) to draw up; **stendersi** vpr (coricarsi) to stretch out, lie down; (estendersi) to extend, stretch
stenogra'fia sf shorthand
sten'tare vi **~ a fare** to find it hard to do, have difficulty doing
'**stento** sm (fatica) difficulty; **stenti** smpl (privazioni) hardship sg, privation sg; **a ~** with difficulty, barely
'**sterco** sm dung
stereo['stereo] ag inv stereo ▷ sm inv (impianto) stereo
'**sterile** ag sterile; (terra) barren; (fig) futile, fruitless
steriliz'zare[sterilid'dzare] vt to sterilize
ster'lina sf pound (sterling)
stermi'nare vt to exterminate, wipe out
stermi'nato, -a ag immense; endless
ster'minio sm extermination, destruction
'**sterno** sm (Anat) breastbone
ste'roide sm steroid
ster'zare[ster'tsare] vt, vi (Aut) to steer; '**sterzo** sm steering; (volante) steering wheel
'**stessi** ecc vb vedi **stare**
'**stesso, -a** ag same; (rafforzativo: in persona, proprio): **il re ~** the king himself o in person ▷ pron **lo(la) ~(a)** the same (one); **i suoi stessi avversari lo ammirano** even his enemies admire him; **fa lo ~** it doesn't matter; **per me è lo ~** it's all the same to me, it doesn't matter to me; vedi **io**; **tu** ecc
ste'sura sf drafting no pl, drawing up no pl; draft
'**stetti** ecc vb vedi **stare**
'**stia** ecc vb vedi **stare**
sti'lare vt to draw up, draft
'**stile** sm style; **stile libero**freestyle; **sti'lista, -i** sm designer
stilo'grafica, -che sf (anche: **penna ~**) fountain pen
'**stima** sf esteem; valuation; assessment, estimate
sti'mare vt (persona) to esteem, hold in high regard; (terreno, casa ecc) to value;

(stabilire in misura approssimativa) to estimate, assess; (ritenere): **~ che** to consider that; **stimarsi fortunato** to consider o.s. (to be) lucky
stimo'lare vt to stimulate; (incitare): **~ qn (a fare)** to spur sb on (to do)
'**stimolo** sm (anche fig) stimulus
'**stingere**['stindʒere] vt, vi (anche: **stingersi**) to fade; '**stinto, -a** pp di **stingere**
sti'pare vt to cram, pack; **stiparsi** vpr (accalcarsi) to crowd, throng
sti'pendio sm salary
'**stipite** sm (di porta, finestra) jamb
stipu'lare vt (redigere) to draw up
sti'rare vt (abito) to iron; (distendere) to stretch; (strappare: muscolo) to strain; **stirarsi** vpr to stretch (o.s.)
stiti'chezza[stiti'kettsa] sf constipation
'**stitico, -a, -ci, -che** ag constipated
'**stiva** sf (di nave) hold
sti'vale sm boot
'**stizza**['stittsa] sf anger, vexation
'**stoffa** sf material, fabric; (fig): **aver la ~ di** to have the makings of
'**stomaco, -chi** sm stomach; **dare di ~** to vomit, be sick
sto'nato, -a ag (persona) off-key; (strumento) off-key, out of tune
stop sm inv (Tel) stop; (Aut: cartello) stop sign; (: fanalino d'arresto) brake-light
storcere['stortʃere] vt to twist; **storcersi** vpr to writhe, twist; **~ il naso** (fig) to turn up one's nose; **storcersi la caviglia** to twist one's ankle
stor'dire vt (intontire) to stun, daze; **stor'dito, -a** ag stunned
'**storia** sf (scienza, avvenimenti) history; (racconto, bugia) story; (faccenda, questione) business no pl; (pretesto) excuse, pretext; **storie** sfpl (smancerie) fuss sg; '**storico, -a, -ci, -che** ag historic(al) ▷ sm historian
stori'one sm (Zool) sturgeon
'**stormo** sm (di uccelli) flock
'**storpio, -a** ag crippled, maimed
'**storsi** ecc vb vedi **storcere**
'**storta** sf (distorsione) sprain, twist
'**storto, -a** pp di **storcere** ▷ ag (chiodo) twisted, bent; (gamba, quadro) crooked
sto'viglie[sto'viʎʎe] sfpl dishes pl, crockery
'**strabico, -a, -ci, -che** ag squint-eyed; (occhi) squint
strac'chino[strak'kino] sm type of soft cheese
stracci'are[strat'tʃare] vt to tear; **stracciarsi** vpr to tear
'**straccio, -a, -ci, -ce**[strat'tʃo] ag **carta straccia** waste paper ▷ sm rag; (per pulire)

cloth, duster; **stracci** smpl (peg: indumenti) rags; **si è ridotto a uno ~** he's worn himself out; **non ha uno ~ di lavoro** he's not got a job of any sort

'**strada** sf road; (di città) street; (cammino, via, fig) way; **che ~ devo prendere per andare a ...?** which road do I take for ...?; **farsi ~** (fig) to do well for o.s.; **essere fuori ~** (fig) to be on the wrong track; **~ facendo** on the way; **strada senza uscita** dead end; **stra'dale** ag road cpd

strafalci'one [strafal'tʃone] sm blunder, howler

stra'fare vi to overdo it

strafot'tente ag **è ~** he doesn't give a damn, he couldn't care less

'strage ['stradʒe] sf massacre, slaughter

stralu'nato, -a ag (occhi) rolling; (persona) beside o.s., very upset

'strambo, -a ag strange, queer

strampa'lato, -a ag odd, eccentric

stra'nezza [stra'nettsa] sf strangeness

strango'lare vt to strangle

strani'ero, -a ag foreign ▷ sm/f foreigner

Attenzione! In inglese esiste la parola stranger, che però significa sconosciuto oppure estraneo.

'strano, -a ag strange, odd

straordi'nario, -a ag extraordinary; (treno ecc) special ▷ sm (lavoro) overtime

strapi'ombo sm overhanging rock; **a ~** overhanging

strap'pare vt (gen) to tear, rip; (pagina ecc) to tear off, tear out; (sradicare) to pull up; (togliere): **~ qc a qn** to snatch sth from sb; (fig) to wrest sth from sb; **strapparsi** vpr (lacerarsi) to rip, tear; (rompersi) to break; **strapparsi un muscolo** to tear a muscle; '**strappo** sm pull, tug; tear, rip; **fare uno strappo alla regola** to make an exception to the rule; **strappo muscolare** torn muscle

strari'pare vi to overflow

'strascico, -chi ['straʃʃiko] sm (di abito) train; (conseguenza) after-effect

strata'gemma, -i [strata'dʒemma] sm stratagem

strate'gia, -'gie [strate'dʒia] sf strategy; **stra'tegico, -a, -ci, -che** ag strategic

'strato sm layer; (rivestimento) coat, coating; (Geo, fig) stratum; (Meteor) stratus; **strato d'ozono** ozone layer

strat'tone sm tug, jerk; **dare uno ~ a qc** to tug o jerk sth, give sth a tug o jerk

strava'gante ag odd, eccentric

stra'volto, -a pp di stravolgere

'strazio ['stratsjo] sm torture; (fig: cosa fatta male): **essere uno ~** to be appalling

'strega, -ghe sf witch

stre'gare vt to bewitch

stre'gone sm (mago) wizard; (di tribù) witch doctor

strepi'toso, -a ag clamorous, deafening; (fig: successo) resounding

stres'sante ag stressful

stres'sato, -a ag under stress

stretch [stretʃ] ag inv stretch

'stretta sf (di mano) grasp; (finanziaria) squeeze; (fig: dolore, turbamento) pang; **una ~ di mano** a handshake; **essere alle strette** to have one's back to the wall; vedi anche **stretto**

stretta'mente av tightly; (rigorosamente) strictly

'stretto, -a pp di stringere ▷ ag (corridoio, limiti) narrow; (gonna, scarpe, nodo, curva) tight; (intimo: parente, amico) close; (rigoroso: osservanza) strict; (preciso: significato) precise, exact ▷ sm (braccio di mare) strait; **a denti stretti** with clenched teeth; **lo ~ necessario** the bare minimum; **stret'toia** sf bottleneck; (fig) tricky situation

stri'ato, -a ag streaked

'stridulo, -a ag shrill

stril'lare vt, vi to scream, shriek; '**strillo** sm scream, shriek

strimin'zito, -a [strimin'tsito] ag (misero) shabby; (molto magro) skinny

strimpel'lare vt (Mus) to strum

'stringa, -ghe sf lace

strin'gato, -a ag (fig) concise

'stringere ['strindʒere] vt (avvicinare due cose) to press (together), squeeze (together); (tenere stretto) to hold tight, clasp, clutch; (pugno, mascella, denti) to clench; (labbra) to compress; (avvitare) to tighten; (abito) to take in; (scarpe) to pinch, be tight for; (fig: concludere: patto) to make; (: accelerare: passo, tempo) to quicken ▷ vi (essere stretto) to be tight; (tempo: incalzare) to be pressing

'strinsi ecc vb vedi **stringere**

'striscia, -sce ['striʃʃa] sf (di carta, tessuto ecc) strip; (riga) stripe; **strisce (pedonali)** zebra crossing sg

strisci'are [striʃʃare] vt (piedi) to drag; (muro, macchina) to graze ▷ vi to crawl, creep

'striscio ['striʃʃo] sm graze; (Med) smear; **colpire di ~** to graze

strisci'one [striʃ'ʃone] sm banner

strito'lare vt to grind

striz'zare [strit'tsare] vt (panni) to wring (out); **~ l'occhio** to wink

'strofa sf strophe

strofi'naccio [strofi'nattʃo] sm duster, cloth; (per piatti) dishcloth; (per pavimenti)

floorcloth

strofi'nare vt to rub

stron'care vt to break off; (fig: ribellione) to suppress, put down; (: film, libro) to tear to pieces

'stronzo ['strontso] sm (sterco) turd; (fig fam!: persona) shit (!)

stroz'zare [strot'tsare] vt (soffocare) to choke, strangle

struccarsi vpr to remove one's make-up

strumen'tale ag (Mus) instrumental

strumentaliz'zare [strumentalid'dzare] vt to exploit, use to one's own ends

stru'mento sm (arnese, fig) instrument, tool; (Mus) instrument; ~ **a corda** o **ad arco/a fiato** stringed/wind instrument

'strutto sm lard

strut'tura sf structure

'struzzo ['struttso] sm ostrich

stuc'care vt (muro) to plaster; (vetro) to putty; (decorare con stucchi) to stucco

'stucco, -chi sm plaster; (da vetri) putty; (ornamentale) stucco; **rimanere di ~** (fig) to be dumbfounded

stu'dente, -'essa sm/f student; (scolaro) pupil, schoolboy/girl

studi'are vt to study

'studio sm studying; (ricerca, saggio, stanza) study; (di professionista) office; (di artista, Cinema, TV, Radio) studio; **studi** smpl (Ins) studies; **studio medico** doctor's surgery (BRIT) o office (US)

studi'oso, -a ag studious, hard-working ▷ sm/f scholar

'stufa sf stove; **stufa elettrica** electric fire o heater

stu'fare vt (Cuc) to stew; (fig: fam) to bore; **stufarsi** vpr (fam): **stufarsi (di)** (fig) to get fed up (with); **stufo, -a** (fam) ag **essere stufo di** to be fed up with, be sick and tired of

stu'oia sf mat

stupefa'cente [stupefa'tʃɛnte] ag stunning, astounding ▷ sm drug, narcotic

stupe'fatto, -a pp di **stupefare**

stu'pendo, -a ag marvellous, wonderful

stupi'daggine [stupi'daddʒine] sf stupid thing (to do o say)

stupidità sf stupidity

'stupido, -a ag stupid

stu'pire vt to amaze, stun ▷ vi **stupirsi; ~ (di)** to be amazed (at), be stunned (by)

stu'pore sm amazement, astonishment

stu'prare vt to rape

'stupro sm rape

stu'rare vt (lavandino) to clear

stuzzica'denti [stuttsika'dɛnti] sm toothpick

stuzzi'care [stuttsi'kare] vt (ferita ecc)

to poke (at), prod (at); (fig) to tease; (: appetito) to whet; (: curiosità) to stimulate; **~ i denti** to pick one's teeth

 PAROLA CHIAVE

su (su +il = **sul**, su +lo = **sullo**, su +l' = **sull'**, su +la = **sulla**, su +i = **sui**, su +gli = **sugli**, su +le = **sulle**) prep **1** (gen) on; (moto) on(to); (in cima a) on (top of); **mettilo sul tavolo** put it on the table; **un paesino sul mare** a village by the sea

2 (argomento) about, on; **un libro su Cesare** a book on o about Caesar

3 (circa) about; **costerà sui 3 milioni** it will cost about 3 million; **una ragazza sui 17 anni** a girl of about 17 (years of age)

4: su misura made to measure; **su richiesta** on request; **3 casi su dieci** 3 cases out of 10

▷ av **1** (in alto, verso l'alto) up; **vieni su** come on up; **guarda su** look up; **su le mani!** hands up!; **in su** (verso l'alto) up(wards); (in poi) onwards; **dai 20 anni in su** from the age of 20 onwards

2 (addosso) on; **cos'hai su?** what have you got on?

▷ escl come on!; **su coraggio!** come on, cheer up!

su'bacqueo, -a ag underwater ▷ sm skin-diver

sub'buglio [sub'buʎʎo] sm confusion, turmoil

'subdolo, -a ag underhand, sneaky

suben'trare vi: **~ a qn in qc** to take over sth from sb

su'bire vt to suffer, endure

'subito av immediately, at once, straight away

subodo'rare vt (insidia ecc) to smell, suspect

subordi'nato, -a ag subordinate; (dipendente): **~ a** dependent on, subject to

suc'cedere [sut'tʃɛdere] vi (prendere il posto di qn): **~ a** to succeed; (venire dopo): **~ a** to follow; (accadere) to happen; **cos'è successo?** what happened?; **succes'sivo, -a** ag successive; **suc'cesso, -a** pp di **succedere** ▷ sm (esito) outcome; (buona riuscita) success; **di successo** (libro, personaggio) successful

succhi'are [suk'kjare] vt to suck (up); **succhi'otto** sm (per bambino) dummy

succhi'otto [suk'kjɔtto] sm dummy (BRIT), pacifier (US), comforter (US)

suc'cinto, -a [sut'tʃinto] ag (discorso) succinct; (abito) brief

'succo, -chi sm juice; (fig) essence, gist;

succo di frutta/pomodoro fruit/tomato juice

succur'sale sf branch (office)

sud sm south ▷ ag inv south; (lato) south, southern

Su'dafrica sm **il ~** South Africa; **sudafri'cano, -a** ag, sm/f South African

Suda'merica sm **il ~** South America

su'dare vi to perspire, sweat; **~ freddo** to come out in a cold sweat

su'dato, -a ag (persona, mani) sweaty; (fig: denaro) hard-earned ▷ sf (anche fig) sweat; **una vittoria sudata** a hard-won victory; **ho fatto una bella sudata per finirlo in tempo** it was a real sweat to get it finished in time

suddi'videre vt to subdivide

su'dest sm south-east

'sudicio, -a, -ci, -ce ['suditʃo] ag dirty, filthy

su'dore sm perspiration, sweat

su'dovest sm south-west

suffici'ente [suffi'tʃɛnte] ag enough, sufficient; (borioso) self-important; (Ins) satisfactory; **suffici'enza** sf self-importance; pass mark; **a sufficienza** enough; **ne ho avuto a sufficienza!** I've had enough of this!

suf'fisso sm (Ling) suffix

suggeri'mento [suddʒeri'mento] sm suggestion; (consiglio) piece of advice, advice no pl

sugge'rire [suddʒe'rire] vt (risposta) to tell; (consigliare) to advise; (proporre) to suggest; (Teatro) to prompt

suggestio'nare [suddʒestjo'nare] vt to influence

sugges'tivo, -a [suddʒes'tivo] ag (paesaggio) evocative; (teoria) interesting, attractive

'sughero ['sugero] sm cork

'sugo, -ghi sm (succo) juice; (di carne) gravy; (condimento) sauce; (fig) gist, essence

sui'cida, -i, -e [sui'tʃida] ag suicidal ▷ sm/f suicide

suici'darsi [suitʃi'darsi] vpr to commit suicide

sui'cidio [sui'tʃidjo] sm suicide

su'ino, -a ag **carne suina** pork ▷ sm pig

sul'tano, -a sm/f sultan/sultana

'suo (f **'sua**, pl **'sue, su'oi**) det **il ~, la sua** ecc (di lui) his; (di lei) her; (di esso) its; (con valore indefinito) one's, his/her; (anche: **S~**: forma di cortesia) your ▷ pron **il ~, la sua** ecc his; hers; yours; **i ~i** his (o her o one's o your) family

su'ocero, -a ['swɔtʃero] sm/f father/mother-in-law

su'ola sf (di scarpa) sole

su'olo sm (terreno) ground; (terra) soil

suo'nare vt (Mus) to play; (campana) to ring; (ore) to strike; (clacson, allarme) to sound ▷ vi to play; (telefono, campana) to ring; (ore) to strike; (clacson, fig: parole) to sound

suone'ria sf alarm

su'ono sm sound

su'ora sf (Rel) sister

'super sf (anche: **benzina ~**) ≈ four-star (petrol) (BRIT), premium (US)

supe'rare vt (oltrepassare: limite) to exceed, surpass; (percorrere) to cover; (attraversare: fiume) to cross; (sorpassare: veicolo) to overtake; (fig: essere più bravo di) to surpass, outdo; (: difficoltà) to overcome; (: esame) to get through; **~ qn in altezza/peso** to be taller/heavier than sb; **ha superato la cinquantina** he's over fifty (years of age)

su'perbia sf pride; **su'perbo, -a** ag proud; (fig) magnificent, superb

superfici'ale [superfi'tʃale] ag superficial

super'ficie, -ci [super'fitʃe] sf surface

su'perfluo, -a ag superfluous

superi'ore ag (piano, arto, classi) upper; (più elevato: temperatura, livello) **~ (a)** higher (than); (migliore): **~ (a)** superior (to)

superla'tivo, -a ag, sm superlative

supermer'cato sm supermarket

su'perstite ag surviving ▷ sm/f survivor

superstizi'one [superstit'tsjone] sf superstition; **superstizi'oso, -a** ag superstitious

super'strada sf ≈ (toll-free) motorway

su'pino, -a ag supine

supplemen'tare ag extra; (treno) relief cpd; (entrate) additional

supple'mento sm supplement

sup'plente sm/f temporary member of staff, supply (o substitute) teacher

'supplica, -che sf (preghiera) plea; (domanda scritta) petition, request

suppli'care vt to implore, beseech

sup'plizio [sup'plittsjo] sm torture

sup'pongo, sup'poni ecc vb vedi **suppore**

sup'porre vt to suppose

sup'porto sm (sostegno) support

sup'posta sf (Med) suppository

su'premo, -a ag supreme

surge'lare [surdʒe'lare] vt to (deep-)freeze

surge'lato, -a [surdʒe'lato] ag (deep-)frozen ▷ smpl **i surgelati** frozen food sg

sur'plus sm inv (Econ) surplus

surriscal'dare vt to overheat

suscet'tibile [suʃʃet'tibile] ag (sensibile) touchy, sensitive

susci'tare [suʃʃi'tare] vt to provoke,

arouse

su'sina sf plum

susseguirsi vpr to follow one another

sus'sidio sm subsidy; **sussidi didattici** teaching aids

sussul'tare vi to shudder

sussur'rare vt, vi to whisper, murmur; **sus'surro** sm whisper, murmur

svagarsi vpr to amuse o.s.; to enjoy o.s.

'svago, -ghi sm (riposo) relaxation; (ricreazione) amusement; (passatempo) pastime

svaligi'are [zvali'dʒare] vt to rob, burgle (BRIT), burglarize (US)

svalu'tarsi vpr (Econ) to be devalued

svalutazi'one sf devaluation

sva'nire vi to disappear, vanish

svantaggi'ato, -a [zvantad'dʒato] ag at a disadvantage

svan'taggio [zvan'taddʒo] sm disadvantage; (inconveniente) drawback, disadvantage

svari'ato, -a ag varied; various

'svastica sf swastika

sve'dese ag Swedish ▷ sm/f Swede ▷ sm (Ling) Swedish

'sveglia ['zveʎʎa] sf waking up; (orologio) alarm (clock); **sveglia telefonica** alarm call

svegli'are [zveʎ'ʎare] vt to wake up; (fig) to awaken, arouse; **svegliarsi** vpr to wake up; (fig) to be revived, reawaken; **vorrei essere svegliato alle 7, per favore** could I have an alarm call at 7 am, please?

'sveglio, -a ['zveʎʎo] ag awake; (fig) quick-witted

sve'lare vt to reveal

'svelto, -a ag (passo) quick; (mente) quick, alert; **alla svelta** quickly

'svendere vt to sell off, clear

'svendita sf (Comm) (clearance) sale

'svengo ecc vb vedi **svenire**

sveni'mento sm fainting fit, faint

sve'nire vi to faint

sven'tare vt to foil, thwart

sven'tato, -a ag (distratto) scatterbrained; (imprudente) rash

svento'lare vt, vi to wave, flutter

sven'tura sf misfortune

sverrò ecc vb vedi **svenire**

sves'tire vt to undress; **svestirsi** vpr to get undressed

'Svezia ['zvettsja] sf **la ~** Sweden

svi'are vt to divert; (fig) to lead astray

svi'gnarsela [zviɲ'ɲarsela] vpr to slip away, sneak off

svilup'pare vt to develop; **svilupparsi** vpr to develop; **può ~ questo rullino?** can you develop this film?

svi'luppo sm development

'svincolo sm (stradale) motorway (BRIT) o expressway (US) intersection

'svista sf oversight

svi'tare vt to unscrew

'Svizzera ['zvittsera] sf **la ~** Switzerland

'svizzero, -a ['zvittsero] ag, sm/f Swiss

svogli'ato, -a [zvoʎ'ʎato] ag listless; (pigro) lazy

'svolgere ['zvɔldʒere] vt to unwind; (srotolare) to unroll; (fig: argomento) to develop; (: piano, programma) to carry out; **svolgersi** vpr to unwind; to unroll; (fig: aver luogo) to take place; (: procedere) to go on

'svolsi ecc vb vedi **svolgere**

'svolta sf (atto) turning no pl; (curva) turn, bend; (fig) turning-point

svol'tare vi to turn

svuo'tare vt to empty (out)

T, t [ti] *sf o m inv (lettera)* T, t; **T come Taranto** ≈ T for Tommy

t *abbr* = **tonnellata**

tabacche'ria [tabakke'ria] *sf* tobacconist's (shop)

ta'bacco, -chi *sm* tobacco

ta'bella *sf (tavola)* table; *(elenco)* list

tabel'lone *sm (pubblicitario)* billboard; *(con orario)* timetable board

TAC *sigla f (Med: = Tomografia Assiale Computerizzata)* CAT

tac'chino [tak'kino] *sm* turkey

'tacco, -chi *sm* heel; **tacchi a spillo** stiletto heels

taccu'ino *sm* notebook

ta'cere [ta'tʃere] *vi* to be silent o quiet; *(smettere di parlare)* to fall silent ▷ *vt* to keep to oneself, say nothing about; **far ~ qn** to make sb be quiet; *(fig)* to silence sb

ta'chimetro [ta'kimetro] *sm* speedometer

'tacqui *ecc vb vedi* **tacere**

ta'fano *sm* horsefly

'taglia ['taʎʎa] *sf (statura)* height; *(misura)* size; *(riscatto)* ransom; *(ricompensa)* reward; **taglia forte** *(di abito)* large size

taglia'carte [taʎʎa'karte] *sm inv* paperknife

tagli'ando [taʎ'ʎando] *sm* coupon

tagli'are [taʎ'ʎare] *vt* to cut; *(recidere, interrompere)* to cut off; *(intersecare)* to cut across, intersect; *(carne)* to carve; *(vini)* to blend ▷ *vi* to cut; *(prendere una scorciatoia)* to take a short-cut; **tagliarsi** *vpr* to cut o.s.; **mi sono tagliato** I've cut myself; **~ corto** *(fig)* to cut short; **~ la corda** *(fig)* to sneak off; **~ i ponti (con)** *(fig)* to break off relations (with); **~ la strada a qn** to cut across sb; **mi sono tagliato** I've cut myself

taglia'telle [taʎʎa'tɛlle] *sfpl* tagliatelle *pl*

taglia'unghie [taʎʎa'ungje] *sm inv* nail clippers *pl*

tagli'ente [taʎ'ʎɛnte] *ag* sharp

'taglio ['taʎʎo] *sm* cutting *no pl*; cut; *(parte tagliente)* cutting edge; *(di abito)* cut, style; *(di stoffa: lunghezza)* length; *(di vini)* blending; **di ~** on edge, edgeways; **banconote di piccolo/grosso ~** notes of small/large denomination; **taglio cesareo** Caesarean section

tailan'dese *ag, sm/f, sm* Thai

Tai'landia *sf* **la ~** Thailand

'talco *sm* talcum powder

 PAROLA CHIAVE

'tale *det* **1** *(simile, così grande)* such; **un(a) tale …** such (a) …; **non accetto tali discorsi** I won't allow such talk; **è di una tale arroganza** he is so arrogant; **fa una tale confusione!** he makes such a mess! **2** *(persona o cosa indeterminata)* such-and-such; **il giorno tale all'ora tale** on such-and-such a day at such-and-such a time; **la tal persona** that person; **ha telefonato una tale Giovanna** somebody called Giovanna phoned

3 *(nelle similitudini)*: **tale … tale** like … like; **tale padre tale figlio** like father, like son; **hai il vestito tale quale il mio** your dress is just o exactly like mine

▷ *pron (indefinito: persona)*: **un(a) tale** someone; **quel (o quella) tale** that person, that man (o woman); **il tal dei tali** what's-his-name

tale'bano *sm* Taliban

ta'lento *sm* talent

talis'mano *sm* talisman

tallon'cino [tallon'tʃino] *sm* counterfoil

tal'lone *sm* heel

tal'mente *av* so

'talpa *sf* (*Zool*) mole

tal'volta *av* sometimes, at times

tambu'rello *sm* tambourine

tam'buro *sm* drum

Ta'migi [ta'midʒi] *sm* **il ~** the Thames

tampo'nare *vt* (*otturare*) to plug; (*urtare: macchina*) to crash o ram into

tam'pone *sm* (*Med*) wad, pad; (*per timbri*) ink-pad; (*respingente*) buffer; **tampone assorbente** tampon

'tana *sf* lair, den

'tanga *sm inv* G-string

tan'gente [tan'dʒɛnte] *ag* (*Mat*): **~ a** tangential to ▷ *sf* tangent; (*quota*) share

tangenzi'ale [tandʒen'tsjale] *sf* (*Aut*) bypass

'tanica *sf* (*contenitore*) jerry can

⊙ **PAROLA CHIAVE**

'tanto, -a *det* **1** (*molto: quantità*) a lot of, much; (*: numero*) a lot of, many; (*così tanto: quantità*) so much, such a lot of; (*: numero*) so many, such a lot of; **tante volte** so many times, so often; **tanti auguri!** all the best!; **tante grazie** many thanks; **tanto tempo** so long, such a long time; **ogni tanti chilometri** every so many kilometres

2: **tanto ... quanto** (*quantità*) as much ... as; (*numero*) as many ... as; **ho tanta pazienza quanta ne hai tu** I have as much patience as you have o as you; **ha tanti amici quanti nemici** he has as many friends as he has enemies

3 (*rafforzativo*) such; **ho aspettato per tanto tempo** I waited so long o for such a long time

▷ *pron* **1** (*molto*) much, a lot; (*così tanto*) so much, such a lot; **tanti, e** many, a lot; so many, such a lot; **credevo ce ne fosse tanto** I thought there was (such) a lot, I thought there was plenty

2: **tanto quanto** (*denaro*) as much as; (*cioccolatini*) as many as; **ne ho tanto quanto basta** I have as much as I need; **due volte tanto** twice as much

3 (*indeterminato*) so much; **tanto per l'affitto, tanto per il gas** so much for the rent, so much for the gas; **costa un tanto al metro** it costs so much per metre; **di tanto in tanto, ogni tanto** every so often; **tanto vale che ...** I (o we ecc) may as well ...; **tanto meglio!** so much the better!; **tanto peggio per lui!** so much the worse for him!

▷ *av* **1** (*molto*) very; **vengo tanto volentieri** I'd be very glad to come; **non ci vuole tanto a capirlo** it doesn't take much to understand it

2 (*così tanto: con ag, av*) so; (*: con vb*) so much, such a lot; **è tanto bella!** she's so beautiful!; **non urlare tanto** don't shout so much; **sto tanto meglio adesso** I'm so much better now; **tanto ... che** so ... (that); **tanto ... da** so ... as

3: **tanto ... quanto** as ... as; **conosco tanto Carlo quanto suo padre** I know both Carlo and his father; **non è poi tanto complicato quanto sembri** it's not as difficult as it seems; **tanto più insisti, tanto più non mollerà** the more you insist, the more stubborn he'll be; **quanto più ... tanto meno** the more ... the less

4 (*solamente*) just; **tanto per cambiare/ scherzare** just for a change/a joke; **una volta tanto** for once

5 (*a lungo*) (for) long

▷ *cong* after all

'tappa *sf* (*luogo di sosta, fermata*) stop, halt; (*parte di un percorso*) stage, leg; (*Sport*) lap; **a tappe** in stages

tap'pare *vt* to plug, stop up; (*bottiglia*) to cork; **tapparsi** *vpr* **tapparsi in casa** to shut o.s. up at home; **tapparsi la bocca** to shut up; **tapparsi le orecchie** to turn a deaf ear

tappa'rella *sf* rolling shutter

tappe'tino *sm* (*per auto*) car mat; **tappetino antiscivolo** (*da bagno*) non-slip mat

tap'peto *sm* carpet; (*anche*: **tappetino**) rug; (*Sport*): **andare al ~** to go down for the count; **mettere sul ~** (*fig*) to bring up for discussion

tappez'zare [tappet'tsare] *vt* (*con carta*) to paper; (*rivestire*): **~ qc (di)** to cover sth (with); **tappezze'ria** *sf* (*tessuto*) tapestry; (*carta da parati*) wallpaper; (*arte*) upholstery; **far da tappezzeria** (*fig*) to be a wallflower

'tappo *sm* stopper; (*in sughero*) cork

tar'dare *vi* to be late ▷ *vt* to delay; **~ a fare** to delay doing

'tardi *av* late; **più ~** later (on); **al più ~** at the latest; **sul ~** (*verso sera*) late in the day; **far ~** to be late; (*restare alzato*) to stay up late; **è troppo ~** it's too late

'targa, -ghe *sf* plate; (*Aut*) number (BRIT) o license (US) plate; **tar'ghetta** *sf* (*su bagaglio*) name tag; (*su porta*) nameplate

ta'riffa *sf* (*gen*) rate, tariff; (*di trasporti*) fare; (*elenco*) price list; tariff

'tarlo *sm* woodworm

'**tarma** sf moth

tarocchi smpl (gioco) tarot sg

tarta'ruga, -ghe sf tortoise; (di mare) turtle; (materiale) tortoiseshell

tar'tina sf canapé

tar'tufo sm (Bot) truffle

'**tasca, -sche** sf pocket; **tas'cabile** ag (libro) pocket cpd

'**tassa** sf (imposta) tax; (doganale) duty; (per iscrizione: a scuola ecc) fee; **tassa di circolazione** road tax; **tassa di soggiorno** tourist tax

tas'sare vt to tax; to levy a duty on

tas'sello sm plug; wedge

tassì sm inv = **taxi**; **tas'sista, -i, -e** sm/f taxi driver

'**tasso** sm (di natalità, d'interesse ecc) rate; (Bot) yew; (Zool) badger; **tasso di cambio/d'interesse** rate of exchange/interest

tas'tare vt to feel; ~ **il terreno** (fig) to see how the land lies

tasti'era sf keyboard

'**tasto** sm key; (tatto) touch, feel

tas'toni av **procedere (a)** ~ to grope one's way forward

'**tatto** sm (senso) touch; (fig) tact; **duro al** ~ hard to the touch; **aver** ~ to be tactful, have tact

tatu'aggio [tatu'addʒo] sm tattooing; (disegno) tattoo

tatu'are vt to tattoo

'**tavola** sf table; (asse) plank, board; (lastra) tablet; (quadro) panel (painting); (illustrazione) plate; **tavola calda** snack bar; **tavola rotonda** (fig) round table; **tavola a vela** windsurfer

tavo'letta sf tablet, bar; **a** ~ (Aut) flat out

tavo'lino sm small table; (scrivania) desk

'**tavolo** sm table; **un** ~ **per 4 per favore** a table for 4, please

'**taxi** sm inv taxi; **può chiamarmi un** ~ **per favore?** can you call me a taxi, please?

'**tazza** ['tattsa] sf cup; **una** ~ **di caffè/tè** a cup of coffee/tea; **tazza da tè/caffè** tea/coffee cup

TBC abbr f (= tubercolosi) TB

te pron (soggetto: in forme comparative, oggetto) you

tè sm inv tea; (trattenimento) tea party

tea'trale ag theatrical

te'atro sm theatre

techno ['tɛkno] ag inv (musica) techno

'**tecnica, -che** sf technique; (tecnologia) technology

'**tecnico, -a, -ci, -che** ag technical ▷ sm/f technician

tecnolo'gia [teknolo'dʒia] sf technology

te'desco, -a, -schi, -sche ag, sm/f, sm German

te'game sm (Cuc) pan

'**tegola** sf tile

tei'era sf teapot

tel. abbr (= telefono) tel.

'**tela** sf (tessuto) cloth; (per vele, quadri) canvas; (dipinto) canvas, painting; **di** ~ (calzoni) (heavy) cotton cpd; (scarpe, borsa) canvas cpd; **tela cerata** oilcloth

te'laio sm (apparecchio) loom; (struttura) frame

tele'camera sf television camera

teleco'mando sm remote control

tele'cronaca sf television report

telefo'nare vi to telephone, ring; to make a phone call ▷ vt to telephone; ~ **a** to phone up, ring up, call up

telefo'nata sf (telephone) call; ~ **a carico del destinatario** reverse charge (BRIT) o collect (US) call

tele'fonico, -a, -ci, -che ag (tele)phone cpd

telefon'ino sm mobile phone

te'lefono sm telephone; **telefono a gettoni** ≈ pay phone

telegior'nale [teledʒor'nale] sm television news (programme)

tele'gramma, -i sm telegram

tele'lavoro sm teleworking

Tele'pass® sm inv automatic payment card for use on Italian motorways

telepa'tia sf telepathy

teles'copio sm telescope

teleselezi'one [teleselet'sjone] sf direct dialling

telespetta'tore, -'trice sm/f (television) viewer

tele'vendita sf teleshopping

televisi'one sf television

televi'sore sm television set

'**tema, -i** sm theme; (Ins) essay, composition

te'mere vt to fear, be afraid of; (essere sensibile a: freddo, calore) to be sensitive to ▷ vi to be afraid; (essere preoccupato): ~ **per** to worry about, fear for; ~ **di/che** to be afraid of/that

temperama'tite sm inv pencil sharpener

tempera'mento sm temperament

tempera'tura sf temperature

tempe'rino sm penknife

tem'pesta sf storm; **tempesta di sabbia/neve** sand/snowstorm

'**tempia** sf (Anat) temple

'**tempio** sm (edificio) temple

'**tempo** sm (Meteor) weather; (cronologico) time; (epoca) time, times pl; (di film, gioco: parte) part; (Mus) time; (: battuta) beat; (Ling) tense; **che** ~ **fa?** what's the weather like?; **un** ~ once; ~ **fa** some time ago; **al** ~

stesso o **a un ~** at the same time; **per ~** early; **ha fatto il suo ~ it** it has had its day; **primo/secondo ~** (*Teatro*) first/second part; (*Sport*) first/second half; **in ~ utile** in due time o course; **a ~ pieno** full-time; **tempo libero** free time

tempo'rale ag temporal ▷ sm (*Meteor*) (thunder)storm

tempo'raneo, -a ag temporary

te'nace [te'natʃe] ag strong, tough; (*fig*) tenacious

te'naglie [te'naʎʎe] sfpl pincers pl

'tenda sf (*riparo*) awning; (*di finestra*) curtain; (*per campeggio ecc*) tent

ten'denza [ten'dɛntsa] sf tendency; (*orientamento*) trend; **avere ~ a** o **per qc** to have a bent for sth

'tendere vt (*allungare al massimo*) to stretch, draw tight; (*porgere: mano*) to hold out; (*fig: trappola*) to lay, set ▷ vi **~ a qc/a fare** to tend towards sth/to do; **~ l'orecchio** to prick up one's ears; **il tempo tende al caldo** the weather is getting hot; **un blu che tende al verde** a greenish blue

'tendine sm tendon, sinew

ten'done sm (*da circo*) tent

'tenebre sfpl darkness sg

te'nente sm lieutenant

te'nere vt to hold; (*conservare, mantenere*) to keep; (*ritenere, considerare*) to consider; (*spazio: occupare*) to take up, occupy; (*seguire: strada*) to keep to ▷ vi to hold; (*colori*) to be fast; (*dare importanza*): **~ a** to care about; **~ a fare** to want to do, be keen to do; **tenersi** vpr (*stare in una determinata posizione*) to stand; (*stimarsi*) to consider o.s.; (*aggrapparsi*): **tenersi a** to hold on to; (*attenersi*): **tenersi a** to stick to; **~ una conferenza** to give a lecture; **~ conto di qc** to take sth into consideration; **~ presente qc** to bear sth in mind

'tenero, -a ag tender; (*pietra, cera, colore*) soft; (*fig*) tender, loving

'tengo ecc vb vedi **tenere**

'tenni ecc vb vedi **tenere**

'tennis sm tennis

ten'nista, -i, e sm/f tennis player

te'nore sm (*tono*) tone; (*Mus*) tenor; **tenore di vita** (*livello*) standard of living

tensi'one sf tension

ten'tare vt (*indurre*) to tempt; (*provare*): **~ qc/di fare** to attempt o try sth/to do; **tenta'tivo** sm attempt; **tentazi'one** sf temptation

tenten'nare vi to shake, be unsteady; (*fig*) to hesitate, waver

ten'toni av **andare a ~** (*anche fig*) to grope one's way

'tenue ag (*sottile*) fine; (*colore*) soft; (*fig*)

slender, slight

te'nuta sf (*capacità*) capacity; (*divisa*) uniform; (*abito*) dress; (*Agr*) estate; **a ~ d'aria** airtight; **tenuta di strada** roadholding power

teolo'gia [teolo'dʒia] sf theology

teo'ria sf theory

te'pore sm warmth

tep'pista, -i sm hooligan

tera'pia sf therapy; **terapia intensiva** intensive care

tergicris'tallo [terdʒikris'tallo] sm windscreen (*BRIT*) o windshield (*US*) wiper

tergiver'sare [terdʒiver'sare] vi to shilly-shally

ter'male ag thermal; **stazione** sf **~** spa

'terme sfpl thermal baths

termi'nale ag, sm terminal

termi'nare vt to end; (*lavoro*) to finish ▷ vi to end

'termine sm term; (*fine, estremità*) end; (*di territorio*) boundary, limit; **contratto a ~** (*Comm*) forward contract; **a breve/lungo ~** short-/long-term; **parlare senza mezzi termini** to talk frankly, not to mince one's words

ter'mometro sm thermometer

'termos sm inv = **thermos®**

termosi'fone sm radiator

ter'mostato sm thermostat

'terra sf (*gen, Elettr*) earth; (*sostanza*) soil, earth; (*opposto al mare*) land no pl; (*regione, paese*) land; (*argilla*) clay; **terre** sfpl (*possedimento*) lands, land sg; **a** o **per ~** (*stato*) on the ground (o floor); (*moto*) to the ground, down; **mettere a ~** (*Elettr*) to earth

terra'cotta sf terracotta; **vasellame** sm **di ~** earthenware

terra'ferma sf dry land, terra firma; (*continente*) mainland

ter'razza [ter'rattsa] sf terrace

ter'razzo [ter'rattso] sm = **terrazza**

terre'moto sm earthquake

ter'reno, -a ag (*vita, beni*) earthly ▷ sm (*suolo, fig*) ground; (*Comm*) land no pl, plot (of land); site; (*Sport, Mil*) field

ter'restre ag (*superficie*) of the earth, earth's; (*di terra: battaglia, animale*) land cpd; (*Rel*) earthly, worldly

ter'ribile ag terrible, dreadful

terrifi'cante ag terrifying

ter'rina sf tureen

territori'ale ag territorial

terri'torio sm territory

ter'rore sm terror; **terro'rismo** sm terrorism; **terro'rista, -i, e** sm/f terrorist

terroriz'zare [terrorid'dzare] vt to terrorize

terza ['tɛrtsa] sf (Scol: elementare) ≈ third year at primary school; (: media) ≈ second year at secondary school; (: superiore) ≈ fifth year at secondary school; (Aut) third gear

ter'zino [ter'tsino] sm (Calcio) fullback, back

'terzo, -a ['tɛrtso] ag third ▷ sm (frazione) third; (Dir) third party; **terza pagina** (Stampa) Arts page; **terzi** smpl (altri) others, other people

'teschio ['tɛskjo] sm skull

'tesi[1] sf thesis; **tesi di laurea** degree thesis

'tesi[2] ecc vb vedi **tendere**

'teso, -a pp di **tendere** ▷ ag (tirato) taut, tight; (fig) tense

te'soro sm treasure; **il Ministero del T~** the Treasury

'tessera sf (documento) card

tes'suto sm fabric, material; (Biol) tissue

test ['tɛst] sm inv test

'testa sf head; (di cose: estremità, parte anteriore) head, front; **di ~** (vettura ecc) front; **tenere ~ a qn** (nemico ecc) to stand up to sb; **fare di ~ propria** to go one's own way; **in ~** (Sport) in the lead; **~ o croce?** heads or tails?; **avere la ~ dura** to be stubborn; **testa d'aglio** bulb of garlic; **testa di serie** (Tennis) seed, seeded player

testa'mento sm (atto) will; **l'Antico/il Nuovo T~** (Rel) the Old/New Testament

tes'tardo, -a ag stubborn, pig-headed

tes'tata sf (parte anteriore) head; (intestazione) heading

tes'ticolo sm testicle

testi'mone sm/f (Dir) witness; **testimone oculare** eye witness

testimoni'are vt to testify; (fig) to bear witness to, testify to ▷ vi to give evidence, testify

'testo sm text; **fare ~** (opera, autore) to be authoritative; **questo libro non fa ~** this book is not essential reading

tes'tuggine [tes'tuddʒine] sf tortoise; (di mare) turtle

'tetano sm (Med) tetanus

'tetto sm roof; **tet'toia** sf roofing; canopy

tettuccio [tet'tuttʃo] sm **~ apribile** (Aut) sunroof

'Tevere sm **il ~** the Tiber

TG, Tg abbr = **telegiornale**

'thermos® ['tɛrmos] sm inv vacuum o Thermos® flask

ti pron (dav lo, la, li, le, ne diventa **te**) ▷ pron (oggetto) you; (complemento di termine) (to) you; (riflessivo) yourself

'Tibet sm **il ~** Tibet

'tibia sf tibia, shinbone

tic sm inv tic, (nervous) twitch; (fig) mannerism

ticchet'tio [tikket'tio] sm (di macchina da scrivere) clatter; (di orologio) ticking; (della pioggia) patter

'ticket sm inv (su farmaci) prescription charge

ti'ene ecc vb vedi **tenere**

ti'epido, -a ag lukewarm, tepid

'tifo sm (Med) typhus; (fig): **fare il ~ per** to be a fan of

ti'fone sm typhoon

ti'foso, -a sm/f (Sport ecc) fan

tigi [ti'dʒi] sm inv TV news

'tiglio ['tiʎʎo] sm lime (tree), linden (tree)

'tigre sf tiger

tim'brare vt to stamp; (annullare: francobolli) to postmark; **~ il cartellino** to clock in

'timbro sm stamp; (Mus) timbre, tone

'timido, -a ag shy; timid

'timo sm thyme

ti'mone sm (Naut) rudder

ti'more sm (paura) fear; (rispetto) awe

'timpano sm (Anat) eardrum; (Mus)

'tingere ['tindʒere] vt to dye

'tinsi ecc vb vedi **tingere**

'tinta sf (materia colorante) dye; (colore) colour, shade

tintin'nare vi to tinkle

tinto'ria sf (lavasecco) dry cleaner's (shop)

tin'tura sf (operazione) dyeing; (colorante) dye; **tintura di iodio** tincture of iodine

'tipico, -a, -ci, -che ag typical

'tipo sm type; (genere) kind, type; (fam) chap, fellow; **che ~ di...?** what kind of ...?

tipogra'fia sf typography; (procedimento) letterpress (printing); (officina) printing house

TIR sigla m (= Transports Internationaux Routiers) International Heavy Goods Vehicle

ti'rare vt (gen) to pull; (estrarre): **~ qc da** to take o pull sth out of; to get sth out of; to extract sth from; (chiudere: tenda ecc) to draw, pull; (tracciare, disegnare) to draw, trace; (lanciare: sasso, palla) to throw; (stampare) to print; (pistola, freccia) to fire ▷ vi (pipa, camino) to draw; (vento) to blow; (abito) to be tight; (fare fuoco) to fire; (fare del tiro, Calcio) to shoot; **~ avanti** vi to struggle on ▷ vt to keep going; **~ fuori** (estrarre) to take out, pull out; **~ giù** (abbassare) to bring down, to lower; (da scaffale ecc.) to take down; **~ su** to pull up; (capelli) to put up; (fig: bambino) to bring up; **tirarsi** vpr **tirarsi indietro** to draw back; (fig) to back out; **~ a indovinare** to take a guess; **~ sul prezzo** to bargain; **tirar dritto** to keep right on going; **tirati su!** (fig) cheer up!; **~ via** (togliere) to take off

tira'tura sf (azione) printing; (di libro) (print) run; (di giornale) circulation

'tirchio, -a ['tirkjo] ag mean, stingy

'tiro sm shooting no pl, firing no pl; (colpo, sparo) shot; (di palla: lancio) throwing no pl; throw; (fig) trick; **cavallo da ~** draught (BRIT) o draft (US) horse; **tiro a segno** target shooting; (luogo) shooting range; **tiro con l'arco** archery

tiro'cinio [tiro'tʃinjo] sm apprenticeship; (professionale) training

ti'roide sf thyroid (gland)

Tir'reno sm **il (mar) ~** the Tyrrhenian Sea

ti'sana sf herb tea

tito'lare sm/f incumbent; (proprietario) owner; (Calcio) regular player

'titolo sm title; (di giornale) headline; (diploma) qualification; (Comm) security; (: azione) share; **a che ~?** for what reason?; **a ~ di amicizia** out of friendship; **a ~ di premio** as a prize; **titolo di credito** share; **titoli di stato** government securities; **titoli di testa** (Cinema) credits

titu'bante ag hesitant, irresolute

toast [toust] sm inv toasted sandwich (generally with ham and cheese)

toc'cante ag touching

toc'care vt to touch; (tastare) to feel; (fig: riguardare) to concern; (: commuovere) to touch, move; (: pungere) to hurt, wound; (: far cenno a: argomento) to touch on, mention ▷ vi **~ a** (accadere) to happen to; (spettare) to be up to; **~ (il fondo)** (in acqua) to touch the bottom; **tocca a te difenderci** it's up to you to defend us; **a chi tocca?** whose turn is it?; **mi toccò pagare** I had to pay

toccherò ecc [tokke'rɔ] vb vedi **toccare**

'togliere ['tɔʎʎere] vt (rimuovere) to take away (o off), remove; (riprendere, non concedere più) to take away, remove; (Mat) to take away, subtract; **~ qc a qn** to take sth (away) from sb; **ciò non toglie che** nevertheless, be that as it may; **togliersi il cappello** to take off one's hat

toi'lette [twa'lɛt] sf inv toilet; (mobile) dressing table; **dov'è la ~?** where's the toilet?

'Tokyo sf Tokyo

'tolgo ecc vb vedi **togliere**

tolle'rare vt to tolerate

'tolsi ecc vb vedi **togliere**

'tomba sf tomb

tom'bino sm manhole cover

'tombola sf (gioco) tombola; (ruzzolone) tumble

'tondo, -a ag round

'tonfo sm splash; (rumore sordo) thud; (caduta): **fare un ~** to take a tumble

tonifi'care vt (muscoli, pelle) to tone up; (irrobustire) to invigorate, brace

tonnel'lata sf ton

'tonno sm tuna (fish)

'tono sm (gen) tone; (Mus: di pezzo) key; (di colore) shade, tone

ton'silla sf tonsil

'tonto, -a ag dull, stupid

to'pazio [to'pattsjo] sm topaz

'topo sm mouse

'toppa sf (serratura) keyhole; (pezza) patch

to'race [to'ratʃe] sm chest

'torba sf peat

'torcere ['tɔrtʃere] vt to twist; **torcersi** vpr to twist, writhe

'torcia, -ce ['tɔrtʃa] sf torch; **torcia elettrica** torch (BRIT), flashlight (US)

torci'collo [tortʃi'kɔllo] sm stiff neck

'tordo sm thrush

To'rino sf Turin

tor'menta sf snowstorm

tormen'tare vt to torment; **tormentarsi** vpr to fret, worry o.s.

tor'nado sm tornado

tor'nante sm hairpin bend

tor'nare vi to return, go (o come) back; (ridiventare: anche fig) to become (again); (riuscire giusto, esatto: conto) to work out; (risultare) to turn out (to be), prove (to be); **~ utile** to prove o turn out (to be) useful; **~ a casa** to go (o come) home; **torno a casa martedì** I'm going home on Tuesday

tor'neo sm tournament

'tornio sm lathe

'toro sm bull; (dello zodiaco): **T~** Taurus

'torre sf tower; (Scacchi) rook, castle; **torre di controllo** (Aer) control tower

tor'rente sm torrent

torri'one sm keep

tor'rone sm nougat

'torsi ecc vb vedi **torcere**

torsi'one sf twisting; torsion

'torso sm torso, trunk; (Arte) torso

'torsolo sm (di cavolo ecc) stump; (di frutta) core

'torta sf cake

tortel'lini smpl (Cuc) tortellini

'torto, -a pp di **torcere** ▷ ag (ritorto) twisted; (storto) twisted, crooked ▷ sm (ingiustizia) wrong; (colpa) fault; **a ~** wrongly; **aver ~** to be wrong

tor'tora sf turtle dove

tor'tura sf torture; **tortu'rare** vt to torture

to'sare vt (pecora) to shear; (siepe) to clip

Tos'cana sf **la ~** Tuscany

'tosse sf cough; **ho la ~** I've got a cough

'tossico, -a, -ci, -che ag toxic

tossicodipen'dente sm/f drug addict

tos'sire vi to cough

tosta'pane sm inv toaster

to'tale ag, sm total

toto'calcio [toto'kaltʃo] sm gambling pool betting on football results, ≈ (football) pools pl (BRIT)

to'vaglia [to'vaʎʎa] sf tablecloth; **tovagli'olo** sm napkin

tra prep (di due persone, cose) between; (di più persone, cose) among(st); (tempo: entro) within, in; **~ 5 giorni** in 5 days' time; **sia detto ~ noi ...** between you and me ...; **litigano ~ (di) loro** they're fighting amongst themselves; **~ breve** soon; **~ sé e sé** (parlare ecc) to oneself

traboc'care vi to overflow

traboc'chetto [trabok'ketto] sm (fig) trap

'traccia, -ce ['trattʃa] sf (segno, striscia) trail, track; (orma) tracks pl; (residuo, testimonianza) trace, sign; (abbozzo) outline

tracci'are [trat'tʃare] vt to trace, mark (out); (disegnare) to draw; (fig: abbozzare) to outline

tra'chea [tra'kɛa] sf windpipe, trachea

tra'colla sf shoulder strap; **borsa a ~** shoulder bag

tradi'mento sm betrayal; (Dir, Mil) treason

tra'dire vt to betray; (coniuge) to be unfaithful to; (doveri: mancare) to fail in; (rivelare) to give away, reveal; **tradirsi** vpr to give o.s. away

tradizio'nale [tradittsjo'nale] ag traditional

tradizi'one [tradit'tsjone] sf tradition

tra'durre vt to translate; (spiegare) to render, convey; **me lo può ~?** can you translate this for me?; **traduzi'one** sf translation

'trae vb vedi **trarre**

traffi'cante sm/f dealer; (peg) trafficker

traffi'care vi (commerciare): **~ (in)** to trade (in), deal (in); (affaccendarsi) to busy o.s. ▷ vt (peg) to traffic in

'traffico, -ci sm traffic; (commercio) trade, traffic; **traffico di armi/droga** arms/drug trafficking

tra'gedia [tra'dʒedja] sf tragedy

'traggo ecc vb vedi **trarre**

tra'ghetto [tra'getto] sm ferry(boat)

'tragico, -a, -ci, -che ['tradʒiko] ag tragic

tra'gitto [tra'dʒitto] sm (passaggio) crossing; (viaggio) journey

tragu'ardo sm (Sport) finishing line; (fig) goal, aim

'trai ecc vb vedi **trarre**

traiet'toria sf trajectory

trai'nare vt to drag, haul; (rimorchiare) to tow

tralasci'are [tralaʃ'ʃare] vt (studi) to neglect; (dettagli) to leave out, omit

tra'liccio [tra'littʃo] sm (Elettr) pylon

tram sm inv tram

'trama sf (filo) weft, woof; (fig: argomento, maneggio) plot

traman'dare vt to pass on, hand down

tram'busto sm turmoil

tramez'zino [tramed'dzino] sm sandwich

'tramite prep through

tramon'tare vi to set, go down; **tra'monto** sm setting; (del sole) sunset

trampo'lino sm (per tuffi) springboard, diving board; (per lo sci) ski-jump

tra'nello sm trap

'tranne prep except (for), but (for); **~ che** unless

tranquil'lante sm (Med) tranquillizer

tranquillità sf calm, stillness; quietness; peace of mind

tranquilliz'zare [trankwillid'dzare] vt to reassure

> Attenzione! In inglese esiste il verbo to tranquillize, che però significa "calmare con un tranquillante".

tran'quillo, -a ag calm, quiet; (bambino, scolaro) quiet; (sereno) with one's mind at rest; **sta' ~** don't worry

transazi'one [transat'tsjone] sf compromise; (Dir) settlement; (Comm) transaction, deal

tran'senna sf barrier

transgenico, -a, -ci, -che [trans'dʒeniko] ag genetically modified

tran'sigere [tran'sidʒere] vi (venire a patti) to compromise, come to an agreement

transi'tabile ag passable

transi'tare vi to pass

transi'tivo, -a ag transitive

'transito sm transit; **di ~ (merci)** in transit; (stazione) transit cpd; **"divieto di ~"** "no entry"

'trapano sm (utensile) drill; (Med) trepan

trape'lare vi to leak, ooze; (fig) to leak out

tra'pezio [tra'pɛttsjo] sm (Mat) trapezium; (attrezzo ginnico) trapeze

trapian'tare vt to transplant; **trapi'anto** sm transplanting; (Med) transplant; **trapianto cardiaco** heart transplant

'trappola sf trap

tra'punta sf quilt

'trarre vt to draw, pull; (portare) to take; (prendere, tirare fuori) to take (out), draw; (derivare) to obtain; **~ origine da qc** to have its origins o originate in sth

trasa'lire vi to start, jump

trasan'dato, -a ag shabby

trasci'nare [traʃʃi'nare] vt to drag; **trascinarsi** vpr to drag o.s. along; (fig) to drag on

tras'correre vt (tempo) to spend, pass ▷ vi to pass

tras'crivere vt to transcribe

trascu'rare vt to neglect; (non considerare) to disregard

trasferi'mento sm transfer; (trasloco) removal, move; **trasferimento di chiamata** (Tel) call forwarding

trasfe'rire vt to transfer; **trasferirsi** vpr to move; **tras'ferta** sf transfer; (indennità) travelling expenses pl; (Sport) away game

trasfor'mare vt to transform, change; **trasformarsi** vpr to be transformed; **trasformarsi in qc** to turn into sth; **trasforma'tore** sm (Elec) transformer

trasfusi'one sf (Med) transfusion

trasgre'dire vt to disobey, contravene

traslo'care vt to move, transfer; **tras'loco, -chi** sm removal

tras'mettere vt (passare): **~ qc a qn** to pass sth on to sb; (mandare) to send; (Tecn, Tel, Med) to transmit; (TV, Radio) to broadcast; **trasmissi'one** sf (gen, Fisica, Tecn) transmission; (passaggio) transmission, passing on; (TV, Radio) broadcast

traspa'rente ag transparent

traspor'tare vt to carry, move; (merce) to transport, convey; **lasciarsi ~ (da qc)** (fig) to let o.s. be carried away (by sth); **tras'porto** sm transport

'trassi ecc vb vedi **trarre**

trasver'sale ag transverse, cross(-); running at right angles

'tratta sf (Econ) draft; (di persone): **la ~ delle bianche** the white slave trade

tratta'mento sm treatment; (servizio) service

trat'tare vt (gen) to treat; (commerciare) to deal in; (svolgere: argomento) to discuss, deal with; (negoziare) to negotiate ▷ vi **~ di** to deal with; **~ con** (persona) to deal with; **si tratta di ...** it's about ...

tratte'nere vt (far rimanere: persona) to detain; (intrattenere: ospiti) to entertain; (tenere, frenare, reprimere) to hold back, keep back; (astenersi dal consegnare) to hold, keep; (detrarre: somma) to deduct; **trattenersi** vpr (astenersi) to restrain o.s., stop o.s.; (soffermarsi) to stay, remain

trat'tino sm dash; (in parole composte) hyphen

'tratto, -a pp di **trarre** ▷ sm (di penna, matita) stroke; (parte) part, piece; (di strada) stretch; (di mare, cielo) expanse; (di tempo) period (of time)

trat'tore sm tractor

tratto'ria sf restaurant

'trauma, -i sm trauma

tra'vaglio [tra'vaʎʎo] sm (angoscia) pain, suffering; (Med) pains pl

trava'sare vt to decant

tra'versa sf (trave) crosspiece; (via) side street; (Ferr) sleeper (BRIT), (railroad) tie (US); (Calcio) crossbar

traver'sata sf crossing; (Aer) flight, trip; **quanto dura la ~?** how long does the crossing take?

traver'sie sfpl mishaps, misfortunes

tra'verso, -a ag oblique; **di ~** ag askew ▷ av sideways; **andare di ~** (cibo) to go down the wrong way; **guardare di ~** to look askance at

travesti'mento sm disguise

travestirsi vpr to disguise o.s.

tra'volgere [tra'vɔldʒere] vt to sweep away, carry away; (fig) to overwhelm

tre num three

'treccia, -ce ['trettʃa] sf plait, braid

tre'cento [tre'tʃɛnto] num three hundred ▷ sm **il T~** the fourteenth century

'tredici ['treditʃi] num thirteen

'tregua sf truce; (fig) respite

tre'mare vi **~ di** (freddo ecc) to shiver o tremble with; (paura, rabbia) to shake o tremble with

tre'mendo, -a ag terrible, awful

> Attenzione! In inglese esiste la parola tremendous, che però significa enorme oppure fantastico, strepitoso.

'tremito sm trembling no pl; shaking no pl; shivering no pl

'treno sm train; **è questo il ~ per...?** is this the train for ...?; **treno di gomme** set of tyres (BRIT) o tires (US); **treno merci** goods o freight train; **treno viaggiatori** passenger train

○ **TRENI**
○
○
○ There are various types of train in
○ Italy. For short journeys there are
○ the "Regionali" (R), which generally
○ operate within a particular region,
○ and the "Interregionali" (IR), which
○ operate beyond regional boundaries.
○ Medium- and long-distance passenger
○ journeys are carried out by "Intercity" (I)
○ and "Eurocity" (EC) trains. The "Eurostar"
○ service (ES) offers fast connections
○ between the major Italian cities. Night
○ services are operated by "Intercity
○ Notte" (ICN), "Euronight" (EN) and by
○ "Espressi" (EXP).

'trenta num thirty; **tren'tesimo, -a** num thirtieth; **tren'tina** sf **una trentina (di)** thirty or so, about thirty

'trepidante *ag* anxious

tri'angolo *sm* triangle

tribù *sf inv* tribe

tri'buna *sf* (*podio*) platform; (*in aule ecc*) gallery; (*di stadio*) stand

tribu'nale *sm* court

tri'ciclo [tri'tʃiklo] *sm* tricycle

tri'foglio [tri'fɔʎʎo] *sm* clover

'triglia ['triʎʎa] *sf* red mullet

tri'mestre *sm* period of three months; (*Ins*) term, quarter (*us*); (*Comm*) quarter

trin'cea [trin'tʃea] *sf* trench

trion'fare *vi* to triumph, win; **~ su** to triumph over, overcome; **tri'onfo** *sm* triumph

tripli'care *vt* to triple

'triplo, -a *ag* triple; treble ▷ *sm* **il ~ (di)** three times as much (as); **la spesa è tripla** it costs three times as much

'trippa *sf* (*Cuc*) tripe

'triste *ag* sad; (*luogo*) dreary, gloomy

tri'tare *vt* to mince, grind (*us*)

trivi'ale *ag* vulgar, low

tro'feo *sm* trophy

'tromba *sf* (*Mus*) trumpet; (*Aut*) horn; **tromba d'aria** whirlwind; **tromba delle scale** stairwell

trom'bone *sm* trombone

trom'bosi *sf* thrombosis

tron'care *vt* to cut off; (*spezzare*) to break off

'tronco, -a, -chi, -che *ag* cut off; broken off; (*Ling*) truncated; (*fig*) cut short ▷ *sm* (*Bot, Anat*) trunk; (*fig: tratto*) section; **licenziare qn in ~** to fire sb on the spot

'trono *sm* throne

tropi'cale *ag* tropical

PAROLA CHIAVE

'troppo, -a *det* (*in eccesso: quantità*) too much; (*: numero*) too many; **c'era troppa gente** there were too many people; **fa troppo caldo** it's too hot

▷ *pron* (*in eccesso: quantità*) too much; (*: numero*) too many; **ne hai messo troppo** you've put in too much; **meglio troppi che pochi** better too many than too few

▷ *av* (*eccessivamente: con ag, av*) too; (*: con vb*) too much; **troppo amaro/tardi** too bitter/late; **lavora troppo** he works too much; **costa troppo** it costs too much; **di troppo** too much; too many; **qualche tazza di troppo** a few cups too many; **2 euro di troppo** 2 euros too much; **essere di troppo** to be in the way

'trota *sf* trout

'trottola *sf* spinning top

tro'vare *vt* to find; (*giudicare*): **trovo che** I find *o* think that; **trovarsi** *vpr* (*reciproco: incontrarsi*) to meet; (*essere, stare*) to be; (*arrivare, capitare*) to find o.s.; **non trovo più il portafoglio** I can't find my wallet; **andare a ~ qn** to go and see sb; **~ qn colpevole** to find sb guilty; **trovarsi bene** (*in un luogo, con qn*) to get on well

truc'care *vt* (*falsare*) to fake; (*attore ecc*) to make up; (*travestire*) to disguise; (*Sport*) to fix; (*Aut*) to soup up; **truccarsi** *vpr* to make up (one's face)

'trucco, -chi *sm* trick; (*cosmesi*) make-up

'truffa *sf* fraud, swindle; **truf'fare** *vt* to swindle, cheat

truffa'tore, -'trice *sm/f* swindler, cheat

'truppa *sf* troop

tu *pron* you; **tu stesso(a)** you yourself; **dare del tu a qn** to address sb as "tu"

'tubo *sm* tube; pipe; **tubo digerente** (*Anat*) alimentary canal, digestive tract; **tubo di scappamento** (*Aut*) exhaust pipe

tuffarsi *vpr* to plunge, dive

'tuffo *sm* dive; (*breve bagno*) dip

tuli'pano *sm* tulip

tu'more *sm* (*Med*) tumour

Tuni'sia *sf* **la ~** Tunisia

'tuo, *pl* **'tua, tu'oi, 'tue**) *det* **il ~, la tua** *ecc* your ▷ *pron* **il ~, la tua** *ecc* yours

tuo'nare *vi* to thunder; **tuona** it is thundering, there's some thunder

tu'ono *sm* thunder

tu'orlo *sm* yolk

tur'bante *sm* turban

tur'bare *vt* to disturb, trouble

tur'bato, -a *ag* upset; (*preoccupato, ansioso*) anxious

turbo'lenza [turbo'lentsa] *sf* turbulence

tur'chese [tur'kese] *sf* turquoise

Tur'chia [tur'kia] *sf* **la ~** Turkey

'turco, -a, -chi, -che *ag* Turkish ▷ *sm/f* Turk/Turkish woman ▷ *sm* (*Ling*) Turkish; **parlare ~** (*fig*) to talk double-dutch

tu'rismo *sm* tourism; tourist industry; **tu'rista, -i, -e** *sm/f* tourist; **turismo sessuale** sex tourism; **tu'ristico, -a, -ci, -che** *ag* tourist *cpd*

'turno *sm* turn; (*di lavoro*) shift; **di ~** (*soldato, medico, custode*) on duty; **a ~** (*rispondere*) in turn; (*lavorare*) in shifts; **fare a ~ a fare qc** to take turns to do sth; **è il suo ~** it's your (*o* his *ecc* turn)

'turpe *ag* filthy, vile

'tuta *sf* overalls *pl*; (*Sport*) tracksuit

tu'tela *sf* (*Dir: di minore*) guardianship; (*: protezione*) protection; (*difesa*) defence

tutta'via *cong* nevertheless, yet

○ **PAROLA CHIAVE**

'tutto, -a *det* **1** (*intero*) all; **tutto il latte**
all the milk; **tutta la notte** all night, the
whole night; **tutto il libro** the whole book;
tutta una bottiglia a whole bottle
2 (*pl, collettivo*) all; every; **tutti i libri** all the
books; **tutte le notti** every night; **tutti i
venerdì** every Friday; **tutti gli uomini** all
the men; (*collettivo*) all men; **tutto l'anno**
all year long; **tutti e due** both *o* each of us
(*o* them *o* you); **tutti e cinque** all five of us
(*o* them *o* you)
3 (*completamente*): **era tutta sporca**
she was all dirty; **tremava tutto** he was
trembling all over; **è tutta sua madre**
she's just *o* exactly like her mother
4: **a tutt'oggi** so far, up till now; **a tutta
velocità** at full *o* top speed
▷ *pron* **1** (*ogni cosa*) everything, all;
(*qualsiasi cosa*) anything; **ha mangiato
tutto** he's eaten everything; **tutto
considerato** all things considered; **in
tutto: 5 euro in tutto** 5 euros in all; **in
tutto eravamo 50** there were 50 of us
in all
2: **tutti, e** (*ognuno*) all, everybody;
vengono tutti they are all coming,
everybody's coming; **tutti quanti** all and
sundry
▷ *av* (*completamente*) entirely, quite; **è
tutto il contrario** it's quite *o* exactly the
opposite; **tutt'al più: saranno stati
tutt'al più una cinquantina** there were
about fifty of them at (the very) most;
tutt'al più possiamo prendere un treno
if the worst comes to the worst we can
take a train; **tutt'altro** on the contrary;
è tutt'altro che felice he's anything but
happy; **tutt'a un tratto** suddenly ▷ *sm* **il
tutto** the whole lot, all of it

tut'tora *av* still
TV [ti'vu] *sf inv* (= *televisione*) TV ▷ *sigla*
= **Treviso**

ubbidi'ente *ag* obedient
ubbi'dire *vi* to obey; **~ a** to obey; (*veicolo,
macchina*) to respond to
ubria'care *vt* **~ qn** to get sb drunk; (*alcool*)
to make sb drunk; (*fig*) to make sb's head
spin *o* reel; **ubriacarsi** *vpr* to get drunk;
ubriacarsi di (*fig*) to become intoxicated
with
ubri'aco, -a, -chi, -che *ag, sm/f* drunk
uc'cello [ut'tʃello] *sm* bird
uc'cidere [ut'tʃidere] *vt* to kill; **uccidersi**
vpr (*suicidarsi*) to kill o.s.; (*perdere la vita*) to
be killed
u'dito *sm* (sense of) hearing
UE *sigla f* (= *Unione Europea*) EU
UEM *sigla f* (= *Unione economica e monetaria*)
EMU
'uffa *escl* tut!
uffici'ale [uffi'tʃale] *ag* official ▷ *sm* (*Amm*)
official, officer; (*Mil*) officer; **~ di stato
civile** registrar
uf'ficio [uf'fitʃo] *sm* (*gen*) office; (*dovere*)
duty; (*mansione*) task, function, job;
(*agenzia*) agency, bureau; (*Rel*) service; **d'~**
ag office *cpd*; official ▷ *av* officially; **ufficio
di collocamento** employment office;
ufficio informazioni information bureau;
ufficio oggetti smarriti lost property
office (*BRIT*), lost and found (*US*); **ufficio
(del) personale** personnel department;

ufficio postale post office
uffici'oso, -a [uffi'tʃoso] *ag* unofficial
uguagli'anza [ugwaʎ'ʎantsa] *sf* equality
uguagli'are [ugwaʎ'ʎare] *vt* to make equal; (*essere uguale*) to equal, be equal to; (*livellare*) to level; **uguagliarsi a** *o* **con qn** (*paragonarsi*) to compare o.s. to sb
ugu'ale *ag* equal; (*identico*) identical, the same; (*uniforme*) level, even ▷ *av* **costano ~** they cost the same; **sono bravi ~** they're equally good
UIL *sigla f* (= Unione Italiana del Lavoro) trade union federation
'ulcera ['ultʃera] *sf* ulcer
U'livo *sm* **l'~** centre-left Italian political grouping
u'livo = **olivo**
ulteri'ore *ag* further
ultima'mente *av* lately, of late
ulti'mare *vt* to finish, complete
'ultimo, -a *ag* (*finale*) last; (*estremo*) farthest, utmost; (*recente: notizia, moda*) latest; (*fig: sommo, fondamentale*) ultimate ▷ *sm/f* last (one); **fino all'~** to the last, until the end; **da ~, in ~** in the end; **abitare all'~ piano** to live on the top floor; **per ~** (*entrare, arrivare*) last
ulu'lare *vi* to howl
umanità *sf* humanity
u'mano, -a *ag* human; (*comprensivo*) humane
umidità *sf* dampness; humidity
'umido, -a *ag* damp; (*mano, occhi*) moist; (*clima*) humid ▷ *sm* dampness, damp; **carne in ~** stew
'umile *ag* humble
umili'are *vt* to humiliate; **umiliarsi** *vpr* to humble o.s.
u'more *sm* (*disposizione d'animo*) mood; (*carattere*) temper; **di buon/cattivo ~** in a good/bad mood
umo'rismo *sm* humour; **avere il senso dell'~** to have a sense of humour; **umo'ristico, -a, -ci, -che** *ag* humorous, funny
u'nanime *ag* unanimous
unci'netto [untʃi'netto] *sm* crochet hook
un'cino [un'tʃino] *sm* hook
undi'cenne [undi'tʃɛnne] *ag, sm/f* eleven-year-old
undi'cesimo, -a [undi'tʃɛzimo] *num* eleventh
'undici ['unditʃi] *num* eleven
'ungere ['undʒere] *vt* to grease, oil; (*Rel*) to anoint; (*fig*) to flatter, butter up
unghe'rese [unge'rese] *ag, sm/f, sm* Hungarian
Unghe'ria [unge'ria] *sf* **l'~** Hungary
'unghia ['ungja] *sf* (*Anat*) nail; (*di animale*)

claw; (*di rapace*) talon; (*di cavallo*) hoof
ungu'ento *sm* ointment
'unico, -a, -ci, -che *ag* (*solo*) only; (*ineguagliabile*) unique; (*singolo: binario*) single; **figlio(a) ~(a)** only son/daughter, only child
unifi'care *vt* to unite, unify; (*sistemi*) to standardize; **unificazi'one** *sf* uniting; unification; standardization
uni'forme *ag* uniform; (*superficie*) even ▷ *sf* (*divisa*) uniform
uni'one *sf* union; (*fig: concordia*) unity, harmony; **Unione europea** European Union; **ex Unione Sovietica** former Soviet Union
u'nire *vt* to unite; (*congiungere*) to join, connect; (: *ingredienti, colori*) to combine; (*in matrimonio*) to unite, join together; **unirsi** *vpr* to unite; (*in matrimonio*) to be joined together; **~ qc a** to unite sth with; to join o connect sth with; to combine sth with; **unirsi a** (*gruppo, società*) to join
unità *sf inv* (*unione, concordia*) unity; (*Mat, Mil, Comm, di misura*) unit; **unità di misura** unit of measurement
u'nito, -a *ag* (*paese*) united; (*amici, famiglia*) close; **in tinta unita** plain, self-coloured
univer'sale *ag* universal; general
università *sf inv* university
uni'verso *sm* universe

⊙ **PAROLA CHIAVE**

'uno, -a (*dav sm* **un** + *C, V*, **uno** + *s impura, gn, pn, ps, x, z; dav sf* **un'** +*V*, **una** + *C*) *art indef* **1** a; (*dav vocale*) an; **un bambino** a child; **una strada** a street; **uno zingaro** a gypsy
2 (*intensivo*): **ho avuto una paura!** I got such a fright!
▷ *pron* **1** one; **prendine uno** take one (of them); **l'uno o l'altro** either (of them); **l'uno e l'altro** both (of them); **aiutarsi l'un l'altro** to help one another o each other; **sono entrati l'uno dopo l'altro** they came in one after the other
2 (*un tale*) someone, somebody
3 (*con valore impersonale*) one, you; **se uno vuole** if one wants, if you want
▷ *num* one; **una mela e due pere** one apple and two pears; **uno più uno fa due** one plus one equals two, one and one are two ▷ *sf* **è l'una** it's one (o'clock)

'unsi *ecc vb vedi* **ungere**
'unto, -a *pp di* **ungere** ▷ *ag* greasy, oily ▷ *sm* grease
u'omo (*pl* **u'omini**) *sm* man; **da ~** (*abito, scarpe*) men's, for men; **uomo d'affari** businessman; **uomo di paglia** stooge;

uomo politico politician; **uomo rana** frogman

u'ovo (pl(f) **u'ova**) sm egg; **uovo affogato/alla coque** poached/boiled egg; **uovo bazzotto/sodo** soft-/hard-boiled egg; **uovo di Pasqua** Easter egg; **uovo in camicia** poached egg; **uova strapazzate/al tegame** scrambled/fried eggs

ura'gano sm hurricane

urba'nistica sf town planning

ur'bano, -a ag urban, city cpd, town cpd; (Tel: chiamata) local; (fig) urbane

ur'gente [ur'dʒɛnte] ag urgent; **ur'genza** sf urgency; **in caso d'urgenza** in (case of) an emergency; **d'urgenza** ag emergency ▷ av urgently, as a matter of urgency

ur'lare vi (persona) to scream, yell; (animale, vento) to howl ▷ vt to scream, yell

'urlo (pl(m) **'urli**, pl(f) **'urla**) sm scream, yell; howl

urrà escl hurrah!

U.R.S.S. abbr f **l'U.R.S.S.** the USSR

ur'tare vt to bump into, knock against; (fig: irritare) to annoy ▷ vi **~ contro** o **in** to bump into, knock against, crash into; (fig: imbattersi) to come up against; **urtarsi** vpr (reciproco: scontrarsi) to collide; (: fig) to clash; (irritarsi) to get annoyed

'U.S.A. ['uza] smpl **gli U.S.A.** the USA

u'sanza [u'zantsa] sf custom; (moda) fashion

u'sare vt to use, employ ▷ vi (servirsi): **~ di** to use; (: diritto) to exercise; (essere di moda) to be fashionable; (essere solito): **~ fare** to be in the habit of doing, be accustomed to doing ▷ vb impers **qui usa così** it's the custom round here; **u'sato, -a** ag used; (consumato) worn; (di seconda mano) used, second-hand ▷ sm second-hand goods pl

u'scire [uʃʃire] vi (gen) to come out; (partire, andare a passeggio, a uno spettacolo ecc) to go out; (essere sorteggiato: numero) to come up; **~ da** (gen) to leave; (posto) to go (o come) out of, leave; (solco, vasca ecc) to come out of; (muro) to stick out of; (competenza ecc) to be outside; (infanzia, adolescenza) to leave behind; (famiglia nobile ecc) to come from; **~ da** o **di casa** to go out; (fig) to leave home; **~ in automobile** to go out in the car, go for a drive; **~ di strada** (Aut) to go off o leave the road

u'scita [uʃʃita] sf (passaggio, varco) exit, way out; (per divertimento) outing; (Econ: somma) expenditure; (Teatro) entrance; (fig: battuta) witty remark; **dov'è l'~?** where's the exit?; **uscita di sicurezza** emergency exit

usi'gnolo [uziɲ'ɲɔlo] sm nightingale

'uso sm (utilizzazione) use; (esercizio) practice; (abitudine) custom; **a ~ di** for (the use of); **d'~** (corrente) in use; **fuori ~** out of use; **uso esterno; per ~ esterno** for external use only

usti'one sf burn

usu'ale ag common, everyday

u'sura sf usury; (logoramento) wear (and tear)

uten'sile sm tool, implement; **utensili da cucina** kitchen utensils

u'tente sm/f user

'utero sm uterus

'utile ag useful ▷ sm (vantaggio) advantage, benefit; (Econ: profitto) profit

utiliz'zare [utilid'dzare] vt to use, make use of, utilize

'uva sf grapes pl; **uva passa** raisins pl; **uva spina** gooseberry

UVA abbr (= ultravioletto prossimo) UVA

UVB abbr (= ultravioletto remoto) UVB

v. abbr (= vedi) v
va, va' vb vedi **andare**
va'cante ag vacant
va'canza[va'kantsa] sf (riposo, ferie) holiday(s) pl (BRIT), vacation (US); (giorno di permesso) day off, holiday; **vacanze** sfpl (periodo di ferie) holidays (BRIT), vacation sg (US); **essere/andare in ~** to be/go on holiday o vacation; **sono qui in ~** I'm on holiday here; **vacanze estive** summer holiday(s) o vacation; **vacanze natalizie** Christmas holidays o vacation

> Attenzione! In inglese esiste la parola vacancy che però indica un posto vacante o una camera disponibile.

'vacca, -che sf cow
vacci'nare[vattʃi'nare] vt to vaccinate
vac'cino[vat'tʃino] sm (Med) vaccine
vacil'lare[vatʃil'lare] vi to sway, wobble; (luce) to flicker; (fig: memoria, coraggio) to be failing, falter
'vacuo, -a ag (fig) empty, vacuous
'vado ecc vb vedi **andare**
vaga'bondo, -a sm/f tramp, vagrant
va'gare vi to wander
vagherò ecc [vage'rɔ] vb vedi **vagare**
va'gina[va'dʒina] sf vagina
'vaglia['vaʎʎa] sm inv money order; **vaglia postale** postal order
vagli'are[vaʎ'ʎare] vt to sift; (fig) to weigh up
'vago, -a, -ghi, -ghe ag vague
va'gone sm (Ferr: per passeggeri) coach; (: per merci) truck, wagon; **vagone letto** sleeper, sleeping car; **vagone ristorante** dining o restaurant car
'vai vb vedi **andare**
vai'olo sm smallpox
va'langa, -ghe sf avalanche
va'lere vi (avere forza, potenza) to have influence; (essere valido) to be valid; (avere vigore, autorità) to hold, apply; (essere capace: poeta, studente) to be good, be able ▷ vt (prezzo, sforzo) to be worth; (corrispondere) to correspond to; (procurare): **~ qc a qn** to earn sb sth; **valersi di** to make use of, take advantage of; **far ~** (autorità ecc) to assert; **vale a dire** that is to say; **~ la pena** to be worth the effort o worth it
'valgo ecc vb vedi **valere**
vali'care vt to cross
'valico, -chi sm (passo) pass
'valido, -a ag valid; (rimedio) effective; (aiuto) real; (persona) worthwhile
vali'getta[vali'dʒetta] sf briefcase; **valigetta ventiquattrore** overnight bag o case
va'ligia, -gie o **ge**[va'lidʒa] sf (suit)case; **fare le valigie** to pack (up)
'valle sf valley; **a ~** (di fiume) downstream; **scendere a ~** to go downhill
va'lore sm (gen) value; (merito) merit, worth; (coraggio) valour, courage; (Comm: titolo) security; **valori** smpl (oggetti preziosi) valuables
valoriz'zare[valorid'dzare] vt (terreno) to develop; (fig) to make the most of
va'luta sf currency, money; (Banca): **~ 15 gennaio** interest to run from January 15th
valu'tare vt (casa, gioiello, fig) to value; (stabilire: peso, entrate, fig) to estimate
'valvola sf (Tecn, Anat) valve; (Elettr) fuse
'valzer['valtser] sm inv waltz
vam'pata sf (di fiamma) blaze; (di calore) blast; (: al viso) flush
vam'piro sm vampire
vanda'lismo sm vandalism
'vandalo sm vandal
vaneggi'are[vaned'dʒare] vi to rave
van'gelo[van'dʒɛlo] sm gospel
va'niglia[va'niʎʎa] sf vanilla
vanità sf vanity; (di promessa) emptiness; (di sforzo) futility; **vani'toso, -a** ag vain, conceited
'vanno vb vedi **andare**
'vano, -a ag vain ▷ sm (spazio) space; (apertura) opening; (stanza) room

van'taggio [van'taddʒo] sm advantage; **essere/portarsi in ~** (Sport) to be in/take the lead; **vantaggi'oso, -a** ag advantageous; favourable

vantarsi vpr **~ (di/di aver fatto)** to boast o brag (about/about having done)

'vanvera sf **a ~** haphazardly; **parlare a ~** to talk nonsense

va'pore sm vapour; (anche: **~ acqueo**) steam; (nave) steamer; **a ~** (turbina ecc) steam cpd; **al ~** (Cuc) steamed

va'rare vt (Naut, fig) to launch; (Dir) to pass

var'care vt to cross

'varco, -chi sm passage; **aprirsi un ~ tra la folla** to push one's way through the crowd

vare'china [vare'kina] sf bleach

vari'abile ag variable; (tempo, umore) changeable, variable ▷ sf (Mat) variable

vari'cella [vari'tʃella] sf chickenpox

vari'coso, -a ag varicose

varietà sf inv variety ▷ sm inv variety show

'vario, -a ag varied; (parecchi: col sostantivo al pl) various; (mutevole: umore) changeable

'varo sm (Naut: fig) launch; (di leggi) passing

varrò ecc vb vedi **valere**

Var'savia sf Warsaw

va'saio sm potter

'vasca, -sche sf basin; **vasca da bagno** bathtub, bath

vas'chetta [vas'ketta] sf (per gelato) tub; (per sviluppare fotografie) dish

vase'lina sf Vaseline®

'vaso sm (recipiente) pot; (: barattolo) jar; (: decorativo) vase; (Anat) vessel; **vaso da fiori** vase; (per piante) flowerpot

vas'soio sm tray

'vasto, -a ag vast, immense

Vati'cano sm **il ~** the Vatican

ve pron, av vedi **vi**

vecchi'aia [vek'kjaja] sf old age

'vecchio, -a ['vɛkkjo] ag old ▷ sm/f old man/woman; **i vecchi** the old

ve'dere vt, vi to see; **vedersi** vpr to meet, see one another; **avere a che ~ con** to have something to do with; **far ~ qc a qn** to show sb sth; **farsi ~** to show o.s.; (farsi vivo) to show one's face; **vedi di non farlo** make sure o see you don't do it; **non (ci) si vede** (è buio ecc) you can't see a thing; **non lo posso ~** (fig) I can't stand him

ve'detta sf (sentinella, posto) look-out; (Naut) patrol boat

'vedovo, -a sm/f widower/widow

vedrò ecc vb vedi **vedere**

ve'duta sf view; **vedute** sfpl (fig: opinioni) views; **di larghe** o **ampie vedute** broad-minded; **di vedute limitate** narrow-minded

vege'tale [vedʒe'tale] ag, sm vegetable

vegetari'ano, -a [vedʒeta'rjano] ag, sm/f vegetarian; **avete piatti vegetariani?** do you have any vegetarian dishes?

vegetazi'one [vedʒetat'tsjone] sf vegetation

'vegeto, -a ['vɛdʒeto] ag (pianta) thriving; (persona) strong, vigorous

'veglia ['veʎʎa] sf wakefulness; (sorveglianza) watch; (trattenimento) evening gathering; **fare la ~ a un malato** to watch over a sick person

vegli'one [veʎ'ʎone] sm ball, dance; **veglione di Capodanno** New Year's Eve party

ve'icolo sm vehicle

'vela sf (Naut: tela) sail; (Sport) sailing

ve'leno sm poison; **vele'noso, -a** ag poisonous

veli'ero sm sailing ship

vel'luto sm velvet; **velluto a coste** cord

'velo sm veil; (tessuto) voile

ve'loce [ve'lotʃe] ag fast, quick ▷ av fast, quickly; **velocità** sf speed; **a forte velocità** at high speed; **velocità di crociera** cruising speed

'vena sf (gen) vein; (filone) vein, seam; (fig: ispirazione) inspiration; (: umore) mood; **essere in ~ di qc** to be in the mood for sth

ve'nale ag (prezzo, valore) market cpd; (fig) venal; mercenary

ven'demmia sf (raccolta) grape harvest; (quantità d'uva) grape crop, grapes pl; (vino ottenuto) vintage

'vendere vt to sell; **"vendesi"** "for sale"

ven'detta sf revenge

vendicarsi vpr **~ (di)** to avenge o.s. (for); (per rancore) to take one's revenge (for); **~ su qn** to revenge o.s. on sb

'vendita sf sale; **la ~** (attività) selling; (smercio) sales pl; **in ~** on sale; **vendita all'asta** sale by auction; **vendita per telefono** telesales sg

vene'rare vt to venerate

venerdì sm inv Friday; **di** o **il ~** on Fridays; **V~ Santo** Good Friday

ve'nereo, -a ag venereal

Ve'nezia [ve'nɛttsja] sf Venice

'vengo ecc vb vedi **venire**

veni'ale ag venial

ve'nire vi to come; (riuscire: dolce, fotografia) to turn out; (come ausiliare: essere): **viene ammirato da tutti** he is admired by everyone; **~ da** to come from; **quanto viene?** how much does it cost?; **far ~** (mandare a chiamare) to send for; **~ giù** to come down; **~ meno** (svenire) to faint; **~ meno a qc** not to fulfil sth; **~ su** to come up; **~ a trovare qn** to come and see sb; **~**

via to come away

'**venni** ecc vb vedi **venire**

ven'taglio [ven'taʎʎo] sm fan

ven'tata sf gust (of wind)

ven'tenne ag **una ragazza ~** a twenty-year-old girl, a girl of twenty

ven'tesimo, -a num twentieth

'venti num twenty

venti'lare vt (stanza) to air, ventilate; (fig: idea, proposta) to air; **ventila'tore** sm ventilator, fan

ven'tina sf **una ~ (di)** around twenty, twenty or so

'vento sm wind

'ventola sf (Aut, Tecn) fan

ven'tosa sf (Zool) sucker; (di gomma) suction pad

ven'toso, -a ag windy

'ventre sm stomach

'vera sf wedding ring

vera'mente av really

ve'randa sf veranda(h)

ver'bale ag verbal ▷ sm (di riunione) minutes pl

'verbo sm (Ling) verb; (parola) word; (Rel): **il V~** the Word

'verde ag, sm green; **essere al ~** to be broke; **verde bottiglia/oliva** bottle/olive green

ver'detto sm verdict

ver'dura sf vegetables pl

'vergine ['verdʒine] sf virgin; (dello zodiaco): **V~** Virgo ▷ ag virgin; (ragazza): **essere ~** to be a virgin

ver'gogna [ver'ɡoɲɲa] sf shame; (timidezza) shyness, embarrassment; **vergo'gnarsi** vpr **vergognarsi (di)** to o feel ashamed (of); to be shy (about), be embarrassed (about); **vergo'gnoso, -a** ag ashamed; (timido) shy, embarrassed; (causa di vergogna: azione) shameful

ve'rifica, -che sf checking no pl, check

verifi'care vt (controllare) to check; (confermare) to confirm, bear out

verità sf inv truth

'verme sm worm

ver'miglio [ver'miʎʎo] sm vermilion, scarlet

ver'nice [ver'nitʃe] sf (colorazione) paint; (trasparente) varnish; (pelle) patent leather; **"~ fresca"** "wet paint"; **vernici'are** vt to paint; to varnish

'vero, -a ag (veridico: fatti, testimonianza) true; (autentico) real ▷ sm (verità) truth; (realtà) (real) life; **un ~ e proprio delinquente** a real criminal, an out-and-out criminal

vero'simile ag likely, probable

verrò ecc vb vedi **venire**

ver'ruca, -che sf wart

versa'mento sm (pagamento) payment; (deposito di denaro) deposit

ver'sante sm slopes pl, side

ver'sare vt (fare uscire: vino, farina) to pour (out); (spargere: lacrime, sangue) to shed; (rovesciare) to spill; (Econ) to pay; (: depositare) to deposit, pay in

versa'tile ag versatile

versi'one sf version; (traduzione) translation

'verso sm (di poesia) verse, line; (di animale, uccello) cry; (direzione) direction; (modo) way; (di foglio di carta) verso; (di moneta) reverse; **versi** smpl (poesia) verse sg; **non c'è ~ di persuaderlo** there's no way of persuading him, he can't be persuaded prep (in direzione di) toward(s); (nei pressi di) near, around (about); (in senso temporale) about, around; (nei confronti di) for; **~ di me** towards me; **~ sera** towards evening

'vertebra sf vertebra

verte'brale ag vertebral; **colonna ~** spinal column, spine

verti'cale ag, sf vertical

'vertice ['vertitʃe] sm summit, top; (Mat) vertex; **conferenza al ~ (Pol)** summit conference

ver'tigine [ver'tidʒine] sf dizziness no pl; dizzy spell; (Med) vertigo; **avere le vertigini** to feel dizzy

ve'scica, -che [veʃʃika] sf (Anat) bladder; (Med) blister

'vescovo sm bishop

'vespa sf wasp

ves'taglia [ves'taʎʎa] sf dressing gown

ves'tire vt (bambino, malato) to dress; (avere indosso) to have on, wear; **vestirsi** vpr to dress, get dressed; **ves'tito, -a** ag dressed ▷ sm garment; (da donna) dress; (da uomo) suit; **vestiti** smpl (indumenti) clothes; **vestito di bianco** dressed in white

veteri'nario, -a ag veterinary ▷ sm veterinary surgeon (BRIT), veterinarian (US), vet

'veto sm inv veto

ve'traio sm glassmaker; glazier

ve'trata sf glass door (o window); (di chiesa) stained glass window

ve'trato, -a ag (porta, finestra) glazed; (che contiene vetro) glass cpd ▷ sf glass door (o window); (di chiesa) stained glass window; **carta vetrata** sandpaper

ve'trina sf (di negozio) (shop) window; (armadio) display cabinet; **vetri'nista, -i, -e** sm/f window dresser

'vetro sm glass; (per finestra, porta) pane (of glass)

'vetta sf peak, summit, top

vet'tura *sf (carrozza)* carriage; *(Ferr)* carriage *(BRIT)*, car *(US)*; *(auto)* car *(BRIT)*, automobile *(US)*

vezzeggia'tivo [vettseddʒa'tivo] *sm (Ling)* term of endearment

vi *(dav lo, la, li, le, ne diventa ve)* pron *(oggetto)* you; *(complemento di termine)* (to) you; *(riflessivo)* yourselves; *(reciproco)* each other ▷ *av (li)* there; *(qui)* here; *(per questo/quel luogo)* through here/there; **vi è/sono** there is/are

'via *sf (gen)* way; *(strada)* street; *(sentiero, pista)* path, track; *(Amm: procedimento)* channels *pl* ▷ *prep (passando per)* via, by way of ▷ *av* away ▷ *escl* go away!; *(suvvia)* come on!; *(Sport)* go! ▷ *sm (Sport)* starting signal; **in ~ di guarigione** on the road to recovery; **per ~ di** *(a causa di)* because of, on account of; **in o per ~** on the way; **per ~ aerea** by air; *(lettere)* by airmail; **andare/essere ~** to go/be away; **~ ~ che** *(a mano a mano)* as; **dare il ~** *(Sport)* to give the starting signal; **dare il ~ a** *(fig)* to start; **in ~ provvisoria** provisionally; **Via lattea** *(Astr)* Milky Way; **via di mezzo** middle course; **via d'uscita** *(fig)* way out

via'dotto *sm* viaduct

viaggi'are [viad'dʒare] *vi* to travel; **viaggia'tore, -'trice** *ag* travelling ▷ *sm* traveller; *(passeggero)* passenger

vi'aggio ['vjaddʒo] *sm* travel(ling); *(tragitto)* journey, trip; **buon ~!** have a good trip!; **com'è andato il ~?** how was your journey?; **il ~ dura due ore** the journey takes two hours; **viaggio di nozze** honeymoon; **siamo in ~ di nozze** we're on honeymoon

vi'ale *sm* avenue

via'vai *sm* coming and going, bustle

vi'brare *vi* to vibrate

'vice ['vitʃe] *sm/f* deputy

vi'cenda [vi'tʃenda] *sf* event; **a ~** in turn

vice'versa [vitʃe'vɛrsa] *av* vice versa; **da Roma a Pisa e ~** from Rome to Pisa and back

vici'nanza [vitʃi'nantsa] *sf* nearness, closeness

vi'cino, -a [vi'tʃino] *ag (gen)* near; *(nello spazio)* near, nearby; *(accanto)* next; *(nel tempo)* near, close at hand ▷ *sm/f* neighbour ▷ *av* near, close; **da ~** *(guardare)* close up; *(esaminare, seguire)* closely; *(conoscere)* well, intimately; **~ a** near (to), close to; *(accanto a)* beside; **c'è una banca qui ~?** is there a bank nearby?; **~ di casa** neighbour

'vicolo *sm* alley; **vicolo cieco** blind alley

'video *sm inv (TV: schermo)* screen; **video'camera** *sf* camcorder;

videocas'setta *sf* videocassette; **videoclip** [video'klip] *sm inv* videoclip; **videogi'oco, -chi** [video'dʒɔko] *sm* video game; **videoregistra'tore** *sm* video (recorder); **videote'lefono** *sm* videophone

'vidi *ecc vb vedi* **vedere**

vie'tare *vt* to forbid; *(Amm)* to prohibit; **~ a qn di fare** to forbid sb to do; to prohibit sb from doing; **"vietato fumare/l'ingresso"** "no smoking/admittance"

vie'tato, -a *ag (vedi vb)* forbidden; prohibited; banned; **"~ fumare/l'ingresso"** "no smoking/admittance"; **~ ai minori di 14/18 anni** prohibited to children under 14/18; **"senso ~"** *(Aut)* "no entry"; **"sosta vietata"** *(Aut)* "no parking"

Viet'nam *sm* **il ~** Vietnam; **vietna'mita, -i, -e** *ag, sm/f, sm* Vietnamese *inv*

vi'gente [vi'dʒɛnte] *ag* in force

'vigile ['vidʒile] *ag* watchful ▷ *sm (anche:* **~ urbano)** policeman *(in towns)*; **vigile del fuoco** fireman

vi'gilia [vi'dʒilja] *sf (giorno antecedente)* eve; **la ~ di Natale** Christmas Eve

vigli'acco, -a, -chi, -che [viʎ'ʎakko] *ag* cowardly ▷ *sm/f* coward

vi'gneto [viɲ'ɲeto] *sm* vineyard

vi'gnetta [viɲ'ɲetta] *sf* cartoon

vi'gore *sm* vigour; *(Dir)* **essere/entrare in ~** to be in/come into force

'vile *ag (spregevole)* low, mean, base; *(codardo)* cowardly

'villa *sf* villa

vil'laggio [vil'laddʒo] *sm* village; **villaggio turistico** holiday village

vil'lano, -a *ag* rude, ill-mannered

villeggia'tura [villeddʒa'tura] *sf* holiday(s) *pl (BRIT)*, vacation *(US)*

vil'letta *sf*, **vil'lino** ▷ *sm* small house (with a garden), cottage

'vimini *smpl* **di ~** wicker

'vincere ['vintʃere] *vt (in guerra, al gioco, a una gara)* to defeat, beat; *(premio, guerra, partita)* to win; *(fig)* to overcome, conquer ▷ *vi* to win; **~ qn in bellezza** to be better-looking than sb; **vinci'tore** *sm* winner; *(Mil)* victor

vi'nicolo, -a *ag* wine *cpd*

'vino *sm* wine; **vino bianco/rosato/rosso** white/rosé/red wine; **vino da pasto** table wine

'vinsi *ecc vb vedi* **vincere**

vi'ola *sf (Bot)* violet; *(Mus)* viola ▷ *ag, sm inv (colore)* purple

vio'lare *vt (chiesa)* to desecrate, violate; *(giuramento, legge)* to violate

violen'tare *vt* to use violence on; *(donna)* to rape

vio'lento, -a *ag* violent; vio'lenza *sf* violence; violenza carnale rape

vio'letta *sf* (Bot) violet

vio'letto, -a *ag*, *sm* (colore) violet

violi'nista, -i, -e *sm/f* violinist

vio'lino *sm* violin

violon'cello [violon'tʃello] *sm* cello

vi'ottolo *sm* path, track

vip [vip] *sigla m* (= very important person) VIP

'vipera *sf* viper, adder

vi'rare *vi* (Naut, Aer) to turn; (Fot) to tone; ~ di bordo (Naut) to tack

'virgola *sf* (Ling) comma; (Mat) point; virgo'lette *sfpl* inverted commas, quotation marks

vi'rile *ag* (proprio dell'uomo) masculine; (non puerile, da uomo) manly, virile

virtù *sf inv* virtue; in o per ~ di by virtue of, by

virtu'ale *ag* virtual

'virus *sm inv* (anche Inform) virus

'viscere ['viʃʃere] *sfpl* (di animale) entrails pl; (fig) bowels pl

'vischio ['viskjo] *sm* (Bot) mistletoe; (pania) birdlime

'viscido, -a ['viʃʃido] *ag* slimy

vi'sibile *ag* visible

visibilità *sf* visibility

visi'era *sf* (di elmo) visor; (di berretto) peak

visi'one *sf* vision; prendere ~ di qc to examine sth, look sth over; prima/ seconda ~ (Cinema) first/second showing

'visita *sf* visit; (Med) visit, call; (: esame) examination; visita guidata guided tour; a che ora comincia la ~ guidata? what time does the guided tour start?; visita medica medical examination; visi'tare *vt* to visit; (Med) to visit, call on; (: esaminare) to examine; visita'tore, -'trice *sm/f* visitor

vi'sivo, -a *ag* visual

'viso *sm* face

vi'sone *sm* mink

'vispo, -a *ag* quick, lively

'vissi *ecc* *vb vedi* vivere

'vista *sf* (facoltà) (eye)sight; (fatto di vedere): la ~ di the sight of; (veduta) view; sparare a ~ to shoot on sight; in ~ in sight; perdere qn di ~ to lose sight of sb; (fig) to lose touch with sb; a ~ d'occhio as far as the eye can see; (fig) before one's very eyes; far ~ di fare to pretend to do

'visto, -a *pp di* vedere ▷ *sm* visa; ~ che seeing (that)

vis'toso, -a *ag* gaudy, garish; (ingente) considerable

visu'ale *ag* visual

'vita *sf* life; (Anat) waist; a ~ for life

vi'tale *ag* vital

vita'mina *sf* vitamin

'vite *sf* (Bot) vine; (Tecn) screw

vi'tello *sm* (Zool) calf; (carne) veal; (pelle) calfskin

'vittima *sf* victim

'vitto *sm* food; (in un albergo ecc) board; vitto e alloggio board and lodging

vit'toria *sf* victory

'viva *escl* ~ il re! long live the king!

vi'vace [vi'vatʃe] *ag* (vivo, animato) lively; (: mente) lively, sharp; (colore) bright

vi'vaio *sm* (di pesci) hatchery; (Agr) nursery

vivavoce [viva'votʃe] *sm inv* (dispositivo) loudspeaker; mettere il ~ to switch on the loudspeaker

vi'vente *ag* living, alive; i viventi the living

'vivere *vi* to live ▷ *vt* to live; (passare: brutto momento) to live through, go through; (sentire: gioie, pene di qn) to share ▷ *sm* life; (anche: modo di ~) way of life; viveri *smpl* (cibo) food sg, provisions; ~ di to live on

'vivido, -a *ag* (colore) vivid, bright

vivisezi'one [viviset'tsjone] *sf* vivisection

'vivo, -a *ag* (vivente) alive, living; (: animale) live; (fig) lively; (: colore) bright, brilliant; i vivi the living; ~ e vegeto hale and hearty; farsi ~ to show one's face; to be heard from; ritrarre dal ~ to paint from life; pungere qn nel ~ (fig) to cut sb to the quick

vivrò *ecc* *vb vedi* vivere

vizi'are [vit'tsjare] *vt* (bambino) to spoil; (corrompere moralmente) to corrupt; vizi'ato, -a *ag* spoilt; (aria, acqua) polluted

'vizio ['vittsjo] *sm* (morale) vice; (cattiva abitudine) bad habit; (imperfezione) flaw, defect; (errore) fault, mistake

V.le *abbr* = viale

vocabo'lario *sm* (dizionario) dictionary; (lessico) vocabulary

vo'cabolo *sm* word

vo'cale *ag* vocal ▷ *sf* vowel

vocazi'one [vokat'tsjone] *sf* vocation; (fig) natural bent

'voce ['votʃe] *sf* voice; (diceria) rumour; (di un elenco, in bilancio) item; aver ~ in capitolo (fig) to have a say in the matter

'voga *sf* (Naut) rowing; (usanza): essere in ~ to be in fashion o in vogue

vo'gare *vi* to row

vogherò *ecc* [voge'rɔ] *vb vedi* vogare

'voglia ['vɔʎʎa] *sf* desire, wish; (macchia) birthmark; aver ~ di qc/di fare to feel like sth/like doing; (più forte) to want sth/to do

'voglio *ecc* ['vɔʎʎo] *vb vedi* volere

'voi *pron* you; voi'altri *pron* you

vo'lante *ag* flying ▷ *sm* (steering) wheel

volan'tino *sm* leaflet

vo'lare *vi* (uccello, aereo, fig) to fly; (cappello)

to blow away o off, fly away o off; **~ via** to fly away o off

vo'latile ag (Chim) volatile ▷ sm (Zool) bird

volente'roso, -a ag willing

volenti'eri av willingly; **"~"** "with pleasure", "I'd be glad to"

 PAROLA CHIAVE

vo'lere sm will, wish(es); **contro il volere di** against the wishes of; **per volere di qn** in obedience to sb's will o wishes

▷ vt **1** (esigere, desiderare) to want; **voler fare/che qn faccia** to want to do/sb to do; **volete del caffè?** would you like o do you want some coffee?; **vorrei questo/fare** I would o I'd like this/to do; **come vuoi** as you like; **senza volere** (inavvertitamente) without meaning to, unintentionally

2 (consentire): **vogliate attendere, per piacere** please wait; **vogliamo andare?** shall we go?; **vuole essere così gentile da ...?** would you be so kind as to ...?; **non ha voluto ricevermi** he wouldn't see me

3: **volerci** (essere necessario: materiale, attenzione) to need; (: tempo) to take; **quanta farina ci vuole per questa torta?** how much flour do you need for this cake?; **ci vuole un'ora per arrivare a Venezia** it takes an hour to get to Venice

4: **voler bene a qn** (amore) to love sb; (affetto) to be fond of sb, like sb very much; **voler male a qn** to dislike sb; **volerne a qn** to bear sb a grudge; **voler dire** to mean

vol'gare ag vulgar

voli'era sf aviary

voli'tivo, -a ag strong-willed

'volli ecc vb vedi volere

'volo sm flight; **al ~: colpire qc al ~** to hit sth as it flies past; **capire al ~** to understand straight away; **volo charter** charter flight; **volo di linea** scheduled flight

volontà sf will; **a ~** (mangiare, bere) as much as one likes; **buona/cattiva ~** goodwill/ lack of goodwill

volon'tario, -a ag voluntary ▷ sm (Mil) volunteer

'volpe sf fox

'volta sf (momento, circostanza) time; (turno, giro) turn; (curva) turn, bend; (Archit) vault; (direzione): **partire alla ~ di** to set off for; **a mia** (o **tua** ecc) **~** in turn; **una ~** once; **una ~ sola** only once; **due volte** twice; **una cosa per ~** one thing at a time; **una ~ per tutte** once and for all; **a volte** at times, sometimes; **una ~ che** (temporale) once;

(causale) since; **3 volte 4** 3 times 4

volta'faccia [volta'fattʃa] sm inv (fig) volte-face

vol'taggio [vol'taddʒo] sm (Elettr) voltage

vol'tare vt to turn; (girare: moneta) to turn over; (rigirare) to turn round ▷ vi to turn; **voltarsi** vpr to turn; to turn over; to turn round

voltas'tomaco sm nausea; (fig) disgust

'volto, -a pp di **volgere** ▷ sm face

vo'lubile ag changeable, fickle

vo'lume sm volume

vomi'tare vt, vi to vomit; **'vomito** sm vomiting no pl; vomit

'vongola sf clam

vo'race [vo'ratʃe] ag voracious, greedy

vo'ragine [vo'radʒine] sf abyss, chasm

vorrò ecc vb vedi volere

'vortice ['vortitʃe] sm whirlwind; whirlpool; (fig) whirl

'vostro, -a det il(la) **~(a)** ecc your ▷ pron il(la) **~(a)** ecc yours

vo'tante sm/f voter

vo'tare vi to vote ▷ vt (sottoporre a votazione) to take a vote on; (approvare) to vote for; (Rel): **~ qc a** to dedicate sth to

'voto sm (Pol) vote; (Ins) mark; (Rel) vow; (: offerta) votive offering; **aver voti belli/ brutti** (Ins) to get good/bad marks

vs. abbr (Comm) = **vostro**

vul'cano sm volcano

vulne'rabile ag vulnerable

vu'oi, vu'ole vb vedi volere

vuo'tare vt to empty; **vuotarsi** vpr to empty

vu'oto, -a ag empty; (fig: privo): **~ di** (senso ecc) devoid of ▷ sm empty space, gap; (spazio in bianco) blank; (Fisica) vacuum; (fig: mancanza) gap, void; **a mani vuote** empty-handed; **vuoto d'aria** air pocket; **vuoto a rendere** returnable bottle

W X

'wafer ['vafer] *sm inv* (*Cuc, Elettr*) wafer
'water ['wɔːtər] *sm inv* toilet
watt [vat] *sm inv* watt
W.C. *sm inv* WC
web [ueb] *sm* **il ~** the Web; **cercare nel ~** to search the Web ▷ *ag inv* **pagina ~** web page
'weekend ['wiːkend] *sm inv* weekend
'western ['wɛstern] *ag* (*Cinema*) cowboy *cpd* ▷ *sm inv* western, cowboy film; **western all'italiana** spaghetti western
'whisky ['wiski] *sm inv* whisky
'windsurf ['windsəːf] *sm inv* (*tavola*) windsurfer; (*sport*) windsurfing
'würstel ['vyrstəl] *sm inv* frankfurter

xe'nofobo, -a [kse'nɔfobo] *ag* xenophobic ▷ *sm/f* xenophobe
xi'lofono [ksi'lɔfono] *sm* xylophone

Y Z

yacht [jɔt] sm inv yacht
'yoga ['jɔga] ag inv, sm yoga (cpd)
yogurt ['jɔgurt] sm inv yog(h)urt

zabai'one [dzaba'jone] sm dessert made of egg yolks, sugar and marsala
zaf'fata [tsaf'fata] sf (tanfo) stench
zaffe'rano [dzaffe'rano] sm saffron
zaf'firo [dzaf'firo] sm sapphire
'zaino ['dzaino] sm rucksack
'zampa ['tsampa] sf (di animale: gamba) leg; (: piede) paw; **a quattro zampe** on all fours
zampil'lare [tsampil'lare] vi to gush, spurt
zan'zara [dzan'dzara] sf mosquito; **zanzari'era** sf mosquito net
'zappa ['tsappa] sf hoe
'zapping ['tsapiŋ] sm (TV) channel-hopping
zar, za'rina [tsar, tsa'rina] sm/f tsar/tsarina
'zattera ['dzattera] sf raft
'zebra ['dzɛbra] sf zebra; **zebre** sfpl (Aut) zebra crossing sg (BRIT), crosswalk sg (US)
'zecca, -che ['tsekka] sf (Zool) tick; (officina di monete) mint
'zelo ['dzɛlo] sm zeal
'zenzero ['dzendzero] sm ginger
'zeppa ['tseppa] sf wedge
'zeppo, -a ['tseppo] ag ~ **di** crammed o packed with
zer'bino [dzer'bino] sm doormat
'zero ['dzɛro] sm zero, nought; **vincere per**

tre a ~ (*Sport*) to win three-nil

'zia ['tsia] *sf* aunt

zibel'lino [dzibel'lino] *sm* sable

'zigomo ['dzigomo] *sm* cheekbone

zig'zag [dzig'dzag] *sm inv* zigzag; **andare a ~** to zigzag

Zimbabwe [tsim'babwe] *sm* **lo ~** Zimbabwe

'zinco ['dzinko] *sm* zinc

'zingaro, -a ['dzingaro] *sm/f* gipsy

'zio ['tsio] (*pl* **'zii**) *sm* uncle

zip'pare *vt* (*Inform: file*) to zip

zi'tella [dzi'tella] *sf* spinster; (*peg*) old maid

'zitto, -a ['tsitto] *ag* quiet, silent; **sta' ~!** be quiet!

'zoccolo ['tsɔkkolo] *sm* (*calzatura*) clog; (*di cavallo ecc*) hoof; (*basamento*) base; plinth

zodia'cale [dzodia'kale] *ag* zodiac *cpd*; **segno ~** sign of the zodiac

zo'diaco [dzo'diako] *sm* zodiac

'zolfo ['tsolfo] *sm* sulphur

'zolla ['dzɔlla] *sf* clod (of earth)

zol'letta [dzol'letta] *sf* sugar lump

'zona ['dzɔna] *sf* zone, area; **zona di depressione** (*Meteor*) trough of low pressure; **zona disco** (*Aut*) ≈ meter zone; **zona industriale** industrial estate; **zona pedonale** pedestrian precinct; **zona verde** (*di abitato*) green area

'zonzo ['dzondzo]: **a ~** *av*, **andare a ~** to wander about, stroll about

zoo ['dzɔo] *sm inv* zoo

zoolo'gia [dzoolo'dʒia] *sf* zoology

zoppi'care [tsoppi'kare] *vi* to limp; to be shaky, rickety

'zoppo, -a ['tsɔppo] *ag* lame; (*fig: mobile*) shaky, rickety

Z.T.L. *sigla f* (= *Zona a Traffico Limitato*) *controlled traffic zone*

'zucca, -che ['tsukka] *sf* (*Bot*) marrow; pumpkin

zucche'rare [tsukke'rare] *vt* to put sugar in; **zucche'rato, -a** *ag* sweet, sweetened

zuccheri'era [tsukke'rjɛra] *sf* sugar bowl

'zucchero ['tsukkero] *sm* sugar; **zucchero di canna** cane sugar; **zucchero filato** candy floss, cotton candy (*us*)

zuc'china [tsuk'kina] *sf* courgette (BRIT), zucchini (*us*)

'zuffa ['tsuffa] *sf* brawl

'zuppa ['tsuppa] *sf* soup; (*fig*) mixture, muddle; **zuppa inglese** (*Cuc*) *dessert made with sponge cake, custard and chocolate,* ≈ trifle (BRIT)

'zuppo, -a ['tsuppo] *ag* **~ (di)** drenched (with), soaked (with)

A [eɪ] n (Mus) la m

O **KEYWORD**

a [ə] (before vowel or silent h **an**) indef art **1** un (uno + s impure, gn, pn, ps, x, z), una f (un' + vowel); **a book** un libro; **a mirror** uno specchio; **an apple** una mela; **she's a doctor** è medico
2 (instead of the number "one") un(o), f una; **a year ago** un anno fa; **a hundred/thousand** etc **pounds** cento/mille etc sterline
3 (in expressing ratios, prices etc) a, per; **3 a day/week** 3 al giorno/alla settimana; **10 km an hour** 10 km all'ora; **£5 a person** 5 sterline a persona or per persona

A.A. n abbr (= Alcoholics Anonymous) AA; (BRIT: = Automobile Association) ≈ A.C.I. m
A.A.A. (US) n abbr (= American Automobile Association) ≈ A.C.I. m
aback [ə'bæk] adv **to be taken ~** essere sbalordito(-a)
abandon [ə'bændən] vt abbandonare ▷ n **with ~** sfrenatamente, spensieratamente
abattoir ['æbətwɑ:ʳ] (BRIT) n mattatoio
abbey ['æbɪ] n abbazia, badia
abbreviation [əbri:vɪ'eɪʃən] n abbreviazione f

abdomen ['æbdəmən] n addome m
abduct [æb'dʌkt] vt rapire
abide [ə'baɪd] vt **I can't ~ it/him** non lo posso soffrire or sopportare; **abide by** vt fus conformarsi a
ability [ə'bɪlɪtɪ] n abilità f inv
able ['eɪbl] adj capace; **to be ~ to do sth** essere capace di fare qc, poter fare qc
abnormal [æb'nɔ:məl] adj anormale
aboard [ə'bɔ:d] adv a bordo ▷ prep a bordo di
abolish [ə'bɔlɪʃ] vt abolire
abolition [æbəu'lɪʃən] n abolizione f
abort [ə'bɔ:t] vt abortire; **abortion** [ə'bɔ:ʃən] n aborto; **to have an abortion** abortire

O **KEYWORD**

about [ə'baut] adv **1** (approximately) circa, quasi; **about a hundred/thousand** etc un centinaio/migliaio etc, circa cento/mille etc; **it takes about 10 hours** ci vogliono circa 10 ore; **at about 2 o'clock** verso le 2; **I've just about finished** ho quasi finito
2 (referring to place) qua e là, in giro; **to leave things lying about** lasciare delle cose in giro; **to run about** correre qua e là; **to walk about** camminare
3: **to be about to do sth** stare per fare qc
▷ prep **1** (relating to) su, di; **a book about London** un libro su Londra; **what is it about?** di che si tratta?; (book, film etc) di cosa tratta?; **we talked about it** ne abbiamo parlato; **what or how about doing this?** che ne dici di fare questo?
2 (referring to place): **to walk about the town** camminare per la città; **her clothes were scattered about the room** i suoi vestiti erano sparsi or in giro per tutta la stanza

above [ə'bʌv] adv, prep sopra; **mentioned ~** suddetto; **~ all** soprattutto
abroad [ə'brɔ:d] adv all'estero
abrupt [ə'brʌpt] adj (sudden) improvviso(-a); (gruff, blunt) brusco(-a)
abscess ['æbsɪs] n ascesso
absence ['æbsəns] n assenza
absent ['æbsənt] adj assente; **absent-minded** adj distratto(-a)
absolute ['æbsəlu:t] adj assoluto(-a); **absolutely** [-'lu:tlɪ] adv assolutamente
absorb [əb'zɔ:b] vt assorbire; **to be ~ed in a book** essere immerso in un libro; **absorbent cotton** [əb'zɔ:bənt-] (US) n cotone m idrofilo; **absorbing** adj avvincente, molto interessante
abstain [əb'steɪn] vi **to ~ (from)**

astenersi (da)

abstract ['æbstrækt] *adj* astratto(-a)

absurd [əb'sə:d] *adj* assurdo(-a)

abundance [ə'bʌndəns] *n* abbondanza

abundant [ə'bʌndənt] *adj* abbondante

abuse [*n* ə'bju:s, *vb* ə'bju:z] *n* abuso; (*insults*) ingiurie *fpl* ▷ *vt* abusare di; **abusive** *adj* ingiurioso(-a)

abysmal [ə'bɪzməl] *adj* spaventoso(-a)

academic [ækə'dɛmɪk] *adj* accademico(-a); (*pej: issue*) puramente formale ▷ *n* universitario(-a); **academic year** *n* anno accademico

academy [ə'kædəmɪ] *n* (*learned body*) accademia; (*school*) scuola privata; **academy of music** *n* conservatorio

accelerate [æk'sɛləreɪt] *vt, vi* accelerare; **acceleration** *n* accelerazione *f*; **accelerator** *n* acceleratore *m*

accent ['æksɛnt] *n* accento

accept [ək'sɛpt] *vt* accettare; **acceptable** *adj* accettabile; **acceptance** *n* accettazione *f*

access ['æksɛs] *n* accesso; **accessible** [æk'sɛsɪbl] *adj* accessibile

accessory [æk'sɛsərɪ] *n* accessorio; (*Law*): ~ **to** complice *m/f* di

accident ['æksɪdənt] *n* incidente *m*; (*chance*) caso; **I've had an ~** ho avuto un incidente; **by ~** per caso; **accidental** [-'dɛntl] *adj* accidentale; **accidentally** [-'dɛntəlɪ] *adv* per caso; **Accident and Emergency Department** *n* (BRIT) pronto soccorso; **accident insurance** *n* assicurazione *f* contro gli infortuni

acclaim [ə'kleɪm] *n* acclamazione *f*

accommodate [ə'kɔmədeɪt] *vt* alloggiare; (*oblige, help*) favorire

accommodation [əkɔmə'deɪʃən] (*US* **accommodations**) *n* alloggio

accompaniment [ə'kʌmpənɪmənt] *n* accompagnamento

accompany [ə'kʌmpənɪ] *vt* accompagnare

accomplice [ə'kʌmplɪs] *n* complice *m/f*

accomplish [ə'kʌmplɪʃ] *vt* compiere; (*goal*) raggiungere; **accomplishment** *n* compimento; realizzazione *f*

accord [ə'kɔ:d] *n* accordo ▷ *vt* accordare; **of his own ~** di propria iniziativa; **accordance** *n* **in accordance with** in conformità con; **according: according to** *prep* secondo; **accordingly** *adv* in conformità

account [ə'kaunt] *n* (*Comm*) conto; (*report*) descrizione *f*; **~s** *npl* (*Comm*) conti *mpl*; **of no ~** di nessuna importanza; **on ~** in acconto; **on no ~** per nessun motivo; **on ~ of** a causa di; **to take into ~, take**

~ of tener conto di; **account for** *vt fus* spiegare; giustificare; **accountable** *adj* **accountable (to)** responsabile (verso); **accountant** [ə'kauntənt] *n* ragioniere(-a); **account number** *n* numero di conto

accumulate [ə'kju:mjuleɪt] *vt* accumulare ▷ *vi* accumularsi

accuracy ['ækjurəsɪ] *n* precisione *f*

accurate ['ækjurɪt] *adj* preciso(-a); **accurately** *adv* precisamente

accusation [ækju'zeɪʃən] *n* accusa

accuse [ə'kju:z] *vt* accusare; **accused** *n* accusato(-a)

accustomed [ə'kʌstəmd] *adj* **~ to** abituato(-a) a

ace [eɪs] *n* asso

ache [eɪk] *n* male *m*, dolore *m* ▷ *vi* (*be sore*) far male, dolere; **my head ~s** mi fa male la testa

achieve [ə'tʃi:v] *vt* (*aim*) raggiungere; (*victory, success*) ottenere; **achievement** *n* compimento; successo

acid ['æsɪd] *adj* acido(-a) ▷ *n* acido

acknowledge [ək'nɔlɪdʒ] *vt* (*letter: also*: **~ receipt of**) confermare la ricevuta di; (*fact*) riconoscere; **acknowledgement** *n* conferma; riconoscimento

acne ['æknɪ] *n* acne *f*

acorn ['eɪkɔ:n] *n* ghianda

acoustic [ə'ku:stɪk] *adj* acustico(-a)

acquaintance [ə'kweɪntəns] *n* conoscenza; (*person*) conoscente *m/f*

acquire [ə'kwaɪə'] *vt* acquistare; **acquisition** [ækwɪ'zɪʃən] *n* acquisto

acquit [ə'kwɪt] *vt* assolvere; **to ~ o.s. well** comportarsi bene

acre ['eɪkə'] *n* acro, ≈ 4047 m²

acronym ['ækrənɪm] *n* acronimo

across [ə'krɔs] *prep* (*on the other side*) dall'altra parte di; (*crosswise*) attraverso ▷ *adv* dall'altra parte; in larghezza; **to run/ swim ~** attraversare di corsa/a nuoto; **~ from** di fronte a

acrylic [ə'krɪlɪk] *adj* acrilico(-a)

act [ækt] *n* atto; (*in music-hall etc*) numero; (*Law*) decreto ▷ *vi* agire; (*Theatre*) recitare; (*pretend*) fingere ▷ *vt* (*part*) recitare; **to ~ as** agire da; **act up** (*inf*) *vi* (*person*) comportarsi male; (*knee, back, injury*) fare male; (*machine*) non funzionare; **acting** *adj* che fa le funzioni di ▷ *n* (*of actor*) recitazione *f*; (*activity*): **to do some acting** fare del teatro (*or* del cinema)

action ['ækʃən] *n* azione *f*; (*Mil*) combattimento; (*Law*) processo; **out of ~** fuori combattimento; fuori servizio; **to take ~** agire; **action replay** *n* (*TV*) replay *m inv*

activate ['æktɪveɪt] vt (*mechanism*) attivare

active ['æktɪv] adj attivo(-a); **actively** adv (*participate*) attivamente; (*discourage, dislike*) vivamente

activist ['æktɪvɪst] n attivista m/f

activity [æk'tɪvɪtɪ] n attività f inv; **activity holiday** n vacanza organizzata con attività ricreative per ragazzi

actor ['æktə^r] n attore m

actress ['æktrɪs] n attrice f

actual ['æktjuəl] adj reale, effettivo(-a)

Be careful not to translate *actual* by the Italian word *attuale*.

actually ['æktjuəlɪ] adv veramente; (*even*) addirittura

Be careful not to translate *actually* by the Italian word *attualmente*.

acupuncture ['ækjupʌŋktʃə^r] n agopuntura

acute [ə'kju:t] adj acuto(-a); (*mind, person*) perspicace

ad [æd] n abbr = **advertisement**

A.D. adv abbr (= *Anno Domini*) d.C.

adamant ['ædəmənt] adj irremovibile

adapt [ə'dæpt] vt adattare ▷ vi **to ~ (to)** adattarsi (a); **adapter, adaptor** n (*Elec*) adattatore m

add [æd] vt aggiungere ▷ vi **to ~ to** (*increase*) aumentare; **add up** vt (*figures*) addizionare ▷ vi (*fig*): **it doesn't ~ up** non ha senso; **add up to** vt fus (*Math*) ammontare a; (*fig: mean*) significare; **it doesn't ~ up to much** non è un granché

addict ['ædɪkt] n tossicomane m/f; (*fig*) fanatico(-a); **addicted** [ə'dɪktɪd] adj **to be addicted to** (*drink etc*) essere dedito(-a) a; (*fig: football etc*) essere tifoso(-a) di; **addiction** [ə'dɪkʃən] n (*Med*) tossicodipendenza; **addictive** [ə'dɪktɪv] adj che dà assuefazione

addition [ə'dɪʃən] n addizione f; (*thing added*) aggiunta; **in ~** inoltre; **in ~ to** oltre; **additional** adj supplementare

additive ['ædɪtɪv] n additivo

address [ə'drɛs] n indirizzo; (*talk*) discorso ▷ vt indirizzare; (*speak to*) fare un discorso a; (*issue*) affrontare; **my ~ is ...** il mio indirizzo è ...; **address book** n rubrica

adequate ['ædɪkwɪt] adj adeguato(-a), sufficiente

adhere [əd'hɪə^r] vi **to ~ to** aderire a; (*fig: rule, decision*) seguire

adhesive [əd'hi:zɪv] n adesivo; **adhesive tape** n (*BRIT: for parcels etc*) nastro adesivo; (*US Med*) cerotto adesivo

adjacent [ə'dʒeɪsənt] adj adiacente; **~ to** accanto a

adjective ['ædʒɛktɪv] n aggettivo

adjoining [ə'dʒɔɪnɪŋ] adj accanto inv, adiacente

adjourn [ə'dʒə:n] vt rimandare ▷ vi essere aggiornato(-a)

adjust [ə'dʒʌst] vt aggiustare; (*change*) rettificare ▷ vi **to ~ (to)** adattarsi (a); **adjustable** adj regolabile; **adjustment** n (*Psych*) adattamento; (*of machine*) regolazione f; (*of prices, wages*) modifica

administer [əd'mɪnɪstə^r] vt amministrare; (*justice, drug*) somministrare; **administration** [ədmɪnɪs'treɪʃən] n amministrazione f; **administrative** [əd'mɪnɪstrətɪv] adj amministrativo(-a)

administrator [əd'mɪnɪstreɪtə^r] n amministratore(-trice)

admiral ['ædmərəl] n ammiraglio

admiration [ædmə'reɪʃən] n ammirazione f

admire [əd'maɪə^r] vt ammirare; **admirer** n ammiratore(-trice)

admission [əd'mɪʃən] n ammissione f; (*to exhibition, nightclub etc*) ingresso; (*confession*) confessione f

admit [əd'mɪt] vt ammettere; far entrare; (*agree*) riconoscere; **admit to** vt fus riconoscere; **admittance** n ingresso; **admittedly** adv bisogna pur riconoscere (che)

adolescent [ædəu'lɛsnt] adj, n adolescente m/f

adopt [ə'dɔpt] vt adottare; **adopted** adj adottivo(-a); **adoption** [ə'dɔpʃən] n adozione f

adore [ə'dɔ:^r] vt adorare

adorn [ə'dɔ:n] vt ornare

Adriatic [eɪdrɪ'ætɪk] n **the ~ (Sea)** il mare Adriatico, l'Adriatico

adrift [ə'drɪft] adv alla deriva

adult ['ædʌlt] adj adulto(-a); (*work, education*) per adulti ▷ n adulto(-a); **adult education** n scuola per adulti

adultery [ə'dʌltərɪ] n adulterio

advance [əd'vɑ:ns] n avanzamento; (*money*) anticipo ▷ adj (*booking etc*) in anticipo ▷ vt (*money*) anticipare ▷ vi avanzare; **in ~** in anticipo; **do I need to book in ~?** occorre che prenoti in anticipo?; **advanced** adj avanzato(-a); (*Scol: studies*) superiore

advantage [əd'vɑ:ntɪdʒ] n (*also Tennis*) vantaggio; **to take ~ of** approfittarsi di

advent ['ædvənt] n avvento; (*Rel*): **A~** Avvento

adventure [əd'vɛntʃə^r] n avventura; **adventurous** [əd'vɛntʃərəs] adj avventuroso(-a)

adverb ['ædvə:b] n avverbio

adversary ['ædvəsərɪ] n avversario(-a)
adverse ['ædvə:s] adj avverso(-a)
advert ['ædvə:t] (BRIT) n abbr
= **advertisement**
advertise ['ædvətaɪz] vi, vt fare pubblicità
or réclame (a); fare un'inserzione (per
vendere); **to ~ for** (staff) mettere un
annuncio sul giornale per trovare;
advertisement [əd'və:tɪsmənt] n
(Comm) réclame f inv, pubblicità f inv; (in
classified ads) inserzione f; **advertiser** n
azienda che reclamizza un prodotto; (in
newspaper) inserzionista m/f; **advertising**
['ædvətaɪzɪŋ] n pubblicità
advice [əd'vaɪs] n consigli mpl; **piece of ~**
consiglio; **to take legal ~** consultare un
avvocato
advisable [əd'vaɪzəbl] adj consigliabile
advise [əd'vaɪz] vt consigliare; **to ~ sb of
sth** informare qn di qc; **to ~ sb against
sth/doing sth** sconsigliare qc a qn/a qn
di fare qc; **adviser** n consigliere(-a); (in
business) consulente m/f, consigliere(-a);
advisory [-ərɪ] adj consultivo(-a)
advocate [n 'ædvəkɪt, vb 'ædvəkeɪt]
n (upholder) sostenitore(-trice); (Law)
avvocato (difensore) ▷ vt propugnare
Aegean [ɪ'dʒɪːən] n **the ~ (Sea)** il mar
Egeo, l'Egeo
aerial ['ɛərɪəl] n antenna ▷ adj aereo(-a)
aerobics [ɛə'rəubɪks] n aerobica
aeroplane ['ɛərəpleɪn] (BRIT) n aeroplano
aerosol ['ɛərəsɔl] (BRIT) n aerosol m inv
affair [ə'fɛəʳ] n affare m; (also: **love ~**)
relazione f amorosa; **~s** (business) affari
affect [ə'fɛkt] vt toccare; (influence)
influire su, incidere su; (feign) fingere;
affected adj affettato(-a); **affection**
[ə'fɛkʃən] n affezione f; **affectionate** adj
affettuoso(-a)
afflict [ə'flɪkt] vt affliggere
affluent ['æfluənt] adj ricco(-a); **the ~
society** la società del benessere
afford [ə'fɔːd] vt permettersi; (provide)
fornire; **affordable** adj (che ha un prezzo)
abbordabile
Afghanistan [æf'gænɪstɑːn] n Afganistan
m
afraid [ə'freɪd] adj impaurito(-a); **to be ~
of** or **to/that** aver paura di/che; **I am ~
so/not** ho paura di sì/no
Africa ['æfrɪkə] n Africa; **African** adj, n
africano(-a); **African-American** adj, n
afroamericano(-a)
after ['ɑːftəʳ] prep, adv dopo ▷ conj dopo
che; **what/who are you ~?** che/chi
cerca?; **~ he left/having done** dopo
che se ne fu andato/dopo aver fatto; **to
name sb ~ sb** dare a qn il nome di qn; **it's**

twenty ~ eight (US) sono le otto e venti;
to ask ~ sb chiedere di qn; **~ all** dopo
tutto; **~ you!** dopo di lei!; **after-effects**
npl conseguenze fpl; (of illness) postumi
mpl; **aftermath** n conseguenze fpl; **in
the aftermath of** nel periodo dopo;
afternoon n pomeriggio; **after-shave
(lotion)** ['ɑːftəʃeɪv-] n dopobarba m inv;
aftersun (lotion/cream) n doposole m
inv; **afterwards** (US **afterward**) adv dopo
again [ə'gɛn] adv di nuovo; **to begin/see ~**
ricominciare/rivedere; **not ... ~** non ... più;
~ and ~ ripetutamente
against [ə'gɛnst] prep contro
age [eɪdʒ] n età f inv ▷ vt, vi invecchiare;
it's been ~s since sono secoli che; **he is
20 years of ~** ha 20 anni; **to come of ~**
diventare maggiorenne; **~d 10** di 10 anni;
the ~d ['eɪdʒɪd] gli anziani; **age group** n
generazione f; **age limit** n limite m d'età
agency ['eɪdʒənsɪ] n agenzia
agenda [ə'dʒɛndə] n ordine m del giorno
agent ['eɪdʒənt] n agente m
aggravate ['ægrəveɪt] vt aggravare;
(person) irritare
aggression [ə'grɛʃən] n aggressione f
aggressive [ə'grɛsɪv] adj aggressivo(-a)
agile ['ædʒaɪl] adj agile
agitated ['ædʒɪteɪtɪd] adj agitato(-a),
turbato(-a)
AGM n abbr = **annual general meeting**
ago [ə'gəu] adv **2 days ~** 2 giorni fa; **not
long ~** poco tempo fa; **how long ~?**
quanto tempo fa?
agony ['ægənɪ] n dolore m atroce; **to be in
~** avere dolori atroci
agree [ə'griː] vt (price) pattuire ▷ vi **to
~ (with)** essere d'accordo (con); (Ling)
concordare (con); **to ~ to sth/to do sth**
accettare qc/di fare qc; **to ~ that** (admit)
ammettere che; **to ~ on sth** accordarsi su
qc; **garlic doesn't ~ with me** l'aglio non
mi va; **agreeable** adj gradevole; (willing)
disposto(-a); **agreed** adj (time, place)
stabilito(-a); **agreement** n accordo; **in
agreement** d'accordo
agricultural [ægrɪ'kʌltʃərəl] adj
agricolo(-a)
agriculture ['ægrɪkʌltʃəʳ] n agricoltura
ahead [ə'hɛd] adv avanti; davanti; **~ of**
davanti a; (fig: schedule etc) in anticipo su;
~ of time in anticipo; **go right** or **straight
~** tiri diritto
aid [eɪd] n aiuto ▷ vt aiutare; **in ~ of** a
favore di
aide [eɪd] n (person) aiutante m/f
AIDS [eɪdz] n abbr (= acquired immune
deficiency syndrome) AIDS f
ailing ['eɪlɪŋ] adj sofferente; (fig: economy,

industry etc) in difficoltà
ailment['eɪlmənt] *n* indisposizione *f*
aim[eɪm] *vt* **to ~ sth at** (*such as gun*) mirare qc a; puntare qc a; (*camera*) rivolgere qc a; (*missile*) lanciare qc contro ▷ *vi* (*also:* **to take ~**) prendere la mira ▷ *n* mira; **to ~ at** mirare; **to ~ to do** aver l'intenzione di fare
ain't[eɪnt] (*inf*) = **am not**; **aren't**; **isn't**
air[ɛəʳ] *n* aria ▷ *vt* (*room*) arieggiare; (*clothes*) far prendere aria a; (*grievances, ideas*) esprimere pubblicamente ▷ *cpd* (*currents*) d'aria; (*attack*) aereo(-a); **to throw sth into the ~** lanciare qc in aria; **by ~** (*travel*) in aereo; **on the ~** (*Radio, TV*) in onda; **airbag** *n* airbag *m inv*; **airbed** (BRIT) *n* materassino; **airborne** ['ɛəbɔːn] *adj* (*plane*) in volo; (*troops*) aerotrasportato(-a); **as soon as the plane was airborne** appena l'aereo ebbe decollato; **air-conditioned** *adj* con or ad aria condizionata; **air conditioning** *n* condizionamento d'aria; **aircraft** *n inv* apparecchio; **airfield** *n* campo d'aviazione; **Air Force** *n* aviazione *f* militare; **air hostess** *n* hostess *f inv*; **airing cupboard**['ɛərɪŋ-] *n* armadio riscaldato per asciugare panni.; **airlift** *n* ponte *m* aereo; **airline** *n* linea aerea; **airliner** *n* aereo di linea; **airmail** *n* **by airmail** per via aerea; **airplane** (US) *n* aeroplano; **airport** *n* aeroporto; **air raid** *n* incursione *f* aerea; **airsick** *adj* **to be airsick** soffrire di mal d'aria; **airspace** *n* spazio aereo; **airstrip** *n* pista d'atterraggio; **air terminal** *n* air-terminal *m inv*; **airtight** *adj* ermetico(-a); **air-traffic controller** *n* controllore *m* del traffico aereo; **airy** *adj* arioso(-a); (*manners*) noncurante
aisle[aɪl] *n* (*of church*) navata laterale; navata centrale; (*of plane*) corridoio; **aisle seat** *n* (*on plane*) posto sul corridoio
ajar[ə'dʒɑːʳ] *adj* socchiuso(-a)
à la carte[ɑːlɑː'kɑːt] *adv* alla carta
alarm[ə'lɑːm] *n* allarme *m* ▷ *vt* allarmare; **alarm call** *n* (*in hotel etc*) sveglia; **could I have an alarm call at 7 am, please?** vorrei essere svegliato alle 7, per favore; **alarm clock** *n* sveglia; **alarmed** (*person*) allarmato(-a); (*house, car etc*) dotato(-a) di allarme; **alarming** *adj* allarmante, preoccupante
Albania[æl'beɪnɪə] *n* Albania
albeit[ɔːl'biːɪt] *conj* sebbene + *sub*, benché + *sub*
album['ælbəm] *n* album *m inv*
alcohol['ælkəhɔl] *n* alcool *m*; **alcohol-free** *adj* analcolico(-a); **alcoholic**[-'hɔlɪk] *adj* alcolico(-a) ▷ *n* alcolizzato(-a)

alcove['ælkəuv] *n* alcova
ale[eɪl] *n* birra
alert[ə'ləːt] *adj* vigile ▷ *n* allarme *m* ▷ *vt* avvertire; mettere in guardia; **on the ~** all'erta
algebra['ældʒɪbrə] *n* algebra
Algeria[æl'dʒɪərɪə] *n* Algeria
alias['eɪlɪəs] *adv* alias ▷ *n* pseudonimo, falso nome *m*
alibi['ælɪbaɪ] *n* alibi *m inv*
alien['eɪlɪən] *n* straniero(-a); (*extraterrestrial*) alieno(-a) ▷ *adj* **~ (to)** estraneo(-a) (a); **alienate** *vt* alienare
alight[ə'laɪt] *adj* acceso(-a) ▷ *vi* scendere; (*bird*) posarsi
align[ə'laɪn] *vt* allineare
alike[ə'laɪk] *adj* simile ▷ *adv* sia … sia; **to look ~** assomigliarsi
alive[ə'laɪv] *adj* vivo(-a); (*lively*) vivace

⭕ KEYWORD

all[ɔːl] *adj* tutto(-a); **all day** tutto il giorno; **all night** tutta la notte; **all men** tutti gli uomini; **all five came** sono venuti tutti e cinque; **all the books** tutti i libri; **all the food** tutto il cibo; **all the time** sempre; tutto il tempo; **all his life** tutta la vita ▷ *pron* 1 tutto(-a); **I ate it all, I ate all of it** l'ho mangiato tutto; **all of us went** tutti noi siamo andati; **all of the boys went** tutti i ragazzi sono andati
2 (*in phrases*): **above all** soprattutto; **after all** dopotutto; **at all: not at all** (*in answer to question*) niente affatto; (*in answer to thanks*) prego!, di niente!, s'immagini!; **I'm not at all tired** non sono affatto stanco(-a); **anything at all will do** andrà bene qualsiasi cosa; **all in all** tutto sommato
▷ *adv* **all alone** tutto(-a) solo(-a); **it's not as hard as all that** non è poi così difficile; **all the more/the better** tanto più/meglio; **all but** quasi; **the score is two all** il punteggio è di due a due

Allah['ælə] *n* Allah *m*
allegation[ælɪ'geɪʃən] *n* asserzione *f*
alleged[ə'lɛdʒd] *adj* presunto(-a); **allegedly**[ə'lɛdʒɪdlɪ] *adv* secondo quanto si asserisce
allegiance[ə'liːdʒəns] *n* fedeltà
allergic[ə'ləːdʒɪk] *adj* **~ to** allergico(-a) a; **I'm ~ to penicillin** sono allergico alla penicillina
allergy['ælədʒɪ] *n* allergia
alleviate[ə'liːvɪeɪt] *vt* sollevare
alley['ælɪ] *n* vicolo
alliance[ə'laɪəns] *n* alleanza

allied ['ælaɪd] adj alleato(-a)
alligator ['ælɪgeɪtəʳ] n alligatore m
all-in ['ɔːlɪn] adj (BRIT: also adv: charge) tutto compreso
allocate ['æləkeɪt] vt assegnare
allot [ə'lɔt] vt assegnare
all-out ['ɔːlaut] adj (effort etc) totale ▷ adv to go all out for mettercela tutta per
allow [ə'lau] vt (practice, behaviour) permettere; (sum to spend etc) accordare; (sum, time estimated) dare; (concede): to ~ that ammettere che; to ~ sb to do permettere a qn di fare; he is ~ed to lo può fare; allow for vt fus tener conto di; allowance n (money received) assegno; indennità f inv; (Tax) detrazione f di imposta; to make allowances for tener conto di
all right adv (feel, work) bene; (as answer) va bene
ally ['ælaɪ] n alleato
almighty [ɔːl'maɪtɪ] adj onnipotente; (row etc) colossale
almond ['ɑːmənd] n mandorla
almost ['ɔːlməust] adv quasi
alone [ə'ləun] adj, adv solo(-a); to leave sb ~ lasciare qn in pace; to leave sth ~ lasciare stare qc; let ~ ... figuriamoci poi ..., tanto meno ...
along [ə'lɔŋ] prep lungo ▷ adv is he coming ~? viene con noi?; he was limping ~ veniva zoppicando; ~ with insieme con; all ~ (all the time) sempre, fin dall'inizio; alongside prep accanto a; lungo ▷ adv accanto
aloof [ə'luːf] adj distaccato(-a) ▷ adv to stand ~ tenersi a distanza or in disparte
aloud [ə'laud] adv ad alta voce
alphabet ['ælfəbet] n alfabeto
Alps [ælps] npl the ~ le Alpi
already [ɔːl'redɪ] adv già
alright [ɔːl'raɪt] (BRIT) adv = all right
also ['ɔːlsəu] adv anche
altar ['ɔltəʳ] n altare m
alter ['ɔltəʳ] vt, vi alterare; alteration [ɔltə'reɪʃən] n modificazione f, alterazione f; alterations (Sewing, Archit) modifiche fpl; timetable subject to alteration orario soggetto a variazioni
alternate [adj ɔl'təːnɪt, vb 'ɔltə:neɪt] adj alterno(-a); (us: plan etc) alternativo(-a) ▷ vi to ~ (with) alternarsi (a); on ~ days ogni due giorni
alternative [ɔl'təːnətɪv] adj alternativo(-a) ▷ n (choice) alternativa; alternatively adv alternatively one could ... come alternativa si potrebbe ...
although [ɔːl'ðəu] conj benché + sub, sebbene + sub

altitude ['æltɪtjuːd] n altitudine f
altogether [ɔːltə'geðəʳ] adv del tutto, completamente; (on the whole) tutto considerato; (in all) in tutto
aluminium [ælju'mɪnɪəm] (BRIT), aluminum [ə'luːmɪnəm] (us) n alluminio
always ['ɔːlweɪz] adv sempre
Alzheimer's (disease) ['æltshaɪməz-] n (malattia di) Alzheimer
am [æm] vb see be
amalgamate [ə'mælgəmeɪt] vt amalgamare ▷ vi amalgamarsi
amass [ə'mæs] vt ammassare
amateur ['æmətəʳ] n dilettante m/f ▷ adj (Sport) dilettante
amaze [ə'meɪz] vt stupire; amazed adj sbalordito(-a); to be amazed (at) essere sbalordito (da); amazement n stupore m; amazing adj sorprendente, sbalorditivo(-a)
Amazon ['æməzən] n (Mythology) Amazzone f; (river): the ~ il Rio delle Amazzoni ▷ cpd (basin, jungle) amazzonico(-a)
ambassador [æm'bæsədəʳ] n ambasciatore(-trice)
amber ['æmbəʳ] n ambra; at ~ (BRIT Aut) giallo
ambiguous [æm'bɪgjuəs] adj ambiguo(-a)
ambition [æm'bɪʃən] n ambizione f; ambitious [æm'bɪʃəs] adj ambizioso(-a)
ambulance ['æmbjuləns] n ambulanza; call an ~! chiamate un'ambulanza!
ambush ['æmbuʃ] n imboscata
amen ['ɑː'men] excl così sia, amen
amend [ə'mend] vt (law) emendare; (text) correggere; to make ~s fare ammenda; amendment n emendamento; correzione f
amenities [ə'miːnɪtɪz] npl attrezzature fpl ricreative e culturali
America [ə'merɪkə] n America; American adj, n americano(-a); American football n (BRIT) football m americano
amicable ['æmɪkəbl] adj amichevole
amid(st) [ə'mɪd(st)] prep in mezzo a
ammunition [æmju'nɪʃən] n munizioni fpl
amnesty ['æmnɪstɪ] n amnistia; to grant an ~ to concedere l'amnistia a, amnistiare
among(st) [ə'mʌŋ(st)] prep fra, tra, in mezzo a
amount [ə'maunt] n somma; ammontare m; quantità f inv ▷ vi to ~ to (total) ammontare a; (be same as) essere come
amp(ère) ['æmpεəʳ] n ampère m inv
ample ['æmpl] adj ampio(-a); spazioso(-a); (enough): this is ~ questo è più che sufficiente

amplifier['æmplifaɪə'] *n* amplificatore *m*

amputate['æmpjuteɪt] *vt* amputare

Amtrak['æmtræk] (*us*) *n* società ferroviaria americana

amuse[ə'mjuːz] *vt* divertire; **amusement** *n* divertimento; **amusement arcade** *n* sala giochi; **amusement park** *n* luna park *m inv*

amusing[ə'mjuːzɪŋ] *adj* divertente

an[æn] *indef art see* **a**

anaemia[ə'niːmɪə] (*us* **anemia**) *n* anemia

anaemic[ə'niːmɪk] (*us* **anemic**) *adj* anemico(-a)

anaesthetic[ænɪs'θεtɪk] (*us* **anesthetic**) *adj* anestetico(-a) ▷ *n* anestetico

analog(ue)['ænəlɔg] *adj* (*watch, computer*) analogico(-a)

analogy[ə'nælədʒɪ] *n* analogia; **to draw an ~ between** fare un'analogia tra

analyse['ænəlaɪz] (*us* **analyze**) *vt* analizzare; **analysis**[ə'næləsɪs] (*pl* **analyses**) *n* analisi *f inv*; **analyst** ['ænəlɪst] *n* (*Pol etc*) analista *m/f*; (*us*) (psic)analista *m/f*

analyze['ænəlaɪz] (*us*) *vt* = **analyse**

anarchy['ænəkɪ] *n* anarchia

anatomy[ə'nætəmɪ] *n* anatomia

ancestor['ænsɪstə'] *n* antenato(-a)

anchor['æŋkə'] *n* ancora ▷ *vi* (*also:* **to drop ~**) gettare l'ancora ▷ *vt* ancorare; **to weigh ~** salpare *or* levare l'ancora

anchovy['æntʃəvɪ] *n* acciuga

ancient['eɪnʃənt] *adj* antico(-a); (*person, car*) vecchissimo(-a)

and[ænd] *conj* e; (*often ed before vowel*): **~ so on** e così via; **try ~ come** cerca di venire; **he talked ~ talked** non la finiva di parlare; **better ~ better** sempre meglio

Andes['ændiːz] *npl* **the ~** le Ande

anemia *etc* [ə'niːmɪə] (*us*) = **anaemia** *etc*

anesthetic[ænɪs'θεtɪk] (*us*) *adj, n* = **anaesthetic**

angel['eɪndʒəl] *n* angelo

anger['æŋgə'] *n* rabbia

angina[æn'dʒaɪnə] *n* angina pectoris

angle['æŋgl] *n* angolo; **from their ~** dal loro punto di vista

angler['æŋglə'] *n* pescatore *m* con la lenza

Anglican['æŋglɪkən] *adj, n* anglicano(-a)

angling['æŋglɪŋ] *n* pesca con la lenza

angrily['æŋgrɪlɪ] *adv* con rabbia

angry['æŋgrɪ] *adj* arrabbiato(-a), furioso(-a); (*wound*) infiammato(-a); **to be ~ with sb/at sth** essere in collera con qn/per qc; **to get ~** arrabbiarsi; **to make sb ~** fare arrabbiare qn

anguish['æŋgwɪʃ] *n* angoscia

animal['ænɪməl] *adj* animale ▷ *n* animale *m*

animated['ænɪmeɪtɪd] *adj* animato(-a)

animation[ænɪ'meɪʃən] *n* animazione *f*

aniseed['ænɪsiːd] *n* semi *mpl* di anice

ankle['æŋkl] *n* caviglia

annex[*n* ə'nεks, *vb* ə'nεks] *n* (*BRIT: also:* **~e**) (edificio) annesso ▷ *vt* annettere

anniversary[ænɪ'vəːsərɪ] *n* anniversario

announce[ə'nauns] *vt* annunciare; **announcement** *n* annuncio; (*letter, card*) partecipazione *f*; **announcer** *n* (*Radio, TV: between programmes*) annunciatore(-trice); (*: in a programme*) presentatore(-trice)

annoy[ə'nɔɪ] *vt* dare fastidio a; **don't get ~ed!** non irritarti!; **annoying** *adj* noioso(-a)

annual['ænjuəl] *adj* annuale ▷ *n* (*Bot*) pianta annua; (*book*) annuario; **annually** *adv* annualmente

annum['ænəm] *n see* **per**

anonymous[ə'nɔnɪməs] *adj* anonimo(-a)

anorak['ænəræk] *n* giacca a vento

anorexia[ænə'rεksɪə] *n* (*Med: also:* **~ nervosa**) anoressia

anorexic[ænə'rεksɪk] *adj, n* anoressico(-a)

another[ə'nʌðə'] *adj* **~ book** (*one more*) un altro libro, ancora un libro; (*a different one*) un altro libro ▷ *pron* un altro(un'altra), ancora uno(-a); *see also* **one**

answer['ɑːnsə'] *n* risposta; soluzione *f* ▷ *vi* rispondere ▷ *vt* (*reply to*) rispondere a; (*problem*) risolvere; (*prayer*) esaudire; **in ~ to your letter** in risposta alla sua lettera; **to ~ the phone** rispondere (al telefono); **to ~ the bell** rispondere al campanello; **to ~ the door** aprire la porta; **answer back** *vi* ribattere; **answerphone** *n* (*esp BRIT*) segreteria telefonica

ant[ænt] *n* formica

Antarctic[ænt'ɑːktɪk] *n* **the ~** l'Antartide *f*

antelope['æntɪləup] *n* antilope *f*

antenatal['æntɪ'neɪtl] *adj* prenatale

antenna[æn'tεnə, -niː] (*pl* **antennae**) *n* antenna

anthem['ænθəm] *n* **national ~** inno nazionale

anthology[æn'θɔlədʒɪ] *n* antologia

anthrax['ænθræks] *n* antrace *m*

anthropology[ænθrə'pɔlədʒɪ] *n* antropologia

anti[ænti] *prefix* anti; **antibiotic** ['æntɪbaɪ'ɔtɪk] *n* antibiotico; **antibody** ['æntɪbɔdɪ] *n* anticorpo

anticipate[æn'tɪsɪpeɪt] *vt* prevedere; pregustare; (*wishes, request*) prevenire; **anticipation**[æntɪsɪ'peɪʃən] *n* anticipazione *f*; (*expectation*) aspettative *fpl*

anticlimax['æntɪ'klaɪmæks] *n* **it was an ~** fu una completa delusione

anticlockwise [ˈæntɪˈklɔkwaɪz] adj, adv in senso antiorario

antics [ˈæntɪks] npl buffonerie fpl

anti: **antidote** [ˈæntɪdəut] n antidoto; **antifreeze** [ˈæntɪˈfriːz] n anticongelante m; **anti-globalization** [æntɪgləʊbəlaɪˈzeɪʃən] n antiglobalizzazione f; **antihistamine** [æntɪˈhɪstəmɪn] n antistaminico; **antiperspirant** [ˈæntɪˈpəːspərənt] adj antitraspirante

antique [ænˈtiːk] n antichità f inv ▷ adj antico(-a); **antique shop** n negozio d'antichità

antiseptic [æntɪˈsɛptɪk] n antisettico

antisocial [ˈæntɪˈsəʊʃəl] adj asociale

antlers [ˈæntləz] npl palchi mpl

anxiety [æŋˈzaɪətɪ] n ansia; (keenness): ~ **to do** smania di fare

anxious [ˈæŋkʃəs] adj ansioso(-a), inquieto(-a); (worrying) angosciante; (keen): ~ **to do/that** impaziente di fare/che + sub

○ KEYWORD

any [ˈɛnɪ] adj 1 (in questions etc): **have you any butter?** hai del burro?, hai un po' di burro?; **have you any children?** hai bambini?; **if there are any tickets left** se ci sono ancora (dei) biglietti, se c'è ancora qualche biglietto
2 (with negative): **I haven't any money/books** non ho soldi/libri
3 (no matter which) qualsiasi, qualunque; **choose any book you like** scegli un libro qualsiasi
4 (in phrases): **in any case** in ogni caso; **any day now** da un giorno all'altro; **at any moment** in qualsiasi momento, da un momento all'altro; **at any rate** ad ogni modo
▷ pron 1 (in questions, with negative): **have you got any?** ne hai?; **can any of you sing?** qualcuno di voi sa cantare?; **I haven't any (of them)** non ne ho
2 (no matter which one(s)): **take any of those books (you like)** prendi uno qualsiasi di quei libri
▷ adv 1 (in questions etc): **do you want any more soup/sandwiches?** vuoi ancora un po' di minestra/degli altri panini?; **are you feeling any better?** ti senti meglio?
2 (with negative): **I can't hear him any more** non lo sento più; **don't wait any longer** non aspettare più

any: **anybody** [ˈɛnɪbɔdɪ] pron (in questions etc) qualcuno, nessuno; (with negative) nessuno; (no matter who) chiunque; **can you see anybody?** vedi qualcuno or nessuno?; **if anybody should phone ...** se telefona qualcuno ...; **I can't see anybody** non vedo nessuno; **anybody could do it** chiunque potrebbe farlo; **anyhow** [ˈɛnɪhau] adv (at any rate) ad ogni modo, comunque; (haphazard): **do it anyhow you like** fallo come ti pare; **I shall go anyhow** ci andrò lo stesso or comunque; **she leaves things just anyhow** lascia tutto come capita; **anyone** [ˈɛnɪwʌn] pron = **anybody**; **anything** [ˈɛnɪθɪŋ] pron (in question etc) qualcosa, niente; (with negative) niente; (no matter what): **you can say anything you like** puoi dire quello che ti pare; **can you see anything?** vedi niente or qualcosa?; **if anything happens to me ...** se mi dovesse succedere qualcosa ...; **I can't see anything** non vedo niente; **anything will do** va bene qualsiasi cosa or tutto; **anytime** adv in qualunque momento; quando vuole; **anyway** [ˈɛnɪweɪ] adv (at any rate) ad ogni modo, comunque; (besides) ad ogni modo; **anywhere** [ˈɛnɪwɛər] adv (in questions etc) da qualche parte; (with negative) da nessuna parte; (no matter where) da qualsiasi or qualunque parte, dovunque; **can you see him anywhere?** lo vedi da qualche parte?; **I can't see him anywhere** non lo vedo da nessuna parte; **anywhere in the world** dovunque nel mondo

apart [əˈpɑːt] adv (to one side) a parte; (separately) separatamente; **with one's legs ~** con le gambe divaricate; **10 miles ~** a 10 miglia di distanza (l'uno dall'altro); **to take ~** smontare; **~ from** a parte, eccetto

apartment [əˈpɑːtmənt] (us) n appartamento; (room) locale m; **apartment building** (us) n stabile m, caseggiato

apathy [ˈæpəθɪ] n apatia

ape [eɪp] n scimmia ▷ vt scimmiottare

aperitif [əˈpɛrɪtiːf] n aperitivo

aperture [ˈæpətʃjuər] n apertura

APEX n abbr (= advance purchase excursion) APEX m inv

apologize [əˈpɔlədʒaɪz] vi **to ~ (for sth to sb)** scusarsi (di qc a qn), chiedere scusa (a qn per qc)

apology [əˈpɔlədʒɪ] n scuse fpl

apostrophe [əˈpɔstrəfɪ] n (sign) apostrofo

appal [əˈpɔːl] (us **appall**) vt scioccare; **appalling** adj spaventoso(-a)

apparatus [æpəˈreɪtəs] n apparato; (in gymnasium) attrezzatura

apparent [əˈpærənt] adj evidente; **apparently** adv evidentemente

appeal [əˈpiːl] vi (Law) appellarsi alla legge ▷ n (Law) appello; (request) richiesta; (charm) attrattiva; **to ~ for** chiedere (con insistenza); **to ~ to** (person) appellarsi a; (thing) piacere a; **it doesn't ~ to me** mi dice poco; **appealing** adj (nice) attraente

appear [əˈpɪəʳ] vi apparire; (Law) comparire; (publication) essere pubblicato(-a); (seem) sembrare; **it would ~ that** sembra che; **appearance** n apparizione f; apparenza; (look, aspect) aspetto

appendicitis [əpɛndɪˈsaɪtɪs] n appendicite f

appendix [əˈpɛndɪks] (pl **appendices**) n appendice f

appetite [ˈæpɪtaɪt] n appetito

appetizer [ˈæpɪtaɪzəʳ] n stuzzichino

applaud [əˈplɔːd] vt, vi applaudire

applause [əˈplɔːz] n applauso

apple [ˈæpl] n mela; **apple pie** n torta di mele

appliance [əˈplaɪəns] n apparecchio

applicable [əˈplɪkəbl] adj applicabile; **to be ~ to** essere valido per; **the law is ~ from January** la legge entrerà in vigore in gennaio

applicant [ˈæplɪkənt] n candidato(-a)

application [æplɪˈkeɪʃən] n applicazione f; (for a job, a grant etc) domanda; **application form** n modulo per la domanda

apply [əˈplaɪ] vt **to ~ (to)** (paint, ointment) dare (a); (theory, technique) applicare (a) ▷ vi **to ~ to** (ask) rivolgersi a; (be suitable for, relevant to) riguardare, riferirsi a; **to ~ (for)** (permit, grant, job) fare domanda (per); **to ~ o.s. to** dedicarsi a

appoint [əˈpɔɪnt] vt nominare; **appointment** n nomina; (arrangement to meet) appuntamento; **I have an appointment (with) ...** ho un appuntamento (con) ...; **I'd like to make an appointment (with)** vorrei prendere un appuntamento (con)

appraisal [əˈpreɪzl] n valutazione f

appreciate [əˈpriːʃɪeɪt] vt (like) apprezzare; (be grateful for) essere riconoscente di; (be aware of) rendersi conto di ▷ vi (Finance) aumentare; **I'd ~ your help** ti sono grato per l'aiuto; **appreciation** [əpriːʃɪˈeɪʃən] n apprezzamento; (Finance) aumento del valore

apprehension [æprɪˈhɛnʃən] n (fear) inquietudine f

apprehensive [æprɪˈhɛnsɪv] adj apprensivo(-a)

apprentice [əˈprɛntɪs] n apprendista m/f

approach [əˈprəʊtʃ] vi avvicinarsi ▷ vt (come near) avvicinarsi a; (ask, apply to) rivolgersi a; (subject, passer-by) avvicinare ▷ n approccio; accesso; (to problem) modo di affrontare

appropriate [adj əˈprəʊprɪɪt, vb əˈprəʊprɪeɪt] adj appropriato(-a), adatto(-a) ▷ vt (take) appropriarsi

approval [əˈpruːvəl] n approvazione f; **on ~** (Comm) in prova, in esame

approve [əˈpruːv] vt, vi approvare; **approve of** vt fus approvare

approximate [əˈprɔksɪmɪt] adj approssimativo(-a); **approximately** adv circa

Apr. abbr (= April) apr.

apricot [ˈeɪprɪkɔt] n albicocca

April [ˈeɪprəl] n aprile m; **~ fool!** pesce d'aprile!; **April Fools' Day** n vedi nota nel riquadro

---

● **APRIL FOOLS' DAY**

● **April Fool's Day** è il primo aprile, il giorno degli scherzi e delle burle. Il nome deriva dal fatto che, se una persona cade nella trappola che gli è stata tesa, fa la figura del "fool", cioè dello sciocco. Tradizionalmente, gli scherzi vengono fatti entro mezzogiorno.

---

apron [ˈeɪprən] n grembiule m

apt [æpt] adj (suitable) adatto(-a); (able) capace; (likely): **to be ~ to do** avere tendenza a fare

aquarium [əˈkwɛərɪəm] n acquario

Aquarius [əˈkwɛərɪəs] n Acquario

Arab [ˈærəb] adj, n arabo(-a)

Arabia [əˈreɪbɪə] n Arabia; **Arabian** [əˈreɪbɪən] adj arabo(-a); **Arabic** [ˈærəbɪk] adj arabico(-a), arabo(-a) ▷ n arabo; **Arabic numerals** n numeri mpl arabi, numerazione f araba

arbitrary [ˈɑːbɪtrərɪ] adj arbitrario(-a)

arbitration [ɑːbɪˈtreɪʃən] n (Law) arbitrato; (Industry) arbitraggio

arc [ɑːk] n arco

arcade [ɑːˈkeɪd] n portico; (passage with shops) galleria

arch [ɑːtʃ] n arco; (of foot) arco plantare ▷ vt inarcare

archaeology [ɑːkɪˈɔlədʒɪ] (us **archeology**) n archeologia

archbishop [ɑːtʃˈbɪʃəp] n arcivescovo

archeology etc [ɑːkɪˈɔlədʒɪ] (us) = **archaeology** etc

architect [ˈɑːkɪtɛkt] n architetto; **architectural** [ɑːkɪˈtɛktʃərəl] adj architettonico(-a); **architecture** [ˈɑːkɪtɛktʃəʳ] n architettura

archive ['ɑːkaɪv] n (often pl: also Comput)
archivio

Arctic ['ɑːktɪk] adj artico(-a) ▷ n **the ~**
l'Artico

are [ɑːʳ] vb see **be**

area ['ɛərɪə] n (Geom) area; (zone) zona; (:
smaller) settore m; **area code** (us) n (Tel)
prefisso

arena [əˈriːnə] n arena

aren't [ɑːnt] = **are not**

Argentina [ɑːdʒənˈtiːnə] n Argentina;
Argentinian [-ˈtɪnɪən] adj, n
argentino(-a)

arguably ['ɑːgjuəblɪ] adv **it is ~ ...** si può
sostenere che sia ...

argue ['ɑːgjuː] vi (quarrel) litigare; (reason)
ragionare; **to ~ that** sostenere che

argument ['ɑːgjumənt] n (reasons)
argomento; (quarrel) lite f

Aries ['ɛərɪz] n Ariete m

arise [əˈraɪz] (pt **arose**, pp **arisen**) vi
(opportunity, problem) presentarsi

arithmetic [əˈrɪθmətɪk] n aritmetica

arm [ɑːm] n braccio ▷ vt armare; **~s** npl
(weapons) armi fpl; **~ in ~** a braccetto;
armchair n poltrona

armed [ɑːmd] adj armato(-a); **armed
robbery** n rapina a mano armata

armour ['ɑːməʳ] (us **armor**) n armatura;
(Mil: tanks) mezzi mpl blindati

armpit ['ɑːmpɪt] n ascella

armrest ['ɑːmrɛst] n bracciolo

army ['ɑːmɪ] n esercito

A road n strada statale

aroma [əˈrəumə] n aroma; **aromatherapy**
n aromaterapia

arose [əˈrəuz] pt of **arise**

around [əˈraund] adv attorno, intorno
▷ prep intorno a; (fig: about): **~ £5/3 o'clock**
circa 5 sterline/le 3; **is he ~?** è in giro?

arouse [əˈrauz] vt (sleeper) svegliare;
(curiosity, passions) suscitare

arrange [əˈreɪndʒ] vt sistemare;
(programme) preparare; **to ~ to do
sth** mettersi d'accordo per fare qc;
arrangement n sistemazione f;
(agreement) accordo; **arrangements** npl
(plans) progetti mpl, piani mpl

array [əˈreɪ] n **~ of** fila di

arrears [əˈrɪəz] npl arretrati mpl; **to be in
~ with one's rent** essere in arretrato con
l'affitto

arrest [əˈrɛst] vt arrestare; (sb's attention)
attirare ▷ n arresto; **under ~** in arresto

arrival [əˈraɪvəl] n arrivo; (person)
arrivato(-a); **a new ~** un nuovo venuto;
(baby) un neonato

arrive [əˈraɪv] vi arrivare; **what time does
the train from Rome ~?** a che ora arriva il
treno da Roma?; **arrive at** vt fus arrivare a

arrogance ['ærəgəns] n arroganza

arrogant ['ærəgənt] adj arrogante

arrow ['ærəu] n freccia

arse [ɑːs] (inf!) n culo (!)

arson ['ɑːsn] n incendio doloso

art [ɑːt] n arte f; (craft) mestiere m; **art
college** n scuola di belle arti

artery ['ɑːtərɪ] n arteria

art gallery n galleria d'arte

arthritis [ɑːˈθraɪtɪs] n artrite f

artichoke ['ɑːtɪtʃəuk] n carciofo;
Jerusalem ~ topinambur m inv

article ['ɑːtɪkl] n articolo

articulate [adj ɑːˈtɪkjulɪt, vb ɑːˈtɪkjuleɪt]
adj (person) che si esprime forbitamente;
(speech) articolato(-a) ▷ vi articolare

artificial [ɑːtɪˈfɪʃəl] adj artificiale

artist ['ɑːtɪst] n artista m/f; **artistic**
[ɑːˈtɪstɪk] adj artistico(-a)

art school n scuola d'arte

KEYWORD

as [æz] conj **1** (referring to time) mentre;
as the years went by col passare degli
anni; **he came in as I was leaving**
arrivò mentre stavo uscendo; **as from
tomorrow** da domani

2 (in comparisons): **as big as** grande come;
twice as big as due volte più grande di;
as much/many as tanto quanto/tanti
quanti; **as soon as possible** prima
possibile

3 (since, because) dal momento che,
siccome

4 (referring to manner, way) come; **do as
you wish** fa' come vuoi; **as she said** come
ha detto lei

5 (concerning): **as for** or **to that** per quanto
riguarda or quanto a quello

6: **as if** or **as though** come se; **he looked
as if he was ill** sembrava stare male; see
also **long**; **such**; **well**

▷ prep **he works as a driver** fa l'autista; **as
chairman of the company he ...** come
presidente della compagnia lui ...; **he gave
me it as a present** me lo ha regalato

a.s.a.p. abbr = **as soon as possible**

asbestos [æzˈbɛstəs] n asbesto, amianto

ascent [əˈsɛnt] n salita

ash [æʃ] n (dust) cenere f; (wood, tree)
frassino

ashamed [əˈʃeɪmd] adj vergognoso(-a); **to
be ~ of** vergognarsi di

ashore [əˈʃɔːʳ] adv a terra

ashtray ['æʃtreɪ] n portacenere m

Ash Wednesday n mercoledì m inv delle

Ceneri

Asia ['eɪʃə] n Asia; **Asian** adj, n asiatico(-a)

aside [ə'saɪd] adv da parte ▷ n a parte m

ask [ɑːsk] vt (question) domandare; (invite) invitare; **to ~ sb sth/sb to do sth** chiedere qc a qn/a qn di fare qc; **to ~ sb about sth** chiedere a qn di qc; **to ~ (sb) a question** fare una domanda (a qn); **to ~ sb out to dinner** invitare qn a mangiare fuori; **ask for** vt fus chiedere; (trouble etc) cercare

asleep [ə'sliːp] adj addormentato(-a); **to be ~** dormire; **to fall ~** addormentarsi

asparagus [əs'pærəgəs] n asparagi mpl

aspect ['æspɛkt] n aspetto

aspirations [æspə'reɪʃənz] npl aspirazioni fpl

aspire [əs'paɪəʳ] vi **to ~ to** aspirare a

aspirin ['æsprɪn] n aspirina

ass [æs] n asino; (inf) scemo(-a); (us: inf!) culo (!)

assassin [ə'sæsɪn] n assassino; **assassinate** [ə'sæsɪneɪt] vt assassinare

assault [ə'sɔːlt] n (Mil) assalto; (gen: attack) aggressione f ▷ vt assaltare; aggredire; (sexually) violentare

assemble [ə'sɛmbl] vt riunire; (Tech) montare ▷ vi riunirsi

assembly [ə'sɛmblɪ] n (meeting) assemblea; (construction) montaggio

assert [ə'səːt] vt asserire; (insist on) far valere; **assertion** [ə'səːʃən] n asserzione f

assess [ə'sɛs] vt valutare; **assessment** n valutazione f

asset ['æsɛt] n vantaggio; **~s** npl (Finance: of individual) beni mpl; (: of company) attivo

assign [ə'saɪn] vt **to ~ (to)** (task) assegnare (a); (resources) riservare (a); (cause, meaning) attribuire (a); **to ~ a date to sth** fissare la data di qc; **assignment** n compito

assist [ə'sɪst] vt assistere, aiutare; **assistance** n assistenza, aiuto; **assistant** n assistente m/f; (BRIT: also: **shop assistant**) commesso(-a)

associate [adj, n ə'səʊʃiːt, vb ə'səʊʃieɪt] adj associato(-a); (member) aggiunto(-a) ▷ n collega m/f ▷ vt associare ▷ vi **to ~ with sb** frequentare qn

association [əsəʊsɪ'eɪʃən] n associazione f

assorted [ə'sɔːtɪd] adj assortito(-a)

assortment [ə'sɔːtmənt] n assortimento

assume [ə'sjuːm] vt supporre; (responsibilities etc) assumere; (attitude, name) prendere

assumption [ə'sʌmpʃən] n supposizione f, ipotesi f inv; (of power) assunzione f

assurance [ə'ʃuərəns] n assicurazione f; (self-confidence) fiducia in se stesso

assure [ə'ʃuəʳ] vt assicurare

asterisk ['æstərɪsk] n asterisco

asthma ['æsmə] n asma

astonish [ə'stɔnɪʃ] vt stupire; **astonished** adj stupito(-a), sorpreso(-a); **to be astonished (at)** essere stupito(-a) (da); **astonishing** adj sorprendente, stupefacente; **I find it astonishing that ...** mi stupisce che ...; **astonishment** n stupore m

astound [ə'staund] vt sbalordire

astray [ə'streɪ] adv **to go ~** smarrirsi; **to lead ~** portare sulla cattiva strada

astrology [əs'trɔlədʒɪ] n astrologia

astronaut ['æstrənɔːt] n astronauta m/f

astronomer [əs'trɔnəməʳ] n astronomo(-a)

astronomical [æstrə'nɔmɪkl] adj astronomico(-a)

astronomy [əs'trɔnəmɪ] n astronomia

astute [əs'tjuːt] adj astuto(-a)

asylum [ə'saɪləm] n (politico) asilo; (per malati) manicomio

KEYWORD

at [æt] prep **1** (referring to position, direction) a; **at the top** in cima; **at the desk** al banco, alla scrivania; **at home/school** a casa/scuola; **at the baker's** dal panettiere; **to look at sth** guardare qc; **to throw sth at sb** lanciare qc a qn
2 (referring to time) a; **at 4 o'clock** alle 4; **at night** di notte; **at Christmas** a Natale; **at times** a volte
3 (referring to rates, speed etc) a; **at £1 a kilo** a 1 sterlina al chilo; **two at a time** due alla volta, due per volta; **at 50 km/h** a 50 km/h
4 (referring to manner): **at a stroke** d'un solo colpo; **at peace** in pace
5 (referring to activity): **to be at work** essere al lavoro; **to play at cowboys** giocare ai cowboy; **to be good at sth/doing sth** essere bravo in qc/fare qc
6 (referring to cause): **shocked/surprised/annoyed at sth** colpito da/sorpreso da/arrabbiato per qc; **I went at his suggestion** ci sono andato dietro suo consiglio

ate [eɪt] pt of **eat**

atheist ['eɪθɪɪst] n ateo(-a)

Athens ['æθɪnz] n Atene f

athlete ['æθliːt] n atleta m/f

athletic [æθ'lɛtɪk] adj atletico(-a); **athletics** n atletica

Atlantic [ət'læntɪk] adj atlantico(-a) ▷ n **the ~ (Ocean)** l'Atlantico, l'Oceano Atlantico

atlas ['ætləs] n atlante m

A.T.M. n abbr (= automated telling machine) cassa automatica prelievi, sportello automatico

atmosphere ['ætməsfɪəʳ] n atmosfera

atom ['ætəm] n atomo; **atomic** [ə'tɔmɪk] adj atomico(-a); **atom(ic) bomb** n bomba atomica

A to Z® n (map) stradario

atrocity [ə'trɔsɪtɪ] n atrocità f inv

attach [ə'tætʃ] vt attaccare; (document, letter) allegare; (importance etc) attribuire; **to be ~ed to sb/sth** (to like) essere affezionato(-a) a qn/qc; **attachment** [ə'tætʃmənt] n (tool) accessorio; (love): **attachment (to)** affetto (per)

attack [ə'tæk] vt attaccare; (person) aggredire; (task etc) iniziare; (problem) affrontare ▷ n attacco; **heart ~** infarto; **attacker** n aggressore m

attain [ə'teɪn] vt (also: **to ~ to**) arrivare a, raggiungere

attempt [ə'tɛmpt] n tentativo ▷ vt tentare; **to make an ~ on sb's life** attentare alla vita di qn

attend [ə'tɛnd] vt frequentare; (meeting, talk) andare a; (patient) assistere; **attend to** vt fus (needs, affairs etc) prendersi cura di; (customer) occuparsi di; **attendance** n (being present) presenza; (people present) gente f presente; **attendant** n custode m/f; persona di servizio ▷ adj concomitante

Be careful not to translate **attend** by the Italian word **attendere**.

attention [ə'tɛnʃən] n attenzione f ▷ excl (Mil) attenti!; **for the ~ of** (Admin) per l'attenzione di

attic ['ætɪk] n soffitta

attitude ['ætɪtjuːd] n atteggiamento; posa

attorney [ə'təːnɪ] n (lawyer) avvocato; (having proxy) mandatario; **Attorney General** n (BRIT) Procuratore m Generale; (US) Ministro della Giustizia

attract [ə'trækt] vt attirare; **attraction** [ə'trækʃən] n (gen pl: pleasant things) attrattiva; (Physics, fig: towards sth) attrazione f; **attractive** adj attraente

attribute [n ə'trɪbjuːt, vb ə'trɪbjuːt] n attributo ▷ vt **to ~ sth to** attribuire qc a

aubergine ['əubəʒiːn] n melanzana

auburn ['ɔːbən] adj tizianesco(-a)

auction ['ɔːkʃən] n (also: **sale by ~**) asta ▷ vt (also: **to sell by ~**) vendere all'asta; (also: **to put up for ~**) mettere all'asta

audible ['ɔːdɪbl] adj udibile

audience ['ɔːdɪəns] n (people) pubblico; spettatori mpl; ascoltatori mpl; (interview) udienza

audit ['ɔːdɪt] vt rivedere, verificare

audition [ɔː'dɪʃən] n audizione f

auditor ['ɔːdɪtəʳ] n revisore m

auditorium [ɔːdɪ'tɔːrɪəm] n sala, auditorio

Aug. abbr (= August) ago., ag.

August ['ɔːgəst] n agosto

aunt [ɑːnt] n zia; **auntie** n zietta; **aunty** n zietta

au pair ['əu'pɛəʳ] n (also: **~ girl**) (ragazza f) alla pari inv

aura ['ɔːrə] n aura

austerity [ɔs'tɛrɪtɪ] n austerità f inv

Australia [ɔs'treɪlɪə] n Australia; **Australian** adj, n australiano(-a)

Austria ['ɔstrɪə] n Austria; **Austrian** adj, n austriaco(-a)

authentic [ɔː'θɛntɪk] adj autentico(-a)

author ['ɔːθəʳ] n autore(-trice)

authority [ɔː'θɔrɪtɪ] n autorità f inv; (permission) autorizzazione f; **the authorities** npl (government etc) le autorità

authorize ['ɔːθəraɪz] vt autorizzare

auto ['ɔːtəu] (US) n auto f inv; **autobiography** [ɔːtəbaɪ'ɔgrəfɪ] n autobiografia; **autograph** ['ɔːtəgrɑːf] n autografo ▷ vt firmare; **automatic** [ɔːtə'mætɪk] adj automatico(-a) ▷ n (gun) arma automatica; (washing machine) lavatrice f automatica; (car) automobile f con cambio automatico; **automatically** adv automaticamente; **automobile** ['ɔːtəməbiːl] (US) n automobile f; **autonomous** [ɔː'tɔnəməs] adj autonomo(-a); **autonomy** [ɔː'tɔnəmɪ] n autonomia

autumn ['ɔːtəm] n autunno

auxiliary [ɔːg'zɪlɪərɪ] adj ausiliario(-a) ▷ n ausiliare m/f

avail [ə'veɪl] vt **to ~ o.s. of** servirsi di; approfittarsi di ▷ n **to no ~** inutilmente

availability [əveɪlə'bɪlɪtɪ] n disponibilità

available [ə'veɪləbl] adj disponibile

avalanche ['ævəlɑːnʃ] n valanga

Ave. abbr = **avenue**

avenue ['ævənjuː] n viale m; (fig) strada, via

average ['ævərɪdʒ] n media ▷ adj medio(-a) ▷ vt (a certain figure) fare di or in media; **on ~** in media

avert [ə'vəːt] vt evitare, prevenire; (one's eyes) distogliere

avid ['ævɪd] adj (supporter etc) accanito(-a)

avocado [ævə'kɑːdəu] n (BRIT: also: **~ pear**) avocado m inv

avoid [ə'vɔɪd] vt evitare

await [ə'weɪt] vt aspettare

awake [ə'weɪk] (pt awoke, pp awoken, awaked) adj sveglio(-a) ▷ vt svegliare ▷ vi svegliarsi

award [ə'wɔːd] n premio; (Law) risarcimento ▷ vt assegnare; (Law: damages) accordare

aware [ə'wɛə^r] adj ~ **of** (conscious) conscio(-a) di; (informed) informato(-a) di; **to become ~ of** accorgersi di; **awareness** n consapevolezza

away [ə'weɪ] adj, adv via; lontano(-a); **two kilometres ~** a due chilometri di distanza; **two hours ~ by car** a due ore di distanza in macchina; **the holiday was two weeks ~** mancavano due settimane alle vacanze; **he's ~ for a week** è andato via per una settimana; **to take ~** togliere; **he was working/pedalling** etc ~ (la particella indica la continuità e l'energia dell'azione) lavorava/pedalava etc più che poteva; **to fade/wither** etc ~ (la particella rinforza l'idea della diminuzione)

awe [ɔː] n timore m; **awesome** adj imponente

awful ['ɔːfəl] adj terribile; **an ~ lot of** un mucchio di; **awfully** adv (very) terribilmente

awkward ['ɔːkwəd] adj (clumsy) goffo(-a); (inconvenient) scomodo(-a); (embarrassing) imbarazzante

awoke [ə'wəuk] pt of **awake**

awoken [ə'wəukn] pp of **awake**

axe [æks] (US **ax**) n scure f ▷ vt (project etc) abolire; (jobs) sopprimere

axle ['æksl] n (also: **~-tree**) asse m

ay(e) [aɪ] excl (yes) sì

azalea [ə'zeɪlɪə] n azalea

B [biː] n (Mus) si m

B.A. n abbr = **Bachelor of Arts**

baby ['beɪbɪ] n bambino(-a); **baby carriage** (US) n carrozzina; **baby-sit** vi fare il (or la) baby-sitter; **baby-sitter** n baby-sitter m/f inv; **baby wipe** n salvietta umidificata

bachelor ['bætʃələ^r] n scapolo; **B~ of Arts/ Science** ≈ laureato(-a) in lettere/scienze

back [bæk] n (of person, horse) dorso, schiena; (as opposed to front) dietro; (of hand) dorso; (of train) coda; (of chair) schienale m; (of page) rovescio; (of book) retro; (Football) difensore m ▷ vt (candidate) appoggiare; (horse: at races) puntare su; (car) guidare a marcia indietro ▷ vi indietreggiare; (car etc) fare marcia indietro ▷ cpd posteriore, di dietro; (Aut: seat, wheels) posteriore ▷ adv (not forward) indietro; (returned): **he's ~** è tornato; **he ran ~** tornò indietro di corsa; (restitution): **throw the ball ~** ritira la palla; **can I have it ~?** posso riaverlo?; (again): **he called ~** ha richiamato; **back down** vi fare marcia indietro; **back out** vi (of promise) tirarsi indietro; **back up** vt (support) appoggiare, sostenere; (Comput) fare una copia di riserva di; **backache** n mal m di schiena; **backbencher** (BRIT) n membro del Parlamento senza potere amministrativo;

backbone n spina dorsale; **back door** n porta sul retro; **backfire** vi (Aut) dar ritorni di fiamma; (plans) fallire; **backgammon** n tavola reale; **background** n sfondo; (of events) background m inv; (basic knowledge) base f; (experience) esperienza; **family background** ambiente m familiare; **backing** n (fig) appoggio; **backlog** n **backlog of work** lavoro arretrato; **backpack** n zaino; **backpacker** n chi viaggia con zaino e sacco a pelo; **backslash** n backslash m inv, barra obliqua inversa; **backstage** adv nel retroscena; **backstroke** n nuoto sul dorso; **backup** adj (train, plane) supplementare; (Comput) di riserva ▷ n (support) appoggio, sostegno; (also: **backup file**) file m inv di riserva; **backward** adj (movement) indietro inv; (person) tardivo(-a); (country) arretrato(-a); **backwards** adv indietro; (fall, walk) all'indietro; **backyard** n cortile m dietro la casa

bacon ['beɪkən] n pancetta

bacteria [bæk'tɪərɪə] npl batteri mpl

bad [bæd] adj cattivo(-a); (accident, injury) brutto(-a); (meat, food) andato(-a) a male; **his ~ leg** la sua gamba malata; **to go ~** andare a male

badge [bædʒ] n insegna; (of policeman) stemma m

badger ['bædʒəʳ] n tasso

badly ['bædlɪ] adv (work, dress etc) male; **~ wounded** gravemente ferito; **he needs it ~** ne ha un gran bisogno

bad-mannered [bæd'mænəd] adj maleducato(-a), sgarbato(-a)

badminton ['bædmɪntən] n badminton m

bad-tempered ['bæd'tɛmpəd] adj irritabile; di malumore

bag [bæg] n sacco; (handbag etc) borsa; **~s of** (inf: lots of) un sacco di; **baggage** n bagagli mpl; **baggage allowance** n franchigia f bagaglio inv; **baggage reclaim** n ritiro m bagaglio inv; **baggy** adj largo(-a), sformato(-a); **bagpipes** npl cornamusa

bail [beɪl] n cauzione f ▷ vt (prisoner: also: **grant ~ to**) concedere la libertà provvisoria su cauzione a; (boat: also: **~ out**) aggottare; **on ~** in libertà provvisoria su cauzione

bait [beɪt] n esca ▷ vt (hook) innescare; (trap) munire di esca; (fig) tormentare

bake [beɪk] vt cuocere al forno ▷ vi cuocersi al forno; **baked beans** [-biːnz] npl fagioli mpl in salsa di pomodoro; **baked potato** n patata cotta al forno con la buccia; **baker** n fornaio(-a), panettiere(-a); **bakery** n panetteria;

baking n cottura (al forno); **baking powder** n lievito in polvere

balance ['bæləns] n equilibrio; (Comm: sum) bilancio; (remainder) resto; (scales) bilancia ▷ vt tenere in equilibrio; (budget) far quadrare; (account) pareggiare; (compensate) contrappesare; **~ of trade/payments** bilancia commerciale/dei pagamenti; **balanced** adj (personality, diet) equilibrato(-a); **balance sheet** n bilancio

balcony ['bælkənɪ] n balcone m; (in theatre) balconata; **do you have a room with a ~?** avete una camera con balcone?

bald [bɔːld] adj calvo(-a); (tyre) liscio(-a)

Balearics [bælɪ'ærɪks] npl **the ~** le Baleari fpl

ball [bɔːl] n palla; (football) pallone m; (for golf) pallina; (of wool, string) gomitolo; (dance) ballo; **to play ~** (fig) stare al gioco

ballerina [bælə'riːnə] n ballerina

ballet ['bæleɪ] n balletto; **ballet dancer** n ballerino(-a) classico(-a)

balloon [bə'luːn] n pallone m

ballot ['bælət] n scrutinio

ballpoint (pen) ['bɔːlpɔɪnt(-)] n penna a sfera

ballroom ['bɔːlrum] n sala da ballo

Baltic ['bɔːltɪk] adj, n **the ~ Sea** il (mar) Baltico

bamboo [bæm'buː] n bambù m

ban [bæn] n interdizione f ▷ vt interdire

banana [bə'nɑːnə] n banana

band [bænd] n banda; (at a dance) orchestra; (Mil) fanfara

bandage ['bændɪdʒ] n benda, fascia

Band-Aid® ['bændeɪd] (US) n cerotto

B. & B. n abbr = **bed and breakfast**

bandit ['bændɪt] n bandito

bang [bæŋ] n (of door) lo sbattere; (of gun, blow) colpo ▷ vt battere (violentemente); (door) sbattere ▷ vi scoppiare; sbattere

Bangladesh [bɑːŋglə'dɛʃ] n Bangladesh m

bangle ['bæŋgl] n braccialetto

bangs [bæŋz] (US) npl (fringe) frangia, frangetta

banish ['bænɪʃ] vt bandire

banister(s) ['bænɪstə(z)] n(pl) ringhiera

banjo ['bændʒəu] (pl **banjoes** or **banjos**) n banjo m inv

bank [bæŋk] n banca, banco; (of river, lake) riva, sponda; (of earth) banco ▷ vi (Aviat) inclinarsi in virata; **bank on** vt fus contare su; **bank account** n conto in banca; **bank balance** n saldo; **a healthy bank balance** un solido conto in banca; **bank card** n carta f assegni inv; **bank charges** npl (BRIT) spese fpl bancarie; **banker** n banchiere m; **bank holiday** (BRIT) n giorno di festa; vedi nota nel riquadro; **banking**

n attività bancaria; professione *f* di banchiere; **bank manager** *n* direttore *m* di banca; **banknote** *n* banconota

● **BANK HOLIDAY**
●
● Una **bank holiday**, in Gran Bretagna,
● è una giornata in cui banche e molti
● negozi sono chiusi. Generalmente le
● **bank holidays** cadono di lunedì e molti
● ne approfittano per fare una breve
● vacanza fuori città.

bankrupt ['bæŋkrʌpt] *adj* fallito(-a); **to go ~** fallire; **bankruptcy** *n* fallimento
bank statement *n* estratto conto
banner ['bænə^r] *n* striscione *m*
bannister(s) ['bænɪstə(z)] *n(pl)* see **banister(s)**
banquet ['bæŋkwɪt] *n* banchetto
baptism ['bæptɪzəm] *n* battesimo
baptize [bæp'taɪz] *vt* battezzare
bar [bɑː^r] *n* (*place*) bar *m inv*; (*counter*) banco; (*rod*) barra; (*of window etc*) sbarra; (*of chocolate*) tavoletta; (*fig*) ostacolo; restrizione *f*; (*Mus*) battuta ▷ *vt* (*road, window*) sbarrare; (*person*) escludere; (*activity*) interdire; **~ of soap** saponetta; **the B~** (*Law*) l'Ordine *m* degli avvocati; **behind ~s** (*prisoner*) dietro le sbarre; **~ none** senza eccezione
barbaric [bɑː'bærɪk] *adj* barbarico(-a)
barbecue ['bɑːbɪkjuː] *n* barbecue *m inv*
barbed wire ['bɑːbd-] *n* filo spinato
barber ['bɑːbə^r] *n* barbiere *m*; **barber's (shop)** (*US* **barber (shop)**) *n* barbiere *m*
bar code *n* (*on goods*) codice *m* a barre
bare [bɛə^r] *adj* nudo(-a) ▷ *vt* scoprire, denudare; (*teeth*) mostrare; **the ~ necessities** lo stretto necessario; **barefoot** *adj, adv* scalzo(-a); **barely** *adv* appena
bargain ['bɑːgɪn] *n* (*transaction*) contratto; (*good buy*) affare *m* ▷ *vi* trattare; **into the ~** per giunta; **bargain for** *vt fus* **he got more than he ~ed for** gli è andata peggio di quel che si aspettasse
barge [bɑːdʒ] *n* chiatta; **barge in** *vi* (*walk in*) piombare dentro; (*interrupt talk*) intromettersi a sproposito
bark [bɑːk] *n* (*of tree*) corteccia; (*of dog*) abbaio ▷ *vi* abbaiare
barley ['bɑːlɪ] *n* orzo
barmaid ['bɑːmeɪd] *n* cameriera al banco
barman ['bɑːmən] (*irreg*) *n* barista *m*
barn [bɑːn] *n* granaio
barometer [bə'rɒmɪtə^r] *n* barometro
baron ['bærən] *n* barone *m*; **baroness** *n* baronessa

barracks ['bærəks] *npl* caserma
barrage ['bærɑːʒ] *n* (*Mil, dam*) sbarramento; (*fig*) fiume *m*
barrel ['bærəl] *n* barile *m*; (*of gun*) canna
barren ['bærən] *adj* sterile; (*soil*) arido(-a)
barrette [bə'rɛt] (*US*) *n* fermaglio per capelli
barricade [bærɪ'keɪd] *n* barricata
barrier ['bærɪə^r] *n* barriera
barring ['bɑːrɪŋ] *prep* salvo
barrister ['bærɪstə^r] (*BRIT*) *n* avvocato(-essa) (*con diritto di parlare davanti a tutte le corti*)
barrow ['bærəʊ] *n* (*cart*) carriola
bartender ['bɑːtɛndə^r] (*US*) *n* barista *m*
base [beɪs] *n* base *f* ▷ *vt* **to ~ sth on** basare qc su ▷ *adj* vile
baseball ['beɪsbɔːl] *n* baseball *m*; **baseball cap** *n* berretto da baseball
basement ['beɪsmənt] *n* seminterrato; (*of shop*) interrato
bases[1] ['beɪsiːz] *npl of* **basis**
bases[2] ['beɪsɪz] *npl of* **base**
bash [bæʃ] (*inf*) *vt* picchiare
basic ['beɪsɪk] *adj* rudimentale; essenziale; sostanzialmente; **basics** *npl* **the basics** l'essenziale *m*
basically [-lɪ] *adv* fondamentalmente; sostanzialmente; **basics** *npl* **the basics** l'essenziale *m*
basil ['bæzl] *n* basilico
basin ['beɪsn] *n* (*vessel: also Geo*) bacino; (*also*: **wash~**) lavabo
basis ['beɪsɪs] (*pl* **bases**) *n* base *f*; **on a part-time ~** part-time; **on a trial ~** in prova
basket ['bɑːskɪt] *n* cesta; (*smaller*) cestino; (*with handle*) paniere *m*; **basketball** *n* pallacanestro *f*
bass [beɪs] *n* (*Mus*) basso
bastard ['bɑːstəd] *n* bastardo(-a); (*inf!*) stronzo (!)
bat [bæt] *n* pipistrello; (*for baseball etc*) mazza; (*BRIT: for table tennis*) racchetta ▷ *vt* **he didn't ~ an eyelid** non battè ciglio
batch [bætʃ] *n* (*of bread*) infornata; (*of papers*) cumulo
bath [bɑːθ] *n* bagno; (*bathtub*) vasca da bagno ▷ *vt* far fare il bagno a; **to have a ~** fare un bagno; *see also* **baths**
bathe [beɪð] *vi* fare il bagno ▷ *vt* (*wound*) lavare
bathing ['beɪðɪŋ] *n* bagni *mpl*; **bathing costume** (*US* **bathing suit**) *n* costume *m* da bagno
bath: bathrobe ['bɑːθrəʊb] *n* accappatoio; **bathroom** ['bɑːθrʊm] *n* stanza da bagno; **baths** [bɑːðz] *npl* bagni *mpl* pubblici; **bath towel** *n* asciugamano da bagno; **bathtub** *n* (*vasca da*) bagno
baton ['bætən] *n* (*Mus*) bacchetta;

(*Athletics*) testimone *m*; (*club*) manganello
batter ['bætə^r] *vt* battere ▷ *n* pastetta;
battered *adj* (*hat*) sformato(-a); (*pan*)
ammaccato(-a)
battery ['bætərɪ] *n* batteria; (*of torch*) pila;
battery farming *n* allevamento in batteria
battle ['bætl] *n* battaglia ▷ *vi* battagliare,
lottare; **battlefield** *n* campo di battaglia
bay [beɪ] *n* (*of sea*) baia; **to hold sb at ~**
tenere qn a bada
bazaar [bə'zɑː^r] *n* bazar *m inv*; vendita di
beneficenza
BBC *n abbr* (= British Broadcasting
Corporation) rete nazionale di radiotelevisione
in Gran Bretagna

● **BBC**
●
●
● La **BBC** è l'azienda statale che fornisce
● il servizio radiofonico e televisivo in
● Gran Bretagna. Ha due reti televisive
● terrestri (BBC1 e BBC2), e cinque
● stazioni radiofoniche nazionali. Oggi
● la BBC ha anche diverse stazioni
● digitali radiofoniche e televisive. Da
● molti anni fornisce inoltre un servizio
● di intrattenimento e informazione
● internazionale, il "BBC World Service",
● trasmesso in tutto il mondo.

B.C. *adv abbr* (= *before Christ*) a.C.

○ **KEYWORD**

be [biː] (*pt* **was, were**, *pp* **been**) *aux vb* **1**
(*with present participle: forming continuous
tenses*): **what are you doing?** che fa?, che
sta facendo?; **they're coming tomorrow**
vengono domani; **I've been waiting for
her for hours** sono ore che l'aspetto
2 (*with pp: forming passives*) essere; **to be
killed** essere *or* venire ucciso(-a); **the box
had been opened** la scatola era stata
aperta; **the thief was nowhere to be
seen** il ladro non si trovava da nessuna
parte
3 (*in tag questions*): **it was fun, wasn't it?** è
stato divertente, no?; **he's good-looking,
isn't he?** è un bell'uomo, vero?; **she's
back, is she?** così è tornata, eh?
4 (+ *to* + *infinitive*): **the house is
to be sold** abbiamo *or* hanno *etc*
intenzione di vendere casa; **you're to
be congratulated for all your work**
dovremo farvi i complimenti per tutto il
vostro lavoro; **he's not to open it** non
deve aprirlo
▷ *vb* + *complement* **1** (*gen*) essere; **I'm
English** sono inglese; **I'm tired** sono

stanco(-a); **I'm hot/cold** ho caldo/freddo;
he's a doctor è medico; **2 and 2 are 4** 2
più 2 fa 4; **be careful!** sta attento(-a)!; **be
good** sii buono(-a)
2 (*of health*) stare; **how are you?** come
sta?; **he's very ill** sta molto male
3 (*of age*) **how old are you?** quanti anni
hai?; **I'm sixteen (years old)** ho sedici
anni
4 (*cost*) costare; **how much was the
meal?** quant'era *or* quanto costava il
pranzo?; **that'll be £5, please** (fa) 5
sterline, per favore
▷ *vi* **1** (*exist, occur etc*) essere, esistere; **the
best singer that ever was** il migliore
cantante mai esistito *or* di tutti i tempi; **be
that as it may** comunque sia, sia come
sia; **so be it** sia pure, e sia
2 (*referring to place*) essere, trovarsi; **I won't
be here tomorrow** non ci sarò domani;
Edinburgh is in Scotland Edimburgo si
trova in Scozia
3 (*referring to movement*): **where have you
been?** dov'è stato?; **I've been to China**
sono stato in Cina
▷ *impers vb* **1** (*referring to time, distance*)
essere; **it's 5 o'clock** sono le 5; **it's the
28th of April** è il 28 aprile; **it's 10 km to
the village** di qui al paese sono 10 km
2 (*referring to the weather*) fare; **it's too
hot/cold** fa troppo caldo/freddo; **it's
windy** c'è vento
3 (*emphatic*): **it's me** sono io; **it was Maria
who paid the bill** è stata Maria che ha
pagato il conto

beach [biːtʃ] *n* spiaggia ▷ *vt* tirare in secco
beacon ['biːkən] *n* (*lighthouse*) faro;
(*marker*) segnale *m*
bead [biːd] *n* perlina; **~s** *npl* (*necklace*)
collana
beak [biːk] *n* becco
beam [biːm] *n* trave *f*; (*of light*) raggio ▷ *vi*
brillare
bean [biːn] *n* fagiolo; (*of coffee*) chicco;
runner ~ fagiolino; **beansprouts** *npl*
germogli *mpl* di soia
bear [bɛə^r] (*pt* **bore**, *pp* **borne**) *n* orso ▷ *vt*
portare; (*endure*) sopportare; (*produce*)
generare ▷ *vi* **to ~ right/left** piegare a
destra/sinistra
beard [bɪəd] *n* barba
bearer ['bɛərə^r] *n* portatore *m*
bearing ['bɛərɪŋ] *n* portamento;
(*connection*) rapporto
beast [biːst] *n* bestia
beat [biːt] (*pt* **beat**, *pp* **beaten**) *n* colpo;
(*of heart*) battito; (*Mus*) tempo; battuta;
(*of policeman*) giro ▷ *vt* battere; (*eggs,*

cream) sbattere ▷ *vi* battere; **off the ~en track** fuori mano; **~ it!** (*inf*) fila!, fuori dai piedi!; **beat up** *vt* (*person*) picchiare; (*eggs*) sbattere; **beating** *n* bastonata

beautiful ['bju:tɪful] *adj* bello(-a); **beautifully** *adv* splendidamente

beauty ['bju:tɪ] *n* bellezza; **beauty parlour** [-'pɑ:lə^r] (*us* **beauty parlor**) *n* salone *m* di bellezza; **beauty salon** *n* istituto di bellezza; **beauty spot** (*BRIT*) *n* (*Tourism*) luogo pittoresco

beaver ['bi:və^r] *n* castoro

became [bɪ'keɪm] *pt of* **become**

because [bɪ'kɔz] *conj* perché; **~ of** a causa di

beckon ['bɛkən] *vt* (*also:* **~ to**) chiamare con un cenno

become [bɪ'kʌm] (*irreg: like* **come**) *vt* diventare; **to ~ fat/thin** ingrassarsi/ dimagrire

bed [bɛd] *n* letto; (*of flowers*) aiuola; (*of coal, clay*) strato; **single/double ~** letto a una piazza/a due piazze *or* matrimoniale; **bed and breakfast** *n* (*place*) ≈ pensione f familiare; (*terms*) camera con colazione; *vedi nota nel riquadro*; **bedclothes** ['bɛdkləuðz] *npl* biancheria e coperte *fpl* da letto; **bedding** *n* coperte e lenzuola *fpl*; **bed linen** *n* biancheria da letto; **bedroom** *n* camera da letto; **bedside** *n* **at sb's bedside** al capezzale di qn; **bedside lamp** *n* lampada da comodino; **bedside table** *n* comodino; **bedsit(ter)** (*BRIT*) *n* monolocale *m*; **bedspread** *n* copriletto; **bedtime** *n* **it's bedtime** è ora di andare a letto

● **BED AND BREAKFAST**

● I **bed and breakfasts**, anche **B & Bs**,
● sono piccole pensioni a conduzione
● familiare, più economiche rispetto agli
● alberghi, dove al mattino viene servita
● la tradizionale colazione all'inglese.

bee [bi:] *n* ape *f*

beech [bi:tʃ] *n* faggio

beef [bi:f] *n* manzo; **roast ~** arrosto di manzo; **beefburger** *n* hamburger *m inv*; **Beefeater** *n* guardia della Torre di Londra

been [bi:n] *pp of* **be**

beer [bɪə^r] *n* birra; **beer garden** *n* (*BRIT*) giardino (*di pub*)

beet [bi:t] (*us*) *n* (*also:* **red ~**) barbabietola rossa

beetle ['bi:tl] *n* scarafaggio; coleottero

beetroot ['bi:tru:t] (*BRIT*) *n* barbabietola

before [bɪ'fɔ:^r] *prep* (*in time*) prima di; (*in space*) davanti a ▷ *conj* prima che + *sub*; prima di ▷ *adv* prima; **~ going** prima di andare; **~ she goes** prima che vada; **the week ~** la settimana prima; **I've seen it ~** l'ho già visto; **I've never seen it ~** la prima volta che lo vedo; **beforehand** *adv* in anticipo

beg [bɛg] *vi* chiedere l'elemosina ▷ *vt* (*also:* **~ for**) chiedere in elemosina; (*favour*) chiedere; **to ~ sb to do** pregare qn di fare

began [bɪ'gæn] *pt of* **begin**

beggar ['bɛgə^r] *n* mendicante *m/f*

begin [bɪ'gɪn] (*pt* **began**, *pp* **begun**) *vt*, *vi* cominciare; **to ~ doing** *or* **to do sth** incominciare *or* iniziare a fare qc; **beginner** *n* principiante *m/f*; **beginning** *n* inizio, principio

begun [bɪ'gʌn] *pp of* **begin**

behalf [bɪ'hɑ:f] *n* **on ~ of** per conto di; a nome di

behave [bɪ'heɪv] *vi* comportarsi; (*well: also:* **~ o.s.**) comportarsi bene; **behaviour** [bɪ'heɪvjə^r] (*us* **behavior**) *n* comportamento, condotta

behind [bɪ'haɪnd] *prep* dietro; (*followed by pronoun*) dietro di; (*time*) in ritardo con ▷ *adv* dietro; (*leave, stay*) indietro ▷ *n* didietro; **to be ~ (schedule)** essere in ritardo rispetto al programma; **~ the scenes** (*fig*) dietro le quinte

beige [beɪʒ] *adj* beige *inv*

Beijing ['beɪ'dʒɪŋ] *n* Pechino *f*

being ['bi:ɪŋ] *n* essere *m*

belated [bɪ'leɪtɪd] *adj* tardo(-a)

belch [bɛltʃ] *vi* ruttare ▷ *vt* (*gen: belch out: smoke etc*) eruttare

Belgian ['bɛldʒən] *adj*, *n* belga *m/f*

Belgium ['bɛldʒəm] *n* Belgio

belief [bɪ'li:f] *n* (*opinion*) opinione *f*, convinzione *f*; (*trust, faith*) fede *f*

believe [bɪ'li:v] *vt*, *vi* credere; **to ~ in** (*God*) credere in; (*ghosts*) credere a; (*method*) avere fiducia in; **believer** *n* (*Rel*) credente *m/f*; (*in idea, activity*): **to be a believer in** credere in

bell [bɛl] *n* campana; (*small, on door, electric*) campanello

bellboy ['bɛlbɔɪ], (*us* **bellhop**) 'bɛlhɔp] *n* ragazzo d'albergo, fattorino d'albergo

bellow ['bɛləu] *vi* muggire

bell pepper (*esp us*) *n* peperone *m*

belly ['bɛlɪ] *n* pancia; **belly button** *n* ombelico

belong [bɪ'lɔŋ] *vi* **to ~ to** appartenere a; (*club etc*) essere socio di; **this book ~s here** questo libro va qui; **belongings** *npl* cose *fpl*, roba

beloved [bɪ'lʌvɪd] *adj* adorato(-a)

below [bɪ'ləu] *prep* sotto, al di sotto di ▷ *adv* sotto, di sotto; giù; **see ~** vedi sotto *or* oltre

belt [bɛlt] *n* cintura; (*Tech*) cinghia ▷ *vt* (*thrash*) picchiare ▷ *vi* (*inf*) filarsela; **beltway** (*US*) *n* (*Aut: ring road*) circonvallazione *f*; (: *motorway*) autostrada

bemused [bɪ'mjuːzd] *adj* perplesso(-a), stupito(-a)

bench [bɛntʃ] *n* panca; (*in workshop, Pol*) banco; **the B~** (*Law*) la Corte

bend [bɛnd] (*pt, pp* **bent**) *vt* curvare; (*leg, arm*) piegare ▷ *vi* curvarsi; piegarsi ▷ *n* (*BRIT: in road*) curva; (*in pipe, river*) gomito; **bend down** *vi* chinarsi; **bend over** *vi* piegarsi

beneath [bɪ'niːθ] *prep* sotto, al di sotto di; (*unworthy of*) indegno(-a) di ▷ *adv* sotto, di sotto

beneficial [bɛnɪ'fɪʃəl] *adj* che fa bene; vantaggioso(-a)

benefit ['bɛnɪfɪt] *n* beneficio, vantaggio; (*allowance of money*) indennità *f inv* ▷ *vt* far bene a ▷ *vi* **he'll ~ from it** ne trarrà beneficio *or* profitto

benign [bɪ'naɪn] *adj* (*person, smile*) benevolo(-a); (*Med*) benigno(-a)

bent [bɛnt] *pt, pp of* **bend** ▷ *n* inclinazione *f* ▷ *adj* (*inf: dishonest*) losco(-a); **to be ~ on** essere deciso(-a) a

bereaved [bɪ'riːvd] *n* **the ~** i familiari in lutto

beret ['bɛreɪ] *n* berretto

Berlin [bəː'lɪn] *n* Berlino *f*

Bermuda [bəː'mjuːdə] *n* le Bermude

berry ['bɛrɪ] *n* bacca

berth [bəːθ] *n* (*bed*) cuccetta; (*for ship*) ormeggio ▷ *vi* (*in harbour*) entrare in porto; (*at anchor*) gettare l'ancora

beside [bɪ'saɪd] *prep* accanto a; **to be ~ o.s. (with anger)** essere fuori di sé (dalla rabbia); **that's ~ the point** non c'entra; **besides** [bɪ'saɪdz] *adv* inoltre, per di più ▷ *prep* oltre a; a parte

best [bɛst] *adj* migliore ▷ *adv* meglio; **the ~ part of** (*quantity*) la maggior parte di; **at ~** tutt'al più; **to make the ~ of sth** cavare il meglio possibile da qc; **to do one's ~** fare del proprio meglio; **to the ~ of my knowledge** per quel che ne so; **to the ~ of my ability** al massimo delle mie capacità; **best-before date** *n* scadenza; **best man** (*irreg*) *n* testimone *m* dello sposo; **bestseller** *n* bestseller *m inv*

bet [bɛt] (*pt, pp* **bet** *or* **betted**) *n* scommessa ▷ *vt, vi* scommettere; **to ~ sb sth** scommettere qc con qn

betray [bɪ'treɪ] *vt* tradire

better ['bɛtəʳ] *adj* migliore ▷ *adv* meglio ▷ *vt* migliorare ▷ *n* **to get the ~ of** avere la meglio su; **you had ~ do it** è meglio che lo

faccia; **he thought ~ of it** cambiò idea; **to get ~** migliorare

betting ['bɛtɪŋ] *n* scommesse *fpl*; **betting shop** (*BRIT*) *n* ufficio dell'allibratore

between [bɪ'twiːn] *prep* tra ▷ *adv* in mezzo, nel mezzo

beverage ['bɛvərɪdʒ] *n* bevanda

beware [bɪ'wɛəʳ] *vt, vi* **to ~ (of)** stare attento(-a) (a); **"~ of the dog"** "attenti al cane"

bewildered [bɪ'wɪldəd] *adj* sconcertato(-a), confuso(-a)

beyond [bɪ'jɔnd] *prep* (*in space*) oltre; (*exceeding*) al di sopra di ▷ *adv* di là; **~ doubt** senza dubbio; **~ repair** irreparabile

bias ['baɪəs] *n* (*prejudice*) pregiudizio; (*preference*) preferenza; **bias(s)ed** *adj* parziale

bib [bɪb] *n* bavaglino

Bible ['baɪbl] *n* Bibbia

bicarbonate of soda [baɪ'kɑːbənɪt-] *n* bicarbonato (di sodio)

biceps ['baɪsɛps] *n* bicipite *m*

bicycle ['baɪsɪkl] *n* bicicletta; **bicycle pump** *n* pompa della bicicletta

bid [bɪd] (*pt* **bade** *or* **bid**, *pp* **bidden** *or* **bid**) *n* offerta; (*attempt*) tentativo ▷ *vi* fare un'offerta ▷ *vt* fare un'offerta di; **to ~ sb good day** dire buon giorno a qn; **bidder** *n* **the highest bidder** il maggior offerente

bidet ['biːdeɪ] *n* bidè *m inv*

big [bɪg] *adj* grande; grosso(-a); **Big Apple** *n vedi nota nel riquadro*; **bigheaded** ['bɪg'hɛdɪd] *adj* presuntuoso(-a); **big toe** *n* alluce *m*

● **BIG APPLE**
●
● Tutti sanno che **The Big Apple**, la
● Grande Mela, è New York ("apple"
● in gergo significa grande città), ma
● sicuramente i soprannomi di altre città
● americane non sono così conosciuti.
● Chicago è soprannominata "the Windy
● City" perché è ventosa, New Orleans
● si chiama "the Big Easy" per il modo di
● vivere tranquillo e rilassato dei suoi
● abitanti, e l'industria automobilistica
● ha fatto sì che Detroit fosse
● soprannominata "Motown".

bike [baɪk] *n* bici *f inv*; **bike lane** *n* pista ciclabile

bikini [bɪ'kiːnɪ] *n* bikini *m inv*

bilateral [baɪ'lætərl] *adj* bilaterale

bilingual [baɪ'lɪŋgwəl] *adj* bilingue

bill [bɪl] *n* conto; (*Pol*) atto; (*US: banknote*) banconota; (*of bird*) becco; (*of show*) locandina; **can I have the ~, please** il

conto, per favore; **put it on my ~** lo metta
sul mio conto; **"post no ~s"** "divieto di
affissione"; **to fit** or **fill the ~** (fig) fare al
caso; **billboard** n tabellone m; **billfold**
['bɪlfəʊld] (us) n portafoglio
billiards ['bɪljədz] n biliardo
billion ['bɪljən] num (BRIT) bilione m; (us)
miliardo
bin [bɪn] n (for coal, rubbish) bidone m; (for
bread) cassetta; (dustbin) pattumiera; (litter
bin) cestino
bind [baɪnd] (pt, pp **bound**) vt legare;
(oblige) obbligare ▷ n (inf) scocciatura
binge [bɪndʒ] (inf) n **to go on a ~** fare
baldoria
bingo ['bɪŋgəʊ] n gioco simile alla tombola
binoculars [bɪ'nɔkjuləz] npl binocolo
bio... ['baɪə'...] prefix; **biochemistry**
n biochimica; **biodegradable** adj
biodegradabile; **biography** [baɪ'ɔgrəfɪ]
n biografia; **biological** adj biologico(-a);
biology [baɪ'ɔlədʒɪ] n biologia
birch [bə:tʃ] n betulla
bird [bə:d] n uccello; (BRIT: inf: girl)
bambola; **bird of prey** n (uccello) rapace
m; **birdwatching** n birdwatching m
Biro® ['baɪrəʊ] n biro® f inv
birth [bə:θ] n nascita; **to give ~ to**
partorire; **birth certificate** n certificato
di nascita; **birth control** n controllo
delle nascite; contraccezione f; **birthday**
n compleanno ▷ cpd di compleanno;
birthmark n voglia; **birthplace** n luogo
di nascita
biscuit ['bɪskɪt] (BRIT) n biscotto
bishop ['bɪʃəp] n vescovo
bistro ['bi:strəʊ] n bistrò m inv
bit [bɪt] pt of **bite** ▷ n pezzo; (Comput) bit
m inv; (of horse) morso; **a ~ of** un po' di; **a ~
mad** un po' matto; **a ~ by ~** a poco a poco
bitch [bɪtʃ] n (dog) cagna; (inf!) vacca
bite [baɪt] (pt, pp **bit, bitten**) vt, vi mordere;
(insect) pungere ▷ n morso; (insect bite)
puntura; (mouthful) boccone m; **let's have
a ~ to eat** mangiamo un boccone; **to ~
one's nails** mangiarsi le unghie
bitten ['bɪtn] pp of **bite**
bitter ['bɪtər] adj amaro(-a); (wind, criticism)
pungente ▷ n (BRIT: beer) birra amara
bizarre [bɪ'zɑ:r] adj bizzarro(-a)
black [blæk] adj nero(-a) ▷ n nero;
(person): **B~** negro(-a) ▷ vt (BRIT Industry)
boicottare; **to give sb a ~ eye** fare un
occhio nero a qn; **in the ~** (bank account)
in attivo; **black out** vi (faint) svenire;
blackberry n mora; **blackbird** n merlo;
blackboard n lavagna; **black coffee** n
caffè m inv nero; **blackcurrant** n ribes
m inv; **black ice** n strato trasparente

di ghiaccio; **blackmail** n ricatto ▷ vt
ricattare; **black market** n mercato nero;
blackout n oscuramento; (TV, Radio)
interruzione f delle trasmissioni; (fainting)
svenimento; **black pepper** n pepe m nero;
black pudding n sanguinaccio; **Black
Sea** n **the Black Sea** il Mar Nero
bladder ['blædər] n vescica
blade [bleɪd] n lama; (of oar) pala; **~ of
grass** filo d'erba
blame [bleɪm] n colpa ▷ vt **to ~ sb/sth for
sth** dare la colpa di qc a qn/qc; **who's to ~?**
chi è colpevole?
bland [blænd] adj mite; (taste) blando(-a)
blank [blæŋk] adj bianco(-a); (look)
distratto(-a) ▷ n spazio vuoto; (cartridge)
cartuccia a salve
blanket ['blæŋkɪt] n coperta
blast [blɑ:st] n (of wind) raffica; (of bomb
etc) esplosione f ▷ vt far saltare
blatant ['bleɪtənt] adj flagrante
blaze [bleɪz] n (fire) incendio; (fig)
vampata; splendore m ▷ vi (fire) ardere,
fiammeggiare; (guns) sparare senza sosta;
(fig: eyes) ardere ▷ vt **to ~ a trail** (fig)
tracciare una via nuova; **in a ~ of publicity**
circondato da grande pubblicità
blazer ['bleɪzər] n blazer m inv
bleach [bli:tʃ] n (also: **household ~**)
varechina ▷ vt (material) candeggiare;
bleachers (us) npl (Sport) posti mpl di
gradinata
bleak [bli:k] adj tetro(-a)
bled [blɛd] pt, pp of **bleed**
bleed [bli:d] (pt, pp **bled**) vi sanguinare;
my nose is ~ing mi viene fuori sangue
dal naso
blemish ['blɛmɪʃ] n macchia
blend [blɛnd] n miscela ▷ vt mescolare
▷ vi (colours etc: also: **~ in**) armonizzare;
blender n (Culin) frullatore m
bless [blɛs] (pt, pp **blessed** or **blest**) vt
benedire; **~ you!** (after sneeze) salute!;
blessing n benedizione f; fortuna
blew [blu:] pt of **blow**
blight [blaɪt] vt (hopes etc) deludere; (life)
rovinare
blind [blaɪnd] adj cieco(-a) ▷ n (for window)
avvolgibile m; (Venetian blind) veneziana
▷ vt accecare; **the ~** npl i ciechi; **blind
alley** n vicolo cieco; **blindfold** n benda
▷ adj, adv bendato(-a) ▷ vt bendare gli
occhi a
blink [blɪŋk] vi battere gli occhi; (light)
lampeggiare
bliss [blɪs] n estasi f
blister ['blɪstər] n (on skin) vescica; (on
paintwork) bolla ▷ vi (paint) coprirsi di bolle
blizzard ['blɪzəd] n bufera di neve

bloated ['bləutɪd] adj gonfio(-a)

blob [blɔb] n (drop) goccia; (stain, spot) macchia

block [blɔk] n blocco; (in pipes) ingombro; (toy) cubo; (of buildings) isolato ▷ vt bloccare; **the sink is ~ed** il lavandino è otturato; **block up** vt bloccare; (pipe) ingorgare, intasare; **blockade** [-'keɪd] n blocco; **blockage** n ostacolo; **blockbuster** n (film, book) grande successo; **block capitals** npl stampatello; **block letters** npl stampatello

bloke [bləuk] (BRIT: inf) n tizio

blond(e) [blɔnd] adj, n biondo(-a)

blood [blʌd] n sangue m; **blood donor** n donatore(-trice) di sangue; **blood group** n gruppo sanguigno; **blood poisoning** n setticemia; **blood pressure** n pressione f sanguigna; **bloodshed** n spargimento di sangue; **bloodshot** adj **bloodshot eyes** occhi iniettati di sangue; **bloodstream** n flusso del sangue; **blood test** n analisi f inv del sangue; **blood transfusion** n trasfusione f di sangue; **blood type** n gruppo sanguigno; **blood vessel** n vaso sanguigno; **bloody** adj (fight) sanguinoso(-a); (nose) sanguinante; (BRIT: inf!): **this bloody ...** questo maledetto ...; **bloody awful/good** (inf!) veramente terribile/forte

bloom [bluːm] n fiore m ▷ vi (tree) essere in fiore; (flower) aprirsi

blossom ['blɔsəm] n fiore m; (with pl sense) fiori mpl ▷ vi essere in fiore

blot [blɔt] n macchia ▷ vt macchiare

blouse [blauz] n (feminine garment) camicetta

blow [bləu] (pt **blew**, pp **blown**) n colpo ▷ vi soffiare ▷ vt (fuse) far saltare; (instrument) suonare; **to ~ one's nose** soffiarsi il naso; **to ~ a whistle** fischiare; **blow away** vt portare via; **blow out** vi scoppiare; **blow up** vi saltare in aria ▷ vt far saltare in aria; (tyre) gonfiare; (Phot) ingrandire; **blow-dry** n messa in piega a föhn

blown [bləun] pp of **blow**

blue [bluː] adj azzurro(-a); (depressed) giù inv; **~ film/joke** film/barzelletta pornografico(-a); **out of the ~** (fig) all'improvviso; **bluebell** n giacinto dei boschi; **blueberry** n mirtillo; **blue cheese** n formaggio tipo gorgonzola; **blues** npl **the blues** (Mus) il blues; **to have the blues** (inf: feeling) essere a terra; **bluetit** n cinciarella

bluff [blʌf] vi bluffare ▷ n bluff m inv ▷ adj (person) brusco(-a); **to call sb's ~** mettere alla prova il bluff di qn

blunder ['blʌndəʳ] n abbaglio ▷ vi prendere un abbaglio

blunt [blʌnt] adj smussato(-a); spuntato(-a); (person) brusco(-a)

blur [bləːʳ] n forma indistinta ▷ vt offuscare; **blurred** adj (photo) mosso(-a); (TV) sfuocato(-a)

blush [blʌʃ] vi arrossire ▷ n rossore m; **blusher** n fard m inv

board [bɔːd] n tavola; (on wall) tabellone m; (committee) consiglio, comitato; (in firm) consiglio d'amministrazione; (Naut, Aviat): **on ~** a bordo ▷ vt (ship) salire a bordo di; (train) salire su; **full ~** (BRIT) pensione completa; **half ~** (BRIT) mezza pensione; **~ and lodging** vitto e alloggio; **which goes by the ~** (fig) che viene abbandonato; **board game** n gioco da tavolo; **boarding card** n = **boarding pass**; **boarding pass** n (Aviat, Naut) carta d'imbarco; **boarding school** n collegio; **board room** n sala del consiglio

boast [bəust] vi **to ~ (about or of)** vantarsi (di)

boat [bəut] n nave f; (small) barca

bob [bɔb] vi (boat, cork on water: also: **~ up and down**) andare su e giù

bobby pin ['bɔbɪ-] (US) n fermaglio per capelli

body ['bɔdɪ] n corpo; (of car) carrozzeria; (of plane) fusoliera; (fig: group) gruppo; (: organization) organizzazione f; (: quantity) quantità f inv; **body-building** n culturismo; **bodyguard** n guardia del corpo; **bodywork** n carrozzeria

bog [bɔg] n palude f ▷ vt **to get ~ged down** (fig) impantanarsi

bogus ['bəugəs] adj falso(-a); finto(-a)

boil [bɔɪl] vt, vi bollire ▷ n (Med) foruncolo; **to come to the** (BRIT) or **a** (US) **~** raggiungere l'ebollizione; **boil over** vi traboccare (bollendo); **boiled egg** n uovo alla coque; **boiled potatoes** npl patate fpl bollite or lesse; **boiler** n caldaia; **boiling** adj bollente; **I'm boiling (hot)** (inf) sto morendo di caldo; **boiling point** n punto di ebollizione

bold [bəuld] adj audace; (child) impudente; (colour) deciso(-a)

Bolivia [bə'lɪvɪə] n Bolivia

Bolivian [bə'lɪvɪən] adj, n boliviano(-a)

bollard ['bɔləd] (BRIT) n (Aut) colonnina luminosa

bolt [bəult] n chiavistello; (with nut) bullone m ▷ adv **~ upright** diritto(-a) come un fuso ▷ vt serrare; (also: **~ together**) imbullonare; (food) mangiare in fretta ▷ vi scappare via

bomb [bɔm] n bomba ▷ vt bombardare;

bombard [bɔm'bɑːd] *vt* bombardare; **bomber** *n* (*Aviat*) bombardiere *m*; **bomb scare** *n* stato di allarme (*per sospetta presenza di una bomba*)

bond [bɔnd] *n* legame *m*; (*binding promise, Finance*) obbligazione *f*; (*Comm*): **in ~** in attesa di sdoganamento

bone [bəun] *n* osso; (*of fish*) spina, lisca ▷ *vt* disossare; togliere le spine a

bonfire ['bɔnfaɪə²] *n* falò *m inv*

bonnet ['bɔnɪt] *n* cuffia; (*BRIT: of car*) cofano

bonus ['bəunəs] *n* premio; (*fig*) sovrappiù *m inv*

boo [buː] *excl* ba! ▷ *vt* fischiare

book [buk] *n* libro; (*of stamps etc*) blocchetto ▷ *vt* (*ticket, seat, room*) prenotare; (*driver*) multare; (*football player*) ammonire; **~s** *npl* (*Comm*) conti *mpl*; **I'd like to ~ a double room** vorrei prenotare una camera doppia; **I ~ed a table in the name of ...** ho prenotato un tavolo al nome di...; **book in** *vi* (*BRIT: at hotel*) prendere una camera; **book up** *vt* riservare, prenotare; **the hotel is ~ed up** l'albergo è al completo; **all seats are ~ed up** è tutto esaurito; **bookcase** *n* scaffale *m*; **booking** (*BRIT*) prenotazione *f*; **I confirmed my booking by fax/e-mail** ho confermato la mia prenotazione tramite fax/e-mail; **booking office** (*BRIT*) *n* (*Rail*) biglietteria; (*Theatre*) botteghino; **book-keeping** *n* contabilità; **booklet** *n* libricino; **bookmaker** *n* allibratore *m*; **bookmark** (*also Comput*) *n* segnalibro ▷ *vt* (*Comput*) mettere un segnalibro a; (*Internet Explorer*) aggiungere a "Preferiti"; **bookseller** *n* libraio; **bookshelf** *n* mensola (per libri); **bookshop, bookstore** *n* libreria

boom [buːm] *n* (*noise*) rimbombo; (*in prices etc*) boom *m inv* ▷ *vi* rimbombare; andare a gonfie vele

boost [buːst] *n* spinta ▷ *vt* spingere

boot [buːt] *n* stivale *m*; (*for hiking*) scarpone *m* da montagna; (*for football etc*) scarpa; (*BRIT: of car*) portabagagli *m inv* ▷ *vt* (*Comput*) inizializzare; **to ~** (*in addition*) per giunta, in più

booth [buːð] *n* cabina; (*at fair*) baraccone *m*

booze [buːz] (*inf*) *n* alcool *m*

border ['bɔːdə²] *n* orlo; margine *m*; (*of a country*) frontiera; (*for flowers*) aiuola (laterale) ▷ *vt* (*road*) costeggiare; (*another country*): edge **~ on** confinare con; **the B~s** la zona di confine tra l'Inghilterra e la Scozia; **borderline** *n* (*fig*): **on the borderline** incerto(-a)

bore [bɔː²] *pt of* **bear** ▷ *vt* (*hole etc*)

scavare; (*person*) annoiare ▷ *n* (*person*) seccatore(-trice); (*of gun*) calibro; **bored** *adj* annoiato(-a); **to be bored** annoiarsi; **he's bored to tears** *or* **to death** è annoiato a morte; **boredom** *n* noia

boring ['bɔːrɪŋ] *adj* noioso(-a)

born [bɔːn] *adj* **to be ~** nascere; **I was ~ in 1960** sono nato nel 1960

borne [bɔːn] *pp of* **bear**

borough ['bʌrə] *n* comune *m*

borrow ['bɔrəu] *vt* **to ~ sth (from sb)** prendere in prestito qc (da qn)

Bosnia(-Herzegovina) ['bɔznɪə(hɛrzə'gəuviːnə)] *n* Bosnia-Erzegovina; **Bosnian** ['bɔznɪən] *n, adj* bosniaco(-a) *m/f*

bosom ['buzəm] *n* petto; (*fig*) seno

boss [bɔs] *n* capo ▷ *vt* comandare; **bossy** *adj* prepotente

both [bəuθ] *adj* entrambi(-e), tutt'e due ▷ *pron* **~ of them** entrambi(-e); **~ of us went, we ~ went** ci siamo andati tutt'e due ▷ *adv* **they sell ~ meat and poultry** vendono insieme la carne ed il pollame

bother ['bɔðə²] *vt* (*worry*) preoccupare; (*annoy*) infastidire ▷ *vi* (*also: ~ o.s.*) preoccuparsi ▷ *n* **it is a ~ to have to do** è una seccatura dover fare; **it was no ~** non c'era problema; **to ~ doing sth** darsi la pena di fare qc

bottle ['bɔtl] *n* bottiglia; (*baby's*) biberon *m inv* ▷ *vt* imbottigliare; **bottle bank** *n* contenitore *m* per la raccolta del vetro; **bottle-opener** *n* apribottiglie *m inv*

bottom ['bɔtəm] *n* fondo; (*buttocks*) sedere *m* ▷ *adj* più basso(-a); ultimo(-a); **at the ~ of** in fondo a

bought [bɔːt] *pt, pp of* **buy**

boulder ['bəuldə²] *n* masso (tondeggiante)

bounce [bauns] *vi* (*ball*) rimbalzare; (*cheque*) essere restituito(-a) ▷ *vt* far rimbalzare ▷ *n* (*rebound*) rimbalzo; **bouncer** (*inf*) *n* buttafuori *m inv*

bound [baund] *pt, pp of* **bind** ▷ *n* (*gen pl*) limite *m*; (*leap*) salto ▷ *vi* saltare ▷ *vt* (*limit*) delimitare ▷ *adj* **~ by law** obbligato(-a) per legge; **to be ~ to do sth** (*obliged*) essere costretto(-a) a fare qc; **he's ~ to fail** (*likely*) fallirà di certo; **~ for** diretto(-a) a; **out of ~s** il cui accesso è vietato

boundary ['baundrɪ] *n* confine *m*

bouquet ['bukeɪ] *n* bouquet *m inv*

bourbon ['buəbən] (*US*) *n* (*also: ~ whiskey*) bourbon *m inv*

bout [baut] *n* periodo; (*of malaria etc*) attacco; (*Boxing etc*) incontro

boutique [buː'tiːk] *n* boutique *f inv*

bow¹ [bəu] *n* nodo; (*weapon*) arco; (*Mus*) archetto

bow²[bau] n (with body) inchino; (Naut: also: ~s) prua ▷ vi inchinarsi; (yield): **to ~ to** or **before** sottomettersi a

bowels['bauəlz] npl intestini mpl; (fig) viscere fpl

bowl[bəul] n (for eating) scodella; (for washing) bacino; (ball) boccia ▷ vi servire (la palla); (Cricket) **bowler**['bəulər] n (Cricket, Baseball) lanciatore m; (BRIT: also: **bowler hat**) bombetta; **bowling**['bəulɪŋ] n (game) gioco delle bocce; **bowling alley** n pista da bowling; **bowling green** n campo di bocce; **bowls**[bəulz] n gioco delle bocce

bow tie n cravatta a farfalla

box[bɔks] n scatola; (also: **cardboard ~**) cartone m; (Theatre) palco ▷ vt inscatolare ▷ vi fare del pugilato; **boxer** n (person) pugile m; **boxer shorts**['bɔksəʃɔːts] pl n boxer; **a pair of boxer shorts** un paio di boxer; **boxing** n (Sport) pugilato; **Boxing Day**(BRIT) n ≈ Santo Stefano; vedi nota nel riquadro; **boxing gloves** npl guantoni mpl da pugile; **boxing ring** n ring m inv; **box office** n biglietteria

● **BOXING DAY**
●
● Il **Boxing Day** è un giorno di festa e
● cade in genere il 26 dicembre. Prende
● il nome dalla tradizionale usanza di
● donare pacchi regalo natalizi, chiamati
● "Christmas boxes", a fornitori e
● dipendenti.

boy[bɔɪ] n ragazzo

boycott['bɔɪkɔt] n boicottaggio ▷ vt boicottare

boyfriend['bɔɪfrɛnd] n ragazzo

bra[brɑː] n reggipetto, reggiseno

brace[breɪs] n (on teeth) apparecchio correttore; (tool) trapano ▷ vt rinforzare, sostenere; **~s**(BRIT) npl (Dress) bretelle fpl; **to ~ o.s.** (also fig) tenersi forte

bracelet['breɪslɪt] n braccialetto

bracket['brækɪt] n (Tech) mensola; (group) gruppo; (Typ) parentesi f inv ▷ vt mettere fra parentesi

brag[bræg] vi vantarsi

braid[breɪd] n (trimming) passamano; (of hair) treccia

brain[breɪn] n cervello; **~s** npl (intelligence) cervella fpl; **he's got ~s** è intelligente

braise[breɪz] vt brasare

brake[breɪk] n (on vehicle) freno ▷ vi frenare; **brake light** n (fanalino dello) stop m inv

bran[bræn] n crusca

branch[brɑːntʃ] n ramo; (Comm)

succursale f; **branch off** vi diramarsi; **branch out** vi (fig) intraprendere una nuova attività

brand[brænd] n marca; (fig) tipo ▷ vt (cattle) marcare (a ferro rovente); **brand name** n marca; **brand-new** adj nuovo(-a) di zecca

brandy['brændɪ] n brandy m inv

brash[bræʃ] adj sfacciato(-a)

brass[brɑːs] n ottone m; **the ~** (Mus) gli ottoni; **brass band** n fanfara

brat[bræt] (pej) n marmocchio, monello(-a)

brave[breɪv] adj coraggioso(-a) ▷ vt affrontare; **bravery** n coraggio

brawl[brɔːl] n rissa

Brazil[brə'zɪl] n Brasile m; **Brazilian** adj, n brasiliano(-a)

breach[briːtʃ] vt aprire una breccia in ▷ n (gap) breccia, varco; (breaking): **~ of contract** rottura di contratto; **~ of the peace** violazione f dell'ordine pubblico

bread[brɛd] n pane m; **breadbin** n cassetta f portapane inv; **breadbox**(US) n cassetta f portapane inv; **breadcrumbs** npl briciole fpl; (Culin) pangrattato

breadth[brɛtθ] n larghezza; (fig: of knowledge etc) ampiezza

break[breɪk] (pt broke, pp broken) vt rompere; (law) violare; (record) battere ▷ vi rompersi; (storm) scoppiare; (weather) cambiare; (dawn) spuntare; (news) saltare fuori ▷ n (gap) breccia; (fracture) rottura; (rest, also Scol) intervallo; (: short) pausa; (chance) possibilità f inv; **to ~ one's leg etc** rompersi la gamba ecc; **to ~ the news to sb** comunicare per primo la notizia a qn; **to ~ even** coprire le spese; **to ~ free** or **loose** spezzare i legami; **to ~ open** (door etc) sfondare; **break down** vt (figures, data) analizzare ▷ vi (person) avere un esaurimento (nervoso); (Aut) guastarsi; **my car has broken down** mi si è rotta la macchina; **break in** vt (horse etc) domare ▷ vi (burglar) fare irruzione; (interrupt) interrompere; **break into** vt fus (house) fare irruzione in; **break off** vi (speaker) interrompersi; (branch) troncarsi; **break out** vi evadere; (war, fight) scoppiare; **to ~ out in spots** coprirsi di macchie; **break up** vi (ship) sfondarsi; (meeting) sciogliersi; (crowd) disperdersi; (marriage) andare a pezzi; (Scol) chiudere ▷ vt fare a pezzi, spaccare; (fight etc) interrompere, far cessare; **breakdown** n (Aut) guasto; (in communications) interruzione f; (of marriage) rottura; (Med: also: **nervous breakdown**) esaurimento nervoso; (of statistics) resoconto; **breakdown truck,**

breakdown van n carro m attrezzi inv
breakfast['brɛkfəst] n colazione f; **what time is ~?** a che ora è servita la colazione?
break break-in n irruzione f;
  breakthrough n (fig) passo avanti
breast[brɛst] n (of woman) seno; (chest, Culin) petto; **breast-feed**(irreg: like **feed**) vt, vi allattare (al seno); **breast-stroke** n nuoto a rana
breath[brɛθ] n respiro; **out of ~** senza fiato
Breathalyser®['brɛθəlaɪzər] (BRIT) n alcoltest m inv
breathe[briːð] vt, vi respirare; **breathe in** vt respirare ▷ vi inspirare; **breathe out** vt, vi espirare; **breathing** n respiro, respirazione f
breath: breathless['brɛθlɪs] adj senza fiato; breathtaking['brɛθteɪkɪŋ] adj mozzafiato inv; **breath test** n ≈ prova del palloncino
bred[brɛd] pt, pp of **breed**
breed[briːd] (pt, pp **bred**) vt allevare ▷ vi riprodursi ▷ n razza; (type, class) varietà f inv
breeze[briːz] n brezza
breezy['briːzɪ] adj allegro(-a), ventilato(-a)
brew[bruː] vt (tea) fare un infuso di; (beer) fare ▷ vi (storm, fig: trouble etc) prepararsi; **brewery** n fabbrica di birra
bribe[braɪb] n bustarella f ▷ vt comprare; **bribery** n corruzione f
bric-a-brac['brɪkəbræk] n bric-a-brac m
brick[brɪk] n mattone m; **bricklayer** n muratore m
bride[braɪd] n sposa; **bridegroom** n sposo; **bridesmaid** n damigella d'onore
bridge[brɪdʒ] n ponte m; (Naut) ponte di comando; (of nose) dorso; (Cards) bridge m inv ▷ vt (fig: gap) colmare
bridle['braɪdl] n briglia
brief[briːf] adj breve ▷ n (Law) comparsa f; (gen) istruzioni fpl ▷ vt mettere al corrente; **~s** npl (underwear) mutande fpl; **briefcase** n cartella; **briefing** n briefing m inv; **briefly** adv (glance) di sfuggita; (explain, say) brevemente
brigadier[brɪgəˈdɪər] n generale m di brigata
bright[braɪt] adj luminoso(-a); (clever) sveglio(-a); (lively) vivace
brilliant['brɪljənt] adj brillante; (light, smile) radioso(-a); (inf) splendido(-a)
brim[brɪm] n orlo
brine[braɪn] n (Culin) salamoia
bring[brɪŋ] (pt, pp **brought**) vt portare; **bring about** vt causare; **bring back** vt riportare; **bring down** vt portare giù; abbattere; **bring in** vt (person)

fare entrare; (object) portare; (Pol: bill) presentare; (: legislation) introdurre; (Law: verdict) emettere; (produce: income) rendere; **bring on** vt (illness, attack) causare, provocare; (player, substitute) far scendere in campo; **bring out** vt tirar fuori; (meaning) mettere in evidenza; (book, album) far uscire; **bring up** vt (carry up) portare su; (child) allevare; (question) introdurre; (food: vomit) rimettere, rigurgitare
brink[brɪŋk] n orlo
brisk[brɪsk] adj (manner) spiccio(-a); (trade) vivace; (pace) svelto(-a)
bristle['brɪsl] n setola ▷ vi rizzarsi; **bristling with** irto(-a) di
Brit[brɪt] n abbr (inf: = British person) britannico(-a)
Britain['brɪtən] n (also: **Great ~**) Gran Bretagna
British['brɪtɪʃ] adj britannico(-a); **British Isles** npl Isole Britanniche
Briton['brɪtən] n britannico(-a)
brittle['brɪtl] adj fragile
broad[brɔːd] adj largo(-a); (distinction) generale; (accent) spiccato(-a); **in ~ daylight** in pieno giorno; **broadband** adj (Comput) a banda larga ▷ n banda larga; **broad bean** n fava; **broadcast** (pt, pp **broadcast**) n trasmissione f ▷ vt trasmettere per radio (or per television) ▷ vi fare una trasmissione; **broaden** vt allargare ▷ vi allargarsi; **broadly** adv (fig) in generale; **broad-minded** adj di mente aperta
broccoli['brɔkəlɪ] n broccoli mpl
brochure['brəʊʃjuər] n dépliant m inv
broil[brɔɪl] vt cuocere a fuoco vivo
broiler['brɔɪlər] (us) n (grill) griglia
broke[brəʊk] pt of **break** ▷ adj (inf) squattrinato(-a)
broken['brəʊkn] pp of **break** ▷ adj rotto(-a); **a ~ leg** una gamba rotta; **in ~ English** in un inglese stentato
broker['brəʊkər] n agente m
bronchitis[brɔŋˈkaɪtɪs] n bronchite f
bronze[brɔnz] n bronzo
brooch[brəʊtʃ] n spilla
brood[bruːd] n covata ▷ vi (person) rimuginare
broom[brum] n scopa; (Bot) ginestra
Bros. abbr (= Brothers) F.lli
broth[brɔθ] n brodo
brothel['brɔθl] n bordello
brother['brʌðər] n fratello; **brother-in-law** n cognato
brought[brɔːt] pt, pp of **bring**
brow[brau] n fronte f; (rare, gen: eyebrow) sopracciglio; (of hill) cima

brown [braun] *adj* bruno(-a), marrone;
(*tanned*) abbronzato(-a) ▷ *n* (*colour*) color
m bruno *or* marrone ▷ *vt* (*Culin*) rosolare;
brown bread *n* pane *m* integrale, pane
nero

Brownie ['braunɪ] *n* giovane
esploratrice *f*

brown rice *n* riso greggio

brown sugar *n* zucchero greggio

browse [brauz] *vi* (*among books*) curiosare
fra i libri; **to ~ through a book** sfogliare un
libro; **browser** *n* (*Comput*) browser *m inv*

bruise [bru:z] *n* (*on person*) livido ▷ *vt* farsi
un livido a

brunette [bru:'nɛt] *n* bruna

brush [brʌʃ] *n* spazzola; (*for painting,
shaving*) pennello; (*quarrel*) schermaglia
▷ *vt* spazzolare; (*also*: **~ against**) sfiorare

Brussels ['brʌslz] *n* Bruxelles *f*

Brussels sprout [spraut] *n* cavolo di
Bruxelles

brutal ['bru:tl] *adj* brutale

B.Sc. *n abbr* (*Univ*) = **Bachelor of Science**

BSE *n abbr* (= *bovine spongiform
encephalopathy*) encefalite *f* bovina
spongiforme

bubble ['bʌbl] *n* bolla ▷ *vi* ribollire; (*sparkle:
fig*) essere effervescente; **bubble bath**
n bagnoschiuma *m inv*; **bubble gum** *n*
gomma americana

buck [bʌk] *n* maschio (*di camoscio,
caprone, coniglio ecc*); (*us: inf*) dollaro ▷ *vi*
sgroppare; **to pass the ~ to sb** scaricare
(su di qn) la propria responsabilità

bucket ['bʌkɪt] *n* secchio

buckle ['bʌkl] *n* fibbia ▷ *vt* allacciare ▷ *vi*
(*wheel etc*) piegarsi

bud [bʌd] *n* gemma; (*of flower*) bocciolo ▷ *vi*
germogliare; (*flower*) sbocciare

Buddhism ['budɪzəm] *n* buddismo

Buddhist ['budɪst] *adj, n* buddista (*m/f*)

buddy ['bʌdɪ] (*us*) *n* compagno

budge [bʌdʒ] *vt* scostare; (*fig*) smuovere
▷ *vi* spostarsi; smuoversi

budgerigar ['bʌdʒərɪgɑ:'] *n*
pappagallino

budget ['bʌdʒɪt] *n* bilancio preventivo ▷ *vi*
to ~ for sth fare il bilancio per qc

budgie ['bʌdʒɪ] *n* = **budgerigar**

buff [bʌf] *adj* color camoscio ▷ *n* (*inf:
enthusiast*) appassionato(-a)

buffalo ['bʌfələu] (*pl* **buffalo** *or* **buffaloes**)
n bufalo; (*us*) bisonte *m*

buffer ['bʌfə'] *n* respingente *m*; (*Comput*)
memoria tampone, buffer *m inv*

buffet[1] ['bufeɪ] *vt* sferzare

buffet[2] ['bufeɪ] *n* (*food*, BRIT: *bar*) buffet
m inv; **buffet car** (BRIT) *n* (*Rail*) ≈ servizio
ristoro

bug [bʌg] *n* (*esp us: insect*) insetto; (*Comput,
fig: germ*) virus *m inv*; (*spy device*) microfono
spia ▷ *vt* mettere sotto controllo; (*inf:
annoy*) scocciare

buggy ['bʌgɪ] *n* (*baby buggy*) passeggino

build [bɪld] (*pt, pp* **built**) *n* (*of person*)
corporatura ▷ *vt* costruire; **build up**
vt accumulare; aumentare; **builder** *n*
costruttore *m*; **building** *n* costruzione *f*;
edificio; (*industry*) edilizia; **building site**
n cantiere *m* di costruzione; **building
society** (BRIT) *n* società *f inv* immobiliare

built [bɪlt] *pt, pp of* **build**; **built-in** *adj*
(*cupboard*) a muro; (*device*) incorporato(-a);
built-up area *adj* **built-up area** abitato

bulb [bʌlb] *n* (*Bot*) bulbo; (*Elec*) lampadina

Bulgaria [bʌl'gɛərɪə] *n* Bulgaria;
Bulgarian *adj* bulgaro(-a) ▷ *n*
bulgaro(-a); (*Ling*) bulgaro

bulge [bʌldʒ] *n* rigonfiamento ▷ *vi*
essere protuberante *or* rigonfio(-a); **to
be bulging with** essere pieno(-a) *or*
zeppo(-a) di

bulimia [bə'lɪmɪə] *n* bulimia

bulimic [bju:'lɪmɪk] *adj, n* bulimico(-a)

bulk [bʌlk] *n* massa, volume *m*; **in ~** a
pacchi *or* cassette *etc*; (*Comm*) all'ingrosso;
the ~ of il grosso di; **bulky** *adj* grosso(-a),
voluminoso(-a)

bull [bul] *n* toro; (*male elephant, whale*)
maschio

bulldozer ['buldəuzə'] *n* bulldozer *m inv*

bullet ['bulɪt] *n* pallottola

bulletin ['bulɪtɪn] *n* bollettino; **bulletin
board** *n* (*Comput*) bulletin board *m inv*

bullfight ['bulfaɪt] *n* corrida; **bullfighter**
n torero; **bullfighting** *n* tauromachia

bully ['bulɪ] *n* prepotente *m* ▷ *vt* angariare;
(*frighten*) intimidire

bum [bʌm] (*inf*) *n* (*backside*) culo; (*tramp*)
vagabondo(-a)

bumblebee ['bʌmblbi:] *n* bombo

bump [bʌmp] *n* (*in car*) piccolo
tamponamento; (*jolt*) scossa; (*on road etc*)
protuberanza; (*on head*) bernoccolo ▷ *vt*
battere; **bump into** *vt fus* scontrarsi con;
(*person*) imbattersi in; **bumper** *n* paraurti
m inv ▷ *adj* **bumper harvest** raccolto
eccezionale; **bumpy** ['bʌmpɪ] *adj* (*road*)
dissestato(-a)

bun [bʌn] *n* focaccia; (*of hair*) crocchia

bunch [bʌntʃ] *n* (*of flowers, keys*) mazzo;
(*of bananas*) casco; (*of people*) gruppo; **~ of
grapes** grappolo d'uva; **~es** *npl* (*in hair*)
codine *fpl*

bundle ['bʌndl] *n* fascio ▷ *vt* (*also*: **~ up**)
legare in un fascio; (*put*): **to ~ sth/sb into**
spingere qc/qn in

bungalow ['bʌngələu] *n* bungalow *m inv*

bungee jumping [ˈbʌndʒiːˈdʒʌmpɪŋ] *n* salto nel vuoto da ponti, grattacieli etc con un cavo fissato alla caviglia

bunion [ˈbʌnjən] *n* callo (al piede)

bunk [bʌŋk] *n* cuccetta; **bunk beds** *npl* letti *mpl* a castello

bunker [ˈbʌŋkər] *n* (coal store) ripostiglio per il carbone; (Mil, Golf) bunker *m inv*

bunny [ˈbʌnɪ] *n* (also: ~ **rabbit**) coniglietto

buoy [bɔɪ] *n* boa; **buoyant** *adj* galleggiante; (fig) vivace

burden [ˈbəːdn] *n* carico, fardello ▷ *vt* **to ~ sb with** caricare qn di

bureau [bjuəˈrəu] (pl **bureaux**) *n* (BRIT: writing desk) scrivania; (US: chest of drawers) cassettone *m*; (office) ufficio, agenzia

bureaucracy [bjuəˈrɔkrəsɪ] *n* burocrazia

bureaucrat [ˈbjuərəkræt] *n* burocrate *m/f*

bureau de change [-dəˈʃɑ̃ʒ] (pl **bureaux de change**) *n* cambiavalute *m inv*

bureaux [bjuəˈrəuz] *npl of* **bureau**

burger [ˈbəːgər] *n* hamburger *m inv*

burglar [ˈbəːglər] *n* scassinatore *m*; **burglar alarm** *n* campanello antifurto; **burglary** *n* furto con scasso

burial [ˈbɛrɪəl] *n* sepoltura

burn [bəːn] (pt, pp **burned** or **burnt**) *vt, vi* bruciare ▷ *n* bruciatura, scottatura; **burn down** *vt* distruggere col fuoco; **burn out** *vt* (writer etc): **to ~ o.s. out** esaurirsi; **burning** *adj* in fiamme; (sand) che scotta; (ambition) bruciante

Burns Night *n* vedi nota nel riquadro

● **BURNS NIGHT**
●
● **Burns Night** è la festa celebrata il 25
● gennaio per commemorare il poeta
● scozzese Robert Burns (1759-1796). Gli
● scozzesi festeggiano questa data con
● una cena, la "Burns supper", a base di
● "haggis", piatto tradizionale scozzese,
● e whisky.

burnt [bəːnt] pt, pp of **burn**

burp [bəːp] (inf) *n* rutto ▷ *vi* ruttare

burrow [ˈbʌrəu] *n* tana ▷ *vt* scavare

burst [bəːst] (pt, pp **burst**) *vt* far scoppiare ▷ *vi* esplodere; (tyre) scoppiare ▷ *n* scoppio; (also: ~ **pipe**) rottura nel tubo, perdita; **a ~ of speed** uno scatto di velocità; **to ~ into flames/tears** scoppiare in fiamme/lacrime; **to ~ out laughing** scoppiare a ridere; **to be ~ing with** scoppiare di; **burst into** *vt fus* (room etc) irrompere in

bury [ˈbɛrɪ] *vt* seppellire

bus [bʌs] (pl **buses**) *n* autobus *m inv*; **bus conductor** *n* autista *m/f* (dell'autobus)

bush [buʃ] *n* cespuglio; (scrub land) macchia; **to beat about the ~** menare il cane per l'aia

business [ˈbɪznɪs] *n* (matter) affare *m*; (trading) affari *mpl*; (firm) azienda; (job, duty) lavoro; **to be away on ~** essere andato via per affari; **it's none of my ~** questo non mi riguarda; **he means ~** non scherza; **business class** *n* (Aer) business class *f*; **businesslike** *adj* serio(-a), efficiente; **businessman** (irreg) *n* uomo d'affari; **business trip** *n* viaggio d'affari; **businesswoman** (irreg) *n* donna d'affari

busker [ˈbʌskər] (BRIT) *n* suonatore(-trice) ambulante

bus: **bus pass** *n* tessera dell'autobus; **bus shelter** *n* pensilina (alla fermata dell'autobus); **bus station** *n* stazione *f* delle corriere, autostazione *f*; **bus-stop** *n* fermata d'autobus

bust [bʌst] *n* busto; (Anat) seno ▷ *adj* (inf: broken) rotto(-a); **to go ~** fallire

bustling [ˈbʌslɪŋ] *adj* movimentato(-a)

busy [ˈbɪzɪ] *adj* occupato(-a); (shop, street) molto frequentato(-a) ▷ *vt* **to ~ o.s.** darsi da fare; **busy signal** (US) *n* (Tel) segnale *m* di occupato

 KEYWORD

but [bʌt] *conj* ma; **I'd love to come, but I'm busy** vorrei tanto venire, ma ho da fare
▷ *prep* (apart from, except) eccetto, tranne, meno; **he was nothing but trouble** non dava altro che guai; **no-one but him can do it** nessuno può farlo tranne lui; **but for you/your help** se non fosse per te/per il tuo aiuto; **anything but that** tutto ma non questo
▷ *adv* (just, only) solo, soltanto; **she's but a child** è solo una bambina; **had I but known** se solo avessi saputo; **I can but try** tentar non nuoce; **all but finished** quasi finito

butcher [ˈbutʃər] *n* macellaio ▷ *vt* macellare; **butcher's (shop)** *n* macelleria

butler [ˈbʌtlər] *n* maggiordomo

butt [bʌt] *n* (cask) grossa botte *f*; (of gun) calcio; (of cigarette) mozzicone *m*; (BRIT: fig: target) oggetto ▷ *vt* cozzare

butter [ˈbʌtər] *n* burro ▷ *vt* imburrare; **buttercup** *n* ranuncolo

butterfly [ˈbʌtəflaɪ] *n* farfalla; (Swimming: also: ~ **stroke**) (nuoto a) farfalla

buttocks [ˈbʌtəks] *npl* natiche *fpl*

button [ˈbʌtn] *n* bottone *m*; (US: badge)

distinctivo ▷ *vt* (*also:* ~ **up**) abbottonare ▷ *vi* abbottonarsi

buy [baɪ] (*pt, pp* **bought**) *vt* comprare ▷ *n* acquisto; **where can I ~ some postcards?** dove posso comprare delle cartoline?; **to ~ sb sth/sth from sb** comprare qc per qn/qc da qn; **to ~ sb a drink** offrire da bere a qn; **buy out** *vt* (*business*) rilevare; **buy up** *vt* accaparrare; **buyer** *n* compratore(-trice)

buzz [bʌz] *n* ronzio; (*inf: phone call*) colpo di telefono ▷ *vi* ronzare; **buzzer** [ˈbʌzəʳ] *n* cicalino

 KEYWORD

by [baɪ] *prep* **1** (*referring to cause, agent*) da; **killed by lightning** ucciso da un fulmine; **surrounded by a fence** circondato da uno steccato; **a painting by Picasso** un quadro di Picasso

2 (*referring to method, manner, means*): **by bus/car/train** in autobus/macchina/treno, con l'autobus/la macchina/il treno; **to pay by cheque** pagare con (un) assegno; **by moonlight** al chiaro di luna; **by saving hard, he ...** risparmiando molto, lui ...

3 (*via, through*) per; **we came by Dover** siamo venuti via Dover

4 (*close to, past*) accanto a; **the house by the river** la casa sul fiume; **a holiday by the sea** una vacanza al mare; **she sat by his bed** si sedette accanto al suo letto; **she rushed by me** mi è passata accanto correndo; **I go by the post office every day** passo davanti all'ufficio postale ogni giorno

5 (*not later than*) per, entro; **by 4 o'clock** per *or* entro le 4; **by this time tomorrow** domani a quest'ora; **by the time I got here it was too late** quando sono arrivato era ormai troppo tardi

6 (*during*): **by day/night** di giorno/notte

7 (*amount*) a; **by the kilo/metre** a chili/metri; **paid by the hour** pagato all'ora; **one by one** uno per uno; **little by little** a poco a poco

8 (*Math, measure*): **to divide/multiply by 3** dividere/moltiplicare per 3; **it's broader by a metre** è un metro più largo, è più largo di un metro

9 (*according to*) per; **to play by the rules** attenersi alle regole; **it's all right by me** per me va bene

10: **(all) by oneself** *etc* (tutto(-a)) solo(-a); **he did it (all) by himself** lo ha fatto (tutto) da solo

11: **by the way** a proposito; **this wasn't**

my idea by the way tra l'altro l'idea non è stata mia

▷ *adv* **1** *see* **go**; **pass** *etc*

2: **by and by** (*in past*) poco dopo; (*in future*) fra breve; **by and large** nel complesso

bye(-bye) [ˈbaɪˈbaɪ] *excl* ciao!, arrivederci!

by-election [ˈbaɪɪlɛkʃən] (*BRIT*) *n* elezione *f* straordinaria

bypass [ˈbaɪpɑːs] *n* circonvallazione *f*; (*Med*) by-pass *m inv* ▷ *vt* fare una deviazione intorno a

byte [baɪt] *n* (*Comput*) byte *m inv*, bicarattere *m*

C

C [si:] n (Mus) do

cab [kæb] n taxi m inv; (of train, truck) cabina

cabaret ['kæbəreɪ] n cabaret m inv

cabbage ['kæbɪdʒ] n cavolo

cabin ['kæbɪn] n capanna; (on ship) cabina; **cabin crew** n equipaggio

cabinet ['kæbɪnɪt] n (Pol) consiglio dei ministri; (furniture) armadietto; (also: **display ~**) vetrinetta; **cabinet minister** n ministro (membro del Consiglio)

cable ['keɪbl] n cavo; fune f; (Tel) cablogramma m ▷ vt telegrafare; **cable car** n funivia; **cable television** n televisione f via cavo

cactus ['kæktəs] (pl cacti) n cactus m inv

café ['kæfeɪ] n caffè m inv

cafeteria [kæfɪ'tɪərɪə] n self-service m inv

caffein(e) ['kæfiːn] n caffeina

cage [keɪdʒ] n gabbia

cagoule [kə'guːl] n K-way® m inv

cake [keɪk] n (large) torta; (small) pasticcino; **cake of soap** n saponetta

calcium ['kælsɪəm] n calcio

calculate ['kælkjuleɪt] vt calcolare; **calculation** [-'leɪʃən] n calcolo; **calculator** n calcolatrice f

calendar ['kæləndər] n calendario

calf [kɑːf] (pl **calves**) n (of cow) vitello; (of other animals) piccolo; (also: **~skin**) (pelle f di) vitello; (Anat) polpaccio

calibre ['kælɪbər] (us **caliber**) n calibro

call [kɔːl] vt (gen: also Tel) chiamare; (meeting) indire ▷ vi chiamare; (visit: also: **~ in, ~ round**) passare ▷ n (shout) grido, urlo; (Tel) telefonata; **to be ~ed** (person, object) chiamarsi; **can you ~ back later?** può richiamare più tardi?; **can I make a ~ from here?** posso telefonare da qui?; **to be on ~** essere a disposizione; **call back** vi (return) ritornare; (Tel) ritelefonare, richiamare; **call for** vt fus richiedere; (fetch) passare a prendere; **call in** vt (doctor, expert, police) chiamare, far venire; **call off** vt disdire; **call on** vt fus (visit) passare da; (appeal to) chiedere a; **call out** vi (in pain) urlare; (to person) chiamare; **call up** vt (Mil) richiamare; (Tel) telefonare a; **callbox** (BRIT) n cabina telefonica; **call centre** (US **call center**) n centro informazioni telefoniche; **caller** n persona che chiama, visitatore(-trice)

callous ['kæləs] adj indurito(-a), insensibile

calm [kɑːm] adj calmo(-a) ▷ n calma ▷ vt calmare; **calm down** vi calmarsi ▷ vt calmare; **calmly** adv con calma

Calor gas® ['kælər-] n butano

calorie ['kælərɪ] n caloria

calves [kɑːvz] npl of **calf**

camcorder ['kæmkɔːdər] n camcorder f inv

came [keɪm] pt of **come**

camel ['kæməl] n cammello

camera ['kæmərə] n macchina fotografica; (Cinema, TV) cinepresa; **in ~** a porte chiuse; **cameraman** (irreg) n cameraman m inv

camouflage ['kæməflɑːʒ] n (Mil, Zool) mimetizzazione f ▷ vt mimetizzare

camp [kæmp] n campeggio; (Mil) campo ▷ vi accamparsi ▷ adj effeminato(-a)

campaign [kæm'peɪn] n (Mil, Pol etc) campagna ▷ vi (also fig) fare una campagna; **campaigner** n **campaigner for** fautore(-trice) di; **campaigner against** oppositore(-trice) di

camp: **campbed** n (BRIT) brandina; **camper** ['kæmpər] n campeggiatore(-trice); (vehicle) camper m inv; **campground** (US) n campeggio; **camping** ['kæmpɪŋ] n campeggio; **to go camping** andare in campeggio; **campsite** ['kæmpsaɪt] n campeggio

campus ['kæmpəs] n campus m inv

can¹ [kæn] n (of milk) scatola; (of oil) bidone m; (of water) tanica; (tin) scatola ▷ vt

mettere in scatola

 KEYWORD

can² [kæn] (*negative* **cannot, can't**, *conditional and pt* **could**) *aux vb* **1** (*be able to*) potere; **I can't go any further** non posso andare oltre; **you can do it if you try** sei in grado di farlo — basta provarci; **I'll help you all I can** ti aiuterò come potrò; **I can't see you** non ti vedo **2** (*know how to*) sapere, essere capace di; **I can swim** so nuotare; **can you speak French?** parla francese? **3** (*may*) potere; **could I have a word with you?** posso parlarle un momento? **4** (*expressing disbelief, puzzlement etc*): **it can't be true!** non può essere vero!; **what can he want?** cosa può mai volere? **5** (*expressing possibility, suggestion etc*): **he could be in the library** può darsi che sia in biblioteca; **she could have been delayed** può aver avuto un contrattempo

Canada ['kænədə] *n* Canada *m*; **Canadian** [kə'neɪdɪən] *adj, n* canadese *m/f*
canal [kə'næl] *n* canale *m*
canary [kə'nɛərɪ] *n* canarino
Canary Islands, Canaries [kə'nɛərɪz] *npl* **the ~** le (isole) Canarie
cancel ['kænsəl] *vt* annullare; (*train*) sopprimere; (*cross out*) cancellare; **I want to ~ my booking** vorrei disdire la mia prenotazione; **cancellation** [-'leɪʃən] *n* annullamento; soppressione *f*; cancellazione *f*; (*Tourism*) prenotazione *f* annullata
cancer ['kænsə^r] *n* cancro
Cancer ['kænsə^r] *n* (*sign*) Cancro
candidate ['kændɪdeɪt] *n* candidato(-a)
candle ['kændl] *n* candela; (*in church*) cero; **candlestick** *n* bugia; (*bigger, ornate*) candeliere *m*
candy ['kændɪ] *n* zucchero candito; (*us*) caramella; caramelle *fpl*; **candy bar** (*us*) *n* lungo biscotto, in genere ricoperto di cioccolata; **candyfloss** ['kændɪflɒs] *n* (*BRIT*) zucchero filato
cane [keɪn] *n* canna; (*for furniture*) bambù *m*; (*stick*) verga ▷ *vt* (*BRIT Scol*) punire a colpi di verga
canister ['kænɪstə^r] *n* scatola metallica
cannabis ['kænəbɪs] *n* canapa indiana
canned [kænd] *adj* (*food*) in scatola
cannon ['kænən] (*pl* **cannon** *or* **cannons**) *n* (*gun*) cannone *m*
cannot ['kænɔt] = **can not**

canoe [kə'nuː] *n* canoa; **canoeing** *n* canottaggio
canon ['kænən] *n* (*clergyman*) canonico; (*standard*) canone *m*
can-opener ['kænəupnə^r] *n* apriscatole *m inv*
can't [kænt] = **can not**
canteen [kæn'tiːn] *n* mensa; (*BRIT: of cutlery*) portaposate *m inv*

> Be careful not to translate *canteen* by the Italian word *cantina*.

canter ['kæntə^r] *vi* andare al piccolo galoppo
canvas ['kænvəs] *n* tela
canvass ['kænvəs] *vi* (*Pol*): **to ~ for** raccogliere voti per ▷ *vt* fare un sondaggio di
canyon ['kænjən] *n* canyon *m inv*
cap [kæp] *n* (*hat*) berretto; (*of pen*) coperchio; (*of bottle, toy gun*) tappo; (*contraceptive*) diaframma *m* ▷ *vt* (*outdo*) superare; (*limit*) fissare un tetto a(a)
capability [keɪpə'bɪlɪtɪ] *n* capacità *f inv*, abilità *f inv*
capable ['keɪpəbl] *adj* capace
capacity [kə'pæsɪtɪ] *n* capacità *f inv*; (*of lift etc*) capienza
cape [keɪp] *n* (*garment*) cappa; (*Geo*) capo
caper ['keɪpə^r] *n* (*Culin*) cappero; (*prank*) scherzetto
capital ['kæpɪtl] *n* (*also: ~ city*) capitale *f*; (*money*) capitale *m*; (*also: ~ letter*) (lettera) maiuscola; **capitalism** *n* capitalismo; **capitalist** *adj, n* capitalista *m/f*; **capital punishment** *n* pena capitale
Capitol ['kæpɪtl] *n* **the ~** il Campidoglio
Capricorn ['kæprɪkɔːn] *n* Capricorno
capsize [kæp'saɪz] *vt* capovolgere ▷ *vi* capovolgersi
capsule ['kæpsjuːl] *n* capsula
captain ['kæptɪn] *n* capitano
caption ['kæpʃən] *n* leggenda
captivity [kæp'tɪvɪtɪ] *n* cattività
capture ['kæptʃə^r] *vt* catturare; (*Comput*) registrare ▷ *n* cattura; (*data*) registrazione *f* or rilevazione *f* di dati
car [kaː^r] *n* (*Aut*) macchina, automobile *f*; (*Rail*) vagone *m*
carafe [kə'ræf] *n* caraffa
caramel ['kærəməl] *n* caramello
carat ['kærət] *n* carato; **18 ~ gold** oro a 18 carati
caravan ['kærəvæn] *n* (*BRIT*) roulotte *f inv*; (*of camels*) carovana; **caravan site** (*BRIT*) *n* campeggio per roulotte
carbohydrate [kaːbəu'haɪdreɪt] *n* carboidrato
carbon ['kaːbən] *n* carbonio; **carbon dioxide** [-daɪ'ɒksaɪd] *n* diossido di

carbonio; **carbon monoxide** [-mɔ'nɔksaɪd] n monossido di carbonio
car boot sale n vedi nota nel riquadro

● **CAR BOOT SALE**
●
● Il **car boot sale** è un mercatino
● dell'usato molto popolare in Gran
● Bretagna. Normalmente ha luogo in
● un parcheggio o in un grande spiazzo,
● e la merce viene in genere esposta nei
● bagagliai, in inglese appunto "boots",
● aperti delle macchine.

carburettor [kɑ:bju'rɛtər] (US **carburetor**) n carburatore m
card [kɑ:d] n carta; (visiting card etc) biglietto; (Christmas card etc) cartolina; **cardboard** n cartone m; **card game** n gioco di carte
cardigan ['kɑ:dɪgən] n cardigan m inv
cardinal ['kɑ:dɪnl] adj cardinale ▷ n cardinale m
cardphone ['kɑ:dfəun] n telefono a scheda
care [kɛər] n cura, attenzione f; (worry) preoccupazione f ▷ vi **to ~ about** curarsi di; (thing, idea) interessarsi di; **~ of** presso; **in sb's ~** alle cure di qn; **to take ~ (to do)** fare attenzione (a fare); **to take ~ of** curarsi di; (bill, problem) occuparsi di; **I don't ~** non me ne importa; **I couldn't ~ less** non m'interessa affatto; **care for** vt fus aver cura di; (like) volere bene a
career [kə'rɪər] n carriera ▷ vi (also: **~ along**) andare di (gran) carriera
care: **carefree** ['kɛəfri:] adj sgombro(-a) di preoccupazioni; **careful** ['kɛəful] adj attento(-a); (cautious) cauto(-a); **(be) careful!** attenzione!; **carefully** adv con cura; cautamente; **caregiver** (US) n (professional) badante m/f; (unpaid) persona che si prende cura di un parente malato o anziano; **careless** ['kɛəlɪs] adj negligente; (heedless) spensierato(-a); **carelessness** n negligenza; mancanza di tatto; **carer** ['kɛərər] n assistente m/f (di persone malata o handicappata); **caretaker** ['kɛəteɪkər] n custode m
car-ferry ['kɑ:fɛri] n traghetto
cargo ['kɑ:gəu] (pl **cargoes**) n carico
car hire n autonoleggio
Caribbean [kærɪ'bi:ən] adj **the ~ Sea** il Mar dei Caraibi
caring ['kɛərɪŋ] adj (person) premuroso(-a); (society, organization) umanitario(-a)
carnation [kɑ:'neɪʃən] n garofano
carnival ['kɑ:nɪvəl] n (public celebration) carnevale m; (US: funfair) luna park m inv

carol ['kærəl] n **Christmas ~** canto di Natale
carousel [kærə'sɛl] (US) n giostra
car park (BRIT) n parcheggio
carpenter ['kɑ:pɪntər] n carpentiere m
carpet ['kɑ:pɪt] n tappeto ▷ vt coprire con tappeto
car rental (US) n autonoleggio
carriage ['kærɪdʒ] n vettura; (of goods) trasporto; **carriageway** (BRIT) n (part of road) carreggiata
carrier ['kærɪər] n (of disease) portatore(-trice); (Comm) impresa di trasporti; **carrier bag** (BRIT) n sacchetto
carrot ['kærət] n carota
carry ['kæri] vt (person) portare; (: vehicle) trasportare; (involve: responsibilities etc) comportare; (Med) essere portatore(-trice) di ▷ vi (sound) farsi sentire; **to be** or **get carried away** (fig) entusiasmarsi; **carry on** vi **to ~ on with sth/doing** continuare qc/a fare ▷ vt mandare avanti; **carry out** vt (orders) eseguire; (investigation) svolgere
cart [kɑ:t] n carro ▷ vt (inf) trascinare
carton ['kɑ:tən] n (box) scatola di cartone; (of yogurt) cartone m; (of cigarettes) stecca
cartoon [kɑ:'tu:n] n (Press) disegno umoristico; (comic strip) fumetto; (Cinema) disegno animato
cartridge ['kɑ:trɪdʒ] n (for gun, pen) cartuccia; (music tape) cassetta
carve [kɑ:v] vt (meat) trinciare; (wood, stone) intagliare; **carving** n (in wood etc) scultura
car wash n lavaggio auto
case [keɪs] n caso; (Law) causa, processo; (box) scatola; (BRIT: also: **suit~**) valigia; **in ~ of** in caso di; **in ~ he** caso mai lui; **in any ~** in ogni caso; **just in ~** in caso di bisogno
cash [kæʃ] n denaro; (coins, notes) denaro liquido ▷ vt incassare; **I haven't got any ~** non ho contanti; **to pay (in) ~** pagare in contanti; **~ on delivery** pagamento alla consegna; **cashback** n (discount) sconto; (at supermarket etc) anticipo di contanti ottenuto presso la cassa di un negozio tramite una carta di debito; **cash card** (BRIT) n tesserino di prelievo; **cash desk** (BRIT) n cassa; **cash dispenser** (BRIT) n sportello automatico
cashew [kæ'ʃu:] n (also: **~ nut**) anacardio
cashier [kæ'ʃɪər] n cassiere(-a)
cashmere ['kæʃmɪər] n cachemire m
cash point n sportello bancario automatico, Bancomat® m inv
cash register n registratore m di cassa
casino [kə'si:nəu] n casinò m inv
casket ['kɑ:skɪt] n cofanetto; (US: coffin) bara

casserole ['kæsərəul] n casseruola; (food): **chicken ~** pollo in casseruola

cassette [kæ'sɛt] n cassetta; **cassette player** n riproduttore m a cassette

cast [kɑːst] (pt, pp **cast**) vt (throw) gettare; (metal) gettare, fondere; (Theatre): **to ~ sb as Hamlet** scegliere qn per la parte di Amleto ▷ n (Theatre) cast m inv; (also: **plaster ~**) ingessatura; **to ~ one's vote** votare, dare il voto; **cast off** vi (Naut) salpare; (Knitting) calare

castanets [kæstə'nɛts] npl castagnette fpl

caster sugar ['kɑːstə^r-] (BRIT) n zucchero semolato

cast-iron ['kɑːstaɪən] adj (lit) di ghisa; (fig: case) di ferro

castle ['kɑːsl] n castello

casual ['kæʒjul] adj (chance) casuale, fortuito(-a); (: work etc) avventizio(-a); (unconcerned) noncurante, indifferente; **~ wear** casual m

casualty ['kæʒjultɪ] n ferito(-a); (dead) morto(-a), vittima; (Med: department) pronto soccorso

cat [kæt] n gatto

catalogue ['kætəlɔg] (US **catalog**) n catalogo ▷ vt catalogare

catalytic converter [kætəlɪtɪk-] n marmitta catalitica, catalizzatore m

cataract ['kætərækt] n (also Med) cateratta

catarrh [kə'tɑː^r] n catarro

catastrophe [kə'tæstrəfɪ] n catastrofe f

catch [kætʃ] (pt, pp **caught**) vt prendere; (ball) afferrare; (surprise: person) sorprendere; (attention) attirare; (comment, whisper) cogliere; (person) raggiungere ▷ vi (fire) prendere ▷ n (fish etc caught) retata; (of ball) presa; (trick) inganno; (Tech) gancio; (game) catch m inv; **to ~ fire** prendere fuoco; **to ~ sight of** scorgere; **catch up** vi mettersi in pari ▷ vt (also: **~ up with**) raggiungere; **catching** ['kætʃɪŋ] adj (Med) contagioso(-a)

category ['kætɪgərɪ] n categoria

cater ['keɪtə^r] vt, vi **for** (BRIT: needs) provvedere a; (: readers, consumers) incontrare i gusti di; (Comm: provide food) provvedere alla ristorazione di

caterpillar ['kætəpɪlə^r] n bruco

cathedral [kə'θiːdrəl] n cattedrale f, duomo

Catholic ['kæθəlɪk] adj, n (Rel) cattolico(-a)

Catseye® ['kæts'aɪ] (BRIT) n (Aut) catarifrangente m

cattle ['kætl] npl bestiame m, bestie fpl

catwalk ['kætwɔːk] n passerella

caught [kɔːt] pt, pp of **catch**

cauliflower ['kɔlɪflauə^r] n cavolfiore m

cause [kɔːz] n causa ▷ vt causare

caution ['kɔːʃən] n prudenza; (warning) avvertimento ▷ vt avvertire; ammonire; **cautious** ['kɔːʃəs] adj cauto(-a), prudente

cave [keɪv] n caverna, grotta; **cave in** vi (roof etc) crollare

caviar(e) ['kævɪɑː^r] n caviale m

cavity ['kævɪtɪ] n cavità f inv

cc abbr = **cubic centimetres**; **carbon copy**

CCTV n abbr (= closed-circuit television) televisione f a circuito chiuso

CD abbr (disc) CD m inv; (player) lettore m CD inv; **CD player** n lettore m CD; **CD-ROM** [-rɔm] n abbr CD-ROM m inv

cease [siːs] vt, vi cessare; **ceasefire** n cessate il fuoco m inv

cedar ['siːdə^r] n cedro

ceilidh ['keɪlɪ] n festa con musiche e danze popolari scozzesi o irlandesi

ceiling ['siːlɪŋ] n soffitto; (on wages etc) tetto

celebrate ['sɛlɪbreɪt] vt, vi celebrare; **celebration** [-'breɪʃən] n celebrazione f

celebrity [sɪ'lɛbrɪtɪ] n celebrità f inv

celery ['sɛlərɪ] n sedano

cell [sɛl] n cella; (of revolutionaries, Biol) cellula; (Elec) elemento (di batteria)

cellar ['sɛlə^r] n sottosuolo; cantina

cello ['tʃɛləu] n violoncello

Cellophane® ['sɛləfeɪn] n cellophane® m

cellphone ['sɛləfeɪn] n cellulare m

Celsius ['sɛlsɪəs] adj Celsius inv

Celtic ['kɛltɪk, 'sɛltɪk] adj celtico(-a)

cement [sə'mɛnt] n cemento

cemetery ['sɛmɪtrɪ] n cimitero

censor ['sɛnsə^r] n censore m ▷ vt censurare; **censorship** n censura

census ['sɛnsəs] n censimento

cent [sɛnt] n (US: coin) centesimo (= 1.100 di un dollaro); (unit of euro) centesimo; see also **per**

centenary [sɛn'tiːnərɪ] n centenario

centennial [sɛn'tɛnɪəl] (US) n centenario

center ['sɛntə^r] (US) n, vt = **centre**

centi... [sɛntɪ] prefix: **centigrade** ['sɛntɪgreɪd] adj centigrado(-a); **centimetre** ['sɛntɪmiːtə^r] (US **centimeter**) n centimetro; **centipede** ['sɛntɪpiːd] n centopiedi m inv

central ['sɛntrəl] adj centrale; **Central America** n America centrale; **central heating** n riscaldamento centrale; **central reservation** n (BRIT Aut) banchina f spartitraffico inv

centre ['sɛntə^r] (US **center**) n centro ▷ vt centrare; **centre-forward** n (Sport) centroavanti m inv; **centre-half** n (Sport) centromediano

century ['sɛntjurɪ] n secolo; **twentieth ~**

ventesimo secolo

CEO n abbr = **chief executive officer**

ceramic ['sɪ'ræmɪk] adj ceramico(-a)

cereal ['sɪːrɪəl] n cereale m

ceremony ['serɪmənɪ] n cerimonia; **to stand on ~** fare complimenti

certain ['səːtən] adj certo(-a); **to make ~ of** assicurarsi di; **for ~** per certo, di sicuro; **certainly** adv certamente, certo; **certainty** n certezza

certificate [sə'tɪfɪkɪt] n certificato; diploma m

certify ['səːtɪfaɪ] vt certificare; (award diploma to) conferire un diploma a; (declare insane) dichiarare pazzo(-a)

cf. abbr (= compare) cfr.

CFC n (= chlorofluorocarbon) CFC m inv

chain [tʃeɪn] n catena ▷ vt (also: **~ up**) incatenare; **chain-smoke** vi fumare una sigaretta dopo l'altra

chair [tʃɛəʳ] n sedia; (armchair) poltrona; (of university) cattedra; (of meeting) presidenza ▷ vt (meeting) presiedere; **chairlift** n seggiovia; **chairman** (irreg) n presidente m; **chairperson** n presidente(-essa); **chairwoman** (irreg) n presidentessa

chalet ['ʃæleɪ] n chalet m inv

chalk [tʃɔːk] n gesso; **chalkboard** (us) n lavagna

challenge ['tʃælɪndʒ] n sfida ▷ vt sfidare; (statement, right) mettere in dubbio; **to ~ sb to do** sfidare qn a fare; **challenging** adj (task) impegnativo(-a); (look) di sfida

chamber ['tʃeɪmbəʳ] n camera; **chambermaid** n cameriera

champagne [ʃæm'peɪn] n champagne m inv

champion ['tʃæmpɪən] n campione(-essa); **championship** n campionato

chance [tʃɑːns] n caso; (opportunity) occasione f; (likelihood) possibilità f inv ▷ vt **to ~ it** rischiare, provarci ▷ adj fortuito(-a); **to take a ~** rischiare; **by ~** per caso

chancellor ['tʃɑːnsələʳ] n cancelliere m; **Chancellor of the Exchequer** [-ɪks'tʃɛkəʳ] (BRIT) n Cancelliere dello Scacchiere

chandelier [ʃændə'lɪəʳ] n lampadario

change [tʃeɪndʒ] vt cambiare; (transform): **to ~ sb into** trasformare qn in ▷ vi cambiare; (change one's clothes) cambiarsi; (be transformed): **to ~ into** trasformarsi in ▷ n cambiamento; (of clothes) cambio; (money returned) resto; (coins) spiccioli; **where can I ~ some money?** dove posso cambiare dei soldi?; **to ~ one's mind** cambiare idea; **keep the ~!** tenga pure il resto!; **sorry, I don't have any ~** mi dispiace, non ho spiccioli; **for a ~** tanto per

cambiare; **change over** vi (from sth to sth) passare; (players etc) scambiarsi (di posto o di campo) ▷ vt cambiare; **changeable** adj (weather) variabile; **change machine** n distributore automatico di monete; **changing room** n (BRIT: in shop) camerino; (: Sport) spogliatoio

channel ['tʃænl] n canale m; (of river, sea) alveo ▷ vt canalizzare; **Channel Tunnel** n **the Channel Tunnel** il tunnel sotto la Manica

chant [tʃɑːnt] n canto; salmodia ▷ vt cantare; salmodiare

chaos ['keɪɔs] n caos m

chaotic [keɪ'ɔtɪk] adj caotico(-a)

chap [tʃæp] (BRIT: inf) n (man) tipo

chapel ['tʃæpəl] n cappella

chapped [tʃæpt] adj (skin, lips) screpolato(-a)

chapter ['tʃæptəʳ] n capitolo

character ['kærɪktəʳ] n carattere m; (in novel, film) personaggio; **characteristic** [-'rɪstɪk] adj caratteristico(-a) ▷ n caratteristica; **characterize** ['kærɪktəraɪz] vt caratterizzare; (describe): **to characterize (as)** descrivere (come)

charcoal ['tʃɑːkəul] n carbone m di legna

charge [tʃɑːdʒ] n accusa; (cost) prezzo; (responsibility) responsabilità ▷ vt (gun, battery, Mil: enemy) caricare; (customer) fare pagare a; (sum) fare pagare; (Law): **to ~ sb (with)** accusare qn (di) ▷ vi (gen with: up, along etc) lanciarsi; **charge card** n carta f clienti inv; **charger** n (also: **battery charger**) caricabatterie m inv; (old: warhorse) destriero

charismatic [kærɪz'mætɪk] adj carismatico(-a)

charity ['tʃærɪtɪ] n carità; (organization) opera pia; **charity shop** n (BRIT) negozi che vendono articoli di seconda mano e devolvono il ricavato in beneficenza

charm [tʃɑːm] n fascino; (on bracelet) ciondolo ▷ vt affascinare, incantare; **charming** adj affascinante

chart [tʃɑːt] n tabella; grafico; (map) carta nautica ▷ vt fare una carta nautica di; **~s** npl (Mus) hit parade f

charter ['tʃɑːtəʳ] vt (plane) noleggiare ▷ n (document) carta; **chartered accountant** ['tʃɑːtəd-] (BRIT) n ragioniere(-a) professionista; **charter flight** n volo m charter inv

chase [tʃeɪs] vt inseguire; (also: **~ away**) cacciare ▷ n caccia

chat [tʃæt] vi (also: **have a ~**) chiacchierare ▷ n chiacchierata; **chat up** vt (BRIT inf: girl) abbordare; **chat room** n (Internet) chat room f inv; **chat show** (BRIT) n talk show *m inv*

chatter ['tʃætə'] *vi (person)* ciarlare; *(bird)* cinguettare; *(teeth)* battere ▷ *n* ciarle *fpl*; cinguettio

chauffeur ['ʃəufə'] *n* autista *m*

chauvinist ['ʃəuvɪnɪst] *n (male chauvinist)* maschilista *m*; *(nationalist)* sciovinista *m/f*

cheap [tʃiːp] *adj* economico(-a); *(joke)* grossolano(-a); *(poor quality)* di cattiva qualità ▷ *adv* a buon mercato; **can you recommend a ~ hotel/restaurant, please?** potrebbe indicarmi un albergo/ ristorante non troppo caro?; **cheap day return** *n* biglietto ridotto di andata e ritorno valido in giornata; **cheaply** *adv* a buon prezzo, a buon mercato

cheat [tʃiːt] *vi* imbrogliare; *(at school)* copiare ▷ *vt* ingannare ▷ *n* imbroglione *m*; **to ~ sb out of sth** defraudare qn di qc; **cheat on** *vt fus (husband, wife)* tradire

Chechnya [tʃɪtʃ'njaː] *n* Cecenia

check [tʃɛk] *vt* verificare; *(passport, ticket)* controllare; *(halt)* fermare; *(restrain)* contenere ▷ *n* verifica; controllo; *(curb)* freno; *(us: bill)* conto; *(pattern: gen pl)* quadretti *mpl*; *(us)* = **cheque** ▷ *adj (pattern, cloth)* a quadretti; **check in** *vi (in hotel)* registrare; *(at airport)* presentarsi all'accettazione ▷ *vt (luggage)* depositare; **check off** *vt* segnare; **check out** *vi (in hotel)* saldare il conto; **check up** *vi* **to ~ up (on sth)** investigare (qc); **to ~ up on sb** informarsi sul conto di qn; **checkbook** *(us)* *n* = **chequebook; checked** *adj* a quadretti; **checkers** *(us)* *n* dama; **check-in** *(also:* **check-in desk***: at airport)* check-in *m inv*, accettazione *f* (bagagli *inv*); **checking account** *(us)* *n* conto corrente; **checklist** *n* lista di controllo; **checkmate** *n* scaccomatto; **checkout** *n (in supermarket)* cassa; **checkpoint** *n* posto di blocco; **checkroom** *(us)* *n* deposito *m* bagagli *inv*; **checkup** *n (Med)* controllo medico

cheddar ['tʃɛdə'] *n* formaggio duro di latte di mucca di colore bianco o arancione

cheek [tʃiːk] *n* guancia; *(impudence)* faccia tosta; **cheekbone** *n* zigomo; **cheeky** *adj* sfacciato(-a)

cheer [tʃɪə'] *vt* applaudire; *(gladden)* rallegrare ▷ *vi* applaudire ▷ *n* grido (di incoraggiamento); **cheer up** *vi* rallegrarsi, farsi animo ▷ *vt* rallegrare; **cheerful** *adj* allegro(-a)

cheerio ['tʃɪərɪ'əu] *(BRIT) excl* ciao!

cheerleader ['tʃɪəliːdə'] *n* cheerleader *f inv*

cheese [tʃiːz] *n* formaggio; **cheeseburger**

n cheeseburger *m inv*; **cheesecake** *n* specie di torta di ricotta, a volte con frutta

chef [ʃɛf] *n* capocuoco

chemical ['kɛmɪkəl] *adj* chimico(-a) ▷ *n* prodotto chimico

chemist ['kɛmɪst] *n (BRIT: pharmacist)* farmacista *m/f*; *(scientist)* chimico(-a); **chemistry** *n* chimica; **chemist's (shop)** *(BRIT) n* farmacia

cheque [tʃɛk] *(us* **check***) n* assegno; **chequebook** *n* libretto degli assegni; **cheque card** *n* carta *f* assegni *inv*

cherry ['tʃɛrɪ] *n* ciliegia; *(also: ~ tree)* ciliegio

chess [tʃɛs] *n* scacchi *mpl*

chest [tʃɛst] *n* petto; *(box)* cassa

chestnut ['tʃɛsnʌt] *n* castagna; *(also: ~ tree)* castagno

chest of drawers *n* cassettone *m*

chew [tʃuː] *vt* masticare; **chewing gum** *n* chewing gum *m*

chic [ʃiːk] *adj* elegante

chick [tʃɪk] *n* pulcino; *(inf)* pollastrella

chicken ['tʃɪkɪn] *n* pollo; *(inf: coward)* coniglio; **chicken out** *(inf) vi* avere fifa; **chickenpox** *n* varicella

chickpea ['tʃɪkpiː] *n* cece *m*

chief [tʃiːf] *n* capo ▷ *adj* principale; **chief executive (officer)** *n* direttore *m* generale; **chiefly** *adv* per lo più, soprattutto

child [tʃaɪld] *(pl* **children***) n* bambino(-a); **child abuse** *n* molestie *fpl* a minori; **child benefit** *n (BRIT)* ≈ assegni *mpl* familiari; **childbirth** *n* parto; **child-care** *n* il badare ai bambini; **childhood** *n* infanzia; **childish** *adj* puerile; **child minder** [-'maɪndə'] *(BRIT) n* bambinaia; **children** ['tʃɪldrən] *npl of* **child**

Chile ['tʃɪlɪ] *n* Cile *m*

Chilean ['tʃɪlɪən] *adj, n* cileno(-a)

chill [tʃɪl] *n* freddo; *(Med)* infreddatura ▷ *vt* raffreddare; **chill out** *(esp us) vi (inf)* darsi una calmata

chil(l)i ['tʃɪlɪ] *n* peperoncino

chilly ['tʃɪlɪ] *adj* freddo(-a), fresco(-a); **to feel ~** sentirsi infreddolito(-a)

chimney ['tʃɪmnɪ] *n* camino

chimpanzee [tʃɪmpæn'ziː] *n* scimpanzé *m inv*

chin [tʃɪn] *n* mento

China ['tʃaɪnə] *n* Cina

china ['tʃaɪnə] *n* porcellana

Chinese [tʃaɪ'niːz] *adj* cinese ▷ *n inv* cinese *m/f*; *(Ling)* cinese *m*

chip [tʃɪp] *n (gen pl: Culin)* patatina fritta; *(: us: also:* **potato ~***)* patatina; *(of wood, glass, stone)* scheggia; *(also:* **micro~***)* chip *m inv* ▷ *vt (cup, plate)* scheggiare; **chip**

shop n (BRIT) vedi nota nel riquadro

● CHIP SHOP
●
● I **chip shops**, anche chiamati "fish
● and chip shops", sono friggitorie che
● vendono principalmente filetti di pesce
● impanati e patatine fritte.

chiropodist [kɪ'rɔpədɪst] (BRIT) n pedicure m/f inv
chisel ['tʃɪzl] n cesello
chives [tʃaɪvz] npl erba cipollina
chlorine ['klɔːriːn] n cloro
choc-ice ['tʃɔkaɪs] n (BRIT) gelato ricoperto al cioccolato
chocolate ['tʃɔklɪt] ▷ n (substance) cioccolato, cioccolata; (drink) cioccolata; (a sweet) cioccolatino
choice [tʃɔɪs] n scelta ▷ adj scelto(-a)
choir ['kwaɪəʳ] n coro
choke [tʃəuk] vi soffocare ▷ vt soffocare; (block): **to be ~d with** essere intasato(-a) di ▷ n (Aut) valvola dell'aria
cholesterol [kə'lestərɔl] n colesterolo
choose [tʃuːz] (pt chose,, pp chosen) vt scegliere; **to ~ to do** decidere di fare; preferire fare
chop [tʃɔp] vt (wood) spaccare; (Culin: also: ~ up) tritare ▷ n (Culin) costoletta; **chop down** vt (tree) abbattere; **chop off** vt tagliare; **chopsticks** ['tʃɔpstɪks] npl bastoncini mpl cinesi
chord [kɔːd] n (Mus) accordo
chore [tʃɔːʳ] n faccenda; **household ~s** faccende fpl domestiche
chorus ['kɔːrəs] n coro; (repeated part of song: also fig) ritornello
chose [tʃəuz] pt of choose
chosen ['tʃəuzn] pp of choose
Christ [kraɪst] n Cristo
christen ['krɪsn] vt battezzare; **christening** n battesimo
Christian ['krɪstɪən] adj, n cristiano(-a); **Christianity** [-'ænɪtɪ] n cristianesimo; **Christian name** n nome m (di battesimo)
Christmas ['krɪsməs] n Natale m; **Merry ~!** Buon Natale!; **Christmas card** n cartolina di Natale; **Christmas carol** n canto natalizio; **Christmas Day** n il giorno di Natale; **Christmas Eve** n la vigilia di Natale; **Christmas pudding** n (esp BRIT) specie di budino con frutta secca, spezie e brandy; **Christmas tree** n albero di Natale
chrome [krəum] n cromo
chronic ['krɔnɪk] adj cronico(-a)
chrysanthemum [krɪ'sænθəməm] n crisantemo

chubby ['tʃʌbɪ] adj paffuto(-a)
chuck [tʃʌk] (inf) vt buttare, gettare; (BRIT: also: ~ up) piantare; **chuck out** vt buttar fuori
chuckle ['tʃʌkl] vi ridere sommessamente
chum [tʃʌm] n compagno(-a)
chunk [tʃʌŋk] n pezzo
church [tʃəːtʃ] n chiesa; **churchyard** n sagrato
churn [tʃəːn] n (for butter) zangola; (for milk) bidone m
chute [ʃuːt] n (also: **rubbish ~**) canale m di scarico; (BRIT: children's slide) scivolo
chutney ['tʃʌtnɪ] n salsa piccante (di frutta, zucchero e spezie)
CIA (US) n abbr (= Central Intelligence Agency) CIA f
CID (BRIT) n abbr (= Criminal Investigation Department) ≈ polizia giudiziaria
cider ['saɪdəʳ] n sidro
cigar [sɪ'gɑːʳ] n sigaro
cigarette [sɪgə'ret] n sigaretta; **cigarette lighter** n accendino
cinema ['sɪnəmə] n cinema m inv
cinnamon ['sɪnəmən] n cannella
circle ['səːkl] n cerchio; (of friends etc) circolo; (in cinema) galleria ▷ vi girare in circolo ▷ vt (surround) circondare; (move round) girare intorno a
circuit ['səːkɪt] n circuito
circular ['səːkjuləʳ] adj circolare ▷ n circolare f
circulate ['səːkjuleɪt] vi circolare ▷ vt far circolare; **circulation** [-'leɪʃən] n circolazione f; (of newspaper) tiratura
circumstances ['səːkəmstənsɪz] npl circostanze fpl; (financial condition) condizioni fpl finanziarie
circus ['səːkəs] n circo
cite [saɪt] vt citare
citizen ['sɪtɪzn] n (of country) cittadino(-a); (of town) abitante m/f; **citizenship** n cittadinanza
citrus fruits ['sɪtrəs-] npl agrumi mpl
city ['sɪtɪ] n città f inv; **the C~** la Città di Londra (centro commerciale); **city centre** n centro della città; **city technology college** n (BRIT) istituto tecnico superiore (finanziato dall'industria)
civic ['sɪvɪk] adj civico(-a)
civil ['sɪvɪl] adj civile; **civilian** [sɪ'vɪlɪən] adj, n borghese m/f
civilization [sɪvɪlaɪ'zeɪʃən] n civiltà f inv
civilized ['sɪvɪlaɪzd] adj civilizzato(-a); (fig) cortese
civil: **civil law** n codice m, civile; (study) diritto civile; **civil rights** npl diritti mpl civili; **civil servant** n impiegato(-a) statale; **Civil Service** n amministrazione f

statale; **civil war** n guerra civile
CJD abbr (= Creutzfeld Jacob disease) malattia di Creutzfeldt-Jacob
claim [kleɪm] vt (assert): **to ~ (that)/to be** sostenere (che)/di essere; (credit, rights etc) rivendicare; (damages) richiedere ▷ vi (for insurance) fare una domanda d'indennizzo ▷ n pretesa; rivendicazione f; richiesta; **claim form** n (gen) modulo di richiesta; (for expenses) modulo di rimborso spese
clam [klæm] n vongola
clamp [klæmp] n pinza; morsa ▷ vt stringere con una morsa; (Aut: wheel) applicare i ceppi bloccaruote a
clan [klæn] n clan m inv
clap [klæp] vi applaudire
claret ['klærət] n vino di Bordeaux
clarify ['klærɪfaɪ] vt chiarificare, chiarire
clarinet [klærɪ'nɛt] n clarinetto
clarity ['klærɪtɪ] n clarità
clash [klæʃ] n frastuono; (fig) scontro ▷ vi scontrarsi; cozzare
clasp [klɑːsp] n (hold) stretta; (of necklace, bag) fermaglio, fibbia ▷ vt stringere
class [klɑːs] n classe f ▷ vt classificare
classic ['klæsɪk] adj classico(-a) ▷ n classico; **classical** adj classico(-a)
classification [klæsɪfɪ'keɪʃən] n classificazione f
classify ['klæsɪfaɪ] vt classificare
classmate ['klɑːsmeɪt] n compagno(-a) di classe
classroom ['klɑːsrum] n aula
classy ['klɑːsɪ] adj (inf) chic inv, elegante
clatter ['klætəʳ] n tintinnio; scalpitio ▷ vi tintinnare; scalpitare
clause [klɔːz] n clausola; (Ling) proposizione f
claustrophobic [klɔːstrə'fəubɪk] adj claustrofobico(-a)
claw [klɔː] n (of bird of prey) artiglio; (of lobster) pinza
clay [kleɪ] n argilla
clean [kliːn] adj pulito(-a); (clear, smooth) liscio(-a) ▷ vt pulire; **clean up** vt (also fig) ripulire; **cleaner** n (person) donna delle pulizie; **cleaner's** n (also: **dry cleaner's**) tintoria; **cleaning** n pulizia
cleanser ['klɛnzəʳ] n detergente m
clear [klɪəʳ] adj chiaro(-a); (glass etc) trasparente; (road, way) libero(-a); (conscience) pulito(-a) ▷ vt sgombrare; liberare; (table) sparecchiare; (cheque) fare la compensazione di; (Law: suspect) discolpare; (obstacle) superare ▷ vi (weather) rasserenarsi; (fog) andarsene ▷ adv **~ of** distante da; **clear away** vt (things, clothes etc) mettere a posto; **to ~ away the dishes** sparecchiare la tavola;

clear up vt mettere in ordine; (mystery) risolvere; **clearance** n (removal) sgombro; (permission) autorizzazione f, permesso; **clear-cut** adj ben delineato(-a), distinto(-a); **clearing** n radura; **clearly** adv chiaramente; **clearway** (BRIT) n strada con divieto di sosta
clench [klɛntʃ] vt stringere
clergy ['klɜːdʒɪ] n clero
clerk [klɑːk, (US) klɜːrk] n (BRIT) impiegato(-a); (US) commesso(-a)
clever ['klɛvəʳ] adj (mentally) intelligente; (deft, skilful) abile; (device, arrangement) ingegnoso(-a)
cliché ['kliːʃeɪ] n cliché m inv
click [klɪk] vi scattare ▷ vt (heels etc) battere; (tongue) far schioccare
client ['klaɪənt] n cliente m/f
cliff [klɪf] n scogliera scoscesa, rupe f
climate ['klaɪmɪt] n clima m
climax ['klaɪmæks] n culmine m; (sexual) orgasmo
climb [klaɪm] vi salire; (clamber) arrampicarsi ▷ vt salire; (Climbing) scalare ▷ n salita; arrampicata; scalata; **climb down** vi scendere; (BRIT fig) far marcia indietro; **climber** n rocciatore(-trice); alpinista m/f; **climbing** n alpinismo
clinch [klɪntʃ] vt (deal) concludere
cling [klɪŋ] (pt, pp clung) vi **to ~ (to)** aggrapparsi (a); (of clothes) aderire strettamente (a)
Clingfilm® ['klɪŋfɪlm] n pellicola trasparente (per alimenti)
clinic ['klɪnɪk] n clinica
clip [klɪp] n (for hair) forcina; (also: **paper ~**) graffetta; (TV, Cinema) sequenza ▷ vt attaccare insieme; (hair, nails) tagliare; (hedge) tosare; **clipping** n (from newspaper) ritaglio
cloak [kləuk] n mantello ▷ vt avvolgere; **cloakroom** n (for coats etc) guardaroba m inv; (BRIT: W.C.) gabinetti mpl
clock [klɔk] n orologio; **clock in** or **on** vi timbrare il cartellino (all'entrata); **clock off** or **out** vi timbrare il cartellino (all'uscita); **clockwise** adv in senso orario; **clockwork** n movimento or meccanismo a orologeria ▷ adj a molla
clog [klɔg] n zoccolo ▷ vt intasare ▷ vi (also: **~ up**) intasarsi, bloccarsi
clone [kləun] n clone m
close¹ [kləus] adj **~ (to)** vicino(-a) (a); (watch, link, relative) stretto(-a); (examination) attento(-a); (contest) combattuto(-a); (weather) afoso(-a) ▷ adv vicino, dappresso; **~ to** vicino a; **~ by**, **at hand** a portata di mano; **a ~ friend** un amico intimo; **to have a ~ shave** (fig)

scamparla bella

close² [kləʊz] vt chiudere ▷ vi (shop etc) chiudere; (lid, door etc) chiudersi; (end) finire ▷ n (end) fine f; **what time do you ~?** a che ora chiudete?; **close down** vi cessare (definitivamente); **closed** adj chiuso(-a)

closely ['kləʊslɪ] adv (examine, watch) da vicino; (related) strettamente

closet ['klɒzɪt] n (cupboard) armadio

close-up ['kləʊsʌp] n primo piano

closing time n orario di chiusura

closure ['kləʊʒəʳ] n chiusura

clot [klɒt] n (also: **blood ~**) coagulo; (inf: idiot) scemo(-a) ▷ vi coagularsi

cloth [klɒθ] n (material) tessuto, stoffa; (rag) strofinaccio

clothes [kləʊðz] npl abiti mpl, vestiti mpl; **clothes line** n corda (per stendere il bucato); **clothes peg** (us **clothes pin**) n molletta

clothing ['kləʊðɪŋ] n = **clothes**

cloud [klaʊd] n nuvola; **cloud over** vi rannuvolarsi; (fig) offuscarsi; **cloudy** adj nuvoloso(-a); (liquid) torbido(-a)

clove [kləʊv] n chiodo di garofano; **clove of garlic** n spicchio d'aglio

clown [klaʊn] n pagliaccio ▷ vi (also: ~ **about**, ~ **around**) fare il pagliaccio

club [klʌb] n (society) club m inv, circolo; (weapon, Golf) mazza ▷ vt bastonare ▷ vi **to ~ together** associarsi; **~s** npl (Cards) fiori mpl; **club class** n (Aviat) classe f club inv

clue [kluː] n indizio; (in crosswords) definizione f; **I haven't a ~** non ho la minima idea

clump [klʌmp] n (of flowers, trees) gruppo; (of grass) ciuffo

clumsy ['klʌmzɪ] adj goffo(-a)

clung [klʌŋ] pt, pp of **cling**

cluster ['klʌstəʳ] n gruppo ▷ vi raggrupparsi

clutch [klʌtʃ] n (grip, grasp) presa, stretta; (Aut) frizione f ▷ vt afferrare, stringere forte

cm abbr (= centimetre) cm

Co. abbr = **county**; **company**

c/o abbr (= care of) presso

coach [kəʊtʃ] n (bus) pullman m inv; (horse-drawn, of train) carrozza; (Sport) allenatore(-trice); (tutor) chi dà ripetizioni ▷ vt allenare; dare ripetizioni a; **coach station** (BRIT) n stazione f delle corriere; **coach trip** n viaggio in pullman

coal [kəʊl] n carbone m

coalition [kəʊə'lɪʃən] n coalizione f

coarse [kɔːs] adj (salt, sand etc) grosso(-a); (cloth, person) rozzo(-a)

coast [kəʊst] n costa ▷ vi (with cycle etc) scendere a ruota libera; **coastal** adj costiero(-a); **coastguard** n guardia costiera; **coastline** n linea costiera

coat [kəʊt] n cappotto; (of animal) pelo; (of paint) mano f ▷ vt coprire; **coat hanger** n attaccapanni m inv; **coating** n rivestimento

coax [kəʊks] vt indurre (con moine)

cob [kɒb] n see **corn**

cobbled ['kɒbld] adj ~ **street** strada pavimentata a ciottoli

cobweb ['kɒbwɛb] n ragnatela

cocaine [kə'keɪn] n cocaina

cock [kɒk] n (rooster) gallo; (male bird) maschio ▷ vt (gun) armare; **cockerel** n galletto

cockney ['kɒknɪ] n cockney m/f inv (abitante dei quartieri popolari dell'East End di Londra)

cockpit ['kɒkpɪt] n abitacolo

cockroach ['kɒkrəʊtʃ] n blatta

cocktail ['kɒkteɪl] n cocktail m inv

cocoa ['kəʊkəʊ] n cacao

coconut ['kəʊkənʌt] n noce f di cocco

cod [kɒd] n merluzzo

C.O.D. abbr = **cash on delivery**

code [kəʊd] n codice m

coeducational ['kəʊɛdju'keɪʃənl] adj misto(-a)

coffee ['kɒfɪ] n caffè m inv; **coffee bar** (BRIT) n caffè m inv; **coffee bean** n grano or chicco di caffè; **coffee break** n pausa per il caffè; **coffee maker** n bollitore m per il caffè; **coffeepot** n caffettiera; **coffee shop** n ≈ caffè m inv; **coffee table** n tavolino

coffin ['kɒfɪn] n bara

cog [kɒg] n dente m

cognac ['kɒnjæk] n cognac m inv

coherent [kəʊ'hɪərənt] adj coerente

coil [kɔɪl] n rotolo; (Elec) bobina; (contraceptive) spirale f ▷ vt avvolgere

coin [kɔɪn] n moneta ▷ vt (word) coniare

coincide [kəʊɪn'saɪd] vi coincidere; **coincidence** [kəʊ'ɪnsɪdəns] n combinazione f

Coke® [kəʊk] n coca

coke [kəʊk] n coke m

colander ['kɒləndəʳ] n colino

cold [kəʊld] adj freddo(-a) ▷ n freddo; (Med) raffreddore m; **it's ~** fa freddo; **to be ~** (person) aver freddo; (object) essere freddo(-a); **to catch ~** prendere freddo; **to catch a ~** prendere un raffreddore; **in ~ blood** a sangue freddo; **cold sore** n erpete m

coleslaw ['kəʊlslɔː] n insalata di cavolo bianco

colic ['kɒlɪk] n colica

collaborate [kə'læbəreɪt] vi collaborare
collapse [kə'læps] vi crollare ▷ n crollo;
(Med) collasso
collar ['kɒlər] n (of coat, shirt) colletto; (of
dog, cat) collare m; **collarbone** n clavicola
colleague ['kɒliːɡ] n collega m/f
collect [kə'lɛkt] vt (gen) raccogliere; (as
a hobby) fare collezione di; (BRIT: call and
pick up) prendere; (money owed, pension)
riscuotere; (donations, subscriptions) fare
una colletta di ▷ vi adunarsi, riunirsi;
ammucchiarsi; **to call ~** (US Tel) fare
una chiamata a carico del destinatario;
collection [kə'lɛkʃən] n raccolta;
collezione f; (for money) colletta; **collective**
adj collettivo(-a) ▷ n collettivo; **collector**
[kə'lɛktər] n collezionista m/f
college ['kɒlɪdʒ] n college m inv; (of
technology etc) istituto superiore
collide [kə'laɪd] vi **to ~ with** scontrarsi
(con)
collision [kə'lɪʒən] n collisione f, scontro
cologne [kə'ləun] n (also: **eau de ~**) acqua
di colonia
Colombia [kə'lɒmbɪə] n Colombia;
Colombian adj, n colombiano(-a)
colon ['kəulən] n (sign) due punti mpl;
(Med) colon m inv
colonel ['kəːnl] n colonnello
colonial [kə'ləunɪəl] adj coloniale
colony ['kɒlənɪ] n colonia
colour etc ['kʌlər] (US **color**) n colore
m ▷ vt colorare; (tint, dye) tingere; (fig:
affect) influenzare ▷ vi (blush) arrossire;
colour in vt colorare; **colour-blind** adj
daltonico(-a); **coloured** adj (photo) a
colori; (person) di colore; **colour film** n
(for camera) pellicola a colori; **colourful**
adj pieno(-a) di colore, a vivaci colori;
(personality) colorato(-a); **colouring** n
(substance) colorante m; (complexion)
colorito; **colour television** n televisione
f a colori
column ['kɒləm] n colonna
coma ['kəumə] n coma m inv
comb [kəum] n pettine m ▷ vt (hair)
pettinare; (area) battere a tappeto
combat ['kɒmbæt] n combattimento ▷ vt
combattere, lottare contro
combination [kɒmbɪ'neɪʃən] n
combinazione f
combine [vb kəm'baɪn, n 'kɒmbaɪn] vt
to ~ (with) combinare (con); (one quality
with another) unire (a) ▷ vi unirsi; (Chem)
combinarsi ▷ n (Econ) associazione f
come [kʌm] (pt **came**, pp **come**) vi venire;
arrivare; **to ~ to** (decision etc) raggiungere;
I've ~ to like him ha cominciato a
piacermi; **to ~ undone** slacciarsi; **to ~**
loose allentarsi; **come across** vt fus
trovare per caso; **come along** vi (pupil,
work) fare progressi; **~ along!** avanti!,
andiamo!, forza!; **come back** vi ritornare;
come down vi scendere; (prices) calare;
(buildings) essere demolito(-a); **come from**
vt fus venire da; provenire da; **come in** vi
entrare; **come off** vi (button) staccarsi;
(stain) andar via; (attempt) riuscire; **come**
on vi (pupil, work, project) fare progressi;
(lights) accendersi; (electricity) entrare in
funzione; **~ on!** avanti!, andiamo!, forza!;
come out vi uscire; (stain) andare via;
come round vi (after faint, operation)
riprendere conoscenza, rinvenire; **come**
to vi rinvenire; **come up** vi (sun) salire;
(problem) sorgere; (event) essere in arrivo;
(in conversation) saltar fuori; **come up with**
vt fus **he came up with an idea** venne
fuori con un'idea
comeback ['kʌmbæk] n (Theatre etc)
ritorno
comedian [kə'miːdɪən] n comico
comedy ['kɒmɪdɪ] n commedia
comet ['kɒmɪt] n cometa
comfort ['kʌmfət] n comodità f inv,
benessere m; (relief) consolazione f,
conforto ▷ vt consolare, confortare;
comfortable adj comodo(-a); (financially)
agiato(-a); **comfort station** (US) n
gabinetti mpl
comic ['kɒmɪk] adj (also: **~al**) comico(-a)
▷ n comico; (BRIT: magazine) giornaletto;
comic book (US) n giornalino (a fumetti);
comic strip n fumetto
comma ['kɒmə] n virgola
command [kə'mɑːnd] n ordine m,
comando; (Mil: authority) comando;
(mastery) padronanza ▷ vt comandare;
to ~ sb to do ordinare a qn di fare;
commander n capo; (Mil) comandante m
commemorate [kə'mɛməreɪt] vt
commemorare
commence [kə'mɛns] vt, vi cominciare;
commencement (US) n (Univ) cerimonia
di consegna dei diplomi
commend [kə'mɛnd] vt lodare;
raccomandare
comment ['kɒmɛnt] n commento ▷ vi **to**
~ (on) fare commenti (su); **commentary**
['kɒməntərɪ] n commentario; (Sport)
radiocronaca; telecronaca; **commentator**
['kɒmənteɪtər] n commentatore(-trice);
radiocronista m/f; telecronista m/f
commerce ['kɒməːs] n commercio
commercial [kə'məːʃəl] adj commerciale
▷ n (TV, Radio: advertisement) pubblicità
f inv; **commercial break** n intervallo
pubblicitario

commission [kə'mɪʃən] n commissione
f ▷ vt (work of art) commissionare; **out
of ~** (Naut) in disarmo; **commissioner** n
(Police) questore m
commit [kə'mɪt] vt (act) commettere;
(to sb's care) affidare; **to ~ o.s. to do**
impegnarsi (a fare); **to ~ suicide** suicidarsi;
commitment n impegno; promessa
committee [kə'mɪtɪ] n comitato
commodity [kə'mɔdɪtɪ] n prodotto,
articolo
common ['kɔmən] adj comune; (pej)
volgare; (usual) normale ▷ n terreno
comune; **the C~s** npl la Camera
dei Comuni; **in ~** in comune; **commonly**
adv comunemente, usualmente;
commonplace adj banale, ordinario(-a);
Commons npl (BRIT Pol): **the (House
of) Commons** la Camera dei Comuni;
common sense n buon senso;
Commonwealth n **the Commonwealth**
il Commonwealth

● COMMONWEALTH
●
● Il **Commonwealth** è un'associazione
● di stati sovrani indipendenti e di
● alcuni territori annessi che facevano
● parte dell'antico Impero Britannico.
● Nel 1931 questi assunsero il nome
● di "Commonwealth of Nations",
● denominazione successivamente
● semplificata in "Commonwealth".
● Attualmente gli stati del
● "Commonwealth" riconoscono ancora il
● proprio capo di stato.

communal ['kɔmju:nl] adj (for common
use) pubblico(-a)
commune [n 'kɔmju:n, vb kə'mju:n] n
(group) comune f ▷ vi **to ~ with** mettersi in
comunione con
communicate [kə'mju:nɪkeɪt] vt
comunicare, trasmettere ▷ vi **to ~ with**
comunicare (con)
communication [kəmju:nɪ'keɪʃən] n
comunicazione f
communion [kə'mju:nɪən] n (also: **Holy
C~**) comunione f
communism ['kɔmjunɪzəm] n
comunismo; **communist** adj, n
comunista m/f
community [kə'mju:nɪtɪ] n comunità f
inv; **community centre** (US **community
center**) n circolo ricreativo; **community
service** n (BRIT) ≈ lavoro sostitutivo
commute [kə'mju:t] vi fare il pendolare
▷ vt (Law) commutare; **commuter** n
pendolare m/f

compact [adj kəm'pækt, n 'kɔmpækt]
adj compatto(-a) ▷ n (also: **powder
~**) portacipria m inv; **compact disc** n
compact disc m inv; **compact disc player**
n lettore m CD inv
companion [kəm'pænɪən] n
compagno(-a)
company ['kʌmpənɪ] n (also Comm,
Mil, Theatre) compagnia; **to keep sb ~**
tenere compagnia a qn; **company car**
n macchina (di proprietà) della ditta;
company director n amministratore m,
consigliere m di amministrazione
comparable ['kɔmpərəbl] adj simile
comparative [kəm'pærətɪv] adj
relativo(-a); (adjective etc) comparativo(-a);
comparatively adv relativamente
compare [kəm'pɛəʳ] vt **to ~ sth/sb
with/to** confrontare qc/qn con/a ▷ vi
to ~ (with) reggere il confronto (con);
comparison [-'pærɪsn] n confronto; **in
comparison (with)** in confronto (a)
compartment [kəm'pɑːtmənt] n
compartimento; (Rail) scompartimento; **a
non-smoking ~** uno scompartimento per
non-fumatori
compass ['kʌmpəs] n bussola; **~es** npl
(Math) compasso
compassion [kəm'pæʃən] n compassione
f
compatible [kəm'pætɪbl] adj compatibile
compel [kəm'pɛl] vt costringere,
obbligare; **compelling** adj (fig: argument)
irresistibile
compensate ['kɔmpənseɪt] vt risarcire
▷ vi **to ~ for** compensare; **compensation**
[-'seɪʃən] n compensazione f; (money)
risarcimento
compete [kəm'pi:t] vi (take part)
concorrere; (vie): **to ~ with** fare
concorrenza (a)
competent ['kɔmpɪtənt] adj competente
competition [kɔmpɪ'tɪʃən] n gara;
concorso; (Econ) concorrenza
competitive [kəm'petɪtɪv] adj (Econ)
concorrenziale; (sport) agonistico(-a);
(person) che ha spirito di competizione; che
ha spirito agonistico
competitor [kəm'petɪtəʳ] n concorrente
m/f
complacent [kəm'pleɪsnt] adj
compiaciuto(-a) di sé
complain [kəm'pleɪn] vi lagnarsi,
lamentarsi; **complaint** n lamento; (in
shop etc) reclamo; (Med) malattia
complement [n 'kɔmplɪmənt, vb
'kɔmplɪment] n complemento; (especially
of ship's crew etc) effettivo ▷ vt (enhance)
accompagnarsi bene a; **complementary**

[kɔmplɪˈmɛntərɪ] adj complementare
complete [kəmˈpliːt] adj completo(-a)
▷ vt completare; (a form) riempire;
completely adv completamente;
completion n completamento
complex [ˈkɔmplɛks] adj complesso(-a)
▷ n (Psych, of buildings etc) complesso
complexion [kəmˈplɛkʃən] n (of face)
carnagione f
compliance [kəmˈplaɪəns] n
acquiescenza; **in ~ with** (orders, wishes etc)
in conformità con
complicate [ˈkɔmplɪkeɪt] vt complicare;
complicated adj complicato(-a);
complication [-ˈkeɪʃən] n complicazione f
compliment [n ˈkɔmplɪmənt, vb
ˈkɔmplɪmɛnt] n complimento ▷ vt fare
un complimento a; **complimentary**
[-ˈmɛntərɪ] adj complimentoso(-a),
elogiativo(-a); (free) in omaggio
comply [kəmˈplaɪ] vi **to ~ with** assentire
a; conformarsi a
component [kəmˈpəʊnənt] adj
componente ▷ n componente m
compose [kəmˈpəʊz] vt (form): **to be ~d
of** essere composto di; (music, poem etc)
comporre; **to ~ o.s.** ricomporsi; **composer**
n (Mus) compositore(-trice); **composition**
[kɔmpəˈzɪʃən] n composizione f
composure [kəmˈpəʊʒə*] n calma
compound [ˈkɔmpaʊnd] n (Chem, Ling)
composto; (enclosure) recinto ▷ adj
composto(-a)
comprehension [kɔmprɪˈhɛnʃən] n
comprensione f
comprehensive [kɔmprɪˈhɛnsɪv] adj
completo(-a); **comprehensive (school)**
(BRIT) n scuola secondaria aperta a tutti

> Be careful not to translate
> **comprehensive** by the Italian word
> **comprensivo**.

compress [vb kəmˈprɛs, n ˈkɔmprɛs] vt
comprimere ▷ n (Med) compressa
comprise [kəmˈpraɪz] vt (also: **be ~d**)
comprendere
compromise [ˈkɔmprəmaɪz] n
compromesso ▷ vt compromettere ▷ vi
venire a un compromesso
compulsive [kəmˈpʌlsɪv] adj (liar, gambler)
che non riesce a controllarsi; (viewing,
reading) cui non si può fare a meno
compulsory [kəmˈpʌlsərɪ] adj
obbligatorio(-a)
computer [kəmˈpjuːtə*] n computer
m inv, elaboratore m elettronico;
computer game n gioco per computer;
computer-generated adj realizzato(-a)
al computer; **computerize** vt
computerizzare; **computer programmer**

n programmatore(-trice); **computer
programming** n programmazione
f di computer; **computer science** n
informatica; **computer studies** npl
informatica; **computing** n informatica
con [kɔn] (inf) vt truffare ▷ n truffa
conceal [kənˈsiːl] vt nascondere
concede [kənˈsiːd] vt ammettere
conceited [kənˈsiːtɪd] adj
presuntuoso(-a), vanitoso(-a)
conceive [kənˈsiːv] vt concepire ▷ vi
concepire un bambino
concentrate [ˈkɔnsəntreɪt] vi
concentrarsi ▷ vt concentrare
concentration [kɔnsənˈtreɪʃən] n
concentrazione f
concept [ˈkɔnsɛpt] n concetto
concern [kənˈsəːn] n affare m; (Comm)
azienda, ditta; (anxiety) preoccupazione
f ▷ vt riguardare; **to be ~ed (about)**
preoccuparsi (di); **concerning** prep
riguardo a, circa
concert [ˈkɔnsət] n concerto; **concert
hall** n sala da concerti
concerto [kənˈtʃəːtəʊ] n concerto
concession [kənˈsɛʃən] n concessione f
concise [kənˈsaɪs] adj conciso(-a)
conclude [kənˈkluːd] vt concludere;
conclusion [-ˈkluːʒən] n conclusione f
concrete [ˈkɔnkriːt] n calcestruzzo ▷ adj
concreto(-a), di calcestruzzo
concussion [kənˈkʌʃən] n commozione
f cerebrale
condemn [kənˈdɛm] vt condannare;
(building) dichiarare pericoloso(-a)
condensation [kɔndɛnˈseɪʃən] n
condensazione f
condense [kənˈdɛns] vi condensarsi ▷ vt
condensare
condition [kənˈdɪʃən] n condizione f;
(Med) malattia ▷ vt condizionare; **on ~
that** a condizione che + sub, a condizione
di; **conditional** adj condizionale; **to
be conditional upon** dipendere da;
conditioner n (for hair) balsamo; (for
fabrics) ammorbidente m
condo [ˈkɔndəʊ] (US) n abbr (inf)
= **condominium**
condom [ˈkɔndəm] n preservativo
condominium [kɔndəˈmɪnɪəm] (US) n
condominio
condone [kənˈdəʊn] vt condonare
conduct [n ˈkɔndʌkt, vb kənˈdʌkt]
n condotta ▷ vt condurre; (manage)
dirigere; amministrare; (Mus) dirigere;
to ~ o.s. comportarsi; **conducted tour**
[kənˈdʌktɪd-] n gita accompagnata;
conductor n (of orchestra) direttore m
d'orchestra; (on bus) bigliettaio; (US: on

train) controllore *m*; (*Elec*) conduttore *m*

cone [kəʊn] *n* cono; (*Bot*) pigna; (*traffic cone*) birillo

confectionery [kən'fɛkʃənrɪ] *n* dolciumi *mpl*

confer [kən'fəː'] *vt* **to ~ sth on** conferire qc a ▷ *vi* conferire

conference ['kɔnfərns] *n* congresso

confess [kən'fɛs] *vt* confessare, ammettere ▷ *vi* confessare; **confession** [kən'fɛʃən] *n* confessione *f*

confide [kən'faɪd] *vi* **to ~ in** confidarsi con

confidence ['kɔnfɪdns] *n* confidenza; (*trust*) fiducia; (*self-assurance*) sicurezza di sé; **in ~** (*speak, write*) in confidenza, confidenzialmente; **confident** *adj* sicuro(-a), sicuro(-a) di sé; **confidential** [kɔnfɪ'dɛnʃəl] *adj* riservato(-a), confidenziale

confine [kən'faɪn] *vt* limitare; (*shut up*) rinchiudere; **confined** *adj* (*space*) ristretto(-a)

confirm [kən'fəːm] *vt* confermare; **confirmation** [kɔnfə'meɪʃən] *n* conferma; (*Rel*) cresima

confiscate ['kɔnfɪskeɪt] *vt* confiscare

conflict [*n* 'kɔnflɪkt, *vb* kən'flɪkt] *n* conflitto ▷ *vi* essere in conflitto

conform [kən'fɔːm] *vi* **to ~ to** conformarsi (a)

confront [kən'frʌnt] *vt* (*enemy, danger*) affrontare; **confrontation** [kɔnfrən'teɪʃən] *n* scontro

confuse [kən'fjuːz] *vt* (*one thing with another*) confondere; **confused** *adj* confuso(-a); **confusing** *adj* che fa confondere; **confusion** [-'fjuːʒən] *n* confusione *f*

congestion [kən'dʒɛstʃən] *n* congestione *f*

congratulate [kən'grætjuleɪt] *vt* **to ~ sb (on)** congratularsi con qn (per *or* di); **congratulations** [-'leɪʃənz] *npl* auguri *mpl*; (*on success*) complimenti *mpl*, congratulazioni *fpl*

congregation [kɔŋgrɪ'geɪʃən] *n* congregazione *f*

congress ['kɔŋgrɛs] *n* congresso; **congressman** (*irreg: us*) *n* membro del Congresso; **congresswoman** (*irreg: us*) *n* (donna) membro del Congresso

conifer ['kɔnɪfə'] *n* conifero

conjugate ['kɔndʒugeɪt] *vt* coniugare

conjugation [kɔndʒə'geɪʃən] *n* coniugazione *f*

conjunction [kən'dʒʌŋkʃən] *n* congiunzione *f*

conjure ['kʌndʒə'] *vi* fare giochi di prestigio

connect [kə'nɛkt] *vt* connettere, collegare; (*Elec, Tel*) collegare; (*fig*) associare ▷ *vi* (*train*): **to ~ with** essere in coincidenza con; **to be ~ed with** (*associated*) aver rapporti con; **connecting flight** *n* volo in coincidenza; **connection** [-ʃən] ▷ *n* relazione *f*, rapporto; (*Elec*) connessione *f*; (*train, plane*) coincidenza; (*Tel*) collegamento

conquer ['kɔŋkə'] *vt* conquistare; (*feelings*) vincere

conquest ['kɔŋkwɛst] *n* conquista

cons [kɔnz] *npl see* **convenience**; **pro**

conscience ['kɔnʃəns] *n* coscienza

conscientious [kɔnʃɪ'ɛnʃəs] *adj* coscienzioso(-a)

conscious ['kɔnʃəs] *adj* consapevole; (*Med*) cosciente; **consciousness** *n* consapevolezza; coscienza

consecutive [kən'sɛkjutɪv] *adj* consecutivo(-a); **on 3 ~ occasions** 3 volte di fila

consensus [kən'sɛnsəs] *n* consenso; **the ~ of opinion** l'opinione *f* unanime *or* comune

consent [kən'sɛnt] *n* consenso ▷ *vi* **to ~ (to)** acconsentire (a)

consequence ['kɔnsɪkwəns] *n* conseguenza, risultato; importanza

consequently ['kɔnsɪkwəntlɪ] *adv* di conseguenza, dunque

conservation [kɔnsə'veɪʃən] *n* conservazione *f*

conservative [kən'sə:vətɪv] *adj* conservatore(-trice); (*cautious*) cauto(-a); **Conservative** (*BRIT*) *adj, n* (*Pol*) conservatore(-trice)

conservatory [kən'sə:vətrɪ] *n* (*greenhouse*) serra; (*Mus*) conservatorio

consider [kən'sɪdə'] *vt* considerare; (*take into account*) tener conto di; **to ~ doing sth** considerare la possibilità di fare qc; **considerable** [kən'sɪdərəbl] *adj* considerevole, notevole; **considerably** *adv* notevolmente, decisamente; **considerate** [kən'sɪdərɪt] *adj* premuroso(-a); **consideration** [kənsɪdə'reɪʃən] *n* considerazione *f*; **considering** [kən'sɪdərɪŋ] *prep* in considerazione di

consignment [kən'saɪnmənt] *n* (*of goods*) consegna; spedizione *f*

consist [kən'sɪst] *vi* **to ~ of** constare di, essere composto(-a) di

consistency [kən'sɪstənsɪ] *n* consistenza; (*fig*) coerenza

consistent [kən'sɪstənt] *adj* coerente

consolation [kɔnsə'leɪʃən] *n* consolazione *f*

console[1] [kən'səul] *vt* consolare

console² ['kɒnsəul] n quadro di comando
consonant ['kɒnsənənt] n consonante f
conspicuous [kən'spɪkjuəs] adj cospicuo(-a)
conspiracy [kən'spɪrəsɪ] n congiura, cospirazione f
constable ['kʌnstəbl] (BRIT) n ≈ poliziotto, agente m di polizia; **chief ~** ≈ questore m
constant ['kɒnstənt] adj costante, continuo(-a); **constantly** adv costantemente; continuamente
constipated ['kɒnstɪpeɪtɪd] adj stitico(-a); **constipation** [kɒnstɪ'peɪʃən] n stitichezza
constituency [kən'stɪtjuənsɪ] n collegio elettorale
constitute ['kɒnstɪtjuːt] vt costituire
constitution [kɒnstɪ'tjuːʃən] n costituzione f
constraint [kən'streɪnt] n costrizione f
construct [kən'strʌkt] vt costruire; **construction** [-ʃən] n costruzione f; **constructive** adj costruttivo(-a)
consul ['kɒnsl] n console m; **consulate** ['kɒnsjulɪt] n consolato
consult [kən'sʌlt] vt consultare; **consultant** n (Med) consulente m medico; (other specialist) consulente; **consultation** [-'teɪʃən] n (Med) consulto; (discussion) consultazione f; **consulting room** [kən'sʌltɪŋ-] (BRIT) n ambulatorio
consume [kən'sjuːm] vt consumare; **consumer** n consumatore(-trice)
consumption [kən'sʌmpʃən] n consumo
cont. abbr = **continued**
contact ['kɒntækt] n contatto; (person) conoscenza ▷ vt mettersi in contatto con; **contact lenses** npl lenti fpl a contatto
contagious [kən'teɪdʒəs] adj (also fig) contagioso(-a)
contain [kən'teɪn] vt contenere; **to ~ o.s.** contenersi; **container** n recipiente m; (for shipping etc) container m inv
contaminate [kən'tæmɪneɪt] vt contaminare
cont'd abbr = **continued**
contemplate ['kɒntəmpleɪt] vt contemplare; (consider) pensare a (or di)
contemporary [kən'tɛmpərərɪ] adj, n contemporaneo(-a)
contempt [kən'tɛmpt] n disprezzo; **~ of court** (Law) oltraggio alla Corte
contend [kən'tɛnd] vt **to ~ that** sostenere che ▷ vi **to ~ with** lottare contro
content¹ ['kɒntɛnt] n contenuto; **~s** npl (of box, case etc) contenuto; **(table of) ~s** indice m
content² [kən'tɛnt] adj contento(-a), soddisfatto(-a) ▷ vt contentare, soddisfare; **contented** adj contento(-a), soddisfatto(-a)
contest [n 'kɒntɛst, vb kən'tɛst] n lotta; (competition) gara, concorso ▷ vt contestare; impugnare; (compete for) essere in lizza per; **contestant** [kən'tɛstənt] n concorrente m/f; (in fight) avversario(-a)
context ['kɒntɛkst] n contesto
continent ['kɒntɪnənt] n continente m; **the C~** (BRIT) l'Europa continentale; **continental** [-'nɛntl] adj continentale; **continental breakfast** n colazione f all'europea (senza piatti caldi); **continental quilt** (BRIT) n piumino
continual [kən'tɪnjuəl] adj continuo(-a); **continually** adv di continuo
continue [kən'tɪnjuː] vi continuare ▷ vt continuare; (start again) riprendere
continuity [kɒntɪ'njuːɪtɪ] n continuità; (TV, Cinema) (ordine m della) sceneggiatura
continuous [kən'tɪnjuəs] adj continuo(-a), ininterrotto(-a); **continuous assessment** n (BRIT) valutazione f continua; **continuously** adv (repeatedly) continuamente; (uninterruptedly) ininterrottamente
contour ['kɒntuə'] n contorno, profilo; (also: **~ line**) curva di livello
contraception [kɒntrə'sɛpʃən] n contraccezione f
contraceptive [kɒntrə'sɛptɪv] adj contraccettivo(-a) ▷ n contraccettivo
contract [n 'kɒntrækt, vb kən'trækt] n contratto ▷ vi (become smaller) contrarsi; (Comm) **to ~ to do sth** fare un contratto per fare qc ▷ vt (illness) contrarre; **contractor** n imprenditore m
contradict [kɒntrə'dɪkt] vt contraddire; **contradiction** [kɒntrə'dɪkʃən] n contraddizione f; **to be in contradiction with** discordare con
contrary¹ ['kɒntrərɪ] adj contrario(-a); (unfavourable) avverso(-a), contrario(-a) ▷ n contrario; **on the ~** al contrario; **unless you hear to the ~** salvo contrordine
contrary² [kən'trɛərɪ] adj (perverse) bisbetico(-a)
contrast [n 'kɒntrɑːst, vb kən'trɑːst] n contrasto ▷ vt mettere in contrasto; **in ~ to** contrariamente a
contribute [kən'trɪbjuːt] vi contribuire ▷ vt **to ~ £10/an article to** dare 10 sterline/un articolo a; **to ~ to** contribuire a; (newspaper) scrivere per; **contribution** [kɒntrɪ'bjuːʃən] n contributo; **contributor** n (to newspaper) collaboratore(-trice)

control [kən'trəul] vt controllare; (firm, operation etc) dirigere ▷ n controllo; **~s** npl (of vehicle etc) comandi mpl; (governmental) controlli mpl; **under ~** sotto controllo; **to be in ~ of** avere il controllo di; **to go out of ~** (car) non rispondere ai comandi; (situation) sfuggire di mano; **control tower** n (Aviat) torre f di controllo

controversial [kɒntrə'və:ʃl] adj controverso(-a), polemico(-a)

controversy ['kɒntrəvə:sɪ] n controversia, polemica

convenience [kən'vi:nɪəns] n comodità f inv; **at your ~** a suo comodo; **all modern ~s** (BRIT), **all mod cons** tutte le comodità moderne

convenient [kən'vi:nɪənt] adj comodo(-a)

> Be careful not to translate **convenient** by the Italian word **conveniente**.

convent ['kɒnvənt] n convento

convention [kən'vɛnʃən] n convenzione f; (meeting) convegno; **conventional** adj convenzionale

conversation [kɒnvə'seɪʃən] n conversazione f

conversely [kɒn'və:slɪ] adv al contrario, per contro

conversion [kən'və:ʃən] n conversione f; (BRIT: of house) trasformazione f, rimodernamento

convert [vb kən'və:t, n 'kɒnvə:t] vt (Comm, Rel) convertire; (alter) trasformare ▷ n convertito(-a); **convertible** n macchina decappottabile

convey [kən'veɪ] vt trasportare; (thanks) comunicare; (idea) dare; **conveyor belt** [kən'veɪə'-] n nastro trasportatore

convict [vb kən'vɪkt, n 'kɒnvɪkt] vt dichiarare colpevole ▷ n carcerato(-a); **conviction** [-ʃən] n condanna; (belief) convinzione f

convince [kən'vɪns] vt convincere, persuadere; **convinced** adj **convinced of/that** convinto(-a) di/che; **convincing** adj convincente

convoy ['kɒnvɔɪ] n convoglio

cook [kuk] vt cucinare, cuocere ▷ vi cuocere; (person) cucinare ▷ n cuoco(-a); **cook book** n libro di cucina; **cooker** n fornello, cucina; **cookery** n cucina; **cookery book** (BRIT) n = **cook book**; **cookie** (US) n biscotto; **cooking** n cucina

cool [ku:l] adj fresco(-a); (not afraid, calm) calmo(-a); (unfriendly) freddo(-a) ▷ vt raffreddare; (room) rinfrescare ▷ vi (water) raffreddarsi; (air) rinfrescarsi; **cool down** vi raffreddarsi; (fig: person, situation) calmarsi; **cool off** vi (become

calmer) calmarsi; (lose enthusiasm) perdere interesse

cop [kɒp] (inf) n sbirro

cope [kəup] vi **to ~ with** (problems) far fronte a

copper ['kɒpə'] n rame m; (inf: policeman) sbirro

copy ['kɒpɪ] n copia ▷ vt copiare; **copyright** n diritto d'autore

coral ['kɒrəl] n corallo

cord [kɔ:d] n corda; (Elec) filo; **~s** npl (trousers) calzoni mpl (di velluto) a coste; **cordless** adj senza cavo

corduroy ['kɔ:dərɔɪ] n fustagno

core [kɔ:'] n (of fruit) torsolo; (of organization etc) cuore m ▷ vt estrarre il torsolo da

coriander [kɒrɪ'ændə'] n coriandolo

cork [kɔ:k] n sughero; (of bottle) tappo; **corkscrew** n cavatappi m inv

corn [kɔ:n] n (BRIT: wheat) grano; (US: maize) granturco; (on foot) callo; **~ on the cob** (Culin) pannocchia cotta

corned beef ['kɔ:nd-] n carne f di manzo in scatola

corner ['kɔ:nə'] n angolo; (Aut) curva ▷ vt intrappolare; mettere con le spalle al muro; (Comm: market) accaparrare ▷ vi prendere una curva

corner shop (BRIT) piccolo negozio di generi alimentari

cornflakes ['kɔ:nfleɪks] npl fiocchi mpl di granturco

cornflour ['kɔ:nflauə'] (BRIT) n farina finissima di granturco

cornstarch ['kɔ:nsta:tʃ] (US) n = **cornflour**

Cornwall ['kɔ:nwəl] n Cornovaglia

coronary ['kɒrənərɪ] n **~ (thrombosis)** trombosi f coronaria

coronation [kɒrə'neɪʃən] n incoronazione f

coroner ['kɒrənə'] n magistrato incaricato di indagare la causa di morte in circostanze sospette

corporal ['kɔ:pərl] n caporalmaggiore m ▷ adj **~ punishment** pena corporale

corporate ['kɔ:pərɪt] adj costituito(-a) (in corporazione), comune

corporation [kɔ:pə'reɪʃən] n (of town) consiglio comunale; (Comm) ente m

corps [kɔ:', pl kɔ:z] n inv corpo

corpse [kɔ:ps] n cadavere m

correct [kə'rɛkt] adj (accurate) corretto(-a), esatto(-a); (proper) corretto(-a) ▷ vt correggere; **correction** [-ʃən] n correzione f

correspond [kɒrɪs'pɒnd] vi corrispondere; **correspondence** n corrispondenza; **correspondent** n corrispondente m/f; **corresponding** adj corrispondente

corridor ['kɔrɪdɔ:ʳ] n corridoio
corrode [kə'rəud] vt corrodere ▷ vi corrodersi
corrupt [kə'rʌpt] adj corrotto(-a); (Comput) alterato(-a) ▷ vt corrompere; **corruption** n corruzione f
Corsica ['kɔ:sɪkə] n Corsica
cosmetic [kɔz'mɛtɪk] n cosmetico ▷ adj (fig: measure etc) superficiale; **cosmetic surgery** n chirurgia plastica
cosmopolitan [kɔzmə'pɔlɪtn] adj cosmopolita
cost [kɔst] (pt, pp cost) n costo ▷ vt costare; (find out the cost of) stabilire il prezzo di; **~s** npl (Comm, Law) spese fpl; **how much does it ~?** quanto costa?; **at all ~s** a ogni costo
co-star ['kəustɑ:ʳ] n attore/trice della stessa importanza del protagonista
Costa Rica ['kɔstə'ri:kə] n Costa Rica
costly ['kɔstlɪ] adj costoso(-a), caro(-a)
cost of living adj **~ allowance** indennità f inv di contingenza
costume ['kɔstju:m] n costume m; (lady's suit) tailleur m inv; (BRIT: also: **swimming ~**) costume m da bagno
cosy ['kəuzɪ] (US **cozy**) adj intimo(-a); **I'm very ~ here** sto proprio bene qui
cot [kɔt] n (BRIT: child's) lettino; (US: campbed) brandina
cottage ['kɔtɪdʒ] n cottage m inv; **cottage cheese** n fiocchi mpl di latte magro
cotton ['kɔtn] n cotone m; **cotton on** vi (inf): **to ~ on (to sth)** afferrare (qc); **cotton bud** n (BRIT) cotton fioc® m inv; **cotton candy** (US) n zucchero filato; **cotton wool** (BRIT) n cotone idrofilo
couch [kautʃ] n sofà m inv
cough [kɔf] vi tossire ▷ n tosse f; **I've got a ~** ho la tosse; **cough mixture, cough syrup** n sciroppo per la tosse
could [kud] pt of **can²**
couldn't = **could not**
council ['kaunsl] n consiglio; **city or town ~** consiglio comunale; **council estate** (BRIT) n quartiere m di case popolari; **council house** (BRIT) n casa popolare; **councillor** (US **councilor**) n consigliere(-a); **council tax** n (BRIT) tassa comunale sulla proprietà
counsel ['kaunsl] n avvocato; consultazione f ▷ vt consigliare; **counselling** (US **counseling**) n (Psych) assistenza psicologica; **counsellor** (US **counselor**) n consigliere(-a); (US) avvocato
count [kaunt] vt, vi contare ▷ n (of votes etc) conteggio; (of pollen etc) livello; (nobleman) conte m; **count in** (inf) vt includere; **~ me**

in ci sto anch'io; **count on** vt fus contare su; **countdown** n conto alla rovescia
counter ['kauntəʳ] n banco ▷ vt opporsi a ▷ adv **~ to** contro; in opposizione a; **counter clockwise** [-'klɔkwaɪz] (US) adv in senso antiorario
counterfeit ['kauntəfɪt] n contraffazione f, falso ▷ vt contraffare, falsificare ▷ adj falso(-a)
counterpart ['kauntəpɑ:t] n (of document etc) copia; (of person) corrispondente m/f
countess ['kauntɪs] n contessa
countless ['kauntlɪs] adj innumerevole
country ['kʌntrɪ] n paese m; (native land) patria; (as opposed to town) campagna; (region) regione f; **country and western (music)** n musica country e western, country m; **country house** n villa in campagna; **countryside** n campagna
county ['kauntɪ] n contea
coup [ku:] (pl **coups**) n colpo; (also: **~ d'état**) colpo di Stato
couple ['kʌpl] n coppia; **a ~ of** un paio di
coupon ['ku:pɔn] n buono; (detachable form) coupon m inv
courage ['kʌrɪdʒ] n coraggio; **courageous** adj coraggioso(-a)
courgette [kuə'ʒɛt] (BRIT) n zucchina
courier ['kurɪəʳ] n corriere m; (for tourists) guida
course [kɔ:s] n corso; (of ship) rotta; (for golf) campo; (part of meal) piatto; **of ~** senz'altro, naturalmente; **~ of action** modo d'agire; **a ~ of treatment** (Med) una cura
court [kɔ:t] n corte f; (Tennis) campo ▷ vt (woman) fare la corte a; **to take to ~** citare in tribunale
courtesy ['kə:təsɪ] n cortesia; **(by) ~ of** per gentile concessione di; **courtesy bus, courtesy coach** n autobus m inv gratuito (di hotel, aeroporto)
court: **court-house** (US) n palazzo di giustizia; **courtroom** n tribunale m; **courtyard** n cortile m
cousin ['kʌzn] n cugino(-a); **first ~** cugino di primo grado
cover ['kʌvəʳ] vt coprire; (book, table) rivestire; (include) comprendere; (Press) fare un servizio su ▷ n (of pan) coperchio; (over furniture) fodera; (of bed) copriletto; (of book) copertina; (shelter) riparo; (Comm, Insurance, of spy) copertura; **~s** npl (on bed) lenzuola fpl e coperte fpl; **to take ~** (shelter) ripararsi; **under ~** al riparo; **under ~ of darkness** protetto dall'oscurità; **under separate ~** (Comm) a parte, in plico separato; **cover up** vi **to ~ up for sb** coprire qn; **coverage** n (Press, Radio,

TV): **to give full coverage to sth** fare un ampio servizio su qc; **cover charge** *n* coperto; **cover-up** *n* occultamento (di informazioni)

cow [kau] *n* vacca ▷ *vt* (*person*) intimidire

coward ['kauəd] *n* vigliacco(-a); **cowardly** *adj* vigliacco(-a)

cowboy ['kaubɔɪ] *n* cow-boy *m inv*

cozy ['kəuzɪ] (*US*) *adj* = **cosy**

crab [kræb] *n* granchio

crack [kræk] *n* fessura, crepa; incrinatura; (*noise*) schiocco; (: *of gun*) scoppio; (*drug*) crack *m inv* ▷ *vt* spaccare; incrinare; (*whip*) schioccare; (*nut*) schiacciare; (*problem*) risolvere; (*code*) decifrare ▷ *adj* (*troops*) fuori classe; **to ~ a joke** fare una battuta; **crack down on** *vt fus* porre freno a; **cracked** *adj* (*inf*) matto(-a); **cracker** *n* cracker *m inv*; petardo

crackle ['krækl] *vi* crepitare

cradle ['kreɪdl] *n* culla

craft [krɑːft] *n* mestiere *m*; (*cunning*) astuzia; (*boat*) naviglio; **craftsman** (*irreg*) *n* artigiano; **craftsmanship** *n* abilità

cram [kræm] *vt* (*fill*): **to ~ sth with** riempire qc di; (*put*): **to ~ sth into** stipare qc in ▷ *vi* (*for exams*) prepararsi (in gran fretta)

cramp [kræmp] *n* crampo; **I've got ~ in my leg** ho un crampo alla gamba; **cramped** *adj* ristretto(-a)

cranberry ['krænbərɪ] *n* mirtillo

crane [kreɪn] *n* gru *f inv*

crap [kræp] *n* (*infl*) fesserie *fpl*; **to have a ~ cacare** (!)

crash [kræʃ] *n* fragore *m*; (*of car*) incidente *m*; (*of plane*) caduta; (*of business etc*) crollo ▷ *vt* fracassare ▷ *vi* (*plane*) fracassarsi; (*car*) avere un incidente; (*two cars*) scontrarsi; (*business etc*) fallire, andare in rovina; **crash course** *n* corso intensivo; **crash helmet** *n* casco

crate [kreɪt] *n* cassa

crave [kreɪv] *vt*, *vi* **to ~ (for)** desiderare ardentemente

crawl [krɔːl] *vi* strisciare carponi; (*vehicle*) avanzare lentamente ▷ *n* (*Swimming*) crawl *m*

crayfish ['kreɪfɪʃ] *n inv* (*freshwater*) gambero (d'acqua dolce); (*saltwater*) gambero

crayon ['kreɪən] *n* matita colorata

craze [kreɪz] *n* mania

crazy ['kreɪzɪ] *adj* matto(-a); (*inf: keen*): **~ about sb** pazzo(-a) di qn; **~ about sth** matto(-a) per qc

creak [kriːk] *vi* cigolare, scricchiolare

cream [kriːm] *n* crema; (*fresh*) panna ▷ *adj* (*colour*) color crema *inv*; **cream cheese** *n* formaggio fresco; **creamy** *adj* cremoso(-a)

crease [kriːs] *n* grinza; (*deliberate*) piega ▷ *vt* sgualcire ▷ *vi* sgualcirsi

create [kriː'eɪt] *vt* creare; **creation** [-ʃən] *n* creazione *f*; **creative** *adj* creativo(-a); **creator** *n* creatore(-trice)

creature ['kriːtʃəʳ] *n* creatura

crèche [krɛʃ] *n* asilo infantile

credentials [krɪ'dɛnʃlz] *npl* credenziali *fpl*

credibility [krɛdɪ'bɪlɪtɪ] *n* credibilità

credible ['krɛdɪbl] *adj* credibile; (*witness, source*) attendibile

credit ['krɛdɪt] *n* credito; onore *m* ▷ *vt* (*Comm*) accreditare; (*believe: also:* **give ~ to**) credere, prestar fede a; **~s** *npl* (*Cinema*) titoli *mpl*; **to ~ sb with** (*fig*) attribuire a qn; **to be in ~** (*person*) essere creditore(-trice); (*bank account*) essere coperto(-a); **credit card** *n* carta di credito; **do you take credit cards?** accettate carte di credito?

creek [kriːk] *n* insenatura; (*US*) piccolo fiume *m*

creep [kriːp] (*pt, pp* **crept**) *vi* avanzare furtivamente (*o pian piano*)

cremate [krɪ'meɪt] *vt* cremare

crematorium [krɛmə'tɔːrɪəm] (*pl* **crematoria**) *n* forno crematorio

crept [krɛpt] *pt, pp of* **creep**

crescent ['krɛsnt] *n* (*shape*) mezzaluna; (*street*) strada semicircolare

cress [krɛs] *n* crescione *m*

crest [krɛst] *n* cresta; (*of coat of arms*) cimiero

crew [kruː] *n* equipaggio; **crew-neck** *n* girocollo

crib [krɪb] *n* culla ▷ *vt* (*inf*) copiare

cricket ['krɪkɪt] *n* (*insect*) grillo; (*game*) cricket *m*; **cricketer** *n* giocatore *m* di cricket

crime [kraɪm] *n* crimine *m*; **criminal** ['krɪmɪnl] *adj*, *n* criminale *m/f*

crimson ['krɪmzn] *adj* color cremisi *inv*

cringe [krɪndʒ] *vi* acquattarsi; (*in embarrassment*) sentirsi sprofondare

cripple ['krɪpl] *n* zoppo(-a) ▷ *vt* azzoppare

crisis ['kraɪsɪs] (*pl* **crises**) *n* crisi *f inv*

crisp [krɪsp] *adj* croccante; (*fig*) frizzante; vivace; deciso(-a); **crispy** *adj* croccante

criterion [kraɪ'tɪərɪən] (*pl* **criteria**) *n* criterio

critic ['krɪtɪk] *n* critico; **critical** *adj* critico(-a); **criticism** ['krɪtɪsɪzm] *n* critica; **criticize** ['krɪtɪsaɪz] *vt* criticare

Croat ['krəuæt] *adj*, *n* = **Croatian**

Croatia [krəu'eɪʃə] *n* Croazia; **Croatian** *adj* croato(-a) ▷ *n* croato(-a); (*Ling*) croato

crockery ['krɔkərɪ] *n* vasellame *m*

crocodile ['krɔkədaɪl] *n* coccodrillo

crocus ['krəukəs] n croco
croissant ['krwɑs] n brioche f inv, croissant m inv
crook [kruk] n truffatore m; (of shepherd) bastone m; **crooked** ['krukɪd] adj curvo(-a), storto(-a); (action) disonesto(-a)
crop [krɔp] n (produce) coltivazione f; (amount produced) raccolto; (riding crop) frustino ▷ vt (hair) rapare; **crop up** vi presentarsi
cross [krɔs] n croce f; (Biol) incrocio ▷ vt (street etc) attraversare; (arms, legs, Biol) incrociare; (cheque) sbarrare ▷ adj di cattivo umore; **cross off** vt cancellare (tirando una riga con la penna); **cross out** vt cancellare; **cross over** vi attraversare; **cross-Channel ferry** ['krɔs'tʃænl-] n traghetto che attraversa la Manica; **crosscountry (race)** n cross-country m inv; **crossing** n incrocio; (sea passage) traversata; (also: **pedestrian crossing**) passaggio pedonale; **how long does the crossing take?** quanto dura la traversata?; **crossing guard** (US) n dipendente comunale che aiuta i bambini ad attraversare la strada; **crossroads** n incrocio; **crosswalk** (US) n strisce fpl pedonali, passaggio pedonale; **crossword** n cruciverba m inv
crotch [krɔtʃ] n (Anat) inforcatura; (of garment) pattina
crouch [krautʃ] vi acquattarsi; rannicchiarsi
crouton ['kru:tɔn] n crostino
crow [krəu] n (bird) cornacchia; (of cock) canto del gallo ▷ vi (cock) cantare
crowd [kraud] n folla ▷ vt affollare, stipare ▷ vi to ~ **round/in** affollarsi intorno a/in; **crowded** adj affollato(-a); **crowded with** stipato(-a) di
crown [kraun] n corona; (of head) calotta cranica; (of hat) cocuzzolo; (of hill) cima ▷ vt incoronare; (fig: career) coronare; **crown jewels** npl gioielli mpl della Corona
crucial ['kru:ʃl] adj cruciale, decisivo(-a)
crucifix ['kru:sɪfɪks] n crocifisso
crude [kru:d] adj (materials) greggio(-a), non raffinato(-a); (fig: basic) crudo(-a), primitivo(-a); (: vulgar) rozzo(-a), grossolano(-a); **crude (oil)** n (petrolio) greggio
cruel ['kruəl] adj crudele; **cruelty** n crudeltà f inv
cruise [kru:z] n crociera ▷ vi andare a velocità di crociera; (taxi) circolare
crumb [krʌm] n briciola
crumble ['krʌmbl] vt sbriciolare ▷ vi sbriciolarsi; (plaster etc) sgretolarsi; (land, earth) franare; (building, fig) crollare
crumpet ['krʌmpɪt] n specie di frittella

crumple ['krʌmpl] vt raggrinzare, spiegazzare
crunch [krʌntʃ] vt sgranocchiare; (underfoot) scricchiolare ▷ n (fig) punto or momento cruciale; **crunchy** adj croccante
crush [krʌʃ] n folla; (love): **to have a ~ on sb** avere una cotta per qn; (drink): **lemon ~** spremuta di limone ▷ vt schiacciare; (crumple) squalcire
crust [krʌst] n crosta; **crusty** adj (bread) croccante; (person) brontolone(-a); (remark) brusco(-a)
crutch [krʌtʃ] n gruccia
cry [kraɪ] vi piangere; (shout) urlare ▷ n urlo, grido; **cry out** vi, vt gridare
crystal ['krɪstl] n cristallo
cub [kʌb] n cucciolo; (also: ~ **scout**) lupetto
Cuba ['kju:bə] n Cuba
Cuban ['kju:bən] adj, n cubano(-a)
cube [kju:b] n cubo ▷ vt (Math) elevare al cubo; **cubic** adj cubico(-a); (metre, foot) cubo(-a)
cubicle ['kju:bɪkl] n scompartimento separato; cabina
cuckoo ['kuku:] n cucù m inv
cucumber ['kju:kʌmbəʳ] n cetriolo
cuddle ['kʌdl] vt abbracciare, coccolare ▷ vi abbracciarsi
cue [kju:] n (snooker cue) stecca; (Theatre etc) segnale m
cuff [kʌf] n (BRIT: of shirt, coat etc) polsino; (US: of trousers) risvolto; **off the ~** improvvisando; **cufflinks** npl gemelli mpl
cuisine [kwɪ'zi:n] n cucina
cul-de-sac ['kʌldəsæk] n vicolo cieco
cull [kʌl] vt (ideas etc) scegliere ▷ n (of animals) abbattimento selettivo
culminate ['kʌlmɪneɪt] vi **to ~ in** culminare con
culprit ['kʌlprɪt] n colpevole m/f
cult [kʌlt] n culto
cultivate ['kʌltɪveɪt] vt (also fig) coltivare
cultural ['kʌltʃərəl] adj culturale
culture ['kʌltʃəʳ] n (also fig) cultura
cumin ['kʌmɪn] n (spice) cumino
cunning ['kʌnɪŋ] n astuzia, furberia ▷ adj astuto(-a), furbo(-a)
cup [kʌp] n tazza; (prize, of bra) coppa
cupboard ['kʌbəd] n armadio
cup final n (BRIT Football) finale f di coppa
curator [kjuə'reɪtəʳ] n direttore m (di museo ecc)
curb [kə:b] vt tenere a freno ▷ n freno; (US) bordo del marciapiede
curdle ['kə:dl] vi cagliare
cure [kjuəʳ] vt guarire; (Culin) trattare; affumicare; essiccare ▷ n rimedio
curfew ['kə:fju:] n coprifuoco
curiosity [kjuərɪ'ɔsɪtɪ] n curiosità

curious ['kjʊərɪəs] *adj* curioso(-a)

curl [kəːl] *n* riccio ▷ *vt* ondulare; (*tightly*) arricciare ▷ *vi* arricciarsi; **curl up** *vi* rannicchiarsi; **curler** *n* bigodino; **curly** ['kəːlɪ] *adj* ricciuto(-a)

currant ['kʌrnt] *n* (*dried*) sultanina; (*bush, fruit*) ribes *m inv*

currency ['kʌrnsɪ] *n* moneta; **to gain ~** (*fig*) acquistare larga diffusione

current ['kʌrnt] *adj* corrente ▷ *n* corrente *f*; **current account** (*BRIT*) *n* conto corrente; **current affairs** *npl* attualità *fpl*; **currently** *adv* attualmente

curriculum [kə'rɪkjʊləm] (*pl* **curriculums** or **curricula**) *n* curriculum *m inv*; **curriculum vitae** [-'viːtaɪ] *n* curriculum vitae *m inv*

curry ['kʌrɪ] *n* curry *m inv* ▷ *vt* **to ~ favour with** cercare di attirarsi i favori di; **curry powder** *n* curry *m*

curse [kəːs] *vt* maledire ▷ *vi* bestemmiare ▷ *n* maledizione *f*; bestemmia

cursor ['kəːsəʳ] *n* (*Comput*) cursore *m*

curt [kəːt] *adj* secco(-a)

curtain ['kəːtn] *n* tenda; (*Theatre*) sipario

curve [kəːv] *n* curva ▷ *vi* curvarsi; **curved** *adj* curvo(-a)

cushion ['kʊʃən] *n* cuscino ▷ *vt* (*shock*) fare da cuscinetto a

custard ['kʌstəd] *n* (*for pouring*) crema

custody ['kʌstədɪ] *n* (*of child*) tutela; **to take into ~** (*suspect*) mettere in detenzione preventiva

custom ['kʌstəm] *n* costume *m*, consuetudine *f*; (*Comm*) clientela

customer ['kʌstəməʳ] *n* cliente *m/f*

customized ['kʌstəmaɪzd] *adj* (*car etc*) fuoriserie *inv*

customs ['kʌstəmz] *npl* dogana; **customs officer** *n* doganiere *m*

cut [kʌt] (*pt, pp* **cut**) *vt* tagliare; (*shape, make*) intagliare; (*reduce*) ridurre ▷ *vt* tagliare ▷ *n* taglio; (*in salary etc*) riduzione *f*; **I've ~ myself** mi sono tagliato; **to ~ a tooth** mettere un dente; **cut back** *vt* (*plants*) tagliare; (*production, expenditure*) ridurre; **cut down** *vt* (*tree etc*) abbattere ▷ *vt fus* (*also: ~ down on*) ridurre; **cut off** *vt* tagliare; (*fig*) isolare; **cut out** *vt* tagliare fuori; eliminare; ritagliare; **cut up** *vt* tagliare a pezzi; **cutback** *n* riduzione *f*

cute [kjuːt] *adj* (*sweet*) carino(-a)

cutlery ['kʌtlərɪ] *n* posate *fpl*

cutlet ['kʌtlɪt] *n* costoletta; (*nut etc cutlet*) cotoletta vegetariana

cut: **cut-price** (*BRIT*) *adj* a prezzo ridotto; **cut-rate** (*US*) *adj* = **cut-price**; **cutting** ['kʌtɪŋ] *adj* tagliente ▷ *n* (*from newspaper*) ritaglio (di giornale); (*from plant*) talea

CV *n abbr* = **curriculum vitae**

cwt *abbr* = **hundredweight(s)**

cybercafé ['saɪbəkaefeɪ] *n* cybercaffè *m inv*

cyberspace ['saɪbəspeɪs] *n* ciberspazio

cycle ['saɪkl] *n* ciclo; (*bicycle*) bicicletta ▷ *vi* andare in bicicletta; **cycle hire** *n* noleggio *m* biciclette *inv*; **cycle lane** *n* pista ciclabile; **cycle path** *n* pista ciclabile; **cycling** ['saɪklɪŋ] *n* ciclismo; **cyclist** ['saɪklɪst] *n* ciclista *m/f*

cyclone ['saɪkləun] *n* ciclone *m*

cylinder ['sɪlɪndəʳ] *n* cilindro

cymbal ['sɪmbl] *n* piatto

cynical ['sɪnɪkl] *adj* cinico(-a)

Cypriot ['sɪprɪət] *adj*, *n* cipriota (*m/f*)

Cyprus ['saɪprəs] *n* Cipro

cyst [sɪst] *n* cisti *f inv*; **cystitis** [sɪs'taɪtɪs] *n* cistite *f*

czar [zɑːʳ] *n* zar *m inv*

Czech [tʃɛk] *adj* ceco(-a) ▷ *n* ceco(-a); (*Ling*) ceco; **Czech Republic** *n* **the Czech Republic** la Repubblica Ceca

D [di:] *n* (*Mus*) re *m*

dab [dæb] *vt* (*eyes, wound*) tamponare; (*paint, cream*) applicare (con leggeri colpetti)

dad, daddy [dæd, 'dædɪ] *n* babbo, papà *m inv*

daffodil ['dæfədɪl] *n* trombone *m*, giunchiglia

daft [dɑ:ft] *adj* sciocco(-a)

dagger ['dægəʳ] *n* pugnale *m*

daily ['deɪlɪ] *adj* quotidiano(-a), giornaliero(-a) ▷ *n* quotidiano ▷ *adv* tutti i giorni

dairy ['dɛərɪ] *n* (*BRIT: shop*) latteria; (*on farm*) caseificio ▷ *adj* caseario(-a); **dairy produce** *npl* latticini *mpl*

daisy ['deɪzɪ] *n* margherita

dam [dæm] *n* diga ▷ *vt* sbarrare; costruire dighe su

damage ['dæmɪdʒ] *n* danno, danni *mpl*; (*fig*) danno ▷ *vt* danneggiare; **~s** *npl* (*Law*) danni

damn [dæm] *vt* condannare; (*curse*) maledire ▷ *n* (*inf*): **I don't give a ~** non me ne frega niente ▷ *adj* (*inf: also:* **~ed**): **this ~ ...** questo maledetto ...; **~ it!** accidenti!

damp [dæmp] *adj* umido(-a), umido ▷ *vt* (*also:* **~en**: *cloth, rag*) inumidire, bagnare; (: *enthusiasm etc*) spegnere

dance [dɑ:ns] *n* danza, ballo; (*ball*) ballo ▷ *vi* ballare; **dance floor** *n* pista da ballo; **dancer** *n* danzatore(-trice); (*professional*) ballerino(-a); **dancing** ['dɑ:nsɪŋ] *n* danza, ballo

dandelion ['dændɪlaɪən] *n* dente *m* di leone

dandruff ['dændrəf] *n* forfora

Dane [deɪn] *n* danese *m/f*

danger ['deɪndʒəʳ] *n* pericolo; **there is a ~ of fire** c'è pericolo di incendio; **in ~** in pericolo; **he was in ~ of falling** rischiava di cadere; **dangerous** *adj* pericoloso(-a)

dangle ['dæŋgl] *vt* dondolare; (*fig*) far balenare ▷ *vi* pendolare

Danish ['deɪnɪʃ] *adj* danese ▷ *n* (*Ling*) danese *m*

dare [dɛəʳ] *vt*: **to ~ sb to do** sfidare qn a fare ▷ *vi*: **to ~ to do sth** osare fare qc; **I ~ say** (*I suppose*) immagino (che); **daring** *adj* audace, ardito(-a) ▷ *n* audacia

dark [dɑ:k] *adj* (*night, room*) buio(-a), scuro(-a); (*colour, complexion*) scuro(-a); (*fig*) cupo(-a), tetro(-a), nero(-a) ▷ *n*: **in the ~** al buio; **in the ~ about** (*fig*) all'oscuro di; **after ~** a notte fatta; **darken** *vt* (*colour*) scurire ▷ *vi* (*sky, room*) oscurarsi; **darkness** *n* oscurità, buio; **darkroom** *n* camera oscura

darling ['dɑ:lɪŋ] *adj* caro(-a) ▷ *n* tesoro

dart [dɑ:t] *n* freccetta; (*Sewing*) pince *f inv* ▷ *vi*: **to ~ towards** precipitarsi verso; **to ~ away/along** sfrecciare via/lungo; **dartboard** *n* bersaglio (per freccette); **darts** *n* tiro al bersaglio (con freccette)

dash [dæʃ] *n* (*sign*) lineetta; (*small quantity*) punta ▷ *vt* (*missile*) gettare; (*hopes*) infrangere ▷ *vi*: **to ~ towards** precipitarsi verso

dashboard ['dæʃbɔ:d] *n* (*Aut*) cruscotto

data ['deɪtə] *npl* dati *mpl*; **database** *n* base *f* di dati, data base *m inv*; **data processing** *n* elaborazione *f* (elettronica) dei dati

date [deɪt] *n* data; appuntamento; (*fruit*) dattero ▷ *vt* datare; (*person*) uscire con; **what's the ~ today?** quanti ne abbiamo oggi?; **~ of birth** data di nascita; **to ~** (*until now*) fino a oggi; **dated** *adj* passato(-a) di moda

daughter ['dɔ:təʳ] *n* figlia; **daughter-in-law** *n* nuora

daunting ['dɔ:ntɪŋ] *adj* non invidiabile

dawn [dɔ:n] *n* alba ▷ *vi* (*day*) spuntare; (*fig*): **it ~ed on him that ...** gli è venuto in mente che ...

day [deɪ] *n* giorno; (*as duration*) giornata; (*period of time, age*) tempo, epoca; **the ~ before** il giorno avanti *or* prima; **the ~ after, the following ~** il giorno dopo *or* seguente; **the ~ after tomorrow** dopodomani; **the ~ before yester~** l'altroieri; **by ~** di giorno; **day-care centre** *n* scuola materna; **daydream** *vi* sognare a occhi aperti; **daylight** *n* luce *f* del giorno; **day return** (BRIT) *n* biglietto giornaliero di andata e ritorno; **daytime** *n* giorno; **day-to-day** *adj* (*life, organization*) quotidiano(-a); **day trip** *n* gita (di un giorno)

dazed [deɪzd] *adj* stordito(-a)

dazzle ['dæzl] *vt* abbagliare; **dazzling** *adj* (*light*) abbagliante; (*colour*) violento(-a); (*smile*) smagliante

DC *abbr* (= *direct current*) c.c.

dead [dɛd] *adj* morto(-a); (*numb*) intirizzito(-a); (*telephone*) muto(-a); (*battery*) scarico(-a) ▷ *adv* assolutamente, perfettamente ▷ *npl* **the ~** i morti; **he was shot ~** fu colpito a morte; **~ tired** stanco(-a) morto(-a); **to stop ~** fermarsi di colpo; **dead end** *n* vicolo cieco; **deadline** *n* scadenza; **deadly** *adj* mortale; (*weapon, poison*) micidiale; **Dead Sea** *n* **the Dead Sea** il mar Morto

deaf [dɛf] *adj* sordo(-a); **deafen** *vt* assordare; **deafening** *adj* fragoroso(-a), assordante

deal [di:l] (*pt, pp* **dealt**) *n* accordo; (*business deal*) affare *m* ▷ *vt* (*blow, cards*) dare; **a great ~ (of)** molto(-a); **deal with** *vt fus* (*Comm*) fare affari con, trattare con; (*handle*) occuparsi di; (*be about: book etc*) trattare di; **dealer** *n* commerciante *m/f*; **dealings** *npl* (*Comm*) relazioni *fpl*; (*relations*) rapporti *mpl*

dealt [dɛlt] *pt, pp of* **deal**

dean [di:n] *n* (*Rel*) decano; (*Scol*) preside *m* di facoltà (*or* di collegio)

dear [dɪə^r] *adj* caro(-a) ▷ *n* **my ~** caro mio/ cara mia ▷ *excl* **~ me!** Dio mio!; **D~ Sir/ Madam** (*in letter*) Egregio Signore/Egregia Signora; **D~ Mr/Mrs X** Gentile Signor/ Signora X; **dearly** *adv* (*love*) moltissimo; (*pay*) a caro prezzo

death [dɛθ] *n* morte *f*; (*Admin*) decesso; **death penalty** *n* pena di morte; **death sentence** *n* condanna a morte

debate [dɪ'beɪt] *n* dibattito ▷ *vt* dibattere; discutere

debit ['dɛbɪt] *n* debito ▷ *vt* **to ~ a sum to sb** *or* **to sb's account** addebitare una somma a qn; **debit card** *n* carta di debito

debris ['dɛbriː] *n* detriti *mpl*

debt [dɛt] *n* debito; **to be in ~** essere indebitato(-a)

debut ['deɪbjuː] *n* debutto

Dec. *abbr* (= *December*) dic.

decade ['dɛkeɪd] *n* decennio

decaffeinated [dɪ'kæfɪneɪtɪd] *adj* decaffeinato(-a)

decay [dɪ'keɪ] *n* decadimento; (*also:* **tooth ~**) carie *f* ▷ *vi* (*rot*) imputridire

deceased [dɪ'siːst] *n* defunto(-a)

deceit [dɪ'siːt] *n* inganno; **deceive** [dɪ'siːv] *vt* ingannare

December [dɪ'sɛmbə^r] *n* dicembre *m*

decency ['diːsənsɪ] *n* decenza

decent ['diːsənt] *adj* decente; (*respectable*) per bene; (*kind*) gentile

deception [dɪ'sɛpʃən] *n* inganno

deceptive [dɪ'sɛptɪv] *adj* ingannevole

decide [dɪ'saɪd] *vt* (*person*) far prendere una decisione a; (*question, argument*) risolvere, decidere ▷ *vi* decidere, decidersi; **to ~ to do/that** decidere di fare/che; **to ~ on** decidere per

decimal ['dɛsɪməl] *adj* decimale ▷ *n* decimale *m*

decision [dɪ'sɪʒən] *n* decisione *f*

decisive [dɪ'saɪsɪv] *adj* decisivo(-a); (*person*) deciso(-a)

deck [dɛk] *n* (*Naut*) ponte *m*; (*of bus*): **top ~** imperiale *m*; (*record deck*) piatto; (*of cards*) mazzo; **deckchair** *n* sedia a sdraio

declaration [dɛklə'reɪʃən] *n* dichiarazione *f*

declare [dɪ'klɛə^r] *vt* dichiarare

decline [dɪ'klaɪn] *n* (*decay*) declino; (*lessening*) ribasso ▷ *vt* declinare; rifiutare ▷ *vi* declinare; diminuire

decorate ['dɛkəreɪt] *vt* (*adorn, give a medal to*) decorare; (*paint and paper*) tinteggiare e tappezzare; **decoration** [-'reɪʃən] *n* (*medal etc, adornment*) decorazione *f*; **decorator** *n* decoratore *m*

decrease [*n* 'diːkriːs, *vb* diːˈkriːs] *n* diminuzione *f* ▷ *vt, vi* diminuire

decree [dɪ'kriː] *n* decreto

dedicate ['dɛdɪkeɪt] *vt* consacrare; (*book etc*) dedicare; **dedicated** *adj* coscienzioso(-a); (*Comput*) specializzato(-a), dedicato(-a); **dedication** [dɛdɪ'keɪʃən] *n* (*devotion*) dedizione *f*; (*in book etc*) dedica

deduce [dɪ'djuːs] *vt* dedurre

deduct [dɪ'dʌkt] *vt* **to ~ sth from** dedurre qc (da); **deduction** [dɪ'dʌkʃən] *n* deduzione *f*

deed [diːd] *n* azione *f*, atto; (*Law*) atto

deem [diːm] *vt* (*formal*) giudicare, ritenere; **to ~ it wise to do** ritenere prudente fare

deep [diːp] *adj* profondo(-a); **4 metres ~** profondo(-a) 4 metri ▷ *adv* **spectators stood 20 ~** c'erano 20 file di spettatori; **how ~ is the water?** quanto è profonda l'acqua?; **deep-fry** *vt* friggere in olio

abbondante; **deeply** adv profondamente
deer [dɪəʳ] n inv **the ~** i cervidi; **(red) ~**
cervo; **(fallow) ~** daino; **roe ~** capriolo
default [dɪ'fɔːlt] n (Comput: also: **~ value**)
default m inv; **by ~** (Sport) per abbandono
defeat [dɪ'fiːt] n sconfitta ▷ vt (team,
opponents) sconfiggere
defect [n 'diːfɛkt, vb dɪ'fɛkt] n difetto ▷ vi
to ~ to the enemy passare al nemico;
defective [dɪ'fɛktɪv] adj difettoso(-a)
defence [dɪ'fɛns] (US **defense**) n difesa
defend [dɪ'fɛnd] vt difendere; **defendant**
n imputato(-a); **defender** n difensore(-a)
defense [dɪ'fɛns] (US) n = **defence**
defensive [dɪ'fɛnsɪv] adj difensivo(-a) ▷ n
on the ~ sulla difensiva
defer [dɪ'fɜːʳ] vt (postpone) differire,
rinviare
defiance [dɪ'faɪəns] n sfida; **in ~ of**
a dispetto di; **defiant** [dɪ'faɪənt] adj
(attitude) di sfida; (person) ribelle
deficiency [dɪ'fɪʃənsɪ] n deficienza;
carenza; **deficient** adj deficiente;
insufficiente; **to be deficient in** mancare
di
deficit ['dɛfɪsɪt] n deficit m inv
define [dɪ'faɪn] vt definire
definite ['dɛfɪnɪt] adj (fixed) definito(-a),
preciso(-a); (clear, obvious) ben definito(-a),
esatto(-a); (Ling) determinativo(-a); **he
was ~ about it** ne era sicuro; **definitely**
adv indubbiamente
definition [dɛfɪ'nɪʃən] n definizione f
deflate [diː'fleɪt] vt sgonfiare
deflect [dɪ'flɛkt] vt deflettere, deviare
defraud [dɪ'frɔːd] vt defraudare
defrost [diː'frɒst] vt (fridge) disgelare
defuse [diː'fjuːz] vt disinnescare; (fig)
distendere
defy [dɪ'faɪ] vt sfidare; (efforts etc) resistere
a; **it defies description** supera ogni
descrizione
degree [dɪ'griː] n grado; (Scol) laurea
(universitaria); **a first ~ in maths** una
laurea in matematica; **by ~s** (gradually)
gradualmente, a poco a poco; **to some ~/
a certain ~** fino a un certo punto, in certa misura
dehydrated [diːhaɪ'dreɪtɪd] adj
disidratato(-a); (milk, eggs) in polvere
de-icer [diː'aɪsəʳ] n sbrinatore m
delay [dɪ'leɪ] vt ritardare ▷ vi **to ~ (in
doing sth)** ritardare (a fare qc) ▷ n ritardo;
to be ~ed subire un ritardo; (person) essere
trattenuto(-a)
delegate [n 'dɛlɪgɪt, vb 'dɛlɪgeɪt] n
delegato(-a) ▷ vt delegare
delete [dɪ'liːt] vt cancellare
deli ['dɛlɪ] n = **delicatessen**
deliberate [adj dɪ'lɪbərɪt, vb dɪ'lɪbəreɪt]

adj (intentional) intenzionale; (slow)
misurato(-a) ▷ vi deliberare, riflettere;
deliberately adv (on purpose)
deliberatamente
delicacy ['dɛlɪkəsɪ] n delicatezza
delicate ['dɛlɪkɪt] adj delicato(-a)
delicatessen [dɛlɪkə'tɛsn] n ≈ salumeria
delicious [dɪ'lɪʃəs] adj delizioso(-a),
squisito(-a)
delight [dɪ'laɪt] n delizia, gran piacere m
▷ vt dilettare; **to take (a) ~ in** dilettarsi
in; **delighted** adj **delighted (at** or
with) contentissimo(-a) (di), felice (di);
delighted to do felice di fare; **delightful**
adj delizioso(-a), incantevole
delinquent [dɪ'lɪŋkwənt] adj, n
delinquente m/f
deliver [dɪ'lɪvəʳ] vt (mail) distribuire;
(goods) consegnare; (speech) pronunciare;
(Med) far partorire; **delivery** n
distribuzione f; consegna; (of speaker)
dizione f; (Med) parto
delusion [dɪ'luːʒən] n illusione f
de luxe [də'lʌks] adj di lusso
delve [dɛlv] vi **to ~ into** frugare in; (subject)
far ricerche in
demand [dɪ'mɑːnd] vt richiedere;
(rights) rivendicare ▷ n domanda; (claim)
rivendicazione f; **in ~** ricercato(-a),
richiesto(-a); **on ~** a richiesta;
demanding adj (boss) esigente; (work)
impegnativo(-a)
demise [dɪ'maɪz] n decesso
demo ['dɛməu] (inf) n abbr
(= demonstration) manifestazione f
democracy [dɪ'mɔkrəsɪ] n
democrazia; **democrat** ['dɛməkræt]
n democratico(-a); **democratic**
[dɛmə'krætɪk] adj democratico(-a)
demolish [dɪ'mɔlɪʃ] vt demolire
demolition [dɛmə'lɪʃən] n demolizione f
demon ['diːmən] n (also fig) demonio ▷ cpd
a ~ squash player un mago dello squash;
a ~ driver un guidatore folle
demonstrate ['dɛmənstreɪt] vt
dimostrare, provare ▷ vi dimostrare,
manifestare; **demonstration** [-'streɪʃən]
n dimostrazione f; (Pol) dimostrazione,
manifestazione f; **demonstrator**
n (Pol) dimostrante m/f; (Comm)
dimostratore(-trice)
demote [dɪ'məut] vt far retrocedere
den [dɛn] n tana, covo; (room) buco
denial [dɪ'naɪəl] n diniego; rifiuto
denim ['dɛnɪm] n tessuto di cotone
ritorto; **~s** npl (jeans) blue jeans mpl
Denmark ['dɛnmɑːk] n Danimarca
denomination [dɪnɒmɪ'neɪʃən] n (money)
valore m; (Rel) confessione f

denounce [dɪˈnaʊns] vt denunciare
dense [dɛns] adj fitto(-a); (smoke)
denso(-a); (inf: person) ottuso(-a), duro(-a)
density [ˈdɛnsɪtɪ] n densità f inv
dent [dɛnt] n ammaccatura ▷ vt (also:
make a ~ in) ammaccare
dental [ˈdɛntl] adj dentale; **dental floss**
[-flɔs] n filo interdentale; **dental surgery**
n ambulatorio del dentista
dentist [ˈdɛntɪst] n dentista m/f
dentures [ˈdɛntʃəz] npl dentiera
deny [dɪˈnaɪ] vt negare; (refuse) rifiutare
deodorant [diːˈəudərənt] n deodorante m
depart [dɪˈpɑːt] vi partire; **to ~ from** (fig)
deviare da
department [dɪˈpɑːtmənt] n (Comm)
reparto; (Scol) sezione f, dipartimento;
(Pol) ministero; **department store** n
grande magazzino
departure [dɪˈpɑːtʃər] n partenza; (fig): **~
from** deviazione f da; **a new ~** una svolta
(decisiva); **departure lounge** n (at airport)
sala d'attesa
depend [dɪˈpɛnd] vi **to ~ on** dipendere
da; (rely on) contare su; **it ~s** dipende;
~ing on the result ... a seconda del
risultato ...; **dependant** n persona a
carico; **dependent** adj **to be dependent
on** dipendere da; (child, relative) essere a
carico di ▷ n = **dependant**
depict [dɪˈpɪkt] vt (in picture) dipingere; (in
words) descrivere
deport [dɪˈpɔːt] vt deportare; espellere
deposit [dɪˈpɔzɪt] n (Comm, Geo) deposito;
(of ore, oil) giacimento; (Chem) sedimento;
(part payment) acconto; (for hired goods
etc) cauzione f ▷ vt depositare; dare in
acconto; mettere or lasciare in deposito;
deposit account n conto vincolato
depot [ˈdɛpəu] n deposito; (us) stazione f
ferroviaria
depreciate [dɪˈpriːʃɪeɪt] vi svalutarsi
depress [dɪˈprɛs] vt deprimere; (price,
wages) abbassare; (press down) premere;
depressed adj (person) depresso(-a),
abbattuto(-a); (price) in ribasso; (industry)
in crisi; **depressing** adj deprimente;
depression [dɪˈprɛʃən] n depressione f
deprive [dɪˈpraɪv] vt **to ~ sb of** privare qn
di; **deprived** adj disgraziato(-a)
dept. abbr = **department**
depth [dɛpθ] n profondità f inv; **in the ~s of**
nel profondo di; nel cuore di; **out of one's
~** (in water) dove non si tocca; (fig) a disagio
deputy [ˈdɛpjutɪ] adj **~ head** (brit Scol)
vicepreside m/f ▷ n (assistant) vice m/f inv;
(us: also: **~ sheriff**) vice-sceriffo
derail [dɪˈreɪl] vt **to be ~ed** deragliare
derelict [ˈdɛrɪlɪkt] adj abbandonato(-a)

derive [dɪˈraɪv] vt **to ~ sth from** derivare
qc da; trarre qc da ▷ vi **to ~ from** derivare
da
descend [dɪˈsɛnd] vt, vi discendere,
scendere; **to ~ from** discendere da; **to ~ to**
(lying, begging) abbassarsi a; **descendant**
n discendente m/f; **descent** [dɪˈsɛnt] n
discesa; (origin) discendenza, famiglia
describe [dɪsˈkraɪb] vt descrivere;
description [-ˈkrɪpʃən] n descrizione f;
(sort) genere m, specie f
desert [n ˈdɛzət, vb dɪˈzəːt] n deserto ▷ vt
lasciare, abbandonare ▷ vi (Mil) disertare;
deserted [dɪˈzəːtɪd] adj deserto(-a)
deserve [dɪˈzəːv] vt meritare
design [dɪˈzaɪn] n (art, sketch) disegno;
(layout, shape) linea; (pattern) fantasia;
(intention) intenzione f ▷ vt disegnare;
progettare
designate vt [vb ˈdɛzɪgneɪt, adj ˈdɛzɪgnɪt]
designare ▷ adj designato(-a)
designer [dɪˈzaɪnər] n (Art, Tech)
disegnatore(-trice); (of fashion) modellista
m/f
desirable [dɪˈzaɪərəbl] adj desiderabile; **it
is ~ that** è opportuno che + sub
desire [dɪˈzaɪər] n desiderio, voglia ▷ vt
desiderare, volere
desk [dɛsk] n (in office) scrivania; (for pupil)
banco; (brit: in shop, restaurant) cassa; (in
hotel) ricevimento; (at airport) accettazione
f; **desk-top publishing** n desktop
publishing m
despair [dɪsˈpɛər] n disperazione f ▷ vi **to ~
of** disperare di
despatch [dɪsˈpætʃ] n, vt = **dispatch**
desperate [ˈdɛspərɪt] adj disperato(-a);
(fugitive) capace di tutto; **to be ~ for
sth/to do** volere disperatamente qc/fare;
desperately adv disperatamente;
(very) terribilmente, estremamente;
desperation [dɛspəˈreɪʃən] n
disperazione f
despise [dɪsˈpaɪz] vt disprezzare, sdegnare
despite [dɪsˈpaɪt] prep malgrado, a
dispetto di, nonostante
dessert [dɪˈzəːt] n dolce m; frutta;
dessertspoon n cucchiaio da dolci
destination [dɛstɪˈneɪʃən] n destinazione
f
destined [ˈdɛstɪnd] adj **to be ~ to do/for**
essere destinato(-a) a fare/per
destiny [ˈdɛstɪnɪ] n destino
destroy [dɪsˈtrɔɪ] vt distruggere
destruction [dɪsˈtrʌkʃən] n distruzione f
destructive [dɪsˈtrʌktɪv] adj
distruttivo(-a)
detach [dɪˈtætʃ] vt staccare, distaccare;
detached adj (attitude) distante;

detached house n villa
detail ['di:teɪl] n particolare m, dettaglio
▷ vt dettagliare, particolareggiare;
in ~ nei particolari; **detailed** adj
particolareggiato(-a)
detain [dɪ'teɪn] vt trattenere; (in captivity)
detenere
detect [dɪ'tɛkt] vt scoprire, scorgere; (Med,
Police, Radar etc) individuare; **detection**
[dɪ'tɛkʃən] n scoperta; individuazione
f; **detective** n investigatore(-trice);
detective story n giallo
detention [dɪ'tɛnʃən] n detenzione f; (Scol)
permanenza forzata per punizione
deter [dɪ'tə:ʳ] vt dissuadere
detergent [dɪ'tə:dʒənt] n detersivo
deteriorate [dɪ'tɪərɪəreɪt] vi deteriorarsi
determination [dɪtə:mɪ'neɪʃən] n
determinazione f
determine [dɪ'tə:mɪn] vt determinare;
determined adj (person) risoluto(-a),
deciso(-a); **determined to do** deciso(-a)
a fare
deterrent [dɪ'tɛrənt] n deterrente m; **to
act as a ~** fungere da deterrente
detest [dɪ'tɛst] vt detestare
detour ['di:tuəʳ] n deviazione f
detract [dɪ'trækt] vi **to ~ from** detrarre da
detrimental [dɛtrɪ'mɛntl] adj **~ to**
dannoso(-a) a, nocivo(-a) a
devastating ['dɛvəsteɪtɪŋ] adj
devastatore(-trice), sconvolgente
develop [dɪ'vɛləp] vt sviluppare; (habit)
prendere (gradualmente) ▷ vi svilupparsi;
(facts, symptoms: appear) manifestarsi,
rivelarsi; **can you ~ this film?** può
sviluppare questo rullino?; **developing
country** n paese m in via di sviluppo;
development n sviluppo
device [dɪ'vaɪs] n (apparatus) congegno
devil ['dɛvl] n diavolo; demonio
devious ['di:vɪəs] adj (person) subdolo(-a)
devise [dɪ'vaɪz] vt escogitare, concepire
devote [dɪ'vəut] vt **to ~ sth to** dedicare qc
a; **devoted** adj devoto(-a); **to be devoted
to sb** essere molto affezionato(-a) a qn;
devotion [dɪ'vəuʃən] n devozione f,
attaccamento; (Rel) atto di devozione,
preghiera
devour [dɪ'vauəʳ] vt divorare
devout [dɪ'vaut] adj pio(-a), devoto(-a)
dew [dju:] n rugiada
diabetes [daɪə'bi:ti:z] n diabete m
diabetic [daɪə'bɛtɪk] adj, n diabetico(-a)
diagnose [daɪəg'nəuz] vt diagnosticare
diagnosis [daɪəg'nəusɪs] (pl **diagnoses**) n
diagnosi f inv
diagonal [daɪ'ægənl] adj diagonale ▷ n
diagonale f

diagram ['daɪəgræm] n diagramma m
dial ['daɪəl] n quadrante m; (on radio)
lancetta; (on telephone) disco combinatore
▷ vt (number) fare
dialect ['daɪəlɛkt] n dialetto
dialling code, (us **area code**) n prefisso;
what's the ~ for Paris? qual è il prefisso
telefonico di Parigi?
dialling tone ['daɪəlɪŋ-] (us **dial tone**) n
segnale m di linea libera
dialogue ['daɪəlɔg] (us **dialog**) n dialogo
diameter [daɪ'æmɪtəʳ] n diametro
diamond ['daɪəmənd] n diamante m;
(shape) rombo; ~**s** npl (Cards) quadri mpl
diaper ['daɪəpəʳ] (us) n pannolino
diarrhoea [daɪə'ri:ə] (us **diarrhea**) n
diarrea
diary ['daɪərɪ] n (daily account) diario; (book)
agenda
dice [daɪs] n inv dado ▷ vt (Culin) tagliare
a dadini
dictate [dɪk'teɪt] vt dettare; **dictation**
[dɪk'teɪʃən] n dettatura; (Scol) dettato
dictator [dɪk'teɪtəʳ] n dittatore m
dictionary ['dɪkʃənrɪ] n dizionario
did [dɪd] pt of **do**
didn't [dɪdnt] = **did not**
die [daɪ] vi morire; **to be dying for sth/to
do sth** morire dalla voglia di qc/di fare
qc; **die down** vi abbassarsi; **die out** vi
estinguersi
diesel ['di:zəl] n (vehicle) diesel m inv
diet ['daɪət] n alimentazione f; (restricted
food) dieta ▷ vi (also: **be on a ~**) stare a
dieta
differ ['dɪfəʳ] vi **to ~ from sth** differire
da qc, essere diverso(-a) da qc; **to ~
from sb over sth** essere in disaccordo
con qn su qc; **difference** n differenza;
(disagreement) screzio; **different** adj
diverso(-a); **differentiate** [-'rɛnʃɪeɪt] vi
to differentiate between discriminare
or fare differenza fra; **differently** adv
diversamente
difficult ['dɪfɪkəlt] adj difficile; **difficulty** n
difficoltà f inv
dig [dɪg] (pt, pp **dug**) vt (hole) scavare;
(garden) vangare ▷ n (prod) gomitata;
(archaeological) scavo; (fig) frecciata; **dig
up** vt (tree etc) sradicare; (information)
scavare fuori
digest [vb daɪ'dʒɛst, n 'daɪdʒɛst] vt digerire
▷ n compendio; **digestion** [dɪ'dʒɛstʃən] n
digestione f
digit ['dɪdʒɪt] n cifra; (finger) dito; **digital**
adj digitale; **digital camera** n macchina
fotografica digitale; **digital TV** n
televisione f digitale
dignified ['dɪgnɪfaɪd] adj dignitoso(-a)

dignity ['dɪgnɪtɪ] n dignità
digs [dɪgz] (BRIT: inf) npl camera ammobiliata
dilemma [daɪ'lɛmə] n dilemma m
dill [dɪl] n aneto
dilute [daɪ'luːt] vt diluire; (with water) annacquare
dim [dɪm] adj (light) debole; (shape etc) vago(-a); (room) in penombra; (inf: person) tonto(-a) ▷ vt (light) abbassare
dime [daɪm] (US) n = 10 cents
dimension [daɪ'mɛnʃən] n dimensione f
diminish [dɪ'mɪnɪʃ] vt, vi diminuire
din [dɪn] n chiasso, fracasso
dine [daɪn] vi pranzare; **diner** n (person) cliente m/f; (US: place) tavola calda
dinghy ['dɪŋgɪ] n battello pneumatico; (also: **rubber ~**) gommone m
dingy ['dɪndʒɪ] adj grigio(-a)
dining car ['daɪnɪŋ-] (BRIT) n vagone m ristorante
dining room n sala da pranzo
dining table n tavolo da pranzo
dinner ['dɪnə'] n (lunch) pranzo; (evening meal) cena; (public) banchetto; **dinner jacket** n smoking m inv; **dinner party** n cena; **dinner time** n ora di pranzo (or cena)
dinosaur ['daɪnəsɔː'] n dinosauro
dip [dɪp] n discesa; (in sea) bagno; (Culin) salsetta ▷ vt immergere; bagnare; (BRIT Aut: lights) abbassare ▷ vi abbassarsi
diploma [dɪ'pləumə] n diploma m
diplomacy [dɪ'pləuməsɪ] n diplomazia
diplomat ['dɪpləmæt] n diplomatico; **diplomatic** [dɪplə'mætɪk] adj diplomatico(-a)
dipstick ['dɪpstɪk] n (Aut) indicatore m di livello dell'olio
dire [daɪə'] adj terribile; estremo(-a)
direct [daɪ'rɛkt] adj diretto(-a) ▷ vt dirigere; (order) **to ~ sb to do sth** dare direttive a qn di fare qc ▷ adv direttamente; **can you ~ me to ...?** mi può indicare la strada per ...?; **direct debit** n (Banking) addebito effettuato per ordine di un cliente di banca
direction [dɪ'rɛkʃən] n direzione f; ~**s** npl (advice) chiarimenti mpl; **sense of ~** senso dell'orientamento; ~**s for use** istruzioni fpl
directly [dɪ'rɛktlɪ] adv (in straight line) direttamente; (at once) subito
director [dɪ'rɛktə'] n direttore(-trice), amministratore(-trice); (Theatre, Cinema) regista m/f
directory [dɪ'rɛktərɪ] n elenco; **directory enquiries** (US **directory assistance**) n informazioni fpl elenco abbonati inv
dirt [dəːt] n sporcizia; immondizia; (earth)

terra; **dirty** adj sporco(-a) ▷ vt sporcare
disability [dɪsə'bɪlɪtɪ] n invalidità f inv; (Law) incapacità f inv
disabled [dɪs'eɪbld] adj invalido(-a); (mentally) ritardato(-a) ▷ npl **the ~** gli invalidi
disadvantage [dɪsəd'vɑːntɪdʒ] n svantaggio
disagree [dɪsə'griː] vi (differ) discordare; (be against, think otherwise): **to ~ (with)** essere in disaccordo (con), dissentire (da); **disagreeable** adj sgradevole; (person) antipatico(-a); **disagreement** n disaccordo; (argument) dissapore m
disappear [dɪsə'pɪə'] vi scomparire; **disappearance** n scomparsa
disappoint [dɪsə'pɔɪnt] vt deludere; **disappointed** adj deluso(-a); **disappointing** adj deludente; **disappointment** n delusione f
disapproval [dɪsə'pruːvəl] n disapprovazione f
disapprove [dɪsə'pruːv] vi **to ~ of** disapprovare
disarm [dɪs'ɑːm] vt disarmare; **disarmament** n disarmo
disaster [dɪ'zɑːstə'] n disastro; **disastrous** [dɪ'zɑːstrəs] adj disastroso(-a)
disbelief ['dɪsbə'liːf] n incredulità
disc [dɪsk] n disco; (Comput) = **disk**
discard [dɪs'kɑːd] vt (old things) scartare; (fig) abbandonare
discharge [vb dɪs'tʃɑːdʒ, n 'dɪstʃɑːdʒ] vt (duties) compiere; (Elec, waste etc) scaricare; (Med) emettere; (patient) dimettere; (employee) licenziare; (soldier) congedare; (defendant) liberare ▷ n (Elec) scarica; (Med) emissione f; (dismissal) licenziamento; congedo; liberazione f
discipline ['dɪsɪplɪn] n disciplina ▷ vt disciplinare; (punish) punire
disc jockey n disc jockey m inv
disclose [dɪs'kləuz] vt rivelare, svelare
disco [dɪs'kəu] n abbr discoteca
discoloured [dɪs'kʌləd] (US **discolored**) adj scolorito(-a), ingiallito(-a)
discomfort [dɪs'kʌmfət] n disagio; (lack of comfort) scomodità f inv
disconnect [dɪskə'nɛkt] vt sconnettere, staccare; (Elec, Radio) staccare; (gas, water) chiudere
discontent [dɪskən'tɛnt] n scontentezza
discontinue [dɪskən'tɪnjuː] vt smettere, cessare; **"~d"** (Comm) "fuori produzione"
discount [n 'dɪskaunt, vb dɪs'kaunt] n sconto ▷ vt scontare; (idea) non badare a; **are there ~s for students?** ci sono sconti

per studenti?

discourage [dɪsˈkʌrɪdʒ] vt scoraggiare

discover [dɪsˈkʌvəʳ] vt scoprire; **discovery** n scoperta

discredit [dɪsˈkrɛdɪt] vt screditare; mettere in dubbio

discreet [dɪˈskriːt] adj discreto(-a)

discrepancy [dɪˈskrɛpənsɪ] n discrepanza

discretion [dɪˈskrɛʃən] n discrezione f; **use your own ~** giudichi lei

discriminate [dɪˈskrɪmɪneɪt] vi **to ~ between** distinguere tra; **to ~ against** discriminare contro; **discrimination** [-ˈneɪʃən] n discriminazione f; (judgment) discernimento

discuss [dɪˈskʌs] vt discutere; (debate) dibattere; **discussion** [dɪˈskʌʃən] n discussione f

disease [dɪˈziːz] n malattia

disembark [dɪsɪmˈbɑːk] vt, vi sbarcare

disgrace [dɪsˈɡreɪs] n vergogna; (disfavour) disgrazia ▷ vt disonorare, far cadere in disgrazia; **disgraceful** adj scandaloso(-a), vergognoso(-a)

disgruntled [dɪsˈɡrʌntld] adj scontento(-a), di cattivo umore

disguise [dɪsˈɡaɪz] n travestimento ▷ vt **to ~ (as)** travestire (da); **in ~** travestito(-a)

disgust [dɪsˈɡʌst] n disgusto, nausea ▷ vt disgustare, far schifo a; **disgusted** [dɪsˈɡʌstɪd] adj indignato(-a); **disgusting** [dɪsˈɡʌstɪŋ] adj disgustoso(-a), ripugnante

dish [dɪʃ] n piatto; **to do** or **wash the ~es** fare i piatti; **dishcloth** n strofinaccio

dishonest [dɪsˈɔnɪst] adj disonesto(-a)

dishtowel [ˈdɪʃtauəl] (us) n strofinaccio dei piatti

dishwasher [ˈdɪʃwɔʃəʳ] n lavastoviglie f inv

disillusion [dɪsɪˈluːʒən] vt disilludere, disingannare

disinfectant [dɪsɪnˈfɛktənt] n disinfettante m

disintegrate [dɪsˈɪntɪɡreɪt] vi disintegrarsi

disk [dɪsk] n (Comput) disco; **single-/double-sided ~** disco a facciata singola/doppia; **disk drive** n lettore m; **diskette** (us) n = **disk**

dislike [dɪsˈlaɪk] n antipatia, avversione f; (gen pl) cosa che non piace ▷ vt **he ~s it** non gli piace

dislocate [ˈdɪsləkeɪt] vt slogare

disloyal [dɪsˈlɔɪəl] adj sleale

dismal [ˈdɪzml] adj triste, cupo(-a)

dismantle [dɪsˈmæntl] vt (machine) smontare

dismay [dɪsˈmeɪ] n costernazione f ▷ vt sgomentare

dismiss [dɪsˈmɪs] vt congedare; (employee) licenziare; (idea) scacciare; (Law) respingere; **dismissal** n congedo; licenziamento

disobedient [dɪsəˈbiːdɪənt] adj disubbidiente

disobey [dɪsəˈbeɪ] vt disubbidire a

disorder [dɪsˈɔːdəʳ] n disordine m; (rioting) tumulto; (Med) disturbo

disorganized [dɪsˈɔːɡənaɪzd] adj (person, life) disorganizzato(-a); (system, meeting) male organizzato(-a)

disown [dɪsˈəun] vt rinnegare

dispatch [dɪsˈpætʃ] vt spedire, inviare ▷ n spedizione f, invio; (Mil, Press) dispaccio

dispel [dɪsˈpɛl] vt dissipare, scacciare

dispense [dɪsˈpɛns] vt distribuire, amministrare; **dispense with** vt fus fare a meno di; **dispenser** n (container) distributore m

disperse [dɪsˈpəːs] vt disperdere; (knowledge) disseminare ▷ vi disperdersi

display [dɪsˈpleɪ] n esposizione f; (of feeling etc) manifestazione f; (screen) schermo ▷ vt mostrare; (goods) esporre; (pej) ostentare

displease [dɪsˈpliːz] vt dispiacere a, scontentare; **~d with** scontento di

disposable [dɪsˈpəuzəbl] adj (pack etc) a perdere; (income) disponibile

disposal [dɪsˈpəuzl] n eliminazione f; (of property) cessione f; **at one's ~** alla sua disposizione

dispose [dɪsˈpəuz] vi **~ of** sbarazzarsi di; **disposition** [-ˈzɪʃən] n disposizione f; (temperament) carattere m

disproportionate [dɪsprəˈpɔːʃənət] adj sproporzionato(-a)

dispute [dɪsˈpjuːt] n disputa; (also: **industrial ~**) controversia (sindacale) ▷ vt contestare; (matter) discutere; (victory) disputare

disqualify [dɪsˈkwɔlɪfaɪ] vt (Sport) squalificare; **to ~ sb from sth/from doing** rendere qn incapace a qc/a fare; squalificare qn da qc/da fare; **to ~ sb from driving** ritirare la patente a qn

disregard [dɪsrɪˈɡɑːd] vt non far caso a, non badare a

disrupt [dɪsˈrʌpt] vt disturbare; (meeting) scompiglio in; **disruption** [dɪsˈrʌpʃən] n disordine m; interruzione f

dissatisfaction [dɪssætɪsˈfækʃən] n scontentezza, insoddisfazione f

dissatisfied [dɪsˈsætɪsfaɪd] adj **~ (with)** scontento(a) or insoddisfatto(a) (di)

dissect [dɪˈsɛkt] vt sezionare

dissent [dɪˈsɛnt] *n* dissenso
dissertation [dɪsəˈteɪʃən] *n* tesi *f inv*, dissertazione *f*
dissolve [dɪˈzɔlv] *vt* dissolvere, sciogliere; (*Pol, marriage etc*) sciogliere ▷ *vi* dissolversi, sciogliersi
distance [ˈdɪstns] *n* distanza; **in the ~** in lontananza
distant [ˈdɪstnt] *adj* lontano(-a), distante; (*manner*) riservato(-a), freddo(-a)
distil [dɪsˈtɪl] (*US* **distill**) *vt* distillare; **distillery** *n* distilleria
distinct [dɪsˈtɪŋkt] *adj* distinto(-a); **as ~ from** a differenza di; **distinction** [dɪsˈtɪŋkʃən] *n* distinzione *f*; (*in exam*) lode *f*; **distinctive** *adj* distintivo(-a)
distinguish [dɪsˈtɪŋgwɪʃ] *vt* distinguere; discernere; **distinguished** *adj* (*eminent*) eminente
distort [dɪsˈtɔːt] *vt* distorcere; (*Tech*) deformare
distract [dɪsˈtrækt] *vt* distrarre; **distracted** *adj* distratto(-a); **distraction** [dɪsˈtrækʃən] *n* distrazione *f*
distraught [dɪsˈtrɔːt] *adj* stravolto(-a)
distress [dɪsˈtrɛs] *n* angoscia ▷ *vt* affliggere; **distressing** *adj* doloroso(-a)
distribute [dɪsˈtrɪbjuːt] *vt* distribuire; **distribution** [-ˈbjuːʃən] *n* distribuzione *f*; **distributor** *n* distributore *m*
district [ˈdɪstrɪkt] *n* (*of country*) regione *f*; (*of town*) quartiere *m*; (*Admin*) distretto; **district attorney** (*US*) *n* ≈ sostituto procuratore *m* della Repubblica
distrust [dɪsˈtrʌst] *n* diffidenza, sfiducia ▷ *vt* non aver fiducia in
disturb [dɪsˈtəːb] *vt* disturbare; **disturbance** *n* disturbo; (*political etc*) disordini *mpl*; **disturbed** *adj* (*worried, upset*) turbato(-a); **emotionally disturbed** con turbe emotive; **disturbing** *adj* sconvolgente
ditch [dɪtʃ] *n* fossa ▷ *vt* (*inf*) piantare in asso
ditto [ˈdɪtəu] *adv* idem
dive [daɪv] *n* tuffo; (*of submarine*) immersione *f* ▷ *vi* tuffarsi; immergersi; **diver** *n* tuffatore(-trice), palombaro
diverse [daɪˈvəːs] *adj* vario(-a)
diversion [daɪˈvəːʃən] *n* (*BRIT Aut*) deviazione *f*; (*distraction*) divertimento
diversity [daɪˈvəːsɪtɪ] *n* diversità *f inv*, varietà *f inv*
divert [daɪˈvəːt] *vt* deviare
divide [dɪˈvaɪd] *vt* dividere; (*separate*) separare ▷ *vi* dividersi; **divided highway** (*US*) *n* strada a doppia carreggiata
divine [dɪˈvaɪn] *adj* divino(-a)
diving [ˈdaɪvɪŋ] *n* tuffo; **diving board** *n* trampolino
division [dɪˈvɪʒən] *n* divisione *f*; separazione *f*; (*esp Football*) serie *f*
divorce [dɪˈvɔːs] *n* divorzio ▷ *vt* divorziare da; (*dissociate*) separare; **divorced** *adj* divorziato(-a); **divorcee** [-ˈsiː] *n* divorziato(-a)
D.I.Y. (*BRIT*) *n abbr* = **do-it-yourself**
dizzy [ˈdɪzɪ] *adj* **to feel ~** avere il capogiro
DJ *n abbr* = **disc jockey**
DNA *n abbr* (= deoxyribonucleic acid) DNA *m*; **DNA test** *n* test *m inv* del DNA

 KEYWORD

do [duː] (*pt* **did**, *pp* **done**) *n* (*inf: party etc*) festa; **it was rather a grand do** è stato un ricevimento piuttosto importante ▷ *vb* **1** (*in negative constructions: non tradotto*): **I don't understand** non capisco
2 (*to form questions: non tradotto*): **didn't you know?** non lo sapevi?; **why didn't you come?** perché non sei venuto?
3 (*for emphasis, in polite expressions*): **she does seem rather late** sembra essere piuttosto in ritardo; **do sit down** si accomodi la prego, prego si sieda; **do take care!** mi raccomando, sta attento!
4 (*used to avoid repeating vb*): **she swims better than I do** lei nuota meglio di me; **do you agree? — yes, I do/no, I don't** sei d'accordo? — sì/no; **she lives in Glasgow — so do I** lei vive a Glasgow — anch'io; **he asked me to help him and I did** mi ha chiesto di aiutarlo ed io l'ho fatto
5 (*in question tags*): **you like him, don't you?** ti piace, vero?; **I don't know him, do I?** non lo conosco, vero?
▷ *vt* (*gen, carry out, perform etc*) fare; **what are you doing tonight?** che fa stasera?; **to do the cooking** cucinare; **to do the washing-up** fare i piatti; **to do one's teeth** lavarsi i denti; **to do one's hair/nails** farsi i capelli/le unghie; **the car was doing 100** la macchina faceva i 100 all'ora
▷ *vi* **1** (*act, behave*) fare; **do as I do** faccia come me, faccia come faccio io
2 (*get on, fare*) andare; **he's doing well/badly at school** va bene/male a scuola; **how do you do?** piacere!
3 (*suit*) andare bene; **this room will do** questa stanza va bene
4 (*be sufficient*) bastare; **will £10 do?** basteranno 10 sterline?; **that'll do** basta così; **that'll do!** (*in annoyance*) ora basta!; **to make do (with)** arrangiarsi (con)
do away with *vt fus* (*kill*) far fuori; (*abolish*) abolire

do up vt (laces) allacciare; (dress, buttons) abbottonare; (renovate: room, house) rimettere a nuovo, rifare

do with vt fus (need) aver bisogno di; (be connected): **what has it got to do with you?** e tu che c'entri?; **I won't have anything to do with it** non voglio avere niente a che farci; **it has to do with money** si tratta di soldi

do without vi fare senza ▷ vt fus fare a meno di

dock [dɔk] n (Naut) bacino; (Law) banco degli imputati ▷ vi entrare in bacino; (Space) agganciarsi; **~s** npl (Naut) dock m inv

doctor ['dɔktər] n medico(-a); (Ph.D. etc) dottore(-essa) ▷ vt (drink etc) adulterare; **call a ~!** chiamate un dottore!; **Doctor of Philosophy** n dottorato di ricerca; (person) titolare m/f di un dottorato di ricerca

document ['dɔkjumənt] n documento; **documentary** [-'mɛntərɪ] adj (evidence) documentato(-a) ▷ n documentario; **documentation** [dɔkjumən'teɪʃən] n documentazione f

dodge [dɔdʒ] n trucco; schivata ▷ vt schivare, eludere

dodgy ['dɔdʒɪ] adj (inf: uncertain) rischioso(-a); (untrustworthy) sospetto(-a)

does [dʌz] vb see **do**

doesn't ['dʌznt] = **does not**

dog [dɔg] n cane m ▷ vt (follow closely) pedinare; (fig: memory etc) perseguitare; **doggy bag** n sacchetto per gli avanzi (da portare a casa)

do-it-yourself ['duːɪtjɔː'sɛlf] n il far da sé

dole [dəul] (BRIT) n sussidio di disoccupazione; **to be on the ~** vivere del sussidio

doll [dɔl] n bambola

dollar ['dɔlər] n dollaro

dolphin ['dɔlfɪn] n delfino

dome [dəum] n cupola

domestic [də'mɛstɪk] adj (duty, happiness, animal) domestico(-a); (policy, affairs, flights) nazionale; **domestic appliance** n elettrodomestico

dominant ['dɔmɪnənt] adj dominante

dominate ['dɔmɪneɪt] vt dominare

domino ['dɔmɪnəu] (pl **dominoes**) n domino; **dominoes** n (game) gioco del domino

donate [də'neɪt] vt donare; **donation** [də'neɪʃən] n donazione f

done [dʌn] pp of **do**

donkey ['dɔŋkɪ] n asino

donor ['dəunər] n donatore(-trice); **donor card** n tessera di donatore di organi

don't [dəunt] = **do not**

donut ['dəunʌt] (US) n = **doughnut**

doodle ['duːdl] vi scarabocchiare

doom [duːm] n destino; rovina ▷ vt **to be ~ed (to failure)** essere predestinato(-a) (a fallire)

door [dɔːr] n porta; **doorbell** n campanello; **door handle** n maniglia; **doorknob** ['dɔːnɔb] n pomello, maniglia; **doorstep** n gradino della porta; **doorway** n porta

dope [dəup] n (inf: drugs) roba ▷ vt (horse etc) drogare

dormitory ['dɔːmɪtrɪ] n dormitorio; (US) casa dello studente

DOS [dɔs] n abbr (= disk operating system) DOS m

dosage ['dəusɪdʒ] n posologia

dose [dəus] n dose f; (bout) attacco

dot [dɔt] n punto; macchiolina ▷ vt **~ted with** punteggiato(-a) di; **on the ~** in punto; **dotted line** ['dɔtɪd-] n linea punteggiata

double ['dʌbl] adj doppio(-a) ▷ adv (twice): **to cost ~ sth** costare il doppio (di qc) ▷ n sosia m inv ▷ vt raddoppiare; (fold) piegare doppio or in due ▷ vi raddoppiarsi; **at the ~** (BRIT), **on the ~** a passo di corsa; **double back** vi (person) tornare sui propri passi; **double bass** n contrabbasso; **double bed** n letto matrimoniale; **double-check** vt, vi ricontrollare; **double-click** vi (Comput) fare doppio click; **double-cross** vt fare il doppio gioco con; **doubledecker** n autobus m inv a due piani; **double glazing** (BRIT) n doppi vetri mpl; **double room** n camera matrimoniale; **doubles** n (Tennis) doppio; **double yellow lines** npl (BRIT: Aut) linea gialla doppia continua che segnala il divieto di sosta

doubt [daut] n dubbio ▷ vt dubitare di; **to ~ that** dubitare che + sub; **doubtful** adj dubbioso(-a), incerto(-a); (person) equivoco(-a); **doubtless** adv indubbiamente

dough [dəu] n pasta, impasto; **doughnut** (US **donut**) n bombolone m

dove [dʌv] n colombo/a

down [daun] n piume fpl ▷ adv giù, di sotto ▷ prep giù per ▷ vt (inf: drink) scolarsi; **~ with X!** abbasso X!; **down-and-out** n barbone m/f; **downfall** n caduta; rovina; **downhill** adv **to go downhill** andare in discesa; (fig) lasciarsi andare; andare a rotoli

Downing Street ['daʊnɪŋ-] *n* **lo ~** *residenza del primo ministro inglese*

● **DOWNING STREET**
●
● Al numero 10 di **Downing Street**, nel
● quartiere di Westminster a Londra, si
● trova la residenza del primo ministro
● inglese, al numero 11 quella del
● **Chancellor of the Exchequer**.

down: **download** *vt* (*Comput*) scaricare; **downright** *adj* franco(-a); (*refusal*) assoluto(-a)

Down's syndrome *n* sindrome *f* di Down
down: **downstairs** *adv* di sotto; al piano inferiore; **down-to-earth** *adj* pratico(-a); (*US*: *call-up*) leva ▷ *vt* downtown *adv* in città; **down under** *adv* (*Australia etc*) agli antipodi; **downward** ['daʊnwəd] *adj*, *adv* in giù, in discesa; **downwards** ['daʊnwədz] *adv* = **downward**

doz. *abbr* = **dozen**
doze [dəʊz] *vi* sonnecchiare
dozen ['dʌzn] *n* dozzina; **a ~ books** una dozzina di libri; **~s of** decine *fpl* di
Dr. *abbr* (= *doctor*) dott.; (*in street names*) = **drive**

drab [dræb] *adj* tetro(-a), grigio(-a)
draft [drɑːft] *n* abbozzo; (*Pol*) bozza; (*Comm*) tratta; (*US*: *call-up*) leva ▷ *vt* abbozzare; *see also* **draught**

drag [dræg] *vt* trascinare; (*river*) dragare ▷ *vi* trascinarsi ▷ *n* (*inf*) noioso(-a); noia, fatica; (*women's clothing*): **in ~** travestito (da donna)

dragon ['drægən] *n* drago
dragonfly ['drægənflaɪ] *n* libellula
drain [dreɪn] *n* (*for sewage*) fogna; (*on resources*) salasso ▷ *vt* (*land, marshes*) prosciugare; (*vegetables*) scolare ▷ *vi* (*water*) defluire (via); **drainage** *n* prosciugamento; fognatura; **drainpipe** *n* tubo di scarico

drama ['drɑːmə] *n* (*art*) dramma *m*, teatro; (*play*) commedia; (*event*) dramma; **dramatic** [drə'mætɪk] *adj* drammatico(-a)

drank [dræŋk] *pt of* **drink**
drape [dreɪp] *vt* drappeggiare; **~s** (*US*) *npl* (*curtains*) tende *fpl*
drastic ['dræstɪk] *adj* drastico(-a)
draught [drɑːft] (*US* **draft**) *n* corrente *f* d'aria; (*Naut*) pescaggio; **on ~** (*beer*) alla spina; **draught beer** *n* birra alla spina; **draughts** (*BRIT*) *n* (*gioco della*) dama
draw [drɔː] (*pt* **drew**, *pp* **drawn**) *vt* tirare; (*take out*) estrarre; (*attract*) attirare; (*picture*) disegnare; (*line, circle*) tracciare;

(*money*) ritirare ▷ *vi* (*Sport*) pareggiare ▷ *n* pareggio; (*in lottery*) estrazione *f*; **to ~ near** avvicinarsi; **draw out** *vi* (*lengthen*) allungarsi ▷ *vt* (*money*) ritirare; **draw up** *vi* (*stop*) arrestarsi, fermarsi ▷ *vt* (*chair*) avvicinare; (*document*) compilare; **drawback** *n* svantaggio, inconveniente *m*
drawer [drɔːʳ] *n* cassetto
drawing ['drɔːɪŋ] *n* disegno; **drawing pin** (*BRIT*) *n* puntina da disegno; **drawing room** *n* salotto
drawn [drɔːn] *pp of* **draw**
dread [drɛd] *n* terrore *m* ▷ *vt* tremare all'idea di; **dreadful** *adj* terribile
dream [driːm] (*pt, pp* **dreamed** *or* **dreamt**) *n* sogno ▷ *vt, vi* sognare; **dreamer** *n* sognatore(-trice)
dreamt [drɛmt] *pt, pp of* **dream**
dreary ['drɪərɪ] *adj* tetro(-a); monotono(-a)
drench [drɛntʃ] *vt* inzuppare
dress [drɛs] *n* vestito; (*no pl: clothing*) abbigliamento ▷ *vt* vestire; (*wound*) fasciare ▷ *vi* vestirsi; **to get ~ed** vestirsi; **dress up** *vi* vestirsi a festa; (*in fancy dress*) vestirsi in costume; **dress circle** (*BRIT*) *n* prima galleria; **dresser** *n* (*BRIT*: *cupboard*) credenza; (*US*) cassettone *m*; **dressing** *n* (*Med*) benda; (*Culin*) condimento; **dressing gown** (*BRIT*) *n* vestaglia; **dressing room** *n* (*Theatre*) camerino; (*Sport*) spogliatoio; **dressing table** *n* toilette *f* inv; **dressmaker** *n* sarta
drew [druː] *pt of* **draw**
dribble ['drɪbl] *vi* (*baby*) sbavare ▷ *vt* (*ball*) dribblare
dried [draɪd] *adj* (*fruit, beans*) secco(-a); (*eggs, milk*) in polvere
drier ['draɪəʳ] *n* = **dryer**
drift [drɪft] *n* (*of current etc*) direzione *f*; forza; (*of snow*) cumulo; turbine *m*; (*general meaning*) senso ▷ *vi* (*boat*) essere trasportato(-a) dalla corrente; (*sand, snow*) ammucchiarsi
drill [drɪl] *n* trapano; (*Mil*) esercitazione *f* ▷ *vt* trapanare; (*troops*) addestrare ▷ *vi* (*for oil*) fare trivellazioni
drink [drɪŋk] (*pt* **drank**, *pp* **drunk**) *n* bevanda, bibita; (*alcoholic drink*) bicchierino; (*sip*) sorso ▷ *vt, vi* bere; **to have a ~** bere qualcosa; **would you like a ~?** vuoi qualcosa da bere?; **a ~ of water** un po' d'acqua; **drink-driving** *n* guida in stato di ebbrezza; **drinker** *n* bevitore(-trice); **drinking water** *n* acqua potabile
drip [drɪp] *n* goccia; gocciolamento; (*Med*) fleboclisi *f* inv ▷ *vi* gocciolare; (*tap*) sgocciolare

drive [draɪv] (pt **drove**, pp **driven**) n passeggiata or giro in macchina; (also: **~way**) viale m d'accesso; (energy) energia; (campaign) campagna; (also: **disk ~**) lettore m ▷ vt guidare; (nail) piantare; (push) cacciare, spingere; (Tech: motor) azionare; far funzionare ▷ vi (Aut: at controls) guidare; (: travel) andare in macchina; **left-/right-hand ~** guida a sinistra/destra; **to ~ sb mad** far impazzire qn; **drive out** vt (force out) cacciare, mandare via; **drive-in** (esp us) adj, n drive-in (m inv)

driven ['drɪvn] pp of **drive**

driver ['draɪvə'] n conducente m/f; (of taxi) tassista m; (chauffeur: of bus) autista m/f; **driver's license** (us) n patente f di guida

driveway ['draɪvweɪ] n viale m d'accesso

driving ['draɪvɪŋ] n guida; **driving instructor** n istruttore(-trice) di scuola guida; **driving lesson** n lezione f di guida; **driving licence** (BRIT) n patente f di guida; **driving test** n esame m di guida

drizzle ['drɪzl] n pioggerella

droop [druːp] vi (flower) appassire; (head, shoulders) chinarsi

drop [drɔp] n (of water) goccia; (lessening) diminuzione f; (fall) caduta ▷ vt lasciare cadere; (voice, eyes, price) abbassare; (set down from car) far scendere; (name from list) lasciare fuori ▷ vi cascare; (wind) abbassarsi; **drop in** vi (inf: visit): **to ~ in (on)** fare un salto (da), passare (da); **drop off** vi (sleep) addormentarsi ▷ vt (passenger) far scendere; **drop out** vi (withdraw) ritirarsi; (student etc) smettere di studiare

drought [draut] n siccità f inv

drove [drəuv] pt of **drive**

drown [draun] vt affogare; (fig: noise) soffocare ▷ vi affogare

drowsy ['drauzɪ] adj sonnolento(-a), assonnato(-a)

drug [drʌɡ] n farmaco; (narcotic) droga ▷ vt drogare; **to be on ~s** drogarsi; (Med) prendere medicinali; **hard/soft ~s** droghe pesanti/leggere; **drug addict** n tossicomane m/f; **drug dealer** n trafficante m/f di droga; **druggist** (us) n persona che gestisce un drugstore; **drugstore** (us) n drugstore m inv

drum [drʌm] n tamburo; (for oil, petrol) fusto ▷ vi tamburellare; **~s** npl (set of drums) batteria; **drummer** n batterista m/f

drunk [drʌŋk] pp of **drink** ▷ adj ubriaco(-a); ebbro(-a) ▷ n (also: **~ard**) ubriacone(-a); **drunken** adj ubriaco(-a); da ubriaco

dry [draɪ] adj secco(-a); (day, clothes) asciutto(-a) ▷ vt seccare; (clothes, hair, hands) asciugare ▷ vi asciugarsi; **dry off** vi asciugarsi ▷ vt asciugare; **dry up** vi seccarsi; **dry-cleaner's** n lavasecco m inv; **dry-cleaning** n pulitura a secco; **dryer** n (for hair) föhn m inv, asciugacapelli m inv; (for clothes) asciugabiancheria; (us: spin-dryer) centrifuga

DSS n abbr (= Department of Social Security) ministero della Previdenza sociale

DTP n abbr (= desk-top publishing) desktop publishing m inv

dual ['djuəl] adj doppio(-a); **dual carriageway** (BRIT) n strada a doppia carreggiata

dubious ['djuːbɪəs] adj dubbio(-a)

Dublin ['dʌblɪn] n Dublino f

duck [dʌk] n anatra ▷ vi abbassare la testa

due [djuː] adj dovuto(-a); (expected) atteso(-a); (fitting) giusto(-a) ▷ n dovuto ▷ adv **~ north** diritto verso nord

duel ['djuəl] n duello

duet [djuːˈɛt] n duetto

dug [dʌɡ] pt, pp of **dig**

duke [djuːk] n duca m

dull [dʌl] adj (light) debole; (boring) noioso(-a); (slow-witted) ottuso(-a); (sound, pain) sordo(-a); (weather, day) fosco(-a), scuro(-a) ▷ vt (pain, grief) attutire; (mind, senses) intorpidire

dumb [dʌm] adj muto(-a); (pej) stupido(-a)

dummy ['dʌmɪ] n (tailor's model) manichino; (Tech, Comm) riproduzione f; (BRIT: for baby) tettarella ▷ adj falso(-a), finto(-a)

dump [dʌmp] n (also: **rubbish ~**) discarica di rifiuti; (inf: place) buco ▷ vt (put down) scaricare; mettere giù; (get rid of) buttar via

dumpling ['dʌmplɪŋ] n specie di gnocco

dune [djuːn] n duna

dungarees [dʌŋɡəˈriːz] npl tuta

dungeon ['dʌndʒən] n prigione f sotterranea

duplex ['djuːplɛks] (us) n (house) casa con muro divisorio in comune con un'altra; (apartment) appartamento su due piani

duplicate (n 'djuːplɪkət, vb 'djuːplɪkeɪt) n doppio ▷ vt duplicare; **in ~** in doppia copia

durable ['djuərəbl] adj durevole; (clothes, metal) resistente

duration [djuəˈreɪʃən] n durata

during ['djuərɪŋ] prep durante, nel corso di

dusk [dʌsk] n crepuscolo

dust [dʌst] n polvere f ▷ vt (furniture) spolverare; (cake etc): **to ~ with** cospargere con; **dustbin** (BRIT) n pattumiera; **duster** n straccio per la polvere; **dustman** (irreg: BRIT) n netturbino; **dustpan** n pattumiera; **dusty** adj polveroso(-a)

Dutch [dʌtʃ] *adj* olandese ▷ *n* (*Ling*) olandese *m*; **the ~** *npl* gli Olandesi; **to go ~** (*inf*) fare alla romana; **Dutchman, Dutchwoman** (*irreg*) *n* olandese *m/f*

duty ['dju:tɪ] *n* dovere *m*; (*tax*) dazio, tassa; **on ~** di servizio; **off ~** libero(-a), fuori servizio; **duty-free** *adj* esente da dazio

duvet ['du:veɪ] (*BRIT*) *n* piumino, piumone *m*

DVD *n abbr* (= *digital versatile or video disk*) DVD *m inv*; **DVD player** *n* lettore *m* DVD

dwarf [dwɔ:f] *n* nano(-a) ▷ *vt* far apparire piccolo

dwell [dwel] (*pt, pp* **dwelt**) *vi* dimorare; **dwell on** *vt fus* indugiare su

dwelt [dwelt] *pt, pp of* **dwell**

dwindle ['dwɪndl] *vi* diminuire

dye [daɪ] *n* tinta ▷ *vt* tingere

dying ['daɪɪŋ] *adj* morente, moribondo(-a)

dynamic [daɪ'næmɪk] *adj* dinamico(-a)

dynamite ['daɪnəmaɪt] *n* dinamite *f*

dyslexia [dɪs'lɛksɪə] *n* dislessia

dyslexic [dɪs'lɛksɪk] *adj, n* dislessico(-a)

E [i:] *n* (*Mus*) mi *m*

E111 *n abbr* (*also:* **form ~**) E111 (*modulo CEE per rimborso spese mediche*)

each [i:tʃ] *adj* ogni, ciascuno(-a) ▷ *pron* ciascuno(-a), ognuno(-a); **~ one** ognuno(-a); **~ other** *si or ci etc*; **they hate ~ other** si odiano (l'un l'altro); **you are jealous of ~ other** siete gelosi l'uno dell'altro; **they have 2 books ~** hanno 2 libri ciascuno

eager ['i:gə'] *adj* impaziente, desideroso(-a); ardente; **to be ~ for** essere desideroso di, aver gran voglia di

eagle ['i:gl] *n* aquila

ear [ɪə'] *n* orecchio; (*of corn*) pannocchia; **earache** *n* mal *m* d'orecchi; **eardrum** *n* timpano

earl [ə:l] (*BRIT*) *n* conte *m*

earlier ['ə:lɪə'] *adj* precedente ▷ *adv* prima

early ['ə:lɪ] *adv* presto, di buon'ora; (*ahead of time*) in anticipo ▷ *adj* (*near the beginning*) primo(-a); (*sooner than expected*) prematuro(-a); (*quick: reply*) veloce; **at an ~ hour** di buon'ora; **to have an ~ night** andare a letto presto; **in the ~** *or* **~ in the spring/19th century** all'inizio della primavera/dell'Ottocento; **early retirement** *n* ritiro anticipato

earmark ['ɪəma:k] *vt* **to ~ sth for** destinare qc a

earn [əːn] vt guadagnare; (rest, reward) meritare

earnest ['əːnɪst] adj serio(-a); **in ~** sul serio

earnings ['əːnɪŋz] npl guadagni mpl; (salary) stipendio

ear: **earphones** ['ɪəfəʊnz] npl cuffia; **earplugs** npl tappi mpl per le orecchie; **earring** ['ɪərɪŋ] n orecchino

earth [əːθ] n terra ▷ vt (BRIT Elec) mettere a terra; **earthquake** n terremoto

ease [iːz] n agio, comodo ▷ vt (soothe) calmare; (loosen) allentare; **to ~ sth out/in** tirare fuori/infilare qc con delicatezza; facilitare l'uscita/l'entrata di qc; **at ~ a** proprio agio; (Mil) a riposo

easily ['iːzɪlɪ] adv facilmente

east [iːst] n est m ▷ adj dell'est ▷ adv a oriente; **the E~** l'Oriente m; (Pol) l'Est; **eastbound** ['iːstbaʊnd] adj (traffic) diretto(-a) a est; (carriageway) che porta a est

Easter ['iːstər] n Pasqua; **Easter egg** n uovo di Pasqua

eastern ['iːstən] adj orientale, d'oriente; dell'est

Easter Sunday n domenica di Pasqua

easy ['iːzɪ] adj facile; (manner) disinvolto(-a) ▷ adv **to take it** or **things ~** prendersela con calma; **easy-going** adj accomodante

eat [iːt] (pt **ate**, pp **eaten**) vt, vi mangiare; **can we have something to ~?** possiamo mangiare qualcosa?; **eat out** vi mangiare fuori

eavesdrop ['iːvzdrɔp] vi **to ~ (on a conversation)** origliare (una conversazione)

e-book ['iːbuk] n libro elettronico

e-business ['iːbɪznɪs] n (company) azienda che opera in Internet; (commerce) commercio elettronico

EC n abbr (= European Community) CE f

eccentric [ɪk'sɛntrɪk] adj, n eccentrico(-a)

echo ['ɛkəʊ] (pl **echoes**) n eco m or f ▷ vt ripetere; fare eco a ▷ vi echeggiare; dare un eco

eclipse [ɪ'klɪps] n eclissi f inv

eco-friendly [iːkəʊ'frɛndlɪ] adj ecologico(-a)

ecological [iːkə'lɔdʒɪkəl] adj ecologico(-a)

ecology [ɪ'kɔlədʒɪ] n ecologia

e-commerce [iːkɔmə:s] n commercio elettronico

economic [iːkə'nɔmɪk] adj economico(-a); **economical** adj economico(-a); (person) economo(-a); **economics** n economia ▷ npl lato finanziario

economist [ɪ'kɔnəmɪst] n economista m/f

economize [ɪ'kɔnəmaɪz] vi risparmiare, fare economia

economy [ɪ'kɔnəmɪ] n economia; **economy class** n (Aviat) classe f turistica; **economy class syndrome** n sindrome f della classe economica

ecstasy ['ɛkstəsɪ] n estasi f inv; **ecstatic** [ɛks'tætɪk] adj estatico(-a), in estasi

eczema ['ɛksɪmə] n eczema m

edge [ɛdʒ] n margine m; (of table, plate, cup) orlo; (of knife etc) taglio ▷ vt bordare; **on ~** (fig) = **edgy**; **to edge away from** sgattaiolare da

edgy ['ɛdʒɪ] adj nervoso(-a)

edible ['ɛdɪbl] adj commestibile; (meal) mangiabile

Edinburgh ['ɛdɪnbərə] n Edimburgo f

edit ['ɛdɪt] vt curare; **edition** [ɪ'dɪʃən] n edizione f; **editor** n (in newspaper) redattore(-trice), redattore(-trice) capo; (of sb's work) curatore(-trice); **editorial** [-'tɔːrɪəl] adj redazionale, editoriale ▷ n editoriale m

> Be careful not to translate **editor** by the Italian word **editore**.

educate ['ɛdjukeɪt] vt istruire; educare; **educated** adj istruito(-a)

education [ɛdju'keɪʃən] n educazione f; (schooling) istruzione f; **educational** adj pedagogico(-a); scolastico(-a); istruttivo(-a)

eel [iːl] n anguilla

eerie ['ɪərɪ] adj che fa accapponare la pelle

effect [ɪ'fɛkt] n effetto ▷ vt effettuare; **to take ~** (law) entrare in vigore; (drug) fare effetto; **in ~** effettivamente; **~s** npl (Theat) effetti mpl scenici; (property) effetti mpl; **effective** adj efficace; (actual) effettivo(-a); **effectively** adv efficacemente; effettivamente

efficiency [ɪ'fɪʃənsɪ] n efficienza; rendimento effettivo

efficient [ɪ'fɪʃənt] adj efficiente; **efficiently** adv efficientemente; efficacemente

effort ['ɛfət] n sforzo; **effortless** adj senza sforzo, facile

e.g. adv abbr (= exempli gratia) per esempio, p.es.

egg [ɛg] n uovo; **hard-boiled/soft-boiled ~** uovo sodo/alla coque; **eggcup** n portauovo m inv; **eggplant** (esp US) n melanzana; **eggshell** n guscio d'uovo; **egg white** n albume m, bianco d'uovo; **egg yolk** n tuorlo, rosso (d'uovo)

ego ['iːgəʊ] n ego m inv

Egypt ['iːdʒɪpt] n Egitto; **Egyptian** [ɪ'dʒɪpʃən] adj, n egiziano(-a)

eight [eɪt] num otto; **eighteen** num diciotto; **eighteenth** num diciottesimo(-a); **eighth** [eɪtθ] num

ottavo(-a); **eightieth** ['eɪtɪɪθ] num
ottantesimo(-a); **eighty** num ottanta
Eire ['ɛərə] n Repubblica d'Irlanda
either ['aɪðəʳ] adj l'uno(-a) o l'altro(-a);
(both, each) ciascuno(-a) ▷ pron **~ (of
them)** (o) l'uno(-a) o l'altro(-a) ▷ adv
neanche ▷ conj **~ good or bad** o buono o
cattivo; **on ~ side** su ciascun lato; **I don't
like ~** non mi piace né l'uno né l'altro; **no, I
don't ~** no, neanch'io
eject [ɪ'dʒɛkt] vt espellere; lanciare
elaborate [adj ɪ'læbərɪt, vb ɪ'læbəreɪt]
adj elaborato(-a), minuzioso(-a) ▷ vt
elaborare ▷ vi fornire i particolari
elastic [ɪ'læstɪk] adj elastico(-a) ▷ n
elastico; **elastic band** (BRIT) n elastico
elbow ['ɛlbəu] n gomito
elder ['ɛldəʳ] adj maggiore, più vecchio(-a)
▷ n (tree) sambuco; **one's ~s** i più anziani;
elderly adj anziano(-a) ▷ npl **the elderly**
gli anziani
eldest ['ɛldɪst] adj, n **the ~ (child)** il(la)
maggiore (dei bambini)
elect [ɪ'lɛkt] vt eleggere ▷ adj **the
president ~** il presidente designato; **to ~
to do** decidere di fare; **election** [ɪ'lɛkʃən]
n elezione f; **electoral** [ɪ'lɛktərəl] adj
elettorale; **electorate** n elettorato
electric [ɪ'lɛktrɪk] adj elettrico(-a);
electrical adj elettrico(-a); **electric
blanket** n coperta elettrica; **electric fire**
n stufa elettrica; **electrician** [ɪlɛk'trɪʃən]
n elettricista m; **electricity** [ɪlɛk'trɪsɪtɪ]
n elettricità; **electric shock** n scossa
(elettrica); **electrify** [ɪ'lɛktrɪfaɪ] vt (Rail)
elettrificare; (audience) elettrizzare
electronic [ɪlɛk'trɔnɪk] adj elettronico(-a);
electronic mail n posta elettronica;
electronics n elettronica
elegance ['ɛlɪgəns] n eleganza
elegant ['ɛlɪgənt] adj elegante
element ['ɛlɪmənt] n elemento; (of heater,
kettle etc) resistenza
elementary [ɛlɪ'mɛntərɪ] adj elementare;
elementary school (us) n scuola
elementare
elephant ['ɛlɪfənt] n elefante(-essa)
elevate ['ɛlɪveɪt] vt elevare
elevator ['ɛlɪveɪtəʳ] n elevatore m; (us: lift)
ascensore m
eleven [ɪ'lɛvn] num undici; **eleventh** adj
undicesimo(-a)
eligible ['ɛlɪdʒəbl] adj eleggibile; (for
membership) che ha i requisiti
eliminate [ɪ'lɪmɪneɪt] vt eliminare
elm [ɛlm] n olmo
eloquent ['ɛləkwənt] adj eloquente
else [ɛls] adv altro; **something ~**
qualcos'altro; **somewhere ~** altrove;

everywhere ~ in qualsiasi altro luogo;
nobody ~ nessun altro; **where ~?** in quale
altro luogo?; **little ~** poco altro; **elsewhere**
adv altrove
elusive [ɪ'lu:sɪv] adj elusivo(-a)
e-mail n abbr (= electronic mail) posta
elettronica ▷ vt mandare un messaggio
di posta elettronica a; **e-mail address** n
indirizzo di posta elettronica
embankment [ɪm'bæŋkmənt] n (of road,
railway) terrapieno
embargo [ɪm'ba:gəu] n (pl **embargoes**)
(Comm, Naut) embargo ▷ vt mettere
l'embargo su; **to put an ~ on sth** mettere
l'embargo su qc
embark [ɪm'ba:k] vi **to ~ (on)** imbarcarsi
(su) ▷ vt imbarcare; **to ~ on** (fig)
imbarcarsi in
embarrass [ɪm'bærəs] vt imbarazzare;
embarrassed adj imbarazzato(-a);
embarrassing adj imbarazzante;
embarrassment n imbarazzo
embassy ['ɛmbəsɪ] n ambasciata
embrace [ɪm'breɪs] vt abbracciare ▷ vi
abbracciarsi ▷ n abbraccio
embroider [ɪm'brɔɪdəʳ] vt ricamare;
embroidery n ricamo
embryo ['ɛmbrɪəu] n embrione m
emerald ['ɛmərəld] n smeraldo
emerge [ɪ'mə:dʒ] vi emergere
emergency [ɪ'mə:dʒənsɪ] n emergenza;
in an ~ in caso di emergenza; **emergency
brake** (us) n freno a mano; **emergency
exit** n uscita di sicurezza; **emergency
landing** n atterraggio forzato;
emergency room (us: Med) n pronto
soccorso; **emergency services** npl (fire,
police, ambulance) servizi mpl di pronto
intervento
emigrate ['ɛmɪgreɪt] vi emigrare;
emigration [ɛmɪ'greɪʃən] n emigrazione f
eminent ['ɛmɪnənt] adj eminente
emissions [ɪ'mɪʃənz] npl emissioni fpl
emit [ɪ'mɪt] vt emettere
emotion [ɪ'məuʃən] n emozione f;
emotional adj (person) emotivo(-a);
(scene) commovente; (tone, speech)
carico(-a) d'emozione
emperor ['ɛmpərəʳ] n imperatore m
emphasis ['ɛmfəsɪs] (pl **-ases**) n enfasi f
inv; importanza
emphasize ['ɛmfəsaɪz] vt (word, point)
sottolineare; (feature) mettere in evidenza
empire ['ɛmpaɪəʳ] n impero
employ [ɪm'plɔɪ] vt impiegare; **employee**
[-'i:] n impiegato(-a); **employer** n
principale m/f, datore m di lavoro;
employment n impiego; **employment
agency** n agenzia di collocamento

empower [ɪm'pauəʳ] vt **to ~ sb to do** concedere autorità a qn di fare

empress ['ɛmprɪs] n imperatrice f

emptiness ['ɛmptɪnɪs] n vuoto

empty ['ɛmptɪ] adj vuoto(-a); (threat, promise) vano(-a) ▷ vt vuotare ▷ vi vuotarsi; (liquid) scaricarsi; **empty-handed** adj a mani vuote

EMU n abbr (= economic and monetary union) unione f economica e monetaria

emulsion [ɪ'mʌlʃən] n emulsione f

enable [ɪ'neɪbl] vt **to ~ sb to do** permettere a qn di fare

enamel [ɪ'næməl] n smalto; (also: **~ paint**) vernice f a smalto

enchanting [ɪn'tʃɑːntɪŋ] adj incantevole, affascinante

encl. abbr (= enclosed) all.

enclose [ɪn'kləuz] vt (land) circondare, recingere; (letter etc) **to ~ (with)** allegare (con); **please find ~d** trovi qui accluso

enclosure [ɪn'kləuʒəʳ] n recinto

encore [ɔŋ'kɔːʳ] excl bis ▷ n bis m inv

encounter [ɪn'kauntəʳ] n incontro ▷ vt incontrare

encourage [ɪn'kʌrɪdʒ] vt incoraggiare; **encouragement** n incoraggiamento

encouraging [ɪn'kʌrɪdʒɪŋ] adj incoraggiante

encyclop(a)edia [ɛnsaɪkləu'piːdɪə] n enciclopedia

end [ɛnd] n fine f; (aim) fine m; (of table) bordo estremo; (of pointed object) punta ▷ vt finire; (also: **bring to an ~, put an ~ to**) mettere fine a ▷ vi finire; **in the ~** alla fine; **on ~** (object) ritto(-a); **to stand on ~** (hair) rizzarsi; **for hours on ~** per ore ed ore; **end up** vi **to ~ up in** finire in

endanger [ɪn'deɪndʒəʳ] vt mettere in pericolo

endearing [ɪn'dɪərɪŋ] adj accattivante

endeavour [ɪn'dɛvəʳ] (US **endeavor**) n sforzo, tentativo ▷ vi **to ~ to do** cercare or sforzarsi di fare

ending ['ɛndɪŋ] n fine f, conclusione f; (Ling) desinenza

endless ['ɛndlɪs] adj senza fine

endorse [ɪn'dɔːs] vt (cheque) girare; (approve) approvare, appoggiare; **endorsement** n approvazione f; (on driving licence) contravvenzione registrata sulla patente

endurance [ɪn'djuərəns] n resistenza; pazienza

endure [ɪn'djuəʳ] vt sopportare, resistere a ▷ vi durare

enemy ['ɛnəmɪ] adj, n nemico(-a)

energetic [ɛnə'dʒɛtɪk] adj energico(-a), attivo(-a)

energy ['ɛnədʒɪ] n energia

enforce [ɪn'fɔːs] vt (Law) applicare, far osservare

engaged [ɪn'geɪdʒd] adj (BRIT: busy, in use) occupato(-a); (betrothed) fidanzato(-a); **the line's ~** la linea è occupata; **to get ~** fidanzarsi; **engaged tone** (BRIT) n (Tel) segnale m di occupato

engagement [ɪn'geɪdʒmənt] n impegno, obbligo; appuntamento; (to marry) fidanzamento; **engagement ring** n anello di fidanzamento

engaging [ɪn'geɪdʒɪŋ] adj attraente

engine ['ɛndʒɪn] n (Aut) motore m; (Rail) locomotiva

engineer [ɛndʒɪ'nɪəʳ] n ingegnere m; (BRIT: for repairs) tecnico; (on ship: US: Rail) macchinista m; **engineering** n ingegneria

England ['ɪŋglənd] n Inghilterra

English ['ɪŋglɪʃ] adj inglese ▷ n (Ling) inglese m; **the ~** npl gli Inglesi; **English Channel** n **the English Channel** la Manica; **Englishman** (irreg) n inglese m; **Englishwoman** (irreg) n inglese f

engrave [ɪn'greɪv] vt incidere

engraving [ɪn'greɪvɪŋ] n incisione f

enhance [ɪn'hɑːns] vt accrescere

enjoy [ɪn'dʒɔɪ] vt godere; (have: success, fortune) avere; **to ~ o.s.** godersela, divertirsi; **enjoyable** adj piacevole; **enjoyment** n piacere m, godimento

enlarge [ɪn'lɑːdʒ] vt ingrandire ▷ vi **to ~ on** (subject) dilungarsi su; **enlargement** n (Phot) ingrandimento

enlist [ɪn'lɪst] vt arruolare; (support) procurare ▷ vi arruolarsi

enormous [ɪ'nɔːməs] adj enorme

enough [ɪ'nʌf] adj, n: **~ time/books** assai tempo/libri; **have you got ~?** ne ha abbastanza or a sufficienza? ▷ adv **big ~** abbastanza grande; **he has not worked ~** non ha lavorato abbastanza; **~!** basta!; **that's ~, thanks** basta così, grazie; **I've had ~ of him** ne ho abbastanza di lui; **... which, funnily** or **oddly ~** ... che, strano a dirsi

enquire [ɪn'kwaɪəʳ] vt, vi (esp BRIT) **= inquire**

enquiry [ɪn'kwaɪərɪ] n (esp BRIT) **= inquiry**

enrage [ɪn'reɪdʒ] vt fare arrabbiare

enrich [ɪn'rɪtʃ] vt arricchire

enrol [ɪn'rəul] (US **enroll**) vt iscrivere ▷ vi iscriversi; **enrolment** (US **enrollment**) n iscrizione f

en route [ɔn'ruːt] adv **~ for/from/to** in viaggio per/da/a

en suite [ɔn'swiːt] adj **room with ~**

bathroom camera con bagno

ensure [ɪnˈʃʊəʳ] vt assicurare; garantire

entail [ɪnˈteɪl] vt comportare

enter [ˈɛntəʳ] vt entrare in; (army) arruolarsi in; (competition) partecipare a; (sb for a competition) iscrivere; (write down) registrare; (Comput) inserire ▷ vi entrare

enterprise [ˈɛntəpraɪz] n (undertaking, company) impresa; (spirit) iniziativa; **free ~** liberalismo economico; **private ~** iniziativa privata; **enterprising** [ˈɛntəpraɪzɪŋ] adj intraprendente

entertain [ɛntəˈteɪn] vt divertire; (invite) ricevere; (idea, plan) nutrire; **entertainer** n comico(-a); **entertaining** adj divertente; **entertainment** n (amusement) divertimento; (show) spettacolo

enthusiasm [ɪnˈθuːzɪæzəm] n entusiasmo

enthusiast [ɪnˈθuːzɪæst] n entusiasta m/f; **enthusiastic** [-ˈæstɪk] adj entusiasta, entusiastico(-a); **to be enthusiastic about sth/sb** essere appassionato(-a) di qc/entusiasta di qn

entire [ɪnˈtaɪəʳ] adj intero(-a); **entirely** adv completamente, interamente

entitle [ɪnˈtaɪtl] vt (give right): **to ~ sb to sth/to do** dare diritto a qn a qc/a fare; **entitled** adj (book) che si intitola; **to be entitled to do** avere il diritto di fare

entrance [n ˈɛntrns, vb ɪnˈtrɑːns] n entrata, ingresso; (of person) entrata ▷ vt incantare, rapire; **where's the ~?** dov'è l'entrata?; **to gain ~ to** (university etc) essere ammesso a; **entrance examination** n esame m di ammissione; **entrance fee** n tassa d'iscrizione; (to museum etc) prezzo d'ingresso; **entrance ramp** (us) n (Aut) rampa di accesso; **entrant** [ˈɛntrnt] n partecipante m/f; concorrente m/f

entrepreneur [ɔntrəprəˈnəːʳ] n imprenditore m

entrust [ɪnˈtrʌst] vt **to ~ sth to** affidare qc a

entry [ˈɛntrɪ] n entrata; (way in) entrata, ingresso; (item: on list) iscrizione f; (in dictionary) voce f; **no ~** vietato l'ingresso; (Aut) divieto di accesso; **entry phone** n citofono

envelope [ˈɛnvələup] n busta

envious [ˈɛnvɪəs] adj invidioso(-a)

environment [ɪnˈvaɪərnmənt] n ambiente m; **environmental** [-ˈmɛntl] adj ecologico(-a); ambientale; **environmentally** [ɪnvaɪərənˈmɛntəlɪ] adv **environmentally sound/friendly** che rispetta l'ambiente

envisage [ɪnˈvɪzɪdʒ] vt immaginare;

prevedere

envoy [ˈɛnvɔɪ] n inviato(-a)

envy [ˈɛnvɪ] n invidia ▷ vt invidiare; **to ~ sb sth** invidiare qn per qc

epic [ˈɛpɪk] n poema m epico ▷ adj epico(-a)

epidemic [ɛpɪˈdɛmɪk] n epidemia

epilepsy [ˈɛpɪlɛpsɪ] n epilessia

epileptic [ɛpɪˈlɛptɪk] adj, n epilettico(-a); **epileptic fit** n attacco epilettico

episode [ˈɛpɪsəud] n episodio

equal [ˈiːkwl] adj uguale ▷ n pari m/f inv ▷ vt uguagliare; **~ to** (task) all'altezza di; **equality** [iːˈkwɔlɪtɪ] n uguaglianza; **equalize** vi pareggiare; **equally** adv ugualmente

equation [ɪˈkweɪʃən] n (Math) equazione f

equator [ɪˈkweɪtəʳ] n equatore m

equip [ɪˈkwɪp] vt equipaggiare, attrezzare; **to ~ sb/sth with** fornire qn/qc di; **to be well ~ped** (office etc) essere ben attrezzato(-a); **he is well ~ped for the job** ha i requisiti necessari per quel lavoro; **equipment** n attrezzatura; (electrical etc) apparecchiatura

equivalent [ɪˈkwɪvələnt] adj equivalente ▷ n equivalente m; **to be ~ to** equivalere a

ER abbr (BRIT) = **Elizabeth Regina** (US: Med) = **emergency room**

era [ˈɪərə] n era, età f inv

erase [ɪˈreɪz] vt cancellare; **eraser** n gomma

erect [ɪˈrɛkt] adj eretto(-a) ▷ vt costruire; (assemble) montare; **erection** [ɪˈrɛkʃən] n costruzione f; montaggio; (Physiol) erezione f

ERM n (= Exchange Rate Mechanism) ERM m

erode [ɪˈrəud] vt erodere; (metal) corrodere

erosion [ɪˈrəuʒən] n erosione f

erotic [ɪˈrɔtɪk] adj erotico(-a)

errand [ˈɛrnd] n commissione f

erratic [ɪˈrætɪk] adj imprevedibile; (person, mood) incostante

error [ˈɛrəʳ] n errore m

erupt [ɪˈrʌpt] vi (volcano) mettersi (or essere) in eruzione; (war, crisis) scoppiare; **eruption** [ɪˈrʌpʃən] n eruzione f; scoppio

escalate [ˈɛskəleɪt] vi intensificarsi

escalator [ˈɛskəleɪtəʳ] n scala mobile

escape [ɪˈskeɪp] n evasione f; fuga; (of gas etc) fuga, fuoriuscita ▷ vi fuggire; (from jail) evadere, scappare; (leak) uscire ▷ vt sfuggire a; **to ~ from** (place) fuggire da; (person) sfuggire a

escort [n ˈɛskɔːt, vb ɪˈskɔːt] n scorta; (male companion) cavaliere m ▷ vt scortare; accompagnare

especially [ɪˈspɛʃlɪ] adv specialmente;

soprattutto; espressamente

espionage ['ɛspɪənɑːʒ] n spionaggio

essay ['ɛseɪ] n (Scol) composizione f; (Literature) saggio

essence ['ɛsns] n essenza

essential [ɪ'sɛnʃl] adj essenziale ▷ n elemento essenziale; **essentially** adv essenzialmente; **essentials** npl **the essentials** l'essenziale msg

establish [ɪ'stæblɪʃ] vt stabilire; (business) mettere su; (one's power etc) affermare; **establishment** n stabilimento; **the Establishment** la classe dirigente, l'establishment m

estate [ɪ'steɪt] n proprietà f inv; beni mpl, patrimonio; (BRIT: also: **housing ~**) complesso edilizio; **estate agent** (BRIT) n agente m immobiliare; **estate car** (BRIT) n giardiniera

estimate [n 'ɛstɪmət, vb 'ɛstɪmeɪt] n stima; (Comm) preventivo ▷ vt stimare, valutare

etc abbr (= et cetera) etc., ecc.

eternal [ɪ'təːnl] adj eterno(-a)

eternity [ɪ'təːnɪtɪ] n eternità

ethical ['ɛθɪkl] adj etico(-a), morale; **ethics** ['ɛθɪks] n etica ▷ npl morale f

Ethiopia [iːθɪ'əupɪə] n Etiopia

ethnic ['ɛθnɪk] adj etnico(-a); **ethnic minority** n minoranza etnica

etiquette ['ɛtɪkɛt] n etichetta

EU n abbr (= European Union) UE f

euro ['juərəu] n (currency) euro m inv

Europe ['juərəp] n Europa; **European** [-'piːən] adj, n europeo(-a); **European Community** n Comunità Europea; **European Union** n Unione f europea

Eurostar® ['juərəustɑːʳ] n Eurostar® m inv

evacuate [ɪ'vækjueɪt] vt evacuare

evade [ɪ'veɪd] vt (tax) evadere; (duties etc) sottrarsi a; (person) schivare

evaluate [ɪ'væljueɪt] vt valutare

evaporate [ɪ'væpəreɪt] vi evaporare

eve [iːv] n **on the ~ of** alla vigilia di

even ['iːvn] adj regolare; (number) pari inv ▷ adv anche, perfino; **~ if, ~ though** anche se; **~ more** ancora di più; **~ so** ciò nonostante; **not ~** nemmeno; **to get ~ with sb** dare la pari a qn

evening ['iːvnɪŋ] n sera; (as duration, event) serata; **in the ~** la sera; **evening class** n corso serale; **evening dress** n (woman's) abito da sera; **in evening dress** (man) in abito scuro; (woman) in abito lungo

event [ɪ'vɛnt] n avvenimento; (Sport) gara; **in the ~ of** in caso di; **eventful** adj denso(-a) di eventi

eventual [ɪ'vɛntʃuəl] adj finale

⬛ Be careful not to translate **eventual** by the Italian word **eventuale**.

eventually [ɪ'vɛntʃuəlɪ] adv alla fine

⬛ Be careful not to translate **eventually** by the Italian word **eventualmente**.

ever ['ɛvəʳ] adv mai; (at all times) sempre; **the best ~** il migliore che ci sia mai stato; **have you ~ seen it?** l'ha mai visto?; **~ since** adv da allora ▷ conj sin da quando; **~ so pretty** così bello(-a); **evergreen** n sempreverde m

every ['ɛvrɪ] adj ogni; **~ day** tutti i giorni, ogni giorno; **~ other/third day** ogni due/tre giorni; **~ other car** una macchina su due; **~ now and then** ogni tanto, di quando in quando; **everybody** pron = **everyone**; **everyday** adj quotidiano(-a); di ogni giorno; **everyone** pron ognuno, tutti pl; **everything** pron tutto, ogni cosa; **everywhere** adv (gen) dappertutto; (wherever) ovunque

evict [ɪ'vɪkt] vt sfrattare

evidence ['ɛvɪdns] n (proof) prova; (of witness) testimonianza; (sign) **to show ~ of** dare segni di; **to give ~** deporre

evident ['ɛvɪdnt] adj evidente; **evidently** adv evidentemente

evil ['iːvl] adj cattivo(-a), maligno(-a) ▷ n male m

evoke [ɪ'vəuk] vt evocare

evolution [iːvə'luːʃən] n evoluzione f

evolve [ɪ'vɔlv] vt elaborare ▷ vi svilupparsi, evolversi

ewe [juː] n pecora

ex (inf) [ɛks] n **my ex** il (la) mio(-a) ex

ex- [ɛks] prefix ex

exact [ɪg'zækt] adj esatto(-a) ▷ vt **to ~ sth (from)** estorcere qc (da); esigere qc (da); **exactly** adv esattamente

exaggerate [ɪg'zædʒəreɪt] vt, vi esagerare; **exaggeration** [-'reɪʃən] n esagerazione f

exam [ɪg'zæm] n abbr (Scol) = **examination**

examination [ɪgzæmɪ'neɪʃən] n (Scol) esame m; (Med) controllo

examine [ɪg'zæmɪn] vt esaminare; **examiner** n esaminatore(-trice)

example [ɪg'zɑːmpl] n esempio; **for ~** ad or per esempio

exasperated [ɪg'zɑːspəreɪtɪd] adj esasperato(-a)

excavate ['ɛkskəveɪt] vt scavare

exceed [ɪk'siːd] vt superare; (one's powers, time limit) oltrepassare; **exceedingly** adv eccessivamente

excel [ɪk'sɛl] vi eccellere ▷ vt sorpassare; **to ~ o.s** (BRIT) superare se stesso

excellence ['ɛksələns] n eccellenza

excellent ['ɛksələnt] *adj* eccellente

except [ɪk'sɛpt] *prep (also:* **~ for, ~ing)** salvo, all'infuori di, eccetto ▷ *vt* escludere; **~ if/when** salvo se/quando; **~ that** salvo che; **exception** [ɪk'sɛpʃən] *n* eccezione f; **to take exception to** trovare a ridire su; **exceptional** [ɪk'sɛpʃənl] *adj* eccezionale; **exceptionally** [ɪk'sɛpʃənəlɪ] *adv* eccezionalmente

excerpt ['ɛksəːpt] *n* estratto

excess [ɪk'sɛs] *n* eccesso; **excess baggage** *n* bagaglio in eccedenza; **excessive** *adj* eccessivo(-a)

exchange [ɪks'tʃeɪndʒ] *n* scambio; *(also:* **telephone ~)** centralino ▷ *vt* to **~ (for)** scambiare (con); **could I ~ this, please?** posso cambiarlo, per favore?; **exchange rate** *n* tasso di cambio

excite [ɪk'saɪt] *vt* eccitare; **to get ~d** eccitarsi; **excited** *adj* **to get excited** essere elettrizzato(-a); **excitement** *n* eccitazione f; agitazione f; **exciting** *adj* avventuroso(-a); *(film, book)* appassionante

exclaim [ɪk'skleɪm] *vi* esclamare; **exclamation** [ɛksklə'meɪʃən] *n* esclamazione f; **exclamation mark** (us **exclamation point**) *n* punto esclamativo

exclude [ɪk'skluːd] *vt* escludere

excluding [ɪk'skluːdɪŋ] *prep* **~ VAT** IVA esclusa

exclusion [ɪk'skluːʒən] *n* esclusione f; **to the ~ of** escludendo

exclusive [ɪk'skluːsɪv] *adj* esclusivo(-a); **~ of VAT** I.V.A. esclusa; **exclusively** *adv* esclusivamente

excruciating [ɪk'skruːʃɪeɪtɪŋ] *adj* straziante, atroce

excursion [ɪk'skəːʃən] *n* escursione f, gita

excuse [*n* ɪk'skjuːs, *vb* ɪk'skjuːz] *n* scusa ▷ *vt* scusare; **to ~ sb from** *(activity)* dispensare qn da; **~ me!** mi scusi!; **now, if you will ~ me …** ora, mi scusi ma …

ex-directory ['ɛksdɪ'rɛktərɪ] (BRIT) *adj* *(Tel)* **to be ~** non essere sull'elenco

execute ['ɛksɪkjuːt] *vt* *(prisoner)* giustiziare; *(plan etc)* eseguire; **execution** [ɛksɪ'kjuːʃən] *n* esecuzione f

executive [ɪg'zɛkjutɪv] *n* *(Comm)* dirigente *m*; *(Pol)* esecutivo *m* ▷ *adj* esecutivo(-a)

exempt [ɪg'zɛmpt] *adj* esentato(-a) ▷ *vt* **to ~ sb from** esentare qn da

exercise ['ɛksəsaɪz] *n* *(keep fit)* moto; *(Scol, Mil etc)* esercizio ▷ *vt* esercitare; *(patience)* usare; *(dog)* portar fuori ▷ *vi* *(also:* **take ~)** fare del moto; **exercise book** *n* quaderno

exert [ɪg'zəːt] *vt* esercitare; **to ~ o.s.** sforzarsi; **exertion** [-ʃən] *n* sforzo

exhale [ɛks'heɪl] *vt, vi* espirare

exhaust [ɪg'zɔːst] *n* *(also:* **~ fumes)** scappamento; *(also:* **~ pipe)** tubo di scappamento ▷ *vt* esaurire; **exhausted** *adj* esaurito(-a); **exhaustion** [ɪg'zɔːstʃən] *n* esaurimento; **nervous exhaustion** sovraffaticamento mentale

exhibit [ɪg'zɪbɪt] *n* *(Art)* oggetto esposto; *(Law)* documento *or* oggetto esibito ▷ *vt* esporre; *(courage, skill)* dimostrare; **exhibition** [ɛksɪ'bɪʃən] *n* mostra, esposizione f

exhilarating [ɪg'zɪləreɪtɪŋ] *adj* esilarante; stimolante

exile ['ɛksaɪl] *n* esilio; *(person)* esiliato(-a) ▷ *vt* esiliare

exist [ɪg'zɪst] *vi* esistere; **existence** *n* esistenza; **existing** *adj* esistente

exit ['ɛksɪt] *n* uscita ▷ *vi* *(Theatre, Comput)* uscire; **where's the ~?** dov'è l'uscita?; **exit ramp** (us) *n* *(Aut)* rampa di uscita

exotic [ɪg'zɔtɪk] *adj* esotico(-a)

expand [ɪk'spænd] *vt* espandere; estendere; allargare ▷ *vi* *(business, gas)* espandersi; *(metal)* dilatarsi

expansion [ɪk'spænʃən] *n* *(gen)* espansione f; *(of town, economy)* sviluppo; *(of metal)* dilatazione f

expect [ɪk'spɛkt] *vt* *(anticipate)* prevedere, aspettarsi, prevedere *or* aspettarsi che + *sub*; *(require)* richiedere, esigere; *(suppose)* supporre; *(await, also baby)* aspettare ▷ *vi* **to be ~ing** essere in stato interessante; **to ~ sb to do** aspettarsi che qn faccia; **expectation** [ɛkspɛk'teɪʃən] *n* aspettativa; speranza

expedition [ɛkspə'dɪʃən] *n* spedizione f

expel [ɪk'spɛl] *vt* espellere

expenditure [ɪk'spɛndɪtʃəˊ] *n* spesa

expense [ɪk'spɛns] *n* spesa; *(high cost)* costo; **~s** *npl* *(Comm)* spese *fpl*, indennità *fpl*; **at the ~ of** a spese di; **expense account** *n* conto *m* spese *inv*

expensive [ɪk'spɛnsɪv] *adj* caro(-a), costoso(-a); **it's too ~** è troppo caro

experience [ɪk'spɪərɪəns] *n* esperienza ▷ *vt* *(pleasure)* provare; *(hardship)* soffrire; **experienced** *adj* esperto(-a)

experiment [*n* ɪk'spɛrɪmənt, *vb* ɪk'spɛrɪmɛnt] *n* esperimento, esperienza ▷ *vi* **to ~ (with/on)** fare esperimenti (con/su); **experimental** [ɪkspɛrɪ'mɛntl] *adj* sperimentale; **at the experimental stage** in via di sperimentazione

expert ['ɛkspəːt] *adj, n* esperto(-a); **expertise** [-'tiːz] *n* competenza

expire [ɪk'spaɪəˊ] *vi* *(period of time, licence)* scadere; **expiry** *n* scadenza; **expiry date** *n* *(of medicine, food item)* data di scadenza

explain [ɪk'spleɪn] *vt* spiegare;

explicit | 272

explanation [ɛksplə'neɪʃən] n
spiegazione f
explicit [ɪk'splɪsɪt] adj esplicito(-a)
explode [ɪk'spləʊd] vi esplodere
exploit [n 'ɛksplɔɪt, vb ɪk'splɔɪt] n impresa
▷ vt sfruttare; **exploitation** [-'teɪʃən] n
sfruttamento
explore [ɪk'splɔːʳ] vt esplorare;
(possibilities) esaminare; **explorer** n
esploratore(-trice)
explosion [ɪk'spləʊʒən] n esplosione f;
explosive [ɪk'spləʊsɪv] adj esplosivo(-a)
▷ n esplosivo
export [vb ɛk'spɔːt, n 'ɛkspɔːt] vt
esportare ▷ n esportazione f; articolo
di esportazione ▷ cpd d'esportazione;
exporter n esportatore m
expose [ɪk'spəʊz] vt esporre; (unmask)
smascherare; **exposed** adj (position)
esposto(-a); **exposure** [ɪk'spəʊʒəʳ]
n esposizione f; (Phot) posa; (Med)
assideramento
express [ɪk'sprɛs] adj (definite) chiaro(-a),
espresso(-a); (BRIT: letter etc) espresso
inv ▷ n (train) espresso ▷ vt esprimere;
expression [ɪk'sprɛʃən] n espressione
f; **expressway** (US) n (urban motorway)
autostrada che attraversa la città
exquisite [ɛk'skwɪzɪt] adj squisito(-a)
extend [ɪk'stɛnd] vt (visit) protrarre; (road,
deadline) prolungare; (building) ampliare;
(offer) offrire, porgere ▷ vi (land, period)
estendersi; **extension** [ɪk'stɛnʃən] n (of
road, term) prolungamento; (of contract,
deadline) proroga; (building) annesso;
(to wire, table) prolunga; (telephone)
interno; (: in private house) apparecchio
supplementare; **extension lead** n
prolunga
extensive [ɪk'stɛnsɪv] adj esteso(-a),
ampio(-a); (damage) su larga scala;
(coverage, discussion) esauriente; (use)
grande
extent [ɪk'stɛnt] n estensione f; **to some ~**
fino a un certo punto; **to such an ~ that ...**
a un tal punto che ...; **to what ~?** fino a che
punto?; **to the ~ of ...** fino al punto di ...
exterior [ɛk'stɪərɪəʳ] adj esteriore,
esterno(-a) ▷ n esteriore m, esterno;
aspetto (esteriore)
external [ɛk'stɜːnl] adj esterno(-a),
esteriore
extinct [ɪk'stɪŋkt] adj estinto(-a);
extinction [ɪk'stɪŋkʃən] n estinzione f
extinguish [ɪk'stɪŋgwɪʃ] vt estinguere
extra ['ɛkstrə] adj extra inv, supplementare
▷ adv (in addition) di più ▷ n extra m inv;
(surcharge) supplemento; (Cinema, Theatre)
comparsa

extract [vb ɪk'strækt, n 'ɛkstrækt] vt
estrarre; (money, promise) strappare ▷ n
estratto; (passage) brano
extradite ['ɛkstrədaɪt] vt estradare
extraordinary [ɪk'strɔːdnrɪ] adj
straordinario(-a)
extravagance [ɪk'strævəgəns] n
sperpero; stravaganza
extravagant [ɪk'strævəgənt] adj (lavish)
prodigo(-a); (wasteful) dispendioso(-a)
> Be careful not to translate
extravagant by the Italian word
stravagante.
extreme [ɪk'striːm] adj estremo(-a) ▷ n
estremo; **extremely** adv estremamente
extremist [ɪk'striːmɪst] adj, n estremista
(m/f)
extrovert ['ɛkstrəvəːt] n estroverso(-a)
eye [aɪ] n occhio; (of needle) cruna ▷ vt
osservare; **to keep an ~ on** tenere
d'occhio; **eyeball** n globo dell'occhio;
eyebrow n sopracciglio; **eyedrops** npl
gocce fpl oculari, collirio; **eyelash** n ciglio;
eyelid n palpebra; **eyeliner** n eye-liner
m inv; **eyeshadow** n ombretto; **eyesight**
n vista; **eye witness** n testimone m/f
oculare

F [ɛf] n (Mus) fa m
fabric ['fæbrɪk] n stoffa, tessuto
fabulous ['fæbjuləs] adj favoloso(-a);
(super) favoloso(-a), fantastico(-a)
face [feɪs] n faccia, viso, volto; (expression)
faccia; (of clock) quadrante m; (of building)
facciata ▷ vt essere di fronte a; (facts,
situation) affrontare; **~ down** a faccia in
giù; **to make** or **pull a ~** fare una smorfia;
in the ~ of (difficulties etc) di fronte a; **on
the ~ of it** a prima vista; **~ to ~** faccia a
faccia; **face up to** vt fus affrontare, far
fronte a; **face cloth** (BRIT) n guanto di
spugna; **face pack** n (BRIT) maschera di
bellezza
facial ['feɪʃəl] adj del viso
facilitate [fə'sɪlɪteɪt] vt facilitare
facilities [fə'sɪlɪtɪz] npl attrezzature fpl;
credit ~ facilitazioni fpl di credito
fact [fækt] n fatto; **in ~** in effetti
faction ['fækʃən] n fazione f
factor ['fæktə'] n fattore m; **I'd like a ~ 15
suntan lotion** vorrei una crema solare con
fattore di protezione 15
factory ['fæktərɪ] n fabbrica, stabilimento
Be careful not to translate *factory* by
the Italian word *fattoria*.
factual ['fæktjuəl] adj che si attiene ai fatti
faculty ['fækəltɪ] n facoltà f inv; (us) corpo
insegnante

fad [fæd] n mania; capriccio
fade [feɪd] vi sbiadire, sbiadirsi; (light,
sound, hope) attenuarsi, affievolirsi;
(flower) appassire; **fade away** vi (sound)
affievolirsi
fag [fæg] (BRIT: inf) n (cigarette) cicca
Fahrenheit ['fɑːrənhaɪt] n Fahrenheit
m inv
fail [feɪl] vt (exam) non superare; (candidate)
bocciare; (courage, memory) mancare a
▷ vi fallire; (student) essere respinto(-a);
(eyesight, health, light) venire a mancare; **to
~ to do sth** (neglect) mancare di fare qc; (be
unable) non riuscire a fare qc; **without ~**
senza fallo; certamente; **failing** n difetto
▷ prep in mancanza di; **failure** ['feɪljə'] n
fallimento; (person) fallito(-a); (mechanical
etc) guasto
faint [feɪnt] adj debole; (recollection)
vago(-a); (mark) indistinto(-a) ▷ n (Med)
svenimento ▷ vi svenire; **to feel ~** sentirsi
svenire; **faintest** adj **I haven't the
faintest idea** non ho la più pallida idea;
faintly adv debolmente; vagamente
fair [fɛə'] adj (person, decision) giusto(-a),
equo(-a); (quite large, quite good)
discreto(-a); (hair etc) biondo(-a); (skin,
complexion) chiaro(-a); (weather) bello(-a),
clemente ▷ adv (play) lealmente ▷ n fiera;
(BRIT: funfair) luna park m inv; **fairground** n
luna park m inv; **fair-haired** [fɛə'hɛəd] adj
(person) biondo(-a); **fairly** adv equamente;
(quite) abbastanza; **fairway** n (Golf)
fairway m inv
fairy ['fɛərɪ] n fata; **fairy tale** n fiaba
faith [feɪθ] n fede f; (trust) fiducia; (sect)
religione f, fede f; **faithful** adj fedele;
faithfully adv fedelmente; **yours
faithfully** (BRIT: in letters) distinti saluti
fake [feɪk] n imitazione f; (picture) falso;
(person) impostore(-a) ▷ adj falso(-a)
▷ vt (accounts) falsificare; (illness) fingere;
(painting) contraffare
falcon ['fɔːlkən] n falco, falcone m
fall [fɔːl] (pt **fell**, pp **fallen**) n caduta; (in
temperature) abbassamento; (in price)
ribasso; (us: autumn) autunno ▷ vi cadere;
(temperature, price, night) scendere; **~s** npl
(waterfall) cascate fpl; **to ~ flat** (on one's
face) cadere bocconi; (joke) fare cilecca;
(plan) fallire; **fall apart** vi cadere a pezzi;
fall down vi (person) cadere; (building)
crollare; **fall for** vt fus (person) prendere
una cotta per; **to ~ for a trick** (or a story
etc) cascarci; **fall off** vi cadere; (diminish)
diminuire, abbassarsi; **fall out** vi (hair,
teeth) cadere; (friends etc) litigare; **fall over**
vi cadere; **fall through** vi (plan, project)
fallire

fallen ['fɔːlən] pp of **fall**

fallout ['fɔːlaut] n fall-out m

false [fɔːls] adj falso(-a); **under ~ pretences** con l'inganno; **false alarm** n falso allarme m; **false teeth** (BRIT) npl denti mpl finti

fame [feɪm] n fama, celebrità

familiar [fə'mɪlɪə'] adj familiare; (close) intimo(-a); **to be ~ with** (subject) conoscere; **familiarize** [fə'mɪlɪəraɪz] vt **to familiarize o.s. with** familiarizzare con

family ['fæmɪlɪ] n famiglia; **family doctor** n medico di famiglia; **family planning** n pianificazione f familiare

famine ['fæmɪn] n carestia

famous ['feɪməs] adj famoso(-a)

fan [fæn] n (folding) ventaglio; (Elec) ventilatore m; (person) ammiratore(-trice), tifoso(-a) ▷ vt far vento a; (fire, quarrel) alimentare

fanatic [fə'nætɪk] n fanatico(-a)

fan belt n cinghia del ventilatore

fan club n fan club m inv

fancy ['fænsɪ] n immaginazione f, fantasia; (whim) capriccio ▷ adj (hat) stravagante; (hotel, food) speciale ▷ vt (feel like, want) aver voglia di; (imagine, think) immaginare; **to take a ~ to** incapricciarsi di; **he fancies her** (inf) gli piace; **fancy dress** n costume m (per maschera)

fan heater n (BRIT) stufa ad aria calda

fantasize ['fæntəsaɪz] vi fantasticare, sognare

fantastic [fæn'tæstɪk] adj fantastico(-a)

fantasy ['fæntəsɪ] n fantasia, immaginazione f; fantasticheria; chimera

fanzine ['fænziːn] n rivista specialistica (per appassionati)

FAQs abbr (= frequently asked questions) FAQ fpl

far [fɑː'] adj lontano(-a) ▷ adv lontano; (much, greatly) molto; **is it ~ from here?** è molto lontano da qui?; **how ~?** quanto lontano?; (referring to activity etc) fino a dove?; **how ~ is the town centre?** quanto dista il centro da qui?; **~ away, ~ off** lontano, distante; **~ better** assai migliore; **~ from** lontano da; **by ~** di gran lunga; **go as ~ as the farm** vada fino alla fattoria; **as ~ as I know** per quel che so

farce [fɑːs] n farsa

fare [fɛə'] n (on trains, buses) tariffa; (in taxi) prezzo della corsa; (food) vitto, cibo; **half ~** metà tariffa; **full ~** tariffa intera

Far East n **the ~** l'Estremo Oriente m

farewell [fɛə'wɛl] excl, n addio

farm [fɑːm] n fattoria, podere m ▷ vt coltivare; **farmer** n coltivatore(-trice), agricoltore(-trice); **farmhouse** n fattoria;

farming n (gen) agricoltura; (of crops) coltivazione f; (of animals) allevamento; **farmyard** n aia

far-reaching [fɑː'riːtʃɪŋ] adj di vasta portata

fart [fɑːt] (inf!) vi scoreggiare (!)

farther ['fɑːðə'] adv più lontano ▷ adj più lontano(-a)

farthest ['fɑːðɪst] superl of **far**

fascinate ['fæsɪneɪt] vt affascinare; **fascinated** adj affascinato(-a); **fascinating** adj affascinante; **fascination** [-'neɪʃən] n fascino

fascist ['fæʃɪst] adj, n fascista (m/f)

fashion ['fæʃən] n moda; (manner) maniera, modo ▷ vt foggiare, formare; **in ~** alla moda; **out of ~** passato(-a) di moda; **fashionable** adj alla moda, di moda; **fashion show** n sfilata di moda

fast [fɑːst] adj rapido(-a), svelto(-a), veloce; (clock): **to be ~** andare avanti; (dye, colour) solido(-a) ▷ adv rapidamente; (stuck, held) saldamente ▷ n digiuno ▷ vi digiunare; **~ asleep** profondamente addormentato

fasten ['fɑːsn] vt chiudere, fissare; (coat) abbottonare, allacciare ▷ vi chiudersi, fissarsi; abbottonarsi, allacciarsi

fast food n fast food m

fat [fæt] adj grasso(-a); (book, profit etc) grosso(-a) ▷ n grasso

fatal ['feɪtl] adj fatale; mortale; disastroso(-a); **fatality** [fə'tælɪtɪ] n (road death etc) morto(-a), vittima; **fatally** adv a morte

fate [feɪt] n destino; (of person) sorte f

father ['fɑːðə'] n padre m; **Father Christmas** n Babbo Natale; **father-in-law** n suocero

fatigue [fə'tiːg] n stanchezza

fattening ['fætnɪŋ] adj (food) che fa ingrassare

fatty ['fætɪ] adj (food) grasso(-a) ▷ n (inf) ciccione(-a)

faucet ['fɔːsɪt] (US) n rubinetto

fault [fɔːlt] n colpa; (Tennis) fallo; (defect) difetto; (Geo) faglia ▷ vt criticare; **it's my ~** è colpa mia; **to find ~ with** trovare da ridire su; **at ~** in fallo; **faulty** adj difettoso(-a)

fauna ['fɔːnə] n fauna

favour etc ['feɪvə'] (US **favor**) n favore m ▷ vt (proposition) favorire, essere favorevole a; (pupil etc) favorire; (team, horse) dare per vincente; **to do sb a ~** fare un favore or una cortesia a qn; **to find ~ with** (person) entrare nelle buone grazie di; (: suggestion) avere l'approvazione di; **in ~ of** in favore di; **favourable** adj favorevole; **favourite** [-rɪt] adj, n favorito(-a)

fawn [fɔːn] n daino ▷ adj (also: **~-coloured**) marrone chiaro inv ▷ vi **to ~ (up)on** adulare servilmente

fax [fæks] n (document) facsimile m inv, telecopia; (machine) telecopiatrice f ▷ vt telecopiare, trasmettere in facsimile

FBI (us) n abbr (= Federal Bureau of Investigation) F.B.I. f

fear [fɪər] n paura, timore m ▷ vt aver paura di, temere; **for ~ of** per paura di; **fearful** adj pauroso(-a); (sight, noise) terribile, spaventoso(-a); **fearless** adj intrepido(-a), senza paura

feasible ['fiːzəbl] adj possibile, realizzabile

feast [fiːst] n festa, banchetto; (Rel: also: **~ day**) festa ▷ vi banchettare

feat [fiːt] n impresa, fatto insigne

feather ['fɛðər] n penna

feature ['fiːtʃər] n caratteristica; (Press, TV) articolo ▷ vt (film) avere come protagonista ▷ vi figurare; **~s** npl (of face) fisionomia; **feature film** n film m inv principale

Feb. [fɛb] abbr (= February) feb

February ['fɛbruərɪ] n febbraio

fed [fɛd] pt, pp of **feed**

federal ['fɛdərəl] adj federale

federation [fɛdə'reɪʃən] n federazione f

fed up adj **to be ~** essere stufo(-a)

fee [fiː] n pagamento; (of doctor, lawyer) onorario; (for examination) tassa d'esame; **school ~s** tasse fpl scolastiche

feeble ['fiːbl] adj debole

feed [fiːd] (pt, pp **fed**) n (of baby) pappa; (of animal) mangime m; (on printer) meccanismo di alimentazione ▷ vt nutrire; (baby) allattare; (horse etc) dare da mangiare a; (fire, machine) alimentare; (data, information) **to ~ into** inserire in; **feedback** n feed-back m

feel [fiːl] (pt, pp **felt**) n consistenza; (sense of touch) tatto ▷ vt toccare; palpare; tastare; (cold, pain, anger) sentire; (think, believe): **to ~ (that)** pensare che; **to ~ hungry/cold** aver fame/freddo; **to ~ lonely/better** sentirsi solo/meglio; **I don't ~ well** non mi sento bene; **it ~s soft** è morbido al tatto; **to ~ like** (want) aver voglia di; **to ~ about** or **around for** cercare a tastoni; **feeling** n sensazione f; (emotion) sentimento

feet [fiːt] npl of **foot**

fell [fɛl] pt of **fall** ▷ vt (tree) abbattere

fellow ['fɛləu] n individuo, tipo; compagno; (of learned society) membro cpd; **fellow citizen** n concittadino(-a); **fellow countryman** (irreg) n compatriota m; **fellow men** npl simili mpl; **fellowship** n associazione f; compagnia; specie di borsa di studio universitaria

felony ['fɛlənɪ] n reato, crimine m

felt [fɛlt] pt, pp of **feel** ▷ n feltro

female ['fiːmeɪl] n (Zool) femmina; (pej: woman) donna, femmina ▷ adj (Biol, Elec) femmina inv; (sex, character) femminile; (vote etc) di donne

feminine ['fɛmɪnɪn] adj femminile

feminist ['fɛmɪnɪst] n femminista m/f

fence [fɛns] n recinto ▷ vt (also: **~ in**) recingere ▷ vi (Sport) tirare di scherma; **fencing** n (Sport) scherma

fend [fɛnd] vi **to ~ for o.s.** arrangiarsi; **fend off** vt (attack, questions) respingere, difendersi da

fender ['fɛndər] n parafuoco; (on boat) parabordo; (us) parafango; paraurti m inv

fennel ['fɛnl] n finocchio

ferment [vb fə'mɛnt, n 'fəːmɛnt] vi fermentare ▷ n (fig) agitazione f, eccitazione f

fern [fəːn] n felce f

ferocious [fə'rəuʃəs] adj feroce

ferret ['fɛrɪt] n furetto

ferry ['fɛrɪ] n (small) traghetto m; (large: also: **~boat**) nave f traghetto inv ▷ vt traghettare

fertile ['fəːtaɪl] adj fertile; (Biol) fecondo(-a); **fertilize** ['fəːtɪlaɪz] vt fertilizzare; fecondare; **fertilizer** ['fəːtɪlaɪzə] n fertilizzante m

festival ['fɛstɪvəl] n (Rel) festa; (Art, Mus) festival m inv

festive ['fɛstɪv] adj di festa; **the ~ season** (BRIT: Christmas) il periodo delle feste

fetch [fɛtʃ] vt andare a prendere; (sell for) essere venduto(-a) per

fête [feɪt] n festa

fetus ['fiːtəs] (us) n = **foetus**

feud [fjuːd] n contesa, lotta

fever ['fiːvər] n febbre f; **feverish** adj febbrile

few [fjuː] adj pochi(-e); **a ~** adj qualche inv ▷ pron alcuni(-e); **fewer** adj meno inv, meno numerosi(-e); **fewest** adj il minor numero di

fiancé [fɪ'ãːŋseɪ] n fidanzato; **fiancée** n fidanzata

fiasco [fɪ'æskəu] n fiasco

fib [fɪb] n piccola bugia

fibre ['faɪbər] (us **fiber**) n fibra; **Fibreglass®** ['faɪbəglɑːs] (us **fiberglass**) n fibra di vetro

fickle ['fɪkl] adj incostante, capriccioso(-a)

fiction ['fɪkʃən] n narrativa, romanzi mpl; (sth made up) finzione f; **fictional** adj immaginario(-a)

fiddle ['fɪdl] n (Mus) violino; (cheating) imbroglio; truffa ▷ vt (BRIT: accounts) falsificare, falsare; **fiddle with** vt fus gingillarsi con

fidelity [fɪ'dɛlɪtɪ] n fedeltà; (*accuracy*) esattezza

field [fiːld] n campo; **field marshal** n feldmaresciallo

fierce [fɪəs] adj (*animal, person, fighting*) feroce; (*loyalty*) assoluto(-a); (*wind*) furioso(-a); (*heat*) intenso(-a)

fifteen [fɪf'tiːn] num quindici; **fifteenth** num quindicesimo(-a)

fifth [fɪfθ] num quinto(-a)

fiftieth ['fɪftɪɪθ] num cinquantesimo(-a)

fifty ['fɪftɪ] num cinquanta; **fifty-fifty** adj **a fifty-fifty chance** una possibilità su due ▷ adv fifty-fifty, metà per ciascuno

fig [fɪg] n fico

fight [faɪt] (pt, pp **fought**) n zuffa, rissa; (*Mil*) battaglia, combattimento; (*against cancer etc*) lotta ▷ vt (*person*) azzuffarsi con; (*enemy: also Mil*) combattere; (*cancer, alcoholism, emotion*) lottare contro, combattere; (*election*) partecipare a ▷ vi combattere; **fight back** vi difendersi; (*Sport, after illness*) riprendersi ▷ vt (*tears*) ricacciare; **fight off** vt (*attack, attacker*) respingere; (*disease, sleep, urge*) lottare contro; **fighting** n combattimento

figure ['fɪgə'] n figura; (*number, cipher*) cifra ▷ vt (*think: esp US*) pensare ▷ vi (*appear*) figurare; **figure out** vt riuscire a capire; calcolare

file [faɪl] n (*tool*) lima; (*dossier*) incartamento; (*folder*) cartellina; (*Comput*) archivio; (*row*) fila ▷ vt (*nails, wood*) limare; (*papers*) archiviare; (*Law: claim*) presentare; passare agli atti; **filing cabinet** ['faɪlɪŋ-] n casellario

Filipino [fɪlɪ'piːnəu] n filippino(-a); (*Ling*) tagal m

fill [fɪl] vt riempire; (*job*) coprire ▷ n **to eat one's ~** mangiare a sazietà; **fill in** vt (*hole*) riempire; (*form*) compilare; **fill out** vt (*form, receipt*) riempire; **fill up** vt riempire; **~ it up, please** (*Aut*) il pieno, per favore

fillet ['fɪlɪt] n filetto; **fillet steak** n bistecca di filetto

filling ['fɪlɪŋ] n (*Culin*) impasto, ripieno; (*for tooth*) otturazione f; **filling station** n stazione f di rifornimento

film [fɪlm] n (*Cinema*) film m inv; (*Phot*) pellicola, rullino; (*of powder, liquid*) sottile strato ▷ vt, vi girare; **I'd like a 36-exposure ~** vorrei un rullino da 36 pose; **film star** n divo(-a) dello schermo

filter ['fɪltə'] n filtro ▷ vt filtrare; **filter lane** (*BRIT*) n (*Aut*) corsia di svincolo

filth [fɪlθ] n sporcizia; **filthy** adj lordo(-a), sozzo(-a); (*language*) osceno(-a)

fin [fɪn] n (*of fish*) pinna

final ['faɪnl] adj finale, ultimo(-a); definitivo(-a) ▷ n (*Sport*) finale f; **~s** npl (*Scol*) esami mpl finali; **finale** [fɪ'nɑːlɪ] n finale m; **finalist** ['faɪnəlɪst] n (*Sport*) finalista m/f; **finalize** ['faɪnəlaɪz] vt mettere a punto; **finally** ['faɪnəlɪ] adv (*lastly*) alla fine; (*eventually*) finalmente

finance [faɪ'næns] n finanza; (*capital*) capitale m ▷ vt finanziare; **~s** npl (*funds*) finanze fpl; **financial** [faɪ'nænʃəl] adj finanziario(-a); **financial year** n anno finanziario, esercizio finanziario

find [faɪnd] (pt, pp **found**) vt trovare; (*lost object*) ritrovare ▷ n trovata, scoperta; **to ~ sb guilty** (*Law*) giudicare qn colpevole; **find out** vt (*truth, secret*) scoprire; (*person*) cogliere in fallo; **to ~ out about** informarsi su; (*by chance*) scoprire; **findings** npl (*Law*) sentenza, conclusioni fpl; (*of report*) conclusioni

fine [faɪn] adj bello(-a); ottimo(-a); (*thin, subtle*) fine ▷ adv (*well*) molto bene ▷ n (*Law*) multa ▷ vt (*Law*) multare; **to be ~** (*person*) stare bene; (*weather*) far bello; **fine arts** npl belle arti fpl

finger ['fɪŋgə'] n dito ▷ vt toccare, tastare; **little/index ~** mignolo/(dito) indice m; **fingernail** n unghia; **fingerprint** n impronta digitale; **fingertip** n punta del dito

finish ['fɪnɪʃ] n fine f; (*polish etc*) finitura ▷ vt, vi finire; **when does the show ~?** quando finisce lo spettacolo?; **to ~ doing sth** finire di fare qc; **to ~ third** arrivare terzo(-a); **finish off** vt compiere; (*kill*) uccidere; **finish up** vi, vt finire

Finland ['fɪnlənd] n Finlandia; **Finn** [fɪn] n finlandese m/f; **Finnish** adj finlandese ▷ n (*Ling*) finlandese m

fir [fəː'] n abete m

fire [faɪə'] n fuoco; (*destructive*) incendio; (*gas fire, electric fire*) stufa ▷ vt (*gun*) far fuoco con; (*arrow*) sparare; (*fig*) infiammare; (*inf: dismiss*) licenziare ▷ vi sparare, far fuoco; **~! al** fuoco!; **on ~** in fiamme; **fire alarm** n allarme m d'incendio; **firearm** n arma da fuoco; **fire brigade** [-brɪ'geɪd] (*US* **fire department**) n (corpo dei) pompieri mpl; **fire engine** n autopompa; **fire escape** n scala di sicurezza; **fire exit** n uscita di sicurezza; **fire extinguisher** [-ɪk'stɪŋgwɪʃə'] n estintore m; **fireman** (*irreg*) n pompiere m; **fireplace** n focolare m; **fire station** n caserma dei pompieri; **firetruck** (*US*) n **= fire engine**; **firewall** n (*Internet*) firewall m inv; **firewood** n legna da ardere; **fireworks** npl fuochi mpl d'artificio

firm [fəːm] adj fermo(-a) ▷ n ditta,

azienda; **firmly** adv fermamente
first [fɜːst] adj primo(-a) ▷ adv (before others) il primo, la prima; (before other things) per primo; (when listing reasons etc) per prima cosa ▷ n (person: in race) primo(-a); (BRIT Scol) laurea con lode; (Aut) prima; **at ~** dapprima, all'inizio; **~ of all** prima di tutto; **first aid** n pronto soccorso; **first-aid kit** n cassetta pronto soccorso; **first-class** adj di prima classe; **first-hand** adj di prima mano; **first lady** (US) n moglie f del presidente; **firstly** adv in primo luogo; **first name** n prenome m; **first-rate** adj di prima qualità, ottimo(-a)
fiscal ['fɪskəl] adj fiscale; **fiscal year** n anno fiscale
fish [fɪʃ] n inv pesce m ▷ vt (river, area) pescare in ▷ vi pescare; **to go ~ing** andare a pesca; **fish and chip shop** n see **chip shop**; **fisherman** (irreg) n pescatore m; **fish fingers** (BRIT) npl bastoncini mpl di pesce (surgelati); **fishing** n pesca; **fishing boat** n barca da pesca; **fishing line** n lenza; **fishmonger** n pescivendolo; **fishmonger's (shop)** (BRIT) n pescheria; **fish sticks** (US) npl = **fish fingers**; **fishy** (inf) adj (tale, story) sospetto(-a)
fist [fɪst] n pugno
fit [fɪt] adj (Med, Sport) in forma; (proper) adatto(-a), appropriato(-a); conveniente ▷ vt (clothes) stare bene a; (put in, attach) mettere; installare; (equip) fornire, equipaggiare ▷ vi (clothes) stare bene; (parts) andare bene, adattarsi; (in space, gap) entrare ▷ n (Med) accesso, attacco; **~ to** in grado di; **~ for** adatto(-a) a, degno(-a) di; **a ~ of anger** un accesso d'ira; **this dress is a good ~** questo vestito sta bene; **by ~s and starts** a sbalzi; **fit in** vi accordarsi; adattarsi; **fitness** n (Med) forma fisica; **fitted** adj **fitted cupboards** armadi mpl a muro; **fitted carpet** moquette f inv; **fitted kitchen** (BRIT) cucina componibile; **fitting** adj appropriato(-a) ▷ n (of dress) prova; (of piece of equipment) montaggio, aggiustaggio; **fitting room** n camerino; **fittings** npl (in building) impianti mpl
five [faɪv] num cinque; **fiver** (inf) n (BRIT) biglietto da cinque sterline; (US) biglietto da cinque dollari
fix [fɪks] vt fissare; (mend) riparare; (meal, drink) preparare ▷ n **to be in a ~** essere nei guai; **fix up** vt (meeting) fissare; **to ~ sb up with sth** procurare qc a qn; **fixed** [fɪkst] adj (prices etc) fisso(-a); **fixture** ['fɪkstʃər] n impianto (fisso); (Sport) incontro (del calendario sportivo)
fizzy ['fɪzɪ] adj frizzante; gassato(-a)
flag [flæg] n bandiera; (also: **~stone**) pietra

da lastricare ▷ vi stancarsi; affievolirsi; **flagpole** ['flæɡpəʊl] n albero
flair [fleər] n (for business etc) fiuto; (for languages etc) facilità; (style) stile m
flak [flæk] n (Mil) fuoco d'artiglieria; (inf: criticism) critiche fpl
flake [fleɪk] n (of rust, paint) scaglia; (of snow, soap powder) fiocco ▷ vi (also: **~ off**) sfaldarsi
flamboyant [flæm'bɔɪənt] adj sgargiante
flame [fleɪm] n fiamma
flamingo [flə'mɪŋɡəʊ] n fenicottero, fiammingo
flammable ['flæməbl] adj infiammabile
flan [flæn] (BRIT) n flan m inv
flank [flæŋk] n fianco ▷ vt fiancheggiare
flannel ['flænl] n (BRIT: also: **face ~**) guanto di spugna; (fabric) flanella
flap [flæp] n (of pocket) patta; (of envelope) lembo ▷ vt (wings) battere ▷ vi (sail, flag) sbattere; (inf: also: **be in a ~**) essere in agitazione
flare [fleər] n razzo; (in skirt etc) svasatura; **~s** (trousers) pantaloni mpl a zampa d'elefante; **flare up** vi andare in fiamme; (fig: person) infiammarsi di rabbia; (: revolt) scoppiare
flash [flæʃ] n vampata; (also: **news ~**) notizia f lampo inv; (Phot) flash m inv ▷ vt accendere e spegnere; (send: message) trasmettere; (: look, smile) lanciare ▷ vi brillare; (light on ambulance, eyes etc) lampeggiare; **in a ~** in un lampo; **to ~ one's headlights** lampeggiare; **he ~ed by** or **past** ci passò davanti come un lampo; **flashback** n flashback m inv; **flashbulb** n cubo m flash inv; **flashlight** n lampadina tascabile
flask [flɑːsk] n fiasco; (also: **vacuum ~**) Thermos® m inv
flat [flæt] adj piatto(-a); (tyre) sgonfio(-a), a terra; (battery) scarico(-a); (beer) svampito(-a); (denial) netto(-a); (Mus) bemolle inv; (: voice) stonato(-a); (rate, fee) unico(-a) ▷ n (BRIT: rooms) appartamento; (Aut) pneumatico sgonfio; (Mus) bemolle m; **to work ~ out** lavorare a più non posso; **flatten** vt (also: **flatten out**) appiattire; (building, city) spianare
flatter ['flætər] vt lusingare; **flattering** adj lusinghiero(-a); (dress) che dona
flaunt [flɔːnt] vt fare mostra di
flavour etc ['fleɪvər] (US **flavor**) n gusto ▷ vt insaporire, aggiungere sapore a; **what ~s do you have?** che gusti avete?; **strawberry-~ed** al gusto di fragola; **flavouring** n essenza (artificiale)
flaw [flɔː] n difetto; **flawless** adj senza difetti

flea [fliː] n pulce f; **flea market** n mercato delle pulci

flee [fliː] (pt, pp **fled**) vt fuggire da ▷ vi fuggire, scappare

fleece [fliːs] n vello ▷ vt (inf) pelare

fleet [fliːt] n flotta; (of lorries etc) convoglio; parco

fleeting ['fliːtɪŋ] adj fugace, fuggitivo(-a); (visit) volante

Flemish ['flɛmɪʃ] adj fiammingo(-a)

flesh [flɛʃ] n carne f; (of fruit) polpa

flew [fluː] pt of **fly**

flex [flɛks] n filo (flessibile) ▷ vt flettere; (muscles) contrarre; **flexibility** n flessibilità; **flexible** adj flessibile; **flexitime** ['flɛksɪtaɪm] n orario flessibile

flick [flɪk] n colpetto; scarto ▷ vt dare un colpetto a; **flick through** vt fus sfogliare

flicker ['flɪkər] vi tremolare

flies [flaɪz] npl of **fly**

flight [flaɪt] n volo; (escape) fuga; (also: ~ of steps) scalinata; **flight attendant** (US) n steward m inv, hostess f inv

flimsy ['flɪmzɪ] adj (shoes, clothes) leggero(-a); (building) poco solido(-a); (excuse) che non regge

flinch [flɪntʃ] vi ritirarsi; **to ~ from** tirarsi indietro di fronte a

fling [flɪŋ] (pt, pp **flung**) vt lanciare, gettare

flint [flɪnt] n selce f; (in lighter) pietrina

flip [flɪp] vt (switch) far scattare; (coin) lanciare in aria

flip-flops ['flɪpflɔps] npl (esp BRIT: sandals) infradito mpl

flipper ['flɪpər] n pinna

flirt [fləːt] vi flirtare ▷ n civetta

float [fləut] n galleggiante m; (in procession) carro; (money) somma ▷ vi galleggiare

flock [flɔk] n (of sheep, Rel) gregge m; (of birds) stormo ▷ vi **to ~ to** accorrere in massa a

flood [flʌd] n alluvione m; (of letters etc) marea ▷ vt allagare; (people) invadere ▷ vi (place) allagarsi; (people): **to ~ into** riversarsi in; **flooding** n inondazione f; **floodlight** n riflettore m ▷ vt illuminare a giorno

floor [flɔːr] n pavimento; (storey) piano; (of sea, valley) fondo ▷ vt (blow) atterrare; (: question) ridurre al silenzio; **which ~ is it on?** a che piano si trova?; **ground ~** (BRIT), **first ~** (US) pianterreno; **first ~** (BRIT), **second ~** (US) primo piano; **floorboard** n tavellone m di legno; **flooring** n (floor) pavimento; (material) materiale m per pavimentazioni; **floor show** n spettacolo di varietà

flop [flɔp] n fiasco ▷ vi far fiasco; (fall)

lasciarsi cadere; **floppy** ['flɔpɪ] adj floscio(-a), molle

floral ['flɔːrl] adj floreale

Florence ['flɔrəns] n Firenze f

Florentine ['flɔrəntaɪn] adj fiorentino(-a)

florist ['flɔrɪst] n fioraio(-a); **florist's (shop)** n fioraio(-a)

flotation [fləu'teɪʃən] n (Comm) lancio

flour ['flauər] n farina

flourish ['flʌrɪʃ] vi fiorire ▷ n (bold gesture): **with a ~** con ostentazione

flow [fləu] n flusso; circolazione f ▷ vi fluire; (traffic, blood in veins) circolare; (hair) scendere

flower ['flauər] n fiore m ▷ vi fiorire; **flower bed** n aiuola; **flowerpot** n vaso da fiori

flown [fləun] pp of **fly**

fl. oz. abbr = **fluid ounce**

flu [fluː] n influenza

fluctuate ['flʌktjueɪt] vi fluttuare, oscillare

fluent ['fluːənt] adj (speech) facile, sciolto(-a); corrente; **he speaks ~ Italian, he's ~ in Italian** parla l'italiano correntemente

fluff [flʌf] n lanugine f; **fluffy** adj lanuginoso(-a); (toy) di peluche

fluid ['fluːɪd] adj fluido(-a) ▷ n fluido; **fluid ounce** (BRIT) = 0.028 l; 0.05 pints

fluke [fluːk] (inf) n colpo di fortuna

flung [flʌŋ] pt, pp of **fling**

fluorescent [fluə'rɛsnt] adj fluorescente

fluoride ['fluəraɪd] n fluoruro

flurry ['flʌrɪ] n (of snow) tempesta; **a ~ of activity** uno scoppio di attività

flush [flʌʃ] n rossore m; (fig: of youth, beauty etc) rigoglio, pieno vigore ▷ vt ripulire con un getto d'acqua ▷ vi arrossire ▷ adj **~ with** a livello di, pari a; **to ~ the toilet** tirare l'acqua

flute [fluːt] n flauto

flutter ['flʌtər] n agitazione f; (of wings) battito ▷ vi (bird) battere le ali

fly [flaɪ] (pt **flew**, pp **flown**) n (insect) mosca; (on trousers: also: **flies**) chiusura ▷ vt pilotare; (passengers, cargo) trasportare (in aereo); (distances) percorrere ▷ vi volare; (passengers) andare in aereo; (escape) fuggire; (flag) sventolare; **fly away** vi volar via; **fly-drive** n **fly-drive holiday** fly and drive m inv; **flying** n (activity) aviazione f; (action) volo ▷ adj **flying visit** visita volante; **with flying colours** con risultati brillanti; **flying saucer** n disco volante; **flyover** (BRIT) n (bridge) cavalcavia m inv

FM abbr (= frequency modulation) FM

foal [fəul] n puledro

foam [fəum] n schiuma; (also: **~ rubber**)

gommapiuma® ▷ vi schiumare; (*soapy water*) fare la schiuma

focus ['fəukəs] (*pl* **focuses**) *n* fuoco; (*of interest*) centro ▷ vt (*field glasses etc*) mettere a fuoco ▷ vi **to ~ on** (*with camera*) mettere a fuoco; (*person*) fissare lo sguardo su; **in ~** a fuoco; **out of ~** sfocato(-a)

foetus ['fiːtəs] (*US* **fetus**) *n* feto

fog [fɔg] *n* nebbia; **foggy** *adj* **it's foggy** c'è nebbia; **fog lamp** (*US* **fog light**) *n* (*Aut*) faro *m* antinebbia *inv*

foil [fɔɪl] *vt* confondere, frustrare ▷ *n* lamina di metallo; (*kitchen foil*) foglio di alluminio; (*Fencing*) fioretto; **to act as a ~ to** (*fig*) far risaltare

fold [fəuld] *n* (*bend, crease*) piega; (*Agr*) ovile *m*; (*fig*) gregge *m* ▷ vt piegare; (*arms*) incrociare; **fold up** *vi* (*map, bed, table*) piegarsi; (*business*) crollare ▷ vt (*map etc*) piegare, ripiegare; **folder** *n* (*for papers*) cartella; cartellina; **folding** *adj* (*chair, bed*) pieghevole

foliage ['fəulɪɪdʒ] *n* fogliame *m*

folk [fəuk] *npl* gente *f* ▷ *adj* popolare; **~s** *npl* (*family*) famiglia; **folklore** ['fəuklɔːʳ] *n* folclore *m*; **folk music** *n* musica folk *inv*; **folk song** *n* canto popolare

follow ['fɔləu] *vt* seguire ▷ *vi* seguire; (*result*) conseguire, risultare; **to ~ suit** fare lo stesso; **follow up** *vt* (*letter, offer*) fare seguito a; (*case*) seguire; **follower** *n* seguace *m/f*, discepolo(-a); **following** *adj* seguente ▷ *n* seguito, discepoli *mpl*; **follow-up** *n* seguito

fond [fɔnd] *adj* (*memory, look*) tenero(-a), affettuoso(-a); **to be ~ of sb** volere bene a qn; **he's ~ of walking** gli piace fare camminate

food [fuːd] *n* cibo; **food mixer** *n* frullatore *m*; **food poisoning** *n* intossicazione *f*; **food processor** [-'prəusesə] *n* tritatutto *m inv* elettrico; **food stamp** (*US*) *n* buono alimentare dato agli indigenti

fool [fuːl] *n* sciocco(-a); (*Culin*) frullato ▷ vt ingannare ▷ vi (*gen: fool around*) fare lo sciocco; **fool about**, **fool around** *vi* (*waste time*) perdere tempo; **foolish** *adj* scemo(-a), stupido(-a); imprudente; **foolproof** *adj* (*plan etc*) sicurissimo(-a)

foot [fut] (*pl* **feet**) *n* piede *m*; (*measure*) piede (= 304 *mm*; 12 *inches*); (*of animal*) zampa ▷ vt (*bill*) pagare; **on ~** a piedi; **footage** *n* (*Cinema: length*) ≈ metraggio; (: *material*) sequenza; **foot-and-mouth (disease)** [futənd'mauθ-] *n* afta epizootica; **football** *n* pallone *m*; (*sport: BRIT*) calcio; (: *US*) football *m* americano; **footballer** *n* (*BRIT*) = **football player**; **football match** *n* (*BRIT*) partita di calcio;

football player *n* (*BRIT: also:* **footballer**) calciatore *m*; (*US*) giocatore *m* di football americano; **footbridge** *n* passerella; **foothills** *npl* contrafforti *fpl*; **foothold** *n* punto d'appoggio; **footing** *n* (*fig*) posizione *f*; **to lose one's footing** mettere un piede in fallo; **footnote** *n* nota (a piè di pagina); **footpath** *n* sentiero; (*in street*) marciapiede *m*; **footprint** *n* orma, impronta; **footstep** *n* passo; (*footprint*) orma, impronta; **footwear** *n* calzatura

KEYWORD

for [fɔːʳ] *prep* **1** (*indicating destination, intention, purpose*) per; **the train for London** il treno per Londra; **he went for the paper** è andato a prendere il giornale; **it's time for lunch** è ora di pranzo; **what's it for?** a che serve?; **what for?** (*why*) perché?

2 (*on behalf of, representing*) per; **to work for sb/sth** lavorare per qn/qc; **I'll ask him for you** glielo chiederò a nome tuo; **G for George** G come George

3 (*because of*) per, a causa di; **for this reason** per questo motivo

4 (*with regard to*) per; **it's cold for July** è freddo per luglio; **for everyone who voted yes, 50 voted no** per ogni voto a favore ce n'erano 50 contro

5 (*in exchange for*) per; **I sold it for £5** l'ho venduto per 5 sterline

6 (*in favour of*) per, a favore di; **are you for or against us?** è con noi o contro di noi?; **I'm all for it** sono completamente a favore

7 (*referring to distance, time*) per; **there are roadworks for 5 km** ci sono lavori in corso per 5 km; **he was away for 2 years** è stato via per 2 anni; **she will be away for a month** starà via un mese; **it hasn't rained for 3 weeks** non piove da 3 settimane; **can you do it for tomorrow?** può farlo per domani?

8 (*with infinitive clauses*): **it is not for me to decide** non sta a me decidere; **it would be best for you to leave** sarebbe meglio che lei se ne andasse; **there is still time for you to do it** ha ancora tempo per farlo; **for this to be possible ...** perché ciò sia possibile ...

9 (*in spite of*) nonostante; **for all his complaints, he's very fond of her** nonostante tutte le sue lamentele, le vuole molto bene

▷ *conj* (*since, as: rather formal*) dal momento che, poiché

forbid [fə'bɪd] (*pt* **forbad(e)**, *pp* **forbidden**)

vt vietare, interdire; **to ~ sb to do sth**
proibire a qn di fare qc; **forbidden** *pt of*
forbid ▷ *adj* (*food*) proibito(-a); (*area,*
territory) vietato(-a); (*word, subject*) tabù *inv*
force [fɔ:s] *n* forza ▷ *vt* forzare; **forced**
adj forzato(-a); **forceful** *adj* forte,
vigoroso(-a)
ford [fɔ:d] *n* guado
fore [fɔ:ʳ] *n* **to come to the ~** mettersi
in evidenza; **forearm** ['fɔ:rɑ:m] *n*
avambraccio; **forecast** ['fɔ:kɑ:st] (*irreg:*
like **cast**) *n* previsione *f* ▷ *vt* prevedere;
forecourt ['fɔ:kɔ:t] *n* (*of garage*) corte *f*
esterna; **forefinger** ['fɔ:fɪŋɡəʳ] *n* (*dito*)
indice *m*; **forefront** ['fɔ:frʌnt] *n* **in**
the forefront of all'avanguardia in;
foreground
['fɔ:ɡraund] *n* primo piano; **forehead**
['fɔrɪd] *n* fronte *f*
foreign ['fɔrɪn] *adj* straniero(-a); (*trade*)
estero(-a); (*object, matter*) estraneo(-a);
foreign currency *n* valuta estera;
foreigner *n* straniero(-a); **foreign**
exchange *n* cambio con l'estero;
(*currency*) valuta estera; **Foreign Office**
(BRIT) *n* Ministero degli Esteri; **Foreign**
Secretary (BRIT) *n* ministro degli Affari
esteri
fore: **foreman** ['fɔ:mən] (*irreg*) *n*
caposquadra *m*; **foremost** ['fɔ:məust]
adj principale; più in vista ▷ *adv* **first and**
foremost innanzitutto; **forename** *n*
nome *m* di battesimo
forensic [fə'rɛnsɪk] *adj* **~ medicine**
medicina legale
foresee [fɔ:'si:] (*irreg: like* **see**) *vt*
prevedere; **foreseeable** *adj* prevedibile
forest ['fɔrɪst] *n* foresta; **forestry**
['fɔrɪstrɪ] *n* silvicoltura
forever [fə'rɛvəʳ] *adv* per sempre;
(*endlessly*) sempre, di continuo
foreword ['fɔ:wə:d] *n* prefazione *f*
forfeit ['fɔ:fɪt] *vt* perdere; (*one's happiness,*
health) giocarsi
forgave [fə'ɡeɪv] *pt of* **forgive**
forge [fɔ:dʒ] *n* fucina ▷ *vt* (*signature,*
money) contraffare, falsificare; (*wrought*
iron) fucinare, foggiare; **forger** *n*
contraffattore *m*; **forgery** *n* falso;
(*activity*) contraffazione *f*
forget [fə'ɡɛt] (*pt* **forgot**, *pp* **forgotten**)
vt, vi dimenticare; **I've forgotten my**
key/passport ho dimenticato la chiave/il
passaporto; **forgetful** *adj* di corta
memoria; **forgetful of** dimentico(-a) di
forgive [fə'ɡɪv] (*pt* **forgave**, *pp* **forgiven**)
vt perdonare; **to ~ sb for sth** perdonare
qc a qn
forgot [fə'ɡɔt] *pt of* **forget**

forgotten [fə'ɡɔtn] *pp of* **forget**
fork [fɔ:k] *n* (*for eating*) forchetta; (*for*
gardening) forca; (*of roads, rivers, railways*)
biforcazione *f* ▷ *vi* (*road etc*) biforcarsi
forlorn [fə'lɔ:n] *adj* (*person*) sconsolato(-a);
(*place*) abbandonato(-a); (*attempt*)
disperato(-a); (*hope*) vano(-a)
form [fɔ:m] *n* forma; (*Scol*) classe *f*;
(*questionnaire*) scheda ▷ *vt* formare; **in top**
~ in gran forma
formal ['fɔ:məl] *adj* formale; (*gardens*)
simmetrico(-a), regolare; **formality**
[fɔ:'mælɪtɪ] *n* formalità *f inv*
format ['fɔ:mæt] *n* formato ▷ *vt* (*Comput*)
formattare
formation [fɔ:'meɪʃən] *n* formazione *f*
former ['fɔ:məʳ] *adj* vecchio(-a); (*before n*)
ex *inv* (*before n*); **the ~ ... the latter** quello
... questo; **formerly** *adv* in passato
formidable ['fɔ:mɪdəbl] *adj* formidabile
formula ['fɔ:mjulə] *n* formula
fort [fɔ:t] *n* forte *m*
forthcoming [fɔ:θ'kʌmɪŋ] *adj* (*event*)
prossimo(-a); (*help*) disponibile; (*character*)
aperto(-a), comunicativo(-a)
fortieth ['fɔ:tɪɪθ] *num* quarantesimo(-a)
fortify ['fɔ:tɪfaɪ] *vt* (*city*) fortificare;
(*person*) armare
fortnight ['fɔ:tnaɪt] (BRIT) *n* quindici
giorni *mpl*, due settimane *fpl*; **fortnightly**
adj bimensile ▷ *adv* ogni quindici giorni
fortress ['fɔ:trɪs] *n* fortezza, rocca
fortunate ['fɔ:tʃənɪt] *adj* fortunato(-a); **it**
is ~ that è una fortuna che; **fortunately**
adv fortunatamente
fortune ['fɔ:tʃən] *n* fortuna; **fortune-**
teller *n* indovino(-a)
forty ['fɔ:tɪ] *num* quaranta
forum ['fɔ:rəm] *n* foro
forward ['fɔ:wəd] *adj* (*ahead of schedule*)
in anticipo; (*movement, position*) in avanti;
(*not shy*) aperto(-a), diretto(-a) ▷ *n* (*Sport*)
avanti *m inv* ▷ *vt* (*letter*) inoltrare; (*parcel,*
goods) spedire; (*career, plans*) promuovere,
appoggiare; **to move ~** avanzare;
forwarding address *n* nuovo recapito cui
spedire la posta; **forward(s)** *adv* avanti;
forward slash *n* barra obliqua
fossil ['fɔsl] *adj* fossile ▷ *n* fossile *m*
foster ['fɔstəʳ] *vt* incoraggiare, nutrire;
(*child*) avere in affidamento; **foster child**
n bambino(-a) preso(-a) in affidamento;
foster mother *n* madre *f* affidataria
fought [fɔ:t] *pt, pp of* **fight**
foul [faul] *adj* (*smell, food, temper etc*)
cattivo(-a); (*weather*) brutto(-a); (*language*)
osceno(-a) ▷ *n* (*Sport*) fallo ▷ *vt* sporcare;
foul play *n* (*Law*): **the police suspect**
foul play la polizia sospetta un atto

criminale
found [faʊnd] *pt, pp of* **find** ▷ *vt (establish)*
fondare; **foundation** [-'deɪʃən] *n*
(act) fondazione *f*; *(base)* base *f*; *(also:*
foundation cream) fondo tinta;
foundations *npl (of building)* fondamenta
fpl
founder ['faʊndəʳ] *n* fondatore(-trice) ▷ *vi*
affondare
fountain ['faʊntɪn] *n* fontana; **fountain
pen** *n* penna stilografica
four [fɔːʳ] *num* quattro; **on all ~s** a
carponi; **four-letter word** ['fɔːlɛtə-] *n*
parolaccia; **four-poster** *n (also:* **four-
poster bed**) letto a quattro colonne;
fourteen *num* quattordici; **fourteenth**
num quattordicesimo(-a); **fourth** *num*
quarto(-a); **four-wheel drive** ['fɔːwiːl-] *n*
(Aut): **with four-wheel drive** con quattro
ruote motrici
fowl [faʊl] *n* pollame *m*; volatile *m*
fox [fɔks] *n* volpe *f* ▷ *vt* confondere
foyer ['fɔɪeɪ] *n* atrio; *(Theatre)* ridotto
fraction ['frækʃən] *n* frazione *f*
fracture ['fræktʃəʳ] *n* frattura
fragile ['frædʒaɪl] *adj* fragile
fragment ['frægmənt] *n* frammento
fragrance ['freɪgrəns] *n* fragranza,
profumo
frail [freɪl] *adj* debole, delicato(-a)
frame [freɪm] *n (of building)* armatura,
(of human, animal) ossatura, corpo; *(of
picture)* cornice *f*; *(of door, window)* telaio;
(of spectacles: also: **~s**) montatura ▷ *vt*
(picture) incorniciare; **framework** *n*
struttura
France [frɑːns] *n* Francia
franchise ['fræntʃaɪz] *n (Pol)* diritto di
voto; *(Comm)* concessione *f*
frank [fræŋk] *adj* franco(-a), aperto(-a)
▷ *vt (letter)* affrancare; **frankly** *adv*
francamente, sinceramente
frantic ['fræntɪk] *adj* frenetico(-a)
fraud [frɔːd] *n* truffa; *(Law)* frode *f*; *(person)*
impostore(-trice)
fraught [frɔːt] *adj* **~ with** pieno(-a) di,
intriso(-a) da
fray [freɪ] *vt* logorare ▷ *vi* logorarsi
freak [friːk] *n* fenomeno, mostro
freckle ['frɛkl] *n* lentiggine *f*
free [friː] *adj* libero(-a); *(gratis)* gratuito(-a)
▷ *vt (prisoner, jammed person)* liberare;
(jammed object) districare; **is this seat ~?**
è libero questo posto?; **~ of charge, for
~** gratuitamente; **freedom** ['friːdəm]
n libertà; **Freefone®** *n* numero verde;
free gift *n* regalo, omaggio; **free kick** *n*
calcio libero; **freelance** *adj* indipendente;
freely *adv* liberamente; *(liberally)*

281 | **frivolous**

liberalmente; **Freepost®** *n* affrancatura
a carico del destinatario; **free-range** *adj*
(hen) ruspante; *(eggs)* di gallina ruspante;
freeway *(US) n* superstrada; **free will** *n*
libero arbitrio; **of one's own free will** di
spontanea volontà
freeze [friːz] *(pt* **froze**, *pp* **frozen**) *vi* gelare
▷ *vt* gelare; *(food)* congelare; *(prices,
salaries)* bloccare ▷ *n* gelo; blocco; **freezer**
n congelatore *m*; **freezing** ['friːzɪŋ] *adj*
(wind, weather) gelido(-a); **freezing point**
n punto di congelamento; **3 degrees
below freezing point** 3 gradi sotto zero
freight [freɪt] *n (goods)* merce *f*, merci
fpl; *(money charged)* spese *fpl* di trasporto;
freight train *(US) n* treno *m* merci *inv*
French [frɛntʃ] *adj* francese ▷ *n (Ling)*
francese *m*; **the ~** *npl* i Francesi; **French
bean** *n* fagiolino; **French bread** *n*
baguette *f inv*; **French dressing** *n (Culin)*
condimento per insalata; **French fried
potatoes** *(US* **French fries**) *npl* patate
fpl fritte; **Frenchman** *(irreg) n* francese
m; **French stick** *n* baguette *f inv*; **French
window** *n* portafinestra; **Frenchwoman**
(irreg) n francese *f*
frenzy ['frɛnzɪ] *n* frenesia
frequency ['friːkwənsɪ] *n* frequenza
frequent [*adj* 'friːkwənt, *vb* frɪ'kwɛnt] *adj*
frequente ▷ *vt* frequentare; **frequently**
adv frequentemente, spesso
fresh [frɛʃ] *adj* fresco(-a); *(new)* nuovo(-a);
(cheeky) sfacciato(-a); **freshen** *vi*
(wind, air) rinfrescare; **freshen up** *vi*
rinfrescarsi; **fresher** *(BRIT: inf) n (Scol)*
matricola; **freshly** *adv* di recente, di
fresco; **freshman** *(irreg: US) n* = **fresher**;
freshwater *adj (fish)* d'acqua dolce
fret [frɛt] *vi* agitarsi, affliggersi
Fri. *abbr (= Friday)* ven.
friction ['frɪkʃən] *n* frizione *f*, attrito
Friday ['fraɪdɪ] *n* venerdì *m inv*
fridge [frɪdʒ] *(BRIT) n* frigo, frigorifero
fried [fraɪd] *pt, pp of* **fry** ▷ *adj* fritto(-a)
friend [frɛnd] *n* amico(-a); **friendly** *adj*
amichevole; **friendship** *n* amicizia
fries [fraɪz] *(esp US) npl* patate *fpl* fritte
frigate ['frɪgɪt] *n (Naut: modern)* fregata
fright [fraɪt] *n* paura, spavento; **to take ~**
spaventarsi; **frighten** *vt* spaventare, far
paura a; **frightened** *adj* spaventato(-a);
frightening *adj* spaventoso(-a),
pauroso(-a); **frightful** *adj* orribile
frill [frɪl] *n* balza
fringe [frɪndʒ] *n (decoration:* BRIT: *of hair)*
frangia; *(edge: of forest etc)* margine *m*
Frisbee® ['frɪzbɪ] *n* frisbee *m inv*
fritter ['frɪtəʳ] *n* frittella
frivolous ['frɪvələs] *adj* frivolo(-a)

fro [frəu] *see* **to**

frock [frɔk] *n* vestito

frog [frɔg] *n* rana; **frogman** (*irreg*) *n* uomo *m* rana *inv*

 KEYWORD

from [frɔm] *prep* **1** (*indicating starting place, origin etc*) da; **where do you come from?**, **where are you from?** da dove viene?, di dov'è?; **from London to Glasgow** da Londra a Glasgow; **a letter from my sister** una lettera da mia sorella; **tell him from me that ...** gli dica da parte mia che ...
2 (*indicating time*) da; **from one o'clock to** or **until** or **till two** dall'una alle due; **from January (on)** da gennaio, a partire da gennaio
3 (*indicating distance*) da; **the hotel is 1 km from the beach** l'albergo è a 1 km dalla spiaggia
4 (*indicating price, number etc*) da; **prices range from £10 to £50** i prezzi vanno dalle 10 alle 50 sterline
5 (*indicating difference*) da; **he can't tell red from green** non sa distinguere il rosso dal verde
6 (*because of, on the basis of*): **from what he says** da quanto dice lui; **weak from hunger** debole per la fame

front [frʌnt] *n* (*of house, dress*) davanti *m inv*; (*of train*) testa; (*of book*) copertina; (*promenade: also:* **sea ~**) lungomare *m*; (*Mil, Pol, Meteor*) fronte *m*; (*fig: appearances*) fronte *f* ▷ *adj* primo(-a); anteriore, davanti *inv*; **in ~ of** davanti a; **front door** *n* porta d'entrata; (*of car*) sportello anteriore; **frontier** ['frʌntɪəʳ] *n* frontiera; **front page** *n* prima pagina; **front-wheel drive** ['frʌntwiːl-] *n* trasmissione *f* anteriore

frost [frɔst] *n* gelo; (*also:* **hoar~**) brina; **frostbite** *n* congelamento; **frosting** (*us*) *n* (*on cake*) glassa; **frosty** *adj* (*weather, look*) gelido(-a)

froth ['frɔθ] *n* spuma; schiuma

frown [fraun] *vi* acclgliarsi

froze [frəuz] *pt of* **freeze**

frozen ['frəuzn] *pp of* **freeze**

fruit [fruːt] *n inv* (*also fig*) frutto; (*collectively*) frutta; **fruit juice** *n* succo di frutta; **fruit machine** (BRIT) *n* macchina *f* mangiasoldi *inv*; **fruit salad** *n* macedonia

frustrate [frʌs'treɪt] *vt* frustrare; **frustrated** *adj* frustrato(-a)

fry [fraɪ] (*pt, pp* **fried**) *vt* friggere; *see also* **small**; **frying pan** *n* padella

ft. *abbr* = **foot**; **feet**

fudge [fʌdʒ] *n* (*Culin*) specie di caramella a base di latte, burro e zucchero

fuel [fjuəl] *n* (*for heating*) combustibile *m*; (*for propelling*) carburante *m*; **fuel tank** *n* deposito *m* nafta *inv*; (*on vehicle*) serbatoio (della benzina)

fulfil [ful'fɪl] *vt* (*function*) compiere; (*order*) eseguire; (*wish, desire*) soddisfare, appagare

full [ful] *adj* pieno(-a); (*details, skirt*) ampio(-a) ▷ *adv* **to know ~ well that** sapere benissimo che; **I'm ~ (up)** sono sazio; **a ~ two hours** due ore intere; **at ~ speed** a tutta velocità; **in ~** per intero; **full-length** *adj* (*film*) a lungometraggio; (*coat, novel*) lungo(-a); (*portrait*) in piedi; **full moon** *n* luna piena; **full-scale** *adj* (*attack, war*) su larga scala; (*model*) in grandezza naturale; **full stop** *n* punto; **full-time** *adj, adv* (*work*) a tempo pieno; **fully** *adv* interamente, pienamente, completamente; (*at least*) almeno

fumble ['fʌmbl] *vi* **to ~ with sth** armeggiare con qc

fume [fjuːm] *vi* essere furioso(-a); **fumes** *npl* esalazioni *fpl*, vapori *mpl*

fun [fʌn] *n* divertimento, spasso; **to have ~** divertirsi; **for ~** per scherzo; **to make ~ of** prendersi gioco di

function ['fʌŋkʃən] *n* funzione *f*; cerimonia, ricevimento ▷ *vi* funzionare

fund [fʌnd] *n* fondo, cassa; (*source*) fondo; (*store*) riserva; **~s** *npl* (*money*) fondi *mpl*

fundamental [fʌndə'mɛntl] *adj* fondamentale

funeral ['fjuːnərəl] *n* funerale *m*; **funeral director** *n* impresario di pompe funebri; **funeral parlour** [-'pɑːləʳ] *n* impresa di pompe funebri

funfair ['fʌnfɛəʳ] *n* luna park *m inv*

fungus ['fʌŋgəs] (*pl* **fungi**) *n* fungo; (*mould*) muffa

funnel ['fʌnl] *n* imbuto; (*of ship*) ciminiera

funny ['fʌnɪ] *adj* divertente, buffo(-a); (*strange*) strano(-a), bizzarro(-a)

fur [fəːʳ] *n* pelo; pelliccia; (BRIT: *in kettle etc*) deposito calcare; **fur coat** *n* pelliccia

furious ['fjuərɪəs] *adj* furioso(-a); (*effort*) accanito(-a)

furnish ['fəːnɪʃ] *vt* ammobiliare; (*supply*) fornire; **furnishings** *npl* mobili *mpl*, mobilia

furniture ['fəːnɪtʃəʳ] *n* mobili *mpl*; **piece of ~** mobile *m*

furry ['fəːrɪ] *adj* (*animal*) peloso(-a)

further ['fəːðəʳ] *adj* supplementare, altro(-a); nuovo(-a); più lontano(-a) ▷ *adv* più lontano; (*more*) di più; (*moreover*) inoltre ▷ *vt* favorire, promuovere; **further**

education n ≈ corsi mpl di formazione;
college of further education istituto
statale con corsi specializzati (di formazione
professionale, aggiornamento professionale
ecc); **furthermore** [fə:ðə'mɔː^r] adv inoltre,
per di più

furthest ['fə:ðɪst] superl of **far**

fury ['fjʊərɪ] n furore m

fuse [fjuːz] (us **fuze**) n fusibile m; (for bomb
etc) miccia, spoletta ▷ vt fondere ▷ vi
fondersi; **to ~ the lights** (BRIT Elec) far
saltare i fusibili; **fuse box** n cassetta dei
fusibili

fusion ['fjuːʒən] n fusione f

fuss [fʌs] n agitazione f; (complaining) storie
fpl; **to make a ~** fare delle storie; **fussy** adj
(person) puntiglioso(-a), esigente; che fa le
storie; (dress) carico(-a) di fronzoli; (style)
elaborato(-a)

future ['fjuːtʃə^r] adj futuro(-a) ▷ n futuro,
avvenire m; (Ling) futuro; **in ~** in futuro; **~s**
npl (Comm) operazioni fpl a termine

fuze [fjuːz] (us) = **fuse**

fuzzy ['fʌzɪ] adj (Phot) indistinto(-a),
sfocato(-a); (hair) crespo(-a)

G [dʒiː] n (Mus) sol m

g. abbr (= gram, gravity) g.

gadget ['gædʒɪt] n aggeggio

Gaelic ['geɪlɪk] adj gaelico(-a) ▷ n (Ling)
gaelico

gag [gæg] n bavaglio; (joke) facezia,
scherzo ▷ vt imbavagliare

gain [geɪn] n guadagno, profitto ▷ vt
guadagnare ▷ vi (clock, watch) andare
avanti; (benefit): **to ~ (from)** trarre
beneficio (da); **to ~ 3lbs (in weight)**
aumentare di 3 libbre; **to ~ on sb** (in race
etc) guadagnare su qn

gal. abbr = **gallon**

gala ['gɑːlə] n gala; **swimming ~**
manifestazione f di nuoto

galaxy ['gæləksɪ] n galassia

gale [geɪl] n vento forte; burrasca

gall bladder ['gɔːl-] n cistifellea

gallery ['gælərɪ] n galleria

gallon ['gælən] n gallone m (= 8 pints; BRIT
= 4.543l; US = 3.785l)

gallop ['gæləp] n galoppo ▷ vi galoppare

gallstone ['gɔːlstəun] n calcolo biliare

gamble ['gæmbl] n azzardo, rischio
calcolato ▷ vt, vi giocare; **to ~ on** (fig)
giocare su; **gambler** n giocatore(-trice)
d'azzardo; **gambling** n gioco d'azzardo

game [geɪm] n gioco; (event) partita;
(Tennis) game m inv; (Culin, Hunting)

selvaggina ▷ adj (ready): **to be ~ (for sth/ to do)** essere pronto(-a) (a qc a fare); **big ~** selvaggina grossa; **~s** npl (Scol) attività fpl sportive; **big ~** selvaggina grossa; **games console** [geɪmz-] n console f inv dei videogame; **game show** ['geɪmʃəu] n gioco a premi

gammon ['gæmən] n (bacon) quarto di maiale; (ham) prosciutto affumicato

gang [gæŋ] n banda, squadra ▷ vi **to ~ up on sb** far combutta contro qn

gangster ['gæŋstəʳ] n gangster m inv

gap [gæp] n (space) buco; (in time) intervallo; (difference): **~ (between)** divario (tra)

gape [geɪp] vi (person) restare a bocca aperta; (shirt, hole) essere spalancato(-a)

gap year n (Scol) anno di pausa durante il quale gli studenti viaggiano o lavorano

garage ['gærɑ:ʒ] n garage m inv; **garage sale** n vendita di oggetti usati nel garage di un privato

garbage ['gɑ:bɪdʒ] (US) n immondizie fpl, rifiuti mpl; (inf) sciocchezze fpl; **garbage can** (US) n bidone m della spazzatura; **garbage collector** (US) n spazzino(-a)

garden ['gɑ:dn] n giardino; **~s** npl (public park) giardini pubblici; **garden centre** n vivaio; **gardener** n giardiniere(-a); **gardening** n giardinaggio

garlic ['gɑ:lɪk] n aglio

garment ['gɑ:mənt] n indumento

garnish ['gɑ:nɪʃ] vt (food) guarnire

garrison ['gærɪsn] n guarnigione f

gas [gæs] n gas m inv; (US: gasoline) benzina ▷ vt asfissiare con il gas; **I can smell ~** sento odore di gas; **gas cooker** (BRIT) n cucina a gas; **gas cylinder** n bombola del gas; **gas fire** (BRIT) n radiatore m a gas

gasket ['gæskɪt] n (Aut) guarnizione f

gasoline ['gæsəli:n] (US) n benzina

gasp [gɑ:sp] n respiro affannoso, ansito ▷ vi ansare, ansimare; (in surprise) restare senza fiato

gas: **gas pedal** (esp US) n pedale m dell'acceleratore; **gas station** (US) n distributore m di benzina; **gas tank** (US) n (Aut) serbatoio (di benzina)

gate [geɪt] n cancello; (at airport) uscita

gateau ['gætəu, -z] (pl gateaux) n torta

gatecrash ['geɪtkræʃ] (BRIT) vt partecipare senza invito a

gateway ['geɪtweɪ] n porta

gather ['gæðəʳ] vt (flowers, fruit) cogliere; (pick up) raccogliere; (assemble) radunare; raccogliere; (understand) capire; (Sewing) increspare ▷ vi (assemble) radunarsi; **to ~ speed** acquistare velocità; **gathering** n adunanza

gauge [geɪdʒ] n (instrument) indicatore m ▷ vt misurare; (fig) valutare

gave [geɪv] pt of **give**

gay [geɪ] adj (homosexual) omosessuale; (cheerful) gaio(-a), allegro(-a); (colour) vivace, vivo(-a)

gaze [geɪz] n sguardo fisso ▷ vi **to ~ at** guardare fisso

GB abbr = **Great Britain**

GCSE (BRIT) n abbr General Certificate of Secondary Education

gear [gɪəʳ] n attrezzi mpl, equipaggiamento; (Tech) ingranaggio; (Aut) marcia ▷ vt (fig: adapt): **to ~ sth to** adattare qc a; **in top** or (US) **high/low ~** in quarta (or quinta)/seconda; **in ~** in marcia; **gear up** vi **to ~ up (to do)** prepararsi (a fare); **gear box** n scatola del cambio; **gear lever** n leva del cambio; **gear shift** (US), **gear stick** (BRIT) n = **gear lever**

geese [gi:s] npl of **goose**

gel [dʒɛl] n gel m inv

gem [dʒɛm] n gemma

Gemini ['dʒɛmɪnaɪ] n Gemelli mpl

gender ['dʒɛndəʳ] n genere m

gene [dʒi:n] n (Biol) gene m

general ['dʒɛnərl] n generale m ▷ adj generale; **in ~** in genere; **general anaesthetic** (US **general anesthetic**) n anestesia totale; **general election** n elezioni fpl generali; **generalize** vi generalizzare; **generally** adv generalmente; **general practitioner** n medico generico; **general store** n emporio

generate ['dʒɛnəreɪt] vt generare

generation [dʒɛnə'reɪʃən] n generazione f

generator ['dʒɛnəreɪtəʳ] n generatore m

generosity [dʒɛnə'rɔsɪtɪ] n generosità f

generous ['dʒɛnərəs] adj generoso(-a); (copious) abbondante

genetic [dʒɪ'nɛtɪk] adj genetico(-a); **~ engineering** ingegneria genetica; **genetically modified** adj geneticamente modificato(-a), transgenico(-a); **genetics** n genetica

Geneva [dʒɪ'ni:və] n Ginevra

genitals ['dʒɛnɪtlz] npl genitali mpl

genius ['dʒi:nɪəs] n genio

Genoa ['dʒɛnəuə] n Genova

gent [dʒɛnt] n abbr = **gentleman**

gentle ['dʒɛntl] adj delicato(-a); (person) dolce

> Be careful not to translate **gentle** by the Italian word **gentile**.

gentleman ['dʒɛntlmən] (irreg) n signore m; (well-bred man) gentiluomo

gently ['dʒɛntlɪ] adv delicatamente

gents [dʒɛnts] n W.C. m (per signori)

genuine ['dʒɛnjuɪn] adj autentico(-a); sincero(-a); **genuinely** adv genuinamente

geographic(al) [dʒɪə'græfɪk(l)] adj geografico(-a)

geography [dʒɪ'ɔgrəfɪ] n geografia

geology [dʒɪ'ɔlədʒɪ] n geologia

geometry [dʒɪ'ɔmətrɪ] n geometria

geranium [dʒɪ'reɪnjəm] n geranio

geriatric [dʒɛrɪ'ætrɪk] adj geriatrico(-a)

germ [dʒə:m] n (Med) microbo; (Biol, fig) germe m

German ['dʒə:mən] adj tedesco(-a) ▷ n tedesco(-a); (Ling) tedesco; **German measles** (BRIT) n rosolia

Germany ['dʒə:mənɪ] n Germania

gesture ['dʒɛstjəʳ] n gesto

KEYWORD

get [gɛt] (pt, pp **got**, (us) pp **gotten**) vi 1 (become, be) diventare, farsi; **to get old** invecchiare; **to get tired** stancarsi; **to get drunk** ubriacarsi; **to get killed** venire or rimanere ucciso(-a); **when do I get paid?** quando mi pagate?; **it's getting late** si sta facendo tardi

2 (go): **to get to/from** andare a/da; **to get home** arrivare or tornare a casa; **how did you get here?** come sei venuto?

3 (begin) mettersi a, cominciare a; **to get to know sb** incominciare a conoscere qn; **let's get going** or **started** muoviamoci

4 (modal aux vb): **you've got to do it** devi farlo

▷ vt 1: **to get sth done** (do) fare qc; (have done) far fare qc; **to get one's hair cut** farsi tagliare i capelli; **to get sb to do sth** far fare qc a qn

2 (obtain: money, permission, results) ottenere; (find: job, flat) trovare; (fetch: person, doctor) chiamare; (: object) prendere; **to get sth for sb** prendere or procurare qc a qn; **get me Mr Jones, please** (Tel) mi passi il signor Jones, per favore; **can I get you a drink?** le posso offrire da bere?

3 (receive: present, letter, prize) ricevere; (acquire: reputation) farsi; **how much did you get for the painting?** quanto le hanno dato per il quadro?

4 (catch) prendere; (hit: target etc) colpire; **to get sb by the arm/throat** afferrare qn per un braccio/alla gola; **get him!** prendetelo!

5 (take, move) portare; **to get sth to sb** far avere qc a qn; **do you think we'll get it through the door?** pensi che riusciremo a farlo passare per la porta?

6 (catch, take: plane, bus etc) prendere; **where do we get the ferry to …?** dove si prende il traghetto per …?

7 (understand) afferrare; (hear) sentire; **I've got it!** ci sono arrivato!, ci sono!; **I'm sorry, I didn't get your name** scusi, non ho capito (or sentito) il suo nome

8 (have, possess): **to have got** avere; **how many have you got?** quanti ne ha?

get along vi (agree) andare d'accordo; (depart) andarsene; (manage) = **get by**

get at vt fus (attack) prendersela con; (reach) raggiungere, arrivare a

get away vi partire, andarsene; (escape) scappare

get away with vt fus cavarsela; farla franca

get back vi (return) ritornare, tornare ▷ vt riottenere, riavere; **when do we get back?** quando ritorniamo?

get by vi (pass) passare; (manage) farcela

get down vi, vt fus scendere ▷ vt far scendere; (depress) buttare giù

get down to vt fus (work) mettersi a (fare)

get in vi entrare; (train) arrivare; (arrive home) ritornare, tornare

get into vt fus entrare in; **to get into a rage** incavolarsi

get off vi (from train etc) scendere; (depart: person, car) andare via; (escape) cavarsela ▷ vt (remove: clothes, stain) levare ▷ vt fus (train, bus) scendere da; **where do I get off?** dove devo scendere?

get on vi (at exam etc) andare; (agree): **to get on (with)** andare d'accordo (con) ▷ vt fus montare in; (horse) montare su

get out vi uscire; (of vehicle) scendere ▷ vt tirar fuori, far uscire

get out of vt fus uscire da; (duty etc) evitare

get over vt fus (illness) riaversi da

get round vt fus aggirare; (fig: person) rigirare

get through vi (Tel) avere la linea

get through to vt fus (Tel) parlare a

get together vi riunirsi ▷ vt raccogliere; (people) adunare

get up vi (rise) alzarsi ▷ vt fus salire su per

get up to vt fus (reach) raggiungere; (prank etc) fare

getaway ['gɛtəweɪ] n fuga

Ghana ['gɑːnə] n Ghana m

ghastly ['gɑːstlɪ] adj orribile, orrendo(-a); (pale) spettrale

ghetto ['gɛtəu] n ghetto

ghost [gəust] n fantasma m, spettro

giant ['dʒaɪənt] n gigante m ▷ adj gigantesco(-a), enorme

gift [gɪft] n regalo; (*donation, ability*) dono; **gifted** adj dotato(-a); **gift shop** (US **gift store**) n negozio di souvenir

gift token, gift voucher n buono m omaggio inv

gig [gɪg] n (*inf: of musician*) serata

gigabyte [gɪːgəbaɪt] n gigabyte m inv

gigantic [dʒaɪˈgæntɪk] adj gigantesco(-a)

giggle [ˈgɪgl] vi ridere scioccamente

gills [gɪlz] npl (*of fish*) branchie fpl

gilt [gɪlt] n doratura ▷ adj dorato(-a)

gimmick [ˈgɪmɪk] n trucco

gin [dʒɪn] n (*liquor*) gin m inv

ginger [ˈdʒɪndʒəʳ] n zenzero

gipsy [ˈdʒɪpsɪ] n zingaro(-a)

giraffe [dʒɪˈrɑːf] n giraffa

girl [gəːl] n ragazza, ragazzina; (*young unmarried woman*) signorina; (*daughter*) figlia, figliola; **girlfriend** n (*of girl*) amica; (*of boy*) ragazza; **Girl Scout** (US) n Giovane Esploratrice f

gist [dʒɪst] n succo

give [gɪv] (*pt* **gave**, *pp* **given**) vt dare ▷ vi cedere; **to ~ sb sth**, **~ sth to sb** dare qc a qn; **I'll ~ you £5 for it** te lo pago 5 sterline; **to ~ a cry/sigh** emettere un grido/sospiro; **to ~ a speech** fare un discorso; **give away** vt dare via; (*disclose*) rivelare; (*bride*) condurre all'altare; **give back** vt rendere; **give in** vi cedere ▷ vt consegnare; **give out** vt distribuire; annunciare; **give up** vi rinunciare ▷ vt rinunciare a; **to ~ up smoking** smettere di fumare; **to ~ o.s. up** arrendersi

given [ˈgɪvn] pp of **give** ▷ adj (*fixed: time, amount*) dato(-a), determinato(-a) ▷ conj **~ (that) ...** dato che ...; **~ the circumstances ...** date le circostanze ...

glacier [ˈglæsɪəʳ] n ghiacciaio

glad [glæd] adj lieto(-a), contento(-a); **gladly** [ˈglædlɪ] adv volentieri

glamorous [ˈglæmərəs] adj affascinante, seducente

glamour [ˈglæməʳ] (US **glamor**) n fascino

glance [glɑːns] n occhiata, sguardo ▷ vi **to ~ at** dare un'occhiata a; **to ~ off** (*bullet*) rimbalzare su

gland [glænd] n ghiandola

glare [glɛəʳ] n (*of anger*) sguardo furioso; (*of light*) riverbero, luce f abbagliante; (*of publicity*) chiasso ▷ vi abbagliare; **to ~ at** guardare male; **glaring** adj (*mistake*) madornale

glass [glɑːs] n (*substance*) vetro; (*tumbler*) bicchiere m; **~es** npl (*spectacles*) occhiali mpl

glaze [gleɪz] vt (*door*) fornire di vetri; (*pottery*) smaltare ▷ n smalto

gleam [gliːm] vi luccicare

glen [glɛn] n valletta

glide [glaɪd] vi scivolare; (*Aviat, birds*) planare; **glider** n (*Aviat*) aliante m

glimmer [ˈglɪməʳ] n barlume m

glimpse [glɪmps] n impressione f fugace ▷ vt vedere al volo

glint [glɪnt] vi luccicare

glisten [ˈglɪsn] vi luccicare

glitter [ˈglɪtəʳ] vi scintillare

global [ˈgləʊbl] adj globale; **global warming** n effetto m serra inv

globe [gləʊb] n globo, sfera

gloom [gluːm] n oscurità, buio; (*sadness*) tristezza, malinconia; **gloomy** adj scuro(-a), fosco(-a), triste

glorious [ˈglɔːrɪəs] adj glorioso(-a), magnifico(-a)

glory [ˈglɔːrɪ] n gloria; splendore m

gloss [glɔs] n (*shine*) lucentezza; (*also: ~ paint*) vernice f a olio

glossary [ˈglɔsərɪ] n glossario

glossy [ˈglɔsɪ] adj lucente

glove [glʌv] n guanto; **glove compartment** n (*Aut*) vano portaoggetti

glow [gləʊ] vi ardere; (*face*) essere luminoso(-a)

glucose [ˈgluːkəʊs] n glucosio

glue [gluː] n colla ▷ vt incollare

GM adj abbr (= *genetically modified*) geneticamente modificato(-a)

gm abbr = **gram**

GMO n abbr (= *genetically modified organism*) OGM m inv

GMT abbr (= *Greenwich Mean Time*) T.M.G.

gnaw [nɔː] vt rodere

go [gəʊ] (*pt* **went**, *pp* **gone**) (*pl* **goes**) vi andare; (*depart*) partire, andarsene; (*work*) funzionare; (*time*) passare; (*break etc*) rompersi; (*be sold*): **to go for £10** essere venduto per 10 sterline; (*fit, suit*): **to go with** andare bene con; (*become*): **to go pale** diventare pallido(-a); **to go mouldy** ammuffire ▷ n **to have a go (at)** provare; **to be on the go** essere in moto; **whose go is it?** a chi tocca?; **he's going to do** sta per fare; **to go for a walk** andare a fare una passeggiata; **to go dancing/shopping** andare a ballare/fare la spesa; **just then the bell went** proprio allora suonò il campanello; **how did it go?** com'è andato?; **to go round the back/by the shop** passare da dietro/davanti al negozio; **go ahead** vi andare avanti; **go away** vi partire, andarsene; **go back** vi tornare, ritornare; **go by** vi (*years, time*) scorrere ▷ vt fus attenersi a, seguire (alla lettera); prestar fede a; **go down** vi scendere; (*ship*) affondare; (*sun*) tramontare ▷ vt fus scendere; **go for** vt fus (*fetch*) andare a prendere; (*like*) andar matto(-a) per; (*attack*) attaccare; saltare addosso a; **go in** *vi* entrare; **go into** *vt fus* entrare in; (*investigate*) indagare, esaminare; (*embark on*) lanciarsi in; **go off** *vi* partire, andar via; (*food*) guastarsi; (*explode*) esplodere, scoppiare; (*event*) passare ▷ *vt fus* **I've ~ne off chocolate** la cioccolata non mi piace più; **the gun went off** il fucile si scaricò; **go on** *vi* continuare; (*happen*) succedere; **to ~ on doing** continuare a fare; **go out** *vi* uscire; (*couple*) **they went out for 3 years** sono stati insieme per 3 anni; (*fire, light*) spegnersi; **go over** *vi* (*ship*) ribaltarsi ▷ *vt fus* (*check*) esaminare; **go past** *vi* passare ▷ *vt fus* passare davanti a; **go round** *vi* (*circulate: news, rumour*) circolare; (*revolve*) girare; (*visit*): **to ~ round (to sb's)** passare (da qn); (*make a detour*): **to ~ round (by)** passare (per); (*suffice*) bastare (per tutti); **go through** *vt fus* (*town etc*) attraversare; (*files, papers*) passare in rassegna; (*examine: list etc*) leggere da cima a fondo; **go up** *vi* salire; **go with** *vt fus* (*accompany*) accompagnare; **go without** *vt fus* fare a meno di

go-ahead ['gəuəhed] *adj* intraprendente ▷ *n* via *m*

goal [gəul] *n* (*Sport*) gol *m*, rete *f*; (: *place*) porta; (*fig: aim*) fine *m*, scopo; **goalkeeper** *n* portiere *m*; **goal-post** *n* palo (della porta)

goat [gəut] *n* capra

gobble ['gɔbl] *vt* (*also*: **~ down, ~ up**) ingoiare

god [gɔd] *n* dio; **G~** Dio; **godchild** *n* figlioccio(-a); **goddaughter** *n* figlioccia; **goddess** *n* dea; **godfather** *n* padrino; **godmother** *n* madrina; **godson** *n* figlioccio

goggles ['gɔglz] *npl* occhiali *mpl* (di protezione)

going ['gəuiŋ] *n* (*conditions*) andare *m*, stato del terreno ▷ *adj* **the ~ rate** la tariffa in vigore

gold [gəuld] *n* oro ▷ *adj* d'oro; **golden** *adj* (*made of gold*) d'oro; (*gold in colour*) dorato(-a); **goldfish** *n* pesce *m* dorato or rosso; **goldmine** *n* (*also fig*) miniera d'oro; **gold-plated** *adj* placcato(-a) oro *inv*

golf [gɔlf] *n* golf *m*; **golf ball** *n* (*for game*) pallina da golf; (*on typewriter*) pallina; **golf club** *n* circolo di golf; (*stick*) bastone *m* or mazza da golf; **golf course** *n* campo di golf; **golfer** *n* giocatore(-trice) di golf

gone [gɔn] *pp of* **go** ▷ *adj* partito(-a)

gong [gɔŋ] *n* gong *m inv*

good [gud] *adj* buono(-a); (*kind*) buono(-a), gentile; (*child*) bravo(-a) ▷ *n* bene *m*; **~s** *npl* (*Comm etc*) beni *mpl*; merci *fpl*; **~!** bene!, ottimo!; **to be ~ at** essere bravo(-a) in; **to be ~ for** andare bene per; **it's ~ for you** fa bene; **would you be ~ enough to …?** avrebbe la gentilezza di …?; **a ~ deal (of)** molto(-a), una buona quantità (di); **a ~ many** molti(-e); **to make ~** (*loss, damage*) compensare; **it's no ~ complaining** brontolare non serve a niente; **for ~** per sempre, definitivamente; **~ morning!** buon giorno!; **~ afternoon/evening!** buona sera!; **~ night!** buona notte!; **goodbye** *excl* arrivederci!; **Good Friday** *n* Venerdì Santo; **good-looking** *adj* bello(-a); **good-natured** *adj* affabile; **goodness** *n* (*of person*) bontà; **for goodness sake!** per amor di Dio!; **goodness gracious!** santo cielo!, mamma mia!; **goods train** (*BRIT*) *n* treno *m* merci *inv*; **goodwill** *n* amicizia, benevolenza

goose [gu:s] (*pl* **geese**) *n* oca

gooseberry ['guzbəri] *n* uva spina; **to play ~** (*BRIT*) tenere la candela

goose bumps, goose pimples *npl* pelle *f* d'oca

gorge [gɔ:dʒ] *n* gola ▷ *vt* **to ~ o.s. (on)** ingozzarsi (di)

gorgeous ['gɔ:dʒəs] *adj* magnifico(-a)

gorilla [gə'rilə] *n* gorilla *m inv*

gosh (*inf*) [gɔʃ] *excl* perdinci!

gospel ['gɔspl] *n* vangelo

gossip ['gɔsip] *n* chiacchiere *fpl*; pettegolezzi *mpl*; (*person*) pettegolo(-a) ▷ *vi* chiacchierare; **gossip column** *n* cronaca mondana

got [gɔt] *pt, pp of* **get**

gotten ['gɔtn] (*US*) *pp of* **get**

gourmet ['guəmei] *n* buongustaio(-a)

govern ['gʌvən] *vt* governare; **government** ['gʌvnmənt] *n* governo; **governor** ['gʌvənər] *n* (*of state, bank*) governatore *m*; (*of school, hospital*) amministratore *m*; (*BRIT: of prison*) direttore(-trice)

gown [gaun] *n* vestito lungo; (*of teacher, BRIT: of judge*) toga

G.P. *n abbr* = **general practitioner**

grab [græb] *vt* afferrare, arraffare; (*property, power*) impadronirsi di ▷ *vi* **to ~ at** cercare di afferrare

grace [greis] *n* grazia ▷ *vt* onorare; **5 days' ~** dilazione *f* di 5 giorni; **graceful** *adj* elegante, aggraziato(-a); **gracious** ['greiʃəs] *adj* grazioso(-a), misericordioso(-a)

grade [greid] *n* (*Comm*) qualità *f inv*; classe *f*; categoria; (*in hierarchy*) grado; (*Scol: mark*) voto; (*US: school class*) classe ▷ *vt* classificare; ordinare; graduare; **grade**

crossing (US) n passaggio a livello; **grade school** (US) n scuola elementare
gradient ['greɪdɪənt] n pendenza, inclinazione f
gradual ['grædjuəl] adj graduale; **gradually** adv man mano, a poco a poco
graduate [n 'grædjuɪt, vb 'grædjueɪt] n (of university) laureato(-a); (US: of high school) diplomato(-a) ▷ vi laurearsi; diplomarsi; **graduation** [-'eɪʃən] n (ceremony) consegna delle lauree (or dei diplomi)
graffiti [grə'fiːtɪ] npl graffiti mpl
graft [grɑːft] n (Agr, Med) innesto; (bribery) corruzione f; (BRIT: hard work): **it's hard** - è un lavoraccio ▷ vt innestare
grain [greɪn] n grano; (of sand) granello; (of wood) venatura
gram [græm] n grammo
grammar ['græmə'] n grammatica; **grammar school** (BRIT) n ≈ liceo
gramme [græm] n = **gram**
gran (inf) [græn] n (BRIT) nonna
grand [grænd] adj grande, magnifico(-a); grandioso(-a); **grandad** (inf) n = **granddad**; **grandchild** (pl -**children**) n nipote m; **granddad** (inf) n nonno; **granddaughter** n nipote f; **grandfather** n nonno; **grandma** (inf) n nonna; **grandmother** n nonna; **grandpa** (inf) n = **granddad**; **grandparents** npl nonni mpl; **grand piano** n pianoforte m a coda; **Grand Prix** ['grɑ̃'priː] n (Aut) Gran Premio, Grand Prix m inv; **grandson** n nipote m
granite ['grænɪt] n granito
granny ['grænɪ] (inf) n nonna
grant [grɑːnt] vt accordare; (a request) accogliere; (admit) ammettere, concedere ▷ n (Scol) borsa; (Admin) sussidio, sovvenzione f; **to take sth for ~ed** dare qc per scontato; **to take sb for ~ed** dare per scontata la presenza di qn
grape [greɪp] n chicco d'uva, acino
grapefruit ['greɪpfruːt] n pompelmo
graph [grɑːf] n grafico; **graphic** adj grafico(-a); (vivid) vivido(-a); **graphics** n grafica ▷ npl illustrazioni fpl
grasp [grɑːsp] vt afferrare ▷ n (grip) presa; (fig) potere m; comprensione f
grass [grɑːs] n erba; **grasshopper** n cavalletta
grate [greɪt] n graticola (del focolare) ▷ vi cigolare, stridere ▷ vt (Culin) grattugiare
grateful ['greɪtful] adj grato(-a), riconoscente
grater ['greɪtə'] n grattugia
gratitude ['grætɪtjuːd] n gratitudine f
grave [greɪv] n tomba ▷ adj grave, serio(-a)

gravel ['grævl] n ghiaia
gravestone ['greɪvstəun] n pietra tombale
graveyard ['greɪvjɑːd] n cimitero
gravity ['grævɪtɪ] n (Physics) gravità; pesantezza; (seriousness) gravità, serietà
gravy ['greɪvɪ] n intingolo della carne; salsa
gray [greɪ] adj = **grey**
graze [greɪz] vi pascolare, pascere ▷ vt (touch lightly) sfiorare; (scrape) escoriare ▷ n (Med) escoriazione f
grease [griːs] n (fat) grasso; (lubricant) lubrificante m ▷ vt ingrassare; lubrificare; **greasy** adj grasso(-a), untuoso(-a)
great [greɪt] adj grande; (inf) magnifico(-a), meraviglioso(-a); **Great Britain** n Gran Bretagna; **great-grandfather** n bisnonno; **great-grandmother** n bisnonna; **greatly** adv molto
Greece [griːs] n Grecia
greed [griːd] n (also: ~**iness**) avarizia; (for food) golosità, ghiottoneria; **greedy** adj avido(-a); goloso(-a), ghiotto(-a)
Greek [griːk] adj greco(-a) ▷ n greco(-a); (Ling) greco
green [griːn] adj verde; (inexperienced) inesperto(-a), ingenuo(-a) ▷ n verde m; (stretch of grass) prato; (on golf course) green m inv; ~**s** npl (vegetables) verdura; **green card** n (BRIT Aut) carta verde; (US Admin) permesso di soggiorno e di lavoro; **greengage** ['griːngeɪdʒ] n susina Regina Claudia; **greengrocer** (BRIT) n fruttivendolo(-a), erbivendolo(-a); **greenhouse** n serra; **greenhouse effect** n effetto serra
Greenland ['griːnlənd] n Groenlandia
green salad n insalata verde
greet [griːt] vt salutare; **greeting** n saluto; **greeting(s) card** n cartolina d'auguri
grew [gruː] pt of **grow**
grey [greɪ] (US **gray**) adj grigio(-a); **grey-haired** adj dai capelli grigi; **greyhound** n levriere m
grid [grɪd] n grata; (Elec) rete f; **gridlock** ['grɪdlɔk] n (traffic jam) paralisi f inv del traffico; **gridlocked** adj paralizzato(-a) dal traffico; (talks etc) in fase di stallo
grief [griːf] n dolore m
grievance ['griːvəns] n lagnanza
grieve [griːv] vi addolorarsi; rattristarsi ▷ vt addolorare; **to ~ for sb** (dead person) piangere qn
grill [grɪl] n (on cooker) griglia; (also: **mixed ~**) grigliata mista ▷ vt (BRIT) cuocere ai ferri; (inf: question) interrogare senza sosta
grille [grɪl] n grata; (Aut) griglia

grim [grɪm] *adj* sinistro(-a), brutto(-a)

grime [graɪm] *n* sudiciume *m*

grin [grɪn] *n* sorriso smagliante ▷ *vi* fare un gran sorriso

grind [graɪnd] (*pt, pp* **ground**) *vt* macinare; (*make sharp*) arrotare ▷ *n* (*work*) sgobbata

grip [grɪp] *n* impugnatura; presa; (*holdall*) borsa da viaggio ▷ *vt* (*object*) afferrare; (*attention*) catturare; **to come to ~s with** affrontare; cercare di risolvere; **gripping** ['grɪpɪŋ] *adj* avvincente

grit [grɪt] *n* ghiaia; (*courage*) fegato ▷ *vt* (*road*) coprire di sabbia; **to ~ one's teeth** stringere i denti

grits [grɪts] (*us*) *npl* macinato grosso (di avena *etc*)

groan [grəun] *n* gemito ▷ *vi* gemere

grocer ['grəusəʳ] *n* negoziante *m* di generi alimentari; **groceries** *npl* provviste *fpl*; **grocer's (shop)** *n* negozio di (generi) alimentari

grocery ['grəusərɪ] *n* (*shop*) (negozio di) alimentari

groin [grɔɪn] *n* inguine *m*

groom [gruːm] *n* palafreniere *m*; (*also:* **bride~**) sposo ▷ *vt* (*horse*) strigliare; (*fig*): **to ~ sb for** avviare qn a; **well-~ed** (*person*) curato(-a)

groove [gruːv] *n* scanalatura, solco

grope [grəup] *vi* **to ~ for** cercare a tastoni

gross [grəus] *adj* grossolano(-a); (*Comm*) lordo(-a); **grossly** *adv* (*greatly*) molto

grotesque [grəu'tesk] *adj* grottesco(-a)

ground [graund] *pt, pp of* **grind** ▷ *n* suolo, terra; (*land*) terreno; (*Sport*) campo; (*reason: gen pl*) ragione *f*; (*us: also:* **~ wire**) terra ▷ *vt* (*plane*) tenere a terra; (*us Elec*) mettere la presa a terra a; **~s** *npl* (*of coffee etc*) fondi *mpl*; (*gardens etc*) terreno, giardini *mpl*; **on/to the ~** per/a terra; **to gain/lose ~** guadagnare/perdere terreno; **ground floor** *n* pianterreno; **groundsheet** (*brit*) *n* telone *m* impermeabile; **groundwork** *n* preparazione *f*

group [gruːp] *n* gruppo ▷ *vt* (*also:* **~ together**) raggruppare ▷ *vi* (*also:* **~ together**) raggrupparsi

grouse [graus] *n inv* (*bird*) tetraone *m* ▷ *vi* (*complain*) brontolare

grovel ['grɔvl] *vi* (*fig*): **to ~ (before)** strisciare (di fronte a)

grow [grəu] (*pt* **grew**, *pp* **grown**) *vi* crescere; (*increase*) aumentare; (*develop*) svilupparsi; (*become*): **to ~ rich/weak** arricchirsi/indebolirsi ▷ *vt* coltivare, far crescere; **grow on** *vt fus* **that painting is ~ing on me** quel quadro più lo guardo più mi piace; **grow up** *vi* farsi grande, crescere

growl [graul] *vi* ringhiare

grown [grəun] *pp of* **grow**; **grown-up** *n* adulto(-a), grande *m/f*

growth [grəuθ] *n* crescita, sviluppo; (*what has grown*) crescita; (*Med*) escrescenza, tumore *m*

grub [grʌb] *n* larva; (*inf: food*) roba (da mangiare)

grubby ['grʌbɪ] *adj* sporco(-a)

grudge [grʌdʒ] *n* rancore *m* ▷ *vt* **to ~ sb sth** dare qc a qn di malavoglia; invidiare qc a qn; **to bear sb a ~ (for)** serbar rancore a qn (per)

gruelling ['gruəlɪŋ] (*us* **grueling**) *adj* estenuante

gruesome ['gruːsəm] *adj* orribile

grumble ['grʌmbl] *vi* brontolare, lagnarsi

grumpy ['grʌmpɪ] *adj* scorbutico(-a)

grunt [grʌnt] *vi* grugnire

guarantee [gærən'tiː] *n* garanzia ▷ *vt* garantire

guard [gɑːd] *n* guardia; (*one man*) guardia, sentinella; (*brit Rail*) capotreno; (*on machine*) schermo protettivo; (*also:* **fire~**) parafuoco ▷ *vt* fare la guardia a; (*protect*): **to ~ (against)** proteggere (da); **to be on one's ~** stare in guardia; **guardian** *n* custode *m/f*; (*of minor*) tutore(-trice)

guerrilla [gə'rɪlə] *n* guerrigliero

guess [gɛs] *vi* indovinare ▷ *vt* indovinare; (*us*) credere, pensare ▷ *n* **to take** *or* **have a ~** provare a indovinare

guest [gɛst] *n* ospite *m/f*; (*in hotel*) cliente *m/f*; **guest house** *n* pensione *f*; **guest room** *n* camera degli ospiti

guidance ['gaɪdəns] *n* guida, direzione *f*

guide [gaɪd] *n* (*person, book etc*) guida; (*brit: also:* **girl ~**) giovane esploratrice *f* ▷ *vt* guidare; **is there an English-speaking ~?** c'è una guida che parla inglese?; **guidebook** *n* guida; **do you have a guidebook in English?** avete una guida in inglese?; **guide dog** *n* cane *m* guida *inv*; **guided tour** *n* visita guidata; **what time does the guided tour start?** a che ora comincia la visita guidata?; **guidelines** *npl* (*fig*) indicazioni *fpl*, linee *fpl* direttive

guild [gɪld] *n* arte *f*, corporazione *f*; associazione *f*

guilt [gɪlt] *n* colpevolezza; **guilty** *adj* colpevole

guinea pig ['gɪnɪ-] *n* cavia

guitar [gɪ'tɑːʳ] *n* chitarra; **guitarist** *n* chitarrista *m/f*

gulf [gʌlf] *n* golfo; (*abyss*) abisso

gull [gʌl] *n* gabbiano

gulp [gʌlp] *vi* deglutire; (*from emotion*) avere il nodo in gola ▷ *vt* (*also:* **~ down**) tracannare, inghiottire

gum [gʌm] n (Anat) gengiva; (glue) colla; (also: **~drop**) caramella gommosa; (also: **chewing ~**) chewing-gum m inv ▷ vt **to ~ (together)** incollare

gun [gʌn] n fucile m; (small) pistola, rivoltella; (rifle) carabina; (shotgun) fucile da caccia; (cannon) cannone m; **gunfire** n spari mpl; **gunman** (irreg) n bandito armato; **gunpoint** n **at gunpoint** sotto minaccia di fucile; **gunpowder** n polvere f da sparo; **gunshot** n sparo

gush [gʌʃ] vi sgorgare; (fig) abbandonarsi ad effusioni

gust [gʌst] n (of wind) raffica; (of smoke) buffata

gut [gʌt] n intestino, budello; **~s** npl (Anat) interiora fpl; (courage) fegato

gutter ['gʌtər] n (of roof) grondaia; (in street) cunetta

guy [gaɪ] n (inf: man) tipo, elemento; (also: **~rope**) cavo or corda di fissaggio; (figure) effigie di Guy Fawkes

Guy Fawkes Night [-'fɔːks-] n (BRIT) vedi nota nel riquadro

gym [dʒɪm] n (also: **~nasium**) palestra; (also: **~nastics**) ginnastica; **gymnasium** [dʒɪm'neɪzɪəm] n palestra; **gymnast** ['dʒɪmnæst] n ginnasta m/f; **gymnastics** [-'næstɪks] n, npl ginnastica; **gym shoes** npl scarpe fpl da ginnastica

gynaecologist [gaɪnɪ'kɔlədʒɪst] (US **gynecologist**) n ginecologo(-a)

gypsy ['dʒɪpsɪ] n = **gipsy**

haberdashery ['hæbə'dæʃərɪ] (BRIT) n merceria

habit ['hæbɪt] n abitudine f; (costume) abito; (Rel) tonaca

habitat ['hæbɪtæt] n habitat m inv

hack [hæk] vt tagliare, fare a pezzi ▷ n (pej: writer) scribacchino(-a); **hacker** ['hækər] n (Comput) pirata m informatico

had [hæd] pt, pp of **have**

haddock ['hædək] (pl **haddock** or **haddocks**) n eglefino

hadn't ['hædnt] = **had not**

haemorrhage ['hɛmərɪdʒ] (US **hemorrhage**) n emorragia

haemorrhoids ['hɛmərɔɪdz] (US **hemorrhoids**) npl emorroidi fpl

haggle ['hægl] vi mercanteggiare

Hague [heɪg] n **The ~** L'Aia

hail [heɪl] n grandine f; (of criticism etc) pioggia ▷ vt (call) chiamare; (flag down: taxi) fermare; (greet) salutare ▷ vi grandinare; **hailstone** n chicco di grandine

hair [hɛər] n capelli mpl; (single hair: on head) capello; (: on body) pelo; **to do one's ~** pettinarsi; **hairband** ['hɛəbænd] n (elastic) fascia per i capelli; (rigid) cerchietto; **hairbrush** n spazzola per capelli; **haircut** n taglio di capelli; **hairdo** ['hɛəduː] n acconciatura, pettinatura;

hairdresser n parrucchiere(-a); **hairdresser's** n parrucchiere(-a); **hair dryer** n asciugacapelli m inv; **hair gel** n gel m inv per capelli; **hair spray** n lacca per capelli; **hairstyle** n pettinatura, acconciatura; **hairy** adj irsuto(-a), peloso(-a); (inf: frightening) spaventoso(-a)

hake [heɪk] (pl **hake** or **hakes**) n nasello

half [hɑːf] (pl **halves**) n mezzo, metà f inv ▷ adj mezzo(-a) ▷ adv a mezzo, a metà; **~ an hour** mezz'ora; **~ a dozen** mezza dozzina; **~ a pound** mezza libbra; **two and a ~** due e mezzo; **a week and a ~** una settimana e mezza; **~ (of it)** la metà; **~ (of)** la metà di; **to cut sth in ~** tagliare qc in due; **~ asleep** mezzo(-a) addormentato(-a); **half board** (BRIT) n mezza pensione; **half-brother** n fratellastro; **half day** n mezza giornata; **half fare** n tariffa a metà prezzo; **half-hearted** adj tiepido(-a); **half-hour** n mezz'ora; **half-price** adj, adv a metà prezzo; **half term** (BRIT) n (Scol) vacanza a or di metà trimestre; **half-time** n (Sport) intervallo; **halfway** adv a metà strada

hall [hɔːl] n sala, salone m; (entrance way) entrata

hallmark ['hɔːlmɑːk] n marchio di garanzia; (fig) caratteristica

hallo [hə'ləu] excl = **hello**

hall of residence (BRIT) n casa dello studente

Halloween [hæləu'iːn] n vigilia d'Ognissanti

○ **HALLOWEEN**

○
○ Negli Stati Uniti e in Gran Bretagna il
○ 31 ottobre si festeggia **Halloween**, la
○ notte delle streghe e dei fantasmi. I
○ bambini, travestiti da fantasmi, streghe
○ o mostri, bussano alle porte e ricevono
○ dolci e piccoli doni.

hallucination [həluːsɪ'neɪʃən] n allucinazione f

hallway ['hɔːlweɪ] n corridoio; (entrance) ingresso

halo ['heɪləu] n (of saint etc) aureola

halt [hɔːlt] n fermata ▷ vt fermare ▷ vi fermarsi

halve [hɑːv] vt (apple etc) dividere a metà; (expense) ridurre di metà

halves [hɑːvz] npl of **half**

ham [hæm] n prosciutto

hamburger ['hæmbəːgəʳ] n hamburger m inv

hamlet ['hæmlɪt] n paesetto

hammer ['hæməʳ] n martello ▷ vt martellare ▷ vi **to ~ on** or **at the door** picchiare alla porta

hammock ['hæmək] n amaca

hamper ['hæmpəʳ] vt impedire ▷ n cesta

hamster ['hæmstəʳ] n criceto

hamstring ['hæmstrɪŋ] n (Anat) tendine m del ginocchio

hand [hænd] n mano f; (of clock) lancetta; (handwriting) scrittura; (at cards) mano; (: game) partita; (worker) operaio(-a) ▷ vt dare, passare; **to give sb a ~** dare una mano a qn; **at ~** a portata di mano; **in ~** a disposizione; (work) in corso; **on ~** (person) disponibile; (services) pronto(-a) a intervenire; **to ~** (information etc) a portata di mano; **on the one ~ ...,** **on the other ~** da un lato ..., dall'altro; **hand down** vt passare giù; (tradition, heirloom) tramandare; (US: sentence, verdict) emettere; **hand in** vt consegnare; **hand out** vt distribuire; **hand over** vt passare; cedere; **handbag** n borsetta; **hand baggage** n bagaglio a mano; **handbook** n manuale m; **handbrake** n freno a mano; **handcuffs** npl manette fpl; **handful** n manciata, pugno

handicap ['hændɪkæp] n handicap m inv ▷ vt handicappare; **to be physically ~ped** essere handicappato(-a); **to be mentally ~ped** essere un(a) handicappato(-a) mentale

handkerchief ['hæŋkətʃɪf] n fazzoletto

handle ['hændl] n (of door etc) maniglia; (of cup etc) ansa; (of knife etc) impugnatura; (of saucepan) manico; (for winding) manovella ▷ vt toccare, maneggiare; (deal with) occuparsi di; (treat: people) trattare; **"~ with care"** "fragile"; **to fly off the ~** (fig) perdere le staffe, uscire dai gangheri; **handlebar(s)** n(pl) manubrio

hand: hand luggage n bagagli mpl a mano; **handmade** adj fatto(-a) a mano; **handout** n (money, food) elemosina; (leaflet) volantino; (at lecture) prospetto

handsome ['hænsəm] adj bello(-a); (profit, fortune) considerevole

handwriting ['hændraɪtɪŋ] n scrittura

handy ['hændɪ] adj (person) bravo(-a); (close at hand) a portata di mano; (convenient) comodo(-a)

hang [hæŋ] (pt, pp **hung**) vt appendere; (criminal: pt, pp **hanged**) impiccare ▷ vi (painting) essere appeso(-a); (hair) scendere; (drapery) cadere; **to get the ~ of sth** (inf) capire come qc funziona; **hang about** or **around** vi bighellonare, ciondolare; **hang down** vi ricadere; **hang on** vi (wait) aspettare; **hang out** vt (washing) stendere (fuori); (inf: live) stare ▷ vi penzolare, pendere; **hang round** vi = **hang around**; **hang up** vi (Tel) riattaccare ▷ vt appendere

hanger ['hæŋə^r] n gruccia

hang-gliding ['-glaɪdɪŋ] n volo col deltaplano

hangover ['hæŋəuvə^r] n (after drinking) postumi mpl di sbornia

hankie ['hæŋkɪ] n abbr = **handkerchief**

happen ['hæpən] vi accadere, succedere; (chance): **to ~ to do sth** fare qc per caso; **what ~ed?** cos'è successo?; **as it ~s** guarda caso

happily ['hæpɪlɪ] adv felicemente; fortunatamente

happiness ['hæpɪnɪs] n felicità, contentezza

happy ['hæpɪ] adj felice, contento(-a); **~ with** (arrangements etc) soddisfatto(-a) di; **to be ~ to do** (willing) fare volentieri; **~ birthday!** buon compleanno!

harass ['hærəs] vt molestare; **harassment** n molestia

harbour ['hɑːbə^r] (US **harbor**) n porto ▷ vt (hope, fear) nutrire; (criminal) dare rifugio a

hard [hɑːd] adj duro(-a) ▷ adv (work) sodo; (think, try) bene; **to look ~ at** guardare fissamente; esaminare attentamente; **no ~ feelings!** senza rancore!; **to be ~ of hearing** essere duro(-a) d'orecchio; **to be ~ done by** essere trattato(-a) ingiustamente; **hardback** n libro rilegato; **hardboard** n legno precompresso; **hard disk** n (Comput) disco rigido; **harden** vt, vi indurire

hardly ['hɑːdlɪ] adv (scarcely) appena; **it's ~ the case** non è proprio il caso; **~ anyone/ anywhere** quasi nessuno/da nessuna parte; **~ ever** quasi mai

hard: **hardship** ['hɑːdʃɪp] n avversità f inv; privazioni fpl; **hard shoulder** (BRIT) n (Aut) corsia d'emergenza; **hard-up** (inf) adj al verde; **hardware** ['hɑːdwɛə^r] n ferramenta fpl; (Comput) hardware m; (Mil) armamenti mpl; **hardware shop** (US **hardware store**) n (negozio di) ferramenta fpl; **hard-working** [-'wə:kɪŋ] adj lavoratore(-trice)

hardy ['hɑːdɪ] adj robusto(-a); (plant) resistente al gelo

hare [hɛə^r] n lepre f

harm [hɑːm] n male m; (wrong) danno ▷ vt (person) fare male a; (thing) danneggiare; **out of ~'s way** al sicuro; **harmful** adj dannoso(-a); **harmless** adj innocuo(-a), inoffensivo(-a)

harmony ['hɑːmənɪ] n armonia

harness ['hɑːnɪs] n (for horse) bardatura, finimenti mpl; (for child) briglie fpl; (safety harness) imbracatura ▷ vt (horse) bardare; (resources) sfruttare

harp [hɑːp] n arpa ▷ vi **to ~ on about** insistere tediosamente su

harsh [hɑːʃ] adj (life, winter) duro(-a); (judge, criticism) severo(-a); (sound) rauco(-a); (light) violento(-a)

harvest ['hɑːvɪst] n raccolto; (of grapes) vendemmia ▷ vt fare il raccolto di, raccogliere; vendemmiare

has [hæz] vb see **have**

hasn't ['hæznt] = **has not**

hassle ['hæsl] (inf) n sacco di problemi

haste [heɪst] n fretta; precipitazione f; **hasten** ['heɪsn] vt affrettare ▷ vi **to hasten (to)** affrettarsi (a); **hastily** adv in fretta; precipitosamente; **hasty** adj affrettato(-a), precipitoso(-a)

hat [hæt] n cappello

hatch [hætʃ] n (Naut: also: **~way**) boccaporto; (also: **service ~**) portello di servizio ▷ vi (bird) uscire dal guscio; (egg) schiudersi

hatchback ['hætʃbæk] n (Aut) tre (or cinque) porte f inv

hate [heɪt] vt odiare, detestare ▷ n odio; **hatred** ['heɪtrɪd] n odio

haul [hɔːl] vt trascinare, tirare ▷ n (of fish) pescata; (of stolen goods etc) bottino

haunt [hɔːnt] vt (fear) pervadere; (person) frequentare ▷ n rifugio; **this house is ~ed** questa casa è abitata da un fantasma; **haunted** adj (castle etc) abitato(-a) dai fantasmi or dagli spiriti; (look) ossessionato(-a), tormentato(-a)

 KEYWORD

have [hæv] (pt, pp **had**) aux vb **1** (gen) avere; essere; **to have arrived/gone** essere arrivato(-a)/andato(-a); **to have eaten/slept** avere mangiato/dormito; **he has been kind/promoted** è stato gentile/promosso; **having finished** or **when he had finished, he left** dopo aver finito, se n'è andato

2 (in tag questions): **you've done it, haven't you?** l'ha fatto, (non è) vero?; **he hasn't done it, has he?** non l'ha fatto, vero?

3 (in short answers and questions): **you've made a mistake — no I haven't/so I have** ha fatto un errore — ma no, niente affatto/sì, è vero; **we haven't paid — yes we have!** non abbiamo pagato — ma sì che abbiamo pagato!

▷ modal aux vb (be obliged): **to have (got) to do sth** dover fare qc; **I haven't got**

or **I don't have to wear glasses** non ho bisogno di portare gli occhiali
▷ vt 1 (*possess, obtain*) avere; **he has (got) blue eyes/dark hair** ha gli occhi azzurri/i capelli scuri; **do you have** or **have you got a car/phone?** ha la macchina/il telefono?; **may I have your address?** potrebbe darmi il suo indirizzo?; **you can have it for £5** te lo lascio per 5 sterline
2 (+ *noun: take, hold etc*): **to have breakfast/a swim/a bath** fare colazione/una nuotata/un bagno; **to have lunch** pranzare; **to have dinner** cenare; **to have a drink** bere qualcosa; **to have a cigarette** fumare una sigaretta
3: **to have sth done** far fare qc; **to have one's hair cut** farsi tagliare i capelli; **to have sb do sth** far fare qc a qn
4 (*experience, suffer*) avere; **to have a cold/flu** avere il raffreddore/l'influenza; **she had her bag stolen** le hanno rubato la borsa
5 (*inf: dupe*): **you've been had!** ci sei cascato!
have out vt **to have it out with sb** (*settle a problem etc*) mettere le cose in chiaro con qn

haven ['heɪvn] n porto; (*fig*) rifugio
haven't ['hævnt] = **have not**
havoc ['hævək] n caos m
Hawaii [həˈwaɪː] n le Hawaii
hawk [hɔːk] n falco
hawthorn ['hɔːθɔːn] n biancospino
hay [heɪ] n fieno; **hay fever** n febbre f da fieno; **haystack** ['heɪstæk] n pagliaio
hazard ['hæzəd] n azzardo, ventura; pericolo, rischio ▷ vt (*guess etc*) azzardare; **hazardous** adj pericoloso(-a); **hazard warning lights** npl (*Aut*) luci fpl di emergenza
haze [heɪz] n foschia
hazel ['heɪzl] n (*tree*) nocciolo ▷ adj (*eyes*) (*color*) nocciola inv; **hazelnut** ['heɪzlnʌt] n nocciola
hazy ['heɪzɪ] adj fosco(-a); (*idea*) vago(-a)
he [hiː] pron lui, egli; **it is he who ...** è lui che ...
head [hɛd] n testa; (*leader*) capo; (*of school*) preside m/f ▷ vt (*list*) essere in testa a; (*group*) essere a capo di; **~s or tails** testa (o croce), pari (o dispari); **~ first** a capofitto, di testa; **~ over heels in love** pazzamente innamorato(-a); **to ~ the ball** colpire una palla di testa; **head for** vt fus dirigersi verso; **head off** vt (*threat, danger*) sventare; **headache** n mal m di testa; **heading** n titolo; intestazione f; **headlamp** (*BRIT*) n

= **headlight**; **headlight** n fanale m;
headline n titolo; **head office** n sede f (centrale); **headphones** npl cuffia; **headquarters** npl ufficio centrale; (*Mil*) quartiere m generale; **headroom** n (*in car*) altezza dell'abitacolo; (*under bridge*) altezza limite; **headscarf** n foulard m inv; **headset** n = **headphones**; **headteacher** n (*of primary school*) direttore(-trice); (*of secondary school*) preside m/f; **head waiter** n capocameriere m
heal [hiːl] vt, vi guarire
health [hɛlθ] n salute f; **health care** n assistenza sanitaria; **health centre** (*BRIT*) n poliambulatorio; **health food** n cibo macrobiotico; **Health Service** (*BRIT*) n **the Health Service** ≈ il Servizio Sanitario Statale; **healthy** adj (*person*) sano(-a), in buona salute; (*climate*) salubre; (*appetite, economy etc*) sano(-a)
heap [hiːp] n mucchio ▷ vt (*stones, sand*): **to ~ (up)** ammucchiare; (*plate, sink*): **to ~ sth with** riempire qc di; **~s of** (*inf*) un mucchio di
hear [hɪəʳ] (*pt, pp* **heard**) vt sentire; (*news*) ascoltare ▷ vi sentire; **to ~ about** avere notizie di; sentire parlare di; **to ~ from sb** ricevere notizie da qn
hearing ['hɪərɪŋ] n (*sense*) udito; (*of witnesses*) audizione f; (*of a case*) udienza; **hearing aid** n apparecchio acustico
hearse [həːs] n carro funebre
heart [hɑːt] n cuore m; **~s** npl (*Cards*) cuori mpl; **to lose ~** scoraggiarsi; **to take ~** farsi coraggio; **at ~** in fondo; **by ~** (*learn, know*) a memoria; **heart attack** n attacco di cuore; **heartbeat** n battito del cuore; **heartbroken** adj **to be heartbroken** avere il cuore spezzato; **heartburn** n bruciore m di stomaco; **heart disease** n malattia di cuore
hearth [hɑːθ] n focolare m
heartless ['hɑːtlɪs] adj senza cuore
hearty ['hɑːtɪ] adj caloroso(-a); robusto(-a), sano(-a); vigoroso(-a)
heat [hiːt] n calore m; (*fig*) ardore m; fuoco; (*Sport: also: qualifying ~*) prova eliminatoria ▷ vt scaldare; **heat up** vi (*liquids*) scaldarsi; (*room*) riscaldarsi ▷ vt riscaldare; **heated** adj riscaldato(-a); (*argument*) acceso(-a); **heater** n radiatore m; (*stove*) stufa
heather ['hɛðəʳ] n erica
heating ['hiːtɪŋ] n riscaldamento
heatwave ['hiːtweɪv] n ondata di caldo
heaven ['hɛvn] n paradiso, cielo; **heavenly** adj divino(-a), celeste
heavily ['hɛvɪlɪ] adv pesantemente; (*drink, smoke*) molto

heavy | 294

heavy ['hɛvɪ] adj pesante; (sea) grosso(-a); (rain, blow) forte; (weather) afoso(-a); (drinker, smoker) gran (before noun); **it's too ~** è troppo pesante

Hebrew ['hi:bru:] adj ebreo(-a) ▷ n (Ling) ebraico

hectare ['hɛktɑːʳ] n (BRIT) ettaro

hectic ['hɛktɪk] adj movimentato(-a)

he'd [hi:d] = **he would**; **he had**

hedge [hɛdʒ] n siepe f ▷ vi essere elusivo(-a); **to ~ one's bets** (fig) coprirsi dai rischi

hedgehog ['hɛdʒhɔg] n riccio

heed [hi:d] vt (also: **take ~ of**) badare a, far conto di

heel [hi:l] n (Anat) calcagno; (of shoe) tacco ▷ vt (shoe) rifare i tacchi a

hefty ['hɛftɪ] adj (person) robusto(-a); (parcel) pesante; (profit) grosso(-a)

height [haɪt] n altezza; (high ground) altura; (fig: of glory) apice m; (: of stupidity) colmo; **heighten** vt (fig) accrescere

heir [ɛəʳ] n erede m; **heiress** n erede f

held [hɛld] pt, pp of **hold**

helicopter ['hɛlɪkɔptəʳ] n elicottero

hell [hɛl] n inferno; **~!** (inf) porca miseria!, accidenti!

he'll [hi:l] = **he will**; **he shall**

hello [hə'ləu] excl buon giorno!; ciao! (to sb one addresses as "tu"); (surprise) ma guarda!

helmet ['hɛlmɪt] n casco

help [hɛlp] n aiuto; (charwoman) donna di servizio ▷ vt aiutare; **~!** aiuto!; **can you ~ me?** può aiutarmi?; **~ yourself (to bread)** si serva (del pane); **he can't ~ it** non ci può far niente; **help out** vi aiutare ▷ vt **to ~ sb out** aiutare qn; **helper** n aiutante m/f, assistente m/f; **helpful** adj di grande aiuto; (useful) utile; **helping** n porzione f; **helpless** adj impotente; debole; **helpline** n ≈ telefono amico; (Comm) servizio m informazioni inv (a pagamento)

hem [hɛm] n orlo ▷ vt fare l'orlo a

hemisphere ['hɛmɪsfɪəʳ] n emisfero

hemorrhage ['hɛmərɪdʒ] (US) n = **haemorrhage**

hemorrhoids ['hɛmərɔɪdz] (US) npl = **haemorrhoids**

hen [hɛn] n gallina; (female bird) femmina

hence [hɛns] adv (therefore) dunque; **2 years ~** di qui a 2 anni

hen night n (inf) addio al nubilato

hepatitis [hɛpə'taɪtɪs] n epatite f

her [hə:ʳ] pron (direct) la, l' + vowel; (indirect) le; (stressed, after prep) lei ▷ adj il (la) suo(-a), i (le) suoi (sue); see also **me**; **my**

herb [hə:b] n erba; **herbal** adj di erbe; **herbal tea** n tisana

herd [hə:d] n mandria

here [hɪəʳ] adv qui, qua ▷ excl ehi!; **~!** (at roll call) presente!; **~ is/are** ecco; **~ he/she is** eccolo/eccola

hereditary [hɪ'rɛdɪtrɪ] adj ereditario(-a)

heritage ['hɛrɪtɪdʒ] n eredità; (fig) retaggio

hernia ['hə:nɪə] n ernia

hero ['hɪərəu] (pl **heroes**) n eroe m; **heroic** [hɪ'rəuɪk] adj eroico(-a)

heroin ['hɛrəuɪn] n eroina

heroine ['hɛrəuɪn] n eroina

heron ['hɛrən] n airone m

herring ['hɛrɪŋ] n aringa

hers [hə:z] pron il (la) suo(-a), i (le) suoi (sue); see also **mine**¹

herself [hə:'sɛlf] pron (reflexive) si; (emphatic) lei stessa; (after prep) se stessa, sé; see also **oneself**

he's [hi:z] = **he is**; **he has**

hesitant ['hɛzɪtənt] adj esitante, indeciso(-a)

hesitate ['hɛzɪteɪt] vi **to ~ (about/to do)** esitare (su/a fare); **hesitation** [-'teɪʃən] n esitazione f

heterosexual ['hɛtərəu'sɛksjuəl] adj, n eterosessuale m/f

hexagon ['hɛksəgən] n esagono

hey [heɪ] excl ehi!

heyday ['heɪdeɪ] n **the ~ of** i bei giorni di, l'età d'oro di

HGV n abbr = **heavy goods vehicle**

hi [haɪ] excl ciao!

hibernate ['haɪbəneɪt] vi ibernare

hiccough ['hɪkʌp] vi singhiozzare

hiccup ['hɪkʌp] = **hiccough**

hid [hɪd] pt of **hide**

hidden ['hɪdn] pp of **hide**

hide [haɪd] (pt **hid**, pp **hidden**) n (skin) pelle f ▷ vt **to ~ sth (from sb)** nascondere qc (a qn) ▷ vi **to ~ (from sb)** nascondersi (da qn)

hideous ['hɪdɪəs] adj laido(-a); orribile

hiding ['haɪdɪŋ] n (beating) bastonata; **to be in ~** (concealed) tenersi nascosto(-a)

hi-fi ['haɪfaɪ] n stereo ▷ adj ad alta fedeltà, hi-fi inv

high [haɪ] adj alto(-a); (speed, respect, number) grande; (wind) forte; (voice) acuto(-a) ▷ adv alto, in alto; **20m ~** alto(-a) 20m; **highchair** n seggiolone m; **high-class** adj (neighbourhood) elegante; (hotel) di prim'ordine; (person) di gran classe; (food) raffinato(-a); **higher education** n studi mpl superiori; **high heels** npl (heels) tacchi mpl alti; (shoes) scarpe fpl con i tacchi alti; **high jump** n (Sport) salto in alto; **the Highlands** le Highlands scozzesi; **highlight** n (fig: of event) momento culminante; (in hair) colpo di sole ▷ vt mettere in evidenza; **highlights** npl (in hair) colpi mpl di sole; **highlighter** n (pen) evidenziatore m; **highly** adv molto; **to speak highly of** parlare molto bene di; **highness** n **Her Highness** Sua Altezza; **high-rise** n (also: **high-rise block, high-rise building**) palazzone m; **high school** n scuola secondaria; (US) istituto superiore d'istruzione; **high season** (BRIT) n alta stagione; **high street** (BRIT) n strada principale; **high-tech** (inf) adj high-tech inv; **highway** ['haɪweɪ] n strada maestra; **Highway Code** (BRIT) n codice m della strada

hijack ['haɪdʒæk] vt dirottare; **hijacker** n dirottatore(-trice)

hike [haɪk] vi fare un'escursione a piedi ▷ n escursione f a piedi; **hiker** n escursionista m/f; **hiking** n escursioni fpl a piedi

hilarious [hɪ'lɛərɪəs] adj (behaviour, event) spassosissimo(-a)

hill [hɪl] n collina, colle m; (fairly high) montagna; (on road) salita; **hillside** n fianco della collina; **hill walking** n escursioni fpl in collina; **hilly** adj collinoso(-a); montagnoso(-a)

him [hɪm] pron (direct) lo, l' + vowel; (indirect) gli; (stressed, after prep) lui; see also **me**; **himself** pron (reflexive) si; (emphatic) lui stesso; (after prep) se stesso, sé; see also **oneself**

hind [haɪnd] adj posteriore ▷ n cerva

hinder ['hɪndər] vt ostacolare

hindsight ['haɪndsaɪt] n **with ~** con il senno di poi

Hindu ['hɪnduː] n indù m/f inv; **Hinduism** n (Rel) induismo

hinge [hɪndʒ] n cardine m ▷ vi (fig): **to ~ on** dipendere da

hint [hɪnt] n (suggestion) allusione f; (advice) consiglio; (sign) accenno ▷ vt **to ~ that** lasciar capire che ▷ vi **to ~ at** alludere a

hip [hɪp] n anca, fianco

hippie ['hɪpɪ] n hippy m/f inv

hippo ['hɪpəʊ] (pl **hippos**) n ippopotamo

hippopotamus [hɪpə'pɔtəməs] (pl **hippopotamuses** or **hippopotami**) n ippopotamo

hippy ['hɪpɪ] n = **hippie**

hire ['haɪər] vt (BRIT: car, equipment) noleggiare; (worker) assumere, dare lavoro a ▷ n nolo, noleggio; **for ~** da nolo; (taxi) libero(-a); **I'd like to ~ a car** vorrei noleggiare una macchina; **hire(d) car** (BRIT) n macchina a nolo; **hire purchase** (BRIT) n acquisto (or vendita) rateale

his [hɪz] adj, pron il (la) suo (sua), i (le) suoi (sue); see also **my**; **mine¹**

Hispanic [hɪs'pænɪk] adj ispanico(-a)

hiss [hɪs] vi fischiare; (cat, snake) sibilare

historian [hɪ'stɔːrɪən] n storico(-a)

historic(al) [hɪ'stɔrɪk(l)] adj storico(-a)

history ['hɪstərɪ] n storia

hit [hɪt] (pt, pp **hit**) vt colpire, picchiare; (knock against) battere; (reach: target) raggiungere; (collide with: car) urtare contro; (fig: affect) colpire; (find: problem etc) incontrare ▷ n colpo; (success, song) successo; **to ~ it off with sb** andare molto d'accordo con qn; **hit back** vi **to ~ back at sb** restituire il colpo a qn

hitch [hɪtʃ] vt (fasten) attaccare; (also: **~ up**) tirare su ▷ n (difficulty) intoppo, difficoltà f inv; **to ~ a lift** fare l'autostop; **hitch-hike** vi fare l'autostop; **hitch-hiker** n autostoppista m/f; **hitch-hiking** n autostop m

hi-tech ['haɪtɛk] adj high-tech inv

hitman ['hɪtmæn] (irreg) n (inf) sicario

HIV abbr **~-negative/-positive** adj sieronegativo(-a)/sieropositivo(-a)

hive [haɪv] n alveare m

hoard [hɔːd] n (of food) provviste fpl; (of money) gruzzolo ▷ vt ammassare

hoarse [hɔːs] adj rauco(-a)

hoax [həʊks] n scherzo; falso allarme

hob [hɔb] n piastra (con fornelli)

hobble ['hɔbl] vi zoppicare

hobby ['hɔbɪ] n hobby m inv, passatempo

hobo ['həʊbəʊ] (US) n vagabondo

hockey ['hɔkɪ] n hockey m; **hockey stick** n bastone m da hockey

hog [hɔg] n maiale m ▷ vt (fig) arraffare; **to go the whole ~** farlo fino in fondo

Hogmanay [hɔgmə'neɪ] n (Scottish) ≈ San Silvestro

hoist [hɔɪst] n paranco ▷ vt issare

hold [həʊld] (pt, pp **held**) vt tenere; (contain) contenere; (keep back) trattenere; (believe) mantenere; considerare; (possess) avere, possedere; detenere ▷ vi (withstand pressure) tenere; (be valid) essere valido(-a) ▷ n presa; (control): **to have a ~ over** avere controllo su; (Naut) stiva; **~ the line!** (Tel) resti in linea!; **to ~ one's own** (fig) difendersi bene; **to catch** or **get (a) ~ of** afferrare; **hold back** vt trattenere; (secret) tenere celato(-a); **hold on** vi tener fermo; (wait) aspettare; **~ on!** (Tel) resti in linea!; **hold out** vt offrire ▷ vi (resist) resistere; **hold up** vt (raise) alzare; (support) sostenere; (delay) ritardare; (rob) assaltare; **holdall** (BRIT) n borsone m; **holder** n (container) contenitore m; (of ticket, title) possessore/posseditrice; (of office etc) incaricato(-a); (of record) detentore(-trice)

hole [həʊl] n buco, buca

holiday ['hɔlədɪ] n vacanza; (day off)
giorno di vacanza; (public) giorno festivo;
on ~ in vacanza; **I'm on ~ here** sono qui
in vacanza; **holiday camp** (BRIT) n (also:
holiday centre) ≈ villaggio (di vacanze);
holiday job n (BRIT) ≈ lavoro estivo;
holiday-maker (BRIT) n villeggiante m/f;
holiday resort n luogo di villeggiatura
Holland ['hɔlənd] n Olanda
hollow ['hɔləu] adj cavo(-a); (container,
claim) vuoto(-a); (laugh, sound) cupo(-a) ▷ n
cavità f inv; (in land) valletta, depressione f
▷ vt **to ~ out** scavare
holly ['hɔlɪ] n agrifoglio
Hollywood ['hɔlɪwud] n Hollywood f
holocaust ['hɔləkɔːst] n olocausto
holy ['həulɪ] adj santo(-a); (bread, ground)
benedetto(-a), consacrato(-a)
home [həum] n casa; (country) patria;
(institution) casa, ricovero ▷ cpd familiare;
(cooking etc) casalingo(-a); (Econ, Pol)
nazionale, interno(-a); (Sport) di casa ▷ adv
a casa; in patria; (right in: nail etc) fino in
fondo; **at ~** a casa; (in situation) a proprio
agio; **to go** or **come ~** tornare a casa (or
in patria); **make yourself at ~** si metta
a suo agio; **home address** n indirizzo
di casa; **homeland** n patria; **homeless**
adj senza tetto; spatriato(-a); **homely**
adj semplice, alla buona; accogliente;
home-made adj casalingo(-a); **home
match** n partita in casa; **Home Office**
(BRIT) n ministero degli Interni; **home
owner** n proprietario(-a) di casa; **home
page** n (Comput) home page f inv; **Home
Secretary** (BRIT) n ministro degli Interni;
homesick adj **to be homesick** avere la
nostalgia; **home town** n città f inv natale;
homework n compiti mpl (per casa)
homicide ['hɔmɪsaɪd] (US) n omicidio
homoeopathic [həumɪə'pæθɪk] (US
homeopathic) adj omeopatico(-a)
homoeopathy [həumɪ'ɔpəθɪ] (US
homeopathy) n omeopatia
homosexual [hɔməu'sɛksjuəl] adj, n
omosessuale m/f
honest ['ɔnɪst] adj onesto(-a);
sincero(-a); **honestly** adv onestamente;
sinceramente; **honesty** n onestà
honey ['hʌnɪ] n miele m; **honeymoon**
n luna di miele, viaggio di nozze; **we're
on honeymoon** siamo in luna di miele;
honeysuckle n (Bot) caprifoglio
Hong Kong ['hɔŋ'kɔŋ] n Hong Kong f
honorary ['ɔnərərɪ] adj onorario(-a); (duty,
title) onorifico(-a)
honour ['ɔnəʳ] (US **honor**) vt onorare ▷ n
onore m; **honourable** (US **honorable**) adj
onorevole; **honours degree** n (Scol) laurea

specializzata
hood [hud] n cappuccio; (on cooker) cappa;
(BRIT Aut) capote f; (US Aut) cofano
hoof [huːf] (pl **hooves**) n zoccolo
hook [huk] n gancio; (for fishing) amo ▷ vt
uncinare; (dress) agganciare
hooligan ['huːlɪgən] n giovinastro,
teppista m
hoop [huːp] n cerchio
hooray [huː'reɪ] excl = **hurray**
hoot [huːt] vi (Aut) suonare il clacson;
(siren) ululare; (owl) gufare
Hoover® ['huːvəʳ] (BRIT) n aspirapolvere m
inv ▷ vt **hoover** pulire con l'aspirapolvere
hooves [huːvz] npl of **hoof**
hop [hɔp] vi saltellare, saltare; (on one foot)
saltare su una gamba
hope [həup] vt **to ~ that/to do** sperare
che/di fare ▷ vi sperare ▷ n speranza;
I ~ so/not spero di sì/no; **hopeful** adj
(person) pieno(-a) di speranza; (situation)
promettente; **hopefully** adv con
speranza; **hopefully he will recover**
speriamo che si riprenda; **hopeless** adj
senza speranza, disperato(-a); (useless)
inutile
hops [hɔps] npl luppoli mpl
horizon [hə'raɪzn] n orizzonte m;
horizontal [hɔrɪ'zɔntl] adj orizzontale
hormone ['hɔːməun] n ormone m
horn [hɔːn] n (Zool, Mus) corno; (Aut)
clacson m inv
horoscope ['hɔrəskəup] n oroscopo
horrendous [hə'rɛndəs] adj orrendo(-a)
horrible ['hɔrɪbl] adj orribile, tremendo(-a)
horrid ['hɔrɪd] adj orrido(-a); (person)
odioso(-a)
horrific [hɔ'rɪfɪk] adj (accident)
spaventoso(-a); (film) orripilante
horrifying ['hɔrɪfaɪɪŋ] adj terrificante
horror ['hɔrəʳ] n orrore m; **horror film** n
film m inv dell'orrore
hors d'œuvre [ɔː'dəːvrə] n antipasto
horse [hɔːs] n cavallo; **horseback: on
horseback** adj, adv a cavallo; **horse
chestnut** n ippocastano; **horsepower** n
cavallo (vapore); **horse-racing** n ippica;
horseradish n rafano; **horse riding** n
(BRIT) equitazione f
hose [həuz] n (also: **~pipe**) tubo; (also:
garden ~) tubo per annaffiare
hospital ['hɔspɪtl] n ospedale m; **where's
the nearest ~?** dov'è l'ospedale più vicino?
hospitality [hɔspɪ'tælɪtɪ] n ospitalità
host [həust] n ospite m; (Rel) ostia; (large
number): **a ~ of** una schiera di
hostage ['hɔstɪdʒ] n ostaggio(-a)
hostel ['hɔstl] n ostello; (also: **youth ~**)
ostello della gioventù

hostess ['həustɪs] n ospite f; (BRIT: air hostess) hostess f inv

hostile ['hɒstaɪl] adj ostile

hostility [hɒ'stɪlɪtɪ] n ostilità f inv

hot [hɒt] adj caldo(-a); (as opposed to only warm) molto caldo(-a); (spicy) piccante; (fig) accanito(-a); ardente; violento(-a), focoso(-a); **to be ~** (person) aver caldo; (object) essere caldo(-a); (weather) far caldo; **hot dog** n hot dog m inv

hotel [həu'tɛl] n albergo

hot-water bottle [hɒt'wɔːtə-] n borsa dell'acqua calda

hound [haund] vt perseguitare ▷ n segugio

hour ['auər] n ora; **hourly** adj all'ora

house [n haus, pl 'hauzɪz] [vb hauz] n (also: firm) casa; (Pol) camera; (Theatre) sala; pubblico; spettacolo; (dynasty) casata ▷ vt (person) ospitare, alloggiare; **on the ~** (fig) offerto(-a) dalla casa; **household** n famiglia; casa; **householder** n padrone(-a) di casa; (head of house) capofamiglia m/f; **housekeeper** n governante f; **housekeeping** n (work) governo della casa; (money) soldi mpl per le spese di casa; **housewife** (irreg) n massaia, casalinga; **house wine** n vino della casa; **housework** n faccende fpl domestiche

housing ['hauzɪŋ] n alloggio; **housing development** (BRIT), **housing estate** n zona residenziale con case popolari e/o private

hover ['hɒvər] vi (bird) librarsi; **hovercraft** n hovercraft m inv

how [hau] adv come; **~ are you?** come sta?; **~ do you do?** piacere!; **~ far is it to the river?** quanto è lontano il fiume?; **~ long have you been here?** da quando è qui?; **~ lovely!/awful!** che bello!/orrore!; **~ many?** quanti(-e)?; **~ much?** quanto(-a)?; **~ much milk?** quanto latte?; **~ many people?** quante persone?; **~ old are you?** quanti anni ha?

however [hau'ɛvər] adv in qualsiasi modo or maniera che; (+ adjective) per quanto + sub; (in questions) come ▷ conj comunque, però

howl [haul] vi ululare; (baby, person) urlare

H.P. abbr = **hire purchase**; **horsepower**

h.p. n abbr = **H.P**

HQ n, abbr = **headquarters**

hr(s) abbr (= hour(s)) h

HTML abbr (= hypertext markup language) HTML m inv

hubcap ['hʌbkæp] n coprimozzo

huddle ['hʌdl] vi **to ~ together** rannicchiarsi l'uno contro l'altro

huff [hʌf] n **in a ~** stizzito(-a)

hug [hʌg] vt abbracciare; (shore, kerb) stringere

huge [hjuːdʒ] adj enorme, immenso(-a)

hull [hʌl] n (of ship) scafo

hum [hʌm] vt (tune) canticchiare ▷ vi canticchiare; (insect, plane, tool) ronzare

human ['hjuːmən] (irreg) adj umano(-a) ▷ n essere m umano

humane [hjuː'meɪn] adj umanitario(-a)

humanitarian [hjuːmænɪ'tɛərɪən] adj umanitario(-a)

humanity [hjuː'mænɪtɪ] n umanità

human rights npl diritti mpl dell'uomo

humble ['hʌmbl] adj umile, modesto(-a) ▷ vt umiliare

humid ['hjuːmɪd] adj umido(-a); **humidity** [hjuː'mɪdɪtɪ] n umidità

humiliate [hjuː'mɪlɪeɪt] vt umiliare; **humiliating** adj umiliante; **humiliation** [-'eɪʃən] n umiliazione f

hummus ['huməs] n purè di ceci

humorous ['hjuːmərəs] adj umoristico(-a); (person) buffo(-a)

humour ['hjuːmər] (US **humor**) n umore m ▷ vt accontentare

hump [hʌmp] n gobba

hunch [hʌntʃ] n (premonition) intuizione f

hundred ['hʌndrəd] num cento; **~s of** centinaia fpl di; **hundredth** [-ɪdθ] num centesimo(-a)

hung [hʌŋ] pt, pp of **hang**

Hungarian [hʌŋ'gɛərɪən] adj ungherese ▷ n ungherese m/f; (Ling) ungherese m

Hungary ['hʌŋgərɪ] n Ungheria

hunger ['hʌŋgər] n fame f ▷ vi **to ~ for** desiderare ardentemente

hungry ['hʌŋgrɪ] adj affamato(-a); **to be ~** aver fame

hunt [hʌnt] vt (seek) cercare; (Sport) cacciare ▷ vi **to ~ (for)** andare a caccia (di) ▷ n caccia; **hunter** n cacciatore m; **hunting** n caccia

hurdle ['həːdl] n (Sport, fig) ostacolo

hurl [həːl] vt lanciare con violenza

hurrah [hu'rɑː] excl = **hurray**

hurray [hu'reɪ] excl urra!, evviva!

hurricane ['hʌrɪkən] n uragano

hurry ['hʌrɪ] n fretta ▷ vi (also: ~ up) affrettarsi ▷ vt (also: ~ up: person) affrettare; (work) far in fretta; **to be in a ~** aver fretta; **hurry up** vi sbrigarsi

hurt [həːt] (pt, pp **hurt**) vt (cause pain to) far male a; (injure, fig) ferire ▷ vi far male

husband ['hʌzbənd] n marito

hush [hʌʃ] n silenzio, calma ▷ vt zittire

husky ['hʌskɪ] adj roco(-a) ▷ n cane m eschimese

hut [hʌt] n rifugio; (shed) ripostiglio

hyacinth ['haɪəsɪnθ] n giacinto

hydrangea [haɪˈdreɪnʒə] n ortensia
hydrofoil [ˈhaɪdrəʊfɔɪl] n aliscafo
hydrogen [ˈhaɪdrədʒən] n idrogeno
hygiene [ˈhaɪdʒiːn] n igiene f; **hygienic**
[haɪˈdʒiːnɪk] adj igienico(-a)
hymn [hɪm] n inno; cantica
hype [haɪp] (inf) n campagna pubblicitaria
hyphen [ˈhaɪfn] n trattino
hypnotize [ˈhɪpnətaɪz] vt ipnotizzare
hypocrite [ˈhɪpəkrɪt] n ipocrita m/f
hypocritical [hɪpəˈkrɪtɪkl] adj ipocrita
hypothesis [haɪˈpɒθɪsɪs] (pl **hypotheses**)
n ipotesi f inv
hysterical [hɪˈsterɪkl] adj isterico(-a)
hysterics [hɪˈsterɪks] npl accesso di
isteria; (laughter) attacco di riso

I [aɪ] pron io
ice [aɪs] n ghiaccio; (on road) gelo; (ice
cream) gelato ▷ vt (cake) glassare ▷ vi
(also: ~ over) ghiacciare; (also: ~ up)
gelare; **iceberg** n iceberg m inv; **ice
cream** n gelato; **ice cube** n cubetto
di ghiaccio; **ice hockey** n hockey m su
ghiaccio
Iceland [ˈaɪslənd] n Islanda; **Icelander** n
islandese m/f; **Icelandic** [aɪsˈlændɪk] adj
islandese ▷ n (Ling) islandese m
ice: ice lolly (BRIT) n ghiacciolo; **ice rink**
n pista di pattinaggio; **ice skating** n
pattinaggio sul ghiaccio
icing [ˈaɪsɪŋ] n (Culin) glassa; **icing sugar**
(BRIT) n zucchero a velo
icon [ˈaɪkɒn] n icona
icy [ˈaɪsɪ] adj ghiacciato(-a); (weather,
temperature) gelido(-a)
I'd [aɪd] = **I would**; **I had**
ID card n = **identity card**
idea [aɪˈdɪə] n idea
ideal [aɪˈdɪəl] adj ideale ▷ n ideale m;
ideally [aɪˈdɪəlɪ] adv perfettamente,
assolutamente; **ideally the book
should have ...** l'ideale sarebbe che il
libro avesse ...
identical [aɪˈdentɪkl] adj identico(-a)
identification [aɪdentɪfɪˈkeɪʃən] n
identificazione f; **(means of) ~** carta

d'identità

identify [aɪ'dɛntɪfaɪ] vt identificare

identity [aɪ'dɛntɪtɪ] n identità f inv;
identity card n carta d'identità

ideology [aɪdɪ'ɔlədʒɪ] n ideologia

idiom ['ɪdɪəm] n idioma m; (phrase)
espressione f idiomatica

idiot ['ɪdɪət] n idiota m/f

idle ['aɪdl] adj inattivo(-a); (lazy) pigro(-a),
ozioso(-a); (unemployed) disoccupato(-a);
(question, pleasures) ozioso(-a) ▷ vi (engine)
girare al minimo

idol ['aɪdl] n idolo

idyllic [ɪ'dɪlɪk] adj idillico(-a)

i.e. adv abbr (= that is) cioè

if [ɪf] conj se; **if I were you ...** se fossi in te
..., io al tuo posto ...; **if so** se è così; **if not** se
no; **if only** se solo o soltanto

ignite [ɪg'naɪt] vt accendere ▷ vi
accendersi

ignition [ɪg'nɪʃən] n (Aut) accensione f; **to
switch on/off the ~** accendere/spegnere
il motore

ignorance ['ɪgnərəns] n ignoranza; **to
keep sb in ~ of sth** tenere qn all'oscuro
di qc

ignorant ['ɪgnərənt] adj ignorante; **to be
~ of** (subject) essere ignorante in; (events)
essere ignaro(-a) di

ignore [ɪg'nɔːʳ] vt non tener conto di;
(person, fact) ignorare

I'll [aɪl] = **I will; I shall**

ill [ɪl] adj (sick) malato(-a); (bad) cattivo(-a)
▷ n male m ▷ adv **to speak** etc **~ of sb**
parlare etc male di qn; **to take** or **be taken
~** ammalarsi

illegal [ɪ'liːgl] adj illegale

illegible [ɪ'lɛdʒɪbl] adj illeggibile

illegitimate [ɪlɪ'dʒɪtɪmət] adj
illegittimo(-a)

ill health n problemi mpl di salute

illiterate [ɪ'lɪtərət] adj analfabeta,
illetterato(-a); (letter) scorretto(-a)

illness ['ɪlnɪs] n malattia

illuminate [ɪ'luːmɪneɪt] vt illuminare

illusion [ɪ'luːʒən] n illusione f

illustrate ['ɪləstreɪt] vt illustrare

illustration [ɪlə'streɪʃən] n illustrazione f

I'm [aɪm] = **I am**

image ['ɪmɪdʒ] n immagine f; (public face)
immagine (pubblica)

imaginary [ɪ'mædʒɪnərɪ] adj
immaginario(-a)

imagination [ɪmædʒɪ'neɪʃən] n
immaginazione f, fantasia

imaginative [ɪ'mædʒɪnətɪv] adj
immaginoso(-a)

imagine [ɪ'mædʒɪn] vt immaginare

imbalance [ɪm'bæləns] n squilibrio

imitate ['ɪmɪteɪt] vt imitare; **imitation**
[-'teɪʃən] n imitazione f

immaculate [ɪ'mækjulət] adj
immacolato(-a); (dress, appearance)
impeccabile

immature [ɪmə'tjuəʳ] adj immaturo(-a)

immediate [ɪ'miːdɪət] adj immediato(-a);
immediately adv (at once) subito,
immediatamente; **immediately next to**
proprio accanto a

immense [ɪ'mɛns] adj immenso(-a);
enorme; **immensely** adv
immensamente

immerse [ɪ'məːs] vt immergere

immigrant ['ɪmɪgrənt] n immigrante
m/f; immigrato(-a); **immigration**
[ɪmɪ'greɪʃən] n immigrazione f

imminent ['ɪmɪnənt] adj imminente

immoral [ɪ'mɔrl] adj immorale

immortal [ɪ'mɔːtl] adj, n immortale m/f

immune [ɪ'mjuːn] adj **~ (to)** immune
(da); **immune system** n sistema m
immunitario

immunize ['ɪmjunaɪz] vt immunizzare

impact ['ɪmpækt] n impatto

impair [ɪm'pɛəʳ] vt danneggiare

impartial [ɪm'pɑːʃl] adj imparziale

impatience [ɪm'peɪʃəns] n impazienza

impatient [ɪm'peɪʃənt] adj impaziente; **to
get** or **grow ~** perdere la pazienza

impeccable [ɪm'pɛkəbl] adj impeccabile

impending [ɪm'pɛndɪŋ] adj imminente

imperative [ɪm'pɛrətɪv] adj
imperativo(-a); necessario(-a), urgente;
(voice) imperioso(-a)

imperfect [ɪm'pəːfɪkt] adj imperfetto(-a);
(goods etc) difettoso(-a) ▷ n (Ling: also: ~
tense) imperfetto

imperial [ɪm'pɪərɪəl] adj imperiale;
(measure) legale

impersonal [ɪm'pəːsənl] adj
impersonale

impersonate [ɪm'pəːsəneɪt] vt
impersonare; (Theatre) fare la mimica di

impetus ['ɪmpɪtəs] n impeto

implant [ɪm'plɑːnt] vt (Med) innestare;
(fig: idea, principle) inculcare

implement [n 'ɪmplɪmənt, vb 'ɪmplɪmɛnt]
n attrezzo; (for cooking) utensile m ▷ vt
effettuare

implicate ['ɪmplɪkeɪt] vt implicare

implication [ɪmplɪ'keɪʃən] n implicazione
f; **by ~** implicitamente

implicit [ɪm'plɪsɪt] adj implicito(-a);
(complete) completo(-a)

imply [ɪm'plaɪ] vt insinuare; suggerire

impolite [ɪmpə'laɪt] adj scortese

import [vb ɪm'pɔːt, n 'ɪmpɔːt] vt importare
▷ n (Comm) importazione f

importance [ɪmˈpɔːtns] n importanza
important [ɪmˈpɔːtnt] adj importante;
it's not ~ non ha importanza
importer [ɪmˈpɔːtəʳ] n
importatore(-trice)
impose [ɪmˈpəʊz] vt imporre ▷ vi **to ~
on sb** sfruttare la bontà di qn; **imposing**
[ɪmˈpəʊzɪŋ] adj imponente
impossible [ɪmˈpɔsɪbl] adj impossibile
impotent [ˈɪmpətnt] adj impotente
impoverished [ɪmˈpɔvərɪʃt] adj
impoverito(-a)
impractical [ɪmˈpræktɪkl] adj non
pratico(-a)
impress [ɪmˈprɛs] vt impressionare; (mark)
imprimere, stampare; **to ~ sth on sb** far
capire qc a qn
impression [ɪmˈprɛʃən] n impressione
f; **to be under the ~ that** avere
l'impressione che
impressive [ɪmˈprɛsɪv] adj notevole
imprison [ɪmˈprɪzn] vt imprigionare;
imprisonment n imprigionamento
improbable [ɪmˈprɔbəbl] adj improbabile;
(excuse) inverosimile
improper [ɪmˈprɔpəʳ] adj scorretto(-a);
(unsuitable) inadatto(-a), improprio(-a);
sconveniente, indecente
improve [ɪmˈpruːv] vt migliorare ▷ vi
migliorare; (pupil etc) fare progressi;
improvement n miglioramento;
progresso
improvise [ˈɪmprəvaɪz] vt, vi improvvisare
impulse [ˈɪmpʌls] n impulso; **on ~**
d'impulso, impulsivamente; **impulsive**
[ɪmˈpʌlsɪv] adj impulsivo(-a)

 KEYWORD

in [ɪn] prep **1** (indicating place, position) in;
in the house/garden in casa/giardino;
in the box nella scatola; **in the fridge**
nel frigorifero; **I have it in my hand** ce
l'ho in mano; **in town/the country** in
città/campagna; **in school** a scuola; **in
here/there** qui/lì dentro
2 (with place names: of town, region,
country): **in London** a Londra; **in England**
in Inghilterra; **in the United States** negli
Stati Uniti; **in Yorkshire** nello Yorkshire
3 (indicating time: during, in the space of) in;
in spring/summer in primavera/estate;
in 1988 nel 1988; **in May** in o a maggio; **I'll
see you in July** ci vediamo a luglio; **in the
afternoon** nel pomeriggio; **at 4 o'clock
in the afternoon** alle 4 del pomeriggio;
I did it in 3 hours/days l'ho fatto in 3
ore/giorni; **I'll see you in 2 weeks** or **in 2
weeks' time** ci vediamo tra 2 settimane

4 (indicating manner etc) a; **in a loud/soft
voice** a voce alta/bassa; **in pencil** a
matita; **in English/French** in inglese/
francese; **the boy in the blue shirt** il
ragazzo con la camicia blu
5 (indicating circumstances): **in the sun**
al sole; **in the shade** all'ombra; **in the
rain** sotto la pioggia; **a rise in prices** un
aumento dei prezzi
6 (indicating mood, state): **in tears** in
lacrime; **in anger** per la rabbia; **in
despair** disperato(-a); **in good condition**
in buono stato, in buone condizioni; **to
live in luxury** vivere nel lusso
7 (with ratios, numbers): **1 in 10** 1 su 10;
20 pence in the pound 20 pence per
sterlina; **they lined up in twos** si misero
in fila a due a due
8 (referring to people, works) in; **the
disease is common in children** la
malattia è comune nei bambini; **in (the
works of) Dickens** in Dickens
9 (indicating profession etc) in; **to be in
teaching** fare l'insegnante, insegnare; **to
be in publishing** essere nell'editoria
10 (after superlative) di; **the best in the
class** il migliore della classe
11 (with present participle): **in saying this**
dicendo questo, nel dire questo
▷ adv **to be in** (person: at home, work)
esserci; (train, ship, plane) essere
arrivato(-a); (in fashion) essere di moda; **to
ask sb in** invitare qn ad entrare; **to run/
limp etc in** entrare di corsa/zoppicando
etc
▷ n **the ins and outs of the problem**
tutti i particolari del problema

inability [ɪnəˈbɪlɪtɪ] n **~ (to do)** incapacità
(di fare)
inaccurate [ɪnˈækjurət] adj inesatto(-a),
impreciso(-a)
inadequate [ɪnˈædɪkwət] adj
insufficiente
inadvertently [ɪnədˈvəːtntlɪ] adv senza
volerlo
inappropriate [ɪnəˈprəupriət] adj
non adatto(-a); (word, expression)
improprio(-a)
inaugurate [ɪˈnɔːgjureɪt] vt inaugurare;
(president, official) insediare
Inc. (US) abbr (= incorporated) S.A.
incapable [ɪnˈkeɪpəbl] adj incapace
incense [n ˈɪnsɛns, vb ɪnˈsɛns] n incenso
▷ vt (anger) infuriare
incentive [ɪnˈsɛntɪv] n incentivo
inch [ɪntʃ] n pollice m (25 mm, 12 in a foot);
within an ~ of a un pelo da; **he didn't give
an ~** non ha ceduto di un millimetro

incidence ['ɪnsɪdns] n (of crime, disease) incidenza

incident ['ɪnsɪdnt] n incidente m; (in book) episodio

incidentally [ɪnsɪ'dɛntəlɪ] adv (by the way) a proposito

inclination [ɪnklɪ'neɪʃən] n inclinazione f

incline [n 'ɪnklaɪn, vb ɪn'klaɪn] n pendenza, pendio ▷ vt inclinare ▷ vi (surface) essere inclinato(-a); **to be ~d to do** tendere a fare; essere propenso(-a) a fare

include [ɪn'kluːd] vt includere, comprendere; **is service ~d?** il servizio è compreso?; **including** prep compreso(-a), incluso(-a); **inclusion** [ɪn'kluːʒən] n inclusione f; **inclusive** [ɪn'kluːsɪv] adj incluso(-a), compreso(-a); **inclusive of tax** etc tasse etc comprese

income ['ɪnkʌm] n reddito; **income support** n (BRIT) sussidio di indigenza or povertà; **income tax** n imposta sul reddito

incoming ['ɪnkʌmɪŋ] adj (flight, mail) in arrivo; (government) subentrante; (tide) montante

incompatible [ɪnkəm'pætɪbl] adj incompatibile

incompetence [ɪn'kɔmpɪtns] n incompetenza, incapacità

incompetent [ɪn'kɔmpɪtnt] adj incompetente, incapace

incomplete [ɪnkəm'pliːt] adj incompleto(-a)

inconsistent [ɪnkən'sɪstənt] adj incoerente; **~ with** non coerente con

inconvenience [ɪnkən'viːnjəns] n inconveniente m; (trouble) disturbo ▷ vt disturbare

inconvenient [ɪnkən'viːnjənt] adj scomodo(-a)

incorporate [ɪn'kɔːpəreɪt] vt incorporare; (contain) contenere

incorrect [ɪnkə'rɛkt] adj scorretto(-a); (statement) inesatto(-a)

increase [n 'ɪnkriːs, vb ɪn'kriːs] n aumento ▷ vi, vt aumentare; **increasingly** adv sempre più

incredible [ɪn'krɛdɪbl] adj incredibile; **incredibly** adv incredibilmente

incur [ɪn'kəː] vt (expenses) incorrere; (anger, risk) esporsi a; (debt) contrarre; (loss) subire

indecent [ɪn'diːsnt] adj indecente

indeed [ɪn'diːd] adv infatti; veramente; **yes ~!** certamente!

indefinitely [ɪn'dɛfɪnɪtlɪ] adv (wait) indefinitamente

independence [ɪndɪ'pɛndns] n indipendenza; **Independence Day** (US) n vedi nota nel riquadro

● **INDEPENDENCE DAY**
●
● Negli Stati Uniti il 4 luglio si festeggia
● l'**Independence Day**, giorno in
● cui, nel 1776, 13 colonie britanniche
● proclamarono la propria indipendenza
● dalla Gran Bretagna ed entrarono
● ufficialmente a far parte degli Stati Uniti
● d'America.

independent [ɪndɪ'pɛndənt] adj indipendente; **independent school** n (BRIT) istituto scolastico indipendente che si autofinanzia

index ['ɪndɛks] (pl **indexes**) n (in book) indice m; (: in library etc) catalogo; (pl **indices**: ratio, sign) indice m

India ['ɪndɪə] n India; **Indian** adj, n indiano(-a)

indicate ['ɪndɪkeɪt] vt indicare; **indication** [-'keɪʃən] n indicazione f, segno; **indicative** [ɪn'dɪkətɪv] adj **indicative of** indicativo(-a) di; **indicator** ['ɪndɪkeɪtə'] n indicatore m; (Aut) freccia

indices ['ɪndɪsiːz] npl of **index**

indict [ɪn'daɪt] vt accusare; **indictment** [ɪn'daɪtmənt] n accusa

indifference [ɪn'dɪfrəns] n indifferenza

indifferent [ɪn'dɪfrənt] adj indifferente; (poor) mediocre

indigenous [ɪn'dɪdʒɪnəs] adj indigeno(-a)

indigestion [ɪndɪ'dʒɛstʃən] n indigestione f

indignant [ɪn'dɪgnənt] adj **~ (at sth/with sb)** indignato(-a) (per qc/contro qn)

indirect [ɪndɪ'rɛkt] adj indiretto(-a)

indispensable [ɪndɪ'spɛnsəbl] adj indispensabile

individual [ɪndɪ'vɪdjuəl] n individuo ▷ adj individuale; (characteristic) particolare, originale; **individually** adv singolarmente, uno(-a) per uno(-a)

Indonesia [ɪndə'niːzɪə] n Indonesia

indoor ['ɪndɔː'] adj da interno; (plant) d'appartamento; (swimming pool) coperto(-a); (sport, games) fatto(-a) al coperto; **indoors** [ɪn'dɔːz] adv all'interno

induce [ɪn'djuːs] vt persuadere; (bring about, Med) provocare

indulge [ɪn'dʌldʒ] vt (whim) compiacere, soddisfare; (child) viziare ▷ vi **to ~ in sth** concedersi qc; abbandonarsi a qc; **indulgent** adj indulgente

industrial [ɪn'dʌstrɪəl] adj industriale; (injury) sul lavoro; **industrial estate** (BRIT) n zona industriale; **industrialist**

[ɪn'dʌstrɪəlɪst] n industriale m; **industrial park** (US) n = **industrial estate**

industry ['ɪndəstrɪ] n industria; (diligence) operosità

inefficient [ɪnɪ'fɪʃənt] adj inefficiente

inequality [ɪnɪ'kwɔlɪtɪ] n ineguaglianza

inevitable [ɪn'ɛvɪtəbl] adj inevitabile; **inevitably** adv inevitabilmente

inexpensive [ɪnɪk'spɛnsɪv] adj poco costoso(-a)

inexperienced [ɪnɪks'pɪərɪənst] adj inesperto(-a), senza esperienza

inexplicable [ɪnɪk'splɪkəbl] adj inesplicabile

infamous ['ɪnfəməs] adj infame

infant ['ɪnfənt] n bambino(-a)

infantry ['ɪnfəntrɪ] n fanteria

infant school n (BRIT) scuola elementare (per bambini dall'età di 5 a 7 anni)

infect [ɪn'fɛkt] vt infettare; **infection** [ɪn'fɛkʃən] n infezione f; **infectious** [ɪn'fɛkʃəs] adj (disease) infettivo(-a), contagioso(-a); (person: fig: enthusiasm) contagioso(-a)

infer [ɪn'fəː'] vt inferire, dedurre

inferior [ɪn'fɪərɪəʳ] adj inferiore; (goods) di qualità scadente ▷ n inferiore m/f; (in rank) subalterno(-a)

infertile [ɪn'fəːtaɪl] adj sterile

infertility [ɪnfəː'tɪlɪtɪ] n sterilità

infested [ɪn'fɛstɪd] adj ~ **(with)** infestato(-a) (di)

infinite ['ɪnfɪnɪt] adj infinito(-a); **infinitely** adv infinitamente

infirmary [ɪn'fəːmərɪ] n ospedale m; (in school, factory) infermeria

inflamed [ɪn'fleɪmd] adj infiammato(-a)

inflammation [ɪnflə'meɪʃən] n infiammazione f

inflatable [ɪn'fleɪtəbl] adj gonfiabile

inflate [ɪn'fleɪt] vt (tyre, balloon) gonfiare; (fig) esagerare; gonfiare; **inflation** [ɪn'fleɪʃən] n (Econ) inflazione f

inflexible [ɪn'flɛksɪbl] adj inflessibile, rigido(-a)

inflict [ɪn'flɪkt] vt **to ~ on** infliggere a

influence ['ɪnfluəns] n influenza ▷ vt influenzare; **under the ~ of alcohol** sotto l'effetto dell'alcool; **influential** [ɪnflu'ɛnʃl] adj influente

influx ['ɪnflʌks] n afflusso

info (inf) ['ɪnfəu] n = **information**

inform [ɪn'fɔːm] vt **to ~ sb (of)** informare qn (di) ▷ vi **to ~ on sb** denunciare qn

informal [ɪn'fɔːml] adj informale; (announcement, invitation) non ufficiale

information [ɪnfə'meɪʃən] n informazioni fpl; particolari mpl; **a piece of ~** un'informazione; **information office** n

ufficio m informazioni inv; **information technology** n informatica

informative [ɪn'fɔːmətɪv] adj istruttivo(-a)

infra-red [ɪnfrə'rɛd] adj infrarosso(-a)

infrastructure ['ɪnfrəstrʌktʃəʳ] n infrastruttura

infrequent [ɪn'friːkwənt] adj infrequente, raro(-a)

infuriate [ɪn'fjuərɪeɪt] vt rendere furioso(-a)

infuriating [ɪn'fjuərɪeɪtɪŋ] adj molto irritante

ingenious [ɪn'dʒiːnjəs] adj ingegnoso(-a)

ingredient [ɪn'griːdɪənt] n ingrediente m; elemento

inhabit [ɪn'hæbɪt] vt abitare; **inhabitant** [ɪn'hæbɪtnt] n abitante m/f

inhale [ɪn'heɪl] vt inalare ▷ vi (in smoking) aspirare; **inhaler** n inalatore m

inherent [ɪn'hɪərənt] adj ~ **(in or to)** inerente (a)

inherit [ɪn'hɛrɪt] vt ereditare; **inheritance** n eredità

inhibit [ɪn'hɪbɪt] vt (Psych) inibire; **inhibition** [-'bɪʃən] n inibizione f

initial [ɪ'nɪʃl] adj iniziale ▷ n iniziale f ▷ vt siglare; **~s** npl (of name) iniziali fpl; (as signature) sigla; **initially** adv inizialmente, all'inizio

initiate [ɪ'nɪʃɪeɪt] vt (start) avviare; intraprendere; iniziare; (person) iniziare; **to ~ sb into a secret** mettere qn a parte di un segreto; **to ~ proceedings against sb** (Law) intentare causa contro qn

initiative [ɪ'nɪʃətɪv] n iniziativa

inject [ɪn'dʒɛkt] vt (liquid) iniettare; (patient): **to ~ sb with sth** fare a qn un'iniezione di qc; (funds) immettere; **injection** [ɪn'dʒɛkʃən] n iniezione f, puntura

injure ['ɪndʒəʳ] vt ferire; (damage: reputation etc) nuocere a; **injured** adj ferito(-a); **injury** ['ɪndʒərɪ] n ferita

injustice [ɪn'dʒʌstɪs] n ingiustizia

ink [ɪŋk] n inchiostro; **ink-jet printer** ['ɪŋkdʒɛt-] n stampante f a getto d'inchiostro

inland [adj 'ɪnlənd, adv ɪn'lænd] adj interno(-a) ▷ adv all'interno; **Inland Revenue** (BRIT) n Fisco

in-laws ['ɪnlɔːz] npl suoceri mpl; famiglia del marito (or della moglie)

inmate ['ɪnmeɪt] n (in prison) carcerato(-a); (in asylum) ricoverato(-a)

inn [ɪn] n locanda

inner ['ɪnəʳ] adj interno(-a), interiore; **inner-city** n centro di una zona urbana

inning ['ɪnɪŋ] n (US: Baseball) ripresa; **~s**

(*Cricket*) turno di battuta

innocence ['ɪnəsns] *n* innocenza

innocent ['ɪnəsnt] *adj* innocente

innovation [ɪnəu'veɪʃən] *n* innovazione *f*

innovative ['ɪnəu'veɪtɪv] *adj* innovativo(-a)

in-patient ['ɪnpeɪʃənt] *n* ricoverato(-a)

input ['ɪnput] *n* input *m*

inquest ['ɪnkwest] *n* inchiesta

inquire [ɪn'kwaɪəʳ] *vi* informarsi ▷ *vt* domandare, informarsi su; **inquiry** *n* domanda; (*Law*) indagine *f*, investigazione *f*, **"inquiries"** "informazioni"

ins. *abbr* = **inches**

insane [ɪn'seɪn] *adj* matto(-a), pazzo(-a); (*Med*) alienato(-a)

insanity [ɪn'sænɪtɪ] *n* follia; (*Med*) alienazione *f* mentale

insect ['ɪnsekt] *n* insetto; **insect repellent** *n* insettifugo

insecure [ɪnsɪ'kjuəʳ] *adj* malsicuro(-a); (*person*) insicuro(-a)

insecurity [ɪnsɪ'kjuərɪtɪ] *n* mancanza di sicurezza

insensitive [ɪn'sensɪtɪv] *adj* insensibile

insert [ɪn'sɜːt] *vt* inserire, introdurre

inside ['ɪn'saɪd] *n* interno, parte *f* interiore ▷ *adj* interno(-a), interiore ▷ *adv* dentro, all'interno ▷ *prep* dentro, all'interno di; (*of time*): **~ 10 minutes** entro 10 minuti; **inside lane** *n* (*Aut*) corsia di marcia; **inside out** *adv* (*turn*) a rovescio; (*know*) in fondo

insight ['ɪnsaɪt] *n* acume *m*, perspicacia; (*glimpse, idea*) percezione *f*

insignificant [ɪnsɪg'nɪfɪknt] *adj* insignificante

insincere [ɪnsɪn'sɪəʳ] *adj* insincero(-a)

insist [ɪn'sɪst] *vi* insistere; **to ~ on doing** insistere per fare; **to ~ that** insistere perché + *sub*; (*claim*) sostenere che; **insistent** *adj* insistente

insomnia [ɪn'sɔmnɪə] *n* insonnia

inspect [ɪn'spekt] *vt* ispezionare; (*BRIT: ticket*) controllare; **inspection** [ɪn'spekʃən] *n* ispezione *f*, controllo; **inspector** *n* ispettore(-trice); (*BRIT: on buses, trains*) controllore *m*

inspiration [ɪnspə'reɪʃən] *n* ispirazione *f*; **inspire** [ɪn'spaɪəʳ] *vt* ispirare; **inspiring** *adj* stimolante

instability [ɪnstə'bɪlɪtɪ] *n* instabilità

install [ɪn'stɔːl] (*US* **instal**) *vt* installare; **installation** [ɪnstə'leɪʃən] *n* installazione *f*

instalment [ɪn'stɔːlmənt] (*US* **installment**) *n* rata; (*of TV serial etc*) puntata; **in ~s** (*pay*) a rate; (*receive*) una parte per volta; (: *publication*) a fascicoli

instance ['ɪnstəns] *n* esempio, caso; **for ~**

per *or* ad esempio; **in the first ~** in primo luogo

instant ['ɪnstənt] *n* istante *m*, attimo ▷ *adj* immediato(-a); urgente; (*coffee, food*) in polvere; **instantly** *adv* immediatamente, subito

instead [ɪn'sted] *adv* invece; **~ of** invece di

instinct ['ɪnstɪŋkt] *n* istinto; **instinctive** *adj* istintivo(-a)

institute ['ɪnstɪtjuːt] *n* istituto ▷ *vt* istituire, stabilire; (*inquiry*) avviare; (*proceedings*) iniziare

institution [ɪnstɪ'tjuːʃən] *n* istituzione *f*; (*educational institution, mental institution*) istituto

instruct [ɪn'strʌkt] *vt* **to ~ sb in sth** insegnare qc a qn; **to ~ sb to do** dare ordini a qn di fare; **instruction** [ɪn'strʌkʃən] *n* istruzione *f*; **instructions (for use)** istruzioni per l'uso; **instructor** *n* istruttore(-trice); (*for skiing*) maestro(-a)

instrument ['ɪnstrəmənt] *n* strumento; **instrumental** [-'mentl] *adj* (*Mus*) strumentale; **to be instrumental in** essere d'aiuto in

insufficient [ɪnsə'fɪʃənt] *adj* insufficiente

insulate ['ɪnsjuleɪt] *vt* isolare; **insulation** [-'leɪʃən] *n* isolamento

insulin ['ɪnsjulɪn] *n* insulina

insult [*n* 'ɪnsʌlt, *vb* ɪn'sʌlt] *n* insulto, affronto ▷ *vt* insultare; **insulting** *adj* offensivo(-a), ingiurioso(-a)

insurance [ɪn'ʃuərəns] *n* assicurazione *f*; **fire/life ~** assicurazione contro gli incendi/sulla vita; **insurance company** *n* società di assicurazioni; **insurance policy** *n* polizza d'assicurazione

insure [ɪn'ʃuəʳ] *vt* assicurare

intact [ɪn'tækt] *adj* intatto(-a)

intake ['ɪnteɪk] *n* (*Tech*) immissione *f*; (*of food*) consumo; (*BRIT: of pupils etc*) afflusso

integral ['ɪntɪgrəl] *adj* integrale; (*part*) integrante

integrate ['ɪntɪgreɪt] *vt* integrare ▷ *vi* integrarsi

integrity [ɪn'tegrɪtɪ] *n* integrità

intellect ['ɪntəlekt] *n* intelletto; **intellectual** [-'lektjuəl] *adj, n* intellettuale *m/f*

intelligence [ɪn'telɪdʒəns] *n* intelligenza; (*Mil etc*) informazioni *fpl*

intelligent [ɪn'telɪdʒənt] *adj* intelligente

intend [ɪn'tend] *vt* (*gift etc*): **to ~ sth for** destinare qc a; **to ~ to do** aver l'intenzione di fare

intense [ɪn'tens] *adj* intenso(-a); (*person*) di forti sentimenti

intensify [ɪn'tensɪfaɪ] *vt* intensificare

intensity [ɪn'tensɪtɪ] *n* intensità

intensive [ɪnˈtɛnsɪv] adj intensivo(-a);
intensive care n terapia intensiva;
intensive care unit (ICU) n reparto
terapia intensiva
intent [ɪnˈtɛnt] n intenzione f ▷ adj **~ (on)**
intento(-a) (a), immerso(-a) (in); **to all ~s
and purposes** a tutti gli effetti; **to be ~ on
doing sth** essere deciso a fare qc
intention [ɪnˈtɛnʃən] n intenzione
f; **intentional** adj intenzionale,
deliberato(-a)
interact [ɪntərˈækt] vi interagire;
interaction [ɪntərˈækʃən] n azione f
reciproca, interazione f; **interactive** adj
(Comput) interattivo(-a)
intercept [ɪntəˈsɛpt] vt intercettare;
(person) fermare
interchange [ˈɪntətʃeɪndʒ] n (exchange)
scambio; (on motorway) incrocio
pluridirezionale
intercourse [ˈɪntəkɔːs] n rapporti mpl
interest [ˈɪntrɪst] n interesse m; (Comm:
stake, share) interessi mpl ▷ vt interessare;
interested adj interessato(-a); **to be
interested in** interessarsi di; **interesting**
adj interessante; **interest rate** n tasso di
interesse
interface [ˈɪntəfeɪs] n (Comput) interfaccia
interfere [ɪntəˈfɪəʳ] vi **to ~ in** (quarrel, other
people's business) immischiarsi in; **to ~ with**
(object) toccare; (plans, duty) interferire
con; **interference** [ɪntəˈfɪərəns] n
interferenza
interim [ˈɪntərɪm] adj provvisorio(-a) ▷ n
in the ~ nel frattempo
interior [ɪnˈtɪərɪəʳ] n interno; (of
country) entroterra ▷ adj interno(-a);
(minister) degli Interni; **interior design** n
architettura d'interni
intermediate [ɪntəˈmiːdɪət] adj
intermedio(-a)
intermission [ɪntəˈmɪʃən] n pausa;
(Theatre, Cinema) intermissione f, intervallo
intern [vb ɪnˈtəːn, n ˈɪntəːn] vt internare
▷ n (US) medico interno
internal [ɪnˈtəːnl] adj interno(-a); **Internal
Revenue Service** (US) n Fisco
international [ɪntəˈnæʃənl] adj
internazionale ▷ n (BRIT Sport) incontro
internazionale
Internet [ˈɪntənɛt] n **the ~** Internet f;
Internet café n cybercaffè m inv; **Internet
Service Provider** n Provider m inv;
Internet user n utente m/f Internet
interpret [ɪnˈtəːprɪt] vt interpretare
▷ vi fare da interprete; **interpretation**
[ɪntəːprɪˈteɪʃən] n interpretazione f;
interpreter n interprete m/f; **could you
act as an interpreter for us?** ci potrebbe

fare da interprete?
interrogate [ɪnˈtɛrəʊgeɪt] vt interrogare;
interrogation [-ˈgeɪʃən] n interrogazione
f; (of suspect etc) interrogatorio
interrogative [ɪntəˈrɔgətɪv] adj
interrogativo(-a) ▷ n (Ling) interrogativo
interrupt [ɪntəˈrʌpt] vt, vi interrompere;
interruption [-ˈrʌpʃən] n interruzione f
intersection [ɪntəˈsɛkʃən] n intersezione
f; (of roads) incrocio
interstate [ˈɪntəsteɪt] (US) n fra stati
interval [ˈɪntəvl] n intervallo; **at ~s** a
intervalli
intervene [ɪntəˈviːn] vi (time) intercorrere;
(event, person) intervenire
interview [ˈɪntəvjuː] n (Radio, TV
etc) intervista; (for job) colloquio ▷ vt
intervistare; avere un colloquio con;
interviewer n intervistatore(-trice)
intimate [adj ˈɪntɪmət, vb ˈɪntɪmeɪt] adj
intimo(-a); (knowledge) profondo(-a) ▷ vt
lasciar capire
intimidate [ɪnˈtɪmɪdeɪt] vt intimidire,
intimorire
intimidating [ɪnˈtɪmɪdeɪtɪŋ] adj (sight)
spaventoso(-a); (appearance, figure)
minaccioso(-a)
into [ˈɪntuː] prep dentro, in; **come ~ the
house** entra in casa; **he worked late ~ the
night** lavorò fino a tarda notte; **~ Italian**
in italiano
intolerant [ɪnˈtɔlərnt] adj **~ of**
intollerante di
intranet [ˈɪntrənɛt] n intranet f
intransitive [ɪnˈtrænsɪtɪv] adj
intransitivo(-a)
intricate [ˈɪntrɪkət] adj intricato(-a),
complicato(-a)
intrigue [ɪnˈtriːg] n intrigo ▷ vt
affascinare; **intriguing** adj affascinante
introduce [ɪntrəˈdjuːs] vt introdurre;
to ~ sb (to sb) presentare qn (a qn); **to
~ sb to** (pastime, technique) iniziare qn a;
introduction [-ˈdʌkʃən] n introduzione
f; (of person) presentazione f; (to new
experience) iniziazione f; **introductory** adj
introduttivo(-a)
intrude [ɪnˈtruːd] vi (person): **to ~ (on)**
intromettersi (in); **intruder** n intruso(-a)
intuition [ɪntjuːˈɪʃən] n intuizione f
inundate [ˈɪnʌndeɪt] vt **to ~ with**
inondare di
invade [ɪnˈveɪd] vt invadere
invalid [n ˈɪnvəlɪd, adj ɪnˈvælɪd] n
malato(-a); (with disability) invalido(-a)
▷ adj (not valid) invalido(-a), non valido(-a)
invaluable [ɪnˈvæljuəbl] adj prezioso(-a);
inestimabile
invariably [ɪnˈvɛərɪəblɪ] adv

invariabilmente; sempre

invasion [ɪnˈveɪʒən] n invasione f

invent [ɪnˈvɛnt] vt inventare; **invention** [ɪnˈvɛnʃən] n invenzione f; **inventor** n inventore m

inventory [ˈɪnvəntrɪ] n inventario

inverted commas [ɪnˈvəːtɪd-] npl virgolette fpl

invest [ɪnˈvɛst] vt investire ▷ vi **to ~ (in)** investire (in)

investigate [ɪnˈvɛstɪgeɪt] vt investigare, indagare; (crime) fare indagini su; **investigation** [-ˈgeɪʃən] n investigazione f; (of crime) indagine f

investigator [ɪnˈvɛstɪgeɪtər] n investigatore(-trice); **a private ~** un investigatore privato, un detective

investment [ɪnˈvɛstmənt] n investimento

investor [ɪnˈvɛstər] n investitore(-trice); azionista m/f

invisible [ɪnˈvɪzɪbl] adj invisibile

invitation [ɪnvɪˈteɪʃən] n invito

invite [ɪnˈvaɪt] vt invitare; (opinions etc) sollecitare; **inviting** adj invitante, attraente

invoice [ˈɪnvɔɪs] n fattura ▷ vt fatturare

involve [ɪnˈvɔlv] vt (entail) richiedere, comportare; (associate): **to ~ sb (in)** implicare qn (in); coinvolgere qn (in); **involved** adj involuto(-a), complesso(-a); **to be involved in** essere coinvolto(-a) in; **involvement** n implicazione f; coinvolgimento

inward [ˈɪnwəd] adj (movement) verso l'interno; (thought, feeling) interiore, intimo(-a); **inward(s)** adv verso l'interno

IQ n abbr (= intelligence quotient) quoziente m d'intelligenza

IRA n abbr (= Irish Republican Army) IRA f

Iran [ɪˈrɑːn] n Iran m; **Iranian** adj, n iraniano(-a)

Iraq [ɪˈrɑːk] n Iraq m; **Iraqi** adj, n iracheno(-a)

Ireland [ˈaɪələnd] n Irlanda

iris [ˈaɪrɪs] (pl **irises**) n iride f; (Bot) giaggiolo, iride

Irish [ˈaɪrɪʃ] adj irlandese ▷ npl **the ~** gli Irlandesi; **Irishman** (irreg) n irlandese m; **Irish Sea** n Mar m d'Irlanda; **Irishwoman** (irreg) n irlandese f

iron [ˈaɪən] n ferro; (for clothes) ferro da stiro ▷ adj di or in ferro ▷ vt (clothes) stirare

ironic(al) [aɪˈrɔnɪk(l)] adj ironico(-a); **ironically** adv ironicamente

ironing [ˈaɪənɪŋ] n (act) stirare m; (clothes) roba da stirare; **ironing board** n asse f da stiro

irony [ˈaɪrənɪ] n ironia

irrational [ɪˈræʃənl] adj irrazionale

irregular [ɪˈrɛgjulər] adj irregolare

irrelevant [ɪˈrɛləvənt] adj non pertinente

irresistible [ɪrɪˈzɪstɪbl] adj irresistibile

irresponsible [ɪrɪˈspɔnsɪbl] adj irresponsabile

irrigation [ɪrɪˈgeɪʃən] n irrigazione f

irritable [ˈɪrɪtəbl] adj irritabile

irritate [ˈɪrɪteɪt] vt irritare; **irritating** adj (person, sound etc) irritante; **irritation** [-ˈteɪʃən] n irritazione f

IRS (US) n abbr = **Internal Revenue Service**

is [ɪz] vb see **be**

ISDN n abbr (= Integrated Services Digital Network) I.S.D.N. f

Islam [ˈɪzlɑːm] n Islam m; **Islamic** [ɪzˈlæmɪk] adj islamico(-a)

island [ˈaɪlənd] n isola; **islander** n isolano(-a)

isle [aɪl] n isola

isn't [ˈɪznt] = **is not**

isolated [ˈaɪsəleɪtɪd] adj isolato(-a)

isolation [aɪsəˈleɪʃən] n isolamento

ISP n abbr (= Internet Service Provider) provider m inv

Israel [ˈɪzreɪl] n Israele m; **Israeli** [ɪzˈreɪlɪ] adj, n israeliano(-a)

issue [ˈɪʃjuː] n questione f, problema m; (of banknotes etc) emissione f; (of newspaper etc) numero ▷ vt (statement) rilasciare; (rations, equipment) distribuire; (book) pubblicare; (banknotes, cheques, stamps) emettere; **at ~** in gioco, in discussione; **to take ~ with sb (over sth)** prendere posizione contro qn (riguardo a qc); **to make an ~ of sth** fare un problema di qc

KEYWORD

it [ɪt] pron **1** (specific: subject) esso(-a); (: direct object) lo (la), l'; (: indirect object) gli (le); **where's my book? — it's on the table** dov'è il mio libro? — è sulla tavola; **I can't find it** non lo (or la) trovo; **give it to me** dammelo (or dammela); **about/from/ of it** ne; **I spoke to him about it** gliene ho parlato; **what did you learn from it?** quale insegnamento ne hai tratto?; **I'm proud of it** ne sono fiero; **did you go to it?** ci sei andato?; **put the book in it** mettici il libro

2 (impers): **it's raining** piove; **it's Friday tomorrow** domani è venerdì; **it's 6 o'clock** sono le 6; **who is it? — it's me** chi è? — sono io

IT n abbr see **information technology**

Italian [ɪˈtæljən] adj italiano(-a) ▷ n

italiano(-a); (*Ling*) italiano; **the ~s** gli
Italiani; **what's the ~ (word) for ...?** come
si dice in italiano ...?
italics [ɪ'tælɪks] *npl* corsivo
Italy ['ɪtəlɪ] *n* Italia
itch [ɪtʃ] *n* prurito ▷ *vi* (*person*) avere il
prurito; (*part of body*) prudere; **to ~ to do
sth** aver una gran voglia di fare qc; **itchy**
adj che prude; **to be itchy = to itch**
it'd ['ɪtd] = **it would; it had**
item ['aɪtəm] *n* articolo; (*on agenda*) punto;
(*also:* **news ~**) notizia
itinerary [aɪ'tɪnərərɪ] *n* itinerario
it'll ['ɪtl] = **it will; it shall**
its [ɪts] *adj* il (la) suo(-a), i (le) suoi (sue)
it's [ɪts] = **it is; it has**
itself [ɪt'sɛlf] *pron* (*emphatic*) esso(-a)
stesso(-a); (*reflexive*) si
ITV (*BRIT*) *n abbr* (= *Independent Television*)
rete televisiva in concorrenza con la BBC
I've [aɪv] = **I have**
ivory ['aɪvərɪ] *n* avorio
ivy ['aɪvɪ] *n* edera

jab [dʒæb] *vt* dare colpetti a ▷ *n* (*Med:
inf*) puntura; **to ~ sth into** affondare or
piantare qc dentro
jack [dʒæk] *n* (*Aut*) cricco; (*Cards*) fante *m*
jacket ['dʒækɪt] *n* giacca; (*of book*)
copertura; **jacket potato** *n* patata cotta al
forno con la buccia
jackpot ['dʒækpɔt] *n* primo premio (in
denaro)
Jacuzzi® [dʒə'kuːzɪ] *n* vasca per
idromassaggio Jacuzzi®
jagged ['dʒægɪd] *adj* seghettato(-a); (*cliffs
etc*) frastagliato(-a)
jail [dʒeɪl] *n* prigione *f* ▷ *vt* mandare in
prigione; **jail sentence** *n* condanna al
carcere
jam [dʒæm] *n* marmellata; (*also:* **traffic
~**) ingorgo; (*inf*) pasticcio ▷ *vt* (*passage
etc*) ingombrare, ostacolare; (*mechanism,
drawer etc*) bloccare; (*Radio*) disturbare con
interferenze ▷ *vi* incepparsi; **to ~ sth into**
forzare qc dentro; infilare qc a forza dentro
Jamaica [dʒə'meɪkə] *n* Giamaica
jammed [dʒæmd] *adj* (*door*) bloccato(-a);
(*rifle, printer*) inceppato(-a)
Jan. *abbr* (= *January*) gen., genn.
janitor ['dʒænɪtə*] *n* (*caretaker*) portiere *m*;
(*: Scol*) bidello
January ['dʒænjuərɪ] *n* gennaio
Japan [dʒə'pæn] *n* Giappone *m*; **Japanese**

[dʒæpə'niːz] adj giapponese ▷ n inv giapponese m/f; (Ling) giapponese m

jar [dʒɑːʳ] n (glass) barattolo, vasetto ▷ vi (sound) stridere; (colours etc) stonare

jargon ['dʒɑːɡən] n gergo

javelin ['dʒævlɪn] n giavellotto

jaw [dʒɔː] n mascella

jazz [dʒæz] n jazz m

jealous ['dʒɛləs] adj geloso(-a); **jealousy** n gelosia

jeans [dʒiːnz] npl (blue-)jeans mpl

Jello® ['dʒɛləʊ] (us) n gelatina di frutta

jelly ['dʒɛlɪ] n gelatina; **jellyfish** n medusa

jeopardize ['dʒɛpədaɪz] vt mettere in pericolo

jerk [dʒəːk] n sobbalzo, scossa; sussulto; (inf: idiot) tonto(-a) ▷ vt dare una scossa a ▷ vi (vehicles) sobbalzare

jersey ['dʒəːzɪ] n Jersey m

jersey ['dʒəːzɪ] n maglia; (fabric) jersey m

Jesus ['dʒiːzəs] n Gesù m

jet [dʒɛt] n (of gas, liquid) getto; (Aviat) aviogetto; **jet lag** n (problemi mpl dovuti allo) sbalzo dei fusi orari; **jet-ski** vi acquascooter m inv

jetty ['dʒɛtɪ] n molo

Jew [dʒuː] n ebreo

jewel ['dʒuːəl] n gioiello; **jeweller** (us **jeweler**) n orefice m, gioielliere(-a); **jeweller's (shop)** (us **jewelry store**) n oreficeria, gioielleria; **jewellery** (us **jewelry**) n gioielli mpl

Jewish ['dʒuːɪʃ] adj ebreo(-a), ebraico(-a)

jigsaw ['dʒɪɡsɔː] n (also: ~ puzzle) puzzle m inv

job [dʒɔb] n lavoro; (employment) impiego, posto; **it's not my ~** (duty) non è compito mio; **it's a good ~ that ...** meno male che ...; **just the ~!** proprio quello che ci vuole; **job centre** (BRIT) n ufficio di collocamento; **jobless** adj senza lavoro, disoccupato(-a)

jockey ['dʒɔkɪ] n fantino, jockey m inv ▷ vi **to ~ for position** manovrare per una posizione di vantaggio

jog [dʒɔg] vt urtare ▷ vi (Sport) fare footing, fare jogging; **to ~ sb's memory** rinfrescare la memoria a qn; **to ~ along** trottare; (fig) andare avanti piano piano; **jogging** n footing m, jogging m

join [dʒɔɪn] vt unire, congiungere; (become member of) iscriversi a; (meet) raggiungere; riunirsi a ▷ vi (roads, rivers) confluire ▷ n giuntura; **join in** vi partecipare ▷ vt fus unirsi a; **join up** vi incontrarsi; (Mil) arruolarsi

joiner ['dʒɔɪnəʳ] (BRIT) n falegname m

joint [dʒɔɪnt] n (Tech) giuntura; giunto; (Anat) articolazione f, giuntura; (BRIT Culin) arrosto; (inf: place) locale m; (: of cannabis) spinello ▷ adj comune; **joint account** n (at bank etc) conto in partecipazione, conto comune; **jointly** adv in comune, insieme

joke [dʒəʊk] n scherzo; (funny story) barzelletta; (also: **practical ~**) beffa ▷ vi scherzare; **to play a ~ on sb** fare uno scherzo a qn; **joker** n (Cards) matta, jolly m inv

jolly ['dʒɔlɪ] adj allegro(-a), gioioso(-a) ▷ adv (BRIT: inf) veramente, proprio

jolt [dʒəʊlt] n scossa, sobbalzo ▷ vt urtare

Jordan ['dʒɔːdən] n (country) Giordania; (river) Giordano

journal ['dʒəːnl] n giornale m; rivista; diario; **journalism** n giornalismo; **journalist** n giornalista m/f

journey ['dʒəːnɪ] n viaggio; (distance covered) tragitto; **how was your ~?** com'è andato il viaggio?; **the ~ takes two hours** il viaggio dura due ore

joy [dʒɔɪ] n gioia; **joyrider** n chi ruba un'auto per farvi un giro; **joy stick** n (Aviat) barra di comando; (Comput) joystick m inv

Jr abbr = **junior**

judge [dʒʌdʒ] n giudice m/f ▷ vt giudicare

judo ['dʒuːdəʊ] n judo

jug [dʒʌg] n brocca, bricco

juggle ['dʒʌgl] vi fare giochi di destrezza; **juggler** n giocoliere(-a)

juice [dʒuːs] n succo; **juicy** ['dʒuːsɪ] adj succoso(-a)

Jul. abbr (= July) lug., lu.

July [dʒuː'laɪ] n luglio

jumble ['dʒʌmbl] n miscuglio ▷ vt (also: ~ up) mischiare; **jumble sale** (BRIT) n vendita di beneficenza

● **JUMBLE SALE**
●
● Una **jumble sale** è un mercatino di
● oggetti di seconda mano organizzato
● in chiese, scuole o in circoli ricreativi,
● i cui proventi vengono devoluti in
● beneficenza.

jumbo ['dʒʌmbəʊ] adj ~ **jet** jumbo-jet m inv; ~ **size** formato gigante

jump [dʒʌmp] vi saltare, balzare; (start) sobbalzare; (increase) rincarare ▷ vt saltare ▷ n salto, balzo; sobbalzo

jumper ['dʒʌmpəʳ] n (BRIT: pullover) maglione m, pullover m inv; (us: dress) scamiciato

jumper cables (us) npl = **jump leads**

jump leads (BRIT) npl cavi mpl per batteria

Jun. abbr = **junior**

junction ['dʒʌŋkʃən] n (BRIT: of roads) incrocio; (of rails) nodo ferroviario

June [dʒu:n] n giugno

jungle ['dʒʌŋgl] n giungla

junior ['dʒu:nɪəʳ] adj, n **he's ~ to me by 2 years, he's my ~ by 2 years** è più giovane di me (di 2 anni); **he's ~ to me** (seniority) è al di sotto di me, ho più anzianità di lui; **junior high school** (US) n scuola media (da 12 a 15 anni); **junior school** (BRIT) n scuola elementare (da 8 a 11 anni)

junk [dʒʌŋk] n cianfrusaglie fpl; (cheap goods) robaccia; **junk food** n porcherie fpl

junkie ['dʒʌŋkɪ] (inf) n drogato(-a)

junk mail n stampe fpl pubblicitarie

Jupiter ['dʒu:pɪtəʳ] n (planet) Giove m

jurisdiction [dʒuərɪs'dɪkʃən] n giurisdizione f; **it falls** or **comes within/outside our ~** è/non è di nostra competenza

jury ['dʒuərɪ] n giuria

just [dʒʌst] adj giusto(-a) ▷ adv **he's ~ done it/left** lo ha appena fatto/è appena partito; **~ right** proprio giusto; **~ 2 o'clock** le 2 precise; **she's ~ as clever as you** è in gamba proprio quanto te; **it's ~ as well that ...** meno male che ...; **~ as I arrived** proprio mentre arrivavo; **it was ~ before/ enough/here** era poco prima/appena assai/proprio qui; **it's ~ me** sono solo io; **~ missed/caught** appena perso/preso; **~ listen to this!** senta un po' questo!

justice ['dʒʌstɪs] n giustizia

justification [dʒʌstɪfɪ'keɪʃən] n giustificazione f; (Typ) giustezza

justify ['dʒʌstɪfaɪ] vt giustificare

jut [dʒʌt] vi (also: **~ out**) sporgersi

juvenile ['dʒu:vənaɪl] adj giovane, giovanile; (court) dei minorenni; (books) per ragazzi ▷ n giovane m/f, minorenne m/f

K abbr (= one thousand) mille; (= kilobyte) K

kangaroo [kæŋgə'ru:] n canguro

karaoke [ka:rə'əukɪ] n karaoke m inv

karate [kə'ra:tɪ] n karatè m

kebab [kə'bæb] n spiedino

keel [ki:l] n chiglia; **on an even ~** (fig) in uno stato normale

keen [ki:n] adj (interest, desire) vivo(-a); (eye, intelligence) acuto(-a); (competition) serrato(-a); (edge) affilato(-a); (eager) entusiasta; **to be ~ to do** or **on doing sth** avere una gran voglia di fare qc; **to be ~ on sth** essere appassionato(-a) di qc; **to be ~ on sb** avere un debole per qn

keep [ki:p] (pt, pp **kept**) vt tenere; (hold back) trattenere; (feed: one's family etc) mantenere, sostentare; (a promise) mantenere; (chickens, bees, pigs etc) allevare ▷ vi (food) mantenersi; (remain: in a certain state or place) restare ▷ n (of castle) maschio; (food etc): **enough for his ~** abbastanza per vitto e alloggio; (inf): **for ~s** per sempre; **to ~ doing sth** continuare a fare qc; fare qc di continuo; **to ~ sb from doing** impedire a qn di fare; **to ~ sb busy/a place tidy** tenere qn occupato(-a)/un luogo in ordine; **to ~ sth to o.s.** tenere qc per sé; **to ~ sth (back) from sb** celare qc a qn; **to ~ time** (clock) andar bene; **keep away** vt **to ~ sth/sb away from sb**

tenere qc/qn lontano da qn ▷ vi **to ~ away
(from)** stare lontano (da); **keep back**
vt (crowds, tears, money) trattenere ▷ vi
tenersi indietro; **keep off** vt (dog, person)
tenere lontano da ▷ vi stare alla larga; **~
your hands off!** non toccare!, giù le mani!;
"~ off the grass" "non calpestare l'erba";
keep on vi **to ~ on doing** continuare
a fare; **to ~ on (about sth)** continuare
a insistere (su qc); **keep out** vt tener
fuori; **"~ out"** "vietato l'accesso"; **keep
up** vt continuare, mantenere ▷ vi **to ~ up
with** tener dietro a, andare di pari passo
con; (work etc) farcela a seguire; **keeper**
n custode m/f, guardiano(-a); **keeping**
n (care) custodia; **in keeping with** in
armonia con; in accordo con

kennel ['kɛnl] n canile m; **~s** npl canile
m; **to put a dog in ~s** mettere un cane al
canile

Kenya ['kɛnjə] n Kenia m
kept [kɛpt] pt, pp of **keep**
kerb [kə:b] (BRIT) n orlo del marciapiede
kerosene ['kɛrəsi:n] n cherosene m
ketchup ['kɛtʃəp] n ketchup m inv
kettle ['kɛtl] n bollitore m
key [ki:] n (gen, Mus) chiave f; (of piano,
typewriter) tasto ▷ adj chiave inv ▷ vt (also:
~ in) digitare; **can I have my ~?** posso
avere la mia chiave?; **keyboard** n tastiera;
keyhole n buco della serratura; **keyring**
n portachiavi m inv

kg abbr (= kilogram) Kg
khaki ['ka:kɪ] adj cachi ▷ n cachi m
kick [kɪk] vt calciare, dare calci a; (inf: habit
etc) liberarsi di ▷ vi (horse) tirar calci ▷ n
calcio; (thrill): **he does it for ~s** lo fa giusto
per il piacere di farlo; **kick-off** vi (Sport)
dare il primo calcio; **kick-off** n (Sport)
calcio d'inizio

kid [kɪd] n (inf: child) ragazzino(-a); (animal,
leather) capretto ▷ vi (inf) scherzare
kidnap ['kɪdnæp] vt rapire, sequestrare;
kidnapping n sequestro (di persona)
kidney ['kɪdnɪ] n (Anat) rene m; (Culin)
rognone m; **kidney bean** n fagiolo
borlotto

kill [kɪl] vt uccidere, ammazzare ▷ n
uccisione f; **killer** n uccisore m, killer m
inv; assassino(-a); **killing** n assassinio; **to
make a killing** (inf) fare un bel colpo
kiln [kɪln] n forno
kilo ['ki:ləu] n chilo; **kilobyte** n
(Comput) kilobyte m inv; **kilogram(me)**
['kɪləugræm] n chilogrammo; **kilometre**
['kɪləmi:tə'] (US **kilometer**) n chilometro;
kilowatt ['kɪləuwɔt] n chilowatt m inv
kilt [kɪlt] n gonnellino scozzese
kin [kɪn] n see **next**; **kith**

kind [kaɪnd] adj gentile, buono(-a) ▷ n
sorta, specie f; (species) genere m; **what
~ of ...?** che tipo di ...?; **to be two of a ~**
essere molto simili; **in ~** (Comm) in natura
kindergarten ['kɪndəga:tn] n giardino
d'infanzia
kindly ['kaɪndlɪ] adj pieno(-a) di
bontà, benevolo(-a) ▷ adv con bontà,
gentilmente; **will you ~ ...** vuole ... per
favore
kindness ['kaɪndnɪs] n bontà, gentilezza
king [kɪŋ] n re m inv; **kingdom** n regno,
reame m; **kingfisher** n martin m inv
pescatore; **king-size(d) bed** n letto
king-size
kiosk ['ki:ɔsk] n edicola, chiosco; (BRIT Tel)
cabina (telefonica)
kipper ['kɪpə'] n aringa affumicata
kiss [kɪs] n bacio ▷ vt baciare; **to ~ (each
other)** baciarsi; **kiss of life** n respirazione
f bocca a bocca
kit [kɪt] n equipaggiamento, corredo; (set of
tools etc) attrezzi mpl; (for assembly) scatola
di montaggio
kitchen ['kɪtʃɪn] n cucina
kite [kaɪt] n (toy) aquilone m
kitten ['kɪtn] n gattino(-a), micino(-a)
kiwi ['ki:wi:] n (also: **~ fruit**) kiwi m inv
km abbr (= kilometre) km
km/h abbr (= kilometres per hour) km/h
knack [næk] n **to have the ~ of** avere
l'abilità di
knee [ni:] n ginocchio; **kneecap** n rotula
kneel [ni:l] (pt, pp knelt) vi (also: **~ down**)
inginocchiarsi
knelt [nɛlt] pt, pp of **kneel**
knew [nju:] pt of **know**
knickers ['nɪkəz] (BRIT) npl mutandine fpl
knife [naɪf] (pl **knives**) n coltello ▷ vt
accoltellare, dare una coltellata a
knight [naɪt] n cavaliere m; (Chess) cavallo
knit [nɪt] vt fare a maglia ▷ vi lavorare a
maglia; (broken bones) saldarsi; **to ~ one's
brows** aggrottare le sopracciglia; **knitting**
n lavoro a maglia; **knitting needle** n ferro
(da calza); **knitwear** n maglieria
knives [naɪvz] npl of **knife**
knob [nɔb] n bottone m; manopola
knock [nɔk] vt colpire; urtare; (fig: inf)
criticare ▷ vi (at door etc): **to ~ at/on**
bussare a ▷ n bussata; colpo, botta;
knock down vt abbattere; **knock off** vi
(inf: finish) smettere (di lavorare) ▷ vt (from
price) far abbassare; (inf: steal) sgraffignare;
knock out vt stendere; (Boxing) mettere
K.O.; (defeat) battere; **knock over** vt
(person) investire; (object) far cadere;
knockout n (Boxing) knock out m inv ▷ cpd
a eliminazione

knot [nɔt] n nodo ▷ vt annodare
know [nəu] (pt **knew**, pp **known**) vt
sapere; (person, author, place) conoscere;
I don't ~ non lo so; **do you ~ where
I can ...?** sa dove posso ...?; **to ~ how
to do** sapere fare; **to ~ about** or **of
sth/sb** conoscere qc/qn; **know-
all** n sapientone(-a); **know-how** n
tecnica; pratica; **knowing** adj (look etc)
d'intesa; **knowingly** adv (purposely)
consapevolmente; (smile, look) con aria
d'intesa; **know-it-all** (us) n = **know-all**
knowledge ['nɔlɪdʒ] n consapevolezza;
(learning) conoscenza, sapere m;
knowledgeable adj ben informato(-a)
known [nəun] pp of **know**
knuckle ['nʌkl] n nocca
koala [kəu'ɑːlə] n (also: **~ bear**) koala m inv
Koran [kɔ'rɑːn] n Corano
Korea [kə'rɪə] n Corea; **Korean** adj, n
coreano(-a)
kosher ['kəuʃəʳ] adj kasher inv
Kosovar, Kosovan ['kɔsəvaʳ, 'kɔsəvən]
adj kosovaro(-a)
Kosovo ['kusəvəu] n Kosovo
Kremlin ['kremlɪn] n **the ~** il Cremlino
Kuwait [ku'weɪt] n Kuwait m

L (BRIT) abbr = **learner driver**
l. abbr (= litre) l
lab [læb] n abbr (= laboratory) laboratorio
label ['leɪbl] n etichetta, cartellino; (brand:
of record) casa ▷ vt etichettare
labor etc ['leɪbəʳ] (us) = **labour** etc
laboratory [lə'bɔrətərɪ] n laboratorio
Labor Day (us) n festa del lavoro

● **LABOR DAY**
●
● Negli Stati Uniti e nel Canada il **Labor**
● **Day**, la festa del lavoro, cade il primo
● lunedì di settembre, contrariamente a
● quanto accade nella maggior parte dei
● paesi europei dove tale celebrazione ha
● luogo il primo maggio.

labor union (us) n sindacato
labour ['leɪbəʳ] (us **labor**) n (task) lavoro;
(workmen) manodopera; (Med): **to be in
~** avere le doglie ▷ vi **to ~ (at)** lavorare
duro(a); **L~, the L~ party** (BRIT) il partito
laburista, i laburisti; **hard ~** lavori mpl
forzati; **labourer** n manovale m; **farm
labourer** lavoratore m agricolo
lace [leɪs] n merletto, pizzo; (of shoe etc)
laccio ▷ vt (shoe: also: **~ up**) allacciare
lack [læk] n mancanza ▷ vt mancare di;
through or **for ~ of** per mancanza di; **to be**

~ing mancare; **to be ~ing in** mancare di
lacquer ['lækə^r] n lacca
lacy ['leɪsɪ] adj (like lace) che sembra un pizzo
lad [læd] n ragazzo, giovanotto
ladder ['lædə^r] n scala; (BRIT: in tights) smagliatura
ladle ['leɪdl] n mestolo
lady ['leɪdɪ] n signora; dama; **L~ Smith** lady Smith; **the ladies' (room)** i gabinetti per signore; **ladybird** (US **ladybug**) n coccinella
lag [læg] n (of time) lasso, intervallo ▷ vi (also: **~ behind**) trascinarsi ▷ vt (pipes) rivestire di materiale isolante
lager ['lɑːgə^r] n lager m inv
lagoon [lə'guːn] n laguna
laid [leɪd] pt, pp of **lay**; **laid back** (inf) adj rilassato(-a), tranquillo(-a)
lain [leɪn] pp of **lie**
lake [leɪk] n lago
lamb [læm] n agnello
lame [leɪm] adj zoppo(-a); (excuse etc) zoppicante
lament [lə'mɛnt] n lamento ▷ vt lamentare, piangere
lamp [læmp] n lampada; **lamppost** ['læmppəust] (BRIT) n lampione m; **lampshade** ['læmpʃeɪd] n paralume m
land [lænd] n (as opposed to sea) terra (ferma); (country) paese m; (soil) terreno; suolo; (estate) terreni mpl, terre fpl ▷ vi (from ship) sbarcare; (Aviat) atterrare; (fig: fall) cadere ▷ vt (passengers) sbarcare; (goods) scaricare; **to ~ sb with sth** affibbiare qc a qn; **landing** n atterraggio; (of staircase) pianerottolo; **landing card** n carta di sbarco; **landlady** n padrona or proprietaria di casa; **landlord** n padrone m or proprietario di casa; (of pub etc) padrone m; **landmark** n punto di riferimento; (fig) pietra miliare; **landowner** n proprietario(-a) terriero(-a); **landscape** n paesaggio; **landslide** n (Geo) frana; (fig: Pol) valanga
lane [leɪn] n stradina; (Aut, in race) corsia; **"get in ~"** "immettersi in corsia"
language ['læŋgwɪdʒ] n lingua; (way one speaks) linguaggio; **what ~s do you speak?** che lingue parla?; **bad ~** linguaggio volgare; **language laboratory** n laboratorio linguistico
lantern ['læntn] n lanterna
lap [læp] n (of track) giro; (of body): **in or on one's ~** in grembo ▷ vt (also: **~ up**) papparsi, leccare ▷ vi (waves) sciabordare
lapel [lə'pɛl] n risvolto
lapse [læps] n lapsus m inv; (longer) caduta ▷ vi (law) cadere; (membership, contract) scadere; **to ~ into bad habits** pigliare cattive abitudini; **~ of time** spazio di tempo
laptop (computer) ['læptɔp-] n laptop m inv
lard [lɑːd] n lardo
larder ['lɑːdə^r] n dispensa
large [lɑːdʒ] adj grande; (person, animal) grosso(-a); **at ~** (free) in libertà; (generally) in generale; nell'insieme; **largely** adv in gran parte; **large-scale** adj (map, drawing etc) in grande scala; (reforms, business activities) su vasta scala
lark [lɑːk] n (bird) allodola; (joke) scherzo, gioco
laryngitis [lærɪn'dʒaɪtɪs] n laringite f
lasagne [lə'zænjə] n lasagne fpl
laser ['leɪzə^r] n laser m; **laser printer** n stampante f laser inv
lash [læʃ] n frustata; (also: **eye~**) ciglio ▷ vt frustare; (tie): **to ~ to/together** legare a insieme; **lash out** vi **to ~ out (at** or **against sb)** attaccare violentemente (qn)
lass [læs] n ragazza
last [lɑːst] adj ultimo(-a); (week, month, year) scorso(-a), passato(-a) ▷ adv per ultimo ▷ vi durare; **~ week** la settimana scorsa; **~ night** ieri sera, la notte scorsa; **at ~** finalmente, alla fine; **~ but one** penultimo(-a); **lastly** adv infine, per finire; **last-minute** adj fatto(-a) (or preso(-a) etc) all'ultimo momento
latch [lætʃ] n chiavistello; **latch onto** vt fus (cling to: person) attaccarsi a, appiccicarsi a; (: idea) afferrare, capire
late [leɪt] adj (not on time) in ritardo; (far on in day etc) tardi inv; tardo(-a); (former) ex; (dead) defunto(-a) ▷ adv tardi; (behind time, schedule) in ritardo; **sorry I'm ~** scusi il ritardo; **the flight is two hours ~** il volo ha due ore di ritardo; **it's too ~** è troppo tardi; **of ~** di recente; **in the ~ afternoon** nel tardo pomeriggio; **in ~ May** verso la fine di maggio; **latecomer** n ritardatario(-a); **lately** adv recentemente; **later** ['leɪtə^r] adj (date etc) posteriore; (version etc) successivo(-a) ▷ adv più tardi; **later on** più avanti; **latest** ['leɪtɪst] adj ultimo(-a), più recente; **at the latest** al più tardi
lather ['lɑːðə^r] n schiuma di sapone ▷ vt insaponare
Latin ['lætɪn] n latino ▷ adj latino(-a); **Latin America** n America Latina; **Latin American** adj sudamericano(-a)
latitude ['lætɪtjuːd] n latitudine f; (fig) libertà d'azione
latter ['lætə^r] adj secondo(-a), più recente ▷ n **the ~** quest'ultimo, il secondo
laugh [lɑːf] n risata ▷ vi ridere; **laugh at**

launch | 312

vt fus (misfortune etc) ridere di; **laughter** *n*
riso; risate *fpl*

launch [lɔ:ntʃ] *n (of rocket, Comm)* lancio;
(of new ship) varo; *(also: **motor ~**)* lancia
▷ *vt (rocket, Comm)* lanciare; *(ship, plan)*
varare; **launch into** *vt fus* lanciarsi in

launder [ˈlɔ:ndəʳ] *vt* lavare e stirare

Launderette® [lɔ:nˈdrɛt] *(BRIT)* *n*
lavanderia (automatica)

Laundromat® [ˈlɔ:ndrəmæt] *(US)* *n*
lavanderia automatica

laundry [ˈlɔ:ndrɪ] *n* lavanderia; *(clothes)*
biancheria; *(: dirty)* panni *mpl* da lavare

lava [ˈlɑ:və] *n* lava

lavatory [ˈlævətərɪ] *n* gabinetto

lavender [ˈlævəndəʳ] *n* lavanda

lavish [ˈlævɪʃ] *adj* rilassato(-a), abbondante;
(giving freely): **~ with** prodigo(-a) di,
largo(-a) in ▷ *vt* **to ~ sth on sb** colmare
qn di qc

law [lɔ:] *n* legge *f*; **civil/criminal ~** diritto
civile/penale; **lawful** *adj* legale, lecito(-a);
lawless *adj* che non conosce nessuna
legge

lawn [lɔ:n] *n* tappeto erboso; **lawnmower**
n tosaerba *m or f inv*

lawsuit [ˈlɔ:su:t] *n* processo, causa

lawyer [ˈlɔ:jəʳ] *n (for sales, wills
etc)* ≈ notaio; *(partner, in court)*
≈ avvocato(-essa)

lax [læks] *adj* rilassato(-a), negligente

laxative [ˈlæksətɪv] *n* lassativo

lay [leɪ] *(pt, pp **laid**)* *pt of **lie*** ▷ *adj* laico(-a);
(not expert) profano(-a) ▷ *vt* posare,
mettere; *(eggs)* fare; *(trap)* tendere;
(plans) fare, elaborare; **to ~ the table**
apparecchiare la tavola; **lay down** *vt*
mettere giù; *(rules etc)* formulare, fissare;
to ~ down the law dettar legge; **to ~
down one's life** dare la propria vita;
lay off *vt (workers)* licenziare; **lay on**
vt (provide) fornire; **lay out** *vt (display)*
presentare, disporre; **lay-by** *(BRIT)* *n*
piazzola (di sosta)

layer [ˈleɪəʳ] *n* strato

layman [ˈleɪmən] *(irreg)* *n* laico; profano

layout [ˈleɪaut] *n* lay-out *m inv*,
disposizione *f*; *(Press)* impaginazione *f*

lazy [ˈleɪzɪ] *adj* pigro(-a)

lb. *abbr* = **pound** *(weight)*

lead¹ [li:d] *(pt, pp **led**)* *n (front position)*
posizione *f* di testa; *(distance, time ahead)*
vantaggio; *(clue)* indizio; *(Elec)* filo
(elettrico); *(for dog)* guinzaglio; *(Theatre)*
parte *f* principale ▷ *vt* guidare, condurre;
(induce) indurre; *(be leader of)* essere a capo
di ▷ *vi* condurre; *(Sport)* essere in testa; **in
the ~** in testa; **to ~ the way** fare strada;
lead up to *vt fus* portare a

lead² [lɛd] *n (metal)* piombo; *(in pencil)* mina

leader [ˈli:dəʳ] *n* capo; leader *m inv*; *(in
newspaper)* articolo di fondo; *(Sport)* chi è in
testa; **leadership** *n* direzione *f*; capacità
di comando

lead-free [ˈlɛdfri:] *adj* senza piombo

leading [ˈli:dɪŋ] *adj* primo(-a), principale

lead singer *n* cantante alla testa di un
gruppo

leaf [li:f] *(pl **leaves**)* *n* foglia ▷ *vi* **to ~
through sth** sfogliare qc; **to turn over a
new ~** cambiar vita

leaflet [ˈli:flɪt] *n* dépliant *m inv*; *(Pol, Rel)*
volantino

league [li:g] *n* lega; *(Football)* campionato;
to be in ~ with essere in lega con

leak [li:k] *n (out)* fuga; *(in)* infiltrazione
f; *(security leak)* fuga d'informazioni ▷ *vi
(roof, bucket)* perdere; *(liquid)* uscire; *(shoes)*
lasciar passare l'acqua ▷ *vt (information)*
divulgare

lean [li:n] *(pt, pp **leaned** or **leant**)* *adj*
magro(-a) ▷ *vt* **to ~ sth on sth** appoggiare
qc su qc ▷ *vi (slope)* pendere; *(rest)*: **to
~ against** appoggiarsi contro; essere
appoggiato(-a) a; **to ~ on** appoggiarsi a;
lean forward *vi* sporgersi in avanti; **lean
over** *vi* inclinarsi; **leaning** *n* **leaning
(towards)** propensione *f* (per)

leant [lɛnt] *pt, pp of **lean***

leap [li:p] *(pt, pp **leaped** or **leapt**)* *n* salto,
balzo ▷ *vi* saltare, balzare

leapt [lɛpt] *pt, pp of **leap***

leap year *n* anno bisestile

learn [lə:n] *(pt, pp **learned** or **learnt**)* *vt,
vi* imparare; **to ~ about sth** *(hear, read)*
apprendere qc; **to ~ to do sth** imparare
a fare qc; **learner** *n* principiante
m/f; apprendista *m/f*; *(BRIT: also: **learner
driver**)* guidatore(-a) principiante;
learning *n* erudizione *f*, sapienza

learnt [lə:nt] *pt, pp of **learn***

lease [li:s] *n* contratto d'affitto ▷ *vt*
affittare

leash [li:ʃ] *n* guinzaglio

least [li:st] *adj* **the ~** *(+ noun)* il (la) più
piccolo(-a), il (la) minimo(-a); *(smallest
amount of)* il (la) meno ▷ *adv (+ verb)* meno;
the ~ *(+ adjective)*: **~ beautiful girl** la
ragazza meno bella; **the ~ possible effort**
il minimo sforzo possibile; **I have the
~ money** ho meno denaro di tutti; **at ~**
almeno; **not in the ~** affatto, per nulla

leather [ˈlɛðəʳ] *n* cuoio

leave [li:v] *(pt, pp **left**)* *vt* lasciare; *(go away
from)* partire da ▷ *vi* partire, andarsene;
(bus, train) partire ▷ *n (time off)* congedo;
(Mil, consent) licenza; **what time does the
train/bus ~?** a che ora parte il treno/

l'autobus?; **to be left** rimanere; **there's some milk left over** c'è rimasto del latte; **on ~** in congedo; **leave behind** vt (person, object) lasciare; (: forget) dimenticare; **leave out** vt omettere, tralasciare

leaves [liːvz] npl of **leaf**

Lebanon ['lɛbənən] n Libano

lecture ['lɛktʃəʳ] n conferenza; (Scol) lezione f ▷ vi fare conferenze; fare lezioni ▷ vt (scold): **to ~ sb on** or **about sth** rimproverare qn or fare una ramanzina a qn per qc; **to give a ~ on** tenere una conferenza su; **lecture hall** n aula magna; **lecturer** ['lɛktʃərəʳ] (BRIT) n (at university) professore(-essa), docente m/f; **lecture theatre** n = **lecture hall**

led [lɛd] pt, pp of **lead**

ledge [lɛdʒ] n (of window) davanzale m; (on wall etc) sporgenza; (of mountain) cornice f, cengia

leek [liːk] n porro

left [lɛft] pt, pp of **leave** ▷ adj sinistro(-a) ▷ adv a sinistra ▷ n sinistra; **on the ~, to the ~** a sinistra; **the L~** (Pol) la sinistra; **left-hand** adj **the left-hand side** il lato sinistro; **left-hand drive** adj guida a sinistra; **left-handed** adj mancino(-a); **left-luggage locker** n armadietto per deposito bagagli; **left-luggage (office)** (BRIT) n deposito m bagagli inv; **left-overs** npl avanzi mpl, resti mpl; **left-wing** adj (Pol) di sinistra

leg [lɛg] n gamba; (of animal) zampa; (of furniture) piede m; (Culin: of chicken) coscia; (of journey) tappa; **1st/2nd ~** (Sport) partita di andata/ritorno

legacy ['lɛgəsɪ] n eredità f inv

legal ['liːgl] adj legale; **legal holiday** (US) n giorno festivo, festa nazionale; **legalize** vt legalizzare; **legally** adv legalmente; **legally binding** legalmente vincolante

legend ['lɛdʒənd] n leggenda; **legendary** ['lɛdʒəndərɪ] adj leggendario(-a)

leggings ['lɛgɪŋz] npl ghette fpl

legible ['lɛdʒəbl] adj leggibile

legislation [lɛdʒɪs'leɪʃən] n legislazione f

legislative ['lɛdʒɪslətɪv] adj legislativo(-a)

legitimate [lɪ'dʒɪtɪmət] adj legittimo(-a)

leisure ['lɛʒəʳ] n agio, tempo libero; ricreazioni fpl; **at ~** con comodo; **leisure centre** n centro di ricreazione; **leisurely** adj tranquillo(-a), fatto(-a) con comodo or senza fretta

lemon ['lɛmən] n limone m; **lemonade** [-'neɪd] n limonata; **lemon tea** n tè m inv al limone

lend [lɛnd] (pt, pp lent) vt **to ~ sth (to sb)** prestare qc (a qn); **could you ~ me some**

money? mi può prestare dei soldi?

length [lɛŋθ] n lunghezza; (distance) distanza; (section: of road, pipe etc) pezzo, tratto; (of time) periodo; **at ~** (at last) finalmente, alla fine; (lengthily) a lungo; **lengthen** vt allungare, prolungare ▷ vi allungarsi; **lengthways** adv per il lungo; **lengthy** adj molto lungo(-a)

lens [lɛnz] n lente f; (of camera) obiettivo

Lent [lɛnt] n Quaresima

lent [lɛnt] pt, pp of **lend**

lentil ['lɛntl] n lenticchia

Leo ['liːəu] n Leone m

leopard ['lɛpəd] n leopardo

leotard ['liːətɑːd] n calzamaglia

leprosy ['lɛprəsɪ] n lebbra

lesbian ['lɛzbɪən] n lesbica

less [lɛs] adj, pron, adv meno ▷ prep **~ tax/10% discount** meno tasse/il 10% di sconto; **~ than ever** meno che mai; **~ than half** meno della metà; **~ and ~** sempre meno; **the ~ he works ...** meno lavora ...; **lessen** ['lɛsn] vi diminuire, attenuarsi ▷ vt diminuire, ridurre; **lesser** ['lɛsəʳ] adj minore, più piccolo(-a); **to a lesser extent** in grado or misura minore

lesson ['lɛsn] n lezione f; **to teach sb a ~** dare una lezione a qn

let [lɛt] (pt, pp let) vt lasciare; (BRIT: lease) dare in affitto; **to ~ sb do sth** lasciar fare qc a qn, lasciare che qn faccia qc; **to ~ sb know sth** far sapere qc a qn; **~'s go** andiamo; **~ him come** lo lasci venire; **"to ~"** "affittasi"; **let down** vt (lower) abbassare; (dress) allungare; (hair) sciogliere; (tyre) sgonfiare; (disappoint) deludere; **let in** vt lasciare entrare; (visitor etc) far entrare; **let off** vt (allow to go) lasciare andare; (firework etc) far partire; **let out** vt lasciare uscire; (scream) emettere

lethal ['liːθl] adj letale, mortale

letter ['lɛtəʳ] n lettera; **letterbox** (BRIT) n buca delle lettere

lettuce ['lɛtɪs] n lattuga, insalata

leukaemia [luː'kiːmɪə] (US **leukemia**) n leucemia

level ['lɛvl] adj piatto(-a), piano(-a); orizzontale ▷ adv **to draw ~ with** mettersi alla pari di ▷ n livello ▷ vt livellare, spianare; **to be ~ with** essere alla pari di; **level crossing** (BRIT) n passaggio a livello

lever ['liːvəʳ] n leva; **leverage** n **leverage (on** or **with)** forza (su); (fig) ascendente m (su)

levy ['lɛvɪ] n tassa, imposta ▷ vt imporre

liability [laɪə'bɪlətɪ] n responsabilità f inv; (handicap) peso

liable ['laɪəbl] adj (subject): **~ to**

soggetto(-a) a; passibile di; (*responsible*):
~ **for** responsabile (di); (*likely*): ~ **to do**
propenso(-a) a fare

liaise [lɪ:ˈeɪz] *vi* **to ~ (with)** mantenere i
contatti (con)

liar [ˈlaɪəʳ] *n* bugiardo(-a)

liberal [ˈlɪbərl] *adj* liberale;
(*generous*): **to be ~ with** distribuire
liberalmente; **Liberal Democrat** *n*
liberaldemocratico(-a)

liberate [ˈlɪbəreɪt] *vt* liberare

liberation [lɪbəˈreɪʃən] *n* liberazione *f*

liberty [ˈlɪbətɪ] *n* libertà *f inv*; **at ~** (*criminal*)
in libertà; **at ~ to do** libero(-a) di fare

Libra [ˈliːbrə] *n* Bilancia

librarian [laɪˈbreərɪən] *n* bibliotecario(-a)

library [ˈlaɪbrərɪ] *n* biblioteca

Libya [ˈlɪbɪə] *n* Libia

lice [laɪs] *npl of* **louse**

licence [ˈlaɪsns] (*us* **license**) *n*
autorizzazione *f*, permesso; (*Comm*)
licenza; (*Radio, TV*) canone *m*,
abbonamento; (*also*: **driving ~**: *us*: *also*:
driver's license) patente *f* di guida;
(*excessive freedom*) licenza

license [ˈlaɪsns] *n* (*us*) = **licence** ▷ *vt* dare
una licenza a; **licensed** *adj* (*for alcohol*) che
ha la licenza di vendere bibite alcoliche;
license plate (*esp us*) *n* (*Aut*) targa
(automobilistica); **licensing hours** (*BRIT*)
npl orario d'apertura (*di un pub*)

lick [lɪk] *vt* leccare; (*inf: defeat*) stracciare;
to ~ one's lips (*fig*) leccarsi i baffi

lid [lɪd] *n* coperchio; (*eyelid*) palpebra

lie [laɪ] (*pt* **lay**, *pp* **lain**) *vi* (*rest*) giacere, star
disteso(-a); (*of object: be situated*) trovarsi,
essere; (*tell lies*: *pt*, *pp* **lied**) mentire, dire
bugie ▷ *n* bugia, menzogna; **to ~ low** (*fig*)
latitare; **lie about** *or* **around** *vi* (*things*)
essere in giro; (*person*) bighellonare; **lie
down** *vi* stendersi, sdraiarsi

Liechtenstein [ˈlɪktənstaɪn] *n*
Liechtenstein *m*

lie-in [ˈlaɪɪn] (*BRIT*) *n* **to have a ~** rimanere
a letto

lieutenant [lɛfˈtɛnənt, (*us*) lu:ˈtɛnənt] *n*
tenente *m*

life [laɪf] (*pl* **lives**) *n* vita ▷ *cpd* di vita; della
vita; a vita; **to come to ~** rianimarsi; **life
assurance** (*BRIT*) *n* = **life insurance**;
lifeboat *n* scialuppa di salvataggio;
lifeguard *n* bagnino; **life insurance**
n assicurazione *f* sulla vita; **life jacket**
n giubbotto di salvataggio; **lifelike**
adj verosimile; rassomigliante; **life
preserver** [-prɪˈzə:vəʳ] (*us*) *n* salvagente
m; giubbotto di salvataggio; **life
sentence** *n* ergastolo; **lifestyle** *n* stile *m*
di vita; **lifetime** *n* **in his lifetime** durante

la sua vita; **once in a lifetime** una volta
nella vita

lift [lɪft] *vt* sollevare; (*ban, rule*) levare ▷ *vi*
(*fog*) alzarsi ▷ *n* (*BRIT: elevator*) ascensore
m; **to give sb a ~** (*BRIT*) dare un passaggio
a qn; **can you give me a ~ to the station?**
può darmi un passaggio fino alla stazione?;
lift up *vt* sollevare, alzare; **lift-off** *n*
decollo

light [laɪt] (*pt*, *pp* **lighted** *or* **lit**) *n* luce *f*,
lume *m*; (*daylight*) luce *f*, giorno; (*lamp*)
lampada; (*Aut: rear light*) luce *f* di posizione;
(: *headlamp*) fanale *m*; (*for cigarette etc*):
have you got a ~? ha da accendere?;
~s *npl* (*Aut: traffic lights*) semaforo *vt*
(*candle, cigarette, fire*) accendere; (*room*):
to be lit by essere illuminato(-a) da *adj*
(*room, colour*) chiaro(-a); (*not heavy, also
fig*) leggero(-a); **to come to ~** venire alla
luce, emergere; **light up** *vi* illuminarsi
▷ *vt* illuminare; **light bulb** *n* lampadina;
lighten *vt* (*make less heavy*) alleggerire;
lighter *n* (*also*: **cigarette lighter**)
accendino; **light-hearted** *adj* gioioso(-a),
gaio(-a); **lighthouse** *n* faro; **lighting** *n*
illuminazione *f*; **lightly** *adv* leggermente;
to get off lightly cavarsela a buon
mercato

lightning [ˈlaɪtnɪŋ] *n* lampo, fulmine *m*

lightweight [ˈlaɪtweɪt] *adj* (*suit*)
leggero(-a) ▷ *n* (*Boxing*) peso leggero

like [laɪk] *vt* (*person*) volere bene a;
(*activity, object, food*): **I ~ swimming/
that book/chocolate** mi piace
nuotare/quel libro/il cioccolato ▷ *prep*
come ▷ *adj* simile, uguale ▷ *n* **the ~**
uno(-a) uguale; **his ~s and dis~s** i suoi
gusti; **I would ~, I'd ~** mi piacerebbe,
vorrei; **would you ~ a coffee?**
gradirebbe un caffè?; **to be/look ~
sb/sth** somigliare a qn/qc; **what does
it look/taste ~?** che aspetto/gusto ha?;
what does it sound ~? come fa?; **that's
just ~ him** è proprio da lui; **do it ~ this**
fallo così; **it is nothing ~ ...** non è affatto
come ...; **likeable** *adj* simpatico(-a)

likelihood [ˈlaɪklɪhud] *n* probabilità

likely [ˈlaɪklɪ] *adj* probabile; plausibile;
he's ~ to leave probabilmente partirà, è
probabile che parta; **not ~!** neanche per
sogno!

likewise [ˈlaɪkwaɪz] *adv* similmente, nello
stesso modo

liking [ˈlaɪkɪŋ] *n* **~ (for)** debole *m* (per); **to
be to sb's ~** piacere a qn

lilac [ˈlaɪlək] *n* lilla *m inv*

Lilo® [ˈlaɪləu] *n* materassino gonfiabile

lily [ˈlɪlɪ] *n* giglio

limb [lɪm] *n* arto

limbo ['lɪmbəʊ] n **to be in ~** (fig) essere lasciato(-a) nel dimenticatoio

lime [laɪm] n (tree) tiglio; (fruit) limetta; (Geo) calce f

limelight ['laɪmlaɪt] n **in the ~** (fig) alla ribalta, in vista

limestone ['laɪmstəʊn] n pietra calcarea; (Geo) calcare m

limit ['lɪmɪt] n limite m ▷ vt limitare; **limited** adj limitato(-a), ristretto(-a); **to be limited to** limitarsi a

limousine ['lɪməziːn] n limousine f inv

limp [lɪmp] n **to have a ~** ▷ vi zoppicare ▷ adj floscio(-a), flaccido(-a)

line [laɪn] n linea; (rope) corda; (for fishing) lenza; (wire) filo; (of poem) verso; (row, series) fila, riga; coda; (on face) ruga ▷ vt (clothes): **to ~ (with)** foderare (di); (box): **to ~ (with)** rivestire or foderare (di); (trees, crowd) fiancheggiare; **~ of business** settore m or ramo d'attività; **in ~ with** in linea con; **line up** vi allinearsi, mettersi in fila ▷ vt mettere in fila; (event, celebration) preparare

linear ['lɪnɪə'] adj lineare

linen ['lɪnɪn] n biancheria, panni mpl; (cloth) tela di lino

liner ['laɪnə'] n nave f di linea; (for bin) sacchetto

line-up ['laɪnʌp] n allineamento, fila; (Sport) formazione f di gioco

linger ['lɪŋgə'] vi attardarsi; indugiare; (smell, tradition) persistere

lingerie ['lænʒəriː] n biancheria intima femminile

linguist ['lɪŋgwɪst] n linguista m/f; poliglotta m/f; **linguistic** adj linguistico(-a)

lining ['laɪnɪŋ] n fodera

link [lɪŋk] n (of a chain) anello; (relationship) legame m; (connection) collegamento ▷ vt collegare, unire, congiungere; (associate): **to ~ with** or **to** collegare a; **~s** npl (Golf) pista or terreno da golf; **link up** vt collegare, unire ▷ vi riunirsi; associarsi

lion ['laɪən] n leone m; **lioness** n leonessa

lip [lɪp] n labbro; (of cup etc) orlo; **lip-read** vi leggere sulle labbra; **lip salve** [-sælv] n burro di cacao; **lipstick** n rossetto

liqueur [lɪ'kjuə'] n liquore m

liquid ['lɪkwɪd] n liquido ▷ adj liquido(-a); **liquidizer** n frullatore m (a brocca)

liquor ['lɪkə'] n alcool m; **liquor store** (US) n negozio di liquori

Lisbon ['lɪzbən] n Lisbona

lisp [lɪsp] n pronuncia blesa della "s"

list [lɪst] n lista, elenco ▷ vt (write down) mettere in lista; fare una lista di;

(enumerate) elencare

listen ['lɪsn] vi ascoltare; **to ~ to** ascoltare; **listener** n ascoltatore(-trice)

lit [lɪt] pt, pp of **light**

liter ['liːtə'] (US) n = **litre**

literacy ['lɪtərəsɪ] n il sapere leggere e scrivere

literal ['lɪtərl] adj letterale; **literally** adv alla lettera, letteralmente

literary ['lɪtərərɪ] adj letterario(-a)

literate ['lɪtərət] adj che sa leggere e scrivere

literature ['lɪtərɪtʃə'] n letteratura; (brochures etc) materiale m

litre ['liːtə'] (US **liter**) n litro

litter ['lɪtə'] n (rubbish) rifiuti mpl; (young animals) figliata; **litter bin** (BRIT) n cestino per rifiuti; **littered** adj **littered with** coperto(-a) di

little ['lɪtl] adj (small) piccolo(-a); (not much) poco(-a) ▷ adv poco; **a ~** un po' (di); **a ~ bit** un pochino; **~ by ~** a poco a poco; **little finger** n mignolo

live¹ [lɪv] vi vivere; (reside) vivere, abitare; **where do you ~?** dove abita?; **live together** vi vivere insieme, convivere; **live up to** vt fus tener fede a, non venir meno a

live² [laɪv] adj (animal) vivo(-a); (wire) sotto tensione; (bullet, missile) inesploso(-a); (broadcast) diretto(-a); (performance) dal vivo

livelihood ['laɪvlɪhud] n mezzi mpl di sostentamento

lively ['laɪvlɪ] adj vivace, vivo(-a)

liven up ['laɪvn ʌp] vt (discussion, evening) animare ▷ vi ravvivarsi

liver ['lɪvə'] n fegato

lives [laɪvz] npl of **life**

livestock ['laɪvstɔk] n bestiame m

living ['lɪvɪŋ] adj vivo(-a), vivente ▷ n **to earn** or **make a ~** guadagnarsi la vita; **living room** n soggiorno

lizard ['lɪzəd] n lucertola

load [ləud] n (weight) peso; (thing carried) carico ▷ vt (also: **~ up**): **to ~ (with)** (lorry, ship) caricare (di); (gun, camera, Comput) caricare (con); **a ~ of**, **~s of** (fig) un sacco di; **loaded** adj (vehicle): **loaded (with)** carico(-a) (di); (question) capzioso(-a); (inf: rich) carico(-a) di soldi

loaf [ləuf] (pl **loaves**) n pane m, pagnotta

loan [ləun] n prestito ▷ vt dare in prestito; **on ~** in prestito

loathe [ləuð] vt detestare, aborrire

loaves [ləuvz] npl of **loaf**

lobby ['lɔbɪ] n atrio, vestibolo; (Pol: pressure group) gruppo di pressione ▷ vt fare pressione su

lobster ['lɔbstə'] n aragosta
local ['ləukl] adj locale ▷ n (BRIT: pub)
≈ bar m inv all'angolo; **the ~s** npl (local inhabitants) la gente della zona; **local anaesthetic** n anestesia locale; **local authority** n ente m locale; **local government** n amministrazione f locale; **locally** ['ləukəlɪ] adv da queste parti; nel vicinato
locate [ləu'keɪt] vt (find) trovare; (situate) collocare; situare
location [ləu'keɪʃən] n posizione f; **on ~** (Cinema) all'esterno
loch [lɔx] n lago
lock [lɔk] n (of door, box) serratura; (of canal) chiusa; (of hair) ciocca, riccio ▷ vt (with key) chiudere a chiave ▷ vi (door etc) chiudersi; (wheels) bloccarsi, incepparsi; **lock in** vt chiudere dentro (a chiave); **lock out** vt chiudere fuori; **lock up** vt (criminal, mental patient) rinchiudere; (house) chiudere (a chiave) ▷ vi chiudere tutto (a chiave)
locker ['lɔkə'] n armadietto; **locker-room** (us) n (Sport) spogliatoio
locksmith ['lɔksmɪθ] n magnano
locomotive [ləukə'məutɪv] n locomotiva
lodge [lɔdʒ] n casetta, portineria; (hunting lodge) casino di caccia ▷ vi (person): **to ~ (with)** essere a pensione (presso or da); (bullet etc) conficcarsi ▷ vt (appeal etc) presentare, fare; **to ~ a complaint** presentare un reclamo; **lodger** n affittuario(-a); (with room and meals) pensionante m/f
lodging ['lɔdʒɪŋ] n alloggio; see also **board**
loft [lɔft] n solaio, soffitta
log [lɔg] n (of wood) ceppo; (also: **~book**: Naut, Aviat) diario di bordo; (Aut) libretto di circolazione ▷ vt registrare; **log in** vi (Comput) aprire una sessione (con codice di riconoscimento); **log off** vi (Comput) terminare una sessione
logic ['lɔdʒɪk] n logica; **logical** adj logico(-a)
logo ['ləugəu] n logo m inv
lollipop ['lɔlɪpɔp] n lecca lecca m inv
lolly ['lɔlɪ] (inf) n lecca lecca m inv; (also: **ice ~**) ghiacciolo; (money) grana
London ['lʌndən] n Londra; **Londoner** n londinese m/f
lone [ləun] adj solitario(-a)
loneliness ['ləunlɪnɪs] n solitudine f, isolamento
lonely ['ləunlɪ] adj solo(-a); solitario(-a), isolato(-a)
long [lɔŋ] adj lungo(-a) ▷ adv a lungo,

per molto tempo ▷ vi **to ~ for sth/to do** desiderare qc/di fare, non veder l'ora di aver qc/di fare; **so** or **as ~ as** (while) finché; (provided that) sempre che + sub; **don't be ~!** fai presto!; **how ~ is this river/course?** quanto è lungo questo fiume/corso?; **6 metres ~** lungo 6 metri; **6 months ~** che dura 6 mesi, di 6 mesi; **all night ~** tutta la notte; **he no ~er comes** non viene più; **~ before** molto tempo prima; **before ~** (+future) presto, fra poco; (+past) poco tempo dopo; **at ~ last** finalmente; **long-distance** adj (race) di fondo; (call) interurbano(-a); **long-haul** ['lɔŋhɔːl] adj (flight) a lunga percorrenza inv; **longing** n desiderio, voglia, brama
longitude ['lɔŋgɪtjuːd] n longitudine f
long: **long jump** n salto in lungo; **long-life** adj (milk) a lunga conservazione; (batteries) di lunga durata; **long-sighted** adj presbite; **long-standing** adj di vecchia data; **long-term** adj a lungo termine
loo [luː] (BRIT: inf) n W.C. m inv, cesso
look [luk] vi guardare; (seem) sembrare, parere; (building etc): **to ~ south/on to the sea** dare a sud/sul mare ▷ n sguardo; (appearance) aspetto, aria; **~s** npl (good looks) bellezza; **look after** vt fus occuparsi di, prendere cura di; (keep an eye on) guardare, badare a; **look around** vi guardarsi intorno; **look at** vt fus guardare; **look back** vi **to ~ back on** (event etc) ripensare a; **look down on** vt fus (fig) guardare dall'alto, disprezzare; **look for** vt fus cercare; **we're ~ing for a hotel/restaurant** stiamo cercando un albergo/ristorante; **look forward to** vt fus non veder l'ora di; (in letters): **we ~ forward to hearing from you** in attesa di una vostra gentile risposta; **look into** vt fus esaminare; **look out** vi (beware): **to ~ out (for)** stare in guardia (per); **look out for** vt fus cercare; **look round** vi (turn) girarsi, voltarsi; (in shop) dare un'occhiata; **look through** vt fus (papers, book) scorrere; (telescope) guardare attraverso; **look up** vi alzare gli occhi; (improve) migliorare ▷ vt (word) cercare; (friend) andare a trovare; **look up to** vt fus avere rispetto per; **lookout** n posto d'osservazione; guardia; **to be on the lookout (for)** stare in guardia (per)
loom [luːm] n telaio ▷ vi (also: **~ up**) apparire minaccioso(-a); (event) essere imminente
loony ['luːnɪ] (inf) n pazzo(-a)
loop [luːp] n cappio ▷ vt **to ~ sth round sth** passare qc intorno a qc; **loophole** n

via d'uscita; scappatoia
loose [luːs] *adj* (*knot*) sciolto(-a); (*screw*) allentato(-a); (*stone*) cadente; (*clothes*) ampio(-a), largo(-a); (*animal*) in libertà, scappato(-a); (*life, morals*) dissoluto(-a) ▷ *n* **to be on the ~** essere in libertà; **loosely** *adv* senza stringere; approssimativamente; **loosen** *vt* sciogliere; (*belt etc*) allentare
loot [luːt] *n* bottino ▷ *vt* saccheggiare
lop-sided ['lɔp'saɪdɪd] *adj* non equilibrato(-a), asimmetrico(-a)
lord [lɔːd] *n* signore *m*; **L~ Smith** lord Smith; **the L~** il Signore; **good L~!** buon Dio!; **the (House of) L~s** (*BRIT*) la Camera dei Lord
lorry ['lɔrɪ] (*BRIT*) *n* camion *m inv*; **lorry driver** (*BRIT*) *n* camionista *m*
lose [luːz] (*pt, pp* **lost**) *vt* perdere ▷ *vi* perdere; **I've lost my wallet/passport** ho perso il portafoglio/passaporto; **to ~ (time)** (*clock*) ritardare; **lose out** *vi* rimetterci; **loser** *n* perdente *m/f*
loss [lɔs] *n* perdita; **to be at a ~** essere perplesso(-a)
lost [lɔst] *pt, pp di* **lose** ▷ *adj* perduto(-a); **I'm ~** mi sono perso; **lost property** (*US* **lost and found**) *n* oggetti *mpl* smarriti
lot [lɔt] *n* (*at auctions*) lotto; (*destiny*) destino, sorte *f*; **the ~** tutto(-a) quanto(-a); tutti(-e) quanti(-e); **a ~** molto(-a); **a ~ of** una gran quantità di, un sacco di; **~s of** molto(-a); **to draw ~s (for sth)** tirare a sorte (per qc)
lotion ['ləʊʃən] *n* lozione *f*
lottery ['lɔtərɪ] *n* lotteria
loud [laʊd] *adj* forte, alto(-a); (*gaudy*) vistoso(-a), sgargiante ▷ *adv* (*speak etc*) forte; **out ~** (*read etc*) ad alta voce; **loudly** *adv* fortemente, ad alta voce; **loudspeaker** *n* altoparlante *m*
lounge [laʊndʒ] *n* salotto, soggiorno; (*at airport, station*) sala d'attesa; (*BRIT: also: ~ bar*) bar *m inv* con servizio a tavolino ▷ *vi* oziare
louse [laʊs] (*pl* **lice**) *n* pidocchio
lousy ['laʊzɪ] (*inf*) *adj* orrendo(-a), schifoso(-a); **to feel ~** stare da cani
love [lʌv] *n* amore *m* ▷ *vt* amare; voler bene a; **to ~ to do: I ~ to do** mi piace fare; **to be/fall in ~ with** essere innamorato(-a)/innamorarsi di; **to make ~** fare l'amore; **"15 ~"** (*Tennis*) "15 a zero"; **love affair** *n* relazione *f*; **love life** *n* vita sentimentale
lovely ['lʌvlɪ] *adj* bello(-a); (*delicious: smell, meal*) buono(-a)
lover ['lʌvər] *n* amante *m/f*; (*person in love*) innamorato(-a); (*amateur*): **a ~ of** un(-un')

amante di; un(-un') appassionato(-a) di
loving ['lʌvɪŋ] *adj* affettuoso(-a)
low [ləʊ] *adj* basso(-a) ▷ *adv* in basso ▷ *n* (*Meteor*) depressione *f*; **to be ~ on** (*supplies etc*) avere scarsità di; **to feel ~** sentirsi giù; **low-alcohol** *adj* a basso contenuto alcolico; **low-calorie** *adj* a basso contenuto calorico
lower ['ləʊər] *adj* (*bottom: of 2 things*) più basso; (*less important*) meno importante ▷ *vt* calare; (*prices, eyes, voice*) abbassare
low-fat ['ləʊ'fæt] *adj* magro(-a)
loyal ['lɔɪəl] *adj* fedele, leale; **loyalty** *n* fedeltà, lealtà; **loyalty card** *n* carta che offre sconti a clienti abituali
L.P. *n abbr* = **long-playing record**
L-plates ['elpleɪts] (*BRIT*) *npl* contrassegno P principiante
Lt *abbr* (= *lieutenant*) Ten.
Ltd *abbr* (= *limited*) ≈ S.r.l.
luck [lʌk] *n* fortuna, sorte *f*; **bad ~** sfortuna, mala sorte; **good ~!** buona fortuna!; **luckily** *adv* fortunatamente, per fortuna; **lucky** *adj* fortunato(-a); (*number etc*) che porta fortuna
lucrative ['luːkrətɪv] *adj* lucrativo(-a), lucroso(-a), profittevole
ludicrous ['luːdɪkrəs] *adj* ridicolo(-a)
luggage ['lʌgɪdʒ] *n* bagagli *mpl*; **our ~ hasn't arrived** i nostri bagagli non sono arrivati; **luggage rack** *n* portabagagli *m inv*
lukewarm ['luːkwɔːm] *adj* tiepido(-a)
lull [lʌl] *n* intervallo di calma ▷ *vt* **to ~ sb to sleep** cullare qn finché si addormenta
lullaby ['lʌləbaɪ] *n* ninnananna
lumber ['lʌmbər] *n* (*wood*) legname *m*; (*junk*) roba vecchia
luminous ['luːmɪnəs] *adj* luminoso(-a)
lump [lʌmp] *n* pezzo; (*in sauce*) grumo; (*swelling*) gonfiore *m*; (*also:* **sugar ~**) zolletta ▷ *vt* (*also:* **~ together**) riunire, mettere insieme; **lump sum** *n* somma globale; **lumpy** *adj* (*sauce*) pieno(-a) di grumi; (*bed*) bitorzoluto(-a)
lunatic ['luːnətɪk] *adj* pazzo(-a), matto(-a)
lunch [lʌntʃ] *n* pranzo, colazione *f*; **lunch break** *n* intervallo del pranzo; **lunch time** *n* ora di pranzo
lung [lʌŋ] *n* polmone *m*
lure [luər] *n* richiamo; lusinga ▷ *vt* attirare (con l'inganno)
lurk [ləːk] *vi* stare in agguato
lush [lʌʃ] *adj* lussureggiante
lust [lʌst] *n* lussuria; cupidigia; desiderio; (*fig*): **~ for** sete *f* di
Luxembourg ['lʌksəmbəːg] *n* (*state*) Lussemburgo *m*; (*city*) Lussemburgo *f*

luxurious [lʌgˈzjuərɪəs] *adj* sontuoso(-a), di lusso
luxury [ˈlʌkʃərɪ] *n* lusso ▷ *cpd* di lusso
Be careful not to translate *luxury* by the Italian word *lussuria*.
Lycra® [ˈlaɪkrə] *n* lycra® *f inv*
lying [ˈlaɪɪŋ] *n* bugie *fpl*, menzogne *fpl* ▷ *adj* bugiardo(-a)
lyrics [ˈlɪrɪks] *npl* (*of song*) parole *fpl*

m. *abbr* = **metre**; **mile**; **million**
M.A. *abbr* = **Master of Arts**
ma (*inf*) [mɑː] *n* mamma
mac [mæk] (*BRIT*) *n* impermeabile *m*
macaroni [mækəˈrəʊnɪ] *n* maccheroni *mpl*
Macedonia [mæsɪˈdəʊnɪə] *n* Macedonia; **Macedonian** [mæsɪˈdəʊnɪən] *adj* macedone ▷ *n* macedone *m/f*; (*Ling*) macedone *m*
machine [məˈʃiːn] *n* macchina ▷ *vt* (*Tech*) lavorare a macchina; (*dress etc*) cucire a macchina; **machine gun** *n* mitragliatrice *f*; **machinery** *n* macchinario, macchine *fpl*; (*fig*) macchina; **machine washable** *adj* lavabile in lavatrice
macho [ˈmætʃəʊ] *adj* macho *inv*
mackerel [ˈmækrl] *n inv* sgombro
mackintosh [ˈmækɪntɔʃ] (*BRIT*) *n* impermeabile *m*
mad [mæd] *adj* matto(-a), pazzo(-a); (*foolish*) sciocco(-a); (*angry*) furioso(-a); **to be ~ about** (*keen*) andare pazzo(-a) per
Madagascar [mædəˈgæskəʳ] *n* Madagascar *m*
madam [ˈmædəm] *n* signora
mad cow disease *n* encefalite *f* bovina spongiforme
made [meɪd] *pt, pp of* **make**; **made-to-measure** (*BRIT*) *adj* fatto(-a) su

misura; **made-up** ['meɪdʌp] adj (story) inventato(-a)

madly ['mædlɪ] adv follemente

madman ['mædmən] (irreg) n pazzo, alienato

madness ['mædnɪs] n pazzia

Madrid [mə'drɪd] n Madrid f

Mafia ['mæfɪə] n mafia f

mag [mæg] n abbr (BRIT inf) = **magazine** (Press)

magazine [mægə'ziːn] n (Press) rivista; (Radio, TV) rubrica

> Be careful not to translate *magazine* by the Italian word *magazzino*.

maggot ['mægət] n baco, verme m

magic ['mædʒɪk] n magia ▷ adj magico(-a); **magical** adj magico(-a); **magician** [mə'dʒɪʃən] n mago(-a)

magistrate ['mædʒɪstreɪt] n magistrato; giudice m/f

magnet ['mægnɪt] n magnete m, calamita; **magnetic** [-'nɛtɪk] adj magnetico(-a)

magnificent [mæg'nɪfɪsnt] adj magnifico(-a)

magnify ['mægnɪfaɪ] vt ingrandire; **magnifying glass** n lente f d'ingrandimento

magpie ['mægpaɪ] n gazza

mahogany [mə'hɔgənɪ] n mogano

maid [meɪd] n domestica; (in hotel) cameriera

maiden name ['meɪdn-] n nome m da nubile or da ragazza

mail [meɪl] n posta ▷ vt spedire (per posta); **mailbox** (US) n cassetta delle lettere; **mailing list** n elenco d'indirizzi; **mailman** (irreg; US) n portalettere m inv, postino; **mail-order** n vendita (or acquisto) per corrispondenza

main [meɪn] adj principale ▷ n (pipe) conduttura principale; **main course** n (Culin) piatto principale, piatto forte; **mainland** n continente m; **mainly** adv principalmente, soprattutto; **main road** n strada principale; **mainstream** n (fig) corrente f principale; **main street** n strada principale

maintain [meɪn'teɪn] vt mantenere; (affirm) sostenere; **maintenance** ['meɪntənəns] n manutenzione f; (alimony) alimenti mpl

maisonette [meɪzə'nɛt] n (BRIT) appartamento a due piani

maize [meɪz] n granturco, mais m

majesty ['mædʒɪstɪ] n maestà f inv

major ['meɪdʒəʳ] n (Mil) maggiore m ▷ adj (greater, Mus) maggiore; (in importance) principale, importante

Majorca [mə'jɔːkə] n Maiorca

majority [mə'dʒɔrɪtɪ] n maggioranza

make [meɪk] (pt, pp **made**) vt fare; (manufacture) fare, fabbricare; (cause to be): **to ~ sb sad** etc rendere qn triste etc; (force): **to ~ sb do sth** costringere qn a fare qc, far fare qc a qn; (equal): **2 and 2 ~ 4** 2 più 2 fa 4 ▷ n fabbricazione f; (brand) marca; **to ~ a fool of sb** far fare a qn la figura dello scemo; **to ~ a profit** realizzare un profitto; **to ~ a loss** subire una perdita; **to ~ it** (arrive) arrivare; (achieve sth) farcela; **what time do you ~ it?** che ora fai?; **to ~ do with** arrangiarsi con; **make off** vi svignarsela; **make out** vt (write out) scrivere; (: cheque) emettere; (understand) capire; (see) distinguere; (: numbers) decifrare; **make up** vt (constitute) formare; (invent) inventare; (parcel) fare ▷ vi conciliarsi; (with cosmetics) truccarsi; **make up for** vt fus compensare; ricuperare; **makeover** ['meɪkəʊvəʳ] n (change of image) cambiamento di immagine; (of room, house) trasformazione f; **maker** n (of programme etc) creatore (-trice); (manufacturer) fabbricante m; **makeshift** adj improvvisato(-a); **make-up** n trucco

making ['meɪkɪŋ] n (fig): **in the ~** in formazione; **to have the ~s of** (actor, athlete etc) avere la stoffa di

malaria [mə'lɛərɪə] n malaria

Malaysia [mə'leɪzɪə] n Malaysia

male [meɪl] n (Biol) maschio ▷ adj maschile; maschio(-a)

malicious [mə'lɪʃəs] adj malevolo(-a); (Law) doloso(-a)

malignant [mə'lɪgnənt] adj (Med) maligno(-a)

mall [mɔːl] n (also: **shopping ~**) centro commerciale

mallet ['mælɪt] n maglio

malnutrition [mælnjuː'trɪʃən] n denutrizione f

malpractice [mæl'præktɪs] n prevaricazione f; negligenza

malt [mɔːlt] n malto

Malta ['mɔːltə] n Malta; **Maltese** [mɔː'tiːz] adj, n (pl inv) maltese (m/f); (Ling) maltese m

mammal ['mæml] n mammifero

mammoth ['mæməθ] adj enorme, gigantesco(-a)

man [mæn] (pl **men**) n uomo ▷ vt fornire d'uomini; stare a; **an old ~** un vecchio; **~ and wife** marito e moglie

manage ['mænɪdʒ] vi farcela ▷ vt (be in charge of) occuparsi di; gestire; **to ~ to do sth** riuscire a far qc; **manageable** adj maneggevole; fattibile; **management** n amministrazione f, direzione f; **manager** n direttore m; (of shop, restaurant) gerente m; (of artist, Sport) manager m inv; **manageress** [-ə'rɛs] n direttrice f; gerente f; **managerial** [-ə'dʒɪərɪəl] adj dirigenziale; **managing director** n amministratore m delegato

mandarin ['mændərɪn] n (person, fruit) mandarino

mandate ['mændeɪt] n mandato

mandatory ['mændətərɪ] adj obbligatorio(-a), ingiuntivo(-a)

mane [meɪn] n criniera

mangetout ['mɔnʒ'tuː] n pisello dolce, taccola

mango ['mæŋɡəʊ] (pl **mangoes**) n mango

man: **manhole** ['mænhəʊl] n botola stradale; **manhood** ['mænhʊd] n età virile; virilità

mania ['meɪnɪə] n mania; **maniac** ['meɪnɪæk] n maniaco(-a)

manic ['mænɪk] adj (behaviour, activity) maniacale

manicure ['mænɪkjʊəʳ] n manicure f inv

manifest ['mænɪfɛst] vt manifestare ▷ adj manifesto(-a), palese

manifesto [mænɪ'fɛstəʊ] n manifesto

manipulate [mə'nɪpjʊleɪt] vt manipolare

man: **mankind** [mæn'kaɪnd] n umanità, genere m umano; **manly** ['mænlɪ] adj virile; coraggioso(-a); **man-made** adj sintetico(-a); artificiale

manner ['mænəʳ] n maniera, modo; (behaviour) modo di fare; (type, sort): **all ~ of things** ogni genere di cosa; **~s** npl (conduct) maniere fpl; **bad ~s** maleducazione f

manoeuvre [mə'nuːvəʳ] (US **maneuver**) vt manovrare ▷ vi far manovre ▷ n manovra

manpower ['mænpaʊəʳ] n manodopera

mansion ['mænʃən] n casa signorile

manslaughter ['mænslɔːtəʳ] n omicidio preterintenzionale

mantelpiece ['mæntlpiːs] n mensola del caminetto

manual ['mænjʊəl] adj manuale ▷ n manuale m

manufacture [mænju'fæktʃəʳ] vt fabbricare ▷ n fabbricazione f, manifattura; **manufacturer** n fabbricante m

manure [mə'njuəʳ] n concime m

manuscript ['mænjuskrɪpt] n manoscritto

many ['mɛnɪ] adj molti(-e) ▷ pron molti(-e); **a great ~** moltissimi(-e), un gran numero (di); **~ a time** molte volte

map [mæp] n carta (geografica); (of city)

cartina; **can you show it to me on the ~?** può indicarmelo sulla cartina?

maple ['meɪpl] n acero

mar [mɑːʳ] vt sciupare

Mar. abbr (= March) mar.

marathon ['mærəθən] n maratona

marble ['mɑːbl] n marmo; (toy) pallina, bilia

March [mɑːtʃ] n marzo

march [mɑːtʃ] vi marciare; sfilare ▷ n marcia

mare [mɛəʳ] n giumenta

margarine [mɑːdʒə'riːn] n margarina

margin ['mɑːdʒɪn] n margine m; **marginal** adj marginale; **marginal seat** (Pol) seggio elettorale ottenuto con una stretta maggioranza; **marginally** adv (bigger, better) lievemente, di poco; (different) un po'

marigold ['mærɪɡəʊld] n calendola

marijuana [mærɪ'wɑːnə] n marijuana

marina [mə'riːnə] n marina

marinade n [mærɪ'neɪd] marinata ▷ vt ['mærɪneɪd] = **marinate**

marinate ['mærɪneɪt] vt marinare

marine [mə'riːn] adj (animal, plant) marino(-a); (forces, engineering) marittimo(-a) ▷ n (BRIT) fante m di marina; (US) marine m inv

marital ['mærɪtl] adj maritale, coniugale; **marital status** n stato civile

maritime ['mærɪtaɪm] adj marittimo(-a)

marjoram ['mɑːdʒərəm] n maggiorana

mark [mɑːk] n segno; (stain) macchia; (of skid etc) traccia; (BRIT Scol) voto; (Sport) bersaglio; (currency) marco ▷ vt segnare; (stain) macchiare; (indicate) indicare; (BRIT Scol) dare un voto a; correggere; **to ~ time** segnare il passo; **marked** adj spiccato(-a), chiaro(-a); **marker** n (sign) segno; (bookmark) segnalibro

market ['mɑːkɪt] n mercato ▷ vt (Comm) mettere in vendita; **marketing** n marketing m; **marketplace** n (piazza del) mercato; (world of trade) piazza, mercato; **market research** n indagine f o ricerca di mercato

marmalade ['mɑːməleɪd] n marmellata d'arance

maroon [mə'ruːn] vt (also fig): **to be ~ed (in** or **at)** essere abbandonato(-a) (in) ▷ adj bordeaux inv

marquee [mɑː'kiː] n padiglione m

marriage ['mærɪdʒ] n matrimonio; **marriage certificate** n certificato di matrimonio

married ['mærɪd] adj sposato(-a); (life, love) coniugale, matrimoniale

marrow ['mærəʊ] n midollo; (vegetable) zucca

marry ['mærɪ] vt sposare, sposarsi con; (vicar, priest etc) dare in matrimonio ▷ vi (also: **get married**) sposarsi

Mars [mɑːz] n (planet) Marte m

marsh [mɑːʃ] n palude f

marshal ['mɑːʃl] n maresciallo; (us: fire) capo; (: police) capitano ▷ vt (thoughts, support) ordinare; (soldiers) adunare

martyr ['mɑːtər] n martire m/f

marvel ['mɑːvl] n meraviglia ▷ vi to ~ **(at)** meravigliarsi (di); **marvellous** (us **marvelous**) adj meraviglioso(-a)

Marxism ['mɑːksɪzəm] n marxismo

Marxist ['mɑːksɪst] adj, n marxista m/f

marzipan ['mɑːzɪpæn] n marzapane m

mascara [mæs'kɑːrə] n mascara m

mascot ['mæskət] n mascotte f inv

masculine ['mæskjulɪn] adj maschile; (woman) mascolino(-a)

mash [mæʃ] vt passare, schiacciare; **mashed potatoes** npl purè m di patate

mask [mɑːsk] n maschera ▷ vt mascherare

mason ['meɪsn] n (also: **stone~**) scalpellino; (also: **free~**) massone m; **masonry** n muratura

mass [mæs] n moltitudine f, massa; (Physics) massa; (Rel) messa ▷ cpd di massa ▷ vi ammassarsi; **the ~es** npl (ordinary people) le masse; **~es of** (inf) una montagna di

massacre ['mæsəkər] n massacro

massage ['mæsɑːʒ] n massaggio

massive ['mæsɪv] adj enorme, massiccio(-a)

mass media npl mass media mpl

mass-produce ['mæsprə'djuːs] vt produrre in serie

mast [mɑːst] n albero

master ['mɑːstər] n padrone m; (Art etc, teacher: in primary school) maestro; (: in secondary school) professore m; (title for boys): **M~ X** Signorino X ▷ vt domare; (learn) imparare a fondo; (understand) conoscere a fondo; **mastermind** n mente f superiore ▷ vt essere il cervello di; **Master of Arts/Science** n Master m inv in lettere/scienze; **masterpiece** n capolavoro

masturbate ['mæstəbeɪt] vi masturbare

mat [mæt] n stuoia; (also: **door~**) stoino, zerbino; (also: **table ~**) sottopiatto ▷ adj = **matt**

match [mætʃ] n fiammifero; (game) partita, incontro; (fig) uguale m/f; matrimonio; partito ▷ vt intonare; (go well with) andare benissimo con; (equal) uguagliare; (correspond to) corrispondere a; (pair: also: **~ up**) accoppiare ▷ vi combaciare; **to be a good ~** andare bene; **matchbox** n scatola per fiammiferi; **matching** adj ben assortito(-a)

mate [meɪt] n compagno(-a) di lavoro; (inf: friend) amico(-a); (animal) compagno(-a); (in merchant navy) secondo ▷ vi accoppiarsi

material [mə'tɪərɪəl] n (substance) materiale m, materia; (cloth) stoffa ▷ adj materiale; **~s** npl (equipment) materiali mpl

materialize [mə'tɪərɪəlaɪz] vi materializzarsi, realizzarsi

maternal [mə'təːnl] adj materno(-a)

maternity [mə'təːnɪtɪ] n maternità; **maternity hospital** n ≈ clinica ostetrica; **maternity leave** n congedo di maternità

math [mæθ] (us) n = **maths**

mathematical [mæθə'mætɪkl] adj matematico(-a)

mathematician [mæθəmə'tɪʃən] n matematico(-a)

mathematics [mæθə'mætɪks] n matematica

maths [mæθs] (us **math**) n matematica

matinée ['mætɪneɪ] n matinée f inv

matron ['meɪtrən] n (in hospital) capoinfermiera; (in school) infermiera

matt [mæt] adj opaco(-a)

matter ['mætər] n questione f; (Physics) materia, sostanza; (content) contenuto; (Med: pus) pus m ▷ vi importare; **it doesn't ~** non importa; (I don't mind) non fa niente; **what's the ~?** che cosa c'è?; **no ~ what** qualsiasi cosa accada; **as a ~ of course** come cosa naturale; **as a ~ of fact** in verità; **~s** npl (affairs) questioni

mattress ['mætrɪs] n materasso

mature [mə'tjuər] adj maturo(-a); (cheese) stagionato(-a) ▷ vi maturare; stagionare; **mature student** n studente universitario che ha più di 25 anni; **maturity** n maturità

maul [mɔːl] vt lacerare

mauve [məuv] adj malva inv

max abbr = **maximum**

maximize ['mæksɪmaɪz] vt (profits etc) massimizzare; (chances) aumentare al massimo

maximum ['mæksɪməm] (pl **maxima**) adj massimo(-a) ▷ n massimo

May [meɪ] n maggio

may [meɪ] (conditional **might**) vi (indicating possibility): **he ~ come** può darsi che venga; (be allowed to): **~ I smoke?** posso fumare?; (wishes): **~ God bless you!** Dio la benedica!; **you ~ as well go** tanto vale che tu te ne vada

maybe ['meɪbiː] adv forse, può darsi; **~ he'll ...** può darsi che lui ... + sub, forse lui ...

May Day n il primo maggio

mayhem ['meɪhɛm] n cagnara

mayonnaise [meɪə'neɪz] n maionese f

mayor [mɛəʳ] n sindaco; **mayoress** n sindaco (donna); moglie f del sindaco

maze [meɪz] n labirinto, dedalo

MD n abbr (= Doctor of Medicine) titolo di studio; (Comm) see **managing director**

me [miː] pron mi, m' + vowel or silent "h"; (stressed, after prep) me; **he heard me** mi ha or m'ha sentito; **give me a book** dammi (or mi dia) un libro; **it's me** sono io; **with me** con me; **without me** senza di me

meadow ['mɛdəʊ] n prato

meagre ['miːgəʳ] (US **meager**) adj magro(-a)

meal [miːl] n pasto; (flour) farina; **mealtime** n l'ora di mangiare

mean [miːn] (pt, pp **meant**) adj (with money) avaro(-a), gretto(-a); (unkind) meschino(-a), maligno(-a); (shabby) misero(-a); (average) medio(-a) ▷ vt (signify) significare, voler dire; (intend) **to ~ to do** aver l'intenzione di fare ▷ n mezzo; (Math) media; **~s** npl (way, money) mezzi mpl; **by ~s of** per mezzo di; **by all ~s** ma certo, prego; **to be ~t for** essere destinato(-a) a; **do you ~ it?** dice sul serio?; **what do you ~?** che cosa vuol dire?

meaning ['miːnɪŋ] n significato, senso; **meaningful** adj significativo(-a); **meaningless** adj senza senso

meant [mɛnt] pt, pp of **mean**

meantime ['miːntaɪm] adv (also: **in the ~**) nel frattempo

meanwhile ['miːnwaɪl] adv nel frattempo

measles ['miːzlz] n morbillo

measure ['mɛʒəʳ] vt, vi misurare ▷ n misura; (also: **tape ~**) metro

measurement ['mɛʒəmənt] n (act) misurazione f; (measure) misura; **chest/hip ~** giro petto/fianchi; **to take sb's ~s** prendere le misure di qn

meat [miːt] n carne f; **I don't eat ~** non mangio carne; **cold ~** affettato; **meatball** n polpetta di carne

Mecca ['mɛkə] n (also fig) la Mecca

mechanic [mɪ'kænɪk] n meccanico; **can you send a ~?** può mandare un meccanico?; **mechanical** adj meccanico(-a)

mechanism ['mɛkənɪzəm] n meccanismo

medal ['mɛdl] n medaglia; **medallist** (US **medalist**) n (Sport): **to be a gold medallist** essere medaglia d'oro

meddle ['mɛdl] vi **to ~ in** immischiarsi in, mettere le mani in; **to ~ with** toccare

media ['miːdɪə] npl media mpl

mediaeval [mɛdɪ'iːvl] adj = **medieval**

mediate ['miːdɪeɪt] vi fare da mediatore(-trice)

medical ['mɛdɪkl] adj medico(-a) ▷ n visita medica; **medical certificate** n certificato medico

medicated ['mɛdɪkeɪtɪd] adj medicato(-a)

medication [mɛdɪ'keɪʃən] n medicinali mpl, farmaci mpl

medicine ['mɛdsɪn] n medicina

medieval [mɛdɪ'iːvl] adj medievale

mediocre [miːdɪ'əʊkəʳ] adj mediocre

meditate ['mɛdɪteɪt] vi **to ~ (on)** meditare (su)

meditation [mɛdɪ'teɪʃən] n meditazione f

Mediterranean [mɛdɪtə'reɪnɪən] adj mediterraneo(-a); **the ~ (Sea)** il (mare) Mediterraneo

medium ['miːdɪəm] (pl **media**) adj medio(-a) ▷ n (means) mezzo; (pl **mediums**: person) medium m inv; **medium-sized** adj (tin etc) di grandezza media; (clothes) di taglia media; **medium wave** n onde fpl medie

meek [miːk] adj dolce, umile

meet [miːt] (pt, pp **met**) vt incontrare; (for the first time) fare la conoscenza di; (go and fetch) andare a prendere; (fig) affrontare, soddisfare; raggiungere ▷ vi incontrarsi; (in session) riunirsi; (join: objects) unirsi; **nice to ~ you** piacere (di conoscerla); **meet up** vi **to ~ up with sb** incontrare qn; **meet with** vt fus incontrare; **meeting** n incontro; (session: of club etc) riunione f; (interview) intervista; **she's at a meeting** (Comm) è in riunione; **meeting place** n luogo d'incontro

megabyte ['mɛgəbaɪt] n (Comput) megabyte m inv

megaphone ['mɛgəfəʊn] n megafono

melancholy ['mɛlənkəlɪ] n malinconia ▷ adj malinconico(-a)

melody ['mɛlədɪ] n melodia

melon ['mɛlən] n melone m

melt [mɛlt] vi (gen) sciogliersi, struggersi; (metals) fondersi ▷ vt sciogliere, struggere; fondere

member ['mɛmbəʳ] n membro; **Member of Congress** (US) n membro del Congresso; **Member of Parliament** (BRIT) n deputato(-a); **Member of the European Parliament** (BRIT) n eurodeputato(-a); **Member of the Scottish Parliament** (BRIT) n deputato(-a) del Parlamento scozzese; **membership** n iscrizione f, (numero d')iscritti mpl, membri mpl; **membership card** n tessera (di iscrizione)

memento [mə'mɛntəʊ] n ricordo, souvenir m inv

memo ['mɛməʊ] n appunto; (Comm etc) comunicazione f di servizio

memorable ['mɛmərəbl] adj memorabile

memorandum [mɛməˈrændəm] (pl
memoranda) n appunto; (Comm etc)
comunicazione f di servizio
memorial [mɪˈmɔːrɪəl] n
monumento commemorativo ▷ adj
commemorativo(-a)
memorize [ˈmɛməraɪz] vt memorizzare
memory [ˈmɛmərɪ] n (also Comput)
memoria; (recollection) ricordo
men [mɛn] npl of **man**
menace [ˈmɛnəs] n minaccia ▷ vt
minacciare
mend [mɛnd] vt aggiustare, riparare;
(darn) rammendare ▷ n **on the ~** in via di
guarigione
meningitis [mɛnɪnˈdʒaɪtɪs] n meningite f
menopause [ˈmɛnəupɔːz] n menopausa
men's room n **the men's room** (esp US) la
toilette degli uomini
menstruation [mɛnstruˈeɪʃən] n
mestruazione f
menswear [ˈmɛnzwɛəʳ] n abbigliamento
maschile
mental [ˈmɛntl] adj mentale; **mental
hospital** n ospedale m psichiatrico;
mentality [mɛnˈtælɪtɪ] n mentalità
f inv; **mentally** adv **to be mentally
handicapped** essere minorato psichico
menthol [ˈmɛnθɒl] n mentolo
mention [ˈmɛnʃən] n menzione f ▷ vt
menzionare, far menzione di; **don't ~ it!**
non c'è di che!, prego!
menu [ˈmɛnjuː] n (set menu, Comput) menù
m inv; (printed) carta; **could we see the ~?**
ci può portare il menù?
MEP n abbr = **Member of the European
Parliament**
mercenary [ˈmɜːsɪnərɪ] adj venale ▷ n
mercenario
merchandise [ˈmɜːtʃəndaɪz] n merci fpl
merchant [ˈmɜːtʃənt] n mercante m,
commerciante m; **merchant navy** (US
merchant marine) n marina mercantile
merciless [ˈmɜːsɪlɪs] adj spietato(-a)
mercury [ˈmɜːkjurɪ] n mercurio
mercy [ˈmɜːsɪ] n pietà; (Rel) misericordia;
at the ~ of alla mercé di
mere [mɪəʳ] adj semplice; **by a ~
chance** per mero caso; **merely** adv
semplicemente, non … che
merge [mɜːdʒ] vt unire ▷ vi fondersi,
unirsi; (Comm) fondersi; **merger** n (Comm)
fusione f
meringue [məˈræŋ] n meringa
merit [ˈmɛrɪt] n merito, valore m ▷ vt
meritare
mermaid [ˈmɜːmeɪd] n sirena
merry [ˈmɛrɪ] adj gaio(-a), allegro(-a); **M~
Christmas!** Buon Natale!; **merry-go-**

round n carosello
mesh [mɛʃ] n maglia; rete f
mess [mɛs] n confusione f, disordine m;
(fig) pasticcio; (dirt) sporcizia; (Mil) mensa;
mess about or **around** (inf) vi trastullarsi;
mess with (inf) vt fus (challenge, confront)
litigare con; (drugs, drinks) abusare di;
mess up vt sporcare; fare un pasticcio di;
rovinare
message [ˈmɛsɪdʒ] n messaggio; **can I
leave a ~?** posso lasciare un messaggio?;
are there any ~s for me? ci sono
messaggi per me?
messenger [ˈmɛsɪndʒəʳ] n
messaggero(-a)
Messrs [ˈmɛsəz] abbr (on letters) Spett.
messy [ˈmɛsɪ] adj sporco(-a),
disordinato(-a)
met [mɛt] pt, pp of **meet**
metabolism [mɛˈtæbəlɪzəm] n
metabolismo
metal [ˈmɛtl] n metallo; **metallic** [-ˈtælɪk]
adj metallico(-a)
metaphor [ˈmɛtəfəʳ] n metafora
meteor [ˈmiːtɪəʳ] n meteora; **meteorite**
[ˈmiːtɪəraɪt] n meteorite m
meteorology [miːtɪəˈrɔlədʒɪ] n
meteorologia
meter [ˈmiːtəʳ] n (instrument) contatore
m; (parking meter) parchimetro; (US: unit)
= **metre**
method [ˈmɛθəd] n metodo; **methodical**
[mɪˈθɒdɪkl] adj metodico(-a)
meths [mɛθs] (BRIT) n alcool m denaturato
meticulous [mɛˈtɪkjuləs] adj
meticoloso(-a)
metre [ˈmiːtəʳ] (US **meter**) n metro
metric [ˈmɛtrɪk] adj metrico(-a)
metro [ˈmɛtrəu] n metro m inv
metropolitan [mɛtrəˈpɔlɪtən] adj
metropolitano(-a)
Mexican [ˈmɛksɪkən] adj, n messicano(-a)
Mexico [ˈmɛksɪkəu] n Messico
mg abbr (= milligram) mg
mice [maɪs] npl of **mouse**
micro... [ˈmaɪkrəu] prefix micro…;
microchip n microcircuito integrato;
microphone n microfono; **microscope**
n microscopio; **microwave** n (also:
microwave oven) forno a microonde
mid [mɪd] adj **~ May** metà maggio; **~
afternoon** metà pomeriggio; **in ~ air** a
mezz'aria; **midday** n mezzogiorno
middle [ˈmɪdl] n mezzo; centro; (waist)
vita ▷ adj di mezzo; **in the ~ of the night**
nel bel mezzo della notte; **middle-aged**
adj di mezza età; **Middle Ages** npl **the
Middle Ages** il Medioevo; **middle-class**
adj ≈ borghese; **Middle East** n Medio

Oriente m; **middle name** n secondo nome m; **middle school** n (US) scuola media per ragazzi dagli 11 ai 14 anni; (BRIT) scuola media per ragazzi dagli 8 o 9 ai 12 o 13 anni

midge [mɪdʒ] n moscerino

midget ['mɪdʒɪt] n nano(-a)

midnight ['mɪdnaɪt] n mezzanotte f

midst [mɪdst] n **in the ~ of** in mezzo a

midsummer [mɪd'sʌmər] n mezza or piena estate f

midway [mɪd'weɪ] adj, adv **~ (between)** a mezza strada (fra); **~ (through)** a metà (di)

midweek [mɪd'wiːk] adv a metà settimana

midwife ['mɪdwaɪf] (pl **midwives**) n levatrice f

midwinter [mɪd'wɪntər] n pieno inverno

might [maɪt] vb see **may** ▷ n potere m, forza; **mighty** adj forte, potente

migraine ['miːɡreɪn] n emicrania

migrant ['maɪɡrənt] adj (bird) migratore(-trice); (worker) emigrato(-a)

migrate [maɪ'ɡreɪt] vi (bird) migrare; (person) emigrare

migration [maɪ'ɡreɪʃən] n migrazione f

mike [maɪk] n abbr (= microphone) microfono

Milan [mɪ'læn] n Milano f

mild [maɪld] adj mite; (person, voice) dolce; (flavour) delicato(-a); (illness) leggero(-a); (interest) blando(-a) ▷ n (beer) birra leggera; **mildly** ['maɪldlɪ] adv mitemente; dolcemente; delicatamente; leggermente; blandamente; **to put it mildly** a dire poco

mile [maɪl] n miglio; **mileage** n distanza in miglia, ≈ chilometraggio; **mileometer** [maɪ'lɔmɪtər] n ≈ contachilometri m inv; **milestone** ['maɪlstəun] n pietra miliare

military ['mɪlɪtərɪ] adj militare

militia [mɪ'lɪʃə] n milizia

milk [mɪlk] n latte m ▷ vt (cow) mungere; (fig) sfruttare; **milk chocolate** n cioccolato al latte; **milkman** (irreg) n lattaio; **milky** adj lattiginoso(-a); (colour) latteo(-a)

mill [mɪl] n mulino; (small: for coffee, pepper etc) macinino; (factory) fabbrica; (spinning mill) filatura ▷ vt macinare ▷ vi (also: ~ about) brulicare

millennium [mɪ'lɛnɪəm] (pl **millenniums** or **millennia**) n millennio

milli... ['mɪlɪ] prefix: **milligram(me)** (US **milliliter**) n millilitro; **millimetre** (US **millimeter**) n millimetro

million ['mɪljən] num milione m; **millionaire** n milionario, ≈ miliardario; **millionth** num milionesimo(-a)

milometer [maɪ'lɔmɪtər] n = **mileometer**

mime [maɪm] n mimo ▷ vt, vi mimare

mimic ['mɪmɪk] n imitatore(-trice) ▷ vt fare la mimica di

min. abbr = **minute(s)**; **minimum**

mince [mɪns] vt tritare, macinare ▷ n (BRIT Culin) carne f tritata or macinata; **mincemeat** n frutta secca tritata per uso in pasticceria; (US) carne f tritata or macinata; **mince pie** n specie di torta con frutta secca

mind [maɪnd] n mente f ▷ vt (attend to, look after) badare a, occuparsi di; (be careful) fare attenzione a, stare attento(-a) a; (object to): **I don't ~ the noise** il rumore non mi dà alcun fastidio; **I don't ~** non m'importa; **do you ~ if ...?** le dispiace se...?; **it is on my ~** mi preoccupa; **to my ~** secondo me, a mio parere; **to be out of one's ~** essere uscito(-a) di mente; **to keep** or **bear sth in ~** non dimenticare qc; **to make up one's ~** decidersi; **~ you, ...** sì, però va detto che ...; **never ~** non importa, non fa niente; (don't worry) non preoccuparti; **"~ the step"** "attenzione allo scalino"; **mindless** adj idiota

mine¹ [maɪn] pron il (la) mio(-a); (pl) i (le) miei (mei); **that book is ~** quel libro è mio; **yours is red, ~ is green** il tuo è rosso, il mio è verde; **a friend of ~** un mio amico

mine² [maɪn] n miniera; (explosive) mina ▷ vt (coal) estrarre; (ship, beach) minare; **minefield** n (also fig) campo minato; **miner** ['maɪnər] n minatore m

mineral ['mɪnərəl] adj minerale ▷ n minerale m; **mineral water** n acqua minerale

mingle ['mɪŋɡl] vi **to ~ with** mescolarsi a, mischiarsi con

miniature ['mɪnətʃər] adj in miniatura ▷ n miniatura

minibar ['mɪnɪbɑːr] n minibar m inv

minibus ['mɪnɪbʌs] n minibus m inv

minicab ['mɪnɪkæb] n (BRIT) ≈ taxi m inv

minimal ['mɪnɪml] adj minimo(-a)

minimize ['mɪnɪmaɪz] vt minimizzare

minimum ['mɪnɪməm] (pl **minima**) n minimo ▷ adj minimo(-a)

mining ['maɪnɪŋ] n industria mineraria

miniskirt ['mɪnɪskəːt] n minigonna

minister ['mɪnɪstər] n (BRIT Pol) ministro; (Rel) pastore m

ministry ['mɪnɪstrɪ] n ministero

minor ['maɪnər] adj minore, di poca importanza; (Mus) minore ▷ n (Law) minorenne m/f

Minorca [mɪ'nɔːkə] n Minorca

minority [maɪ'nɔrɪtɪ] n minoranza

mint [mɪnt] n (plant) menta; (sweet) pasticca di menta ▷ vt (coins) battere; **the (Royal) M~** (BRIT), **the (US) M~** (US)

la Zecca; **in ~ condition** come nuovo(-a)
di zecca
minus ['maɪnəs] n (also: **~ sign**) segno
meno ▷ prep meno
minute [adj maɪ'njuːt, n 'mɪnɪt] adj
minuscolo(-a); (detail) minuzioso(-a) ▷ n
minuto; **~s** npl (of meeting) verbale m
miracle ['mɪrəkl] n miracolo
miraculous [mɪ'rækjuləs] adj
miracoloso(-a)
mirage ['mɪrɑːʒ] n miraggio
mirror ['mɪrər] n specchio; (in car)
specchietto
misbehave [mɪsbɪ'heɪv] vi comportarsi
male
misc. abbr = **miscellaneous**; **miscarriage**
['mɪskærɪdʒ] n (Med) aborto spontaneo;
miscarriage of justice errore m
giudiziario
miscellaneous [mɪsɪ'leɪnɪəs] adj (items)
vario(-a); (selection) misto(-a)
mischief ['mɪstʃɪf] n (naughtiness)
birichineria; (maliciousness) malizia;
mischievous adj birichino(-a)
misconception ['mɪskən'sɛpʃən] n idea
sbagliata
misconduct [mɪs'kɒndʌkt] n cattiva
condotta; **professional ~** reato
professionale
miser ['maɪzər] n avaro
miserable ['mɪzərəbl] adj infelice;
(wretched) miserabile; (weather)
deprimente; (offer, failure) misero(-a)
misery ['mɪzərɪ] n (unhappiness) tristezza;
(wretchedness) miseria
misfortune [mɪs'fɔːtʃən] n sfortuna
misgiving [mɪs'gɪvɪŋ] n apprensione f; **to
have ~s about** avere dei dubbi per quanto
riguarda
misguided [mɪs'gaɪdɪd] adj sbagliato(-a),
poco giudizioso(-a)
mishap ['mɪshæp] n disgrazia
misinterpret [mɪsɪn'təːprɪt] vt
interpretare male
misjudge [mɪs'dʒʌdʒ] vt giudicare male
mislay [mɪs'leɪ] (irreg) vt smarrire
mislead [mɪs'liːd] (irreg) vt sviare;
misleading adj ingannevole
misplace [mɪs'pleɪs] vt smarrire
misprint ['mɪsprɪnt] n errore m di stampa
misrepresent [mɪsrɛprɪ'zɛnt] vt travisare
Miss [mɪs] n Signorina
miss [mɪs] vt (fail to get) perdere; (fail to
hit) mancare; (fail to see) **you can't ~ it**
non puoi non vederlo; (regret the absence
of): **I ~ him** sento la sua mancanza ▷ vi
mancare ▷ n (shot) colpo mancato; **we
~ed our train** abbiamo perso il treno;
miss out (BRIT) vt omettere; **miss out on**

vt fus (fun, party) perdersi; (chance, bargain)
lasciarsi sfuggire
missile ['mɪsaɪl] n (Mil) missile m; (object
thrown) proiettile m
missing ['mɪsɪŋ] adj perso(-a),
smarrito(-a); (person) scomparso(-a); (:
after disaster, Mil) disperso(-a); (removed)
mancante; **to be ~** mancare
mission ['mɪʃən] n missione f; **missionary**
n missionario(-a)
misspell [mɪs'spɛl] vt (irreg: like **spell**)
sbagliare l'ortografia di
mist [mɪst] n nebbia, foschia ▷ vi (also: **~
over**, **~ up**) annebbiarsi; (: BRIT: windows)
appannarsi
mistake [mɪs'teɪk] (irreg: like **take**) n
sbaglio, errore m ▷ vt sbagliarsi di;
fraintendere; **to make a ~** fare uno
sbaglio, sbagliare; **there must be some
~** ci dev'essere un errore; **by ~** per sbaglio;
to ~ for prendere per; **mistaken** pp of
mistake ▷ adj (idea etc) sbagliato(-a); **to
be mistaken** sbagliarsi
mister ['mɪstər] (inf) n signore m; see **Mr**
mistletoe ['mɪsltəu] n vischio
mistook [mɪs'tuk] pt of **mistake**
mistress ['mɪstrɪs] n padrona; (lover)
amante f; (BRIT Scol) insegnante f
mistrust [mɪs'trʌst] vt diffidare di
misty ['mɪstɪ] adj nebbioso(-a),
brumoso(-a)
misunderstand [mɪsʌndə'stænd]
(irreg) vt, vi capire male, fraintendere;
misunderstanding n malinteso,
equivoco; **there's been a
misunderstanding** c'è stato un malinteso
misunderstood [mɪsʌndə'stud] pt, pp of
misunderstand
misuse [n mɪs'juːs, vb mɪs'juːz] n cattivo
uso; (of power) abuso ▷ vt far cattivo uso
di; abusare di
mitt(en) ['mɪt(n)] n mezzo guanto;
manopola
mix [mɪks] vt mescolare ▷ vi (people): **to ~
with** avere a che fare con ▷ n mescolanza;
preparato; **mix up** vt mescolare; (confuse)
confondere; **mixed** adj misto(-a); **mixed
grill** n (BRIT) misto alla griglia; **mixed
salad** n insalata mista; **mixed-up** adj
(confused) confuso(-a); **mixer** n (for food:
electric) frullatore m; (: hand) frullino;
(person): **he is a good mixer** è molto
socievole; **mixture** n mescolanza; (blend:
of tobacco etc) miscela; (Med) sciroppo;
mix-up n confusione f
ml abbr (= millilitre(s)) ml
mm abbr (= millimetre) mm
moan [məun] n gemito ▷ vi (inf: complain):
to ~ (about) lamentarsi (di)

moat [məut] n fossato

mob [mɔb] n calca ▷ vt accalcarsi intorno a

mobile ['məubaɪl] adj mobile ▷ n (decoration) mobile m; **mobile home** n grande roulotte f inv (utilizzata come domicilio); **mobile phone** n telefono portatile, telefonino

mobility [məu'bɪlɪtɪ] n mobilità; (of applicant) disponibilità a viaggiare

mobilize ['məubɪlaɪz] vt mobilitare ▷ vi mobilitarsi

mock [mɔk] vt deridere, burlarsi di ▷ adj falso(-a); **~s** npl (BRIT: Scol: inf) simulazione f degli esami; **mockery** n derisione f; **to make a mockery of** burlarsi di; (exam) rendere una farsa

mod cons ['mɔd'kɔnz] npl abbr (BRIT) = **modern conveniences**; see **convenience**

mode [məud] n modo

model ['mɔdl] n modello; (person: for fashion) indossatore(-trice); (: for artist) modello(-a) ▷ adj (small-scale: railway etc) in miniatura; (child, factory) modello inv ▷ vt modellare ▷ vi fare l'indossatore (or l'indossatrice); **to ~ clothes** presentare degli abiti

modem ['məudɛm] n modem m inv

moderate [adj 'mɔdərət, vb 'mɔdəreɪt] adj moderato(-a) ▷ vi moderarsi, placarsi ▷ vt moderare

moderation [mɔdə'reɪʃən] n moderazione f, misura; **in ~** in quantità moderata, con moderazione

modern ['mɔdən] adj moderno(-a); **mod cons** comodità fpl moderne; **modernize** vt modernizzare; **modern languages** npl lingue fpl moderne

modest ['mɔdɪst] adj modesto(-a); **modesty** n modestia

modification [mɔdɪfɪ'keɪʃən] n modificazione f; **to make ~s** fare or apportare delle modifiche

modify ['mɔdɪfaɪ] vt modificare

module ['mɔdjuːl] n modulo

mohair ['məuhɛəʳ] n mohair m

Mohammed [məu'hæmɪd] n Maometto

moist [mɔɪst] adj umido(-a); **moisture** ['mɔɪstʃəʳ] n umidità; (on glass) goccioline fpl di vapore; **moisturizer** ['mɔɪstʃəraɪzəʳ] n idratante f

mold etc [məuld] n, vt = **mould**

mole [məul] n (animal, fig) talpa; (spot) neo

molecule ['mɔlɪkjuːl] n molecola

molest [məu'lɛst] vt molestare

molten ['məultən] adj fuso(-a)

mom [mɔm] (us) n = **mum**

moment ['məumənt] n momento, istante m; **at that ~** in quel momento; **at**

the ~ al momento, in questo momento; **momentarily** ['məuməntərɪlɪ] adv per un momento; (us: very soon) da un momento all'altro; **momentary** adj momentaneo(-a), passeggero(-a); **momentous** [-'mɛntəs] adj di grande importanza

momentum [məu'mɛntəm] n (Physics) momento; (fig) impeto; **to gather ~** aumentare di velocità

mommy ['mɔmɪ] (us) n = **mummy**

Mon. abbr (= Monday) lun.

Monaco ['mɔnəkəu] n Principato di Monaco

monarch ['mɔnək] n monarca m; **monarchy** n monarchia

monastery ['mɔnəstərɪ] n monastero

Monday ['mʌndɪ] n lunedì m inv

monetary ['mʌnɪtərɪ] adj monetario(-a)

money ['mʌnɪ] n denaro, soldi mpl; **I haven't got any ~** non ho soldi; **money belt** n marsupio (per soldi); **money order** n vaglia m inv

mongrel ['mʌŋgrəl] n (dog) cane m bastardo

monitor ['mɔnɪtəʳ] n (TV, Comput) monitor m inv ▷ vt controllare

monk [mʌŋk] n monaco

monkey ['mʌŋkɪ] n scimmia

monologue ['mɔnəlɔg] n monologo

monopoly [mə'nɔpəlɪ] n monopolio

monosodium glutamate [mɔnə'səudɪəm'gluːtəmeɪt] n glutammato di sodio

monotonous [mə'nɔtənəs] adj monotono(-a)

monsoon [mɔn'suːn] n monsone m

monster ['mɔnstəʳ] n mostro

month [mʌnθ] n mese m; **monthly** adj mensile ▷ adv al mese; ogni mese

monument ['mɔnjumənt] n monumento

mood [muːd] n umore m; **to be in a good/bad ~** essere di buon/cattivo umore; **moody** adj (variable) capriccioso(-a), lunatico(-a); (sullen) imbronciato(-a)

moon [muːn] n luna; **moonlight** n chiaro di luna

moor [muəʳ] n brughiera ▷ vt (ship) ormeggiare ▷ vi ormeggiarsi

moose [muːs] n inv alce m

mop [mɔp] n lavapavimenti m inv; (also: ~ of hair) zazzera ▷ vt lavare con lo straccio; (face) asciugare; **mop up** vt asciugare con uno straccio

mope [məup] vi fare il broncio

moped ['məupɛd] n (BRIT) ciclomotore m

moral ['mɔrl] adj morale ▷ n morale f; **~s** npl (principles) moralità

morale [mɔ'rɑːl] n morale m

morality [məˈrælɪtɪ] n moralità
morbid [ˈmɔːbɪd] adj morboso(-a)

○ KEYWORD

more [mɔːʳ] adj **1** (greater in number etc)
più; **more people/letters than we
expected** più persone/lettere di quante
ne aspettavamo; **I have more wine/
money than you** ho più vino/soldi di te;
I have more wine than beer ho più vino
che birra
2 (additional) altro(-a), ancora; **do you
want (some) more tea?** vuole dell'altro
tè?, vuole ancora del tè?; **I have no** or **I
don't have any more money** non ho
più soldi
▷ pron **1** (greater amount) più; **more than 10**
più di 10; **it cost more than we expected**
ha costato più di quanto ci aspettavamo
2 (further or additional amount) ancora;
is there any more? ce n'è ancora?;
there's no more non ce n'è più; **a little
more** ancora un po'; **many/much more**
molti(-e)/molto(-a) di più
▷ adv **more dangerous/easily (than)**
più pericoloso/facilmente (di); **more and
more** sempre di più; **more and more
difficult** sempre più difficile; **more or less**
più o meno; **more than ever** più che mai

moreover [mɔːˈrəuvəʳ] adv inoltre, di più
morgue [mɔːg] n obitorio
morning [ˈmɔːnɪŋ] n mattina, mattino;
(duration) mattinata ▷ cpd del mattino;
in the ~ la mattina; **7 o'clock in the ~** le 7
di or della mattina; **morning sickness** n
nausee fpl mattutine
Moroccan [məˈrɔkən] adj, n
marocchino(-a)
Morocco [məˈrɔkəu] n Marocco
moron [ˈmɔːrɔn] (inf) n deficiente m/f
morphine [ˈmɔːfiːn] n morfina
morris dancing n vedi nota nel riquadro

◉ MORRIS DANCING

Il **morris dancing** è una danza
folcloristica inglese tradizionalmente
riservata agli uomini. Vestiti di bianco
e con dei campanelli attaccati alle
caviglie, i ballerini eseguono una danza
tenendo in mano dei fazzoletti bianchi
e lunghi bastoni. Questa danza è molto
popolare nelle feste paesane.

Morse [mɔːs] n (also: **~ code**) alfabeto
Morse
mortal [ˈmɔːtl] adj mortale ▷ n mortale m

mortar [ˈmɔːtəʳ] n (Constr) malta; (dish)
mortaio
mortgage [ˈmɔːgɪdʒ] n ipoteca; (loan)
prestito ipotecario ▷ vt ipotecare
mortician [mɔːˈtɪʃən] (US) n impresario di
pompe funebri
mortified [ˈmɔːtɪfaɪd] adj umiliato(-a)
mortuary [ˈmɔːtjuərɪ] n camera
mortuaria; obitorio
mosaic [məuˈzeɪɪk] n mosaico
Moscow [ˈmɔskəu] n Mosca
Moslem [ˈmɔzləm] adj, n = **Muslim**
mosque [mɔsk] n moschea
mosquito [mɔsˈkiːtəu] (pl **mosquitoes**)
n zanzara
moss [mɔs] n muschio
most [məust] adj (almost all) la maggior
parte di; (largest, greatest): **who has (the)
~ money?** chi ha più soldi di tutti? ▷ pron
la maggior parte ▷ adv più; (work, sleep
etc) di più; (very) molto, estremamente;
the ~ (also: **+ adjective**) il(-la) più; **~ of** la
maggior parte di; **~ of them** quasi tutti; **I
saw the ~** ho visto più io; **at the (very)
~** al massimo; **to make the ~ of** trarre il
massimo vantaggio da; **a ~ interesting
book** un libro estremamente interessante;
mostly adv per lo più
MOT (BRIT) n abbr = **Ministry of
Transport**; **the ~ (test)** revisione annuale
obbligatoria degli autoveicoli
motel [məuˈtɛl] n motel m inv
moth [mɔθ] n farfalla notturna; tarma
mother [ˈmʌðəʳ] n madre f ▷ vt (care
for) fare da madre a; **motherhood** n
maternità; **mother-in-law** n suocera;
mother-of-pearl [mʌðərəvˈpəːl] n
madreperla; **Mother's Day** n la festa della
mamma; **mother-to-be** [mʌðətəˈbiː]
n futura mamma; **mother tongue** n
madrelingua
motif [məuˈtiːf] n motivo
motion [ˈməuʃən] n movimento, moto;
(gesture) gesto; (at meeting) mozione f ▷ vt,
vi **to ~ (to) sb to do** fare cenno a qn di
fare; **motionless** adj immobile; **motion
picture** n film m inv
motivate [ˈməutɪveɪt] vt (act, decision)
dare origine a, motivare; (person) spingere
motivation [məutɪˈveɪʃən] n motivazione
f
motive [ˈməutɪv] n motivo
motor [ˈməutəʳ] n motore m;
(BRIT: inf: vehicle) macchina ▷ cpd
automobilistico(-a); **motorbike** n moto f
inv; **motorboat** n motoscafo; **motorcar**
(BRIT) n automobile f; **motorcycle**
n motocicletta; **motorcyclist** n
motociclista m/f; **motoring** (BRIT) n

turismo automobilistico; **motorist** n automobilista m/f; **motor racing** (BRIT) n corse fpl automobilistiche; **motorway** (BRIT) n autostrada

motto ['mɔtəu] (pl **mottoes**) n motto

mould [məuld] (US **mold**) n forma, stampo; (mildew) muffa ▷ vt formare; (fig) foggiare; **mouldy** adj ammuffito(-a); (smell) di muffa

mound [maund] n rialzo, collinetta; (heap) mucchio

mount [maunt] n (Geo) monte m ▷ vt montare; (horse) montare a ▷ vi (increase) aumentare; **mount up** vi (build up) accumularsi

mountain ['mauntin] n montagna ▷ cpd di montagna; **mountain bike** n mountain bike f inv; **mountaineer** [-'niə^r] n alpinista m/f; **mountaineering** [-'niəriŋ] n alpinismo; **mountainous** adj montagnoso(-a); **mountain range** n catena montuosa

mourn [mɔ:n] vt piangere, lamentare ▷ vi **to ~ (for sb)** piangere (la morte di qn); **mourner** n parente m/f o amico(-a) del defunto; **mourning** n lutto; **in mourning** in lutto

mouse [maus] (pl **mice**) n topo; (Comput) mouse m inv; **mouse mat, mouse pad** n (Comput) tappetino del mouse

moussaka [mu'sɑːkə] n moussaka

mousse [mu:s] n mousse f inv

moustache [məs'tɑːʃ] (US **mustache**) n baffi mpl

mouth [mauθ, pl mauðz] n bocca; (of river) bocca, foce f; (opening) orifizio; **mouthful** n boccata; **mouth organ** n armonica; **mouthpiece** n (Mus) imboccatura, bocchino; (spokesman) portavoce m/f inv; **mouthwash** n collutorio

move [mu:v] n (movement) movimento; (in game) mossa; (: turn to play) turno; (change: of house) trasloco; (: of job) cambiamento ▷ vt muovere; (change position of) spostare; (emotionally) commuovere; (Pol: resolution etc) proporre ▷ vi (gen) muoversi, spostarsi; (also: ~ **house**) cambiar casa, traslocare; **to get a ~ on** affrettarsi, sbrigarsi; **can you ~ your car, please?** può spostare la macchina, per favore?; **to ~ sb to do sth** indurre or spingere qn a fare qc; **to ~ towards** andare verso; **move back** vi (return) ritornare; **move in** vi (to a house) entrare (in una nuova casa); (police etc) intervenire; **move off** vi partire; **move on** vi riprendere la strada; **move out** vi (of house) sgombrare; **move over** vi spostarsi; **move up** vi avanzare; **movement** ['mu:vmənt] n (gen)

movimento; (gesture) gesto; (of stars, water, physical) moto

movie ['mu:vi] n film m inv; **the ~s** il cinema; **movie theater** (US) n cinema m inv

moving ['mu:viŋ] adj mobile; (causing emotion) commovente

mow [məu] (pt **mowed**, pp **mowed** or **mown**) vt (grass) tagliare; (corn) mietere; **mower** n (also: **lawnmower**) tagliaerba m inv

Mozambique [məuzəm'bi:k] n Mozambico

MP n abbr = **Member of Parliament**

MP3 n abbr M3; **MP3 player** n lettore m MP3

mpg n abbr = **miles per gallon** (30 mpg = 9.4 l. per 100 km)

m.p.h. n abbr = **miles per hour** (60 m.p.h = 96 km/h)

Mr ['mistə^r] (US **Mr.**) n **Mr X** Signor X, Sig. X

Mrs ['misiz] (US **Mrs.**) n **Mrs X** Signora X, Sig.ra X

Ms [miz] (US **Ms.**) n = **Miss or Mrs**; **Ms X** ≈ Signora X, ≈ Sig.ra X

● **Ms**
●
● In inglese si usa **Ms** al posto di "Mrs"
● (Signora) o "Miss" (Signorina) per evitare
● la distinzione tradizionale tra le donne
● sposate e quelle nubili.

MSP n abbr = **Member of the Scottish Parliament**

Mt abbr (Geo: = mount) M.

 KEYWORD

much [mʌtʃ] adj, pron molto(-a); **he's done so much work** ha lavorato così tanto; **I have as much money as you** ho tanti soldi quanti ne hai tu; **how much is it?** quant'è?; **it costs too much** costa troppo; **as much as you want** quanto vuoi ▷ adv 1 (greatly) molto, tanto; **thank you very much** molte grazie; **he's very much the gentleman** è il vero gentiluomo; **I read as much as I can** leggo quanto posso; **as much as you** tanto quanto te 2 (by far) molto; **it's much the biggest company in Europe** è di gran lunga la più grossa società in Europa 3 (almost) grossomodo, praticamente; **they're much the same** sono praticamente uguali

muck [mʌk] n (dirt) sporcizia; **muck up** (inf) vt (ruin) rovinare; **mucky** adj (dirty) sporco(-a), lordo(-a)

mucus ['mjuːkəs] n muco

mud [mʌd] n fango

muddle ['mʌdl] n confusione f, disordine m; pasticcio ▷ vt (also: **~ up**) confondere

muddy ['mʌdɪ] adj fangoso(-a)

mudguard ['mʌdgɑːd] n parafango

muesli ['mjuːzlɪ] n muesli m

muffin ['mʌfɪn] n specie di pasticcino soffice da tè

muffled ['mʌfld] adj smorzato(-a), attutito(-a)

muffler ['mʌflər] (us) n (Aut) marmitta; (: on motorbike) silenziatore m

mug [mʌg] n (cup) tazzone m; (for beer) boccale m; (inf: face) muso; (: fool) scemo(-a) ▷ vt (assault) assalire; **mugger** ['mʌgər] n aggressore m; **mugging** n assalto

muggy ['mʌgɪ] adj afoso(-a)

mule [mjuːl] n mulo

multicoloured ['mʌltɪkʌləd] (us **multicolored**) adj multicolore, variopinto(-a)

multimedia ['mʌltɪ'miːdɪə] adj multimedia inv

multinational [mʌltɪ'næʃənl] adj, n multinazionale (f)

multiple ['mʌltɪpl] adj multiplo(-a), molteplice ▷ n multiplo; **multiple choice (test)** n esercizi mpl a scelta multipla; **multiple sclerosis** [-sklɪ'rəusɪs] n sclerosi f a placche

multiplex cinema ['mʌltɪpleks-] n cinema m inv multisala inv

multiplication [mʌltɪplɪ'keɪʃən] n moltiplicazione f

multiply ['mʌltɪplaɪ] vt moltiplicare ▷ vi moltiplicarsi

multistorey ['mʌltɪ'stɔːrɪ] (brit) adj (building, car park) a più piani

mum [mʌm] (brit: inf) n mamma ▷ adj **to keep ~** non aprire bocca

mumble ['mʌmbl] vt, vi borbottare

mummy ['mʌmɪ] n (brit: mother) mamma; (embalmed) mummia

mumps [mʌmps] n orecchioni mpl

munch [mʌntʃ] vt, vi sgranocchiare

municipal [mjuː'nɪsɪpl] adj municipale

mural ['mjuərl] n dipinto murale

murder ['məːdər] n assassinio, omicidio ▷ vt assassinare; **murderer** n omicida m, assassino

murky ['məːkɪ] adj tenebroso(-a)

murmur ['məːmər] n mormorio ▷ vt, vi mormorare

muscle ['mʌsl] n muscolo; (fig) forza; **muscular** ['mʌskjulər] adj muscolare; (person, arm) muscoloso(-a)

329 | myth

museum [mjuː'zɪəm] n museo

mushroom ['mʌʃrum] n fungo ▷ vi crescere in fretta

music ['mjuːzɪk] n musica; **musical** adj musicale; (person) portato(-a) per la musica ▷ n (show) commedia musicale; **musical instrument** n strumento musicale; **musician** [-'zɪʃən] n musicista m/f

Muslim ['mʌzlɪm] adj, n musulmano(-a)

muslin ['mʌzlɪn] n mussola

mussel ['mʌsl] n cozza

must [mʌst] aux vb (obligation): **I ~ do it** devo farlo; (probability): **he ~ be there by now** dovrebbe essere arrivato ormai; **I ~ have made a mistake** devo essermi sbagliato ▷ n **it's a ~** è d'obbligo

mustache ['mʌstæʃ] (us) n = **moustache**

mustard ['mʌstəd] n senape f, mostarda

mustn't ['mʌsnt] = **must not**

mute [mjuːt] adj, n muto(-a)

mutilate ['mjuːtɪleɪt] vt mutilare

mutiny ['mjuːtɪnɪ] n ammutinamento

mutter ['mʌtər] vt, vi borbottare, brontolare

mutton ['mʌtn] n carne f di montone

mutual ['mjuːtʃuəl] adj mutuo(-a), reciproco(-a)

muzzle ['mʌzl] n muso; (protective device) museruola; (of gun) bocca ▷ vt mettere la museruola a

my [maɪ] adj il (la) mio(-a); (pl) i (le) miei (mie); **my house** la mia casa; **my books** i miei libri; **my brother** mio fratello; **I've washed my hair/cut my finger** mi sono lavato i capelli/tagliato il dito

myself [maɪ'self] pron (reflexive) mi; (emphatic) io stesso(-a); (after prep) me; see also **oneself**

mysterious [mɪs'tɪərɪəs] adj misterioso(-a)

mystery ['mɪstərɪ] n mistero

mystical ['mɪstɪkəl] adj mistico(-a)

mystify ['mɪstɪfaɪ] vt mistificare; (puzzle) confondere

myth [mɪθ] n mito; **mythology** [mɪ'θɔlədʒɪ] n mitologia

n/a abbr = **not applicable**

nag [næg] vt tormentare ▷ vi brontolare in continuazione

nail [neɪl] n (human) unghia; (metal) chiodo ▷ vt inchiodare; **to ~ sb down to (doing) sth** costringere qn a (fare) qc; **nailbrush** n spazzolino da or per unghie; **nailfile** n lima da or per unghie; **nail polish** n smalto da or per unghie; **nail polish remover** n acetone m, solvente m; **nail scissors** npl forbici fpl da or per unghie; **nail varnish** (BRIT) n = **nail polish**

naïve [naɪ'iːv] adj ingenuo(-a)

naked ['neɪkɪd] adj nudo(-a)

name [neɪm] n nome m; (reputation) nome, reputazione f ▷ vt (baby etc) chiamare; (plant, illness) nominare; (person, object) identificare; (price, date) fissare; **what's your ~?** come si chiama?; **by ~** di nome; **she knows them all by ~** li conosce tutti per nome; **namely** adv cioè

nanny ['nænɪ] n bambinaia

nap [næp] n (sleep) pisolino; (of cloth) peluria; **to be caught ~ping** essere preso alla sprovvista

napkin ['næpkɪn] n (also: **table ~**) tovagliolo

nappy ['næpɪ] (BRIT) n pannolino

narcotics [nɑː'kɔtɪkz] npl (drugs) narcotici, stupefacenti mpl

narrative ['nærətɪv] n narrativa

narrator [nə'reɪtəʳ] n narratore(-trice)

narrow ['nærəu] adj stretto(-a); (fig) limitato(-a), ristretto(-a) ▷ vi restringersi; **to have a ~ escape** farcela per un pelo; **narrow down** vt (search, investigation, possibilities) restringere; (list) ridurre; **narrowly** adv per un pelo; (time) per poco; **narrow-minded** adj meschino(-a)

nasal ['neɪzl] adj nasale

nasty ['nɑːstɪ] adj (person, remark: unpleasant) cattivo(-a); (: rude) villano(-a); (smell, wound, situation) brutto(-a)

nation ['neɪʃən] n nazione f

national ['næʃənl] adj nazionale ▷ n cittadino(-a); **national anthem** n inno nazionale; **national dress** n costume m nazionale; **National Health Service** (BRIT) n servizio nazionale di assistenza sanitaria, ≈ S.S.N. m; **National Insurance** (BRIT) n ≈ Previdenza Sociale; **nationalist** adj, n nazionalista (m/f); **nationality** ['næliti] n nazionalità f inv; **nationalize** vt nazionalizzare; **national park** n parco nazionale; **National Trust** n sovrintendenza ai beni culturali e ambientali

● **NATIONAL TRUST**
●
● Fondato nel 1895, il **National Trust** è
● un'organizzazione che si occupa della
● tutela e della salvaguardia di luoghi
● di interesse storico o ambientale nel
● Regno Unito.

nationwide ['neɪʃənwaɪd] adj diffuso(-a) in tutto il paese ▷ adv in tutto il paese

native ['neɪtɪv] n abitante m/f del paese ▷ adj indigeno(-a); (country) natio(-a); (ability) innato(-a); **a ~ of Russia** un nativo della Russia; **a ~ speaker of French** una persona di madrelingua francese; **Native American** n discendente di tribù dell'America settentrionale

NATO ['neɪtəu] n abbr (= North Atlantic Treaty Organization) N.A.T.O. f

natural ['nætʃrəl] adj naturale; (ability) innato(-a); (manner) semplice; **natural gas** n gas m metano; **natural history** n storia naturale; **naturally** adv naturalmente; (by nature: gifted) di natura; **natural resources** npl risorse fpl naturali

nature ['neɪtʃəʳ] n natura; (character) natura, indole f; **by ~** di natura; **nature reserve** n (BRIT) parco naturale

naughty ['nɔːtɪ] adj (child) birichino(-a), cattivello(-a); (story, film) spinto(-a)

nausea ['nɔːsɪə] n (Med) nausea; (fig: disgust) schifo

naval ['neɪvl] *adj* navale

navel ['neɪvl] *n* ombelico

navigate ['nævɪgeɪt] *vt* percorrere navigando ▷ *vi* navigare; (*Aut*) fare da navigatore; **navigation** [-'geɪʃən] *n* navigazione *f*

navy ['neɪvɪ] *n* marina

Nazi ['nɑːtsɪ] *n* nazista *m/f*

NB *abbr* (= *nota bene*) N.B.

near [nɪər] *adj* vicino(-a); (*relation*) prossimo(-a) ▷ *adv* vicino ▷ *prep* (*also*: **~ to**) vicino a, presso; (: *time*) verso ▷ *vt* avvicinarsi a; **nearby** [nɪə'baɪ] *adj* vicino(-a) ▷ *adv* vicino; **is there a bank nearby?** c'è una banca qui vicino?; **nearly** *adv* quasi; **I nearly fell** per poco non sono caduto; **near-sighted** [nɪə'saɪtɪd] *adj* miope

neat [niːt] *adj* (*person, room*) ordinato(-a); (*work*) pulito(-a); (*solution, plan*) ben indovinato(-a), azzeccato(-a); (*spirits*) liscio(-a); **neatly** *adv* con ordine; (*skilfully*) abilmente

necessarily ['nesɪsrɪlɪ] *adv* necessariamente

necessary ['nesɪsrɪ] *adj* necessario(-a)

necessity [nɪ'sesɪtɪ] *n* necessità *f inv*

neck [nɛk] *n* collo; (*of garment*) colletto ▷ *vi* (*inf*) pomiciare, sbaciucchiarsi; **~ and ~** testa a testa; **necklace** ['nɛklɪs] *n* collana; **necktie** ['nɛktaɪ] *n* cravatta

nectarine ['nɛktərɪn] *n* nocepesca

need [niːd] *n* bisogno ▷ *vt* aver bisogno di; **do you ~ anything?** ha bisogno di qualcosa?; **to ~ to do** dover fare; aver bisogno di fare; **you don't ~ to go** non devi andare, non c'è bisogno che tu vada

needle ['niːdl] *n* ago; (*on record player*) puntina ▷ *vt* punzecchiare

needless ['niːdlɪs] *adj* inutile

needlework ['niːdlwəːk] *n* cucito

needn't ['niːdnt] = **need not**

needy ['niːdɪ] *adj* bisognoso(-a)

negative ['nɛgətɪv] *n* (*Ling*) negazione *f*; (*Phot*) negativo ▷ *adj* negativo(-a)

neglect [nɪ'glɛkt] *vt* trascurare ▷ *n* (*of person, duty*) negligenza; (*of child, house etc*) scarsa cura; **state of ~** stato di abbandono

negotiate [nɪ'gəuʃɪeɪt] *vi* **to ~ (with)** negoziare (con) ▷ *vt* (*Comm*) negoziare; (*obstacle*) superare; **negotiations** [nɪgəuʃɪ'eɪʃənz] *pl n* trattative *fpl*, negoziati *mpl*

negotiator [nɪ'gəuʃɪeɪtər] *n* negoziatore(-trice)

neighbour ['neɪbər] (*us* **neighbor**) *n* vicino(-a); **neighbourhood** *n* vicinato; **neighbouring** *adj* vicino(-a)

neither ['naɪðər] *adj, pron* né l'uno(-a) né l'altro(-a), nessuno(-a) dei (delle) due ▷ *conj* neanche, nemmeno, neppure ▷ *adv* **~ good nor bad** né buono né cattivo; **I didn't move and ~ did Claude** io non mi mossi e nemmeno Claude; **..., ~ did I refuse** ..., ma non ho nemmeno rifiutato

neon ['niːɔn] *n* neon *m*

Nepal [nɪ'pɔːl] *n* Nepal *m*

nephew ['nɛvjuː] *n* nipote *m*

nerve [nəːv] *n* nervo; (*fig*) coraggio; (*impudence*) faccia tosta; **~s** (*nervousness*) nervosi; **a fit of ~s** una crisi di nervi

nervous ['nəːvəs] *adj* nervoso(-a); (*anxious*) agitato(-a), in apprensione; **nervous breakdown** *n* esaurimento nervoso

nest [nɛst] *n* nido ▷ *vi* fare il nido, nidificare

net [nɛt] *n* rete *f* ▷ *adj* netto(-a) ▷ *vt* (*fish etc*) prendere con la rete; (*profit*) ricavare un utile netto di; **the N~** (*Internet*) Internet *f*; **netball** *n* specie di pallacanestro

Netherlands ['nɛðələndz] *npl* **the ~** i Paesi Bassi

nett [nɛt] *adj* = **net**

nettle ['nɛtl] *n* ortica

network ['nɛtwəːk] *n* rete *f*

neurotic [njuə'rɔtɪk] *adj, n* nevrotico(-a)

neuter ['njuːtər] *adj* neutro(-a) ▷ *vt* (*cat etc*) castrare

neutral ['njuːtrəl] *adj* neutro(-a); (*person, nation*) neutrale ▷ *n* (*Aut*): **in ~** in folle

never ['nɛvər] *adv* (*non...*) mai; **I've ~ been to Spain** non sono mai stato in Spagna; **~ again** mai più; **I'll ~ go there again** non ci vado più; **~ in my life** mai in vita mia; *see also* **mind**; **never-ending** *adj* interminabile; **nevertheless** [nɛvəðə'lɛs] *adv* tuttavia, ciò nonostante, ciò nondimeno

new [njuː] *adj* nuovo(-a); (*brand new*) nuovo(-a) di zecca; **New Age** *n* New Age *f inv*; **newborn** *adj* neonato(-a); **newcomer** ['njuːkʌmər] *n* nuovo(-a) venuto(-a); **newly** *adv* di recente

news [njuːz] *n* notizie *fpl*; (*Radio*) giornale *m* radio; (*TV*) telegiornale *m*; **a piece of ~** una notizia; **news agency** *n* agenzia di stampa; **newsagent** (*BRIT*) *n* giornalaio; **newscaster** *n* (*Radio, TV*) annunciatore(-trice); **news dealer** (*US*) *n* = **newsagent**; **newsletter** *n* bollettino; **newspaper** *n* giornale *m*; **newsreader** *n* = **newscaster**

newt [njuːt] *n* tritone *m*

New Year *n* Anno Nuovo; **New Year's Day** *n* il Capodanno; **New Year's Eve** *n* la vigilia di Capodanno

New York [-'jɔːk] n New York f
New Zealand [-'ziːlənd] n Nuova Zelanda;
New Zealander n neozelandese m/f
next [nɛkst] adj prossimo(-a) ▷ adv
accanto; (in time) dopo; **the ~ day** il giorno
dopo, l'indomani; **~ time** la prossima
volta; **~ year** l'anno prossimo; **when do
we meet ~?** quando ci rincontriamo?; **~
to** accanto a; **~ to nothing** quasi niente;
~ please! (avanti) il prossimo!; **next door**
adv, adj accanto inv; **next-of-kin** n parente
m/f prossimo(-a)
NHS n abbr = **National Health Service**
nibble ['nɪbl] vt mordicchiare
nice [naɪs] adj (holiday, trip) piacevole; (flat,
picture) bello(-a); (person) simpatico(-a),
gentile; **nicely** adv bene
niche [niːʃ] n (Archit) nicchia
nick [nɪk] n taglietto; tacca ▷ vt (inf)
rubare; **in the ~ of time** appena in tempo
nickel ['nɪkl] n nichel m; (US) moneta da
cinque centesimi di dollaro
nickname ['nɪkneɪm] n
soprannome m
nicotine ['nɪkətiːn] n nicotina
niece [niːs] n nipote f
Nigeria [naɪ'dʒɪərɪə] n Nigeria
night [naɪt] n notte f; (evening) sera; **at
~ la sera; by ~** di notte; **the ~ before
last** l'altro ieri notte (or sera); **night
club** n locale m notturno; **nightdress**
n camicia da notte; **nightie** ['naɪtɪ] n
= **nightdress**; **nightlife** ['naɪtlaɪf] n vita
notturna; **nightly** ['naɪtlɪ] adj di ogni
notte or sera; (by night) notturno(-a)
▷ adv ogni notte or sera; **nightmare**
['naɪtmɛəʳ] n incubo
night: **night school** n scuola serale; **night
shift** n turno di notte; **night-time** n
notte f
nil [nɪl] n nulla m; (BRIT Sport) zero
nine [naɪn] num nove; **nineteen** num
diciannove; **nineteenth** [naɪn'tiːnθ] num
diciannovesimo(-a); **ninetieth** ['naɪntɪɪθ]
num novantesimo(-a); **ninety** num
novanta; **ninth** [naɪnθ] num nono(-a)
nip [nɪp] vt pizzicare; (bite) mordere
nipple ['nɪpl] n (Anat) capezzolo
nitrogen ['naɪtrədʒən] n azoto

⬤ KEYWORD

no [nəu] (pl **noes**) adv (opposite of "yes") no;
are you coming? — no (I'm not) viene?
— no (non vengo); **would you like some
more? — no thank you** ne vuole ancora
un po'? — no, grazie
▷ adj (not any) nessuno(-a); **I have no
money/time/books** non ho soldi/

tempo/libri; **no student would have
done it** nessuno studente lo avrebbe
fatto; **"no parking"** "divieto di sosta"; **"no
smoking"** "vietato fumare"
▷ n no m inv

nobility [nəu'bɪlɪtɪ] n nobiltà
noble ['nəubl] adj nobile
nobody ['nəubədɪ] pron nessuno
nod [nɔd] vi accennare col capo, fare un
cenno; (in agreement) annuire con un cenno
del capo; (sleep) sonnecchiare ▷ vt **to ~
one's head** fare di sì col capo ▷ n cenno;
nod off vi assopirsi
noise [nɔɪz] n rumore m; (din, racket)
chiasso; **I can't sleep for the ~** non riesco
a dormire a causa del rumore; **noisy**
adj (street, car) rumoroso(-a); (person)
chiassoso(-a)
nominal ['nɔmɪnl] adj nominale; (rent)
simbolico(-a)
nominate ['nɔmɪneɪt] vt (propose)
proporre come candidato; (elect)
nominare; **nomination** [nɔmɪ'neɪʃən]
n nomina; candidatura; **nominee**
[nɔmɪ'niː] n persona nominata,
candidato(-a)
none [nʌn] pron (not one thing) niente;
(not one person) nessuno(-a); **~ of you**
nessuno(-a) di voi; **I've ~ left** non ne ho
più; **he's ~ the worse for it** non ne ha
risentito
nonetheless [nʌnðə'lɛs] adv
nondimeno
non-fiction [nɔn'fɪkʃən] n saggistica
nonsense ['nɔnsəns] n sciocchezze fpl
non: **non-smoker** n non fumatore(-trice);
non-smoking adj (person) che non fuma;
(area, section) per non fumatori; **non-stick**
adj antiaderente, antiadesivo(-a)
noodles ['nuːdlz] npl taglierini mpl
noon [nuːn] n mezzogiorno
no-one ['nəuwʌn] pron = **nobody**
nor [nɔːʳ] conj = **neither** ▷ adv see **neither**
norm [nɔːm] n norma
normal ['nɔːml] adj normale; **normally**
adv normalmente
north [nɔːθ] n nord m, settentrione m
▷ adj nord inv, del nord, settentrionale
▷ adv verso nord; **North America** n
America del Nord; **North American**
adj, n nordamericano(-a); **northbound**
['nɔːθbaund] adj (traffic) diretto(-a)
a nord; (carriageway) nord inv; **north-
east** n nord-est m; **northeastern** adj
nordorientale; **northern** ['nɔːðən] adj del
nord, settentrionale; **Northern Ireland**
n Irlanda del Nord; **North Korea** n Corea
del Nord; **North Pole** n Polo Nord; **North**

Sea n Mare m del Nord; **north-west**
n nord-ovest m; **northwestern** adj
nordoccidentale

Norway ['nɔːweɪ] n Norvegia; **Norwegian**
[nɔːˈwiːdʒən] adj norvegese ▷ n
norvegese m/f; (Ling) norvegese m

nose [nəuz] n naso; (of animal) muso
▷ vi **to ~ about** aggirarsi; **nosebleed** n
emorragia nasale; **nosey** (inf) adj = **nosy**

nostalgia [nɔsˈtældʒɪə] n nostalgia

nostalgic [nɔsˈtældʒɪk] adj
nostalgico(-a)

nostril ['nɔstrɪl] n narice f; (of horse)
frogia

nosy ['nəuzɪ] (inf) adj curioso(-a)

not [nɔt] adv non; **he is ~ or isn't here** non
è qui, non c'è; **you must ~ or you mustn't
do that** non devi fare quello; **it's too late,
isn't it or is it ~?** è troppo tardi, vero?; **~
that I don't like him** non che (lui) non mi
piaccia; **~ yet/now** non ancora/ora; see
also **all**; **only**

notable ['nəutəbl] adj notevole; **notably**
['nəutəblɪ] adv (markedly) notevolmente;
(particularly) in particolare

notch [nɔtʃ] n tacca; (in saw) dente m

note [nəut] n nota; (letter, banknote)
biglietto ▷ vt (also: **~ down**) prendere
nota di; **to take ~s** prendere appunti;
notebook n taccuino; **noted** ['nəutɪd]
adj celebre; **notepad** n bloc-notes m inv;
notepaper n carta da lettere

nothing ['nʌθɪŋ] n nulla m, niente m;
(zero) zero; **he does ~** non fa niente; **~
new/much** etc niente di nuovo/speciale
etc; **for ~** per niente

notice ['nəutɪs] n avviso; (of leaving)
preavviso ▷ vt notare, accorgersi di; **to
take ~ of** fare attenzione a; **to bring sth
to sb's ~** far notare qc a qn; **at short ~**
con un breve preavviso; **until further ~**
fino a nuovo avviso; **to hand in one's ~**
licenziarsi; **noticeable** adj evidente

notify ['nəutɪfaɪ] vt **to ~ sth to sb** far
sapere qc a qn; **to ~ sb of sth** avvisare qn
di qc

notion ['nəuʃən] n idea; (concept) nozione
f; **~s** npl (us: haberdashery) merceria

notorious [nəuˈtɔːrɪəs] adj
famigerato(-a)

notwithstanding [nɔtwɪθˈstændɪŋ] adv
nondimeno ▷ prep nonostante, malgrado

nought [nɔːt] n zero

noun [naun] n nome m, sostantivo

nourish ['nʌrɪʃ] vt nutrire; **nourishment**
n nutrimento

Nov. abbr (= November) nov.

novel ['nɔvl] n romanzo ▷ adj nuovo(-a);
novelist n romanziere(-a); **novelty** n

novità f inv

November [nəuˈvɛmbəʳ] n novembre m

novice ['nɔvɪs] n principiante m/f; (Rel)
novizio(-a)

now [nau] adv ora, adesso ▷ conj **~
(that)** adesso che, ora che; **by ~** ormai;
just ~ proprio ora; **right ~** subito,
immediatamente; **~ and then, ~ and
again** ogni tanto; **from ~ on** da ora in poi;
nowadays ['nauədeɪz] adv oggidì

nowhere ['nəuwɛəʳ] adv in nessun luogo,
da nessuna parte

nozzle ['nɔzl] n (of hose etc) boccaglio; (of
fire extinguisher) lancia

nr abbr (BRIT) = **near**

nuclear ['njuːklɪəʳ] adj nucleare

nucleus ['njuːklɪəs] (pl **nuclei**) n nucleo

nude [njuːd] adj nudo(-a) ▷ n (Art) nudo;
in the ~ tutto(-a) nudo(-a)

nudge [nʌdʒ] vt dare una gomitata a

nudist ['njuːdɪst] n nudista m/f

nudity ['njuːdɪtɪ] n nudità

nuisance ['njuːsns] n **it's a ~** è una
seccatura; **he's a ~** è uno scocciatore

numb [nʌm] adj **~ (with)** intorpidito(-a)
(da); (with fear) impietrito(-a) (da); **~ with
cold** intirizzito(-a) (dal freddo)

number ['nʌmbəʳ] n numero ▷ vt
numerare; (include) contare; **a ~ of** un
certo numero di; **to be ~ed among** venire
annoverato(-a) tra; **they were 10 in ~**
erano in tutto 10; **number plate** (BRIT)
n (Aut) targa; **Number Ten** n (BRIT: = 10
Downing Street) residenza del Primo Ministro
del Regno Unito

numerical [njuːˈmɛrɪkl] adj
numerico(-a)

numerous ['njuːmərəs] adj
numeroso(-a)

nun [nʌn] n suora, monaca

nurse [nəːs] n infermiere(-a); (also:
~maid) bambinaia ▷ vt (patient, cold)
curare; (baby: BRIT) cullare; (: US) allattare,
dare il latte a

nursery ['nəːsərɪ] n (room) camera dei
bambini; (institution) asilo; (for plants)
vivaio; **nursery rhyme** n filastrocca;
nursery school n scuola materna;
nursery slope (BRIT) n (Ski) pista per
principianti

nursing ['nəːsɪŋ] n (profession)
professione f di infermiere (or di
infermiera); (care) cura; **nursing home** n
casa di cura

nurture ['nəːtʃəʳ] vt allevare; nutrire

nut [nʌt] n (of metal) dado; (fruit) noce f

nutmeg ['nʌtmɛg] n noce f moscata

nutrient ['njuːtrɪənt] adj nutriente ▷ n
sostanza nutritiva

nutrition [njuːˈtrɪʃən] *n* nutrizione *f*
nutritious [njuːˈtrɪʃəs] *adj* nutriente
nuts [nʌts] (*inf*) *adj* matto(-a)
NVQ *n abbr* (BRIT) = **National Vocational Qualification**
nylon [ˈnaɪlɔn] *n* nailon *m* ▷ *adj* di nailon

oak [əuk] *n* quercia ▷ *adj* di quercia
O.A.P. (BRIT) *n*, *abbr* = **old age pensioner**
oar [ɔːʳ] *n* remo
oasis [əuˈeɪsɪs] (*pl* **oases**) *n* oasi *f inv*
oath [əuθ] *n* giuramento; (*swear word*) bestemmia
oatmeal [ˈəutmiːl] *n* farina d'avena
oats [əuts] *npl* avena
obedience [əˈbiːdɪəns] *n* ubbidienza
obedient [əˈbiːdɪənt] *adj* ubbidiente
obese [əuˈbiːs] *adj* obeso(-a)
obesity [əuˈbiːsɪtɪ] *n* obesità
obey [əˈbeɪ] *vt* ubbidire a; (*instructions, regulations*) osservare
obituary [əˈbɪtjuərɪ] *n* necrologia
object [*n* ˈɔbdʒɪkt, *vb* əbˈdʒɛkt] *n* oggetto; (*purpose*) scopo, intento; (*Ling*) complemento oggetto ▷ *vi* **to ~ to** (*attitude*) disapprovare; (*proposal*) protestare contro, sollevare delle obiezioni contro; **expense is no ~** non si bada a spese; **to ~ that** obiettare che; **objection** [əbˈdʒɛkʃən] *n* obiezione *f*; **objective** *n* obiettivo
obligation [ɔblɪˈɡeɪʃən] *n* obbligo, dovere *m*; **without ~** senza impegno
obligatory [əˈblɪɡətərɪ] *adj* obbligatorio(-a)
oblige [əˈblaɪdʒ] *vt* (*force*): **to ~ sb to do** costringere qn a fare; (*do a favour*) fare una

cortesia a; **to be ~d to sb for sth** essere
grato a qn per qc

oblique [ə'bli:k] *adj* obliquo(-a); (*allusion*)
indiretto(-a)

obliterate [ə'blɪtəreɪt] *vt* cancellare

oblivious [ə'blɪvɪəs] *adj* **~ of** incurante di;
inconscio(-a) di

oblong ['ɔblɔŋ] *adj* oblungo(-a) ▷ *n*
rettangolo

obnoxious [əb'nɔkʃəs] *adj* odioso(-a);
(*smell*) disgustoso(-a), ripugnante

oboe ['əubəu] *n* oboe *m*

obscene [əb'si:n] *adj* osceno(-a)

obscure [əb'skjuə'] *adj* oscuro(-a) ▷ *vt*
oscurare; (*hide: sense*) nascondere

observant [əb'zə:vnt] *adj* attento(-a)

> Be careful not to translate *observant*
> by the Italian word *osservante*.

observation [ɔbzə'veɪʃən] *n* osservazione
f; (*by police etc*) sorveglianza

observatory [əb'zə:vətrɪ] *n*
osservatorio

observe [əb'zə:v] *vt* osservare;
(*remark*) fare osservare; **observer** *n*
osservatore(-trice)

obsess [əb'sɛs] *vt* ossessionare; **obsession**
[əb'sɛʃən] *n* ossessione *f*; **obsessive** *adj*
ossessivo(-a)

obsolete ['ɔbsəliːt] *adj* obsoleto(-a)

obstacle ['ɔbstəkl] *n* ostacolo

obstinate ['ɔbstɪnɪt] *adj* ostinato(-a)

obstruct [əb'strʌkt] *vt* (*block*) ostruire,
ostacolare; (*halt*) fermare; (*hinder*)
impedire; **obstruction** [əb'strʌkʃən] *n*
ostruzione *f*; ostacolo

obtain [əb'teɪn] *vt* ottenere

obvious ['ɔbvɪəs] *adj* ovvio(-a), evidente;
obviously *adv* ovviamente; certo

occasion [ə'keɪʒən] *n* occasione *f*;
(*event*) avvenimento; **occasional** *adj*
occasionale; **occasionally** *adv* ogni
tanto

occult [ɔ'kʌlt] *adj* occulto(-a) ▷ *n* **the ~**
l'occulto

occupant ['ɔkjupənt] *n* occupante *m/f*; (*of
boat, car etc*) persona a bordo

occupation [ɔkju'peɪʃən] *n* occupazione *f*;
(*job*) mestiere *m*, professione *f*

occupy ['ɔkjupaɪ] *vt* occupare; **to ~ o.s. in
doing** occuparsi a fare

occur [ə'kə:'] *vi* succedere, capitare; **to ~
to sb** venire in mente a qn; **occurrence** *n*
caso, fatto; presenza

> Be careful not to translate *occur* by
> the Italian word *occorrere*.

ocean ['əuʃən] *n* oceano

o'clock [ə'klɔk] *adv* **it is 5 o'clock** sono le 5

Oct. *abbr* (= *October*) ott.

October [ɔk'təubə'] *n* ottobre *m*

octopus ['ɔktəpəs] *n* polpo, piovra

odd [ɔd] *adj* (*strange*) strano(-a),
bizzarro(-a); (*number*) dispari *inv*; (*not of a
set*) spaiato(-a); **60~** 60 e oltre; **at ~ times**
di tanto in tanto; **the ~ one out** l'eccezione
f; **oddly** *adv* stranamente; **odds** *npl* (*in
betting*) quota

odometer [ɔ'dɔmɪtə'] *n* odometro

odour ['əudə'] (*US* **odor**) *n* odore *m*;
(*unpleasant*) cattivo odore

 KEYWORD

of [ɔv, əv] *prep* **1** (*gen*) di; **a boy of 10** un
ragazzo di 10 anni; **a friend of ours** un
nostro amico; **that was kind of you** è
stato molto gentile da parte sua
2 (*expressing quantity, amount, dates etc*)
di; **a kilo of flour** un chilo di farina; **how
much of this do you need?** quanto gliene
serve?; **there were 3 of them** (*people*)
erano in 3; (*objects*) ce n'erano 3; **3 of us
went** 3 di noi sono andati; **the 5th of July**
il 5 luglio
3 (*from, out of*) di, in; **of made of wood**
(fatto) di *or* in legno

 KEYWORD

off [ɔf] *adv* **1** (*distance, time*): **it's a long way
off** è lontano; **the game is 3 days off** la
partita è tra 3 giorni
2 (*departure, removal*) via; **to go off to
Paris** andarsene a Parigi; **I must be off**
devo andare via; **to take off one's coat**
togliersi il cappotto; **the button came off**
il bottone è venuto via *or* si è staccato; **10%
off** con lo sconto del 10%
3 (*not at work*): **to have a day off** avere un
giorno libero; **to be off sick** essere assente
per malattia
▷ *adj* (*engine*) spento(-a); (*tap*) chiuso(-a);
(*cancelled*) sospeso(-a); (*BRIT: food*)
andato(-a) a male; **on the off chance**
nel caso; **to have an off day** non essere
in forma
▷ *prep* **1** (*motion, removal etc*) da; (*distant
from*) a poca distanza da; **a street off the
square** una strada che parte dalla piazza
2: **to be off meat** non mangiare più la
carne

offence [ə'fɛns] (*US* **offense**) *n* (*Law*)
contravvenzione *f*; (: *more serious*) reato; **to
take ~ at** offendersi per

offend [ə'fɛnd] *vt* (*person*) offendere;
offender *n* delinquente *m/f*; (*against
regulations*) contravventore(-trice)

offense [ə'fɛns] (*US*) *n* = **offence**

offensive [əˈfɛnsɪv] adj offensivo(-a); (smell etc) sgradevole, ripugnante ▷ n (Mil) offensiva

offer [ˈɔfəʳ] n offerta, proposta ▷ vt offrire; **"on ~"** (Comm) "in offerta speciale"

offhand [ɔfˈhænd] adj disinvolto(-a), noncurante ▷ adv su due piedi

office [ˈɔfɪs] n (place) ufficio; (position) carica; **doctor's ~** (us) studio; **to take ~** entrare in carica; **office block** (us **office building**) n complesso di uffici; **office hours** npl orario d'ufficio; (us Med) orario di visite

officer [ˈɔfɪsəʳ] n (Mil etc) ufficiale m; (also: **police ~**) agente m di polizia; (of organization) funzionario

office worker n impiegato(-a) d'ufficio

official [əˈfɪʃl] adj (authorized) ufficiale ▷ n ufficiale m; (civil servant) impiegato m statale; funzionario

off-licence (BRIT) n (shop) spaccio di bevande alcoliche; **off-line** adj, adv (Comput) off-line inv, fuori linea; (: switched off) spento(-a); **off-peak** adj (ticket, heating etc) a tariffa ridotta; (time) non di punta; **off-putting** (BRIT) adj sgradevole, antipatico(-a); **off-season** adj, adv fuori stagione; **offset** [ˈɔfsɛt] (irreg) vt (counteract) controbilanciare, compensare; **offshore** [ɔfˈʃɔːʳ] adj (breeze) di terra; (island) vicino alla costa; (fishing) costiero(-a); **offside** [ˈɔfˈsaɪd] adj (Sport) fuori gioco; (Aut: in Britain) destro(-a); (: in Italy etc) sinistro(-a); **offspring** [ˈɔfsprɪŋ] n inv prole f, discendenza

often [ˈɔfn] adv spesso; **how ~ do you go?** quanto spesso ci vai?

oh [əu] excl oh!

oil [ɔɪl] n olio; (petroleum) petrolio; (for central heating) nafta ▷ vt (machine) lubrificare; **oil filter** n (Aut) filtro dell'olio; **oil painting** n quadro a olio; **oil refinery** n raffineria di petrolio; **oil rig** n derrick m inv; (at sea) piattaforma per trivellazioni subacquee; **oil slick** n chiazza d'olio; **oil tanker** n (ship) petroliera; (truck) autocisterna per petrolio; **oil well** n pozzo petrolifero; **oily** adj unto(-a), oleoso(-a); (food) grasso(-a)

ointment [ˈɔɪntmənt] n unguento

O.K. [ˈəuˈkeɪ] excl d'accordo! ▷ adj non male inv ▷ vt approvare; **is it O.K.?, are you O.K.?** tutto bene?

old [əuld] adj vecchio(-a); (ancient) antico(-a), vecchio(-a); (person) vecchio(-a), anziano(-a); **how ~ are you?** quanti anni ha?; **he's 10 years ~** ha 10 anni; **~er brother** fratello maggiore; **old age** n

vecchiaia; **old-age pension** [ˈəuldeɪdʒ-] n (BRIT) pensione f di vecchiaia; **old-age pensioner** (BRIT) n pensionato(-a); **old-fashioned** adj antiquato(-a), fuori moda; (person) all'antica; **old people's home** n ricovero per anziani

olive [ˈɔlɪv] n (fruit) oliva; (tree) olivo ▷ adj (also: **~-green**) verde oliva inv; **olive oil** n olio d'oliva

Olympic [əuˈlɪmpɪk] adj olimpico(-a); **the ~ Games, the ~s** i giochi olimpici, le Olimpiadi

omelet(te) [ˈɔmlɪt] n omelette f inv

omen [ˈəumən] n presagio, augurio

ominous [ˈɔmɪnəs] adj minaccioso(-a); (event) di malaugurio

omit [əuˈmɪt] vt omettere

 KEYWORD

on [ɔn] prep 1 (indicating position) su; **on the wall** sulla parete; **on the left** a or sulla sinistra
2 (indicating means, method, condition etc): **on foot** a piedi; **on the train/plane** in treno/aereo; **on the telephone** al telefono; **on the radio/television** alla radio/televisione; **to be on drugs** drogarsi; **on holiday** in vacanza
3 (of time): **on Friday** venerdì; **on Fridays** il or di venerdì; **on June 20th** il 20 giugno; **on Friday, June 20th** venerdì, 20 giugno; **a week on Friday** venerdì a otto; **on his arrival** al suo arrivo; **on seeing this** vedendo ciò
4 (about, concerning) su, di; **information on train services** informazioni sui collegamenti ferroviari; **a book on Goldoni/physics** un libro su Goldoni/di or sulla fisica
▷ adv 1 (referring to dress, covering): **to have one's coat on** avere indosso il cappotto; **to put one's coat on** mettersi il cappotto; **what's she got on?** cosa indossa?; **she put her boots/gloves/hat on** si mise gli stivali/i guanti/il cappello; **screw the lid on tightly** avvita bene il coperchio
2 (further, continuously): **to walk on, go on** etc continuare, proseguire etc; **to read on** continuare a leggere; **on and off** ogni tanto
▷ adj 1 (in operation: machine, TV, light) acceso(-a); (: tap) aperto(-a); (: brake) inserito(-a); **is the meeting still on?** (in progress) la riunione è ancora in corso?; (not cancelled) è confermato l'incontro?; **there's a good film on at the cinema** danno un buon film al cinema

2 (inf): **that's not on!** (not acceptable) non si fa così!; (not possible) non se ne parla neanche!

once [wʌns] adv una volta ▷ conj non appena, quando; **~ he had left/it was done** dopo che se n'era andato/fu fatto; **at ~** subito; (simultaneously) a un tempo; **~ a week** una volta per settimana; **~ more** ancora una volta; **~ and for all** una volta per sempre; **~ upon a time** c'era una volta
oncoming ['ɒnkʌmɪŋ] adj (traffic) che viene in senso opposto

KEYWORD

one [wʌn] num uno(-a); **one hundred and fifty** centocinquanta; **one day** un giorno ▷ adj 1 (sole) unico(-a); **the one book which** l'unico libro che; **the one man who** l'unico che
2 (same) stesso(-a); **they came in the one car** sono venuti nella stessa macchina ▷ pron 1: **this one** questo(-a); **that one** quello(-a); **I've already got one/a red one** ne ho già uno/uno rosso; **one by one** uno per uno
2: **one another** l'un l'altro; **to look at one another** guardarsi; **to help one another** aiutarsi l'un l'altro or a vicenda
3 (impersonal) si; **one never knows** non si sa mai; **to cut one's finger** tagliarsi un dito; **one needs to eat** bisogna mangiare

one: **one-off** (BRIT: inf) n fatto eccezionale
oneself [wʌn'sɛlf] pron (reflexive) si; (after prep) se stesso(-a), sé; **to do sth (by) ~** fare qc da sé; **to hurt ~** farsi male; **to keep sth for ~** tenere qc per sé; **to talk to ~** parlare da solo
one: **one-shot** [wʌn'ʃɒt] (US) n = **one-off**; **one-sided** adj (argument) unilaterale; **one-to-one** adj (relationship) univoco(-a); **one-way** adj (street, traffic) a senso unico
ongoing ['ɒngəʊɪŋ] adj in corso; in attuazione
onion ['ʌnjən] n cipolla
on-line ['ɒnlaɪn] adj, adv (Comput) on-line inv
onlooker ['ɒnlʊkəʳ] n spettatore(-trice)
only ['əʊnlɪ] adv solo, soltanto ▷ adj solo(-a), unico(-a) ▷ conj solo che, ma; **an ~ child** un figlio unico; **not ~ ... but also** non solo ... ma anche
on-screen [ɒn'skriːn] adj sullo schermo inv
onset ['ɒnsɛt] n inizio
onto ['ɒntu] prep = **on to**
onward(s) ['ɒnwəd(z)] adv (move) in avanti; **from that time onward(s)** da

quella volta in poi
oops [ʊps] excl ops! (esprime rincrescimento per un piccolo contrattempo); **~-a-daisy!** oplà!
ooze [uːz] vi stillare
opaque [əʊ'peɪk] adj opaco(-a)
open ['əʊpn] adj aperto(-a); (road) libero(-a); (meeting) pubblico(-a) ▷ vt aprire ▷ vi (eyes, door, debate) aprirsi; (flower) sbocciare; (shop, bank, museum) aprire; (book etc: commence) cominciare; **is it ~ to the public?** è aperto al pubblico?; **in the ~ (air)** all'aperto; **what time do you ~?** a che ora aprite?; **open up** vt aprire; (blocked road) sgombrare ▷ vi (shop, business) aprire; **open-air** adj all'aperto; **opening** adj (speech) di apertura ▷ n apertura; (opportunity) occasione f, opportunità f inv; sbocco; **opening hours** npl orario d'apertura; **open learning** n sistema educativo secondo il quale lo studente ha maggior controllo e gestione delle modalità di apprendimento; **openly** adv apertamente; **open-minded** adj che ha la mente aperta; **open-necked** adj col collo slacciato; **open-plan** adj senza pareti divisorie; **Open University** n (BRIT) vedi nota nel riquadro

● **OPEN UNIVERSITY**
●
● La **Open University**, fondata in Gran
● Bretagna nel 1969, organizza corsi
● di laurea per corrispondenza o via
● Internet. Alcune lezioni possono venir
● seguite per radio o alla televisione e
● vengono organizzati regolari corsi
● estivi.

opera ['ɒpərə] n opera; **opera house** n opera; **opera singer** n cantante m/f d'opera or lirico(-a)
operate ['ɒpəreɪt] vt (machine) azionare, far funzionare; (system) usare ▷ vi funzionare; (drug) essere efficace; **to ~ on sb (for)** (Med) operare qn (di)
operating room (US) n = **operating theatre**
operating theatre n (Med) sala operatoria
operation [ɒpə'reɪʃən] n operazione f; **to be in ~** (machine) essere in azione or funzionamento; (system) essere in vigore; **to have an ~** (Med) subire un'operazione; **operational** adj in funzione; d'esercizio
operative ['ɒpərətɪv] adj (measure) operativo(-a)
operator ['ɒpəreɪtəʳ] n (of machine) operatore(-trice); (Tel) centralinista m/f

opinion [ə'pɪnɪən] n opinione f, parere m; **in my ~** secondo me, a mio avviso; **opinion poll** n sondaggio di opinioni

opponent [ə'pəunənt] n avversario(-a)

opportunity [ɔpə'tjuːnɪtɪ] n opportunità f inv, occasione f; **to take the ~ of doing** cogliere l'occasione per fare

oppose [ə'pəuz] vt opporsi a; **~d to** contrario(-a) a; **as ~d to** in contrasto con

opposite ['ɔpəzɪt] adj opposto(-a); (house etc) di fronte ▷ adv di fronte, dirimpetto ▷ prep di fronte a ▷ n **the ~** il contrario, l'opposto; **the ~ sex** l'altro sesso

opposition [ɔpə'zɪʃən] n opposizione f

oppress [ə'prɛs] vt opprimere

opt [ɔpt] vi **to ~ for** optare per; **to ~ to do** scegliere di fare; **opt out** vi **to ~ out of** ritirarsi da

optician [ɔp'tɪʃən] n ottico

optimism ['ɔptɪmɪzəm] n ottimismo

optimist ['ɔptɪmɪst] n ottimista m/f; **optimistic** [-'mɪstɪk] adj ottimistico(-a)

optimum ['ɔptɪməm] adj ottimale

option ['ɔpʃən] n scelta; (Scol) materia facoltativa; (Comm) opzione f; **optional** adj facoltativo(-a); (Comm) a scelta

or [ɔːᵣ] conj o, oppure; (with negative): **he hasn't seen or heard anything** non ha visto né sentito niente; **or else** se no, altrimenti; oppure

oral ['ɔːrəl] adj orale ▷ n esame m orale

orange ['ɔrɪndʒ] n (fruit) arancia ▷ adj arancione; **orange juice** n succo d'arancia; **orange squash** n succo d'arancia (da diluire con l'acqua)

orbit ['ɔːbɪt] n orbita ▷ vt orbitare intorno a

orchard ['ɔːtʃəd] n frutteto

orchestra ['ɔːkɪstrə] n orchestra; (us: seating) platea

orchid ['ɔːkɪd] n orchidea

ordeal [ɔː'diːl] n prova, travaglio

order ['ɔːdəᵣ] n ordine m; (Comm) ordinazione f ▷ vt ordinare; **can I ~ now, please?** posso ordinare, per favore?; **in ~** in ordine; (of document) in regola; **in (working) ~** funzionante; **in ~ to do** per fare; **in ~ that** affinché + sub; **on ~** (Comm) in ordinazione; **out of ~** non in ordine; (not working) guasto; **to ~ sb to do** ordinare a qn di fare; **order form** n modulo d'ordinazione; **orderly** n (Mil) attendente m; (Med) inserviente m ▷ adj (room) in ordine; (mind) metodico(-a); (person) ordinato(-a), metodico(-a)

ordinary ['ɔːdnrɪ] adj normale, comune; (pej) mediocre; **out of the ~** diverso dal solito, fuori dell'ordinario

ore [ɔːᵣ] n minerale m grezzo

oregano [ɔrɪ'gɑːnəu] n origano

organ ['ɔːgən] n organo; **organic** [ɔː'gænɪk] adj organico(-a); (of food) biologico(-a); **organism** n organismo

organization [ɔːgənaɪ'zeɪʃən] n organizzazione f

organize ['ɔːgənaɪz] vt organizzare; **to get ~d** organizzarsi; **organized** ['ɔː gənaɪzd] adj organizzato(-a); **organizer** n organizzatore(-trice)

orgasm ['ɔːgæzəm] n orgasmo

orgy ['ɔːdʒɪ] n orgia

oriental [ɔːrɪ'ɛntl] adj, n orientale m/f

orientation [ɔːrɪen'teɪʃən] n orientamento

origin ['ɔrɪdʒɪn] n origine f

original [ə'rɪdʒɪnl] adj originale; (earliest) originario(-a) ▷ n originale m; **originally** adv (at first) all'inizio

originate [ə'rɪdʒɪneɪt] vi **to ~ from** essere originario(-a) di; (suggestion) provenire da; **to ~ in** avere origine in

Orkneys ['ɔːknɪz] npl **the ~** (also: **the Orkney Islands**) le Orcadi

ornament ['ɔːnəmənt] n ornamento; (trinket) ninnolo; **ornamental** [-'mɛntl] adj ornamentale

ornate [ɔː'neɪt] adj molto ornato(-a)

orphan ['ɔːfn] n orfano(-a)

orthodox ['ɔːθədɔks] adj ortodosso(-a)

orthopaedic [ɔːθə'piːdɪk] (us **orthopedic**) adj ortopedico(-a)

osteopath ['ɔstɪəpæθ] n specialista m/f di osteopatia

ostrich ['ɔstrɪtʃ] n struzzo

other ['ʌðəᵣ] adj altro(-a) ▷ pron **the ~ (one)** l'altro(-a); **~s** (other people) altri mpl; **~ than** altro che; a parte; **otherwise** adv, conj altrimenti

otter ['ɔtəᵣ] n lontra

ouch [autʃ] excl ohi!, ahi!

ought [ɔːt] (pt **ought**) aux vb **I ~ to do it** dovrei farlo; **this ~ to have been corrected** questo avrebbe dovuto essere corretto; **he ~ to win** dovrebbe vincere

ounce [auns] n oncia (= 28.35 g, 16 in a pound)

our ['auəᵣ] adj il (la) nostro(-a); (pl) i (le) nostri(-e); see also **my**; **ours** pron il (la) nostro(-a); (pl) i (le) nostri(-e); see also **mine**; **ourselves** pron pl (reflexive) ci; (after preposition) noi; (emphatic) noi stessi(-e); see also **oneself**

oust [aust] vt cacciare, espellere

out [aut] adv (gen) fuori; **~ here/there** qui/là fuori; **to speak ~ loud** parlare forte; **to have a night ~** uscire una sera; **the boat was 10 km ~** la barca era a 10 km dalla costa; **3 days ~ from Plym~h** a 3 giorni da Plymouth; **~ of** (*outside*) fuori di; (*because of*) per; **~ of 10** su 10; **~ of petrol** senza benzina; **outback** ['autbæk] *n* (*in Australia*) interno, entroterra; **outbound** *adj* **outbound (for** *or* **from)** in partenza (per *or* da); **outbreak** ['autbreɪk] *n* scoppio; epidemia; **outburst** ['autbɜːst] *n* scoppio; **outcast** ['autkɑːst] *n* esule *m/f*; (*socially*) paria *m inv*; **outcome** ['autkʌm] *n* esito, risultato; **outcry** ['autkraɪ] *n* protesta, clamore *m*; **outdated** [aut'deɪtɪd] *adj* (*custom, clothes*) fuori moda; (*idea*) sorpassato(-a); **outdoor** [aut'dɔːʳ] *adj* all'aperto; **outdoors** *adv* fuori; all'aria aperta

outer ['autəʳ] *adj* esteriore; **outer space** *n* spazio cosmico

outfit ['autfɪt] *n* (*clothes*) completo; (: *for sport*) tenuta

out: **outgoing** ['autɡəʊɪŋ] *adj* (*character*) socievole; **outgoings** (BRIT) *npl* (*expenses*) spese *fpl*, uscite *fpl*; **outhouse** ['authaus] *n* costruzione *f* annessa

outing ['autɪŋ] *n* gita; escursione *f*

out: **outlaw** ['autlɔː] *n* fuorilegge *m/f* ▷ *vt* bandire; **outlay** ['autleɪ] *n* spese *fpl*; (*investment*) sborsa, spesa; **outlet** ['autlet] *n* (*for liquid etc*) sbocco, scarico; (*us Elec*) presa di corrente; (*also*: **retail outlet**) punto di vendita; **outline** ['autlaɪn] *n* contorno, profilo; (*summary*) abbozzo, grandi linee *fpl* ▷ *vt* (*fig*) descrivere a grandi linee; **outlook** ['autluk] *n* prospettiva, vista; **outnumber** [aut'nʌmbəʳ] *vt* superare in numero; **out-of-date** *adj* (*passport*) scaduto(-a); (*clothes*) fuori moda *inv*; **out-of-doors** [autəv'dɔːz] *adv* all'aperto; **out-of-the-way** *adj* (*place*) fuori mano *inv*; **out-of-town** [autəv'taun] *adj* (*shopping centre etc*) fuori città; **outpatient** ['autpeɪʃənt] *n* paziente *m/f* esterno(-a); **outpost** ['autpəust] *n* avamposto; **output** ['autput] *n* produzione *f*; (*Comput*) output *m inv*

outrage ['autreɪdʒ] *n* oltraggio; scandalo ▷ *vt* oltraggiare; **outrageous** [-'reɪdʒəs] *adj* oltraggioso(-a), scandaloso(-a)

outright [*adv* aut'raɪt, *adj* 'autraɪt] *adv* completamente; schiettamente; apertamente; sul colpo ▷ *adj* completo(-a), schietto(-a) e netto(-a)

outset ['autset] *n* inizio

outside [aut'saɪd] *n* esterno, esteriore *m* ▷ *adj* esterno(-a), esteriore ▷ *adv* fuori, all'esterno ▷ *prep* fuori di, all'esterno di; **at the ~** (*fig*) al massimo; **outside lane** *n* (*Aut*) corsia di sorpasso; **outside line** *n* (*Tel*) linea esterna; **outsider** *n* (*in race etc*) outsider *m inv*; (*stranger*) estraneo(-a)

out: **outsize** ['autsaɪz] *adj* (*clothes*) per taglie forti; **outskirts** ['autskɜːts] *npl* sobborghi *mpl*; **outspoken** [aut'spəukən] *adj* molto franco(-a); **outstanding** [aut'stændɪŋ] *adj* eccezionale, di rilievo; (*unfinished*) non completo(-a); non evaso(-a); non regolato(-a)

outward ['autwəd] *adj* (*sign, appearances*) esteriore; (*journey*) d'andata; **outwards** ['autwədz] *adv* (*esp* BRIT) = **outward**

outweigh [aut'weɪ] *vt* avere maggior peso di

oval ['əuvl] *adj* ovale ▷ *n* ovale *m*

ovary ['əuvərɪ] *n* ovaia

oven ['ʌvn] *n* forno; **oven glove** *n* guanto da forno; **ovenproof** *adj* da forno; **oven-ready** *adj* pronto(-a) da infornare

over ['əuvəʳ] *adv* al di sopra ▷ *adj* (*or adv*) (*finished*) finito(-a), terminato(-a); (*too*) troppo; (*remaining*) che avanza ▷ *prep* su; sopra; (*above*) al di sopra di; (*on the other side of*) di là di; (*more than*) più di; (*during*) durante; **~ here** qui; **~ there** là; **all ~** (*everywhere*) dappertutto; (*finished*) tutto(-a) finito(-a); **~ and ~ (again)** più e più volte; **~ above** oltre (a); **to ask sb ~** invitare qn (a passare)

overall [*adj, n* 'əuvərɔːl, *adv* əuvər'ɔːl] *adj* totale ▷ *n* (BRIT) grembiule *m* ▷ *adv* nell'insieme, complessivamente; **~s** *npl* (*worker's overalls*) tuta (da lavoro)

overboard ['əuvəbɔːd] *adv* (*Naut*) fuori bordo, in mare

overcame [əuvə'keɪm] *pt of* **overcome**

overcast ['əuvəkɑːst] *adj* (*sky*) coperto(-a)

overcharge [əuvə'tʃɑːdʒ] *vt* **to ~ sb for sth** far pagare troppo caro a qn per qc

overcoat ['əuvəkəut] *n* soprabito, cappotto

overcome [əuvə'kʌm] (*irreg*) *vt* superare; sopraffare

over: **overcrowded** [əuvə'kraudɪd] *adj* sovraffollato(-a); **overdo** [əuvə'duː] (*irreg*) *vt* esagerare; (*overcook*) cuocere troppo; **overdone** [əuvə'dʌn] *adj* troppo cotto(-a); **overdose** ['əuvədəus] *n* dose *f* eccessiva; **overdraft** ['əuvədrɑːft] *n* scoperto (di conto); **overdrawn** [əuvə'drɔːn] *adj* (*account*) scoperto(-a); **overdue** [əuvə'djuː] *adj* in ritardo; **overestimate** [əuvər'estɪmeɪt] *vt* sopravvalutare

overflow [*vb* əuvə'fləu, *n* 'əuvəfləu] *vi* traboccare ▷ *n* (*also*: **~ pipe**) troppopieno

overgrown [əuvə'ɡrəun] *adj* (*garden*) ricoperto(-a) di vegetazione

overhaul [*vb* əuvə'hɔːl, *n* 'əuvəhɔːl] *vt* revisionare ▷ *n* revisione *f*

overhead [*adv* əuvə'hed, *adj, n* 'əuvəhed] *adv* di sopra ▷ *adj* aereo(-a); (*lighting*)

verticale ▷ n (US) = **overheads**;
overhead projector n lavagna luminosa;
overheads npl spese fpl generali

over: **overhear** [əuvəˈhɪəʳ] vt (irreg) vt sentire
(per caso); **overheat** [əuvəˈhiːt] vi (engine)
surriscaldare; **overland** adj, adv per via di
terra; **overlap** [əuvəˈlæp] vi sovrapporsi;
overleaf [əuvəˈliːf] adv a tergo; **overload**
[əuvəˈləud] vt sovraccaricare; **overlook**
[əuvəˈluk] vt (have view of) dare su; (miss)
trascurare; (forgive) passare sopra a

overnight [əuvəˈnaɪt] adv (happen)
durante la notte; (fig) tutto ad un tratto
▷ adj di notte; **he stayed there ~** ci ha
passato la notte; **overnight bag** n borsa
da viaggio

overpass [ˈəuvəpɑːs] n cavalcavia m inv

overpower [əuvəˈpauəʳ] vt sopraffare;
overpowering adj irresistibile; (heat,
stench) soffocante

over: **overreact** [əuvəriːˈækt] vi reagire
in modo esagerato; **overrule** [əuvəˈruːl]
vt (decision) annullare; (claim) respingere;
overrun [əuvəˈrʌn] (irreg: like run) vt
(country) invadere; (time limit) superare

overseas [əuvəˈsiːz] adv oltremare;
(abroad) all'estero ▷ adj (trade) estero(-a);
(visitor) straniero(-a)

oversee [əuvəˈsiː] vt irreg sorvegliare

overshadow [əuvəˈʃædəu] vt far ombra
su; (fig) eclissare

oversight [ˈəuvəsaɪt] n omissione f, svista

oversleep [əuvəˈsliːp] (irreg) vt dormire
troppo a lungo

overspend [əuvəˈspɛnd] vi irreg spendere
troppo; **we have overspent by 5000
dollars** abbiamo speso 5000 dollari di
troppo

overt [əuˈvəːt] adj palese

overtake [əuvəˈteɪk] (irreg) vt sorpassare

over: **overthrow** [əuvəˈθrəu] (irreg)
vt (government) rovesciare; **overtime**
[ˈəuvətaɪm] n (lavoro) straordinario

overtook [əuvəˈtuk] pt of **overtake**

over: **overturn** [əuvəˈtəːn] vt rovesciare
▷ vi rovesciarsi; **overweight** [əuvəˈweɪt]
adj (person) troppo grasso(-a); **overwhelm**
[əuvəˈwɛlm] vt sopraffare; sommergere;
schiacciare; **overwhelming** adj (victory,
defeat) schiacciante; (heat, desire)
intenso(-a)

ow [au] excl ahi!

owe [əu] vt **to ~ sb sth, to ~ sth to sb**
dovere qc a qn; **how much do I ~ you?**
quanto le devo?; **owing to** prep a causa di

owl [aul] n gufo

own [əun] vt possedere ▷ adj proprio(-a);
a room of my ~ la mia propria camera; **to
get one's ~ back** vendicarsi; **on one's ~**
tutto(-a) solo(-a); **own up** vi confessare;
owner n proprietario(-a); **ownership** n
possesso

ox [ɔks] (pl **oxen**) n bue m

Oxbridge [ˈɔksbrɪdʒ] n le università di
Oxford e/o Cambridge

oxen [ˈɔksn] npl of **ox**

oxygen [ˈɔksɪdʒən] n ossigeno

oyster [ˈɔɪstəʳ] n ostrica

oz. abbr = **ounce(s)**

ozone [ˈəuzəun] n ozono; **ozone friendly**
adj che non danneggia l'ozono; **ozone
layer** n fascia d'ozono

p [pi:] *abbr* = **penny; pence**
P.A. *n abbr* = **personal assistant; public address system**
p.a. *abbr* = **per annum**
pace [peɪs] *n* passo; (*speed*) passo; velocità ▷ *vi* **to ~ up and down** camminare su e giù; **to keep ~ with** camminare di pari passo a; (*events*) tenersi al corrente di; **pacemaker** *n* (*Med*) segnapasso; (*Sport: also:* **pace setter**) battistrada *m inv*
Pacific [pə'sɪfɪk] *n* **the ~ (Ocean)** il Pacifico, l'Oceano Pacifico
pacifier ['pæsɪfaɪə'] (*US*) *n* (*dummy*) succhiotto, ciuccio (*col*)
pack [pæk] *n* pacco; (*US: of cigarettes*) pacchetto; (*backpack*) zaino; (*of hounds*) muta; (*of thieves etc*) banda; (*of cards*) mazzo ▷ *vt* (*in suitcase etc*) mettere; (*box*) riempire; (*cram*) stipare, pigiare; **to ~ (one's bags)** fare la valigia; **to ~ sb off** spedire via qn; **~ it in!** (*inf*) dacci un taglio!; **pack in** (*BRIT inf*) *vi* (*watch, car*) guastarsi ▷ *vt* mollare, piantare; **~ it in!** piantala!; **pack up** *vi* (*BRIT inf: machine*) guastarsi; (: *person*) far fagotto ▷ *vt* (*belongings, clothes*) mettere in una valigia; (*goods, presents*) imballare
package ['pækɪdʒ] *n* pacco; balla; (*also:* **~ deal**) pacchetto; forfait *m inv*; **package holiday** *n* vacanza organizzata; **package tour** *n* viaggio organizzato
packaging ['pækɪdʒɪŋ] *n* confezione *f*, imballo
packed [pækt] *adj* (*crowded*) affollato(-a); **packed lunch** *n* pranzo al sacco
packet ['pækɪt] *n* pacchetto
packing ['pækɪŋ] *n* imballaggio
pact [pækt] *n* patto, accordo; trattato
pad [pæd] *n* blocco; (*to prevent friction*) cuscinetto; (*inf: flat*) appartamentino ▷ *vt* imbottire; **padded** *adj* imbottito(-a)
paddle ['pædl] *n* (*oar*) pagaia; (*US: for table tennis*) racchetta da ping-pong ▷ *vi* sguazzare ▷ *vt* **to ~ a canoe** *etc* vogare con la pagaia; **paddling pool** (*BRIT*) *n* piscina per bambini
paddock ['pædək] *n* prato recintato; (*at racecourse*) paddock *m inv*
padlock ['pædlɔk] *n* lucchetto
paedophile ['pi:dəufaɪl] (*US* **pedophile**) *adj*, *n* pedofilo(-a)
page [peɪdʒ] *n* pagina; (*also:* **~ boy**) paggio ▷ *vt* (*in hotel etc*) (far) chiamare
pager ['peɪdʒə'] *n* (*Tel*) cercapersone *m inv*
paid [peɪd] *pt, pp of* **pay** ▷ *adj* (*work, official*) rimunerato(-a); **to put ~ to** (*BRIT*) mettere fine a
pain [peɪn] *n* dolore *m*; **to be in ~** soffrire, aver male; **to take ~s to do** mettercela tutta per fare; **painful** *adj* doloroso(-a), che fa male; difficile, penoso(-a); **painkiller** *n* antalgico, antidolorifico; **painstaking** ['peɪnzteɪkɪŋ] *adj* (*person*) sollecito(-a); (*work*) accurato(-a)
paint [peɪnt] *n* vernice *f*, colore *m* ▷ *vt* dipingere; (*walls, door etc*) verniciare; **to ~ the door blue** verniciare la porta di azzurro; **paintbrush** *n* pennello; **painter** *n* (*artist*) pittore *m*; (*decorator*) imbianchino; **painting** *n* pittura; verniciatura; (*picture*) dipinto, quadro
pair [peə'] *n* (*of shoes, gloves etc*) paio; (*of people*) coppia; duo *m inv*; **a ~ of scissors/trousers** un paio di forbici/pantaloni
pajamas [pɪ'dʒɑːməz] (*US*) *npl* pigiama *m*
Pakistan [pɑːkɪ'stɑːn] *n* Pakistan *m*; **Pakistani** *adj*, *n* pakistano(-a)
pal [pæl] (*inf*) *n* amico(-a), compagno(-a)
palace ['pæləs] *n* palazzo
pale [peɪl] *adj* pallido(-a) ▷ *n* **to be beyond the ~** aver oltrepassato ogni limite
Palestine ['pælɪstaɪn] *n* Palestina; **Palestinian** [-'tɪnɪən] *adj*, *n* palestinese *m/f*
palm [pɑːm] *n* (*Anat*) palma, palmo; (*also:* **~ tree**) palma ▷ *vt* **to ~ sth off on sb** (*inf*) rifilare qc a qn
pamper ['pæmpə'] *vt* viziare, coccolare
pamphlet ['pæmflət] *n* dépliant *m inv*

pan [pæn] n (also: **sauce~**) casseruola; (also: **frying ~**) padella

pancake ['pænkeɪk] n frittella

panda ['pændə] n panda m inv

pane [peɪn] n vetro

panel ['pænl] n (of wood, cloth etc) pannello; (Radio, TV) giuria

panhandler ['pænhændlə'] (US) n (inf) accattone(-a)

panic ['pænɪk] n panico ▷ vi perdere il sangue freddo

panorama [pænə'rɑ:mə] n panorama m

pansy ['pænzɪ] n (Bot) viola del pensiero, pensée f inv; (inf: pej) femminuccia

pant [pænt] vi ansare

panther ['pænθə'] n pantera

panties ['pæntɪz] npl slip m, mutandine f pl

pantomime ['pæntəmaɪm] (BRIT) n pantomima

● **PANTOMIME**

In Gran Bretagna la **pantomime** è una sorta di libera interpretazione delle favole più conosciute, che vengono messe in scena a teatro durante il periodo natalizio. È uno spettacolo per tutta la famiglia che prevede la partecipazione del pubblico.

pants [pænts] npl mutande f pl, slip m; (US: trousers) pantaloni mpl

paper ['peɪpə'] n carta; (also: **wall~**) carta da parati, tappezzeria; (also: **news~**) giornale m; (study, article) saggio; (exam) prova scritta ▷ adj di carta ▷ vt tappezzare; **~s** npl (also: **identity ~s**) carte f pl, documenti mpl; **paperback** n tascabile m; edizione f economica; **paper bag** n sacchetto di carta; **paper clip** n graffetta, clip f inv; **paper shop** n (BRIT) giornalaio (negozio); **paperwork** n lavoro amministrativo

paprika ['pæprɪkə] n paprica

par [pɑ:'] n parità, pari f; (Golf) norma; **on a ~ with** alla pari con

paracetamol [pærə'si:təmɔl] (BRIT) n paracetamolo

parachute ['pærəʃu:t] n paracadute m inv

parade [pə'reɪd] n parata ▷ vt (fig) fare sfoggio di ▷ vi sfilare in parata

paradise ['pærədaɪs] n paradiso

paradox ['pærədɔks] n paradosso

paraffin ['pærəfɪn] (BRIT) n **~ (oil)** paraffina

paragraph ['pærəgrɑ:f] n paragrafo

parallel ['pærəlɛl] adj parallelo(-a); (fig) analogo(-a) ▷ n (line) parallela; (fig, Geo) parallelo

paralysed ['pærəlaɪzd] adj paralizzato(-a)

paralysis [pə'rælɪsɪs] n paralisi f inv

paramedic [pærə'mɛdɪk] n paramedico

paranoid ['pærənɔɪd] adj paranoico(-a)

parasite ['pærəsaɪt] n parassita m

parcel ['pɑ:sl] n pacco, pacchetto ▷ vt (also: **~ up**) impaccare

pardon ['pɑ:dn] n perdono; grazia ▷ vt perdonare; (Law) graziare; **~ me!** mi scusi!; **I beg your ~!** scusi!; **I beg your ~?** (BRIT), **~ me?** (US) prego?

parent ['pɛərənt] n genitore m; **~s** npl (mother and father) genitori mpl; **parental** [pə'rɛntl] adj dei genitori

> Be careful not to translate **parent** by the Italian word **parente**.

Paris ['pærɪs] n Parigi f

parish ['pærɪʃ] n parrocchia; (BRIT: civil) ≈ municipio

Parisian [pə'rɪzɪən] adj, n parigino(-a)

park [pɑ:k] n parco ▷ vt, vi parcheggiare; **can I ~ here?** posso parcheggiare qui?

parking ['pɑ:kɪŋ] n parcheggio; **"no ~"** "sosta vietata"; **parking lot** (US) n posteggio, parcheggio; **parking meter** n parchimetro; **parking ticket** n multa per sosta vietata

parkway ['pɑ:kweɪ] (US) n viale m

parliament ['pɑ:ləmənt] n parlamento; **parliamentary** [pɑ:lə'mɛntərɪ] adj parlamentare

Parmesan [pɑ:mɪ'zæn] n (also: **~ cheese**) parmigiano

parole [pə'rəul] n **on ~** in libertà per buona condotta

parrot ['pærət] n pappagallo

parsley ['pɑ:slɪ] n prezzemolo

parsnip ['pɑ:snɪp] n pastinaca

parson ['pɑ:sn] n prete m; (Church of England) parroco

part [pɑ:t] n parte f; (of machine) pezzo; (US: in hair) scriminatura ▷ adj in parte ▷ adv = **partly** ▷ vt separare ▷ vi (people) separarsi; **to take ~ in** prendere parte a; **for my ~** per parte mia; **to take sth in good ~** prendere bene qc; **to take sb's ~** parteggiare per or prendere le parti di qn; **for the most ~** in generale; nella maggior parte dei casi; **part with** vt fus separarsi da; rinunciare a

partial ['pɑ:ʃl] adj parziale; **to be ~ to** avere un debole per

participant [pɑ:'tɪsɪpənt] n **~ (in)** partecipante m/f (a)

participate [pɑ:'tɪsɪpeɪt] vi **to ~ (in)** prendere parte (a), partecipare (a)

particle ['pɑ:tɪkl] n particella

particular [pə'tɪkjulə'] adj particolare;

speciale; (*fussy*) difficile; meticoloso(-a);
in ~ in particolare, particolarmente;
particularly adv particolarmente; in
particolare; **particulars** npl particolari
mpl, dettagli mpl; (*information*)
informazioni fpl

parting ['pɑːtɪŋ] n separazione f; (BRIT: *in
hair*) scriminatura ▷ adj d'addio

partition [pɑː'tɪʃən] n (*Pol*) partizione f;
(*wall*) tramezzo

partly ['pɑːtlɪ] adv parzialmente; in parte

partner ['pɑːtnə'] n (*Comm*) socio(-a);
(*wife, husband etc, Sport*) compagno(-a);
(*at dance*) cavaliere/dama; **partnership** n
associazione f; (*Comm*) società f inv

part of speech n parte f del discorso

partridge ['pɑːtrɪdʒ] n pernice f

part-time ['pɑːt'taɪm] adj, adv a orario
ridotto

party ['pɑːtɪ] n (*Pol*) partito; (*group*)
gruppo; (*Law*) parte f; (*celebration*)
ricevimento; serata; festa ▷ cpd (*Pol*) del
partito, di partito

pass [pɑːs] vt (*gen*) passare; (*place*) passare
davanti a; (*exam*) passare, superare;
(*candidate*) promuovere; (*overtake, surpass*)
sorpassare, superare; (*approve*) approvare
▷ vi passare ▷ n (*permit*) lasciapassare
m inv; permesso; (*in mountains*) passo,
gola; (*Sport*) passaggio; (*Scol*): **to get a ~**
prendere la sufficienza; **could you ~ the
salt/oil, please?** mi passa il sale/l'olio,
per favore?; **to ~ sth through a hole** etc
far passare qc attraverso un buco etc; **to
make a ~ at sb** (*inf*) fare delle proposte or
delle avances a qn; **pass away** vi morire;
pass by vi passare ▷ vt trascurare; **pass
on** vt passare; **pass out** vi svenire; **pass
over** vi (*die*) spirare ▷ vt lasciare da parte;
pass up vt (*opportunity*) lasciarsi sfuggire,
perdere; **passable** adj (*road*) praticabile;
(*work*) accettabile

passage ['pæsɪdʒ] n (*gen*) passaggio; (*also:
~way*) corridoio; (*in book*) brano, passo; (*by
boat*) traversata

passenger ['pæsɪndʒə'] n passeggero(-a)

passer-by [pɑːsə'baɪ] n passante m/f

passing place n (*Aut*) piazzola di sosta

passion ['pæʃən] n passione f; amore
m; **passionate** adj appassionato(-a);
passion fruit n frutto della passione

passive ['pæsɪv] adj (*also Ling*) passivo(-a)

passport ['pɑːspɔːt] n passaporto;
passport control n controllo m
passaporti inv; **passport office** n ufficio
m, passaporti inv

password ['pɑːswəːd] n parola d'ordine

past [pɑːst] prep (*further than*) oltre, di là di;
dopo; (*later than*) dopo ▷ adj passato(-a);

(*president etc*) ex inv ▷ n passato; **he's ~
forty** ha più di quarant'anni; **ten ~ eight** le
otto e dieci; **for the ~ few days** da qualche
giorno; in questi ultimi giorni; **to run ~**
passare di corsa

pasta ['pæstə] n pasta

paste [peɪst] n (*glue*) colla; (*Culin*) pâté m
inv; pasta ▷ vt collare

pastel ['pæstl] adj pastello inv

pasteurized ['pæstəraɪzd] adj
pastorizzato(-a)

pastime ['pɑːstaɪm] n passatempo

pastor ['pɑːstə'] n pastore m

past participle [-'pɑːtɪsɪpl] n (*Ling*)
participio passato

pastry ['peɪstrɪ] n pasta

pasture ['pɑːstʃə'] n pascolo

pasty¹ ['pæstɪ] n pasticcio di carne

pasty² ['peɪstɪ] adj (*face etc*) smorto(-a)

pat [pæt] vt accarezzare, dare un colpetto
(affettuoso) a

patch [pætʃ] n (*of material, on tyre*) toppa;
(*eye patch*) benda; (*spot*) macchia ▷ vt
(*clothes*) rattoppare; **(to go through) a
bad ~** (attraversare) un brutto periodo;
patchy adj irregolare

pâté ['pæteɪ] n pâté m inv

patent ['peɪtnt] n brevetto ▷ vt brevettare
▷ adj patente, manifesto(-a)

paternal [pə'təːnl] adj paterno(-a)

paternity leave [pə'təːnɪtɪ-] n congedo
di paternità

path [pɑːθ] n sentiero, viottolo; viale
m; (*fig*) via, strada; (*of planet, missile*)
traiettoria

pathetic [pə'θɛtɪk] adj (*pitiful*)
patetico(-a); (*very bad*) penoso(-a)

pathway ['pɑːθweɪ] n sentiero

patience ['peɪʃns] n pazienza; (BRIT *Cards*)
solitario

patient ['peɪʃnt] n paziente m/f,
malato(-a) ▷ adj paziente

patio ['pætɪəu] n terrazza

patriotic [pætrɪ'ɔtɪk] adj patriottico(-a)

patrol [pə'trəul] n pattuglia ▷ vt
pattugliare; **patrol car** n autoradio f inv
(della polizia)

patron ['peɪtrən] n (*in shop*) cliente m/f; (*of
charity*) benefattore(-trice); **~ of the arts**
mecenate m/f

patronizing ['pætrənaɪzɪŋ] adj
condiscendente

pattern ['pætən] n modello; (*design*)
disegno, motivo; **patterned** adj a disegni,
a motivi; (*material*) fantasia inv

pause [pɔːz] n pausa ▷ vi fare una pausa,
arrestarsi

pave [peɪv] vt pavimentare; **to ~ the way
for** aprire la via a

pavement ['peɪvmənt] (BRIT) n
marciapiede m
  ▪ Be careful not to translate **pavement**
  by the Italian word **pavimento**.
pavilion [pə'vɪlɪən] n (Sport) edificio
annesso a campo sportivo
paving ['peɪvɪŋ] n pavimentazione f
paw [pɔː] n zampa
pawn [pɔːn] n (Chess) pedone m; (fig)
pedina ▷ vt dare in pegno; **pawn broker** n
prestatore m su pegno
pay [peɪ] (pt, pp **paid**) n stipendio; paga
▷ vt pagare ▷ vi (be profitable) rendere;
can I ~ by credit card? posso pagare
con la carta di credito?; **to ~ attention
(to)** fare attenzione (a); **to ~ sb a visit**
far visita a qn; **to ~ one's respects to sb**
porgere i propri rispetti a qn; **pay back** vt
rimborsare; **pay for** vt fus pagare; **pay
in** vt versare; **pay off** vt (debt) saldare;
(person) pagare; (employee) pagare e
licenziare ▷ vi (scheme, decision) dare
dei frutti; **pay out** vt (money) sborsare,
tirar fuori; (rope) far allentare; **pay up** vt
saldare; **payable** adj pagabile; **pay day**
n giorno di paga; **pay envelope** (US) n
= **pay packet**; **payment** n pagamento;
versamento; saldo; **payout** n pagamento;
(in competition) premio; **pay packet** (BRIT)
n busta f paga inv; **pay phone** n cabina
telefonica; **payroll** n ruolo (organico); **pay
slip** n foglio m paga inv; **pay television** n
televisione f a pagamento, pay-tv f inv
PC n abbr = **personal computer** ▷ adv abbr
= **politically correct**
p.c. abbr = **per cent**
PDA n abbr (= personal digital assistant) PDA
m inv
PE n abbr (= physical education) ed. fisica
pea [piː] n pisello
peace [piːs] n pace f; **peaceful** adj
pacifico(-a), calmo(-a)
peach [piːtʃ] n pesca
peacock ['piːkɔk] n pavone m
peak [piːk] n (of mountain) cima, vetta;
(mountain itself) picco; (of cap) visiera; (fig)
apice m, culmine m; **peak hours** npl ore
fpl di punta
peanut ['piːnʌt] n arachide f, nocciolina
americana; **peanut butter** n burro dei
arachidi
pear [pɛər] n pera
pearl [pəːl] n perla
peasant ['pɛznt] n contadino(-a)
peat [piːt] n torba
pebble ['pɛbl] n ciottolo
peck [pɛk] vt (also: ~ **at**) beccare ▷ n colpo
di becco; (kiss) bacetto; **peckish** (BRIT: inf)
adj **I feel peckish** ho un languorino

peculiar [pɪ'kjuːlɪər] adj strano(-a),
bizzarro(-a); peculiare; **~ to** peculiare di
pedal ['pɛdl] n pedale m ▷ vi pedalare
pedalo ['pɛdələu] n pedalò m inv
pedestal ['pɛdəstl] n piedestallo
pedestrian [pɪ'dɛstrɪən] n pedone(-a)
▷ adj pedonale; (fig) prosaico(-a),
pedestre; **pedestrian crossing** (BRIT) n
passaggio pedonale; **pedestrianized**
adj **a pedestrianized street** una zona
pedonalizzata; **pedestrian precinct**
(BRIT), **pedestrian zone** (US) n zona
pedonale
pedigree ['pɛdɪgriː] n (of animal) pedigree
m inv; (fig) background m inv ▷ cpd (animal)
di razza
pedophile ['piːdəufaɪl] (US) n
= **paedophile**
pee [piː] (inf) vi pisciare
peek [piːk] vi guardare furtivamente
peel [piːl] n buccia; (of orange, lemon) scorza
▷ vt sbucciare ▷ vi (paint etc) staccarsi
peep [piːp] n (BRIT: look) sguardo furtivo,
sbirciata; (sound) pigolio ▷ vi (BRIT)
guardare furtivamente
peer [pɪər] vi **to ~ at** scrutare ▷ n (noble)
pari m inv; (equal) pari m/f inv, uguale m/f;
(contemporary) contemporaneo(-a)
peg [pɛg] n caviglia; (for coat etc)
attaccapanni m inv; (BRIT: also: **clothes ~**)
molletta
pelican ['pɛlɪkən] n pellicano; **pelican
crossing** (BRIT) n (Aut) attraversamento
pedonale con semaforo a controllo manuale
pelt [pɛlt] vt **to ~ sb (with)** bombardare qn
(con) ▷ vi (rain) piovere a dirotto; (inf: run)
filare ▷ n pelle f
pelvis ['pɛlvɪs] n pelvi f inv, bacino
pen [pɛn] n penna; (for sheep) recinto
penalty ['pɛnltɪ] n penalità f inv;
sanzione f penale; (fine) ammenda; (Sport)
penalizzazione f
pence [pɛns] (BRIT) npl of **penny**
pencil ['pɛnsl] n matita; **pencil in**
vt scrivere a matita; **pencil case** n
astuccio per matite; **pencil sharpener** n
temperamatite m inv
pendant ['pɛndnt] n pendaglio
pending ['pɛndɪŋ] prep in attesa di ▷ adj
in sospeso
penetrate ['pɛnɪtreɪt] vt penetrare
penfriend ['pɛnfrɛnd] (BRIT) n
corrispondente m/f
penguin ['pɛŋgwɪn] n pinguino
penicillin [pɛnɪ'sɪlɪn] n penicillina
peninsula [pə'nɪnsjulə] n penisola
penis ['piːnɪs] n pene m
penitentiary [pɛnɪ'tɛnʃərɪ] (US) n carcere
m

penknife ['pɛnnaɪf] n temperino
penniless ['pɛnɪlɪs] adj senza un soldo
penny ['pɛnɪ] (pl **pennies** or **pence**) (BRIT) n penny m; (US) centesimo
penpal ['pɛnpæl] n corrispondente m/f
pension ['pɛnʃən] n pensione f; **pensioner** (BRIT) n pensionato(-a)
pentagon ['pɛntəgən] n pentagono; **the P~** (US Pol) il Pentagono
penthouse ['pɛnthaus] n appartamento (di lusso) nell'attico
penultimate [pɪ'nʌltɪmət] adj penultimo(-a)
people ['piːpl] npl gente f; persone fpl; (citizens) popolo ▷ n (nation, race) popolo; **4/several ~ came** 4/parecchie persone sono venute; **~ say that ...** si dice che ...
pepper ['pɛpə'] n pepe m; (vegetable) peperone m ▷ vt (fig): **to ~ with** spruzzare di; **peppermint** n (sweet) pasticca di menta
per [pə:'] prep per; a; **~ hour** all'ora; **~ kilo** etc il chilo etc; **~ day** al giorno
perceive [pə'siːv] vt percepire; (notice) accorgersi di
per cent adv per cento
percentage [pə'sɛntɪdʒ] n percentuale f
perception [pə'sɛpʃən] n percezione f; sensibilità; perspicacia
perch [pə:tʃ] n (fish) pesce m persico; (for bird) sostegno, ramo ▷ vi appollaiarsi
percussion [pə'kʌʃən] n percussione f; (Mus) strumenti mpl a percussione
perfect [adj, n 'pə:fɪkt, vb pə'fɛkt] adj perfetto(-a) ▷ n (also: **~ tense**) perfetto, passato prossimo ▷ vt perfezionare; mettere a punto; **perfection** [pə'fɛkʃən] n perfezione f; **perfectly** adv perfettamente, alla perfezione
perform [pə'fɔ:m] vt (carry out) eseguire, fare; (symphony etc) suonare; (play, ballet) dare; (opera) fare ▷ vi suonare; recitare; **performance** n esecuzione f; (at theatre etc) rappresentazione f, spettacolo; (of an artist) interpretazione f; (of player etc) performance f; (of car, engine) prestazione f; **performer** n artista m/f
perfume ['pə:fjuːm] n profumo
perhaps [pə'hæps] adv forse
perimeter [pə'rɪmɪtə'] n perimetro
period ['pɪərɪəd] n periodo; (History) epoca; (Scol) lezione f; (full stop) punto; (Med) mestruazioni fpl ▷ adj (costume, furniture) d'epoca; **periodical** [-'ɔdɪkl] n periodico; **periodically** adv periodicamente
perish ['pɛrɪʃ] vi perire, morire; (decay) deteriorarsi
perjury ['pə:dʒərɪ] n spergiuro
perk [pə:k] (inf) n vantaggio

perm [pə:m] n (for hair) permanente f
permanent ['pə:mənənt] adj permanente; **permanently** adv definitivamente
permission [pə'mɪʃən] n permesso
permit [n 'pə:mɪt, vb pə'mɪt] n permesso ▷ vt permettere; **to ~ sb to do** permettere a qn di fare
perplex [pə'plɛks] vt lasciare perplesso(-a)
persecute ['pə:sɪkjuːt] vt perseguitare
persecution [pə:sɪ'kjuːʃən] n persecuzione f
persevere [pə:sɪ'vɪə'] vi perseverare
Persian ['pə:ʃən] adj persiano(-a) ▷ n (Ling) persiano; **the (~) Gulf** n il Golfo Persico
persist [pə'sɪst] vi **to ~ (in doing)** persistere (nel fare); ostinarsi (a fare); **persistent** adj persistente; ostinato(-a)
person ['pə:sn] n persona; **in ~** di or in persona, personalmente; **personal** adj personale; individuale; **personal assistant** n segretaria personale; **personal computer** n personal computer m inv; **personality** [-'nælɪtɪ] n personalità f inv; **personally** adv personalmente; **to take sth personally** prendere qc come una critica personale; **personal organizer** n (Filofax®) Fulltime®; (electronic) agenda elettronica; **personal stereo** n Walkman® m inv
personnel [pə:sə'nɛl] n personale m
perspective [pə'spɛktɪv] n prospettiva
perspiration [pə:spɪ'reɪʃən] n traspirazione f, sudore m
persuade [pə'sweɪd] vt **to ~ sb to do sth** persuadere qn a fare qc
persuasion [pə'sweɪʒən] n persuasione f; (creed) convinzione f, credo
persuasive [pə'sweɪsɪv] adj persuasivo(-a)
perverse [pə'və:s] adj perverso(-a)
pervert [n 'pə:və:t, vb pə'və:t] n pervertito(-a) ▷ vt pervertire
pessimism ['pɛsɪmɪzəm] n pessimismo
pessimist ['pɛsɪmɪst] n pessimista m/f; **pessimistic** [-'mɪstɪk] adj pessimistico(-a)
pest [pɛst] n animale m (or insetto) pestifero; (fig) peste f
pester ['pɛstə'] vt tormentare, molestare
pesticide ['pɛstɪsaɪd] n pesticida m
pet [pɛt] n animale m domestico ▷ cpd favorito(-a) ▷ vt accarezzare; **teacher's ~** favorito(-a) del maestro
petal ['pɛtl] n petalo
petite [pə'tiːt] adj piccolo(-a) e aggraziato(-a)
petition [pə'tɪʃən] n petizione f
petrified ['pɛtrɪfaɪd] adj (fig) morto(-a) di paura

petrol ['pɛtrəl] (BRIT) n benzina; **two/four-star ~** ≈ benzina normale/super; **I've run out of ~** sono rimasto senza benzina

> Be careful not to translate *petrol* by the Italian word *petrolio*.

petroleum [pə'trəʊliəm] n petrolio
petrol: **petrol pump** (BRIT) n (in car, at garage) pompa di benzina; **petrol station** (BRIT) n stazione f di rifornimento; **petrol tank** (BRIT) n serbatoio della benzina
petticoat ['pɛtɪkəʊt] n sottana
petty ['pɛtɪ] adj (mean) meschino(-a); (unimportant) insignificante
pew [pju:] n panca (di chiesa)
pewter ['pju:tə'] n peltro
phantom ['fæntəm] n fantasma m
pharmacist ['fɑ:məsɪst] n farmacista m/f
pharmacy ['fɑ:məsɪ] n farmacia
phase [feɪz] n fase f, periodo; **phase in** vt introdurre gradualmente; **phase out** vt (machinery) eliminare gradualmente; (product) ritirare gradualmente; (job, subsidy) abolire gradualmente
Ph.D. n abbr = **Doctor of Philosophy**
pheasant ['fɛznt] n fagiano
phenomena [fə'nɔmɪnə] npl of **phenomenon**
phenomenal [fɪ'nɔmɪnl] adj fenomenale
phenomenon [fə'nɔmɪnən] (pl **phenomena**) n fenomeno
Philippines ['fɪlɪpi:nz] npl **the ~** le Filippine
philosopher [fɪ'lɔsəfə'] n filosofo(-a)
philosophical [fɪlə'sɔfɪkl] adj filosofico(-a)
philosophy [fɪ'lɔsəfɪ] n filosofia
phlegm [flɛm] n flemma
phobia ['fəʊbjə] n fobia
phone [fəʊn] n telefono ▷ vt telefonare; **to be on the ~** avere il telefono; (be calling) essere al telefono; **phone back** vt, vi richiamare; **phone up** vt telefonare a ▷ vi telefonare; **phone book** n guida del telefono, elenco telefonico; **phone booth** n = **phone box**; **phone box** n cabina telefonica; **phone call** n telefonata; **phonecard** n scheda telefonica; **phone number** n numero di telefono
phonetics [fə'nɛtɪks] n fonetica
phoney ['fəʊnɪ] adj falso(-a), fasullo(-a)
photo ['fəʊtəʊ] n foto f inv
photo... ['fəʊtəʊ] prefix: **photo album** n (new) album m inv per fotografie; (containing photos) album m inv delle fotografie; **photocopier** n fotocopiatrice f; **photocopy** n fotocopia ▷ vt fotocopiare
photograph ['fəʊtəgræf] n fotografia ▷ vt fotografare; **photographer** [fə'tɔgrəfə']

n fotografo; **photography** [fə'tɔgrəfɪ] n fotografia
phrase [freɪz] n espressione f; (Ling) locuzione f; (Mus) frase f ▷ vt esprimere; **phrase book** n vocabolarietto
physical ['fɪzɪkl] adj fisico(-a); **physical education** n educazione f fisica; **physically** adv fisicamente
physician [fɪ'zɪʃən] n medico
physicist ['fɪzɪsɪst] n fisico
physics ['fɪzɪks] n fisica
physiotherapist [fɪzɪəʊ'θɛrəpɪst] n fisioterapista m/f
physiotherapy [fɪzɪəʊ'θɛrəpɪ] n fisioterapia
physique [fɪ'zi:k] n fisico; costituzione f
pianist ['pi:ənɪst] n pianista m/f
piano [pɪ'ænəʊ] n pianoforte m
pick [pɪk] n (tool: also: **~-axe**) piccone m ▷ vt scegliere; (gather) cogliere; (remove) togliere; (lock) far scattare; **take your ~** scelga; **the ~ of** il fior fiore di; **to ~ one's nose** mettersi le dita nel naso; **to ~ one's teeth** pulirsi i denti con lo stuzzicadenti; **to ~ a quarrel** attaccar briga; **pick on** vt fus (person) avercela con; **pick out** vt scegliere; (distinguish) distinguere; **pick up** vi (improve) migliorarsi ▷ vt raccogliere; (Police, Radio) prendere; (collect) passare a prendere; (Aut: give lift to) far salire; (person: for sexual encounter) rimorchiare; (learn) imparare; **to ~ up speed** acquistare velocità; **to ~ o.s. up** rialzarsi
pickle ['pɪkl] n (also: **~s**: as condiment) sottaceti mpl; (fig: mess) pasticcio ▷ vt mettere sottaceto; mettere in salamoia
pickpocket ['pɪkpɔkɪt] n borsaiolo
pick-up ['pɪkʌp] n (BRIT: on record player) pick-up m inv; (small truck: also: **~ truck**, **~ van**) camioncino
picnic ['pɪknɪk] n picnic m inv; **picnic area** n area per il picnic
picture ['pɪktʃə'] n quadro; (painting) pittura; (photograph) foto(grafia); (drawing) disegno; (film) film m inv ▷ vt raffigurarsi; **~s** (BRIT) npl (cinema): **the ~s** il cinema; **would you take a ~ of us, please?** può farci una foto, per favore?; **picture frame** n cornice m inv; **picture messaging** n picture messaging m, invio di messaggini con disegni
picturesque [pɪktʃə'rɛsk] adj pittoresco(-a)
pie [paɪ] n torta; (of meat) pasticcio
piece [pi:s] n pezzo; (of land) appezzamento; (item): **a ~ of furniture/advice** un mobile/consiglio ▷ vt **to ~ together** mettere insieme; **to take to ~s** smontare

pie chart n grafico a torta
pier [pɪəʳ] n molo; (of bridge etc) pila
pierce [pɪəs] vt forare; (with arrow etc) trafiggere; **pierced** adj **I've got pierced ears** ho i buchi per gli orecchini
pig [pɪg] n maiale m, porco
pigeon ['pɪdʒən] n piccione m
piggy bank ['pɪgɪ-] n salvadanaro
pigsty ['pɪgstaɪ] n porcile m
pigtail ['pɪgteɪl] n treccina
pike [paɪk] n (fish) luccio
pilchard ['pɪltʃəd] n specie di sardina
pile [paɪl] n (pillar, of books) pila; (heap) mucchio; (of carpet) pelo; **to ~ into** (car) stiparsi or ammucchiarsi in; **pile up** vt ammucchiare ▷ vi ammucchiarsi; **piles** [paɪlz] npl emorroidi fpl; **pile-up** ['paɪlʌp] n (Aut) tamponamento a catena
pilgrimage ['pɪlgrɪmɪdʒ] n pellegrinaggio
pill [pɪl] n pillola; **the ~** la pillola
pillar ['pɪləʳ] n colonna
pillow ['pɪləu] n guanciale m; **pillowcase** n federa
pilot ['paɪlət] n pilota m/f ▷ cpd (scheme etc) pilota inv ▷ vt pilotare; **pilot light** n fiamma pilota
pimple ['pɪmpl] n foruncolo
pin [pɪn] n spillo; (Tech) perno ▷ vt attaccare con uno spillo; **~s and needles** formicolio; **to ~ sb down** (fig) obbligare qn a pronunziarsi; **to ~ sth on sb** (fig) addossare la colpa di qc a qn
PIN n abbr (= personal identification number) codice m segreto
pinafore ['pɪnəfɔːʳ] n (also: **~ dress**) grembiule m (senza maniche)
pinch [pɪntʃ] n pizzicotto, pizzico ▷ vt pizzicare; (inf: steal) grattare; **at a ~** in caso di bisogno
pine [paɪn] n (also: **~ tree**) pino ▷ vi **to ~ for** struggersi dal desiderio di
pineapple ['paɪnæpl] n ananas m inv
ping [pɪŋ] n (noise) tintinnio; **ping-pong®** n ping-pong® m
pink [pɪŋk] adj rosa inv ▷ n (colour) rosa m inv; (Bot) garofano
pinpoint ['pɪnpɔɪnt] vt indicare con precisione
pint [paɪnt] n pinta (BRIT = 0.57l; US = 0.47l); (BRIT: inf) ≈ birra da mezzo
pioneer [paɪə'nɪəʳ] n pioniere(-a)
pious ['paɪəs] adj pio(-a)
pip [pɪp] n (seed) seme m; (BRIT: time signal on radio) segnale m orario
pipe [paɪp] n tubo; (for smoking) pipa ▷ vt portare per mezzo di tubazione; **pipeline** n conduttura; (for oil) oleodotto; **piper** n piffero; suonatore(-trice) di cornamusa
pirate ['paɪərət] n pirata m ▷ vt riprodurre abusivamente

Pisces ['paɪsiːz] n Pesci mpl
piss [pɪs] (inf) vi pisciare; **pissed** (inf) adj (drunk) ubriaco fradicio(-a)
pistol ['pɪstl] n pistola
piston ['pɪstən] n pistone m
pit [pɪt] n buca, fossa; (also: **coal ~**) miniera; (quarry) cava ▷ vt **to ~ sb against sb** opporre qn a qn
pitch [pɪtʃ] n (BRIT Sport) campo; (Mus) tono; (tar) pece f; (fig) grado, punto ▷ vt (throw) lanciare ▷ vi (fall) cascare; **to ~ a tent** piantare una tenda; **pitch-black** adj nero(-a) come la pece
pitfall ['pɪtfɔːl] n trappola
pith [pɪθ] n (of plant) midollo; (of orange) parte f interna della scorza; (fig) essenza, succo; vigore m
pitiful ['pɪtɪful] adj (touching) pietoso(-a)
pity ['pɪtɪ] n pietà ▷ vt aver pietà di; **what a ~!** che peccato!
pizza ['piːtsə] n pizza
placard ['plækaːd] n affisso
place [pleɪs] n posto, luogo; (proper position, rank, seat) posto; (house) casa, alloggio; (home): **at/to his ~** a casa sua ▷ vt (object) posare, mettere; (identify) riconoscere; individuare; **to take ~** aver luogo; succedere; **to change ~s with sb** scambiare il posto con qn; **out of ~** (not suitable) inopportuno(-a); **in the first ~** in primo luogo; **to ~ an order** dare un'ordinazione; **to be ~d** (in race, exam) classificarsi; **place mat** n sottopiatto; (in linen etc) tovaglietta; **placement** n collocamento; (job) lavoro
placid ['plæsɪd] adj placido(-a), calmo(-a)
plague [pleɪg] n peste f ▷ vt tormentare
plaice [pleɪs] n inv varietà di platessa
plain [pleɪn] adj (clear) chiaro(-a), palese; (simple) semplice; (frank) franco(-a), aperto(-a); (not handsome) bruttino(-a); (without seasoning etc) scondito(-a); naturale; (in one colour) tinta unita inv ▷ adv francamente, chiaramente ▷ n pianura; **plain chocolate** n cioccolato fondente; **plainly** adv chiaramente; (frankly) francamente
plaintiff ['pleɪntɪf] n attore(-trice)
plait [plæt] n treccia
plan [plæn] n pianta; (scheme) progetto, piano ▷ vt (think in advance) progettare; (prepare) organizzare ▷ vi far piani or progetti; **to ~ to do** progettare di fare
plane [pleɪn] n (Aviat) aereo; (tree) platano; (tool) pialla; (Art, Math etc) piano ▷ adj piano(-a), piatto(-a) ▷ vt (with tool) piallare
planet ['plænɪt] n pianeta m
plank [plæŋk] n tavola, asse f

planning ['plænɪŋ] n progettazione f;
family ~ pianificazione f delle nascite
plant [plɑːnt] n pianta; (machinery)
impianto; (factory) fabbrica ▷ vt piantare;
(bomb) mettere
plantation [plæn'teɪʃən] n piantagione f
plaque [plæk] n placca
plaster ['plɑːstəʳ] n intonaco; (also: **~
of Paris**) gesso; (BRIT: also: **sticking ~**)
cerotto ▷ vt intonacare; ingessare; (cover):
to ~ with coprire di; **plaster cast** n (Med)
ingessatura, gesso; (model, statue) modello
in gesso
plastic ['plæstɪk] n plastica ▷ adj (made
of plastic) di or in plastica; **plastic bag** n
sacchetto di plastica; **plastic surgery** n
chirurgia plastica
plate [pleɪt] n (dish) piatto; (in book) tavola;
(dental plate) dentiera; **gold/silver ~**
vasellame m d'oro/d'argento
plateau ['plætəʊ] (pl **plateaus** or
plateaux) n altipiano
platform ['plætfɔːm] n (stage, at meeting)
palco; (Rail) marciapiede m; (BRIT: of bus)
piattaforma; **which ~ does the train for
Rome go from?** da che binario parte il
treno per Roma?
platinum ['plætɪnəm] n platino
platoon [plə'tuːn] n plotone m
platter ['plætəʳ] n piatto
plausible ['plɔːzɪbl] adj plausibile,
credibile; (person) convincente
play [pleɪ] n gioco; (Theatre) commedia
▷ vt (game) giocare a; (team, opponent)
giocare contro; (instrument, piece of music)
suonare; (record, tape) ascoltare; (role,
part) interpretare ▷ vi giocare; suonare;
recitare; **to ~ safe** giocare sul sicuro;
play back vt riascoltare, risentire;
play up vi (cause trouble) fare i capricci;
player n giocatore(-trice); (Theatre)
attore(-trice); (Mus) musicista m/f;
playful adj giocoso(-a); **playground** n
(in school) cortile m per la ricreazione; (in
park) parco m giochi inv; **playgroup** n
giardino d'infanzia; **playing card** n carta
da gioco; **playing field** n campo sportivo;
playschool n = **playgroup; playtime**
n (Scol) ricreazione f; **playwright** n
drammaturgo(-a)
plc abbr (= public limited company) società
per azioni a responsabilità limitata quotata
in borsa
plea [pliː] n (request) preghiera, domanda;
(Law) (argomento di) difesa
plead [pliːd] vt patrocinare; (give as excuse)
addurre a pretesto ▷ vi (Law) perorare la
causa; (beg): **to ~ with sb** implorare qn
pleasant ['plɛznt] adj piacevole, gradevole

please [pliːz] excl per piacere!, per favore!;
(acceptance): **yes, ~** sì, grazie ▷ vt piacere
a ▷ vi piacere; (think fit): **do as you ~**
faccia come le pare; **~ yourself!** come ti
(or le) pare!; **pleased** adj **pleased (with)**
contento(-a) (di); **pleased to meet you!**
piacere!
pleasure ['plɛʒəʳ] n piacere m; **"it's a ~"**
"prego"
pleat [pliːt] n piega
pledge [plɛdʒ] n pegno; (promise)
promessa ▷ vt impegnare; promettere
plentiful ['plɛntɪful] adj abbondante,
copioso(-a)
plenty ['plɛntɪ] n **~ of** tanto(-a), molto(-a);
un'abbondanza di
pliers ['plaɪəz] npl pinza
plight [plaɪt] n situazione f critica
plod [plɔd] vi camminare a stento; (fig)
sgobbare
plonk [plɔŋk] (inf) n (BRIT: wine) vino da
poco ▷ vt **to ~ sth down** buttare giù qc
bruscamente
plot [plɔt] n congiura, cospirazione f; (of
story, play) trama; (of land) lotto ▷ vt (mark
out) fare la pianta di; rilevare; (: diagram etc)
tracciare; (conspire) congiurare, cospirare
▷ vi congiurare
plough [plaʊ] (US **plow**) n aratro ▷ vt
(earth) arare; **to ~ money into** (company
etc) investire danaro in; **ploughman's
lunch** ['plaʊmənz-] (BRIT) n pasto a base di
pane, formaggio e birra
plow [plaʊ] (US) = **plough**
ploy [plɔɪ] n stratagemma m
pluck [plʌk] vt (fruit) cogliere; (musical
instrument) pizzicare; (bird) spennare;
(hairs) togliere ▷ n coraggio, fegato; **to ~
up courage** farsi coraggio
plug [plʌg] n tappo; (Elec) spina; (Aut: also:
spark(ing) ~) candela ▷ vt (hole) tappare;
(inf: advertise) spingere; **plug in** vt (Elec)
attaccare a una presa; **plughole** n (BRIT)
scarico
plum [plʌm] n (fruit) susina
plumber ['plʌməʳ] n idraulico
plumbing ['plʌmɪŋ] n (trade) lavoro di
idraulico; (piping) tubature fpl
plummet ['plʌmɪt] vi **to ~ (down)** cadere
a piombo
plump [plʌmp] adj grassoccio(-a) ▷ vi **to ~
for** (inf: choose) decidersi per
plunge [plʌndʒ] n tuffo; (fig) caduta ▷ vt
immergere ▷ vi (fall) cadere, precipitare;
(dive) tuffarsi; **to take the ~** saltare il fosso
plural ['pluərl] adj plurale ▷ n plurale m
plus [plʌs] n (also: **~ sign**) segno più ▷ prep
più; **ten/twenty ~** più di dieci/venti
ply [plaɪ] vt (a trade) esercitare ▷ vi (ship)

fare il servizio ▷ n (of wool, rope) capo; **to ~ sb with drink** dare di bere continuamente a qn; **plywood** n legno compensato

P.M. n abbr = **prime minister**

p.m. adv abbr (= post meridiem) del pomeriggio

PMS n abbr (= premenstrual syndrome) sindrome f premestruale

PMT n abbr (= premenstrual tension) sindrome f premestruale

pneumatic drill [nju:'mætɪk-] n martello pneumatico

pneumonia [nju:'məʊnɪə] n polmonite f

poach [pəʊtʃ] vt (cook: egg) affogare; (: fish) cuocere in bianco; (steal) cacciare (or pescare) di frodo ▷ vi fare il bracconiere; **poached** adj (egg) affogato(-a)

P.O. Box n = **Post Office Box**

pocket ['pɔkɪt] n tasca ▷ vt intascare; **to be out of ~** (BRIT) rimetterci; **pocketbook** (US) n (wallet) portafoglio; **pocket money** n paghetta, settimana

pod [pɔd] n guscio

podiatrist [pɔ'di:ətrɪst] (US) n callista m/f, pedicure m/f

podium ['pəʊdɪəm] n podio

poem ['pəʊɪm] n poesia

poet ['pəʊɪt] n poeta/essa; **poetic** [-'ɛtɪk] adj poetico(-a); **poetry** n poesia

poignant ['pɔɪnjənt] adj struggente

point [pɔɪnt] n (gen) punto; (tip: of needle etc) punta; (in time) punto, momento; (Scol) voto; (main idea, important part) nocciolo; (Elec) presa di corrente; (also: **decimal ~**): **2 ~ 3 (2.3)** 2 virgola 3 (2,3) ▷ vt (show) indicare; (gun etc) puntare qc contro ▷ vi **to ~ at** mostrare a dito; **~s** npl (Aut) puntine fpl; (Rail) scambio; **to be on the ~ of doing sth** essere sul punto di or stare per fare qc; **to make a ~** fare un'osservazione; **to get/miss the ~** capire/non capire; **to come to the ~** venire al fatto; **there's no ~ in doing** è inutile (fare); **point out** vt far notare; **point-blank** adv (also: **at point-blank range**) a bruciapelo; (fig) categoricamente; **pointed** adj (shape) aguzzo(-a), appuntito(-a); (remark) specifico(-a); **pointer** n (needle) lancetta; (fig) indicazione f, consiglio; **pointless** adj inutile, vano(-a); **point of view** n punto di vista

poison ['pɔɪzn] n veleno ▷ vt avvelenare; **poisonous** adj velenoso(-a)

poke [pəʊk] vt (fire) attizzare; (jab with finger, stick etc) punzecchiare; (put): **to ~ sth in(to)** spingere qc dentro; **poke about** or **around** vi frugare; **poke out** vi (stick out) sporger fuori

poker ['pəʊkər] n attizzatoio; (Cards) poker m

Poland ['pəʊlənd] n Polonia

polar ['pəʊlər] adj polare; **polar bear** n orso bianco

Pole [pəʊl] n polacco(-a)

pole [pəʊl] n (of wood) palo; (Elec, Geo) polo; **pole bean** (US) n (runner bean) fagiolino; **pole vault** n salto con l'asta

police [pə'li:s] n polizia ▷ vt mantenere l'ordine in; **police car** n macchina della polizia; **police constable** (BRIT) n agente m di polizia; **police force** n corpo di polizia, polizia; **policeman** (irreg) n poliziotto, agente m di polizia; **police officer** n = **police constable**; **police station** n posto di polizia; **policewoman** (irreg) n donna f poliziotto inv

policy ['pɔlɪsɪ] n politica; (also: **insurance ~**) polizza (d'assicurazione)

polio ['pəʊlɪəʊ] n polio f

Polish ['pəʊlɪʃ] adj polacco(-a) ▷ n (Ling) polacco

polish ['pɔlɪʃ] n (for shoes) lucido; (for floor) cera; (for nails) smalto; (shine) lucentezza, lustro; (fig: refinement) raffinatezza ▷ vt lucidare; (fig: improve) raffinare; **polish off** vt (food) mangiarsi; **polished** adj (fig) raffinato(-a)

polite [pə'laɪt] adj cortese; **politeness** n cortesia

political [pə'lɪtɪkl] adj politico(-a); **politically** adv politicamente; **politically correct** politicamente corretto(-a)

politician [pɔlɪ'tɪʃən] n politico

politics ['pɔlɪtɪks] n politica ▷ npl (views, policies) idee fpl politiche

poll [pəʊl] n scrutinio; (votes cast) voti mpl; (also: **opinion ~**) sondaggio (d'opinioni) ▷ vt ottenere

pollen ['pɔlən] n polline m

polling station ['pəʊlɪŋ-] (BRIT) n sezione f elettorale

pollute [pə'lu:t] vt inquinare

pollution [pə'lu:ʃən] n inquinamento

polo ['pəʊləʊ] n polo; **polo-neck** n collo alto; (also: **polo-neck sweater**) dolcevita ▷ adj a collo alto; **polo shirt** n polo f inv

polyester [pɔlɪ'ɛstər] n poliestere m

polystyrene [pɔlɪ'staɪri:n] n polistirolo

polythene ['pɔlɪθi:n] n politene m; **polythene bag** n sacco di plastica

pomegranate ['pɔmɪgrænɪt] n melagrana

pompous ['pɔmpəs] adj pomposo(-a)

pond [pɔnd] n pozza; stagno

ponder ['pɔndər] vt ponderare, riflettere su

pony ['pəʊnɪ] n pony m inv; **ponytail** n coda di cavallo; **pony trekking**

[-trɛkɪŋ] (BRIT) n escursione f a cavallo

poodle ['puːdl] n barboncino, barbone m

pool [puːl] n (puddle) pozza; (pond) stagno; (also: **swimming ~**) piscina; (fig: of light) cerchio; (billiards) specie di biliardo a buca ▷ vt mettere in comune; **~s** npl (football pools) ≈ totocalcio; **typing ~** servizio comune di dattilografia

poor [puəʳ] adj povero(-a); (mediocre) mediocre, cattivo(-a) ▷ npl **the ~** i poveri; **~ in** povero(-a) di; **poorly** adv poveramente; male ▷ adj indisposto(-a), malato(-a)

pop [pɒp] n (noise) schiocco; (Mus) musica pop; (drink) bibita gasata; (US: inf: father) babbo ▷ vt (put) mettere (in fretta) ▷ vi scoppiare; (cork) schioccare; **pop in** vi passare; **pop out** vi fare un salto fuori; **popcorn** n pop-corn m

poplar ['pɒpləʳ] n pioppo

popper ['pɒpəʳ] n bottone m a pressione

poppy ['pɒpɪ] n papavero

Popsicle® ['pɒpsɪkl] (US) n (ice lolly) ghiacciolo

pop star n pop star f inv

popular ['pɒpjuləʳ] adj popolare; (fashionable) in voga; **popularity** [-'lærɪtɪ] n popolarità

population [pɒpju'leɪʃən] n popolazione f

porcelain ['pɔːslɪn] n porcellana

porch [pɔːtʃ] n veranda

pore [pɔːʳ] n poro ▷ vi **to ~ over** essere immerso(-a) in

pork [pɔːk] n carne f di maiale; **pork chop** n braciola or costoletta di maiale; **pork pie** n (BRIT: Culin) pasticcio di maiale in crosta

porn [pɔːn] (inf) n pornografia ▷ adj porno inv; **pornographic** [pɔːnə'græfɪk] adj pornografico(-a); **pornography** [pɔː'nɔɡrəfɪ] n pornografia

porridge ['pɒrɪdʒ] n porridge m

port [pɔːt] n (gen, wine) porto; (Naut: left side) babordo

portable ['pɔːtəbl] adj portatile

porter ['pɔːtəʳ] n (for luggage) facchino, portabagagli m inv; (doorkeeper) portiere m, portinaio

portfolio [pɔːt'fəʊlɪəʊ] n (case) cartella; (Pol, Finance) portafoglio; (of artist) raccolta dei propri lavori

portion ['pɔːʃən] n porzione f

port of call n (porto di) scalo

portrait ['pɔːtreɪt] n ritratto

portray [pɔː'treɪ] vt fare il ritratto di; (character on stage) rappresentare; (in writing) ritrarre

Portugal ['pɔːtjuɡl] n Portogallo

Portuguese [pɔːtjuˈɡiːz] adj portoghese ▷ n inv portoghese m/f; (Ling) portoghese m

pose [pəʊz] n posa ▷ vi posare; (pretend): **to ~ as** atteggiarsi a, posare a ▷ vt porre

posh [pɒʃ] (inf) adj elegante; (family) per bene

position [pə'zɪʃən] n posizione f; (job) posto ▷ vt sistemare

positive ['pɒzɪtɪv] adj positivo(-a); (certain) sicuro(-a), certo(-a); (definite) preciso(-a), definitivo(-a); **positively** adv (affirmatively, enthusiastically) positivamente; (decisively) decisamente; (really) assolutamente

possess [pə'zɛs] vt possedere; **possession** [pə'zɛʃən] n possesso; **possessions** npl (belongings) beni mpl; **possessive** adj possessivo(-a)

possibility [pɒsɪ'bɪlɪtɪ] n possibilità f inv

possible ['pɒsɪbl] adj possibile; **as big as ~** il più grande possibile; **possibly** ['pɒsɪblɪ] adv (perhaps) forse; **if you possibly can** se le è possibile; **I cannot possibly come** proprio non posso venire

post [pəʊst] n (BRIT) posta; (: collection) levata; (job, situation) posto; (Mil) postazione f; (pole) palo ▷ vt (BRIT: send by post) imbucare; (: appoint): **to ~ to** assegnare a; **where can I ~ these cards?** dove posso imbucare queste cartoline?; **postage** n affrancatura; **postal** adj postale; **postal order** n vaglia m inv postale; **postbox** (BRIT) n cassetta postale; **postcard** n cartolina; **postcode** n (BRIT) codice m (di avviamento) postale

poster ['pəʊstəʳ] n manifesto, affisso

postgraduate ['pəʊst'ɡrædjuət] n laureato/a che continua gli studi

postman ['pəʊstmən] (irreg) n postino

postmark ['pəʊstmɑːk] n bollo or timbro postale

post-mortem [-'mɔːtəm] n autopsia

post office n (building) ufficio postale; (organization): **the Post Office** ≈ le Poste e Telecomunicazioni

postpone [pəs'pəʊn] vt rinviare

posture ['pɒstʃəʳ] n portamento; (pose) posa, atteggiamento

postwoman ['pəʊstwumən] (BRIT: irreg) n postina

pot [pɒt] n (for cooking) pentola, casseruola; (teapot) teiera; (coffeepot) caffettiera; (for plants, jam) vaso; (inf: marijuana) erba ▷ vt (plant) piantare in vaso; **a ~ of tea for two** tè per due; **to go to ~** (inf: work, performance) andare in malora

potato [pə'teɪtəʊ] (pl **potatoes**) n patata; **potato peeler** n sbucciapatate m inv

potent ['pəʊtnt] adj potente, forte

potential [pə'tɛnʃl] adj potenziale ▷ n possibilità fpl

pothole ['pɒthəʊl] n (in road) buca; (BRIT:

underground) caverna

pot plant n pianta in vaso

potter ['pɒtə^r] n vasaio ▷ vi **to ~ around, ~ about** (BRIT) lavoracchiare; **pottery** n ceramiche fpl; (*factory*) fabbrica di ceramiche

potty ['pɒtɪ] adj (*inf: mad*) tocco(-a) ▷ n (*child's*) vasino

pouch [pautʃ] n borsa; (*Zool*) marsupio

poultry ['pəultrɪ] n pollame m

pounce [pauns] vi **to ~ (on)** piombare (su)

pound [paund] n (*weight*) libbra; (*money*) (lira) sterlina ▷ vt (*beat*) battere; (*crush*) pestare, polverizzare ▷ vi (*beat*) battere, martellare; **pound sterling** n sterlina (inglese)

pour [pɔː^r] vt versare ▷ vi riversarsi; (*rain*) piovere a dirotto; **pour in** vi affluire in gran quantità; **pour out** vi (*people*) uscire a fiumi ▷ vt vuotare; versare; (*fig*) sfogare; **pouring** adj **pouring rain** pioggia torrenziale

pout [paut] vi sporgere le labbra; fare il broncio

poverty ['pɒvətɪ] n povertà, miseria

powder ['paudə^r] n polvere f ▷ vt **to ~ one's face** incipriarsi il viso; **powdered milk** n latte m in polvere

power ['pauə^r] n (*strength*) potenza, forza; (*ability, Pol: of party, leader*) potere m; (*Elec*) corrente f; **to be in ~** (*Pol etc*) essere al potere; **power cut** (BRIT) n interruzione f or mancanza di corrente; **power failure** n interruzione f della corrente elettrica; **powerful** adj potente, forte; **powerless** adj impotente; **powerless to do** impossibilitato(-a) a fare; **power point** (BRIT) n presa di corrente; **power station** n centrale f elettrica

p.p. abbr = **per procurationem**; **p.p.J. Smith** per J. Smith; (= *pages*) p.p.

PR abbr = **public relations**

practical ['præktɪkl] adj pratico(-a); **practical joke** n beffa; **practically** adv praticamente

practice ['præktɪs] n pratica; (*of profession*) esercizio; (*at football etc*) allenamento; (*business*) gabinetto; clientela ▷ vt, vi (*us*) = **practise**; **in ~** (*in reality*) in pratica; **out of ~** fuori esercizio

practise ['præktɪs] (*US* **practice**) vt (*work at: piano, one's backhand etc*) esercitarsi a; (*train for: skiing, running etc*) allenarsi a; (*a sport, religion*) praticare; (*method*) usare; (*profession*) esercitare ▷ vi esercitarsi; (*train*) allenarsi; (*lawyer, doctor*) esercitare; **practising** adj (*Christian etc*) praticante; (*lawyer*) che esercita la professione

practitioner [præk'tɪʃənə^r] n

professionista m/f

pragmatic [præg'mætɪk] adj pragmatico(-a)

prairie ['prɛərɪ] n prateria

praise [preɪz] n elogio, lode f ▷ vt elogiare, lodare

pram [præm] (BRIT) n carrozzina

prank [præŋk] n burla

prawn [prɔːn] n gamberetto; **prawn cocktail** n cocktail m inv di gamberetti

pray [preɪ] vi pregare; **prayer** [prɛə^r] n preghiera

preach [priːtʃ] vt, vi predicare; **preacher** n predicatore(-trice); (*US: minister*) pastore m

precarious [prɪ'kɛərɪəs] adj precario(-a)

precaution [prɪ'kɔːʃən] n precauzione f

precede [prɪ'siːd] vt precedere; **precedent** ['prɛsɪdənt] n precedente m; **preceding** [prɪ'siːdɪŋ] adj precedente

precinct ['priːsɪŋkt] (*US*) n circoscrizione f

precious ['prɛʃəs] adj prezioso(-a)

precise [prɪ'saɪs] adj preciso(-a); **precisely** adv precisamente

precision [prɪ'sɪʒən] n precisione f

predator ['prɛdətə^r] n predatore m

predecessor ['priːdɪsɛsə^r] n predecessore(-a)

predicament [prɪ'dɪkəmənt] n situazione f difficile

predict [prɪ'dɪkt] vt predire; **predictable** adj prevedibile; **prediction** [prɪ'dɪkʃən] n predizione f

predominantly [prɪ'dɒmɪnəntlɪ] adv in maggior parte; soprattutto

preface ['prɛfəs] n prefazione f

prefect ['priːfɛkt] n (BRIT: in school) studente(-essa) con funzioni disciplinari; (*French etc, Admin*) prefetto

prefer [prɪ'fəː^r] vt preferire; **to ~ doing** or **to do** preferire fare; **preferable** ['prɛfrəbl] adj preferibile; **preferably** ['prɛfrəblɪ] adv preferibilmente; **preference** ['prɛfrəns] n preferenza

prefix ['priːfɪks] n prefisso

pregnancy ['prɛgnənsɪ] n gravidanza

pregnant ['prɛgnənt] adj incinta ag

prehistoric ['priːhɪs'tɔrɪk] adj preistorico(-a)

prejudice ['prɛdʒudɪs] n pregiudizio; (*harm*) torto, danno; **prejudiced** adj **prejudiced (against)** prevenuto(-a) (contro); **prejudiced (in favour of)** ben disposto(-a) (verso)

preliminary [prɪ'lɪmɪnərɪ] adj preliminare

prelude ['prɛljuːd] n preludio

premature ['prɛmətʃuə^r] adj prematuro(-a)

premier ['prɛmɪə^r] adj primo(-a) ▷ n (*Pol*) primo ministro

première ['prɛmɪɛəʳ] *n* prima
Premier League *n* ≈ serie A
premises ['prɛmɪsɪz] *npl* locale *m*; **on the
~** sul posto; **business ~** locali commerciali
premium ['priːmɪəm] *n* premio; **to be at a
~** essere ricercatissimo
premonition [prɛməˈnɪʃən] *n*
premonizione *f*
preoccupied [priːˈɔkjupaɪd] *adj*
preoccupato(-a)
prepaid [priːˈpeɪd] *adj* pagato(-a) in
anticipo
preparation [prɛpəˈreɪʃən] *n*
preparazione *f*; **~s** *npl* (*for trip, war*)
preparativi *mpl*
preparatory school [prɪˈpærətərɪ-] *n*
scuola elementare privata
prepare [prɪˈpeəʳ] *vt* preparare ▷ *vi* **to ~
for** prepararsi a; **~d to** pronto(-a) a
preposition [prɛpəˈzɪʃən] *n* preposizione *f*
prep school *n* = **preparatory school**
prerequisite [priːˈrɛkwɪzɪt] *n* requisito
indispensabile
preschool ['priːˈskuːl] *adj* (*age*)
prescolastico(-a); (*child*) in età
prescolastica
prescribe [prɪˈskraɪb] *vt* (*Med*) prescrivere
prescription [prɪˈskrɪpʃən] *n* prescrizione
f; (*Med*) ricetta; **could you write me a ~?**
mi può fare una ricetta medica?
presence ['prɛzns] *n* presenza; **~ of mind**
presenza di spirito
present [*adj, n* 'prɛznt, *vb* prɪˈzɛnt] *adj*
presente; (*wife, residence, job*) attuale ▷ *n*
(*actuality*): **the ~** il presente; (*gift*) regalo
▷ *vt* presentare; (*give*): **to ~ sb with sth**
offrire qc a qn; **to give sb a ~** fare un regalo
a qn; **at ~** al momento; **presentable**
[prɪˈzɛntəbl] *adj* presentabile;
presentation [-ˈteɪʃən] *n* presentazione *f*;
(*ceremony*) consegna ufficiale; **present-
day** *adj* attuale, d'oggigiorno; **presenter**
n (*Radio, TV*) presentatore(-trice);
presently *adv* (*soon*) fra poco, presto; (*at
present*) al momento; **present participle**
n participio presente
preservation [prɛzəˈveɪʃən] *n*
preservazione *f*, conservazione *f*
preservative [prɪˈzəːvətɪv] *n* conservante
m
preserve [prɪˈzəːv] *vt* (*keep safe*)
preservare, proteggere; (*maintain*)
conservare; (*food*) mettere in conserva ▷ *n*
(*often pl: jam*) marmellata; (: *fruit*) frutta
sciroppata
preside [prɪˈzaɪd] *vi* **to ~ (over)** presiedere
(a)
president ['prɛzɪdənt] *n* presidente *m*;
presidential [-ˈdɛnʃl] *adj* presidenziale

press [prɛs] *n* (*newspapers etc*): **the P~** la
stampa; (*tool, machine*) pressa; (*for wine*)
torchio ▷ *vt* (*push*) premere, pigiare;
(*squeeze*) spremere; (: *hand*) stringere;
(*clothes: iron*) stirare; (*pursue*) incalzare;
(*insist*): **to ~ sth on sb** far accettare qc da
qn ▷ *vi* premere; accalcare; **we are ~ed
for time** ci manca il tempo; **to ~ for sth**
insistere per avere qc; **press conference**
n conferenza *f* stampa *inv*; **pressing** *adj*
urgente; **press stud** (BRIT) *n* bottone *m*
a pressione; **press-up** (BRIT) *n* flessione *f*
sulle braccia
pressure ['prɛʃəʳ] *n* pressione *f*; **to put ~
on sb (to do)** mettere qn sotto pressione
(affinché faccia); **pressure cooker** *n*
pentola a pressione; **pressure group** *n*
gruppo di pressione
prestige [prɛsˈtiːʒ] *n* prestigio
prestigious [prɛsˈtɪdʒəs] *adj*
prestigioso(-a)
presumably [prɪˈzjuːməblɪ] *adv*
presumibilmente
presume [prɪˈzjuːm] *vt* supporre
pretence [prɪˈtɛns] (US **pretense**) *n* (*claim*)
pretesa; **to make a ~ of doing** far finta di
fare; **under false ~s** con l'inganno
pretend [prɪˈtɛnd] *vt* (*feign*) fingere ▷ *vi* far
finta; **to ~ to do** far finta di fare
pretense [prɪˈtɛns] (US) *n* = **pretence**
pretentious [prɪˈtɛnʃəs] *adj*
pretenzioso(-a)
pretext ['priːtɛkst] *n* pretesto
pretty ['prɪtɪ] *adj* grazioso(-a), carino(-a)
▷ *adv* abbastanza, assai
prevail [prɪˈveɪl] *vi* (*win, be usual*)
prevalere; (*persuade*): **to ~ (up)on sb to
do** persuadere qn a fare; **prevailing** *adj*
dominante
prevalent ['prɛvələnt] *adj* (*belief*)
predominante; (*customs*) diffuso(-a);
(*fashion*) corrente; (*disease*) comune
prevent [prɪˈvɛnt] *vt* **to ~ sb from doing**
impedire a qn di fare; **to ~ sth from
happening** impedire che qc succeda;
prevention [-ˈvɛnʃən] *n* prevenzione *f*;
preventive *adj* preventivo(-a)
preview ['priːvjuː] *n* (*of film*) anteprima
previous ['priːvɪəs] *adj* precedente;
anteriore; **previously** *adv* prima
prey [preɪ] *n* preda ▷ *vi* **to ~ on** far preda
di; **it was ~ing on his mind** lo stava
ossessionando
price [praɪs] *n* prezzo ▷ *vt* (*goods*) fissare
il prezzo di; valutare; **priceless** *adj*
inapprezzabile; **price list** *n* listino (dei)
prezzi
prick [prɪk] *n* puntura ▷ *vt* pungere; **to ~
up one's ears** drizzare gli orecchi

prickly ['prɪklɪ] *adj* spinoso(-a)
pride [praɪd] *n* orgoglio; superbia ▷ *vt* **to ~ o.s. on** essere orgoglioso(-a) di, vantarsi di
priest [pri:st] *n* prete *m*, sacerdote *m*
primarily ['praɪmərɪlɪ] *adv* principalmente, essenzialmente
primary ['praɪmərɪ] *adj* primario(-a); (*first in importance*) primo(-a) ▷ *n* (*US*: *election*) primarie *fpl*; **primary school** (*BRIT*) *n* scuola elementare
prime [praɪm] *adj* primario(-a), fondamentale; (*excellent*) di prima qualità ▷ *vt* (*wood*) preparare; (*fig*) mettere al corrente ▷ *n* **in the ~ of life** nel fiore della vita; **Prime Minister** *n* primo ministro
primitive ['prɪmɪtɪv] *adj* primitivo(-a)
primrose ['prɪmrəuz] *n* primavera
prince [prɪns] *n* principe *m*
princess [prɪn'sɛs] *n* principessa
principal ['prɪnsɪpl] *adj* principale ▷ *n* (*headmaster*) preside *m*; **principally** *adv* principalmente
principle ['prɪnsɪpl] *n* principio; **in ~** in linea di principio; **on ~** per principio
print [prɪnt] *n* (*mark*) impronta; (*letters*) caratteri *mpl*; (*fabric*) tessuto stampato; (*Art, Phot*) stampa ▷ *vt* imprimere; (*publish*) stampare, pubblicare; (*write in capitals*) scrivere in stampatello; **out of ~** esaurito(-a); **print out** *vt* (*Comput*) stampare; **printer** *n* tipografo; (*machine*) stampante *f*; **printout** *n* tabulato
prior ['praɪə^r] *adj* precedente; (*claim etc*) più importante; **~ to doing** prima di fare
priority [praɪ'ɔrɪtɪ] *n* priorità *f inv*; precedenza
prison ['prɪzn] *n* prigione *f* ▷ *cpd* (*system*) carcerario(-a); (*conditions, food*) nelle *or* delle prigioni; **prisoner** *n* prigioniero(-a); **prisoner-of-war** *n* prigioniero(-a) di guerra
pristine ['prɪsti:n] *adj* immacolato(-a)
privacy ['prɪvəsɪ] *n* solitudine *f*, intimità
private ['praɪvɪt] *adj* privato(-a); personale ▷ *n* soldato semplice; **"~"** (*on envelope*) "riservata"; (*on door*) "privato"; **in ~** in privato; **privately** *adv* in privato; (*within oneself*) dentro di sé; **private property** *n* proprietà privata; **private school** *n* scuola privata
privatize ['praɪvɪtaɪz] *vt* privatizzare
privilege ['prɪvɪlɪdʒ] *n* privilegio
prize [praɪz] *n* premio ▷ *adj* (*example, idiot*) perfetto(-a); (*bull, novel*) premiato(-a) ▷ *vt* apprezzare, pregiare; **prize-giving** *n* premiazione *f*; **prizewinner** *n* premiato(-a)
pro [prəu] *n* (*Sport*) professionista *m/f* ▷ *prep* pro; **the ~s and cons** il pro e il contro
probability [prɔbə'bɪlɪtɪ] *n* probabilità *f inv*; **in all ~** con tutta probabilità
probable ['prɔbəbl] *adj* probabile
probably ['prɔbəblɪ] *adv* probabilmente
probation [prə'beɪʃən] *n* **on ~** (*employee*) in prova; (*Law*) in libertà vigilata
probe [prəub] *n* (*Med, Space*) sonda; (*enquiry*) indagine *f*, investigazione *f* ▷ *vt* sondare, esplorare; indagare
problem ['prɔbləm] *n* problema *m*
procedure [prə'si:dʒə^r] *n* (*Admin, Law*) procedura; (*method*) metodo, procedimento
proceed [prə'si:d] *vi* (*go forward*) avanzare, andare avanti; (*go about it*) procedere; (*continue*): **to ~ (with)** continuare; **to ~ to** andare a; passare a; **to ~ to do** mettersi a fare; **proceedings** *npl* misure *fpl*; (*Law*) procedimento; (*meeting*) riunione *f*; (*records*) rendiconti *mpl*; atti *mpl*; **proceeds** ['prəusi:dz] *npl* profitto, incasso
process ['prəusɛs] *n* processo; (*method*) metodo, sistema *m* ▷ *vt* trattare; (*information*) elaborare
procession [prə'sɛʃən] *n* processione *f*, corteo; **funeral ~** corteo funebre
proclaim [prə'kleɪm] *vt* proclamare, dichiarare
prod [prɔd] *vt* dare un colpetto a; pungolare ▷ *n* colpetto
produce [*n* 'prɔdju:s, *vb* prə'dju:s] *n* (*Agr*) prodotto, prodotti *mpl* ▷ *vt* produrre; (*show*) esibire, mostrare; (*cause*) cagionare, causare; **producer** *n* (*Theatre*) regista *m/f*; (*Agr, Cinema*) produttore *m*
product ['prɔdʌkt] *n* prodotto; **production** [prə'dʌkʃən] *n* produzione *f*; **productive** [prə'dʌktɪv] *adj* produttivo(-a); **productivity** [prɔdʌk'tɪvɪtɪ] *n* produttività
Prof. *abbr* (= *professor*) Prof.
profession [prə'fɛʃən] *n* professione *f*; **professional** *n* professionista *m/f* ▷ *adj* professionale; (*work*) da professionista
professor [prə'fɛsə^r] *n* professore *m* (*titolare di una cattedra*); (*US*) professore(-essa)
profile ['prəufaɪl] *n* profilo
profit ['prɔfɪt] *n* profitto; beneficio ▷ *vi* **to ~ (by** *or* **from)** approfittare (di); **profitable** *adj* redditizio(-a)
profound [prə'faund] *adj* profondo(-a)
programme ['prəugræm] (*US* **program**) *n* programma *m* ▷ *vt* programmare; **programmer** (*US* **programer**) *n* programmatore(-trice); **programming** (*US* **programing**) *n* programmazione *f*
progress [*n* 'prəugrɛs, *vb* prə'grɛs] *n*

progresso ▷ vi avanzare, procedere;
in ~ in corso; **to make ~** far progressi;
progressive [-'grɛsɪv] adj progressivo(-a);
(person) progressista
prohibit [prə'hɪbɪt] vt proibire, vietare
project [n 'prɔdʒɛkt, vb prə'dʒɛkt] n (plan)
piano; (venture) progetto; (Scol) studio
▷ vt proiettare ▷ vi (stick out) sporgere;
projection [prə'dʒɛkʃən] n proiezione
f; sporgenza; **projector** [prə'dʒɛktəʳ] n
proiettore m
prolific [prə'lɪfɪk] adj (artist etc)
fecondo(-a)
prolong [prə'lɔŋ] vt prolungare
prom [prɔm] n abbr = **promenade**; (us:
ball) ballo studentesco

● **PROM**
●
● In Gran Bretagna i **Proms**, o
● "promenade concerts", sono concerti di
● musica classica, i più noti dei quali sono
● eseguiti nella prestigiosa **Royal Albert**
● **Hall** a Londra. Si chiamano così perché
● un tempo il pubblico seguiva i concerti
● in piedi, passeggiando (in inglese
● "promenade" voleva dire, appunto,
● passeggiata). Negli Stati Uniti, invece,
● con **prom**, si intende l'annuale ballo
● studentesco di un'università o di una
● scuola secondaria.

promenade [prɔmə'nɑːd] n (by sea)
lungomare m
prominent ['prɔmɪnənt] adj
(standing out) prominente; (important)
importante
promiscuous [prə'mɪskjuəs] adj (sexually)
di facili costumi
promise ['prɔmɪs] n promessa ▷ vt,
vi promettere; **to ~ sb sth, ~ sth to sb**
promettere qc a qn; **to ~ (sb) that/to
do sth** promettere (a qn) che/di fare qc;
promising adj promettente
promote [prə'məut] vt promuovere;
(venture, event) organizzare; **promotion**
[-'məuʃən] n promozione f
prompt [prɔmpt] adj rapido(-a),
svelto(-a); puntuale; (reply) sollecito(-a)
▷ adv (punctually) in punto ▷ n (Comput)
prompt m ▷ vt incitare; provocare;
(Theatre) suggerire a; **to ~ sb to do** incitare
qn a fare; **promptly** adv prontamente;
puntualmente
prone [prəun] adj (lying) prono(-a); **~ to**
propenso(-a) a, incline a
prong [prɔŋ] n rebbio, punta
pronoun ['prəunaun] n pronome m
pronounce [prə'nauns] vt pronunciare;

how do you ~ it? come si pronuncia?
pronunciation [prənʌnsɪ'eɪʃən] n
pronuncia
proof [pruːf] n prova; (of book) bozza; (Phot)
provino ▷ adj **~ against** a prova di
prop [prɔp] n sostegno, appoggio ▷ vt
(also: **~ up**) sostenere, appoggiare; (lean):
to ~ sth against appoggiare qc contro
or a; **~s** oggetti m inv di scena; **prop up** vt
sostenere, appoggiare
propaganda [prɔpə'gændə] n
propaganda
propeller [prə'pɛləʳ] n elica
proper ['prɔpəʳ] adj (suited, right)
adatto(-a), appropriato(-a); (seemly)
decente; (authentic) vero(-a); (inf: real:
noun) + vero(-a) e proprio(-a); **properly**
['prɔpəlɪ] adv (eat, study) bene; (behave)
come si deve; **proper noun** n nome m
proprio
property ['prɔpətɪ] n (things owned) beni
mpl; (land, building) proprietà f inv; (Chem
etc: quality) proprietà
prophecy ['prɔfɪsɪ] n profezia
prophet ['prɔfɪt] n profeta m
proportion [prə'pɔːʃən] n proporzione f;
(share) parte f; **~s** npl (size) proporzioni fpl;
proportional adj proporzionale
proposal [prə'pəuzl] n proposta; (plan)
progetto; (of marriage) proposta di
matrimonio
propose [prə'pəuz] vt proporre, suggerire
▷ vi fare una proposta di matrimonio; **to
~ to do** proporsi di fare, aver l'intenzione
di fare
proposition [prɔpə'zɪʃən] n proposizione
f; (offer) proposta
proprietor [prə'praɪətəʳ] n
proprietario(-a)
prose [prəuz] n prosa
prosecute ['prɔsɪkjuːt] vt processare;
prosecution [-'kjuːʃən] n processo;
(accusing side) accusa; **prosecutor** n (also:
public prosecutor) ≈ procuratore m della
Repubblica
prospect [n 'prɔspɛkt, vb prə'spɛkt] n
prospettiva; (hope) speranza ▷ vi **to ~ for**
cercare; **~s** npl (for work etc) prospettive
fpl; **prospective** [-'spɛktɪv] adj possibile;
futuro(-a)
prospectus [prə'spɛktəs] n prospetto,
programma m
prosper ['prɔspə] vi prosperare;
prosperity [prɔ'spɛrɪtɪ] n prosperità;
prosperous adj prospero(-a)
prostitute ['prɔstɪtjuːt] n prostituta;
male ~ uomo che si prostituisce
protect [prə'tɛkt] vt proteggere,
salvaguardare; **protection** n protezione f;

protective adj protettivo(-a)
protein ['prəuti:n] n proteina
protest [n 'prəutɛst, vb prə'tɛst] n protesta
▷ vt, vi protestare
Protestant ['prɔtɪstənt] adj, n protestante
m/f
protester [prə'tɛstər] n dimostrante m/f
protractor [prə'træktər] n (Geom)
goniometro
proud [praud] adj fiero(-a), orgoglioso(-a);
superbo(-a); (pej) superbo(-a)
prove [pru:v] vt provare, dimostrare ▷ vi
to ~ (to be) correct etc risultare vero(-a)
etc; **to ~ o.s.** mostrare le proprie capacità
proverb ['prɔvə:b] n proverbio
provide [prə'vaɪd] vt fornire, provvedere;
to ~ sb with sth fornire or provvedere qn di
qc; **provide for** vt fus provvedere a; (future
event) prevedere; **provided** conj **provided
(that)** purché + sub, a condizione che +
sub; **providing** [prə'vaɪdɪŋ] conj purché
+sub, a condizione che +sub
province ['prɔvɪns] n provincia;
provincial [prə'vɪnʃəl] adj provinciale
provision [prə'vɪʒən] n (supply) riserva;
(supplying) provvista; rifornimento;
(stipulation) condizione f; **~s** npl
(food) provviste fpl; **provisional** adj
provvisorio(-a)
provocative [prə'vɔkətɪv] adj (aggressive)
provocatorio(-a); (thought-provoking)
stimolante; (seductive) provocante
provoke [prə'vəuk] vt provocare; incitare
prowl [praul] vi (also: **~ about, ~ around**)
aggirarsi ▷ n **to be on the ~** aggirarsi
proximity [prɔk'sɪmɪtɪ] n prossimità
proxy ['prɔksɪ] n **by ~** per procura
prudent ['pru:dnt] adj prudente
prune [pru:n] n prugna secca ▷ vt potare
pry [praɪ] vi **to ~ into** ficcare il naso in
PS abbr (= postscript) P.S.
pseudonym ['sju:dənɪm] n pseudonimo
psychiatric [saɪkɪ'ætrɪk] adj
psichiatrico(-a)
psychiatrist [saɪ'kaɪətrɪst] n psichiatra
m/f
psychic ['saɪkɪk] adj (also: **~al**) psichico(-a);
(person) dotato(-a) di qualità telepatiche
psychoanalysis [saɪkəuə'nælɪsɪs, -sɪ:z]
(pl -ses) n psicanalisi f inv
psychological [saɪkə'lɔdʒɪkl] adj
psicologico(-a)
psychologist [saɪ'kɔlədʒɪst] n
psicologo(-a)
psychology [saɪ'kɔlədʒɪ] n psicologia
psychotherapy [saɪkəu'θɛrəpɪ] n
psicoterapia
pt abbr (= pint; point) pt.
PTO abbr (= please turn over) v.r.

355 | pull

pub [pʌb] n abbr (= public house) pub m inv
puberty ['pju:bətɪ] n pubertà
public ['pʌblɪk] adj pubblico(-a) ▷ n
pubblico; **in ~** in pubblico
publication [pʌblɪ'keɪʃən] n
pubblicazione f
public: public company n società f inv
per azioni (costituita tramite pubblica
sottoscrizione); **public convenience** (BRIT)
n gabinetti mpl; **public holiday** n giorno
festivo, festa nazionale; **public house**
(BRIT) n pub m inv
publicity [pʌb'lɪsɪtɪ] n pubblicità
publicize ['pʌblɪsaɪz] vt rendere
pubblico(-a)
public: public limited company n
≈ società per azioni a responsabilità
limitata (quotata in Borsa); **publicly**
['pʌblɪklɪ] adv pubblicamente; **public
opinion** n opinione f pubblica; **public
relations** n pubbliche relazioni fpl; **public
school** n (BRIT) scuola privata; (US) scuola
statale; **public transport** n mezzi mpl
pubblici
publish ['pʌblɪʃ] vt pubblicare; **publisher** n
editore m; **publishing** n (industry) editoria;
(of a book) pubblicazione f
pub lunch n pranzo semplice ed economico
servito nei pub
pudding ['pudɪŋ] n budino; (BRIT:
dessert) dolce m; **black ~,** (US) **blood ~**
sanguinaccio
puddle ['pʌdl] n pozza, pozzanghera
Puerto Rico ['pwə:təu'ri:kəu] n Portorico
puff [pʌf] n sbuffo ▷ vt **to ~ one's pipe**
tirare sboccate di fumo ▷ vi (pant) ansare;
puff pastry n pasta sfoglia
pull [pul] n (tug): **to give sth a ~** tirare su
qc ▷ vt tirare; (muscle) strappare; (trigger)
premere ▷ vi tirare; **to ~ to pieces** fare
a pezzi; **to ~ one's punches** (Boxing)
risparmiare l'avversario; **to ~ one's
weight** dare il proprio contributo; **to ~
o.s. together** ricomporsi, riprendersi;
to ~ sb's leg prendere in giro qn; **pull
apart** vt (break) fare a pezzi; **pull away** vi
(move off: vehicle) muoversi, partire; (boat)
staccarsi dal molo, salpare; (draw back:
person) indietreggiare; **pull back** vt (lever
etc) tirare indietro; (curtains) aprire ▷ vi
(from confrontation etc) tirarsi indietro; (Mil:
withdraw) ritirarsi; **pull down** vt (house)
demolire; (tree) abbattere; **pull in** vi (Aut:
at the kerb) accostarsi; (Rail) entrare in
stazione; **pull off** vt (clothes) togliere;
(deal etc) portare a compimento; **pull out**
vi partire; (Aut: come out of line) spostarsi
sulla mezzeria ▷ vt staccare; far uscire;
(withdraw) ritirare; **pull over** vi (Aut)

accostare; **pull up** vi (stop) fermarsi ▷ vt
(raise) sollevare; (uproot) sradicare
pulley ['pulɪ] n puleggia, carrucola
pullover ['puləʊvə'] n pullover m inv
pulp [pʌlp] n (of fruit) polpa
pulpit ['pulpɪt] n pulpito
pulse [pʌls] n polso; (Bot) legume m; ~s npl
(Culin) legumi mpl
puma ['pjuːmə] n puma m inv
pump [pʌmp] n pompa; (shoe) scarpetta
▷ vt pompare; **pump up** vt gonfiare
pumpkin ['pʌmpkɪn] n zucca
pun [pʌn] n gioco di parole
punch [pʌntʃ] n (blow) pugno; (tool)
punzone m; (drink) ponce m ▷ vt (hit): **to ~
sb/sth** dare un pugno a qn/qc; **punch-up**
(BRIT: inf) n rissa
punctual ['pʌŋktjuəl] adj puntuale
punctuation [pʌŋktjuˈeɪʃən] n
interpunzione f, punteggiatura
puncture ['pʌŋktʃə'] n foratura ▷ vt forare
Be careful not to translate *puncture*
by the Italian word *puntura*.
punish ['pʌnɪʃ] vt punire; **punishment** n
punizione f
punk [pʌŋk] n (also: ~ **rocker**) punk m/f inv;
(also: ~ **rock**) musica punk, punk rock m;
(US: inf: hoodlum) teppista m
pup [pʌp] n cucciolo(-a)
pupil ['pjuːpl] n allievo(-a); (Anat) pupilla
puppet ['pʌpɪt] n burattino
puppy ['pʌpɪ] n cucciolo(-a), cagnolino(-a)
purchase ['pəːtʃɪs] n acquisto, compera
▷ vt comprare
pure [pjuə'] adj puro(-a); **purely** ['pjuəlɪ]
adv puramente
purify ['pjuərɪfaɪ] vt purificare
purity ['pjuərɪtɪ] n purezza
purple ['pəːpl] adj di porpora; viola inv
purpose ['pəːpəs] n intenzione f, scopo; **on**
~ apposta
purr [pəː'] vi fare le fusa
purse [pəːs] n (BRIT) borsellino; (US)
borsetta ▷ vt contrarre
pursue [pəˈsjuː] vt inseguire; (fig: activity
etc) continuare con; (: aim etc) perseguire
pursuit [pəˈsjuːt] n inseguimento; (fig)
ricerca; (pastime) passatempo
pus [pʌs] n pus m
push [puʃ] n spinta; (effort) grande
sforzo; (drive) energia ▷ vt spingere;
(button) premere; (thrust): **to ~ sth (into)**
ficcare qc (in); (fig) fare pubblicità a ▷ vi
spingere; premere; **to ~ for** (fig) insistere
per; **push in** vi introdursi a forza; **push
off** (inf) vi filare; **push on** vi (continue)
continuare; **push over** vt far cadere; **push
through** vi farsi largo spingendo ▷ vt
(measure) far approvare; **pushchair** (BRIT)

n passeggino; **pusher** n (drug pusher)
spacciatore(-trice); **push-up** (US) n (press-
up) flessione f sulle braccia
pussy(-cat) ['pusɪ(-)] (inf) n micio
put [put] (pt, pp **put**) vt mettere, porre;
(say) dire, esprimere; (a question) fare;
(estimate) stimare; **put away** vt (return)
mettere a posto; **put back** vt (replace)
rimettere (a posto); (postpone) rinviare;
(delay) ritardare; **put by** vt (money)
mettere da parte; **put down** vt (parcel
etc) posare, mettere giù; (pay) versare;
(in writing) mettere per iscritto; (revolt,
animal) sopprimere; (attribute) attribuire;
put forward vt (ideas) avanzare,
proporre; **put in** vt (application, complaint)
presentare; (time, effort) mettere; **put
off** vt (postpone) rimandare, rinviare;
(discourage) dissuadere; **put on** vt (clothes,
lipstick etc) mettere; (light etc) accendere;
(play etc) mettere in scena; (food, meal)
mettere su; (brake) mettere; **to ~ on
weight** ingrassare; **to ~ on airs** darsi
delle arie; **put out** vt mettere fuori; (one's
hand) porgere; (light etc) spegnere; (person:
inconvenience) scomodare; **put through**
vt (Tel: call) passare; (: person) mettere in
comunicazione; (plan) far approvare; **put
up** vt (raise) sollevare, alzare; (: umbrella)
aprire; (: tent) montare; (pin up) affiggere;
(hang) appendere; (build) costruire, erigere;
(increase) aumentare; (accommodate)
alloggiare; **put aside** vt (lay down: book
etc) mettere da una parte, posare; (save)
mettere da parte; (in shop) tenere da
parte; **put together** vt mettere insieme,
riunire; (assemble: furniture) montare; (:
meal) improvvisare; **put up with** vt fus
sopportare
putt [pʌt] n colpo leggero; **putting green**
n green m inv; campo da putting
puzzle ['pʌzl] n enigma m, mistero;
(jigsaw) puzzle m; (also: **crossword ~**)
parole fpl incrociate, cruciverba m inv ▷ vt
confondere, rendere perplesso(-a) ▷ vi
scervellarsi; **puzzled** adj perplesso(-a);
puzzling adj (question) poco chiaro(-a);
(attitude, set of instructions) incomprensibile
pyjamas [pɪˈdʒɑːməz] (BRIT) npl pigiama m
pylon ['paɪlən] n pilone m
pyramid ['pɪrəmɪd] n piramide f
Pyrenees [pɪrɪˈniːz] npl **the ~** i Pirenei

q

quack [kwæk] n (of duck) qua qua m inv; (pej: doctor) dottoruccio(-a)

quadruple [kwɔ'drupl] vt quadruplicare ▷ vi quadruplicarsi

quail [kweɪl] n (Zool) quaglia ▷ vi (person): **to ~ at** or **before** perdersi d'animo davanti a

quaint [kweɪnt] adj bizzarro(-a); (old-fashioned) antiquato(-a); grazioso(-a), pittoresco(-a)

quake [kweɪk] vi tremare ▷ n abbr = **earthquake**

qualification [kwɔlɪfɪ'keɪʃən] n (degree etc) qualifica, titolo; (ability) competenza, qualificazione f; (limitation) riserva, restrizione f

qualified ['kwɔlɪfaɪd] adj qualificato(-a); (able): **~ to** competente in, qualificato(-a) a; (limited) condizionato(-a)

qualify ['kwɔlɪfaɪ] vt abilitare; (limit: statement) modificare, precisare ▷ vi **to ~ (as)** qualificarsi (come); **to ~ (for)** acquistare i requisiti necessari (per); (Sport) qualificarsi (per or a)

quality ['kwɔlɪtɪ] n qualità f inv

qualm [kwɑːm] n dubbio; scrupolo

quantify ['kwɔntɪfaɪ] vt quantificare

quantity ['kwɔntɪtɪ] n quantità f inv

quarantine ['kwɔrntiːn] n quarantena

quarrel ['kwɔrəl] n lite f, disputa ▷ vi litigare

quarry ['kwɔrɪ] n (for stone) cava; (animal) preda

quart [kwɔːt] n ≈ litro

quarter ['kwɔːtəʳ] n quarto; (us: coin) quarto di dollaro; (of year) trimestre m; (district) quartiere m ▷ vt dividere in quattro; (Mil) alloggiare; **~s** npl (living quarters) alloggio; (Mil) alloggi mpl, quadrato; **a ~ of an hour** un quarto d'ora; **quarter final** n quarto di finale; **quarterly** adj trimestrale ▷ adv trimestralmente

quartet(te) [kwɔː'tɛt] n quartetto

quartz [kwɔːts] n quarzo

quay [kiː] n (also: **~side**) banchina

queasy ['kwiːzɪ] adj (stomach) delicato(-a); **to feel ~** aver la nausea

queen [kwiːn] n (gen) regina; (Cards etc) regina, donna

queer [kwɪəʳ] adj strano(-a), curioso(-a) ▷ n (inf) finocchio

quench [kwɛntʃ] vt **to ~ one's thirst** dissetarsi

query ['kwɪərɪ] n domanda, questione f ▷ vt mettere in questione

quest [kwɛst] n cerca, ricerca

question ['kwɛstʃən] n domanda, questione f ▷ vt (person) interrogare; (plan, idea) mettere in questione or in dubbio; **it's a ~ of doing** si tratta di fare; **beyond ~** fuori di dubbio; **out of the ~** fuori discussione, impossibile; **questionable** adj discutibile; **question mark** n punto interrogativo; **questionnaire** [kwɛstʃə'nɛəʳ] n questionario

queue [kjuː] (BRIT) n coda, fila ▷ vi fare la coda

quiche [kiːʃ] n torta salata a base di uova, formaggio, prosciutto o altro

quick [kwɪk] adj rapido(-a), veloce; (reply) pronto(-a); (mind) pronto(-a), acuto(-a) ▷ n **cut to the ~** (fig) toccato(-a) sul vivo; **be ~!** fa presto!; **quickly** adv rapidamente, velocemente

quid [kwɪd] (BRIT: inf) n inv sterlina

quiet ['kwaɪət] adj tranquillo(-a), quieto(-a); (ceremony) semplice ▷ n tranquillità, calma ▷ vt, vi (us) = **quieten**; **keep ~!** sta zitto!; **quieten** (also: **quieten down**) vi calmarsi, chetarsi ▷ vt calmare, chetare; **quietly** adv tranquillamente, calmamente, sommessamente

quilt [kwɪlt] n trapunta; (continental quilt) piumino

quirky ['kwəːkɪ] adj stravagante

quit [kwɪt] (pt, pp **quit** or **quitted**) vt mollare; (premises) lasciare, partire da ▷ vi (give up) mollare; (resign) dimettersi

quite [kwaɪt] *adv* (*rather*) assai; (*entirely*) completamente, del tutto; **I ~ understand** capisco perfettamente; **that's not ~ big enough** non è proprio sufficiente; **~ a few of them** non pochi di loro; **~ (so)!** esatto!

quits [kwɪts] *adj* **~ (with)** pari (con); **let's call it ~** adesso siamo pari

quiver ['kwɪvə'] *vi* tremare, fremere

quiz [kwɪz] *n* (*game*) quiz *m inv*; indovinello ▷ *vt* interrogare

quota ['kwəʊtə] *n* quota

quotation [kwəʊ'teɪʃən] *n* citazione *f*; (*of shares etc*) quotazione *f*; (*estimate*) preventivo; **quotation marks** *npl* virgolette *fpl*

quote [kwəʊt] *n* citazione *f* ▷ *vt* (*sentence*) citare; (*price*) dare, fissare; (*shares*) quotare ▷ *vi* **to ~ from** citare; **~s** *npl* = **quotation marks**

rabbi ['ræbaɪ] *n* rabbino

rabbit ['ræbɪt] *n* coniglio

rabies ['reɪbiːz] *n* rabbia

RAC (BRIT) *n abbr* = **Royal Automobile Club**

rac(c)oon [rə'kuːn] *n* procione *m*

race [reɪs] *n* razza; (*competition, rush*) corsa ▷ *vt* (*horse*) far correre ▷ *vi* correre; (*engine*) imballarsi; **race car** (US) *n* = **racing car**; **racecourse** *n* campo di corse, ippodromo; **racehorse** *n* cavallo da corsa; **racetrack** *n* pista

racial ['reɪʃl] *adj* razziale

racing ['reɪsɪŋ] *n* corsa; **racing car** (BRIT) *n* macchina da corsa; **racing driver** (BRIT) *n* corridore *m* automobilista

racism ['reɪsɪzəm] *n* razzismo; **racist** *adj*, *n* razzista *m/f*

rack [ræk] *n* rastrelliera; (*also*: **luggage ~**) rete *f*, portabagagli *m inv*; (*also*: **roof ~**) portabagagli; (*dish rack*) scolapiatti *m inv* ▷ *vt* **~ed by** torturato(-a) da; **to ~ one's brains** scervellarsi

racket ['rækɪt] *n* (*for tennis*) racchetta; (*noise*) fracasso; baccano; (*swindle*) imbroglio, truffa; (*organized crime*) racket *m inv*

racquet ['rækɪt] *n* racchetta

radar ['reɪdɑː'] *n* radar *m*

radiation [reɪdɪ'eɪʃən] *n* irradiamento;

(radioactive) radiazione f
radiator ['reɪdɪeɪtər] n radiatore m
radical ['rædɪkl] adj radicale
radio ['reɪdɪəu] n radio f inv; **on the ~** alla radio; **radioactive** [reɪdɪəu'æktɪv] adj radioattivo(-a); **radio station** n stazione f radio inv
radish ['rædɪʃ] n ravanello
RAF n abbr = **Royal Air Force**
raffle ['ræfl] n lotteria
raft [rɑːft] n zattera; (also: **life ~**) zattera di salvataggio
rag [ræg] n straccio, cencio; (pej: newspaper) giornalaccio, bandiera; (for charity) iniziativa studentesca a scopo benefico; **~s** npl (torn clothes) stracci mpl, brandelli mpl
rage [reɪdʒ] n (fury) collera, furia ▷ vi (person) andare su tutte le furie; (storm) infuriare; **it's all the ~** fa furore
ragged ['rægɪd] adj (edge) irregolare; (clothes) logoro(-a); (appearance) pezzente
raid [reɪd] n (Mil) incursione f; (criminal) rapina; (by police) irruzione f ▷ vt fare un'incursione in; rapinare; fare irruzione in
rail [reɪl] n (on stair) ringhiera; (on bridge, balcony) parapetto; (of ship) battagliola; **railcard** n (BRIT) tessera di riduzione ferroviaria; **railing(s)** n(pl) ringhiere fpl; **railroad** (US) n = **railway**; **railway** (BRIT: irreg) n ferrovia; **railway line** (BRIT) n linea ferroviaria; **railway station** (BRIT) n stazione f ferroviaria
rain [reɪn] n pioggia ▷ vi piovere; **in the ~** sotto la pioggia; **it's ~ing** piove; **rainbow** n arcobaleno; **raincoat** n impermeabile m; **raindrop** n goccia di pioggia; **rainfall** n pioggia; (measurement) piovosità; **rainforest** n foresta pluviale; **rainy** adj piovoso(-a)
raise [reɪz] n aumento ▷ vt (lift) alzare; sollevare; (increase) aumentare; (a protest, doubt, question) sollevare; (cattle, family) allevare; (crop) coltivare; (army, funds) raccogliere; (loan) ottenere; **to ~ one's voice** alzare la voce
raisin ['reɪzn] n uva secca
rake [reɪk] n (tool) rastrello ▷ vt (garden) rastrellare
rally ['rælɪ] n (Pol etc) riunione f; (Aut) rally m inv; (Tennis) scambio ▷ vt riunire, radunare ▷ vi (sick person, Stock Exchange) riprendersi
RAM [ræm] n abbr (= random access memory) memoria ad accesso casuale
ram [ræm] n montone m, ariete m ▷ vt conficcare; (crash into) cozzare, sbattere contro; percuotere; speronare
Ramadan [ræmə'dæn] n Ramadan m inv

ramble ['ræmbl] n escursione f ▷ vi (pej: also: ~ **on**) divagare; **rambler** n escursionista m/f; (Bot) rosa rampicante; **rambling** adj (speech) sconnesso(-a); (house) tutto(-a) a nicchie e corridoi; (Bot) rampicante
ramp [ræmp] n rampa; **on/off ~** (US Aut) raccordo di entrata/uscita
rampage [ræm'peɪdʒ] n **to go on the ~** scatenarsi in modo violento
ran [ræn] pt of **run**
ranch [rɑːntʃ] n ranch m inv
random ['rændəm] adj fatto(-a) or detto(-a) per caso; (Comput, Math) casuale ▷ n **at ~** a casaccio
rang [ræŋ] pt of **ring**
range [reɪndʒ] n (of mountains) catena; (of missile, voice) portata; (of proposals, products) gamma; (Mil: also: **shooting ~**) campo di tiro; (also: **kitchen ~**) fornello, cucina economica ▷ vt disporre ▷ vi **to ~ over** coprire; **to ~ from ... to** andare da ... a
ranger ['reɪndʒər] n guardia forestale
rank [ræŋk] n fila; (status, Mil) grado; (BRIT: also: **taxi ~**) posteggio di taxi ▷ vi **to ~ among** essere tra ▷ adj puzzolente; vero(-a) e proprio(-a); **the ~ and file** (fig) la gran massa
ransom ['rænsəm] n riscatto; **to hold sb to ~** (fig) esercitare pressione su qn
rant [rænt] vi vociare
rap [ræp] vt bussare a; picchiare su ▷ n (music) rap m inv
rape [reɪp] n violenza carnale, stupro; (Bot) ravizzone m ▷ vt violentare
rapid ['ræpɪd] adj rapido(-a); **rapidly** adv rapidamente; **rapids** npl (Geo) rapida
rapist ['reɪpɪst] n violentatore m
rapport [ræ'pɔːr] n rapporto
rare [rɛər] adj raro(-a); (Culin: steak) al sangue; **rarely** ['rɛəlɪ] adv raramente
rash [ræʃ] adj imprudente, sconsiderato(-a) ▷ n (Med) eruzione f; (of events etc) scoppio
rasher ['ræʃər] n fetta sottile (di lardo or prosciutto)
raspberry ['rɑːzbərɪ] n lampone m
rat [ræt] n ratto
rate [reɪt] n (proportion) tasso, percentuale f; (speed) velocità f inv; (price) tariffa ▷ vt giudicare; stimare; **~s** npl (BRIT: property tax) imposte fpl comunali; (fees) tariffe fpl; **to ~ sb/sth as** valutare qn/qc come
rather ['rɑːðər] adv piuttosto; **it's ~ expensive** è piuttosto caro; (too) è un po' caro; **there's ~ a lot** ce n'è parecchio; **I would** or **I'd ~ go** preferirei andare
rating ['reɪtɪŋ] n (assessment) valutazione f; (score) punteggio di merito; **~s** npl (Radio,

TV) indice *m* di ascolto
ratio ['reɪʃɪəu] *n* proporzione *f*, rapporto
ration ['ræʃən] *n (gen pl)* razioni *fpl* ▷ *vt*
razionare; **~s** *npl* razioni *fpl*
rational ['ræʃənl] *adj* razionale,
ragionevole; *(solution, reasoning)* logico(-a)
rattle ['rætl] *n* tintinnio; *(louder)* strepito;
(for baby) sonaglino ▷ *vi* risuonare,
tintinnare; fare un rumore di ferraglia ▷ *vt*
scuotere (con strepito)
rave [reɪv] *vi (in anger)* infuriarsi; *(with
enthusiasm)* andare in estasi; *(Med)* delirare
▷ *n (BRIT: inf: party)* rave *m inv*
raven ['reɪvən] *n* corvo
ravine [rə'viːn] *n* burrone *m*
raw [rɔː] *adj (uncooked)* crudo(-a); *(not
processed)* greggio(-a); *(sore)* vivo(-a);
(inexperienced) inesperto(-a); *(weather, day)*
gelido(-a)
ray [reɪ] *n* raggio; **a ~ of hope** un barlume
di speranza
razor ['reɪzər] *n* rasoio; **razor blade** *n* lama
di rasoio
Rd *abbr* = **road**
re [riː] *prep* con riferimento a
RE *n abbr (BRIT Mil:* = *Royal Engineers)* ≈ G.
M. *(Genio Militare)*; *(BRIT)* = **religious
education**
reach [riːtʃ] *n* portata; *(of river etc)* tratto
▷ *vt* raggiungere; arrivare a ▷ *vi* stendersi;
out of/within ~ fuori/a portata di mano;
within ~ of the shops/station vicino ai
negozi/alla stazione; **reach out** *vt* (hand)
allungare ▷ *vi* **to ~ out for** stendere la
mano per prendere
react [riː'ækt] *vi* reagire; **reaction**
[-'ækʃən] *n* reazione *f*; **reactor** [riː'æktər]
n reattore *m*
read [riːd, *pt, pp* rɛd] *(pt, pp* **read)** *vi* leggere
▷ *vt* leggere; *(understand)* intendere,
interpretare; *(study)* studiare; **read
out** *vt* leggere ad alta voce; **reader** *n*
lettore(-trice); *(BRIT: at university)* professore
con funzioni preminenti di ricerca
readily ['redɪlɪ] *adv* volentieri; *(easily)*
facilmente; *(quickly)* prontamente
reading ['riːdɪŋ] *n* lettura; *(understanding)*
interpretazione *f*; *(on instrument)*
indicazione *f*
ready ['redɪ] *adj* pronto(-a); *(willing)*
pronto(-a), disposto(-a); *(available)*
disponibile ▷ *n* **at the ~** *(Mil)* pronto a
sparare; **when will my photos be ~?**
quando saranno pronte le mie foto?; **to
get ~** *vi* prepararsi ▷ *vt* preparare; **ready-
made** *adj* prefabbricato(-a); *(clothes)*
confezionato(-a)
real [rɪəl] *adj* reale; vero(-a); **in ~ terms**
in realtà; **real ale** *n* birra ad effervescenza

naturale; **real estate** *n* beni *mpl* immobili;
realistic [-'lɪstɪk] *adj* realistico(-a);
reality [riː'ælɪtɪ] *n* realtà *f inv*
realization [rɪəlaɪ'zeɪʃən] *n* presa di
coscienza; realizzazione *f*
realize ['rɪəlaɪz] *vt (understand)* rendersi
conto di
really ['rɪəlɪ] *adv* veramente, davvero; **~!**
(indicating annoyance) oh, insomma!
realm [relm] *n* reame *m*, regno
Realtor® ['rɪəltɔːr] *(US)* *n* agente *m*
immobiliare
reappear [riːə'pɪər] *vi* ricomparire,
riapparire
rear [rɪər] *adj* di dietro; *(Aut: wheel etc)*
posteriore ▷ *n* di dietro, parte *f* posteriore
▷ *vt (cattle, family)* allevare ▷ *vi (also: ~ up*:
animal) impennarsi
rearrange [riːə'reɪndʒ] *vt* riordinare
rear: **rear-view mirror** ['rɪəvjuː-] *n (Aut)*
specchio retrovisore; **rear-wheel drive** *n*
trazione *fpl* posteriore
reason ['riːzn] *n* ragione *f*; *(cause, motive)*
ragione, motivo ▷ *vi* **to ~ with sb** far
ragionare qn; **it stands to ~ that** è
ovvio che; **reasonable** *adj* ragionevole;
(not bad) accettabile; **reasonably**
adv ragionevolmente; **reasoning** *n*
ragionamento
reassurance [riːə'ʃuərəns] *n*
rassicurazione *f*
reassure [riːə'ʃuər] *vt* rassicurare; **to ~ sb
of** rassicurare qn di *or* su
rebate ['riːbeɪt] *n (on tax etc)* sgravio
rebel [*n* 'rɛbl, *vb* rɪ'bɛl] *n* ribelle *m/f*
▷ *vi* ribellarsi; **rebellion** *n* ribellione *f*;
rebellious *adj* ribelle
rebuild [riː'bɪld] *vt irreg* ricostruire
recall [rɪ'kɔːl] *vt* richiamare; *(remember)*
ricordare, richiamare alla mente ▷ *n*
richiamo
rec'd *abbr* = **received**
receipt [rɪ'siːt] *n (document)* ricevuta; *(act
of receiving)* ricevimento; **~s** *npl (Comm)*
introiti *mpl*; **can I have a ~, please?** posso
avere una ricevuta, per favore?
receive [rɪ'siːv] *vt* ricevere; *(guest)*
ricevere, accogliere; **receiver** [rɪ'siː-
vər] *n (Tel)* ricevitore *m*; *(Radio, TV)*
apparecchio ricevente; *(of stolen goods)*
ricettatore(-trice); *(Comm)* curatore *m*
fallimentare
recent ['riːsnt] *adj* recente; **recently** *adv*
recentemente
reception [rɪ'sɛpʃən] *n* ricevimento;
(welcome) accoglienza; *(TV etc)* ricezione
f; **reception desk** *n (in hotel)* reception *f*
inv; *(in hospital, at doctor's)* accettazione *f*;
(in offices etc) portineria; **receptionist** *n*

receptionist m/f inv

recession [rɪ'sɛʃən] n recessione f

recharge [riː'tʃɑːdʒ] vt (battery) ricaricare

recipe ['rɛsɪpɪ] n ricetta

recipient [rɪ'sɪpɪənt] n beneficiario(-a); (of letter) destinatario(-a)

recital [rɪ'saɪtl] n recital m inv

recite [rɪ'saɪt] vt (poem) recitare

reckless ['rɛkləs] adj (driver etc) spericolato(-a); (spending) folle

reckon ['rɛkən] vt (count) calcolare; (think): **I ~ that ...** penso che ...

reclaim [rɪ'kleɪm] vt (demand back) richiedere, reclamare; (land) bonificare; (materials) recuperare

recline [rɪ'klaɪn] vi stare sdraiato(-a)

recognition [rɛkəg'nɪʃən] n riconoscimento; **transformed beyond ~** irriconoscibile

recognize ['rɛkəgnaɪz] vt **to ~ (by/as)** riconoscere (a o/da/come)

recollection [rɛkə'lɛkʃən] n ricordo

recommend [rɛkə'mɛnd] vt raccomandare; (advise) consigliare; **can you ~ a good restaurant?** mi può consigliare un buon ristorante?; **recommendation** [rɛkəmɛn'deɪʃən] n raccomandazione f; consiglio

reconcile ['rɛkənsaɪl] vt (two people) riconciliare; (two facts) conciliare, quadrare; **to ~ o.s. to** rassegnarsi a

reconsider [riːkən'sɪdəʳ] vt riconsiderare

reconstruct [riːkən'strʌkt] vt ricostruire

record [n 'rɛkɔːd, vb rɪ'kɔːd] n ricordo, documento; (of meeting etc) nota, verbale m; (register) registro; (file) pratica, dossier m inv; (Comput) record m inv; (also: **criminal ~**) fedina penale sporca; (Mus: disc) disco; (Sport) record m inv, primato ▷ vt (set down) prendere nota di, registrare; (Mus: song etc) registrare; **in ~ time** a tempo di record; **off the ~** adj ufficioso(-a) ▷ adv ufficiosamente; **recorded delivery** (BRIT) n (Post): **recorded delivery letter** etc lettera etc raccomandata; **recorder** n (Mus) flauto diritto; **recording** n (Mus) registrazione f; **record player** n giradischi m inv

recount [rɪ'kaunt] vt raccontare, narrare

recover [rɪ'kʌvəʳ] vt ricuperare ▷ vi **to ~ (from)** riprendersi (da); **recovery** [rɪ'kʌvərɪ] n ricupero; ristabilimento; ripresa

⬛ Be careful not to translate **recover** by the Italian word **ricoverare**.

recreate [riː'krieɪt] vt ricreare

recreation [rɛkrɪ'eɪʃən] n ricreazione f; svago; **recreational drug** [rɛkrɪ'eɪʃənl-] n sostanza stupefacente usata a scopo ricreativo;

recreational vehicle (US) n camper m inv

recruit [rɪ'kruːt] n recluta; (in company) nuovo(-a) assunto(-a) ▷ vt reclutare; **recruitment** n reclutamento

rectangle ['rɛktæŋgl] n rettangolo; **rectangular** [-'tæŋgjuləʳ] adj rettangolare

rectify ['rɛktɪfaɪ] vt (error) rettificare; (omission) riparare

rector ['rɛktəʳ] n (Rel) parroco (anglicano)

recur [rɪ'kəːʳ] vi riaccadere; (symptoms) ripresentarsi; **recurring** adj (Math) periodico(-a)

recyclable [riː'saɪkləbl] adj riciclabile

recycle [riː'saɪkl] vt riciclare

recycling [riː'saɪklɪŋ] n riciclaggio

red [rɛd] n rosso; (Pol: pej) rosso(-a) ▷ adj rosso(-a); **in the ~** (account) scoperto; (business) in deficit; **Red Cross** n Croce f Rossa; **redcurrant** n ribes m inv

redeem [rɪ'diːm] vt (debt) riscattare; (sth in pawn) ritirare; (fig, also Rel) redimere

red: **red-haired** [-'hɛəd] adj dai capelli rossi; **redhead** ['rɛdhɛd] n rosso(-a); **red-hot** adj arroventato(-a); **red light** n **to go through a red light** (Aut) passare col rosso; **red-light district** ['rɛdlaɪt-] n quartiere m a luci rosse; **red meat** n carne f rossa

reduce [rɪ'djuːs] vt ridurre; (lower) ridurre, abbassare; **"~ speed now"** (Aut) "rallentare"; **at a ~d price** scontato(-a); **reduced** (decreased) ridotto(-a); **at a reduced price** a prezzo ribassato or ridotto; **"greatly reduced prices"** "grandi ribassi"; **reduction** [rɪ'dʌkʃən] n riduzione f; (of price) ribasso; (discount) sconto; **is there a reduction for children/ students?** ci sono riduzioni per i bambini/ gli studenti?

redundancy [rɪ'dʌndənsɪ] n licenziamento

redundant [rɪ'dʌndnt] adj (worker) licenziato(-a); (detail, object) superfluo(-a); **to be made ~** essere licenziato (per eccesso di personale)

reed [riːd] n (Bot) canna; (Mus: of clarinet etc) ancia

reef [riːf] n (at sea) scogliera

reel [riːl] n bobina, rocchetto; (Fishing) mulinello; (Cinema) rotolo; (dance) danza veloce scozzese ▷ vi (sway) barcollare

ref [rɛf] (inf) n abbr (= referee) arbitro

refectory [rɪ'fɛktərɪ] n refettorio

refer [rɪ'fəːʳ] vt **to ~ sth to** (dispute, decision) deferire qc a; **to ~ sb to** (inquirer, Med: patient) indirizzare qn a; (reader: to text) rimandare qn a ▷ vi **to ~ to** (allude to) accennare a; (consult) rivolgersi a

referee [rɛfə'riː] n arbitro; (BRIT: for job application) referenza ▷ vt arbitrare

reference ['rɛfrəns] n riferimento; (mention) menzione f, allusione f; (for job application) referenza; **with ~ to** (Comm: in letter) in or con riferimento a; **reference number** n numero di riferimento

refill [vb riː'fɪl, n 'riː'fɪl] vt riempire di nuovo; (pen, lighter etc) ricaricare ▷ n (for pen etc) ricambio

refine [rɪ'faɪn] vt raffinare; **refined** adj (person, taste) raffinato(-a); **refinery** n raffineria

reflect [rɪ'flɛkt] vt (light, image) riflettere; (fig) rispecchiare ▷ vi (think) riflettere, considerare; **it ~s badly/well on him** si ripercuote su di lui in senso negativo/positivo; **reflection** [-'flɛkʃən] n riflessione f; (image) riflesso; (criticism): **reflection on** giudizio su; attacco a; **on reflection** pensandoci sopra

reflex ['riːflɛks] adj riflesso(-a) ▷ n riflesso

reform [rɪ'fɔːm] n (of sinner etc) correzione f; (of law etc) riforma ▷ vt correggere; riformare

refrain [rɪ'freɪn] vi **to ~ from doing** trattenersi dal fare ▷ n ritornello

refresh [rɪ'frɛʃ] vt rinfrescare; (food, sleep) ristorare; **refreshing** adj (drink) rinfrescante; (sleep) riposante, ristoratore(-trice); **refreshments** npl rinfreschi mpl

refrigerator [rɪ'frɪdʒəreɪtəʳ] n frigorifero

refuel [riː'fjuəl] vi far rifornimento (di carburante)

refuge ['rɛfjuːdʒ] n rifugio; **to take ~ in** rifugiarsi in; **refugee** [rɛfju'dʒiː] n rifugiato(-a), profugo(-a)

refund [n 'riː'fʌnd, vb riː'fʌnd] n rimborso ▷ vt rimborsare

refurbish [riː'fəːbɪʃ] vt rimettere a nuovo

refusal [rɪ'fjuːzəl] n rifiuto; **to have first ~ on** avere il diritto d'opzione su

refuse¹ [n 'rɛfjuːs, vb rɪ'fjuːz] n rifiuti mpl ▷ vt, vi rifiutare; **to ~ to do** rifiutare di fare

regain [rɪ'geɪn] vt riguadagnare; riacquistare, ricuperare

regard [rɪ'gɑːd] n riguardo, stima ▷ vt considerare, stimare; **to give one's ~s to** porgere i suoi saluti a; **"with kindest ~s"** "cordiali saluti"; **regarding** prep riguardo a, per quanto riguarda; **regardless** adv lo stesso; **regardless of** a dispetto di, nonostante

regenerate [rɪ'dʒɛnəreɪt] vt rigenerare

reggae ['rɛgeɪ] n reggae m

regiment ['rɛdʒɪmənt] n reggimento

region ['riːdʒən] n regione f; **in the ~ of** (fig) all'incirca di; **regional** adj regionale

register ['rɛdʒɪstəʳ] n registro; (also: **electoral ~**) lista elettorale ▷ vt registrare; (vehicle) immatricolare; (letter) assicurare; (instrument) segnare ▷ vi iscriversi; (at hotel) firmare il registro; (make impression) entrare in testa; **registered** (BRIT) adj (letter) assicurato(-a)

registrar ['rɛdʒɪstrɑːʳ] n ufficiale m di stato civile; segretario

registration [rɛdʒɪs'treɪʃən] n (act) registrazione f; iscrizione f; (Aut: also: ~ **number**) numero di targa

registry office (BRIT) n anagrafe f; **to get married in a ~** ≈ sposarsi in municipio

regret [rɪ'grɛt] n rimpianto, rincrescimento ▷ vt rimpiangere; **regrettable** adj deplorevole

regular ['rɛgjuləʳ] adj regolare; (usual) abituale, normale; (soldier) dell'esercito regolare ▷ n (client etc) cliente m/f abituale; **regularly** adv regolarmente

regulate ['rɛgjuleɪt] vt regolare; **regulation** [-'leɪʃən] n regolazione f; (rule) regola, regolamento

rehabilitation ['riːhəbɪlɪ'teɪʃən] n (of offender) riabilitazione f; (of disabled) riadattamento

rehearsal [rɪ'həːsəl] n prova

rehearse [rɪ'həːs] vt provare

reign [reɪn] n regno ▷ vi regnare

reimburse [riːɪm'bəːs] vt rimborsare

rein [reɪn] n (for horse) briglia

reincarnation [riːɪnkɑː'neɪʃən] n reincarnazione f

reindeer ['reɪndɪəʳ] n inv renna

reinforce [riːɪn'fɔːs] vt rinforzare; **reinforcements** npl (Mil) rinforzi mpl

reinstate [riːɪn'steɪt] vt reintegrare

reject [n 'riːdʒɛkt, vb rɪ'dʒɛkt] n (Comm) scarto ▷ vt rifiutare, respingere; (Comm: goods) scartare; **rejection** [rɪ'dʒɛkʃən] n rifiuto

rejoice [rɪ'dʒɔɪs] vi **to ~ (at or over)** provare diletto in

relate [rɪ'leɪt] vt (tell) raccontare; (connect) collegare ▷ vi **to ~ to** (connect) riferirsi a; (get on with) stabilire un rapporto con; **relating to** che riguarda, rispetto a; **related** adj **related (to)** imparentato(-a) (con); collegato(-a) or connesso(-a) (a)

relation [rɪ'leɪʃən] n (person) parente m/f; (link) rapporto, relazione f; **~s** npl (relatives) parenti mpl; **relationship** n rapporto; (personal ties) rapporti mpl, relazioni fpl; (also: **family relationship**) legami mpl di parentela

relative ['rɛlətɪv] n parente m/f ▷ adj relativo(-a); (respective) rispettivo(-a); **relatively** adv relativamente; (fairly, *rather)* abbastanza

relax [rɪˈlæks] *vi* rilasciarsi; (*person: unwind*) rilassarsi ▷ *vt* rilasciare; (*mind, person*) rilassare; **relaxation** [riːlækˈseɪʃən] *n* rilasciamento; rilassamento; (*entertainment*) ricreazione *f*, svago; **relaxed** *adj* rilassato(-a); **relaxing** *adj* rilassante

relay [ˈriːleɪ] *n* (*Sport*) corsa a staffetta ▷ *vt* (*message*) trasmettere

release [rɪˈliːs] *n* (*from prison*) rilascio; (*from obligation*) liberazione *f*; (*of gas etc*) emissione *f*; (*of film etc*) distribuzione *f*; (*record*) disco; (*device*) disinnesto ▷ *vt* (*prisoner*) rilasciare; (*from obligation, wreckage etc*) liberare; (*book, film*) fare uscire; (*news*) rendere pubblico(-a); (*gas etc*) emettere; (*Tech: catch, spring etc*) disinnestare

relegate [ˈrɛləgeɪt] *vt* relegare; (*BRIT Sport*): **to be ~d** essere retrocesso(-a)

relent [rɪˈlɛnt] *vi* cedere; **relentless** *adj* implacabile

relevant [ˈrɛləvənt] *adj* pertinente; (*chapter*) in questione; **~ to** pertinente a

▌ Be careful not to translate **relevant** by the Italian word **rilevante**.

reliable [rɪˈlaɪəbl] *adj* (*person, firm*) fidato(-a), che dà affidamento; (*method*) sicuro(-a); (*machine*) affidabile

relic [ˈrɛlɪk] *n* (*Rel*) reliquia; (*of the past*) resto

relief [rɪˈliːf] *n* (*from pain, anxiety*) sollievo; (*help, supplies*) soccorsi *mpl*; (*Art, Geo*) rilievo

relieve [rɪˈliːv] *vt* (*pain, patient*) sollevare; (*bring help*) soccorrere; (*take over from: gen*) sostituire; (: *guard*) rilevare; **to ~ sb of sth** (*load*) alleggerire qn di qc; **to ~ o.s.** fare i propri bisogni; **relieved** *adj* sollevato(-a); **to be relieved that ...** essere sollevato(-a) (dal fatto) che ...; **I'm relieved to hear it** mi hai tolto un peso con questa notizia

religion [rɪˈlɪdʒən] *n* religione *f*

religious [rɪˈlɪdʒəs] *adj* religioso(-a); **religious education** *n* religione *f*

relish [ˈrɛlɪʃ] *n* (*Culin*) condimento; (*enjoyment*) gran piacere *m* ▷ *vt* (*food etc*) godere; **to ~ doing** adorare fare

relocate [ˈriːləʊkeɪt] *vt* trasferire ▷ *vi* trasferirsi

reluctance [rɪˈlʌktəns] *n* riluttanza

reluctant [rɪˈlʌktənt] *adj* riluttante, mal disposto(-a); **reluctantly** *adv* di mala voglia, a malincuore

rely [rɪˈlaɪ]: **to ~ on** *vt fus* contare su; (*be dependent*) dipendere da

remain [rɪˈmeɪn] *vi* restare, rimanere; **remainder** *n* resto; (*Comm*) rimanenza; **remaining** *adj* che rimane; **remains** *npl*

resti *mpl*

remand [rɪˈmɑːnd] *n* **on ~** in detenzione preventiva ▷ *vt* **to ~ in custody** rinviare in carcere; trattenere a disposizione della legge

remark [rɪˈmɑːk] *n* osservazione *f* ▷ *vt* osservare, dire; **remarkable** *adj* notevole; eccezionale

remarry [riːˈmærɪ] *vi* risposarsi

remedy [ˈrɛmədɪ] *n* **~ (for)** rimedio (per) ▷ *vt* rimediare a

remember [rɪˈmɛmbəʳ] *vt* ricordare, ricordarsi di; **~ me to him** salutalo da parte mia; **Remembrance Day** [rɪˈmɛmbrəns-] *n* 11 novembre, giorno della commemorazione dei caduti in guerra

● **REMEMBRANCE DAY**

● In Gran Bretagna, il **Remembrance Day** è un giorno di commemorazione dei caduti in guerra. Si celebra ogni anno la domenica più vicina all'11 novembre, anniversario della firma dell'armistizio con la Germania nel 1918.

remind [rɪˈmaɪnd] *vt* **to ~ sb of sth** ricordare qc a qn; **to ~ sb to do** ricordare a qn di fare; **reminder** *n* richiamo; (*note etc*) promemoria *m inv*

reminiscent [rɛmɪˈnɪsnt] *adj* **~ of** che fa pensare a, che richiama

remnant [ˈrɛmnənt] *n* resto, avanzo

remorse [rɪˈmɔːs] *n* rimorso

remote [rɪˈməʊt] *adj* remoto(-a), lontano(-a); (*person*) distaccato(-a); **remote control** *n* telecomando; **remotely** *adv* remotamente; (*slightly*) vagamente

removal [rɪˈmuːvəl] *n* (*taking away*) rimozione *f*; soppressione *f*; (*BRIT: from house*) trasloco; (*from office: dismissal*) destituzione *f*; (*Med*) ablazione *f*; **removal man** (*irreg*) *n* (*BRIT*) addetto ai traslochi; **removal van** (*BRIT*) *n* furgone *m* per traslochi

remove [rɪˈmuːv] *vt* togliere, rimuovere; (*employee*) destituire; (*stain*) far sparire; (*doubt, abuse*) sopprimere, eliminare

Renaissance [rɪˈneɪsɑːns] *n* **the ~** il Rinascimento

rename [riːˈneɪm] *vt* ribattezzare

render [ˈrɛndəʳ] *vt* rendere

rendezvous [ˈrɒndɪvuː] *n* appuntamento; (*place*) luogo d'incontro; (*meeting*) incontro

renew [rɪˈnjuː] *vt* rinnovare; (*negotiations*) riprendere

renovate [ˈrɛnəveɪt] *vt* rinnovare; (*art work*) restaurare

renowned [rɪ'naund] adj rinomato(-a)
rent [rɛnt] n affitto ▷ vt (take for rent)
prendere in affitto; (also: ~ **out**) dare in
affitto; **rental** n (for television, car) fitto
reorganize [riː'ɔːgənaɪz] vt riorganizzare
rep [rɛp] n abbr (Comm: = representative)
rappresentante m/f; (Theatre: = repertory)
teatro di repertorio
repair [rɪ'pɛər] n riparazione f ▷ vt
riparare; **in good/bad ~** in buone/cattive
condizioni; **where can I get this ~ed?**
dove lo posso far riparare?; **repair kit** n
corredo per riparazioni
repay [riː'peɪ] (irreg) vt (money, creditor)
rimborsare, ripagare; (sb's efforts)
ricompensare; (favour) ricambiare;
repayment n pagamento; rimborso
repeat [rɪ'piːt] n (Radio, TV) replica ▷ vt
ripetere; (pattern) riprodurre; (promise,
attack, also Comm: order) rinnovare
▷ vi ripetere; **can you ~ that, please?**
può ripetere, per favore?; **repeatedly**
adv ripetutamente, spesso; **repeat
prescription** n (BRIT) ricetta ripetibile
repellent [rɪ'pɛlənt] adj repellente ▷ n
insect ~ prodotto m anti-insetti inv
repercussions [riːpə'kʌʃənz] npl
ripercussioni fpl
repetition [rɛpɪ'tɪʃən] n ripetizione f
repetitive [rɪ'pɛtɪtɪv] adj (movement) che
si ripete; (work) monotono(-a); (speech)
pieno(-a) di ripetizioni
replace [rɪ'pleɪs] vt (put back) rimettere
a posto; (take the place of) sostituire;
replacement n rimessa; sostituzione f;
(person) sostituto(-a)
replay ['riːpleɪ] n (of match) partita
ripetuta; (of tape, film) replay m inv
replica ['rɛplɪkə] n replica, copia
reply [rɪ'plaɪ] n risposta ▷ vi rispondere
report [rɪ'pɔːt] n rapporto; (Press etc)
cronaca; (BRIT: also: **school ~**) pagella; (of
gun) sparo ▷ vt riportare; (Press etc) fare
una cronaca su; (bring to notice: occurrence)
segnalare; (: person) denunciare ▷ vi (make
a report) fare un rapporto (or una cronaca);
(present o.s.): **to ~ (to sb)** presentarsi (a
qn); **I'd like to ~ a theft** vorrei denunciare
un furto; **report card** (US, Scottish) n
pagella; **reportedly** adv stando a quanto
si dice; **he reportedly told them to
…** avrebbe detto loro di …; **reporter** n
reporter m inv
represent [rɛprɪ'zɛnt] vt rappresentare;
representation [-'teɪʃən] n
rappresentazione f; (petition)
rappresentanza; **representative** n
rappresentante m/f; (US Pol) deputato(-a)
▷ adj rappresentativo(-a)

repress [rɪ'prɛs] vt reprimere; **repression**
[-'prɛʃən] n repressione f
reprimand ['rɛprɪmɑːnd] n rimprovero
▷ vt rimproverare
reproduce [riːprə'djuːs] vt riprodurre ▷ vi
riprodursi; **reproduction** [-'dʌkʃən] n
riproduzione f
reptile ['rɛptaɪl] n rettile m
republic [rɪ'pʌblɪk] n repubblica;
republican adj, n repubblicano(-a)
reputable ['rɛpjutəbl] adj di buona
reputazione; (occupation) rispettabile
reputation [rɛpju'teɪʃən] n reputazione f
request [rɪ'kwɛst] n domanda; (formal)
richiesta ▷ vt **to ~ (of or from sb)** chiedere
(a qn); **request stop** (BRIT) n (for bus)
fermata facoltativa or a richiesta
require [rɪ'kwaɪər] vt (need: person) aver
bisogno di; (: thing, situation) richiedere;
(want) volere; esigere; (order): **to ~ sb to do
sth** ordinare a qn di fare qc; **requirement**
n esigenza; bisogno; requisito
resat [riː'sæt] pt, pp of **resit**
rescue ['rɛskjuː] n salvataggio; (help)
soccorso ▷ vt salvare
research [rɪ'səːtʃ] n ricerca, ricerche fpl
▷ vt fare ricerche su
resemblance [rɪ'zɛmbləns] n somiglianza
resemble [rɪ'zɛmbl] vt assomigliare a
resent [rɪ'zɛnt] vt risentirsi di; **resentful**
adj pieno(-a) di risentimento; **resentment**
n risentimento
reservation [rɛzə'veɪʃən] n (booking)
prenotazione f; (doubt) dubbio; (protected
area) riserva; (BRIT: on road: also: **central ~**)
spartitraffico m inv; **reservation desk** (US)
n (in hotel) reception f inv
reserve [rɪ'zəːv] n riserva ▷ vt (seats etc)
prenotare; **reserved** adj (shy) riservato(-a)
reservoir ['rɛzəvwɑː'] n serbatoio
residence ['rɛzɪdəns] n residenza;
residence permit (BRIT) n permesso di
soggiorno
resident ['rɛzɪdənt] n residente m/f; (in
hotel) cliente m/f fisso(-a) ▷ adj residente;
(doctor) fisso(-a); (course, college) a tempo
pieno con pernottamento; **residential** [-
'dɛnʃəl] adj di residenza; (area) residenziale
residue ['rɛzɪdjuː] n resto; (Chem, Physics)
residuo
resign [rɪ'zaɪn] vt (one's post) dimettersi da
▷ vi dimettersi; **to ~ o.s. to** rassegnarsi a;
resignation [rɛzɪg'neɪʃən] n dimissioni
fpl; rassegnazione f
resin ['rɛzɪn] n resina
resist [rɪ'zɪst] vt resistere a; **resistance** n
resistenza
resit ['riːsɪt] (BRIT) (pt, pp **resat**) vt (exam)
ripresentarsi a; (subject) ridare l'esame di

▷ n **he's got his French ~ on Friday** deve ridare l'esame di francese venerdì
resolution [rɛzə'luːʃən] n risoluzione f
resolve [rɪ'zɔlv] n risoluzione f ▷ vi (decide): **to ~ to do** decidere di fare ▷ vt (problem) risolvere
resort [rɪ'zɔːt] n (town) stazione f; (recourse) ricorso ▷ vi **to ~ to** aver ricorso a; **in the last ~** come ultima risorsa
resource [rɪ'sɔːs] n risorsa; **resourceful** adj pieno(-a) di risorse, intraprendente
respect [rɪs'pɛkt] n rispetto ▷ vt rispettare; **respectable** adj rispettabile; **respectful** adj rispettoso(-a); **respective** [rɪs'pɛktɪv] adj rispettivo(-a); **respectively** adv rispettivamente
respite ['rɛspaɪt] n respiro, tregua
respond [rɪs'pɔnd] vi rispondere; **response** [rɪs'pɔns] n risposta
responsibility [rɪspɔnsɪ'bɪlɪtɪ] n responsabilità f inv
responsible [rɪs'pɔnsɪbl] adj (trustworthy) fidato(-a); (job) di (grande) responsabilità; **~ (for)** responsabile (di); **responsibly** adv responsabilmente
responsive [rɪs'pɔnsɪv] adj che reagisce
rest [rɛst] n riposo; (stop) sosta, pausa; (Mus) pausa; (object: to support sth) appoggio, sostegno; (remainder) resto, avanzi mpl ▷ vi riposarsi; (remain) rimanere, restare; (be supported): **to ~ on** appoggiarsi su ▷ vt (far) riposare; (lean): **to ~ sth on/against** appoggiare qc su/contro; **the ~ of them** gli altri; **it ~s with him to decide** sta a lui decidere
restaurant ['rɛstərɔŋ] n ristorante m; **restaurant car** (BRIT) n vagone m ristorante
restless ['rɛstlɪs] adj agitato(-a), irrequieto(-a)
restoration [rɛstə'reɪʃən] n restauro; restituzione f
restore [rɪ'stɔːʳ] vt (building, to power) restaurare; (sth stolen) restituire; (peace, health) ristorare
restrain [rɪs'treɪn] vt (feeling, growth) contenere, frenare; (person): **to ~ (from doing)** trattenere (dal fare); **restraint** n (restriction) limitazione f; (moderation) ritegno; (of style) contenutezza
restrict [rɪs'trɪkt] vt restringere, limitare; **restriction** [-kʃən] n **restriction (on)** restrizione f (di), limitazione f
rest room (US) n toletta
restructure [riː'strʌktʃəʳ] vt ristrutturare
result [rɪ'zʌlt] n risultato ▷ vi **to ~ in** avere per risultato; **as a ~ of** in or di conseguenza a, in seguito a
resume [rɪ'zjuːm] vt, vi (work, journey) riprendere

résumé ['reɪzjumeɪ] n riassunto; (US) curriculum m inv vitae
resuscitate [rɪ'sʌsɪteɪt] vt (Med) risuscitare
retail ['riːteɪl] adj, adv al minuto ▷ vt vendere al minuto; **retailer** n commerciante m/f al minuto, dettagliante m/f
retain [rɪ'teɪn] vt (keep) tenere, serbare
retaliation [rɪtælɪ'eɪʃən] n rappresaglie fpl
retarded [rɪ'tɑːdɪd] adj ritardato(-a)
retire [rɪ'taɪəʳ] vi (give up work) andare in pensione; (withdraw) ritirarsi, andarsene; (go to bed) andare a letto, ritirarsi; **retired** adj (person) pensionato(-a); **retirement** n pensione f; (act) pensionamento
retort [rɪ'tɔːt] vi rimbeccare
retreat [rɪ'triːt] n ritirata; (place) rifugio ▷ vi battere in ritirata
retrieve [rɪ'triːv] vt (sth lost) ricuperare, ritrovare; (situation, honour) salvare; (error, loss) rimediare a
retrospect ['rɛtrəspɛkt] n **in ~** guardando indietro; **retrospective** [-'spɛktɪv] adj retrospettivo(-a); (law) retroattivo(-a)
return [rɪ'təːn] n (going or coming back) ritorno; (of sth stolen etc) restituzione f; (Finance: from land, shares) profitto, reddito ▷ cpd (journey, match) di ritorno; (BRIT: ticket) di andata e ritorno ▷ vi tornare, ritornare ▷ vt rendere, restituire; (bring back) riportare; (send back) mandare indietro; (put back) rimettere; (Pol: candidate) eleggere; **~s** npl (Comm) incassi mpl; profitti mpl; **in ~ (for)** in cambio (di); **by ~ of post** a stretto giro di posta; **many happy ~s (of the day)!** cento di questi giorni!; **return ticket** n (esp BRIT) biglietto di andata e ritorno
reunion [riː'juːnɪən] n riunione f
reunite [riːju'naɪt] vt riunire
revamp ['riː'væmp] vt (firm) riorganizzare
reveal [rɪ'viːl] vt (make known) rivelare, svelare; (display) rivelare, mostrare; **revealing** adj rivelatore(-trice); (dress) scollato(-a)
revel ['rɛvl] vi **to ~ in sth/in doing** dilettarsi di qc/a fare
revelation [rɛvə'leɪʃən] n rivelazione f
revenge [rɪ'vɛndʒ] n vendetta ▷ vt vendicare; **to take ~ on** vendicarsi di
revenue ['rɛvənjuː] n reddito
Reverend ['rɛvərənd] adj (in titles) reverendo(-a)
reversal [rɪ'vəːsl] n capovolgimento
reverse [rɪ'vəːs] n contrario, opposto; (back, defeat) rovescio; (Aut: also: **~ gear**) marcia indietro ▷ adj (order, direction)

contrario(-a), opposto(-a) ▷ vt (turn) invertire, rivoltare; (change) capovolgere, rovesciare; (Law: judgment) cassare; (car) fare marcia indietro con ▷ vi (BRIT Aut, person etc) fare marcia indietro; **reverse-charge call** [rɪ'vəːstʃɑːdʒ-] (BRIT) n (Tel) telefonata con addebito al ricevente; **reversing lights** (BRIT) npl (Aut) luci fpl per la retromarcia

revert [rɪ'vəːt] vi **to ~ to** tornare a

review [rɪ'vjuː] n rivista; (of book, film) recensione f; (of situation) esame m ▷ vt passare in rivista; fare la recensione di; fare il punto di

revise [rɪ'vaɪz] vt (manuscript) rivedere, correggere; (opinion) emendare, modificare; (study: subject, notes) ripassare; **revision** [rɪ'vɪʒən] n revisione f; ripasso

revival [rɪ'vaɪvəl] n ripresa; ristabilimento; (of faith) risveglio

revive [rɪ'vaɪv] vt (person) rianimare; (custom) far rivivere; (hope, courage, economy) ravvivare; (play, fashion) riesumare ▷ vi (person) rianimarsi; (hope) ravvivarsi; (activity) riprendersi

revolt [rɪ'vəult] n rivolta, ribellione f ▷ vi rivoltarsi, ribellarsi ▷ vt (far) rivoltare; **revolting** adj ripugnante

revolution [rɛvə'luːʃən] n rivoluzione f; (of wheel etc) rivoluzione, giro; **revolutionary** adj, n rivoluzionario(-a)

revolve [rɪ'vɒlv] vi girare

revolver [rɪ'vɒlvə] n rivoltella

reward [rɪ'wɔːd] n ricompensa, premio ▷ vt **to ~ (for)** ricompensare (per); **rewarding** adj (fig) gratificante

rewind [riː'waɪnd] (irreg) vt (watch) ricaricare; (ribbon etc) riavvolgere

rewrite [riː'raɪt] vt irreg riscrivere

rheumatism ['ruːmətɪzəm] n reumatismo

rhinoceros [raɪ'nɔsərəs] n rinoceronte m

rhubarb ['ruːbɑːb] n rabarbaro

rhyme [raɪm] n rima; (verse) poesia

rhythm ['rɪðm] n ritmo

rib [rɪb] n (Anat) costola ▷ vt (tease) punzecchiare

ribbon ['rɪbən] n nastro; **in ~s** (torn) a brandelli

rice [raɪs] n riso; **rice pudding** n budino di riso

rich [rɪtʃ] adj ricco(-a); (clothes) sontuoso(-a); (abundant): **~ in** ricco(-a) di

rid [rɪd] (pt, pp **rid**) vt **to ~ sb of** sbarazzare or liberare qn di; **to get ~ of** sbarazzarsi di

riddle ['rɪdl] n (puzzle) indovinello ▷ vt **to be ~d with** (holes) essere crivellato(-a) di; (doubts) essere pieno(-a) di

ride [raɪd] (pt **rode**, pp **ridden**) n (on horse) cavalcata; (outing) passeggiata; (distance covered) cavalcata; corsa ▷ vi (as sport) cavalcare; (go somewhere: on horse, bicycle) andare (a cavallo or in bicicletta etc); (journey: on bicycle, motorcycle, bus) andare, viaggiare ▷ vt (a horse) montare, cavalcare; **to take sb for a ~** (fig) prendere in giro qn; fregare qn; **to ~ a horse/bicycle/camel** montare a cavallo/in bicicletta/in groppa a un cammello; **rider** n cavalcatore(-trice); (in race) fantino; (on bicycle) ciclista m/f; (on motorcycle) motociclista m/f

ridge [rɪdʒ] n (of hill) cresta; (of roof) colmo; (on object) riga (in rilievo)

ridicule ['rɪdɪkjuːl] n ridicolo; scherno ▷ vt mettere in ridicolo; **ridiculous** [rɪ'dɪkjuləs] adj ridicolo(-a)

riding ['raɪdɪŋ] n equitazione f; **riding school** n scuola d'equitazione

rife [raɪf] adj diffuso(-a); **to be ~ with** abbondare di

rifle ['raɪfl] n carabina ▷ vt vuotare

rift [rɪft] n fessura, crepatura; (fig: disagreement) incrinatura, disaccordo

rig [rɪg] n (also: **oil ~**: on land) derrick m inv; (: at sea) piattaforma di trivellazione ▷ vt (election etc) truccare

right [raɪt] adj giusto(-a); (suitable) appropriato(-a); (not left) destro(-a) ▷ n giusto; (title, claim) diritto; (not left) destra ▷ adv (answer) correttamente; (not on the left) a destra ▷ vt raddrizzare; (fig) riparare ▷ excl bene!; **to be ~** (person) aver ragione; (answer) essere giusto(-a) or corretto(-a); **by ~s** di diritto; **on the ~** a destra; **to be in the ~** aver ragione, essere nel giusto; **~ now** proprio adesso; subito; **~ away** subito; **right angle** n angolo retto; **rightful** adj (heir) legittimo(-a); **right-hand** adj **right-hand drive** guida a destra; **the right-hand side** il lato destro; **right-handed** adj (person) che adopera la mano destra; **rightly** adv bene, correttamente; (with reason) a ragione; **right of way** n diritto di passaggio; (Aut) precedenza; **right-wing** adj (Pol) di destra

rigid ['rɪdʒɪd] adj rigido(-a); (principle) rigoroso(-a)

rigorous ['rɪgərəs] adj rigoroso(-a)

rim [rɪm] n orlo; (of spectacles) montatura; (of wheel) cerchione m

rind [raɪnd] n (of bacon) cotenna; (of lemon etc) scorza

ring [rɪŋ] (pt **rang**, pp **rung**) n anello; (of people, objects) cerchio; (of spies) giro; (of smoke etc) spirale m; (arena) pista, arena; (for boxing) ring m inv; (sound of bell) scampanio ▷ vi (person, bell, telephone) suonare; (also: **~ out**: voice, words) risuonare; (Tel) telefonare; (ears) fischiare ▷ vt (BRIT Tel) telefonare a; (: bell, doorbell) suonare; **to give sb a ~** (BRIT Tel) dare un colpo di telefono a qn; **ring back** vt, vi (Tel) richiamare; **ring off** (BRIT) vi (Tel) mettere giù, riattaccare; **ring up** (BRIT) vt (Tel) telefonare a; **ringing tone** (BRIT) n (Tel) segnale m di libero; **ringleader** n (of gang) capobanda m; **ring road** (BRIT) n raccordo anulare

ring tone n suoneria

rink [rɪŋk] n (also: **ice ~**) pista di pattinaggio

rinse [rɪns] n risciacquatura; (hair tint) cachet m inv ▷ vt sciacquare

riot ['raɪət] n sommossa, tumulto; (of colours) orgia ▷ vi tumultuare; **to run ~** creare disordine

rip [rɪp] n strappo ▷ vt strappare ▷ vi strapparsi; **rip off** vt (inf: cheat) fregare; **rip up** vt stracciare

ripe [raɪp] adj (fruit, grain) maturo(-a); (cheese) stagionato(-a)

rip-off ['rɪpɔf] n (inf): **it's a ~!** è un furto!

ripple ['rɪpl] n increspamento, ondulazione f; mormorio ▷ vi incresparsi

rise [raɪz] (pt rose, pp risen) n (slope) salita, pendio; (hill) altura; (increase: in wages: BRIT) aumento; (: in prices, temperature) rialzo, aumento; (fig: to power etc) ascesa ▷ vi alzarsi, levarsi; (prices) aumentare; (waters, river) crescere; (sun, wind, person: from chair, bed) levarsi; (also: ~ up: building) ergersi; (: rebel) insorgere; ribellarsi; (in rank) salire; **to give ~ to** provocare, dare origine a; **to ~ to the occasion** essere all'altezza; **risen** ['rɪzn] pp of **rise**; **rising** adj (increasing: number) sempre crescente; (: prices) in aumento; (tide) montante; (sun, moon) nascente, che sorge

risk [rɪsk] n rischio; pericolo ▷ vt rischiare; **to take** or **run the ~ of doing** correre il rischio di fare; **at ~** in pericolo; **at one's own ~** a proprio rischio e pericolo; **risky** adj rischioso(-a)

rite [raɪt] n rito; **last ~s** l'estrema unzione

ritual ['rɪtjuəl] adj rituale ▷ n rituale m

rival ['raɪvl] n rivale m/f; (in business) concorrente m/f ▷ adj rivale; che fa concorrenza; to be in concorrenza con; **to ~ sb/sth in** competere con qn/qc in; **rivalry** n rivalità; concorrenza

river ['rɪvəʳ] n fiume m ▷ cpd (port, traffic) fluviale; **up/down ~** a monte/valle; **riverbank** n argine m

rivet ['rɪvɪt] n ribattino, rivetto ▷ vt (fig) concentrare, fissare

Riviera [rɪvɪ'ɛərə] n **the (French) ~** la Costa Azzurra; **the Italian ~** la Riviera

road [rəud] n strada; (small) cammino; (in town) via ▷ cpd stradale; **major/minor ~** strada con/senza diritto di precedenza; **which ~ do I take for ...?** che strada devo prendere per andare a...?; **roadblock** n blocco stradale; **road map** n carta stradale; **road rage** n comportamento aggressivo al volante; **road safety** n sicurezza sulle strade; **roadside** n margine m della strada; **roadsign** n cartello stradale; **road tax** n (BRIT) tassa di circolazione; **roadworks** npl lavori mpl stradali

roam [rəum] vi errare, vagabondare

roar [rɔːʳ] n ruggito; (of crowd) tumulto; (of thunder, storm) muggito; (of laughter) scoppio ▷ vi ruggire; tumultuare; muggire; **to ~ with laughter** scoppiare dalle risa; **to do a ~ing trade** fare affari d'oro

roast [rəust] n arrosto ▷ vt arrostire; (coffee) tostare, torrefare; **roast beef** n arrosto di manzo

rob [rɔb] vt (person) rubare; (bank) svaligiare; **to ~ sb of sth** derubare qn di qc; (fig: deprive) privare qn di qc; **robber** n ladro; (armed) rapinatore m; **robbery** n furto; rapina

robe [rəub] n (for ceremony etc) abito; (also: **bath ~**) accappatoio; (US: also: **lap ~**) coperta

robin ['rɔbɪn] n pettirosso

robot ['rəubɔt] n robot m inv

robust [rəu'bʌst] adj robusto(-a); (economy) solido(-a)

rock [rɔk] n (substance) roccia; (boulder) masso; roccia; (in sea) scoglio; (US: pebble) ciottolo; (BRIT: sweet) zucchero candito ▷ vt (swing gently: cradle) dondolare; (: child) cullare; (shake) scrollare, far tremare ▷ vi dondolarsi; scrollarsi, tremare; **on the ~s** (drink) col ghiaccio; (marriage etc) in crisi; **rock and roll** n rock and roll m; **rock climbing** n roccia

rocket ['rɔkɪt] n razzo

rocking chair n sedia a dondolo

rocky ['rɔkɪ] adj (hill) roccioso(-a); (path) sassoso(-a); (marriage etc) instabile

rod [rɔd] n (metallic, Tech) asta; (wooden) bacchetta; (also: **fishing ~**) canna da pesca

rode [rəud] pt of **ride**

rodent ['rəudnt] n roditore m

rogue [rəug] n mascalzone m

role [rəul] n ruolo; **role-model** n modello (di comportamento)

roll [rəul] n rotolo; (of banknotes) mazzo; (also: **bread ~**) panino; (register) lista; (sound: of drums etc) rullo ▷ vt rotolare; (also: **~ up**: string) aggomitolare; (: sleeves) rimboccare; (*cigarettes*) arrotolare; (*eyes*) roteare; (*also*: **~ out**: *pastry*) stendere; (*lawn, road etc*) spianare ▷ *vi* rotolare; (*wheel*) girare; (*drum*) rullare; (*vehicle: also*: **~ along**) avanzare; (*ship*) rollare; **roll over** *vi* rivoltarsi; **roll up** (*inf*) *vi* (*arrive*) arrivare ▷ *vt* (*carpet*) arrotolare; **roller** *n* rullo; (*wheel*) rotella; (*for hair*) bigodino; **Rollerblades®** *npl* pattini *mpl* in linea; **roller coaster** [-'kəʊstəʳ] *n* montagne *fpl* russe; **roller skates** *npl* pattini *mpl* a rotelle; **roller-skating** *n* pattinaggio a rotelle; **to go roller-skating** andare a pattinare (*con i pattini a rotelle*); **rolling pin** *n* matterello

ROM [rɔm] *n abbr* (= *read only memory*) memoria di sola lettura

Roman ['rəʊmən] *adj, n* romano(-a); **Roman Catholic** *adj, n* cattolico(-a)

romance [rə'mæns] *n* storia (*or* avventura *or* film *m inv*) romantico(-a); (*charm*) poesia; (*love affair*) idillio

Romania [rəʊ'meɪnɪə] *n* Romania

Romanian [rəʊ'meɪnɪən] *adj* romeno(-a) ▷ *n* romeno; (*Ling*) romeno

Roman numeral *n* numero romano

romantic [rə'mæntɪk] *adj* romantico(-a); sentimentale

Rome [rəʊm] *n* Roma

roof [ruːf] *n* tetto; (*of tunnel, cave*) volta ▷ *vt* coprire (con un tetto); **~ of the mouth** palato; **roof rack** *n* (*Aut*) portabagagli *m inv*

rook [rʊk] *n* (*bird*) corvo nero; (*Chess*) torre *f*

room [ruːm] *n* (*in house*) stanza; (*bedroom, in hotel*) camera; (*in school etc*) sala; (*space*) posto, spazio; **roommate** *n* compagno(-a) di stanza; **room service** *n* servizio da camera; **roomy** *adj* spazioso(-a); (*garment*) ampio(-a)

rooster ['ruːstəʳ] *n* gallo

root [ruːt] *n* radice *f* ▷ *vi* (*plant, belief*) attecchire

rope [rəʊp] *n* corda, fune *f*; (*Naut*) cavo ▷ *vt* (*box*) legare; (*climbers*) legare in cordata; (*area: also*: **~ off**) isolare cingendo con cordoni; **to know the ~s** (*fig*) conoscere i trucchi del mestiere

rose [rəʊz] *pt* of **rise** ▷ *n* rosa; (*also*: **~ bush**) rosaio; (*on watering can*) rosetta

rosé ['rəʊzeɪ] *n* vino rosato

rosemary ['rəʊzmərɪ] *n* rosmarino

rosy ['rəʊzɪ] *adj* roseo(-a)

rot [rɔt] *n* (*decay*) putrefazione *f*; (*inf: nonsense*) stupidaggini *fpl* ▷ *vt, vi* imputridire, marcire

rota ['rəʊtə] *n* tabella dei turni

rotate [rəʊ'teɪt] *vt* (*revolve*) far girare; (*change round: jobs*) fare a turno ▷ *vi* (*revolve*) girare

rotten ['rɔtn] *adj* (*decayed*) putrido(-a), marcio(-a); (*dishonest*) corrotto(-a); (*inf: bad*) brutto(-a); (*: action*) vigliacco(-a); **to feel ~** (*ill*) sentirsi da cani

rough [rʌf] *adj* (*skin, surface*) ruvido(-a); (*terrain, road*) accidentato(-a); (*voice*) rauco(-a); (*person, manner: coarse*) rozzo(-a), aspro(-a); (*: violent*) brutale; (*district*) malfamato(-a); (*weather*) cattivo(-a); (*sea*) mosso(-a); (*plan*) abbozzato(-a); (*guess*) approssimativo(-a) ▷ *n* (*Golf*) macchia; **to ~ it** far vita dura; **to sleep ~** (*BRIT*) dormire all'addiaccio; **roughly** *adv* (*handle*) rudemente, brutalmente; (*make*) grossolanamente; (*speak*) bruscamente; (*approximately*) approssimativamente

roulette [ruː'lɛt] *n* roulette *f*

round [raʊnd] *adj* rotondo(-a); (*figures*) tondo(-a) ▷ *n* (*BRIT: of toast*) fetta; (*duty: of policeman, milkman etc*) giro; (*: of doctor*) visite *fpl*; (*game: of cards, golf, in competition*) partita; (*of ammunition*) cartuccia; (*Boxing*) round *m inv*; (*of talks*) serie *f inv* ▷ *vt* (*corner*) girare; (*bend*) prendere ▷ *prep* intorno a ▷ *adv* **all ~** tutt'attorno; **to go the long way ~** fare il giro più lungo; **all the year ~** tutto l'anno; **it's just ~ the corner** (*also fig*) è dietro l'angolo; **~ the clock** ininterrottamente; **to go ~ to sb's house** andare da qn; **go ~ the back** passi dietro; **enough to go ~** abbastanza per tutti; **~ of applause** applausi *mpl*; **~ of drinks** giro di bibite; **~ of sandwiches** sandwich *m inv*; **round off** *vt* (*speech etc*) finire; **round up** *vt* radunare; (*criminals*) fare una retata di; (*prices*) arrotondare; **roundabout** *n* (*BRIT Aut*) rotatoria; (*: at fair*) giostra ▷ *adj* (*route, means*) indiretto(-a); **round trip** *n* (*viaggio di*) andata e ritorno; **roundup** *n* raduno; (*of criminals*) retata

rouse [raʊz] *vt* (*wake up*) svegliare; (*stir up*) destare; provocare; risvegliare

route [ruːt] *n* itinerario; (*of bus*) percorso

routine [ruː'tiːn] *adj* (*work*) corrente, abituale; (*procedure*) solito(-a) ▷ *n* (*pej*) routine *f*, tran tran *m*; (*Theatre*) numero

row¹ [rəʊ] *n* (*line*) riga, fila; (*Knitting*) ferro; (*behind one another: of cars, people*) fila; (*in boat*) remata ▷ *vi* (*in boat*) remare; (*as sport*) vogare ▷ *vt* (*boat*) manovrare a remi; **in a ~** (*fig*) di fila

row² [raʊ] *n* (*racket*) baccano, chiasso; (*dispute*) lite *f*; (*scolding*) sgridata ▷ *vi* (*argue*) litigare

rowboat ['rəʊbəʊt] (*US*) *n* barca a remi

rowing ['rəʊɪŋ] *n* canottaggio; **rowing boat** (*BRIT*) *n* barca a remi

royal ['rɔɪəl] *adj* reale; **royalty** ['rɔɪəltɪ] *n* (*royal persons*) (membri *mpl* della) famiglia reale; (*payment: to author*) diritti *mpl* d'autore

rpm *abbr* (= *revolutions per minute*) giri/min.

R.S.V.P. *abbr* (= *répondez s'il vous plaît*) R.S.V.P.

Rt. Hon. (BRIT) *abbr* (= *Right Honourable*) ≈ Onorevole

rub [rʌb] *n* **to give sth a ~** strofinare qc; (*sore place*) massaggiare qc ▷ *vt* strofinare; massaggiare; (*hands: also: ~ together*) sfregarsi; **to ~ sb up** (BRIT) *or* **~ sb the wrong way** (US) lisciare qn contro pelo; **rub in** *vt* (*ointment*) far penetrare (massaggiando *or* frizionando); **rub off** *vi* andare via; **rub out** *vt* cancellare

rubber ['rʌbə^r] *n* gomma; **rubber band** *n* elastico; **rubber gloves** *npl* guanti *mpl* di gomma

rubbish ['rʌbɪʃ] *n* (*from household*) immondizie *fpl*, rifiuti *mpl*; (*fig, pej*) cose *fpl* senza valore; robaccia; sciocchezze *fpl*; **rubbish bin** (BRIT) *n* pattumiera; **rubbish dump** *n* (*in town*) immondezzaio

rubble ['rʌbl] *n* macerie *fpl*; (*smaller*) pietrisco

ruby ['ruːbɪ] *n* rubino

rucksack ['rʌksæk] *n* zaino

rudder ['rʌdə^r] *n* timone *m*

rude [ruːd] *adj* (*impolite: person*) scortese, rozzo(-a); (*: word, manners*) grossolano(-a), rozzo(-a); (*shocking*) indecente

ruffle ['rʌfl] *vt* (*hair*) scompigliare; (*clothes, water*) increspare; (*fig: person*) turbare

rug [rʌg] *n* tappeto; (BRIT: *for knees*) coperta

rugby ['rʌgbɪ] *n* (*also: ~ football*) rugby *m*

rugged ['rʌgɪd] *adj* (*landscape*) aspro(-a); (*features, determination*) duro(-a); (*character*) brusco(-a)

ruin ['ruːɪn] *n* rovina ▷ *vt* rovinare; **~s** *npl* (*of building, castle etc*) rovine *fpl*, ruderi *mpl*

rule [ruːl] *n* regola; (*regulation*) regolamento, regola; (*government*) governo; (*ruler*) riga ▷ *vt* (*country*) governare; (*person*) dominare ▷ *vi* regnare; decidere; (*Law*) dichiarare; **as a ~** normalmente; **rule out** *vt* escludere; **ruler** *n* (*sovereign*) sovrano(-a); (*for measuring*) regolo, riga; **ruling** *adj* (*party*) al potere; (*class*) dirigente ▷ *n* (*Law*) decisione *f*

rum [rʌm] *n* rum *m*

Rumania *etc* [ruːˈmeɪnɪə] *n* = **Romania** *etc*

rumble ['rʌmbl] *n* rimbombo; brontolio ▷ *vi* rimbombare; (*stomach, pipe*) brontolare

rumour ['ruːmə^r] (US **rumor**) *n* voce *f* ▷ *vt* **it is ~ed that** corre voce che

Be careful not to translate *rumour* by the Italian word *rumore*.

rump steak [rʌmp-] *n* bistecca di girello

run [rʌn] (*pt* **ran**, *pp* **run**) *n* corsa; (*outing*) gita (in macchina); (*distance travelled*) percorso, tragitto; (*Ski*) pista; (*Cricket, Baseball*) meta; (*series*) serie *f*; (*Theatre*) periodo di rappresentazione; (*in tights, stockings*) smagliatura ▷ *vt* (*distance*) correre; (*operate: business*) gestire, dirigere; (*: competition, course*) organizzare; (*: hotel*) gestire; (*: house*) governare; (*Comput*) eseguire; (*water, bath*) far scorrere; (*force through: rope, pipe*) **to ~ sth through** far passare qc attraverso; (*pass: hand, finger*): **to ~ sth over** passare qc su; (*Press: feature*) presentare ▷ *vi* correre; (*flee*) scappare; (*pass: road etc*) passare; (*work: machine, factory*) funzionare, andare; (*bus, train: operate*) far servizio; (*: travel*) circolare; (*continue: play, contract*) durare; (*slide: drawer; flow: river, bath*) scorrere; (*colours, washing*) stemperarsi; (*in election*) presentarsi candidato; (*nose*) colare; **there was a ~ on ...** c'era una corsa a ...; **in the long ~** a lungo andare; **on the ~** in fuga; **to ~ a race** partecipare ad una gara; **I'll ~ you to the station** la porto alla stazione; **to ~ a risk** correre un rischio; **run after** *vt fus* (*to catch up*) rincorrere; (*chase*) correre dietro a; **run away** *vi* fuggire; **run down** *vt* (*production*) ridurre gradualmente; (*factory*) rallentare l'attività di; (*Aut*) investire; (*criticize*) criticare; **to be ~ down** (*person: tired*) essere esausto(-a); **run into** *vt fus* (*meet: person*) incontrare per caso; (*: trouble*) incontrare, trovare; (*collide with*) andare a sbattere contro; **run off** *vi* fuggire ▷ *vt* (*water*) far scolare; (*copies*) fare; **run out** *vi* (*person*) uscire di corsa; (*liquid*) colare; (*lease*) scadere; (*money*) esaurirsi; **run out of** *vt fus* rimanere a corto di; **run over** *vt* (*Aut*) investire, mettere sotto ▷ *vt fus* (*revise*) rivedere; **run through** *vt fus* (*instructions*) dare una scorsa a; (*rehearse: play*) riprovare, ripetere; **run up** *vt* (*debt*) lasciar accumulare; **to ~ up against** (*difficulties*) incontrare; **runaway** *adj* (*person*) fuggiasco(-a); (*horse*) in libertà; (*truck*) fuori controllo

rung [rʌŋ] *pp of* **ring** ▷ *n* (*of ladder*) piolo

runner ['rʌnə^r] *n* (*in race*) corridore *m*; (*: horse*) partente *m/f*; (*on sledge*) pattino; (*for drawer etc*) guida; **runner bean** (BRIT) *n* fagiolo rampicante; **runner-up** *n* secondo(-a) arrivato(-a)

running ['rʌnɪŋ] *n* corsa; direzione *f*; organizzazione *f*; funzionamento

▷ adj (water) corrente; (commentary)
simultaneo(-a); **to be in/out of the ~ for
sth** essere/non essere più in lizza per qc; **6
days ~** 6 giorni di seguito
runny ['rʌnɪ] adj che cola
run-up ['rʌnʌp] n **~ to** (election etc) periodo
che precede
runway ['rʌnweɪ] n (Aviat) pista (di
decollo)
rupture ['rʌptʃə'] n (Med) ernia
rural ['rʊərəl] adj rurale
rush [rʌʃ] n corsa precipitosa; (hurry)
furia, fretta; (sudden demand): **~ for** corsa
a; (current) flusso; (of emotion) impeto;
(Bot) giunco ▷ vt mandare or spedire
velocemente; (attack: town etc) prendere
d'assalto ▷ vi precipitarsi; **rush hour** n
ora di punta
Russia ['rʌʃə] n Russia; **Russian** adj
russo(-a) ▷ n russo(-a); (Ling) russo
rust [rʌst] n ruggine f ▷ vi arrugginirsi
rusty ['rʌstɪ] adj arrugginito(-a)
ruthless ['ruːθlɪs] adj spietato(-a)
RV abbr (= revised version) versione riveduta
della Bibbia ▷ n abbr (US) see **recreational
vehicle**
rye [raɪ] n segale f

S

Sabbath ['sæbəθ] n (Jewish) sabato;
(Christian) domenica
sabotage ['sæbətɑːʒ] n sabotaggio ▷ vt
sabotare
saccharin(e) ['sækərɪn] n saccarina
sachet ['sæʃeɪ] n bustina
sack [sæk] n (bag) sacco ▷ vt (dismiss)
licenziare, mandare a spasso; (plunder)
saccheggiare; **to get the ~** essere
mandato a spasso
sacred ['seɪkrɪd] adj sacro(-a)
sacrifice ['sækrɪfaɪs] n sacrificio ▷ vt
sacrificare
sad [sæd] adj triste
saddle ['sædl] n sella ▷ vt (horse) sellare; **to
be ~d with sth** (inf) avere qc sulle spalle
sadistic [sə'dɪstɪk] adj sadico(-a)
sadly ['sædlɪ] adv tristemente; (regrettably)
sfortunatamente; **~ lacking in**
penosamente privo di
sadness ['sædnɪs] n tristezza
s.a.e. n abbr (= stamped addressed envelope)
busta affrancata e con indirizzo
safari [sə'fɑːrɪ] n safari m inv
safe [seɪf] adj sicuro(-a); (out of danger)
salvo(-a), al sicuro; (cautious) prudente
▷ n cassaforte f; **~ from** al sicuro da; **~
and sound** sano(-a) e salvo(-a); **(just) to
be on the ~ side** per non correre rischi;
could you put this in the ~, please? lo

potrebbe mettere nella cassaforte, per favore?; **safely** adv sicuramente; sano(-a) e salvo(-a); prudentemente; **safe sex** n sesso sicuro

safety ['seɪftɪ] n sicurezza; **safety belt** n cintura di sicurezza; **safety pin** n spilla di sicurezza

saffron ['sæfrən] n zafferano

sag [sæg] vi incurvarsi; afflosciarsi

sage [seɪdʒ] n (herb) salvia; (man) saggio

Sagittarius [sædʒɪ'tɛərɪəs] n Sagittario

Sahara [sə'hɑːrə] n **the ~ (Desert)** il (deserto del) Sahara

said [sɛd] pt, pp of **say**

sail [seɪl] n (on boat) vela; (trip): **to go for a ~** fare un giro in barca a vela ▷ vt (boat) condurre, governare ▷ vi (travel: ship) navigare; (: passenger) viaggiare per mare; (set off) salpare; (sport) fare della vela; **they ~ed into Genoa** entrarono nel porto di Genova; **sailboat** (US) n barca a vela; **sailing** n (sport) vela; **to go sailing** fare della vela; **sailing boat** n barca a vela; **sailor** n marinaio

saint [seɪnt] n santo(-a)

sake [seɪk] n **for the ~ of** per, per amore di

salad ['sæləd] n insalata; **salad cream** (BRIT) n (tipo di) maionese f; **salad dressing** n condimento per insalata

salami [sə'lɑːmɪ] n salame m

salary ['sælərɪ] n stipendio

sale [seɪl] n vendita; (at reduced prices) svendita, liquidazione f; (auction) vendita all'asta; **"for ~"** "in vendita"; **on ~** in vendita; **on ~ or return** da vendere o rimandare; **~s** npl (total amount sold) vendite fpl; **sales assistant** (US **sales clerk**) n commesso(-a); **salesman/ woman** (irreg) n commesso(-a); (representative) rappresentante m/f; **salesperson** (irreg) n (in shop) commesso; (representative) rappresentante m/f di commercio; **sales rep** n rappresentante m/f di commercio

saline ['seɪlaɪn] adj salino(-a)

saliva [sə'laɪvə] n saliva

salmon ['sæmən] n inv salmone m

salon ['sælɔn] n (hairdressing salon) parrucchiere(-a); (beauty salon) salone m di bellezza

saloon [sə'luːn] n (US) saloon m inv, bar m inv; (BRIT: Aut) berlina; (ship's lounge) salone m

salt [sɔlt] n sale m ▷ vt salare; **saltwater** adj di mare; **salty** adj salato(-a)

salute [sə'luːt] n saluto ▷ vt salutare

salvage ['sælvɪdʒ] n (saving) salvataggio; (things saved) beni mpl salvati or recuperati ▷ vt salvare, mettere in salvo

Salvation Army [sæl'veɪʃən-] n Esercito della Salvezza

same [seɪm] adj stesso(-a), medesimo(-a) ▷ pron **the ~** lo (la) stesso(-a), gli (le) stessi(-e); **the ~ book as** lo stesso libro di (o che); **at the ~ time** allo stesso tempo; **all** or **just the ~** tuttavia; **to do the ~ as sb** fare come qn; **the ~ to you!** altrettanto a te!

sample ['sɑːmpl] n campione m ▷ vt (food) assaggiare; (wine) degustare

sanction ['sæŋkʃən] n sanzione f ▷ vt sancire, sanzionare; **~s** npl (Pol) sanzioni fpl

sanctuary ['sæŋktjuərɪ] n (holy place) santuario; (refuge) rifugio; (for wildlife) riserva

sand [sænd] n sabbia ▷ vt (also: ~ **down**) cartavetrare

sandal ['sændl] n sandalo

sand: sandbox ['sændbɔks] (US) n = **sandpit**; **sandcastle** ['sændkɑːsl] n castello di sabbia; **sand dune** n duna di sabbia; **sandpaper** ['sændpeɪpə'] n carta vetrata; **sandpit** ['sændpɪt] n (for children) buca di sabbia; **sands** npl spiaggia; **sandstone** ['sændstəun] n arenaria

sandwich ['sændwɪtʃ] n tramezzino, panino, sandwich m inv ▷ vt: **~ed between** incastrato(-a) fra; **cheese/ham ~** sandwich al formaggio/prosciutto

sandy ['sændɪ] adj sabbioso(-a); (colour) color sabbia inv, biondo(-a) rossiccio(-a)

sane [seɪn] adj (person) sano(-a) di mente; (outlook) sensato(-a)

sang [sæŋ] pt of **sing**

sanitary towel ['sænɪtərɪ-] (US **sanitary napkin**) n assorbente m (igienico)

sanity ['sænɪtɪ] n sanità mentale; (common sense) buon senso

sank [sæŋk] pt of **sink**

Santa Claus [sæntə'klɔːz] n Babbo Natale

sap [sæp] n (of plants) linfa ▷ vt (strength) fiaccare

sapphire ['sæfaɪə'] n zaffiro

sarcasm ['sɑːkæzm] n sarcasmo

sarcastic [sɑː'kæstɪk] adj sarcastico(-a); **to be ~** fare del sarcasmo

sardine [sɑː'diːn] n sardina

Sardinia [sɑː'dɪnɪə] n Sardegna

SASE (US) n abbr (= self-addressed stamped envelope) busta affrancata e con indirizzo

sat [sæt] pt, pp of **sit**

Sat. abbr (= Saturday) sab.

satchel ['sætʃl] n cartella

satellite ['sætəlaɪt] adj satellite ▷ n satellite m; **satellite dish** n antenna parabolica; **satellite television** n televisione f via satellite

satin ['sætɪn] n raso ▷ adj di raso

satire ['sætaɪəʳ] n satira

satisfaction [sætɪs'fækʃən] n soddisfazione f

satisfactory [sætɪs'fæktərɪ] adj soddisfacente

satisfied ['sætɪsfaɪd] adj (customer) soddisfatto(-a); **to be ~ (with sth)** essere soddisfatto(-a) (di qc)

satisfy ['sætɪsfaɪ] vt soddisfare; (convince) convincere

Saturday ['sætədɪ] n sabato

sauce [sɔːs] n salsa; (containing meat, fish) sugo; **saucepan** n casseruola

saucer ['sɔːsəʳ] n sottocoppa m, piattino

Saudi Arabia ['saudɪ-] n Arabia Saudita

sauna ['sɔːnə] n sauna

sausage ['sɒsɪdʒ] n salsiccia; **sausage roll** n rotolo di pasta sfoglia ripieno di salsiccia

sautéed ['səuteɪd] adj saltato(-a)

savage ['sævɪdʒ] adj (cruel, fierce) selvaggio(-a), feroce; (primitive) primitivo(-a) ▷ n selvaggio(-a) ▷ vt attaccare selvaggiamente

save [seɪv] vt (person, belongings, Comput) salvare; (money) risparmiare, mettere da parte; (time) risparmiare; (food) conservare; (avoid: trouble) evitare; (Sport) parare ▷ vi (also: **~ up**) economizzare ▷ n (Sport) parata ▷ prep salvo, a eccezione di

savings ['seɪvɪŋz] npl (money) risparmi mpl; **savings account** n libretto di risparmio; **savings and loan association** (US) n ≈ società di credito immobiliare

savoury ['seɪvərɪ] (US **savory**) adj (dish: not sweet) salato(-a)

saw [sɔː] (pt **sawed**, pp **sawed** or **sawn**) pt of **see** ▷ n (tool) sega ▷ vt segare; **sawdust** n segatura

sawn [sɔːn] pp of **saw**

saxophone ['sæksəfəun] n sassofono

say [seɪ] (pt, pp **said**) n **to have one's ~** fare sentire il proprio parere; **to have a** or **some ~** avere voce in capitolo ▷ vt dire; **could you ~ that again?** potrebbe ripeterlo?; **that goes without ~ing** va da sé; **saying** n proverbio, detto

scab [skæb] n crosta; (pej) crumiro(-a)

scaffolding ['skæfəldɪŋ] n impalcatura

scald [skɔːld] vt scottatura ▷ vt scottare

scale [skeɪl] n scala; (of fish) squama ▷ vt (mountain) scalare; **~s** npl (for weighing) bilancia; **on a large ~** su vasta scala; **~ of charges** tariffa

scallion ['skæljən] n cipolla; (US: shallot) scalogna; (: leek) porro

scallop ['skɒləp] n (Zool) pettine m; (Sewing) smerlo

scalp [skælp] n cuoio capelluto ▷ vt scotennare

scalpel ['skælpl] n bisturi m inv

scam [skæm] n (inf) truffa

scampi ['skæmpɪ] npl scampi mpl

scan [skæn] vt scrutare; (glance at quickly) scorrere, dare un'occhiata a; (TV) analizzare; (Radar) esplorare ▷ n (Med) ecografia

scandal ['skændl] n scandalo; (gossip) pettegolezzi mpl

Scandinavia [skændɪ'neɪvɪə] n Scandinavia; **Scandinavian** adj, n scandinavo(-a)

scanner ['skænəʳ] n (Radar, Med) scanner m inv

scapegoat ['skeɪpɡəut] n capro espiatorio

scar [skɑː] n cicatrice f ▷ vt sfregiare

scarce [skɛəs] adj scarso(-a); (copy, edition) raro(-a); **to make o.s. ~** (inf) squagliarsela; **scarcely** adv appena

scare [skɛəʳ] n spavento; panico ▷ vt spaventare, atterrire; **there was a bomb ~ at the bank** hanno evacuato la banca per paura di un attentato dinamitardo; **to ~ sb stiff** spaventare a morte qn; **scarecrow** n spaventapasseri m inv; **scared** adj **to be scared** aver paura

scarf [skɑːf] (pl **scarves** or **scarfs**) n (long) sciarpa; (square) fazzoletto da testa, foulard m inv

scarlet ['skɑːlɪt] adj scarlatto(-a)

scarves [skɑːvz] npl of **scarf**

scary ['skɛərɪ] adj che spaventa

scatter ['skætəʳ] vt spargere; (crowd) disperdere ▷ vi disperdersi

scenario [sɪ'nɑːrɪəu] n (Theatre, Cinema) copione m; (fig) situazione f

scene [siːn] n (Theatre, fig etc) scena; (of crime, accident) scena, luogo; (sight, view) vista, veduta; **scenery** n (Theatre) scenario; (landscape) panorama m; **scenic** adj scenico(-a); panoramico(-a)

scent [sɛnt] n profumo; (sense of smell) olfatto, odorato; (fig: track) pista

sceptical ['skɛptɪkəl] (US **skeptical**) adj scettico(-a)

schedule ['ʃɛdjuːl, (US) 'skɛdjuːl] n programma m, piano; (of trains) orario; (of prices etc) lista, tabella ▷ vt fissare; **on ~** in orario; **to be ahead of/behind ~** essere in anticipo/ritardo sul previsto; **scheduled flight** n volo di linea

scheme [skiːm] n piano, progetto; (method) sistema m; (dishonest plan, plot) intrigo, trama; (arrangement) disposizione f, sistemazione f; (pension scheme etc) programma m ▷ vi fare progetti; (intrigue) complottare

schizophrenic [skɪtsə'frɛnɪk] adj, n

schizofrenico(-a)

scholar ['skɔlə'] n (expert) studioso(-a); **scholarship** n erudizione f; (grant) borsa di studio

school [sku:l] n (primary, secondary) scuola; (university: US) università f inv ▷ cpd scolare, scolastico(-a) ▷ vt (animal) addestrare; **schoolbook** n libro scolastico; **schoolboy** n scolaro; **school children** npl scolari mpl; **schoolgirl** n scolara; **schooling** n istruzione f; **schoolteacher** n insegnante m/f, docente m/f; (primary) maestro(-a)

science ['saɪəns] n scienza; **science fiction** n fantascienza; **scientific** [-'tɪfɪk] adj scientifico(-a); **scientist** n scienziato(-a)

sci-fi ['saɪfaɪ] n abbr (inf) = **science fiction**

scissors ['sɪzəz] npl forbici fpl

scold [skəuld] vt rimproverare

scone [skɔn] n focaccina da tè

scoop [sku:p] n mestolo; (for ice cream) cucchiaio dosatore; (Press) colpo giornalistico, notizia (in) esclusiva

scooter ['sku:tə'] n (motor cycle) motoretta, scooter m inv; (toy) monopattino

scope [skəup] n (capacity: of plan, undertaking) portata; (: of person) capacità fpl; (opportunity) possibilità fpl

scorching ['skɔ:tʃɪŋ] adj cocente, scottante

score [skɔ:'] n punti mpl, punteggio; (Mus) partitura, spartito; (twenty) venti ▷ vt (goal, point) segnare, fare; (success) ottenere ▷ vi segnare; (Football) fare un goal; (keep score) segnare i punti; ~s of (very many) un sacco di; **on that** ▷ a questo riguardo; **to ~ 6 out of 10** prendere 6 su 10; **score out** vt cancellare con un segno; **scoreboard** n tabellone m segnapunti; **scorer** n marcatore(-trice); (keeping score) segnapunti m inv

scorn [skɔ:n] n disprezzo ▷ vt disprezzare

Scorpio ['skɔ:pɪəu] n Scorpione m

scorpion ['skɔ:pɪən] n scorpione m

Scot [skɔt] n scozzese m/f

Scotch tape® n scotch® m

Scotland ['skɔtlənd] n Scozia

Scots [skɔts] adj scozzese; **Scotsman** (irreg) n scozzese m; **Scotswoman** (irreg) n scozzese f; **Scottish** ['skɔtɪʃ] adj scozzese; **Scottish Parliament** n Parlamento scozzese

scout [skaut] n (Mil) esploratore m; (also: **boy ~**) giovane esploratore, scout m inv

scowl [skaul] vi accigliarsi, aggrottare le sopracciglia; **to ~ at** guardare torvo

scramble ['skræmbl] n arrampicata ▷ vi inerpicarsi; **to ~ out** etc uscire etc in fretta; **to ~ for** azzuffarsi per; **scrambled eggs** npl uova fpl strapazzate

scrap [skræp] n pezzo, pezzetto; (fight) zuffa; (also: **~ iron**) rottami mpl di ferro, ferraglia ▷ vt demolire; (fig) scartare ▷ vi **to ~ (with sb)** fare a botte (con qn); **~s** npl (waste) scarti mpl; **scrapbook** n album m inv di ritagli

scrape [skreɪp] vt, vi raschiare, grattare ▷ n **to get into a ~** cacciarsi in un guaio

scrap paper n cartaccia

scratch [skrætʃ] n graffio ▷ cpd **~ team** squadra raccogliticcia ▷ vt graffiare, rigare ▷ vi grattare; (paint, car) graffiare; **to start from ~** cominciare or partire da zero; **to be up to ~** essere all'altezza; **scratch card** n (BRIT) cartolina f gratta e vinci

scream [skri:m] n grido, urlo ▷ vi urlare, gridare

screen [skri:n] n schermo; (fig) muro, cortina, velo ▷ vt schermare, fare schermo a; (from the wind etc) riparare; (film) proiettare; (book) adattare per lo schermo; (candidates etc) selezionare; **screening** n (Med) dépistage m inv; **screenplay** n sceneggiatura; **screen saver** n (Comput) screen saver m inv

screw [skru:] n vite f ▷ vt avvitare; **screw up** vt (paper etc) spiegazzare; (inf: ruin) rovinare; **to ~ up one's eyes** strizzare gli occhi; **screwdriver** n cacciavite m

scribble ['skrɪbl] n scarabocchio ▷ vt scribacchiare in fretta ▷ vi scarabocchiare

script [skrɪpt] n (Cinema etc) copione m; (in exam) elaborato or compito d'esame

scroll [skrəul] n rotolo di carta

scrub [skrʌb] n (land) boscaglia ▷ vt pulire strofinando; (reject) annullare

scruffy ['skrʌfɪ] adj sciatto(-a)

scrum(mage) ['skrʌm(ɪdʒ)] n mischia

scrutiny ['skru:tɪnɪ] n esame m accurato

scuba diving ['sku:bə-] n immersioni fpl subacquee

sculptor ['skʌlptə'] n scultore m

sculpture ['skʌlptʃə'] n scultura

scum [skʌm] n schiuma; (pej: people) feccia

scurry ['skʌrɪ] vi sgambare, affrettarsi

sea [si:] n mare m ▷ cpd marino(-a), del mare; (bird, fish) di mare; (route, transport) marittimo(-a); **by ~** (travel) per mare; **on the ~** (boat) in mare; (town) di mare; **to be all at ~** (fig) non sapere che pesci pigliare; **out to ~** al largo; **(out) at ~** in mare; **seafood** n frutti mpl di mare; **sea front** n lungomare m; **seagull** n gabbiano

seal [si:l] n (animal) foca; (stamp) sigillo;

(*impression*) impronta del sigillo ▷ vt sigillare; **seal off** vt (*close*) sigillare; (*forbid entry to*) bloccare l'accesso a

sea level n livello del mare

seam [si:m] n cucitura; (*of coal*) filone m

search [sə:tʃ] n ricerca; (*Law: at sb's home*) perquisizione f ▷ vt frugare ▷ vi ricercare; **in ~ of** alla ricerca di; **search engine** n (*Comput*) motore m di ricerca; **search party** n squadra di soccorso

sea: seashore ['si:ʃɔː'] n spiaggia; **seasick** ['si:sɪk] adj che soffre il mal di mare; **seaside** ['si:saɪd] n spiaggia; **seaside resort** n stazione f balneare

season ['si:zn] n stagione f ▷ vt condire, insaporire; **seasonal** adj stagionale; **seasoning** n condimento; **season ticket** n abbonamento

seat [si:t] n sedile m; (*in bus, train: place*) posto; (*Parliament*) seggio; (*buttocks*) didietro; (*of trousers*) fondo ▷ vt far sedere; (*have room for*) avere or essere fornito(-a) di posti a sedere per; **I'd like to book two ~s** vorrei prenotare due posti; **to be ~ed** essere seduto(-a); **seat belt** n cintura di sicurezza; **seating** n posti mpl a sedere

sea: sea water n acqua di mare; **seaweed** ['si:wi:d] n alghe fpl

sec. abbr = **second(s)**

secluded [sɪ'klu:dɪd] adj isolato(-a), appartato(-a)

second ['sɛkənd] num secondo(-a) ▷ adv (*in race etc*) al secondo posto ▷ n (*unit of time*) secondo; (*Aut: also: ~ gear*) seconda; (*Comm: imperfect*) scarto; (*BRIT: Scol: degree*) laurea con punteggio discreto ▷ vt (*motion*) appoggiare; **secondary** adj secondario(-a); **secondary school** n scuola secondaria; **second-class** adj di seconda classe ▷ adv in seconda classe; **secondhand** adj di seconda mano, usato(-a); **secondly** adv in secondo luogo; **second-rate** adj scadente; **second thoughts** npl ripensamenti mpl; **on second thoughts** (*BRIT*) or **thought** (*US*) ripensandoci bene

secrecy ['si:krəsɪ] n segretezza

secret ['si:krɪt] adj segreto(-a) ▷ n segreto; **in ~** in segreto

secretary ['sɛkrətrɪ] n segretario(-a); **S~ of State (for)** (*BRIT: Pol*) ministro (di)

secretive ['si:krətɪv] adj riservato(-a)

secret service n servizi mpl segreti

sect [sɛkt] n setta

section ['sɛkʃən] n sezione f

sector ['sɛktə'] n settore m

secular ['sɛkjulə'] adj secolare

secure [sɪ'kjuə'] adj sicuro(-a); (*firmly fixed*) assicurato(-a), ben fermato(-a); (*in safe place*) al sicuro ▷ vt (*fix*) fissare, assicurare; (*get*) ottenere, assicurarsi; **securities** npl (*Stock Exchange*) titoli mpl

security [sɪ'kjuərɪtɪ] n sicurezza; (*for loan*) garanzia; **security guard** n guardia giurata

sedan [sə'dæn] (*US*) n (*Aut*) berlina

sedate [sɪ'deɪt] adj posato(-a), calmo(-a) ▷ vt calmare

sedative ['sɛdɪtɪv] n sedativo, calmante m

seduce [sɪ'dju:s] vt sedurre; **seductive** [-'dʌktɪv] adj seducente

see [si:] (*pt* **saw**, *pp* **seen**) vt vedere; (*accompany*): **to ~ sb to the door** accompagnare qn alla porta ▷ vi vedere; (*understand*) capire ▷ n sede f vescovile; **to ~ that** (*ensure*) badare che + sub, fare in modo che + sub; **~ you soon!** a presto!; **see off** vt salutare alla partenza; **see out** vt (*take to the door*) accompagnare alla porta; **see through** vt portare a termine ▷ vt fus non lasciarsi ingannare da; **see to** vt fus occuparsi di

seed [si:d] n seme m; (*fig*) germe m; (*Tennis etc*) testa di serie; **to go to ~** fare seme; (*fig*) scadere

seeing ['si:ɪŋ] conj **~ (that)** visto che

seek [si:k] (*pt, pp* **sought**) vt cercare

seem [si:m] vi sembrare, parere; **there ~s to be ...** sembra che ci sia ...; **seemingly** adv apparentemente

seen [si:n] pp of **see**

seesaw ['si:sɔ:] n altalena a bilico

segment ['sɛgmənt] n segmento

segregate ['sɛgrɪgeɪt] vt segregare, isolare

seize [si:z] vt (*grasp*) afferrare; (*take possession of*) impadronirsi di; (*Law*) sequestrare

seizure ['si:ʒə'] n (*Med*) attacco; (*Law*) confisca, sequestro

seldom ['sɛldəm] adv raramente

select [sɪ'lɛkt] adj scelto(-a) ▷ vt scegliere, selezionare; **selection** [-'lɛkʃən] n selezione f, scelta; **selective** adj selettivo(-a)

self [sɛlf] n **the ~** l'io m ▷ prefix auto...; **self-assured** adj sicuro(-a) di sé; **self-catering** (*BRIT*) adj in cui ci si cucina da sé; **self-centred** (*US* **self-centered**) adj egocentrico(-a); **self-confidence** n sicurezza di sé; **self-confident** adj sicuro(-a) di sé; **self-conscious** adj timido(-a); **self-contained** (*BRIT*) adj (*flat*) indipendente; **self-control** n autocontrollo; **self-defence** (*US* **self-defense**) n autodifesa; (*Law*) legittima difesa; **self-drive** adj (*BRIT: rented car*) senza autista; **self-employed** adj che lavora in proprio; **self-esteem** n amor proprio m; **self-indulgent** adj indulgente verso se stesso(-a); **self-interest** n interesse m personale; **selfish** adj egoista; **self-pity** n autocommiserazione f; **self-raising** (us **self-rising**) adj **self-raising flour** miscela di farina e lievito; **self-respect** n rispetto di sé, amor proprio; **self-service** n autoservizio, self-service m

sell [sɛl] (pt, pp **sold**) vt vendere ▷ vi vendersi; **to ~ at** or **for 1000 euros** essere in vendita a 1000 euro; **sell off** vt svendere, liquidare; **sell out** vi **to ~ out (of sth)** esaurire (qc); **the tickets are all sold out** i biglietti sono esauriti; **sell-by date** ['sɛlbaɪ-] n data di scadenza; **seller** n venditore(-trice)

Sellotape® ['sɛləʊteɪp] (BRIT) n nastro adesivo, scotch® m

selves [sɛlvz] npl of **self**

semester [sɪ'mɛstə^r] (us) n semestre m

semi... ['sɛmɪ] prefix semi...; **semicircle** n semicerchio; **semidetached (house)** [sɛmɪdɪ'tætʃt-] (BRIT) n casa gemella; **semi-final** n semifinale f

seminar ['sɛmɪnɑː^r] n seminario

semi-skimmed ['sɛmɪ'skɪmd] adj (milk) parzialmente scremato(-a)

senate ['sɛnɪt] n senato; **senator** n senatore(-trice)

send [sɛnd] (pt, pp **sent**) vt mandare; **send back** vt rimandare; **send for** vt fus mandare a chiamare, far venire; **send in** vt (report, application, resignation) presentare; **send off** vt (goods) spedire; (BRIT: Sport: player) espellere; **send on** vt (BRIT: letter) inoltrare; (luggage etc: in advance) spedire in anticipo; **send out** vt (invitation) diramare; **send up** vt (person, price) far salire; (BRIT: parody) mettere in ridicolo; **sender** n mittente m/f; **send-off** n **to give sb a good send-off** festeggiare la partenza di qn

senile ['siːnaɪl] adj senile

senior ['siːnɪə^r] adj (older) più vecchio(-a); (of higher rank) di grado più elevato; **senior citizen** n persona anziana; **senior high school** (us) n ≈ liceo

sensation [sɛn'seɪʃən] n sensazione f; **sensational** adj sensazionale; (marvellous) eccezionale

sense [sɛns] n senso; (feeling) sensazione f, senso; (meaning) senso, significato; (wisdom) buonsenso ▷ vt sentire, percepire; **it makes ~** ha senso; **senseless** adj sciocco(-a); (unconscious) privo(-a) di sensi; **sense of humour** (BRIT) n senso dell'umorismo

sensible ['sɛnsɪbl] adj sensato(-a), ragionevole

Be careful not to translate **sensible** by the Italian word **sensibile**.

sensitive ['sɛnsɪtɪv] adj sensibile; (skin, question) delicato(-a)

sensual ['sɛnsjuəl] adj sensuale

sensuous ['sɛnsjuəs] adj sensuale

sent [sɛnt] pt, pp of **send**

sentence ['sɛntns] n (Ling) frase f; (Law: judgment) sentenza; (: punishment) condanna ▷ vt **to ~ sb to death/to 5 years** condannare qn a morte/a 5 anni

sentiment ['sɛntɪmənt] n sentimento; (opinion) opinione f; **sentimental** [-'mɛntl] adj sentimentale

Sep. abbr (= September) Sett.

separate [adj 'sɛprɪt, vb 'sɛpəreɪt] adj separato(-a) ▷ vt separare ▷ vi separarsi; **separately** adv separatamente; **separates** npl (clothes) coordinati mpl; **separation** [-'reɪʃən] n separazione f

September [sɛp'tɛmbə^r] n settembre m

septic ['sɛptɪk] adj settico(-a); (wound) infettato(-a); **septic tank** n fossa settica

sequel ['siːkwl] n conseguenza; (of story) seguito; (of film) sequenza

sequence ['siːkwəns] n (series) serie f; (order) ordine m

sequin ['siːkwɪn] n lustrino, paillette f inv

Serb [səːb] adj, n = **Serbian**

Serbia ['səːbɪə] n Serbia

Serbian ['səːbɪən] adj serbo(-a) ▷ n serbo(-a); (Ling) serbo

sergeant ['sɑːdʒənt] n sergente m; (Police) brigadiere m

serial ['sɪərɪəl] n (Press) romanzo a puntate; (Radio, TV) trasmissione f a puntate, serial m inv; **serial killer** n serial-killer m/f inv; **serial number** n numero di serie

series ['sɪəriːz] n inv serie f inv; (Publishing) collana

serious ['sɪərɪəs] adj serio(-a), grave; **seriously** adv seriamente

sermon ['səːmən] n sermone m

servant ['səːvənt] n domestico(-a)

serve [səːv] vt (employer etc) servire, essere a servizio di; (purpose) servire a; (customer, food, meal) servire; (apprenticeship) fare; (prison term) scontare ▷ vi (also Tennis) servire; (be useful): **to ~ as/for/to do** servire da/per/per fare ▷ n (Tennis) servizio; **it ~s him right** ben gli sta, se l'è meritata; **server** n (Comput) server m inv

service ['səːvɪs] n servizio; (Aut: maintenance) assistenza, revisione f ▷ vt (car, washing machine) revisionare; **to be of ~ to sb** essere d'aiuto a qn; **~ included/**

not included servizio compreso/escluso; **~s** (BRIT: *on motorway*) stazione *f* di servizio; (*Mil*): **the S~s** le Forze Armate; **service area** *n* (*on motorway*) area di servizio; **service charge** (BRIT) *n* servizio; **serviceman** (*irreg*) *n* militare *m*; **service station** *n* stazione *f* di servizio

serviette [sɜːvɪˈɛt] (BRIT) *n* tovagliolo

session [ˈsɛʃən] *n* (*sitting*) seduta, sessione *f*; (*Scol*) anno scolastico (*or* accademico)

set [sɛt] (*pt, pp* **set**) *n* serie *f* inv; (*of cutlery etc*) servizio; (*Radio, TV*) apparecchio; (*Tennis*) set *m* inv; (*group of people*) mondo, ambiente *m*; (*Cinema*) scenario; (*Theatre: stage*) scene *fpl*; (: *scenery*) scenario; (*Math*) insieme *m*; (*Hairdressing*) messa in piega ⊳ *adj* (*fixed*) stabilito(-a), determinato(-a); (*ready*) pronto(-a) ⊳ *vt* (*place*) posare, mettere; (*arrange*) sistemare; (*fix*) fissare; (*adjust*) regolare; (*decide: rules etc*) stabilire, fissare ⊳ *vi* (*sun*) tramontare; (*jam, jelly*) rapprendersi; (*concrete*) fare presa; **to be ~ on doing** essere deciso a fare; **to ~ to music** mettere in musica; **to ~ on fire** dare fuoco a; **to ~ free** liberare; **to ~ sth going** mettere in moto qc; **to ~ sail** prendere il mare; **set aside** *vt* mettere da parte; **set down** *vt* (*bus, train*) lasciare; **set in** *vi* (*infection*) svilupparsi; (*complications*) intervenire; **the rain has ~ in for the day** ormai pioverà tutto il giorno; **set off** *vi* partire ⊳ *vt* (*bomb*) far scoppiare; (*cause to start*) mettere in moto; (*show up well*) dare risalto a; **set out** *vi* partire ⊳ *vt* (*arrange*) disporre; (*state*) esporre, presentare; **to ~ out to do** proporsi di fare; **set up** *vt* (*organization*) fondare, costituire; **setback** *n* (*hitch*) contrattempo, inconveniente *m*; **set menu** *n* menù *m* inv fisso

settee [sɛˈtiː] *n* divano, sofà *m* inv

setting [ˈsɛtɪŋ] *n* (*background*) ambiente *m*; (*of controls*) posizione *f*; (*of sun*) tramonto; (*of jewel*) montatura

settle [ˈsɛtl] *vt* (*argument, matter*) appianare; (*accounts*) regolare; (*Med: calm*) calmare ⊳ *vi* (*bird, dust etc*) posarsi; (*sediment*) depositarsi; **to ~ for sth** accontentarsi di qc; **to ~ on sth** decidersi per qc; **settle down** *vi* (*get comfortable*) sistemarsi; (*calm down*) calmarsi; (*get back to normal: situation*) tornare alla normalità; **settle in** *vi* sistemarsi; **settle up** *vi* **to ~ up with sb** regolare i conti con qn; **settlement** *n* (*payment*) pagamento, saldo; (*agreement*) accordo; (*colony*) colonia; (*village etc*) villaggio, comunità *f* inv

setup [ˈsɛtʌp] *n* (*arrangement*) sistemazione *f*; (*situation*) situazione *f*

seven [ˈsɛvn] *num* sette; **seventeen** *num* diciassette; **seventeenth** [sɛvnˈtiːnθ] *num* diciassettesimo(-a); **seventh** *num* settimo(-a); **seventieth** [ˈsɛvntɪɪθ] *num* settantesimo(-a); **seventy** *num* settanta

sever [ˈsɛvəʳ] *vt* recidere, tagliare; (*relations*) troncare

several [ˈsɛvərl] *adj, pron* alcuni(-e), diversi(-e); **~ of us** alcuni di noi

severe [sɪˈvɪəʳ] *adj* severo(-a); (*serious*) serio(-a), grave; (*hard*) duro(-a); (*plain*) semplice, sobrio(-a)

sew [səʊ] (*pt* **sewed**, *pp* **sewn**) *vt, vi* cucire

sewage [ˈsuːɪdʒ] *n* acque *fpl* di scolo

sewer [ˈsuːəʳ] *n* fogna

sewing [ˈsəʊɪŋ] *n* cucitura; cucito; **sewing machine** *n* macchina da cucire

sewn [səʊn] *pp of* **sew**

sex [sɛks] *n* sesso; **to have ~ with** avere rapporti sessuali con; **sexism** [ˈsɛksɪzəm] *n* sessismo; **sexist** *adj, n* sessista *m/f*; **sexual** [ˈsɛksjuəl] *adj* sessuale; **sexual intercourse** *n* rapporti *mpl* sessuali; **sexuality** [sɛksjuˈælɪtɪ] *n* sessualità; **sexy** [ˈsɛksɪ] *adj* provocante, sexy *inv*

shabby [ˈʃæbɪ] *adj* malandato(-a); (*behaviour*) vergognoso(-a)

shack [ʃæk] *n* baracca, capanna

shade [ʃeɪd] *n* ombra; (*for lamp*) paralume *m*; (*of colour*) tonalità *f* inv; (*small quantity*): **a ~ (more/too large)** un po' (di più/ troppo grande) ⊳ *vt* ombreggiare, fare ombra a; **in the ~** all'ombra; **~s** (US) *npl* (*sunglasses*) occhiali *mpl* da sole

shadow [ˈʃædəʊ] *n* ombra ⊳ *vt* (*follow*) pedinare; **shadow cabinet** (BRIT) *n* (*Pol*) governo *m* ombra *inv*

shady [ˈʃeɪdɪ] *adj* ombroso(-a); (*fig: dishonest*) losco(-a), equivoco(-a)

shaft [ʃɑːft] *n* (*of arrow, spear*) asta; (*Aut, Tech*) albero; (*of mine*) pozzo; (*of lift*) tromba; (*of light*) raggio

shake [ʃeɪk] (*pt* **shook**, *pp* **shaken**) *vt* scuotere; (*bottle, cocktail*) agitare ⊳ *vi* tremare; **to ~ one's head** (*in refusal, dismay*) scuotere la testa; **to ~ hands with sb** stringere *or* dare la mano a qn; **shake off** *vt* scrollare (via); (*fig*) sbarazzarsi di; **shake up** *vt* scuotere; **shaky** *adj* (*hand, voice*) tremante; (*building*) traballante

shall [ʃæl] *aux vb* **I ~ go** andrò; **~ I open the door?** apro io la porta?; **I'll get some, ~ I?** ne prendo un po', va bene?

shallow [ˈʃæləʊ] *adj* poco profondo(-a); (*fig*) superficiale

sham [ʃæm] *n* finzione *f*, messinscena; (*jewellery, furniture*) imitazione *f*

shambles [ˈʃæmblz] *n* confusione *f*, baraonda, scompiglio

shame [ʃeɪm] n vergogna ▷ vt far vergognare; **it is a ~ (that/to do)** è un peccato (che + sub/fare); **what a ~!** che peccato!; **shameful** adj vergognoso(-a); **shameless** adj sfrontato(-a); (immodest) spudorato(-a)

shampoo [ʃæm'pu:] n shampoo m inv ▷ vt fare lo shampoo a

shandy ['ʃændɪ] n birra con gassosa

shan't [ʃɑ:nt] = **shall not**

shape [ʃeɪp] n forma ▷ vt formare; (statement) formulare; (sb's ideas) condizionare; **to take ~** prendere forma; **share** [ʃɛəʳ] n (thing received, contribution) parte f; (Comm) azione f ▷ vt dividere; (have in common) condividere, avere in comune; **shareholder** n azionista m/f

shark [ʃɑ:k] n squalo, pescecane m

sharp [ʃɑ:p] adj (razor, knife) affilato(-a); (point) acuto(-a), acuminato(-a); (nose, chin) aguzzo(-a); (outline, contrast) netto(-a); (cold, pain) pungente; (voice) stridulo(-a); (person: quick-witted) sveglio(-a); (: unscrupulous) disonesto(-a); (Mus): **C ~** do diesis ▷ n (Mus) diesis m inv ▷ adv **at 2 o'clock ~** alle due in punto; **sharpen** vt affilare; (pencil) fare la punta a; (fig) acuire; **sharpener** n (also: **pencil sharpener**) temperamatite m inv; **sharply** adv (turn, stop) bruscamente; (stand out, contrast) nettamente; (criticize, retort) duramente, aspramente

shatter ['ʃætəʳ] vt mandare in frantumi, frantumare; (fig: upset) distruggere; (: ruin) rovinare ▷ vi frantumarsi, andare in pezzi; **shattered** adj (grief-stricken) sconvolto(-a); (exhausted) a pezzi, distrutto(-a)

shave [ʃeɪv] vt radere, rasare ▷ vi radersi, farsi la barba ▷ n **to have a ~** farsi la barba; **shaver** n (also: **electric shaver**) rasoio elettrico

shaving cream n crema da barba

shaving foam n = **shaving cream**

shavings ['ʃeɪvɪŋz] npl (of wood etc) trucioli mpl

shawl [ʃɔ:l] n scialle m

she [ʃi:] pron ella, lei; **~-cat** gatta; **~-elephant** elefantessa

sheath [ʃi:θ] n fodero, guaina; (contraceptive) preservativo

shed [ʃɛd] (pt, pp **shed**) n capannone m ▷ vt (leaves, fur etc) perdere; (tears, blood) versare; (workers) liberarsi di

she'd [ʃi:d] = **she had**; **she would**

sheep [ʃi:p] n inv pecora; **sheepdog** n cane m da pastore; **sheepskin** n pelle f di pecora

sheer [ʃɪəʳ] adj (utter) vero(-a)

(e proprio(-a)); (steep) a picco, perpendicolare; (almost transparent) sottile ▷ adv a picco

sheet [ʃi:t] n (on bed) lenzuolo; (of paper) foglio; (of glass, ice) lastra; (of metal) foglio, lamina

sheik(h) [ʃeɪk] n sceicco

shelf [ʃɛlf] (pl **shelves**) n scaffale m, mensola

shell [ʃɛl] n (on beach) conchiglia; (of egg, nut etc) guscio; (explosive) granata; (of building) scheletro ▷ vt (peas) sgranare; (Mil) bombardare

she'll [ʃi:l] = **she will**; **she shall**

shellfish ['ʃɛlfɪʃ] n inv (crab etc) crostaceo; (scallop etc) mollusco; (as food) crostacei; molluschi

shelter ['ʃɛltəʳ] n riparo, rifugio ▷ vt riparare, proteggere; (give lodging to) dare rifugio or asilo a ▷ vi ripararsi, mettersi al riparo; **sheltered** adj riparato(-a)

shelves ['ʃɛlvz] npl of **shelf**

shelving ['ʃɛlvɪŋ] n scaffalature fpl

shepherd ['ʃɛpəd] n pastore m ▷ vt (guide) guidare; **shepherd's pie** (BRIT) n timballo di carne macinata e purè di patate

sheriff ['ʃɛrɪf] (us) n sceriffo

sherry ['ʃɛrɪ] n sherry m inv

she's [ʃi:z] = **she is**; **she has**

Shetland ['ʃɛtlənd] n (also: **the ~s, the ~ Isles**) le isole Shetland, le Shetland

shield [ʃi:ld] n scudo; (trophy) scudetto; (protection) schermo ▷ vt **to ~ (from)** riparare (da), proteggere (da or contro)

shift [ʃɪft] n (change) cambiamento; (of workers) turno ▷ vt spostare, muovere; (remove) rimuovere ▷ vi spostarsi, muoversi

shin [ʃɪn] n tibia

shine [ʃaɪn] (pt, pp **shone**) n splendore m, lucentezza ▷ vi (ri)splendere, brillare ▷ vt far brillare, far risplendere; (torch): **to ~ sth on** puntare qc verso

shingles ['ʃɪŋglz] n (Med) herpes zoster m

shiny ['ʃaɪnɪ] adj lucente, lucido(-a)

ship [ʃɪp] n nave f ▷ vt trasportare (via mare); (send) spedire (via mare); **shipment** n carico; **shipping** n (ships) naviglio; (traffic) navigazione f; **shipwreck** n relitto; (event) naufragio ▷ vt **to be shipwrecked** naufragare, fare naufragio; **shipyard** n cantiere m navale

shirt [ʃə:t] n camicia; **in ~ sleeves** in maniche di camicia

shit [ʃɪt] (infl) excl merda (!)

shiver ['ʃɪvəʳ] n brivido ▷ vi rabbrividire, tremare

shock [ʃɔk] n (impact) urto, colpo; (Elec) scossa; (emotional) colpo, shock m inv;

(*Med*) shock ▷ *vt* colpire, scioccare; scandalizzare; **shocking** *adj* scioccante, traumatizzante; scandaloso(-a)

shoe [ʃuː] (*pt, pp* **shod**) *n* scarpa; (*also:* **horse~**) ferro di cavallo ▷ *vt* (*horse*) ferrare; **shoelace** *n* stringa; **shoe polish** *n* lucido per scarpe; **shoeshop** *n* calzoleria

shone [ʃɔn] *pt, pp of* **shine**

shook [ʃuk] *pt of* **shake**

shoot [ʃuːt] (*pt, pp* **shot**) *n* (*on branch, seedling*) germoglio ▷ *vt* (*game*) cacciare, andare a caccia di; (*person*) sparare a; (*execute*) fucilare; (*film*) girare ▷ *vi* (*with gun*): **to ~ (at)** sparare (a), fare fuoco (su); (*with bow*): **to ~ (at)** tirare (su); (*Football*) sparare, tirare (forte); **shoot down** *vt* (*plane*) abbattere; **shoot up** *vi* (*fig*) salire alle stelle; **shooting** *n* (*shots*) sparatoria; (*Hunting*) caccia

shop [ʃɔp] *n* negozio; (*workshop*) officina ▷ *vi* (*also:* **go ~ping**) fare spese; **shop assistant** (*BRIT*) *n* commesso(-a); **shopkeeper** *n* negoziante *m/f*, bottegaio(-a); **shoplifting** *n* taccheggio; **shopping** *n* (*goods*) spesa, acquisti *mpl*; **shopping bag** *n* borsa per la spesa; **shopping centre** (*US* **shopping center**) *n* centro commerciale; **shopping mall** *n* centro commerciale; **shopping trolley** *n* (*BRIT*) carrello del supermercato; **shop window** *n* vetrina

shore [ʃɔːʳ] *n* (*of sea*) riva, spiaggia; (*of lake*) riva ▷ *vt* **to ~ (up)** puntellare; **on ~** a riva

short [ʃɔːt] *adj* (*not long*) corto(-a); (*soon finished*) breve; (*person*) basso(-a); (*curt*) brusco(-a), secco(-a); (*insufficient*) insufficiente ▷ *n* (*also:* **~ film**) cortometraggio; **to be ~ of sth** essere a corto di *o* mancare di qc; **in ~** in breve; **~ of doing** a meno che non si faccia; **everything ~ of** tutto fuorché; **it is ~ for** è l'abbreviazione *o* il diminutivo di; **to cut ~** (*speech, visit*) accorciare, abbreviare; **to fall ~ of** venir meno a; non soddisfare; **to run ~ of** rimanere senza; **to stop ~** fermarsi di colpo; **to stop ~ of** non arrivare fino a; **shortage** *n* scarsezza, carenza; **shortbread** *n* biscotto di pasta frolla; **shortcoming** *n* difetto; **short(crust) pastry** (*BRIT*) *n* pasta frolla; **shortcut** *n* scorciatoia; **shorten** *vt* accorciare, ridurre; **shortfall** *n* deficit *m*; **shorthand** (*BRIT*) *n* stenografia; **short-lived** *adj* di breve durata; **shortly** *adv* fra poco; **shorts** *npl* (*also:* **a pair of shorts**) i calzoncini; **short-sighted** (*BRIT*) *adj* miope; **short-sleeved** [ˈʃɔːtsliːvd] *adj* a maniche corte; **short story** *n* racconto, novella; **short-tempered** *adj* irascibile;

short-term *adj* (*effect*) di *o* a breve durata; (*borrowing*) a breve scadenza

shot [ʃɔt] *pt, pp of* **shoot** ▷ *n* sparo, colpo; (*try*) prova; (*Football*) tiro; (*injection*) iniezione *f*; (*Phot*) foto *f inv*; **like a ~** come un razzo; (*very readily*) immediatamente; **shotgun** *n* fucile *m* da caccia

should [ʃud] *aux vb* **I ~ go now** dovrei andare ora; **he ~ be there now** dovrebbe essere arrivato ora; **I ~ go if I were you** se fossi in te andrei; **I ~ like to** mi piacerebbe

shoulder [ˈʃəuldəʳ] *n* spalla; (*BRIT: of road*): **hard ~** banchina ▷ *vt* (*fig*) addossarsi, prendere sulle proprie spalle; **shoulder blade** *n* scapola

shouldn't [ˈʃudnt] = **should not**

shout [ʃaut] *n* urlo, grido ▷ *vt* gridare ▷ *vi* (*also:* **~ out**) urlare, gridare

shove [ʃʌv] *vt* spingere; (*inf: put*): **to ~ sth in** ficcare qc in

shovel [ˈʃʌvl] *n* pala ▷ *vt* spalare

show [ʃəu] (*pt* **showed**, *pp* **shown**) *n* (*of emotion*) dimostrazione *f*, manifestazione *f*; (*semblance*) apparenza; (*exhibition*) mostra, esposizione *f*; (*Theatre, Cinema*) spettacolo ▷ *vt* far vedere, mostrare; (*courage etc*) dimostrare, dar prova di; (*exhibit*) esporre ▷ *vi* vedersi, essere visibile; **for ~** per fare scena; **on ~** (*exhibits etc*) esposto(-a); **can you ~ me where it is, please?** può mostrarmi dov'è, per favore?; **show in** *vt* (*person*) far entrare; **show off** *vi* (*pej*) esibirsi, mettersi in mostra ▷ *vt* (*display*) mettere in risalto; (*pej*) mettere in mostra; **show out** *vt* (*person*) accompagnare alla porta; **show up** *vi* (*stand out*) essere ben visibile; (*inf: turn up*) farsi vedere ▷ *vt* mettere in risalto; **show business** *n* industria dello spettacolo

shower [ˈʃauəʳ] *n* (*rain*) acquazzone *m*; (*of stones etc*) pioggia; (*also:* **~bath**) doccia ▷ *vi* fare la doccia ▷ *vt* **to ~ sb with** (*gifts, abuse etc*) coprire qn di; (*missiles*) lanciare contro qn una pioggia di; **to have a ~** fare la doccia; **shower cap** *n* cuffia da doccia; **shower gel** *n* gel *m* doccia inv

showing [ˈʃəuɪŋ] *n* (*of film*) proiezione *f*

show jumping *n* concorso ippico (di salto ad ostacoli)

shown [ʃəun] *pp of* **show**

show: **show-off** (*inf*) *n* (*person*) esibizionista *m/f*; **showroom** *n* sala d'esposizione

shrank [ʃræŋk] *pt of* **shrink**

shred [ʃred] *n* (*gen pl*) brandello ▷ *vt* fare a brandelli; (*Culin*) sminuzzare, tagliuzzare

shrewd [ʃruːd] *adj* astuto(-a), scaltro(-a)

shriek [ʃriːk] *n* strillo ▷ *vi* strillare

shrimp [ʃrimp] *n* gamberetto

shrine [ʃraɪn] n reliquario; (place) santuario

shrink [ʃrɪŋk] (pt **shrank**, pp **shrunk**) vi restringersi; (fig) ridursi; (also: ~ **away**) ritrarsi ▷ vt (wool) far restringere ▷ n (inf: pej) psicanalista m/f; **to ~ from doing sth** rifuggire dal fare qc

shrivel ['ʃrɪvl] (also: ~ **up**) vt raggrinzare, avvizzire ▷ vi raggrinzirsi, avvizzire

shroud [ʃraud] n lenzuolo funebre ▷ vt **~ed in mystery** avvolto(-a) nel mistero

Shrove Tuesday ['ʃrəuv-] n martedì m grasso

shrub [ʃrʌb] n arbusto

shrug [ʃrʌg] n scrollata di spalle ▷ vt, vi **to ~ (one's shoulders)** alzare le spalle, fare spallucce; **shrug off** vt passare sopra a

shrunk [ʃrʌŋk] pp of **shrink**

shudder ['ʃʌdə^r] n brivido ▷ vi rabbrividire

shuffle ['ʃʌfl] vt (cards) mescolare; **to ~ (one's feet)** strascicare i piedi

shun [ʃʌn] vt sfuggire, evitare

shut [ʃʌt] (pt, pp **shut**) vt chiudere ▷ vi chiudersi, chiudere; **shut down** vt, vi chiudere definitivamente; **shut up** vi (inf: keep quiet) stare zitto(-a), fare silenzio ▷ vt (close) chiudere; (silence) far tacere; **shutter** n imposta; (Phot) otturatore m

shuttle ['ʃʌtl] n spola, navetta; (space shuttle) navetta (spaziale); (also: ~ **service**) servizio m navetta inv; **shuttlecock** ['ʃʌtlkɔk] n volano

shy [ʃaɪ] adj timido(-a)

sibling ['sɪblɪŋ] n (formal) fratello/sorella

Sicily ['sɪsɪlɪ] n Sicilia

sick [sɪk] adj (ill) malato(-a); (vomiting): **to be ~** vomitare; (humour) macabro(-a); **to feel ~** avere la nausea; **to be ~ of** (fig) averne abbastanza di; **sickening** adj (fig) disgustoso(-a), rivoltante; **sick leave** n congedo per malattia; **sickly** adj malaticcio(-a); (causing nausea) nauseante; **sickness** n malattia; (vomiting) vomito

side [saɪd] n lato; (of lake) riva; (team) squadra ▷ cpd (door, entrance) laterale ▷ vi **to ~ with sb** parteggiare per qn, prendere le parti di qn; **by the ~ of** a fianco di; (road) sul ciglio di; **~ by ~** fianco a fianco; **from ~ to ~** da una parte all'altra; **to take ~s (with)** schierarsi (con); **sideboard** n credenza; **sideboards** (BRIT), **sideburns** ['saɪdbə:nz] npl (whiskers) basette fpl; **sidelight** n (Aut) luce f di posizione; **sideline** n (Sport) linea laterale; (fig) attività secondaria; **side order** n contorno (pietanza); **side road** n strada secondaria; **side street** n traversa; **sidetrack** vt (fig) distrarre; **sidewalk** (US) n marciapiede m; **sideways** adv (move) di lato, di fianco

siege [si:dʒ] n assedio

sieve [sɪv] n setaccio ▷ vt setacciare

sift [sɪft] vt passare al crivello; (fig) vagliare

sigh [saɪ] n sospiro ▷ vi sospirare

sight [saɪt] n (faculty) vista; (spectacle) spettacolo; (on gun) mira ▷ vt avvistare; **in ~** in vista; **on ~** a vista; **out of ~** non visibile; **sightseeing** n giro turistico; **to go sightseeing** visitare una località

sign [saɪn] n segno; (with hand etc) segno, gesto; (notice) insegna, cartello ▷ vt firmare; (player) ingaggiare; **where do I ~?** dove devo firmare?; **sign for** vt fus (item) firmare per l'accettazione di; **sign in** vi firmare il registro (all'arrivo); **sign on** vi (Mil) arruolarsi; (as unemployed) iscriversi sulla lista (dell'ufficio di collocamento) ▷ vt (Mil) arruolare; (employee) assumere; **sign up** vi (Mil) arruolarsi; (for course) iscriversi ▷ vt (player) ingaggiare; (recruits) reclutare

signal ['sɪgnl] n segnale m ▷ vi segnalare, mettere la freccia ▷ vt (person) fare segno a; (message) comunicare per mezzo di segnali

signature ['sɪgnətʃə^r] n firma

significance [sɪg'nɪfɪkəns] n significato; importanza

significant [sɪg'nɪfɪkənt] adj significativo(-a)

signify ['sɪgnɪfaɪ] vt significare

sign language n linguaggio dei muti

signpost ['saɪnpəust] n cartello indicatore

Sikh [si:k] adj, n sikh (m/f) inv

silence ['saɪlns] n silenzio ▷ vt far tacere, ridurre al silenzio

silent ['saɪlnt] adj silenzioso(-a); (film) muto(-a); **to remain ~** tacere, stare zitto

silhouette [sɪlu:'ɛt] n silhouette f inv

silicon chip ['sɪlɪkən-] n piastrina di silicio

silk [sɪlk] n seta ▷ adj di seta

silly ['sɪlɪ] adj stupido(-a), sciocco(-a)

silver ['sɪlvə^r] n argento; (money) monete da 5, 10, 20 or 50 pence; (also: ~**ware**) argenteria ▷ adj d'argento; **silver-plated** adj argentato(-a)

similar ['sɪmɪlə^r] adj **~ (to)** simile (a); **similarity** [sɪmɪ'lærɪtɪ] n somiglianza, rassomiglianza; **similarly** adv allo stesso modo; così pure

simmer ['sɪmə^r] vi cuocere a fuoco lento

simple ['sɪmpl] adj semplice; **simplicity** [-'plɪsɪtɪ] n semplicità; **simplify** vt semplificare; **simply** adv semplicemente

simulate ['sɪmjuleɪt] vt fingere, simulare

simultaneous [sɪməl'teɪnɪəs] adj simultaneo(-a); **simultaneously** adv simultaneamente, contemporaneamente

sin [sɪn] n peccato ▷ vi peccare

since [sɪns] adv da allora ▷ prep da ▷ conj

(*time*) da quando; (*because*) poiché, dato che; **~ then, ever ~** da allora

sincere [sɪn'sɪəʳ] *adj* sincero(-a); **sincerely** *adv* **yours sincerely** (*in letters*) distinti saluti

sing [sɪŋ] (*pt* **sang**, *pp* **sung**) *vt, vi* cantare

Singapore [sɪŋɡə'pɔːʳ] *n* Singapore *f*

singer ['sɪŋəʳ] *n* cantante *m/f*

singing ['sɪŋɪŋ] *n* canto

single ['sɪŋɡl] *adj* solo(-a), unico(-a); (*unmarried: man*) celibe; (: *woman*) nubile; (*not double*) semplice ▷ *n* (BRIT: *also:* **~ ticket**) biglietto di (sola) andata; (*record*) 45 giri *m*; **~s** *n* (*Tennis*) singolo; **single out** *vt* scegliere; (*distinguish*) distinguere; **single bed** *n* letto singolo; **single file** *n* **in single file** in fila indiana; **single-handed** *adv* senza aiuto, da solo(-a); **single-minded** *adj* tenace, risoluto(-a); **single parent** *n* (*mother*) ragazza *f* madre *inv*; (*father*) ragazzo *m* padre *inv*; **single-parent family** famiglia monoparentale; **single room** *n* camera singola

singular ['sɪŋɡjuləʳ] *adj* (*exceptional*, *Ling*) singolare ▷ *n* (*Ling*) singolare *m*

sinister ['sɪnɪstəʳ] *adj* sinistro(-a)

sink [sɪŋk] (*pt* **sank**, *pp* **sunk**) *n* lavandino, acquaio ▷ *vt* (*ship*) (fare) affondare, colare a picco; (*foundations*) scavare; (*piles etc*): **to ~ sth into** conficcare qc in ▷ *vi* affondare, andare a fondo; (*ground etc*) cedere, avvallarsi; **my heart sank** mi sentii venir meno; **sink in** *vi* penetrare

sinus ['saɪnəs] *n* (*Anat*) seno

sip [sɪp] *n* sorso ▷ *vt* sorseggiare

sir [səʳ] *n* signore *m*; **S~ John Smith** Sir John Smith; **yes ~** sì, signore

siren ['saɪərn] *n* sirena

sirloin ['səːlɔɪn] *n* controfiletto

sister ['sɪstəʳ] *n* sorella; (*nun*) suora; (BRIT: *nurse*) infermiera *f* caposala *inv*; **sister-in-law** *n* cognata

sit [sɪt] (*pt, pp* **sat**) *vi* sedere, sedersi; (*assembly*) essere in seduta; (*for painter*) posare ▷ *vt* (*exam*) sostenere, dare; **sit back** *vi* (*in seat*) appoggiarsi allo schienale; **sit down** *vi* sedersi; **sit on** *vt fus* (*jury, committee*) far parte di; **sit up** *vi* tirarsi su a sedere; (*not go to bed*) stare alzato(-a) fino a tardi

sitcom ['sɪtkɔm] *n abbr* (= *situation comedy*) commedia di situazione; (*TV*) telefilm *m inv* comico d'interni

site [saɪt] *n* posto; (*also:* **building ~**) cantiere *m* ▷ *vt* situare

sitting ['sɪtɪŋ] *n* (*of assembly etc*) seduta; (*in canteen*) turno; **sitting room** *n* soggiorno

situated ['sɪtjueɪtɪd] *adj* situato(-a)

situation [sɪtju'eɪʃən] *n* situazione *f*; (*job*)

lavoro; (*location*) posizione *f*; **"~s vacant"** (BRIT) "offerte *fpl* di impiego"

six [sɪks] *num* sei; **sixteen** *num* sedici; **sixteenth** [sɪks'tiːnθ] *num* sedicesimo(-a); **sixth** *num* sesto(-a); **sixth form** *n* (BRIT) ultimo biennio delle scuole superiori; **sixth-form college** *n* istituto che offre corsi di preparazione all'esame di maturità per ragazzi dai 16 ai 18 anni; **sixtieth** ['sɪkstɪɪθ] *num* sessantesimo(-a) ▷ *pron* (*in series*) sessantesimo; (*fraction*) sessantesimo; **sixty** *num* sessanta

size [saɪz] *n* dimensioni *fpl*; (*of clothing*) taglia, misura; (*of shoes*) numero; (*glue*) colla; **sizeable** *adj* considerevole

sizzle ['sɪzl] *vi* sfrigolare

skate [skeɪt] *n* pattino; (*fish: pl inv*) razza ▷ *vi* pattinare; **skateboard** *n* skateboard *m inv*; **skateboarding** *n* skateboard *m inv*; **skater** *n* pattinatore(-trice); **skating** *n* pattinaggio; **skating rink** *n* pista di pattinaggio

skeleton ['skelɪtn] *n* scheletro

skeptical ['skeptɪkl] (US) *adj* = **sceptical**

sketch [sketʃ] *n* (*drawing*) schizzo, abbozzo; (*Theatre*) scenetta comica, sketch *m inv* ▷ *vt* abbozzare, schizzare

skewer ['skjuːəʳ] *n* spiedo

ski [skiː] *n* sci *m inv* ▷ *vi* sciare; **ski boot** *n* scarpone *m* da sci

skid [skɪd] *n* slittamento ▷ *vi* slittare

ski: skier ['skiːəʳ] *n* sciatore(-trice); **skiing** ['skiːɪŋ] *n* sci *m*

skilful ['skɪlful] (US **skillful**) *adj* abile

ski lift *n* sciovia

skill [skɪl] *n* abilità *f inv*, capacità *f inv*; **skilled** *adj* esperto(-a); (*worker*) qualificato(-a), specializzato(-a)

skim [skɪm] *vt* (*milk*) scremare; (*glide over*) sfiorare ▷ *vi* **to ~ through** (*fig*) scorrere, dare una scorsa a; **skimmed milk** (US **skim milk**) *n* latte *m* scremato

skin [skɪn] *n* pelle *f* ▷ *vt* (*fruit etc*) sbucciare; (*animal*) scuoiare, spellare; **skinhead** *n* skinhead *m/f inv*; **skinny** *adj* molto magro(-a), pelle e ossa *inv*

skip [skɪp] *n* saltello, balzo; (BRIT: *container*) benna ▷ *vi* saltare; (*with rope*) saltare la corda ▷ *vt* saltare

ski: ski pass *n* ski pass *m*; **ski pole** *n* racchetta (da sci)

skipper ['skɪpəʳ] *n* (*Naut, Sport*) capitano

skipping rope ['skɪpɪŋ-] (US **skip rope**) *n* corda per saltare

skirt [skəːt] *n* gonna, sottana ▷ *vt* fiancheggiare, costeggiare

skirting board (BRIT) *n* zoccolo

ski slope *n* pista da sci

ski suit *n* tuta da sci

skull [skʌl] n cranio, teschio

skunk [skʌŋk] n moffetta

sky [skaɪ] n cielo; **skyscraper** n grattacielo

slab [slæb] n lastra; (of cake, cheese) fetta

slack [slæk] adj (loose) allentato(-a); (slow) lento(-a); (careless) negligente; **slacks** npl (trousers) pantaloni mpl

slain [sleɪn] pp of **slay**

slam [slæm] vt (door) sbattere; (throw) scaraventare; (criticize) stroncare ▷ vi sbattere

slander ['slɑːndəʳ] n calunnia; diffamazione f

slang [slæŋ] n gergo, slang m

slant [slɑːnt] n pendenza, inclinazione f; (fig) angolazione f, punto di vista

slap [slæp] n manata, pacca; (on face) schiaffo ▷ vt dare una manata a; schiaffeggiare ▷ adv (directly) in pieno; **~ a coat of paint on it** dagli una mano di vernice

slash [slæʃ] vt tagliare; (face) sfregiare; (fig: prices) ridurre drasticamente, tagliare

slate [sleɪt] n ardesia; (piece) lastra di ardesia ▷ vt (fig: criticize) stroncare, distruggere

slaughter ['slɔːtəʳ] n strage f, massacro ▷ vt (animal) macellare; (people) trucidare, massacrare; **slaughterhouse** n macello, mattatoio

Slav [slɑːv] adj, n slavo(-a)

slave [sleɪv] n schiavo(-a) ▷ vi (also: ~ away) lavorare come uno schiavo; **slavery** n schiavitù f

slay [sleɪ] (pt **slew**, pp **slain**) vt (formal) uccidere

sleazy ['sliːzɪ] adj trasandato(-a)

sled [slɛd] (US) = **sledge**

sledge [slɛdʒ] n slitta

sleek [sliːk] adj (hair, fur) lucido(-a), lucente; (car, boat) slanciato(-a), affusolato(-a)

sleep [sliːp] (pt, pp **slept**) n sonno ▷ vi dormire; **to go to ~** addormentarsi; **sleep in** vi (oversleep) dormire fino a tardi; **sleep together** vi (have sex) andare a letto insieme; **sleeper** n (BRIT) (Rail: on track) traversina; (: train) treno di vagoni letto; **sleeping bag** n sacco a pelo; **sleeping car** n vagone m letto inv, carrozza f letto inv; **sleeping pill** n sonnifero; **sleepover** n notte f che un ragazzino passa da amici; **sleepwalk** vi camminare nel sonno; (as a habit) essere sonnambulo(-a); **sleepy** adj assonnato(-a), sonnolento(-a); (fig) addormentato(-a)

sleet [sliːt] n nevischio

sleeve [sliːv] n manica; (of record) copertina; **sleeveless** adj (garment) senza maniche

sleigh [sleɪ] n slitta

slender ['slɛndəʳ] adj snello(-a), sottile; (not enough) scarso(-a), esiguo(-a)

slept [slɛpt] pt, pp of **sleep**

slew [sluː] pt of **slay** ▷ vi (BRIT) girare

slice [slaɪs] n fetta ▷ vt affettare, tagliare a fette

slick [slɪk] adj (skilful) brillante; (clever) furbo(-a) ▷ n (also: **oil ~**) chiazza di petrolio

slide [slaɪd] (pt, pp **slid**) n scivolone m; (in playground) scivolo; (Phot) diapositiva; (BRIT: also: **hair ~**) fermaglio (per capelli) ▷ vt far scivolare ▷ vi scivolare; **sliding** adj (door) scorrevole

slight [slaɪt] adj (slim) snello(-a), sottile; (frail) delicato(-a), fragile; (trivial) insignificante; (small) piccolo(-a) ▷ n offesa, affronto; **not in the ~est** affatto, neppure per sogno; **slightly** adv lievemente, un po'

slim [slɪm] adj magro(-a), snello(-a) ▷ vi dimagrire; fare (or seguire) una dieta dimagrante; **slimming** ['slɪmɪŋ] adj (diet) dimagrante; (food) ipocalorico(-a)

slimy ['slaɪmɪ] adj (also fig: person) viscido(-a); (covered with mud) melmoso(-a)

sling [slɪŋ] (pt, pp **slung**) n (Med) fascia al collo; (for baby) marsupio ▷ vt lanciare, tirare

slip [slɪp] n scivolata, scivolone m; (mistake) errore m, sbaglio; (underskirt) sottoveste f; (of paper) striscia di carta; tagliando, scontrino ▷ vt (slide) far scivolare ▷ vi (slide) scivolare; (move smoothly): **to ~ into/out of** scivolare in/fuori da; (decline) declinare; **to ~ sth on/off** infilarsi/togliersi qc; **to give sb the ~** sfuggire qn; **a ~ of the tongue** un lapsus linguae; **slip up** vi sbagliarsi

slipper ['slɪpəʳ] n pantofola

slippery ['slɪpərɪ] adj scivoloso(-a)

slip road (BRIT) n (to motorway) rampa di accesso

slit [slɪt] (pt, pp **slit**) n fessura, fenditura; (cut) taglio ▷ vt fendere; tagliare

slog [slɔg] (BRIT) n faticata ▷ vi lavorare con accanimento, sgobbare

slogan ['sləugən] n motto, slogan m inv

slope [sləup] n pendio; (side of mountain) versante m; (ski slope) pista; (of roof) pendenza; (of floor) inclinazione f ▷ vi **to ~ down** declinare; **to ~ up** essere in salita; **sloping** adj inclinato(-a)

sloppy ['slɔpɪ] adj (work) tirato(-a) via; (appearance) sciatto(-a)

slot [slɔt] n fessura ▷ vt **to ~ sth into** infilare qc in; **slot machine** n

(BRIT: *vending machine*) distributore m automatico; (*for gambling*) slot-machine f inv

Slovakia [sləʊ'vækɪə] n Slovacchia

Slovene ['sləʊviːn] adj sloveno(-a) ▷ n sloveno(-a); (*Ling*) sloveno

Slovenia [sləʊ'viːnɪə] n Slovenia; **Slovenian** adj, n = **Slovene**

slow [sləʊ] adj lento(-a); (*watch*): **to be ~** essere indietro ▷ adv lentamente ▷ vt, vi (*also:* **~ down, ~ up**) rallentare; **"~"** (*road sign*) "rallentare"; **slow down** vi rallentare; **slowly** adv lentamente; **slow motion** n **in slow motion** al rallentatore

slug [slʌɡ] n lumaca; (*bullet*) pallottola; **sluggish** adj lento(-a); (*trading*) stagnante

slum [slʌm] n catapecchia

slump [slʌmp] n crollo, caduta; (*economic*) depressione f, crisi f inv ▷ vi crollare

slung [slʌŋ] pt, pp of **sling**

slur [sləːʳ] n (*fig*): **~ (on)** calunnia (su) ▷ vt pronunciare in modo indistinto

sly [slaɪ] adj (*smile, remark*) sornione(-a); (*person*) furbo(-a)

smack [smæk] n (*slap*) pacca; (*on face*) schiaffo ▷ vt schiaffeggiare; (*child*) picchiare ▷ vi **to ~ of** puzzare di

small [smɔːl] adj piccolo(-a); **small ads** (BRIT) npl piccola pubblicità; **small change** n moneta, spiccioli mpl

smart [smɑːt] adj elegante; (*fashionable*) alla moda; (*clever*) intelligente; (*quick*) sveglio(-a) ▷ vi bruciare; **smartcard** ['smɑːtkɑːd] n smartcard f inv, carta intelligente

smash [smæʃ] n (*also:* **~-up**) scontro, collisione f; (*smash hit*) successo m ▷ vt frantumare, fracassare; (*Sport: record*) battere ▷ vi frantumarsi, andare in pezzi; **smashing** (*inf*) adj favoloso(-a), formidabile

smear [smɪəʳ] n macchia; (*Med*) striscio ▷ vt spalmare; (*make dirty*) sporcare; **smear test** n (BRIT Med) Pap-test m inv

smell [smɛl] (pt **smelt** or **smelled**) n odore m; (*sense*) olfatto, odorato ▷ vt sentire (l')odore di ▷ vi (*food etc*): **to ~ (of)** avere odore (di); (*pej*) puzzare, avere un cattivo odore; **smelly** adj puzzolente

smelt [smɛlt] pt, pp of **smell** ▷ vt (*ore*) fondere

smile [smaɪl] n sorriso ▷ vi sorridere

smirk [sməːk] n sorriso furbo; sorriso compiaciuto

smog [smɔɡ] n smog m

smoke [sməʊk] n fumo ▷ vt, vi fumare; **do you mind if I ~?** le dà fastidio se fumo?; **smoke alarm** n rivelatore f di fumo; **smoked** adj (*bacon, glass*) affumicato(-a);

smoker n (*person*) fumatore(-trice); (*Rail*) carrozza per fumatori; **smoking** n fumo; **"no smoking"** (*sign*) "vietato fumare"; **smoky** adj fumoso(-a); (*taste*) affumicato(-a)

smooth [smuːð] adj liscio(-a); (*sauce*) omogeneo(-a); (*flavour, whisky*) amabile; (*movement*) regolare; (*person*) mellifluo(-a) ▷ vt (*also:* **~ out**) lisciare, spianare; (*: difficulties*) appianare

smother ['smʌðəʳ] vt soffocare

SMS abbr (= *short message service*) SMS; **SMS message** n SMS m inv, messaggino

smudge [smʌdʒ] n macchia; sbavatura ▷ vt imbrattare, sporcare

smug [smʌɡ] adj soddisfatto(-a), compiaciuto(-a)

smuggle ['smʌɡl] vt contrabbandare; **smuggling** n contrabbando

snack [snæk] n spuntino; **snack bar** n tavola calda, snack bar m inv

snag [snæɡ] n intoppo, ostacolo imprevisto

snail [sneɪl] n chiocciola

snake [sneɪk] n serpente m

snap [snæp] n (*sound*) schianto, colpo secco; (*photograph*) istantanea ▷ adj improvviso(-a) ▷ vt (far) schioccare; (*break*) spezzare di netto ▷ vi spezzarsi con un rumore secco; (*fig: person*) parlare con tono secco; **to ~ shut** chiudersi di scatto; **snap at** vt fus (*dog*) cercare di mordere; **snap up** vt afferrare; **snapshot** n istantanea

snarl [snɑːl] vi ringhiare

snatch [snætʃ] n (*small amount*) frammento ▷ vt strappare (con violenza); (*fig*) rubare

sneak [sniːk] (pt (US) **snuck**) vi **to ~ in/out** entrare/uscire di nascosto ▷ n spione(-a); **to ~ up on sb** avvicinarsi quatto quatto a qn; **sneakers** npl scarpe fpl da ginnastica

sneer [snɪəʳ] vi sogghignare; **to ~ at** farsi beffe di

sneeze [sniːz] n starnuto ▷ vi starnutire

sniff [snɪf] n fiutata, annusata ▷ vi tirare su col naso ▷ vt fiutare, annusare

snigger ['snɪɡəʳ] vi ridacchiare, ridere sotto i baffi

snip [snɪp] n pezzetto; (*bargain*) (buon) affare m, occasione f ▷ vt tagliare

sniper ['snaɪpəʳ] n (*marksman*) franco tiratore m, cecchino

snob [snɔb] n snob m/f inv

snooker ['snuːkəʳ] n tipo di gioco del biliardo

snoop ['snuːp] vi **to ~ about** curiosare

snooze [snuːz] n sonnellino, pisolino ▷ vi fare un sonnellino

snore [snɔːʳ] vi russare

snorkel ['snɔːkl] n (*of swimmer*) respiratore

m a tubo

snort [snɔːt] *n* sbuffo ▷ *vi* sbuffare

snow [snəʊ] *n* neve *f* ▷ *vi* nevicare; **snowball** *n* palla di neve ▷ *vi* (*fig*) crescere a vista d'occhio; **snowstorm** *n* tormenta

snub [snʌb] *vt* snobbare ▷ *n* offesa, affronto

snug [snʌg] *adj* comodo(-a); (*room, house*) accogliente, comodo(-a)

🔵 **KEYWORD**

so [səʊ] *adv* **1** (*thus, likewise*) così; **if so** se è così, quand'è così; **I didn't do it — you did so!** non l'ho fatto io — sì che l'hai fatto!; **so do I, so am I** *etc* anch'io; **it's 5 o'clock — so it is!** sono le 5 — davvero!; **I hope so** lo spero; **I think so** penso di sì; **so far** finora, fin qui; (*in past*) fino ad allora

2 (*in comparisons etc: to such a degree*) così; **so big (that)** così grande (che); **she's not so clever as her brother** lei non è (così) intelligente come suo fratello

3: so much *adj* tanto(-a) ▷ *adv* tanto; **I've got so much work/money** ho tanto lavoro/tanti soldi; **I love you so much** ti amo tanto; **so many** tanti(-e)

4 (*phrases*): **10 or so** circa 10; **so long!** (*inf: goodbye*) ciao!, ci vediamo!

▷ *conj* **1** (*expressing purpose*): **so as to do** in modo or così da fare; **we hurried so as not to be late** ci affrettammo per non fare tardi; **so (that)** affinché + *sub*, perché + *sub*

2 (*expressing result*): **he didn't arrive so I left** non è venuto così me ne sono andata; **so you see, I could have gone** vedi, sarei potuto andare

soak [səʊk] *vt* inzuppare; (*clothes*) mettere a mollo ▷ *vi* (*clothes etc*) essere a mollo; **soak up** *vt* assorbire; **soaking** *adj* (*also:* **soaking wet**) fradicio(-a)

so-and-so ['səʊənsəʊ] *n* (*somebody*) un tale; **Mr/Mrs ~** signor/signora tal dei tali

soap [səʊp] *n* sapone *m*; **soap opera** *n* soap opera *f inv*; **soap powder** *n* detersivo

soar [sɔːʳ] *vi* volare in alto; (*price etc*) salire alle stelle; (*building*) ergersi

sob [sɔb] *n* singhiozzo ▷ *vi* singhiozzare

sober ['səʊbəʳ] *adj* sobrio(-a); (*not drunk*) non ubriaco(-a); (*moderate*) moderato(-a); **sober up** *vt* far passare la sbornia a ▷ *vi* farsi passare la sbornia

so-called ['səʊ'kɔːld] *adj* cosiddetto(-a)

soccer ['sɔkəʳ] *n* calcio

sociable ['səʊʃəbl] *adj* socievole

social ['səʊʃl] *adj* sociale ▷ *n* festa, serata; **socialism** *n* socialismo; **socialist** *adj, n*

socialista *m/f*; **socialize** *vi* **to socialize (with)** socializzare (con); **social life** *n* vita sociale; **socially** *adv* socialmente, in società; **social security** (*BRIT*) *n* previdenza sociale; **social services** *npl* servizi *mpl* sociali; **social work** *n* servizio sociale; **social worker** *n* assistente *m/f* sociale

society [sə'saɪətɪ] *n* società *f inv*; (*club*) società, associazione *f*; (*also:* **high ~**) alta società

sociology [səʊsɪ'ɔlədʒɪ] *n* sociologia

sock [sɔk] *n* calzino

socket ['sɔkɪt] *n* cavità *f inv*; (*of eye*) orbita; (*BRIT: Elec: also:* **wall ~**) presa di corrente

soda ['səʊdə] *n* (*Chem*) soda; (*also:* **soda water**) acqua di seltz; (*US: also:* **soda pop**) gassosa

sodium ['səʊdɪəm] *n* sodio

sofa ['səʊfə] *n* sofà *m inv*; **sofa bed** *n* divano *m* letto inv

soft [sɔft] *adj* (*not rough*) morbido(-a); (*not hard*) soffice; (*not loud*) sommesso(-a); (*not bright*) tenue; (*kind*) gentile; **soft drink** *n* analcolico; **soft drugs** *npl* droghe *fpl* leggere; **soften** ['sɔfn] *vt* ammorbidire; addolcire; attenuare ▷ *vi* ammorbidirsi; addolcirsi; attenuarsi; **softly** *adv* dolcemente; morbidamente; **software** ['sɔftwɛəʳ] *n* (*Comput*) software *m*

soggy ['sɔgɪ] *adj* inzuppato(-a)

soil [sɔɪl] *n* terreno ▷ *vt* sporcare

solar ['səʊləʳ] *adj* solare; **solar power** *n* energie solare; **solar system** *n* sistema *m* solare

sold [səʊld] *pt, pp of* **sell**

soldier ['səʊldʒəʳ] *n* soldato, militare *m*

sold out *adj* (*Comm*) esaurito(-a)

sole [səʊl] *n* (*of foot*) pianta (del piede); (*of shoe*) suola; (*fish: pl inv*) sogliola ▷ *adj* solo(-a), unico(-a); **solely** *adv* solamente, unicamente; **I will hold you solely responsible** la considererò il solo responsabile

solemn ['sɔləm] *adj* solenne

solicitor [sə'lɪsɪtəʳ] (*BRIT*) *n* (*for wills etc*) ≈ notaio; (*in court*) ≈ avvocato

solid ['sɔlɪd] *adj* solido(-a); (*not hollow*) pieno(-a); (*meal*) sostanzioso(-a) ▷ *n* solido

solitary ['sɔlɪtərɪ] *adj* solitario(-a)

solitude ['sɔlɪtjuːd] *n* solitudine *f*

solo ['səʊləʊ] *n* assolo; **soloist** *n* solista *m/f*

soluble ['sɔljʊbl] *adj* solubile

solution [sə'luːʃən] *n* soluzione *f*

solve [sɔlv] *vt* risolvere

solvent ['sɔlvənt] *adj* (*Comm*) solvibile ▷ *n* (*Chem*) solvente *m*

sombre ['sɔmbə'] (US **somber**) adj
scuro(-a); (mood, person) triste

 KEYWORD

some [sʌm] adj **1** (a certain amount or number
of): **some tea/water/cream** del tè/
dell'acqua/della panna; **some children/
apples** dei bambini/delle mele
2 (certain: in contrasts) certo(-a); **some
people say that ...** alcuni dicono che ...,
certa gente dice che ...
3 (unspecified) un(a) certo(-a), qualche;
some woman was asking for you una
tale chiedeva di lei; **some day** un giorno;
some day next week un giorno della
prossima settimana
▷ pron **1** (a certain number) alcuni(-e),
certi(-e); **I've got some** (books etc) ne ho
alcuni; **some (of them) have been sold**
alcuni sono stati venduti
2 (a certain amount) un po'; **I've got some**
(money, milk) ne ho un po'; **I've read some
of the book** ho letto parte del libro
▷ adv **some 10 people** circa 10 persone

some: **somebody** ['sʌmbədɪ] pron
= **someone**; **somehow** ['sʌmhau] adv
in un modo o nell'altro, in qualche modo;
(for some reason) per qualche ragione;
someone ['sʌmwʌn] pron qualcuno;
someplace ['sʌmpleɪs] (US) adv
= **somewhere**; **something** ['sʌmθɪŋ]
pron qualcosa, qualche cosa; **something
nice** qualcosa di bello; **something to do**
qualcosa da fare; **sometime** ['sʌmtaɪm]
adv (in future) una volta o l'altra; (in past):
sometime last month durante il mese
scorso; **sometimes** ['sʌmtaɪmz] adv
qualche volta; **somewhat** ['sʌmwɔt] adv
piuttosto; **somewhere** ['sʌmwɛə'] adv in
or da qualche parte
son [sʌn] n figlio
song [sɔn] n canzone f
son-in-law ['sʌnɪnlɔː] n genero
soon [suːn] adv presto, fra poco; (early, a
short time after) presto; **~ afterwards** poco
dopo; see also **as**; **sooner** adv (time) prima;
(preference): **I would sooner do** preferirei
fare; **sooner or later** prima o poi
soothe [suːð] vt calmare
sophisticated [sə'fɪstɪkeɪtɪd]
adj sofisticato(-a); raffinato(-a);
complesso(-a)
sophomore ['sɔfəmɔː'] (US) n
studente(-essa) del secondo anno
soprano [sə'prɑːnəu] n (voice) soprano m;
(singer) soprano m/f
sorbet ['sɔːbeɪ] n sorbetto

sordid ['sɔːdɪd] adj sordido(-a)
sore [sɔː'] adj (painful) dolorante ▷ n piaga
sorrow ['sɔrəu] n dolore m
sorry ['sɔrɪ] adj spiacente; (condition,
excuse) misero(-a); **~!** scusa! (or scusi! or
scusate!); **to feel ~ for sb** rincrescersi
per qn
sort [sɔːt] n specie f, genere m; **sort out** vt
(papers) classificare; ordinare; (: letters etc)
smistare; (: problems) risolvere; (Comput)
ordinare
SOS n abbr (= save our souls) S.O.S. m inv
so-so ['səusəu] adv così così
sought [sɔːt] pt, pp of **seek**
soul [səul] n anima
sound [saund] adj (healthy) sano(-a); (safe,
not damaged) solido(-a), in buono stato;
(reliable, not superficial) solido(-a); (sensible)
giudizioso(-a), di buon senso ▷ adv **~
asleep** profondamente addormentato
▷ n suono; (noise) rumore m; (Geo) stretto
▷ vt (alarm) suonare ▷ vi suonare; (fig:
seem) sembrare; **to ~ like** rassomigliare a;
soundtrack n (of film) colonna sonora
soup [suːp] n minestra; brodo; zuppa
sour ['sauə'] adj aspro(-a); (fruit)
acerbo(-a); (milk) acido(-a); (fig)
arcigno(-a); acido(-a); **it's ~ grapes** è
soltanto invidia
source [sɔːs] n fonte f, sorgente f; (fig)
fonte
south [sauθ] n sud m, meridione m,
mezzogiorno ▷ adj del sud, sud inv,
meridionale ▷ adv verso sud; **South
Africa** n Sudafrica m; **South African**
adj, n sudafricano(-a); **South America** n
Sudamerica m, America del sud; **South
American** adj, n sudamericano(-a);
southbound ['sauθbaund] adj (gen)
diretto(-a) a sud; (carriageway) sud
inv; **southeastern** [sauθ'iːstən] adj
sudorientale; **southern** ['sʌðən] adj
del sud, meridionale; esposto(-a) a sud;
South Korea n Corea f del Sud; **South
Pole** n Polo Sud; **southward(s)** adv
verso sud; **south-west** n sud-ovest
m; **southwestern** [sauθ'westən] adj
sudoccidentale
souvenir [suːvə'nɪə'] n ricordo, souvenir
m inv
sovereign ['sɔvrɪn] adj, n sovrano(-a)
sow[1] [səu] (pt **sowed**, pp **sown**) vt
seminare
sow[2] [sau] n scrofa
soya ['sɔɪə] (US **soy**) n **~ bean** n seme m di
soia; **soya sauce** n salsa di soia
spa [spɑː] n (resort) stazione f termale; (US:
also: **health ~**) centro di cure estetiche
space [speɪs] n spazio; (room) posto;

spazio; (*length of time*) intervallo ▷ *cpd*
spaziale ▷ *vt* (*also:* **~ out**) distanziare;
spacecraft *n inv* veicolo spaziale;
spaceship *n* = **spacecraft**
spacious ['speɪʃəs] *adj* spazioso(-a),
ampio(-a)
spade [speɪd] *n* (*tool*) vanga; pala; (*child's*)
paletta; **~s** *npl* (*Cards*) picche *fpl*
spaghetti [spə'gɛtɪ] *n* spaghetti *mpl*
Spain [speɪn] *n* Spagna
spam [spæm] (*Comput*) *n* spamming ▷ *vt*
to ~ sb inviare a qn messaggi pubblicitari
non richiesti via email
span [spæn] *n* (*of bird, plane*) apertura
alare; (*of arch*) campata; (*in time*) periodo;
durata ▷ *vt* attraversare; (*fig*) abbracciare
Spaniard ['spænjəd] *n* spagnolo(-a)
Spanish ['spænɪʃ] *adj* spagnolo(-a) ▷ *n*
(*Ling*) spagnolo; **the ~** *npl* gli Spagnoli
spank [spæŋk] *vt* sculacciare
spanner ['spænəʳ] (*BRIT*) *n* chiave *f* inglese
spare [spɛəʳ] *adj* di riserva, di scorta;
(*surplus*) in più, d'avanzo ▷ *n* (*part*) pezzo
di ricambio ▷ *vt* (*do without*) fare a meno
di; (*afford to give*) concedere; (*refrain from
hurting, using*) risparmiare; **to ~** (*surplus*)
d'avanzo; **spare part** *n* pezzo di ricambio;
spare room *n* stanza degli ospiti; **spare
time** *n* tempo libero; **spare tyre** (*us* **spare
tire**) *n* (*Aut*) gomma di scorta; **spare
wheel** *n* (*Aut*) ruota di scorta
spark [spɑːk] *n* scintilla; **spark(ing) plug**
n candela
sparkle ['spɑːkl] *n* scintillio, sfavillio ▷ *vi*
scintillare, sfavillare
sparrow ['spærəʊ] *n* passero
sparse [spɑːs] *adj* sparso(-a), rado(-a)
spasm ['spæzəm] *n* (*Med*) spasmo; (*fig*)
accesso, attacco
spat [spæt] *pt, pp of* **spit**
spate [speɪt] *n* (*fig*): **~ of** diluvio *or* fiume
m di
spatula ['spætjʊlə] *n* spatola
speak [spiːk] (*pt* **spoke**, *pp* **spoken**) *vt*
(*language*) parlare; (*truth*) dire ▷ *vi* parlare;
I don't ~ Italian non parlo italiano; **do you
~ English?** parla inglese?; **to ~ to sb/of** *or*
about sth parlare a qn/di qc; **can I ~ to ...?**
posso parlare con...?; **~ up!** parla più forte!;
speaker *n* (*in public*) oratore(-trice);
(*also:* **loudspeaker**) altoparlante *m*; (*Pol*):
the Speaker il presidente della Camera dei
Comuni (*BRIT*) *or* dei Rappresentanti (*us*)
spear [spɪəʳ] *n* lancia ▷ *vt* infilzare
special ['spɛʃl] *adj* speciale; **special
delivery** *n* (*Post*): **by special delivery**
per espresso; **special effects** *npl*
(*Cine*) effetti *mpl* speciali; **specialist** *n*
specialista *m/f*; **speciality** [spɛʃɪ'ælɪtɪ]

n specialità *f inv*; **I'd like to try a local
speciality** vorrei assaggiare una specialità
del posto; **specialize** *vi* **to specialize
(in)** specializzarsi (in); **specially** *adv*
specialmente, particolarmente;
special needs *adj* **special needs
children** bambini *mpl* con difficoltà di
apprendimento; **special offer** *n* (*Comm*)
offerta speciale; **special school** *n* (*BRIT*):
scuola speciale (*per portatori di handicap*);
specialty (*us*) *n* = **speciality**
species ['spiːʃɪːz] *n inv* specie *f inv*
specific [spə'sɪfɪk] *adj* specifico(-a);
preciso(-a); **specifically** *adv*
esplicitamente; (*especially*) appositamente
specify ['spɛsɪfaɪ] *vt* specificare, precisare;
unless otherwise specified salvo
indicazioni contrarie
specimen ['spɛsɪmən] *n* esemplare *m*,
modello; (*Med*) campione *m*
speck [spɛk] *n* puntino, macchiolina;
(*particle*) granello
spectacle ['spɛktəkl] *n* spettacolo; **~s**
npl (*glasses*) occhiali *mpl*; **spectacular**
[-'tækjʊləʳ] *adj* spettacolare
spectator [spɛk'teɪtəʳ] *n* spettatore *m*
spectrum ['spɛktrəm] (*pl* **spectra**) *n*
spettro
speculate ['spɛkjʊleɪt] *vi* speculare; (*try to
guess*): **to ~ about** fare ipotesi su
sped [spɛd] *pt, pp of* **speed**
speech [spiːtʃ] *n* (*faculty*) parola; (*talk,
Theatre*) discorso; (*manner of speaking*)
parlata; **speechless** *adj* ammutolito(-a),
muto(-a)
speed [spiːd] *n* velocità *f inv*; (*promptness*)
prontezza; **at full** *or* **top ~** a tutta velocità;
speed up *vi*, *vt* accelerare; **speedboat** *n*
motoscafo; **speeding** *n* (*Aut*) eccesso
di velocità; **speed limit** *n* limite *m* di
velocità; **speedometer** [spɪ'dɔmɪtəʳ] *n*
tachimetro; **speedy** *adj* veloce, rapido(-a);
pronto(-a)
spell [spɛl] (*pt, pp* **spelt** (*BRIT*) *or* **spelled**) *n*
(*also:* **magic ~**) incantesimo; (*period of time*)
(*breve*) periodo ▷ *vt* (*in writing*) scrivere
(*lettera per lettera*); (*aloud*) dire lettera per
lettera; (*fig*) significare; **to cast a ~ on sb**
fare un incantesimo a qn; **he can't ~** fa
errori di ortografia; **spell out** *vt* (*letter by
letter*) dettare lettera per lettera; (*explain*):
to ~ sth out for sb spiegare qc a qn per
filo e per segno; **spellchecker** ['spɛltʃɛkəʳ]
n correttore *m* ortografico; **spelling** *n*
ortografia
spelt [spɛlt] (*BRIT*) *pt, pp of* **spell**
spend [spɛnd] (*pt, pp* **spent**) *vt* (*money*)
spendere; (*time, life*) passare; **spending** *n*
government spending spesa pubblica

spent [spɛnt] *pt, pp of* **spend**

sperm [spə:m] *n* sperma *m*

sphere [sfɪəʳ] *n* sfera

spice [spaɪs] *n* spezia ▷ *vt* aromatizzare

spicy ['spaɪsɪ] *adj* piccante

spider ['spaɪdəʳ] *n* ragno

spike [spaɪk] *n* punta

spill [spɪl] (*pt, pp* **spilt** *or* **spilled**) *vt* versare, rovesciare ▷ *vi* versarsi, rovesciarsi

spin [spɪn] (*pt, pp* **spun**) *n* (*revolution of wheel*) rotazione *f*; (*Aviat*) avvitamento; (*trip in car*) giretto ▷ *vt* (*wool etc*) filare; (*wheel*) far girare ▷ *vi* girare

spinach ['spɪnɪtʃ] *n* spinacio; (*as food*) spinaci *mpl*

spinal ['spaɪnl] *adj* spinale

spin doctor (*inf*) *n* esperto di comunicazioni responsabile dell'immagine di un partito politico

spin-dryer [spɪn'draɪəʳ] (*BRIT*) *n* centrifuga

spine [spaɪn] *n* spina dorsale; (*thorn*) spina

spiral ['spaɪərl] *n* spirale *f* ▷ *vi* (*fig*) salire a spirale

spire ['spaɪəʳ] *n* guglia

spirit ['spɪrɪt] *n* spirito; (*ghost*) spirito, fantasma *m*; (*mood*) stato d'animo, umore *m*; (*courage*) coraggio; **~s** *npl* (*drink*) alcolici *mpl*; **in good ~s** di buon umore

spiritual ['spɪrɪtjuəl] *adj* spirituale

spit [spɪt] (*pt, pp* **spat**) *n* (*for roasting*) spiedo; (*saliva*) sputo; saliva ▷ *vi* sputare; (*fire, fat*) scoppiettare

spite [spaɪt] *n* dispetto ▷ *vt* contrariare, far dispetto a; **in ~ of** nonostante, malgrado; **spiteful** *adj* dispettoso(-a)

splash [splæʃ] *n* spruzzo; (*sound*) splash *m inv*; (*of colour*) schizzo ▷ *vt* spruzzare ▷ *vi* (*also*: **~ about**) sguazzare; **splash out** (*inf*) *vi* (*BRIT*) fare spese folli

splendid ['splɛndɪd] *adj* splendido(-a), magnifico(-a)

splinter ['splɪntəʳ] *n* scheggia ▷ *vi* scheggiarsi

split [splɪt] (*pt, pp* **split**) *n* spaccatura; (*fig: division, quarrel*) scissione *f* ▷ *vt* spaccare; (*party*) dividere; (*work, profits*) spartire, ripartire ▷ *vi* (*divide*) dividersi; **split up** *vi* (*couple*) separarsi, rompere; (*meeting*) sciogliersi

spoil [spɔɪl] (*pt, pp* **spoilt** *or* **spoiled**) *vt* (*damage*) rovinare, guastare; (*mar*) sciupare; (*child*) viziare

spoilt [spɔɪlt] *pt, pp of* **spoil**

spoke [spəuk] *pt of* **speak** ▷ *n* raggio

spoken ['spəukn] *pp of* **speak**

spokesman ['spəuksmən] (*irreg*) *n* portavoce *m inv*

spokesperson ['spəukspə:sn] *n* portavoce *m/f*

spokeswoman ['spəukswumən] (*irreg*) *n* portavoce *f inv*

sponge [spʌndʒ] *n* spugna; (*also*: **~ cake**) pan *m* di spagna ▷ *vt* spugnare, pulire con una spugna ▷ *vi* **to ~ off** *or* **on** scroccare a; **sponge bag** (*BRIT*) *n* nécessaire *m inv*

sponsor ['spɔnsəʳ] *n* (*Radio, TV, Sport etc*) sponsor *m inv*; (*Pol: of bill*) promotore(-trice) ▷ *vt* sponsorizzare; (*bill*) presentare; **sponsorship** *n* sponsorizzazione *f*

spontaneous [spɔn'teɪnɪəs] *adj* spontaneo(-a)

spooky ['spu:kɪ] (*inf*) *adj* che fa accapponare la pelle

spoon [spu:n] *n* cucchiaio; **spoonful** *n* cucchiaiata

sport [spɔ:t] *n* sport *m inv*; (*person*) persona di spirito ▷ *vt* sfoggiare; **sport jacket** (*US*) *n* = **sports jacket**; **sports car** *n* automobile *f* sportiva; **sports centre** (*BRIT*) *n* centro sportivo; **sports jacket** (*BRIT*) *n* giacca sportiva; **sportsman** (*irreg*) *n* sportivo; **sportswear** *n* abiti *mpl* sportivi; **sportswoman** (*irreg*) *n* sportiva; **sporty** *adj* sportivo(-a)

spot [spɔt] *n* punto; (*mark*) macchia; (*dot: on pattern*) pallino; (*pimple*) foruncolo; (*place*) posto; (*Radio, TV*) spot *m inv*; (*small amount*): **a ~ of** un po' di ▷ *vt* (*notice*) individuare, distinguere; **on the ~** sul posto; (*immediately*) su due piedi; (*in difficulty*) nei guai; **spotless** *adj* immacolato(-a); **spotlight** *n* proiettore *m*; (*Aut*) faro ausiliario

spouse [spauz] *n* sposo(-a)

sprain [spreɪn] *n* storta, distorsione *f* ▷ *vt* **to ~ one's ankle** storcersi una caviglia

sprang [spræŋ] *pt of* **spring**

sprawl [sprɔ:l] *vi* sdraiarsi (in modo scomposto); (*place*) estendersi (disordinatamente)

spray [spreɪ] *n* spruzzo; (*container*) nebulizzatore *m*, spray *m inv*; (*of flowers*) mazzetto ▷ *vt* spruzzare; (*crops*) irrorare

spread [sprɛd] (*pt, pp* **spread**) *n* diffusione *f*; (*distribution*) distribuzione *f*; (*Culin*) pasta (da spalmare); (*inf: food*) banchetto ▷ *vt* (*cloth*) stendere, distendere; (*butter etc*) spalmare; (*disease, knowledge*) propagare, diffondere ▷ *vi* stendersi, distendersi; spalmarsi; propagarsi, diffondersi; **spread out** *vi* (*move apart*) separarsi; **spreadsheet** *n* foglio elettronico ad espansione

spree [spri:] *n* **to go on a ~** fare baldoria

spring [sprɪŋ] (*pt* **sprang**, *pp* **sprung**) *n* (*leap*) salto, balzo; (*coiled metal*) molla;

(season) primavera; (of water) sorgente
f ▷ vi saltare, balzare; **spring up** vi
(problem) presentarsi; **spring onion** n
(BRIT) cipollina

sprinkle ['sprıŋkl] vt spruzzare; spargere;
to ~ water etc **on, ~ with water** etc
spruzzare dell'acqua etc su

sprint [sprınt] n scatto ▷ vi scattare

sprung [sprʌŋ] pp of **spring**

spun [spʌn] pt, pp of **spin**

spur [spəːʳ] n sperone m; (fig) sprone m,
incentivo ▷ vt (also: **~ on**) spronare; **on the
~ of the moment** lì per lì

spurt [spəːt] n (of water) getto; (of energy)
scatto ▷ vi sgorgare

spy [spaı] n spia ▷ vi **to ~ on** spiare ▷ vt
(see) scorgere

sq. abbr = **square**

squabble ['skwɒbl] vi bisticciarsi

squad [skwɒd] n (Mil) plotone m; (Police)
squadra

squadron ['skwɒdrn] n (Mil) squadrone m;
(Aviat, Naut) squadriglia

squander ['skwɒndəʳ] vt dissipare

square [skwɛəʳ] n quadrato; (in town)
piazza ▷ adj quadrato(-a); (inf: ideas,
person) di vecchio stampo ▷ vt (arrange)
regolare; (Math) elevare al quadrato;
(reconcile) conciliare; **all ~** pari; **a ~ meal** un
pasto abbondante; **2 metres ~** di 2 metri
per 2; **1 ~ metre** 1 metro quadrato; **square
root** n radice f quadrata

squash [skwɒʃ] n (Sport) squash m; (BRIT:
drink): **lemon/orange ~** sciroppo di
limone/arancia; (US) zucca; (Sport) squash
m ▷ vt schiacciare

squat [skwɒt] adj tarchiato(-a), tozzo(-a)
▷ vi (also: **~ down**) accovacciarsi; **squatter**
n occupante m/f abusivo(-a)

squeak [skwiːk] vi squittire

squeal [skwiːl] vi strillare

squeeze [skwiːz] n pressione f; (also Econ)
stretta ▷ vt premere; (hand, arm) stringere

squid [skwɪd] n calamaro

squint [skwɪnt] vi essere strabico(-a) ▷ n
he has a ~ è strabico

squirm [skwəːm] vi contorcersi

squirrel ['skwɪrəl] n scoiattolo

squirt [skwəːt] vi schizzare; zampillare
▷ vt spruzzare

Sr abbr = **senior**

Sri Lanka [srɪ'læŋkə] n Sri Lanka m

St abbr = **saint**; **street**

stab [stæb] n (with knife etc) pugnalata; (of
pain) fitta; (inf: try): **to have a ~ at (doing)
sth** provare (a fare) qc ▷ vt pugnalare

stability [stə'bɪlɪtɪ] n stabilità

stable ['steɪbl] n (for horses) scuderia; (for
cattle) stalla ▷ adj stabile

stack [stæk] n catasta, pila ▷ vt
accatastare, ammucchiare

stadium ['steɪdɪəm] n stadio

staff [stɑːf] n (work force: gen) personale
m; (: BRIT: Scol) personale insegnante ▷ vt
fornire di personale

stag [stæg] n cervo

stage [steɪdʒ] n palcoscenico; (profession):
the ~ il teatro, la scena; (point) punto;
(platform) palco ▷ vt (play) allestire,
mettere in scena; (demonstration)
organizzare; **in ~s** per gradi; a tappe

stagger ['stægəʳ] vi barcollare ▷ vt (person)
sbalordire; (hours, holidays) scaglionare;
staggering adj (amazing) sbalorditivo(-a)

stagnant ['stægnənt] adj stagnante

stag night, stag party n festa di addio
al celibato

stain [steɪn] n macchia; (colouring)
colorante m ▷ vt macchiare; (wood)
tingere; **stained glass** [steɪnd'glɑːs] n
vetro colorato; **stainless steel** n acciaio
inossidabile

staircase ['stɛəkeɪs] n scale fpl, scala

stairs [stɛəz] npl (flight of stairs) scale fpl,
scala

stairway ['stɛəweɪ] n = **staircase**

stake [steɪk] n palo, piolo; (Comm)
interesse m; (Betting) puntata, scommessa
▷ vt (bet) scommettere; (risk) rischiare; **to
be at ~** essere in gioco

stale [steɪl] adj (bread) raffermo(-a);
(food) stantio(-a); (air) viziato(-a); (beer)
svaporato(-a); (smell) di chiuso

stalk [stɔːk] n gambo, stelo ▷ vt inseguire

stall [stɔːl] n bancarella; (in stable) box m
inv di stalla ▷ vt (Aut) far spegnere; (fig)
bloccare ▷ vi (Aut) spegnersi, fermarsi; (fig)
temporeggiare

stamina ['stæmɪnə] n vigore m, resistenza

stammer ['stæməʳ] n balbuzie f ▷ vi
balbettare

stamp [stæmp] n (postage stamp)
francobollo; (implement) timbro; (mark,
also fig) marchio, impronta; (on document)
bollo; timbro ▷ vi (also: **~ one's foot**)
battere il piede ▷ vt battere; (letter)
affrancare; (mark with a stamp) timbrare;
stamp out vt (fire) estinguere; (crime)
eliminare; (opposition) soffocare; **stamped
addressed envelope** n (BRIT) busta
affrancata e indirizzata

> Be careful not to translate **stamp** the
> Italian word by **stampa**.

stampede [stæm'piːd] n fuggi fuggi m inv

stance [stæns] n posizione f

stand [stænd] (pt, pp **stood**) n (position)
posizione f; (for taxis) posteggio; (structure)
supporto, sostegno; (at exhibition)

stand *m inv*; (*in shop*) banco; (*at market*) bancarella; (*booth*) chiosco; (*Sport*) tribuna ▷ *vi* stare in piedi; (*rise*) alzarsi in piedi; (*be placed*) trovarsi ▷ *vt* (*place*) mettere, porre; (*tolerate, withstand*) resistere, sopportare; (*treat*) offrire; **to make a ~** prendere posizione; **to ~ for parliament** (BRIT) presentarsi come candidato (per il parlamento); **stand back** *vi* prendere le distanze; **stand by** *vi* (*be ready*) tenersi pronto(-a) ▷ *vt fus* (*opinion*) sostenere; **stand down** *vi* (*withdraw*) ritirarsi; **stand for** *vt fus* (*signify*) rappresentare, significare; (*tolerate*) sopportare, tollerare; **stand in for** *vt fus* sostituire; **stand out** *vi* (*be prominent*) spiccare; **stand up** *vi* (*rise*) alzarsi in piedi; **stand up for** *vt fus* difendere; **stand up to** *vt fus* tener testa a, resistere a

standard ['stændəd] *n* modello, standard *m inv*; (*level*) livello; (*flag*) stendardo ▷ *adj* (*size etc*) normale, standard *inv*; **~s** *npl* (*morals*) principi *mpl*, valori *mpl*; **standard of living** *n* livello di vita

stand-by ['stændbaɪ] *n* riserva, sostituto; **to be on ~** (*gen*) tenersi pronto(-a); (*doctor*) essere di guardia; **stand-by ticket** *n* (*Aviat*) biglietto senza garanzia

standing ['stændɪŋ] *adj* diritto(-a), in piedi; (*permanent*) permanente ▷ *n* rango, condizione *f*, posizione *f*; **of many years' ~** che esiste da molti anni; **standing order** (BRIT) *n* (*at bank*) ordine *m* di pagamento (permanente)

stand: standpoint ['stændpɔɪnt] *n* punto di vista; **standstill** ['stændstɪl] *n* **at a standstill** fermo(-a); (*fig*) a un punto morto; **to come to a standstill** fermarsi; giungere a un punto morto

stank [stæŋk] *pt of* **stink**

staple ['steɪpl] *n* (*for papers*) graffetta ▷ *adj* (*food etc*) di base ▷ *vt* cucire

star [stɑːʳ] *n* stella; (*celebrity*) divo(-a) ▷ *vi* **to ~ (in)** essere il (*or* la) protagonista (di) ▷ *vt* (*Cinema*) essere interpretato(-a) da; **the ~s** *npl* (*Astrology*) le stelle

starboard ['stɑːbəd] *n* dritta

starch [stɑːtʃ] *n* amido

stardom ['stɑːdəm] *n* celebrità

stare [stɛəʳ] *n* sguardo fisso ▷ *vi* **to ~ at** fissare

stark [stɑːk] *adj* (*bleak*) desolato(-a) ▷ *adv* **~ naked** completamente nudo(-a)

start [stɑːt] *n* inizio; (*of race*) partenza; (*sudden movement*) sobbalzo; (*advantage*) vantaggio ▷ *vt* cominciare, iniziare; (*car*) mettere in moto ▷ *vi* cominciare; (*on journey*) partire, mettersi in viaggio; (*jump*) sobbalzare; **when does the film ~?**

a che ora comincia il film?; **to ~ doing** *or* **to do sth** (in)cominciare a fare qc; **start off** *vi* cominciare; (*leave*) partire; **start out** *vi* (*begin*) cominciare; (*set out*) partire; **start up** *vi* cominciare; (*car*) avviarsi ▷ *vt* iniziare; (*car*) avviare; **starter** *n* (*Aut*) motorino d'avviamento; (*Sport: official*) starter *m inv*; (BRIT: Culin) primo piatto; **starting point** *n* punto di partenza

startle ['stɑːtl] *vt* far trasalire; **startling** *adj* sorprendente

starvation [stɑː'veɪʃən] *n* fame *f*, inedia

starve [stɑːv] *vi* morire di fame; soffrire la fame ▷ *vt* far morire di fame, affamare

state [steɪt] *n* stato ▷ *vt* dichiarare, affermare; annunciare; **the S~s** (USA) gli Stati Uniti; **to be in a ~** essere agitato(-a); **statement** *n* dichiarazione *f*; **state school** *n* scuola statale; **statesman** (*irreg*) *n* statista *m*

static ['stætɪk] *n* (*Radio*) scariche *fpl* ▷ *adj* statico(-a)

station ['steɪʃən] *n* stazione *f* ▷ *vt* collocare, disporre

stationary ['steɪʃənərɪ] *adj* fermo(-a), immobile

stationer's (shop) *n* cartoleria

stationery ['steɪʃnərɪ] *n* articoli *mpl* di cancelleria

station wagon (US) *n* giardinetta

statistic [stə'tɪstɪk] *n* statistica; **statistics** *n* (*science*) statistica

statue ['stætjuː] *n* statua

stature ['stætʃəʳ] *n* statura

status ['steɪtəs] *n* posizione *f*, condizione *f* sociale; prestigio; stato; **status quo** [-'kwəʊ] *n* **the status quo** lo statu quo

statutory ['stætjutrɪ] *adj* stabilito(-a) dalla legge, statutario(-a)

staunch [stɔːntʃ] *adj* fidato(-a), leale

stay [steɪ] *n* (*period of time*) soggiorno, permanenza ▷ *vi* rimanere; (*reside*) alloggiare, stare; (*spend some time*) trattenersi, soggiornare; **to ~ put** non muoversi; **to ~ the night** fermarsi per la notte; **stay away** *vi* (*from person, building*) stare lontano (*from event*) non andare; **stay behind** *vi* restare indietro; **stay in** *vi* (*at home*) stare in casa; **stay on** *vi* restare, rimanere; **stay out** *vi* (*of house*) rimanere fuori (di casa); **stay up** *vi* (*at night*) rimanere alzato(-a)

steadily ['stedɪlɪ] *adv* (*firmly*) saldamente; (*constantly*) continuamente; (*fixedly*) fisso; (*walk*) con passo sicuro

steady ['stedɪ] *adj* (*not wobbling*) fermo(-a); (*regular*) costante; (*person, character*) serio(-a); (: *calm*) calmo(-a), tranquillo(-a) ▷ *vt* stabilizzare; calmare

steak [steɪk] n (meat) bistecca; (fish) trancia

steal [stiːl] (pt **stole**, pp **stolen**) vt rubare ▷ vi rubare; (move) muoversi furtivamente; **my wallet has been stolen** mi hanno rubato il portafoglio

steam [stiːm] n vapore m ▷ vt (Culin) cuocere a vapore ▷ vi fumare; **steam up** vi (window) appannarsi; **to get ~ed up about sth** (fig) andare in bestia per qc; **steamy** adj (room) pieno(-a) di vapore; (window) appannato(-a)

steel [stiːl] n acciaio ▷ adj di acciaio

steep [stiːp] adj ripido(-a), scosceso(-a); (price) eccessivo(-a) ▷ vt inzuppare; (washing) mettere a mollo

steeple ['stiːpl] n campanile m

steer [stɪəʳ] vt guidare ▷ vi (Naut: person) governare; (car) guidarsi; **steering** n (Aut) sterzo; **steering wheel** n volante m

stem [stɛm] n (of flower, plant) stelo; (of tree) fusto; (of glass) gambo; (of fruit, leaf) picciolo ▷ vt contenere, arginare

step [stɛp] n passo; (stair) gradino, scalino; (action) mossa, azione f ▷ vi **to ~ forward/back** fare un passo avanti/ indietro; **~s** npl (BRIT) = **stepladder**; **to be in/out of ~ (with)** stare/non stare al passo (con); **step down** vi (fig) ritirarsi; **step in** vi fare il proprio ingresso; **step up** vt aumentare; intensificare; **stepbrother** n fratellastro; **stepchild** n figliastro(-a); **stepdaughter** n figliastra; **stepfather** n patrigno; **stepladder** n scala a libretto; **stepmother** n matrigna; **stepsister** n sorellastra; **stepson** n figliastro

stereo ['stɛrɪəʊ] n (system) sistema m stereofonico; (record player) stereo m inv ▷ adj (also: **~phonic**) stereofonico(-a)

stereotype ['stɪərɪətaɪp] n stereotipo

sterile ['stɛraɪl] adj sterile; **sterilize** ['stɛrɪlaɪz] vt sterilizzare

sterling ['stəːlɪŋ] adj (gold, silver) di buona lega ▷ n (Econ) (lira) sterlina; **a pound ~** una lira sterlina

stern [stəːn] adj severo(-a) ▷ n (Naut) poppa

steroid ['stɛrɔɪd] n steroide m

stew [stjuː] n stufato ▷ vt cuocere in umido

steward ['stjuːəd] n (Aviat, Naut, Rail) steward m inv; (in club etc) dispensiere m; **stewardess** n assistente f di volo, hostess f inv

stick [stɪk] (pt, pp **stuck**) n bastone m; (of rhubarb, celery) gambo; (of dynamite) candelotto ▷ vt (glue) attaccare; (thrust): **to ~ sth into** conficcare or piantare or infiggere qc in; (inf: put) ficcare; (inf:

tolerate) sopportare ▷ vi attaccarsi; (remain) restare, rimanere; **stick out** vi sporgere, spuntare; **stick up** vi sporgere, spuntare; **stick up for** vt fus difendere; **sticker** n cartellino adesivo; **sticking plaster** n cerotto adesivo; **stick shift** (US) n (Aut) cambio manuale

sticky ['stɪkɪ] adj attaccaticcio(-a), vischioso(-a); (label) adesivo(-a); (fig: situation) difficile

stiff [stɪf] adj rigido(-a), duro(-a); (muscle) legato(-a), indolenzito(-a); (difficult) difficile, arduo(-a); (cold) freddo(-a), formale; (strong) forte; (high: price) molto alto(-a) ▷ adv **bored ~** annoiato(-a) a morte

stifling ['staɪflɪŋ] adj (heat) soffocante

stigma ['stɪgmə] n (fig) stigma m

stiletto [stɪ'lɛtəʊ] (BRIT) n (also: **~ heel**) tacco a spillo

still [stɪl] adj fermo(-a); silenzioso(-a) ▷ adv (up to this time, even) ancora; (nonetheless) tuttavia, ciò nonostante

stimulate ['stɪmjuleɪt] vt stimolare

stimulus ['stɪmjuləs] (pl **stimuli**) n stimolo

sting [stɪŋ] (pt, pp **stung**) n puntura; (organ) pungiglione m ▷ vt pungere

stink [stɪŋk] (pt **stank**, pp **stunk**) n fetore m, puzzo ▷ vi puzzare

stir [stəːʳ] n agitazione f, clamore m ▷ vt mescolare; (fig) risvegliare ▷ vi muoversi; **stir up** vt provocare, suscitare; **stir-fry** vt saltare in padella ▷ n pietanza al salto

stitch [stɪtʃ] n (Sewing) punto; (Knitting) maglia; (Med) punto (di sutura); (pain) fitta ▷ vt cucire, attaccare; suturare

stock [stɔk] n riserva, provvista; (Comm) giacenza, stock m inv; (Agr) bestiame m; (Culin) brodo; (descent) stirpe f; (Finance) titoli mpl; azioni fpl ▷ adj (fig: reply etc) consueto(-a); classico(-a) ▷ vt (have in stock) avere, vendere; **~s and shares** valori mpl di borsa; **in ~** in magazzino; **out of ~** esaurito(-a); **stockbroker** ['stɔkbrəʊkəʳ] n agente m di cambio; **stock cube** (BRIT) n dado; **stock exchange** n Borsa (valori); **stockholder** ['stɔkhəʊldəʳ] n (Finance) azionista m/f

stocking ['stɔkɪŋ] n calza

stock market n Borsa, mercato finanziario

stole [stəʊl] pt of **steal** ▷ n stola

stolen ['stəʊln] pp of **steal**

stomach ['stʌmək] n stomaco; (belly) pancia ▷ vt sopportare, digerire; **stomachache** n mal m di stomaco

stone [stəʊn] n pietra; (pebble) sasso, ciottolo; (in fruit) nocciolo; (Med) calcolo;

(BRIT: weight) = 6.348 kg; 14 libbre ▷ adj di pietra ▷ vt lapidare; (fruit) togliere il nocciolo a

stood [stʊd] pt, pp of **stand**

stool [stu:l] n sgabello

stoop [stu:p] vi (also: **have a ~**) avere una curvatura; (also: **~ down**) chinarsi, curvarsi

stop [stɔp] n arresto; (stopping place) fermata; (in punctuation) punto ▷ vt arrestare, fermare; (break off) interrompere; (also: **put a ~ to**) porre fine a ▷ vi fermarsi; (rain, noise etc) cessare, finire; **to ~ doing sth** cessare or finire di fare qc; **could you ~ here/at the corner?** può fermarsi qui/all'angolo?; **to ~ dead** fermarsi di colpo; **stop by** vi passare, fare un salto; **stop off** vi sostare brevemente; **stopover** n breve sosta; (Aviat) scalo; **stoppage** ['stɔpɪdʒ] n arresto, fermata; (of pay) trattenuta; (strike) interruzione f del lavoro

storage ['stɔːrɪdʒ] n immagazzinamento

store [stɔː'] n provvista, riserva; (depot) deposito; (BRIT: department store) grande magazzino; (US: shop) negozio ▷ vt immagazzinare; **~s** npl (provisions) rifornimenti mpl, scorte fpl; **in ~** di riserva; in serbo; **storekeeper** (US) n negoziante m/f

storey ['stɔːrɪ] (US **story**) n piano

storm [stɔːm] n tempesta, temporale m, burrasca; uragano ▷ vi (fig) infuriarsi ▷ vt prendere d'assalto; **stormy** adj tempestoso(-a), burrascoso(-a)

story ['stɔːrɪ] n storia; favola; racconto; (US) = **storey**

stout [staʊt] adj solido(-a), robusto(-a); (friend, supporter) tenace; (fat) corpulento(-a), grasso(-a) ▷ n birra scura

stove [stəʊv] n (for cooking) fornello; (: small) fornelletto; (for heating) stufa

straight [streɪt] adj dritto(-a); (frank) onesto(-a), franco(-a); (simple) semplice ▷ adv diritto; (drink) liscio; **to put** or **get ~** mettere in ordine, mettere ordine in; **~ away, ~ off** (at once) immediatamente; **straighten** vt (also: **straighten out**) raddrizzare; **straightforward** adj semplice; onesto(-a), franco(-a)

strain [streɪn] n (Tech) sollecitazione f; (physical) sforzo; (mental) tensione f; (Med) strappo; distorsione f; (streak, trace) tendenza; elemento ▷ vt tendere; (muscle) sforzare; (ankle) storcere; (resources) pesare su; (food) colare; passare; **strained** adj (muscle) stirato(-a); (laugh etc) forzato(-a); (relations) teso(-a); **strainer** n passino, colino

strait [streɪt] n (Geo) stretto; **~s** npl **to be**

in dire ~s (fig) essere nei guai

strand [strænd] n (of thread) filo; **stranded** adj nei guai; senza mezzi di trasporto

strange [streɪndʒ] adj (not known) sconosciuto(-a); (odd) strano(-a), bizzarro(-a); **strangely** adv stranamente; **stranger** n sconosciuto(-a); estraneo(-a)

strangle ['stræŋgl] vt strangolare

strap [stræp] n cinghia; (of slip, dress) spallina, bretella

strategic [strə'tiːdʒɪk] adj strategico(-a)

strategy ['strætɪdʒɪ] n strategia

straw [strɔː] n paglia; (drinking straw) cannuccia; **that's the last ~!** è la goccia che fa traboccare il vaso!

strawberry ['strɔːbərɪ] n fragola

stray [streɪ] adj (animal) randagio(-a); (bullet) vagante; (scattered) sparso(-a) ▷ vi perdersi

streak [striːk] n striscia; (of hair) mèche f inv ▷ vt striare, screziare ▷ vi **to ~ past** passare come un fulmine

stream [striːm] n ruscello; corrente f; (of people, smoke etc) fiume m ▷ vt (Scol) dividere in livelli di rendimento ▷ vi scorrere; **to ~ in/out** entrare/uscire a fiotti

street [striːt] n strada, via; **streetcar** (US) n tram m inv; **street light** n lampione m; **street map** n pianta (di una città); **street plan** n pianta (di una città)

strength [streŋθ] n forza; **strengthen** vt rinforzare; fortificare; consolidare

strenuous ['strenjuəs] adj vigoroso(-a), energico(-a); (tiring) duro(-a), pesante

stress [stres] n (force, pressure) pressione f; (mental strain) tensione f; (accent) accento ▷ vt insistere su, sottolineare; accentare; **stressed** adj (tense: person) stressato(-a); (Ling, Poetry: syllable) accentato(-a); **stressful** adj (job) difficile, stressante

stretch [stretʃ] n (of sand etc) distesa ▷ vi stirarsi; (extend): **to ~ to** or **as far as** estendersi fino a ▷ vt tendere, allungare; (spread) distendere; (fig) spingere (al massimo); **stretch out** vi allungarsi, estendersi ▷ vt (arm etc) allungare, tendere; (to spread) distendere

stretcher ['stretʃə'] n barella, lettiga

strict [strɪkt] adj (severe) rigido(-a), severo(-a); (precise) preciso(-a), stretto(-a); **strictly** adv severamente; rigorosamente; strettamente

stride [straɪd] (pt **strode**, pp **stridden**) n passo lungo ▷ vi camminare a grandi passi

strike [straɪk] (pt, pp **struck**) n sciopero; (of oil etc) scoperta; (attack) attacco ▷ vt colpire; (oil etc) scoprire, trovare; (bargain) fare; (fig): **the thought** or **it ~s me that ...** mi viene in mente che ...

▷ *vi* scioperare; (*attack*) attaccare; (*clock*) suonare; **on ~** (*workers*) in sciopero; **to ~ a match** accendere un fiammifero; **striker** *n* scioperante *m/f*; (*Sport*) attaccante *m*; **striking** *adj* che colpisce

string [strɪŋ] (*pt, pp* **strung**) *n* spago; (*row*) fila; sequenza; catena; (*Mus*) corda ▷ *vt* **to ~ out** disporre di fianco; **to ~ together** (*words, ideas*) mettere insieme; **the ~s** *npl* (*Mus*) gli archi; **to pull ~s for sb** (*fig*) raccomandare qn

strip [strɪp] *n* striscia ▷ *vt* spogliare; (*paint*) togliere; (*also:* **~ down**: *machine*) smontare ▷ *vi* spogliarsi; **strip off** *vt* (*paint etc*) staccare ▷ *vi* (*person*) spogliarsi

stripe [straɪp] *n* striscia, riga; (*Mil, Police*) gallone *m*; **striped** *adj* a strisce *or* righe

stripper ['strɪpəʳ] *n* spogliarellista *m/f*

strip-search ['strɪpsə:tʃ] *vt* **to ~ sb** perquisire qn facendolo(-a) spogliare ▷ *n* perquisizione (*facendo spogliare il perquisto*)

strive [straɪv] (*pt* **strove**, *pp* **striven**) *vi* **~ to do** sforzarsi di fare

strode [strəʊd] *pt of* **stride**

stroke [strəʊk] *n* colpo; (*Swimming*) bracciata; (: *style*) stile *m*; (*Med*) colpo apoplettico ▷ *vt* accarezzare; **at a ~** in un attimo

stroll [strəʊl] *n* giretto, passeggiatina ▷ *vi* andare a spasso; **stroller** (*us*) *n* passeggino

strong [strɒŋ] *adj* (*gen*) forte; (*sturdy: table, fabric etc*) robusto(-a); **they are 50 ~** sono in 50; **stronghold** *n* (*also fig*) roccaforte *f*; **strongly** *adv* fortemente, con forza; energicamente; vivamente

strove [strəʊv] *pt of* **strive**

struck [strʌk] *pt, pp of* **strike**

structure ['strʌktʃəʳ] *n* struttura; (*building*) costruzione *f*, fabbricato

struggle ['strʌgl] *n* lotta ▷ *vi* lottare

strung [strʌŋ] *pt, pp of* **string**

stub [stʌb] *n* mozzicone *m*; (*of ticket etc*) matrice *f*, tallocino ▷ *vt* **to ~ one's toe** urtare *or* sbattere il dito del piede; **stub out** *vt* schiacciare

stubble ['stʌbl] *n* stoppia; (*on chin*) barba ispida

stubborn ['stʌbən] *adj* testardo(-a), ostinato(-a)

stuck [stʌk] *pt, pp of* **stick** ▷ *adj* (*jammed*) bloccato(-a)

stud [stʌd] *n* bottoncino; borchia; (*also:* **~ earring**) orecchino a pressione; (*also:* **~ farm**) scuderia, allevamento di cavalli; (*also:* **~ horse**) stallone *m* ▷ *vt* (*fig*): **~ded with** tempestato(-a) di

student ['stju:dənt] *n* studente(-essa) ▷ *cpd* studentesco(-a); universitario(-a);

degli studenti; **student driver** (*us*) *n* conducente *m/f* principiante; **students' union** *n* (*brit: association*) circolo universitario; (: *building*) sede *f* del circolo universitario

studio ['stju:dɪəʊ] *n* studio; **studio flat** (*us* **studio apartment**) *n* monolocale *m*

study ['stʌdɪ] *n* studio ▷ *vt* studiare; esaminare ▷ *vi* studiare

stuff [stʌf] *n* roba; (*substance*) sostanza, materiale *m* ▷ *vt* imbottire; (*Culin*) farcire; (*dead animal*) impagliare; (*inf: push*) ficcare; **stuffing** *n* imbottitura; (*Culin*) ripieno; **stuffy** *adj* (*room*) mal ventilato(-a), senz'aria; (*ideas*) antiquato(-a)

stumble ['stʌmbl] *vi* inciampare; **to ~ across** (*fig*) imbattersi in

stump [stʌmp] *n* ceppo; (*of limb*) moncone *m* ▷ *vt* **to be ~ed** essere sconcertato(-a)

stun [stʌn] *vt* stordire; (*amaze*) sbalordire

stung [stʌŋ] *pt, pp of* **sting**

stunk [stʌŋk] *pp of* **stink**

stunned [stʌnd] *adj* (*from blow*) stordito(-a); (*amazed, shocked*) sbalordito(-a)

stunning ['stʌnɪŋ] *adj* sbalorditivo(-a); (*girl etc*) fantastico(-a)

stunt [stʌnt] *n* bravata; trucco pubblicitario

stupid ['stju:pɪd] *adj* stupido(-a); **stupidity** [-'pɪdɪtɪ] *n* stupidità *f inv*, stupidaggine *f*

sturdy ['stə:dɪ] *adj* robusto(-a), vigoroso(-a); solido(-a)

stutter ['stʌtəʳ] *n* balbuzie *f* ▷ *vi* balbettare

style [staɪl] *n* stile *m*; (*distinction*) eleganza, classe *f*; **stylish** *adj* elegante; **stylist** *n* **hair stylist** parrucchiere(-a)

sub... [sʌb] *prefix* sub..., sotto...; **subconscious** *adj* subcosciente ▷ *n* subcosciente *m*

subdued [səb'dju:d] *adj* pacato(-a); (*light*) attenuato(-a)

subject [*n* 'sʌbdʒɪkt, *vb* səb'dʒɛkt] *n* soggetto; (*citizen etc*) cittadino(-a); (*Scol*) materia ▷ *vt* **to ~ to** sottomettere a; esporre a; **to be ~ to** (*law*) essere sottomesso(-a) a; (*disease*) essere soggetto(-a) a; **subjective** [-'dʒɛktɪv] *adj* soggettivo(-a); **subject matter** *n* argomento; contenuto

subjunctive [səb'dʒʌŋktɪv] *adj* congiuntivo(-a) ▷ *n* congiuntivo

submarine [sʌbmə'ri:n] *n* sommergibile *m*

submission [səb'mɪʃən] *n* sottomissione *f*; (*claim*) richiesta

submit [səb'mɪt] *vt* sottomettere ▷ *vi* sottomettersi

subordinate [sə'bɔːdɪnət] *adj, n* subordinato(-a)

subscribe [səb'skraɪb] *vi* contribuire; **to ~ to** (*opinion*) approvare, condividere; (*fund*) sottoscrivere a; (*newspaper*) abbonarsi a; essere abbonato(-a) a

subscription [səb'skrɪpʃən] *n* sottoscrizione *f*; abbonamento

subsequent ['sʌbsɪkwənt] *adj* successivo(-a), seguente; conseguente; **subsequently** *adv* in seguito, successivamente

subside [səb'saɪd] *vi* cedere, abbassarsi; (*flood*) decrescere; (*wind*) calmarsi

subsidiary [səb'sɪdɪərɪ] *adj* sussidiario(-a); accessorio(-a) ▷ *n* filiale *f*

subsidize ['sʌbsɪdaɪz] *vt* sovvenzionare

subsidy ['sʌbsɪdɪ] *n* sovvenzione *f*

substance ['sʌbstəns] *n* sostanza

substantial [səb'stænʃl] *adj* solido(-a); (*amount, progress etc*) notevole; (*meal*) sostanzioso(-a)

substitute ['sʌbstɪtjuːt] *n* (*person*) sostituto(-a); (*thing*) succedaneo, surrogato ▷ *vt* **to ~ sth/sb for** sostituire qc/qn a; **substitution** [sʌbstɪ'tjuːʃən] *n* sostituzione *f*

subtle ['sʌtl] *adj* sottile

subtract [səb'trækt] *vt* sottrarre

suburb ['sʌbəːb] *n* sobborgo; **the ~s** la periferia; **suburban** [sə'bəːbən] *adj* suburbano(-a)

subway ['sʌbweɪ] *n* (*US: underground*) metropolitana; (*BRIT: underpass*) sottopassaggio

succeed [sək'siːd] *vi* riuscire; avere successo ▷ *vt* succedere a; **to ~ in doing** riuscire a fare

success [sək'sɛs] *n* successo; **successful** *adj* (*venture*) coronato(-a) da successo, riuscito(-a); **to be successful (in doing)** riuscire (a fare); **successfully** *adv* con successo

succession [sək'sɛʃən] *n* successione *f*

successive [sək'sɛsɪv] *adj* successivo(-a); consecutivo(-a)

successor [sək'sɛsəʳ] *n* successore *m*

succumb [sə'kʌm] *vi* soccombere

such [sʌtʃ] *adj* tale; (*of that kind*): **~ a book** un tale libro, un libro del genere; **~ books** tali libri, libri del genere; (*so much*): **~ courage** tanto coraggio ▷ *adv* talmente, così; **~ a long trip** un viaggio così lungo; **~ a lot of** talmente *or* così tanto(-a); **~ as** (*like*) come; **as ~** come *or* in quanto tale; **such-and-such** *adj* tale (*after noun*)

suck [sʌk] *vt* succhiare; (*breast, bottle*) poppare

Sudan [suː'dɑːn] *n* Sudan *m*

sudden ['sʌdn] *adj* improvviso(-a); **all of a ~** improvvisamente, all'improvviso; **suddenly** *adv* bruscamente, improvvisamente, di colpo

sue [suː] *vt* citare in giudizio

suede [sweɪd] *n* pelle *f* scamosciata

suffer ['sʌfəʳ] *vt* soffrire, patire; (*bear*) sopportare, tollerare ▷ *vi* soffrire; **to ~ from** soffrire di; **suffering** *n* sofferenza

suffice [sə'faɪs] *vi* essere sufficiente, bastare

sufficient [sə'fɪʃənt] *adj* sufficiente; **~ money** abbastanza soldi

suffocate ['sʌfəkeɪt] *vi* (*have difficulty breathing*) soffocare; (*die through lack of air*) asfissiare

sugar ['ʃugəʳ] *n* zucchero ▷ *vt* zuccherare

suggest [sə'dʒɛst] *vt* proporre, suggerire; indicare; **suggestion** [-'dʒɛstʃən] *n* suggerimento, proposta; indicazione *f*

suicide ['suɪsaɪd] *n* (*person*) suicida *m/f*; (*act*) suicidio; *see also* **commit**; **suicide bombing** *n* attentato suicida

suit [suːt] *n* (*man's*) vestito; (*woman's*) completo, tailleur *m inv*; (*Law*) causa; (*Cards*) seme *m*, colore *m* ▷ *vt* andar bene a *or* per; essere adatto(-a) a *or* per; (*adapt*): **to ~ sth to** adattare qc a; **well ~ed** ben assortito(-a); **suitable** *adj* adatto(-a); appropriato(-a); **suitcase** ['suːtkeɪs] *n* valigia

suite [swiːt] *n* (*of rooms*) appartamento; (*Mus*) suite *f inv*; (*furniture*): **bedroom/ dining room ~** arredo *or* mobilia per la camera da letto/sala da pranzo

sulfur ['sʌlfəʳ] (*US*) *n* = **sulphur**

sulk [sʌlk] *vi* fare il broncio

sulphur ['sʌlfəʳ] (*US* **sulfur**) *n* zolfo

sultana [sʌl'tɑːnə] *n* (*fruit*) uva (secca) sultanina

sum [sʌm] *n* somma; (*Scol etc*) addizione *f*; **sum up** *vt, vi* riassumere

summarize ['sʌməraɪz] *vt* riassumere, riepilogare

summary ['sʌmərɪ] *n* riassunto

summer ['sʌməʳ] *n* estate *f* ▷ *cpd* d'estate, estivo(-a); **summer holidays** *npl* vacanze *fpl* estive; **summertime** *n* (*season*) estate *f*

summit ['sʌmɪt] *n* cima, sommità; (*Pol*) vertice *m*

summon ['sʌmən] *vt* chiamare, convocare

Sun. *abbr* (= *Sunday*) dom.

sun [sʌn] *n* sole *m*; **sunbathe** *vi* prendere un bagno di sole; **sunbed** *n* lettino solare; **sunblock** *n* protezione *f* solare totale; **sunburn** *n* (*painful*) scottatura; **sunburned, sunburnt** *adj* abbronzato(-a); (*painfully*) scottato(-a)

Sunday ['sʌndɪ] *n* domenica

Sunday paper n giornale m della domenica

● SUNDAY PAPER

● I **Sunday papers** sono i giornali che escono di domenica. Sono generalmente corredati da supplementi e riviste di argomento culturale, sportivo e di attualità.

sunflower ['sʌnflaʊəʳ] n girasole m
sung [sʌŋ] pp of **sing**
sunglasses ['sʌngla:sɪz] npl occhiali mpl da sole
sunk [sʌŋk] pp of **sink**
sun: sunlight n (luce f del) sole m; **sun lounger** n sedia a sdraio; **sunny** adj assolato(-a), soleggiato(-a); (fig) allegro(-a), felice; **sunrise** n levata del sole, alba; **sun roof** n (Aut) tetto apribile; **sunscreen** n (cream) crema solare protettiva; **sunset** n tramonto; **sunshade** n parasole m; **sunshine** n luce f (del) sole m; **sunstroke** n insolazione f, colpo di sole; **suntan** n abbronzatura; **suntan lotion** n lozione f solare; **suntan oil** n olio solare
super ['su:pəʳ] (inf) adj fantastico(-a)
superb [su:'pə:b] adj magnifico(-a)
superficial [su:pə'fɪʃəl] adj superficiale
superintendent [su:pərɪn'tɛndənt] n direttore(-trice); (Police) ≈ commissario (capo)
superior [su'pɪərɪəʳ] adj, n superiore m/f
superlative [su'pə:lətɪv] adj superlativo(-a), supremo(-a) ▷ n (Ling) superlativo
supermarket ['su:pəma:kɪt] n supermercato
supernatural [su:pə'nætʃərəl] adj soprannaturale ▷ n soprannaturale m
superpower ['su:pəpaʊəʳ] n (Pol) superpotenza
superstition [su:pə'stɪʃən] n superstizione f
superstitious [su:pə'stɪʃəs] adj superstizioso(-a)
superstore ['su:pəstɔ:ʳ] n (BRIT) grande supermercato
supervise ['su:pəvaɪz] vt (person etc) sorvegliare; (organization) soprintendere a; **supervision** [-'vɪʒən] n sorveglianza; supervisione f; **supervisor** n sorvegliante m/f; soprintendente m/f; (in shop) capocommesso(-a)
supper ['sʌpəʳ] n cena
supple ['sʌpl] adj flessibile; agile
supplement [n 'sʌplɪmənt, vb sʌplɪ'mɛnt]

n supplemento ▷ vt completare, integrare
supplier [sə'plaɪəʳ] n fornitore m
supply [sə'plaɪ] vt (provide) fornire; (equip): **to ~ (with)** approvvigionare (di), attrezzare (con) ▷ n riserva, provvista; (supplying) approvvigionamento; (Tech) alimentazione f; **supplies** npl (food) viveri mpl; (Mil) sussistenza
support [sə'pɔ:t] n (moral, financial etc) sostegno, appoggio; (Tech) supporto ▷ vt sostenere; (financially) mantenere; (uphold) sostenere, difendere; **supporter** n (Pol etc) sostenitore(-trice), fautore(-trice); (Sport) tifoso(-a)

▎ Be careful not to translate **support** by the Italian word **sopportare**.

suppose [sə'pəʊz] vt supporre; immaginare; **to be ~d to do** essere tenuto(-a) a fare; **supposedly** [sə'pəʊzɪdlɪ] adv presumibilmente; **supposing** conj se, ammesso che + sub
suppress [sə'prɛs] vt reprimere; sopprimere; occultare
supreme [su'pri:m] adj supremo(-a)
surcharge ['sə:tʃɑ:dʒ] n supplemento
sure [ʃʊəʳ] adj sicuro(-a); (definite, convinced) sicuro(-a), certo(-a); **~!** (of course) senz'altro!, certo!; **~ enough** infatti; **to make ~ of sth/that** assicurarsi di qc/che; **surely** adv sicuramente; certamente
surf [sə:f] n (waves) cavalloni mpl; (foam) spuma
surface ['sə:fɪs] n superficie f ▷ vt (road) asfaltare ▷ vi risalire alla superficie; (fig: news, feeling) venire a galla
surfboard ['sə:fbɔ:d] n tavola per surfing
surfing ['sə:fɪŋ] n surfing m
surge [sə:dʒ] n (strong movement) ondata; (of feeling) impeto ▷ vi gonfiarsi; (people) riversarsi
surgeon ['sə:dʒən] n chirurgo
surgery ['sə:dʒərɪ] n chirurgia; (BRIT: room) studio or gabinetto medico, ambulatorio; (: also: **~ hours**) orario delle visite or di consultazione; **to undergo ~** subire un intervento chirurgico
surname ['sə:neɪm] n cognome m
surpass [sə:'pɑ:s] vt superare
surplus ['sə:pləs] n eccedenza; (Econ) surplus m inv ▷ adj eccedente, d'avanzo
surprise [sə'praɪz] n sorpresa; (astonishment) stupore m ▷ vt sorprendere; stupire; **surprised** [sə'praɪzd] adj (look, smile) sorpreso(-a); **to be surprised** essere sorpreso, sorprendersi; **surprising** adj sorprendente, stupefacente; **surprisingly** adv (easy, helpful) sorprendentemente
surrender [sə'rɛndəʳ] n resa, capitolazione f ▷ vi arrendersi

surround [səˈraʊnd] vt circondare; (Mil etc) accerchiare; **surrounding** adj circostante; **surroundings** npl dintorni mpl; (fig) ambiente m

surveillance [səˈveɪləns] n sorveglianza, controllo

survey [n ˈsɜːveɪ, vb səˈveɪ] n quadro generale; (study) esame m; (in housebuying etc) perizia; (of land) rilevamento, rilievo topografico ▷ vt osservare; esaminare; valutare; rilevare; **surveyor** n perito; geometra m; (of land) agrimensore m

survival [səˈvaɪvl] n sopravvivenza; (relic) reliquia, vestigio

survive [səˈvaɪv] vi sopravvivere ▷ vt sopravvivere a; **survivor** n superstite m/f, sopravvissuto(-a)

suspect [adj, n ˈsʌspekt, vb səsˈpekt] adj sospetto(-a) ▷ n persona sospetta ▷ vt sospettare; (think likely) supporre; (doubt) dubitare

suspend [səsˈpend] vt sospendere; **suspended sentence** n condanna con la condizionale; **suspenders** npl (BRIT) giarrettiere fpl; (US) bretelle fpl

suspense [səsˈpens] n apprensione f; (in film etc) suspense m; **to keep sb in ~** tenere qn in sospeso

suspension [səsˈpenʃən] n (gen Aut) sospensione f; (of driving licence) ritiro temporaneo; **suspension bridge** n ponte m sospeso

suspicion [səsˈpɪʃən] n sospetto; **suspicious** [səsˈpɪʃəs] adj (suspecting) sospettoso(-a); (causing suspicion) sospetto(-a)

sustain [səsˈteɪn] vt sostenere; sopportare; (Law: charge) confermare; (suffer) subire

swallow [ˈswɒləʊ] n (bird) rondine f ▷ vt inghiottire; (fig: story) bere

swam [swæm] pt of **swim**

swamp [swɒmp] n palude f ▷ vt sommergere

swan [swɒn] n cigno

swap [swɒp] vt **to ~ (for)** scambiare (con)

swarm [swɔːm] n sciame m ▷ vi (bees) sciamare; (people) brulicare; (place): **to be ~ing with** brulicare di

sway [sweɪ] vi (tree) ondeggiare; (person) barcollare ▷ vt (influence) influenzare, dominare

swear [sweər] (pt **swore**, pp **sworn**) vi (curse) bestemmiare, imprecare ▷ vt (promise) giurare; **swear in** vt prestare giuramento a; **swearword** n parolaccia

sweat [swet] n sudore m, traspirazione f ▷ vi sudare

sweater [ˈswetər] n maglione m

sweatshirt [ˈswetʃəːt] n felpa

sweaty [ˈsweti] adj sudato(-a), bagnato(-a) di sudore

Swede [swiːd] n svedese m/f

swede [swiːd] n (BRIT) rapa svedese

Sweden [ˈswiːdn] n Svezia; **Swedish** [ˈswiːdɪʃ] adj svedese ▷ n (Ling) svedese m

sweep [swiːp] (pt, pp **swept**) n spazzata; (also: **chimney ~**) spazzacamino ▷ vt spazzare, scopare; (current) spazzare ▷ vi (hand) muoversi con gesto ampio; (wind) infuriare

sweet [swiːt] n (BRIT: pudding) dolce m; (candy) caramella ▷ adj dolce; (fresh) fresco(-a); (fig) piacevole; delicato(-a), grazioso(-a); gentile; **sweetcorn** n granturco dolce; **sweetener** [ˈswiːtnər] n (Culin) dolcificante m; **sweetheart** n innamorato(-a); **sweetshop** n (BRIT) ≈ pasticceria

swell [swel] (pt **swelled**, pp **swollen**, **swelled**) n (of sea) mare m lungo ▷ adj (US: inf: excellent) favoloso(-a) ▷ vt gonfiare, ingrossare; aumentare ▷ vi gonfiarsi, ingrossarsi; (sound) crescere; (also: **~ up**) gonfiarsi; **swelling** n (Med) tumefazione f, gonfiore m

swept [swept] pt, pp of **sweep**

swerve [swəːv] vi deviare; (driver) sterzare; (boxer) scartare

swift [swɪft] n (bird) rondone m ▷ adj rapido(-a), veloce

swim [swɪm] (pt **swam**, pp **swum**) n **to go for a ~** andare a fare una nuotata ▷ vi nuotare; (Sport) fare del nuoto; (head, room) girare ▷ vt (river, channel) attraversare or percorrere a nuoto; (length) nuotare; **swimmer** n nuotatore(-trice); **swimming** n nuoto; **swimming costume** (BRIT) n costume m da bagno; **swimming pool** n piscina; **swimming trunks** npl costume m da bagno (da uomo); **swimsuit** n costume m da bagno

swing [swɪŋ] (pt, pp **swung**) n altalena; (movement) oscillazione f; (Mus) ritmo; swing m ▷ vt dondolare, far oscillare; (also: **~ round**) far girare ▷ vi oscillare, dondolare; (also: **~ round**: object) roteare; (: person) girarsi, voltarsi; **to be in full ~** (activity) essere in piena attività; (party etc) essere nel pieno

swipe card n tessera magnetica

swirl [swəːl] vi turbinare, far mulinello

Swiss [swɪs] adj, n inv svizzero(-a)

switch [swɪtʃ] n (for light, radio etc) interruttore m; (change) cambiamento ▷ vt (change) cambiare; scambiare; **switch off** vt spegnere; **could you ~ off the light?** puoi spegnere la luce?; **switch on**

vt accendere; (*engine, machine*) mettere in moto, avviare; **switchboard** *n* (*Tel*) centralino

Switzerland ['swɪtsələnd] *n* Svizzera

swivel ['swɪvl] *vi* (*also:* **~ round**) girare

swollen ['swəulən] *pp of* **swell**

swoop [swu:p] *n* incursione *f* ▷ *vi* (*also:* **~ down**) scendere in picchiata, piombare

swop [swɔp] *n, vt* = **swap**

sword [sɔ:d] *n* spada; **swordfish** *n* pesce *m* spada *inv*

swore [swɔ:ʳ] *pt of* **swear**

sworn [swɔ:n] *pp of* **swear** ▷ *adj* giurato(-a)

swum [swʌm] *pp of* **swim**

swung [swʌŋ] *pt, pp of* **swing**

syllable ['sɪləbl] *n* sillaba

syllabus ['sɪləbəs] *n* programma *m*

symbol ['sɪmbl] *n* simbolo; **symbolic(al)** [sɪm'bɔlɪk(l)] *adj* simbolico(-a); **to be symbolic(al) of sth** simboleggiare qc

symmetrical [sɪ'mɛtrɪkl] *adj* simmetrico(-a)

symmetry ['sɪmɪtrɪ] *n* simmetria

sympathetic [sɪmpə'θɛtɪk] *adj* (*showing pity*) compassionevole; (*kind*) comprensivo(-a); **~ towards** ben disposto(-a) verso

> Be careful not to translate *sympathetic* by the Italian word *simpatico*.

sympathize ['sɪmpəθaɪz] *vi* **to ~ with** (*person*) compatire; partecipare al dolore di; (*cause*) simpatizzare per

sympathy ['sɪmpəθɪ] *n* compassione *f*

symphony ['sɪmfənɪ] *n* sinfonia

symptom ['sɪmptəm] *n* sintomo; indizio

synagogue ['sɪnəgɔg] *n* sinagoga

syndicate ['sɪndɪkɪt] *n* sindacato

syndrome ['sɪndrəum] *n* sindrome *f*

synonym ['sɪnənɪm] *n* sinonimo

synthetic [sɪn'θɛtɪk] *adj* sintetico(-a)

Syria ['sɪrɪə] *n* Siria

syringe [sɪ'rɪndʒ] *n* siringa

syrup ['sɪrəp] *n* sciroppo; (*also:* **golden ~**) melassa raffinata

system ['sɪstəm] *n* sistema *m*; (*order*) metodo; (*Anat*) organismo; **systematic** [-'mætɪk] *adj* sistematico(-a); metodico(-a); **systems analyst** *n* analista *m* di sistemi

ta [tɑ:] (*BRIT: inf*) *excl* grazie!

tab [tæb] *n* (*loop on coat etc*) laccetto; (*label*) etichetta; **to keep ~s on** (*fig*) tenere d'occhio

table ['teɪbl] *n* tavolo, tavola; (*Math, Chem etc*) tavola ▷ *vt* (*BRIT: motion etc*) presentare; **a ~ for 4, please** un tavolo per 4, per favore; **to lay** *or* **set the ~** apparecchiare *or* preparare la tavola; **tablecloth** *n* tovaglia; **table d'hôte** [tɑ:bl'dəut] *adj* (*meal*) a prezzo fisso; **table lamp** *n* lampada da tavolo; **tablemat** *n* sottopiatto; **tablespoon** *n* cucchiaio da tavola; (*also:* **tablespoonful**: *as measurement*) cucchiaiata

tablet ['tæblɪt] *n* (*Med*) compressa; (*of stone*) targa

table tennis *n* tennis *m* da tavolo, ping-pong® *m*

tabloid ['tæblɔɪd] *n* (*newspaper*) tabloid *m inv* (*giornale illustrato di formato ridotto*); **the ~s, the ~ press** i giornali popolari

taboo [tə'bu:] *adj, n* tabù *m inv*

tack [tæk] *n* (*nail*) bulletta; (*fig*) approccio ▷ *vt* imbullettare; imbastire ▷ *vi* bordeggiare

tackle ['tækl] *n* attrezzatura, equipaggiamento; (*for lifting*) paranco; (*Football*) contrasto; (*Rugby*) placcaggio ▷ *vt* (*difficulty*) affrontare; (*Football*)

contrastare; (*Rugby*) placcare
tacky ['tækɪ] *adj* appiccicaticcio(-a); (*pej*)
scadente
tact [tækt] *n* tatto: **tactful** *adj*
delicato(-a), discreto(-a)
tactics ['tæktɪks] *n, npl* tattica
tactless ['tæktlɪs] *adj* che manca di tatto
tadpole ['tædpəʊl] *n* girino
taffy ['tæfɪ] (*us*) *n* caramella *f* mou *inv*
tag [tæg] *n* etichetta
tail [teɪl] *n* coda; (*of shirt*) falda ▷ *vt* (*follow*)
seguire, pedinare; **~s** *npl* (*formal suit*) frac
m inv
tailor ['teɪlə*r*] *n* sarto
Taiwan [taɪ'wɑːn] *n* Taiwan *m*; **Taiwanese**
[taɪwə'niːz] *adj, n* taiwanese
take [teɪk] (*pt* **took**, *pp* **taken**) *vt* prendere;
(*gain: prize*) ottenere, vincere; (*require:
effort, courage*) occorrere, volerci; (*tolerate*)
accettare, sopportare; (*hold: passengers etc*)
contenere; (*accompany*) accompagnare;
(*bring, carry*) portare; (*exam*) sostenere,
presentarsi a; **to ~ a photo/a shower**
fare una fotografia/una doccia; **I ~ it
that** suppongo che; **take after** *vt fus*
assomigliare a; **take apart** *vt* smontare;
take away *vt* portare via; togliere; **take
back** *vt* (*return*) restituire; riportare; (*one's
words*) ritirare; **take down** *vt* (*building*)
demolire; (*letter etc*) scrivere; **take in**
vt (*deceive*) imbrogliare, abbindolare;
(*understand*) capire; (*include*) comprendere,
includere; (*lodger*) prendere, ospitare;
take off *vi* (*Aviat*) decollare; (*go away*)
andarsene ▷ *vt* (*remove*) togliere; **take
on** *vt* (*work*) accettare, intraprendere;
(*employee*) assumere; (*opponent*) sfidare,
affrontare; **take out** *vt* portare fuori;
(*remove*) togliere; (*licence*) prendere,
ottenere; **to ~ sth out of sth** (*drawer,
pocket etc*) tirare qc fuori da qc; estrarre qc
da qc; **take over** *vt* (*business*) rilevare ▷ *vi*
to ~ over from sb prendere le consegne
or il controllo da qn; **take up** *vt* (*dress*)
accorciare; (*occupy: time, space*) occupare;
(*engage in: hobby etc*) mettersi a; **to ~ sb
up on sth** accettare qc da qn; **takeaway**
(*BRIT*) *n* (*shop etc*) ≈ rosticceria; (*food*)
pasto per asporto; **taken** *pp* of **take**;
takeoff *n* (*Aviat*) decollo; **takeout** (*us*)
n = **takeaway**; **takeover** *n* (*Comm*)
assorbimento; **takings** ['teɪkɪŋz] *npl*
(*Comm*) incasso
talc [tælk] *n* (*also:* **~um powder**) talco
tale [teɪl] *n* racconto, storia; **to tell ~s** (*fig:
to teacher, parent etc*) fare la spia
talent ['tælnt] *n* talento; **talented** *adj* di
talento
talk [tɔːk] *n* discorso; (*gossip*) chiacchiere

fpl; (*conversation*) conversazione *f*;
(*interview*) discussione *f* ▷ *vi* parlare; **~s** *npl*
(*Pol etc*) colloqui *mpl*; **to ~ about** parlare di;
to ~ sb out of/into doing dissuadere qn
da/convincere qn a fare; **to ~ shop** parlare
di lavoro *or* di affari; **talk over** *vt* discutere;
talk show *n* conversazione *f* televisiva,
talk show *m inv*
tall [tɔːl] *adj* alto(-a); **to be 6 feet ~** ≈ essere
alto 1 metro e 80
tambourine [tæmbə'riːn] *n* tamburello
tame [teɪm] *adj* addomesticato(-a); (*fig:
story, style*) insipido(-a), scialbo(-a)
tamper ['tæmpə*r*] *vi* **to ~ with**
manomettere
tampon ['tæmpɒn] *n* tampone *m*
tan [tæn] *n* (*also:* **sun~**) abbronzatura
▷ *vi* abbronzarsi ▷ *adj* (*colour*) marrone
rossiccio *inv*
tandem ['tændəm] *n* tandem *m inv*
tangerine [tændʒə'riːn] *n* mandarino
tangle ['tæŋgl] *n* groviglio; **to get into a ~**
aggrovigliarsi; (*fig*) combinare un pasticcio
tank [tæŋk] *n* serbatoio; (*for fish*) acquario;
(*Mil*) carro armato
tanker ['tæŋkə*r*] *n* (*ship*) nave *f* cisterna *inv*;
(*truck*) autobotte *f*, autocisterna
tanned [tænd] *adj* abbronzato(-a)
tantrum ['tæntrəm] *n* accesso di collera
Tanzania [tænzə'nɪə] *n* Tanzania
tap [tæp] *n* (*on sink etc*) rubinetto; (*gentle
blow*) colpetto ▷ *vt* dare un colpetto a;
(*resources*) sfruttare, utilizzare; (*telephone*)
mettere sotto controllo; **on ~** (*fig:
resources*) a disposizione; **tap dancing** *n*
tip tap *m*
tape [teɪp] *n* nastro; (*also:* **magnetic ~**)
nastro (magnetico); (*sticky tape*) nastro
adesivo ▷ *vt* (*record*) registrare (su nastro);
(*stick*) attaccare con nastro adesivo;
tape measure *n* metro a nastro; **tape
recorder** *n* registratore *m* (a nastro)
tapestry ['tæpɪstrɪ] *n* arazzo; tappezzeria
tar [tɑː*r*] *n* catrame *m*
target ['tɑːgɪt] *n* bersaglio; (*fig: objective*)
obiettivo
tariff ['tærɪf] *n* tariffa
tarmac ['tɑːmæk] *n* (*BRIT: on road*)
macadam *m* al catrame; (*Aviat*) pista di
decollo
tarpaulin [tɑː'pɔːlɪn] *n* tela incatramata
tarragon ['tærəgən] *n* dragoncello
tart [tɑːt] *n* (*Culin*) crostata; (*BRIT: inf:
pej: woman*) sgualdrina ▷ *adj* (*flavour*)
aspro(-a), agro(-a)
tartan ['tɑːtn] *n* tartan *m inv*
tartar(e) sauce *n* salsa tartara
task [tɑːsk] *n* compito; **to take to ~**
rimproverare

taste [teɪst] n gusto; (flavour) sapore m, gusto; (sample) assaggio; (fig: glimpse, idea) idea ▷ vt gustare; (sample) assaggiare ▷ vi **to ~ of** or **like** (fish etc) sapere or avere sapore di; **in good/bad ~** di buon/cattivo gusto; **can I have a ~?** posso assaggiarlo?; **you can ~ the garlic (in it)** (ci) si sente il sapore dell'aglio; **tasteful** adj di buon gusto; **tasteless** adj (food) insipido(-a); (remark) di cattivo gusto; **tasty** adj saporito(-a), gustoso(-a)

tatters ['tætəz] npl **in ~** a brandelli

tattoo [tə'tu:] n tatuaggio; (spectacle) parata militare ▷ vt tatuare

taught [tɔ:t] pt, pp of **teach**

taunt [tɔ:nt] n scherno ▷ vt schernire

Taurus ['tɔ:rəs] n Toro

taut [tɔ:t] adj teso(-a)

tax [tæks] n (on goods) imposta; (on services) tassa; (on income) imposte fpl, tasse fpl ▷ vt tassare; (fig: strain: patience etc) mettere alla prova; **tax-free** adj esente da imposte

taxi ['tæksɪ] n taxi m inv ▷ vi (Aviat) rullare; **can you call me a ~, please?** può chiamarmi un taxi, per favore?; **taxi driver** n tassista m/f; **taxi rank** (BRIT) n = **taxi stand**; **taxi stand** n posteggio dei taxi

tax payer n contribuente m/f

TB n abbr = **tuberculosis**

tea [ti:] n tè m inv; (BRIT: snack: for children) merenda; **high ~** (BRIT) cena leggera (presa nel tardo pomeriggio); **tea bag** n bustina di tè; **tea break** (BRIT) n intervallo per il tè

teach [ti:tʃ] (pt, pp **taught**) vt **to ~ sb sth, ~ sth to sb** insegnare qc a qn ▷ vi insegnare; **teacher** n insegnante m/f; (in secondary school) professore(-essa); (in primary school) maestro(-a); **teaching** n insegnamento

tea: **tea cloth** n (for dishes) strofinaccio; (BRIT: for trolley) tovaglietta da tè; **teacup** ['ti:kʌp] n tazza da tè

tea leaves npl foglie fpl di tè

team [ti:m] n squadra; (of animals) tiro; **team up** vi **to ~ up (with)** mettersi insieme (a)

teapot ['ti:pot] n teiera

tear[1] [tɛəʳ] (pt **tore**, pp **torn**) n strappo ▷ vt strappare ▷ vi strapparsi; **tear apart** vt (also fig) distruggere; **tear down** vt +adv (building, statue) demolire; (poster, flag) tirare giù; **tear off** vt (sheet of paper etc) strappare; (one's clothes) togliersi di dosso; **tear up** vt (sheet of paper etc) strappare

tear[2] [tɪəʳ] n lacrima; **in ~s** in lacrime; **tearful** ['tɪəful] adj piangente, lacrimoso(-a); **tear gas** n gas m lacrimogeno

tearoom ['ti:ru:m] n sala da tè

tease [ti:z] vt canzonare; (unkindly)

tormentare

tea: **teaspoon** n cucchiaino da tè; (also: **teaspoonful:** as measurement) cucchiaino; **teatime** n ora del tè; **tea towel** (BRIT) n strofinaccio (per i piatti)

technical ['tɛknɪkl] adj tecnico(-a)

technician [tɛk'nɪʃən] n tecnico(-a)

technique [tɛk'ni:k] n tecnica

technology [tɛk'nɔlədʒɪ] n tecnologia

teddy (bear) ['tɛdɪ-] n orsacchiotto

tedious ['ti:dɪəs] adj noioso(-a), tedioso(-a)

tee [ti:] n (Golf) tee m inv

teen [ti:n] adj = **teenage** ▷ n (US) = **teenager**

teenage ['ti:neɪdʒ] adj (fashions etc) per giovani, per adolescenti; **teenager** n adolescente m/f

teens [ti:nz] npl **to be in one's ~** essere adolescente

teeth [ti:θ] npl of **tooth**

teetotal ['ti:'təutl] adj astemio(-a)

telecommunications ['tɛlɪkəmju:nɪ'keɪʃənz] n telecomunicazioni fpl

telegram ['tɛlɪgræm] n telegramma m

telegraph pole n palo del telegrafo

telephone ['tɛlɪfəun] n telefono ▷ vt (person) telefonare a; (message) comunicare per telefono; **telephone book** n elenco telefonico; **telephone booth** (BRIT), **telephone box** n cabina telefonica; **telephone call** n telefonata; **telephone directory** n elenco telefonico; **telephone number** n numero di telefono

telesales ['tɛlɪseɪlz] n vendita per telefono

telescope ['tɛlɪskəup] n telescopio

televise ['tɛlɪvaɪz] vt teletrasmettere

television ['tɛlɪvɪʒən] n televisione f; **on ~** alla televisione; **television programme** n programma m televisivo

tell [tɛl] (pt, pp **told**) vt dire; (relate: story) raccontare; (distinguish): **to ~ sth from** distinguere qc da ▷ vi (talk): **to ~ (of)** parlare (di); (have effect) farsi sentire, avere effetto; **to ~ sb to do** dire a qn di fare; **tell off** vt rimproverare, sgridare; **teller** n (in bank) cassiere(-a)

telly ['tɛlɪ] (BRIT: inf) n abbr (= television) tivù f inv

temp [tɛmp] n abbr (= temporary) segretaria temporanea

temper ['tɛmpəʳ] n (nature) carattere m; (mood) umore m; (fit of anger) collera ▷ vt (moderate) moderare; **to be in a ~** essere in collera; **to lose one's ~** andare in collera

temperament ['tɛmprəmənt] n (nature) temperamento; **temperamental** [-'mɛntl] adj capriccioso(-a)

temperature ['tɛmprətʃəʳ] n

temperatura; **to have** or **run a ~** avere la
febbre

temple ['tɛmpl] n (building) tempio; (Anat)
tempia

temporary ['tɛmpərərɪ] adj
temporaneo(-a); (job, worker)
avventizio(-a), temporaneo(-a)

tempt [tɛmpt] vt tentare; **to ~ sb into
doing** indurre qn a fare; **temptation**
[-'teɪʃən] n tentazione f; **tempting** adj
allettante

ten [tɛn] num dieci

tenant ['tɛnənt] n inquilino(-a)

tend [tɛnd] vt badare a, occuparsi di ▷ vi
to ~ to do tendere a fare; **tendency**
['tɛndənsɪ] n tendenza

tender ['tɛndəʳ] adj tenero(-a); (sore)
dolorante ▷ n (Comm: offer) offerta;
(money): **legal ~** moneta in corso legale
▷ vt offrire

tendon ['tɛndən] n tendine m

tenner ['tɛnəʳ] n (BRIT inf) (banconota da)
dieci sterline fpl

tennis ['tɛnɪs] n tennis m; **tennis ball** n
palla da tennis; **tennis court** n campo da
tennis; **tennis match** n partita di tennis;
tennis player n tennista m/f; **tennis
racket** n racchetta da tennis

tenor ['tɛnəʳ] n (Mus) tenore m

tenpin bowling ['tɛnpɪn-] n bowling m

tense [tɛns] adj teso(-a) ▷ n (Ling) tempo

tension ['tɛnʃən] n tensione f

tent [tɛnt] n tenda

tentative ['tɛntətɪv] adj esitante,
incerto(-a); (conclusion) provvisorio(-a)

tenth [tɛnθ] num decimo(-a)

tent: tent peg n picchetto da tenda; **tent
pole** n palo da tenda, montante m

tepid ['tɛpɪd] adj tiepido(-a)

term [tə:m] n termine m; (Scol) trimestre
m; (Law) sessione f ▷ vt chiamare, definire;
~s npl (conditions) condizioni fpl; (Comm)
prezzi mpl, tariffe fpl; **in the short/long ~**
a breve/lunga scadenza; **to be on good ~s
with sb** essere in buoni rapporti con qn; **to
come to ~s with** (problem) affrontare

terminal ['tə:mɪnl] adj finale, terminale;
(disease) terminale ▷ n (Elec) morsetto;
(Comput) terminale m; (Aviat, for oil, ore
etc) terminal m inv; (BRIT: also: **coach ~**)
capolinea m

terminate ['tə:mɪneɪt] vt mettere fine a

termini ['tə:mɪnaɪ] npl of **terminus**

terminology [tə:mɪ'nɔlədʒɪ] n
terminologia

terminus ['tə:mɪnəs] (pl **termini**) n (for
buses) capolinea m; (for trains) stazione f
terminale

terrace ['tɛrəs] n terrazza; (BRIT: row of

houses) fila di case a schiera; **terraced** adj
(garden) a terrazze

terrain [tɛ'reɪn] n terreno

terrestrial [tɪ'rɛstrɪəl] adj (life) terrestre;
(BRIT: channel) terrestre

terrible ['tɛrɪbl] adj terribile; **terribly** adv
terribilmente; (very badly) malissimo

terrier ['tɛrɪəʳ] n terrier m inv

terrific [tə'rɪfɪk] adj incredibile,
fantastico(-a); (wonderful) formidabile,
eccezionale

terrified ['tɛrɪfaɪd] adj atterrito(-a)

terrify ['tɛrɪfaɪ] vt terrorizzare; **terrifying**
adj terrificante

territorial [tɛrɪ'tɔ:rɪəl] adj territoriale

territory ['tɛrɪtərɪ] n territorio

terror ['tɛrəʳ] n terrore m; **terrorism** n
terrorismo; **terrorist** n terrorista m/f

test [tɛst] n (trial, check: of courage etc)
prova; (Med) esame m; (Chem) analisi f inv;
(exam: of intelligence etc) test m inv; (: in
school) compito in classe; (also: **driving ~**)
esame m di guida ▷ vt provare; esaminare;
analizzare; sottoporre ad esame; **to ~ sb in
history** esaminare qn in storia

testicle ['tɛstɪkl] n testicolo

testify ['tɛstɪfaɪ] vi (Law) testimoniare,
deporre; **to ~ to sth** (Law) testimoniare qc;
(gen) comprovare or dimostrare qc

testimony ['tɛstɪmənɪ] n (Law)
testimonianza, deposizione f

test: test match n (Cricket, Rugby) partita
internazionale; **test tube** n provetta

tetanus ['tɛtənəs] n tetano

text [tɛkst] n testo; (on mobile phone) SMS m
inv, messaggino ▷ vt **to ~ sb** (inf) mandare
un SMS a qn; **textbook** n libro di testo

textile ['tɛkstaɪl] n tessile m

text message n (Tel) SMS m inv,
messaggino

text messaging [-'mɛsɪdʒɪŋ] n il
mandarsi SMS

texture ['tɛkstʃəʳ] n tessitura; (of skin,
paper etc) struttura

Thai [taɪ] adj tailandese ▷ n tailandese m/f;
(Ling) tailandese m

Thailand ['taɪlænd] n Tailandia

Thames [tɛmz] n **the ~** il Tamigi

than [ðæn, ðən] conj (in comparisons) che;
(with numerals, pronouns, proper names)
di; **more ~ 10/once** più di 10/una volta; **I
have more/less ~ you** ne ho più/meno
di te; **I have more pens ~ pencils** ho più
penne che matite; **she is older ~ you
think** è più vecchia di quanto tu (non)
pensi

thank [θæŋk] vt ringraziare; **~ you
(very much)** grazie (tante); **~s** npl
ringraziamenti mpl, grazie fpl excl grazie!;

~s to grazie a; **thankfully** *adv* con riconoscenza; con sollievo; **thankfully there were few victims** grazie al cielo ci sono state poche vittime; **Thanksgiving (Day)** *n* giorno del ringraziamento

 KEYWORD

that [ðæt] (*pl* **those**) *adj* (*demonstrative*) quel (quell', quello) *m*; quella (quell') *f*; **that man/woman/book** quell'uomo/quella donna/quel libro; (*not "this"*) quell'uomo/ quella donna/quel libro là; **that one** quello(-a) là
▷ *pron* 1 (*demonstrative*) ciò; (*not "this one"*) quello(-a); **who's that?** chi è?; **what's that?** cos'è quello?; **is that you?** sei tu?; **I prefer this to that** preferisco questo a quello; **that's what he said** questo è ciò che ha detto; **what happened after that?** che è successo dopo?; **that is (to say)** cioè
2 (*relative: direct*) che; (: *indirect*) cui; **the book (that) I read** il libro che ho letto; **the box (that) I put it in** la scatola in cui l'ho messo; **the people (that) I spoke to** le persone con cui *or* con le quali ho parlato
3 (*relative: of time*) in cui; **the day (that) he came** il giorno in cui è venuto
▷ *conj* che; **he thought that I was ill** pensava che io fossi malato
▷ *adv* (*demonstrative*) così; **I can't work that much** non posso lavorare (così) tanto; **that high** così alto; **the wall's about that high and that thick** il muro è alto circa così e spesso circa così

thatched [θætʃt] *adj* (*roof*) di paglia
thaw [θɔː] *n* disgelo ▷ *vi* (*ice*) sciogliersi; (*food*) scongelarsi ▷ *vt* (*food: also:* **~ out**) (fare) scongelare

 KEYWORD

the [ðiː, ðə] *def art* 1 (*gen*) il (lo, l') *m*; la (l') *f*; i (gli) *mpl*; le *fpl*; **the boy/girl/ink** il ragazzo/la ragazza/l'inchiostro; **the books/pencils** i libri/le matite; **the history of the world** la storia del mondo; **give it to the postman** dallo al postino;

I haven't the time/money non ho tempo/soldi; **the rich and the poor** i ricchi e i poveri
2 (*in titles*): **Elizabeth the First** Elisabetta prima; **Peter the Great** Pietro il grande
3 (*in comparisons*): **the more he works, the more he earns** più lavora più guadagna

theatre ['θɪətəʳ] (*us* **theater**) *n* teatro; (*also:* **lecture ~**) aula magna; (*also:* **operating ~**) sala operatoria
theft [θɛft] *n* furto
their [ðɛəʳ] *adj* il (la) loro; (*pl*) i (le) loro; **theirs** *pron* il (la) loro; (*pl*) i (le) loro; *see also* **my; mine**
them [ðɛm, ðəm] *pron* (*direct*) li (le); (*indirect*) gli (loro (*after vb*)); (*stressed, after prep: people*) loro; (: *people, things*) essi(-e); *see also* **me**
theme [θiːm] *n* tema *m*; **theme park** *n* parco di divertimenti (*intorno a un tema centrale*)
themselves [ðəmˈsɛlvz] *pl pron* (*reflexive*) si; (*emphatic*) loro stessi(-e); (*after prep*) se stessi(-e)
then [ðɛn] *adv* (*at that time*) allora; (*next*) poi, dopo; (*and also*) e poi ▷ *conj* (*therefore*) perciò, dunque, quindi ▷ *adj* **the ~ president** il presidente di allora; **by ~** allora; **from ~ on** da allora in poi
theology [θɪˈɒlədʒɪ] *n* teologia
theory ['θɪərɪ] *n* teoria
therapist ['θɛrəpɪst] *n* terapista *m/f*
therapy ['θɛrəpɪ] *n* terapia

 KEYWORD

there [ðɛəʳ] *adv* 1: **there is, there are** c'è, ci sono; **there are 3 of them** (*people*) sono in 3; (*things*) ce ne sono 3; **there is no-one here** non c'è nessuno qui; **there has been an accident** c'è stato un incidente
2 (*referring to place*) là, lì; **up/in/down there** lassù/là dentro/laggiù; **he went there on Friday** ci è andato venerdì; **I want that book there** voglio quel libro là *or* lì; **there he is!** eccolo!
3: **there, there** (*esp to child*) su, su

there: thereabouts [ðɛərəˈbauts] *adv* (*place*) nei pressi, da quelle parti; (*amount*) giù di lì, all'incirca; **thereafter** [ðɛərˈɑːftəʳ] *adv* da allora in poi; **thereby** [ðɛəˈbaɪ] *adv* con ciò; **therefore** ['ðɛəfɔːʳ] *adv* perciò, quindi; **there's** [ðɛəz] = **there is**; **there has**
thermal ['θəːml] *adj* termico(-a)
thermometer [θəˈmɒmɪtəʳ] *n*

termometro

thermostat [ˈθəːməstæt] *n* termostato

these [ðiːz] *pl pron, adj* questi(-e)

thesis [ˈθiːsɪs] (*pl* **theses**) *n* tesi *f inv*

they [ðeɪ] *pl pron* essi (esse); (*people only*) loro; **~ say that …** (*it is said that*) si dice che …; **they'd = they had**; **they would**; **they'll = they shall**; **they will**; **they're = they are**; **they've = they have**

thick [θɪk] *adj* spesso(-a); (*crowd*) compatto(-a); **; they'd = they had**; (*stupid*) ottuso(-a), lento(-a) ▷ *n* **in the ~ of** nel folto di; **it's 20 cm ~** ha uno spessore di 20 cm; **thicken** *vi* ispessire ▷ *vt* ispessire, rendere più denso(-a); **thickness** *n* spessore *m*

thief [θiːf] (*pl* **thieves**) *n* ladro(-a)

thigh [θaɪ] *n* coscia

thin [θɪn] *adj* sottile; (*person*) magro(-a); (*soup*) poco denso(-a) ▷ *vt* **to ~ (down)** (*sauce, paint*) diluire

thing [θɪŋ] *n* cosa; (*object*) oggetto; (*mania*): **to have a ~ about** essere fissato(-a) con; **~s** *npl* (*belongings*) cose *fpl*; **poor ~** poverino(-a); **the best ~ would be to** la cosa migliore sarebbe di; **how are ~s?** come va?

think [θɪŋk] (*pt, pp* **thought**) *vi* pensare, riflettere ▷ *vt* pensare, credere; (*imagine*) immaginare; **to ~ of** pensare a; **what did you ~ of them?** cosa ne ha pensato?; **to ~ about sth/sb** pensare a qc/qn; **I'll ~ about it** ci penserò; **to ~ of doing** pensare di fare; **I ~ so/not** penso di sì/no; **to ~ well of** avere una buona opinione di; **think over** *vt* riflettere su; **think up** *vt* ideare

third [θəːd] *num* terzo(-a) ▷ *n* terzo(-a); (*fraction*) terzo, terza parte *f*; (*Aut*) terza; (BRIT: *Scol: degree*) laurea col minimo dei voti; **thirdly** *adv* in terzo luogo; **third party insurance** (BRIT) *n* assicurazione *f* contro terzi; **Third World** *n* **the Third World** il Terzo Mondo

thirst [θəːst] *n* sete *f*; **thirsty** *adj* (*person*) assetato(-a), che ha sete

thirteen [ˈθəːˈtiːn] *num* tredici; **thirteenth** [-ˈtiːnθ] *num* tredicesimo(-a)

thirtieth [ˈθəːtɪɪθ] *num* trentesimo(-a)

thirty [ˈθəːtɪ] *num* trenta

 KEYWORD

this [ðɪs] (*pl* **these**) *adj* (*demonstrative*) questo(-a); **this man/woman/book** quest'uomo/questa donna/questo libro; (*not "that"*) quest'uomo/questa donna/ questo libro qui; **this one** questo(-a) qui ▷ *pron* (*demonstrative*) questo(-a); (*not "that one"*) questo(-a) qui; **who/what is this?** chi è/che cos'è questo?; **I prefer this to**

that preferisco questo a quello; **this is where I live** io abito qui; **this is what he said** questo è ciò che ha detto; **this is Mr Brown** (*in introductions, photo*) questo è il signor Brown; (*on telephone*) sono il signor Brown

▷ *adv* (*demonstrative*): **this high/long** etc alto/lungo etc così; **I didn't know things were this bad** non sapevo andasse così male

thistle [ˈθɪsl] *n* cardo

thorn [θɔːn] *n* spina

thorough [ˈθʌrə] *adj* (*search*) minuzioso(-a); (*knowledge, research*) approfondito(-a), profondo(-a); (*person*) coscienzioso(-a); (*cleaning*) a fondo; **thoroughly** *adv* (*search*) minuziosamente; (*wash, study*) a fondo; (*very*) assolutamente

those [ðəuz] *pl pron* quelli(-e) ▷ *pl adj* quei (quegli) *mpl*; quelle *fpl*

though [ðəu] *conj* benché, sebbene ▷ *adv* comunque

thought [θɔːt] *pt, pp of* **think** ▷ *n* pensiero; (*opinion*) opinione *f*; **thoughtful** *adj* pensieroso(-a), pensoso(-a); (*considerate*) premuroso(-a); **thoughtless** *adj* sconsiderato(-a); (*behaviour*) scortese

thousand [ˈθauzənd] *num* mille; **one ~** mille; **~s of** migliaia di; **thousandth** *num* millesimo(-a)

thrash [θræʃ] *vt* picchiare; bastonare; (*defeat*) battere

thread [θrɛd] *n* filo; (*of screw*) filetto ▷ *vt* (*needle*) infilare

threat [θrɛt] *n* minaccia; **threaten** *vi* (*storm*) minacciare ▷ *vt* **to threaten sb with/to do** minacciare qn con/di fare; **threatening** *adj* minaccioso(-a)

three [θriː] *num* tre; **three-dimensional** *adj* tridimensionale; (*film*) stereoscopico(-a); **three-piece suite** [ˈθriːpiːs-] *n* salotto comprendente un divano e due poltrone; **three-quarters** *npl* tre quarti *mpl*; **three-quarters full** pieno per tre quarti

threshold [ˈθrɛʃhəuld] *n* soglia

threw [θruː] *pt of* **throw**

thrill [θrɪl] *n* brivido ▷ *vt* (*audience*) elettrizzare; **to be ~ed** (*with gift etc*) essere elettrizzato(-a); **thrilled** *adj* **I was thrilled to get your letter** la tua lettera mi ha fatto veramente piacere; **thriller** *n* thriller *m inv*; **thrilling** *adj* (*book*) pieno(-a) di suspense; (*news, discovery*) elettrizzante

thriving [ˈθraɪvɪŋ] *adj* fiorente

throat [θrəut] *n* gola; **to have a sore ~** avere (un *or* il) mal di gola

throb [θrɔb] *vi* palpitare; pulsare; vibrare

throne [θrəʊn] *n* trono

through [θruː] *prep* attraverso; (*time*) per, durante; (*by means of*) per mezzo di; (*owing to*) a causa di ▷ *adj* (*ticket, train, passage*) diretto(-a) ▷ *adv* attraverso; **to put sb ~ to sb** (*Tel*) passare qn a qn; **to be ~** (*Tel*) ottenere la comunicazione; (*have finished*) essere finito(-a); **"no ~ road"** (BRIT) "strada senza sbocco"; **throughout** *prep* (*place*) dappertutto in; (*time*) per o durante tutto(-a) ▷ *adv* dappertutto; sempre

throw [θrəʊ] (*pt* **threw**, *pp* **thrown**) *n* (*Sport*) lancio, tiro ▷ *vt* tirare, gettare; (*Sport*) lanciare, tirare; (*rider*) disarcionare; (*fig*) confondere; **to ~ a party** dare una festa; **throw away** *vt* gettare o buttare via; **throw in** *vt* (*Sport: ball*) rimettere in gioco; (*include*) aggiungere; **throw off** *vt* sbarazzarsi di; **throw out** *vt* buttare fuori; (*reject*) respingere; **throw up** *vi* vomitare

thru [θruː] (US) *prep, adj, adv* = **through**

thrush [θrʌʃ] *n* tordo

thrust [θrʌst] (*pt, pp* **thrust**) *vt* spingere con forza; (*push in*) conficcare

thud [θʌd] *n* tonfo

thug [θʌg] *n* delinquente *m*

thumb [θʌm] *n* (*Anat*) pollice *m*; **to ~ a lift** fare l'autostop; **thumbtack** (US) *n* puntina da disegno

thump [θʌmp] *n* colpo forte; (*sound*) tonfo ▷ *vt* (*person*) picchiare; (*object*) battere su ▷ *vi* picchiare; battere

thunder [ˈθʌndəʳ] *n* tuono ▷ *vi* tuonare; (*train etc*): **to ~ past** passare con un rombo; **thunderstorm** *n* temporale *m*

Thur(s). *abbr* (= *Thursday*) gio.

Thursday [ˈθəːzdɪ] *n* giovedì *m inv*

thus [ðʌs] *adv* così

thwart [θwɔːt] *vt* contrastare

thyme [taɪm] *n* timo

Tiber [ˈtaɪbəʳ] *n* **the ~** il Tevere

Tibet [tɪˈbɛt] *n* Tibet *m*

tick [tɪk] *n* (*sound: of clock*) tic tac *m inv*; (*mark*) segno; spunta; (*Zool*) zecca; (BRIT: *inf*): **in a ~** in un attimo ▷ *vi* fare tic tac ▷ *vt* spuntare; **tick off** *vt* spuntare; (*person*) sgridare

ticket [ˈtɪkɪt] *n* biglietto; (*in shop: on goods*) etichetta; (*parking ticket*) multa; (*for library*) scheda; **a single/return ~ to ...** un biglietto di sola andata/di andata e ritorno per...; **ticket barrier** *n* (BRIT: *Rail*) cancelletto d'ingresso; **ticket collector** *n* bigliettaio; **ticket inspector** *n* controllore *m*; **ticket machine** *n* distributore *m* di biglietti; **ticket office** *n* biglietteria

tickle [ˈtɪkl] *vt* fare il solletico a; (*fig*) solleticare ▷ *vi* **it ~s** mi (*or* gli *etc*) fa il

solletico; **ticklish** [-lɪʃ] *adj* che soffre il solletico; (*problem*) delicato(-a)

tide [taɪd] *n* marea; (*fig: of events*) corso; **high/low ~** alta/bassa marea

tidy [ˈtaɪdɪ] *adj* (*room*) ordinato(-a), lindo(-a); (*dress, work*) curato(-a), in ordine; (*person*) ordinato(-a) ▷ *vt* (*also: ~ up*) riordinare, mettere in ordine

tie [taɪ] *n* (*string etc*) legaccio; (BRIT: *also:* **neck~**) cravatta; (*fig: link*) legame *m*; (*Sport: draw*) pareggio ▷ *vt* (*parcel*) legare; (*ribbon*) annodare ▷ *vi* (*Sport*) pareggiare; **to ~ sth in a bow** annodare qc; **to ~ a knot in sth** fare un nodo a qc; **tie down** *vt* legare; (*to price etc*) costringere ad accettare; **tie up** *vt* (*parcel, dog*) legare; (*boat*) ormeggiare; (*arrangements*) concludere; **to be ~d up** (*busy*) essere occupato(-a) *or* preso(-a)

tier [tɪəʳ] *n* fila; (*of cake*) piano, strato

tiger [ˈtaɪgəʳ] *n* tigre *f*

tight [taɪt] *adj* (*rope*) teso(-a), tirato(-a); (*money*) poco(-a); (*clothes, budget, bend etc*) stretto(-a); (*control*) severo(-a), fermo(-a); (*inf: drunk*) sbronzo(-a) ▷ *adv* (*squeeze*) fortemente; (*shut*) ermeticamente; **tighten** *vt* (*rope*) tendere; (*screw*) stringere; (*control*) rinforzare ▷ *vi* tendersi; stringersi; **tightly** *adv* (*grasp*) bene, saldamente; **tights** (BRIT) *npl* collant *m inv*

tile [taɪl] *n* (*on roof*) tegola; (*on wall or floor*) piastrella, mattonella

till [tɪl] *n* registratore *m* di cassa ▷ *vt* (*land*) coltivare ▷ *prep, conj* = **until**

tilt [tɪlt] *vt* inclinare, far pendere ▷ *vi* inclinarsi, pendere

timber [ˈtɪmbəʳ] *n* (*material*) legname *m*

time [taɪm] *n* tempo; (*epoch: often pl*) epoca, tempo; (*by clock*) ora; (*moment*) momento; (*occasion*) volta; (*Mus*) tempo ▷ *vt* (*race*) cronometrare; (*programme*) calcolare la durata di; (*fix moment for*) programmare; (*remark etc*) dire (*or* fare) al momento giusto; **a long ~** molto tempo; **what ~ does the museum/shop open?** a che ora apre il museo/negozio?; **for the ~ being** per il momento; **4 at a ~** 4 per *or* alla volta; **from ~ to ~** ogni tanto; **at ~s** a volte; **in ~** (*soon enough*) in tempo; (*after some time*) col tempo; (*Mus*) a tempo; **in a week's ~** fra una settimana; **in no ~** in un attimo; **any ~** in qualsiasi momento; **on ~** puntualmente; **5 ~s 5** 5 volte 5, 5 per 5; **what ~ is it?** che ora è?, che ore sono?; **to have a good ~** divertirsi; **time limit** *n* limite *m* di tempo; **timely** *adj* opportuno(-a); **timer** *n* (*time switch*) temporizzatore *m*; (*in kitchen*) contaminuti *m inv*; **time-share** *adj* **time-share apartment/villa** appartamento/villa in multiproprietà; **timetable** n orario; **time zone** n fuso orario

timid ['tɪmɪd] adj timido(-a); (easily scared) pauroso(-a)

timing ['taɪmɪŋ] n (Sport) cronometraggio; (fig) scelta del momento opportuno

tin [tɪn] n stagno; (also: ~ plate) latta; (container) scatola; (BRIT: can) barattolo (di latta), lattina; **tinfoil** n stagnola

tingle ['tɪŋgl] vi pizzicare

tinker ['tɪŋkər]: ~ with vt fus armeggiare intorno a; cercare di riparare

tinned [tɪnd] (BRIT) adj (food) in scatola

tin opener ['-əʊpnər] (BRIT) n apriscatole m inv

tint [tɪnt] n tinta; **tinted** adj (hair) tinto(-a); (spectacles, glass) colorato(-a)

tiny ['taɪnɪ] adj minuscolo(-a)

tip [tɪp] n (end) punta; (gratuity) mancia; (BRIT: for rubbish) immondezzaio; (advice) suggerimento ⊳ vt (waiter) dare la mancia a; (tilt) inclinare; (overturn: also: ~ over) capovolgere; (empty: also: ~ out) scaricare; **how much should I ~?** quanto devo lasciare di mancia?; **tip off** vt fare una soffiata a

tiptoe ['tɪptəʊ] n **on~** in punta di piedi

tire ['taɪər] n (US) = tyre ⊳ vt stancare ⊳ vi stancarsi; **tired** adj stanco(-a); **to be tired of** essere stanco or stufo di; **tire pressure** (US) n = **tyre pressure**; **tiring** adj faticoso(-a)

tissue ['tɪʃuː] n tessuto; (paper handkerchief) fazzoletto di carta; **tissue paper** n carta velina

tit [tɪt] n (bird) cinciallegra; **to give ~ for tat** rendere pan per focaccia

title ['taɪtl] n titolo

T-junction ['tiː'dʒʌŋkʃən] n incrocio a T

TM abbr = **trademark**

 KEYWORD

to [tuː, tə] prep 1 (direction) a; **to go to France/London/school** andare in Francia/a Londra/a scuola; **to go to Paul's/the doctor's** andare da Paul/dal dottore; **the road to Edinburgh** la strada per Edimburgo; **to the left/right** a sinistra/destra

2 (as far as) (fino) a; **from here to London** da qui a Londra; **to count to 10** contare fino a 10; **from 40 to 50 people** da 40 a 50 persone

3 (with expressions of time): **a quarter to 5** le 5 meno un quarto; **it's twenty to 3** sono le 3 meno venti

4 (for, of): **the key to the front door** la chiave della porta d'ingresso; **a letter to his wife** una lettera per la moglie

5 (expressing indirect object) a; **to give sth to sb** dare qc a qn; **to talk to sb** parlare a qn; **to be a danger to sb/sth** rappresentare un pericolo per qn/qc

6 (in relation to) a; **3 goals to 2** 3 goal a 2; **30 miles to the gallon** ≈ 11 chilometri con un litro

7 (purpose, result): **to come to sb's aid** venire in aiuto a qn; **to sentence sb to death** condannare a morte qn; **to my surprise** con mia sorpresa

⊳ with vb 1 (simple infinitive): **to go/eat** etc andare/mangiare etc

2 (following another vb): **to want/try/ start to do** volere/cercare di/cominciare a fare

3 (with vb omitted): **I don't want to** non voglio (farlo); **you ought to** devi (farlo)

4 (purpose, result) per; **I did it to help you** l'ho fatto per aiutarti

5 (equivalent to relative clause): **I have things to do** ho da fare; **the main thing is to try** la cosa più importante è provare

6 (after adjective etc): **ready to go** pronto a partire; **too old/young to ...** troppo vecchio/giovane per ...

⊳ adv **to push the door to** accostare la porta

toad [təʊd] n rospo; **toadstool** n fungo (velenoso)

toast [təʊst] n (Culin) pane m tostato; (drink, speech) brindisi m inv ⊳ vt (Culin) tostare; (drink to) brindare a; **a piece or slice of ~** una fetta di pane tostato; **toaster** n tostapane m inv

tobacco [tə'bækəʊ] n tabacco

toboggan [tə'bɒgən] n toboga m inv

today [tə'deɪ] adv oggi ⊳ n (also fig) oggi m

toddler ['tɒdlər] n bambino(-a) che impara a camminare

toe [təʊ] n dito del piede; (of shoe) punta; **to ~ the line** (fig) stare in riga, conformarsi; **toenail** n unghia del piede

toffee ['tɒfɪ] n caramella

together [tə'gɛðər] adv insieme; (at same time) allo stesso tempo; **~ with** insieme a

toilet ['tɔɪlət] n (BRIT: lavatory) gabinetto ⊳ cpd (bag, soap etc) da toletta; **where's the ~?** dov'è il bagno?; **toilet bag** n (BRIT) nécessaire m inv da toilette; **toilet paper** n carta igienica; **toiletries** npl articoli mpl da toletta; **toilet roll** n rotolo di carta igienica

token ['təʊkən] n (sign) segno; (substitute coin) gettone m; **book/record/gift ~** (BRIT) buono-libro/disco/regalo

Tokyo ['təʊkjəʊ] n Tokyo f

told [təuld] pt, pp of **tell**

tolerant ['tɔlərnt] adj **~ (of)** tollerante (nei confronti di)

tolerate ['tɔləreit] vt sopportare; (Med, Tech) tollerare

toll [təul] n (tax, charge) pedaggio ▷ vi (bell) suonare; **the accident ~ on the roads** il numero delle vittime della strada; **toll call** (US) n (Tel) (telefonata) interurbana; **toll-free** (US) adj senza addebito, gratuito(-a) ▷ adv gratuitamente; **toll-free number** ≈ numero verde

tomato [tə'ma:təu] (pl **tomatoes**) n pomodoro; **tomato sauce** n salsa di pomodoro

tomb [tu:m] n tomba; **tombstone** ['tu:mstəun] n pietra tombale

tomorrow [tə'mɔrəu] adv domani ▷ n (also fig) domani m inv; **the day after ~** dopodomani; **~ morning** domani mattina

ton [tʌn] n tonnellata; (BRIT: 1016 kg: US: 907 kg: metric 1000 kg); **~s of** (inf) un mucchio or sacco di

tone [təun] n tono ▷ vi (also: **~ in**) intonarsi; **tone down** vt (colour, criticism, sound) attenuare

tongs [tɔŋz] npl tenaglie fpl; (for coal) molle fpl; (for hair) arricciacapelli m inv

tongue [tʌŋ] n lingua; **~ in cheek** (say, speak) ironicamente

tonic ['tɔnik] n (Med) tonico; (also: **~ water**) acqua tonica

tonight [tə'nait] adv stanotte; (this evening) stasera ▷ n questa notte; questa sera

tonne [tʌn] n (BRIT: metric ton) tonnellata

tonsil ['tɔnsl] n tonsilla; **tonsillitis** [-'laitis] n tonsillite f

too [tu:] adv (excessively) troppo; (also) anche; (also: **~ much**) ▷ adv troppo ▷ adj troppo(-a); **~ many** troppi(-e)

took [tuk] pt of **take**

tool [tu:l] n utensile m, attrezzo; **tool box** n cassetta f portautensili; **tool kit** n cassetta di attrezzi

tooth [tu:θ] (pl **teeth**) n (Anat, Tech) dente m; **toothache** n mal m di denti; **toothbrush** n spazzolino da denti; **toothpaste** n dentifricio; **toothpick** n stuzzicadenti m inv

top [tɔp] n (of mountain, page, ladder) cima; (of box, cupboard, table) sopra m inv, parte f superiore; (lid: of box, jar) coperchio; (: of bottle) tappo; (blouse etc) sopra m inv; (toy) trottola ▷ adj più alto(-a); (in rank) primo(-a); (best) migliore ▷ vt (exceed) superare; (be first in) essere in testa a; **on ~ of** sopra, in cima a; (in addition to) oltre a; **from ~ to bottom** da cima a fondo;

top up (US **top off**) vt riempire; (salary) integrare; **top floor** n ultimo piano; **top hat** n cilindro

topic ['tɔpik] n argomento; **topical** adj d'attualità

topless ['tɔplis] adj (bather etc) col seno scoperto

topping ['tɔpiŋ] n (Culin) guarnizione f

topple ['tɔpl] vt rovesciare, far cadere ▷ vi cadere; traballare

torch [tɔ:tʃ] n torcia; (BRIT: electric) lampadina tascabile

tore [tɔ:ʳ] pt of **tear¹**

torment [n 'tɔ:mɛnt, vb tɔ:'mɛnt] n tormento ▷ vt tormentare

torn [tɔ:n] pp of **tear¹**

tornado [tɔ:'neidəu] (pl **tornadoes**) n tornado

torpedo [tɔ:'pi:dəu] (pl **torpedoes**) n siluro

torrent ['tɔrnt] n torrente m; **torrential** [tɔ'rɛnʃl] adj torrenziale

tortoise ['tɔ:təs] n tartaruga

torture ['tɔ:tʃəʳ] n tortura ▷ vt torturare

Tory ['tɔ:ri] (BRIT: Pol) adj dei tories, conservatore(-trice) ▷ n tory m/f inv, conservatore(-trice)

toss [tɔs] vt gettare, lanciare; (one's head) scuotere; **to ~ a coin** fare a testa o croce; **to ~ up for sth** fare a testa o croce per qc; **to ~ and turn** (in bed) girarsi e rigirarsi

total ['təutl] adj totale ▷ n totale m ▷ vt (add up) sommare; (amount to) ammontare a

totalitarian [təutælɪ'tɛəriən] adj totalitario(-a)

totally ['təutəli] adv completamente

touch [tʌtʃ] n tocco; (sense) tatto; (contact) contatto ▷ vt toccare; **a ~ of** (fig) un tocco di; un pizzico di; **to get in ~ with** mettersi in contatto con; **to lose ~** (friends) perdersi di vista; **touch down** vi (on land) atterrare; **touchdown** n atterraggio; (on sea) ammaraggio; (US: Football) meta; **touched** adj commosso(-a); **touching** adj commovente; **touchline** n (Sport) linea laterale; **touch-sensitive** adj sensibile al tatto

tough [tʌf] adj duro(-a); (resistant) resistente

tour ['tuəʳ] n viaggio; (also: **package ~**) viaggio organizzato or tutto compreso; (of town, museum) visita; (by artist) tournée f inv ▷ vt visitare; **tour guide** n guida turistica

tourism ['tuərizəm] n turismo

tourist ['tuərist] n turista m/f ▷ adv (travel) in classe turistica ▷ cpd turistico(-a); **tourist office** n pro loco f inv

tournament ['tuǝnǝmǝnt] *n* torneo
tour operator *n* (BRIT) operatore *m* turistico
tow [tǝu] *vt* rimorchiare; **"on ~"** (BRIT), **"in ~"** (US) "veicolo rimorchiato"; **tow away** *vt* rimorchiare
toward(s) [tǝ'wɔ:d(z)] *prep* verso; (*of attitude*) nei confronti di; (*of purpose*) per
towel ['tauǝl] *n* asciugamano; (*also:* **tea ~**) strofinaccio; **towelling** *n* (*fabric*) spugna
tower ['tauǝʳ] *n* torre *f*; **tower block** (BRIT) *n* palazzone *m*
town [taun] *n* città *f inv*; **to go to ~** andare in città; (*fig*) mettercela tutta; **town centre** *n* centro (città); **town hall** *n* ≈ municipio
tow truck (US) *n* carro *m*, attrezzi *inv*
toxic ['tɔksɪk] *adj* tossico(-a)
toy [tɔɪ] *n* giocattolo; **toy with** *vt fus* giocare con; (*idea*) accarezzare, trastullarsi con; **toyshop** *n* negozio di giocattoli
trace [treɪs] *n* traccia ▷ *vt* (*draw*) tracciare; (*follow*) seguire; (*locate*) rintracciare
track [træk] *n* (*of person, animal*) traccia; (*on tape, Sport, path: gen*) pista; (*: of bullet etc*) traiettoria; (*: of suspect, animal*) pista, tracce *fpl*; (*Rail*) binario, rotaie *fpl* ▷ *vt* seguire le tracce di; **to keep ~ of** seguire; **track down** *vt* (*prey*) scovare; snidare; (*sth lost*) rintracciare; **tracksuit** *n* tuta sportiva
tractor ['træktǝʳ] *n* trattore *m*
trade [treɪd] *n* commercio; (*skill, job*) mestiere *m* ▷ *vi* commerciare ▷ *vt* **to ~ sth (for sth)** barattare qc (con qc); **to ~ with/in** commerciare con/in; **trade in** *vt* (*old car etc*) dare come pagamento parziale; **trademark** *n* marchio di fabbrica; **trader** *n* commerciante *m/f*; **tradesman** (*irreg*) *n* fornitore *m*; (*shopkeeper*) negoziante *m*; **trade union** *n* sindacato
trading ['treɪdɪŋ] *n* commercio
tradition [trǝ'dɪʃǝn] *n* tradizione *f*; **traditional** *adj* tradizionale
traffic ['træfɪk] *n* traffico ▷ *vi* **to ~ in** (*pej: liquor, drugs*) trafficare in; **traffic circle** (US) *n* isola rotatoria; **traffic island** *n* salvagente *m*, isola *f*, spartitraffico *inv*; **traffic jam** *n* ingorgo (del traffico); **traffic lights** *npl* semaforo; **traffic warden** *n* addetto(-a) al controllo del traffico e del parcheggio
tragedy ['trædʒǝdɪ] *n* tragedia
tragic ['trædʒɪk] *adj* tragico(-a)
trail [treɪl] *n* (*tracks*) tracce *fpl*, pista; (*path*) sentiero; (*of smoke etc*) scia ▷ *vt* trascinare,

strascicare; (*follow*) seguire ▷ *vi* essere al traino; (*dress etc*) strusciare; (*plant*) arrampicarsi; strisciare; (*in game*) essere in svantaggio; **trailer** *n* (*Aut*) rimorchio; (*US*) roulotte *f inv*; (*Cinema*) prossimamente *m inv*
train [treɪn] *n* treno; (*of dress*) coda, strascico ▷ *vt* (*apprentice, doctor etc*) formare; (*sportsman*) allenare; (*dog*) addestrare; (*memory*) esercitare; (*point: gun etc*) **to ~ sth on** puntare qc contro ▷ *vi* formarsi; allenarsi; **what time does the ~ from Rome get in?** a che ora arriva il treno da Roma?; **is this the ~ for …?** è questo il treno per…?; **one's ~ of thought** il filo dei propri pensieri
trainee [treɪ'ni:] *n* (*in trade*) apprendista *m/f*; **trainer** *n* (*Sport*) allenatore(-trice); (*: shoe*) scarpa da ginnastica; (*of dogs etc*) addestratore(-trice); **trainers** *npl* (*shoes*) scarpe *fpl* da ginnastica; **training** *n* formazione *f*; allenamento; addestramento; **in training** (*Sport*) in allenamento; **training course** *n* corso di formazione professionale; **training shoes** *npl* scarpe *fpl* da ginnastica
trait [treɪt] *n* tratto
traitor ['treɪtǝʳ] *n* traditore *m*
tram [træm] (BRIT) *n* (*also:* **~car**) tram *m inv*
tramp [træmp] *n* (*person*) vagabondo(-a); (*inf: pej: woman*) sgualdrina
trample ['træmpl] *vt* **to ~ (underfoot)** calpestare
trampoline ['træmpǝli:n] *n* trampolino
tranquil ['træŋkwɪl] *adj* tranquillo(-a); **tranquillizer** (US **tranquilizer**) *n* (*Med*) tranquillante *m*
transaction [træn'zækʃǝn] *n* transazione *f*
transatlantic ['trænzǝt'læntɪk] *adj* transatlantico(-a)
transcript ['trænskrɪpt] *n* trascrizione *f*
transfer [*n* 'trænsfǝʳ, *vb* træns'fǝ:ʳ] *n* (*gen: also Sport*) trasferimento; (*Pol: of power*) passaggio; (*picture, design*) decalcomania; (*: stick-on*) autoadesivo ▷ *vt* trasferire; passare; **to ~ the charges** (BRIT: *Tel*) fare una chiamata a carico del destinatario
transform [træns'fɔ:m] *vt* trasformare; **transformation** *n* trasformazione *f*
transfusion [træns'fju:ʒǝn] *n* trasfusione *f*
transit ['trænzɪt] *n* **in ~** in transito
transition [træn'zɪʃǝn] *n* passaggio, transizione *f*
transitive ['trænzɪtɪv] *adj* (*Ling*) transitivo(-a)
translate [trænz'leɪt] *vt* tradurre; **can**

405 | triumph

you ~ this for me? me lo può tradurre?;
translation [-'leɪʃən] n traduzione f;
translator n traduttore(-trice)
transmission [trænz'mɪʃən] n
trasmissione f
transmit [trænz'mɪt] vt trasmettere;
transmitter n trasmettitore m
transparent [træns'pærnt] adj
trasparente
transplant [vb træns'plɑ:nt, n
'trænsplɑ:nt] vt trapiantare ▷ n (Med)
trapianto
transport [n 'trænspɔ:t, vb træns'pɔ:
t] n trasporto ▷ vt trasportare;
transportation [-'teɪʃən] n (mezzo di)
trasporto
transvestite [trænz'vɛstaɪt] n
travestito(-a)
trap [træp] n (snare, trick) trappola;
(carriage) calesse m ▷ vt prendere in
trappola, intrappolare
trash [træʃ] (pej) n (goods) ciarpame m;
(nonsense) sciocchezze fpl; **trash can** (us) n
secchio della spazzatura
trauma ['trɔ:mə] n trauma m; **traumatic**
[-'mætɪk] adj traumatico(-a)
travel ['trævl] n viaggio; viaggi mpl ▷ vi
viaggiare ▷ vt (distance) percorrere;
travel agency n agenzia (di) viaggi;
travel agent n agente m di viaggio;
travel insurance n assicurazione f
di viaggio; **traveller** (us **traveler**) n
viaggiatore(-trice); **traveller's cheque**
(us **traveler's check**) n assegno turistico;
travelling (us **traveling**) n viaggi mpl;
travel-sick adj **to get travel-sick** (in
vehicle) soffrire di mal d'auto; (in aeroplane)
soffrire di mal d'aria; (in boat) soffrire di mal
di mare; **travel sickness** n mal m d'auto
(or di mare o d'aria)
tray [treɪ] n (for carrying) vassoio; (on desk)
vaschetta
treacherous ['trɛtʃərəs] adj infido(-a)
treacle ['tri:kl] n melassa
tread [trɛd] (pt **trod**, pp **trodden**) n passo;
(sound) rumore m di passi; (of stairs) pedata;
(of tyre) battistrada m inv ▷ vi camminare;
tread on vt fus calpestare
treasure ['trɛʒər] n tesoro ▷ vt (value)
tenere in gran conto, apprezzare molto;
(store) custodire gelosamente; **treasurer**
['trɛʒərər] n tesoriere(-a)
treasury ['trɛʒərɪ] n **the T~** (BRIT), **the T~
Department** (us) il ministero del Tesoro
treat [tri:t] n regalo ▷ vt trattare; (Med)
curare; **to ~ sb to sth** offrire qc a qn;
treatment ['tri:tmənt] n trattamento
treaty ['tri:tɪ] n patto, trattato
treble ['trɛbl] adj triplo(-a), triplice ▷ vt

triplicare ▷ vi triplicarsi
tree [tri:] n albero
trek [trɛk] n escursione f a piedi;
escursione f in macchina; (tiring walk)
camminata sfiancante ▷ vi (as holiday) fare
dell'escursionismo
tremble ['trɛmbl] vi tremare
tremendous [trɪ'mɛndəs] adj (enormous)
enorme; (excellent) fantastico(-a),
strepitoso(-a)

> Be careful not to translate
> **tremendous** by the Italian word
> **tremendo**.

trench [trɛntʃ] n trincea
trend [trɛnd] n (tendency) tendenza; (of
events) corso; (fashion) moda; **trendy** adj
(idea) di moda; (clothes) all'ultima moda
trespass ['trɛspəs] vi **to ~ on** entrare
abusivamente in; **"no ~ing"** "proprietà
privata", "vietato l'accesso"
trial ['traɪəl] n (Law) processo; (test: of
machine etc) collaudo; **on ~** (Law) sotto
processo; **trial period** n periodo di prova
triangle ['traɪæŋgl] n (Math, Mus)
triangolo
triangular [traɪ'æŋgjulə'] adj triangolare
tribe [traɪb] n tribù f inv
tribunal [traɪ'bju:nl] n tribunale m
tribute ['trɪbju:t] n tributo, omaggio; **to
pay ~ to** rendere omaggio a
trick [trɪk] n trucco; (joke) tiro; (Cards) presa
▷ vt imbrogliare, ingannare; **to play a ~
on sb** giocare un tiro a qn; **that should do
the ~** vedrai che funziona
trickle ['trɪkl] n (of water etc) rivolo;
gocciolio ▷ vi gocciolare
tricky ['trɪkɪ] adj difficile, delicato(-a)
tricycle ['traɪsɪkl] n triciclo
trifle ['traɪfl] n sciocchezza; (BRIT: Culin)
≈ zuppa inglese ▷ adv **a ~ long** un po'
lungo
trigger ['trɪgə'] n (of gun) grilletto
trim [trɪm] adj (house, garden) ben
tenuto(-a); (figure) snello(-a) ▷ n (haircut
etc) spuntata, regolata; (embellishment)
finiture fpl; (on car) guarnizioni fpl ▷ vt
spuntare; (decorate): **to ~ (with)** decorare
(con); (Naut: a sail) orientare
trio ['tri:əu] n trio
trip [trɪp] n viaggio; (excursion) gita,
escursione f; (stumble) passo falso ▷ vi
inciampare; (go lightly) camminare con
passo leggero; **on a ~** in viaggio; **trip up** vi
inciampare ▷ vt fare lo sgambetto a
triple ['trɪpl] adj triplo(-a)
triplets ['trɪplɪts] npl bambini(-e)
trigemini(-e)
tripod ['traɪpɔd] n treppiede m
triumph ['traɪʌmf] n trionfo ▷ vi **to**

~ (over) trionfare (su); **triumphant**
[traɪˈʌmfənt] adj trionfante

trivial [ˈtrɪvɪəl] adj insignificante;
(commonplace) banale

> Be careful not to translate **trivial** by
> the Italian word **triviale**.

trod [trɔd] pt of **tread**

trodden [ˈtrɔdn] pp of **tread**

trolley [ˈtrɔlɪ] n carrello

trombone [trɔmˈbəʊn] n trombone m

troop [truːp] n gruppo; (Mil) squadrone m;
~s npl (Mil) truppe fpl

trophy [ˈtrəʊfɪ] n trofeo

tropical [ˈtrɔpɪkl] adj tropicale

trot [trɔt] n trotto ▷ vi trottare; **on the ~**
(BRIT: fig) di fila, uno(-a) dopo l'altro(-a)

trouble [ˈtrʌbl] n difficoltà f inv, problema
m; difficoltà fpl, problemi; (worry)
preoccupazione f; (bother, effort) sforzo;
(Pol) conflitti mpl, disordine m; (Med):
stomach etc **~** disturbi mpl gastrici etc
▷ vt disturbare; (worry) preoccupare ▷ vi
to ~ to do disturbarsi a fare; **~s** npl (Pol
etc) disordini mpl; **to be in ~** avere dei
problemi; **it's no ~!** di niente!; **what's the
~?** cosa c'è che non va?; **I'm sorry to ~ you**
scusi il disturbo; **troubled** adj (person)
preoccupato(-a), inquieto(-a); (epoch, life)
agitato(-a), difficile; **troublemaker** n
elemento disturbatore, agitatore(-trice);
(child) disloco(-a); **troublesome** adj
fastidioso(-a), seccante

trough [trɔf] n (drinking trough)
abbeveratoio; (also: **feeding ~**) trogolo,
mangiatoia; (channel) canale m

trousers [ˈtraʊzəz] npl pantaloni mpl,
calzoni mpl; **short ~** calzoncini mpl

trout [traʊt] n inv trota

trowel [ˈtraʊəl] n cazzuola

truant [ˈtruːənt] (BRIT) n **to play ~**
marinare la scuola

truce [truːs] n tregua

truck [trʌk] n autocarro, camion m inv;
(Rail) carro merci aperto; (for luggage)
carrello m portabagagli inv; **truck driver** n
camionista m/f

true [truː] adj vero(-a); (accurate)
accurato(-a), esatto(-a); (genuine) reale;
(faithful) fedele; **to come ~** avverarsi

truly [ˈtruːlɪ] adv veramente; (truthfully)
sinceramente; (faithfully): **yours ~** (in letter)
distinti saluti

trumpet [ˈtrʌmpɪt] n tromba

trunk [trʌŋk] n (of tree, person) tronco; (of
elephant) proboscide f; (case) baule m; (US:
Aut) bagagliaio; **~s** (also: **swimming ~s**)
calzoncini mpl da bagno

trust [trʌst] n fiducia; (Law)
amministrazione f fiduciaria; (Comm)

trust m inv ▷ vt (rely on) contare su; (hope)
sperare; (entrust): **to ~ sth to sb** affidare qc
a qn; **trusted** adj fidato(-a); **trustworthy**
adj fidato(-a), degno(-a) di fiducia

truth [truːθ, pl truːðz] n verità f inv;
truthful adj (person) sincero(-a);
(description) veritiero(-a), esatto(-a)

try [traɪ] n prova, tentativo; (Rugby) meta
▷ vt (Law) giudicare; (test: also: **~ out**)
provare; (strain) mettere alla prova ▷ vi
provare; **to have a ~** fare un tentativo;
to ~ to do (seek) cercare di fare; **try on**
vt (clothes) provare; **trying** adj (day,
experience) logorante, pesante; (child)
difficile, insopportabile

T-shirt [ˈtiːʃəːt] n maglietta

tub [tʌb] n tinozza; mastello; (bath)
bagno

tube [tjuːb] n tubo; (BRIT: underground)
metropolitana, metrò m inv; (for tyre)
camera d'aria

tuberculosis [tjubəːkjuˈləʊsɪs] n
tubercolosi f inv

tube station (BRIT) n stazione f della
metropolitana

tuck [tʌk] vt (put) mettere; **tuck away** vt
riporre; (building): **to be ~ed away** essere
in un luogo isolato; **tuck in** vt mettere
dentro; (child) rimboccare ▷ vi (eat)
mangiare di buon appetito; abbuffarsi;
tuck shop n negozio di pasticceria (in una
scuola)

Tue(s). abbr (= Tuesday) mar.

Tuesday [ˈtjuːzdɪ] n martedì m inv

tug [tʌg] n (ship) rimorchiatore m ▷ vt
tirare con forza

tuition [tjuːˈɪʃən] n (BRIT) lezioni fpl; (:
private tuition) lezioni fpl private; (US: school
fees) tasse fpl scolastiche

tulip [ˈtjuːlɪp] n tulipano

tumble [ˈtʌmbl] n (fall) capitombolo ▷ vi
capitombolare, ruzzolare; **to ~ to sth**
(inf) realizzare qc; **tumble dryer** (BRIT) n
asciugatrice f

tumbler [ˈtʌmbləʳ] n bicchiere m (senza
stelo)

tummy [ˈtʌmɪ] (inf) n pancia

tumour [ˈtjuːməʳ] (US **tumor**) n tumore m

tuna [ˈtjuːnə] n inv (also: **~ fish**) tonno

tune [tjuːn] n (melody) melodia, aria
▷ vt (Mus) accordare; (Radio, TV, Aut)
regolare, mettere a punto; **to be in/out
of ~** (instrument) essere accordato(-a)/
scordato(-a); (singer) essere intonato(-a)/
stonato(-a); **tune in** vi **to ~ in (to)**
(Radio, TV) sintonizzarsi (su); **tune up** vi
(musician) accordare lo strumento

tunic [ˈtjuːnɪk] n tunica

Tunisia [tjuːˈnɪzɪə] n Tunisia

tunnel ['tʌnl] n galleria ▷ vi scavare una galleria

turbulence ['tə:bjuləns] n (Aviat) turbolenza

turf [tə:f] n terreno erboso; (clod) zolla ▷ vt coprire di zolle erbose

Turin [tjuə'rɪn] n Torino f

Turk [tə:k] n turco(-a)

Turkey ['tə:kɪ] n Turchia

turkey ['tə:kɪ] n tacchino

Turkish ['tə:kɪʃ] adj turco(-a) ▷ n (Ling) turco

turmoil ['tə:mɔɪl] n confusione f, tumulto

turn [tə:n] n giro; (change) cambiamento; (in road) curva; (tendency: of mind, events) tendenza; (performance) numero; (chance) turno; (Med) crisi f inv, attacco ▷ vt girare, voltare; (change): **to ~ sth into** trasformare qc in ▷ vi girare; (person: look back) girarsi, voltarsi; (reverse direction) girare; (change) cambiare; (milk) andare a male; (become) diventare; **a good ~** un buon servizio; **it gave me quite a ~** mi ha fatto prendere un bello spavento; **"no left ~"** (Aut) "divieto di svolta a sinistra"; **it's your ~** tocca a lei; **in ~** a sua volta; a turno; **to take ~s (at sth)** fare (qc) a turno; **~ left/right at the next junction** al prossimo incrocio, giri a sinistra/destra; **turn around** vi (person) girarsi; (rotate) girare ▷ vt (object) girare; **turn away** vi girarsi (dall'altra parte) ▷ vt mandare via; **turn back** vi ritornare, tornare indietro ▷ vt far tornare indietro; (clock) spostare indietro; **turn down** vt (refuse) rifiutare; (reduce) abbassare; (fold) ripiegare; **turn in** vi (inf: go to bed) andare a letto ▷ vt (fold) voltare in dentro; **turn off** vi (from road) girare, voltare ▷ vt (light, radio, engine etc) spegnere; **I can't ~ the heating off** non riesco a spegnere il riscaldamento; **turn on** vt (light, radio etc) accendere; **I can't ~ the heating on** non riesco ad accendere il riscaldamento; **turn out** vt (light, gas) chiudere; spegnere ▷ vi (voters) presentarsi; **to ~ out to be ...** rivelarsi ..., risultare ...; **turn over** vi (person) girarsi ▷ vt girare; **turn round** vi girare; (person) girarsi; **turn to** vt fus **to ~ to sb** girarsi verso qn; **to ~ to sb for help** rivolgersi a qn per aiuto; **turn up** vi (person) arrivare, presentarsi; (lost object) saltar fuori ▷ vt (collar, sound) alzare; **turning** n (in road) curva; **turning point** n (fig) svolta decisiva

turnip ['tə:nɪp] n rapa

turn: turnout ['tə:naut] n presenza, affluenza; **turnover** ['tə:nəuvəʳ] n (Comm) turnover m inv; (Culin): **apple etc turnover** sfogliatella alle melle ecc; **turnstile** ['tə:nstaɪl] n tornella; **turn-up** (BRIT) n (on trousers) risvolto

turquoise ['tə:kwɔɪz] n turchese m ▷ adj turchese

turtle ['tə:tl] n testuggine f; **turtleneck (sweater)** ['tə:tlnɛk-] n maglione m con il collo alto

Tuscany ['tʌskənɪ] n Toscana

tusk [tʌsk] n zanna

tutor ['tju:təʳ] n (in college) docente m/f (responsabile di un gruppo di studenti); (private teacher) precettore m; **tutorial** [-'tɔ:rɪəl] n (Scol) lezione f con discussione (a un gruppo limitato)

tuxedo [tʌk'si:dəu] (US) n smoking m inv

TV [ti:'vi:] n abbr (= television) tivù f inv

tweed [twi:d] n tweed m inv

tweezers ['twi:zəz] npl pinzette fpl

twelfth [twɛlfθ] num dodicesimo(-a)

twelve [twɛlv] num dodici; **at ~ o'clock** alle dodici, a mezzogiorno; (midnight) a mezzanotte

twentieth ['twɛntɪɪθ] num ventesimo(-a)

twenty ['twɛntɪ] num venti

twice [twaɪs] adv due volte; **~ as much** due volte tanto; **~ a week** due volte alla settimana

twig [twɪg] n ramoscello ▷ vt, vi (inf) capire

twilight ['twaɪlaɪt] n crepuscolo

twin [twɪn] adj, n gemello(-a) ▷ vt **to ~ one town with another** fare il gemellaggio di una città con un'altra; **twin(-bedded) room** n stanza con letti gemelli; **twin beds** npl letti mpl gemelli

twinkle ['twɪŋkl] vi scintillare; (eyes) brillare

twist [twɪst] n torsione f; (in wire, flex) piega; (in road) curva; (in story) colpo di scena ▷ vt attorcigliare; (ankle) slogare; (weave) intrecciare; (roll around) arrotolare; (fig) distorcere ▷ vi (road) serpeggiare

twit [twɪt] (inf) n cretino(-a)

twitch [twɪtʃ] n tiratina; (nervous) tic m inv ▷ vi contrarsi

two [tu:] num due; **to put ~ and ~ together** (fig) fare uno più uno

type [taɪp] n (category) genere m; (model) modello; (example) tipo; (Typ) tipo, carattere m ▷ vt (letter etc) battere (a macchina), dattilografare; **typewriter** n macchina da scrivere

typhoid ['taɪfɔɪd] n tifoidea

typhoon [taɪ'fu:n] n tifone m

typical ['tɪpɪkl] adj tipico(-a); **typically** adv tipicamente; **typically, he arrived**

late come al solito è arrivato tardi
typing ['taɪpɪŋ] n dattilografia
typist ['taɪpɪst] n dattilografo(-a)
tyre ['taɪər] (us **tire**) n pneumatico, gomma; **I've got a flat ~** ho una gomma a terra; **tyre pressure** n pressione f (delle gomme)

UFO ['juːfəʊ] n abbr (= unidentified flying object) UFO m inv
Uganda [juːˈgændə] n Uganda
ugly ['ʌglɪ] adj brutto(-a)
UHT abbr (= ultra heat treated) UHT inv, a lunga conservazione
UK n abbr = **United Kingdom**
ulcer ['ʌlsər] n ulcera; (also: **mouth ~**) afta
ultimate ['ʌltɪmət] adj ultimo(-a), finale; (authority) massimo(-a), supremo(-a); **ultimately** adv alla fine; in definitiva, in fin dei conti
ultimatum [ʌltɪˈmeɪtəm, -tə] (pl **ultimatums** or **ultimata**) n ultimatum m inv
ultrasound [ʌltrəˈsaʊnd] n (Med) ultrasuono
ultraviolet ['ʌltrəˈvaɪəlɪt] adj ultravioletto(-a)
umbrella [ʌmˈbrɛlə] n ombrello
umpire ['ʌmpaɪər] n arbitro
UN n abbr (= United Nations) ONU f
unable [ʌnˈeɪbl] adj **to be ~ to** non potere, essere nell'impossibilità di; essere incapace di
unacceptable [ʌnəkˈsɛptəbl] adj (proposal, behaviour) inaccettabile; (price) impossibile
unanimous [juːˈnænɪməs] adj unanime
unarmed [ʌnˈɑːmd] adj (without a weapon)

disarmato(-a); (*combat*) senz'armi
unattended [ʌnəˈtɛndɪd] *adj* (*car, child, luggage*) incustodito(-a)
unattractive [ʌnəˈtræktɪv] *adj* poco attraente
unavailable [ʌnəˈveɪləbl] *adj* (*article, room, book*) non disponibile; (*person*) impegnato(-a)
unavoidable [ʌnəˈvɔɪdəbl] *adj* inevitabile
unaware [ʌnəˈwɛəʳ] *adj* **to be ~ of** non sapere, ignorare; **unawares** *adv* di sorpresa, alla sprovvista
unbearable [ʌnˈbɛərəbl] *adj* insopportabile
unbeatable [ʌnˈbiːtəbl] *adj* imbattibile
unbelievable [ʌnbɪˈliːvəbl] *adj* incredibile
unborn [ʌnˈbɔːn] *adj* non ancora nato(-a)
unbutton [ʌnˈbʌtn] *vt* sbottonare
uncalled-for [ʌnˈkɔːldfɔːʳ] *adj* (*remark*) fuori luogo *inv*; (*action*) ingiustificato(-a)
uncanny [ʌnˈkænɪ] *adj* misterioso(-a), strano(-a)
uncertain [ʌnˈsəːtn] *adj* incerto(-a); dubbio(-a); **uncertainty** *n* incertezza
unchanged [ʌnˈtʃeɪndʒd] *adj* invariato(-a)
uncle [ˈʌŋkl] *n* zio
unclear [ʌnˈklɪəʳ] *adj* non chiaro(-a); **I'm still ~ about what I'm supposed to do** non ho ancora ben capito cosa dovrei fare
uncomfortable [ʌnˈkʌmfətəbl] *adj* scomodo(-a); (*uneasy*) a disagio, agitato(-a); (*unpleasant*) fastidioso(-a)
uncommon [ʌnˈkɔmən] *adj* raro(-a), insolito(-a), non comune
unconditional [ʌnkənˈdɪʃənl] *adj* incondizionato(-a), senza condizioni
unconscious [ʌnˈkɔnʃəs] *adj* privo(-a) di sensi, svenuto(-a); (*unaware*) inconsapevole, inconscio(-a) ▷ *n* **the ~** l'inconscio
uncontrollable [ʌnkənˈtrəuləbl] *adj* incontrollabile; indisciplinato(-a)
unconventional [ʌnkənˈvɛnʃənl] *adj* poco convenzionale
uncover [ʌnˈkʌvəʳ] *vt* scoprire
undecided [ʌndɪˈsaɪdɪd] *adj* indeciso(-a)
undeniable [ʌndɪˈnaɪəbl] *adj* innegabile, indiscutibile
under [ˈʌndəʳ] *prep* sotto; (*less than*) meno di; al disotto di; (*according to*) secondo, in conformità a ▷ *adv* (al) disotto; **~ there** là sotto; **~ repair** in riparazione; **undercover** *adj* segreto(-a), clandestino(-a); **underdone** *adj* (*Culin*) al sangue; (*pej*) poco cotto(-a); **underestimate** *vt* sottovalutare; **undergo** *vt* (*irreg*) subire; (*treatment*) sottoporsi a; **undergraduate** *n* studente(-essa) universitario(-a); **underground** *n* (*BRIT:*

railway) metropolitana; (*Pol*) movimento clandestino ▷ *adj* sotterraneo(-a); (*fig*) clandestino(-a) ▷ *adv* sottoterra; **to go underground** (*fig*) darsi alla macchia; **undergrowth** *n* sottobosco; **underline** *vt* sottolineare; **undermine** *vt* minare; **underneath** [ʌndəˈniːθ] *adv* sotto, disotto ▷ *prep* sotto, al di sotto di; **underpants** *npl* mutande *fpl*, slip *m inv*; **underpass** (*BRIT*) *n* sottopassaggio; **underprivileged** *adj* non abbiente; meno favorito(-a); **underscore** *vt* sottolineare; **undershirt** (*US*) *n* maglietta; **underskirt** (*BRIT*) *n* sottoveste *f*
understand [ʌndəˈstænd] (*irreg: like* **stand**) *vt, vi* capire, comprendere; **I don't ~** non capisco; **I ~ that ...** sento che ...; credo di capire che ...; **understandable** *adj* comprensibile; **understanding** *adj* comprensivo(-a) ▷ *n* comprensione *f*; (*agreement*) accordo
understatement [ʌndəˈsteɪtmənt] *n* **that's an ~!** a dire poco!
understood [ʌndəˈstud] *pt, pp of* **understand** ▷ *adj* inteso(-a); (*implied*) sottinteso(-a)
undertake [ʌndəˈteɪk] (*irreg: like* **take**) *vt* intraprendere; **to ~ to do sth** impegnarsi a fare qc
undertaker [ˈʌndəteɪkəʳ] *n* impresario di pompe funebri
undertaking [ʌndəˈteɪkɪŋ] *n* impresa; (*promise*) promessa
under: underwater [ʌndəˈwɔːtəʳ] *adv* sott'acqua ▷ *adj* subacqueo(-a); **underway** [ʌndəˈweɪ] *adj* **to be underway** essere in corso; **underwear** [ˈʌndəwɛəʳ] *n* biancheria (intima); **underwent** [ʌndəˈwɛnt] *vb see* **undergo**; **underworld** [ˈʌndəwəːld] *n* (*of crime*) malavita
undesirable [ʌndɪˈzaɪərəbl] *adj* sgradevole
undisputed [ʌndɪsˈpjuːtɪd] *adj* indiscusso(-a)
undo [ʌnˈduː] *vt* (*irreg*) disfare
undone [ʌnˈdʌn] *pp of* **undo**; **to come ~** slacciarsi
undoubtedly [ʌnˈdautɪdlɪ] *adv* senza alcun dubbio
undress [ʌnˈdrɛs] *vi* spogliarsi
unearth [ʌnˈəːθ] *vt* dissotterrare; (*fig*) scoprire
uneasy [ʌnˈiːzɪ] *adj* a disagio; (*worried*) preoccupato(-a); (*peace*) precario(-a)
unemployed [ʌnɪmˈplɔɪd] *adj* disoccupato(-a) ▷ *npl* **the ~** i disoccupati
unemployment [ʌnɪmˈplɔɪmənt] *n* disoccupazione *f*; **unemployment**

benefit (us **unemployment compensation**) n sussidio di disoccupazione

unequal [ʌnˈiːkwəl] adj (length, objects) disuguale; (amounts) diverso(-a); (division of labour) ineguale

uneven [ʌnˈiːvn] adj ineguale; irregolare

unexpected [ʌnɪkˈspɛktɪd] adj inatteso(-a), imprevisto(-a); **unexpectedly** adv inaspettatamente

unfair [ʌnˈfɛəʳ] adj ~ **(to)** ingiusto(-a) (nei confronti di)

unfaithful [ʌnˈfeɪθful] adj infedele

unfamiliar [ʌnfəˈmɪlɪəʳ] adj sconosciuto(-a), strano(-a); **to be ~ with** non avere familiarità con

unfashionable [ʌnˈfæʃnəbl] adj (clothes) fuori moda; (district) non alla moda

unfasten [ʌnˈfɑːsn] vt slacciare; sciogliere

unfavourable [ʌnˈfeɪvərəbl] (us **unfavorable**) adj sfavorevole

unfinished [ʌnˈfɪnɪʃt] adj incompleto(-a)

unfit [ʌnˈfɪt] adj (ill) malato(-a), in cattiva salute; (incompetent): ~ **(for)** incompetente (in); (: work, Mil) inabile (a)

unfold [ʌnˈfəuld] vt spiegare ▷ vi (story, plot) svelarsi

unforgettable [ʌnfəˈgɛtəbl] adj indimenticabile

unfortunate [ʌnˈfɔːtʃnət] adj sfortunato(-a); (event, remark) infelice; **unfortunately** adv sfortunatamente, purtroppo

unfriendly [ʌnˈfrɛndlɪ] adj poco amichevole, freddo(-a)

unfurnished [ʌnˈfəːnɪʃt] adj non ammobiliato(-a)

unhappiness [ʌnˈhæpɪnɪs] n infelicità

unhappy [ʌnˈhæpɪ] adj infelice; ~ **about/ with** (arrangements etc) insoddisfatto(-a) di

unhealthy [ʌnˈhɛlθɪ] adj (gen) malsano(-a); (person) malaticcio(-a)

unheard-of [ʌnˈhəːdɔv] adj inaudito(-a), senza precedenti

unhelpful [ʌnˈhɛlpful] adj poco disponibile

unhurt [ʌnˈhəːt] adj illeso(-a)

unidentified [ʌnaɪˈdɛntɪfaɪd] adj non identificato(-a)

uniform [ˈjuːnɪfɔːm] n uniforme f, divisa ▷ adj uniforme

unify [ˈjuːnɪfaɪ] vt unificare

unimportant [ʌnɪmˈpɔːtənt] adj senza importanza, di scarsa importanza

uninhabited [ʌnɪnˈhæbɪtɪd] adj disabitato(-a)

unintentional [ʌnɪnˈtɛnʃənəl] adj involontario(-a)

union [ˈjuːnjən] n unione f; (also: **trade ~**)

sindacato ▷ cpd sindacale, dei sindacati; **Union Jack** n bandiera nazionale britannica

unique [juːˈniːk] adj unico(-a)

unisex [ˈjuːnɪsɛks] adj unisex inv

unit [ˈjuːnɪt] n unità f inv; (section: of furniture etc) elemento; (team, squad) reparto, squadra

unite [juːˈnaɪt] vt unire ▷ vi unirsi; **united** adj unito(-a); unificato(-a); (efforts) congiunto(-a); **United Kingdom** n Regno Unito; **United Nations (Organization)** n (Organizzazione f delle) Nazioni Unite; **United States (of America)** n Stati mpl Uniti (d'America)

unity [ˈjuːnɪtɪ] n unità

universal [juːnɪˈvəːsl] adj universale

universe [ˈjuːnɪvəːs] n universo

university [juːnɪˈvəːsɪtɪ] n università f inv

unjust [ʌnˈdʒʌst] adj ingiusto(-a)

unkind [ʌnˈkaɪnd] adj scortese; crudele

unknown [ʌnˈnəun] adj sconosciuto(-a)

unlawful [ʌnˈlɔːful] adj illecito(-a), illegale

unleaded [ʌnˈlɛdɪd] adj (petrol, fuel) verde, senza piombo

unleash [ʌnˈliːʃ] vt (fig) scatenare

unless [ʌnˈlɛs] conj a meno che (non) + sub

unlike [ʌnˈlaɪk] adj diverso(-a) ▷ prep a differenza di, contrariamente a

unlikely [ʌnˈlaɪklɪ] adj improbabile

unlimited [ʌnˈlɪmɪtɪd] adj illimitato(-a)

unlisted [ʌnˈlɪstɪd] (us) adj (Tel): **to be ~** non essere sull'elenco

unload [ʌnˈləud] vt scaricare

unlock [ʌnˈlɔk] vt aprire

unlucky [ʌnˈlʌkɪ] adj sfortunato(-a); (object, number) che porta sfortuna

unmarried [ʌnˈmærɪd] adj non sposato(-a); (man only) scapolo, celibe; (woman only) nubile

unmistak(e)able [ʌnmɪsˈteɪkəbl] adj inconfondibile

unnatural [ʌnˈnætʃrəl] adj innaturale; contro natura

unnecessary [ʌnˈnɛsəsərɪ] adj inutile, superfluo(-a)

UNO [ˈjuːnəu] n abbr (= United Nations Organization) ONU f

unofficial [ʌnəˈfɪʃl] adj non ufficiale; (strike) non dichiarato(-a) dal sindacato

unpack [ʌnˈpæk] vi disfare la valigia (or le valigie) ▷ vt disfare

unpaid [ʌnˈpeɪd] adj (holiday) non pagato(-a); (work) non retribuito(-a); (bill, debt) da pagare

unpleasant [ʌnˈplɛznt] adj spiacevole

unplug [ʌnˈplʌg] vt staccare

unpopular [ʌnˈpɔpjuləʳ] adj impopolare

unprecedented [ʌnˈprɛsɪdəntɪd] adj senza precedenti

unpredictable [ʌnprɪ'dɪktəbl] *adj*
imprevedibile

unprotected ['ʌnprə'tɛktɪd] *adj* (*sex*) non
protetto(-a)

unqualified [ʌn'kwɔlɪfaɪd] *adj* (*teacher*)
non abilitato(-a); (*success*) assoluto(-a),
senza riserve

unravel [ʌn'rævl] *vt* dipanare, districare

unreal [ʌn'rɪəl] *adj* irreale

unrealistic [ʌnrɪə'lɪstɪk] *adj* non
realistico(-a)

unreasonable [ʌn'ri:znəbl] *adj*
irragionevole

unrelated [ʌnrɪ'leɪtɪd] *adj* **~ (to)** senza
rapporto (con); non imparentato(-a) (con)

unreliable [ʌnrɪ'laɪəbl] *adj* (*person,
machine*) che non dà affidamento; (*news,
source of information*) inattendibile

unrest [ʌn'rɛst] *n* agitazione f

unroll [ʌn'rəul] *vt* srotolare

unruly [ʌn'ru:lɪ] *adj* indisciplinato(-a)

unsafe [ʌn'seɪf] *adj* pericoloso(-a),
rischioso(-a)

unsatisfactory ['ʌnsætɪs'fæktərɪ] *adj*
che lascia a desiderare, insufficiente

unscrew [ʌn'skru:] *vt* svitare

unsettled [ʌn'sɛtld] *adj* (*person*)
turbato(-a); indeciso(-a); (*weather*)
instabile

unsettling [ʌn'sɛtlɪŋ] *adj* inquietante

unsightly [ʌn'saɪtlɪ] *adj* brutto(-a),
sgradevole a vedersi

unskilled [ʌn'skɪld] *adj* non
specializzato(-a)

unspoiled ['ʌn'spɔɪld], **unspoilt**
['ʌn'spɔɪlt] *adj* (*place*) non deturpato(-a)

unstable [ʌn'steɪbl] *adj* (*gen*) instabile;
(*mentally*) squilibrato(-a)

unsteady [ʌn'stɛdɪ] *adj* instabile,
malsicuro(-a)

unsuccessful [ʌnsək'sɛsful] *adj* (*writer,
proposal*) che non ha successo; (*marriage,
attempt*) mal riuscito(-a), fallito(-a); **to be ~**
(*in attempting sth*) non avere successo

unsuitable [ʌn'su:təbl] *adj* inadatto(-a);
inopportuno(-a); sconveniente

unsure [ʌn'ʃuə] *adj* incerto(-a); **to be ~ of
o.s** essere insicuro(-a)

untidy [ʌn'taɪdɪ] *adj* (*room*) in disordine;
(*appearance*) trascurato(-a); (*person*)
disordinato(-a)

untie [ʌn'taɪ] *vt* (*knot, parcel*) disfare;
(*prisoner, dog*) slegare

until [ʌn'tɪl] *prep* fino a; (*after negative*)
prima di ▷ *conj* finché, fino a quando; (*in
past, after negative*) prima che + *sub*, prima
di + *infinitive*; **~ he comes** finché *or* fino a
quando non arriva; **~ now** finora; **~ then**
fino ad allora

untrue [ʌn'tru:] *adj* (*statement*) falso(-a),
non vero(-a)

unused [ʌn'ju:zd] *adj* nuovo(-a)

unusual [ʌn'ju:ʒuəl] *adj* insolito(-a),
eccezionale, raro(-a); **unusually** *adv*
insolitamente

unveil [ʌn'veɪl] *vt* scoprire; svelare

unwanted [ʌn'wɔntɪd] *adj* (*clothing*)
smesso(-a); (*child*) non desiderato(-a)

unwell [ʌn'wɛl] *adj* indisposto(-a); **to feel
~** non sentirsi bene

unwilling [ʌn'wɪlɪŋ] *adj* **to be ~ to do** non
voler fare

unwind [ʌn'waɪnd] (*irreg: like* wind¹) *vt*
svolgere, srotolare ▷ *vi* (*relax*) rilassarsi

unwise [ʌn'waɪz] *adj* poco saggio(-a)

unwittingly [ʌn'wɪtɪŋlɪ] *adv* senza volerlo

unwrap [ʌn'ræp] *vt* disfare; aprire

unzip [ʌn'zɪp] *vt* aprire (la chiusura lampo
di); (*Comput*) dezippare

 KEYWORD

up [ʌp] *prep* **he went up the stairs/the
hill** è salito su per le scale/sulla collina; **the
cat was up a tree** il gatto era su un albero;
they live further up the street vivono un
po' più su nella stessa strada
▷ *adv* **1** (*upwards, higher*) su, in alto; **up in
the sky/the mountains** su nel cielo/in
montagna; **up there** lassù; **up above** su
in alto

2: **to be up** (*out of bed*) essere alzato(-a);
(*prices, level*) essere salito(-a)

3: **up to** (*as far as*) fino a; **up to now** finora

4: **to be up to** (*depending on*): **it's up to
you** sta a lei, dipende da lei; (*equal to*):
he's not up to it (*job, task etc*) non ne è
all'altezza; (*inf: be doing*): **what is he up to?**
cosa sta combinando?

▷ *n* **ups and downs** alti e bassi *mpl*

up-and-coming ['ʌpənd'kʌmɪŋ] *adj*
pieno(-a) di promesse, promettente

upbringing ['ʌpbrɪŋɪŋ] *n* educazione f

update [ʌp'deɪt] *vt* aggiornare

upfront [ʌp'frʌnt] *adj* (*inf*) franco(-a),
aperto(-a) ▷ *adv* (*pay*) subito

upgrade [ʌp'greɪd] *vt* (*house, job*)
migliorare; (*employee*) avanzare di grado

upheaval [ʌp'hi:vl] *n* sconvolgimento;
tumulto

uphill [ʌp'hɪl] *adj* in salita; (*fig: task*) difficile
▷ *adv* **to go ~** andare in salita, salire

upholstery [ʌp'həulstərɪ] *n* tappezzeria

upmarket [ʌp'ma:kɪt] *adj* (*product*) che si
rivolge ad una fascia di mercato superiore

upon [ə'pɔn] *prep* su

upper ['ʌpə'] *adj* superiore ▷ *n* (*of shoe*)

tomaia; **upper-class** adj dell'alta
borghesia
upright ['ʌpraɪt] adj diritto(-a); verticale;
(fig) diritto(-a), onesto(-a)
uprising ['ʌpraɪzɪŋ] n insurrezione f,
rivolta
uproar ['ʌprɔːʳ] n tumulto, clamore m
upset [n 'ʌpset, vb, adj ʌp'set] (irreg:
like **set**) n (to plan etc) contrattempo;
(stomach upset) disturbo ▷ vt (glass etc)
rovesciare; (plan, stomach) scombussolare;
(person: offend) contrariare; (: grieve)
addolorare; sconvolgere ▷ adj
contrariato(-a), addolorato(-a); (stomach)
scombussolato(-a)
upside-down [ʌpsaɪd'daun] adv
sottosopra
upstairs [ʌp'stɛəz] adv, adj di sopra, al
piano superiore ▷ n piano di sopra
up-to-date ['ʌptə'deɪt] adj moderno(-a);
aggiornato(-a)
uptown ['ʌptaun] (US) adv verso i quartieri
residenziali ▷ adj dei quartieri residenziali
upward ['ʌpwəd] adj ascendente; verso
l'alto; **upward(s)** adv in su, verso l'alto
uranium [juə'reɪnɪəm] n uranio
Uranus [juə'reɪnəs] n (planet) Urano
urban ['əːbən] adj urbano(-a)
urge [əːdʒ] n impulso; stimolo; forte
desiderio ▷ vt **to ~ sb to do** esortare qn a
fare, spingere qn a fare; raccomandare a
qn di fare
urgency ['əːdʒənsɪ] n urgenza; (of tone)
insistenza
urgent ['əːdʒənt] adj urgente; (voice)
insistente
urinal ['juərɪnl] n (BRIT: building)
vespasiano; (: vessel) orinale m, pappagallo
urinate ['juərɪneɪt] vi orinare
urine ['juərɪn] n orina
us [ʌs] pron ci; (stressed, after prep) noi; see
also **me**
US(A) n abbr (= United States (of America))
USA mpl
use [n juːs, vb juːz] n uso; impiego,
utilizzazione f ▷ vt usare, utilizzare,
servirsi di; **in ~** in uso; **out of ~** fuori uso; **to
be of ~** essere utile, servire; **it's no ~** non
serve, è inutile; **she ~d to do it** lo faceva
(una volta), era solita farlo; **to be ~d to**
avere l'abitudine di; **use up** vt consumare;
esaurire; **used** adj (object, car) usato(-a);
useful adj utile; **useless** adj inutile;
(person) inetto(-a); **user** n utente m/f;
user-friendly adj (computer) di facile uso
usual ['juːʒuəl] adj solito(-a); **as ~** come
al solito, come d'abitudine; **usually** adv
di solito
utensil [juː'tɛnsl] n utensile m; **kitchen ~s**
utensili da cucina
utility [juː'tɪlɪtɪ] n utilità; (also: **public ~**)
servizio pubblico
utilize ['juːtɪlaɪz] vt utilizzare; sfruttare
utmost ['ʌtməust] adj estremo(-a) ▷ n **to
do one's ~** fare il possibile or di tutto
utter ['ʌtəʳ] adj assoluto(-a), totale ▷ vt
pronunciare, proferire; emettere; **utterly**
adv completamente, del tutto
U-turn ['juː'təːn] n inversione f a U

V

v. *abbr* = **verse**; **versus**; **volt**; (= *vide*) vedi, vedere

vacancy ['veɪkənsɪ] *n* (BRIT: *job*) posto libero; (*room*) stanza libera; **"no vacancies"** "completo"

Be careful not to translate *vacancy* by the Italian word *vacanza*.

vacant ['veɪkənt] *adj* (*job*, *seat etc*) libero(-a); (*expression*) assente

vacate [və'keɪt] *vt* lasciare libero(-a)

vacation [və'keɪʃən] (*esp* US) *n* vacanze *fpl*; **vacationer** (US **vacationist**) *n* vacanziere(-a)

vaccination [væksɪ'neɪʃən] *n* vaccinazione *f*

vaccine ['væksi:n] *n* vaccino

vacuum ['vækjum] *n* vuoto; **vacuum cleaner** *n* aspirapolvere *m inv*

vagina [və'dʒaɪnə] *n* vagina

vague [veɪg] *adj* vago(-a); (*blurred: photo, memory*) sfocato(-a)

vain [veɪn] *adj* (*useless*) inutile, vano(-a); (*conceited*) vanitoso(-a); **in ~** inutilmente, invano

Valentine's Day ['væləntaɪnzdeɪ] *n* San Valentino *m*

valid ['vælɪd] *adj* valido(-a), valevole; (*excuse*) valido(-a)

valley ['vælɪ] *n* valle *f*

valuable ['væljuəbl] *adj* (*jewel*) di (grande) valore; (*time, help*) prezioso(-a); **valuables** *npl* oggetti *mpl* di valore

value ['vælju:] *n* valore *m* ▷ *vt* (*fix price*) valutare, dare un prezzo a; (*cherish*) apprezzare, tenere a; **~s** *npl* (*principles*) valori *mpl*

valve [vælv] *n* valvola

vampire ['væmpaɪər] *n* vampiro

van [væn] *n* (*Aut*) furgone *m*; (BRIT: *Rail*) vagone *m*

vandal ['vændl] *n* vandalo(-a); **vandalism** *n* vandalismo; **vandalize** *vt* vandalizzare

vanilla [və'nɪlə] *n* vaniglia ▷ *cpd* (*ice cream*) alla vaniglia

vanish ['vænɪʃ] *vi* svanire, scomparire

vanity ['vænɪtɪ] *n* vanità

vapour ['veɪpər] (US **vapor**) *n* vapore *m*

variable ['vɛərɪəbl] *adj* variabile; (*mood*) mutevole

variant ['vɛərɪənt] *n* variante *f*

variation [vɛərɪ'eɪʃən] *n* variazione *f*; (*in opinion*) cambiamento

varied ['vɛərɪd] *adj* vario(-a), diverso(-a)

variety [və'raɪətɪ] *n* varietà *f inv*; (*quantity*) quantità, numero

various ['vɛərɪəs] *adj* vario(-a), diverso(-a); (*several*) parecchi(-e), molti(-e)

varnish ['vɑ:nɪʃ] *n* vernice *f*; (*nail varnish*) smalto ▷ *vt* verniciare; mettere lo smalto su

vary ['vɛərɪ] *vt, vi* variare, mutare

vase [vɑ:z] *n* vaso

Vaseline® ['væsɪli:n] *n* vaselina

vast [vɑ:st] *adj* vasto(-a); (*amount, success*) enorme

VAT [væt] *n abbr* (= *value added tax*) I.V.A. *f*

Vatican ['vætɪkən] *n* **the ~** il Vaticano

vault [vɔ:lt] *n* (*of roof*) volta; (*tomb*) tomba; (*in bank*) camera blindata ▷ *vt* (*also: ~ over*) saltare (d'un balzo)

VCR *n abbr* = **video cassette recorder**

VDU *n abbr* = **visual display unit**

veal [vi:l] *n* vitello

veer [vɪər] *vi* girare; virare

vegan ['vi:gən] *n* vegetaliano(-a)

vegetable ['vɛdʒtəbl] *n* verdura, ortaggio ▷ *adj* vegetale

vegetarian [vɛdʒɪ'tɛərɪən] *adj, n* vegetariano(-a); **do you have any ~ dishes?** avete piatti vegetariani?

vegetation [vɛdʒɪ'teɪʃən] *n* vegetazione *f*

vehicle ['vi:ɪkl] *n* veicolo

veil [veɪl] *n* velo

vein [veɪn] *n* vena; (*on leaf*) nervatura

Velcro® ['vɛlkrəu] *n* velcro® *m inv*

velvet ['vɛlvɪt] *n* velluto ▷ *adj* di velluto

vending machine ['vɛndɪŋ-] *n* distributore *m* automatico

vendor ['vɛndər] *n* venditore(-trice)

vengeance ['vɛndʒəns] n vendetta; **with a ~** (fig) davvero; furiosamente
Venice ['vɛnɪs] n Venezia
venison ['vɛnɪsn] n carne f di cervo
venom ['vɛnəm] n veleno
vent [vɛnt] n foro, apertura; (in dress, jacket) spacco ▷ vt (fig: one's feelings) sfogare, dare sfogo a
ventilation [vɛntɪ'leɪʃən] n ventilazione f
venture ['vɛntʃə'] n impresa (rischiosa) ▷ vt rischiare, azzardare ▷ vi avventurarsi; **business ~** iniziativa commerciale
venue ['vɛnjuː] n luogo (designato) per l'incontro
Venus ['viːnəs] n (planet) Venere m
verb [vəːb] n verbo; **verbal** adj verbale; (translation) orale
verdict ['vəːdɪkt] n verdetto
verge [vəːdʒ] (BRIT) n bordo, orlo; **"soft ~s"** (BRIT: Aut) banchine fpl cedevoli; **on the ~ of doing** sul punto di fare
verify ['vɛrɪfaɪ] vt verificare; (prove the truth of) confermare
versatile ['vəːsətaɪl] adj (person) versatile; (machine, tool etc) che si presta a molti usi
verse [vəːs] n versi mpl; (stanza) stanza, strofa; (in bible) versetto
version ['vəːʃən] n versione f
versus ['vəːsəs] prep contro
vertical ['vəːtɪkl] adj verticale ▷ n verticale m
very ['vɛrɪ] adv molto ▷ adj **the ~ book which** proprio il libro che; **the ~ last** proprio l'ultimo; **at the ~ least** almeno; **~ much** moltissimo
vessel ['vɛsl] n (Anat) vaso; (Naut) nave f; (container) recipiente m
vest [vɛst] n (BRIT) maglia; (: sleeveless) canottiera; (US: waistcoat) gilè m inv
vet [vɛt] n abbr (BRIT: = veterinary surgeon) veterinario ▷ vt esaminare minuziosamente
veteran ['vɛtərn] n (also: **war ~**) veterano
veterinary surgeon ['vɛtrɪnərɪ-] (US **veterinarian**) n veterinario
veto ['viːtəu] (pl **vetoes**) n veto ▷ vt opporre il veto a
via ['vaɪə] prep (by way of) via; (by means of) tramite
viable ['vaɪəbl] adj attuabile; vitale
vibrate [vaɪ'breɪt] vi **to ~ (with)** vibrare (di); (resound) risonare (di)
vibration [vaɪ'breɪʃən] n vibrazione f
vicar ['vɪkə'] n pastore m
vice [vaɪs] n (evil) vizio; (Tech) morsa; **vice-chairman** (irreg) n vicepresidente m
vice versa ['vaɪsɪ'vəːsə] adv viceversa
vicinity [vɪ'sɪnɪtɪ] n vicinanze fpl
vicious ['vɪʃəs] adj (remark, dog) cattivo(-a);

(blow) violento(-a)
victim ['vɪktɪm] n vittima
victor ['vɪktə'] n vincitore m
Victorian [vɪk'tɔːrɪən] adj vittoriano(-a)
victorious [vɪk'tɔːrɪəs] adj vittorioso(-a)
victory ['vɪktərɪ] n vittoria
video ['vɪdɪəu] cpd video... ▷ n (video film) video m inv; (also: **~ cassette**) videocassetta; (also: **~ cassette recorder**) videoregistratore m; **video camera** n videocamera; **video (cassette) recorder** n videoregistratore m; **video game** n videogioco; **video shop** n videonoleggio; **video tape** n videotape m inv; **video wall** n schermo m multivideo inv
vie [vaɪ] vi **to ~ with** competere con, rivaleggiare con
Vienna [vɪ'ɛnə] n Vienna
Vietnam [vjɛt'næm] n Vietnam m; **Vietnamese** adj, n inv vietnamita m/f
view [vjuː] n vista, veduta; (opinion) opinione f ▷ vt (look at: also fig) considerare; (house) visitare; **on ~** (in museum etc) esposto(-a); **in full ~ of** sotto gli occhi di; **in ~ of the weather/the fact that** considerato il tempo/che; **in my ~** a mio parere; **viewer** n spettatore(-trice); **viewpoint** n punto di vista; (place) posizione f
vigilant ['vɪdʒɪlənt] adj vigile
vigorous ['vɪgərəs] adj vigoroso(-a)
vile [vaɪl] adj (action) vile; (smell) disgustoso(-a), nauseante; (temper) pessimo(-a)
villa ['vɪlə] n villa
village ['vɪlɪdʒ] n villaggio; **villager** n abitante m/f di villaggio
villain ['vɪlən] n (scoundrel) canaglia; (BRIT: criminal) criminale m; (in novel etc) cattivo
vinaigrette [vɪneɪ'grɛt] n vinaigrette f inv
vine [vaɪn] n vite f; (climbing plant) rampicante m
vinegar ['vɪnɪgə'] n aceto
vineyard ['vɪnjɑːd] n vigna, vigneto
vintage ['vɪntɪdʒ] n (year) annata, produzione f ▷ cpd d'annata
vinyl ['vaɪnl] n vinile m
viola [vɪ'əulə] n viola
violate ['vaɪəleɪt] vt violare
violation [vaɪə'leɪʃən] n violazione f; **in ~ of sth** violando qc
violence ['vaɪələns] n violenza
violent ['vaɪələnt] adj violento(-a)
violet ['vaɪələt] adj (colour) viola inv, violetto(-a) ▷ n (plant) violetta; (colour) violetto
violin [vaɪə'lɪn] n violino
VIP n abbr (= very important person) V.I.P. m/f inv

virgin ['vəːdʒɪn] n vergine f ▷ adj vergine
inv

Virgo ['vəːgəʊ] n (sign) Vergine f

virtual ['vəːtjʊəl] adj effettivo(-a),
vero(-a); (Comput, Physics) virtuale;
(in effect): **it's a ~ impossibility** è
praticamente impossibile; **the ~ leader** il
capo all'atto pratico; **virtually** ['vəːtjʊəlɪ]
adv (almost) praticamente; **virtual reality**
n (Comput) realtà virtuale

virtue ['vəːtjuː] n virtù f inv; (advantage)
pregio, vantaggio; **by ~ of** grazie a

virus ['vaɪərəs] n (also Comput) virus m inv

visa ['viːzə] n visto

vise [vaɪs] (US) n (Tech) = **vice**

visibility [vɪzɪ'bɪlɪtɪ] n visibilità

visible ['vɪzəbl] adj visibile

vision ['vɪʒən] n (sight) vista; (foresight, in
dream) visione f

visit ['vɪzɪt] n visita; (stay) soggiorno ▷ vt
(person: us: also: **~ with**) andare a trovare;
(place) visitare; **visiting hours** npl (in
hospital etc) orario delle visite; **visitor**
n visitatore(-trice); (guest) ospite m/f;
visitor centre (US **visitor center**) n centro
informazioni per visitatori di museo, zoo,
parco ecc

visual ['vɪzjʊəl] adj visivo(-a); visuale;
ottico(-a); **visualize** ['vɪzjʊəlaɪz] vt
immaginare, figurarsi; (foresee) prevedere

vital ['vaɪtl] adj vitale

vitality [vaɪ'tælɪtɪ] n vitalità

vitamin ['vɪtəmɪn] n vitamina

vivid ['vɪvɪd] adj vivido(-a)

V-neck ['viːnɛk] n maglione m con lo
scollo a V

vocabulary [vəʊ'kæbjʊlərɪ] n vocabolario

vocal ['vəʊkl] adj (Mus) vocale;
(communication) verbale

vocational [vəʊ'keɪʃənl] adj professionale

vodka ['vɔdkə] n vodka f inv

vogue [vəʊg] n moda; (popularity)
popolarità, voga

voice [vɔɪs] n voce f ▷ vt (opinion)
esprimere; **voice mail** n servizio di
segreteria telefonica

void [vɔɪd] n vuoto ▷ adj (invalid) nullo(-a);
(empty): **~ of** privo(-a) di

volatile ['vɔlətaɪl] adj volatile; (fig) volubile

volcano [vɔl'keɪnəʊ] n (pl **volcanoes**)
vulcano

volleyball ['vɔlɪbɔːl] n pallavolo f

volt [vəʊlt] n volt m inv; **voltage** n
tensione f, voltaggio

volume ['vɔljuːm] n volume m

voluntarily ['vɔləntrɪlɪ] adv
volontariamente; gratuitamente

voluntary ['vɔləntərɪ] adj volontario(-a);
(unpaid) gratuito(-a), non retribuito(-a)

volunteer [vɔlən'tɪər] n volontario(-a)
▷ vt offrire volontariamente ▷ vi (Mil)
arruolarsi volontario; **to ~ to do** offrire
(volontariamente) di fare

vomit ['vɔmɪt] n vomito ▷ vt, vi vomitare

vote [vəʊt] n voto, suffragio; (cast) voto;
(franchise) diritto di voto ▷ vt **to be ~d
chairman** etc venir eletto presidente etc;
(propose): **to ~ that** approvare la proposta
che ▷ vi votare; **~ of thanks** discorso di
ringraziamento; **voter** n elettore(-trice);
voting n scrutinio

voucher ['vaʊtʃər] n (for meal, petrol etc)
buono

vow [vaʊ] n voto, promessa solenne ▷ vt
to ~ to do/that giurare di fare/che

vowel ['vaʊəl] n vocale f

voyage ['vɔɪɪdʒ] n viaggio per mare,
traversata

vulgar ['vʌlgər] adj volgare

vulnerable ['vʌlnərəbl] adj vulnerabile

vulture ['vʌltʃər] n avvoltoio

W

waddle ['wɔdl] *vi* camminare come una papera

wade [weɪd] *vi* **to ~ through** camminare a stento in; (*fig: book*) leggere con fatica

wafer ['weɪfə'] *n* (*Culin*) cialda

waffle ['wɔfl] *n* (*Culin*) cialda; (*inf*) ciance *fpl* ▷ *vi* cianciare

wag [wæg] *vt* agitare, muovere ▷ *vi* agitarsi

wage [weɪdʒ] *n* (*also*: **~s**) salario, paga ▷ *vt* **to ~ war** fare la guerra

wag(g)on ['wægən] *n* (*horse-drawn*) carro; (BRIT: *Rail*) vagone *m* (merci)

wail [weɪl] *n* gemito; (*of siren*) urlo ▷ *vi* gemere; urlare

waist [weɪst] *n* vita, cintola; **waistcoat** (BRIT) *n* panciotto, gilè *m inv*

wait [weɪt] *n* attesa ▷ *vi* aspettare, attendere; **to lie in ~ for** stare in agguato a; **to ~ for** aspettare; **~ for me, please** aspettami, per favore; **I can't ~ to** (*fig*) non vedo l'ora di; **wait on** *vt fus* servire; **waiter** *n* cameriere *m*; **waiting list** *n* lista di attesa; **waiting room** *n* sala d'aspetto *or* d'attesa; **waitress** *n* cameriera

waive [weɪv] *vt* rinunciare a, abbandonare

wake [weɪk] (*pt* **woke**, **waked**, *pp* **woken**, **waked**) *vt* (*also*: **~ up**) svegliare ▷ *vi* (*also*: **~ up**) svegliarsi ▷ *n* (*for dead person*) veglia funebre; (*Naut*) scia

Wales [weɪlz] *n* Galles *m*

walk [wɔːk] *n* passeggiata; (*short*) giretto; (*gait*) passo, andatura; (*path*) sentiero; (*in park etc*) sentiero, vialetto ▷ *vi* camminare; (*for pleasure, exercise*) passeggiare ▷ *vt* (*distance*) fare *or* percorrere a piedi; (*dog*) accompagnare, portare a passeggiare; **10 minutes' ~ from** 10 minuti di cammino *or* a piedi da; **from all ~s of life** di tutte le condizioni sociali; **walk out** *vi* (*audience*) andarsene; (*workers*) scendere in sciopero; **walker** *n* (*person*) camminatore(-trice); **walkie-talkie** ['wɔːkɪ'tɔːkɪ] *n* walkie-talkie *m inv*; **walking** *n* camminare *m*; **walking shoes** *npl* pedule *fpl*; **walking stick** *n* bastone *m* da passeggio; **Walkman®** ['wɔːkmən] *n* Walkman® *m inv*; **walkway** *n* passaggio pedonale

wall [wɔːl] *n* muro; (*internal, of tunnel, cave*) parete *f*

wallet ['wɔlɪt] *n* portafoglio; **I can't find my ~** non trovo il portafoglio

wallpaper ['wɔːlpeɪpə'] *n* carta da parati ▷ *vt* (*room*) mettere la carta da parati in

walnut ['wɔːlnʌt] *n* noce *f*; (*tree, wood*) noce *m*

walrus ['wɔːlrəs] (*pl* **walrus** *or* **walruses**) *n* tricheco

waltz [wɔːlts] *n* valzer *m inv* ▷ *vi* ballare il valzer

wand [wɔnd] *n* (*also*: **magic ~**) bacchetta (magica)

wander ['wɔndə'] *vi* (*person*) girare senza meta, girovagare; (*thoughts*) vagare ▷ *vt* girovagare per

want [wɔnt] *vt* volere; (*need*) aver bisogno di ▷ *n* **for ~ of** per mancanza di; **wanted** *adj* (*criminal*) ricercato(-a); **"wanted"** (*in adverts*) "cercasi"

war [wɔː'] *n* guerra; **to make ~ (on)** far guerra (a)

ward [wɔːd] *n* (*in hospital: room*) corsia; (: *section*) reparto; (*Pol*) circoscrizione *f*; (*Law*: *child: also*: **~ of court**) pupillo(-a)

warden ['wɔːdn] *n* (*of park, game reserve, youth hostel*) guardiano(-a); (BRIT: *of institution*) direttore(-trice); (BRIT: *also*: **traffic ~**) addetto(-a) al controllo del traffico e del parcheggio

wardrobe ['wɔːdrəub] *n* (*cupboard*) guardaroba *m inv*, armadio; (*clothes*) guardaroba; (*Cinema, Theatre*) costumi *mpl*

warehouse ['wɛəhaus] *n* magazzino

warfare ['wɔːfɛə'] *n* guerra

warhead ['wɔːhɛd] *n* (*Mil*) testata

warm [wɔːm] *adj* caldo(-a); (*thanks, welcome, applause*) caloroso(-a); (*person*) cordiale; **it's ~** fa caldo; **I'm ~** ho caldo; **warm up** *vi* scaldarsi, riscaldarsi

▷ vt scaldare, riscaldare; (engine) far scaldare; **warmly** adv (applaud, welcome) calorosamente; (dress) con abiti pesanti; **warmth** n calore m

warn [wɔ:n] vt **to ~ sb that/(not) to do/of** avvertire or avvisare qn che/di (non) fare/di; **warning** n avvertimento; (notice) avviso; (signal) segnalazione f; **warning light** n spia luminosa

warrant ['wɔrnt] n (voucher) buono; (Law: to arrest) mandato di cattura; (: to search) mandato di perquisizione

warranty ['wɔrənti] n garanzia

warrior ['wɔriə*] n guerriero(-a)

Warsaw ['wɔ:sɔ:] n Varsavia

warship ['wɔ:ʃip] n nave f da guerra

wart [wɔ:t] n verruca

wartime ['wɔ:taim] n **in ~** in tempo di guerra

wary ['wɛəri] adj prudente

was [wɔz] pt of **be**

wash [wɔʃ] vt lavare ▷ vi lavarsi; (sea): **to ~ over/against sth** infrangersi su/contro qc ▷ n lavaggio; (of ship) scia; **to give sth a ~** lavare qc, dare una lavata a qc; **to have a ~** lavarsi; **wash up** vi (BRIT) lavare i piatti; (US) darsi una lavata; **washbasin** (US **washbowl**) n lavabo; **wash cloth** (US) n pezzuola (per lavarsi); **washer** n (Tech) rondella; **washing** n (linen etc) bucato; **washing line** n (BRIT) corda del bucato; **washing machine** n lavatrice f; **washing powder** (BRIT) n detersivo (in polvere)

Washington ['wɔʃiŋtən] n Washington f

wash: washing-up n rigovernatura, lavatura dei piatti; **washing-up liquid** n detersivo liquido (per stoviglie); **washroom** n gabinetto

wasn't ['wɔznt] = **was not**

wasp [wɔsp] n vespa

waste [weist] n spreco; (of time) perdita; (rubbish) rifiuti mpl; (also: **household ~**) immondizie fpl ▷ adj (material) di scarto; (food) avanzato(-a); (land) incolto(-a) ▷ vt sprecare; **waste ground** (BRIT) n terreno incolto or abbandonato; **wastepaper basket** ['weistpeipə-] n cestino per la carta straccia

watch [wɔtʃ] n (also: **wrist ~**) orologio (da polso); (act of watching, vigilance) sorveglianza; (guard: Mil, Naut) guardia; (Naut: spell of duty) quarto ▷ vt (look at) osservare; (: match, programme) guardare; (spy on, guard) sorvegliare, tenere d'occhio; (be careful of) fare attenzione a ▷ vi osservare, guardare; (keep guard) fare or montare la guardia; **watch out** vi fare attenzione; **watchdog** n (also fig) cane m da guardia; **watch strap** n cinturino da

orologio

water ['wɔ:tə*] n acqua ▷ vt (plant) annaffiare ▷ vi (eyes) lacrimare; (mouth): **to make sb's mouth ~** far venire l'acquolina in bocca a qn; **in British ~s** nelle acque territoriali britanniche; **water down** vt (milk) diluire; (fig: story) edulcorare; **watercolour** (US **watercolor**) n acquerello; **watercress** n crescione m; **waterfall** n cascata; **watering can** n annaffiatoio; **watermelon** n anguria, cocomero; **waterproof** adj impermeabile; **water-skiing** n sci m acquatico

watt [wɔt] n watt m inv

wave [weiv] n onda; (of hand) gesto, segno; (in hair) ondulazione f; (fig: surge) ondata ▷ vi fare un cenno con la mano; (branches, grass) ondeggiare; (flag) sventolare ▷ vt (hand) fare un gesto con; (handkerchief) sventolare; (stick) brandire; **wavelength** n lunghezza d'onda

waver ['weivə*] vi esitare; (voice) tremolare

wavy ['weivi] adj ondulato(-a); ondeggiante

wax [wæks] n cera ▷ vt dare la cera a; (car) lucidare ▷ vi (moon) crescere

way [wei] n via, strada; (path, access) passaggio; (distance) distanza; (direction) parte f, direzione f; (manner) modo, stile m; (habit) abitudine f; **which ~? — this —** da che parte or in quale direzione? — da questa parte or per di qua; **on the ~** (en route) per strada; **to be on one's ~** essere in cammino or sulla strada; **to be in the ~** bloccare il passaggio; (fig) essere tra i piedi or d'impiccio; **to go out of one's ~ to do** (fig) mettercela tutta or fare di tutto per fare; **under ~** (project) in corso; **to lose one's ~** perdere la strada; **in a ~** in un certo senso; **in some ~s** sotto certi aspetti; **no ~!** (inf) neanche per idea!; **by the ~** ... a proposito ...; **"~ in"** (BRIT) "entrata", "ingresso"; **"~ out"** (BRIT) "uscita"; **the ~ back** la strada del ritorno; **"give ~"** (BRIT: Aut) "dare la precedenza"

W.C. ['dʌblju:'si:] (BRIT) n W.C. m inv, gabinetto

we [wi:] pl pron noi

weak [wi:k] adj debole; (health) precario(-a); (beam etc) fragile; (tea) leggero(-a); **weaken** vi indebolirsi ▷ vt indebolire; **weakness** n debolezza; (fault) punto debole, difetto; **to have a weakness for** avere un debole per

wealth [wɛlθ] n (money, resources) ricchezza, ricchezze fpl; (of details) abbondanza, profusione f; **wealthy** adj ricco(-a)

weapon ['wɛpən] n arma; **~s of mass**

destruction armi *mpl* di distruzione di massa

wear [wɛə^r] (*pt* **wore**, *pp* **worn**) *n* (*use*) uso; (*damage through use*) logorio, usura; (*clothing*): **sports/baby ~** abbigliamento sportivo/per neonati ▷ *vt* (*clothes*) portare; (*put on*) mettersi; (*damage: through use*) consumare ▷ *vi* (*last*) durare; (*rub etc through*) consumarsi; **evening ~** abiti *mpl* or tenuta da sera; **wear off** *vi* sparire lentamente; **wear out** *vt* consumare; (*person, strength*) esaurire

weary [ˈwɪərɪ] *adj* stanco(-a) ▷ *vi* **to ~ of** stancarsi di

weasel [ˈwiːzl] *n* (*Zool*) donnola

weather [ˈwɛðə^r] *n* tempo ▷ *vt* (*storm, crisis*) superare; **What's the ~ like?** che tempo fa?; **under the ~** (*fig: ill*) poco bene; **weather forecast** *n* previsioni *fpl* del tempo, bollettino meteorologico

weave [wiːv] (*pt* **wove**, *pp* **woven**) *vt* (*cloth*) tessere; (*basket*) intrecciare

web [wɛb] *n* (*of spider*) ragnatela; (*on foot*) palma; (*fabric, also fig*) tessuto; **the (World Wide) W~** la Rete; **web page** (*Comput*) pagina *f* web *inv*; **website** *n* (*Comput*) sito (Internet)

wed [wɛd] (*pt, pp* **wedded**) *vt* sposare ▷ *vi* sposarsi

we'd [wiːd] = **we had**; **we would**

Wed. *abbr* (= *Wednesday*) mer.

wedding [ˈwɛdɪŋ] *n* matrimonio; **wedding anniversary** *n* anniversario di matrimonio; **wedding day** *n* giorno delle nozze or del matrimonio; **wedding dress** *n* abito nuziale; **wedding ring** *n* fede *f*

wedge [wɛdʒ] *n* (*of wood etc*) zeppa; (*of cake*) fetta ▷ *vt* (*fix*) fissare con zeppe; (*pack tightly*) incastrare

Wednesday [ˈwɛdnzdɪ] *n* mercoledì *m inv*

wee [wiː] (*Scottish*) *adj* piccolo(-a)

weed [wiːd] *n* erbaccia ▷ *vt* diserbare; **weedkiller** *n* diserbante *m*

week [wiːk] *n* settimana; **a ~ today/on Friday** oggi/venerdì a otto; **weekday** *n* giorno feriale; (*Comm*) giornata lavorativa; **weekend** *n* fine settimana *m or f inv*, weekend *m inv*; **weekly** *adv* ogni settimana, settimanalmente ▷ *adj* settimanale ▷ *n* settimanale *m*

weep [wiːp] (*pt, pp* **wept**) *vi* (*person*) piangere

weigh [weɪ] *vt, vi* pesare; **to ~ anchor** salpare l'ancora; **weigh up** *vt* valutare

weight [weɪt] *n* peso; **to lose/put on ~** dimagrire/ingrassare; **weightlifting** *n* sollevamento pesi

weir [wɪə^r] *n* diga

weird [wɪəd] *adj* strano(-a), bizzarro(-a);

(*eerie*) soprannaturale

welcome [ˈwɛlkəm] *adj* benvenuto(-a) ▷ *n* accoglienza, benvenuto ▷ *vt* dare il benvenuto a; (*be glad of*) rallegrarsi di; **thank you — you're ~!** grazie — prego!

weld [wɛld] *n* saldatura ▷ *vt* saldare

welfare [ˈwɛlfɛə^r] *n* benessere *m*; **welfare state** *n* stato assistenziale

well [wɛl] *n* pozzo ▷ *adv* bene ▷ *adj* **to be ~** (*person*) stare bene ▷ *excl* allora!; ma!; ebbene!; **as ~** anche; **as ~ as** così come; oltre a; **~ done!** bravo(-a)!; **get ~ soon!** guarisci presto!; **to do ~** andare bene

we'll [wiːl] = **we will**; **we shall**

well: **well-behaved** *adj* ubbidiente; **well-built** *adj* (*person*) ben fatto(-a); **well-dressed** *adj* ben vestito(-a), vestito(-a) bene

wellies (*inf*) [ˈwɛlɪz] *npl* (BRIT) stivali *mpl* di gomma

well: **well-known** *adj* noto(-a), famoso(-a); **well-off** *adj* benestante, danaroso(-a); **well-paid** [wɛlˈpeɪd] *adj* ben pagato(-a)

Welsh [wɛlʃ] *adj* gallese ▷ *n* (*Ling*) gallese *m*; **Welshman** (*irreg*) *n* gallese *m*; **Welshwoman** (*irreg*) *n* gallese *f*

went [wɛnt] *pt of* **go**

wept [wɛpt] *pt, pp of* **weep**

were [wə^r] *pt of* **be**

we're [wɪə^r] = **we are**

weren't [wə:nt] = **were not**

west [wɛst] *n* ovest *m*, occidente *m*, ponente *m* ▷ *adj* (*a*) ovest *inv*, occidentale ▷ *adv* verso ovest; **the W~** l'Occidente *m*; **westbound** [ˈwɛstbaund] *adj* (*traffic*) diretto(-a) a ovest; (*carriageway*) ovest *inv*; **western** *adj* occidentale, dell'ovest ▷ *n* (*Cinema*) western *m inv*; **West Indian** *adj* delle Indie Occidentali ▷ *n* abitante *m/f* delle Indie Occidentali; **West Indies** [-ˈɪndɪz] *npl* Indie *fpl* Occidentali

wet [wɛt] *adj* umido(-a), bagnato(-a); (*soaked*) fradicio(-a); (*rainy*) piovoso(-a) ▷ *n* (BRIT: *Pol*) politico moderato; **to get ~** bagnarsi; **"~ paint"** "vernice fresca"; **wetsuit** *n* tuta da sub

we've [wiːv] = **we have**

whack [wæk] *vt* picchiare, battere

whale [weɪl] *n* (*Zool*) balena

wharf [wɔːf] (*pl* **wharves**) *n* banchina

 KEYWORD

what [wɔt] *adj* **1** (*in direct/indirect questions*) che; quale; **what size is it?** che taglia è?; **what colour is it?** di che colore è?; **what books do you want?** quali or che libri vuole?

2 (*in exclamations*) che; **what a mess!** che

disordine!
▷ pron 1 (*interrogative*) che cosa, cosa, che;
what are you doing? che or (che) cosa
fai?; **what are you talking about?** di
che cosa parli?; **what is it called?** come
si chiama?; **what about me?** e io?; **what
about doing …?** e se facessimo …?
2 (*relative*) ciò che, quello che; **I saw what
you did/was on the table** ho visto quello
che hai fatto/quello che era sul tavolo
3 (*indirect use*) (che) cosa; **he asked me
what she had said** mi ha chiesto che
cosa avesse detto; **tell me what you're
thinking about** dimmi a cosa stai
pensando
▷ excl (*disbelieving*) cosa!, come!

whatever [wɔt'ɛvə] adj ~ **book** qualunque
or qualsiasi libro + sub ▷ pron **do ~ is
necessary/you want** faccia qualunque
or qualsiasi cosa sia necessaria/lei voglia;
~ **happens** qualunque cosa accada; **no
reason ~** or **whatsoever** nessuna ragione
affatto or al mondo; **nothing ~** proprio
niente
whatsoever [wɔtsəu'ɛvə] adj = **whatever**
wheat [wi:t] n grano, frumento
wheel [wi:l] n ruota; (Aut: also: **steering
~**) volante m; (Naut) (ruota del) timone m
▷ vt spingere ▷ vi (birds) roteare; (also: ~
round) girare; **wheelbarrow** n carriola;
wheelchair n sedia a rotelle; **wheel
clamp** n (Aut) morsa che blocca la ruota di
una vettura in sosta vietata
wheeze [wi:z] vi ansimare

 KEYWORD

when [wɛn] adv quando; **when did it
happen?** quando è successo?
▷ conj 1 (at, during, after the time that)
quando; **she was reading when I came
in** quando sono entrato lei leggeva; **that
was when I needed you** era allora che
avevo bisogno di te
2 (on, at which): **on the day when I met
him** il giorno in cui l'ho incontrato; **one
day when it was raining** un giorno che
pioveva
3 (whereas) quando, mentre; **you said I
was wrong when in fact I was right** mi
hai detto che avevo torto, quando in realtà
avevo ragione

whenever [wɛn'ɛvə] adv quando mai
▷ conj quando; (every time that) ogni volta
che
where [wɛə'] adv, conj dove; **this is ~** è qui
che; **whereabouts** adv dove ▷ n **sb's**

whereabouts luogo dove qn si trova;
whereas conj mentre; **whereby** pron per
cui; **wherever** [-'ɛvə'] conj dovunque +
sub; (interrogative) dove mai
whether ['wɛðə'] conj se; **I don't know ~
to accept or not** non so se accettare o no;
it's doubtful ~ è poco probabile che; **~ you
go or not** che lei vada o no

 KEYWORD

which [wɪtʃ] adj 1 (interrogative: direct,
indirect) quale; **which picture do you
want?** quale quadro vuole?; **which one?**
quale?; **which one of you did it?** chi di voi
lo ha fatto?
2: **in which case** nel qual caso
▷ pron 1 (interrogative) quale; **which (of
these) are yours?** quali di questi sono
suoi?; **which of you are coming?** chi di
voi viene?
2 (relative) che; (: indirect) cui, il (la) quale;
**the apple which you ate/which is on
the table** la mela che hai mangiato/che
è sul tavolo; **the chair on which you are
sitting** la sedia sulla quale or su cui sei
seduto; **he said he knew, which is true**
ha detto che lo sapeva, il che è vero; **after
which** dopo di che

whichever [wɪtʃ'ɛvə] adj take ~ **book
you prefer** prenda qualsiasi libro che
preferisce; ~ **book you take** qualsiasi libro
prenda
while [waɪl] n momento ▷ conj mentre;
(as long as) finché; (although) sebbene +
sub; per quanto + sub; **for a ~** per un po'
whilst [waɪlst] conj = **while**
whim [wɪm] n capriccio
whine [waɪn] n gemito ▷ vi gemere;
uggiolare; piagnucolare
whip [wɪp] n frusta; (for riding) frustino;
(Pol: person) capogruppo (che sovrintende
alla disciplina dei colleghi di partito) ▷ vt
frustare; (cream, eggs) sbattere; **whipped
cream** n panna montata
whirl [wə:l] vt (far) girare rapidamente,
(far) turbinare ▷ vi (dancers) volteggiare;
(leaves, water) sollevarsi in vortice
whisk [wɪsk] n (Culin) frusta; frullino ▷ vt
sbattere, frullare; **to ~ sb away** or **off**
portar via qn a tutta velocità
whiskers ['wɪskəz] npl (of animal) baffi mpl;
(of man) favoriti mpl
whisky ['wɪskɪ] (US, Ireland **whiskey**) n
whisky m inv
whisper ['wɪspə'] n sussurro ▷ vt, vi
sussurrare
whistle ['wɪsl] n (sound) fischio; (object)

fischietto ▷ vi fischiare
white [waɪt] *adj* bianco(-a); *(with fear)*
pallido(-a) ▷ *n* bianco; *(person)* bianco(-a);
White House *n* Casa Bianca; **whitewash**
n (paint) bianco di calce ▷ *vt* imbiancare;
(fig) coprire
whiting ['waɪtɪŋ] *n inv (fish)* merlango
Whitsun ['wɪtsn] *n* Pentecoste *f*
whittle ['wɪtl] *vt* **to ~ away, ~ down**
ridurre, tagliare
whizz [wɪz] *vi* **to ~ past** *or* **by** passare
sfrecciando

KEYWORD

who [huː] *pron* **1** *(interrogative)* chi; **who is
it?, who's there?** chi è?
2 *(relative)* che; **the man who spoke to
me** l'uomo che ha parlato con me; **those
who can swim** quelli che sanno nuotare

whoever [huːˈɛvə] *pron* **~ finds it**
chiunque lo trovi; **ask ~ you like** lo chieda
a chiunque vuole; **~ she marries** chiunque
sposerà, non importa chi sposerà; **~ told
you that?** chi mai gliel'ha detto?
whole [həʊl] *adj (complete)* tutto(-a),
completo(-a); *(not broken)* intero(-a),
intatto(-a) ▷ *n (all)*: **the ~ of** tutto(-a) il
(la); *(entire unit)* tutto; *(not broken)* tutto;
the ~ of the town tutta la città, la città
intera; **on the ~, as a ~** nel complesso,
nell'insieme; **wholefood(s)** *n(pl)* cibo
integrale; **wholeheartedly** [həʊlˈhɑː-
tɪdlɪ] *adv* sentitamente, di tutto cuore;
wholemeal *adj (bread, flour)* integrale;
wholesale *n* commercio *or* vendita
all'ingrosso ▷ *adj* all'ingrosso; *(destruction)*
totale; **wholewheat** *adj* = **wholemeal**;
wholly *adv* completamente, del tutto

KEYWORD

whom [huːm] *pron* **1** *(interrogative)* chi;
whom did you see? chi hai visto?; **to
whom did you give it?** a chi lo hai dato?
2 *(relative)* che, *prep* + il (la) quale *(check
syntax of Italian verb used)*; **the man whom
I saw/to whom I spoke** l'uomo che ho
visto/al quale ho parlato

whore [hɔː] *(inf: pej) n* puttana

KEYWORD

whose [huːz] *adj* **1** *(possessive: interrogative)*
di chi; **whose book is this?, whose is
this book?** di chi è questo libro?; **whose
daughter are you?** di chi sei figlia?

2 *(possessive: relative)*: **the man whose
son you rescued** l'uomo il cui figlio hai
salvato; **the girl whose sister you were
speaking to** la ragazza alla cui sorella
stavi parlando
▷ *pron* di chi; **whose is this?** di chi è
questo?; **I know whose it is** so di chi è

KEYWORD

why [waɪ] *adv* perché; **why not?** perché
no?; **why not do it now?** perché non farlo
adesso?
▷ *conj* **I wonder why he said that** mi
chiedo perché l'abbia detto; **that's not
why I'm here** non è questo il motivo per
cui sono qui; **the reason why** il motivo
per cui
▷ *excl (surprise)* ma guarda un po'!;
(remonstrating) ma (via)!; *(explaining)*
ebbene!

wicked ['wɪkɪd] *adj* cattivo(-a),
malvagio(-a); maligno(-a); perfido(-a)
wicket ['wɪkɪt] *n (Cricket)* porta; area tra
le due porte
wide [waɪd] *adj* largo(-a); *(area, knowledge)*
vasto(-a); *(choice)* ampio(-a) ▷ *adv* **to open
~** spalancare; **to shoot ~** tirare a vuoto
or fuori bersaglio; **widely** *adv (differing)*
molto, completamente; *(travelled, spaced)*
molto; *(believed)* generalmente; **widen**
vt allargare, ampliare; **wide open** *adj*
spalancato(-a); **widespread** *adj (belief etc)*
molto *or* assai diffuso(-a)
widow ['wɪdəʊ] *n* vedova; **widower** *n*
vedovo
width [wɪdθ] *n* larghezza
wield [wiːld] *vt (sword)* maneggiare;
(power) esercitare
wife [waɪf] *(pl* **wives)** *n* moglie *f*
wig [wɪg] *n* parrucca
wild [waɪld] *adj* selvatico(-a);
selvaggio(-a); *(sea, weather)*
tempestoso(-a); *(idea, life)* folle;
stravagante; *(applause)* frenetico(-a);
wilderness ['wɪldənɪs] *n* deserto;
wildlife *n* natura; **wildly** *adv*
selvaggiamente; *(applaud)*
freneticamente; *(hit, guess)* a casaccio;
(happy) follemente

KEYWORD

will [wɪl] *(pt, pp* **willed)** *aux vb* **1** *(forming
future tense)*: **I will finish it tomorrow** lo
finirò domani; **I will have finished it by
tomorrow** lo finirò entro domani; **will you
do it? — yes I will/no I won't** lo farai? — sì

(lo farò)/no (non lo farò)
2 (*in conjectures, predictions*): **he will** or **he'll be there by now** dovrebbe essere arrivato ora; **that will be the postman** sarà il postino
3 (*in commands, requests, offers*): **will you be quiet!** vuoi stare zitto?; **will you come?** vieni anche tu?; **will you help me?** mi aiuti?, mi puoi aiutare?; **will you have a cup of tea?** vorrebbe una tazza di tè?; **I won't put up with it!** non lo accetterò!
▷ *vt* **to will sb to do** volere che qn faccia; **he willed himself to go on** continuò grazie a un grande sforzo di volontà ▷ *n* volontà; testamento

willing ['wɪlɪŋ] *adj* volonteroso(-a); **~ to do** disposto(-a) a fare; **willingly** *adv* volentieri
willow ['wɪləʊ] *n* salice *m*
willpower ['wɪlpaʊə*r*] *n* forza di volontà
wilt [wɪlt] *vi* appassire
win [wɪn] (*pt, pp* **won**) *n* (*in sports etc*) vittoria ▷ *vt* (*battle, prize, money*) vincere; (*popularity*) conquistare ▷ *vi* vincere; **win over** *vt* convincere
wince [wɪns] *vi* trasalire
wind[1] [waɪnd] (*pt, pp* **wound**) *vt* attorcigliare; (*wrap*) avvolgere; (*clock, toy*) caricare ▷ *vi* (*road, river*) serpeggiare; **wind down** *vt* (*car window*) abbassare; (*fig: production, business*) diminuire; **wind up** *vt* (*clock*) caricare; (*debate*) concludere
wind[2] [wɪnd] *n* vento; (*Med*) flatulenza; (*breath*) respiro, fiato ▷ *vt* (*take breath away*) far restare senza fiato; **~ power** energia eolica
windfall ['wɪndfɔːl] *n* (*money*) guadagno insperato
winding ['waɪndɪŋ] *adj* (*road*) serpeggiante; (*staircase*) a chiocciola
windmill ['wɪndmɪl] *n* mulino a vento
window ['wɪndəʊ] *n* finestra; (*in car, train, plane*) finestrino; (*in shop etc*) vetrina; (*also:* **~ pane**) vetro; **I'd like a ~ seat** vorrei un posto vicino al finestrino; **window box** *n* cassetta da fiori; **window cleaner** *n* (*person*) pulitore *m* di finestre; **window pane** *n* vetro; **window seat** *n* posto finestrino; **windowsill** *n* davanzale *m*
windscreen ['wɪndskriːn] (*us* **windshield**) *n* parabrezza *m inv*; **windscreen wiper** (*us* **windshield wiper**) *n* tergicristallo
windsurfing ['wɪndsəːfɪŋ] *n* windsurf *m inv*
windy ['wɪndɪ] *adj* ventoso(-a); **it's ~** c'è vento
wine [waɪn] *n* vino; **wine bar** *n* enoteca

(*per degustazione*); **wine glass** *n* bicchiere *m* da vino; **wine list** *n* lista dei vini; **wine tasting** *n* degustazione *f* dei vini
wing [wɪŋ] *n* ala; (*Aut*) fiancata; **wing mirror** *n* (*BRIT*) specchietto retrovisore esterno
wink [wɪŋk] *n* ammiccamento ▷ *vi* ammiccare, fare l'occhiolino; (*light*) baluginare
winner ['wɪnə*r*] *n* vincitore(-trice)
winning ['wɪnɪŋ] *adj* (*team, goal*) vincente; (*smile*) affascinante
winter ['wɪntə*r*] *n* inverno; **winter sports** *npl* sport *mpl* invernali; **wintertime** *n* inverno, stagione *f* invernale
wipe [waɪp] *n* pulita, passata ▷ *vt* pulire (strofinando); (*erase: tape*) cancellare; **wipe out** *vt* (*debt*) pagare, liquidare; (*memory*) cancellare; (*destroy*) annientare; **wipe up** *vt* asciugare
wire [waɪə*r*] *n* filo; (*Elec*) filo elettrico; (*Tel*) telegramma *m* ▷ *vt* (*house*) fare l'impianto elettrico di; (*also:* **~ up**) collegare, allacciare; (*person*) telegrafare a
wiring ['waɪərɪŋ] *n* impianto elettrico
wisdom ['wɪzdəm] *n* saggezza; (*of action*) prudenza; **wisdom tooth** *n* dente *m* del giudizio
wise [waɪz] *adj* saggio(-a); prudente; giudizioso(-a)
wish [wɪʃ] *n* (*desire*) desiderio; (*specific desire*) richiesta ▷ *vt* desiderare, volere; **best ~es** (*on birthday etc*) i migliori auguri; **with best ~es** (*in letter*) cordiali saluti, con i migliori saluti; **to ~ sb goodbye** dire arrivederci a qn; **he ~ed me well** mi augurò di riuscire; **to ~ to do/sb to do** desiderare or volere fare/che qn faccia; **to ~ for** desiderare
wistful ['wɪstful] *adj* malinconico(-a)
wit [wɪt] *n* (*also:* **~s**) intelligenza; presenza di spirito; (*wittiness*) spirito, arguzia; (*person*) bello spirito
witch [wɪtʃ] *n* strega

 KEYWORD

with [wɪð, wɪθ] *prep* **1** (*in the company of*) con; **I was with him** ero con lui; **we stayed with friends** siamo stati da amici; **I'll be with you in a minute** vengo subito
2 (*descriptive*) con; **a room with a view** una stanza con vista sul mare (*or* sulle montagne *etc*); **the man with the grey hat/blue eyes** l'uomo con il cappello grigio/gli occhi blu
3 (*indicating manner, means, cause*): **with tears in her eyes** con le lacrime agli occhi; **red with anger** rosso dalla rabbia; **to**

shake with fear tremare di paura
4 : I'm with you (I understand) la seguo;
to be with it (inf: up-to-date) essere alla
moda; (: alert) essere sveglio(-a)

withdraw [wɪθ'drɔː] (irreg: like draw) vt
ritirare; (money from bank) ritirare; prelevare
▷ vi ritirarsi; withdrawal n ritiro, prelievo;
(of army) ritirata; withdrawal symptoms
n (Med) crisi f di astinenza; withdrawn adj
(person) distaccato(-a)
withdrew [wɪθ'druː] pt of withdraw
wither ['wɪðəʳ] vi appassire
withhold [wɪθ'həʊld] (irreg: like hold)
vt (money) trattenere; (permission): to ~
(from) rifiutare (a); (information): to ~
(from) nascondere (a)
within [wɪð'ɪn] prep all'interno, (in time,
distances) entro ▷ adv all'interno, dentro; ~
reach (of) alla portata (di); ~ sight (of) in
vista (di); ~ a mile of entro un miglio da; ~
the week prima della fine della settimana
without [wɪð'aʊt] prep senza; to go ~ sth
fare a meno di qc
withstand [wɪθ'stænd] (irreg: like stand)
vt resistere a
witness ['wɪtnɪs] n (person, also Law)
testimone m/f ▷ vt (event) essere
testimone di; (document) attestare
l'autenticità di
witty ['wɪtɪ] adj spiritoso(-a)
wives [waɪvz] npl of wife
wizard ['wɪzəd] n mago
wk abbr = week
wobble ['wɔbl] vi tremare; (chair)
traballare
woe [wəʊ] n dolore m; disgrazia
woke [wəʊk] pt of wake
woken ['wəʊkn] pp of wake
wolf [wʊlf] (pl wolves) n lupo
woman ['wʊmən] (pl women) n donna
womb [wuːm] n (Anat) utero
women ['wɪmɪn] npl of woman
won [wʌn] pt, pp of win
wonder ['wʌndəʳ] n meraviglia ▷ vi to ~
whether/why domandarsi se/perché; to
~ at essere sorpreso(-a) di; meravigliarsi
di; to ~ about domandarsi di; pensare
a; it's no ~ that c'è poco or non c'è da
meravigliarsi che + sub; wonderful adj
meraviglioso(-a)
won't [wəʊnt] = will not
wood [wʊd] n legno; (timber) legname m;
(forest) bosco; wooden adj di legno; (fig)
rigido(-a); inespressivo(-a); woodwind npl
(Mus): the woodwind i legni; woodwork
n (craft, subject) falegnameria
wool [wʊl] n lana; to pull the ~ over sb's
eyes (fig) imbrogliare qn; woollen (US

woolen) adj di lana; (industry) laniero(-a);
woolly (US wooly) adj di lana; (fig: ideas)
confuso(-a)
word [wəːd] n parola; (news) notizie fpl
▷ vt esprimere, formulare; in other ~s in
altre parole; to break/keep one's ~ non
mantenere/mantenere la propria parola;
to have ~s with sb avere un diverbio con
qn; wording n formulazione f; word
processing n elaborazione f di testi, word
processing m; word processor n word
processor m inv
wore [wɔːʳ] pt of wear
work [wəːk] n lavoro; (Art, Literature)
opera ▷ vi lavorare; (mechanism, plan etc)
funzionare; (medicine) essere efficace
▷ vt (clay, wood etc) lavorare; (mine etc)
sfruttare; (machine) far funzionare;
(cause: effect, miracle) fare; to be out of
~ essere disoccupato(-a); ~s n (BRIT:
factory) fabbrica npl (of clock, machine)
meccanismo; how does this ~? come
funziona?; the TV isn't ~ing la TV non
funziona; to ~ loose allentarsi; work
out vi (plans etc) riuscire, andare bene
▷ vt (problem) risolvere; (plan) elaborare;
it ~s out at £100 fa 100 sterline; worker
n lavoratore(-trice), operaio(-a); work
experience n (previous jobs) esperienze
fpl lavorative; (student training placement)
tirocinio; workforce n forza lavoro;
working class n classe f operaia;
working week n settimana lavorativa;
workman (irreg) n operaio; work of
art n opera d'arte; workout n (Sport)
allenamento; work permit n permesso
di lavoro; workplace n posto di lavoro;
workshop n officina; (practical session)
gruppo di lavoro; work station n stazione
f di lavoro; work surface n piano di
lavoro; worktop n piano di lavoro
world [wəːld] n mondo ▷ cpd (champion)
del mondo; (power, war) mondiale; to
think the ~ of sb (fig) pensare un gran
bene di qn; World Cup n (Football) Coppa
del Mondo; world-wide adj universale;
World-Wide Web n World Wide Web m
worm [wəːm] n (also: earth~) verme m
worn [wɔːn] pp of wear ▷ adj usato(-a);
worn-out adj (object) consumato(-a),
logoro(-a); (person) sfinito(-a)
worried ['wʌrɪd] adj preoccupato(-a)
worry ['wʌrɪ] n preoccupazione f ▷ vt
preoccupare ▷ vi preoccuparsi; worrying
adj preoccupante
worse [wəːs] adj peggiore ▷ adv, n peggio;
a change for the ~ un peggioramento;
worsen vt, vi peggiorare; worse off adj in
condizioni (economiche) peggiori

worship ['wəːʃɪp] *n* culto ▷ *vt* (*God*) adorare, venerare; (*person*) adorare; **Your W~** (*BRIT: to mayor*) signor sindaco; (*: to judge*) signor giudice

worst [wəːst] *adj* il (la) peggiore ▷ *adv, n* peggio; **at ~** al peggio, per male che vada

worth [wəːθ] *n* valore *m* ▷ *adj* **to be ~** valere; **it's ~ it** ne vale la pena; **it is ~ one's while (to do)** vale la pena (fare); **worthless** *adj* di nessun valore; **worthwhile** *adj* (*activity*) utile; (*cause*) lodevole

worthy ['wəːðɪ] *adj* (*person*) degno(-a); (*motive*) lodevole; **~ of** degno di

 KEYWORD

would [wud] *aux vb* **1** (*conditional tense*): **if you asked him he would do it** se glielo chiedesse lo farebbe; **if you had asked him he would have done it** se glielo avesse chiesto lo avrebbe fatto
2 (*in offers, invitations, requests*): **would you like a biscuit?** vorrebbe *or* vuole un biscotto?; **would you ask him to come in?** lo faccia entrare, per cortesia; **would you open the window please?** apra la finestra, per favore
3 (*in indirect speech*): **I said I would do it** ho detto che l'avrei fatto
4 (*emphatic*): **it would have to snow today!** doveva proprio nevicare oggi!
5 (*insistence*): **she wouldn't do it** non ha voluto farlo
6 (*conjecture*): **it would have been midnight** sarà stato mezzanotte; **it would seem so** sembrerebbe proprio di sì
7 (*indicating habit*): **he would go there on Mondays** andava lì ogni lunedì

wouldn't ['wudnt] = **would not**
wound[1] [waund] *pt, pp of* **wind**[1]
wound[2] [wuːnd] *n* ferita ▷ *vt* ferire
wove [wəuv] *pt of* **weave**
woven ['wəuvn] *pp of* **weave**
wrap [ræp] *vt* avvolgere; (*pack: also: ~ up*) incartare; **wrapper** *n* (*on chocolate*) carta; (*BRIT: of book*) copertina; **wrapping** ['ræpɪŋ] *n* carta; **wrapping paper** *n* carta da pacchi; (*for gift*) carta da regali
wreath [riːθ, *pl* riːðz] *n* corona
wreck [rɛk] *n* (*sea disaster*) naufragio; (*ship*) relitto; (*pej: person*) rottame *m* ▷ *vt* demolire; (*ship*) far naufragare; (*fig*) rovinare; **wreckage** *n* rottami *mpl*; (*of building*) macerie *fpl*; (*of ship*) relitti *mpl*
wren [rɛn] *n* (*Zool*) scricciolo
wrench [rɛntʃ] *n* (*Tech*) chiave *f*; (*tug*) torsione *f* brusca; (*fig*) strazio ▷ *vt*

strappare; storcere; **to ~ sth from** strappare qc a *or* da
wrestle ['rɛsl] *vi* **to ~ (with sb)** lottare (con qn); **wrestler** *n* lottatore(-trice); **wrestling** *n* lotta
wretched ['rɛtʃɪd] *adj* disgraziato(-a); (*inf: weather, holiday*) orrendo(-a), orribile; (*: child, dog*) pestifero(-a)
wriggle ['rɪgl] *vi* (*also: ~ about*) dimenarsi; (*: snake, worm*) serpeggiare, muoversi serpeggiando
wring [rɪŋ] (*pt, pp* **wrung**) *vt* torcere; (*wet clothes*) strizzare; (*fig*): **to ~ sth out of** strappare qc a
wrinkle ['rɪŋkl] *n* (*on skin*) ruga; (*on paper etc*) grinza ▷ *vt* (*nose*) torcere; (*forehead*) corrugare ▷ *vi* (*skin, paint*) raggrinzirsi
wrist [rɪst] *n* polso
write [raɪt] (*pt* **wrote**, *pp* **written**) *vt, vi* scrivere; **write down** *vt* annotare; (*put in writing*) mettere per iscritto; **write off** *vt* (*debt, plan*) cancellare; **write out** *vt* mettere per iscritto; (*cheque, receipt*) scrivere; **write-off** *n* perdita completa; **writer** *n* autore(-trice), scrittore(-trice)
writing ['raɪtɪŋ] *n* scrittura; (*of author*) scritto, opera; **in ~** per iscritto; **writing paper** *n* carta da lettere
written ['rɪtn] *pp of* **write**
wrong [rɒŋ] *adj* sbagliato(-a); (*not suitable*) inadatto(-a); (*wicked*) cattivo(-a); (*unfair*) ingiusto(-a) ▷ *adv* in modo sbagliato, erroneamente ▷ *n* (*injustice*) torto ▷ *vt* fare torto a; **I took a ~ turning** ho sbagliato strada; **you are ~ to do it** ha torto a farlo; **you are ~ about that, you've got it ~** si sbaglia; **to be in the ~** avere torto; **what's ~?** cosa c'è che non va?; **to go ~** (*person*) sbagliarsi; (*plan*) fallire, non riuscire; (*machine*) guastarsi; **wrongly** *adv* (*incorrectly, by mistake*) in modo sbagliato; **wrong number** *n* (*Tel*): **you've got the wrong number** ha sbagliato numero
wrote [rəut] *pt of* **write**
wrung [rʌŋ] *pt, pp of* **wring**
WWW *n abbr* = **World Wide Web**; **the ~** la Rete

XL *abbr* = **extra large**

Xmas ['ɛksməs] *n abbr* = **Christmas**

X-ray ['ɛksreɪ] *n* raggio X; (*photograph*) radiografia ▷ *vt* radiografare

xylophone ['zaɪləfəun] *n* xilofono

yacht [jɔt] *n* panfilo, yacht *m inv*; **yachting** *n* yachting *m*, sport *m* della vela

yard [jɑːd] *n* (*of house etc*) cortile *m*; (*measure*) iarda (= 914 mm; 3 *feet*); **yard sale** (*US*) *n* vendita di oggetti usati nel cortile di una casa privata

yarn [jɑːn] *n* filato; (*tale*) lunga storia

yawn [jɔːn] *n* sbadiglio ▷ *vi* sbadigliare

yd. *abbr* = **yard(s)**

yeah [jɛə] (*inf*) *adv* sì

year [jɪəʳ] *n* anno; (*referring to harvest, wine etc*) annata; **he is 8 ~s old** ha 8 anni; **an eight-~-old child** un(a) bambino(-a) di otto anni; **yearly** *adj* annuale ▷ *adv* annualmente

yearn [jəːn] *vi* **to ~ for sth/to do** desiderare ardentemente qc/di fare

yeast [jiːst] *n* lievito

yell [jɛl] *n* urlo ▷ *vi* urlare

yellow ['jɛləu] *adj* giallo(-a); **Yellow Pages**® *npl* pagine *fpl* gialle

yes [jɛs] *adv* sì ▷ *n* sì *m inv*; **to say/answer ~** dire/rispondere di sì

yesterday ['jestədɪ] *adv* ieri ▷ *n* ieri *m inv*; **~ morning/evening** ieri mattina/sera; **all day ~** ieri per tutta la giornata

yet [jɛt] *adv* ancora; già ▷ *conj* ma, tuttavia; **it is not finished ~** non è ancora finito; **the best ~** finora il

migliore; **as ~** finora
yew [juː] n tasso (albero)
Yiddish ['jɪdɪʃ] n yiddish m
yield [jiːld] n produzione f, resa; reddito
▷ vt produrre, rendere; (surrender)
cedere ▷ vi cedere; (US: Aut) dare la
precedenza
yob(bo) ['jɔb(əu)] n (BRIT inf) bullo
yoga ['jəugə] n yoga m
yog(h)urt ['jəugət] n iogurt m inv
yolk [jəuk] n tuorlo, rosso d'uovo

○ KEYWORD

you [juː] pron **1** (subject) tu; (: polite form) lei;
(: pl) voi; (: very formal) loro; **you Italians
enjoy your food** a voi Italiani piace
mangiare bene; **you and I will go** tu ed io
or lei ed io andiamo
2 (object: direct) ti; la; vi; loro (after vb); (:
indirect) ti; le; vi; loro (after vb); **I know you**
ti or la or vi conosco; **I gave it to you** te
l'ho dato; gliel'ho dato; ve l'ho dato; l'ho
dato loro
3 (stressed, after prep, in comparisons) te; lei;
voi; loro; **I told you to do it** ho detto a TE
(or a LEI etc) di farlo; **she's younger than
you** è più giovane di te (or lei etc)
4 (impers: one) si; **fresh air does you good**
l'aria fresca fa bene; **you never know** non
si sa mai

you'd [juːd] = **you had**; **you would**
you'll [juːl] = **you will**; **you shall**
young [jʌŋ] adj giovane ▷ npl (of animal)
piccoli mpl; (people): **the ~** i giovani, la
gioventù; **youngster** n giovanotto,
ragazzo; (child) bambino(-a)
your [jɔːʳ] adj il (la) tuo(-a) pl, i (le) tuoi
(tue); il (la) suo(-a); (pl) i (le) suoi (sue); il
(la) vostro(-a); (pl) i (le) vostri(-e); il (la)
loro; (pl) i (le) loro; see also **my**
you're [juəʳ] = **you are**
yours [jɔːz] pron il (la) tuo(-a); (pl) i (le)
tuoi (tue); (polite form) il (la) suo(-a); (pl)
i (le) suoi (sue); (pl) il (la) vostro(-a); (pl)
i (le) vostri(-e); (: very formal) il (la) loro;
(pl) i (le) loro; see also **mine**; **faithfully**;
sincerely
yourself [jɔːˈsɛlf] pron (reflexive) ti;
si; (after prep) te; sé; (emphatic) tu
stesso(-a); lei stesso(-a); **yourselves** pl
pron (reflexive) vi; si; (after prep) voi; loro;
(emphatic) voi stessi(-e); loro stessi(-e); see
also **oneself**
youth [juːθ, pl juːðz] n gioventù f; (young
man) giovane m, ragazzo; **youth club** n
centro giovanile; **youthful** adj giovane;
da giovane; giovanile; **youth hostel** n

ostello della gioventù
you've [juːv] = **you have**
Yugoslavia ['juːgəuˈslaːvɪə] n (Hist)
Jugoslavia

Z

zeal [ziːl] *n* zelo; entusiasmo
zebra ['ziːbrə] *n* zebra; **zebra crossing**
(BRIT) *n* (passaggio pedonale a) strisce *fpl*,
zebre *fpl*
zero ['zɪərəu] *n* zero
zest [zɛst] *n* gusto; (*Culin*) buccia
zigzag ['zɪgzæg] *n* zigzag *m inv* ▷ *vi*
zigzagare
Zimbabwe [zɪm'bɑːbwɪ] *n* Zimbabwe *m*
zinc [zɪŋk] *n* zinco
zip [zɪp] *n* (*also:* **~ fastener**, (*US*) **zipper**)
chiusura *for* cerniera *f* lampo *inv* ▷ *vt* (*also:*
~ up) chiudere con una cerniera lampo;
zip code (*US*) *n* codice *m* di avviamento
postale; **zipper** (*US*) *n* cerniera *f* lampo *inv*
zit [zɪt] *n* brufolo
zodiac ['zəudɪæk] *n* zodiaco
zone [zəun] *n* (*also Mil*) zona
zoo [zuː] *n* zoo *m inv*
zoology [zuː'ɔlədʒɪ] *n* zoologia
zoom [zuːm] *vi* **to ~ past** sfrecciare; **zoom
lens** *n* zoom *m inv*, obiettivo a focale
variabile
zucchini [zuː'kiːnɪ] (*US*) *npl* (*courgettes*)
zucchine *fpl*